FEMINISMS

FEMINISMS

an anthology
of literary
theory and
criticism

edited by

robyn r. warhol

and

diane price herndl

rutgers university press · new brunswick, new jersey

Third paperback printing, 1996

Library of Congress Cataloging-in-Publication Data

Feminisms : an anthology of literary theory and criticism / edited by
  Robyn R. Warhol and Diane Price Herndl.
    p. cm.
   Includes bibliographical references and index.
   ISBN 0-8135-1731-1 (cloth) — ISBN 0-8135-1732-X (pbk.)
   1. Feminist literary criticism. 2. Feminism and literature.
  3. Women and literature. I. Warhol, Robyn R., 1955–
  II. Price Herndl, Diane, 1959–
  PN98.W64F366 1991
  809'.89287—dc20   *91-14281*
                                     CIP

British Cataloging-in-Publication information available

CONTENTS

CANON

TRADITION

BODY

DESIRE

READING

DISCOURSE

ETHNICITY

HISTORY

CLASS

MEN

AUTOBIOGRAPHY

ABOUT FEMINISMS

Self-consciousness is one hallmark of contemporary literary scholarship, and feminist criticism is no exception. Indeed, being explicit about the referents of one's pronouns, the origins of one's projects, and the position from which one speaks has become very common among feminists; beginning a book with a personal anecdote is practically obligatory. There are good reasons for this: feminism holds that "the personal *is* political," and as feminists we believe that the traditional academic boundaries between professional and personal experience ought to be undermined.

"We" are Robyn and Diane; we speak as white middle-class heterosexual American feminist academics in our early thirties (to cover a number of the categories feminist criticism has lately been emphasizing as significant to one's reading and speaking position: race, class, sexual orientation, nationality, political positioning, education-level, and age). Colleagues at the University of Vermont since 1989, we two have found that we share passionate interests in fiction, feminism, and quiltmaking; the making of this book has been accompanied by the making of a friendship, and the start of two quilts. The book was built, like so many feminist projects, out of equal parts of frustration and hope.

In the fall of 1989, Diane's first semester at UVM, Robyn was teaching a graduate seminar in "Feminist Theory and Fiction." In our early acquaintance we chatted about the syllabus, about the possibilities it offered and the difficulties it represented. We discussed how hard it was to order books for such a course; the options for texts were so limited. One had either to choose a relatively small anthology, which would represent only part of the whole field of feminist criticism and theory, or one had to require already poor graduate students to spend a fortune buying many books. Even then, much crucial work that had been published in scholarly journals went unrepresented unless one put together extensive "professor publishing packets" with the local copy-store, a labor-intensive and, in these copyright-sensitive days, expensive process that was often botched and usually difficult to read.

We agreed that someone should edit a comprehensive anthology of feminist criticism; we decided to do it ourselves, and—in the spirit of the kinds of feminism modeled by such scholars as Jane Marcus or Sandra M. Gilbert and Susan

Gubar—to do it collaboratively. Over the next several months, we began the intellectual patchwork project that resulted in *Feminisms*.

Most collections of feminist criticism contain twelve to fifteen essays which represent either a particular methodology or are focused on a specific subject. When such anthologies do attempt to represent a variety of methodological approaches, their limited space prevents any attempt at real comprehensiveness. Generally, if an anthology focuses on French feminist theories, it excludes Anglo-American approaches; if it brings together work on minority literature, it leaves out "mainstream" subjects; if it aspires to represent a broad spectrum of perspectives, it usually saves room for a single voice to speak for issues of "race" and perhaps one to speak for "sexual preference." Given the constraints of expense and space in such books, these editorial decisions make perfect sense. *Feminisms* takes advantage of its larger scale to draw upon the collective insights of existing anthologies, bringing together as many current strains of feminist literary theory as possible. This book aspires to give a wide-angle view of what is going on in feminist literary studies in the United States today. Even a book reproducing fifty-eight essays has limits, though; this introductory chapter explains the principles we followed in making our selections.

The title, *Feminisms: An Anthology of Literary Theory and Criticism*, sets out some of the parameters of the anthology's goals. We've used the plural form "feminisms," rather than "feminism," to acknowledge the diversity of motivation, method, and experience among feminist academics. From the outside, "feminism" may appear monolithic, unified, or singularly definable. The more intimately one becomes acquainted with feminist criticism, however, the more one sees the multiplicity of approaches and assumptions inside the movement. While this variety can lead to conflict and competition, it can also be the source of movement, vitality, and genuine learning. Such diversity—if fostered, as it has been in some feminist thought—can be a model for cultural heterogeneity. Our title underscores our commitment to diversity within feminism. By choosing this approach, we take just one of the many positions available within the movement; some feminists do take more aggressive, competitive stances than the one we are adopting here.

Though feminisms are multiple, feminists do share certain beliefs, which we see as the common denominators among the fifty-eight essays reprinted here. Feminist critics generally agree that the oppression of women is a fact of life, that gender leaves its traces in literary texts and on literary history, and that feminist literary criticism plays a worthwhile part in the struggle to end oppression in the world outside of texts. When they turn their attention to social history, most feminists agree that oppression of ethnic and racial minorities, gay men and lesbians, and working class people is closely tied to the oppression of women. Of course, not all feminist critics ground their work in material history. But even when they focus on such comparatively abstract matters as discourse, aesthetics, or the constitution of subjectivity, feminists are always engaged in an explicitly political enterprise, always working to change existing power structures both inside and outside academia. Its overtly political nature is perhaps the single most distinguishing feature of feminist scholarly work.

Attention to gender is another rubric by which feminist criticism can usually be identified. But "gender" is a debatable term: some writers use it to mean biological sex (male/female), whereas others insist upon making a distinction between biology and culture. The latter theorists argue that masculinity and femininity are not predetermined by the body itself, but are constructed within culture. To borrow a vivid illustration of this distinction from Susan Brownmiller: it is female (just as it is male) to grow hair on the legs and in the armpits, but in the United States it is deemed feminine (but not masculine) to shave that hair off. The "female," then, is a matter of sex, the "feminine" a matter of culture. Some feminists depend upon this distinction as a key to combatting "essentialism," or a deterministic view that "biology is destiny." Others embrace the biological facts of femaleness (for example, childbearing, lactation, and menstruation) as potentially liberatory for women, encouraging women to celebrate difference from the male "norm" rather than to discount or denigrate it. Still others (especially those whose work is grounded in the French language, which uses "*féminine*" to mean both "female" and "feminine") resist the binary opposition of sex and gender, arguing that the cultural differences are, after all, instilled on the basis of biological givens. All of these versions of what "gender" means are represented in *Feminisms,* and all are brought to bear here upon literary studies.

We conceive "literary theory and criticism" as the realm of what is taught today in American departments of English. Broadly speaking, we define that realm as "texts." Hence, each of our entries addresses gender-related issues in the study of texts, which may be drawn from traditional "high-culture" literature, from such recently emerging genres as diaries or letters, or from popular forms such as dime-store romance and Hollywood film. The first four sections of the book—"Institutions," "Methodologies," "Canon," and "Tradition"—address the definitions of "literature and criticism" directly, inquiring into the role feminism has played in the task of reshaping the entire field.

Literary studies are not what they were when feminist criticism entered the scene twenty years ago. Indeed, at that time few people were questioning the received definitions of either "literature" or "literary studies," but today both terms demand explanation. One major change brought about chiefly by feminist criticism has been the increasingly interdisciplinary nature of literary studies. Influenced by and participating in Women's Studies, feminists have brought new vitality to the study of literature by introducing to it research done in such fields as sociology, anthropology, history, religion, psychology, political science, and communications. Signs of all these disciplines' influence abound in the primarily literary essays reprinted here.

The book is thus designed for use in courses on criticism and on "women in literature," but it is addressed to many other audiences outside the classroom as well. Because this collection seeks to answer such basic questions as "What is feminist literary theory?" and "What does it mean to do feminist criticism?" it is directed at curious nonfeminist academics as well as at feminists outside of academia looking for correspondences between their own political action and academically applied theory. We have assumed some knowledge of literary history on our readers' part, but we have been careful in our introductions to each section to define terms that are specific to feminism or to literary theory. We hope this will be the book an interdisciplinary reading group could use as an introduction to feminist literary studies, or the book a feminist teacher could hand to the student, colleague, or friend who says "I really like what you're saying about literature and about writing—what can I read to learn more about it?" We hope, too, that *Feminisms* will serve specialists in feminist criticism as a manageable repository of often-quoted and innovative essays representing multiple feminist positions.

We are both feminist teachers, committed to using feminist pedagogy in the classroom. Neither of us is politically reconciled to the position of authority that lecturing from a podium—or editing this anthology—implies. Just as we encourage our students to question us and our assumptions, we invite our readers to question this book's assumptions, its inclusions and exclusions, and its organization. The patchwork here is not the only way these essays could have been pieced together; nor is the material the only selection we could have made.

SELECTING THE PIECES OF FEMINISMS

The concept of *Feminisms*, based as it is upon multiplicity, depends, as we have said, upon accepting heterogeneity within feminist literary studies. This does not mean that we, as editors, position ourselves as "pluralists," or as theorists who think that "anything goes." As independent critics, each of us agrees with some of the pieces in this collection, and each disapproves of others. (Since Diane's work tends to be more "historicist" than Robyn's, Robyn's more "discourse"-oriented than Diane's; and since Diane's work has roots in psychoanalytic theory while Robyn's is influenced by structuralist narratology, the essays Diane likes are not always the same as the ones Robyn likes.) We do, however, believe that each essay here represents a viable—and important—voice in contemporary feminist literary studies that should be heard. Still, we recognize that the diversity of views represented here sometimes leads to irreconcilable logical conflicts. There is no way to force these many voices into a unison performance, or even—in some cases—to make them harmonize. For example, one need only compare Barbara Johnson's and Susan Stanford Friedman's essays on childbirth and abortion tropes, or Jane Marcus's and Shari Benstock's work on Virginia Woolf, to see how disparate the views within feminism can be. For this reason, we have chosen not to evaluate individual positions in our introductions to each section of the book. Rather than poking holes in each writer's argument or declaring any winners in the debate, we have taken every entry on its own terms, trying to summarize briefly what each author has to say and to show the relation each piece holds to the others in its section. In taking this descriptive stance, rather than a prescriptive or evaluative one, we are choosing to avoid what James J. Sosnoski calls "intellectual machismo" (in his essay reprinted in "Institutions"), the kind of power-posturing that prompts endless arguments and inevitably leads either to hegemony or to a paralytic standoff. We are interested in promoting the forward movement of feminist activism, a movement we believe can only occur where difference commands attention, not offhand dismissal or knee-jerk negativism.

Although most of our selections appear in chronological order within sections, we are also resisting any temptations to impose a "progress" model on the development of feminist criticism over the past fifteen years. The order within sections is not intended to imply that the final essays have issued the "final word" on the question. We do not subscribe to "literary Darwinism" (as Olivia Frey has recently called it in an essay in *College English*), or a notion that the "fittest" approaches will survive by eliminating their weaker competitors. We have tried to avoid editorial determinations of "value" or "political correctness"; we do not want to be the arbiters of feminist taste. Our vision of feminist criticism is not as a marketplace where the distinguished individual will rise in importance through special achievement by providing a "better mousetrap" than the next gal. We see it instead as a collective effort, able to absorb and benefit from conflict within the collective. We have left out some movements within feminist criticism that were current in the mid-1970s but that no longer enter the discussions being held today: myth criticism is one example of a formerly popular approach that is not represented in *Feminisms*. While this could suggest that we view these positions as "weaker competitors," our intent is to give a wide-ranging picture of feminist criticism today. We have therefore tried to focus on questions that are still current, debates that are still going on in the early 1990s.

In choosing these previously published essays and book chapters, we followed two basic principles. First, we wanted to reproduce as many as possible of those theoretical statements within feminist criticism that have been repeatedly cited, disputed, and invoked in work written through the 1980s. We have tried to include essays which have, themselves, sparked their own critical debates. Two sections—"Methodologies" and "Reading"—are arranged to promote discussion of the process by which critical essays become embedded in one another, and the ways a feminist critic can summarize (or appropriate) the ideas of others to agree or to argue with them.

Our second principle of selection was to print interesting essays that represent .as many current approaches as possible, regardless of the writers' institutional prominence or fame. These guidelines have resulted in a conglomeration of scholars at many different stages of their careers, though we have, in all cases, selected critics who are still actively pursuing research. We have, in several cases, reprinted essays written early in the careers of critics who have been consistently productive; we do not mean for the pieces here by Myra Jehlen, Jane Marcus, Annette Kolodny, Shoshana Felman, or Sandra M. Gilbert and Susan Gubar to obscure the importance of work they have done since. Indeed, we hope these selections will prompt readers to look into all the writers' later productions.

Having said all this, we do recognize the paradox inherent in setting up what could be seen as a "canon" of feminist criticism. By their nature and function, critical anthologies, like literary anthologies, create canons (as Jane Gallop, among others, has recently been arguing); when they become the basis for syllabi, collections come to define the fields they seek to introduce. While the canonization effect is probably to some degree unavoidable, we have tried our best to subvert it. We hope the diversity of our selections and their organization into sections will emphasize our assertion that this volume does not intend to propose a totalizing definition of feminist criticism, but rather to present various feminisms, a significant number of voices and approaches functioning alongside other feminisms in the academy today.

Those pieces we selected are—with only a few exceptions—uncut; most articles and book chapters appear here in their original forms. We felt it was important for readers to get the full rhetorical thrust of each piece, even though that meant we had space for fewer entries than we might have included, had we used excerpts. Selections from books appearing in *Feminisms* are not meant as substitutes for the whole works; we hope readers will follow through on the citations in our section introductions, to read the entire work. In a few cases we did excerpt parts of book chapters to accommodate constraints of space and of resources available from our press.

The financial constraints upon *Feminisms* have been real and reflect a serious issue facing feminist scholars at work today: How can feminist criticism reject marketplace ethics while still working within the marketplace of the competitive publishing industry? As more and more publishing houses are consolidated or bought by major multinational corporations, even the relatively autonomous university presses are forced to conform, to some extent, to the norms they establish. These norms are increasingly those of the corporate, rather than the academic, world. We have been astonished at the range of fees university presses charge for permission to reprint scholarly work, from nothing more than a credit line to several hundred dollars. Even more dismaying has been our realization that some presses will agree to reduce the price for permission only if authors are willing to waive their part of the profits the fees represent. (We have been gratified, however, to find that many scholars whose fame would warrant hefty fees have generously donated their work in a spirit of collaboration and an appreciation for the goals of this project.) In some cases, even when the author had given up all of her share of the fee, the price was still beyond our means. Therefore, some authors who ought to be represented in *Feminisms* are not; we are sorry, because the presses, not the scholars, are to blame.

To keep the size of the volume within economically feasible limits—and to give it a measure of coherence within diversity—we have narrowed the subject matter of the essays to include chiefly British and North American literature of the nineteenth and tventieth centuries. In doing so, we repeat the gesture of Gilbert and Gubar's 1985 *Norton Anthology of Literature by Women* which (as many have argued) grants disproportionate space to the same periods and nations we feature here. References to certain writers (Charlotte Brontë, Virginia Woolf, Toni Morrison, and Alice Walker) and certain genres (the romance, autobiography, the novel) occur repeatedly here, partly because of our personal interest in those subjects, but partly also to provide various viewpoints on the same material. This choice means that we have omitted important feminist criticism on earlier periods and on literature written in languages other than English. In reprinting pieces from Hélène Cixous, Shoshana Felman, Jane Gallop, Luce Irigaray, and Julia Kristeva, however, we have made some exceptions for writers who have particularly influenced the American critical scene.

In making selections from each critic's corpus, we favored theoretical over purely critical pieces. We looked for work that was explicit about its premises and methods, and that illustrated its theories with specific reference to texts. Of course, the diversity of *Feminisms* means there are exceptions to this rule, too—Kristeva, Cixous, and Irigaray, for instance, write theory without much recourse to practical criticism. But we have steered clear of essays that apply criticism to texts without some self-consciousness about the theories they are using because we wanted to highlight the process and thought behind the practice of feminist literary study.

THE PATTERN OF FEMINISMS

We have made a few references to "Anglo-American" and "French" feminisms, a distinction which will be clearer to those who have read the essays and section introductions in this volume, but which bears some explanation here. In the most general terms, "French feminism" proceeds from the psychoanalytic premises of Freud and Lacan, and adopts or adapts the deconstructive methods of Jacques Derrida. It is "poststructuralist" in that it focuses on discourse and on the constructedness of subjectivity and of representation. By contrast, Anglo-American feminism is generally more interested in history. That can mean literal history (accounts of the lived experience of people in the world) or literary history, or both. Anglo-American feminism tends to focus more than French feminism on the interaction of texts with the extratextual world they simultaneously address and represent.

This simple differentiation between the two is, of course, too schematic; Anglo-American feminists often concern themselves with discourse, French feminists with the world outside of texts. When applied to the essays in this volume, especially, the distinction between French and Anglo-American feminisms becomes blurred. The essays here reveal the many intersections between theories, and show how feminist writers have used various theoretical approaches to understand the mechanisms through which gender operates within texts. We have tried to avoid privileging either approach.

Just as critics can be categorized by identifying their approach as "French" or "Anglo-American," so too can scholars who narrate the history of feminist criticism be divided into two general groups: one approach is to contrast French and Anglo-American feminism with each other, coming down on the French side (as Toril Moi does in *Sexual/Textual Politics*) or the Anglo-American side (as Janet Todd does in *Feminist Literary History*). The other way of talking about feminist criticism is to put French and Anglo-American modes together and narrate their development as a series of "moments" or "phases," as Elaine Showalter does in her essay "A Criticism of Our Own," reprinted here in the "Methodologies" section. Though some sections of *Feminisms* are dominated by critics working in the French mode ("Desire" and "Body," in particular) and others contain chiefly Anglo-American work (especially "Methodologies," "Canon," "Tradition," and "History"), we do not wish to reinforce the oppositions between the two modes. The other seven sections show Anglo-American and French feminisms interacting and complementing each other within certain debates and within the work of individual scholars.

As we tried not to assign national labels to the critics we have reprinted, we also have avoided designating them by methodological orientation. Traditionally, anthologies of criticism are arranged either chronologically or by type of criticism (and, in such collections, "feminist criticism" is usually represented by one or two selections). We found that to try to describe any piece in this collection according to its method (to say, for instance, that something is "Marxist" or "deconstructionist" or "semiotic" criticism) would be greatly to oversimplify and misrepresent the complexity of what each of these feminist critics is doing. Most of these authors combine theoretical approaches in their work; some of them practice an eclecticism that defies categorization. We decided, therefore, to organize the book around a group of concepts that keep coming up in contemporary feminist critical debates.

Each concept that heads a section in *Feminisms* represents the topic of lively discussions among feminists through the 1980s and into the 1990s. Some words that might have been included on such a list ten years ago are not here ("archetype" and "chauvinism" come to mind), because the debates that centered on them seem to have closed down. But the words we chose come from a long list of current possibilities, including "domesticity," "imperialism," "lesbian," "authority," "the subject," "text," "pornography," "femininity," "the gaze," even "woman." All of these concepts—and many others—are subject to discussion today, in terms of what they signify within feminist academic politics and within literary texts and literary history. All of them come up more than once as issues among the selections we have made for this volume. The ideal collection of feminist criticism would devote sections to each of them.

The closest we could come to that ideal was thirteen sections, a number that strikes us as lucky. The introduction to each section explains how we construe its central concept, shows what the relation of each essay to that concept is (from our point of view), and identifies the basic theoretical and methodological assumptions behind each essay's argument. Most pieces could just as easily fit into several other sections of the book; to facilitate discussion of how the issues intersect, we have provided an index, in the back of this volume, suggesting alternative organizations for this material.

The organization of *Feminisms* is ultimately arbitrary—in that way, the volume most strikingly resembles a quilt. We have cut out and stitched together pieces of criticism, and we have laid them out in a pattern that imposes a sense of coherence the pieces themselves might not have fallen into of their own accord. But, like the components of a quilt, those pieces all maintain their own integrity. Pulled together into the fabric of feminist criticism, the pieces acquire a new form and new function in *Feminisms*. We hope our readers will be critical, actively considering the value not just of individual pieces, but of the governing design. We hope, too, that readers who become newly acquainted with these pieces will be moved to go back to the bolts from which they have been cut, to acquire a comfortable familiarity with all the material of feminist criticism and theory.

ACKNOWLEDGMENTS

In this collaboration, we have come to rely a great deal on each other, but without the help of many other people, *Feminisms* could never have happened. We are particularly grateful for the financial support from the University of Vermont Women's Studies program, directed by Joan Smith. That grant, together with the material support that came through Virginia Clark, Chair of the English Department at UVM, enabled us to finish the project in half the time we thought it would take.

Ed White, our research assistant, deserves special appreciation for the rigor and efficiency of the work he did for us. We could ask on Monday for a list of every article ever published in a particular category of feminist criticism, and it would be in our hands by Wednesday. Without his hard work, resourcefulness, and insight, the correspondence and research necessary to a project of this scale would have been unmanageable.

We are grateful, too, to the undergraduate work-study students who helped us with correspondence and manuscript preparation, Willow Older and Mary Thompson. We extend our thanks to Sandy Greiner and Kim McMeekin, who provided willing and efficient secretarial support.

Several people read drafts of our introductions, making suggestions that affected the way we were thinking about what we were doing. For these contributions, we would like to thank Helena Michie, Beth Kowaleski Wallace, Philippe Carrard, and especially Carl Herndl.

Many of the scholars represented in this volume were instrumental in making it possible for us to use their work; our thanks go to Dale Bauer, Catharine R. Stimpson, Annette Kolodny, Jane Marcus, Nancy Armstrong, Myra Jehlen, Gayatri Chakravorty Spivak, Sidonie Smith, Bonnie Zimmerman, Leslie Rabine, Susan Stanford Friedman, Paul Lauter, Linda Kauffman, and Sue Lanser. Their enthusiasm sustained us in sometimes trying circumstances.

Polly Mitchell at the Shelburne Museum was very kind in giving us an afternoon to browse through their quilt collection to find our cover art.

Leslie Mitchner, our editor at Rutgers, cannot be thanked enough for her support, her guidance, and her passion for this project. The rest of the staff at the

Press—Dina Bednarczyk, Adaya Henis, Marilyn Campbell, Stephen D. Mai-
kowski, Barbara Kopel, and John Romer have been super.

Finally, we'd like to dedicate this book to our students, past and present.

—Robyn R. Warhol and Diane Price Herndl
Burlington, Vermont
January 1991

FEMINISMS

institutions

We begin this anthology with "Institutions" and not with a category like "The Self" or "The Individual" as a way of highlighting the emphasis in current feminism on the group and on the systemic nature of women's oppression. In fact, recent work in feminism has begun to see how concepts like "self" or "individual" are themselves constructed within institutions. Institutions establish orderliness, rules, sameness; feminism questions whether that orderliness and sameness has been at the expense of the difference represented by women. The essays in this section explore how women's "otherness" from established patterns has caused their exclusion from various structures of power.

This section could, perhaps, have been called "Otherness"; each of the essays here focuses on how women's difference necessarily disrupts and disturbs the orderliness imposed by male-dominated systems. "Otherness" is itself almost always a matter of institutional definition; insuring homogeneity is often one of the most important tasks of the institution. Difference is excluded, overlooked, forced back into conformity with an artificial norm, or suppressed.

Feminists began this analysis from the outside, as people who had themselves been excluded from and oppressed by educational, religious, and governmental institutions. They tried to understand how oppression had become institutionalized, how it functioned, and how it could be changed. Barbara Ehrenreich and Deirdre English's *Complaints and Disorders: The Sexual Politics of Sickness* examined the medical establishment and its complicity with sexist norms; Phyllis Chesler did the same for the practice of psychiatry in *Women and Madness;* Nancy Chodorow, in *The Reproduction of Mothering*, and Adrienne Rich, in *Of Woman Born*, studied sexist norms in childraising, family structures, and the construction of "compulsory heterosexuality"; Mary Daly's *Beyond God the Father* and *The Church and the Second Sex* questioned the institutional sexism of religion; Catharine MacKinnon has, in numerous articles and *Feminism Unmodified*, examined women's relation to the law and the state; the field of feminist pedagogy has questioned how sexism affects the classroom and the educational system. These examples represent only a fraction of the feminist critique of institutions.

Feminist *literary* criticism has been a part of this challenge, questioning the most basic institutions of literary studies: how we evaluate literature, how we constitute knowledge about it, how its study is determined by the structure of the academy, and how it is separated from other disciplines. Out of the latter concern was born a whole new integrated field of inquiry: Women's Studies. From the other questions have come serious critiques of how literature is taught, why it is taught, and who teaches it. Literary study has been dramatically changed in the last two decades, largely as a result of the feminist critique of it *as* an institution.

It would be possible to argue that all the essays in this anthology are focused on some kind of institution; certainly, the sections on "Methodologies," "The Canon," and "Tradition" are direct questionings of some aspects of the literary/academic enterprise. The essays in this section, though, take on these questions directly as issues of institutionality; literary criticism, literary history, academic evaluation, and even feminist criticism are examined here as systems *per se.* They explore the construction, maintenance, and functioning of literary studies and/in the academy.

All four essays explore literary institutions in relation to some other cultural system: criticism, the history of Western thought, psychoanalysis, literary history, the family, academic advancement, and competitiveness. Each examines the interrelations of these structures and how they support one another; each considers the ways in which sexism institutionalized in one system contributes to sexism in another structure, sometimes even when the second system is deliberately working to avoid it.

Shoshana Felman examines the impact that Western, dichotomized thinking has had on literary criticism and women in "Women and Madness: The Critical Phallacy" (1975). Felman uses Jacques Derrida's analysis of the way that oppositional thinking dominates Western culture (we define things by their opposites, and impose hierarchy upon the opposition: man/woman, sane/insane, speech/silence, same/other) to show that traditional ways of defining woman always subordinate her in the opposition; she is man's "Other" and is therefore what he is not—insane and silent. Felman examines the impact of this opposition upon the critical institution when women begin to speak out, to declare that their point of view is sane; she begins her analysis with two books on women and madness: Phyllis Chesler's *Woman and Madness* and Luce Irigaray's *Speculum de l'autre femme* (part of which is reprinted in this volume). If woman is, by definition, both mad and silent, she asks, "how can the woman as such be speaking in [these books]? Who is speaking here, and who is asserting the otherness of the woman?" Although she cannot answer these two questions in this essay, she does point out that they represent the "major theoretical challenge of all contemporary thought," especially feminist thought. Felman turns from this central problem to a corollary one: how the classification of woman as other, insane, and silent makes its appearance in literary criticism. She uses a story by Balzac, "Adieu," and two critical essays on it to illustrate that readings of realism systematically exclude both women and madness. Traditional literary critique is blind to women, she argues; it is unable to theorize or visualize otherness. Her illustration reveals the difficult task facing the feminist critic: how to work against and from the outside of linguistic and critical institutions so that she will no longer be defined as mad, silent, Other, and invisible.

Jane Tompkins examines how "Otherness" has been excluded by American literary criticism in "Sentimental Power: *Uncle Tom's Cabin* and the Politics of Literary History" (1981). Sentimental novels of the nineteenth century operate according to a different aesthetic and toward a different end from novels of the period written by men, and that difference has led critics to ignore them for decades. What does it mean to compile lists of "American classics" when books like Harriet Beecher Stowe's *Uncle Tom's Cabin* are excluded? Tompkins argues that the sentimental has been systematically left off such lists because of its popularity, and because of its association with the feminine, with feelings. The sentimental novel, which "represents a monumental effort to reorganize culture from the woman's point of view" and attempts to institute a matriarchal society in America, challenges twentieth-century assumptions about the literary institution and men's place in it. Whereas traditional literary criticism has validated the modernist values of innovation and removal from the world of lived experience, sentimental literature explicitly tries to change the world and uses familiar forms, simple language, and recognizable situations to do so. In her study of sentimentality and literary history, Tompkins also examines how women have challenged the institutions of the family and politics. *Uncle Tom's Cabin*, she argues, offers a radically different world-view from that of "high-culture" fiction, and urges a fundamental revision of family and government. Stowe's novel—with its challenge to sexist and racist institutions—provides the ideal site for a challenge to the sexist institution of literary history.

Literary criticism takes place within and is part of a larger institution: the academy. James J. Sosnoski, in "A Mindless Man-driven Theory Machine: Intellectuality, Sexuality, and the Institution of Criticism" (1989), examines criticism as a product of educational and competitive career-oriented systems. Within a structure in which hiring, tenure, and promotion are based on competition, critical debate cannot be a matter of cooperation and collaboration, but must itself be competitive. Literature departments must be able to distinguish among candidates or to provide some grounds on which to make personnel decisions, and those grounds often take the form of a comparison to some ideal career-path, what Sosnoski calls the "Magister Implicatus," a model of the literary career that is consistently modeled on famous men's lives. These institutional pressures to compete, and the related critical institution itself, turn error—holding a mistaken notion—into what he calls "falsificity": a state equivalent to sinfulness, deserving of punishment. He argues that "in the institution of criticism, critical arguments which are judged false are judged so not on purely logical grounds, but on the grounds that they are 'sham, counterfeit, bogus or fake' discourses and therefore punishable." He argues for a new way of thinking about criticism that does not depend on truthfulness and falsehood, but on intuition and feeling, a new critical institution based not on competitiveness but on cooperation and collaboration.

In recent years, the feminist critique of institutions has taken a slightly different, self-reflexive turn. Feminists have begun to question each other and themselves, to examine their methods, goals, and alliances—and their own exclusions and possible oppression. In an essay written fourteen years after Shoshana Felman's, Helena Michie returns to the question of Otherness and feminist criticism. By 1989, when "Not One of the Family: The Repression of the Other Woman in Feminist Theory" was published, feminism had achieved the academic standing to be, arguably, an institution of its own, with its own blindnesses. Michie examines how feminism's reliance on metaphors from two other institutions, psychoanalysis and the family, has excluded a sense of "other women," outsiders, whether defined as outside the family—as sexual threat—or as Other in the sense of being different—third-world, lesbian, or antifeminist, for example. Feminism remains uneasy with Otherness, so the "other woman" is often either displaced or incorporated into sameness, even in feminist texts that explicitly set out to avoid doing so. Analyses of Catharine Stimpson's "Feminism and Feminist Criticism" and two essays by Jane Gallop, "The Monster in the Mirror: The Feminist Critic's Psychoanalysis" and "Annie Leclerc Writing a Letter, with Vermeer," reveal the difficulty of dealing with Otherness in feminist criticism. How can a feminist critic acknowledge Otherness without incorporating, colonizing, or taming it? In other words, how can Otherness remain Other? Michie challenges feminist critics to be careful about how they attempt to include the "other woman" so that they do not merely reinscribe the institution of sameness.

—DPH

WOMEN AND MADNESS
the critical phallacy

~-~

> Silence gives the proper grace to women.
>
> > SOPHOCLES, *AJAX*

> *Dalila:* In argument with men a woman ever
> > Goes by the worse, whatever be her cause.
> *Samson:* For want of words, no doubt, or lack of breath!
>
> > MILTON, *SAMSON AGONISTES*

I. WOMAN AS MADNESS

Is it by chance that hysteria (significantly derived, as is well known, from the Greek word for "uterus") was originally conceived as an exclusively *female* complaint, as the lot and *prerogative* of women? And is it by chance that even today, between women and madness, sociological statistics establish a privileged relation and a definite correlation? "Women," writes Phyllis Chesler, in her book *Women and Madness,* "Women more than men, and in greater numbers than their existence in the general population would predict, are involved in 'careers' as psychiatric patients" [p. xxii]. How is this sociological fact to be analyzed and interpreted? What is the nature of the relationship it implies between women and madness? Supported by extensive documentation, Phyllis Chesler proposes a confrontation between objective data and the subjective testimony of women: laced with the voices of women speaking in the first person—literary excerpts from the novels and autobiographies of woman writers, and word-for-word interviews with female psychiatric patients—the book derives and disputes a "female psychology" conditioned by an oppressive and patriarchal male culture. "It is clear that for a woman to be healthy she must 'adjust' to and accept the behavioral norms for her sex even though these kinds of behavior are generally regarded as less socially desirable. . . . The ethic of mental health is masculine in our culture" [pp. 68–69]. "The *sine qua non* of 'feminine' identity in patriarchal society is the violation of the incest taboo, i.e., the initial and continued 'preference' for Daddy, followed by the approved falling in love and/or marrying of powerful father figures" [p. 138]. From her initial family upbringing throughout her subsequent development, the social role assigned to the woman is that of *serving* an image, authoritative and central, of man: a woman is first and foremost a daughter/a mother/a wife. "What we consider 'madness,' whether it appears in women or in men, is either the acting out of the devalued female role or the total or partial rejection of one's sex-role stereotype" [p. 56].

In contrast to the critical tendency currently in fashion in Europe, through which a certain French circle has allied itself philosophically with the controversial indictments of the English "anti-psychiatry" movement, Phyllis Chesler, although protesting in turn against psychiatry as such, in no way seeks to bestow upon madness the romanticized glamor of political protest and of social and cultural contestation: "It has never been my intention to romanticize madness, or to confuse it with political or cultural revolution" [p. xxiii]. Depressed and terrified women are not about to seize the means of production and reproduction: quite the opposite of rebellion, madness is the impasse confronting those whom cultural conditioning has deprived of the very means of protest or self-affirmation. Far from being a form of contestation, "mental illness" is a *request for help,* a manifestation both of cultural impotence and of political castration. This socially defined help-needing and help-seeking behavior is itself part of female conditioning, ideologically inherent in the behavioral pattern and in the dependent and helpless role assigned to the woman as such.

It is not the material, social, and psychological female condition, but rather the very *status of womanhood* in Western *theoretical* discourse which concerns Luce Irigaray in her recently published book, *Speculum de l'autre femme.* In contrast to Phyllis Chesler, Luce Irigaray interrogates not the empirical voice of women and their subjective testimony, but the key theoretical writings of men—fundamental texts in philosophy and in psychoanalysis—which, in one way or another, involve the concept of femininity. Her study focuses on the text of Freud's (fictive) lecture entitled "On Femininity" and on the feminine metaphors in Plato's myth of the Cave. A psychoanalyst herself, Luce Irigaray adopts the traditional feminist critique of the male-centered orientation and of the anti-feminine bias in psychoanalytical theory; but her elaboration and consolidation of these classical feminist arguments is derived from the current philosophical methods of thinking developed in France by Jacques Derrida and others in their attempt to work out a general critical "deconstruction" of Western metaphysics. According to Derrida's radicalization of the Nietzschean and Heideggerian critiques of traditional philosophy, Western metaphysics is based on the totalitarian principle of so-called "logocentrism," that is, on the repressive predominance of "logos" over "writing," on the privileged status of the present and the consequent valorization of presence. This *presence-to-itself* of a *center* (given the name of Origin, God, Truth, Being, or Reason) centralizes the world through the authority of its self-presence and subordinates to itself, in an agonistic, hierarchical manner, all the other cognizable elements of the same epistemological (or ontological) system. Thus, the metaphysical logic of dichotomous oppositions which dominates philosophical thought (Presence/Absence, Being/Nothingness, Truth/Error, Same/Other, Identity/Difference, etc.) is, in fact, a subtle mechanism of hierarchization which assures the unique valorization of the "positive" pole (that is, of a *single* term) and, consequently, the repressive subordination of all "negativity," the mastery of difference as such. It is by thus examining the mere illusion of duality and the repressive way in which the polarity Masculine/Feminine functions in Western thought so as to privilege a unique term, that Luce Irigaray proceeds to develop her critical argument. Theoretically subordinated to the concept of masculinity, the woman is viewed by the man as *his* opposite, that is to say, as *his* other, the negative of the positive, and not, in her own right, different, other, Otherness itself. Throughout the Platonic metaphors which will come to dominate Western discourse and to act as a vehicle for meaning, Luce Irigaray points out a latent design to exclude the woman from the production of speech, since the woman, and the Other as such, are philosophically subjugated to the logical principle of Identity—Identity being conceived as a solely *masculine* sameness, apprehended as *male* self-presence and consciousness-to-itself. The possibility of a thought which would neither spring from nor return to this masculine Sameness is simply unthinkable. Plato's text thus establishes the repressive systematization of the logic of identity: the privilege of "oneness," of the reproduction of likeness, of the repetition of sameness, of literal meaning, analogy, symmetry, dichotomous oppositions, teleological projects.

Freud, who for the first time freed thought from a certain conception of the present and of presence-to-oneself, whose notions of deferred action, of the unconscious, of the death instinct, and of the repetition compulsion radically undermine the classical logic of identity, remains, nevertheless, himself a prisoner of philosophy when he determines the nature of sexual difference in function of the *a priori* of sameness, that is, of the male phallus. Female sexuality is thus described as an absence (of the masculine presence), as lack, incompleteness, deficiency, envy with respect to the only sexuality in which value resides. This symmetrical conception of otherness is a theoretical blindness to the woman's actual Difference, which is currently asserting itself, and asserting precisely its claim to a new kind of logic and a new type of theoretical reasoning.

A question could be raised: if "the woman" is precisely the Other of any conceivable Western theoretical locus of speech, how can the woman as such be speaking in this book? Who is speaking here, and who is asserting the otherness of the woman? If, as Luce Irigaray suggests, the woman's silence, or the repression of her capacity to speak, are constitutive of philosophy and of theoretical discourse as such, from what theoretical locus is Luce Irigaray herself speaking in order to develop her own theoretical discourse about the woman's exclusion? Is she speaking the language of men, or the silence of women? Is she speaking as a woman, or *in place of* the (silent) woman, *for* the woman, *in the name of* the woman? Is it enough to be a woman in order to *speak as* a woman? Is "speaking as a woman" a fact determined by some biological *condition* or by a strategic, theoretical *position*, by anatomy[1] or by culture? What if "speaking as a woman" were not a simple "natural" fact, could not be taken for granted? With the increasing number of women and men alike who are currently choosing to share in the rising fortune of female misfortune, it has become all too easy to be a speaker "*for* women." But what does "speaking *for* women" imply? What is "to speak *in the name of* the woman?" What, in a general manner, does "speech in the name of" mean? Is it not a precise repetition of the oppressive gesture of *representation*, by means of which, throughout the history of logos, man has reduced the woman to the status of a silent and subordinate object, to something inherently *spoken for?* To "speak in the name of," to "speak *for*," could thus mean, once again, to appropriate and to silence. This important theoretical question about the status of its own discourse and its own "representation" of women, with which any feminist thought has to cope, is not thought out by Luce Irigaray, and thus remains the blind spot of her critical undertaking.

In a sense, the difficulty involved in any feminist enterprise is illustrated by the complementarity, but also by the incompatibility, of the two feminist studies which we have just examined: the works of Phyllis Chesler and Luce Irigaray. The interest of Chesler's book, its overwhelming persuasive power as an outstanding clinical document, lies in the fact that it does *not* speak *for* women: it lets women speak for themselves. Phyllis Chesler accomplishes thus the first symbolical step of the feminist revolution: she *gives voice* to the woman. But she can only do so in a pragmatic, empirical way. As a result, the book's theoretical contribution, although substantial, does not go beyond the classical feminist thought concerning the socio-sexual victimization of women. On the other side of the coin, Irigaray's book has the merit of perceiving the problem on a theoretical level, of trying to think the feminist question through to its logical ends, reminding us that women's oppression exists not only in the material, practical organization of economic, social, medical, and political structures, but also in the very foundations of logos, reasoning, and articulation—in the subtle linguistic procedures and in the logical processes through which meaning itself is produced. It is not clear, however, that statement and utterance here coincide so as to establish actual feminine difference, not only on the thematic, but also on the rhetorical level: although the otherness of the woman is here fully assumed as the subject of the statement, it is not certain whether that otherness can be taken for granted as positively occupying the unthought-out, problematical locus *from which* the statement is being *uttered*.

In the current attempt at a radical questioning and a general "deconstruction" of the whole range of cultural codes, feminism encounters the major theoretical challenge of all contemporary thought. The problem, in fact, is common to the revaluation of madness as well as to the contention of women: how can one speak from the place of the Other? How can the woman be thought about outside of the Masculine/Feminine framework, *other* than as opposed to man, without being subordinated to a primordial masculine model? How can madness, in a similar way, be conceived outside of its dichotomous opposition to sanity, without being subjugated to reason? How can difference as such be thought out as *non-subordinate* to identity? In other words, how can thought break away from the logic of polar oppositions?

In light of these theoretical challenges, and in keeping with the feminist questioning of psychoanalytical and philosophical discourse, it could be instructive to examine the ideological effects of the very production of meaning in the language of literature and in its critical exegesis. We therefore propose here to undertake a reading of a text by Balzac which deals with the woman as well as with madness and to examine the way in which this text, and its portrayal of feminine madness, has been traditionally perceived and commented upon. The text—entitled "Adieu"—is a short story first published in 1830, and later included by Balzac in the volume of *Philosophical Studies* of the *Comédie humaine*.

II. THE REALISTIC INVISIBLE

The story is divided into three parts. The first describes a mysterious domain into which have inadvertently wandered two lost hunters: Philippe de Sucy, a former colonel, and his friend d'Albon, a magistrate. Anxious to find out where they are, they turn to two women, the only human beings in the vicinity, but their questions meet only silence: one of the women, Geneviève, turns out to be a deaf-mute, and the other, an aphasic madwoman whose entire vocabulary consists of the word "adieu." On hearing this word, Philippe faints, recognizing in the madwoman his former mistress Countess Stéphanie de Vandières, who had accompanied him to Russia during the Napoleonic Wars but whom he has not seen again since their separation on the banks of the Berezina River and whose trace he has ever since been unable to recover.

The second part is a flashback to the war episode. Among the collapsing masses of the retreating French army, Stéphanie and Philippe are fighting against unbearable cold, inhuman exhaustion and debilitating hunger, in the midst of the snowy plains. Philippe heroically shields Stéphanie in the hope of crossing the Berezina and of thus reaching and having her reach the safety of the other side, free from the Russian threat. But when it turns out that only two places are left on the life raft, Philippe leaves them to Stéphanie and her husband, the Count of Vandières, sacrificing himself for the latter. The Count, however, never reaches the other side: in a violent jolt during the crossing, he is swept overboard and killed. Stéphanie cries out to Philippe, "Adieu!": it is to be her last lucid word before she loses her reason. For two years thereafter, she continues to be dragged along by the army, the plaything of wretched riffraff. Mad and cast off like an animal, she is discovered one day after the end of the war by her uncle, an elderly doctor, who takes her in and sees to her needs.

The third part describes the combined efforts of the two men—the doctor having been joined by Philippe—to save and to cure Stéphanie. Stéphanie, on seeing Philippe, fails to recognize him: her continuous repetition of the word "adieu" implies no understanding and bears no relation to conscious memory. At the sight of the "stranger" (Philippe), she runs away like a frightened animal. Following the advice of the doctor, Philippe learns how to "tame" Stéphanie by giving her sugar cubes, thus accustoming her to his presence. Philippe still hopes that Stéphanie will some day recognize him. Driven to despair, however, by the long wait, Philippe decides to hasten Stéphanie's recognition of him by subjecting her to a psychodrama designed to restore her memory: he artificially creates a replica of the Russian plains and of the Berezina River; using peasants disguised as soldiers, he theoretically reconstructs and replays before the madwoman's eyes the exact scene of their wartime separation. Stéphanie is thus indeed cured: overwhelmed, she recognizes Philippe, smiles to him, repeats once again "adieu"; but at that very instant she dies.

A current pocket edition of this amazing story (recently published by Gallimard in the "Folio" collection) insures, in two different ways, its critical presentation: the text is preceded and followed by pedagogical commentary—a Preface by Pierre Gascar and a "Notice" by Philippe Berthier—which are supposed to "explain" it and "situate" its importance. It is striking that, of the three chapters which constitute this short story—the discovery of the madwoman in the mysterious domain, the war scene, and the scene of the cure—*both* commentators discuss only one: the chapter depicting the war. The main plot, which consists of the story of a woman's madness (episodes I and III), is somehow completely neglected in favor of the subplot (episode II), a historical narrative whose function is to describe the events which preceded and occasioned the madness. The "explication" thus excludes two things: the madness and the woman. Viewed through the eyes of the two academic critics, "Adieu" becomes a story about the suffering of men in which the real protagonists are none but "the soldiers of the Grand Army." The "Préface" indeed makes a great point of praising Balzac for "the realism, unprecedented in the history of literature, with which the war is here depicted" [p. 9]:[2] "by showing us, in 'Adieu,' the soldiers of the Grand Army haggard, half dead with hunger and cold, draped in rags, surging toward the pontoon bridge thrown across the Berezina, he [Balzac] deals with the myth of military grandeur . . . a blow whose repercussions extend well beyond the post-Napoleonic era" [pp. 10–11]. This supposedly "objective" reading of what is called Balzac's "realism" in fact screens out and disguises an ideological pattern of textual amputations and cuts, in which only a *third* of the text is brought to the reader's attention. "Indeed," concedes the Preface's author, "these scenes do not take up much room in . . . "Adieu," where most of the action occurs subsequent to the historic events which they symbolize. *But they suffice* to give the war its true countenance" [p. 12]. As for the author of the "Notice," he does not even seek to justify the arbitrary, disproportionate cuts underlying his "explication"—by putting forward a *truth* "which suffices": "the *true* countenance of the war. In line with the academic tradition of "selected passages," he proposes, simply and "innocently," literally to *cut up* the text, to *extract* the second chapter, and truly materialize the operation of ideological extirpation with a serene pedagogical confidence: "the second chapter, *which can be isolated from the work* as was the story of Goguelat from the *Country Doctor* (cf. our edition of this novel in Folio) marks the appearance in Balzac's work of the theme of the wartime disappearance of an officer who comes back many years later" [p. 266]. The story is here explicitly summed up as being exclusively that of a man: that of "the wartime disappearnce of *an officer* who comes back many years later." It is, therefore, by no means surprising to see the author of the "Notice" taken aback by the fact—to him incomprehensible—that in its second version this text could have been, as he puts it, "oddly entitled" *A Woman's Duty* [p. 265]. Evident in an abandoned title, but in the text neither seen nor heard, the woman does not belong to the realm of the "explicable"; her claim to commentary is solely an inexplicable piece of knowledge, an unusable article of erudition.

It is just in this manner that the institution of literary criticism pronounces its expert, professional discourse, without even noticing the conspicuousness of its flagrant misogyny. To the *sociological* sexism of the educational system corresponds, in this case, the naive, though by no means innocent, sexism of the exegetical system of *literary analysis*, of the academic and pedagogical fabrication of "literary" and critical discourse. By guiding the reader, through the extirpation of "explicable" facts, to the "correct" perception, to the literal, "proper," so-called "objective" level of textual interpretation, academic criticism conditions the very norms of "legibility." Madness and women, however, turn out to be the two outcasts of the establishment of readability. An ideological conditioning of literary and critical discourse, a political orientation of reading thus affirms itself, not so much through the negative treatment of women as through their total neglect, their pure and simple *omission*. This critical oversight, which appears as a *systematic* blindness to significant facts, functions as a censorship mechanism, as a symbolic eradication of women from the world of literature. It is therefore essential to examine the theoretical presuppositions which permit and sanction this kind of blindness.

We have seen that what is invoked so as to authorize the arbitrariness of the curtailment of the text is the critical concept of Balzac's "realism": the realism of *war,* "unprecedented"—as the Preface puts it—"in the history of literature." In the context of this manly realism, the woman is relegated to non-existence, since she is said to partake of the "unreal": "Beside the Berezina . . . Stéphanie's carriage, blocked among hordes of French soldiers savage with hunger and shock, becomes the *unwonted, almost unreal element* in which the whole absurdity of the situation bursts out" [pp. 11–12]. What, then, is this "realism" the critic here ascribes to Balzac, if not the assumption, not shared by the text, that what happens to men is more important, and/or more "real," than what happens to women? A subtle boundary line, which gives itself as a "natural frontier," is thus traced, in the critical vocabulary, between the realm of the "real" and that of the "unreal," between the category of "realism" and that of the so-called "supernatural": "While Colonel Chabert contains no *supernatural* elements . . . 'Adieu' allots a great deal of space to psychic phenomena, with Stéphanie's madness, and even to parapsychic phenomena, with her death. . . . It is noteworthy . . . that Balzac's short stories . . . devote infinitely more space to the *supernatural,* to the presence of the *invisible* . . . than do his novels. . . . In these four stories where it exists side by side with the most striking *realism, the marvellous* is in fact only represented by the *state of semi-unreality* which the main characters attain through the horror of their ordeal. We here come across . . . the romantic conception of the transfiguring power of suffering" [p. 14–17]. The "supernatural," as everyone knows, cannot be rationally explained and hence should not detain us and does not call for *thought.* Flattened out and banalized into the "edifying conclusion" [p. 17] of the beneficent power of suffering, Stéphanie's madness is *not problematic,* does not deserve to detain us, since it is but a "state of semi-unreality." Realism thus postulates a conception of "nature" and of "reality" which seeks to establish itself, tautologically, as "natural" and as "real." Nothing, indeed, is less neutral than this apparent neutrality; nothing is less "natural" than this frontier which is supposed to separate "the real" from "the unreal" and which in fact delimits only the inside and the outside of an ideological circle: an inside which is *inclusive* of "reason" and men, i.e., "reality" and "nature"; and an outside which is *exclusive* of madness and women, i.e., the "supernatural" and the "unreal." And since the supernatural is linked, as the critic would have it, to "the presence of the invisible" [p. 16], it comes as no surprise to find the woman predestined to be, precisely, *the realistic invisible,* that which realism as such is inherently unable to see.

> It is the whole field of a problematic, which defines and structures the invisible as its definite outside—excluded from the domain of visibility and defined as excluded by the existence and the structure of the problematic field itself. . . . The invisible is defined by the visible as *its* invisible, *its* prohibited sight. . . . To see this invisible . . . requires something quite different from a sharp or attentive eye, it takes an *educated* eye, a revised, renewed way of looking, itself produced by the effect of a "change of terrain" reflected back upon the act of seeing. [Louis Althusser, *Lire le Capital,* I (Paris: Maspero, 1968), pp. 26–28; translation mine; Althusser's italics]

With a "revised" way of looking, "educated" by the "change of terrain" brought about by the feminist interrogation, let us now attempt to reread Balzac's text and to reinterpret its relation to the woman as well as to madness.

III. "SHE? WHO?"

From the very beginning the woman in this text stands out as a problem. The opening pages present the reader with a series of abstract questions concerning a female identity: the two lost hunters are trying to situate themselves, to ascertain the identity of the woman they have just glimpsed in the unknown place into which they have wandered: "Where the devil are we? . . . She, who? . . . Where are we? What is that house? Whose is it? Who are you? Do you live here? . . . But who is this lady? . . . She? Who? . . ." [pp. 148, 156, 159, 164].

The reader, too, cannot get his bearings: deluged with questions, at the same time deprived systematically of information, not really knowing *who* is speaking, much less about whom, he is in turn as *lost* in the text as the two protagonists are in geographical space. The text thus originates in the *loss* of the very conditions of localization and identification, in a general state of confusion from which, in an almost anonymous manner, a recurrent question emerges: "She? Who?" The feminine pronoun preceding any proper denomination, the ambiguous question preceding any informative clarification, this preliminary inquiry takes on an abstractly emphatic and allegorical character, and seems to situate from the start the textual problematic within a systematic search for the nature of feminine identity. From the beginning, however, the question reaches a dead end: addressed to the women themselves, the query meets only silence, since both women here are deprived of the ability to speak. Addressed to others, the question obtains only distant and hypothetical answers: "But who is this lady? . . . It is presumed that she comes from Moulins . . . she is said to be mad. . . . I wouldn't guarantee you the truth of these rumors" [p. 164].

The allegorical question "She? Who?" will thus remain unanswered. The text, nonetheless, will play out the question to its logical end, so as to show in what way it *precludes* any answer, in what way the question is set as a trap. The very *lack of the answer* will then write itself as a *different* question, through which the original question will find itself dislocated, radically shifted and transformed.

"She? Who?" The women cannot respond: mad, they do not understand the men's questions. Nor do the rational men understand the senseless words of the women. But the women, though mad, understand each other. The doctor thus interprets the friendship that seems to unite Stéphanie and the peasant Geneviève: "Here . . . she has found another creature she seems to get along with. It's an idiot peasant-woman. . . . My niece and this poor girl are in a way united by the invisible chain of their common destiny, and by the feeling that causes their madness" [p. 196]. Understanding occurs in this text only on one side *or* the other of the boundary line which, separating silence from speech, distinguishes madness from reason. It is nonetheless striking that the dichotomy Reason/Madness, as well as Speech/Silence, exactly coincides in this text with the dichotomy Men/Women. Women as such are associated both with madness and with silence, whereas men are identified with prerogatives of discourse and of reason. In fact, men appear not only as the possessors, but also as the dispensers, of reason, which they can at will mete out to—or take away from—others. While Philippe and the doctor undertake to "restore Stéphanie's reason," the magistrate, on the other hand, brags: "If you should ever bring a suit to court, *I would make you lose it, even if reason were a hundred per cent on your side*" [p. 150]. The three men in the story in fact symbolically represent—by virtue of their professions: magistrate, doctor, soldier—the power to *act upon* others' reason, in the name of the law, of health, or of force.

With respect to the woman's madness, man's reason reacts by trying to *appropriate* it: in the first place, by claiming to "understand" it, but with an external understanding which reduces the madwoman to a spectacle, to an *object* which can be *known* and *possessed*. "Go on, Sir, leave her alone," the doctor recommends to Philippe, "I know how to live with the dear little creature; I *understand* her madness, I *spy upon* her gestures, I am in on her secrets" [pp. 208–209]. To "spy on" in order to "know"; to "tame" in order to "cure": such are the methods used by masculine reason so as to *objectify* feminine madness, thereby mastering it. If the madwoman is throughout the story seen as and compared to an animal, this pervasive metaphor tells us less about Stéphanie's delirium than about the logic of her therapists. For the object is precisely to capture the animal and to tame it. Thus we see the symbolic import of the initial hunting scene. A metaphorical parody of the episode of the war and of its martial logic ("'Come on, deputy, forward! Double time! Speed up . . . march over the ruts. . . . Come on, march! . . . If you sit down, you're lost'" [pp. 147, 151]), the opening scene of the hunt already symbolically prefigures Philippe's attitude toward Stéphanie: "Come on," cries Philippe from the very first, not yet knowing whom he is talking about, but integrating as a matter of course the woman into his hunter's mentality; "Come on, let's run after the white and black lady! Forward!" [p. 157]. But the hunter's chase will here be but the measure of the flight of his prey.

If masculine reason thus constitutes a scheme to capture and master, indeed, metaphorically *rape* the woman, by the same token, Stéphanie's madness is not contingent on but directly related to her femininity: consisting, precisely, in its loss. Several times Philippe, in fact, explicitly defines Stéphanie's madness as the loss of her womanhood. When the doctor advises him to tame her by feeding her pieces of sugar, Philippe sadly answers: "*When she was a woman*, she had no taste for sweets" [p. 202]. And again, in a burst of sorrow, Philippe cries: "I die a little more every day, every minute! My love is too great! I could bear everything if only, in her madness, she had kept some *semblance of femininity*" [p. 208]. Madness, in other words, is precisely what makes a woman *not a woman*. But what is a "woman"? Woman is a "name," denied in fact to Geneviève in the same way as it is denied to Stéphanie: "Then *a woman*, if such a *name* can be applied to the *undefinable being* who got up from under the bushes, pulled on the cow by its rope" [p. 159]. "Woman" is consequently a "definable being"—chained to a "definition" itself implying a model, a definition commanded by a *logic of resemblance*. Even in the war scene, Stéphanie had already lost her "femininity." "[When] all rolled around herself, *she really resembled nothing*. . . . Was this that *charming woman*, the *glory of her lover*, the *queen of the Parisian ballrooms*? Alas! even the eyes of her most devoted friend could perceive *nothing feminine* left in that heap of linens and rags" [p. 180]. If a "woman" is strictly, exactly, "what *resembles* a woman" ("she really resembled nothing . . . nothing feminine left"), it becomes apparent that "femininity" is much less a "natural" category than a rhetorical one, analogical and metaphorical: a metaphorical category which is explicitly bound, as perceived by Philippe, to a sociosexual stereotype, to the "definable" role of the mistress—"the queen of the Parisian ballrooms." Of course, the "queen" here implies a king; the literal, *proper* meaning of metaphorical femininity, paradoxically enough, turns out to be a masculine property: the "queen of the Parisian ballrooms," "that charming woman," is above all *The glory of her lover.*" "Woman," in other words, is the exact metaphorical measure of the narcissism of man.

The Masculine thus turns out to be the universal equivalent of the opposition: Masculine/Feminine. It is insofar as Masculinity conditions Femininity as its universal equivalent, as what determines and measures its value, that the textual paradox can be created according to which the woman is "madness," while at the same time "madness" is the very "absence of womanhood." The woman is "madness" to the extent that she is Other, *different* from man. But "madness" is the "absence of womanhood" to the extent that "womanhood" is what precisely resembles the Masculine universal equivalent, in the polar division of sexual roles. If so, the woman is "madness" since the woman is *difference;* but "madness" is "non-woman" since madness is the *lack of resemblance.* What the narcissistic economy of the Masculine universal equivalent tries to eliminate, under the label "madness," is nothing other than *feminine difference.*

IV. THE THERAPEUTIC FALLACY

Such is the male narcissistic principle on which the system of reason, with its therapeutic ambition, is based. For, to "restore Stéphanie's reason" signifies, precisely, to reinstate her "femininity": to make her *recognize man,* the "lover" whose "glory" she ought to be. "I'm going to the Bons-Hommes," says Philippe, "to see her, speak to her, *cure* her. . . . Do you think the poor woman would be able to *hear me* and *not recover her reason?*" [p. 197]. In Philippe's mind, "to recover her reason" becomes synonymous with "to hear *me.*" "The cure of the madman," writes Michel Foucault, "is in the reason of the other—his own reason being but the very truth of his madness" [*Histoire de la folie à l'âge classique* (Paris: Gallimard, 1972), p. 540; translation mine]. Stéphanie's cure is in Philippe's reason. The "recovery" of her reason must thus necessarily entail an act of recognition.

> "She doesn't recognize me," cried the colonel in despair.
> "Stéphanie! it's Philippe, your Philippe, Philippe!" [pp. 200–201]
> "Her; not to recognize me, and to run away from me," repeated the colonel. [p. 201]
> "My love," he said, ardently kissing the countess' hands, "I am Philippe." "Come," he added, . . . "Philippe is not dead, he is here, you are sitting on his lap. You are my Stéphanie, and I am your Philippe." "Adieu," she said, "adieu." [p. 207]

Stéphanie's recovery of her "reason," the restoration of her femininity as well as of her identity, depends then, in Philippe's eyes, on her specular recognition of *him*, on her *reflection* of his own name and of his own identity. If the question of female identity remains in the text unanswered, it is simply because it is *never* truly asked: in the guise of asking, "She? Who?", Philippe is in fact always asking "I? Who?"—a false question, the answer to which he believes he knows in advance: "It's Philippe." The question concerning the woman is thereby transformed into the question of a guarantee for men, a question through which nothing is questioned, whose sole function is to insure the validity of its predefined answer: "You are *my* Stéphanie." The use of the possessive adjective makes explicit the act of appropriation focused here on the *proper* names. But it is from Stéphanie's own mouth that Philippe must obtain his proper name, his guarantee of the propriety of his own identity, and of hers: Stéphanie = Philippe, "You are my Stéphanie, and I am your Philippe." In Philippe's eyes, Stéphanie is viewed above all as an object, whose role is to insure, by an interplay of reflections, his own self-sufficiency as a "subject," to serve as a mediator in his own specular relationship with himself. What Philippe pursues in the woman is not a face, but a mirror, which, reflecting his image, will thereby *acknowledge* his narcissistic *self-image*. "Women," writes Virginia Woolf, "have served all these centuries as looking-glasses possessing the magic and delicious power of reflecting the figure of man at twice its natural size." Philippe, as it turns out, desires not *knowledge* of Stéphanie herself but her *acknowledgement* of him: his therapeutic design is to restore her not to *cognition*, but to *recognition*.

To this demand for recognition and for the restoration of identity through language, through the authority of proper names, Stéphanie opposes, in the figure of her madness, the dislocation of any transitive, communicative language, of "propriety" as such, of any correspondence or transparency joining "names" to "things," the blind opacity of a lost signifier unmatched by any signified, the pure recurrent difference of a word detached from both its meaning and its context.

> "Adieu," she said in a soft harmonious voice, but whose melody, impatiently perceived by the expectant hunters, seemed to divulge not the slightest feeling or the least idea. [p. 163]
>
> "Adieu, adieu, adieu!" she said, without her soul's conferring any perceptible inflection upon the word. [p. 200]

To this automatic repetition of senselessness and difference, Philippe in turn will oppose another type of repetition designed precisely to restore resemblance and identity: in order to cure Stéphanie, in order to restore to her demented, dislocated language its nominative and communicative function, he decides to *re-produce* the primal scene of the "adieu" and thus to *re-present* theatrically the errant signifier's lost significance, its proper *signifié*. Without her knowledge, Stéphanie will literally be forced to play herself, to return to her "proper" role. Through the theatrical set-up, everything will end up making sense: and, with all difference thus erased, re-presentation necessarily will bring about the desired re-cognition.

> The baron [de Sucy] had, inspired by a dream, conceived a plan to restore the countess' reason. . . . He devoted the rest of the autumn to the preparation of this immense enterprise. A small river flowed through his park, where

in, the winter, it flooded an extensive marsh which *resembled* . . . the one running along the right bank of the Berezina. The village of Satou, set on a hill, added the final touch to *put this scene of horror in its frame*. . . . The colonel gathered a troop of workers to dig a canal which would represent the voracious river. . . . Thus aided by his memory, Philippe succeeded in *copying* in his park the riverbank where General Elbé had built his bridges. . . . The colonel assembled pieces of debris *similar* to what his fellow sufferers had used to construct their raft. He ravaged his park, in an effort to *complete the illusion* on which he pinned his last hopes. . . . In short, he had forgotten nothing that could reproduce the most horrible of all scenes, and he reached his goal. Toward the beginning of December, when the snow had blanketed the earth with a white coat, he *recognized* the Berezina. This false Russia was of such appalling truth that several of his comrades *recognized* the scene of their former sufferings. Monsieur de Sucy kept the secret of this tragic *representation*. [pp. 209–10]

The cure succeeds. However, so as to fulfill perfectly her "Woman's Duty," to play her role correctly in this theater of the identical, to recognize specularly and reflect perfectly Philippe's "identity," Stéphanie herself must disappear: she has to *die* as *Other*, as a "subject" in her own right. The tragic outcome of the story is inevitable, inscribed as it is from the outset in the very logic of representation inherent in the therapeutic project. Stéphanie will die; Philippe will subsequently commit suicide. If, as ambiguous as it is, the cure turns out to be a murder, this murder, in its narcissistic dialectic, is necessarily suicidal,[3] since, killing Stéphanie in the very enterprise of "saving" her,[4] it is also his own image that Philippe strikes in the mirror.

Through this paradoxical and disconcerting ending, the text subverts and dislocates the logic of representation which it has dramatized through Philippe's endeavor and his failure. Literature thus breaks away from pure representation: when transparency and meaning, "reason" and "representation" are regained, when madness ends, so does the text itself. Literature, in this way, seems to indicate its impuissance to dominate or to recuperate the madness of the signifier from which it speaks, its radical incapacity to master its own signifying repetition, to "tame" its own linguistic difference, to "represent" identity or truth. Like madness and unlike representation, literature can signify but not *make sense*.

Once again, it is amazing to what extent academic criticism, completely unaware of the text's irony, can remain blind to what the text says about itself. It is quite striking to observe to what extent the logic of the unsuspecting "realistic" critic can reproduce, one after the other, all of Philippe's delusions, which the text deconstructs and puts in question. Like Philippe, the "realistic" critic seeks representation, tries, by means of fiction, to reproduce "the real thing," to reconstruct, minutely and exhaustively, the exact historical Berezina scene. Like Philippe, the "realistic" critic is haunted by an obsession with proper names— identity and reference—sharing the same nostalgia for a transparent, transitive, communicative language, where everything possesses, unequivocally, a single meaning which can be consequently mastered and made clear, where each name "represents" a thing, where each signifier, properly and adequately, corresponds both to a signified and to a referent. On the critical as well as on the literary stage, the same attempt is played out to appropriate the signifier and to reduce its differential repetition; we see the same endeavor to do away with difference, the same policing of identities, the same design of mastery, of *sense-control*. For the "realistic" critic, as for Philippe, the readable is designed as a stimulus not for knowledge and cognition, but for acknowledgement and *re-cognition*, not for the *production* of a question, but for the *reproduction* of a foreknown answer—delimited within a pre-existing, pre-defined horizon, where the "truth" to be discovered is reduced to the natural status of a simple *given*, immediately perceptible, directly "representable" through the totally intelligible medium of transparent language. Exactly in the same way as Philippe, the commentators of "Adieu" are in turn taken in by the illusory security of a specularly structured act of recognition. Balzac's text, which applies as much to the "realistic" critic as to Philippe, can itself be read as a kind of preface to its own "Préface," as an ironic reading of its own academic reading.

For, what Philippe *misrecognizes* in his "realistic" recognition of the Berezina is, paradoxically enough, the *real:* the real not as a convergence of reflections, as an effect of mirroring focalization, but as a radically de-centering resistance; the real as, precisely, Other, the unrepresentable as such, the ex-centric residue which the specular relationship of vision cannot embrace.

Along with the illusions of Philippe, the "realistic" critic thus repeats, in turn, his allegorical act of murder, his obliteration of the Other: the critic also, in his own way, *kills the woman*, while killing, at the same time, the question of the text and the text as a question.

But, here again, as in Philippe's case, the murder is incorporated in an enterprise which can be seen as "therapeutic." For in obliterating difference, in erasing from the text the disconcerting and ex-centric features of a woman's madness, the critic seeks to "normalize" the text, to banish and eradicate all trace of violence and anguish, of scandal or insanity, making the text a reassuring, closed retreat whose balance no upheaval can upset, where no convulsion is of any consequence. "To drive these phantoms firmly back into their epoch, to close it upon them, by means of a historical narrative, this seems to have been the writer's intent" ["Préface," p. 8]. By reducing the story to a recognition scheme, familiar, snug and canny, the critic, like Philippe, "cures" the text, precisely of that which in it is incurably and radically uncanny.

From this paradoxical encounter between literature's critical irony and the uncritical naïveté of its critics, from this confrontation in which Balzac's text itself seems to be an ironic reading of its own future reading, the question arises: how *should* we read? How can a reading lead to something other than recognition, "normalization," and "cure"? How can the critical project, in other words, be detached from the therapeutic projection?

This crucial theoretical question, which undermines the foundations of traditional thought and whose importance the feminist writings have helped to bring out, pinpoints at the same time the difficulty of the woman's position in today's critical discourse. If, in our culture, the woman is by definition associated with madness, her problem is how to break out of this (cultural) imposition of madness *without* taking up the critical and therapeutic positions of reason: how to avoid speaking both as *mad* and as *not mad*. The challenge facing the woman today is nothing less than to "re-invent" language, to *re-learn how to speak:* to speak not only against, but outside of the specular phallogocentric structure, to establish a discourse the status of which would no longer be defined by the phallacy of masculine meaning. An old saying would thereby be given new life: today more than ever, changing our minds—changing *the* mind—is a woman's prerogative.

NOTES

1. Freud has thus pronounced his famous verdict on women: "Anatomy is destiny." But this is precisely the focus of the feminist contestation.

2. Quotations from the "Préface," the "Notice" and from Balzac's text are my translations; page numbers refer to the Gallimard/Folio edition; in all quoted passages, italics mine unless otherwise indicated.

3. This suicidal murder is, in fact, a repetition, not only of Philippe's military logic and his attitude throughout the war scene, but also of a specific previous moment in his relationship with Stéphanie. Well before the story's end, Philippe had already been on the point of killing Stéphanie, and himself with her, having, in a moment of despair, given up the hope of her ever recognizing him. The doctor, seeing through Philippe's intentions, had then saved his niece with a perspicacious lie, playing precisely on the specular illusion of the proper name: "'You do not know then,' went on the doctor coldly, hiding his horror, 'that last night in her sleep she said, "Philippe!"'' 'She named me,' cried the baron, letting his pistols drop" [p. 206].

4. Here again, the ambiguous logic of the "savior," in its tragic and heroic narcissism, is prefigured by the war scene. Convinced of his good reason, Philippe characteristically, *imposes* it, by force, on others, so as to "save" them; but ironically and paradoxically, he always saves them in spite of *themselves:* "'Let us save her in spite of herself!' cried Philippe, sweeping up the countess" [p. 182].

WORKS CITED

Balzac, Honoré de. *Adieu (Colonel Chabert, El Verdugo, Adieu, Requisitionnaire).* Ed. Patrick Berthier. Paris: Gallimard/Folio, 1974.

Chesler, Phyllis. *Women and Madness.* New York: Avon Books, 1973.

Irigaray, Luce. *Speculum de l'autre femme.* Paris: Minuit, 1974.

SENTIMENTAL POWER

uncle tom's cabin *and*
the politics of literary history

Once, during a difficult period of my life, I lived in the basement of a house on Forest Street in Hartford, Connecticut, which had belonged to Isabella Beecher Hooker—Harriet Beecher Stowe's half-sister. This woman at one time in her life had believed that the millennium was at hand and that she was destined to be the leader of a new matriarchy.[1] When I lived in that basement, however, I knew nothing of Stowe, or of the Beechers, or of the utopian visions of nineteenth-century American women. I made a reverential visit to the Mark Twain house a few blocks away, took photographs of his study, and completely ignored Stowe's own house—also open to the public—which stood across the lawn. Why should I go? Neither I nor anyone I knew regarded Stowe as a serious writer. At the time, I was giving my first lecture course in the American Renaissance—concentrated exclusively on Hawthorne, Melville, Poe, Emerson, Thoreau, and Whitman—and although *Uncle Tom's Cabin* was written in exactly the same period, and although it is probably the most influential book ever written by an American, I would never have dreamed of including it on my reading list. To begin with, its very popularity would have militated against it; as everybody knew, the classics of American fiction were, with a few exceptions, all succès d'estime.

In 1969, when I lived on Forest Street, the women's movement was just getting underway. It was several years before Chopin's *The Awakening* and Gilman's "The Yellow Wallpaper" would make it onto college reading lists, sandwiched in between Theodore Dreiser and Frank Norris. These women, like some of their male counterparts, had been unpopular in their own time and owed their reputations to the discernment of latter-day critics. Because of their work, it is now respectable to read these writers who, unlike Nathaniel Hawthorne, had to wait several generations for their champions to appear in the literary establishment. But despite the influence of the women's movement, despite the explosion of work in nineteenth-century American social history, and despite the new historicism that is infiltrating literary studies, the women, like Stowe, whose names were household words in the nineteenth century—women such as Susan Warner, Sarah J. Hale, Augusta Evans, Elizabeth Stuart Phelps, her daughter Mary, who took the same name, and Frances Hodgson Burnett—these women remain excluded from the literary canon. And while it has recently become fashionable to study their works as examples of cultural deformation, even critics who have invested their professional careers in that study and who declare themselves feminists still refer to their novels as trash.[2]

My principal target of concern, however, is not feminists who have written on popular women novelists of the nineteenth century, but the male-dominated scholarly tradition that controls both the canon of American literature (from which these novelists are excluded) and the critical perspective that interprets the canon for society. For the tradition of Perry Miller, F. O. Matthiessen, Harry Levin, Richard Chase, R. W. B. Lewis, Yvor Winters, and Henry Nash Smith has prevented even committed feminists from recognizing and asserting the *value* of a powerful and specifically female novelistic tradition. The very grounds on which sentimental fiction has been dismissed by its detractors, grounds which have come to seem universal standards of aesthetic judgment, were established in a struggle to supplant the tradition of evangelical piety and moral commitment these novelists represent. In reaction against their world view, and perhaps even more against their success, twentieth-century critics have taught generations of students to equate popularity with debasement, emotionality with ineffectiveness, religiosity with fakery, domesticity with triviality, and all of these, implicitly, with womanly inferiority.

In this view, sentimental novels written by women in the nineteenth century were responsible for a series of cultural evils whose effects still plague us: the degeneration of American religion from theological rigor to anti-intellectual consumerism, the rationalization of an unjust economic order, the propagation of the debased images of modern mass culture, and the encouragement of self-indulgence and narcissism in literature's most avid readers—women.[3] To the extent that they protested the evils of society, their protest is seen as duplicitous—the product and expression of the very values they pretended to condemn. Unwittingly or not, so the story goes, they were apologists for an oppressive social order. In contrast to male authors such as Thoreau, Whitman, and Melville, who are celebrated as models of intellectual daring and honesty, these women are generally thought to have traded in false stereotypes, dishing out weak-minded pap to nourish the prejudices of an ill-educated and under-employed female readership. Self-deluded and unable to face the harsh facts of a competitive society, they are portrayed as manipulators of a gullible public who kept their readers imprisoned in a dream world of self-justifying clichés. Their fight against the evils of their society was a fixed match from the start.[4]

The thesis I will argue in this chapter is diametrically opposed to these portrayals. It holds that the popular domestic novel of the nineteenth century represents a monumental effort to reorganize culture from the woman's point of view; that this body of work is remarkable for its intellectual complexity, ambition, and resourcefulness; and that, in certain cases, it offers a critique of American society far more devastating than any delivered by better-known critics such as Hawthorne and Melville. Finally, it suggests that the enormous popularity of these novels, which has been cause for suspicion bordering on disgust, is a reason for paying close attention to them. *Uncle Tom's Cabin* was, in almost any terms one can think of, the most important book of the century. It was the first American novel ever to sell over a million copies and its impact is generally thought to have been incalculable. Expressive of and responsible for the values of its time, it also belongs to a genre, the sentimental novel, whose chief characteristic is that it is written by, for, and about women. In this respect, *Uncle Tom's Cabin* is not exceptional but representative. It is the *summa theologica* of nineteenth-century America's religion of domesticity, a brilliant redaction of the culture's favorite story about itself—the story of salvation through motherly love. Out of the ideological materials at their disposal, the sentimental novelists elaborated a myth that gave women the central position of power and authority in the culture; and of these efforts *Uncle Tom's Cabin* is the most dazzling exemplar.

I have used words like "monumental" and "dazzling" to describe Stowe's novel and the tradition of which it is a part because they have for too long been the casualties of a set of critical attitudes that equate intellectual merit with a certain kind of argumentative discourse and certain kinds of subject matter. A long tradition of academic parochialism has enforced this sort of discourse through a series of cultural contrasts: light "feminine" novels vs. tough-minded intellectual treatises; domestic "chattiness" vs. serious thinking; and summarily, the "damned mob of scribbling women" vs. a few giant intellects, unappreciated and misunderstood in their time, struggling manfully against a flood of sentimental rubbish.[5]

The inability of twentieth-century critics either to appreciate the complexity and scope of a novel like Stowe's, or to account for its enormous popular success, stems from their assumptions about the nature and function of literature. In modernist thinking, literature is by definition a form of discourse that has no designs on the world. It does not attempt to change things, but merely to represent them, and it does so in a specifically literary language whose claim to value lies in its uniqueness. Consequently, works whose stated purpose is to influence the course of history, and which therefore employ a language that is not only not unique but common and accessible to everyone, do not qualify as works of art. Literary texts, such as the sentimental novel, that make continual and obvious appeals to the reader's emotions and use technical devices that are distinguished by their utter conventionality, epitomize the opposite of everything that good literature is supposed to be. "For the literary critic," writes J. W. Ward, summing up the dilemma posed by *Uncle Tom's Cabin*, "the problem is how a book so seemingly artless, so lacking in apparent literary talent, was not only an immediate success but has endured."[6]

How deep the problem goes is illustrated dramatically by George F. Whicher's discussion of Stowe's novel in *The Literary History of the United States*. Reflecting the consensus view on what good novels are made of, Whicher writes: "Nothing attributable to Mrs. Stowe or her handiwork can account for the novel's enormous vogue; its author's resources as a purveyor of Sunday-school fiction were not remarkable. She had at most a ready command of broadly conceived melodrama, humor, and pathos, and of these popular elements she compounded her book."[7] At a loss to understand how a book so compounded was able to "convulse a mighty nation," Whicher concludes—incredibly—that Stowe's own explanation that "God wrote it" "solved the paradox." Rather than give up his bias against "melodrama," "pathos," and "Sunday-school fiction," Whicher takes refuge in a solution that, even according to his lights, is patently absurd.[8] And no wonder. The modernistic literary aesthetic cannot account for the unprecedented and persistent popularity of a book like *Uncle Tom's Cabin*, for this novel operates according to principles quite other than those that have been responsible for determining the currently sanctified American literary classics.

It is not my purpose, however, to drag Hawthorne and Melville from their pedestals, nor to claim that the novels of Stowe, Fanny Fern, and Elizabeth Stuart Phelps are good in the same way that *Moby Dick* and *The Scarlet Letter* are; rather, I will argue that the work of the sentimental writers is complex and significant in ways *other than* those that characterize the established masterpieces. I will ask the reader to set aside some familiar categories for evaluating fiction—stylistic intricacy, psychological subtlety, epistemological complexity—and to see the sentimental novel not as an artifice of eternity answerable to certain formal criteria and to certain psychological and philosophical concerns, but as a political enterprise, halfway between sermon and social theory, that both codifies and attempts to mold the values of its time.

The power of a sentimental novel to move its audience depends upon the audience's being in possession of the conceptual categories that constitute character and event. That storehouse of assumptions includes attitudes toward the family and toward social institutions; a definition of power and its relation to individual human feeling; notions of political and social equality; and above all, a set of religious beliefs that organizes and sustains the rest. Once in possession of the system of beliefs that undergirds the patterns of sentimental fiction, it is possible for modern readers to see how its tearful episodes and frequent violations of probability were invested with a structure of meanings that fixed these works, for nineteenth-century readers, not in the realm of fairy tale or escapist fantasy, but in the very bedrock of reality. I do not say that we can read sentimental fiction exactly as Stowe's audience did—that would be impossible—but that we can and should set aside the modernistic prejudices which consign this fiction to oblivion, in order to see how and why it worked for its readers, in its time, with such unexampled effect.

Let us consider the episode in *Uncle Tom's Cabin* most often cited as the epitome of Victorian sentimentalism—the death of little Eva—because it is the kind of incident most offensive to the sensibilities of twentieth-century academic critics. It is on the belief that this incident is nothing more than a sob story that the whole case against sentimentalism rests. Little Eva's death, so the argument goes, like every other sentimental tale, is awash with emotion but does nothing to remedy the evils it deplores. Essentially, it leaves the slave system and the other characters unchanged. This trivializing view of the episode is grounded in assumptions about power and reality so common that we are not even aware they are in force. Thus generations of critics have commented with condescending irony on little Eva's death. But in the system of belief that undergirds Stowe's enterprise, dying is the supreme form of heroism. In *Uncle Tom's Cabin*, death is the equivalent not of defeat but of victory; it brings an access of power, not a loss of it; it is not only the crowning achievement of life, it *is* life, and Stowe's entire presentation of little Eva is designed to dramatize this fact.

Stories like the death of little Eva are compelling for the same reason that the story of Christ's death is compelling; they enact a philosophy, as much political as religious, in which the pure and powerless die to save the powerful and corrupt, and thereby show themselves more powerful than those they save. They enact, in short, a *theory* of power in which the ordinary or "common sense" view of what is efficacious and what is not (a view to which most modern critics are committed) is simply reversed, as the very possibility of social action is made dependent on the action taking place in individual hearts. Little Eva's death enacts the drama of which all the major episodes of the novel are transformations, the idea, central to Christian soteriology, that the highest human calling is to give one's life for another. It presents one version of the ethic of sacrifice on which the entire novel is based and contains in some form all of the motifs that, by their frequent recurrence, constitute the novel's ideological framework.

Little Eva's death, moreover, is also a transformation of a story circulating in the culture at large. It may be found, for example, in a dozen or more versions in the evangelical sermons of the Reverend Dwight Lyman Moody which he preached in Great Britain and Ireland in 1875. In one version it is called "The Child Angel" and it concerns a beautiful golden-haired girl of seven, her father's pride and joy, who dies and, by appearing to him in a dream in which she calls to him from heaven, brings him salvation.[9] The tale shows that by dying even a child can be the instrument of redemption for others, since in death she acquires a spiritual power over those who loved her beyond what she possessed in life.

The power of the dead or the dying to redeem the unregenerate is a major theme of nineteenth-century popular fiction and religious literature. Mothers and children are thought to be uniquely capable of this work. In a sketch entitled "Children," published the year after *Uncle Tom* came out, Stowe writes: "Wouldst thou know, o parent, what is that faith which unlocks heaven? Go not to wrangling polemics, or creeds and forms of theology, but draw to thy bosom thy little one, and read in that clear trusting eye the lesson of eternal life."[10] If children because of their purity and innocence can lead adults to God while living, their spiritual power when they are dead is greater still. Death, Stowe argues in a pamphlet entitled *Ministration of Departed Spirits*, enables the Christian to begin his "real work." God takes people from us sometimes so that their "ministry can act upon us more powerfully from the unseen world."[11]

> The mother would fain electrify the heart of her child. She yearns and burns in vain to make her soul effective on its soul, and to inspire it with a spiritual and holy life; but all her own weaknesses, faults and mortal cares, cramp and confine her till death breaks all fetters; and then, first truly alive, risen, purified, and at rest, she may do calmly, sweetly, and certainly, what, amid the tempest and tossings of her life, she labored for painfully and fitfully.[12]

When the spiritual power of death is combined with the natural sanctity of childhood, the child becomes an angel endowed with salvific force.

Most often, it is the moment of death that saves, when the dying child, glimpsing for a moment the glory of heaven, testifies to the reality of the life to come. Uncle Tom knows that this will happen when little Eva dies, and explains it to Miss Ophelia as follows:

> "You know it says in Scripture, 'At midnight there was a great cry made. Behold the bridegroom cometh.' That's what I'm spectin now, every night, Miss Feely,—and I couldn't sleep out o' hearin', no ways."
> "Why, Uncle Tom, what makes you think so?"
> "Miss Eva, she talks to me. The Lord, he sends his messenger in the soul. I must be thar, Miss Feely; for when that ar blessed child goes into the

kingdom, they'll open the door so wide, we'll all get a look in at the glory, Miss Feely."[13]

Little Eva does not disappoint them. She exclaims at the moment when she passes "from death unto life": "O, love,—joy,—peace!" And her exclamation echoes those of scores of children who die in Victorian fiction and sermon literature with heaven in their eyes. Dickens' Paul Dombey, seeing the face of his dead mother, dies with the words: "The light about the head is shining on me as I go!" The fair, blue-eyed young girl in Lydia Sigourney's *Letters to Mothers*, "death's purple tinge upon her brow," when implored by her mother to utter one last word, whispers "Praise!"[14]

Of course, it could be argued by critics of sentimentalism that the prominence of stories about the deaths of children is precisely what is wrong with the literature of the period; rather than being cited as a source of strength, the presence of such stories in *Uncle Tom's Cabin* could be regarded as an unfortunate concession to the age's fondness for lachrymose scenes. But to dismiss such scenes as "all tears and flapdoodle" is to leave unexplained the popularity of the novels and sermons that are filled with them, unless we choose to believe that a generation of readers was unaccountably moved to tears by matters that are intrinsically silly and trivial. That popularity is better explained, I believe, by the relationship of these scenes to a pervasive cultural myth which invests the suffering and death of an innocent victim with just the kind of power that critics deny to Stowe's novel, the power to work in, and change, the world.

This is the kind of action that little Eva's death in fact performs. It proves its efficacy not through the sudden collapse of the slave system, but through the conversion of Topsy, a motherless, godless black child who has up until that point successfully resisted all attempts to make her "good." Topsy will not be "good" because, never having had a mother's love, she believes that no one can love her. When Eva suggests that Miss Ophelia would love her if only she were good, Topsy cries out: "No; she can't bar me, 'cause I'm a nigger!—she'd's soon have a toad touch her! There can't nobody love niggers, and niggers can't do nothin'! *I* don't care."

> "O, Topsy, poor child, *I* love you!" said Eva, with a sudden burst of feeling, and laying her little thin, white hand on Topsy's shoulder; "I love you, because you haven't had any father, or mother, or friends;—because you've been a poor, abused child! I love you, and I want you to be good. I am very unwell, Topsy, and I think I shan't live a great while; and it really grieves me, to have you be so naughty. I wish you would try to be good, for my sake;—it's only a little while I shall be with you."
>
> The round, keen eyes of the black child were overcast with tears;—large, bright drops rolled heavily down, one by one, and fell on the little white hand. Yes, in that moment, a ray of real belief, a ray of heavenly love, had penetrated the darkness of her heathen soul! She laid her head down between her knees, and wept and sobbed,—while the beautiful child, bending over her, looked like the picture of some bright angel stooping to reclaim a sinner. (XXV, 330–331)

The rhetoric and imagery of this passage—its little white hand, its ray from heaven, bending angel, and plentiful tears—suggest a literary version of the kind of polychrome religious picture that hangs on Sunday-school walls. Words like "kitsch," "camp," and "corny" come to mind. But what is being dramatized here bears no relation to these designations. By giving Topsy her love, Eva initiates a process of redemption whose power, transmitted from heart to heart, can change the entire world. And indeed the process has begun. From that time on, Topsy is "different from what she used to be" (XXVI, 335) (eventually she will go to Africa and become a missionary to her entire race), and Miss Ophelia, who overhears the conversation, is different, too. When little Eva is dead and Topsy cries out "ther an't *nobody* left now," Miss Ophelia answers her in Eva's place:

> "Topsy, you poor child," she said, as she led her into her room, "don't give up! *I* can love you, though I am not like that dear little child. I hope I've learnt something of the love of Christ from her. I can love you; I do, and I'll try to help you to grow up a good Christian girl."
> Miss Ophelia's voice was more than her words, and more than that were the honest tears that fell down her face. From that hour, she acquired an influence over the mind of the destitute child that she never lost. (XXVII, 349)

The tears of Topsy and of Miss Ophelia, which we find easy to ridicule, are the sign of redemption in *Uncle Tom's Cabin;* not words, but the emotions of the heart bespeak a state of grace, and these are known by the sound of a voice, the touch of a hand, but chiefly, in moments of greatest importance, by tears. When Tom lies dying on the plantation on the Red River, the disciples to whom he has preached testify to their conversion by weeping.

> Tears had fallen on that honest, insensible face,—tears of late repentance in the poor, ignorant heathen, whom his dying love and patience had awakened to repentance. . . . (XLI, 485)

Even the bitter and unregenerate Cassy, moved by "the sacrifice that had been made for her," breaks down; "moved by the few last words which the affectionate soul had yet strength to breathe, . . . the dark, despairing woman had wept and prayed" (XLI, 485). When George Shelby, the son of Tom's old master, arrives too late to free him, "tears which did honor to his manly heart fell from the young man's eyes as he bent over his poor friend." And when Tom realizes who is there, "the whole face lighted up, the hard hands clasped, and tears ran down the cheeks" (XLI, 486). The vocabulary of clasping hands and falling tears is one which we associate with emotional exhibitionism, with the overacting that kills off true feeling through exaggeration. But the tears and gestures of Stowe's characters are not in excess of what they feel; if anything they fall short of expressing the experiences they point to—salvation, communion, reconciliation.

If the language of tears seems maudlin and little Eva's death ineffectual, it is because both the tears and the redemption that they signify belong to a conception of the world that is now generally regarded as naive and unrealistic. Topsy's salvation and Miss Ophelia's do not alter the anti-abolitionist majority in the Senate or prevent southern plantation owners and northern investment bankers from doing business to their mutual advantage. Because most modern readers regard such political and economic facts as final, it is difficult for them to take seriously a novel that insists on religious conversion as the necessary precondition for sweeping social change. But in Stowe's understanding of what such change requires, it is the *modern* view that is naive. The political and economic measures that constitute effective action for us, she regards as superficial, mere extensions of the worldly policies that produced the slave system in the first place. Therefore, when Stowe asks the question that is in every reader's mind at the end of the novel—namely, "what can any individual do?"—she recommends not specific alterations in the current political and economic arrangements, but rather a change of heart.

> There is one thing that every individual can do—they can see to it that *they feel right*. An atmosphere of sympathetic influence encircles every human being; and the man or woman who *feels* strongly, healthily and justly, on the great interests of humanity, is a constant benefactor to the human race. See, then, to your sympathies in this matter! Are they in harmony with the sympathies of Christ? or are they swayed and perverted by the sophistries of worldly policy? (XLV, 515)

Stowe is not opposed to concrete measures such as the passage of laws or the formation of political pressure groups, it is just that, by themselves, such actions would be useless. For if slavery *were* to be abolished by these means, the moral conditions that produced slavery in the first place would continue in force. The choice is not between action and inaction, programs and feelings; the choice is between actions that spring from the "sophistries of worldly policy" and those inspired by the "sympathies of Christ." Reality, in Stowe's view, cannot be changed by manipulating the physical environment; it can only be changed by conversion in the spirit because it is the spirit alone that is finally real.

The notion that historical change takes place only through religious conversion, which is a theory of power as old as Christianity itself, is dramatized and vindicated in *Uncle Tom's Cabin* by the novel's insistence that all human events are organized, clarified, and made meaningful by the existence of spiritual realities.[15] The novel is packed with references to the four last things—Heaven, Hell, Death, and Judgment—references which remind the reader constantly that historical events can only be seen for what they are in the light of eternal truths. When St. Clare stands over the grave of little Eva, unable to realize "that it was his Eva that they were hiding from his sight," Stowe interjects, "Nor was it!— not Eva, but only the frail seed of that bright, immortal form with which she shall yet come forth, in the day of the Lord Jesus!" (XVII, 350). And when Legree expresses satisfaction that Tom is dead, she turns to him and says: "Yes, Legree; but who shall shut up that voice in thy soul? that soul, past repentance, past prayer, past hope, in whom the fire that never shall be quenched is already burning!" (XL, 480). These reminders come thick and fast; they are present in Stowe's countless quotations from Scripture—introduced at every possible opportunity, in the narrative, in dialogue, in epigraphs, in quotations from other authors; they are present in the Protestant hymns that thread their way through scene after scene, in asides to the reader, apostrophes to the characters, in quotations from religious poetry, sermons, and prayers, and in long stretches of dialogue and narrative devoted to the discussion of religious matters. Stowe's narrative stipulates a world in which the facts of Christ's death and resurrection and coming day of judgment are never far from our minds because it is only within this frame of reference that she can legitimately have Tom claim, as he dies, "I've got the victory!" (XLI, 486).

The eschatological vision, by putting all individual events in relation to an order that is unchanging, collapses the distinctions among them so that they become interchangeable representations of a single timeless reality. Groups of characters blend into the same character, while the plot abounds with incidents that mirror one another. These features are the features, not of classical nineteenth-century fiction, but of typological narrative. It is this tradition rather than that of the English novel that *Uncle Tom's Cabin* reproduces and extends; for this novel does not simply quote the Bible, it rewrites the Bible as the story of a Negro slave. Formally and philosophically, it stands opposed to works like *Middlemarch* and *The Portrait of a Lady* in which everything depends on human action and decision unfolding in a temporal sequence that withholds revelation until the final moment. The truths that Stowe's narrative conveys can only be reembodied, never discovered, because they are already revealed from the beginning. Therefore, what seem from a modernist point of view to be gross stereotypes in characterization and a needless proliferation of incident, are essential properties of a narrative aimed at demonstrating that human history is a continual reenactment of the sacred drama of redemption. It is the novel's reenactment of this drama that made it irresistible in its day.

Uncle Tom's Cabin retells the culture's central religious myth—the story of the crucifixion—in terms of the nation's greatest political conflict—slavery—and of its most cherished social beliefs—the sanctity of motherhood and the family. It is because Stowe is able to combine so many of the culture's central concerns in a narrative that is immediately accessible to the general population that she is able to move so many people so deeply. The novel's typological organization allows her to present political and social situations both as themselves and as transformations of a religious paradigm which interprets them in a way that readers can both understand and respond to emotionally. For the novel functions both as a means of describing the social world and as a means of changing it. It not only offers an interpretive framework for understanding the culture, and, through the reinforcement of a particular code of values, recommends a strategy for dealing with cultural conflict, but it is itself an agent of that strategy, putting into practice the measures it prescribes. As the religious stereotypes of "Sunday-school fiction" define and organize the elements of social and political life, so the "melodrama" and "pathos" associated with the underlying myth of crucifixion put the reader's heart in the right place with respect to the problems the narrative defines. Hence, rather than making the enduring success of *Uncle Tom's Cabin* inexplicable, these popular elements which puzzled Whicher and have puzzled so many modern scholars—melodrama, pathos, Sunday-school fiction—are the *only* terms in which the book's success can be explained.

The nature of these popular elements also dictates the terms in which any full-scale analysis of *Uncle Tom's Cabin* must be carried out. As I have suggested, its distinguishing features, generically speaking, are not those of the realistic novel, but of typological narrative. Its characters, like the figures in an allegory, do not change or develop, but reveal themselves in response to the demands of a situation. They are not defined primarily by their mental and emotional characteristics—that is to say, psychologically—but soteriologically, according to whether they are saved or damned. The plot, likewise, does not unfold according to Aristotelian standards of probability, but in keeping with the logic of a preordained design, a design which every incident is intended, in one way or another, to enforce.[16] The setting does not so much describe the features of a particular time and place as point to positions on a spiritual map. In *Uncle Tom's Cabin* the presence of realistic detail tends to obscure its highly programmatic nature and to lull readers into thinking that they are in an everyday world of material cause and effect. But what pass for realistic details—the use of dialect, the minute descriptions of domestic activity—are in fact performing a rhetorical function dictated by the novel's ruling paradigm: once that paradigm is perceived, even the homeliest details show up not as the empirically observed facts of human existence but as the expressions of a highly schematic intent.[17]

This schematization has what one might call a totalizing effect on the particulars of the narrative, so that every character in the novel, every scene, and every incident, comes to be apprehended in terms of every *other* character, scene, and incident: all are caught up in a system of endless cross-references in which it is impossible to refer to one without referring to all the rest. To demonstrate what I mean by this kind of narrative organization—a demonstration which will have to stand in lieu of a full-scale reading of the novel—let me show how it works in relation to a single scene. Eva and Tom are seated in the garden of St. Clare's house on the shores of Lake Pontchartrain.

It was Sunday evening, and Eva's Bible lay open on her knee. She read,— "And I saw a sea of glass, mingled with fire."

"Tom," said Eva, suddenly stopping, and pointing to the lake, "there 't is."

"What, Miss Eva?"

"Don't you see,—there?" said the child, pointing to the glassy water, which, as it rose and fell, reflected the golden glow of the sky. "There's a 'sea of glass, mingled with fire.'"

"True enough, Miss Eva," said Tom; and Tom sang—

> *"O, had I the wings of the morning,*
> *I'd fly away to Canaan's shore;*
> *Bright angels should convey me home,*
> *To the new Jerusalem."*

"Where do you suppose new Jerusalem is, Uncle Tom?" said Eva.

"O, up in the clouds, Miss Eva."

"Then I think I see it," said Eva. "Look in those clouds!—they look like great gates of pearl; and you can see beyond them—far, far off—it's all gold. Tom, sing about 'spirits bright.'"

Tom sung the words of a well-known Methodist hymn,

> *"I see a band of spirits bright,*
> *That taste the glories there;*
> *They all are robed in spotless white,*
> *And conquering palms they bear."*

"Uncle Tom, I've seen *them*," said Eva. . . .

"They come to me sometimes in my sleep, those spirits;" and Eva's eyes grew dreamy, and she hummed, in a low voice,

> "They are all robed in spotless white,
> And conquering palms they bear."
> "Uncle Tom," said Eva, "I'm going there."
> "Where, Miss Eva?"
> The child rose, and pointed her little hand to the sky; the glow of evening
> lit her golden hair and flushed cheek with a kind of unearthly radiance, and
> her eyes were bent earnestly on the skies.
> "I'm going there," she said, "to the spirits bright, Tom; I'm going, before
> long." (XXII, 303–307)

The iterative nature of this scene presents in miniature the structure of the whole novel. Eva reads from her Bible about a "sea of glass, mingled with fire," then looks up to find one before her. She reads the words aloud a second time. They remind Tom of a hymn which describes the same vision in a slightly different form (Lake Pontchartrain and the sea of glass become "Canaan's shore" and the "new Jerusalem") and Eva sees what he has sung, this time in the clouds, and offers her own description. Eva asks Tom to sing again and his hymn presents yet another form of the same vision, which Eva again says she has seen: the spirits bright come to her in her sleep. Finally, Eva repeats the last two lines of the hymn and declares that she is going "there"—to the place which has now been referred to a dozen times in this passage. Stowe follows with another description of the golden skies and then with a description of Eva as a spirit bright, and closes the passage with Eva's double reiteration that she is going "there."

The entire scene itself is a re-presentation of others that come before and after. When Eva looks out over Lake Pontchartrain, she sees the "Canaan of liberty" (VII, 70) Eliza saw on the other side of the Ohio River, and the "eternal shore" (XLIII, 499) Eliza and George Harris will reach when they cross Lake Erie in the end. Bodies of water mediate between worlds: the Ohio runs between the slave states and the free; Lake Erie divides the United States from Canada, where runaway slaves cannot be returned to their masters; the Atlantic Ocean divides the North American continent from Africa, where Negroes will have a nation of their own; Lake Pontchartrain shows Eva the heavenly home to which she is going soon; the Mississippi River carries slaves from the relative ease of the middle states to the grinding toil of the southern plantations; the Red River carries Tom to the infernal regions ruled over by Simon Legree. The correspondences between the episodes I have mentioned are themselves based on correspondences between earth and heaven (or hell). Ohio, Canada, and Liberia are related to one another by virtue of their relationship to the one "bright Canaan" for which they stand; the Mississippi River and the Ohio are linked by the Jordan. (Ultimately, there are only three places to be in this story: heaven, hell, or Kentucky, which represents the earthly middle ground in Stowe's geography.)

Characters in the novel are linked to each other in exactly the same way that places are—with reference to a third term that is the source of their identity. The figure of Christ is the common term which unites all of the novel's good characters, who are good precisely in proportion as they are imitations of him. Eva and Tom head the list (she reenacts the last supper and he the crucifixion), but they are also linked to most of the slaves, women, and children in the novel by the characteristics they all share: piety, impressionability, spontaneous affection—and victimization.[18] In this scene, Eva is linked with the "spirits bright" (she later becomes a "bright, immortal form," XXVII, 350) both because she can see them and is soon to join them, and because she, too, always wears white and is elsewhere several times referred to as an an "angel." When Eva dies, she will join her father's mother, who was also named Evangeline, and who herself always wore white, and who, like Eva, is said to be "a direct embodiment and personification of the New Testament" (XIX, 263). And this identification, in its turn, refers back to Uncle Tom who is "all the moral and Christian virtues bound in black morocco, complete" (XIV, 179). The circularity of this train of association is typical of the way the narrative doubles back on itself: later on, Cassy, impersonating the ghost of Legree's saintly mother, will wrap herself in a white sheet.[19]

The scene I have been describing is a node within a network of allusion in which every character and event in the novel has a place. The narrative's rhetorical strength derives in part from the impression it gives of taking every kind of detail in the world into account, from the preparation of breakfast to the orders of the angels, and investing those details with a purpose and a meaning which are both immediately apprehensible and finally significant. The novel reaches out into the reader's world and colonizes it for its own eschatology: that is, it not only incorporates the homely particulars of "Life among the Lowly" into its universal scheme, but it gives them a power and a centrality in that scheme, thereby turning the socio-political order upside down. The totalizing effect of the novel's iterative organization and its doctrine of spiritual redemption are inseparably bound to its political purpose: to bring in the day when the meek—which is to say, women—will inherit the earth.

The specifically political intent of the novel is apparent in its forms of address. Stowe addresses her readers not simply as individuals but as citizens of the United States: "to you, generous, noble-minded men and women, of the South" (XLV, 513), "farmers of Massachusetts, of New Hampshire, of Vermont," "brave and generous men of New York," "and you, mothers of America" (XLV, 514). She speaks to her audience directly in the way the Old Testament prophets spoke to Israel, exhorting, praising, blaming, warning of the wrath to come. "This is an age of the world when nations are trembling and convulsed. A mighty influence is abroad, surging and heaving the world, as with an earthquake. And is America safe? . . . O, Church of Christ, read the signs of the times!" (XLV, 519). Passages like these, descended from the revivalist rhetoric of "Sinners in the Hands of an Angry God," are intended, in the words of a noted scholar, "to direct an imperiled people toward the fulfillment of their destiny, to guide them individually towards salvation, and collectively toward the American city of God."[20]

These words are from Sacvan Bercovitch's *The American Jeremiad,* an influential work of modern scholarship which, although it completely ignores Stowe's novel, makes us aware that *Uncle Tom's Cabin* is a jeremiad in the fullest and truest sense. A jeremiad, in Bercovitch's definition, is "a mode of public exhortation . . . designed to join social criticism to spiritual renewal, public to private identity, the shifting 'signs of the times' to certain traditional metaphors, themes, and symbols."[21] Stowe's novel provides the most obvious and compelling instance of the jeremiad since the Great Awakening, and its exclusion from Bercovitch's book is a striking instance of how totally academic criticism has foreclosed on sentimental fiction; for, because *Uncle Tom's Cabin* is absent from the canon, it isn't "there" to be referred to even when it fulfills a man's theory to perfection. Hence its exclusion from critical discourse is perpetuated automatically, and absence begets itself in a self-confirming cycle of neglect. Nonetheless, Bercovitch's characterization of the jeremiad provides an excellent account of how *Uncle Tom's Cabin* actually worked: among its characters, settings, situations, symbols, and doctrines, the novel establishes a set of correspondences which unite the disparate realms of experience Bercovitch names—social and spiritual, public and private, theological and political—*and*, through the vigor of its representations, attempts to move the nation as a whole toward the vision it proclaims.

The tradition of the jeremiad throws light on *Uncle Tom's Cabin* because Stowe's novel was political in exactly the same way the jeremiad was: both were forms of discourse in which "theology was wedded to politics and politics to the progress of the kingdom of God." [22] The jeremiad strives to persuade its listeners to a providential view of human history which serves, among other things, to maintain the Puritan theocracy in power. Its fusion of theology and politics is not only doctrinal—in that it ties the salvation of the individual to the community's historical enterprise—it is practical as well, for it reflects the interests of Puritan ministers in their bid to retain spiritual and secular authority. The sentimental novel, too, is an act of persuasion aimed at defining social reality; the difference is that the jeremiad represents the interests of Puritan ministers, while the sentimental novel represents the interests of middle-class women. But the relationship between rhetoric and history in both cases is the same. In both cases it is not as if rhetoric and history stand opposed, with rhetoric made up of wish fulfillment and history made up of recalcitrant facts that resist rhetoric's onslaught. Rhetoric *makes* history by shaping reality to the dictates of its political design; it makes history by convincing the people of the world that its description of the world is the true one. The sentimental novelists make their bid for power by positing the kingdom of heaven on earth as a world over which women exercise ultimate control. If history did not take the course these writers recommended, it is not because they were not political, but because they were insufficiently persuasive.

Uncle Tom's Cabin, however, unlike its counterparts in the sentimental tradition, was spectacularly persuasive in conventional political terms: it helped convince a nation to go to war and to free its slaves. But in terms of its own conception of power, a conception it shares with other sentimental fiction, the novel was a political failure. Stowe conceived her book as an instrument for bringing about the day when the world would be ruled not by force, but by Christian love. The novel's deepest political aspirations are expressed only secondarily in its devastating attack on the slave system; the true goal of Stowe's rhetorical undertaking is nothing less than the institution of the kingdom of heaven on earth. Embedded in the world of *Uncle Tom's Cabin*, which is the fallen world of slavery, there appears an idyllic picture, both utopian and Arcadian, of the form human life would assume if Stowe's readers were to heed her moral lesson. In this vision, described in the chapter entitled "The Quaker Settlement," Christian love fulfills itself not in war, but in daily living, and the principle of sacrifice is revealed not in crucifixion, but in motherhood. The form that

Stowe's utopian society takes bears no resemblance to the current social order. Man-made institutions—the church, the courts of law, the legislatures, the economic system—are nowhere in sight. The home is the center of all meaningful activity; women perform the most important tasks; work is carried on in a spirit of mutual cooperation; and the whole is guided by a Christian woman who, through the influence of her "loving words," "gentle moralities," and "motherly loving kindness," rules the world from her rocking chair.

> For why? for twenty years or more, nothing but loving words, and gentle moralities, and motherly loving kindness, had come from that chair,—headaches and heart-aches innumerable had been cured there,—difficulties spiritual and temporal solved there,—all by one good, loving woman, God bless her! (XIII, 163)

The woman in question *is* God in human form. Seated in her kitchen at the head of her table, passing out coffee and cake for breakfast, Rachel Halliday, the millenarian counterpart of little Eva, enacts the redeemed form of the last supper. This is holy communion as it will be under the new dispensation: instead of the breaking of bones, the breaking of bread. The preparation of breakfast exemplifies the way people will work in the ideal society; there will be no competition, no exploitation, no commands. Motivated by self-sacrificing love, and joined to one another by its cohesive power, people will perform their duties willingly and with pleasure: moral suasion will take the place of force.

> All moved obediently to Rachel's gentle "Thee had better," or more gentle "Hadn't thee better?" in the work of getting breakfast. . . . Everything went on so sociably, so quietly, so harmoniously, in the great kitchen,—it seemed so pleasant to every one to do just what they were doing, there was such an atmosphere of mutual confidence and good fellowship everywhere. . . . (XIII, 169–170)

The new matriarchy which Isabella Beecher Hooker had dreamed of leading, pictured here in the Indiana kitchen ("for a breakfast in the luxurious valleys of Indiana is . . . like picking up the rose-leaves and trimming the bushes in Paradise," [XIII, 169]), constitutes the most politically subversive dimension of Stowe's novel, more disruptive and far-reaching in its potential consequences than even the starting of a war or the freeing of slaves. Nor is the ideal of matriarchy simply a daydream; Catherine Beecher, Stowe's elder sister, had offered a ground plan for the realization of such a vision in her *Treatise on Domestic Economy* (1841), which the two sisters republished in an enlarged version entitled *The American Woman's Home* in 1869.[23] Dedicated "To the Women of America, in whose hands rest the real destinies of the republic," this is an instructional book on homemaking in which a wealth of scientific information and practical advice are pointed toward a millenarian goal. Centering on the home, for these women, is not a way of indulging in narcissistic fantasy, as critics have argued,[24] or a turning away from the world into self-absorption and idle reverie; it is the prerequisite of world conquest—defined as the reformation of the human race through proper care and nurturing of its young. Like *Uncle Tom's Cabin*, *The American*

Woman's Home situates the minutiae of domestic life in relation to their soteriological function: "What, then, is the end designed by the family state which Jesus Christ came into this world to secure? It is to provide for the training of our race . . . by means of the self-sacrificing labors of the wise and good . . . with chief reference to a future immortal existence." [25] "The family state," the authors announce at the beginning, "is the aptest earthly illustration of the heavenly kingdom, and . . . woman is its chief minister." [26] In the body of the text, the authors provide women with everything they need to know for the proper establishment and maintenance of home and family, from the construction of furniture ("The [bed] frame is to be fourteen inches from the floor . . . and three inches in thickness. At the head, and at the foot, is to be screwed a notched two-inch board, three inches wide, as in Fig. 8," [30]), to architectural plans, to chapters of instruction on heating, ventilation, lighting, healthful diet, preparation of food, cleanliness, the making and mending of clothes, the care of the sick, the organization of routines, financial management, psychological health, the care of infants, the managing of young children, home amusement, the care of furniture, planting of gardens, the care of domestic animals, the disposal of waste, the cultivation of fruit, and providing for the "Homeless, the Helpless, and the Vicious" (433). After each of these activities has been treated in detail, they conclude by describing the ultimate aim of the domestic enterprise. The founding of a "truly 'Christian family'" will lead to the gathering of a "Christian neighborhood." This "cheering example," they continue,

> would soon spread, and ere long colonies from these prosperous and Christian communities would go forth to shine as "lights of the world" in all the now darkened nations. Thus the "Christian family" and "Christian neighborhood" would become the grand ministry, as they were designed to be, in training our whole race for heaven. [27]

The imperialistic drive behind the encyclopedism and determined practicality of this household manual flatly contradicts the traditional derogations of the American cult of domesticity as a "mirror-phenomenon," "self-immersed" and "self-congratulatory." [28] *The American Woman's Home* is a blueprint for colonizing the world in the name of the "family state" (19) under the leadership of Christian women. What is more, people like Stowe and Catherine Beecher were speaking not simply for a set of moral and religious values. In speaking for the home, they speak for an economy—a household economy—which had supported New England life since its inception. The home, rather than representing a retreat or a refuge from a crass industrial-commercial world, offers an economic *alternative* to that world, one which calls into question the whole structure of American society which was growing up in response to the increase in trade and manufacturing. [29] Stowe's image of a utopian community as presented in Rachel Halliday's kitchen is not simply a Christian dream of communitarian cooperation and harmony; it is a reflection of the real communitarian practices of village life, practices which depended upon cooperation, trust, and a spirit of mutual supportiveness which characterize the Quaker community of Stowe's novel.

One could argue, then, that for all its revolutionary fervor, *Uncle Tom's Cabin* is a conservative book, because it advocates a return to an older way of life—household economy—in the name of the nation's most cherished social and religious beliefs. Even the emphasis on the woman's centrality might be seen as harking back to the "age of homespun" when the essential goods were manufactured in the home and their production was carried out and guided by women. But Stowe's very conservatism—her reliance on established patterns of living and traditional beliefs—is precisely what gives her novel its revolutionary potential. By pushing those beliefs to an extreme and by insisting that they be applied universally, not just to one segregated corner of civil life, but to the conduct of all human affairs, Stowe means to effect a radical transformation of her society. The brilliance of the strategy is that it puts the central affirmations of a culture into the service of a vision that would destroy the present economic and social institutions; by resting her case, absolutely, on the saving power of Christian love and on the sanctity of motherhood and the family, Stowe relocates the center of power in American life, placing it not in the government, nor in the courts of law, nor in the factories, nor in the marketplace, but in the kitchen. And that means that the new society will not be controlled by men, but by women. The image of the home created by Stowe and Beecher in their treatise on domestic science is in no sense a shelter from the stormy blast of economic and political life, a haven from reality divorced from fact which allows the machinery of industrial capitalism to grind on; it is conceived as a dynamic center of activity, physical and spiritual, economic and moral, whose influence spreads out in ever-widening circles. To this activity—and this is the crucial innovation—men are incidental. Although the Beecher sisters pay lip service on occasion to male supremacy, women's roles occupy virtually the whole of their attention and dominate the scene. Male provender is deemphasized in favor of female processing. Men provide the seed, but women bear and raise the children. Men provide the flour, but women bake the bread and get the breakfast. The removal of the male from the center to the periphery of the human sphere is the most radical component of this millenarian scheme, which is rooted so solidly in the most traditional values—religion, motherhood, home, and family. Exactly what position men will occupy in the millennium is specified by a detail inserted casually into Stowe's description of the Indiana kitchen. While the women and children are busy preparing breakfast, Simeon Halliday, the husband and father, stands "in his shirt-sleeves before a little looking-glass in the corner, engaged in the anti-patriarchal operation of shaving" (XIII, 169).

With this detail, so innocently placed, Stowe reconceives the role of men in human history: while Negroes, children, mothers, and grandmothers do the world's primary work, men groom themselves contentedly in a corner. The scene, as critics have noted is often the case in sentimental fiction, is "intimate," the backdrop is "domestic," the tone at times is even "chatty";[30] but the import, as critics have failed to recognize, is world-shaking. The enterprise of sentimental fiction, as Stowe's novel attests, is anything but domestic, in the sense of being limited to purely personal concerns. Its mission, on the contrary, is global and its interests identical with the interests of the race. If the fiction written in the nineteenth century by women whose works sold in the hundreds of thousands has seemed narrow and parochial to the critics of the twentieth century, that narrowness and parochialism belong not to these works nor to the women who wrote them; they are the beholders' share.[31]

NOTES

This chapter is a slightly revised version of the essay that originally appeared in *Glyph, 8.* I would like to thank Sacvan Bercovitch for his editorial suggestions.

1.   Johanna Johnston, *Runaway to Heaven* (Garden City, N.Y.: Doubleday and Co., 1963).

2.   Edward Halsey Foster, for example, prefaces his book-length study *Susan and Anna Warner* (Boston: Twayne Publishers, n.d.), p. 9, by saying: "If one searches nineteenth-century popular fiction for something that has literary value, one searches, by and large, in vain." At the other end of the spectrum stands a critic like Sally Mitchell, whose excellent studies of Victorian women's fiction contain statements that, intentionally or not, conde-scend to the subject matter. For example, in "Sentiment and Suffering: Women's Recreational Reading in the 1860's," *Victorian Studies*, 21, No. 1 (Autumn 1977), p. 34, she says: "Thus, we should see popular novels as emotional analyses, rather than intellectual analyses, of a particular society." The most typical move, however, is to apologize for the poor literary quality of the novels and then to assert that a text is valuable on historical grounds.

3.   Ann Douglas is the foremost of the feminist critics who have accepted this charac-terization of the sentimental writers, and it is to her formulation of the anti-sentimentalist position, *The Feminization of American Culture* (New York: Alfred A. Knopf, 1977), that my arguments throughout are principally addressed. Although her attitude toward the vast quantity of literature written by women between 1820 and 1870 is the one that the male-dominated tradition has always expressed—contempt—Douglas' book is nevertheless extremely important because of its powerful and sustained consideration of this long-neglected body of work. Because Douglas successfully focused critical attention on the cultural centrality of sentimental fiction, forcing the realization that it can no longer be ignored, it is now possible for other critics to put forward a new characterization of these novels and not be dismissed. For these reasons, it seems to me, her work is important.

4.   These attitudes are forcefully articulated by Douglas, p. 9.

5.   The phrase, "a damned mob of scribbling women," coined by Hawthorne in a letter he wrote to his publisher, in 1855, and clearly the product of Hawthorne's own feelings of frustration and envy, comes embedded in a much-quoted passage that has set the tone for criticism of sentimental fiction ever since. As quoted by Fred Lewis Pattee, *The Feminine Fifties* (New York: D. Appleton-Century Co., 1940), p. 110, Hawthorne wrote:

> America is now wholly given over to a d****d mob of scribbling women, and I should have no chance of success while the public taste is occupied with their trash—and should be ashamed of myself if I did succeed. What is the mystery of these innumerable editions of *The Lamplighter*, and other books neither better nor worse? Worse they could not be, and better they need not be, when they sell by the hundred thousand.

6.   J. W. Ward, *Red, White, and Blue: Men, Books, and Ideas in American Culture* (New York: Oxford University Press, 1961), p. 75.

7.   George F. Whicher, "Literature and Conflict," in *The Literary History of the United States*, ed. Robert E. Spiller et al., 3rd ed., rev. (London: Macmillan, 1963), p. 583.

8.   Whicher, in *Literary History*, ed. Spiller, p. 586. Edmund Wilson, despite his some-what sympathetic treatment of Stowe in *Patriotic Gore: Studies in the Literature of the American Civil War* (New York: Oxford University Press, 1966), pp. 5, 32, seems to concur in this opinion, reflecting a characteristic tendency of commentators on the most popular works of sentimental fiction to regard the success of these women as some sort of mysterious erup-tion, inexplicable by natural causes. Henry James gives this attitude its most articulate,

though perhaps least defensible, expression in a remarkable passage from *A Small Boy and Others* (New York: Charles Scribner's Sons, 1913), pp. 159–160, where he describes Stowe's book as really not a book at all but as "a fish, a wonderful 'leaping' fish"—the point being to deny Stowe any role in the process that produced such a wonder:

> Appreciation and judgment, the whole impression, were thus an effect for which there had been no process—any process so related having in other cases *had* to be at some point or other critical; nothing in the guise of a written book, therefore, a book printed, published, sold, bought and "noticed," probably ever reached its mark, the mark of exciting interest, without having at least groped for that goal *as* a book or by the exposure of some literary side. Letters, here, languished unconscious, and Uncle Tom, instead of making even one of the cheap short cuts through the medium in which books breathe, even as fishes in water, went gaily roundabout it altogether, as if a fish, a wonderful "leaping" fish, had simply flown through the air.

9. Reverend Dwight Lyman Moody, "Sermons and Addresses," in *Narrative of Messrs. Moody and Sankey's Labors in Great Britain and Ireland with Eleven Addresses and Lectures in Full* (New York: Anson D. F. Randolph and Co., 1975).

10. Harriet Beecher Stowe, "Children," in *Uncle Sam's Emancipation: Earthly Care, a Heavenly discipline; and other sketches* (Philadelphia: W. P. Hazard, 1853), p. 83.

11. Harriet Beecher Stowe, *Ministration of Departed Spirits* (Boston: American Tract Society, n.d.), pp. 4, 3.

12. Stowe, *Ministration*, p. 3.

13. Harriet Beecher Stowe, *Uncle Tom's Cabin; or, Life Among the Lowly*, ed. Kathryn Kish Sklar (New York: Library of America, 1982), p. 344. All future references to *Uncle Tom's Cabin* will be to this edition; chapter and page numbers are given in parentheses in the text.

14. Charles Dickens, *Dombey and Son* (Boston: Estes and Luriat, 1882), p. 278; Lydia H. Sigourney, *Letters to Mothers* (Hartford: Hudson and Skinner, 1838).

15. Religious conversion as the basis for a new social order was the mainspring of the Christian evangelical movement of the mid-nineteenth century. The emphasis on "feeling," which seems to modern readers to provide no basis whatever for the organization of society, was the key factor in the evangelical theory of reform. See Sandra Sizer's discussions of this phenomenon in *Gospel Hymns and Social Religion* (Philadelphia: Temple University Press, 1978), pp. 52, 59, 70–71, 72. "It is clear from the available literature that prayer, testimony, and exhortation were employed to create a *community* of intense *feeling*, in which individuals underwent similar experiences (centering on conversion) and would thenceforth unite with others in matters of moral decision and social behavior." "People in similar states of feeling, in short, would 'walk together,' would be agreed." "Conversion established individuals in a particular kind of relationship with God, by virtue of which they were automatically members of a social company, alike in interests and feelings." Good order would be preserved by "relying on the spiritual and moral discipline provided by conversion, and on the company of fellow Christians, operating without the coercive force of government."

16. Angus Fletcher, *Allegory, The Theory of a Symbolic Mode* (Ithaca, N.Y.: Cornell University Press, 1964), discusses the characteristic features of allegory in such a way as to make clear the family resemblance between sentimental fiction and the allegorical mode. See particularly, his analyses of character, pp. 35, 60, symbolic action, pp. 150ff., 178, 180, 182, and imagery, p. 171.

17. Fletcher's comment on the presence of naturalistic detail in allegory, pp. 198–199, is pertinent here:

The apparent surface realism of an allegorical agent will recede in importance, as soon as he is felt to take part in a magical plot, as soon as his causal relations to others in that plot are seen to be magically based. This is an important point because there has often been confusion as to the function of the naturalist detail of so much allegory. In terms I have been outlining, this detail now appears not to have a journalistic function; it is more than mere record of observed facts. It serves instead the purposes of magical containment, since the more the allegorist can circumscribe the attributes, metonymic and synecdochic, of his personae, the better he can shape their fictional destiny. Naturalist detail is "cosmic," universalizing, not accidental as it would be in straight journalism.

18.   The associations that link slaves, women, and children are ubiquitous and operate on several levels. Besides being described in the same set of terms, these characters occupy parallel structural positions in the plot. They function chiefly as mediators between God and the unredeemed, so that, e.g., Mrs. Shelby intercedes for Mr. Shelby; Mrs. Bird for Senator Bird; Simon Legree's mother (unsuccessfully) for Simon Legree; little Eva and St. Clare's mother for St. Clare; Tom Loker's mother for Tom Loker; Eliza for George Harris (spiritually, she is the agent of his conversion), and for Harry Harris (physically, she saves him from being sold down the river); and Tom for all the slaves on the Legree plantation (spiritually, he converts them) and for all the slaves of the Shelby plantation (physically, he is the cause of their being set free).

19.   For a parallel example, see Alice Crozier's analysis of the way the lock of hair that little Eva gives Tom becomes transformed into the lock of hair that Simon Legree's mother sent to Simon Legree. *The Novels of Harriet Beecher Stowe* (New York: Oxford University Press, 1969), pp. 29–31.

20.   Sacvan Bercovitch, *The American Jeremiad* (Madison: University of Wisconsin Press, 1978), p. 9.

21.   Bercovitch, p. xi.

22.   Bercovitch, p. xiv.

23.   For an excellent discussion of Beecher's *Treatise* and of the entire cult of domesticity, see Kathryn Kish Sklar, *Catherine Beecher, A Study in American Domesticity* (New York: W. W. Norton and Co., 1976). For other helpful discussions of the topic, see Barbara G. Berg, *The Remembered Gate: Origins of American Feminism, The Woman and the City, 1800–1860* (New York: Oxford University Press, 1978); Sizer; Ronald G. Walters, *The Antislavery Appeal, American Abolitionism after 1830* (Baltimore: The Johns Hopkins University Press, 1976); and Barbara Welter, "The Cult of True Womanhood, 1820–1860," *American Quarterly*, 18 (Summer 1966), pp. 151–174.

24.   For Douglas' charges of narcissism against Stowe and her readers, see *The Feminization of American Culture*, pp. 2, 9, 297, and 300.

25.   Catherine Beecher and Harriet Beecher Stowe, *The American Woman's Home: or, Principles of Domestic Science; Being a Guide to the Formation and Maintenance of Economical, Healthful, Beautiful, and Christian Homes* (New York: J. B. Ford and Co., 1869), p. 18.

26.   Beecher and Stowe, *The American Woman's Home*, p. 19.

27.   Beecher and Stowe, *The American Woman's Home*, pp. 458–459.

28.   These are Douglas' epithets, p. 307.

29.   For a detailed discussion of the changes referred to here, see Christopher Clark, "Household Economy, Market Exchange and the Rise of Capitalism in the Connecticut Valley, 1800–1860," *Journal of Social History*, 13, No. 2 (Winter 1979), pp. 169–189; and Nancy F. Cott, *The Bonds of Womanhood: "Woman's Sphere" in New England, 1780–1835* (New Haven: Yale University Press, 1977).

30.   Douglas, p. 9.

31. In a helpful article in *Signs*, "The Sentimentalists: Promise and Betrayal in the Home," 4, No. 3 (Spring 1979), pp. 434–446, Mary Kelley characterizes the main positions in the debate over the significance of sentimental fiction as follows: (1) the Cowie-Welter thesis, which holds that women's fiction expresses an "ethics of conformity" and accepts the stereotype of the woman as pious, pure, submissive, and dedicated to the home, and (2) the Papashvily-Garrison thesis, which sees sentimental fiction as profoundly subversive of traditional ideas of male authority and female subservience. Kelley locates herself somewhere in between, holding that sentimental novels convey a "contradictory message": "they tried to project an Edenic image," but their own tales "subverted their intentions" by showing how often women were frustrated and defeated in the performance of their heroic roles. My own position is that the sentimental novelists are both conformist and subversive, but not, as Kelley believes, in a self-contradictory way. They used the central myth of their culture—the story of Christ's death for the sins of mankind—as the basis for a new myth which reflected their own interests. They regarded their vision of the Christian home as the fulfillment of the Gospel, "the end . . . which Jesus Christ came into this world to secure," in exactly the same way that the Puritans believed that their mission was to found the "American city of God," and that Christians believe the New Testament to be a fulfillment of the Old. Revolutionary ideologies, typically, announce themselves as the fulfillment of old promises or as a return to a golden age. What I am suggesting here, in short, is that the argument over whether the sentimental novelists were radical or conservative is a false issue. The real problem is how we, in the light of everything that has happened since they wrote, can understand and appreciate their work. See Alexander Cowie, "The Vogue of the Domestic Novel, 1850–1870," *South Atlantic Quarterly*, 41 (October 1942), p. 420; Welter; Helen Waite Papashvily, *All the Happy Endings: A Study of the Domestic Novel in America, the Women Who Wrote It, the Women Who Read It, in the Nineteenth Century* (New York: Harper and Bros., 1956); and Dee Garrison, "Immortal Fiction in the Late Victorian Library," *American Quarterly*, 28 (Spring 1976), pp. 71–80.

JAMES J. SOSNOSKI

A MINDLESS MAN-DRIVEN THEORY MACHINE
intellectuality, sexuality, *and the institution of criticism*

A male perspective, assumed to be 'universal' has dominated fields of knowledge.
GAYLE GREENE AND COPPÉLIA KAHN, *MAKING A DIFFERENCE*

I should hope eventually for the erection of intelligent standards of criticism.
JOHN CROWE RANSOM, 'CRITICISM, INC.'

To be signed with a woman's name doesn't necessarily make a piece of writing feminine. It could quite well be masculine writing, and conversely, the fact that a piece of writing is signed with a man's name does not in itself exclude femininity.
HÉLÈNE CIXOUS, 'CASTRATION OR DECAPITATION?'

The male machine is a special kind of being, different from women, children, and men who don't measure up. He is functional, designed mainly for work. He is programmed to tackle jobs, override obstacles, attack problems, overcome difficulties, and always seize the offensive. He will take on any task that can be presented to him in a competitive framework, and his most important positive reinforcement is victory. . . . this ideology makes competition the guiding principle of moral and intellectual, as well as economic, life. It tells us that the general welfare is served by the self-interested clash of ambitions and ideas.
MARC FEIGEN FASTEAU, *THE MALE MACHINE*

This is an essay about the tie between the institutional construction of intellectuality and the social construction of sexuality. Let me start with error.

Knowing that we do not know is knowledge. And further, knowing that what one thought one knew is no longer believable is the most significant form of knowing. Just as problems, in some sense, precede solutions and questions precede answers, so not-knowing, including not-knowing-one-does-not-know, precedes knowing. This is the precondition upon which an intellectual comes to know. She acknowledges that a problem remains a problem, that an answer does not answer. She acknowledges that she is in error. For her, paradoxically, being in error is not being wrong. Error, in this case, is heuristic. By contrast, the traditional critic, formed by a long anti-intellectual past, insists that what he already thinks will suffice. This is an essay about his willingness not to know.

Indeed, to err is human. We use many words for this contingency. Realizing the inevitability of changing our minds, we speak of making mistakes, being incorrect, finding ourselves wrong, and ridding ourselves of falsehoods. In each case, we offer reasons for changing what we believe, think and/or do. And what would the world be like if we didn't? Cultures change because persons attempt to alter unwelcome states of affairs, to transform errors into questions, to make right what was wrong, to rethink what is false. To be human is to err. Only fools believe they know more than they do not know. This is an essay about resisting change by restricting error.

Error is the state of believing what is untrue, wrong, incorrect, or mistaken. Living with error is not a simple state of affairs. Our use of the word encompasses and often combines a wide range of faults. 'Error' implies 'deviation from truth, accuracy, correctness, right.'[1] It is the broadest term in the following comparisons. On one side of the semantic spectrum, error is understood as 'a blunder, a slip, a *faux pas*, a boner.' These are 'mistakes.' The word 'mistake' suggests an error resulting from 'carelessness, inattention, misunderstanding.' It does not strongly imply wrong-doing. 'Incorrect' mostly means not correct. Since correctness refers to 'adherence to conventionality' (correct behavior), incorrect suggests little more than deviation from convention. It is a comment upon how accurate, precise, or exact one is in performing some predesigned task. 'Wrong,' on the other hand, in its primary sense, means 'not morally right or just; sinful; wicked; immoral' and, in a derived sense, 'not in accordance with an established standard, previous arrangement, given intention.' If you are wrong, it is because you 'oppress, persecute, aggrieve, or abuse someone.' Wrongs are offenses that should be punished. At the other end of the spectrum of error from a mistake is the word 'false,' the most abstract and legal sense of error. 'False,' whose root sense is 'deception,' primarily means 'not true' (as in the phrase 'a false argument,' *WNWD*). Falsehood refers to 'anything that is not in essence that which it purports to be.' When deception is involved, the synonyms for 'false' are 'sham,' 'counterfeit,' 'bogus,' and 'fake.' Given such contrasting ideas of error, it would seem that, when persons are incorrect, it is not because they are sinful; that, when statements are false, it is not because they are immoral. In the institution of criticism, however, these terms appear to be conflated in judgments that incorrect statements are wrong because they are false. This is an essay about a particular conflation of error termed 'falsification.'

In this essay, I focus upon the institutional use of the word 'false' as a term paired with 'true.' In particular, I focus upon the judgment that critical arguments are 'false' as opposed to 'true.' The distinction between an unsound and a sound argument is the only condition upon which literary study as a discipline can be said to 'accumulate knowledge.' Hence, 'falsification,' 'falsifiability,' 'verification,' and 'verifiability' are crucial theoretical concerns. Since, in practice, verification is the result of falsification, I will focus upon the latter.[2] In literary studies, falsification is a judgment that takes the general form of the utterance: 'Professor X is "mistaken/incorrect/wrong" when he . . .' Correlatively, the falsifiability of critical discourse is the condition of possibility for grades, ranks, publications.[3] These uses of the concept false depend upon a belief upon which, in turn, the institution of criticism depends: that a claim about a text can be proven false. Since this belief is an idealization of inquiry and therefore an abstraction of it, I have coined the term 'falsificity' to identify the particular conflation of errors upon which the institution of criticism is based. In short, falsificity is the principle that it is logically wrong (and therefore culpable and punishable) to mistake the incorrect for the correct. I use the term 'wrong' in glossing 'falsificity' to emphasize that, in the institution of criticism, critical arguments which are judged false are judged so not on purely logical grounds but on the grounds that they are 'sham, counterfeit, bogus, or fake' discourses and therefore punishable. False arguments are construed as discourses 'not in essence what they purport to be,' that is, not logical. Since they are proffered as criticism, they are instances of counterfeit discourses. According to the principle of falsificity, to submit as criticism a discourse that is not logical is wrong and hence to be punished—to be marked by an 'F,' to be cast out of editorial houses, to be denied an award. My critique of this principle is that it encourages critics to disagree with each other in ways that do not especially differ from familial quarreling wherein the keeper of the Logos is the Father who chastises his children. This is a paper about the construction of intellectuality as a competitive quarreling.

In this essay, I shall not only try to show that, far from being an impersonal, detached, logical judgment, falsification is a rationalization of academic competition, but, more significantly, that it is a device for maintaining the patriarchal *status quo*. Ordinarily, the identification of error leads to useful changes. (Problems are resolved; thus, a negative state of affairs is changed.) But, paradoxically, changes in a 'system' can be prohibited by defining alternatives to it as errors. (It's wrong, so don't do it!) In the institution of criticism, for example, one is instructed to avoid false arguments, that is, to avoid illogic. This instruction seems thoroughly plausible until one recognizes that, in literary study, the identification of falsehood (illogic) reflects the social construction of the feminine as 'man's specular Other'[4] and thus maintains the patriarchal *status quo*. This is an essay about the oppression of women.

Error can be heuristic. But, falsificity makes error a punishable form of wrongdoing. When we consider that it is a central theoretical assumption in a patriarchal institution hierarchically structured by competition, it can be described as a 'mindless, man-driven theory machine' designed to stamp out alternatives to the system it regulates by regarding them as merely feminine.

THE CONSTRUCTION OF INTELLECTUALITY IN THE INSTITUTION OF CRITICISM

The phrase 'traditional literary criticism' refers to a multitude of critics who differ widely among themselves. It is, nonetheless, a useful phrase because it designates a common form of argumentation. Nor is this an accident of history. The critics who have worked in the 'modern American university,' which, Laurence Veysey argues in his *The Emergence of the American University*, took its shape shortly after the turn of the century, are trained in a common form of argumentation.[5] It is structured by an informal logic whose first articulator was Aristotle. In it, claims are supported by evidence and therefore can be verified. It is requisite in this tradition for critics to discriminate between correct and incorrect readings. For example, in *A Handbook to Literature*, the most widely used of its kind, we read of argumentation that 'its purpose is to convince a reader or hearer by establishing the truth or falsity of a proposition.'

Traditional argumentation has long-standing protocols. Most literary students trained in it, have been fformed by its scholasticism. Dissertations, for example, follow a pattern reminiscent of the treatises of medieval theologians: 'Most rhetoricians recognized five parts for the usual argumentative discourse: *exordium, narratio, confirmatio* or *probatio, refutatio,* and *peroratio*.'[6] Before a traditional critic proves his own case ('confirmatio'), he gives the history of preceding arguments ('narratio') and afterward refutes the likely objections ('refutatio'). Traditional papers, if only in the first footnote, still begin with reviews of the scholarship, most of which is falsified in order to set the stage for the author's view. Footnotes—many of which, as Stephen Nimis points out, have no logical relationship to the argument they footnote[7]—are either formulaic gestures toward verification ('confirmatio') or falsification ('refutatio').

To our post-modern sensibilities, the theory of falsification that provides a basis for traditional criticism is recognizably 'modern.' As I implied above, in this essay the term 'modern' refers to the historical period characterized by the infusion of 'discipline' (in Foucault's sense) into the structure of Western society. By the late nineteenth century, an intellectualized conception of discipline led institutions of higher learning to reorganize along 'disciplinary' lines, which, in turn, led to a significant structural change that produced what is often called the modern or new American university. In Veysey's terms, the rise of the professions led to the development of disciplines of study which led to the creation of departments to house them. For the most part, the organization of a newly formed study as a discipline was modelled on the successful institutionalization of scientific research. Literary studies followed this pattern. Before the turn of the century philology gave literary study the disciplined appearance of a science of literature. Then, literary history did. New Criticism gives us a more recent legacy of attempts to reformulate literary studies as a discipline. The overt intention of New Critical theory, in classics like 'The Intentional *Fallacy*' (my emphasis) or *Theory of Literature*, was to make literary criticism objective, reliable, verifiable, and so on.

But, it is the fact that *men* endeavored to make criticism a discipline along scientific lines that most interests me here. Though women have argued for literary study as a science, the 'canonical' theoretical statements have been made by men. The unselfconscious 'maleness' of their insistence upon a science of criticism is notable. As Gayle Greene and Coppélia Kahn remind us, 'a male perspective, assumed to be "universal," has dominated fields of knowledge.'[8] Literary criticism is no exception. Consider the following remarks of I. A. Richards, John Crowe Ransom, and René Wellek.

Richards wished to put literary criticism on the solid footing of a discipline. As Elmer Borklund points out, he began his career 'by virtually dismissing the entire critical tradition' prior to him.[9]

A few conjectures, a supply of admonitions, many acute isolated observations, some brilliant guesses, much oratory and applied poetry, inexhaustible confusion, a sufficiency of dogma, no small stock of prejudices, whimsies and crochets, a profusion of mysticism, a little genuine speculation, sundry stray inspirations, pregnant hints and *aperçus;* of such as these, it may be said without exaggeration, is extant critical theory composed. [10]

Simultaneously, in America, John Crowe Ransom took a similar view, but couched it in business terms, unwittingly reflecting the extent to which universities had become corporations.

Professors of literature are learned but not critical men. . . . Nevertheless, it is from the professors of literature, in this country the professors of English for the most part, that I should hope eventually for the erection of intelligent standards of criticism. It is their business.

Criticism must become more scientific, or precise and systematic, and this means that it must be developed by the collective and sustained effort of learned persons—which means that its proper seat is in the universities. . . . Rather than occasional criticism by amateurs, I should think the whole enterprise might be seriously taken in hand by professionals. Perhaps I use a distasteful figure, but I have the idea that what we need is Criticism, Inc., or Criticism, Ltd. [11]

Welleck believed that we were still recovering from 'a disaster.' For him, literary criticism, which was 'taken over by politically oriented journalism' during the nineteenth century, became 'degraded to something purely practical, serving temporal ends.' 'The critic,' he laments, 'becomes a middleman, a secretary, even a servant, of the public.' [12] A decade after the publication of *Theory of Literature*, he complained that literary scholars were too much on the defensive:

Our whole society is based on the assumption that we know what is just, and our science on the assumption that we know what is true. Our teaching of literature is actually also based on aesthetic imperatives, even if we feel less definitely bound by them and seem much more hesitant to bring these assumptions out into the open. The disaster of the 'humanities' as far as they are concerned with the arts and literature is due to their timidity in making the very same claims which are made in regard to law and truth. Actually we do make these claims when we teach *Hamlet* or *Paradise Lost* rather than Grace Metalious. . . . But we do so shamefully, apologetically, hesitatingly. There is, contrary to frequent assertions, a very wide agreement on the great classics: the main canon of literature. There is an insuperable gulf between really great art and very bad art: between say 'Lycidas' and a poem on the leading page of the *New York Times*, between Tolstoy's *Master and Man* and a story in *True Confessions*. (pp. 17–18)

He goes on to defend the possibility not only of correct interpretations but also of correct evaluations. Pointing out that, though the complexity of art might make interpretation difficult,

this does not mean that all interpretations are equally right, that there is no possibility of differentiating between them. There are utterly fantastic interpretations, partial, distorted interpretations. We may argue about Bradley's or Dover Wilson's or even Ernest Jones' interpretation of *Hamlet;* but we know that Hamlet was no woman in disguise. The concept of adequacy of

> interpretation leads clearly to the concept of the correctness of judgment. Evaluation grows out of understanding; correct evaluation out of correct understanding. There is a hierarchy of viewpoints implied in the very concept of adequacy of interpretation. Just as there is correct interpretation, at least as an ideal, so there is correct judgment, good judgment. (p. 18)

For Wellek, the only factor that could keep literary criticism from being a 'secretary' to the public was falsification. That we could correctly understand that 'Hamlet was no woman in disguise' would allow us to make the 'good judgment' that *True Confessions* was degrading. For Wellek, the study of literature was *Literaturwissenschaft*, 'systematic knowledge.'

In retrospect, it is remarkable still that the main opponents to New Criticism in the 1960s did not question the view that literary criticism, even though it could not muster exacting objectivity, should be modelled on the sciences. They regarded New Criticism as not scientific enough. Northrop Frye, in his 'Polemical Introduction' to *Anatomy of Criticism*, outflanks the New Critics by arguing the case for a science of Literature rather than for a scientific method of interpretation. E. D. Hirsch's *Validity in Interpretation* critiques the theory of 'the intentional fallacy' by arguing that we can validly determine intention. In the 1960s, when anti–New Critical ferment began, system and method were, nonetheless, privileged terms. The most wide-scale attempt to make criticism into a science belonged to a movement that would have supplanted New Criticism by making its 'scientific' tendencies explicit, namely, structuralism. It is now an often-told tale how structuralism engendered post-structuralism.

To post-structuralist or post-modernist critics, whose intellectual formation is deeply indebted to feminism,[13] traditional or modern theories of criticism are phallo/logocentric.

> Imagine someone (a kind of Monsieur Teste in reverse) who abolishes within himself all barriers, all classes, all exclusions, not by syncretism but by simple discard of that old specter: *logical contradiction;* who mixes every language, even those said to be incompatible; who silently accepts every charge of illogicality, of incongruity; who remains passive in the face of Socratic irony (leading the interlocutor to the supreme disgrace: *self-contradiction*) and legal terrorism (how much penal evidence is based on a psychology of consistency!) Such a man would be the mockery of our society: court, school, asylum, polite conversations would cast him out: who endures contradiction without shame? Now this anti-hero exists. . . .[14]

For the most part, modern criticism is based on the notion that readings can be objective, impersonal and detached, that there is a discipline of literary criticism. Though traditional critics differ widely in their assumptions about interpretation, when contrasted with post-modern critics, they appear similar in their logocentrism. Working within this system, modern critics contend that their readings are demonstrable because textual or contextual evidence can show that rival readings are not logically supported. Since readings that are accepted as 'true' at an earlier moment in time can at a later date be shown to be 'false,' the engine of this system is falsification. New readings supplant old readings. This is a familiar pattern to anyone studying literature. Most critics strive to come up with 'new' readings, and, in order to do so, have to clear their paths by falsifying the previously accepted ones.

In other words, what characterizes modern literary criticism is a principle of falsificity.

INTELLECTUAL SEXUALITY IN THE INSTITUTION OF CRITICISM

Literary criticism is a career. Burton Bledstein tells us in *The Culture of Professionalism* that the idea of a career emerged concomitantly with the rise of the professions in the nineteenth century in contrast to 'a random series of jobs, projects, or businesses providing a livelihood.'[15] It changed the lives of *men* because it articulated *their* aspirations as ambitions (emphasis mine). It involved 'a pre-established total pattern of organized professional activity, with upward movement through recognized preparatory stages, and advancement based on merit bearing honor.' Modern literary criticism was conceived during this period. Like professionals elsewhere, critics make their career patterns discernible in their *curriculum vitae* which require them to list chronologically 'preparatory stages,' 'advancement' in employment, 'honors,' and 'merit'—which, in their case, is signalled by increasing success in placing their work with prestigious publishers. What Bledstein calls a 'vertical' movement characterizes the careers of successful professional critics. For critics, an outstanding career is one in which they earn higher and higher salaries in a succession of jobs at increasingly prestigious institutions. Since the mid-nineteenth century, professional success has been imaged as climbing a ladder of institutional status:

> New expectations displayed themselves in a new style. In a social environment now offering vocational alternatives, young men could criticize, calculate, envision a ladder of advancement, and act with some measure of impunity toward their less flexible elders. Above all, young men could begin thinking in vertical rather than horizontal imagery. They mean, very literally, to move up and away. (p. 176)

Bledstein describes the shift in the sense of the purposefulness of a man's life during the nineteenth century as a shift away from a belief in a 'calling' to a choice of a 'career,' a shift easily discerned in the changing ways ministers, lawyers, doctors, and educators spoke about their professions. A 'calling' was not the choice of an individual, but a career most certainly was. Bledstein's remark that a career was a choice for 'young men' leaves unspoken that women were still 'called.'

The shift Bledstein describes was hierarchically and competitively configured not merely as a change in status and roles provoked by analogies to ladders and races, but also as a change in the social construction of masculinity provoked by images of gentlemen.

> The inner intensity of the new life oriented toward a career stood in contrast to that of the older learned professional life of the eighteenth and early nineteenth centuries. In the earlier period such external attributes of gentle-

> manly behavior as benevolence, duty, virtue, and manners circumscribed the professional experience. Competence, knowledge, and preparation were less important in evaluating the skills of the professional than were dedication to the community, sincerity, trust, permanence, honorable reputation, and righteous behavior. The qualifying credentials of the learned professionals were honesty, decency and civility. (p. 173)

The career professional, by contrast, thought in terms of advancement. The nineteenth-century gentleman gave way to the twentieth-century businessman, who prospered in 'a competitive society in which unrestrained individual self-determination undermined traditional life styles' (p. 174). He is the prototype of the persona Marc Feigen Fasteau calls 'the male machine.'

> The male machine is a special kind of being, different from women, children, and men who don't measure up. He is functional, designed mainly for work. He is programmed to tackle jobs, override obstacles, attack problems, overcome difficulties, and always seize the offensive. He will take on any task that can be presented to him in a competitive framework, and his most important positive reinforcement is victory. . . . this ideology makes competition the guiding principle of moral and intellectual, as well as economic, life. It tells us that the general welfare is served by the self-interested clash of ambitions and ideas.[16]

Bledstein remarks that in the development of nineteenth-century professionalism ambitious men were instrumental in 'structuring our discipline according to a distinct vision—the vertical one of career' (p. ix). From this point of view, the development of literary study matches Bledstein's delineation of the relationship between the growth of the university and the rise of professionalism. To become a literary scholar is to be professionalized, a social process involving the introjection of an 'intellectual competitiveness.' The 'masculine' qualities of exemplary male professors were imitated and became the traits of an idealized career profile. Exemplary male professors became 'role-models' for success within the structure of the academy, a phenomenon which shaped the field of literary study as we now know it.[17] We are the heirs of 'roles' that are explicitly designed for the new gentleman, the businessman.

The history of literary study, for instance, can be understood as the collective biography of exemplary *male* figures: George Marsh, Francis March, Francis Child, Ulrich von Wilamowitz-Moellendorf, Guastave Lanson, I. A. Richards, John Crowe Ransom, Cleanth Brooks, and so on. The criss-crossing movement of their careers influenced the newly developing field of literary study. Its historical development is, in most respects, an account of these critical 'movements' which are usually associated with key men who inspired schools of thought. Figures like Child, Brooks, and Lanson are historically significant because they became exemplary figures. These men were 'exemplary' because in doing what they believed ought to be done, they became examples for others. Modern literary study developed as a profession to the extent that the manner in which a particular man studied literature was widely imitated, to the extent that a man's way of 'doing' criticism or scholarship became a trait in the composite profile of the ideal professor of literature. Invariably, men were the models underlying the ideal profile of the scholar/critic at specific junctures in the development of literary studies. Over time, this idealized career profile became a composite of masculine traits derived from the superimposition of the portrayals of exemplary male scholars. Women working in the academy, in order to succeed in their careers, had to acquire these traits. As Hélène Cixous reminds us, a discourse 'signed with a woman's name doesn't necessarily make a piece of writing feminine. It could quite well be masculine writing.'[18]

Nowadays, to be a professional critic authorized by the institution of criticism still requires submission to an idealized career profile whose masculinity derives from male models. Since this profile is nowhere made explicit as such and *in toto*, I call it the 'Magister Implicatus' to personify and thus concretize the sum total of performances now demanded for accreditation as a professional critic.[19] He is the image we see when we look in the distorted mirror of our resumés. As we currently know him, the Magister Implicatus is a personification of an ideal male career. At present, he stands for the professionalization of the male scholar from the very first examination through various forms of discipline to the final authorization of his work. He is the unified personification of the ways professional critics are taught to portray themselves in official documents—*vitae*, grant applications, course descriptions, and so on.

In his traditional and modern persona, the Magister's power enables or disables any member of the institution who introjects him. He punishes by making us believe we have failed, do not deserve tenure, have not published enough. He is the monster in the male machine, the instrument of self-discipline and self-abnegation. In his traditional guise, he is the personification of the patriarchal institution, the site for training, disciplining, schooling men. He professionalizes the amateur. He governs through our introjection of what the desired outcome of any performance must be if it is to be rewarded. It is his male interests that are served when critics serve their institutions by believing those beliefs that hold it together. An emotional bond to him is a bond to the patriarchal institution. In serving him, one serves it, often while believing he has one's best interests in mind.

The Magister Implicatus is the ghostly patriarchal figure who haunts our job descriptions, our textbooks, our examination committees, and other quarters of the institution of literary criticism. Not surprisingly, given the history of the institution of criticism, his profile is masculine. Because careers allow for professional advances along a ladder of institutional success (degrees, salaries, ranks and so on), the Magister through his exemplariness inspires critics to compete with one another for awards.

It is upon this one trait of the Magister Implicatus, his competitiveness, that I wish to focus your attention.

FALSIFICITY IS INEXTRICABLY LINKED TO COMPETITIVENESS

In the present academy, competitiveness and falsificity are inextricably bound together. Critics are judged according to the extent to which they have successfully argued. The merit of their arguments is measured by the degree to which they have falsified their rival's claims and the degree to which their own arguments are deemed falsifiable. 'And merit is, of course, determined by competition. How else?'[20] The success of a critic is therefore inextricably linked with the extent to which he competes with rival critics.

Competition is usually defined as 'a striving for the same object, position, prize, etc., usually in accordance with certain fixed rules' (*WNWD*). Rule-governed striving is the generating principle of career success. Each juncture of the career path presents to the careerist a goal for which he must compete—a grade, a degree, a job, a promotion, a grant, and so on. In every case, the competitor is judged on the merit of his critical arguments. Hence, if we consider that arguments displace earlier arguments through falsification, then the successful competitor is the successful falsifier. Falsification and competitiveness are inextricable in this system.

As Helen E. Longino points out, 'Competition always involves a contest among individuals seeking the same thing when not all can obtain it.'[21] Some competitions, she argues, are based upon the availability of a single prize. As in a race, there is only one first 'prize.' As a consequence, the differences in abilities of the contestants is the salient factor. Such competitions are staged to establish who is 'the best' in a particular performance. There are many examples in literary criticism—competing for a job, a grant, an award. In other competitions the scarcity of the 'object' sought (the reward) creates a "survival of the fittest' contest and the 'game' has to be played until winners are determined. In literary criticism, competing for publications, jobs, promotions, and salaries has the structure of a 'win/lose' (vs. 'prize') competition. In this type of competition the salient factor is not necessarily ability but perserverance, fortitude, endurance, doggedness, and so on.

When we look at literary criticism as an institution through the lens of competition, that is, when we study the ways in which critical argumentation has been institutionalized as a competition, a peculiar distortion of critical inquiry comes to light. In order to decide between winners and losers in the various career games we all play, administrators, in choosing to focus upon the success of critical arguments, force critics to reify their understanding. Knowledge, as Pierre Bourdieu argues, becomes 'symbolic capital.'[22] What we know has to be quantifiable, measurable and therefore cumulative. We might say that insights have to be converted into information in order to be accumulated. In this system, the goal of criticism is to 'accumulate knowledge,' hence the critic who has accumulated the most knowledge gets the most rewards. Central to this system is falsification.

Let's take a simple example. Jack believes that 'X' is the meaning of poem '1.' He argues his case on the grounds of the beliefs 'A, B, and C' which he takes to be factual. Jill believes that 'y' is the meaning of poem '1.' She argues her case on the grounds of 'a, d, and q.' What are Jack's options? Well, obviously, he could agree. He could say, 'I was mistaken in believing B and C.' If he does so, he admits his reading is false and is no longer eligible for an institutional reward. False arguments are not rewarded. So, in order to maintain his reading, Jack has to say either that d and q are irrelevant or that not-d and not-q are the facts. In other words, to survive the competition among readers, he must maintain his beliefs, otherwise he admits to error and loses status or merit.

In his *Psychology of Intelligence*, Jean Piaget terms the form of intellection I have just described 'assimilation,' namely, the tendency to assimilate all new experiences into the cognitive frameworks one already possesses. He contrasts this mode of intellection to 'accommodation,' wherein inquirers allow new experiences to 'break down' the frameworks they are accustomed to using.[23] It can be safely said that the institution of criticism encourages assimilation. It does not help your career to go around explaining how you are in error.

Considering that the institution of criticism encourages assimilation and therefore falsification as the cognitive strategies best suited to the accumulation of knowledge (information), we might, recalling Cixous's use of 'the proper,' term this cognitive style 'appropriation.'[24] Appropriation is the acquisition of knowledge understood as an entity (identities, samenesses, that is, information); it is the assimilation of concepts into a governing framework. Appropriation is an arrogation, confiscation, seizure of concepts. Ideas can be owned and sold at will. They are proper-ties. A contrasting mode of intellection, like intuition, a term I prefer to the term 'insight,'[25] often involves the in-appropriate, the disconcerting, and so on. Inappropriate because painful, humiliating; disconcerting in forcing one to change one's beliefs. Moreover, intuitions are not appropriatable and thus nothing gets accumulated. Intuitions are unspecifiable.[26] Intuitions are multiple, diverse, *ad hoc*, diffuse, etc. Whereas logical problems have single solutions, intuited problems have plural solutions and often appear illogical.

For post-moderns, thankfully, the veracity of criticism is not a matter of logic. Thought is not single, unified, centered, present. Though I cannot rehearse post-modern critiques of logocentrism here, I believe that I am not alone in thinking that texts do not provide a factual ground to interpretive claims, that writers and readers are discursive subjects who cannot be codified, that distinctions between correct and incorrect are purely conventional, that truth is a signifier like all others. In short, in post-modern theorizing, the very possibility of falsification is thoroughly undermined as a worthwhile intellectual endeavor.

If falsification does not lead to knowledge, then why do we continue to accept it? Obviously, it serves some other purpose. In the case of traditional criticism, the purpose is to regulate competition. Competition always requires rules. Falsification is the governing rule. Thus, modern criticism is no more than a competition governed by an arbitrary rule interpreted by those institutionally empowered to do so. Falsificity is a mechanism of a disciplinary apparatus to regulate competition. In an academic context, 'regulation of competition' refers to the rules that govern the attribution of merit to critical performances. Every competition has to have fixed rules to ensure the result that someone will win. Falsification is a regulating mechanism in the sense that it is like tagging the person who is 'it.' Falsifying reminds one of the fiction boys use in childhood wargames—when an enemy is shot, the victor shouts, 'you're dead!,' moving on to surprise the next opponent. Falsification is a similar device used by successful competitors to establish their progress (over the corpses of rival critics) along the way to winning. In critical games, though rationalized as a reward for possessing 'the best idea' among one's opponents, the competition is for a grade, a degree, a job, a publication, a promotion, a grant, an appointment. The awarding of these prizes in no way guarantees the value of the inquiry. Another irony in this system is that, whereas rules—like falsification—are designed to regulate, to keep under control the aggression involved, they have the effect of increasing it. Falsification, though construed as a regulator, functions only as a measurement of the logicality and frequency of successful counter-claims; hence, it has the effect of multiplying falsifications.

This system intensifies competition and leads to what I call intellectual machismo, the tendency toward an exaggerated expression of competition for the acquisition and appropriation of ideas. It is an exercise of power. In this sense, it is an instance of domination. The instigator, the person who picks the fight, confirms his sense that he is better than his rival often by creating a situation in which the rival, taken by surprise, is overwhelmed. In this scenario knowledge is power. Oddly, since it is an intellectually trivial pursuit, this wargame has the character of a parlor game. The machismic critic scores by knowing the most recent article, the exact date, the most stinging review, the precise reference, the received opinion, and so on. A side effect of these games is that it becomes impossible for the critic whose intellectual style is machismic to admit error. It is regarded as a fault, an embarrassment. This is a ridiculous posture. Ironically, the machismic intellectual, by telling what is obviously a kind of lie, places himself in a ludicrous position if he wishes finally to reach some understanding. Nevertheless, the machismic intellectual's discourse is permeated by utterances like 'Professor X is wrong.' Because, in the institution of criticism, falsification is bound up with the notion of 'wrong-doing,' intellectual machismo has a Rambo effect. The heroic critic is obligated morally to rescue thinkers from the prisons of illogic, to stand up to illogic when no one else cares. He is armed to the teeth with falsifications. Nothing but his self-esteem is left in his wake. He is the supreme falsifier, appropriator, assimilator.

Assimilation, the hallmark of appropriation, mechanizes falsification. When undertaken aggressively, it becomes a machine that falsifies everything in its path. The machine is a simple idea-mower, a handy procrustean mechanism. The machismic intellectual already has a set of beliefs to encompass his world. When he encounters someone else's belief, one of two events occur. Either, the announced belief squares with his own and can be assimilated as a confirmation of what he already believes, in which case verification occurs as a kind of negative falsification (we're right, so they're wrong). Or, as is more often the case, the announced belief does not square with his and is assimilated into his belief system as an error. In the latter instance, the Ramboist (this is, after all, a school of thought that needs a name) finds counter-evidence in his stock of beliefs, or identifies a lapse in logic, or invokes an authority (someone who belives what he believes). In short, since he cannot assimilate a belief that is inconsistent with his belief system, it enters his framework as a false belief. In his Ramboistic wargames, critical arguments are not distinguishable from quarrels. Quarreling is 'a dispute or disagreement, especially one marked by anger and deep resentment' and 'implies heated verbal strife' that 'often suggests continued hostility as a result' (WNWD).

Though arguments are said to be logical, dispassionate, detached, impersonal, objective and so on, and in this sense, can be regarded culturally as 'masculine,' looked at closely, especially in the light of a critique of falsification, they are difficult to distinguish from quarrels. Oddly, the more one examines arguments (intellectual masculinity), the more one finds quarrels (intellectual effeminateness). Similarly, the more one looks at intuition and the confession of error, etc. (intellectual femininity), the more it looks like a strong, incisive, powerful mode of knowing (intellectual virility).

INTELLECTUAL COMPASSION, COMMITMENT, COLLABORATION, CONCURRENCE, AND COMMUNITY

Literary criticism is intellectual work. Unlike work-for-profit, the success of which can be enhanced by competition, intellectual work requires compassion, commitment, collaboration, concurrence, and community. I list these as alternatives to the components of traditional criticism I have critiqued. In this section, I try to articulate my intuitions about them. I admit at the outset that not all of them are obvious alternatives to a competitive system. Collaboration is clearly an alternative to competition, compassion to machismo, intellectual community to scholarly individualism. Once I supply the phrase for which the term stands, it becomes clear that commitment-to-the-public-welfare is an alternative aspiration to self-interested careerism. Concurrence, however, is not the obvious alternative to appropriation. Consequently, in what follows I write about concurrence inchoately, hoping to stir further discussion.

Let me begin with the need for intellectual compassion. Compassion is ordinarily understood as 'sorrow for the sufferings or troubles of another' (*WNWD*) and can be related to the kind of empathy that is necessary for a commitment to collaborative concurrence about painful problems relevant to a community.[27] I contrast it with intellectual machismo. Intellectual compssion allows one intellectual to enter imaginatively into the problems of another. Collaboration depends upon the ability of one intellectual to enter into the pain or suffering that another is attempting to resolve. This contrasts to the kind of intellectual antagonism that competition spawns, which interferes with the resolution of problems.

Problems are not equivalent to puzzles. A problem is frustrating, painful, and difficult; it calls for the articulation of many questions. Each question differs, and therefore questioning requires the breaking down of preconceived frameworks because of the difficulty of formulating the problem in a way that does not simply appropriate it. Collaborative inquiry is not an instance of differing perspectives ultimately coming together in a unified framework. Instead, it seeks intellectual concurrence (rather than appropriation). Concurrence, by which I mean an agreement to join intellectual forces to get something done, is a plausible alternative to appropriation only on the condition that the differences among the researchers are allowed free play. In this form of collaboration, researchers are invited into the group not because they represent the same point of view but because they represent different and even incompatible points of view. Since getting-at-my-truth no longer governs the inquiry, quarrels are abandoned while concurrence is sought because any idea that helps solve the problem helps. Removing contradictions or inconsistencies from one's discourse is less important than resolving the cultural conflicts we call racism, elitism or sexism. Concurrence of this sort is desirable in literary research.[28]

Literary criticism calls for intellectual collaboration. The form of critical collaboration I have been advocating converges upon the apprehension of a problem and the critics involved band together to seek solutions to it. This form of collaboration in literary criticism occurs when a group of differing intellectuals, bound together by the acknowledgment of a textual/cultural problem, concur about a possible reading of it. By concurring, they do not seek conformity; they seek the coincidences among their differences. In this collaboration, concurrences about the problem and the solution are transpersonal. This does not necessarily imply a common ideal or telos holding the group together. Intellectual compassion and care hold the group together. In this form of collaboration, intellectual subject positions are not configured competitively. Differences are crucial. Reading is not an appropriation by an individual; it is the political concurrence of a group.

Inescapably, collaboration is the heart of the practice of literary study, despite the patriarch's insistence upon individualistic readings. How do we therefore explain that we rarely acknowledge it? Maria C. Lugones and Elizabeth V. Spelman note that:

> The desire to excel, the desire to avoid obscurity, and the desire for distinction become definitive of a competitive attitude in a context of opposition and they come, in their turn, to be shaped by this context. For at the heart of the desire to excel in the context of opposition, is the desire to excel not merely in some non-comparative sense, but to excel over others, to better them. . . . The overriding preoccupation is with standing out against the performances of others. . . .
> A competitor qua competitor sustains quite a different conception of herself and others than she would if she were engaged in activities in which it is appropriate to think about other humans as needy or as collaborators.[29]

As they remind us, competition is 'essentially self-centered' (p. 237). It makes 'one's own success and well-being . . . impossible without someone else's failure and/or misery' (p. 241). But, they argue, there is an alternative to the politics of competition—communal excelling.[30]

Collaboration takes place within the polis, the aggregate of communities. An intellectual community is a concurrence of intellectuals. Intellectual communities engender different and sometimes competing collaborations. As Lugones and Spelman write,

> There are contexts in which the desire to avoid obscurity and the desire for excellence are not only compatible with but necessary ingredients of projects that are properly communal. In those cases these desires are incompatible with an individualistic conception of excellence and of the participants in the project. (p. 238)

Though the word 'community' includes the word 'unity,' communities are not unities. Obviously, a notion of community can be deconstructed by pointing out that it implies an essential, central, unity, that it implies the 'presence' of some entity.[31] My concern here is not so much with the aberrations of a metaphysics of presence but with the naive assumption that communities are in fact unities. I do not mean to suggest by privileging the word 'community' that every individual in a community communes, that is, moves through the understanding of common goals and ideals toward identity, sameness. Though the word unfortunately suggests some kind of entity that is unified, it is possible to think of a community as a theatre in which intellectual 'play' is dramatized. In this play, the dramatis personae, each with distinct characteristics uniquely performed, act together toward a resolution of a problem. This is a play of differences that concurrently respond to a problem differentially perceived.[32] In this play, critics enjoy differing subject positions and their characters change, that is, they exchange subject positions. The bond of an intellectual community is intellectual compassion, the imaginative entry into another's problem.

In the terms now under discussion, critical inquiry is the compassionate accommodation of difference. Such inquiries are, by this definition, collaborative. But, to be housed in universities, collaborative inquirers (research groups), must, in some sense, *share* problems with communities. And, ultimately, communities of intellectuals can only legitimize themselves in the institution of criticism to the extent that they inquire into problems characterizing the various public spheres that make up our cultural formation.[33] These are not individualizing possibilities and considering them brings us circuitously back to a consideration of 'theory' (but not a man-driven one). Although falsification cannot and should not be recuperated by post-modern critics, in the context of communal inquiry, it seems foolish, if not impossible, to try to do without the heuristic value of error since problems are related to errors, and to inquire requires error and the breaking apart of preconceptions. Inquiries are written (or, in a grammatological sense, inscribed) as questions. Just as texts are intertexts that encompass myriad cultural formations, so inquiries are texts. Knowing this is theorizing.

Theorizing is not necessarily making theories. Theory-making is patriarchal. Theory is often used as a weapon. Theory is an effective instrument of falsification. And so on. But systematic theories that feed into competitive schemes are only the husk of theorizing. It is in the understanding of a problem through differing intuitions of it that theorizing occurs. Out of these intuitions arises a more general view of critical performance than is available to the solitary scholar. Competition obscures this phenomenon. In a competition among critics, theories become machines of falsification. They are used to refute the assumptions of rival critics. But in a communal inquiry, theorizing is informed by intellectual compassion and arises out of the urgency to end the pain associated with a specific problem. In that endeavor, performances must be made as effective as possible. Theorizing helps.

The precondition of possibility for intellectual compassion, commitment, collaboration, concurrence, and community is the de-masculinization of the Magister Implicatus. Why quarrel?

NOTES

I would like to thank my colleagues Ann Ardis, Dale Bauer, Art Casciato, Susan Jarratt, Kristina Straub, Andy Lakritz of Miami University and Patricia Harkin of Akron University for their intellectual compassion. Because of the intellectual community their concurrence occasions, what I have written is, in most respects, collaborative.

1. All of the quotes in this paragraph are references to *Webster's New World Dictionary*,

hereafter cited as *WNWD*. I have used this dictionary simply because it compares semantically related terms.

2. Though this theorem comes from the philosophy of science (Popper 1968:40), it applies to literary criticism whose disciplinary orientation mimics the institutionalization of scientific research.

3. To give the grade 'F' presupposes that the discourse so assigned is false. The same principle pertains to any grade below 'A+.' This system of 'grading' also pertains to ranking and the unqualified or qualified acceptance or rejection of papers submitted for publication.

4. This is an extension of Luce Irigaray's thematic in Irigaray 1985.

5. Veysey 1965. In this essay, I conflate the terms 'traditional' and 'modern' in a sense that combines Foucault's (1977) delineation of the period of our history dominated by 'discipline' and Lyotard's (1984) suggestion that we are 'post-modern' because the conditions of knowledge production have radically changed. In this context, the reliance on various kinds of warranting in informal logic which Toulmin (1972) sees as the defining characteristic of university studies called disciplines fits well into the notion of 'modern' as the logocentric world-view under critique by 'post-moderns.'

6. Corbett 171: 303.

7. His essay, which is written in English, is ironically entitled, 'Das Fussnoten: das Fundament der Wissenschaft.' It is ironic that a classicist should write this article, since his is among the most heavily footnoted of all fields.

8. Greene and Kahn 1985: 1–2.

9. Borklund 1977: 440.

10. Richards 1925: 6.

11. Ransom 1968: 328–9.

12. Wellek 1967: 3.

13. While deconstruction seems to reign in the news of our profession, post-modern feminism is far more vital. Indeed, post-modern criticism is inconceivable without feminism. Far more important than the deconstruction of literary texts is the politicization of literary study, a project in which feminists have led the way.

14. Barthes 1975: 3.

15. Bledstein 1976: 172.

16. Fasteau 1975: 1.

17. In this section I take an admittedly general look at some aspects of our collective past that can be understood as the historical conditions of the career profile of the literary scholar/critic. Most of my remarks are based on research conducted by the Group for Research into the Institutionalization and Professionalization of Literary Studies (GRIP). Many of the papers published in *The GRIP Report* involve brief historical accounts of exemplary academic figures: George Marsh, Francis Marsh, Francis Child, Ulrich von Wilamowitz-Moellendorf, Gustave Lanson, Cleanth Brooks, and so on. The GRIP collaboration is sponsored by the Society for Critical Exchange, a national organization dedicated to collaborative work in literary theory.

18. Cixous 1981: 52.

19. This paragraph summarizes an essay entitled 'The Magister Implicatus: a configuration of orthodoxy,' originally published in *The GRIP Report*, a revised version of which is included in a volume of GRIP essays under consideration for publication.

20. Longino, 'The ideology of competition,' in Miner and Longino 1987: 253. For detailed discussions of competition and women, see Miner and Longino 1987.

21. Ibid.: 250.

22. Bourdieu 1979: 171–83.

23. Piaget 1963: 8.

24. I draw on Cixous's distinction between the 'proper' and the 'gift' because it succinctly captures the relationship between knowledge and social institutions.

25. I earlier used the term 'insight' in place of the term 'intuition' for rhetorical reasons. Also, for reasons that will become apparent later, I define intuition not in the traditional way as 'the immediate knowing of something without the conscious use of reasoning' (*WNWD*), but as the instantaneous accommodation of unspecifiable differences.

26. I use 'intuition' in roughly Michael Polanyi's sense of 'insight' (Polanyi 1958: 90–1). In his account of intelligence, he focuses upon 'tacit knowledge' which is so complex that it cannot be articulated because the particulars are unspecifiable. Unlike Polanyi, however, I regard the 'unspecifiability' of insight as owing to the relationship between our short- and long-term memories.

27. See Lugones and Spelman 1987 for a detailed discussion of compassion. My use of the term, suggested to me by their essay, differs from theirs.

28. Unlike scientific theories, literary theories are not paradigms for research. Whereas in paradigmatic research theories govern the formulation of questions in the search for sameness, in literary research groups many, even contradictory, theorems can be used in search of differences that might precipitate concurrences. See David Shumway and James Sosnoski, 'Critical protocols,' *The GRIP Report*, vol. 2 (Research in Progress Circulated by the Society for Critical Exchange, 1984).

29. Lugones and Spelman 1987: 236–7.

30. I agree with Lugones and Spelman that competition has its political usefulness and support their contention that groups competing collectively for the welfare of the public can be beneficial. As they point out, while competition is akin to excelling, communal excelling is not destructive in the way that an individual's competing in self-interested ways is. For them, the crucial difference is that in communal excelling, self-interest is regulated by the interests of the group.

31. I am thinking here of Jean-Luc Nancy's work on community in his *La Communauté Désoeuvrée* (1986).

32. One of the topics in Laclau and Mouffe 1985 is the possibility of differences in political action.

33. Without a strong relationship to public spheres, 'intellectuals' are vulnerable to elitism. This is as true of an intellectual who works in a university as it is of any other.

WORKS CITED

Barthes, Roland 1975. *The Pleasure of the Text*. Trans. Richard Miller. New York: Hill and Wang.

Belsey, Catherine 1980. *Critical Practice*. London and New York: Methuen.

Bledstein, Burton J. 1976. *The Culture of Professionalism*. New York: W. W. Norton.

Borklund, Elmer 1977. *Contemporary Literary Critics*. New York: St Martin's Press.

Bourdieu, Pierre 1979. *Outline of a Theory of Practice*. Ed. Jack Goody, trans. Richard Nice. Cambridge: Cambridge University Press.

Cixous, Hélène 1981. 'Castration or decapitation?' Trans. Annette Kuhn. *Signs: Journal of Women in Culture and Society* 7.1 (Autumn): 41–55.

Corbett, Edward P. J. 1971. *Classical Rhetoric for the Modern Student*. New York: Oxford University Press.

Fasteau, Marc Feigen 1975. *The Male Machine*. New York: Dell Publishing Co.

Foucault, Michel 1977. *Discipline and Punish: The Birth of the Prison*. Trans. Alan Sheridan. New York: Vintage.

Frye, Northrop 1957. *Anatomy of Criticism: Four Essays*. Princeton: Princeton University Press.

Greene, Gayle and Kahn, Coppélia 1985. *Making a Difference: Feminist Literary Criticism*. London and New York: Methuen.

Hirsch, Jr, E. D. 1967. *Validity in Interpretation*. New Haven: Yale University Press.

Irigaray, Luce 1985. *Speculum of the Other Woman*. Trans. Gillian G. Gill. Ithaca: Cornell University Press.

Jardine, Alice and Smith, Paul (eds.) 1987. *Men in Feminism*. London and New York: Methuen.

Laclau, Ernesto and Mouffe, Chantal 1985. *Hegemony and Socialist Strategy*. London: Verso.

Lugones, Maria C. and Spelman, Elizabeth V. 1987. 'Competition, compassion and community: models for a feminist ethos,' in Miner and Longino 1987.

Lyotard, Jean-François 1984. *The Postmodern Condition: A Report on Knowledge*. Trans. Geoff Bennington and Brian Massumi. Minneapolis: University of Minnesota Press.

Miner, Valerie and Longino, Helen E. 1987. *Competition: A Feminist Taboo*. New York: The Feminist Press at The City University of New York.

Moi, Toril 1985. *Sexual/Textual Politics: Feminist Literary Theory*. London and New York: Methuen.

Nancy, Jean-Luc 1986. *La Communauté Désoeuvrée*. Paris: Christian Bougois.

Nimis, Stephen 1984. 'Fussnoten: das Fundament der Wissenschaft,' *Arethusa*, 17.2 (Fall): 105–34.

Piaget, Jean 1963. *The Psychology of Intelligence*. Paterson, New Jersey: Littlefield, Adams.

Polanyi, Michael 1958. *Personal Knowledge*. Chicago: University of Chicago Press.

Popper, Karl R. 1968. *The Logic of Scientific Discovery*. New York: Harper and Row.

Ransom, John Crowe 1968. 'Criticism, Inc.,' in *The World's Body*. Baton Rouge: Louisiana State University.

Richards, I. A. 1925. *Principles of Literary Criticism*. New York: Harcourt, Brace and World.

Toulmin, Stephen 1972. *Human Understanding: The Collective Use and Evolution of Concepts*. Princeton: Princeton University Press.

Veysey, Laurence R. 1965. *The Emergence of the American University*. Chicago: University of Chicago Press.

Wellek, René 1967. *Concepts of Criticism*. New Haven: Yale University Press.

Wellek, René and Warren, Austin 1956. *Theory of Literature*. New York: Harcourt, Brace and World.

HELENA MICHIE

NOT ONE OF THE FAMILY

*the repression of the other
woman in feminist theory*

Feminism has come to occupy a contradictory place with regard to the family and to the familial drama at the heart of all psychoanalytic and some sociological accounts of gender. Accused by their critics of being antifamily, feminists have become, in the idiom that will be explored here, home-wreckers. Certainly the dominant metaphors of feminist critiques of society are familial in origin; the world "patriarchy" itself, familiarly ensconced at the center of the feminist lexicon, locates power in literal and metaphorical fatherhood and defines the family as the scene, if not the source, of women's oppression.

There is within feminism, however, a mirror tendency to reclaim the family and to reproduce it in altered form. The figural response to patriarchy is the "sisterhood" invoked as its challenge. The attack, then, comes from within the family, and from within the structuring metaphor that makes intimacy the place of conflict. It is by displacing that conflict generationally, by circumventing the mother and projecting aggression onto a historical, diachronic process, that feminists appropriate for themselves and their sisters the power of teleology and of progress. The struggle of *many* sisters with a *single* father is no simple reenactment of the Oedipal triangle, as it is almost inevitably construed. Criticized repeatedly for its ahistoricism, its synchronicity, and its isolationist insistence on the single child, the Oedipal conflict is disrupted although not dismembered by the introduction of politics and community as they enter onto the familial stage embodied severally as "sisters."

Sisterhood projects a series of daughters who usurp the function and privilege of the father by reproducing themselves. In choosing sisterhood over daughter-hood, feminists have turned their gaze horizontally and have chosen—or tried to choose—to mirror each other and not the father. The axis of symmetry, the mirror of likeness upon which the Oedipal triangle is based, moves, then, from the space between father and daughter to the space(s) between sisters. Perhaps more important, feminist disruption of the symmetry to which the traditional Oedipal triangle accedes mixes the dominant metaphor, renders ungrammatical the word of the father, and exposes the faulty syntax of what Jacques Lacan calls his Law. It is important, however, that syntax, word, and language remain familial matters; the new grammar is still the grammar of the family.

If the clash between sister and father produces the rhetorical energy that fuels feminist practice, it is the relation between the mother and the daughter that has become the locus of the reproduction of feminist psychoanalytic discourse. For American object-relation theorists like Nancy Chodorow as well as neo-Lacanians like Hélène Cixous and Luce Irigaray, it is the problematic bond between mother and daughter that produces language, identity, and a provisional notion of "self" in the little girl. Feminists have, largely, turned their gaze from the Oedipal triangle to the pre-Oedipal period in which the girl struggles with her likeness and unlikeness to her mother before her entrance into and her inscription within the law of the father.

For a variety of historical and political reasons which I will not go into here, feminist literary theorists have followed psychoanalysis in recentering their inquiry around the mother.[1] While very early feminist theorists like Kate Millett struggled with the words of literary and academic fathers, more recent critics and theorists on both sides of the Atlantic have begun to turn their attention to maternal figures, maternal discourse. This discourse has taken many forms and has both figured in and figured almost all major feminist projects. Canonical revision has, for example, frequently been articulated as a search for foremothers; feminist poststructuralists have looked for the place of the mother in producing the *jouissance* that for critics from Roland Barthes to Jacques Derrida in turn produces and disseminates meaning, desire, and language; linguistic theorists have scanned literature and language for marks of *écriture féminine*, the mother tongue, what Cixous so famously refers to as "white ink . . . good mother's milk." Perhaps more fundamentally, motherhood and the maternal body have been seen as the location of language and self, the place where the female subject and the female narrative "I" are produced and reproduced.

As feminist discourse converges on the mother and the sister, it begins to problematize its own central metaphors. Most feminist theorists now acknowledge on some level at least the ambivalence of the mother–daughter relation, the painful tension in the female subject between love and matrophobia, likeness and unlikeness, the need for nurture and the need for separation.[2] Jane Gallop has explored the often-bitter rivalry between sisters for the love of the father, and increasingly, for self-love.[3]

Although theorists locate the causes of tension and rivalry differently— Chodorow, for example, sees matrophobia as a production of patriarchal familial relations, while Gallop seems to see it as an inevitable component of the growth of both mother and daughter—the mother–daughter relation is invoked as much to dramatize and problematize notions of the female self as it is to produce an integrated and integrative notion of female selfhood. No matter how problematized, metaphors of sisterhood and motherhood remain central to the feminist project. "Sister" and "mother" become the vessels that contain, shape, and delimit feminist discourse just as the family as it is now construed contains and shapes the roles and bodies of "real" mothers and sisters.

What about the woman who is not one of this family, the "other woman" who comes from outside to disrupt the home? It is this Other woman who concerns me here; it is she in her many guises for whom this paper attempts to make room. In popular parlance the Other woman is the mistress, the rival, the sexual threat. She is, however, Other in other senses: she is the third-world woman, the lesbian, the antifeminist, the one who is excluded from or resists the embrace of Oedipal sisterhood. While this paper cannot hope to deal effectively with all Other women, cannot even hope to name them since it is the nature of otherness to resist incorporation even by the act of naming, it is the beginning of an exploration of what lies outside what Gallop has called "the pitfall of familial thinking."[4]

The "Other Woman" is a phrase, a name, a non-name, that is beginning to surface in feminist writing and thinking. It finds a place in a veritable litany of popular and academic book titles. To name a few: the best-selling novel, *Other Women*, by Lisa Alther, about the relationship between a female psychologist and a lesbian patient; *The Other Woman: Stories of Two Women and a Man*, an anthology of short stories edited by Susan Koppelman; *The New Other Woman*, by Laurel Richardson, a sociological study of single women who have affairs with married men, and of course, Luce Irigaray's critique of the phallogocentrism of Western metaphysics, *Speculum of the Other Woman*. The very similarity of the titles hints at a problem central to feminist perceptions of otherness; these titles, hardly Other to each other, at once name the Other woman and insert her into familiar sexual tropes.

Feminist unease with Otherness lurks behind issues of title and entitlement; all four of these texts, in their different ways, can be read as strategies to control Otherness, either by its displacement or removal from the speaking subject—the female structuring "I"—or by the incorporation of the other into the family, into sameness. An example of the first rhetorical strategy, *The New Other Woman*, opens, remarkably, with a statement about the author's motives in writing the book that is at once personal and disjunctive. The very first sentence invokes the familiar, improbable fiction of the "friend" who makes possible so many confessional moments: "A friend had been an Other Woman for almost two decades. . . . Her experience was the initial impetus to do the research leading to this book."[5] Literally true or not, the explanation of the book's inception as a response to the situation of a "friend" has the rhetorical effect of projecting otherness onto the life and the body of the other, of establishing a boundary between self and other that is rigorously maintained by sociosexual law, by, in other words, the law that produces and maintains the family. The Other woman, exiled from the family, provides a convenient and articulable space for the exile of Otherness. All that is troubling, adulterous, troublingly adulterous within the family and within the wife can be impersonated by the Other woman.

Speculum of the Other Woman employs an opposite strategy by naming otherness between women only to reproduce it in its more familiar context of heterosexual difference. The "Other" of the title, in both French and English, would seem to modify "Woman" and to hint at the presence of at least two women, other in some sense to each other. In her only discussion of otherness as a category, however—which significantly and tantalizingly takes place in the course of her critique of Freud in female homosexuality—women's sexual identity becomes a matter of identity between women, lesbianism becomes a form of autoeroticism, and women's relations with each other, in the absence of men, become, quite explicitly, the relation of like to like, same to same. While she begins her critique by problematizing the words "like" and "same" by setting them off in quotation marks—"That a woman might desire a woman 'like' herself, someone of the 'same' sex, that she might also have auto- and homosexual appetites, is simply incomprehensible to Freud, and indeed inadmissible"—the quotation marks, those marks of difference, disappear as "same" and "like" get absorbed into the text and into the undifferentiating and capacious trope of sisterhood: "Yet what exhilarating pleasure it is to be partnered with someone like yourself. With a sister, in everyday terms."[6] Sisterhood as "everyday" term, as the infinitely iterated rhetorical move, surfaces here to erase difference between women and to close down its possible orthographic location between ironic quotation marks. Irigaray mirrors Richardson in her need to delimit otherness; like all mirrors, perhaps more vividly like all specula, *Speculum* both reproduces and inverts what it reflects.

If these mirror strategies for the containment of female otherness surface at crucial moments in Richardson and Irigaray, they serve as structures for three important texts of feminist criticism which this paper will discuss in some detail: Catharine Stimpson's "Feminism and Feminist Criticism" and two essays by Jane Gallop—"The Monster in the Mirror: The Feminist Critic's Psychoanalysis" and "Annie Leclerc Writing a Letter, with Vermeer." In examining how these texts simultaneously are and are not about the Other woman, how they make textual space for her entrance onto the scene of feminist criticism and close it off, I necessarily become absorbed by and into the texts of Other women as I absorb them into my paradigms. I hope throughout the process of these close readings of texts of my feminist sisters/mothers to disrupt the very familial metaphor that Harold Bloom suggests is the basis of all re(mis)-reading. To begin to acknowledge the possibility of the Other woman one must work through the texts of other women; to move outside the family is to chart the places made accessible by its idiom. I begin with Catharine Stimpson, who in her role as creator and first editor of *Signs* clearly occupies the place of mother in American feminist critical discourse, and with Jane Gallop, who repeatedly and disingenuously figures herself as daughter, sister, and rival in the field of psychoanalytic and feminist criticism.

Catharine Stimpson's essay is, on first reading, a triumph of the family of feminism, of a marriage not only as its title suggests between feminism and feminist criticism, but between and among a polyphony of feminist voices and enterprises. It summarizes, for an indulgent but perhaps uninformed public, the multiple projects of feminism. As a review essay it promises synthesis and integration. In describing feminism as a "mosaic" of women's voices, it comfortably subsumes differences among feminisms and feminists into a structuring metaphor that sees pattern and beauty in difference. More problematically, perhaps unconsciously, the essay seems at the same time to be a deconstruction of the mosaic, an exploration of the Otherness(es) within feminism. The specter of the Other in what at first reading seems to be a manifesto of pluralist coherence makes its entrances into her text through a series of linguistic slips and shifts. From her invocation of *Jean* Foucault, to whom she refers as "the other Foucault," to her concluding account of the rape of a colleague, another woman at her university, the other is simultaneously invoked and kept at bay.

On the surface, the essay's function is to integrate Otherness, to make it other than Other through a systematic dialectical pluralism that sympathetically includes and mediates among a number of disparate voices. It is also meticulously integrative on a rhetorical level, moving with ease from the personal to the academic to the political and refusing to see any rupture between them. Some of the most successful integrative moments in this essay are its numerous lists, which move lyrically among categories of feminist experience. In describing what she calls the contemporary feminist aesthetic she deliberately mixes genres and styles: "The new woman's culture self-consciously produces a feminist aesthetic that reconciles the flavorful gratuitousness of style with the imperatives of ideology. It appears in posters; clothing, such as T-shirts; demonstrations (those in Italy have a special elegance, verve, and theatricality); fine arts; films, and texts that experiment with a voice both personal and collective, that alludes to ricotta and Adrienne Rich, wool and Virginia Woolf, the domestic and the public."[7] Separated only by semicolons, the objects that make up these lists flow naturally into each other; they are litanies of inclusion, testaments to the graceful ease of feminist bridge-building. They promise a continuum, a seamless fabric: the mosaic naturalized and made fluid. This survey of feminist topography knows and inhabits all spaces, moving with equal freedom from the public world of demonstrations to the private world of wool, from England to (parenthetically) Italy.

The alliteration of the final list-within-a-list "ricotta . . . Rich" "wool . . . Woolf" adds to the incantatory quality of prose based on the most liquid of metonymies and free associative techniques. The movement from ricotta to Rich undermines the potential grammatical impasse of the proper name, while the transmutation of wool into Woolf makes even the canon a matter of feminist weaving. Stimpson's parentheses absorb and contain difference, the foreign, in an expansive and expanding political syntax.

The larger structure of the essay repeats and amplifies the structure of the lists; there is an exhilarating sense of motion throughout as Stimpson moves with ease from topic to topic, from allusion to allusion. The authority of logic, of phallogocentrism, has been replaced with the enabling authority of experience. The essay's assured experiential voice moves with ease from paragraphs about Emily Dickinson to a Yale University computer program named Boris, to the New Testament, to Gertrude Stein. The structure of the essay, like that of the lists, proclaims that within feminism there is no Other, or rather that Otherness can be enveloped in feminism's fertile and nurturant embrace.

It would seem that the fluidity which marks the structure of the essay extends to its pronominal shifts. Apparently untroubled by the pain Monique Wittig and other feminist theorists have reproduced in the engendering of their female narrative "I"'s and "she"'s, Stimpson begins with a historically situated "she": "In 1861, Emily Dickinson cut one of her shard-like poems about language," and moves immediately in the second paragraph to the academically forbidden narrative "I." Indeed, the "she" and the "I" come together in the act of producing the mosaic which structures this essay: "I place Emily Dickinson as the first inlay in the mosaic of my argument to the power of women writers. . . . I do not want to subordinate criticism to feminism, complexities of analysis to the severities of ideology. Neither do I wish to subordinate feminism to criticism. Rather, I seek a 'dialectical mediation between them'" (p. 272). Stimpson, in demonstrating her power to "place," has created a place for the "I" and the "she," the contemporary feminist and the nineteenth-century female poet, to create together. The "I," however, subsumes the "she" in creating both metaphor and mosaic. Like Derrida's "choreographies" of gender, Stimpson's mosaic both disguises and foregrounds the agent and her/his agency; a mosaic, like a dance, is an arrangement of seemingly spontaneous gestures and pieces.

It is not only women who have a place in Stimpson's mosaic. The embedded quotation in the passage just cited—"dialectical mediation between them"— represents the voice of a male, Marxist critic. Stimpson need not have depended on a footnote here; the term "dialectic" is common enough. The quotation marks, like the parentheses around Stimpson's earlier sentence about Italian demonstrations, serve precisely as marks of incorporation. Something foreign, something outside the nuclear family of Anglo-American feminism has been swallowed but left undigested as a testament to the power of feminist inclusion.

If the essay opens with a choreography of positions, of voices, to borrow from Stimpson's remarks about Emily Dickinson, "at once monolithic and polyphonic," it closes with an attempt to simplify and personalize these voices. In the last paragraph of the essay, the "I" reappears for the first time; the paragraph is worth quoting in full:

> I began with a quotation. I wish to end with a difficult anecdote. I was thinking about feminist criticism one night as I was driving home from my university work. On either side of the highway's twelve lanes were oil refineries, with great curved pipes and round towers. I smelled industrial fumes. I saw no green, except for paint and neon signs. Earlier that day, after a meeting, a woman colleague had told me about an experience. She had been raped, at knife-point, in her car, with her son watching. She was in her late twenties, her son only six. She was no Leda, the rapist no swan. To remember that story, to keep it as a fire within consciousness and political will, is the feminism in feminist criticism. Such a memory is a base of our use of language, no matter how skeptical we might be of language's referential power, as feminist criticism annuls powerful cultural arrangements, anneals again the materials of history, and reclaims language's push of joy.

By self-consciously calling attention to the narrative framing of her essay, Stimpson prepared us for both symmetry and teleology. The line "I wish to end with a difficult anecdote" simultaneously reminds us of the quotation with which the piece begins and promises us a change of direction, a movement inward that runs counter to symmetry, perhaps even to coherence. The "I" in "I wish to end" prepares us for its vulnerability; for the first time something is "difficult."

Significantly the "I" is one which both does and does not appear; it announces a violent opening-up (in the sense of both rape and discourse) that does and does not happen. The essay has set itself up for the rape of the author, for the personal to overwhelm the critical, for the "I" that has "placed" Dickinson to lose all control and distance. At the beginning of the paragraph we are made aware for the first time of the narrator's body. "I was thinking . . . I smelled . . . I saw" is both familiar in its integrative movement from thinking to smelling, the intellectual to the sensual, and radically defamiliarizing in its announcement of the presence of the body. Catharine Stimpson's body is the last piece of the mosaic to fall into place. We are prepared to move inward, to violate it, to share its violation, to be moved by it, to move below the surface of the mosaic. At this moment, tentatively embodied by the difficult, the vulnerable narrative "I," we are presented suddenly with a "she." She is the Other woman.

The words "a woman colleague" appear uneasily to us as the narrative "I," reassuring even in its vulnerability—we do, after all, know that the "I" survived, wrote, and is writing—disappears. "She had . . . she was . . . she was" become the sinister mirror burden of a song that began "I was thinking . . . I smelled . . . I saw." The Other woman appears only briefly; she is raped and vanishes. We only know that she is Other, that "she was no Leda." We do not know who she is except that she is not Catharine Stimpson, not Leda. The answer to the question, "Who is this other woman?" does not of course lie in her name or in any facts about her life before or after the rape. What interests me here is who she is not, and how who she is not allows her painful entrance into Stimpson's lyrical text.

The power of Stimpson's feminism depends on the somewhat problematic power of the tropes of analogy and metonymy at work within this final, moving, paragraph. The author remembers the story of the rape of her colleague when she, like her colleague at the time of the rape, is in a car. Stimpson's body positions itself in an act of remembrance and recreation, at the wheel of her car. The author's body, in not being raped as she drives, simultaneously alludes to the body of the woman colleague and allows her the safety to speak for her colleague; the text becomes a witnessing by someone whose speech is made possible because she was not a witness in the usual sense. The "real" witness, the colleague's little boy, cannot speak here of this nightmare amplification and deformation of the primal scene; Stimpson substitutes for the little boy as she substitutes for his mother. The family idiom of feminism allows her to speak what for the family is unspeakable.

On one level, of course, this "difficult" personal/impersonal anecdote acts as a displacement, a way of mediating terror, an attempt to incorporate even the ultimate Otherness of rape into feminist discourse. The Other woman and her body become a test case for the integrative "I," for the warmly integrative yet respectful phrase "woman colleague." The strangely inappropriate phrase "push of joy" that ends this paragraph and this essay brings us back to the beginning where Stimpson quotes the same line from Dickinson. It is too much to say that the rape, through the triumphantly rhetorical ending, has become "a push of joy," that feminist language has been produced by the rape in the act of reproducing it. It is not too much to say that Otherness appears briefly, violently, only to be "reclaimed" by feminism and its language.

It might at this point be useful to recall the beginning of Stimpson's essay, the opening invocation of Dickinson, whose name was the first to be placed in the mosaic. Running counter to the dominant metaphors of connection and coherence is a more troubling set of images that have to do with cutting, pain, and violence. "In 1861 Emily Dickinson cut one of her shard-like poems about language." Dickinson's voice, then, is not easily or unambiguously placed; her poems are "shards"—perhaps bits of mosaic broken into sharpness. Dickinson's voice severs connections even in the act of making them. In this context, Dickinson, the heroine in the romance of literary foremothers who constitute the feminist narrative of literary history, becomes herself Other, not only to the series of editors who tried to remove her shardlike dashes, not only to the patriarchy that kept her imprisoned in her father's house, but to the women who read her, identify her, identify *with* her, write about her, and try to "place" her.

Dickinson joins the colleague whose rape disrupts but is accommodated by the end of this essay to construct a frame that belies the body of Stimpson's argument; both colleague and literary foremother hint at the presence of otherness within the family, be it biological, academic, or literary. If the shardlike frame of Stimpson's essay implicitly undercuts its pronouncements of unity in diversity, the ending of Gallop's "The Monster in the Mirror" explicitly forces us to reread them with a view toward the crevices, cracks, and dislocations that signal the presence of the Other woman. Making familiar a rhetorical closing move out of the family, Gallop repeats in "Monster" the structural strategics of *The Daughter's Seduction*. In *Daughter*, Gallop moves chapter by chapter through the family as she discusses the daughter's struggles with and against her father, her mother, and her sister/rival. The final chapter disturbs the symmetry and intimacy of family relations by invoking otherness within the home in the person of the governess. "Monster" also turns toward the Other woman, offering her the last word. The Other woman of "Monster" is the woman of color, the third-world woman. In a paragraph visually separated from the body of her essay, Gallop concludes with a brief appreciation of Gayatri Spivak's "French Feminism in an International Frame":

> I see a connection between the problem I am pursuing and Spivak's critique of Western feminist theory. She argues that Western elite feminism can only project onto Third World Women. As an antidote to such narcissistic projection, she advocates a new question for feminism to ask. That antidotal question seems equally appropriate to the dilemma I have traced here . . . so I will close with Spivak's words: "However unfeasible and inefficient it may sound, I see no way to avoid insisting that there is a simultaneous other focus: not merely who am I? but who is the Other woman?"[8]

By quoting the Other woman on Otherness, Gallop would seem, in so far as this is possible, to be resisting the domestication of Otherness. She has not only given Spivak the last word, she has given her the last question—and it is one which Gallop will not try to answer. By placing a blank space between the body of the essay and the paragraph in which Spivak's words appear, she refuses the temptation to deny or absorb Otherness; she is, in effect, acknowledging the blank spaces between the pieces in Stimpson's mosaic. This gesture that closes but does not end the debate on Otherness is a gesture toward other answers, the answers of Other women.

Something happens, however, in the move from "Monster" to "Annie Leclerc"; the quotation from Spivak appears in identical form, but this time within the body of the essay. The appearance of the same Other woman in identical guise familiarizes her, makes her part of the family, makes her a Gallop. In quoting something she has already used, Gallop is now, in effect, quoting herself.

In "Annie Leclerc" Gallop structures a critique of the two covers of the *Critical Inquiry* special issue, *Writing and Sexual Difference*, much as I have structured my critique of Stimpson's two framing paragraphs. She looks first at the apparent sexual symmetry between the paintings reproduced on the two covers: "Together they compose a particularly well-articulated illustration of 'writing and sexual difference.' The woman is writing a letter, the man a book. Women write letters—personal, intimate, in relation; men write books—universal, public, in general circulation. The man in the picture is in fact Erasmus, father of our humanist tradition; the woman without a name. In the man's background: books. The woman sits against floral wallpaper."[9] In and between these covers, then, oppositeness, Otherness, will be defined as sexual difference. *Writing and Sexual Difference* will find its place within that difference, between the two covers that represent Man and Woman. The space between these covers is also, however, the space between marital, familial covers; it is a space defined, like heterosexual marriage, as the space between a man and a woman, a place of and constituted by their difference. There is certainly conflict in *Writing and Sexual Difference,* just as there are "differences" in the best-regulated marriage, but the paintings on the covers stand like sentinels to contain difference in its allocated, safe space "between" the sexes.

Gallop's article moves out of this safe space and text into another, more troubling text illustrated by a perhaps even more troubling painting: Annie Leclerc's "La Lettre d'amour," an extended love letter to another woman, and the painting to which the text consistently refers—Vermeer's "Lady Writing a Letter and Her Maidservant." In the painting, a woman is handing a (love?) letter to her maid.

The last five pages of Gallop's article perform an elaborate reading of the painting through Leclerc's text. Gallop's analysis focuses both implicitly and explicitly on the question of the otherness of the maidservant, on the otherness produced by class difference and reproduced as sexual desire in Leclerc's piece. Otherness also permeates the structure of Gallop's essay, which moves metonymically from *Writing and Sexual Difference* and the paintings which frame it to "Lettre d'amour," to the painting, to the Other woman within its frame.

Gallop preserves throughout the sexual dimension of Otherness, its challenge to heterosexual love and to what heterosexuality construes as "sexual difference." She reads Leclerc's desire for the other woman as it is problematized by class difference: "[Leclerc] contemplates the difference between these women [in the painting] and rather than feeling guilt at this difference, rather than feeling pity, she feels desire. She writes 'I love the woman servant . . . oh no, not out of pity, not because I would take up the noble mantle of redressers of wrongs . . . but because I want to touch her, to take her hands, to bury my head in her chest, to smother her cheeks and neck with kisses" (111). Difference, recast, produces desire; class becomes an erotic, a "sexual" difference. The maidservant in the painting, seen through a series of mediating concentric circles, frames, texts, comes to embody desire and the absences and lacks which constitute it.

The concentric nature of this article's textuality repeats itself in the topography of its sexuality. After discussing the possible "problems" with Leclerc's desire for the servant ("there is a long phallic tradition of desire for those with less power and privilege"), Gallop inserts herself and her own desires into the text—parenthetically: "Despite these problems I have with Leclerc's desire for the maid (an erotic attraction to women of another class which I share, I should add), I think it is valuable as a powerful account of just that sort of desire" (111). Gallop places herself last in a chain of desirers who through a series of differences announce their attractions to the maid. Like the woman colleague in Stimpson's essay, Gallop appears only briefly, parenthetically, near the end of the essay.

Gallop's entrance into the text as a narrative "I" simultaneously confirms the maidservant's Otherness, her position as object to a telescopic series of readers and desirers, and announces Gallop's own otherness to her text. Gallop becomes, then, her own sexually disruptive, parenthetically contained Other. Her intrusion into this multiple scene of desire marks her, sets her off in the very act of identifying with Leclerc, with Vermeer, and, with the maid. The "should" of the doubly parenthetical "I should add," foregrounds the problematics of textual self-insertion as effectively as Stimpson's announcement that the closing anecdote of her text will be "difficult." There is coercion in Gallop's "should" that is itself difficult, hard to locate. Who is telling Gallop to confess? Perhaps it is the prescriptive teleology of feminist discourse that demands that a place be made for the "I" and for its (her) desires. Like Stimpson, Gallop promises an "I" only to give us a "she"; like Stimpson the "she" is subsumed under the signature of the "I" as the Other woman becomes other than Other.

Gallop ends this essay, which explores sexual difference as a space between women, with a fragment of the quotation from Spivak with which she ended "Monster" and which she has already placed so securely in the body of this essay. She ends with the "necessarily double and no less urgent questions of feminism: 'not merely who am I? But who is the other woman?'" By repeating Spivak's questions at the end of the essay, Gallop obviously underscores their centrality. By making them central, by placing them in, as it were, her mosaic, she is denying that they are Other. By ending two essays with the words of the same Other woman, she is rendering Spivak's words familiar and welcoming her into the family. The mirror that so frighteningly replicates women in "Monster" is held up to Spivak's face. In looking over Spivak's shoulder, Gallop sees Jane Gallop. The question, "who is the Other woman" transforms itself on the surface of the mirror into the questionable statement "The Other Woman is myself." Gallop's essay, like many rhetorical and political gestures that begin as explorations of Otherness, ends by absorbing Otherness into an increasingly capacious notion of self. It is this capacious and hungry self—most benignly embodied in the metaphor of sisterhood—that feminists must learn to recognize so that they can ultimately recognize the face outside the mirror: the face of the Other woman.

NOTES

1. For a review of recent theoretical explorations of the mother–daughter bond see Marianne Hirsch, "Mothers and Daughters," *Signs* 7, no. 1 (1981), 200–222.

2. Luce Irigaray inscribes the maternal/filial dilemma orthographically by coining the word "in-difference" to describe both the (inevitable?) split between mother and daughter and their non-difference (lack of differentiation). Both underlie surface "indifference." See Luce Irigaray, "When Our Lips Speak Together," *Signs* 6, no. 1 (1983), 71.

3. Jane Gallop, *The Daughter's Seduction* (Ithaca: Cornell Univ. Press, 1982), chap. 5.

4. Gallop, *Daughter's Seduction*, p. xv.

5. Laurel Richardson, *The New Other Woman* (New York: Macmillan, 1985), p. ix.

6. Luce Irigaray, *Speculum of the Other Woman*, trans. Gillian C. Gill (Ithaca: Cornell Univ. Press, 1985), pp. 101, 103.

7. Catharine R. Stimpson, "Feminism and Feminist Criticism," *Massachusetts Review*, 24, no. 2 (1983), 275.

8. Jane Gallop, "The Monster in the Mirror: The Feminist Critic's Psychoanalysis," delivered for the first time at the English institute, Cambridge, Mass., September 1983.

9. Jane Gallop, "Annie Leclerc Writing a Letter, with Vermeer," *October*, Summer 1985, pp. 104, 107.

methodologies

A simple way to distinguish between literary criticism and literary theory might be this: to talk about a particular text—to discuss what it means, how it got produced, what it's worth—is to "do criticism." To talk about doing criticism—to examine what our assumptions are, how our questions get formulated, where our values come from—is to "do theory." American feminists have been doing literary criticism longer than they have been doing theory. The pioneering works of the 1960s and 1970s (many of them cited in the essays reprinted below) tended to concentrate on individual texts; feminist literary scholarship in the 1980s (like all branches of academic literary study) became much more self-conscious, more theoretical.

This section represents part of the conversation about feminist criticism conducted through the 1980s in American departments of English. In choosing to give the section a certain coherence, we have excluded many other conversations about feminist methodology, particularly those that refer more directly to the influence and practice of French feminism and those which grow more directly from structuralism and poststructuralism (later moments in some of those conversations can be found especially in "Desire," "The Body," and "Discourse"). The cross-references tying together these six essays indicate that the writers are directly addressing one another on a common theme: what does it mean to "do feminist literary criticism" at the end of the twentieth century?

The essays appear in the order in which they seem to have been composed, judging from the points on which they answer one another. Their common concerns mark the moment when American feminist critics were moving away from androgyny (or the effacement of gender differentiation) as a standard for art and for scholarship, and were beginning to embrace "difference." That is, from the early part of the decade, these American theorists became increasingly convinced that gender, having a significant impact upon experience, must make important differences in the production and evaluation of literary texts. At issue among these writers are such questions as: Does the difference of gender inhere in the body, or is it culturally constructed? What do the signs of gender difference look like in literary texts? What difference does gender make when a critic undertakes to evaluate a work written by a woman, or one written by a man? How can feminist criticism overcome the double marginalization of lesbian and minority women writers? Should feminist criticism adopt a "pluralist" theoretical stance; does it need "theory" at all? Never achieving anything like closure, the conversation continues today. Each of these essays—"classics" in the field—remains a touchstone for scholars who pursue and reframe these questions.

Myra Jehlen's complex and influential "Archimedes and the Paradox of Feminist Criticism" (1981) begins by interrogating the relationship between feminist criticism and women's studies. Seeing feminism as a stance, a "rethinking" of assumptions, Jehlen questions the advisability of concentrating exclusively on literature written by women, and begins to ask how "ideological" and "appreciative" criticism might come together in feminist study of men's and women's texts. She envisions a "radical comparativism" that would illuminate women's writing as well as allowing the critic to "see the dominant literature whole." Working though the example of nineteenth-century American sentimental fiction, she raises the problems of contradictory aesthetic and ideological values, and proposes a way of exploiting the energy of contradiction by looking at gender and literature in figurative terms, rather than literal ones. After juxtaposing Samuel Richardson's feminocentric novels (that is, novels with female protagonists) with those of the American sentimentalists, Jehlen argues "that [the] interior life, *whether lived by man or woman, is female*," and that "the exterior life, on the other hand, is just as ineluctably male." She analyzes how this pattern gets played out in several novels, and considers this novelistic structure's relation to "basic structures in our society," as well as "the very forms and categories of all our thinking."

Annette Kolodny, in "Dancing Through the Minefield" (1980), treats gender difference as a more literal division between male/misogynist and female/feminist scholars. Kolodny's metaphoric minefield—the academic ground laid with hazards that could destroy the feminist scholar if she treads too heavily—is her warrant for a methodology of pluralism, of choosing freely among the many reading strategies literary theory makes available. Kolodny's argument suggests that the primary task of criticism is to do readings, or find meanings for texts, and she contends that feminist criticism must embrace the possibility that multiple valid readings can be performed on any given work. Similarly open is Kolodny's view of literary value, as she cautions feminist critics against unquestioningly accepting canonized notions of "good" and "bad" literature. Kolodny's three "crucial propositions"—that literary history is a fiction, that we are taught to interpret texts by applying certain learned paradigms, and that we must examine the biases informing our critical methods and judgment—have remained central to American feminist critical practice.

If Jehlen and Kolodny reflect feminism's resistance to a universalized view of all literature as "male," Bonnie Zimmerman takes that resistance a step farther: "Lesbian literary criticism," she says in "What Has Never Been . . ." (1981), "simply restates what feminists already know, that one group cannot name itself 'humanity' or even 'woman.'" Just as feminist critics point out misogynist or androcentric assumptions behind literary criticism at large, Zimmerman here uncovers heterosexist assumptions behind influential feminist projects of the 1970s that suppressed or overlooked lesbian writers and texts. According to Zimmerman, of even more importance to lesbian critics is the development of a unique critical perspective or "at the very least, determining whether or not such a perspective is possible." The challenges for critics trying to make that determination include the difficulty of defining "lesbian" (Is it strictly a sexual term? Does it mean "woman-identified"? Is it an inclusive or exclusive way of referring to women?); the long-standing silence of lesbian voices in literature and in the academy; and the evident lack of a definable lesbian literary tradition.

Zimmerman outlines what lesbian criticism has achieved so far, and calls for some reforms that (interestingly) presage what feminist critics in general would be endorsing by the late 1980s: greater attention to the specificity of texts in particular times and places (a resistance to "ahistoricity"), and a firmer acceptance of differences among women (not just the differences between women and men). Her projected agenda for lesbian criticism—the further discovery of unknown works, the installation of lesbian texts into the feminist canon, the rereading of "great literature" from a lesbian perspective, and the elaboration of a lesbian aesthetic—parallel the broader feminist literary-critical agenda for the 1980s.

That agenda includes a kind of academic activism, and of all the calls-to-action in this volume, the one Jane Marcus makes is perhaps the most contentious. Her "Storming the Toolshed" (1982) revives Kolodny's battlefield metaphor, but revises it, too. Marcus sees the pluralist "relaxation of . . . tensions" among feminists (and between feminists and the academy) as premature. In her memorable phrase, "Dancing shoes will not do. We still need our heavy boots and mine detectors." Beginning by examining the role of literary theory in feminist critical practice, Marcus decries theoreticians' tendency to dismiss the contributions of feminist theorists to literary study. Marcus advocates a form of intellectual affirmative action, as she insists that "our [feminists'] historical losses at their [the male academic establishment's] hands are incalculable. . . . It is up to them to make reparations." She illustrates the radical potential of "lupine" criticism (in which feminist critics metaphorically double as flowers and as wolves) with reference to feminist work on Virginia Woolf, emphasizing especially the "collective and collaborative" studies that challenge conventional notions of individual academic achievement. She also gleefully recounts the tackling of "the two taboo subjects, Woolf's socialist politics and her love of women," thus helping to subvert the received idea of a ladylike, nonfeminist Woolf.

What separates Marcus most distinctly from Jehlen and Kolodny is less her critical program than the tone of her dismissal of pluralism as the model for feminist criticism. Evidently that tone struck Nina Baym, as we see in the last footnote of "The Madwoman and Her Languages: Why I Don't Do Feminist Literary Theory" (1987). Baym and Marcus take the same departure point: Baym begins by saying that "the central issue in academic literary feminism right now is theory itself," which does not diverge far from Marcus's statement that "the most serious issue" is "the division between theory and practice." But rather than endorsing theory as a "power tool" (Marcus's phrase) for feminism, Baym renews Kolodny's plea for pluralism, and asks feminists to return to the "empirically" based study which predated the theoretical revolution in feminist criticism. Baym confronts theoretically based feminist theses that she sees as counterproductive to feminism's goals; for example, she objects to the use Sandra M. Gilbert and Susan Gubar (cited approvingly by Jehlen and Kolodny) make of the "madwoman" as a figure for female authors, rejects the notion of a distinctly "female" language, and repudiates psychoanalytic assumptions she reads as misogynist.

Baym—whose predecessors in this section praise her groundbreaking work on nineteenth-century American women's novels—does not speak from an anti-feminist, but rather an anti-theory (and anti-totalizing) position. Her pluralism recalls Zimmerman's reminder that not all women (nor even all feminists) are alike: as Baym puts it, "a difference more profound for feminism than the male–female difference emerges: the difference between woman and woman."

The differences among feminist critics, and among the theoretical movements they represent, are magnificently chronicled in Elaine Showalter's "A Criticism of Our Own: Autonomy and Assimilation in Afro-American and Feminist Literary Theory" (1989). Since the publication of her influential "Feminist Criticism in the Wilderness" in 1981, Showalter has been one of the primary historians of feminist criticism, proposing categories in which to place all the varieties of feminist projects, and explaining the evolution of those categories within a chronological framework. "A Criticism of Our Own" outlines the dominant feminist methodologies through the 1980s, bringing this section up to date with the concerns feminist literary theorists are addressing now.

Showalter shows that African-American literary criticism and feminist criticism can be seen as having evolved through parallel stages "in our confrontations with the Western literary tradition." Both began "in a separatist cultural aesthetics, born out of participation in a protest movement"; both then moved "to a middle stage of professionalized focus on a specific text-milieu in an alliance with academic literary theory"; and both have recently arrived at "an expanded and pluralistic critical field of expertise on sexual or racial difference." In the case of feminist criticism, Showalter builds upon her earlier versions of its history to delineate six kinds of projects: (1) androgynist poetics, dedicated to effacing gender differences; (2) the feminist critique of male culture; (3) a Female Aesthetic celebrating women's culture; (4) gynocritics, or the study of the tradition(s) of women's writing; (5) gynesic, or poststructuralist feminist criticism, focusing on "the feminine" as a category within culture; and (6) gender theory, which Showalter defines as "the comparative study of sexual difference." Her essay enumerates influential books and essays representing each of these approaches, and attends to figures in such fields as philosophy, psychology, and anthropology whose work has had a significant impact on feminist literary theory. Particularly in its binding issues of race together with issues of gender, "A Criticism of Our Own" could stand by itself as an introduction to the questions about methodology that motivate and dominate the American conversation on feminist criticism today.

—RRW

ARCHIMEDES AND THE PARADOX OF FEMINIST CRITICISM

I

Feminist thinking is really *re*thinking, an examination of the way certain assumptions about women and the female character enter into the fundamental assumptions that organize all our thinking. For instance, assumptions such as the one that makes intuition and reason opposite terms parallel to female and male may have axiomatic force in our culture, but they are precisely what feminists need to question—or be reduced to checking the arithmetic, when the issue lies in the calculus.

Such radical skepticism is an ideal intellectual stance that can generate genuinely new understandings; that is, reconsideration of the relation between female and male can be a way to reconsider that between intuition and reason and ultimately between the whole set of such associated dichotomies: heart and head, nature and history. But it also creates unusual difficulties. Somewhat like Archimedes, who to lift the earth with his lever required someplace else on which to locate himself and his fulcrum, feminists questioning the presumptive order of both nature and history—and thus proposing to remove the ground from under their own feet—would appear to need an alternative base. For as Archimedes had to stand somewhere, one has to assume something in order to reason at all. So if the very axioms of Western thought already incorporate the sexual teleology in question, it seems that, like the Greek philosopher, we have to find a standpoint off this world altogether.

Archimedes never did. However persuasively he established that the earth could be moved from its appointed place, he and the lever remained earthbound and the globe stayed where it was. His story may point another moral, however, just as it points to another science able to harness forces internally and apply energy from within. We could then conclude that what he really needed was a terrestrial fulcrum. My point here, similarly, will be that a terrestrial fulcrum, a standpoint from which we can see our conceptual universe whole but which nonetheless rests firmly on male ground, is what feminists really need. But perhaps because being at once on and off a world seems an improbable feat, the prevailing perspectives of feminist studies have located the scholar one place or the other.

Inside the world of orthodox and therefore male-oriented scholarship, a new category has appeared in the last decade, the category of women. Economics textbooks now draw us our own bell curves, histories of medieval Europe record the esoterica of convents and the stoning of adulterous wives, zoologists calibrate the orgasmic capacities of female chimpanzees. Indeed, whole books on "women in" and "women of" are fast filling in the erstwhile blanks of a questionnaire— one whose questions, however, remain unquestioned. They never asked before what the mother's occupation was, now they do. The meaning of "occupation," or for that matter of "mother," is generally not at issue.

It is precisely the issue, however, for the majority of feminist scholars who have taken what is essentially the opposite approach; rather than appending their findings to the existing literature, they generate a new one altogether in which women are not just another focus but the center of an investigation whose categories and terms are derived from the world of female experience. They respond to the Archimedean dilemma by creating an alternative context, a sort of female enclave apart from the universe of masculinist assumptions. Most "women's studies" have taken this approach and stressed the global, structural character of their separate issues. Women are no longer to be seen as floating in a man's world but as a coherent group, a context in themselves. The problem is that the issues and problems women define from the inside as global, men treat from the outside as insular. Thus, besides the exfoliation of reports on the state of women everywhere and a certain piety on the subject of pronouns, there is little indication of feminist impact on the universe of male discourse. The theoretical cores of the various disciplines remain essentially unchanged, their terms and methods are as always. As always, therefore, the intellectual arts bespeak a world dominated by men, a script that the occasional woman at a podium can hardly revise. Off in the enclaves of women's studies, our basic research lacks the contiguity to force a basic reconsideration of all research, and our encapsulated revisions appear inorganic (or can be made to appear inorganic) to the universal system they mean to address. Archimedes' problem was getting off the world, but ours might be getting back on.

For we have been, perhaps, too successful in constructing an alternative footing. Our world apart, our female intellectual community, becomes increasingly cut off even as it expands. If we have little control over being shunted aside, we may nonetheless render the isolation of women's scholarship more difficult. At least we ought not to accept it, as in a sense we do when we ourselves conflate feminist thought with thinking about women, when we remove ourselves and our lever off this man's world to study the history or the literature, the art or the anatomy of women alone. This essay is about devising a method for an alternative definition of women's studies as the investigation, from women's viewpoint, of everything, thereby finding a way to engage the dominant intellectual systems directly and organically: locating a feminist terrestrial fulcrum. Since feminist thinking is the thinking of an insurgent group that in the nature of things will never possess a world of its own, such engagement would appear a logical necessity.

Logical but also contradictory. To a degree, any analysis that rethinks the most basic assumptions of the thinking it examines is contradictory or at least contrary, for its aim is to question more than to explain and chart. From it we learn not so much the intricacies of how a particular mode of thinking works as the essential points to which it can be reduced. And nowhere is such an adversary rather than appreciative stance more problematical than it is in literary criticism. This is my specific subject here, the perils and uses of a feminist literary criticism that confronts the fundamental axioms of its parent discipline.

What makes feminist literary criticism especially contradictory is the peculiar nature of literature as distinct from the objects of either physical or social scientific study. Unlike these, literature is itself already an interpretation that it is the critic's task to decipher. It is certainly not news that the literary work is biased; indeed that is its value. Critical objectivity enters in only at a second level to provide a reliable reading, though even here many have argued that reading too is an exercise in creative interpretation. On the other hand, while biologists and historians will concede that certain a priori postulates affect their gathering of data, they always maintain that they have tried to correct for bias, attempting, insofar as this is ever possible, to discover the factual, undistorted truth. Therefore expositions of subjectivity are always both relevant and revelatory about the work of biologists and historians. But as a way of judging the literary work per se, exposing its bias is essentially beside the point. Not that literature, as the New Critics once persuaded us, transcends subjectivity or politics. Paradoxically, it is just because the fictional universe is wholly subjective and therefore ideological that the value of its ideology is almost irrelevant to its literary value. The latter instead depends on what might be thought of as the quality of the *apologia*, how successfully the work transforms ideology into ideal, into a myth that works to the extent precisely that it obscures its provenance. Disliking that provenance implies no literary judgment, for a work may be, from my standpoint, quite wrong and even wrongheaded about life and politics and still an extremely successful rendering of its contrary vision. Bad ideas, even ideas so bad that most of humanity rejects them, have been known to make very good literature.

I am not speaking here of what makes a work attractive or meaningful to its audience. The politics of a play, poem, or story may render it quite unreadable or, in the opposite case, enhance its value for particular people and situations. But this poses no critical issue, for what we like, we like and can justify that way; the problem, if we as feminists want to address our whole culture, is to deal with what we do not like but recognize as nonetheless valuable, serious, good. This is a crucial problem at the heart of feminism's wider relevance. No wonder we have tried to avoid it.

One way is to point out that "good" changes its definition according to time and place. This is true, but not true enough. Perhaps only because we participate in this culture even while criticizing it, we do (most of us) finally subscribe to a tradition of the good in art and philosophy that must sometimes be a political embarrassment—and what else could it be, given the entire history of both Western and Eastern civilizations and their often outright dependence on misogyny? Nor is it true enough, I believe, to argue that the really good writers and thinkers unconsciously and sometimes consciously rejected such misogyny. As couched in the analogous interpretation of Shylock as hero because Shakespeare could not really have been anti-Semitic, this argument amounts to second-guessing writers and their works in terms of a provincialism that seems especially hard to maintain in these linguistically and anthropologically conscious times. For such provincialism not only assumes that our view of things is universal and has always been the substance of reality but also that all other and prior representations were insubstantial. So when Shakespeare depicted bastards as scheming subversives, Jews as merchants of flesh, and women as hysterics, he meant none of it but was only using the local idiom. What he meant, thereby demonstrating his universality, was what we mean.

I want to suggest that we gain no benefit from either disclaiming the continuing value of the "great tradition" or reclaiming it as after all an expression of our own viewpoint. On the contrary, we lose by both. In the first instance, we isolate ourselves into irrelevance. In the second—denying, for example, that Shakespeare shared in the conventional prejudices about women—we deny by implication that there is anything necessarily different about a feminist outlook. Thus, discovering that the character of Ophelia will support a feminist interpretation may appear to be a political reading of *Hamlet*, but, in fact, by its exegetical approach it reaffirms the notion that the great traditions are all-encompassing and all-normative, the notion that subsumes women under the heading "mankind."

It seems to me perfectly plausible, however, to see Shakespeare as working within his own ideology that defined bastards, Jews, and women as by nature deformed or inferior, and as understanding the contradictions of that ideology without rejecting its basic tenets—so that, from a feminist standpoint, he was a misogynist—and as being nonetheless a great poet. To be sure, greatness involves a critical penetration of conventions but not necessarily or even frequently a radical rejection of them. If, in his villains, Shakespeare revealed the human being beneath the type, his characterization may have been not a denial of the type but a recognition of the complexity of all identity. The kingly ambition of the bastard, the "white" conscience of the Moor, the father love of the Jew, the woman's manly heart: these complexities are expressed in the terms of the contemporary ideology, and in fact Shakespeare uses these terms the more tellingly for not challenging them at the root.

But the root is what feminists have to be concerned with: what it means not to be a good woman or a bad one but to be a woman at all. Moreover, if a great writer need not be radical, neither need a great radical writer be feminist—but so what? It was only recently that the great Romantic poets conned us into believing that to be a great poet was to tell *the* absolute truth, to be the One prophetic voice for all Mankind. As the philosophy of the Other, feminism has had to reject the very conception of such authority—which, by extension, should permit feminist critics to distinguish between appreciative and political readings.

We should begin, therefore, by acknowledging the separate wholeness of the literary subject, its distinct vision that need not be ours—what the formalists have told us and told us about: its integrity. We need to acknowledge, also, that to respect that integrity by not asking questions of the text that it does not ask itself, to ask the text what questions to ask, will produce the fullest, richest reading. To do justice to Shelley, you do not approach him as you do Swift. But doing justice can be a contrary business, and there are aspects of the text that, as Kate Millett demonstrated,[1] a formalist explication actively obscures. If her intentionally tangential approach violated the terms of Henry Miller's work, for example, it also revealed aspects of the work that the terms had masked. But she would not claim, I think, that her excavation of Miller's underlying assumptions had not done damage to his architecture.

The contradiction between appreciation and political analysis is not peculiar to feminist readings, but those who encountered it in the past did not resolve it either. In fact, they too denied it, or tried to. Sartre, for instance, argued in *What Is Literature?* that a good novel could not propound fascism. But then he also recognized that "the appearance of the work of art is a new event which cannot *be explained* by anterior data."[2] More recently, the Marxist Pierre Macherey has hung on the horns of the same dilemma by maintaining that the literary work is tied inextricably to the life that produces it, but, although not therefore "independent," it is nonetheless "autonomous" in being defined and structured by laws uniquely proper to it.[3] (I cite Sartre and Macherey more or less at random among more or less left-wing critics because theirs is a situation somewhat like that of feminists, though less difficult, many would argue, in that they already have a voice of their own. Perhaps for that reason, the position of black critics in a world dominated by whites would more closely resemble that of women. But at any rate, the large category to which all these belong is that of the literary critic who is also and importantly a critic of her/his society, its political system, and its culture.)

My point is simply that there is no reason to deny the limits of ideological criticism, its reduction of texts that, however, it also illuminates in unique ways. As feminists at odds with our culture, we are at odds also with its literary traditions and need often to talk about texts in terms that the author did not use, may not have been aware of, and might indeed abhor. The trouble is that this necessity goes counter not only to our personal and professional commitment to all serious literature but also to our training as gentlemen and scholars, let alone as Americans, taught to value, above all, value-free scholarship.

Doubtless the possibility of maintaining thereby a sympathetic appreciative critical posture is one of the attractions of dealing only or mainly with women's writings. With such material, ironically, it is possible to avoid political judgment altogether, so that the same approach that for some represents the integration into their work of a political commitment to women can serve Patricia Meyer Spacks to make the point that "criticism need not be political to be aware."[4] She means by this that she will be able to recognize and describe a distinct female culture without evaluating either it or its patriarchal context politically. Of course she understands that all vision is mediated, so that the very selection of texts in which to observe the female imagination is judgment of a kind. But it is not ideological or normative judgment; rather it is an "arbitrary decision" that "reflects the operations of [her] imagination," a personal point of view, a "particular sensibility" with no particular political outlook. The important thing is that her "perception of the problems in every case derived from her reading of the books; the books were not selected to depict preconceived problems."

Spacks seeks in this way to disavow any political bias; but even critics who have chosen a woman-centered approach precisely for its political implications reassure us about their analytical detachment. Ellen Moers stipulates in her preface to *Literary Women* that "the literary women themselves, their language, their concerns, have done the organizing of this book." At the same time she means the book to be "a celebration of the great women who have spoken for us all."[5] Her choice of subject has thus been inspired by feminist thinking, but her approach remains supposedly neutral for she has served only as an informed amanuensis. The uncharacteristic naïveté of this stance is enforced, I think, by Moers's critical ambivalence—her wish, on the one hand, to serve a feminist purpose, and her sense, on the other, that to do so will compromise the study as criticism. So she strikes a stance that should enable her to be, like Spacks, aware but not political. Since in posing a question one already circumscribes the answer, such analytical neutrality is a phantom, however; nor was it even Spacks's goal. Her method of dealing with women separately but traditionally, treating their work as she would the opus of any mainstream school, suits her purpose, which is to define a feminine aesthetic transcending sexual politics. She actively wants to exclude political answers. Moers, seeking to discover the feminist in the feminine, is not as well served by that method; and Elaine Showalter's explicitly feminist study, A Literature of Their Own,[6] suggests that a political criticism may require something like the methodological reverse.

Showalter wrote her book in the hope that it would inspire women to "take strength in their independence to act in the world" and begin to create an autonomous literary universe with a "female tradition" as its "center." Coming at the end of the book, these phrases provide a resonant conclusion, for she has shown women writing in search of a wholeness the world denies them and creating an art whose own wholeness seems a sure ground for future autonomy. But if, in an effort to flesh out this vision, one turns back to earlier discussions, one finds that there she has depicted not actual independence but action despite dependence—and not a self-defined female culture either, but a subculture born out of oppression and either stunted or victorious only at often-fatal cost. Women, she writes at the beginning of the book, form such a "subculture within the framework of a larger society," and "the female literary tradition comes from the still-evolving relationships between women writers and their society." In other words, the meaning of that tradition has been bound up in its dependence. Now, it seems to me that much of what Showalter wants to examine in her study, indeed much of what she does examine, resolves itself into the difference for writers between acting independently as men do and resisting dependence as women do. If her conclusion on the contrary conflates the two, it is because the approach she takes, essentially in common with Spacks and Moers, is not well suited to her more analytical goals.

Like theirs, her book is defined territorially as a description of the circumscribed world of women writers. A Literature of Their Own is thus "an attempt to fill in the terrain between [the Austen peaks, the Brontë cliffs, the Eliot range, and the Woolf hills] and to construct a more reliable map from which to explore the achievements of English women novelists." The trouble is that the map of an enclosed space describes only the territory inside the enclosure. Without knowing the surrounding geography, how are we to evaluate this woman's estate, whose bordering peaks we have measured anyway, not by any internal dimensions, but according to those of Mount Saint Dickens and craggy Hardy? Still less can one envision the circumscribed province as becoming independently global—hence probably the visionary vagueness of Showalter's ending. Instead of a territorial metaphor, her analysis of the world of women as a subculture suggests to me a more fluid imagery of interacting juxtapositions the point of which would be to represent not so much the territory as its defining borders. Indeed, the female territory might well be envisioned as one long border, and independence for women not as a separate country but as open access to the sea.

Women (and perhaps some men not of the universal kind) must deal with their situation as a *pre*condition for writing about it. They have to confront the assumptions that render them a kind of fiction in themselves in that they are defined by others, as components of the language and thought of others. It hardly matters at this prior stage what a woman wants to write; its political nature is implicit in the fact that it is she (a "she") who will do it. All women's writing would thus be congenitally defiant and universally characterized by the blasphemous argument it makes in coming into being. And this would mean that the autonomous individuality of a woman's story or poem is framed by engagement, the engagement of its denial of dependence. We might think of the form this necessary denial takes (however it is individually interpreted, whether conciliatory or assertive) as analogous to genre, in being an issue, not of content, but of the structural formulation of the work's relationship to the inherently formally patriarchal language which is the only language we have.

Heretofore, we have tended to treat the anterior act by which women writers create their creativity as part of their lives as purely psychological, whereas it is also a conceptual and linguistic act: the construction of an enabling relationship with a language that of itself would deny them the ability to use it creatively. This act is part of their work as well and organic to the literature that results. Since men (on the contrary) can assume a natural capacity for creation, they begin there, giving individual shape to an energy with which they are universally gifted. If it is possible, then, to analyze the writings of certain men independently—not those of all men, but only of those members of a society's ruling group whose identity in fact sets the universal norm—this is because their writings come into existence independent of prior individual acts. Women's literature begins to take its individual shape before it is properly literature, which suggests that we should analyze it inclusive of its *ur*-dependence.

In fact, the criticism of women writers has of late more and more focused on the preconditions of their writing as the inspiration not only of its content but also of its form. The writer's self-creation is the primary concern of Sandra Gilbert and Susan Gubar's *The Madwoman in the Attic*,[7] whose very title identifies global (therefore mad) denial as the hot core of women's art. This impressive culmination of what I have called the territorial approach to feminist criticism does with it virtually everything that can be done. In the way of culminations, it delivers us then before a set of problems that cannot be entirely resolved in its terms but that Gilbert and Gubar have uncovered. My earlier questioning can thus become a question: What do we understand about the world, about the whole culture, from our new understanding of the woman's sphere within it? This question looks forward to a development of the study of women in a universal context, but it also has retrospective implications for what we have learned in the female context.

Gilbert and Gubar locate the female territory in its larger context and examine the borders along which the woman writer defined herself. Coming into being— an unnatural being, she must give birth to herself—the female artist commits a double murder. She kills "Milton's bogey" and the specter Virginia Woolf called the "angel in the house," the patriarch and his wife, returning then to an empty universe she will people in her own image. Blasphemy was not until the woman artist was, and the world of women writers is created in sin and extends to a horizon of eternal damnation. For all women must destroy in order to create.

Gilbert and Gubar argue with erudition and passion, and their projection of the woman writer has a definitive ring. It also has a familiar and perhaps a contradictory ring. The artist as mad defiant blasphemer or claustrophobic deviant in a society that denies such a person soulroom is a Romantic image that not only applies also to men but does so in a way that is particularly invidious to women, even more stringently denying them their own identities than earlier ideologies did. That there be contradiction is only right, for when Blake hailed Satan as the hero of *Paradise Lost,* he cast heroism in a newly contradictory mold. Satan is archfiend and Promethean man, individualistic tyrant and revolutionary, architect and supreme wrecker of worlds. It should not be surprising that he is also at once the ultimate, the proto-exploiter of women, and a feminist model. But it does complicate things, as Gilbert and Gubar recognized: Mary Shelley found, in Milton, cosmic misogyny to forbid her creation—and also the model for her rebellion. But then, was her situation not just another version of the general Romantic plight, shared with her friends and relatives, poet-blasphemers all?

No, because she confronted a contradiction that superseded and preceded theirs; she was additionally torn and divided, forbidden to be Satan by Satan as well as by God, ambivalent about being ambivalent. If Satan was both demon and hero to the male poets, he offered women a third possibility, that of Byronic lover and master, therefore a prior choice: feminist assertion or feminine abandon. Here again, women had to act before they could act, choose before they could choose.

But it is just the prior choosing and acting that shape the difference between women's writing and men's that no study of only women's writing can depict. So, for instance, Gilbert and Gubar suggest that the monster in Mary Shelley's *Frankenstein* embodies in his peculiar horror a peculiarly female conception of blasphemy. It may well be, but I do not think we can tell by looking only at *Frankenstein.* At the least we need to go back and look at Satan again, not as a gloss already tending toward *Frankenstein* but as an independent term, an example of what sinful creation is—for a man. Then we need to know what it was for Mary Shelley's fellow Romantics. We might then see the extra dimension of her travail, being able to recognize it because it was extra—outside the requirements of her work and modifying that work in a special way. To reverse the frame of reference, if male critics have consistently missed the woman's aspect of *Frankenstein,* it may be only in part because they are not interested. Another reason could be that in itself the work appears as just another individual treatment of a common Romantic theme. Put simply, then, the issue for a feminist reading of *Frankenstein* is to distinguish its female version of Romanticism: an issue of relatedness and historicity. Women cannot write monologues; there must be two in the world for one woman to exist, and one of them has to be a man.

So in *The Madwoman in the Attic,* building on *Literary Women* and *A Literature of Their Own,* feminist criticism has established the historical relativity of the gender definitions that organize this culture; the patriarchal universe that has always represented itself as absolute has been revealed as man-tailored to a masculine purpose. It is not nature we are looking at in the sexual politics of literature, but history: we know that now because women have rejected the natural order of yin and yang and lived to tell a different tale. I have been arguing that, to read this tale, one needs ultimately to relate it to the myths of the culture it comments on. The converse is also true; in denying the normative universality of men's writing, feminist criticism historicizes it, rendering it precisely, as "men's writing." On the back cover of *The Madwoman in the Attic* Robert Scholes is quoted as having written that "in the future it will be embarrassing to teach Jane Austen, Mary Shelley, the Brontës, George Eliot, Emily Dickinson, and their sisters without consulting this book." Not so embarrassing, one would like to add, as it should be to teach Samuel Richardson, Percy Bysshe Shelley, Charles Dickens, William Makepeace Thackeray, Walt Whitman, and their brothers without consulting a feminist analysis.

Indeed, in suggesting here that women critics adopt a method of radical comparativism, I have in mind as one benefit the possibility of demonstrating thereby the contingency of the dominant male traditions as well. Comparison reverses the territorial image along with its contained methodology and projects instead, as the world of women, something like a long border. The confrontations along that border between, say, *Portrait of a Lady* and *House of Mirth*, two literary worlds created by two gods out of one thematic clay, can light up the outer and most encompassing parameters (perimeters) of both worlds, illuminating the philosophical grounds of the two cosmic models, "natures" that otherwise appear unimpeachably absolute. This border (this no-man's land) might have provided Archimedes himself a standpoint. Through the disengagements, the distancings of comparative analyses, of focusing on the relations between situations rather than on the situations themselves, one might be able to generate the conceptual equivalent of getting off this world and seeing it from the outside. At the same time, comparison also involves engagement by requiring one to identify the specific qualities of each term. The overabstraction of future visions has often been the flip side of nonanalytical descriptions of the present viewed only in its own internal terms. To talk about then and now as focuses of relations may be a way of tempering both misty fantasies and myopic documentations.

Thus the work of a woman—whose proposal to be a writer in itself reveals that female identity is not naturally what it has been assumed to be—may be used comparatively as an external ground for seeing the dominant literature whole. Hers is so fundamental a denial that its outline outlines as well the assumption it confronts. And such comparison works in reverse, too, for juxtaposed with the masculinist assumption we can also see whole the feminist denial and trace its limits. Denial always runs the risk of merely shaping itself in the negative image of what it rejects. If there is any danger that feminism may become trapped, either in winning for women the right to be men or in taking the opposite sentimental tack and celebrating the feminine identity of an oppressed past as ideal womanhood, these extremes can be better avoided when women's assumptions too can be seen down to their structural roots—from the other ground provided by men's writing.

Lest it appear that I am advocating a sort of comparison mongering, let me cite as a model, early blazing a path we have not followed very far, a study that on the surface is not at all comparative. Millett's *Sexual Politics* was all about comparison, however, about the abysses between standpoints, between where men stood to look at women and where women stood to be looked at. Facing these two at the book's starting point was Millett's construction of yet another lookout where a feminist might stand. As criticism per se, *Sexual Politics* may be flawed by its simplifying insistence on a single issue. But as ideological analysis, as model illuminator and "deconstructor," it remains our most powerful work. It is somewhat puzzling that, since then, so little has been written about the dominant literary culture whose ideas and methods of dominance were Millett's major concerns.[8] It may be that the critical shortcomings of so tangential an approach have been too worrisome. Certainly it is in reading the dominant "universal" literature that the contradictions of an ideological criticism become most acute. There are many ways of dealing with contradictions, however, of which only one is to try to resolve them. Another way amounts to joining a contradiction—engaging it not so much for the purpose of overcoming it as to tap its energy. To return one last time to the fulcrum image, a fulcrum is a point at which force is transmitted— the feminist fulcrum is not just any point in the culture where misogyny is manifested but one where misogyny is pivotal or crucial to the whole. The thing to look for in our studies, I believe, is the connection, the meshing of a definition of women and a definition of the world. And insofar as the former is deleterious, the connection will be contradictory; indeed, as the literary examples that follow suggest, one may recognize a point of connection by its contradictions. It will turn out, or I will try to show, that contradictions just such as that between ethical and aesthetic that we have tried to resolve away lest they belie our argument frequently are our firmest and most fruitful grounds. The second part of this essay will attempt to illustrate this use of contradiction through the example of the American sentimental novel, a kind of women's writing in which the contradiction between ideology and criticism would appear well-nigh overwhelming.

II

The problem is all too easily stated: the sentimental novels that were best-sellers in America from the 1820s to the 1870s were written and read mostly by women, constituting an oasis of women's writing in an American tradition otherwise unusually exclusively male. But this oasis holds scant nourishment; in plain words, most of the women's writing is awful. What is a feminist critic to do with it? It is not that as a feminist she must praise women unthinkingly, but there is little point either in her just contributing more witty summaries of improbable plots and descriptions of impossible heroines to enliven the literary histories. There hardly needs a feminist come to tell us that E. D. E. N. Southworth's cautionary tales are a caution; and as to whether Susan Warner's *Wide Wide World* does set "an all-time record for frequency of references to tears and weeping,"[9] there are others already counting. We might do best, with Elizabeth Hardwick, to simply let it alone. In her collection of more or less unknown women's writings,[10] Hardwick selected works that were commendable in their own rights and discarded most of what she read as "so bad I just had to laugh—I wasn't even disappointed. The tradition was just too awful in the nineteenth century."

Still, there it is, the one area of American writing that women have dominated and defined ostensibly in their own image, and it turned out just as the fellows might have predicted. It is gallant but also a little ingenuous of Hardwick to point out that men's sentimental writing was just as bad. For Hawthorne, whose *cri de coeur* against the "damned mob of scribbling women" still resonates in the hearts of his countrymen, did not invent the association between sentimentality and women. The scribbling women themselves did, ascribing their powers to draw readers deep into murky plots and uplift them to heavenly visions to the special gifts of a feminine sensibility. If there is no question of celebrating in the sentimentalists "great women who have spoken for us all," it seems just as clear that they spoke as women to women, and that, if we are to criticize the place of women in this culture, we need to account for the very large place they oc-cupied—and still do; the sentimental mode remains a major aspect of literary commerce, still mostly written and read by women.

Although at bottom either way presents the same contradiction between politics and criticism, the sentimental novel would seem, therefore, to flip the problems encountered in *A Literature of Their Own*, *Literary Women*, and *The Madwoman in the Attic*. The issue there was to uncover new aspects of works and writers that had more or less transcended the limitations of the patriarchal culture—or failed and found tragedy. Inspired by their example, one had nonetheless to temper admiration with critical distance. Here the difficulty lies instead in tempering rejection with a recognition of kinship, kinship one is somewhat hesitant to ac-knowledge in that it rests on a shared subordination in which the sentimental novel appears altogether complicitous. For the sentimentalists were prophets of compliance, to God the patriarch as to his viceroys on earth. Their stories are morality dramas featuring heroines prone at the start to react to unjust treatment by stamping their feet and weeping rebellious tears, but who learn better and in the end find happiness in "unquestioning submission to authority, whether of God or an earthly father figure or society in general." They also find some more substantial rewards, Mammon rising like a fairy godmother to bestow rich hus-bands and fine houses. Conformity is powerful, and Henry Nash Smith's explica-tion of it all has a definitive clarity: "The surrender of inner freedom, the discipline of deviant impulses into rapturous conformity, and the consequent achievement of both worldly success and divine grace merge into a single mythical process, a cosmic success story." [11] If that success is ill-gotten by Smith's lights, it can only appear still more tainted to a feminist critic whose focus makes her acutely aware that the sweet sellout is a woman and the inner freedom of women her first sale. With overgrown conscience and shrunken libido, the senti-mental heroine enumerating her blessings in the many rooms of her husband's mansion is the prototype of that deformed angel Virginia Woolf urged us to kill.

To kill within ourselves, that is. Thus we return to the recognition of kinship that makes it necessary to understand the sentimentalists not only the way critics generally have explained them but also as writers expressing a specifically female response to the patriarchal culture. This is a controversial venture that has re-sulted thus far in (roughly defined) two schools of thought. One of these starts from Hawthorne's charge that the popular novels usurped the place of serious literature. The title of Ann Douglas's *Feminization of American Culture* [12] an-nounces her thesis that the sentimentalists exploited a literary Gresham's law to debase the cultural currency with their feminine coin. But gold is at least hoarded, while this bad money devalued outright Hawthorne's and Melville's good. A tough, iconoclastic, and individualistic masculine high culture, the potential worthy successor of the tough Puritan ethos, was thus routed from the national arena by a conservative femininity that chained the arts to the corners of hearths and to church pews. Henceforth, and still today, a stultifying mass culture has emasculated the American imagination. Douglas does not blame women for this, for she sees them as themselves defined by their society. Even in the exploitation of their destructive power, she thinks, they meant well; nor would she wish for an equivalently simpleminded macho replacement to the feminized culture. But the implied alternative is nonetheless definitely masculine—in a good way, of course: strong, serious, and generously accepting of women who have abjured their feminine sensibilities. Not a hard thing to do, for if the choice is between Susan Warner and Melville, why were we not all born men?

That choice, however, is just the problem, its traditional limits generated by the Archimedean bind of trying to think about new issues in the old terms, when those terms do not merely ignore the new issues but deny them actively and thus force one instead into the old ways, offering choices only among them. The terms here are masculine and feminine as they participate in clusters of value that interpret American history and culture. It has been generally understood among cultural and social historians that the creative force in America is individualistic, active . . . masculine. Perhaps to a fault: Quentin Anderson would have liked the American self less imperially antisocial,[13] and before him Leslie Fiedler worried that its exclusive masculinity excluded heterosexual erotic love.[14] These analysts of American individualism do not necessarily come to judge it the same way, but they define it alike and alike therefore project as its logical opposition conformity, passive compliance, familialism . . . femininity. Huck Finn and Aunt Polly. The critical literature has until now mostly concentrated on Huck Finn, and *The Feminization of American Culture* completes the picture by focusing on Aunt Polly.

In the sense that its features are composed from real facts, "Aunt Polly" may well be a true picture. But her position in the composite American portrait, opposed in her trite conventionality to "his" rugged individualism, is not a function of facts alone but also of an interpretive scheme secured by a set of parallel dichotomies that vouch for one another: Aunt Polly is to Huck as feminine is to masculine; feminine is to masculine as Aunt Polly is to Huck. Only if we pull these apart will we be able to question the separate validity of either.

Potentially even more radically, Nina Baym[15] sets out to reconsider the component terms of the generally accepted dichotomy in the nineteenth century between female conformity and manly individualism, between female social conservatism and masculine rebellion. Representing the other school of thought about sentimentalism, this one in line with recent historical reconsideration of such ridiculed women's movements as temperance and revivalism, she argues that the women novelists too had their reasons. She answers Smith's accusation that the novels' "cosmic success story" pointed an arch-conservative moral by suggesting that for disenfranchised and property-deprived women to acquire wealth, social status, and some measure of control over their domestic environment could be considered a radical achievement, as ruling a husband by virtue of virtue might amount to subversion. As she sees it, "The issue [for the women in the novels] is power and how to live without it." They do not run their society and never hope to, so, short of revolution, no direct action can be taken. Even from their state of total dependence, however, these women can rise to take practical charge of their lives and acquire a significant measure of power by implementing the conservative roles to which the patriarchal society has relegated them. In this light, what Smith terms their "ethos of conformity" takes on another aspect and almost becomes a force for change, all depending on how you look at it.

Which is precisely the problem of this essay, emerging here with unusual clarity because both Smith and Baym approach the material ideologically. Even their descriptions, let alone their interpretations, show the effects of divergent standpoints. Consider how each summarizes the typical sentimental plot. Smith reports that *Wide Wide World* is the tale of "an orphan exposed to poverty and psychological hardships who finally attains economic security and high social status through marriage."[16] Baym reads the same novel as "the story of a young girl who is deprived of the supports she had rightly or wrongly depended on to sustain her throughout life and is faced with the necessity of winning her own way in the world" (p. 19). The second account stresses the role of the girl herself in defining her situation, so that the crux of her story becomes her passage from passivity to active engagement. On the contrary, with an eye to her environment and its use of her, Smith posits her as passive throughout, "exposed" at first, in the end married. Clearly this is not a matter of right or wrong readings but of a politics of vision.

It is as a discussion of the politics of vision that *Woman's Fiction* is perhaps most valuable. Baym has set out to see the novels from a different perspective, and indeed they look different. The impossible piety of the heroine, for instance, Baym views as an assertion of her moral strength against those who consider her an empty vessel, lacking ego and understanding and in need of constant supervision. Typically the heroine starts out sharing this view, taking herself very lightly and looking to the world to coddle and protect her. With each pious stand she takes over the course of the novel, she becomes more self-reliant, until by the end she has "developed a strong conviction of her own worth" (p. 19) and becomes a model for female self-respect. Thus, the heroine's culminating righteousness and its concomitant rewards, that from one viewpoint prove the opportunistic virtues of submission, indicate to Baym a new and quite rare emergence of female power manifested in the avalanche of good things with which the story ends. To Smith those cornucopia endings are the payoff for mindless acquiescence, sweets for the sweet ruining the nation's palate for stronger meat. For Douglas they are a banquet celebrating the women's takeover; a starving Melville is locked out. But for Baym the comfort in which the heroine rests at last is her hard-earned just reward, the sentimental cult of domesticity representing a pragmatic feminism aimed primarily at establishing a place for women under their own rule.

In that spirit, she sees a more grown-up kind of sense than do most critics in the novels' prudishness, pointing out that, when they were written, the Richardsonian model they otherwise followed had become a tale of seduction. The women novelists, she suggests, were "unwilling to accept . . . a concept of woman as inevitable sexual prey" (p. 26); in a world where sexual politics hardly offered women a democratic choice, they preferred to eschew sex altogether rather than be raped. Here again, point of view is all. One recalls that Fiedler had a more ominous reading. According to him, the middle-class ladies who wrote the sentimental fiction had "grown too genteel for sex" but, being female, they still yearned "to see women portrayed as abused and suffering, and the male as crushed and submissive in the end";[17] so they desexed their heroes by causing them to love exceptionally good girls with whom sex was unthinkable.

Without sharing Fiedler's alarm over the state of American manhood, one has to concede that the sentimental novel, with its ethereal heroines and staunchly buttoned heroes, was indeed of a rarefied spirituality. That its typical plot traced, instead of physical seduction, the moral regeneration and all-around strengthening of erstwhile helpless women would appear all to the good; it is surely an improvement for women to cease being portrayed as inevitable victims. But the fact is that the sentimental heroines, perhaps rich as models, are rather poor as characters. Those inner possibilities they discover in becoming self-sufficient seem paradoxically to quench any interior life, so that we nod in both senses of the word when such a heroine "looks to marry a man who is strong, stable and safe." For, "she is canny in her judgment of men, and generally immune to the appeal of a dissolute suitor. When she feels such attraction, she resists it" (p. 41). Quite right, except we actually wish she would not: do we then regret the fragile fair who fell instantly and irrevocably in an earlier literature, or the "graceful deaths that created remorse in all one's tormentors" (p. 25) and in the story some sparks of life?

Baym is well aware of the problem and offers two possible analyses. In the first place, she says, the women novelists never claimed to be writing great literature. They thought of "authorship as a profession rather than a calling, as work and not art. Often the women deliberately and even proudly disavowed membership in an artistic fraternity." So they intentionally traded art for ideology, a matter of political rather than critical significance. "Yet," she adds (and here she is worth quoting at length because she has articulated clearly and forcefully a view that is important in feminist criticism),

> I cannot avoid the belief that "purely" literary criteria, as they have been employed to identify the best American works, have inevitably had a bias in favor of things male—in favor, say of whaling ships rather than the sewing circle as a symbol of the human community; in favor of satires on domineering mothers, shrewish wives, or betraying mistresses rather than tyrannical fathers, abusive husbands, or philandering suitors; displaying an exquisite compassion for the crises of the adolescent male, but altogether impatient with the parallel crises of the female. While not claiming literary greatness for any of the novels introduced in this study, I would like at least to begin to correct such a bias by taking their content seriously. And it is time, perhaps—though this task lies outside my scope here—to reexamine the grounds upon which certain hallowed American classics have been called great. [Pp. 14–15]

On the surface this is an attractive position, and, indeed, much of it is unquestionably valid; but it will not bear a close analysis. She is having it both ways, admitting the artistic limitations of the women's fiction ("I have not unearthed a forgotten Jane Austen or George Eliot, or hit upon even one novel that I would propose to set alongside *The Scarlet Letter*" [p. 14]) and at the same time denying the validity of the criteria that measure those limitations; disclaiming any ambition to reorder the literary canon, and, on second thought, challenging the canon after all—or rather challenging not the canon itself but the grounds for its selection.

There is much reason to reconsider these grounds, and such reconsideration should be one aim of an aggressive feminist criticism. But it has little to do with the problem at hand—the low quality of the women's fiction—that no reconsideration will raise. True, whaling voyages are generally taken more seriously than sewing circles, but it is also true that Melville's treatment of the whale hunt is a more serious affair than the sentimentalists' treatment of sewing circles. And the latter, when treated in the larger terms of the former, do get recognized—for example, Penelope weaving the shroud for Ulysses surrounded by her suitors, or, for that matter, the opening scene of *Middlemarch* in which two young girls quibble over baubles, situations whose resonance not even the most misogynist reader misses.

The first part of the explanation, that the women did not take *themselves* seriously, seems more promising. Baym tells us that they "were expected to write specifically for their own sex and within the tradition of their woman's culture rather than within the Great Tradition"; certainly, "they never presented themselves as followers in the footsteps of Milton or Spenser, seekers after literary immortality, or competitors with the male authors of their own time who were aiming at greatness" (p. 178). With this we come closer to the writing itself and therefore to the sources of its intrinsic success or failure. I want to stress intrinsic here as a way of recalling the distinction between a work as politics—its external significance—and as art. So when seeking to explain the intrinsic failures of the sentimentalists, one needs to look beyond their politics, beyond their relationships with publishers, critics, or audiences, to their relationship to writing as such. Melville wrote without the support of publishers, critics, and audiences—indeed, despite their active discouragement—so those cannot be the crucial elements. He did, however, have himself, he took himself seriously; as Whitman might have said, he *assumed* himself.

Now, no woman can assume herself because she has yet to create herself, and this the sentimentalists, acceding to their society's definition, did not do. To the extent that they began by taking the basic order of things as given, they forswore any claim on the primary vision of art[18] and saw themselves instead as interpreters of the established ethos, its guardians, or even, where needed, its restorers. My point is that, for all their virtual monopoly of the literary marketplace, the women novelists, being themselves conceived by others, were conceptually totally dependent. This means dependent on Melville himself and on the dominant culture of which he, but not they, was a full, albeit an alienated or even a reviled, member. His novel in the sentimental mode could take on sentimentalism because he had an alternative world on which to stand: himself. And although no one would wish on a friendly author the travail that brought forth *Pierre*, there it is nonetheless, the perfect example of what no woman novelist conceiving of herself not as an artist or maker but as a "professional"—read practitioner, implementor, transmitter, follower of a craft—could ever have written. *Pierre* does not know how to be acquiescently sentimental, it can only be *about* sentimentalism. The issue is self-consciousness, and in self-consciousness, it is self. With the example of Melville, we might then reconsider the relationship of the rebel to conventions. The rebel has his conventional definition too—that is, his is one possible interpretation of the conventions—so that he stands fully formed within the culture, at a leading edge. On the other hand, in this society women stand outside any of the definitions of complete being; hence perhaps the appeal to them of a literature of conformity and inclusion—and the extraordinary difficulty, but for the extraordinary few, of serious writing.

Indeed, Baym's defense of the women novelists, like that generally of the lesser achievement of women in any art, seems to me finally unnecessary. If history has treated women badly, it is entirely to be expected that a reduced or distorted female culture, one that is variously discouraged, embittered, obsessively parochial, or self-abnegating, will show it. There is little point then in claiming more than exists or in looking to past achievement as evidence of future promise: at this stage of history, we have the right, I think, simply to assert the promise.

If there is no cause for defensiveness, moreover, it does have its cost. In the case of the sentimental novel, for instance, too much apologia can obscure the hard question Baym implies but does not quite articulate, to wit, why are the ways in which the sentimental novel asserts that women can succeed precisely the ways that it fails as literature? *Is its ideological success tied to its artistic failure?* Is its lack of persuasiveness as art in some way the result of the strong ideological argument it makes for female independence? The issue, it seems, is not merely neglecting art for the sake of politics but actively sacrificing it. Which brings the discussion back to the Douglas thesis that since the sentimentalists universalized (Americanized) a debased feminine culture, the more powerful the women (authors and heroines both), the worse the literature and thereby the consequences for the whole culture. The great appeal of this argument is that it confronts squarely the painful contradiction of women becoming powerful not by overcoming but by exploiting their impotence.

I would like to suggest another possible explanation. The contradiction between the art and the politics of the sentimental novel arises, not surprisingly, at the point where the novelists confronted the tradition in which they were working and, for political reasons, rejected it formally: when they refused to perpetuate the image of the seduced and abandoned heroine and substituted in her stead the good girl who holds out to the happy (bitter or boring) end. The parent tradition is that of the novel of sensibility as it was defined in *Clarissa*. But before *Clarissa*, Richardson wrote *Pamela*, probably the prototype of the female "cosmic success story." Pamela begins powerless and ends up in charge, rewarded for her tenacious virtue (or her virtuous tenacity) by a commodious house, a husband, and all those same comforts of upper middle-class life that crowned the goodness of America's sentimental heroines. Indeed, *Pamela* had helped set up their new world, being the first novel actually printed here—by Benjamin Franklin, who understood both romance and commerce and knew how well they could work together. So did Pamela, of course, a superb pragmatist who not only foils a seducer but also turns him into a very nice husband. She is perhaps not so finely tuned or morally nice as her sentimental descendants, but she is quite as careful

and controlled, as certain of her values, as unwilling to be victimized—and ultimately as triumphant. In contrast, Clarissa is helplessly enamored, seduced, destroyed. She is also the more interesting character and *Clarissa* the more complex
story—can it be that weak victimized women make for better novels?

In the first part of this discussion, I made the point that the madness into
which women artists are characterized as driven by social constraints needs to be
compared with the similar state often attributed to male artists. The same need
arises here, for male protagonists too are generally defeated, and, of course, Clarissa's seducer Lovelace dies along with her. But he is neither weak (in the helpless sense that she is) nor victimized; nor (to name doomed heroes at random) is
Stendhal's Julien Sorel or Melville's Pierre. There is certainly no surprise in the
contrast as such; we expect male characters to be stronger than female. The juxtaposition, however, may be suggesting something not already so evident: that as
the distinctive individual identity of a male character typically is generated by his
defiance, so that of a female character seems to come from her vulnerability,
which thus would be organic to the heroine as a novelistic construct.

It seems reasonable to suppose that the novel, envisioning the encounter of
the individual with his world in the modern idiom, posits as one of its structuring
assumptions (an assumption that transcends the merely thematic, to function
formally) the special form that sexual hierarchy has taken in modern times. The
novel, we know, is organically individualistic: even when it deals with several
equally important individuals, or attacks individualism itself, it is always about
the unitary self versus the others. Moreover, it is about the generation, the becoming, of that self. I want to suggest that this process may be so defined as to
require a definition of female characters that effectively precludes their becoming autonomous, so that indeed they would do so at the risk of the novel's artistic life.

Pamela represents the advent of a new form to deal with such new problems of
the modern era as the transformation of the family and the newly dynamic mode
of social mobility. *Pamela* works these out very well for its heroine, but there is
something wrong in the resolution. Pamela's triumph means the defeat of Mr. B.,
who in his chastened state can hardly be the enterprising, potent entrepreneur
that the rising middle class needs him to be. Her individualism has evolved at
the cost of his; later Freud would develop a special term for such misadventures,
but Richardson must already have known that this was not the way it should be.

At any rate, he resolved this difficulty in his next work simply by raising the
social status of his heroine. Since she was a servant, Pamela's quest for independent selfhood necessarily took a public form. To affirm her value and remain in
possession of her self, Pamela had to assert her equality publicly; to claim herself, she had, in effect, to claim power. But as an established member of the
powerful class, Clarissa is in full possession of its perquisites, notably that of
being taken as honorably marriageable by the lords of her world. Though it is
true that her family's greed for yet more wealth and status precipitates her crisis,
the problems she faces are really not those of upward mobility. Standing at the
other end of that process, she is profoundly unhappy with its results and with the
internal workings of her society. Her story is about the conflict within, the problems that arise inside the middle-class world; and its marvelously suited theater
for exploring these is the self within.

In thus locating itself inside the life of its dominant class, the novel only followed suit after older genres. But what is peculiar to this genre is that it locates the internal problems of its society still deeper inside, inside the self. Richardson's earlier novel had retained an older conception more like that of Defoe, identifying the self externally—hence *Pamela*'s interpretation of romance as commerce. *Clarissa*, on the contrary, now treats commerce in the terms of romance. Pamela had projected her inner world outward and identified her growth as a character with the extension of her power. But this approach tends to vitiate the distinction between the private self and the world out there that is the powerful crux of middle-class identity. *Clarissa* takes that distinction as its theme, and the locale of the novel henceforth is the interior life. I want to propose the thesis that this interior life, *whether lived by man or woman, is female*, so that women characters define themselves and have power only in this realm. Androgyny, in the novel, is a male trait enabling men to act from their male side and feel from their female side.

One common feminist notion is that the patriarchal society suppresses the interior lives of women. In literature, at least, this does not seem altogether true, for indeed the interior lives of female characters are the novel's mainstay. Instead, it is women's ability to act in the public domain that novels suppress, and again Richardson may have shown the way. *Pamela* developed its heroine by reducing its hero (in conventional terms). This compensation was, in fact, inevitable as long as the characters defined themselves the same way, by using and expanding the individualistic potency of the self. Since by this scheme Pamela would be less of a person and a character if she were less active, she had to compete with Mr. B. to the detriment of one of them—to the detriment also of conjugal hierarchy and beyond that, of their society, whose resulting universal competitiveness must become dangerously atomizing and possibly centrifugal. In a middle-class society, however, the family unit is meant to generate coherence, in that the home provides both a base and a terminus for the competitive activity of the marketplace. The self-reliant man necessarily subsumes his family, chief among them his wife, to his own identity; it is in the middle-class society above all that a man's home is his castle. But how can this subsuming be accomplished without denying identity to women altogether and thus seriously undermining their potency as helpmates as well? The problem lies in retaining this potency, that can come only from individualism, without suffering the consequences of its realization in individualistic competition. Tocqueville particularly admired the way this problem had been resolved in America. Women in the New World were free, strong, and independent, but they *voluntarily* stayed home. In other words, their autonomy was realized by being freely abandoned, after which, of course, they ceased to exist as characters—witness their virtual absence from the American novel.

The European novelist, at least the English and the French, either less sanguine about the natural goodness of middle-class values or more embattled with older norms, saw that this voluntary subjugation could be problematical. If women too are people, and people are individualists, might they not rebel? If they succeeded in this, social order would crumble; indeed, they could not succeed because they did not have the power. But the possibility, arising from the most basic terms of middle-class thought and also doomed by the very prevalence of that thought, emerged as the central drama of the modern imagination. It is precisely the drama of the suppressed self, the self who assumes the universal duty of self-realization but finds its individual model in absolute conflict with society. Then as it becomes the more heroically individualistic, the more self-realized, the more it pushes toward inevitable doom. If there is a tragic dimension to the novel, it is here in the doomed encounter between the female self and the middle-class world. This is the encounter Gilbert and Gubar have observed and attributed, too exclusively I think, to women. The lack of a comparative dimension can tend to obscure the distinction between representation and reality, to fuse them so that the female self simply is woman, if woman maligned. But, as Flaubert might have pointed out, many a male novelist has represented at least part of himself as female.

Which is not to suggest that European novelists were champions of women's rights. Their interest lay rather in the metaphorical potential of the female situation to represent the great Problem of modern society, the reconciliation of the private and the public realms, once the cornerstone of the new social and economic order has been laid in their alienation. Such reconciliation is problematical in that the self, granted its freedom, may not willingly accept social control; it may insist on its separate and other privacy, on the integrity of its interior vision. Clarissa wants to be and do otherwise than her world permits, and with that impulse, her inner self comes into view. It grows as she becomes less and less able to project her will, or rather as the incursions against her private self become more ferocious. Who, and what, Clarissa is finally *is* that private world.

I want to stress that in championing her alienated private self, the novel is not taking the side of real women, or even of female characters as female. Recent praise of *Clarissa* as a feminist document, or vindications of its heroine's behavior against her patriarchal oppressors, have not dealt clearly enough with the fact that her creator was a patriarch. If nonetheless he envisioned his heroine in terms with which feminists may sympathize, it is, I believe, because he viewed her as representing not really woman but the interior self, the female interior self in all men—in all men, but especially developed perhaps in writers, whose external role in this society is particularly incommensurate with their vision, who create new worlds but earn sparse recognition or often outright scorn in this one.

It is in this sense, I think, that Emma Bovary was Flaubert, or Anna Karenina, Tolstoy, or Isabel Archer, James. But the way Dorothea Brooke was George Eliot reveals the edge of this common identification between author and heroine, for Eliot, though herself a successful woman, cannot envision Dorothea as equally so.[19] One might suppose that she at least could have imagined her heroine, if not triumphant like Julien Sorel, acting out her doom rather than accepting it. It is one thing for male novelists to assume that women are incapable of effective action, but that women do so as well is more disturbing. I am suggesting that George Eliot was compelled by the form of her story to tell it as she did, that the novel as a genre precludes androgynously heroic women while and indeed *because* it demands androgynous heroes. In other words, the novel demands that the hero have an interior life and that this interior life be metaphorically female. The exterior life, on the other hand, is just as ineluctably male (and the novel has its share of active, manly women). These identifications are not consciously made as being convenient or realistic, in which case they would be vulnerable to conscious change. They are assumed, built into the genre as organic and natural; for, if action were either male or female, we would be back with the potentially castrating Pamela. She, however, bent her considerable force to enter the middle class, endorsing its values wholeheartedly. A similarly active Clarissa, an effective and militant Dorothea, must threaten the entire order of things.

The novel is critical, it examines and even approves the rebellions of Clarissa and Dorothea, but only after signaling its more basic acceptance of an order it locates, beyond political attack, in nature itself. Julien Sorel's alienation, however Napoleonic his aspirations, is associated throughout with the female part of his character; his sensitivity, his inability to accept the life and values his father offers him, these are repeatedly described as feminine traits, and the final act that destroys him bespeaks his feminine nature, much to the dismay of his male friends. In the mirror world of this and other novels, femaleness is not conservative but potentially revolutionary. At the same time, it is by cultural definition incapable of active fulfillment. In taking woman as metaphor for the interior life, then, and—far from suppressing her—expanding hers almost to the exclusion of any other life, the novel both claimed its interior, individualistic, alienated territory and placed the limits of that territory within the structures of the middle-class world it serves. George Eliot could have made Dorothea strong only by challenging these structures or by accepting them and depicting her as manly, thereby telling another story, perhaps *The Bostonians*. And no more than this latter would that story have challenged the conventional notions of feminine and masculine.

There is a third possibility for the novel, which is to return to *Pamela* and close down the alienated interior realm by having Dorothea act not out of internal impulses but in response to social dictates. This is what the sentimental novel does, its heroines realizing themselves in society actively but in full accord with its values and imperatives. This solution to the subversive threat posed by female individualism amounts to reversing the Richardsonian development from *Pamela* to *Clarissa*. We have a precise representation of that reversal—wrought, one is tempted to think, in deference to the greater solidity of the middle-class ethic in this country—in the first American novel, *Charlotte Temple* (1791). Its author, Susanna Rowson, copies the contemporary fashion of *Clarissa*-like stories but then, apparently thinking the better of such downbeat endings, tacks on a *Pamela* conclusion. Charlotte Temple, the disastrously fragile English heroine of the story, is carried off by a soldier en route to America; no sooner carried off than pregnant, no sooner pregnant than abandoned, no sooner abandoned than wandering the icy roads in winter in slippers and a thin shawl. She is charitably taken in to a hospitable fireside only to pass away, leaving an innocent babe and much remorse all around. At this point, however, with one perfectly satisfactory ending in place, Susanna Rowson adds a second.

While neglecting Charlotte, her faithless lover Montraville has fallen in love with New York's most desirable belle, Julia Franklin, an orphaned heiress who is "the very reverse of Charlotte Temple." Julia is strong, healthy, and of independent means and spirit. Her guardian entertains "too high an opinion of her prudence to scrutinize her actions so much as would have been necessary with many young ladies who were not blest with her discretion." Though Montraville has behaved badly toward the hapless Charlotte, he seems to be capable of a New

World redemption. Overcome by guilt at Charlotte's death, he fights a duel to avenge her honor and is dangerously wounded but, more fortunate than Lovelace, is nursed back to health by the discreet Julia. A representative of the new American womanhood, far too sensible to be tempted by rakes, far too clear about the uses of romantic love ever to separate it from marriage, Julia has accomplished the "Pamela" reform. She marries Montraville, and he becomes one of New York's most upright (and affluent) citizens, the fallen seducer risen a husband through the ministrations of a woman who is not merely good but also strong—strong, of course, in being all that she should be. Thus in Julia Franklin the private and the public selves are one, and the novel, with no relation between them to explore and therefore no way or need to envision the private, comes to a speedy end. About Charlotte a far better novel could have and has been written, but about Julia really nothing but exemplary tales for young girls and their spinster aunts. Pioneer mother of sentimental heroines, she deeds them an ability to take care of themselves (by taking care) that Baym rightly applauds from a feminist viewpoint but that effectively does them in as literature. This implies a possibility no less drastic than that the novel, evolved to deal with the psychological and emotional issues of a patriarchal society, may not permit a feminist interpretation.

The possibility that an impotent feminine sensibility is a basic structure of the novel, representing one of the important ways that the novel embodies the basic structures of this society, would suggest more generally that the achievement of female autonomy must have radical implications not only politically but also for the very forms and categories of all our thinking. Yet as students of this thinking, we are not only implicated in it but many of us committed to much of it. Literary criticism especially, because it addresses the best this thinking has produced, exposes this paradox in all its painful complexity—while also revealing the extraordinary possibility of our seeing the old world from a genuinely new perspective.

This analysis of novelistic form has been speculative, of course, a way of setting the issues of women's writing in the context of the whole literature in order to illustrate the uses of a comparative viewpoint as an alternative footing at the critical distance needed for re-vision. It has also been an exercise in joining rather than avoiding the contradiction between ideological and appreciative criticism on the supposition that the crucial issues manifest themselves precisely at the points of contradiction. As a method this has further implications I cannot pursue here. Let me suggest only that to focus on points of contradiction as the places where we can see the whole structure of our world most clearly implies the immanent relativity of all perception and knowledge. Thus, what appears first as a methodological contradiction, then becomes a subject in itself, seems finally to be shaping something like a new epistemology. But then, it is only right that feminism, as rethinking, rethink thinking itself.

NOTES

For their numerous helpful suggestions and suggestive objections, I am grateful to Sacvan Bercovitch, Rachel Blau DuPlessis, Carolyn Heilbrun, Evelyn Keller, Helene Moglen, Sara Ruddick, Catharine Stimpson, and Marilyn Young.

1. Kate Millett, *Sexual Politics* (Garden City, N.Y.: Doubleday & Co., 1970).

2. Jean-Paul Sartre, *What Is Literature?* (New York: Harper Colophon, 1965), p. 40; emphasis in original.

3. Pierre Macherey, *Pour une Théorie de la production littéraire* (Paris: Librairie François Maspero, 1966), pp. 66–68.

4. Patricia Meyer Spacks, *The Female Imagination* (New York: Avon Books, 1976), pp. 5, 6.

5. Ellen Moers, *Literary Women: The Great Writers* (Garden City, N.Y.: Doubleday & Co., 1976), p. xvi.

6. Elaine Showalter, *A Literature of Their Own: British Women Novelists from Brontë to Lessing* (Princeton, N.J.: Princeton University Press, 1977), pp. 11–12, 319.

7. Sandra Gilbert and Susan Gubar, *The Madwoman in the Attic: The Woman Writer and the Nineteenth-Century Literary Imagination* (New Haven, Conn.: Yale University Press, 1979). The chapter referred to at some length in this discussion is chap. 7, "Horror's Twin: Mary Shelley's Monstrous Eve."

8. I want to cite two works, one recently published and one in progress, that do deal with the traditions of male writing. Judith Fetterley in *The Resisting Reader: A Feminist Approach to American Fiction* (Bloomington: Indiana University Press, 1978) writes that women should "resist the view of themselves presented in literature by refusing to believe what they read, and by arguing with it, begin to exorcize the male ideas and attitudes they have absorbed." Lee Edwards in her *Psyche as Hero: Female Heroism and Fictional Form* (Middletown, Conn.: Wesleyan University Press, 1984) expresses the somewhat different but related purpose of reclaiming language and mythology for women. My objections to both these approaches will be clear from the essay. Let me add here only that I also find them nonetheless extremely suggestive and often persuasive.

9. Henry Nash Smith, "The Scribbling Women and the Cosmic Success Story," *Critical Inquiry* 1, no. 1 (September 1974): 49–70.

10. Elizabeth Hardwick, *Rediscovered Fiction by American Women* (New York: Arno Press, 1978).

11. Smith, p. 51.

12. Ann Douglas, *The Feminization of American Culture* (New York: Avon Books, 1978).

13. Quentin Anderson, *The Imperial Self* (New York: Alfred A. Knopf, Inc., 1971).

14. Leslie Fiedler, *Love and Death in the American Novel* (New York: Delta Books, 1966).

15. Nina Baym, *Woman's Fiction: A Guide to Novels by and about Women, 1820–1870* (Ithaca, N.Y.: Cornell University Press, 1978). Page numbers indicated in text.

16. Smith, p. 49.

17. Fiedler, pp. 259–60.

18. I am aware that this analysis assumes a modern psychology of art, that "creation" has not always been the artist's mission, or tacit acceptance of the established ethos considered fatal. But we are here speaking of the nineteenth century, not of all time; and writers who did not challenge their society's values would also not have questioned its fundamental construction of artistic identity as individualistic and as authentically creative.

19. For an illuminating discussion of this phenomenon—of women novelists being unable to imagine female characters as strong as themselves—see Carolyn Heilbrun, "Women Writers and Female Characters: The Failure of Imagination," in *Reinventing Womanhood* (New York: W. W. Norton & Co., 1979), pp. 71–92.

DANCING THROUGH THE MINEFIELD

some observations on the theory, practice, and politics of a feminist literary criticism

Had anyone the prescience, ten years ago, to pose the question of defining a "feminist" literary criticism, she might have been told, in the wake of Mary Ellmann's *Thinking About Women*,[1] that it involved exposing the sexual stereotyping of women in both our literature and our literary criticism and, as well, demonstrating the inadequacy of established critical schools and methods to deal fairly or sensitively with works written by women. In broad outline, such a prediction would have stood well the test of time, and, in fact, Ellmann's book continues to be widely read and to point us in useful directions. What could not have been anticipated in 1969, however, was the catalyzing force of an ideology that, for many of us, helped to bridge the gap between the world as we found it and the world as we wanted it to be. For those of us who studied literature, a previously unspoken sense of exclusion from authorship, and a painfully personal distress at discovering whores, bitches, muses, and heroines dead in childbirth where we had once hoped to discover ourselves, could—for the first time—begin to be understood as more than "a set of disconnected, unrealized private emotions."[2] With a renewed courage to make public our otherwise private discontents, what had once been "felt individually as personal insecurity" came at last to be "viewed collectively as structural inconsistency"[3] within the very disciplines we studied. Following unflinchingly the full implications of Ellmann's percepient observations, and emboldened by the liberating energy of feminist ideology—in all its various forms and guises—feminist criticism very quickly moved beyond merely "expos[ing] sexism in one work of literature after another,"[4] and promised, instead, that we might at last "begin to record new choices in a new literary history."[5] So powerful was that impulse that we experienced it, along with Adrienne Rich, as much "more than a chapter in cultural history": it became, rather, "an act of survival."[6] What was at stake was not so much literature or criticism as such, but the historical, social, and ethical consequences of women's participation in, or exclusion from, either enterprise.

The pace of inquiry these last ten years has been fast and furious—especially after Kate Millett's 1970 analysis of the sexual politics of literature[7] added a note of urgency to what had earlier been Ellmann's sardonic anger—while the diversity of that inquiry easily outstripped all efforts to define feminist literary criticism as either a coherent system or a unified set of methodologies. Under its wide umbrella, everything has been thrown into question: our established canons, our aesthetic criteria, our interpretative strategies, our reading habits, and, most of all, ourselves as critics and as teachers. To delineate its full scope would require nothing less than a book—a book that would be outdated even as it was being composed. For the sake of brevity, therefore, let me attempt only a summary outline.

Perhaps the most obvious success of this new scholarship has been the return to circulation of previously lost or otherwise ignored works by women writers. Following fast upon the initial success of the Feminist Press in reissuing gems such as Rebecca Harding Davis's 1861 novella, *Life in the Iron Mills*, and Charlotte Perkins Gilman's 1892 "The Yellow Wallpaper," published in 1972 and 1973, respectively,[8] commercial trade and reprint houses vied with one another in the reprinting of anthologies of lost texts and, in some cases, in the reprinting of whole series. For those of us in American literature especially, the phenomenon promised a radical reshaping of our concepts of literary history and, at the very least, a new chapter in understanding the development of women's literary traditions. So commercially successful were these reprintings, and so attuned were the reprint houses to the political attitudes of the audiences for which they were offered, that many of us found ourselves wooed to compose critical introductions, which would find in the pages of nineteenth-century domestic and sentimental fictions, some signs of either muted rebellions or overt radicalism, in anticipation of the current wave of "new feminism." In rereading with our students these previously lost works, we inevitably raised perplexing questions as to the reasons for their disappearance from the canons of "major works," and we worried over the aesthetic and critical criteria by which they had been accorded diminished status.

This increased availability of works by women writers led, of course, to an increased interest in what elements, if any, might comprise some sort of unity or connection among them. The possibility that women had developed either a unique, or at least a related tradition of their own, especially intrigued those of us who specialized in one national literature or another, or in historical periods. Nina Baym's recent *Woman's Fiction: A Guide to Novels by and about Women in America, 1820–1870*[9] demonstrates the Americanists' penchant for examining what were once the "best-sellers" of their day, the ranks of the popular fiction writers, among which women took a dominant place throughout the nineteenth century, while the feminist studies of British literature emphasized instead the wealth of women writers who have been regarded as worthy of canonization. Not so much building upon one another's work as clarifying, successively, the parameters of the questions to be posed, Sydney Janet Kaplan, Ellen Moers, Patricia Meyer Spacks, and Elaine Showalter, among many others, concentrated their energies on delineating an internally consistent "body of work" by women that might stand as a female countertradition. For Kaplan, in 1975, this entailed examining women writers' various attempts to portray feminine consciousness and self-consciousness, not as a psychological category, but as a stylistic or rhetorical device.[10] That same year, arguing essentially that literature publicizes the private, Spacks placed her consideration of a "female imagination" within social and historical frames, to conclude that, "for readily discernible historical reasons women

have characteristically concerned themselves with matters more or less peripheral to male concerns," and she attributed to this fact an inevitable difference in
the literary emphases and subject matters of female and male writers.[11] The next
year, Moers's *Literary Women: The Great Writers* focused on the pathways of literary influence that linked the English novel in the hands of women.[12] And, finally,
in 1977, Showalter took up the matter of a "female literary tradition in the English novel from the generation of the Brontës to the present day" by arguing
that, because women in general constitute a kind of "subculture within the
framework of a larger society," the work of women writers, in particular, would
thereby demonstrate a unity of "values, conventions, experiences, and behaviors
impinging on each individual" as she found her sources of "self-expression relative to a dominant [and, by implication, male] society."[13]

At the same time that women writers were being reconsidered and reread,
male writers were similarly subjected to a new feminist scrutiny. The continuing
result—to put ten years of difficult analysis into a single sentence—has been
nothing less than an acute attentiveness to the ways in which certain power relations—usually those in which males wield various forms of influence over females—are inscribed in the texts (both literary and critical), that we have
inherited, not merely as subject matter, but as the unquestioned, often unacknowledged *given* of the culture. Even more important than the new interpretations of individual texts are the probings into the consequences (for women)
of the conventions that inform those texts. For example, in surveying selected
nineteenth- and early twentieth-century British novels which employ what she
calls "the two suitors convention," Jean E. Kennard sought to understand why
and how the structural demands of the convention, even in the hands of women
writers, inevitably work to imply "the inferiority and necessary subordination of
women." Her 1978 study, *Victims of Convention*, points out that the symbolic nature of the marriage which conventionally concludes such novels "indicates the
adjustment of the protagonist to society's value, a condition which is equated
with her maturity." Kennard's concern, however, is with the fact that the structural demands of the form too often sacrifice precisely those "virtues of independence and individuality," or, in other words, the very "qualities we have been
invited to admire in" the heroines.[14] Kennard appropriately cautions us against
drawing from her work any simplistically reductive thesis about the mimetic relations between art and life. Yet her approach nonetheless suggests that what is
important about a fiction is not whether it ends in a death or a marriage, but what
the symbolic demands of that particular conventional ending imply about the
values and beliefs of the world that engendered it.

Her work thus participates in a growing emphasis in feminist literary study on
the fact of literature as a social institution, embedded not only within its own
literary traditions, but also within the particular physical and mental artifacts of
the society from which it comes. Adumbrating Millett's 1970 decision to anchor
her "literary reflections" to a preceding analysis of the historical, social, and economic contexts of sexual politics,[15] more recent work—most notably Lillian
Robinson's—begins with the premise that the process of artistic creation "consists not of ghostly happenings in the head but of a matching of the states and
processes of symbolic models against the states and processes of the wider
world."[16] The power relations inscribed in the form of conventions within our

literary inheritance, these critics argue, reify the encodings of those same power relations in the culture at large. And the critical examination of rhetorical codes becomes, in their hands, the pursuit of ideological codes, because both embody either value systems or the dialectic of competition between value systems. More often than not, these critics also insist upon examining not only the mirroring of life in art, but also the normative impact of art on life. Addressing herself to the popular art available to working women, for example, Robinson is interested in understanding not only "the forms it uses," but, more importantly, "the myths it creates, the influence it exerts." "The way art helps people to order, interpret, mythologize, or dispose of their own experience," she declares, may be "complex and often ambiguous, but it is not impossible to define." [17]

Whether its focus be upon the material or the imaginative contexts of literary invention; single texts or entire canons; the relations between authors, genres, or historical circumstances; lost authors or well-known names, the variety and diversity of all feminist literary criticism finally coheres in its stance of almost defensive rereading. What Adrienne Rich had earlier called "re-vision," that is, "the act of looking back, of seeing with fresh eyes, of entering an old text from a new critical direction," [18] took on a more actively self-protective coloration in 1978, when Judith Fetterley called upon the woman reader to learn to "resist" the sexist designs a text might make upon her—asking her to identify against herself, so to speak, by manipulating her sympathies on behalf of male heroes, but against female shrew or bitch characters. [19] Underpinning a great deal of this critical rereading has been the not-unexpected alliance between feminist literary study and feminist studies in linguistics and language-acquisition. Tillie Olsen's commonsense observation of the danger of "perpetuating—by continued usage—entrenched, centuries-old oppressive power realities, early-on incorporated into language," [20] has been given substantive analysis in the writings of feminists who study "language as a symbolic system closely tied to a patriarchal social structure." Taken together, their work demonstrates "the importance of language in establishing, reflecting, and maintaining an asymmetrical relationship between women and men." [21]

To consider what this implies for the fate of women who essay the craft of language is to ascertain, perhaps for the first time, the real dilemma of the poet who finds her most cherished private experience "hedged by taboos, mined with false-namings." [22] It also explains the dilemma of the male reader who, in opening the pages of a woman's book, finds himself entering a strange and unfamiliar world of symbolic significance. For if, as Nelly Furman insists, neither language use nor language acquisition are "gender-neutral," but are, instead, "imbued with our sex-inflected cultural values"; [23] and if, additionally, reading is a process of "sorting out the structures of signification," [24] in any text, then male readers who find themselves outside of and unfamiliar with the symbolic systems that constitute female experience in women's writings, will necessarily dismiss those systems as undecipherable, meaningless, or trivial. And male professors will find no reason to include such works in the canons of "major authors." At the same time, women writers, coming into a tradition of literary language and conventional forms already appropriated, for centuries, to the purposes of male expression, will be forced virtually to "wrestle" with that language in an effort "to remake it as a language adequate to our conceptual processes." [25] To all of this, feminists concerned with the politics of language and style have been acutely attentive. "Language conceals an invincible adversary," observes French critic Hélène Cixous, "because it's the language of men and their grammar."[26] But equally insistent, as in the work of Sandra M. Gilbert and Susan Gubar, has been the understanding of the need for *all* readers—male and female alike—to learn to penetrate the otherwise unfamiliar universes of symbolic action that comprise women's writings, past and present.[27]

To have attempted so many difficult questions and to have accomplished so much—even acknowledging the inevitable false starts, overlapping, and repetition—in so short a time, should certainly have secured feminist literary criticism an honored berth on that ongoing intellectual journey which we loosely term, in academia, "critical analysis." Instead of being welcomed onto the train, however, we've been forced to negotiate a minefield. The very energy and diversity of our enterprise have rendered us vulnerable to attack on the grounds that we lack both definition and coherence; while our particular attentiveness to the ways in which literature encodes and disseminates cultural value systems calls down upon us imprecations echoing those heaped upon the Marxist critics of an earlier generation. If we are scholars dedicated to rediscovering a lost body of writings by women, then our finds are questioned on aesthetic grounds. And if we are critics, determined to practice revisionist readings, it is claimed that our focus is too narrow, and our results are only distortions or, worse still, polemical misreadings.

The very vehemence of the outcry, coupled with our total dismissal in some quarters,[28] suggests not our deficiencies, however, but the potential magnitude of our challenge. For what we are asking be scrutinized are nothing less than shared cultural assumptions so deeply rooted and so long ingrained that, for the most part, our critical colleagues have ceased to recognize them as such. In other words, what is really being bewailed in the claims that we distort texts or threaten the disappearance of the great Western literary tradition itself[29] is not so much the disappearance of either text or tradition but, instead, the eclipse of that particular *form* of the text, and that particular *shape* of the canon, which previously reified male readers' sense of power and significance in the world. Analogously, by asking whether, as readers, we ought to be "really satisfied by the marriage of Dorothea Brooke to Will Ladislaw? of Shirley Keeldar to Louis Moore?" or whether, as Kennard suggests, we must reckon with the ways in which "the qualities we have been invited to admire in these heroines [have] been sacrificed to structural neatness,"[30] is to raise difficult and profoundly perplexing questions about the ethical implications of our otherwise unquestioned aesthetic pleasures. It is, after all, an imposition of high order to ask the viewer to attend to Ophelia's sufferings in a scene where, before, he'd always so comfortably kept his eye fixed firmly on Hamlet. To understand all this, then, as the real nature of the challenge we have offered and, in consequence, as the motivation for the often overt hostility we've aroused, should help us learn to negotiate the minefield, if not with grace, then with at least a clearer comprehension of its underlying patterns.

The ways in which objections to our work are usually posed, of course, serve to obscure their deeper motivations. But this may, in part, be due to our own reticence at taking full responsibility for the truly radicalizing premises that lie at the theoretical core of all we have so far accomplished. It may be time, therefore, to redirect discussion, forcing our adversaries to deal with the substantive issues and pushing ourselves into a clearer articulation of what, in fact, we are about. Up until now, I fear, we have only piecemeal dealt with the difficulties inherent in challenging the authority of established canons and then justifying the excellence of women's traditions, sometimes in accord with standards to which they have no intrinsic relation.

At the very point at which we must perforce enter the discourse—that is, claiming excellence or importance for our "finds"—all discussion has already, we discover, long ago been closed. "If Kate Chopin were *really* worth reading," an Oxford-trained colleague once assured me, "she'd have lasted—like Shakespeare"; and he then proceeded to vote against the English department's crediting a women's studies seminar I was offering in American women writers. The canon, for him, conferred excellence; Chopin's exclusion demonstrated only her lesser worth. As far as he was concerned, I could no more justify giving English department credit for the study of Chopin than I could dare publicly to question Shakespeare's genius. Through hindsight, I've now come to view that discussion as not only having posed fruitless oppositions, but also as having entirely evaded the much more profound problem lurking just beneath the surface of our disagreement. That is, that the fact of canonization puts any work beyond questions of establishing its merit and, instead, invites students to offer only increasingly more ingenious readings and interpretations, the purpose of which is to validate the greatness already imputed by canonization.

Had I only understood it for what it was then, into this circular and self-serving set of assumptions I might have interjected some statement of my right to question why *any* text is revered and my need to know what it tells us about "how we live, how we have been living, how we have been led to imagine ourselves, [and] how our language has trapped as well as liberated us." [31] The very fact of our critical training within the strictures imposed by an established canon of major works and authors, however, repeatedly deflects us from such questions. Instead, we find ourselves endlessly responding to the *riposte* that the overwhelmingly male presence among canonical authors was only an accident of history—and never intentionally sexist—coupled with claims to the "obvious" aesthetic merit of those canonized texts. It is, as I say, a fruitless exchange, serving more to obscure than to expose the territory being protected and dragging us, again and again, through the minefield.

It is my contention that current hostilities might be transformed into a true dialogue with our critics if we at last made explicit what appear, to this observer, to constitute the three crucial propositions to which our special interests inevitably give rise. They are, moreover, propositions which, if handled with care and intelligence, could breathe new life into now moribund areas of our profession: (1) Literary history (and with that, the historicity of literature) is a fiction; (2) insofar as we are taught how to read, what we engage are not texts but paradigms; and, finally, (3) that since the grounds upon which we assign aesthetic value to texts are never infallible, unchangeable, or universal, we must reexamine not only our aesthetics but, as well, the inherent biases and assumptions informing the critical methods which (in part) shape our aesthetic responses. For the sake of brevity, I won't attempt to offer the full arguments for each but, rather, only sufficient elaboration to demonstrate what I see as their intrinsic relation to the potential scope of and present challenge implied by feminist literary study.

1. *Literary history (and, with that, the historicity of literature) is a fiction.* To begin with, an established canon functions as a model by which to chart the continuities and discontinuities, as well as the influences upon and the interconnections between works, genres, and authors. That model we tend to forget, however, is of our own making. It will take a very different shape, and explain its inclusions and exclusions in very different ways, if the reigning critical ideology believes that new literary forms result from some kind of ongoing internal dialectic within preexisting styles and traditions or if, by contrast, the ideology declares that literary change is dependent upon societal development and thereby determined by upheavals in the social and economic organization of the culture at large.[32] Indeed, whenever in the previous century of English and American literary scholarship one alternative replaced the other, we saw dramatic alterations in canonical "wisdom."

This suggests, then, that our sense of a "literary history" and, by extension, our confidence in a "historical" canon, is rooted not so much in any definitive understanding of the past, as it is in our need to call up and utilize the past on behalf of a better understanding of the present. Thus, to paraphrase David Couzens Hoy, it becomes "necessary to point out that the understanding of art and literature is such an essential aspect of the present's self-understanding that this self-understanding conditions what even gets taken" as comprising that artistic and literary past. To quote Hoy fully, "this continual reinterpretation of the past goes hand in hand with the continual reinterpretation by the present of itself."[33] In our own time, uncertain as to which, if any, model truly accounts for our canonical choices or accurately explains literary history, and pressured further by the feminists' call for some justification of the criteria by which women's writings were largely excluded from both that canon and history, we suffer what Harold Bloom has called "a remarkable dimming" of "our mutual sense of canonical standards."[34]

Into this apparent impasse, feminist literary theorists implicitly introduce the observation that our choices and evaluations of current literature have the effect either of solidifying or of reshaping our sense of the past. The authority of any established canon, after all, is reified by our perception that current work seems to grow, almost inevitably, out of it (even in opposition or rebellion) and is called into question when what we read appears to have little or no relation to what we recognize as coming before. So, were the larger critical community to begin to seriously attend to the recent outpouring of fine literature by women, this would surely be accompanied by a concomitant researching of the past, by literary historians, in order to account for the present phenomenon. In that process, literary history would itself be altered: works by seventeenth- eighteenth-, or nineteenth-century women, to which we had not previously attended, might be given new importance as "precursors" or as prior influences upon present-day authors; while selected male writers might also be granted new prominence as figures whom the women today, or even yesterday, needed to reject. I am arguing, in other words, that the choices we make in the present inevitably alter our sense of the past that led to them.

Related to this is the feminist challenge to that patently mendacious critical fallacy that we read the "classics" in order to reconstruct the past "the way it really was," and that we read Shakespeare and Milton in order to apprehend the meanings that they intended. Short of time machines or miraculous resurrections, there is simply no way to know, precisely or surely, what "really was," what Homer intended when he sang, or Milton when he dictated. Critics more acute than I have already pointed up the impossibility of grounding a reading in the imputation of authorial intention because the further removed the author is from us, so too must be her or his systems of knowledge and belief, points of view, and structures of vision (artistic and otherwise).[35] (I omit here the difficulty of finally either proving or disproving the imputation of intentionality because, inescapably, the only appropriate authority is unavailable: deceased.) What we have really come to mean when we speak of competence in reading historical texts, therefore, is the ability to recognize literary conventions which have survived through time—so as to remain operational in the mind of the reader—and, where these are lacking, the ability to translate (or perhaps transform?) the text's ciphers into more current and recognizable shapes. But we never really reconstruct the past in its own terms. What we gain when we read the "classics," then, is neither Homer's Greece nor George Eliot's England *as they knew it* but, rather, an approximation of an already fictively imputed past made available, though our interpretive strategies, for present concerns. Only by understanding this can we put to rest that recurrent delusion that the "continuing relevance" of the classics serves as "testimony to perennial features of human experience."[36] The only "perennial feature" to which our ability to read and reread texts written in previous centuries testifies is our inventiveness—in the sense that all of literary history is a fiction which we daily recreate as we reread it. What distinguishes feminists in this regard is their desire to alter and extend what we take as historically relevant from out of that vast storehouse of our literary inheritance and, further, feminists' recognition of the storehouse for what it really is: a resource for remodeling our literary history, past, present, and future.

2. *Insofar as we are taught how to read, what we engage are not texts but paradigms.* To pursue the logical consequences of the first proposition leads, however uncomfortably, to the conclusion that we appropriate meaning from a text according to what we need (or desire) or, in other words, according to the critical assumptions or predispositions (conscious or not) that we bring to it. And we appropriate different meanings, or report different gleanings, at different times—even from the same text—according to our changed assumptions, circumstances, and requirements. This, in essence, constitutes the heart of the second proposition. For insofar as literature is itself a social institution, so, too, reading is a highly socialized—or learned—activity. What makes it so exciting, of course, is that it can be constantly relearned and refined, so as to provide either an individual or an entire reading community, over time, with infinite variations of the same text. It *can* provide that, but, I must add, too often it does not. Frequently our reading habits become fixed, so that each successive reading experience functions, in effect, normatively, with one particular kind of novel stylizing our expectations of those to follow, the stylistic devices of any favorite author (or group of authors) alerting us to the presence or absence of those devices in the works of others, and so on. "Once one has read his first poem," Murray Krieger has observed, "he

turns to his second and to the others that will follow thereafter with an increasing series of preconceptions about the sort of activity in which he is indulging. In matters of literary experience, as in other experiences," Krieger concludes, "one is a virgin but once." [37]

For most readers, this is a fairly unconscious process, and not unnaturally, what we are taught to read well and with pleasure, when we are young, predisposes us to certain specific kinds of adult reading tastes. For the professional literary critic, the process may be no different, but it is at least more conscious. Graduate schools, at their best, are training grounds for competing interpretive paradigms or reading techniques: affective stylistics, structuralism, and semiotic analysis, to name only a few of the more recent entries. The delight we learn to take in the mastery of these interpretive strategies is then often mistakenly construed as our delight in reading specific texts, especially in the case of works that would otherwise be unavailable or even offensive to us. In my own graduate career, for example, with superb teachers to guide me, I learned to take great pleasure in *Paradise Lost*, even though as both a Jew and a feminist, I can subscribe neither to its theology nor to its hierarchy of sexual valuation. If, within its own terms (as I have been taught to understand them), the text manipulates my sensibilities and moves me to pleasure—as I will affirm it does—then, at least in part, that must be because, in spite of my real-world alienation from many of its basic tenets, I have been able to enter that text through interpretive strategies which allow me to displace less comfortable observations with others to which I have been taught pleasurably to attend. Though some of my teachers may have called this process "learning to read the text properly," I have now come to see it as learning to effectively manipulate the critical strategies which they taught me so well. Knowing, for example, the poem's debt to epic conventions, I am able to discover in it echoes and reworkings of both lines and situations from Virgil and Homer; placing it within the ongoing Christian debate between Good and Evil, I comprehend both the philosophic and the stylistic significance of Satan's ornate rhetoric as compared to God's majestic simplicity in Book III. But, in each case, an interpretative model, already assumed, had guided my discovery of the evidence for it. [38]

When we consider the implications of these observations for the processes of canon formation and for the assignment of aesthetic value, we find ourselves locked in a chicken-and-egg dilemma, unable easily to distinguish as primary the importance of *what* we read as opposed to *how* we have learned to read it. For, simply put, we read well, and with pleasure, what we already know how to read; and what we know how to read is to a large extent dependent upon what we have already read (works from which we've developed our expectations and learned our interpretive strategies). What we then choose to read—and, by extension, teach and thereby "canonize"—usually follows upon our previous reading. Radical breaks are tiring, demanding, uncomfortable, and sometimes wholly beyond our comprehension.

Though the argument is not usually couched in precisely these terms, a considerable segment of the most recent feminist rereadings of women writers allows the conclusion that, where those authors have dropped out of sight, the reason may be due not to any lack of merit in the work but, instead, to an incapacity of predominantly male readers to properly interpret and appreciate women's texts—due, in large part, to a lack of prior acquaintance. The fictions which women compose about the worlds they inhabit may owe a debt to prior, influential works by other women or, simply enough, to the daily experience of the writer herself or, more usually, to some combination of the two. The reader coming upon such fiction, with knowledge of neither its informing literary traditions nor its real-world contexts, will thereby find himself hard-pressed, though he may recognize the words on the page, to competently decipher its intended meanings. And this is what makes the recent studies by Spacks, Moers, Showalter, Gilbert and Gubar, and others so crucial. For, by attempting to delineate the connections and interrelations that make for a female literary tradition, they provide us invaluable aids for recognizing and understanding the unique literary traditions and sex-related contexts out of which women write.

The (usually male) reader who, both by experience and by reading, has never made acquaintance with those contexts—historically, the lying-in room, the parlor, the nursery, the kitchen, the laundry, and so on—will necessarily lack the capacity to fully interpret the dialogue or action embedded therein; for, as every good novelist knows, the meaning of any character's action or statement is inescapably a function of the specific situation in which it is embedded.[39] Virginia Woolf therefore quite properly anticipated the male reader's disposition to write off what he could not understand, abandoning women's writings as offering "not merely a difference of view, but a view that is weak, or trivial, or sentimental because it differs from his own." In her 1929 essay on "Women and Fiction," Woolf grappled most obviously with the ways in which male writers and male subject matter had already preempted the language of literature. Yet she was also tacitly commenting on the problem of (male) audience and conventional reading expectations when she speculated that the woman writer might well "find that she is perpetually wishing to alter the established values [in literature]—to make serious what appears insignificant to a man, and trivial what is to him important."[40] "The 'competence' necessary for understanding [a] literary message . . . depends upon a great number of codices," after all; as Cesare Segre has pointed out, to be competent, a reader must either share or at least be familiar with, "in addition to the code language . . . the codes of custom, of society, and of conceptions of the world"[41] (what Woolf meant by "values"). Males ignorant of women's "values" or conceptions of the world will necessarily, thereby, be poor readers of works that in any sense recapitulate their codes.

The problem is further exacerbated when the language of the literary text is largely dependent upon figuration. For it can be argued, as Ted Cohen has shown, that while "in general, and with some obvious qualifications . . . all literal use of language is accessible to all whose language it is . . . figurative use can be inaccessible to all but those who share information about one another's knowledge, beliefs, intentions, and attitudes."[42] There was nothing fortuitous, for example, in Charlotte Perkins Gilman's decision to situate the progressive mental breakdown and increasing incapacity of the protagonist of "The Yellow Wallpaper" in an upstairs room that had once served as a nursery (with barred windows, no less). But the reader unacquainted with the ways in which women traditionally inhabited a household might not have taken the initial description of the setting as semantically relevant; and the progressive infantilization of the adult protagonist would thereby lose some of its symbolic implications. Analogously, the contemporary poet who declares, along with Adrienne Rich, the need for "a whole new poetry beginning here" is acknowledging that the materials available for symbolization and figuration from women's contexts will necessarily differ from those that men have traditionally utilized:

> Vision begins to happen in such a life
> as if a woman quietly walked away
> from the argument and jargon in a room
> and sitting down in the kitchen, began turning in her lap
> bits of yarn, calico and velvet scraps,
>
> pulling the tenets of a life together
> with no mere will to mastery,
> only care for the many-lived, unending
> forms in which she finds herself.[43]

What, then, is the fate of the woman writer whose competent reading community is composed only of members of her own sex? And what, then, the response of the male critic who, on first looking into Virginia Woolf or Doris Lessing, finds all of the interpretative strategies at his command inadequate to a full and pleasurable deciphering of their pages? Historically, the result has been the diminished status of women's products and their consequent absence from major canons. Nowadays, however, by pointing out that the act of "interpreting language is no more sexually neutral than language use or the language system itself," feminist students of language, like Nelly Furman, help us better understand the crucial linkage between our gender and our interpretive, or reading, strategies. Insisting upon "the contribution of the . . . reader [in] the active attribution of significance to formal signifiers,"[44] Furman and others promise to shake us all—female and male alike—out of our canonized and conventional aesthetic assumptions.

3. *Since the grounds upon which we assign aesthetic value to texts are never infallible, unchangeable, or universal, we must reexamine not only our aesthetics but, as well, the inherent biases and assumptions informing the critical methods which (in part) shape our aesthetic responses.* I am, on the one hand, arguing that men will be better readers, or appreciators, of women's books when they have read more of them (as women have always been taught to become astute readers of men's texts). On the other hand, it will be noted, the emphasis of my remarks shifts the act of critical judgment from assigning aesthetic valuations to texts and directs it, instead, to ascertaining the adequacy of any interpretive paradigm to a full reading of both female and male writing. My third proposition—and, I admit, perhaps the most controversial—thus calls into question that recurrent tendency in criticism to establish norms for the evaluation of literary works when we might better serve the cause of literature by developing standards for evaluating the adequacy of our critical methods.[45] This does not mean that I wish to discard aesthetic valuation. The choice, as I see it, is not between retaining or discarding aesthetic values; rather, the choice is between having some awareness of what constitutes (at least in part) the bases of our aesthetic responses and going without such an awareness. For it is my view that insofar as aesthetic responsiveness continues to be an integral

aspect of our human response system—in part spontaneous, in part learned and educated—we will inevitably develop theories to help explain, formalize, or even initiate those responses.

In challenging the adequacy of received critical opinion or the imputed excellence of established canons, feminist literary critics are essentially seeking to discover how aesthetic value is assigned in the first place, where it resides (in the text or in the reader), and, most importantly, what validity may really be claimed by our aesthetic "judgments." What ends do those judgments serve, the feminist asks; and what conceptions of the world or ideological stances do they (even if unwittingly) help to perpetuate? In so doing, she points out, among other things, that any response labeled "aesthetic" may as easily designate some immediately experienced moment or event as it may designate a species of nostalgia, a yearning for the components of a simpler past, when the world seemed known or at least understandable. Thus the value accorded an opera or a Shakespeare play may well reside in the viewer's immediate viewing pleasure, or it may reside in the play's nostalgic evocation of a once-comprehensible and ordered world. At the same time, the feminist confronts, for example, the reader who simply cannot entertain the possibility that women's worlds are symbolically rich, the reader who, like the male characters in Susan Glaspell's 1917 short story, "A Jury of Her Peers," has already assumed the innate "insignificance of kitchen things."[46] Such a reader, she knows, will prove himself unable to assign significance to fictions that attend to "kitchen things" and will, instead, judge such fictions as trivial and as aesthetically wanting. For her to take useful issue with such a reader, she must make clear that what appears to be a dispute about aesthetic merit is, in reality, a dispute about the *contexts of judgment;* and what is at issue, then, is the adequacy of the prior assumptions and reading habits brought to bear on the text. To put it bluntly: we have had enough pronouncements of aesthetic valuation for a time; it is now our task to evaluate the imputed norms and normative reading patterns that, in part, led to those pronouncements.

By and large, I think I've made my point. Only to clarify it do I add this coda: when feminists turn their attention to the works of male authors which have traditionally been accorded high aesthetic value and, where warranted, follow Olsen's advice that we assert our "right to say: this is surface, this falsifies reality, this degrades,"[47] such statements do not necessarily mean that we will end up with a diminished canon. To question the source of the aesthetic pleasures we've gained from reading Spenser, Shakespeare, Milton, and so on, does not imply that we must deny those pleasures. It means only that aesthetic response is once more invested with epistemological, ethical, and moral concerns. It means, in other words, that readings of *Paradise Lost* which analyze its complex hierarchal structures but fail to note the implications of gender within that hierarchy; or which insist upon the inherent (or even inspired) perfection of Milton's figurative language but fail to note the consequences, for Eve, of her specifically gender-marked weakness, which, like the flowers to which she attends, requires "propping up"; or which concentrate on the poem's thematic reworking of classical notions of martial and epic prowess into Christian (moral) heroism but fail to note that Eve is stylistically edited out of that process—all such readings, however useful, will no longer be deemed wholly adequate. The pleasures we had earlier learned to take in the poem will not be diminished thereby, but they will become part of an altered reading attentiveness.

These three propositions I believe to be at the theoretical core of most current feminist literary criticism, whether acknowledged as such or not. If I am correct in this, then that criticism represents more than a profoundly skeptical stance toward all other preexisting and contemporaneous schools and methods, and more than an impassioned demand that the variety and variability of women's literary expression be taken into full account, rather than written off as caprice and exception, the irregularity in an otherwise regular design. It represents that locus in literary study where, in unceasing effort, female self-consciousness turns in upon itself, attempting to grasp the deepest conditions of its own unique and multiplicitous realities, in the hope, eventually, of altering the very forms through which the culture perceives, expresses, and knows itself. For, if what the larger women's movement looks for in the future is a transformation of the structures of primarily male power which now order our society, then the feminist literary critic demands that we understand the ways in which those structures have been—and continue to be—reified by our literature and by our literary criticism. Thus, along with other "radical" critics and critical schools, though our focus remains the power of the word to both structure and mirror human experience, our overriding commitment is to a radical alteration—an improvement, we hope—in the nature of that experience.

What distinguishes our work from those similarly oriented "social consciousness" critiques, it is said, is its lack of systematic coherence. Pitted against, for example, psychoanalytic or Marxist readings, which owe a decisive share of their persuasiveness to their apparent internal consistency as a system, the aggregate of feminist literary criticism appears woefully deficient in system, and painfully lacking in program. It is, in fact, from all quarters, the most telling defect alleged against us, the most explosive threat in the minefield. And my own earlier observation that, as of 1976, feminist literary criticism appeared "more like a set of interchangeable strategies than any coherent school or shared goal orientation," has been taken by some as an indictment, by others as a statement of impatience. Neither was intended. I felt then, as I do now, that this would "prove both its strength *and* its weakness,"[48] in the sense that the apparent disarray would leave us vulnerable to the kind of objection I've just alluded to; while the fact of our diversity would finally place us securely where, all along, we should have been: camped out, on the far side of the minefield, with the other pluralists and pluralisms.

In our heart of hearts, of course, most critics are really structuralists (whether or not they accept the label) because what we are seeking are patterns (or structures) that can order and explain the otherwise inchoate; thus, we invent, or believe we discover, relational patternings in the texts we read which promise transcendence from difficulty and perplexity to clarity and coherence. But, as I've tried to argue in these pages, to the imputed "truth" or "accuracy" of these findings, the feminist must oppose the painfully obvious truism that what is attended to in a literary work, and hence what is reported about it, is often determined not so much by the work itself as by the critical technique or aesthetic criteria through which it is filtered or, rather, read and decoded. All the feminist is asserting, then, is her own equivalent right to liberate new (and perhaps different) significances from these same texts; and, at the same time, her right to choose which features of a text she takes as relevant because she is, after all, asking new and different questions of it. In the process, she claims neither definitiveness nor structural completeness for her different readings and reading systems, but only their usefulness in recognizing the particular achievements of woman-as-author and their applicability in conscientiously decoding woman-as-sign.

That these alternate foci of critical attentiveness will render alternate readings or interpretations of the same text—even among feminists—should be no cause for alarm. Such developments illustrate only the pluralist contention that, "in approaching a text of any complexity . . . the reader must choose to emphasize certain aspects which seem to him crucial" and that, "in fact, the variety of readings which we have for many works is a function of the selection of crucial aspects made by the variety of readers." Robert Scholes, from whom I've been quoting, goes so far as to assert that "there is no single 'right' reading for any complex literary work," and, following the Russian formalist school, he observes that "we do not speak of readings that are simply true or false, but of readings that are more or less rich, strategies that are more or less appropriate." [49] Because those who share the term "feminist" nonetheless practice a diversity of critical strategies, leading, in some cases, to quite different readings, we must acknowledge among ourselves that sister critics, "having chosen to tell a different story, may in their interpretation identify different aspects of the meanings conveyed by the same passage." [50]

Adopting a "pluralist" label does not mean, however, that we cease to disagree; it means only that we entertain the possibility that different readings, even of the same text, may be differently useful, even illuminating, within different contexts of inquiry. It means, in effect, that we enter a dialectical process of examining, testing, even trying out the contexts—be they prior critical assumptions or explicitly stated ideological stances (or some combination of the two)—that led to the disparate readings. Not all will be equally acceptable to every one of us, of course, and even those prior assumptions or ideologies that are acceptable may call for further refinement and/or clarification. But, at the very least, because we will have grappled with the assumptions that led to it, we will be better able to articulate *why* we find a particular reading or interpretation adequate or inadequate. This kind of dialectical process, moreover, not only makes us more fully aware of what criticism is, and how it functions; it also gives us access to its future possibilities, making us conscious, as R. P. Blackmur put it, "of what we have done," "of what can be done next, or done again," [51] or, I would add, of what can be done differently. To put it still another way: just because we will no longer tolerate the specifically sexist omissions and oversights of earlier critical schools and methods does not mean that, in their stead, we must establish our own "party line."

In my view, our purpose is not and should not be the formulation of any single reading method or potentially procrustean set of critical procedures nor, even less, the generation of prescriptive categories for some dreamed-of nonsexist literary canon. [52] Instead, as I see it, our task is to initiate nothing less than a playful pluralism responsive to the possibilities of multiple critical schools and methods, but captive of none, recognizing that the many tools needed for our analysis will necessarily be largely inherited and only partly of our own making. Only by employing a plurality of methods will we protect ourselves from the temptation of so oversimplifying any text—and especially those particularly offensive to us—that we render ourselves unresponsive to what Scholes has called "its various systems of meaning and their interaction."[53] Any text we deem worthy of our critical attention is usually, after all, a locus of many and varied kinds of (personal, thematic, stylistic, structural, rhetorical, etc.) relationships. So, whether we tend to treat a text as a *mimesis*, in which words are taken to be recreating or representing viable worlds; or whether we prefer to treat a text as a kind of equation of communication, in which decipherable messages are passed from writers to readers; and whether we locate meaning as inherent in the text, the act of reading, or in some collaboration between reader and text—whatever our predilection, let us not generate from it a straitjacket that limits the scope of possible analysis. Rather, let us generate an ongoing dialogue of competing potential possibilities—among feminists and, as well, between feminist and nonfeminist critics.

The difficulty of what I describe does not escape me. The very idea of pluralism seems to threaten a kind of chaos for the future of literary inquiry while, at the same time, it seems to deny the hope of establishing some basic conceptual model which can organize all data—the hope which always begins any analytical exercise. My effort here, however, has been to demonstrate the essential delusions that inform such objections: If literary inquiry has historically escaped chaos by establishing canons, then it has only substituted one mode of arbitrary action for another—and, in this case, at the expense of half the population. And if feminists openly acknowledge ourselves as pluralists, then we do not give up the search for patterns of opposition and connection—probably the basis of thinking itself; what we give up is simply the arrogance of claiming that our work is either exhaustive or definitive. (It is, after all, the identical arrogance we are asking our nonfeminist colleagues to abandon.) If this kind of pluralism appears to threaten both the present coherence of and the inherited aesthetic criteria for a canon of "greats," then, as I have earlier argued, it is precisely that threat which, alone, can free us from the prejudices, the strictures, and the blind spots of the past. In feminist hands, I would add, it is less a threat than a promise.

What unites and repeatedly invigorates feminist literary criticism, then, is neither dogma nor method but, as I have indicated earlier, an acute and impassioned *attentiveness* to the ways in which primarily male structures of power are inscribed (or encoded) within our literary inheritance; the consequences of that encoding for women—as characters, as readers, and as writers; and, with that, a shared analytic *concern* for the implications of that encoding not only for a better understanding of the past, but also for an improved reordering of the present and future as well. If that *concern* identifies feminist literary criticism as one of the many academic arms of the larger women's movement, then that *attentiveness*, within the halls of academe, poses no less a challenge for change, generating, as it does, the three propositions explored here. The critical pluralism that inevitably follows upon those three propositions, however, bears little resemblance to what Robinson has called "the greatest bourgeois theme of all, the myth of pluralism, with its consequent rejection of ideological commitment as 'too simple' to embrace the (necessarily complex) truth."[54] Only ideological commitment could have gotten us to enter the minefield, putting in jeopardy our careers and our livelihood. Only the power of ideology to transform our conceptual worlds, and the inspiration of that ideology to liberate long-suppressed energies and emotions, can account for our willingness to take on critical tasks that, in an earlier decade, would have been "abandoned in despair or apathy."[55] The fact of differences among us proves only that, despite our shared commitments, we have nonetheless refused to shy away from complexity, preferring rather to openly disagree than to give up either intellectual honesty or hard-won insights.

Finally, I would argue, pluralism informs feminist literary inquiry not simply as a description of what already exists but, more importantly, as the only critical stance consistent with the current status of the larger women's movement. Segmented and variously focused, the different women's organizations neither espouse any single system of analysis nor, as a result, express any wholly shared, consistently articulated ideology. The ensuing loss in effective organization and political clout is a serious one, but it has not been paralyzing; in spite of our differences, we have united to *act* in areas of clear mutual concern (the push for the Equal Rights Amendment is probably the most obvious example). The trade-off, as I see it, has made possible an ongoing and educative dialectic of analysis and proferred solutions, protecting us thereby from the inviting traps of reductionism and dogma. And so long as this dialogue remains active, both our politics and our criticism will be free of dogma—but never, I hope, of feminist ideology, in all its variety. For, "whatever else ideologies may be—projections of unacknowledged fears, disguises for ulterior motives, phatic expressions of group solidarity" (and the women's movement, to date, has certainly been all of these, and more)—whatever ideologies express, they are, as Geertz astutely observes, "most distinctively, maps of problematic social reality and matrices for the creation of collective conscience." And despite the fact that "ideological advocates . . . tend as much to obscure as to clarify the true nature of the problems involved," as Geertz notes, "they at least call attention to their existence and, by polarizing issues, make continued neglect more difficult. Without Marxist attack, there would have been no labor reform; without Black Nationalists, no deliberate speed."[56] Without Seneca Falls, I would add, no enfranchisement of women, and without "consciousness raising," no feminist literary criticism nor, even less, women's studies.

Ideology, however, only truly manifests its power by ordering the *sum* of our actions.[57] If feminist criticism calls anything into question, it must be that dogeared myth of intellectual neutrality. For, what I take to be the underlying spirit, or message, of any consciously ideologically premised criticism—that is, that ideas are important *because* they determine the ways we live, or want to live, in the world—is vitiated by confining those ideas to the study, the classroom, or the pages of our books. To write chapters decrying the sexual stereotyping of women in our literature, while closing our eyes to the sexual harrassment of our women students and colleagues; to display Katherine Hepburn and Rosalind Russell in our courses on "The Image of the Independent Career Women in Film," while managing not to notice the paucity of female administrators on our own campus; to study the women who helped make universal enfranchisement a political reality, while keeping silent about our activist colleagues who are denied promotion or tenure; to include segments on "Women in the Labor Movement" in our American studies or women's studies courses, while remaining willfully ignorant of the department secretary fired for her efforts to organize a clerical workers' union; to glory in the delusions of "merit," "privilege," and "status" which accompany campus life in order to insulate ourselves from the millions of women who labor in poverty—all this is not merely hypocritical; it destroys both the spirit and the meaning of what we are about. It puts us, however unwittingly, in the service of those who laid the minefield in the first place. In my view, it is a fine thing for many of us, individually, to have traversed the minefield; but that happy circumstance will only prove of lasting importance if, together, we expose it for what it is (the male fear of sharing power and significance with women) and deactivate its components, so that others, after us, may literally dance through the minefield.

NOTES

"Dancing Through the Minefield" was the winner of the 1979 Florence Howe Essay Contest, which is sponsored by the Women's Caucus of the Modern Language Association.

Some sections of this essay were composed during the time made available to me by a grant from the Rockefeller Foundation, for which I am most grateful.

1. Mary Ellman, *Thinking About Women* (New York: Harcourt Brace Jovanovich, Harvest, 1968).

2. See Clifford Gertz, "Ideology as a Cultural System," in his *The Interpretation of Cultures: Selected Essays* (New York: Basic Books, 1973), p. 232.

3. Ibid., p. 204.

4. Lillian S. Robinson, "Cultural Criticism and the *Horror Vacui, College English* 33, no. 1 (1972); reprinted as "The Critical Task" in her *Sex, Class, and Culture* (Bloomington: Indiana University Press, 1978), p. 51.

5. Elaine Showalter, *A Literature of Their Own: British Women Novelists From Brontë to Lessing* (Princeton: Princeton University Press, 1977), p. 36.

6. Adrienne Rich, "When We Dead Awaken: Writing as Re-Vision," *College English* 34, no. 1 (October 1972); reprinted in *Adrienne Rich's Poetry*, ed. Barbara Charlesworth Gelpi and Albert Gelpi (New York: W. W. Norton Co., 1975), p. 90.

7. Kate Millett, *Sexual Politics* (Garden City, N.Y.: Doubleday and Co., 1970).

8. Rebecca Harding Davis, *Life in the Iron Mills*, originally published in *The Atlantic Monthly*, April 1861; reprinted with "A Biographical Interpretation" by Tillie Olsen (New York: Feminist Press, 1972). Charlotte Perkins Gilman, "The Yellow Wallpaper," originally published in *The New England Magazine*, May 1892; reprinted with an Afterword by Elaine R. Hedges (New York: Feminist Press, 1973).

9. Nina Baym, *Woman's Fiction: A Guide to Novels by and about Women in America, 1820–1870* (Ithaca: Cornell University Press, 1978).

10. In her *Feminine Consciousness in the Modern British Novel* (Urbana: University of Illinois Press, 1975), p. 3, Sydney Janet Kaplan explains that she is using the term "feminine consciousness" "not simply as some general attitude of women toward their own femininity, and not as something synonymous with a particular sensibility among female writers. I am concerned with it as a literary device: a method of characterization of females in fiction."

11. Patricia Meyer Spacks, *The Female Imagination* (New York: Avon Books, 1975), p. 6.

12. Ellen Moers, *Literary Women: The Great Writers* (Garden City, N.Y.: Doubleday and Co., 1976).

13. Showalter, *A Literature of Their Own*, p. 11.

14. Jean E. Kennard, *Victims of Convention* (Hamden, Conn.: Archon Books, 1978), pp. 164, 18, 14.

15. See Millett, *Sexual Politics*, pt. 3, "The Literary Reflection," pp. 235–361.

16. The phrase is Geertz's, "Ideology as a Cultural System," p. 214.

17. Lillian Robinson, "Criticism—and Self-Criticism," *College English* 36, no. 4 (1974) and "Criticism: Who Needs It?" in *The Uses of Criticism*, ed. A. P. Foulkes (Bern and Frankfurt: Lang, 1976); both reprinted in *Sex, Class, and Culture*, pp. 67, 80.

18. Rich, "When We Dead Awaken," p. 90.

19. Judith Fetterley, *The Resisting Reader: A Feminist Approach to American Fiction* (Bloomington: Indiana University Press, 1978).

20. Tillie Olsen, *Silences* (New York: Delacorte Press/Seymour Lawrence, 1978), pp. 239–240.

21. See Cheris Kramer, Barrie Thorne, and Nancy Henley, "Perspectives on Language and Communication," Review Essay in *Signs* 3, no. 3 (Summer 1978): 646.

22. See Adrienne Rich's discussion of the difficulty in finding authentic language for her experience as a mother in her *Of Woman Born* (New York: W. W. Norton and Co., 1976), p. 15.

23. Nelly Furman, "The Study of Women and Language: Comment on Vol. 3, no. 3" in *Signs* 4, no. 1 (Autumn 1978): 184.

24. Again, my phrasing comes from Geertz, "Thick Description: Toward an Interpretive Theory of Culture" in his *Interpretation of Cultures: Selected Essays* (New York: Basic Books, 1972), p. 9.

25. Julia Penelope Stanley and Susan W. Robbins, "Toward a Feminist Aesthetic," *Chrysalis*, no. 6 (1977): 63.

26. Hélène Cixous, "The Laugh of the Medusa," trans. Keith Cohen and Paula Cohen, *Signs* 1, no. 4 (Summer 1976): 87.

27. In *The Madwoman in the Attic: The Woman Writer and the Nineteenth-Century Literary Imagination* (New Haven: Yale University Press, 1979), Sandra M. Gilbert and Susan Gubar suggest that women's writings are in some sense "palimpsestic" in that their "surface designs conceal or obscure deeper, less accessible (and less socially acceptable) levels of meaning" (p. 73). It is, in their view, an art designed "both to express and to camouflage" (p. 81).

28. Consider, for example, Paul Boyers's reductive and inaccurate generalization that "what distinguishes ordinary books and articles about women from feminist writing is the feminist insistence on asking the same questions of every work and demanding ideologically satisfactory answers to those questions as a means of evaluating it," in his "A Case Against Feminist Criticism," *Partisan Review* 43, no. 4 (1976): 602. It is partly as a result of such misconceptions that we have the paucity of feminist critics who are granted a place in English departments which otherwise pride themselves on the variety of their critical orientations.

29. Ambivalent though he is about the literary continuity that begins with Homer, Harold Bloom nonetheless somewhat ominously prophesies "that the first true break . . . will be brought about in generations to come, if the burgeoning religion of Liberated Woman spreads from its clusters of enthusiasts to dominate the West," in his *A Map of Misreading* (New York: Oxford University Press, 1975), p. 33. On p. 36, he acknowledges that while something "as violent [as] a quarrel would ensue if I expressed my judgment" on Robert Lowell and Norman Mailer, "it would lead to something more intense than quarrels if I expressed my judgment upon . . . the 'literature of Women's Liberation.'"

30. Kennard, *Victims of Convention*, p. 14.

31. Rich, "When We Dead Awaken," p. 90.

32. The first is a proposition currently expressed by some structuralists and formalist critics; the best statement of the second probably appears in Georg Lukacs, *Writer and Critic* (New York: Grosset and Dunlap, 1970), p. 119.

33. David Couzens Hoy, "Hermeneutic Circularity, Indeterminacy, and Incommensurability," *New Literary History* 10, no. 1 (Autumn 1978): 166–67.

34. Bloom, *Map of Misreading;* p. 36.

35. John Dewey offered precisely this argument in 1934 when he insisted that a work of art "is recreated every time it is esthetically experienced. . . . It is absurd to ask what an artist 'really' meant by his product: he himself would find different meanings in it at different days and hours and in different stages of his own development." Further, he explained, "It is simply an impossibility that any one today should experience the Parthenon as the devout Athenian contemporary citizen experienced it, any more than the religious statuary of the twelfth century can mean, esthetically, even to a good Catholic today just what it meant to the worshipers of the old period," in *Art as Experience* (New York: Capricorn Books, 1958), pp. 108–109.

36. Charles Altieri, "The Hermeneutics of Literary Indeterminacy: A Dissent from the New Orthodoxy," *New Literary History* 10, no. 1 (Autumn 1978): 90.

37. Murray Krieger, *Theory of Criticism: A Tradition and Its System* (Baltimore: The Johns Hopkins University Press, 1976), p. 6.

38. See Stanley E. Fish, "Normal Circumstances, Literal Language, Direct Speech Acts, the Ordinary, the Everyday, the Obvious, What Goes without Saying, and Other Special Cases," *Critical Inquiry* 4, no. 4 (Summer 1978): 627–28.

39. Ibid., p. 643.

40. Virginia Woolf, "Women and Fiction," *Granite and Rainbow: Essays* (London: Hogarth, 1958), p. 81.

41. Cesare Segre, "Narrative Structures and Literary History," *Critical Inquiry* 3, no. 2 (Winter 1976): 272–73.

42. Ted Cohen, "Metaphor and the Cultivation of Intimacy," *Critical Inquiry* 5, no. 1 (Autumn 1978): 9.

43. From Adrienne Rich's "Transcendental Etude" in her *The Dream of a Common Language: Poems 1974–1977* (New York: W. W. Norton and Co., 1978), pp. 76–77.

44. Furman, "The Study of Women and Language," p. 184.

45. "A recurrent tendency in criticism is the establishment of false norms for the evaluation of literary works," notes Robert Scholes in his *Structuralism in Literature: An Introduction* (New Haven: Yale University Press, 1974), p. 131.

46. For a full discussion of the Glaspell short story which takes this problem into account, please see my "A Map for Re-Reading: Or, Gender and the Interpretation of Literary Texts," forthcoming in a Special Issue on Narrative, *New Literary History* (1980).

47. Olsen, *Silences*, p. 45.

48. Annette Kolodny, "Literary Criticism," Review Essay in *Signs* 2, no. 2 (Winter 1976): 420.

49. Scholes, *Structuralism in Literature*, p. 144–45. These comments appear within his explication of Tzvetan Todorov's theory of reading.

50. I borrow this concise phrasing of pluralistic modesty from M. H. Abrams's "The Deconstructive Angel," *Critical Inquiry* 3, no. 3 (Spring 1977): 427. Indications of the pluralism that was to mark feminist inquiry were to be found in the diversity of essays collected by Susan Koppelman Cornillon for her early and ground-breaking anthology, *Images of Women in Fiction: Feminist Perspectives* (Bowling Green, Ohio: Bowling Green University Popular Press, 1972).

51. R. P. Blackmur, "A Burden for Critics," *The Hudson Review* 1 (1948): 171. Blackmur, of course, was referring to the way in which criticism makes us conscious of how art

functions; I use his wording here because I am arguing that that same awareness must also be focused on the critical act itself. "Consciousness," he avers, "is the way we feel the critic's burden."

52.   I have earlier elaborated my objection to prescriptive categories for literature in "The Feminist as Literary Critic," Critical Response in *Critical Inquiry* 2, no. 4 (Summer 1976): 827–28.

53.   Scholes, *Structuralism in Literature*, pp. 151–52.

54.   Lillian Robinson, "Dwelling in Decencies: Radical Criticism and the Feminist Perspective," *College English* 32, no. 8 (May 1971); reprinted in *Sex, Class, and Culture*, p. 11.

55.   "Ideology bridges the emotional gap between things as they are and as one would have them be, thus insuring the performance of roles that might otherwise be abandoned in despair or apathy," comments Geertz in "Ideology as a Cultural System," p. 205.

56.   Ibid., p. 220, 205.

57.   I here follow Fredric Jameson's view in *The Prison-House of Language: A Critical Account of Structuralism and Russian Formalism* (Princeton: Princeton University Press, 1974), p. 107, that: "Ideology would seem to be that grillwork of form, convention, and belief which orders our actions."

WHAT HAS NEVER BEEN

an overview of lesbian feminist literary criticism

In the 1970s, a generation of lesbian feminist literary critics came of age. Some, like the lesbian professor in Lynn Strongin's poem, "Sayre,"[1] had been closeted in the profession; many had "come out" as lesbians in the women's liberation movement. As academics and as lesbians, we cautiously began to plait together the strands of our existence: teaching lesbian literature, establishing networks and support groups, and exploring assumptions about a lesbian-focused literary criticism. Beginning with nothing, as we thought, this generation quickly began to expand the limitations of literary scholarship by pointing to what had been for decades "unspeakable"—lesbian existence—thus phrasing, in novelist June Arnold's words, "what has never been."[2] Our process has paralleled the development of feminist literary criticism—and, indeed, pioneering feminist critics and lesbian critics are often one and the same. As women in a male-dominated academy, we explored the way we write and read from a different or "other" perspective. As lesbians in a heterosexist academy, we have continued to explore the impact of "otherness," suggesting dimensions previously ignored and yet necessary to understand fully the female condition and the creative work born from it.

Lesbian critics, in the 1980s, may have more questions than answers, but the questions are important not only to lesbians, but to all feminists teaching and criticizing literature. Does a woman's sexual and affectional preference influence the way she writes, reads, and thinks? Does lesbianism belong in the classroom and in scholarship? Is there a lesbian aesthetic distinct from a feminist aesthetic? What should be the role of the lesbian critic? Can we establish a lesbian "canon" in the way in which feminist critics have established a female canon? Can lesbian feminists develop insights into female creativity that might enrich all literary criticism? Different women, of course, answer these questions in different ways, but one set of assumptions underlies virtually all lesbian criticism: that a woman's identity is not defined only by her relation to a male world and male literary tradition (as feminist critics have demonstrated), that powerful bonds between women are a crucial factor in women's lives, and that the sexual and emotional orientation of a woman profoundly affects her consciousness and thus her creativity. Those critics who have consciously chosen to read as lesbians argue that this perspective can be uniquely liberating and can provide new insights into life and literature because it assigns the lesbian a specific vantage point from which to criticize and analyze the politics, language, and culture of patriarchy:

> We have the whole range of women's experience and the other dimension too, which is the unique viewpoint of the dyke. This extra dimension puts us a step outside of so-called normal life and lets us see how gruesomely abnormal it is. . . . [This perspective] can issue in a world-view that is distinct in history and uniquely liberating.[3]

The purpose of this essay is to analyze the current state of lesbian scholarship, to suggest how lesbians are exercising this unique world view, and to investigate some of the problems, strengths, and future needs of a developing lesbian feminist literary criticism.[4]

One way in which this unique world view takes shape is as a "critical consciousness about heterosexist assumptions."[5] Heterosexism is the set of values and structures that assumes heterosexuality to be the only natural form of sexual and emotional expression, "*the* perceptual screen provided by our [patriarchal] cultural conditioning."[6] Heterosexist assumptions abound in literary texts, such as feminist literary anthologies, that purport to be open-minded about lesbianism. When authors' biographies make special note of husbands, male mentors, and male companions, even when that author was primarily female-identified, but fail to mention the female companions of prominent lesbian writers—that is heterosexism. When anthologists ignore historically significant lesbian writers such as Renée Vivien and Radclyffe Hall—that is heterosexism. When anthologies include only the heterosexual or nonsexual works of a writer like Katherine Philips or Adrienne Rich who is celebrated for her lesbian or homoemotional poetry—that is heterosexism. When a topically organized anthology includes sections on wives, mothers, sex objects, young girls, aging women, and liberated women, but not lesbians—that is heterosexism. Heterosexism in feminist anthologies—like the sexism of androcentric collections—serves to obliterate lesbian existence and maintain the lie that women have searched for emotional and sexual fulfillment only through men—or not at all.

Lesbians have also expressed concern that the absence of lesbian material in women's studies journals such as *Feminist Studies*, *Women's Studies*, and *Women and Literature* indicates heterosexism either by omission or by design. Only in 1979 did lesbian-focused articles appear in *Signs* and *Frontiers*. Most lesbian criticism first appeared in alternative, non-establishment lesbian journals, particularly *Sinister Wisdom* and *Conditions*, which are unfamiliar to many feminist scholars. For example, *Signs*' first review article on literary criticism by Elaine Showalter (1975) makes no mention of lesbianism as a theme or potential critical perspective, not even to point out its absence. Annette Kolodny, in the second review article in *Signs* (1976), does call Jane Rule's *Lesbian Images* "a novelist's challenge to the academy and its accompanying critical community," and further criticizes the homophobia in then-current biographies, calling for "candor and sensitivity" in future work.[7] However, neither this nor subsequent review articles familiarize the reader with "underground" sources of lesbian criticism, some of which had appeared by this time, nor do they explicate lesbianism as a literary theme or critical perspective. Ironically, more articles on lesbian literature have appeared in traditional literary journals than in the women's studies press, just as for years only male critics felt free to mention lesbianism. Possibly, feminist critics continue to feel that they will be identified as "dykes," thus invalidating their work.

The perceptual screen of heterosexism is also evident in most of the acclaimed works of feminist literary criticism. None of the current collections of essays—such as *The Authority of Experience* or *Shakespeare's Sisters*—includes even a token article from a lesbian perspective. Ellen Moers's *Literary Women*, germinal work as it is, is homophobic as well as heterosexist. Lesbians, she points out, appear as monsters, grotesques, and freaks in works by Carson McCullers, Djuna Barnes (her reading of *Nightwood* is at the very least questionable), and Diane Arbus, but she seems to concur in this identification rather than call it into question or explain its historical context. Although her so-called defense of unmarried women writers against the "charge" of lesbianism does criticize the way in which this word has been used as a slur, she neither condemns such antilesbianism nor entertains the possibility that some women writers were, in fact, lesbians. Her chapter on "Loving Heroinism" is virtually textbook heterosexism, assuming as it does that women writers only articulate love for men.[8] Perceptual blinders also mar *The Female Imagination* by Patricia Meyers Spacks which never uses the word "lesbian" (except in the index) or "lover" to describe either the "sexual ambiguity" of the bond between Jane and Helen in *Jane Eyre,* nor Margaret Anderson's relationship with a "beloved older woman." Furthermore, Spacks claims that Gertrude Stein, "whose life lack[ed] real attachments" (a surprise to Alice B. Toklas), also "denied whatever is special to women" (which lesbianism is not?).[9] This latter judgment is particularly ominous because heterosexuals often have difficulty accepting that a lesbian, especially a role-playing "butch," is in fact a woman. More care is demonstrated by Elaine Showalter who, in *A Literature of Their Own,* uncovers the attitudes toward lesbianism held by nineteenth-century writers Eliza Lynn Linton and Mrs. Humphrey Ward. However, she does not integrate lesbian issues into her discussion of the crucial generation of early twentieth-century writers (Virginia Woolf, Vita Sackville-West, Dorothy Richardson, and Rosamond Lehmann among others; Radclyffe Hall is mentioned, but not *The Well of Loneliness*), all of whom wrote about sexual love between women. Her well-taken point that modern British novelists avoid lesbianism might have been balanced, however, by a mention of Maureen Duffy, Sybille Bedford, or Fay Weldon.[10] Finally, Sandra Gilbert and Susan Gubar's *The Madwoman in the Attic* does not even index lesbianism; the lone reference made in the text is to the possibility that "Goblin Market" describes "a covertly (if ambiguously) lesbian world." The authors' tendency to interpret all pairs of female characters as aspects of the self sometimes serves to mask a relationship that a lesbian reader might interpret as bonding or love between women.[11]

Lesbian critics, who as feminists owe much to these critical texts, have had to turn to other resources, first to develop a lesbian canon, and then to establish a lesbian critical perspective. Barbara Grier who, as Gene Damon, reviewed books for the pioneering lesbian journal *The Ladder,* laid the groundwork for this canon with her incomparable, but largely unknown *The Lesbian in Literature: A Bibliography.*[12] Equally obscure was Jeanette Foster's *Sex Variant Women in Literature,* self-published in 1956 after having been rejected by a university press because of its subject matter. An exhaustive chronological account of every reference to love between women from Sappho and Ruth to the fiction of the fifties, *Sex Variant Women* has proven to be an invaluable starting point for lesbian readers and scholars. Out of print almost immediately after its publication and lost to all but a few intrepid souls, it was finally reprinted by Diana Press in 1975.[13] A further resource and gathering point for lesbian critics was the special issue on lesbian writing and publishing in *Margins*, a review of small press publications, which appeared in 1975, the first issue of a literary journal devoted entirely to lesbian writing. In 1976, its editor, Beth Hodges, produced a second special issue, this time in *Sinister Wisdom*.[14] Along with the growing visibility and solidarity of lesbians within the academic profession, and the increased availability of lesbian literature from feminist and mass-market presses, these two journal issues propelled lesbian feminist literary criticism to the surface.[15]

The literary resources available to lesbian critics form only part of the story, for lesbian criticism is equally rooted in political ideology. Although not all lesbian critics are activists, most have been strongly influenced by the politics of lesbian feminism. These politics travel the continuum from civil rights advocacy to separatism; however, most, if not all, lesbian feminists assume that lesbianism is a healthy lifestyle chosen by women in virtually all eras and all cultures, and thus strive to eliminate the stigma historically attached to lesbianism. One way to remove this stigma is to associate lesbianism with positive and desirable attributes, to divert women's attention away from male values and toward an exclusively female communitas. Thus, the influential Radicalesbians' essay, "The Woman-Identified Woman," argues that lesbian feminism assumes "the primacy of women relating to women, of women creating a new consciousness of and with each other. . . . We see ourselves as prime, find our centers inside of ourselves."[16] Many lesbian writers and critics have also been influenced profoundly by the politics of separatism which provides a critique of heterosexuality as a political institution rather than a personal choice, "because relationships between men and women are essentially political, they involve power and dominance."[17] As we shall see, the notion of "woman-identification," that is, the primacy of women bonding with women emotionally and politically, as well as the premises of separatism, that lesbians have a unique and critical place at the margins of patriarchal society, are central to much current lesbian literary criticism.

Unmasking heterosexist assumptions in feminist literary criticism has been an important but hardly primary task for lesbian critics. We are more concerned with the development of a unique lesbian feminist perspective or, at the very least, determining whether or not such a perspective is possible. In order to do so, lesbian critics have had to begin with a special question: "When is a text a 'lesbian text' or its writer a 'lesbian writer'"?[18] Lesbians are faced with this special problem of definition: presumably we know when a writer is a "Victorian writer" or a "Canadian writer." To answer this question, we have to determine how inclusively or exclusively we define "lesbian." Should we limit this appellation to those women for whom sexual experience with other women can be proven? This is an almost impossible historical task, as many have noted, for what constitutes proof? Women have not left obvious markers in their private writings. Furthermore, such a narrow definition "names" lesbianism as an exclu-

sively sexual phenomenon which, many argue, may be an inadequate construction of lesbian experience, both today and in less sexually explicit eras. This
sexual definition of lesbianism also leads to the identification of literature with
life, and thus can be an overly defensive and suspect strategy.

Nevertheless, lesbian criticism continues to be plagued with the problem of
definition. One perspective insists that

> desire must be there and at least somewhat embodied. . . . That carnality
> distinguishes it from gestures of political sympathy for homosexuals and from
> affectionate friendships in which women enjoy each other, support each
> other, and commingle their sense of identity and well-being.[19]

A second perspective, which might be called a school, claims, on the contrary,
that "the very meaning of lesbianism is being expanded in literature, just as it is
being redefined through politics."[20] An articulate spokeswoman for this "expanded meaning" school of criticism is Adrienne Rich, who offers a compelling
inclusive definition of lesbianism:

> I mean the term *lesbian continuum* to include a range—through each woman's
> life and throughout history—of woman-identified experience; not simply the
> fact that a woman has had or consciously desired genital experience with an-
> other woman. If we expand it to embrace many more forms of primary inten-
> sity between and among women, including the sharing of a rich inner life,
> the bonding against male tyranny, the giving and receiving of practical and
> political support . . . we begin to grasp breadths of female history and psy-
> chology which have lain out of reach as a consequence of limited, mostly
> clinical, definitions of "lesbianism."[21]

This definition has the virtue of deemphasizing lesbianism as a static entity
and of suggesting interconnections among the various ways in which women
bond together. However, all inclusive definitions of lesbianism risk blurring the
distinctions between lesbian relationships and non-lesbian female friendships, or
between lesbian identity and female-centered identity. Some lesbian writers
would deny that there are such distinctions, but this position is reductive and of
mixed value to those who are developing lesbian criticism and theory and who
may need limited and precise definitions. In fact, reductionism is a serious problem in lesbian ideology. Too often, we identify lesbian and woman, or feminist;
we equate lesbianism with any close bonds between women or with political
commitment to women. These identifications can be fuzzy and historically questionable, as, for example, in the claim that lesbians have a unique relationship
with nature or (as Rich also has claimed) that all female creativity is lesbian. By
so reducing the meaning of lesbian, we have in effect eliminated lesbianism as a
meaningful category.

A similar problem arises when lesbian theorists redefine lesbianism politically,
equating it with strength, independence, and resistance to patriarchy. This new
political definition then influences the interpretation of literature: "If in a
woman writer's work a sentence refuses to do what it is supposed to do, if there
are strong images of women and if there is a refusal to be linear, the result is

innately lesbian literature."[22] The concept of an "innately" lesbian perspective or aesthetic allows the critic to separate lesbianism from biographical content which is an essential development in lesbian critical theory. Literary interpretation will, of course, be supported by historical and biographical evidence, but perhaps lesbian critics should borrow a few insights from new criticism. If a text lends itself to a lesbian reading, then no amount of biographic "proof" ought to be necessary to establish it as a lesbian text.[23] Barbara Smith, for example, interprets Toni Morrison's *Sula* as a lesbian novel, regardless of the author's affectional preference. But we need to be cautious about what we call "innately" lesbian. Why is circularity or strength limited to lesbians, or, similarly, why is love of nature or creativity? It is certainly not evident that women, let alone lesbians, are "innately" anything. And, although it might require a lesbian perspective to stress the dominant relationship between Nel and Sula ("All that time, all that time, I thought I was missing Jude"), it is difficult to imagine a novel so imbued with heterosexuality as lesbian.

Almost midway between the inclusive and exclusive approaches to a definition of lesbianism lies that of Lillian Faderman in her extraordinary overview, *Surpassing the Love of Man: Romantic Friendship and Love Between Women From the Renaissance to the Present*. Faderman's precise definition of lesbianism provides a conceptual framework for the four hundred years of literary history explored by the text:

> "Lesbian" describes a relationship in which two women's strongest emotions and affections are directed toward each other. Sexual contact may be a part of the relationship to a greater or lesser degree, or it may be entirely absent. By preference the two women spend most of their time together and share most aspects of their lives with each other.[24]

Broader than the exclusive definition of lesbianism—for Faderman argues that not all lesbian relationships may be fully embodied—but narrower than Rich's "lesbian continuum," this definition is both specific and discriminating. The book is slightly marred by a defensive, overexplanatory tone, caused, no doubt, by her attempt to neutralize the "intense charge of the word *lesbian*"; note, for example, that this charged word is omitted from the title.[25] Furthermore, certain problems remain with her framework, as with any that a lesbian critic or historian might establish. The historical relationship between genital sexuality and lesbianism remains unclear, and we cannot identify easily lesbianism outside a monogamous relationship. Nevertheless, despite problems in definition that may be inherent in lesbian studies, the strength of *Surpassing the Love of Men* is partially the precision with which Faderman defines her topic and chooses her texts and subjects.

This problem of definition is exacerbated by the problem of silence. One of the most pervasive themes in lesbian criticism is that woman-identified writers, silenced by a homophobic and misogynistic society, have been forced to adopt coded and obscure language and internal censorship. Emily Dickinson counseled us to "tell all the truth / but tell it slant," and critics are now calculating what price we have paid for slanted truth. The silences of heterosexual women writers may become lies for lesbian writers, as Rich warns: "a life 'in the closet' . . . [may] spread into private life, so that lying (described as *discretion*) becomes an easy way to avoid conflict or complication."[26] Gloria T. Hull recounts the moving story of just such a victim of society, the black lesbian poet Angelina Weld Grimké, whose "convoluted life and thwarted sexuality" marked her slim output of poetry with images of self-abnegation, diminution, sadness, and the wish for death. The lesbian writer who is working class or a woman of color may be particularly isolated, shackled by conventions, and, ultimately, silenced "with [her] real gifts stifled within."[27] What does a lesbian writer do when the words cannot be silenced? Critics are pointing to the codes and strategies for literary survival adopted by many women. For example, Willa Cather may have adopted her characteristic male persona in order to express safely her emotional and erotic feelings for other women.[28] Thus, a writer some critics call antifeminist or at least disappointing may be better appreciated when her lesbianism is taken into account. Similarly, many ask whether Gertrude Stein cultivated obscurity, encoding her lesbianism in order to express hidden feelings and evade potential enemies. Or, on the other hand, Stein may have been always a declared lesbian, but a victim of readers' (and scholars') unwillingness or inability to pay her the close and sympathetic attention she requires.[29]

The silence of "Shakespeare's [lesbian] sister" has meant that modern writers have had little or no tradition with which to nurture themselves. Feminist critics such as Moers, Showalter, and Gilbert and Gubar have demonstrated the extent and significance of a female literary tradition, but the lesbian writer developed her craft alone (and perhaps this is the significance of the title of *the* lesbian novel about novel writing, *The Well of Loneliness*). Elly Bulkin's much-reprinted article on lesbian poetry points out that lesbian poets "have their work shaped by the simple fact of their having begun to write without knowledge of such history and with little or no hope of support from a woman's and/or lesbian writing community."[30] If white women can at least imagine a lesbian literature, the black lesbian writer, as Barbara Smith demonstrates, is even more hampered by the lack of tradition: "Black women are still in the position of having to 'imagine,' discover and verify Black lesbian literature because so little has been written from an avowedly lesbian perspective."[31] Blanche Wiesen Cook points out further that all lesbians are affected by this absence of tradition and role models, or the limiting of role models to Hall's Stephen Gordon. She also reminds us that our lesbian foremothers and networks were not simply lost and forgotten; rather, our past has been "erased," obliterated by the actions of a hostile society.[32]

It would appear then that lesbian critics are faced with a set of problems that make our work particularly delicate and problematic, requiring caution, sensitivity, and flexibility as well as imagination and risk. Lesbian criticism begins with the establishment of the lesbian text: the creation of language out of silence. The critic must first define the term "lesbian" and then determine its applicability to both writer and text, sorting out the relation of literature to life. Her definition of lesbianism will influence the texts she identifies as lesbian, and, except for the growing body of literature written from an explicit lesbian perspective since the development of a lesbian political movement, it is likely that many will disagree with various identifications of lesbian texts. It is not only *Sula* that may provoke controversy, but even the "coded" works of lesbian writers like Gertrude Stein. The critic will need to consider whether a lesbian text is one written by a lesbian (and if so, how do we determine who is a lesbian?), one written about lesbians (which might be by a heterosexual woman or a man), or one that expresses a lesbian "vision" (which has yet to be satisfactorily outlined). But despite the problems raised by definition, silence and coding, and absence of tradition, lesbian critics have begun to develop a critical stance. Often this stance involves peering into shadows, into the spaces between words, into what has been unspoken and barely imagined. It is a perilous critical adventure with results that may violate accepted norms of traditional criticism, but which may also transform our notions of literary possibility.

One of the first tasks of this emerging lesbian criticism has been to provide lesbians with a tradition, even if a retrospective one. Jane Rule, whose *Lesbian Images* appeared about the same time as *Literary Women*, first attempted to establish this tradition.[33] Although her text is problematic, relying overly much on biographical evidence and derivative interpretations and including some questionable writers (such as Dorothy Baker) while omitting others, *Lesbian Images* was a milestone in lesbian criticism. Its importance is partially suggested by the fact that it took five years for another complete book—Faderman's—to appear on lesbian literature. In a review of *Lesbian Images*, I questioned the existence of a lesbian "great tradition" in literature, but now I think I was wrong.[34] Along with Rule, Dolores Klaich in *Woman Plus Woman* and Louise Bernikow in the introduction to *The World Split Open* have explored the possibility of a lesbian tradition,[35] and recent critics such as Faderman and Cook in particular have begun to define that tradition, who belongs to it, and what links the writers who can be identified as lesbians. Cook's review of lesbian literature and culture in the early twentieth century proposes "to analyze the literature and attitudes out of which the present lesbian feminist works have emerged, and to examine the continued denials and invalidation of the lesbian experience."[36] Focusing on the recognized lesbian networks in France and England that included Virginia Woolf, Vita Sackville-West, Ethel Smythe, Gertrude Stein, Radclyffe Hall, Natalie Barney, and Romaine Brooks, Cook provides an important outline of a lesbian cultural tradition and an insightful analysis of the distortions and denials of homophobic scholars, critics, and biographers.

Faderman's *Surpassing the Love of Men*, like her earlier critical articles, ranges more widely through a literary tradition of romantic love between women (whether or not one calls that "lesbian") from the sixteenth to the twentieth centuries. Her thesis is that passionate love between women was labeled neither abnormal nor undesirable—probably because women were perceived to be asexual—until the sexologists led by Krafft-Ebing and Havelock Ellis "morbidified" female friendship around 1900.

Although she does not always clarify the dialectic between idealization and condemnation that is suggested in her text, Faderman's basic theory is quite convincing. Most readers, like myself, will be amazed at the wealth of information about women's same-sex love that Faderman has uncovered. She rescues from heterosexual obscurity Mary Wollstonecraft, Mary Wortley Montagu, Anna Seward, Sarah Orne Jewett, Edith Somerville, "Michael Field," and many others, including the Scottish schoolmistresses whose lesbian libel suit inspired Lillian Hellman's *The Children's Hour*. Faderman has also written on the theme of same-sex love and romantic friendship in poems and letters of Emily Dickinson; in novels by Henry James, Oliver Wendell Holmes, and Henry Wadsworth Longfellow; and in popular magazine fiction of the early twentieth century.[37]

Faderman is preeminent among those critics who are attempting to establish a lesbian tradition by rereading writers of the past previously assumed to be heterosexual or "spinsters." As songwriter Holly Near expresses it: "Lady poet of great acclaim / I have been misreading you / I never knew your poems were meant for me."[38] It is in this area of lesbian scholarship that the most controversy—and some of the most exciting work—occurs. Was Mary Wollstonecraft's passionate love for Fanny Blood, recorded in *Mary, A Fiction*, lesbian? Does Henry James dissect a lesbian relationship in *The Bostonians*? Did Emily Dickinson address many of her love poems to a woman, not a man? How did Virginia Woolf's relationships with Vita Sackville-West and Ethel Smythe affect her literary vision? Not only are some lesbian critics increasingly naming such women and relationships "lesbian," they are also suggesting that criticism cannot fail to take into account the influence of sexual and emotional orientation on literary expression.

In the establishment of a self-conscious literary tradition, certain writers have become focal points both for critics and for lesbians in general, who affirm and celebrate their identity by "naming names," establishing a sense of historical continuity and community through the knowledge that incontrovertibly great women were also lesbians. Foremost among these heroes (or "heras") are the women who created the first self-identified lesbian feminist community in Paris during the early years of the twentieth century. With Natalie Barney at its hub, this circle included such notable writers as Colette, Djuna Barnes, Radclyffe Hall, Renée Vivien, and, peripherally, Gertrude Stein. Contemporary lesbians—literary critics, historians, and lay readers—have been drawn to their mythic and mythmaking presence, seeing in them a vision of lesbian society and culture that may have existed only once before—on the original island of Lesbos.[39] More interest, however, has been paid to their lives so far than to their art. Barnes's portraits of decadent, tormented lesbians and homosexuals in *Nightwood* and silly, salacious ones in *The Ladies Almanack* often prove troublesome to lesbian readers and critics.[40] However, Elaine Marks's perceptive study of French lesbian writers traces a tradition and how it has changed, modified by circumstance and by feminism, from the Sappho of Renée Vivien to the amazons of Monique Wittig.[41]

The problem inherent in reading lesbian literature primarily for role modeling is most evident with Hall—the most notorious of literary lesbians—whose archetypal "butch," Stephen Gordon, has bothered readers since the publication of *The Well of Loneliness*. Although one critic praises it as "the standard by which all subsequent similar works are measured," most contemporary lesbian feminists would, I believe, agree with Faderman's harsh condemnation that it "helped to wreak confusion in young women."[42] Such an extraliterary debate is not limited to lesbian novels and lesbian characters; I am reminded of the intense disappointment expressed by many feminists over George Eliot's disposal of Dorothea Brooke in *Middlemarch*. In both cases, the cry is the same: why haven't these writers provided us with appropriate role models? Cook may be justified in criticizing Hall for creating a narrow and debilitating image for lesbians who follow, but my reading of the novel (and that of Catharine Stimpson in an excellent study of the lesbian novel) convinces me that both Hall's hero and message are highly complex.[43] In looking to writers for a tradition, we need to recognize that the tradition may not always be a happy one. Women like Stephen Gordon exist alongside characters like Molly Bolt, in Rita Mae Brown's *Rubyfruit Jungle*, but lesbians may also question whether or not the incarnation of a "politically correct" but elusive and utopian mythology provides our only appropriate role model.

As with Hall, many readers and critics are strongly antipathetic to Stein, citing her reactionary and antifeminist politics and her role-playing relationship with Alice B. Toklas. However, other critics, by carefully analyzing Stein's actual words, establish, convincingly to my reading, that she did have a lesbian and feminist perspective, calling into question assumptions about coding and masculine role playing. Cynthia Secor, who is developing an exciting lesbian feminist interpretation of Stein, argues that her novel *Ida* attempts to discover what it means to be a female person, and that the author profited from her position on the boundaries of patriarchal society: "Stein's own experience as a lesbian gives her a critical distance that shapes her understanding of the struggle to be one's self. Her own identity is not shaped as she moves into relation with a man." Similarly, Elizabeth Fifer points out that Stein's situation encouraged her to experiment with parody, theatricality, role playing, and "the diversity of ways possible to look at homosexual love and at her love object." Dierdre Vanderlinde finds in *Three Lives* "one of the earliest attempts to find a new language in which to say, 'I, woman-loving woman, exist.'" Catharine Stimpson places more critical emphasis on Stein's use of masculine pronouns and conventional language, but despite what may have been her compromise, Stimpson feels that female bonding in Stein provides her with a private solution to woman's mind–body split.[44]

Along with Stein, Dickinson's woman-identification has drawn the most attention from recent critics, and has generated considerable controversy between lesbian and other feminist critics. Faderman insists that Dickinson's love for women must be considered homosexual, and that critics must take into account her sexuality (or affectionality). Like most critics who accept this lesbian identification of Dickinson, she points to Susan Gilbert Dickinson as Emily's primary romantic and sexual passion. Both Faderman and Bernikow thus argue that Dickinson's "muse" was sometimes a female figure as well as a male.[45] Some of this work can be justifiably criticized for too closely identifying literature with life; however, by altering our awareness of what is *possible*—namely, that Dickinson's poetry was inspired by her love for a woman—we also can transform our response to the poetry. Paula Bennett daringly suggests that Dickinson's use of crumbs, jewels, pebbles, and similar objects was an attempt to create "clitoral imagery." In a controversial paper on the subject, Nadean Bishop argues forcefully that the poet's marriage poems must be reread in light of what she considers to have been Dickinson's consummated sexual relationship with her sister-in-law.[46]

The establishment of a lesbian literary tradition, a "canon," as my lengthy discussion suggests, has been the primary task of critics writing from a lesbian feminist perspective. But it is not the only focus to emerge. For example, lesbian critics, like feminist critics in the early seventies, have begun to analyze the images, stereotypes, and mythic presence of lesbians in fiction by or about lesbians. Bertha Harris, a major novelist as well as a provocative and trailblazing critic, considers the lesbian to be the prototype of the monster and "the quintessence of all that is female; and female enraged . . . a lesbian is . . . that which has been unspeakable about women." [47] Harris offers this monstrous lesbian as a female archetype who subverts traditional notions of female submissiveness, passivity, and virtue. Her "tooth-and-claw" image of the lesbian is ironically similar to that of Ellen Moers, although from a lesbian rather than heterosexual point of view. But the very fact that Moers presents the lesbian-as-monster in a derogatory context and Harris in a celebratory one suggests that there is an important dialectic between how the lesbian articulates herself and how she is articulated and objectified by others. Popular culture, in particular, exposes the objectifying purpose of the lesbian-as-monster image, such as the lesbian vampire first created by Joseph Sheridan LeFanu's 1871 ghost story "Carmilla," and revived in early 1970s "B" films as a symbolic attack on women's struggle for self-identity. [48] Other critics also have analyzed the negative symbolic appearance of the lesbian in literature. Ann Allen Shockley, reviewing black lesbian characters in American fiction, notes that "within these works exists an undercurrent of hostility, trepidation, subtlety, shadiness, and in some instances, ignorance culling forth homophobic stereotypes." [49] Homophobic stereotypes are also what Judith McDaniel and Maureen Brady find in abundance in recent commercial fiction (such as *Kinflicks*, *A Sea Change*, *Some Do*, and *How to Save Your Own Life*) by avowedly feminist novelists. Although individuals might disagree with McDaniel and Brady's severe criticism of specific novels, their overall argument is unimpeachable. Contemporary feminist fiction, by perpetuating stereotyped characters and themes (such as the punishment theme so dear to pre-feminist lesbian literature), serves to "disempower the lesbian." [50] Lesbian, as well as heterosexual, writers present the lesbian as Other, as Julia Penelope Stanley discovered in prefeminist fiction: "The lesbian character creates for herself a mythology of darkness, a world in which she moves through dreams and shadows." [51] Lesbian critics may wish to avoid this analysis of the lesbian as Other because we no longer wish to dwell upon the cultural violence done against us. Yet this area must be explored until we strip these stereotypes of their inhibiting and dehumanizing presence in our popular culture and social mythology.

Lesbian critics have also delved into the area of stylistics and literary theory. If we have been silenced for centuries and speak an oppressor's tongue, then liberation for the lesbian must begin with language. Some writers may have reconciled their internal censor with their speech by writing in code, but many critics maintain that modern lesbian writers, because they are uniquely alienated from the patriarchy, experiment with its literary style and form. Julia Penelope Stanley and Susan Wolfe, considering such diverse writers as Virginia Woolf, Gertrude Stein, Kate Millett, and Elana Dykewoman, claim that "a feminist aesthetic, as it emerges out of women's evolution, grounds itself in female consciousness and in the unrelenting language of process and change." [52] In this article, the authors do not call their feminist aesthetic a lesbian feminist aesthetic, although all the writers they discuss are, in fact, lesbians. Susan Wolfe later confronted this fact: "Few women who continue to identify with men can risk the male censure of 'women's style,' and few escape the male perspective long enough to attempt it."[53] Through examples from Kate Millett, Jill Johnston, and Monique Wittig, she illustrates her contention that lesbian literature is characterized by the use of the continuous present, unconventional grammar, and neologism; and that it breaks boundaries between art and the world, between events and our perceptions of them, and between past, present, and the dream world. It is, as even the proponents of this theory admit, highly debatable that all lesbian writers are modernists, or that all modernists are lesbians. If Virginia Woolf wrote in non-linear, stream-of-consciousness style because she was a lesbian (or "woman-identified") how does one explain Dorothy Richardson whose *Pilgrimage*, despite one lesbian relationship, is primarily heterosexual? If both Woolf and Richardson can be called "feminist" stylists, then how does one explain the nonlinear experimentation of James Joyce or Alain Robbe-Grillet, for example? The holes that presently exist in this theory should not, however, detract from the highly suggestive overlap between experimental and lesbian writers. Nor should we ignore the clear evidence that many contemporary, self-conscious lesbian writers (such as Wittig, Johnston, Bertha Harris and June Arnold) are choosing an experimental style as well as content.

This development of a self-conscious lesbian literature and literary theory in recent years has led a number of critics to investigate the unifying themes and values of current literature. Such an attempt has been made by Elly Bulkin, who traces the various sources of contemporary lesbian poetry, analyzes "the range of lesbian voices," and advises feminist teachers how to teach lesbian poetry. Mary Carruthers, in asking why so much contemporary feminist poetry is also lesbian, observes that the "lesbian love celebrated in contemporary women's poetry requires an affirmation of the value of femaleness, women's bodies, women's sexuality—in women's language."[54] Jane Gurko and Sally Gearhart compare contemporary lesbian and gay male literature, attempting to discern to what extent one or the other transforms heterosexual ideology. They claim that, unlike gay male literature, lesbian literature "does express a revolutionary model of sexuality which in its structure, its content, and its practice defies the fundamental violent assumptions of patriarchal culture."[55] There is a danger in this attempt to establish a characteristic lesbian vision or literary value system, one that is well illustrated by this article. In an attempt to say *this* is what defines a lesbian literature, we are easily tempted to read selectively, omitting what is foreign to our theories. Most contemporary lesbian literature does embrace a rhetoric of nonviolence, but this is not universally true; for example, M. F. Beal's *Angel Dance* is a lesbian hard-boiled detective novel and Monique Wittig's *Le Corps lesbien* is infused with a violent eroticism that is, nonetheless, intensely nonpatriarchal. Violence, role playing, disaffection, unhappiness, suicide, and self-hatred, to name a few "taboo" subjects, all exist within the lesbian culture, and a useful criticism will have to effectively analyze these as *lesbian* themes and issues, regardless of ideological purity.

Lesbian feminist criticism faces a number of concerns that must be addressed as it grows in force and clarity. Among these concerns is the fact that this criticism is dominated by the politics of lesbian separatism. This is exemplified by the following statement from *Sinister Wisdom*, a journal that has developed a consistent and articulate separatist politics, that

> 'lesbian consciousness' is really a point of view, a view from the boundary. And in a sense every time a woman draws a circle around her psyche, saying 'this is a room of *my own*.' and then writes from within that 'room,' she's inhabiting lesbian consciousness.[56]

The value of separatism which, I believe, has always provided the most exciting theoretical developments in lesbian ideology, is precisely this marginality: lesbian existence "on the periphery of patriarchy."[57] Separatism provides criticism, as it did for lesbian politics, a cutting edge and radical energy that keeps us moving forward rather than backward either from fear or complacency. Those critics who maintain a consciously chosen position on the boundaries (and not one imposed by a hostile society) help to keep lesbian and feminist criticism radical and provocative, preventing both from becoming another arm of the established truth. At the same time, however, it is essential that separatist criticism does not itself become an orthodoxy, and thus repetitive, empty, and resistant to change. Lesbian criticism, as Kolodny has argued about feminist criticism, has more to gain from resisting dogma than from monotheism.[58] Understandably, those critics and scholars willing to identify themselves publicly as lesbians also have tended to hold radical politics of marginality. Exposing one's self to public scrutiny as a lesbian may in fact entail marginality through denial of tenure or loss of job, and those lesbians willing to risk these consequences usually have a political position that justifies their risk. However, to me it seems imperative that lesbian criticism develop diversity in theory and approach. Much as lesbians, even more than heterosexual feminists, may mistrust systems of thought developed by and associated with men and male values, we may, in fact, enrich our work through the insights of Marxist, structuralist, semiotic, or even psychoanalytic criticism. Perhaps "male" systems of thought are incompatible with a lesbian literary vision, but we will not know until we attempt to integrate these ideas into our work.[59]

Similarly, lesbian criticism and cultural theory in general can only gain by developing a greater specificity, historically and culturally. We have tended to write and act as if lesbian experience—which is perceived as that of a contemporary, white, middle-class feminist—is universal and unchanging. Although most lesbians know that this is not the case, we too often forget to apply rigorous historical and cross-cultural tools to our scholarship. Much of this ahistoricity occurs around the shifting definitions of lesbianism from one era and one culture to another. To state simply that Wollstonecraft "was" a lesbian because she passionately loved Fanny Blood, or Susan B. Anthony was a lesbian because she wrote amorous letters to Anna Dickinson, without accounting for historical circumstances, may serve to distort or dislocate the actual meaning of these women's lives (just as it is distorting to *deny* their love for women). There are also notable differences among the institution of the *berdache* (the adoption by one sex of the opposite gender role) in Native American tribes; *faute de mieux* lesbian activity tolerated in France (as in Colette's *Claudine* novels); idyllic romantic friendships (such as that of the famous Ladies of Llangollen); and contemporary self-conscious lesbianism. I do believe that there is a common structure—a lesbian "essence"—that may be located in all these specific historical existences, just as we may speak of a widespread, perhaps universal, structure of marriage or the family. However, in each of these cases—lesbianism, marriage, the family— careful attention to history teaches us that differences are as significant as similarities, and vital information about female survival may be found in the different ways in which women have responded to their historical situation. This tendency toward simplistic universalism is accompanied by what I see as a dangerous development of biological determinism and a curious revival of the nineteenth-century feminist notion of female (now lesbian) moral superiority—that women are uniquely caring and superior to inherently violent males. Although only an undertone in some criticism and literature, any such sociobiological impulse should be questioned at every appearance.

The denial of meaningful differences among women is being challenged, particularly around the issue of racism. Bulkin has raised criticisms about the racism of white lesbian feminist theory. She has written that

> if I can put together—or think someone else can put together—a viable piece of feminist criticism or theory whose base is the thought and writing of white women/lesbians and expect that an analysis of racism can be tacked on or dealt with later as a useful addition, it is a measure of the extent to which I partake of that white privilege.[60]

Implicit in the criticism of Bulkin and other antiracist writers is the belief that lesbians, because of our experience of stigma and exclusion from the feminist mainstream, ought to be particularly sensitive to the dynamic between oppression and oppressing. White lesbians who are concerned about eradicating racism in criticism and theory have been greatly influenced as well by the work of several black lesbian feminist literary critics, such as Gloria T. Hull, Barbara Smith, and Lorraine Bethel.[61] Such concern is not yet present over the issue of class, although the historical association of lesbianism with upper-class values has often been used by left-wing political groups and governments to deny legitimacy to homosexual rights and needs. Lesbian critics studying the Barney circle, for example, might analyze the historical connections between lesbianism and class status. Lesbian critics might also develop comparisons among the literatures of various nationalities because the lesbian canon is of necessity cross-national. We have barely explored the differences between American, English, French, and German lesbian literature (although *Surpassing the Love of Men* draws some distinctions), let alone non-Western literature. The paucity of lesbian scholars trained in these literatures has so far prevented the development of a truly international lesbian literary canon.

As lesbian criticism matures, we may anticipate the development of ongoing and compelling political and practical concerns. At this time, for example, lesbians are still defining and discovering texts. We are certainly not as badly off as we were in the early seventies when the only lesbian novels in print were *The Well of Loneliness, Rubyfruit Jungle,* and Isabel Miller's *Patience and Sarah.* However, texts published prior to 1970 are still difficult to find, and even *The Well of Loneliness* is intermittently available at the whim of publishers. Furthermore, the demise of

Diana Press and the apparent slowdown of Daughters (two of the most active lesbian publishing houses) leaves many major works unavailable, possibly forever. As the boom in gay literature subsides, teachers of literature will find it very difficult to unearth teachable texts. Scholars have the excellent Arno Press series, *Homosexuality: Lesbians and Gay Men in Society, History, and Literature,* but, as Faderman's monumental scholarship reveals, far more lesbian literature exists than anyone has suspected. This literature needs to be unearthed, analyzed, explicated, perhaps translated, and made available to readers.

As lesbian critics, we also need to address the exclusion of lesbian literature from not merely the traditional, but also the feminist canon. Little lesbian literature has been integrated into the mainstream of feminist texts, as evidenced by what is criticized, collected, and taught. It is a matter of serious concern that lesbian literature is omitted from anthologies or included in mere token amounts, or that critical works and Modern Language Association panels still exclude lesbianism. It may as yet be possible for heterosexual feminists to claim ignorance about lesbian literature; however, lesbian critics should make it impossible for that claim to stand much longer. Lesbianism is still perceived as a minor and somewhat discomforting variation within the female life cycle, when it is mentioned at all. Just as we need to integrate lesbian material and perspectives into the traditional and feminist canons, we might also apply lesbian theory to traditional literature. Feminists have not only pointed out the sexism in many canonical works, but have also provided creative and influential rereadings of these works; similarly lesbians might contribute to the rereading of these works; similarly lesbians might contribute to the rereading of the classics. For example, *The Bostonians,* an obvious text, has been reread often from a lesbian perspective, and we could reinterpret D. H. Lawrence's anti-feminism or Doris Lessing's compromised feminism (particularly in *The Golden Notebook*) by relating these attitudes to their fear of or discomfort with lesbianism. Other texts or selections of texts—such as Rossetti's "Goblin Market" or the relationship between Lucy Snowe and Ginevra Fanshawe in *Villette*—might reveal a subtext that could be called lesbian. Just as few texts escape a feminist re-vision, few might invade a lesbian transformation.

This last point—that there is a way in which we might "review" literature as lesbians—brings me to my conclusion. In a brief period of a few years, critics have begun to demonstrate the existence of a distinct lesbian aesthetic, just as feminists have outlined elements of a female aesthetic. Certain components of this aesthetic or critical perspective are clear:

> Perhaps lesbian feminist criticism [or literature, I would add] is a political or thematic perspective, a kind of imagination that can see beyond the barriers of heterosexuality, role stereotypes, patterns of language and culture that may be repressive to female sexuality and expression.[62]

A lesbian artist very likely would express herself differently about sexuality, the body, and relationships. But are there other—less obvious—unifying themes, ideas, and imagery that might define a lesbian text or subtext? How, for example, does the lesbian's sense of outlaw status affect her literary vision? Might lesbian writing, because of the lesbian's position on the boundaries, be characterized by a particular sense of freedom and flexibility or, rather, by images of violently imposed barriers, the closet? Or, in fact, is there a dialectic between freedom and imprisonment unique to lesbian writing? Do lesbians have a special perception of suffering and stigma, as so much prefeminist literature seems to suggest? What about the "muse," the female symbol of literary creativity: do women writers create a lesbian relationship with their muse as May Sarton asserts? If so, do those writers who choose a female muse experience a freedom from inhibition because of that fact, or might there be a lack of creative tension in such a figurative same-sex relationship? I feel on solid ground in asserting that there are certain topics and themes that define lesbian culture, and that we are beginning to define a lesbian symbolism. Lesbian literature may present a unified tradition of thematic concerns such as that of unrequited longing, a longing of almost cosmic totality because the love object is denied not by circumstance or chance, but by necessity. The tension between romantic love and genital sexuality takes a particular form in woman-to-woman relationships, often articulated through musings on the difference between purity and impurity (culminating in Colette's study of variant sexuality, *The Pure and the Impure*). Lesbian literature approaches the theme of development or the quest in a manner different from that of men or heterosexual women. Lesbian literature, as lesbian culture in general, is particularly flexible on issues of gender and role identification; even *The Well of Loneliness* hints at the tragedy of rigid gender roles. Because of this flexibility, lesbian artists and writers have always been fascinated with costuming, because dress is an external manifestation of gender roles lesbians often reject.[63] As we read and reread literature from a lesbian perspective, I am confident we will continue to expand our understanding of the lesbian literary tradition and a lesbian aesthetic.

This essay has suggested the vigor of lesbian criticism and its value to all feminists in raising awareness of entrenched heterosexism in existing texts, clarifying the lesbian traditions in literature through scholarship and reinterpretation, pointing out barriers that have stood in the way of free lesbian expression, explicating the recurring themes and values of lesbian literature, and exposing the dehumanizing stereotypes of lesbians in our culture. Many of the issues that face lesbian critics—resisting dogma, expanding the canon, creating a non-racist and non-classist critical vision, transforming our readings of traditional texts, and exploring new methodologies—are the interests of all feminist critics. Because feminism concerns itself with the removal of limitations and impediments in the way of female imagination, and lesbian criticism helps to expand our notions of what is *possible* for women, then all women would grow by adopting for themselves a lesbian vision. Disenfranchised groups have had to adopt a double-vision for survival; one of the political transformations of recent decades has been the realization that enfranchised groups—men, whites, heterosexuals, the middle class—would do well to adopt that double-vision for the survival of us all. Lesbian literary criticism simply restates what feminists already know, that one group cannot name itself "humanity" or even "woman": "We're not trying to become part of the old order misnamed 'universal' which has tabooed us; we are transforming the meaning of 'universality.'"[64] Whether lesbian criticism will survive depends as much upon the external social climate as it does upon the creativity and skill of its practitioners. If political attacks on gay rights and freedom grow; if the so-called Moral Majority wins its fight to eliminate gay teachers and texts from the schools (it would be foolhardy to believe they will exempt universities); and if the academy, including feminist teachers and scholars, fails to support lesbian scholars, eradicate heterosexist values and assumptions, and incorporate the insights of lesbian scholarship into the mainstream; then current lesbian criticism will probably suffer the same fate as did Jeanette Foster's *Sex Variant Women* in the fifties. Lesbian or heterosexual, we will all suffer from that loss.

NOTES

An earlier version of this paper was presented at the first annual convention of the National Women's Studies Association, Lawrence, Kansas, May 1979.

1. Lynn Strongin, "Sayre," in *Rising Tides: Twentieth-Century American Women Poets*, ed. Laura Chester and Sharon Barba (New York: Washington Square Press, 1973), p. 317.

2. June Arnold, "Lesbian Fiction," Special Issue on Lesbian Writing and Publishing, *Sinister Wisdom* 2 (Fall 1976): 28.

3. Sandy Boucher, "Lesbian Artists," Special Issue on Lesbian Art and Artists, *Heresies* 3 (Fall 1977): 48.

4. This survey is limited to published and unpublished essays in literary criticism that present a perspective either sympathetic to lesbianism or those explicitly lesbian in orientation. It is limited to *literature* and to theoretical articles (not book reviews). The sexual preference of the authors is, for the most part, irrelevant; this is an analysis of lesbian feminist *ideas*, not authors. Although the network of lesbian critics is well developed, some major unpublished papers may have escaped my attention.

5. Elly Bulkin, "'Kissing Against the Light': A Look at Lesbian Poetry," *Radical Teacher* 10 (December 1978): 8. This article was reprinted in *College English* and *Women's Studies Newsletter;* an expanded version is available from the Lesbian-Feminist Study Clearinghouse, Women's Studies Program, University of Pittsburgh, Pittsburgh, Pennsylvania 15260.

6. Julia Penelope [Stanley], "The Articulation of Bias: Hoof in Mouth Disease," paper presented at the 1979 convention of the National Council of Teachers of English, San Francisco, November 1979, pp. 4–5. On the same panel, I presented a paper on "Heterosexism in Literary Anthologies," which develops some of the points of this paragraph.

7. Annette Kolodny, "Literary Criticism: Review Essay," *Signs* 2, no. 2 (Winter 1976): 416, 419.

8. Ellen Moers, *Literary Women: The Great Writers* (Garden City, N.Y.: Doubleday & Co., 1976), pp. 108–9, 145.

9. Patricia Meyer Spacks, *The Female Imagination* (New York: Avon Books, 1975), pp. 89, 214, 363.

10. Elaine Showalter, *A Literature of Their Own: British Women Novelists From Brontë to Lessing* (Princeton: Princeton University Press, 1977), pp. 178, 229, 316.

11. Sandra M. Gilbert and Susan Gubar, *The Madwoman in the Attic: The Woman Writer and the Nineteenth-Century Literary Imagination* (New Haven: Yale University Press, 1979), p. 567. Regarding another issue—their analysis of Emily Dickinson's poem no. 1722—Nadean Bishop says, "It is hard to fathom how Sandra Gilbert and Susan Gubar could take this erotic representation of lesbian love-making to be an 'image of the chaste moon goddess Diana,' who does not have hand or tender tongue or inspire incredulity." See Nadean Bishop, "Renunciation in the Bridal Poems of Emily Dickinson," paper presented at the National Women's Studies Association, Bloomington, Indiana, 16–20 May 1980. One other

major critical study, Judith Fetterley's *The Resisting Reader: a Feminist Approach to American Fiction* (Bloomington: Indiana University Press, 1978), is uniquely sensitive to lesbianism in its interpretation of *The Bostonians*.

12.   Gene Damon, Jan Watson, and Robin Jordan, *The Lesbian in Literature: A Bibliography* (1967; reprinted., Reno, Nev.: Naiad Press, 1975).

13.   Jeannette Foster, *Sex Variant Women in Literature* (1956; reprinted., Baltimore: Diana Press, 1975). See also, Karla Jay, "The X-Rated Bibliographer: A Spy in the House of Sex," in *Lavender Culture,* ed. Karla Jay and Allen Young (New York: Harcourt Brace Jovanovich, 1978), pp. 257–61.

14.   Beth Hodges, ed., Special Issue on Lesbian Writing and Publishing, *Margins* 23 (August 1975). Beth Hodges, ed., Special Issue on Lesbian Literature and Publishing, *Sinister Wisdom* 2 (Fall 1976).

15.   In addition, networks of lesbian critics, teachers, and scholars were established through panels at the Modern Language Association's annual conventions and at the Lesbian Writers' Conference in Chicago, which began in 1974 and continued for several years. Currently, networking continues through conferences, journals, and other institutionalized outlets. The Lesbian-Feminist Study Clearinghouse reprints articles, bibliographies, and syllabi pertinent to lesbian studies. See note 5 for the address. The Lesbian Herstory Archives collects all material documenting lesbian lives past or present; their address is P.O. Box 1258, New York, New York 10001. *Matrices*, "A Lesbian-Feminist Research Newsletter," is a network of information about research projects, reference materials, calls for papers, bibliographies, and so forth. There are several regional editors; the managing editor is Bobby Lacy, 4000 Randolph, Lincoln, Nebraska 68510.

16.   Radicalesbians, "The Woman-Identified Woman," in *Radical Feminism,* ed. Anne Koedt, Ellen Levine, and Anita Rapone (New York; Quadrangle, 1973). This article is extensively reprinted in women's studies anthologies.

17.   Charlotte Bunch, "Lesbians in Revolt," in *Lesbianism and the Women's Movement,* ed. Nancy Myron and Charlotte Bunch (Baltimore: Diana Press, 1975), p. 30.

18.   Susan Sniader Lanser, "Speaking in Tongues: *Ladies Almanack* and the Language of Celebration," *Frontiers* 4, no. 3 (Fall 1979): 39.

19.   Catharine R. Stimpson, "Zero Degree Deviancy: A Study of the Lesbian Novel," in this volume, p. 301.

20.   Barbara Smith "Toward a Black Feminist Criticism," *Conditions: Two* 1, no. 2 (October 1977): 39. It is sometimes overlooked that Smith's pathbreaking article on black feminist criticism is also a lesbian feminist analysis.

21.   Adrienne Rich, "Compulsory Heterosexuality and Lesbian Existence," *Signs* 5, no. 4 (Summer 1980): 648–49.

22.   Bertha Harris, quoted by Smith, "Toward a Black Feminist Criticism," p. 33.

23.   Supportive historical and biographical information about women writers can be found in a number of recent articles, in addition to those cited elsewhere in this paper. See, for example, Judith Schwarz, "*Yellow Clover:* Katherine Lee Bates and Katherine Coman," pp. 59–67; Josephine Donovan, "The Unpublished Love Poems of Sarah Orne Jewett," pp. 26–31; and Margaret Cruikshank, "Geraldine Jewsbury and Jane Carlyle," pp. 60–64, all in Special Issue on Lesbian History, *Frontiers* 4, no. 3 (Fall 1979).

24.   Lillian Faderman, *Surpassing the Love of Men: Romantic Friendship and Love Between Women From the Renaissance to the Present* (New York: William Morrow and Co., 1981), pp. 17–18.

25.   Adrienne Rich, "'It Is the Lesbian in Us . . . ,'" in *On Lies, Secrets, and Silence* (New York: W. W. Norton & Co., 1979), p. 202.

26.   Rich, "Women and Honor: Some Notes on Lying (1975)," in *On Lies, Secrets, and Silence,* p. 190.

27.   Gloria T. Hull, "'Under the Days': The Buried Life and Poetry of Angelina Weld Grimké," The Black Women's Issue, *Conditions: Five* 2, no. 2 (Autumn 1979): 23, 20.

28. Joanna Russ, "To Write 'Like a Woman': Transformations of Identity in Willa Cather," paper presented at the MLA convention, in San Francisco, December 1979. On coding in other writers, see also, Ann Cothran and Diane Griffin Crowder, "An Optical Thirst for Invisible Water: Image Structure, Codes and Recoding in Colette's *The Pure and the Impure*," paper presented at the MLA convention, New York, December 1978; and Annette Kolodny, "The Lady's Not For Spurning: Kate Millett and the Critics," *Contemporary Literature* 17, no. 4. 541–62.

29. Two male critics—Edmund Wilson and Robert Bridgman—first suggested the connection between Stein's obscurity and her lesbianism. Jane Rule in *Lesbian Images* and Dolores Klaich in *Woman Plus Woman* (see note 35) both follow their analysis. Cynthia Secor has argued that Stein did declare her lesbianism in her writing ("Can We Call Gertrude Stein a Non-Declared Lesbian Writer?") in a paper presented at the MLA convention, San Francisco, December 1979. For more on Stein, see note 44.

30. Bulkin, "'Kissing Against the Light,'" p. 8.

31. Smith, "Toward a Black Feminist Criticism," p. 39.

32. Blanche Wiesen Cook, "'Women Alone Stir My Imagination': Lesbianism and the Cultural Tradition," *Signs* 4, no. 4 (Summer 1979): 718–39. A curious example of contemporary denial of lesbianism—the obliteration of the lesbian tradition such as it is—is found in Judith Hallett, "Sappho and Her Social Context: Sense and Sensuality," *Signs* 4, no. 3 (Spring 1979): 447–64. Sappho, of course, personifies "lesbian existence," indeed lesbian *possibility*, as well as female poetic creativity. Hallett, however, essentially denies Sappho's love for women with her conclusion that "she did not represent herself in her verses as having expressed homosexual feelings physically." One might certainly argue that no other possible interpretation can exist for Sappho's "He is more than a hero" (Mary Barnard's translation). Eva Stigers, in "Romantic Sensuality, Poetic Sense: A Response to Hallett on Sappho" (same issue, pp. 464–71), contends that Sappho "chose female homosexual love as the vehicle because lesbian love offered the most receptive setting for romantic *eros*." This interpretation may more accurately reflect the perspective of the nineteenth-century romantic poets who rediscovered Sappho. However, Stiger's argument that Sappho used lesbian love to create an alternate world in which male values are not dominant and in which to explore the female experience provides a starting point for a feminist analysis of Sappho's influence on her modern lesbian followers. A fine exposition of this "Sappho model" in French lesbian literature is provided by Elaine Marks in her essay "Lesbian Intertextuality" (see note 41).

33. Jane Rule, *Lesbian Images* (Garden City, N.Y.; Doubleday & Co., 1975).

34. Bonnie Zimmerman, "The New Tradition," *Sinister Wisdom* 2 (Fall 1976): 34–41.

35. Dolores Klaich, *Woman Plus Woman: Attitudes Toward Lesbianism* (New York: William Morrow, 1974); Louise Bernikow, *The World Split Open: Four Centuries of Women Poets in England and America, 1552–1950* (New York: Vintage Books, 1974).

36. Cook, "Women Alone Stir My Imagination," p. 720.

37. See Lillian Faderman's articles: "The Morbidification of Love Between Women by Nineteenth-Century Sexologists," *Journal of Homosexuality* 4, no. 1 (Fall 1978): 73–90; "Emily Dickinson's Letters to Sue Gilbert," *Massachusetts Review* 18, no. 2 (Summer 1977): 197–225; "Emily Dickinson's Homoerotic Poetry," *Higginson Journal* 18 (1978): 19–27; "Female Same-Sex Relationships in Novels by Longfellow, Holmes, and James," *New England Quarterly* 60, no. 3 (September 1978): 309–32; and "Lesbian Magazine Fiction in the Early Twentieth Century," *Journal of Popular Culture* 11, no. 4 (Spring 1978): 800–17.

38. Holly Near, "Imagine My Surprise," on *Imagine My Surprise!* (Redwood Records, 1978).

39. See Klaich, chap. 6. Also, see Bertha Harris, "The More Profound Nationality of their Lesbianism: Lesbian Society in Paris in the 1920's," *Amazon Expedition* (New York: Times Change Press, 1973), pp. 77–88; and Gayle Rubin's Introduction to Renée Vivien's: *A Woman Appeared to Me*, trans. Jeanette Foster (Reno, Nev.: Naiad Press, 1976).

40. For example, see Lanser, "Speaking in Tongues."

41. Marks, "Lesbian Intertexuality," in *Homosexualities and French Literature*, ed. George Stambolian and Elaine Marks (Ithaca, N.Y.: Cornell University Press, 1979), pp. 353–77.

42. Lillian Faderman and Ann Williams, "Radclyffe Hall and the Lesbian Image," *Conditions: One* 1, no. 1 (April 1977): 40; and Sybil Korff Vincent, "Nothing Fails Like Success: Radclyffe Hall's *The Well of Loneliness*," unpublished paper.

43. Stimpson, "Zero Degree Deviancy," pp. 8–17.

44. Cynthia Secor, "*Ida*, A Great American Novel," *Twentieth-Century Literature* 24, no. 1 (Spring 1978): 99; Elizabeth Fifer, "Is Flesh Advisable: The Interior Theater of Gertrude Stein," *Signs* 4, no. 3 (Spring 1979): 478; Dierdre Vanderlinde, "Gertrude Stein: Three Lives," paper presented at MLA convention, San Francisco, December 1979, p. 10; and Catharine Stimpson, "The Mind, and Body and Gertrude Stein," *Critical Inquiry* 3, no. 3 (Spring 1977): 489–506. Like Stimpson on Stein, Lanser, in "Speaking in Tongues," suggests that Djuna Barnes in *Ladies Almanack* "writes through the lesbian body, celebrating not the abstraction of a sexual preference, but female sexuality and its lesbian expression."

45. Lillian Faderman and Louise Bernikow, "Comment on Joanne Feit Diehl's "'Come Slowly—Eden,'" *Signs* 4, no. 1 (Autumn 1978): 188–95. For another perspective on woman as muse, see my paper, "'The Dark Eye Beaming': George Eliot, Sara Hennell and the Female Muse" (presented at MLA convention, "George Eliot and the Female Tradition," 1980); and Arlene Raven and Ruth Iskin, "Through the Peephole: Toward a Lesbian Sensibility in Art," *Chrysalis* no. 4, pp. 19–31. Contemporary lesbian interpretations of Dickinson were anticipated by Rebecca Patterson in *The Riddle of Emily Dickinson* (Boston: Houghton Mifflin, 1951).

46. Paula Bennett, "The Language of Love: Emily Dickinson's Homoerotic Poetry," *Gai Saber* 1, no. 1 (Spring 1977): 13–17; Bennett, "Emily Dickinson and the Value of Isolation," *Dickinson Studies* 36 (1979): 13–17; Bennett's paper presented at the MLA, 1979; and Bishop, "Renunciation in the Bridal Poems."

47. Bertha Harris, "*What we mean to say:* Notes Toward Defining the Nature of Lesbian Literature," *Heresies* 3 (Fall 1977): 7–8. Also, Harris, "The Purification of Monstrosity: The Lesbian as Literature," paper presented at the MLA convention, New York, Dec. 1974.

48. Bonnie Zimmerman, "'Daughters of Darkness': Lesbian Vampires," *Jump Cut* no. 24–25 (March 1981): 23–24. See also, Jane Caputi, "'Jaws': Fish Stories and Patriarchal Myth," *Sinister Wisdom* 7 (Fall 1978): 66–81.

49. Ann Allen Shockley, "The Black Lesbian in American Literature: An Overview," *Conditions: Five* 2: no. 2 (Autumn 1979): 136.

50. Maureen Brady and Judith McDaniel, "Lesbians in the Mainstream: Images of Lesbians in Recent Commercial Fiction," *Conditions: Six* 2, no. 3 (Summer 1980): 83.

51. Julia Penelope Stanley, "Uninhabited Angels: Metaphors for Love," *Margins* 23 (August 1975): 8.

52. Julia Penelope Stanley and Susan J. Wolfe, "Toward a Feminist Aesthetic," *Chrysalis*, no. 6, p. 66.

53. Susan J. Wolfe, "Stylistic Experimentation in Millett, Johnston, and Wittig," paper presented at the MLA convention, New York, December 1978, p. 3. On lesbian stylistics, see Lanser, "Speaking in Tongues"; and Martha Rosenfield, "Linguistic Experimentation in Monique Wittig's *Le Corps lesbien*," paper presented at the MLA convention, 1978.

54. Mary Carruthers, "Imagining Women: Notes Toward a Feminist Poetic," *Massachusetts Review* 20, no. 2 (Summer 1979): 301.

55. Jane Gurko and Sally Gearhart, "The Sword and the Vessel Versus the Lake on the

Lake: A Lesbian Model of Nonviolent Rhetoric," paper presented at the MLA convention, 1979, p. 3.

56. Harriet Desmoines, "Notes for a Magazine II," *Sinister Wisdom* 1, no. 1 (July 1976): 29.

57. Wolfe, "Stylistic Experimentation," p. 16.

58. Annette Kolodny, "Dancing Through the Minefield: Some Observations on the Theory, Practice, and Politics of a Feminist Literary Criticism," *Feminist Studies* 6, no. 1 (Spring 1980): 1–25; in this volume under "Methodologies."

59. For example, a panel at the 1980 MLA convention (Houston), "Literary History and the New Histories of Sexuality," presented gay and lesbian perspectives on contemporary French philosophies.

60. Elly Bulkin, "Racism and Writing: Some Implications for White Lesbian Critics," *Sinister Wisdom* 13 (Spring 1980): 16.

61. See Lorraine Bethel, "'This Infinity of Conscious Pain': Zora Neale Hurston and the Black Female Literary Tradition" and Gloria T. Hull, "Researching Alice Dunbar-Nelson: A Personal and Literary Perspective," both in *All the Women Are White, All the Blacks Are Men, But Some of Us Are Brave: Black Women's Studies,* ed. Gloria T. Hull, Patricia Bell Scott, and Barbara Smith (Old Westbury, N.Y.: Feminist Press, 1982); and Cheryl Clarke, et al., "Conversations and Questions: Black Women on Black Women Writers," *Conditions: Nine* 3, no. 3 (1983): 88–137.

62. Judith McDaniel, "Lesbians and Literature," *Sinister Wisdom* 2 (Fall 1976): 2.

63. Susan Gubar, "Blessings in Disguise: Cross-Dressing as Re-Dressing for Female Modernists," *Massachusetts Review* 22, no. 3 (1981): 477–508.

64. Elly Bulkin, "An Interview with Adrienne Rich: Part II," *Conditions: Two* (1977): 58.

JANE MARCUS

STORMING THE TOOLSHED

I. FEMINIST SCHOLARS AND LITERARY THEORY

Sections II and III of this article reflect their occasions. "Lupine Criticism" was given as a talk at the Modern Language Association (MLA) meeting in San Francisco in 1979. Florence Howe chaired the session with panelists Mary Helen Washington, Sydney Janet Kaplan, Suzanne Juhasz, and Tillie Olsen.[1] There was a large and enthusiastic audience, and the session was remarkable historically for discussion of race, class, and sexual identity, particularly lesbianism, and for vocal criticism and participation from the audience. The sparse audience for feminist sessions the following year in Houston, the current debate in the National Women's Studies Association over the primacy of the issues of racism and lesbian identity,[2] and the concurrent minimization of differences in feminist literary criticism itself by Annette Kolodny and others in recent issues of *Feminist Studies*[3] make it imperative that we reexamine our history. It was, after all, a playful but serious prediction made in "Lupine Criticism" that aggressive, historical feminist scholarship on Virginia Woolf might cease if the practitioners became absorbed into the academy and stopped combining political activism and the position of "outsidership" with their scholarly work.

In "Dancing through the Minefield," Kolodny's liberal relaxation of the tensions among us and the tensions between feminists and the academy reflects a similar relaxation on the part of historians and political activists. What this does is to isolate Marxist feminists and lesbians on the barricades while "good girl" feminists fold their tents and slip quietly into the establishment. There is a battlefield (race, class, and sexual identity) within each one of us, another battlefield where we wage these wars with our own feminist colleagues (as in *Signs*), and a third battlefield where we defend ourselves from male onslaughts both on our work and on the laws that govern our lives as women in society. It is far too early to tear down the barricades. Dancing shoes will not do. We still need our heavy boots and mine detectors.

The most serious issue facing feminist critics today is that which divides the profession as a whole, the division between theory and practice. Leaning on the Greeks, our culture still posits philosophy, music, and mathematics as the highest forms of intellectual endeavor. They have been the fields most zealously guarded against female incursion, the fields where it has been most difficult for women to gain training. The English composer Dame Ethel Smyth defended herself from criticism of her battles for status and position among women musicians: she could not withdraw from the world to compose, to act the artist who simply cultivates her own garden, she said, when someone had locked up all the tools.[4] Literary theory is a branch of philosophy. Its most vigorous practitioners in the United States have been male. It is no historical accident that the hegemony of the theoreticians and the valorization of theory itself parallels the rise of feminist criticism. While we have been doing literary housekeeping, they have been gazing at the stars. They refuse to bear the burden of the sins of their literary fathers or to make amends for centuries of critical abuse of women writers involving the loss, destruction, bowdlerization, or misevaluation of women's texts, diaries, letters, and biographies.

When feminist critics first forced open the toolshed, they polished and sharpened the rusty spades and hoes and rakes men long since had discarded. They learned history, textual criticism, biography, the recovery of manuscripts. They began to search for and reprint women's works and to study the image of woman in Western art. Many moved into linguistics to get at the origins of oppression in language, while others worked to find the writing of women of color.[5] We were all forced to become historians and biographers and to train ourselves in those disciplines. We devoured theories of female psychology, anthropology, and myth to broaden our grasp of the work of women artists. The more materialist and particular the labor of feminist critics became, the more abstract and antimaterialist became the work of the men (they left in Europe the Marxist origins of structuralism and deconstruction). The more we spoke in moral indignation and anger, the more Parnassian were the whispers of male theorists. If the last conference of the School of Criticism and Theory is any model to go by,[6] soon they will have retreated so far from life and literature that they will be analyzing the songs of birds in the garden of Paradise (Adamic only).

Geoffrey Hartman claims for the theorists that literary criticism is in the wilderness.[7] While one may grant that Hartman's manner is a distinct imitation of John the Baptist, one must point out that the theorists are not in the wilderness at all but in a labyrinthine garden with high hedges they have constructed themselves. The arrogance of the metaphor indicates the cause of their isolation. If there is one true word in literary criticism and they are the precursors of their master's voice, the profession is lost. But historians of our difficult era will have little doubt about the social origins of the idea of born-again literary critics. I am reminded of the words of the Victorian aesthetician, Vernon Lee, in a letter to Ethel Smyth. It was bad enough to be a voice crying in the wilderness, she said, but a female philosopher was a "vox clamans" in the closet.[8]

There are some feminist theorists of note, among whom one may cite especially the work of Gayatri Spivak in literature and Julia Lesage in film criticism.[9] Lesage and her colleagues on the film journal *Jump-Cut* have, in fact, made the most revolutionary breakthrough in feminist theory and practice by trying to effect a rapprochement between the left and lesbians. The lesbian-feminist special issue of *Jump-Cut* is a tour de force of brilliant and ground-breaking essays and includes an editorial in which the male editors attempt to deal with what we may call "reparations" for the long battles of the sexes. The writing and publication of these essays is a hopeful sign, but not a victory, until feminist critics who are neither left nor lesbian read and debate these issues and bring them into the classroom.

There were no feminist critics speaking at the first meeting of the School of Criticism and Theory at Northwestern University in the spring of 1981, though the intelligent response of Mary Douglas, the anthropologist, to one of the more reactionary papers, was the highlight of the conference.[10] Protest at the omission of feminists was met by the response that there *are* no feminist theorists, at least none whom the men find "interesting." If there is as yet no feminist critical theory that men find interesting, there is no reason to suppose that it is not at this very moment being written, nor is there any reason to suppose that men will ever be as interested as we are in developments in our own field. Recent critical books attacking the hegemony of the theorists ignore both feminists and Marxists or give them a light cuff, while the heavy blows are aimed at theorists of their own sex. We are excluded from their discourse (theorizing is a male activity); consequently no intellectual intercourse can take place. Even a Marxist critic like Frederic Jameson is loyal to the old boys.[11]

Just as Virginia Woolf predicted both the birth of Shakespeare's sister and our work for her arrival, so one may also predict the birth of the feminist critic of genius. She must reject with Virginia Woolf the patriarchal view of literature as a competition with prizes of "ornamental pots" from the headmaster. The feminist critic is always at odds with the headmaster. She is, as Adrienne Rich argues, "disloyal" to civilization.[12] She must refuse the ornamental pot, even if it is very fashionable and made in France. She must break the measuring rod, even if it is finely calibrated in the literary laboratories at Yale. We shall have a theory of our own when our practice develops it. "Masterpieces are not single and solitary births," Woolf wrote in *A Room of One's Own*, "they are the outcome of many years of thinking in common, of thinking by the body of the people, so that the experience of the mass is behind the single voice." Woolf was discussing Shakespeare as the product of history. But her socialist analysis can be extended to criticism as well. By her analysis one can imagine that there were many little Geoffrey Hartmans before there was one big Geoffrey Hartman, as in literature there were many little Shakespeares before the master himself.[13]

We have already produced feminist critics to match their male counterparts: Mary Ellman, Kate Millett, Ellen Moers, Elaine Showalter. Sandra Gilbert and Susan Gubar can outdo Harold Bloom at his own game; Gayatri Spivak speaks as an equal among the French deconstructionists; Julia Lesage challenges film theory. Many lesser-known feminists have worked steadily for new readings and new values in their own fields. But even if we were to construct the feminist super-critic from the collective voice of all of them, it is doubtful that the self-appointed priesthood would find her analysis interesting. I suspect that this literary amazon is even now slouching toward Ephesus to be born—the critic who will deliver us from slavery to the canon, from racist, sexist, and classist misreadings. But one can be sure that, welcome as she will be among us, the chosen critics will see her as a false messiah.

I do not think we should surrender easily. It is they and their fathers who excluded and oppressed us and our mothers, they who decided to exclude women

writers from what was taught, women students from who was taught. Our historical losses at their hands are incalculable. It is not up to us to beg them to find our
work interesting. It is up to them to make reparations: to establish secure
women's studies departments, black studies departments, chairs of feminist literary criticism and women's history, to read the work of women and black writers,
and to teach it.

After this digression upon theory I would like to return to the subject of the rest
of this article. If "Lupine Criticism" is an example of a battle within a small area
of literary criticism, fought among one's peers, "One Cheer for Democracy, or
Talking Back to Quentin Bell" is a direct confrontation with Virginia Woolf's
nephew, official biographer, and owner of her literary estate. In his essay,
"Bloomsbury and the Vulgar Passions," given on a lecture tour of the United
States and published in *Critical Inquiry*, Bell once again mocks Virginia Woolf's
Three Guineas for its feminism and pacifism.[14] He minimizes her contribution to
political thought by comparing it unfavorably to a pamphlet by his father, Clive
Bell, as well as E. M. Forster's "Two Cheers for Democracy" and *A Passage to
India*. I admire Bell's *Bloomsbury*[15] and am grateful, as are other Woolf scholars,
for the painstaking work of his biography and for the publication of the letters
and diaries. Because we are dependent on the estate for permission to publish, it
has been difficult for Woolf scholars to take issue with his analysis without jeopar-
dizing their careers. The year 1982 is the centenary of Virginia Woolf's birth. In
the thirties she predicted that in fifty years men would allow women writers free
speech. Could she have imagined this deadlock in criticism, this "separate but
equal" free speech as it now exists in literary criticism, where feminist critics are
excluded from discourse with male theorists?[16] She suffered from these same exclusions herself, was chastised for her feminism all her life, and continues to be
chastised after her death. She died, I believe, in an ethical torment over her pacifism in a terrible war. It seems only natural to take up her weapons. Our first
target is the shed where the power tools of literary theory have been kept. There
is no doubt that in the hands of feminist critics they will transform the study of
literature.

II. LUPINE CRITICISM

It is amusing to imagine what Virginia Woolf would think of an MLA meeting.
You know how she despised lectures and did not believe that literature should be
taught to middle-class students. She herself only lectured to women and working-
class people. She gave lectures to women students and fellow professional women,
to the Workers' Education League and the Working Women's Cooperative Guild.
She refused offers to lecture to men, to men's colleges and universities, and to
male-dominated institutions. While she was in Italy, studying Mussolini's fascism first hand, she refused, with a simple and defiant No, her government's
offer of a Companion of Honour, wanting no companionship whatever with the
concerns of the British Empire. She refused a degree from Manchester University, and, much to the horror of the editor of her letters, Nigel Nicolson, she
even refused quite proudly to give the prestigious Clark Lectures at Cambridge,

despite the fact that she was the first woman invited to do so. Her editor feels that this act "only weakened the cause of women in general" and confesses he cannot understand why the only prize she ever accepted was a woman's prize, the Femina Vie Heureuse prize for *To the Lighthouse*.[17]

We all know why she did it, and why, if she were here today, she would accept the Florence Howe Award for her essays on women writers and refuse any other honors. Lecturing, she wrote, "incites the most debased of human passions—vanity, ostentation, self-assertion, and the desire to convert." We confess all these sins and more; feminist literary criticism seems to demand them at the moment just for defense. "Why not create a new form of society founded on poverty and equality?" Woolf asked. "Why not bring together people so that they can talk, without mounting platforms or reading papers or wearing expensive clothes or eating expensive food? Would not such a society be worth, even as a form of education, all the papers on art and literature that have ever been read since the world began? Why not abolish prigs and prophets? Why not invent human intercourse?"[18]

In the last decade, the Commission on Women and the Women's Caucus of the MLA, with Florence Howe at the helm, and also a vast community of women scholars working together have undertaken the enormous task of revaluating women's work, uncovering forgotten lives and books, reprinting our own literature. Virginia Woolf is our model for this task. We—I say ostentatiously, self-assertively, with some vanity, and a veritable passion to make converts—in this very room are inventing "human intercourse."

Writers like Tillie Olsen and Adrienne Rich have inspired us, not only with their creative work but with their theoretical and historical essays. They continue the work in which Virginia Woolf as a feminist literary critic was engaged, a historical process she called "thinking back through our mothers."[19] Woolf would take a particular delight in what Mary Helen Washington and her colleagues are doing on black and Third World women writers. She would applaud with Suzanne Juhasz the women poets who tell the truth. Loving Katherine Mansfield as she did, and Elizabeth Robins, the forgotten feminist who influenced both Mansfield and Woolf herself, she would rub her hands with glee that Sydney Kaplan and her feminist colleagues are delivering Mansfield's ghost from the hands of the lugubrious Middleton Murry.

We in a new generation of feminist Virginia Woolf criticism have also had the advantage of collective and collaborative work, and we have sustained each other in many trials. Whenever two or three of us are gathered together sharing notes on manuscripts and letters, we feel what Virginia Woolf described in her meetings with her Greek teacher, Janet Case, and with Margaret Llewelyn Davies of the Working Women's Cooperative Guild; we are at "the heart of the women's republic."[20] It is an open secret that Virginia Woolf's literary estate is hostile to feminist critics. There are two taboo subjects: on one hand her lesbian identity, woman-centered life, and feminist work, and on the other, her socialist politics. If you wish to discover the truth regarding these issues, you will have a long, hard struggle. In that struggle you will find the sisterhood of feminist Woolf scholarship.

It all began with Ellen Hawkes's review, "The Virgin in the Bell Biography."

She was duly denounced from the pulpit of the English Institute but, despite excommunication, has had a great influence. A group of feminist Woolf scholars protested her expulsion and organized a conference at Santa Cruz. Here Madeline Moore brought together many feminists—Sara Ruddick, Tillie Olsen, and Florence Howe among them. Madeline Moore published many of the papers in a 1977 special issue of *Women's Studies.*[21]

The MLA Woolf Seminar has been notably feminist in its papers during the last five years. At one meeting, for example, Margaret Comstock chaired a session on *Between the Acts* with papers by Judy Little and Diane Gillespie, later published in *Women and Literature.* Feminists, including Kate Ellis and Ellen Hawkes, spoke at the Princeton Woolf Conference organized by Joanna Lipking. And at the Bucknell Woolf Conference in 1977, Carolyn Heilbrun, Eve Merriam, and the late Ellen Moers spoke. (Here let me note that Ellen Moers's death diminishes us all; *Literary Women* has provided us with tools and structures for building feminist literary criticism.) These conferences and seminars cemented scholarly friendships and set new directions for Woolf studies.

The publication of Woolf's letters and diaries has greatly facilitated our work. Yet the manuscripts of the novels retain the utmost fascination. We organized a special issue of the *Bulletin of the New York Public Library* with papers from the MLA Woolf Seminar on *The Years,* including Grace Radin's rendering of "two enormous chunks" of material removed from the galleys just before it went to press, Sallie Sears's essay on sexuality, and Margaret Comstock's "The Loudspeaker and the Human Voice" on the politics of the novel. Woolf's "Professions for Women" turned out to be three times the length and feminist strength of the version published by Leonard Woolf in *Collected Essays.* It has been reprinted by the New York Public Library in Mitchell Leaska's edition of *The Pargiters.*[22]

The original speech "Professions for Women" was delivered in January 1931, to a group of professional women. Preceding Virginia Woolf on the platform was Dame Ethel Smyth, the great English lesbian-feminist composer. Virginia Woolf's pacifism always receded when she spoke as a feminist. Her violent feelings came pouring out in her description of Ethel Smyth: "She is of the race of the pioneers: She is among the ice-breakers, the window-smashers, the indomitable and irresistible armoured tanks who climbed the rough ground; went first; drew the enemy's fire and left a pathway for those who came after her. I never knew whether to be angry that such heroic pertinacity was called for, or glad that it had the chance of showing itself."[23]

In our field the ice breakers and window smashers have been Tillie Olsen, Adrienne Rich, Florence Howe, Ellen Moers, and Carolyn Heilbrun. Our work has been made possible because they drew the enemy's fire. Like Virginia Woolf, we acknowledge our debt, half in anger that such belligerence is necessary, half in gladness that they have fought so well. For the last five years much feminist work on Woolf has appeared in *Virginia Woolf Miscellany,* edited, among others, by the indomitable J. J. Wilson at Sonoma State University. The Fall 1979 issue of *Twentieth-Century Literature* contains splendid and important work by feminists: Ellen Hawkes's edition of Woolf's early utopian feminist fantasy, "Friendships Gallery," written for Violet Dickinson; Susan Squier and Louise De Salvo's edition of an early forty-four-page unpublished story about a woman historian; Madeline Moore's edition of the Orlando manuscripts; and Brenda Silver's edition of two very important late manuscripts called "Anon" and "The Reader."[24]

Doubtless I have left out much new work, but this list itself is an impressive example of the comradeship and collective effort of feminist Woolf scholarship. You will note that all this work is American. We have escaped the domination of the Leavises' point of view that still prevents many British readers from seeing Woolf as anything but "elitist" and "mad." The exception is Michele Barrett's edition of Woolf's *Women and Writing*.[25]

Quentin Bell has announced that the "bottom of the barrel" has been reached in Woolf manuscripts, but we are not finished yet. There is a great deal of literary housekeeping to be done. Virginia Woolf wrote to Ethel Smyth about her own struggle for recognition as a composer, "Somehow the big apples come to the top of the basket. But of course I realize that the musicians' apple lies longest at the bottom and has the hardest struggle to rise."[26] I find these "Granny Smyth" apples to be tart and tasty indeed and am editing Dame Ethel's letters to Virginia Woolf.

What feminist scholars have found in the apples at the bottom of the barrel is a taste of the two taboo subjects, Woolf's socialist politics and her love of women. When the fifth volume of her letters was published, reviewers rushed to reassure readers that Woolf did not really mean it when she wrote to Ethel Smyth, "Women alone stir my imagination."[27] Nigel Nicolson insisted to me that Woolf was only joking. While Quentin Bell is ready to admit privately that *Letter to a Young Poet* and "Thoughts on Peace in an Air Raid" are "more Marxist than the Marxists," his public lecture, "Bloomsbury and the Vulgar Passions," dismisses *Three Guineas* as silly and unimportant.[28]

Quentin Bell is not amused by feminist criticism of Virginia Woolf. He has invented a name for us. He calls us "lupines." There is a particular variety of flower, the lupine, that grows in the American West, covering the rocky slopes of the Big Horns, the Tetons, and the Wind River Mountains in July. It is electric blue, startlingly erect, and extremely hardy. Perhaps we feminist Woolf critics can survive the patronizing label of British cultural imperialism by appropriating it ourselves. During the struggle for woman suffrage, a patronizing journalist called the most militant of the activists "Suffragettes." After a few weeks of smoldering rage at the insult, the women simply pinned that badge to their own breasts and wore it proudly.

In *Three Guineas* Virginia Woolf suggests that women might wear a tuft of horsehair on the left shoulder to indicate motherhood, as a response to male military decorations. Lupine criticism is obviously here to stay. We might as well accept the label and wear it proudly. If the proliferation and hardiness of the flower is any indication of our tenacity, we have a great future. We have not yet ceased to be "prigs and prophetesses," but we have made a start at inventing human intercourse.

Yet achievement and even struggle in common do not come easily. The first of our two volumes of feminist criticism on Virginia Woolf was finished in 1977, but we were unable to find an American publisher. The essays have circulated among feminist critics and have been cited in books and articles in print for years. Because University of Nebraska Press bought the book from Macmillan/London, the price in America is very high.[29] These incontrovertible economic facts are not lost on young scholars. Virginia Woolf founded the Hogarth Press in order to publish what she wanted to write. Feminists often feel forced by economic realities to choose other methodologies and structures that will ensure sympathetic readings from university presses. We may be as middle class as Virginia Woolf, but few of us have the economic security her aunt Caroline Emelia Stephen's legacy gave her. The samizdat circulation among networks of feminist critics works only in a system where repression is equal. If all the members are unemployed or underemployed, unpublished or unrecognized, sisterhood flourishes, and sharing is a source of strength. When we all compete for one job or when one lupine grows bigger and bluer than her sisters with unnatural fertilizers from the establishment, the ranks thin out. Times are hard and getting harder.

Being an outsider is a lonely life. Virginia Woolf proposed a *Society of Outsiders*. Lupine criticism, I think, will only flourish in the collective and in the wild. In captivity, in the rarefied hothouse atmosphere of current academic criticism, it may wither and die. From my last climbing trip in the Wind Rivers, I brought back some wild lupines and carefully transplanted them. My mother warned me that Chicago clay would stifle them, and she was right. Garden lupines are very pretty, and doubtless our colleagues would find us less offensive in the cultivated state. The British label was meant as an insult, and it might be an adjective as well as a noun. If we are going to wear it, sister lupines, let us wear it with wild Woolfian abandon.

III. ONE CHEER FOR DEMOCRACY, OR TALKING BACK TO QUENTIN BELL

Quentin Bell, largely responsible for making the Bloomsbury bed, now refuses to lie in it. In his book on Bloomsbury and his biography of his aunt, he provided readers with the materials for what he now calls "false generalizations."[30] "Bloomsbury and the Vulgar Passions" is a deliberately mystifying title that does not clarify the politics of the period but muddies the waters even more.

Virginia Woolf's clear understanding of the role of the intellectual in relation to the revolution is evident in her title *Three Guineas*.[31] She wants women and the working classes to unite against the war, but she does not presume to speak for any but her own class and sex. In "The Leaning Tower" and *Letter to a Young Poet*[32] she insists on organization in one's own class and has faith that the working class can produce its own leaders. Her title, a deliberate play on Brecht's *Threepenny Opera*, exposes the economic origins of the social problems she discusses. Neither pence nor pounds can accurately describe the contributions expected of a woman in her position. Over the years American academics have shared her frustrating experience, signing petitions and writing checks to help in the civil rights movement and the movement to stop the war in Vietnam. Like her, they sought to relieve social ills by imagining free universities like the one Woolf describes in *Three Guineas*.[33] Current feminism grew out of women's effort to find a place in movements for social change which assumed that race and class and the present war were more important than sex grievances. Woolf was the first to identify the enemy openly as "patriarchy."

Why does Bell choose Keynes's elitist phrase for an essay calculated to reduce the political power of *Three Guineas* to an entirely personal cause? If *Three Guineas* is merely an aunt's elegy for a dead nephew, as Bell argues, is not such ferocious grief a "vulgar passion" too? The phrase is not Bell's; it is the phrase of a man he admires, Maynard Keynes. It is a Victorian upper-class phrase. Few members of Margaret Llewelyn Davies's Working Women's Cooperative Guild would know what it means.[34] The phrase itself is heavy with ambiguity, and it is used by Bell in both positive and negative ways. Curiously, it works to the disadvantage of Virginia Woolf either way. It is men like his father, Keynes, and Forster who remain intellectually above the vulgar passions when Bell considers it correct to be so, and men again who are responsive to the vulgar passions of a nation at war, when this is the attitude he admires.

There is a famous point in Bell's biography of Virginia Woolf when the reader, swept along by the swift flow of prose, brisk and cool like an English trout stream in spring, is suddenly thrown into white water. Bell bursts into capital letters. The reader is on the rocks. "But were we then to scuttle like frightened spinsters before the Fascist thugs? She belonged, inescapably, to the Victorian world of Empire, Class and Privilege. Her gift was for the pursuit of shadows, for the ghostly whispers of the mind and for Pythian incomprehensibility, when what was needed was the swift and lucid phrase that could reach the ears of unemployed working men or Trades Union officials."[35] To the generation of thirties intellectuals (John Lehmann was one, and Woolf wrote her scathing *Letter to a Young Poet* to him), Virginia Woolf was "a fragile middle-aged poetess, a sexless Sappho," and "a distressed gentlewoman caught in a tempest." Bell recalls his "despair" as he urged the Rodmell Labour Party to adopt a resolution supporting the United Front, when Virginia, who was the local party secretary, turned the debate from the question. He does not call her a skilled politician for manipulating the meeting, on pacifist principle, away from patriotic militarism. He says, indeed, that she was closer to the feeling of "the masses" than he was. "I wanted to talk politics, the masses wanted to talk about the vicar's wife."[36]

But, I venture, it was precisely her "swift and lucid phrases" that annoyed him, for she spoke to the Workers' Education Association, and she wrote in the *Daily Worker* of a different kind of united front: while the capitalist, imperialist patriarchs were waging their wars, workers should join women in an assault on culture. "Trespass," she urged them, on the sacred precincts of home front institutions while the warriors are in the field. She was arguing for total subversion of the world of empire, class, and privilege. And among the shadows she pursued most vigorously were upper-class, young, male "missionaries to the masses." Take off those "pro-proletarian spectacles," she urged the generation of Auden, Spender, Lehmann, and Bell; if you really want to make the revolution, you must empty your pockets of your fathers' money, you must convert the men of your *own* class.[37] Virginia Woolf took as hard a line on the role of the intellectual in the class struggle as did Lenin or Trotsky. Its ethical imperative is even improved by the addition of feminism to the socialist-pacifist position. Quentin Bell's objections are honest ones, and there were many who agreed with him. He is infuriated by her feminism and enraged by her pacifism, and he fights back like a man.

It is dirty fighting to be sure. She is dead and cannot respond like the "Lapland Witch" Gerald Brenan says she was.[38] E. M. Forster was a dirty fighter, too.

He said in his Rede Lecture that Woolf was not a great writer because "she had no great cause at heart." [39] But we have already put *A Room of One's Own* and *Three Guineas* on the shelf next to Milton, Wollstonecraft, Mill, and Swift, and where is Forster's "Two Cheers for Democracy"? It is an embarrassment. Forster said he would give up his country before he would give up his friend. But that was not at issue. Nobody was asking him to give up his friend. And *Three Guineas* has some antifascist feminist thuggery of its own. One thing it does not have is "Pythian incomprehensibility." It is a Cassandracry in the crowd of thirties' political pamphlets. No spinsterish whispers either. The loudspeaker blares for all to hear, a withering revolutionary feminist analysis of fascism. The Hitlers and Mussolinis have no monopoly on fascism, she says. The origin of fascism is the patriarchal family. And "the daughters of educated men" had better root it out of the hearts of their English brothers before the latter rush off to fight foreign fascism.

Men on the left were horrified. But the argument that elements of fascism lurk behind patriarchal power struggles is still too radical for people. It was the subject of Lina Wertmuller's shattering feminist film *Seven Beauties*, and all the Bettelheims came out with their battering rams and big guns to remind us of how long it will be before men will "tolerate free speech in women." [40]

During the period covered by the fifth volume of Woolf's letters (1932–35), the political and personal insults that she had received from men were creating the deep sense of grievance that finally burst out in *The Years* and *Three Guineas*. [41] *The Years* itself is the most brilliant indictment in modern literature of the world of empire, class, and privilege, of capitalism and patriarchy. Structurally it is exciting, too, in its portrait of the artist as charwoman of the world. *The Years* was to have been a new form of her opera for the oppressed, alternating chapters of fact and fiction. The documentaries have been reprinted in *The Pargiters*. [42] It is too bad that Leonard talked her out of it. He was fearful of mixing fact and fiction. Her fearlessness went into the writing of both books. But she was justifiably terrified of what the male critics would say.

It is doubtful that she would have predicted her nephew's continuing hostility to *Three Guineas*. I believe there is a direct line in English history from the Clapham Sect to Bloomsbury. The anonymous reviewer in the *Times Literary Supplement* who called Virginia Woolf "the best pamphleteer in England" [43] was (consciously or unconsciously) echoing the very words applied to the antislavery pamphlets of her great-grandfather, James Stephen. That Virginia Woolf should have added feminism to the Stephen family causes is the most natural development in the world. [44] Her pacifism was not a "temporary" phenomenon but a firmly held principle of a tripartite political philosophy. It was largely derived from the important and neglected influence of her Quaker aunt, Caroline Emelia Stephen, described by Quaker historians as almost single-handedly responsible for the revival of the practically moribund English Society of Friends in the late nineteenth century. [45] It is true, as Bell says, that she modified her position at the last, actually wanted to join the fire wardens, and appears to have been willing to defend her beleaguered country in "Thoughts on Peace in an Air Raid." I have described these changes of attitude elsewhere. [46]

Bell's essay is written in response to yet another season of bad press for Bloomsbury. Virginia Woolf wrote to him during an earlier one, stating "Bloomsbury is having a very bad press at the moment; so please take up your hammer and chisel and sculpt a great flaming Goddess to put them all to shame."[47] There was certainly a family precedent. When Fitzjames Stephen was hounded out of office for prejudicing the jury in the Maybrick case after a lifetime of legal bullying and misogyny as the "Giant Grim," Leslie Stephen took up his hammer and chisel and sculpted a genial friendly giant in his biography of his brother. Virginia Stephen herself had participated in Maitland's biography of her father, largely to offset the influence of her Aunt Caroline, who had mountains of evidence that the great man had a terrible temper.[48]

Did Bell perhaps agree with Mirsky's dismissal of Bloomsbury and Virginia Woolf in *The Intelligentsia of Great Britain*,[49] the "bad press" referred to? He took up his hammer and chisel but produced no "great flaming Goddess" but a "sexless Sappho," a "distressed gentlewoman caught in a tempest." I suspect in the end we will all come to see Bell's "sexless Sappho" as a true portrait of the artist who equated chastity with creativity. But she will not do as a portrait of the so- cialist/pacifist/feminist, the "outsider" who "spat out" *Three Guineas* as an origi- nal contribution to an analysis of the origins of fascism in the patriarchal family. If she began the book as an elegy for Bell's brother, Julian, there is nothing un- usual to her method in that, for all her work is elegy. Even *A Room of One's Own* is a female elegy written in a college courtyard for the female writers of the past. The narrator has been denied access to the library which contains the manu- scripts of the two great male elegies in poetry and prose, Milton's *Lycidas* and Thackeray's *Henry Esmond*, and so she is driven to invent the female elegy. If grieving for Julian Bell's death in Spain forced her to the conclusion that she must speak directly to women of her class, to the mothers, sisters, and wives of the war makers, the public effect of a private sorrow is impressive.

But *Three Guineas* is a stubbornly feminist elegy, singing the sorrows of women under patriarchy, relentlessly repeating itself as history has repeated itself, trying to establish a feminist ethics. To my mind, and to the minds of other feminists, *Three Guineas* is the pure historical product of the Clapham Sect reform move- ment. It owes much to the "rational mysticism" of Caroline Emelia Stephen's *The Light Arising*.[50] But if the historian can free himself of sex bias, he will see *Three Guineas* in relation to Bertrand Russell's philosophy and to G. E. Moore's *Principia Ethica*. In fact it might be seen as "Principia Ethica Femina," volume 1.[51]

If Woolf later, in "Thoughts on Peace in an Air Raid," admitted woman's com- plicity in war and concluded that "we must compensate the man for his gun,"[52] she did not suggest how. Bell thinks she has come close to the vulgar passions (which are now positive) in this essay, and he is disposed to grant her some credit.[53] I thought so too in 1976. But I am now disposed to think that "Thoughts on Peace in an Air Raid" is just what the title suggests, a defensive position taken under extreme pressure. The militant feminism of *Three Guineas*, its equally militant pacifism, socialism, and antifascism, are "saddening" and "exas- perating" to Bell. Many European and American feminist historians are studying the forms of Italian and German fascism and their relation to the patriarchal fam- ily, marriage, and the treatment of women and children, and they have found Woolf's pamphlet a strikingly original and eerily correct analysis.[54] I believe Bell labors under the misconception that feminism is not political—a major mis- take—as well as under minor misconceptions that pacifism in World War II was not a respectable political stance (it was certainly not popular) and that Virginia Woolf could not have been much of a socialist because she did not work in Labour Party Committees or associate with the working classes. Even when Bell imagines a committee meeting he sees only Mr. A., Mr. B., Mr. C., Mr. D., and the chairman. I seem to recall that the committee meeting which caused his admirable prose style to flood the gates was chaired by his aunt, Mrs. W., and she prevented him from passing his resolution. It is a long time to hold a grudge.

It is a failure of the imagination to support that all pacifists were, like Clive Bell, ad hoc peaceniks for a particular war. Quakers, like Caroline Stephen and Violet Dickinson, Virginia's early mentors, were opposed to all wars.

It seems oddly un-English and more like an American pragmatist or utilitarian argument to judge the quality of a pamphlet by its contemporary effectiveness. James Stephen turned out antislavery pamphlets that failed to stop the slavers. But it was not until he had been dead many years that his son finally got an antislavery bill through Parliament. How much immediate effect did Mill's *Subjection of Women* have? Women did not get the vote until 1928, and the condition of women is still not by any means satisfactory. *Three Guineas* is still read (and this might be a better measure of "effectiveness") by those who hunger for its message, who feel as guilty as Woolf did about fighting for feminism when atrocities and wars demand one's attention. Seeking for the deepest cause of imperialist and capitalist war, she found it in male aggression. She was saddened, but urged women to stop encouraging aggression. I wish she had been more successful.

If effectiveness is the criterion of a pamphlet's success, is there any way of measuring the success of *Three Guineas* in keeping America out of the war when it was published in the *Atlantic* as "Women Must Weep or Unite against the War"? I suppose it is just as possible to imagine that her pamphlet had that power as to assert that Forster's *A Passage to India* had an immense influence in dissuading Britons from their imperialist passions.[55] I do not share Bell's enthusiasm for *A Passage to India*. It seems so pale and liberal compared to the radical anti-imperialism and anticapitalism of *Mrs. Dalloway* or *The Years*. Virginia Woolf once described Mrs. Humphry Ward's novels as hanging in the lumber room of literature like the mantles of our aunts, covered with beads and bugles. Well, there is something about E. M. Forster's novels reminiscent of our unmarried uncles' silk pajamas, something elegant, but rather effete. They have not worn well. And Woolf's novels get harder and tougher year by year, ethically unyielding and morally challenging.

Any member of the Women's International League for Peace and Freedom or the Women's Cooperative Guild, as well as many left-wing feminists and many socialists, would have seen Virginia Woolf's ideology as more powerful than the liberalism of Keynes or Forster. For those readers, *Three Guineas* is not forced or unsatisfactory. It was not at the time, as Bell implies, nor is it now, a political irrelevance.[56] It is hard to believe that the world is as neatly divided into hawks and doves as Bell would have us believe and that one changes feathers over every war. Some of us imagine Virginia Woolf as a great blue heron anyway, and she describes herself as a misfit, an outsider. As for her ability to feel the vulgar passions, to hear the demotic voice, let him read the song of the caretaker's children in *The Years*. It is the voice of the colonial chickens come home to roost. The full measure of *Three Guineas*'s effect is yet to be weighed, for it deals with older, more universal, and more deeply rooted social ills than the Spanish fascism that prompted it. Her intent reminds me of a surrealist poem by Laura Riding:

> She opens the heads of her brothers
> And lets out the aeroplanes
> "Now," she says, "you will be able to think better." [57]

NOTES

1. Two of the papers delivered at that meeting have since been published: Mary Helen Washington, "New Lives and New Letters: Black Women Writers at the End of the Seventies," *College English* 43, no. 1 (January 1981): 1–11; and Florence Howe, "Those We Still Don't Read," *College English* 43, no. 1 (January 1981): 12–16.

2. See *Women's Studies Quarterly* 9, no. 3 (Fall 1981), particularly the reprint of speeches by Adrienne Rich, "Disobedience Is What the NWSA Is Potentially About," pp. 4–6; and Audre Lorde, "The Uses of Anger," pp. 7–10.

3. See Annette Kolodny, "Dancing through the Minefield: Some Observations on the Theory, Practice, and Politics of a Feminist Literary Criticism," *Feminist Studies* 6, no. 1 (Spring 1980): 1–25; and Judith Gardiner's response, "Marching through Our Field," *Feminist Studies* 8.3 (1982): 629–75. Gardiner distinguishes between liberal, radical, and socialist feminist critics. Gayatri Spivak's unpublished "A Response to Annette Kolodny" (Department of English, University of Texas at Austin, 1980) is an even stronger critique of Kolodny's position. She writes: "To embrace pluralism (as Kolodny recommends) is to espouse the politics of the masculinist establishment. Pluralism is the method employed by the *central* authorities to neutralize opposition by seeming to accept it. The gesture of pluralism on the part of the *marginal* can only mean capitulation to the center."

4. Dame Ethel Smyth's story of her struggle against the masculine establishment in music is told in *Female Pipings in Eden* (London: Peter Davies, 1934). A revival of Dame Ethel's work has begun: several papers were delivered at the First National Congress on Women and Music at New York University in March 1981; her memoirs have been reprinted, *Impressions That Remained* (New York: Da Capo Press, 1981), with a new introduction by Ronald Crichton; and De Capo Press (1980) has also reprinted the score of her *Mass in D* for solo, chorus, and orchestra, with a new introduction by Jane Bernstein.

5. See Gloria T. Hull, Patricia Bell Scott, and Barbara Smith, eds., *But Some of Us Are Brave: Black Women's Studies* (Old Westbury, N.Y.: Feminist Press, 1981).

6. The conference, entitled "A Controversy of Critics," was sponsored by the School of Criticism and Theory at Northwestern University in May 1981.

7. Geoffrey Hartman, *Criticism in the Wilderness: The Study of Literature Today* (New Haven, Conn.: Yale University Press, 1980).

8. Quoted by Ethel Smyth in *Maurice Baring* (London: Heinemann, 1937), p. 206.

9. See Gayatri Spivak, "Feminism and Critical Theory," *Women's Studies International Quarterly* 1, no. 3 (1978): 241–46, and "Three Feminist Readings: McCullers, Drabble, and Habermas," *Union Seminary Quarterly Review* 35, no. 1–2 (Fall–Winter 1978–79): 15–38. The most important essays by Julia Lesage are "Subversive Fantasy in *Celine and Julie Go Boating*," *Jump-Cut* 24–25 (March 1981): 36–43, which deals with the semiotics of body language and domestic space, "Dialectical, Revolutionary, Feminist," *Jump-Cut* 20 (May 1979): 20–23, and "Artful Racism, Artful Rape: D. W. Griffith's *Broken Blossoms*," *Jump-Cut* 26 (May 1981). See also the entire lesbian feminist special issue of *Jump-Cut* (24–25 [March 1981]), especially its bibliography, p. 21; Ruby Rich's analysis of the

teacher in girls' schools playing the roles of "good cop" and "bad cop" in her study of *Maedchen in Uniform,* "From Repressive Tolerance to Erotic Liberation," pp. 44–50; and Bonnie Zimmerman's discussion of lesbian vampire films, "Daughters of Darkness: Lesbian Vampires," pp. 23–24.

10. Julia Lesage uses Mary Douglas's *Purity and Danger: An Analysis of Concepts of Pollution and Taboo* (London: Routledge & Kegan Paul, 1966) as a theoretical construct for the analysis of *Celine and Julie Go Boating* (see n. 9 above): this theory was also very useful to Marina Warner in her analysis of female heroism in *Joan of Arc* (New York: Alfred A. Knopf, Inc., 1981).

11. See Gerald Graff's *Poetic Statement and Critical Dogma* (Evanston, Ill.: Northwestern University Press, 1970), and *Literature against Itself* (Chicago: University of Chicago Press, 1979); Frank Lentricchia's *After the New Criticism* (Chicago: University of Chicago Press, 1980); Fredric Jameson's *The Political Unconscious: Narrative as a Socially Symbolic Act* (Ithaca, N.Y.: Cornell University Press, 1981); and Terry Eagleton's "The Idealism of American Criticism," *New Left Review* 127 (May–June 1981): 53–65, which reviews Lentricchia and Jameson and surveys the field. Eagleton notes that these critics refuse to discuss gender and maintain sexist attitudes, but his own review does not mention the brilliant work done by feminist critics in the United States in the last decade, nor has Eagleton's work itself deviated from male discourse despite its Marxism. If Annette Kolodny's espousal of the pluralist position from the margin may be seen as a capitulation to a misogynist power structure, Jameson's Marxist pluralism, in its refusal to deal with gender, should show those tempted to follow Kolodny's lead that male bonding transcends theoretical enmities and is more primary among American critics than the issues that divide them intellectually.

12. Rich (n. 2 above), p. 5.

13. Virginia Woolf, *A Room of One's Own* (New York: Harcourt, Brace and World 1929: reprint ed. 1957), pp. 68–69, 110.

14. Quentin Bell, "Bloomsbury and the Vulgar Passions," *Critical Inquiry* 6, no. 2 (Winter 1979): 239–56.

15. Quentin Bell, *Bloomsbury* (London: Weidenfeld & Nicolson, 1968).

16. Recent contributions to feminist critical theory include: Myra Jehlen, "Archimedes and the Paradox of Feminist Criticism," *Signs: Journal of Women in Culture and Society* 6, no. 4 (Summer 1981): 575–601; and Nina Baym, "Melodramas of Beset Manhood: How Theories of American Fiction Exclude Women Authors," *American Quarterly* 33, no. 2 (Summer 1981): 123–39. In press is a special issue of *Critical Inquiry* (8, no. 2 [Winter 1981]) edited by Elizabeth Abel called "Writing and Sexual Difference," with essays by Elaine Showalter, Mary Jacobus, Margaret Homans, Susan Gubar, Nancy Vickers, Nina Auerbach, Annette Kolodny, Froma Zeitlin, Judith Gardiner, Catharine Stimpson, and Gayatri Spivak.

17. Nigel Nicolson's introduction to *The Letters of Virginia Woolf, 1932–1935,* vol. 5, *The Sickle Side of the Moon,* ed. Nigel Nicolson and Joanne Trautmann (New York: Harcourt Brace Jovanovich, 1979), pp. xi–xvii, is a sustained attack on Woolf's politics and feminism. Carolyn Heilbrun's feminist review of this volume appears in *Virginia Woolf Miscellany* 14 (Spring 1980): 4; and Nicolson's reply in *Virginia Woolf Miscellany* 16 (Spring 1981): 5. See also Jane Marcus, review of *Sickle Side of the Moon,* ed. Nicolson and Trautmann, *Chicago Tribune Book World* (November 4, 1979).

18. Virginia Woolf, "Why?" in *The Death of the Moth* (New York: Harcourt Brace, 1942), pp. 227–34.

19. Woolf, *A Room of One's Own,* p. 79. See also Jane Marcus, ed., *New Feminist Essays on Virginia Woolf* (London: Macmillan, 1981), pp. 1–30.

20. Virginia Woolf, *The Diary of Virginia Woolf,* ed. Anne Olivier Bell (New York: Harcourt Brace Jovanovich, 1977), p. 146.

21. Ellen Hawkes, "The Virgin in the Bell Biography," *Twentieth-Century Literature* 20 (April 1974): 96–113; and Hawkes, "A Form of One's Own," *Mosaic* 8, no. 1 (1974): 77–90.

22. See *Bulletin of the New York Public Library* 80, no. 2 (Winter 1977); and Virginia Woolf, *The Pargiters*, ed. Mitchell Leaska (New York: New York Public Library and Readex Books, 1977).

23. Woolf, *The Pargiters*, p. xxciii.

24. See *Twentieth-Century Literature* 25, no. 3–4 (Fall–Winter 1979). The collection was conceived and edited by Lucio Ruotolo at Stanford University.

25. Virginia Woolf, *Women and Writing*, ed. Michele Barrett (London: Women's Press, 1979), also published in 1980 by Harcourt Brace Jovanovich.

26. Virginia Woolf, *The Letters of Virginia Woolf, 1929–1931*, vol. 4, *A Reflection of the Other Person*, ed. Nigel Nicolson and Joanne Trautmann (New York: Harcourt Brace Jovanovich, 1978), p. 348.

27. Ibid., p. 203.

28. Bell, "Bloomsbury and the Vulgar Passions," pp. 239–56.

29. See *New Feminist Essays on Virginia Woolf*, ed. Jane Marcus (Lincoln: University of Nebraska Press, 1981). The second volume of *New Feminist Essays on Virginia Woolf*, ed. Jane Marcus (Lincoln: University of Nebraska Press, in press) will contain Martine Stemerick's "The Madonna's Clay Feet," part of a University of Texas Ph.D. dissertation based on unpublished manuscripts, including essays by Julia Stephen. Alice Fox, an Elizabethan scholar, has written an essay called "Virginia Liked Elizabeth." Also included are Beverly Schlack's "Fathers in General: The Patriarchy in Virgina Woolf's Fiction"; "1897: Virginia Woolf at Fifteen" by Louise DeSalvo; Evelyn Haller's "Isis Unveiled: Virginia Woolf's Use of Egyptian Myth"; and "Political Aesthetics: The Feminine Realism of Virginia Woolf and Dorothy Richardson" by Diane Gillespie. Ann McLaughlin contributes "An Uneasy Sisterhood: Woolf and Katherine Mansfield." Emily Jensen's lesbian reading of "Mrs. Dalloway's Respectable Suicide" is included, as is Louise DeSalvo's "Tinder and Flint," a study of Vita Sackville-West and Woolf, and Susan Squier's "A Track of One's Own." Sally Sears adds a close reading of *Between the Acts* in "Theater of War"; and the collection contains Carolyn Heilbrun's "Virginia Woolf in Her Fifties." Political scientist Naomi Black contributes "Virginia Woolf and the Women's Movement"; and I have reprinted "No More Horses: Virginia Woolf on Art and Propaganda" (from *Women's Studies* 4, no. 2–3 [1977]: 265–90) to give a perspective on Woolf's politics.

30. Bell, *Bloomsbury* (n. 15 above); Quentin Bell, *Virginia Woolf* 2 vols. (London: Hogarth Press, 1972); and Bell, "Bloomsbury and the Vulgar Passions" (n. 14 above).

31. Virginia Woolf, *Three Guineas* (London: Hogarth Press, 1939).

32. Virginia Woolf, "The Leaning Tower," in *The Moment and Other Essays* (New York: Harcourt Brace, 1948), pp. 128–54; and Woolf, *Letter to a Young Poet*, Letters Series no. 8 (London: Hogarth Press, 1939).

33. See Adrienne Rich, "Toward a Woman-centered University," in *On Lies, Secrets, and Silence: Selected Prose, 1966–1978* (New York: W. W. Norton & Co., 1979), pp. 125–55.

34. Virginia Woolf was a life-long member and shared its socialist, feminist, and pacifist politics. See Marcus, "No More Horses: Virginia Woolf on Art and Propaganda"; and Black, in Marcus, ed., *New Feminist Essays on Virginia Woolf*, vol. 2.

35. Bell, *Virginia Woolf*, 2:186.

36. Ibid.

37. Woolf, "The Leaning Tower," p. 154.

38. Gerald Brenan, *Personal Record, 1920–1972* (London: Jonathan Cape, 1974).

39. E. M. Forster, *Virginia Woolf, the Rede Lecture, 1941* (Cambridge: Cambridge University Press, 1942).

40. See Bruno Bettelheim, "Surviving," in *Surviving and Other Essays* (New York: Alfred A. Knopf, Inc., 1979), pp. 275–314; see also pp. 20–23.

41. See Nicolson's attack on Woolf's politics in the introduction to *The Letters of Virginia Woolf, 1932–1935*, vol. 5, *The Sickle Side of the Moon* (n. 17 above), pp. xi–xvii.

42. Woolf, *The Pargiters*.

43. Virginia Woolf, *A Writer's Diary* (New York: Harcourt Brace Jovanovich, 1953), p. 234.

44. The Stephen family background is discussed in Stemerick (n. 29 above); and in Jane Marcus, "Niece of a Nun," in *Virginia Woolf: A Feminist Slant*, ed. Jane Marcus (Lincoln: University of Nebraska Press, 1983).

45. Catherine Smith discusses Caroline Stephen in her study of English women mystics (Bucknell University, English Department, in preparation). See also Smith, "Jane Lead: The Feminist Mind and Art of a Seventeenth Century Protestant Mystic," in *Women of Spirit: Female Leadership in the Jewish and Christian Tradition*, ed. Rosemary Reuther and Eleanor McLaughlin (New York: Simon & Schuster, 1979), pp. 184–85. Robert Tod is preparing a biography for the English Society of Friends' Quaker biography series (Haverford College, in preparation); and see also Jane Marcus, "A Nun and Her Niece: Virginia Woolf, Caroline Stephen, and the Cloistered Imagination" (paper presented at the Virginia Woolf Society meeting at the Modern Language Association, New York, 1981).

46. Bell, "Bloomsbury." See also Marcus, "No More Horses: Virginia Woolf on Art and Propaganda" (n. 29 above).

47. Woolf, *Letters*, 5:383.

48. Woolf, *Letters*, 1:148, 151–52, 165, 180.

49. Dmitry Mirsky, *The Intelligentsia of Great Britain*, trans. Alec Brown (New York: Conici, Friede, 1935).

50. Caroline Emelia Stephen, *The Light Arising: Thoughts on the Central Radiance* (Cambridge: W. Heffer & Sons, 1908).

51. Jaakko Hintinkka's "Virginia Woolf and Our Knowledge of the External World," *Journal of Aesthetics and Art Criticism* 38, no. 1 (Fall 1979): 5–14 is relevant here.

52. Virginia Woolf, "Thoughts on Peace in an Air Raid," in *The Death of the Moth* (New York: Harcourt Brace, 1942), pp. 243–48.

53. Bell, "Bloomsbury and the Vulgar Passions."

54. See Maria-Antonietta Macciocchi's translated work, "Female Sexuality in Fascist Ideology," *Feminist Review* 1 (1979): 59–82.

55. Bell, "Bloomsbury and the Vulgar Passions."

56. Ibid.

57. Laura Riding, "In the Beginning," *Collected Poetry of Laura Riding* (New York: Random House, 1938), p. 358.

THE MADWOMAN AND HER LANGUAGES
why i don't do feminist literary theory

Perhaps the central issue in academic literary feminism right now is theory itself. "Early" academic literary feminism—if one may use this word for an enterprise only launched in the early 1970s—developed along two clear paths. First, a pragmatic, empirical attempt to look at women—in society or in texts—as images in literature, as authors, as readers; second, a visionary attempt to describe women's writing in a reconstructed future, an attempt in which description often merged with exhortation. Theory developed later, mainly in response to what Elaine Showalter has described as an androcentric "critical community increasingly theoretical in its interests and indifferent to women's writing."[1] In other words, feminist theory addresses an audience of prestigious male academics and attempts to win its respect. It succeeds, so far as I can see, only when it ignores or dismisses the earlier paths of feminist literary study as "naive" and grounds its own theories in those currently in vogue with the men who make theory: deconstruction, for example, or Marxism. These grounding theories manifest more than mere indifference to women's writing; they are irretrievably misogynist. As a result of building on misogynist foundations, feminist theorists mainly excoriate their deviating sisters.

Feminism has always been bifurcated by contention between pluralists and legalists. Pluralists anticipate the unexpected, encourage diversity; legalists locate the correct position and marshal women within the ranks. As for recent literary theory, it is deeply legalistic and judgmental. Infractions—the wrong theory, theoretical errors, or insouciant disregard for theoretical implications—are crimes. Pluralists "dance"; theorists "storm" or "march."[2] Literary theories—in striking contrast to scientific theories—are designed to constrain what may allowably be said or discovered. Such totalizing by feminist theorists reproduces *to the letter* the appropriation of women's experience by men, substituting only the appropriation and naming of that experience by a subset of women: themselves.[3] Such structural repetition undermines the feminist project.

It is easier to totalize when one restricts application of theories to texts already sanctioned by the academy. These restrictions, however, elide such difficult matters as the relation of the canon to standards of "literariness,"[4] or of gender to genre. There is nothing natural or universal about "creative writing." Women or men in western society undertaking to produce what they hope will be viewed as "serious" writing do so in complicated, culturally mediated ways. "Seriousness" as a criterion of literary merit, for one obvious example, implies a profound Victorian patriarchal didacticism, and is often used to denigrate the popular women's genres. Still, no matter how our standards change in future, to name a work as "literary" will always endow it with a degree of artifice that must inevitably traverse and confuse any hypothesized necessary, immutable relation between "women writing" and "writing by women."

Present feminist theory encourages us, as a chief means of expanding the concept of the literary, to study private—hence presumably "natural"—writings of women. But even diaries and letters are written according to rules. And such "expansion" could well be understood rather as a contraction of the idea of writing, and an iteration of the stereotype of woman as a wholly private, purely expressive being. Such reinscription, indeed incarceration, of women in the private sphere seems to me an ominous countertrend in an era notable for dramatic entry of women into hitherto all-male preserves of public activity: not to mime men but to save our own lives *from* men. More specific to literature, the trend involves rendering invisible the public forms in which women have long written and continue to write so well. We neglect the writings—as writings—of (for example) Hannah Arendt, Margaret Mead, Suzanne Langer, and Rachel Carson. Indeed, we neglect all "non-imaginative" discourse: feature writing, journalism, scientific works both professional and popular, philosophical essays, legal briefs, advertising. At the root of the neglect, simply, is the desire to maintain "difference," for all current theory requires sexual difference as its ground. The title of a special issue of the androcentric journal *Critical Inquiry*, "Writing and Sexual Difference," made this assumption clear, and it appropriated the feminist label for theories that necessarily assumed differences fully known. Differences abound; but what they are, how they are constituted, what they entail, and whether they must be constant, seem to me above all questions that a feminist might ask, questions that are least adequately answered. Today's feminist literary theory makes asking an act of empirical anti-theory, and hence a heresy. It is finally more concerned to be theoretical than to be feminist. It speaks from the position of the *castrata*.

To accept woman as castrated is to evince a "hegemonic" mindset that recapitulates and hence capitulates to fear, dislike, and contempt of women. What will concern me in the rest of this essay are some foci of misogyny in present theory. I concentrate on four recurrent motifs, which I name: the madwoman; a female language; the father; the mother.

I. THE MADWOMAN

The name comes from Sandra M. Gilbert and Susan Gubar's impressive and influential study of nineteenth-century British women writers, *The Madwoman in the Attic*.[5] Their book applies traditional close-reading and image-study techniques to the texts of already-canonized nineteenth-century women writers, in search of a sign of the writers'—presumably shared—biographical situation as writers. It assumes, then, that a sign will be found, and finds it in the recurrent figure of the madwoman. Literary achievement for the nineteenth-century woman, they claim, was psychologically costly because it required defiance of the misogynist strictures and structures of Victorian patriarchy. Defiance had to be hidden; suppressed, it smoldered as a pure rage revealed in the furious madwoman who disrupts or ruptures so many women's texts. Gilbert and Gubar derived this theory of the woman writer from Harold Bloom's "anxiety of influence." That theory had created authorship as an exclusively male phenomenon, wherein would-be-powerful poet sons struggled to overthrow, while avowing loyalty to, already-powerful poet fathers. Possibly, its ulterior motive was to eliminate women from the canon; possibly, the hostile male tradition against which Gilbert and Gubar found their madwomen authors struggling in what they labelled an "anxiety of authorship" was, at least partly, hypostatized in the work they took as their starting point. Possibly, however, Bloom simply expressed traditional misogyny in contemporary terms.

Gilbert and Gubar modified Bloom in one important way. His approach was ahistorical, imposing a quasi-Freudian father and son conflict on literary history as a function of the ineluctable nature of the (male) poet's psyche. The "anxiety of authorship," however, is advanced as a historical concept, a fruitfully accurate description of the state of literature and attitudes toward it in a particular place at a particular time. But though advanced as a historical fact, the anxiety of authorship, except for Emily Dickinson, is demonstrated only by intra-textual evidence; thus *The Madwoman in the Attic* assumes the existence of the historical and literary situation which its textual readings require. Strikingly absent, too, from consideration of the historical moment in the analysis is the appearance among women of a realizable ambition to become professional writers. Traditionally hermeneutic, Gilbert and Gubar concentrate on a hidden message—female anxiety of authorship—while reading past the surface evidence that their studies provide for the arrival of the woman professional author.

The madwoman who names Gilbert and Gubar's book is the nonlingual Bertha Mason from *Jane Eyre*. Gilbert and Gubar read her as "Jane's truest and darkest double . . . the ferocious secret self Jane has been trying to repress" (360). Jane, then—though Gilbert and Gubar do not explicitly say this—must be a vision of woman as she might in future become, rather than any woman presently existing, since women presently existing contain the madwoman within their psyche. While seeing this figure as Jane's alter ego as well as Brontë's, Gilbert and Gubar find little redemptive about her, and considering the way she is described, this is no wonder. "In the deep shade, at the further end of the room, a figure ran backwards and forwards. What it was, whether beast or human being, one could not, at first sight, tell; it grovelled, seemingly, on all fours; it snatched and growled like some wild animal; but it was covered with clothing, and a quantity of dark, grizzled hair, wild as a mane, hid its head and face." Further on, Jane notes how "the clothed hyena rose up, and stood tall on its hind feet" (chapter 26).

I can't ignore the work Brontë has put into defining Bertha out of humanity. Not a scintilla of recognition of Bertha's likeness to herself disturbs Jane's consciousness, or fashions an ironic narrator discourse by which she might be corrected. The creature is wholly hateful, and no wonder: she has *stolen Jane's man*.

Jane's rage against Rochester, one might say, is deflected to what a feminist might well see as an innocent victim. The woman rather than the man becomes her adversary; that woman's death is as necessary for Jane's liberation as is Rochester's blinding. How, then, do Gilbert and Gubar "read" a woman's death as a good thing for women? It seems to me that they have been so far convinced by Brontë's rhetoric as not to see Bertha as a woman. "She" is simply the figuration of anger, at once true and false—true to the situation of women in patriarchy, but since patriarchy is a false system, witness to its falseness. Her disappearance will simply mark the passing of a false order, not the passing of a female subject. Gilbert and Gubar are not, to be sure, entirely happy with the novel's denouement, suggesting that "Brontë was unable clearly to envision viable solutions to the problem of patriarchal oppression" (369), but they refer here to the unfortunate damage inflicted on Rochester. They do not doubt that Bertha's elimination from the fiction is a pure good.

II. A FEMALE LANGUAGE

Among Charlotte Brontë's outrages on her madwoman is the denial of ability to speak; Bertha will never get to tell her own story (Jean Rhys corrected this in *Wide Sargasso Sea*). But, simultaneously influential with Gilbert and Gubar's work, French feminist literary theory appears to accept the figure of the madwoman as redemptive. She is taken to be not what women have regrettably been made by a contemptuous and oppressive culture, but what women either essentially are, or have fortunately been allowed to remain, in a society that brackets but cannot obliterate the innate disruptive, revolutionary force of the female. Since society is bad, this force is good. The madwoman, articulating "otherness," becomes the subject. But, so long silent, what will she say, and how will she say it? A theory of uniquely female language emerges. Descriptions and prescriptions result from a common procedure: features of the dominant language, masculine because dominant, are identified; opposite features are advanced as appropriate for women.

Christiane Makward, one of the important translators of and commentators on French feminism, describes the female language: "open, nonlinear, unfinished, fluid, exploded, fragmented, polysemic, attempting to speak the body i.e., the unconscious, involving silence, incorporating the simultaneity of life as opposed to or clearly different from pre-conceived, oriented, masterly or 'didactic' languages."[6] The women usually associated with this idea are Hélène Cixous and Luce Irigaray, both trained as psychoanalysts by Jacques Lacan, their world-view marked with his patriarchism. While they sometimes attempt to write in the style they recommend, both agree that such a language has never existed before. It is not a language that socially marked "women" have used in the past because such socially marked women are not "true" women at all. A student of the nineteenth-century concept of true womanhood experiences an odd sense of time warp: application of the theory demonstrates, mainly, the absence of "woman" from "women's" writing. The theory is also applied by certain especially ingenious critics to discover the mandated language in canonical women's texts via deconstruction.[7] Deconstruction, however, is a procedure whose vocabulary, shared by nonfeminists and men, yields identical results no matter whose texts it analyzes.

More often the theory is an agenda for the way women might or should write in future; to me it seems a guarantee of continued oppression. The most militant theorists do not use the language they call for; the theory incorporates wholly traditional notions of the feminine. Domna C. Stanton, another sponsor of French feminist theory in this country, writes, "recurring identification of the female in *écriture féminine* with madness, antireason, primitive darkness, mystery" represents a "revalorization of traditional 'feminine' stereotypes."[8] Makward, again, writes that "the theory of femininity is dangerously close to repeating in 'deconstructive' language the traditional assumptions." It is an essentialist definition making women "incapable of speaking as a woman; therefore, the most female course of action is to observe an hour of silence, or to scream. . . . Women are resigning themselves to silence, and to nonspeech. The speech of the other will then swallow them up, will speak *for* them."[9]

Actually, "women" are not resigning themselves to silence and nonspeech; we cannot afford to, and as we enter the public arena in increasing numbers we are not silent, and we do not (publicly) scream. Wishing to speak *to effect*, we use rational sequential discourse and, evidently, we use it well. Have we, then, chosen to become *men*? Before assenting, consider that this open, non-linear, exploded, fragmented, polysemic idea of our speech is congruent with the idea of the hopelessly irrational, disorganized, "weaker sex" desired by the masculine Other. The theory leads to a language that is intensely private, politically ineffectual, designed to fail. Women entering public life, whether as Supreme Court justices or organizers of tenant's unions, disprove the theory empirically, and, indeed, would follow it at their peril. They leave "advanced" theorists of women's literature far in the rear, expose their theory as an esoteric luxury. Of course, along with relegating "woman" to uselessness, the theory affirms belles-lettres as an elite pastime.

Feminists reacting to this theory maintain that nothing inherently bars us from the use of common speech, denying the argument that the "mother tongue" is really an alien, "father" tongue. In one essay, Hélène Cixous announces: "Too bad for [men] if they fall apart upon discovering that women aren't men, or that the mother doesn't have one. But isn't this fear convenient for them? Wouldn't the worst be, isn't the worst, in truth, that women aren't castrated?"[10] Cixous's identification of language with castration derives from the Lacanian reading of Freud's late version of the Oedipus complex, in which the threat of castration becomes the instrument of male socialization. Cixous's suggestion here is quite different from her assertions elsewhere that women really are castrated and hence, having nothing to lose, must remain unreconstructedly asocial.

In their recent essay "Sexual Linguistics,"[11] Gilbert and Gubar propose that twentieth-century women's writing has been shaped by our need to contend with the "intensified misogyny with which male writers greeted the entrance of women into the literary marketplace" (a belated greeting, by the way, since women have dominated the market since the mid-nineteenth century); this, along with men's anxiety over the loss of their own literary language, Latin, the father tongue (another tardy awareness, since men have used English as their primary literary language since the seventeenth century), forced women into fantasies of "alternative speech." Such fantasies have dominated women's writing since the turn of the century and consist in a subterranean celebration of the real state of affairs, which is that it is women, not men, who have the primary relation to language (the mother tongue). Thus, men and women's writing alike in this century represents sharply differentiated recognitions, however distorted, of the linguistic as well as biological primacy of the mother.

In this intriguing argument, it is now men not women who experience anxieties of authorship; women not men who own the language; nevertheless, Gilbert and Gubar can only see women's writings as compensatory and competitive fantasies. Men are ceded possession of the very language that is the woman's domain, women driven into a defensive posture. I would respond that if women are "really" primary in the essentialist way that Gilbert and Gubar describe them, then the historical phenomena described could not have happened; that it need not happen (history is always contingent, anyhow, not necessary); and finally, most crucially, that it did not happen so massively that we must identify the form of twentieth-century women's writing with it.

As alternative linguistic fantasists, women are not distinguishable from male modernists (of course their content is different, but their language is not); and modernism is only one kind of feminine practice in the twentieth century. The idea of an alternative language is as much an apotheosis of the modernist creed as a residue of exclusion from modernism. Emily Dickinson (no longer the cowering recluse of *The Madwoman in the Attic*) appears in "Sexual Linguistics" as the great celebrant of maternal witchcraft; but while granting that she may be the strongest womanist poet in English, we cannot deny that she has been perceived by many excellent critics as a precursor of modernism in her private, expressive, self-communing verse. Virginia Woolf and Gertrude Stein, other prime instances in the new Gilbert and Gubar argument, are also as modernist as they are feminist. We can view modernism, in short, as the creation as much of women as of men writers, a view which the gender-differentiating theory Gilbert and Gubar employ cannot encompass. My point would not be that there are no differences; but that when you start with a theory of difference, you can't see anything but. And when you start with a *misogynist* theory of difference, you are likely to force women into shapes that many may find unnatural or uncongenial. Such women also have voices. If they—we—are drowned out or denied, what has our theory accomplished except to divide woman from woman?

Another way of viewing modernism is not as something new in our century, but as the culmination of entrepreneurial, self-oriented individualism that, in the nineteenth century, was identified by many popular women writers as especially masculine, controlled by selfish and self-aggrandizing commercial motives, involving a will to power, a drive to omnipotence, and the like. Against such values, nineteenth-century women (at least in America) fashioned a "female" ethic—not of private, alternative musings, but of domestic responsibility and communal action apart from self. Nineteenth-century popular American women writers, including feminists, were vitally concerned to gain access to the public sphere in order to transform it by their social and domestic idealism; for this goal, none other than the language in use could possibly serve. Therefore, they availed themselves of it; nor did they have any doubt that it was "their" language as much as it was men's. Hence, we might identify a linguistic tradition of woman's writing precisely by its reappropriation of the mother tongue, its emergence from privatism with an implicit claim that this powerful language is ours as much as it is men's.

And yet again, Elizabeth Hampstead's excellent work *Read This Only to Yourself: The Private Writings of Midwestern Women*,[12] shows that nineteenth-century working-class women, unaffected by pretensions to "literariness" and uninterested in public discourse, wrote letters and diaries in a way opposite to that enjoined by any theories of women's language that have subsequently emerged to locate and, I believe, enforce sexual difference.

III. THE FATHER

It becomes clear that the theory of women's language is closely tied to a theory of the feminine personality; and because Freud is the originator of modern psychological theorizing on the feminine, an encounter with Freud might seem unavoidable. Yet we live in an age in which Freud is much questioned. As science, of course, his theories have yet to win respectability. As cure, his methods do no better than chance. As a body of philosophical writings, his works are shot through with inconsistencies and vaguenesses. And from various sources within the profession he founded, there are now serious doubts expressed about his integrity. What cannot be doubted, however, is the profound misogyny that underlies his descriptions of and prescriptions for women.

Thus, one would think that he could have been ignored by feminists interested in a theoretical base for their own forays into a theory of women's writing. On the contrary, however, literary feminist theorists have elevated him (and Lacan, his up-to-date surrogate) and in so doing have probably given his ideas new currency and prestige. To my perception (and at the risk of undercutting my own position I have to say it) this attachment to Freud—assuming that it is not simply opportunistic—manifests precisely that masochism that Freud and his followers identified with the female. We are most "daddy's girl" when we seek— as Jane Gallop not long ago expressed it—to seduce him.[13] Our attempt to seduce him, or our compliance with his attempt to seduce us, guarantees his authority. If Freud is right, there is no feminism.

Observing the Lacanian basis of contemporary French feminist theory, Christiane Makward roots "the problem of the feminine" in psychoanalytic theory because "the vast majority of those critics and writers—female or male—which [sic] have attempted to rationalize their perception of the different in the relation of women to language have done so on the basis of neo-Freudian postulates."[14] The key phrase here is "perception of the different." The most important questions (to me) for research and analysis—what differences there "really" are, how they are constituted, and what they "signify," not to mention the problematic role of language in the very framing of the questions—are all bypassed by this axiomatic assumption of known, immutable difference. To the extent that any idea of a recuperated future, no matter how modest, is an inalienable part of the concept of "feminism," we have here a program that, despite its claims, must be named antifeminist.

The program is not unique to French feminists, with their particular historical relation to Lacan. In England, Juliet Mitchell has been a strong exponent of the need to retain Freud in a feminist vision of the female personality, and in this country the more recent work of Nancy Chodorow has had a striking impact on feminist literary criticism.[15] Chodorow argued that the questions "why do women want to be mothers?" and "why do they raise daughters who want to be mothers in turn?" could not be accounted for by any combination of biological marking and upbringing, but required an intrapsychic, specifically Freudian explanation. She proposed that girls failed to separate from their mothers because the mothers failed to separate from them with a resulting fluidity of boundary between self and others. In effect, Chodorow answered her questions by adducing the stereotyped notion of the female personality, which, to be sure, she rearticulated in somewhat more timely language; in so doing she gave that stereotype a new efficacy in the construction of a feminine reality. Despite the comments of feminist psychologists that at best Chodorow's was an untested hypothesis, this theory must have satisfied a need among literary feminist critics, for it has inspired numerous readings of women writers based on the assumption of their less organized, more connected and fluid personalities.

It is certainly no secret that the historical Freud was both misogynist and antifeminist. It is demonstrable, too, that the misogynist and antifeminist tendencies in Freud's writings became much more pronounced in his work after World War I, when he broke with many of his followers because of his new emphasis on the castration complex. The post–World War I malaise, exacerbated by the relatively rapid emancipation of women after 1920, manifested itself in his case by defection and dissent of his followers precisely on the question of the feminine; by the virtual disappearance of that kind of female patient who had made his reputation and on whom, therefore, he depended (the hysteric, who did indeed use "body language" as her means of speaking); and by the appearance of women psychoanalysts. One might say that the obedient daughter who could only speak with and through her body, and who was released into speech by Freud thus becoming his creation, gave way to or was supplanted by the rebellious daughter who dared to match him word for word. Her rebellion, of course, was no more than the representation of herself as an equal, rejecting his stewardship, his fatherhood. It is not really surprising that Freud reacted with a marked intensification of his ideas about female inferiority, but he might have done differently.

For example, the Oedipus complex (itself, now, an ever more problematic concept) shifted attention from the boy's loving attachment to his mother to his fearful relation with his father. The mother was altered from the subject of a compelling heterosexual love to the object of a same-sex rivalry. And the castration complex, introduced to explain how the Oedipus complex came to an end, made it impossible for girls, who cannot be castrated, to become adults.[16] "In the absence of fear of castration the chief motive is lacking which leads boys to surmount the Oedipus complex," Freud wrote in "Femininity" (1933). "Girls remain in it for an indeterminate length of time; they demolish it late and, even so, incompletely. In these circumstances the formation of the super-ego must suffer; it cannot attain the strength and independence which give it its cultural significance, and feminists are not pleased when we point out to them the effects of this factor upon the average feminine character."[17] Freud's gibe at the feminists makes his purpose clear; he catches feminists in the double bind, denying that they are women, and asserting that, as women, these feminists cannot be the rational beings they claim to be, capable of original thought. It was part of Freud's intellectual *machismo* to reserve original thought for the male; that is a reservation still immensely powerful in all academia.

Freud's late writing—"Some Psychical Consequences of the Anatomical Distinction between the Sexes" (1925), "Female Sexuality" (1931), and "Femininity" (an essay added to the *New Introductory Lectures* in 1933)—greatly exaggerated his never slight attention to the penis. Not having a penis is a *lack*, an objectively real *inferiority*, a castration *in fact*.[18] The little girl on first seeing a little boy's penis is instantly struck with her shame and inferiority while the boy regards the naked little girl with "horror at the mutilated creature or triumphant contempt for her."[19] Those without the penis can never be initiated into the culture's higher life, nor contribute to it. The aims of therapy are different according to the genital apparatus of the patient: those with a penis are helped to enter the world, those with a vagina are taught to "resign" themselves to marginality. Any woman's attempt to overcome feelings of inferiority vis-à-vis men is interpreted as the wish for a penis which, "unrealizable," is, or can be, the "beginning of a psychosis."[20] Of course this is all a fantasy; yet claiming that fantasy overrode the real world, Freud advanced this fantastic difference as the legitimizing basis of every sexist stereotype and proscription. This fantasy, or so it seems to me, is too patently useful, too crassly interested, and too culturally sophisticated, to qualify as an emanation from the Unconscious.

Lacan too—or perhaps, Lacan even more. At least Freud knew that his "laws" of human development were mostly broken; his livelihood depended on the broken law. Lacan's laws are unbreakable, and he is hence a far less "forgiving" father than Freud. With Lacan, we are always and forever outside. Lacan's deployment of the castration complex as the basis of the model for the symbolic order into which children—boys—are initiated, takes one particularly "sexist" element in Freud's rich system (which contained many ungendered insights) and makes it the whole story. Lacan claimed throughout his career that he had rescued Freud from a dated biologism by reformulating his theory as linguistics, but he resorted to biologism shamelessly when it suited him. Thus, in his 1972 seminar, produced in an ambience not unlike that faced by Freud in the 1920s—the growth of feminism, the arrival of female analysts as competition—he *pronounced* women into silence:

> There is no woman but excluded by the nature of things which is the nature of words, and it has to be said that if there is one thing about which women themselves are complaining at the moment, it's well and truly that—it's just that they don't know what they are saying, which is all the difference between them and me.[21]

Them and me: the difference (since women are clearly doing just what Lacan's theory says they can't do) is not how women act but what they essentially are and cannot help but be. Lacan's defenders, including Juliet Mitchell and Jacqueline Rose, have claimed that he was attempting, here and elsewhere in his attacks on the French feminists, to counter their return to an overt biologism and a worship of the Eternal Feminine. But I find linguistic essentialism no improvement on the biological. Lacan's ideas of women belong neither to his realms of the real nor the symbolic, but to his imaginary. Both Freud and Lacan make haste to correct the fantasies of *others* that their own prevail. Not truth, but power, is the issue.

IV. THE MOTHER

In attempting to save Freud for feminism (to save him more generally for today's world), many have turned to the concept of the pre-Oedipal mother and proposed her to balance the Oedipal father in the life-history of the child. But it seems to me that the pre-Oedipal mother plays, in such thinking, the role that patriarchs always allot to mothers: she shores up the father. Since the aim is to help out Freud rather than to help out women, such a result may have been inherent in the project.

The very term pre-Oedipal suggests the primacy of the Oedipal phase. Why not call the Oedipal phase the "post-Cerean"? Even more bizarre is the coinage "phallic mother," which suggests that the child responds to the pre-Oedipal mother only because she or he believes that the mother has a penis. The pre-Oedipal mother is rudely rejected when the child discovers the mother's appalling "lack," such rejection indicating that the attachment to the mother was based on fantasy, now to be rectified by the Oedipal phase. In a word, the child was never "really" attached to the mother, only fantasized such an attachment; the "real" attachment was always to the father.

The concept also affirms the mother's disappearance as agent and subject from the child's life early on—by age five if development is "normal." And, while allowing influence, it limits it to a global, non-verbal or pre-verbal, endlessly supportive, passively nurturing presence. Here is one source for the idea of the *adult* woman's language as unbounded, polysemous, and the like—a residual memory of our mother in the days before we understood her language, that is, in the days before we had a language of our own. Many feminists celebrate the mother's body fluids as her "language."

Of course we all know, in our rational moments, that the mother's influence lasts far beyond the age of five. But even if we were to grant its waning at that age, we surely know that the mother's role in the child's earliest life is not so simple as this pre-Oedipal model makes it out to be. (At least we who have been mothers know.) To take the matter of most concern for literary theory, we know that the mother is the language teacher, and begins her task before the child is even a year old; normal children in all cultures are thoroughly verbal though not yet fully syntactical by the age of three. And there is—*pace* Lacan—no sudden break, no startling initiation into the order dominated or constructed by language; language from the first is part of the child's relation to the mother. What purpose does the theory of an exclusively nonverbal stage serve? It minimizes the mother.

As the mother's influence on children of both sexes persists long beyond the age of five, so does that influence on a maturing child become yet more complex, albeit increasingly diluted, encompassing many activities that patriarchal rhetoric attributes to the father. Mothers make children into human and social beings through a continuous process in which instruction and nurturance are indistinguishable. No doubt, the social world into which our mothers initiated us, and into which we initiate our sons and daughters, is dominated by men and supported by a rationalizing symbol system; but it differs crucially from the patriarchal social world of Freud and Lacan, in that mothers are demonstrably unlike the mothers of their theories.

Pre-Oedipal, then, is an interested fantasy of the maternal. Its purpose—to contain and confine mothers and hence women within the field of the irrational—is evident; to espouse such a fantasy is to accede to a male appropriation of the mother and her language. Why do feminists do it? Perhaps it is no more than hegemonic fatigue. I offer two other possibilities: first, women feel the same fear and jealousy of the mother that appears in part to underlie Freud's writing (this is the thesis of Dorothy Dinnerstein's *The Mermaid and the Minotaur*);[22] second, a theory in which women have had nothing to do with the world is comforting and inspiring. To put this somewhat differently: the Freudian and the feminist agendas may coincide because feminists do not like their mothers, or because feminists prefer to endow women with a revolutionary power that we cannot have if we have been part of the system all along. To say this is not to blame the victim, but rather to question our ability to carry, after so many centuries of implication, any pure revitalizing force. Our powers are limited, and our agendas for change will have to take internal limitation into account.

These issues are sharply evident in recent feminist literary work on mothers and daughters. It provides testimony, often unwitting and in contradiction to its stated intentions, of the deep-seated hostility of daughters to mothers. (Mothers do not speak of daughters in this discourse.) Adrienne Rich's *Of Woman Born* excoriates the male establishment for forcing the *role* of motherhood on women while denying us the *experience* of it, but is strikingly cold when not silent on the writer's own mother. Nor does Rich's poetry speak to her mother, committed to women though it may be.[23] Even at the moment when the daughter-writer or daughter-feminist claims that she is seeking the mother in order to make strengthening contact she reveals that the mother she seeks is not *her* mother, but another mother, preferably an imaginary mother. Perhaps feminism has become confused with maturation.

In much criticism, it is the pre-Oedipal mother who is looked for, sought not to combat patriarchy, but to defend against the real mother. Here, for example, from *The Lost Tradition*, a collection of essays on the mother-daughter relation (all written from the standpoint of daughters): "confronting the Terrible Mother in order to move beyond the entanglements of the mother/daughter relationship . . . claiming her as metaphor for the sources of our own creative powers, women are creating new self-configurations in which the mother is no longer the necessary comfort but the seed of a new being, and in which we are no longer the protected child but the carriers of the new woman whose birth is our own."[24] We have made the mother our child, we are self-mothered, we move beyond the entanglements of our real mother by imprisoning her in metaphor. The Terrible Mother is called on to perform a matricide.

Karen Elias-Button also comments that the mothers portrayed in contemporary fiction by women "seem to have little existence apart from their children and dread their daughters' independence as if it means their own death."[25] If works with such images were written by men, no feminist would hesitate to label them projections: how like a male to imagine that his mother has no life except in him! "The most disturbing villain in recent women's fiction is not the selfish or oppressive male but instead the bad mother."[26] The author may "dispose of" fear of the mother "by rendering the mother so repulsive or ridiculous that the reader must reject her as her fictional daughter does. Another tactic is for the author to kill the mother in the course of the narrative."[27] The matricidal impulse could not be plainer. Moving into the past, we find that today's women writers join a long tradition. The mothers of fictional heroines in the period ending with Jane Austen "are usually bad and living, or good and dead."[28] "The women novelists of the period from Fanny Burney to Mrs. Gaskell and George Eliot create very few positive images of motherhood."[29] Real mothers—of Harriet Martineau, George Eliot, Emily Dickinson, Ellen Glasgow, Edith Wharton, Willa Cather—all are faulted by their daughters for failing them, and these daughters are taken at their word by today's feminist daughter-critic.

Think, now, for a moment, about Jane Eyre and Bertha Mason. Who, after all, might Bertha Mason be—she to whom Rochester *is already married*? *Jane Eyre* is replete with images of ferocious female power and Jane turns to Rochester, at first, as to a refuge. That refuge is sullied by the presence in the nest of another woman, who is made repulsive and ridiculous so that the reader must reject her; and is killed before the narrative is out, so that the daughter can replace her. Even Gilbert and Gubar perform an unconscious matricide when they define a literary tradition, "handed down not from one woman to another but from the stern literary 'fathers' of patriarchy to all their 'inferiorized' female descendents" (*Madwoman*, 50). Evidently by the time of the Brontës and George Eliot there were literary mothers available; either these nineteenth-century women rejected them as Jane rejected Bertha; or Gilbert and Gubar forgot about them as they were caught up in the challenge of producing a respectable (fathered rather than mothered) feminist literary theory.

A difference more profound for feminism than the male–female difference emerges: the difference between woman and woman. If the speaking woman sees other women as her mother, sees herself but not her mother as a woman, then she can see her mother (other women) only as men or monsters. There is no future for a commonality of women if we cannot traverse the generations. One sees only here and there signs of something different. Julia Kristeva says that we must challenge "the myth of the archaic mother"[30] in order for women to enter society as participant beings—but her language is aggressive toward the myth, not its patriarchal perpetrators; Dinnerstein writes that one must come to see the "first parent" as "no more and no less than a fellow creature."[31] Dinnerstein seems sentimental here, but her point is crucial. It goes beyond her own Freudian emphasis to imply that the family model of daddy, mommy, and me, is inimical to the human future. And, since the family triangle, and its inevitable oddly-named "romance," is the veritable nurturing ground of patriarchy, it "must" be abandoned before there can be a "true" feminist theory. It has probably never existed in reality; one can wonder what a theory deliberately developed from childhood fantasies describes other than childish fantasies, and how such a theory serves feminist intentions.

Indeed, whether children "see" the world as Freudians say they do is something we will never know so long as Freudian scholars are the only ones to ask the question.

I am, evidently, a pluralist. Essays in feminist journals are permeated with musts and shoulds,[32] with homily and exhortation and a fractiousness that at most puts "sisterhood" under erasure and at least means that the totalizing assumptions of theory are fictions. In the late sixties, feminism was called "women's liberation." It seemed to promise us that we could, at last, try to be and do what we wanted; it proposed that women could help each other to become what they wanted. "Women's liberation" didn't suggest we all had to be one thing. To find oneself again a conscript, within a decade, is sad.

NOTES

1. Elaine Showalter, "Feminist Criticism in the Wilderness," *Critical Inquiry*, 8 (1981), 181.

2. I borrow these terms from Wendy Martin, *An American Triptych: Ann Bradstreet, Emily Dickinson, Adrienne Rich* (Chapel Hill: University of North Carolina Press, 1983), p. 229. These terms do not apply to theories as such, but to styles that appear to override theories.

3. These words were originally written before the appalling account of life in the French Mouvement Libération des Femmes—a feminist ideal for many literary theorists—appeared in *Signs*. See Dorothy Kaufmann-McCall, "Politics of Difference: The Women's Movement in France from May 1968 to Mitterand," *Signs*, 9 (1983), 282–93.

4. See Lillian S. Robinson, "Treason our Text: Feminist Challenges to the Literary Canon," *Tulsa Studies in Women's Literature*, 2 (1983), 83–98.

5. Sandra M. Gilbert and Susan Gubar, *The Madwoman in the Attic: The Woman Writer and the Nineteenth-Century Imagination* (New Haven: Yale University Press, 1979). Subsequent references are cited parenthetically in the text.

6. Christiane Makward, "To Be or Not to Be . . . a Feminist Speaker," in *The Future of Difference*, eds. Alice Jardine and Hester Eisenstein (Boston: G. K. Hall, 1980), p. 96.

7. Mary Jacobus, "The Questions of Language: Men or Maxims and *The Mill on the Floss*," *Critical Inquiry* 8 (1981), 222.

8. Domna C. Stanton, "Language and Revolution: The Franco-American Disconnection," in *The Future of Difference*, p. 86.

9. Makward, p. 100.

10. Hélène Cixous, "The Laugh of the Medusa," *Signs*, 1 (1976), 885. As Diane Griffin Crowder, an expert on Cixous, has recently observed in a review in *Tulsa Studies*, "Cixous is not a feminist in any sense that the American movement would recognize." *Tulsa Studies in Women's Literature*, 4 (1985), 149. This being patently the case, the zeal of American literary feminists to put her at the apex of feminist theory is all the more puzzling.

11. Sandra M. Gilbert and Susan Gubar, "Sexual Linguistics," *New Literary History*, 16 (1985), 515–43.

12. Elizabeth Hampsten, *Read This Only to Yourself: The Private Writings of Midwestern Women* (Bloomington: Indiana University Press, 1982).

13. Jane Gallop, *The Daughter's Seduction: Feminism and Psychoanalysis* (Ithaca, N.Y.: Cornell University Press, 1982). A young literary-academic feminist of my acquaintance tells me that most feminists of her generation are feminists precisely because they recognize the abjectness of their attitudes toward men. That recognition has been the starting point for many of us; but a theory that valorizes or prescribes abjectness seems to me to confuse the starting point with the end.

14. Makward, p. 102.

15. Nancy Chodorow, *The Reproduction of Mothering* (Berkeley and Los Angeles: University of California Press, 1976). Another influential book of the same sort is Carol Gilligan, *In a Different Voice* (Cambridge, Mass.: Harvard University Press, 1982). Both of these works have had more impact on feminist literary studies than in their own social science fields, largely because the evidence on which their arguments are based are, by social science standards, deplorably weak.

16. The real Freudian scandal, however—one to shame a feminist advocate of a meeting of feminism and psychoanalysis—is the substitution of the Oedipus complex for the seduction theory on the grounds that it would be impossible for all those women (and men) to have been telling the truth when they testified to childhood sexual abuse. What we are learning of child abuse these days exposes this uncharacteristic eruption of "common sense" into Freud's discourse as a dreadful hypocrisy. And indeed, the logic of this replacement was always poor—much like saying that it would be impossible for all those cases of tuberculosis to have been caused by the same bacteria.

17. Sigmund Freud, "Femininity," in *Psychoanalysis and Feminism*, ed. Juliet Mitchell (New York: Pantheon, 1974), p. 88.

18. Sigmund Freud, "Analysis Terminable and Interminable," in *The Collected Writings of Sigmund Freud*, 5 (London: Hogarth Press, 1953–1974), p. 356.

19. Sigmund Freud, "Some Psychical Consequences of the Anatomical Distinction Between the Sexes," in *Psychoanalysis and Feminism*, p. 191. Note that for Freud there is only "the" distinction. I hope it is clear that my argument does not deny differences; I stress the plural. I believe that differences are multiple, variable, and largely unresearched and not understood; therefore any theory based on only one is pernicious.

20. Freud, "Analysis Terminable and Interminable," p. 357.

21. Quoted in Juliet Mitchell and Jacqueline Rose, eds., *Feminine Psychology: Jacques Lacan and the école freudienne* (New York: Norton, 1982), p. 144.

22. Dorothy Dinnerstein, *The Mermaid and the Minotaur: Sexual Arrangements and Human Malaise* (New York: Harper, 1976).

23. Adrienne Rich, *Of Woman Born* (New York: Norton, 1976).

24. Karen Elias-Button, "The Muse as Medusa," in *The Lost Tradition: Mothers and Daughters in Literature*, eds. Cathy N. Davidson and E. M. Broner (New York: Ungar, 1980), p. 205.

25. Elias-Button, p. 192.

26. Judith Kegan Gardiner, "On Female Identity and Writing By Women," *Critical Inquiry*, 8 (1981), 356.

27. Ibid.

28. Janet Todd, *Women's Friendship in Literature* (New York: Columbia University Press, 1980), p. 2.

29. Susan Peck MacDonald, "Jane Austen and the Tradition of the Absent Mother," in *The Lost Tradition*, p. 58.

30. Julia Kristeva, "Women's Time," *Signs*, 7 (1981), 29.

31. Dinnerstein, p. 164.

32. See Jane Marcus in her attack on pluralism, "Storming the Toolshed," *Signs*, 7 (1982), 622–40, especially p. 626: "she must . . . she must . . . she must." If that *she* is *me*, somebody (once again) is telling me what I "*must*" do to be a true woman, and that somebody is asserting (not incidentally) her own monopoly on truth as she does so. I've been here before.

A CRITICISM OF OUR OWN

autonomy and assimilation in afro-american and feminist literary theory

THE OTHER WOMAN

In the summer of 1985, I was one of the speakers at the annual conference on literary theory at Georgetown University. On the first morning, a distinguished Marxist theorist was introduced, and as he began to read his paper, there appeared from the other side of the stage a slender young woman in a leotard and long skirt who looked like a ballet dancer. Positioning herself a few feet from the speaker, she whirled into motion, waving her fingers and hands, wordlessly moving her lips, alternating smiles and frowns. There were murmurs in the audience; what could this mean? Was it a protest against academic conferences? A Feifferesque prayer to the muse of criticism? A celebratory performance of the Althusserian two-step? Of course, as we soon realized, it was nothing so dramatic or strange. Georgetown had hired this young woman from an organization called Deaf Pride to translate all the papers into sign language for the hearing-impaired.

Yet from the perspective of the audience, this performance soon began to look like a guerrilla theatre of sexual difference which had been staged especially for our benefit. After the first ten minutes, it became impossible simply to *listen* to the famous man, immobilized behind the podium. Our eyes were drawn instead to the nameless woman, and to the eloquent body language into which she mutely translated his words. In this context, her signs seemed uncannily feminine and Other, as if we were watching a Kristevan ambassador from the semiotic, or the ghost of a Freudian hysteric back from the beyond. Anna O. is alive and well in Georgetown!

The feminist implications of this arrangement were increasingly emphasized, moreover, throughout the first day of the conference, because, although the young woman reached ever more dazzling heights of ingenuity, mobility, and grace, not one of the three white male theorists who addressed us took any notice of her presence. No one introduced her; no one alluded to her. It was as if they could not see her. She had become transparent, like the female medium of the symbolists who, according to Mary Ann Caws, "served up the sign, conveying it with fidelity, patience, and absolute personal silence. She herself was patiently ruled out."[1]

Sitting in the audience that first morning, I wondered what would happen when *I* was introduced as the fourth speaker. I had wild fantasies that George-town would provide a bearded male interpreter who would translate my paper into the rhetoric of deconstruction. (It turned out that there were two young women who alternated the task of interpretation. This does not seem to be a man's job.) I wondered too how I should speak from the position of power as the "theorist" when I also identified with the silent, transparent woman? The pres-ence of the other woman was a return of the repressed paradox of female authority, the paradox Jane Gallop describes as fraudulence: "A woman theoreti-cian is already an exile; expatriated from her *langue maternelle*, she speaks a pater-nal language; she presumes to a fraudulent power."[2] The translator seemed to represent not only the *langue maternelle*, the feminine other side of discourse, but also the Other Woman of feminist discourse, the woman outside of academia in the "real world," or the Third World, to whom a Feminist critic is responsible, just as she is responsible to the standards and conventions of criticism.[3] Gayatri Chakravorty Spivak has reminded us that she must always be acknowledged in our work: "Who is the other woman? How am I naming her? How does she name me?"[4]

At the Georgetown conference, my awareness of the Other Woman was shared by the other women on the program; all of us, in our presentations, introduced the interpreter, and changed our lectures in order to work with her presence. Yet the only male speaker who took notice of the interpreter was Houston Baker. By the time he spoke on the second day, Baker had learned enough sign lan-guage to produce a virtuoso translation of the beginning of his own talk, and to work with the translator in a playful duet.

The Georgetown conference was not the first time that Afro-American and feminist critics have found ourselves on the same side of otherness, but it was certainly one of the most dramatic. For those of us who work within "opposi-tional" or cultural criticisms—black, socialist, feminist, or gay—questions of the critic's double consciousness, double audience, and double role come with the territory and arise every day. They are not just the sort of global questions Terry Eagleton poses in *Literary Theory,* as to whether an analysis of the Lacanian imaginary can help welfare mothers, but more mundane problems of ethnicity and ethics: how we will answer the mail, how we will conduct ourselves in the classroom or on the podium, and how we will act not only in symbolic relation-ships but also in real encounters with constituencies inside and outside of academia.

In this essay, I briefly sketch out the parallel histories of Afro-American and feminist literary criticism and theory over the past twenty-five years, in order to learn from our mutual experience in relation to the dominant culture. This may seem like a strange moment for such a project. In both feminist and Afro-American criticism, the Other Woman, the silenced partner, has been the black woman, and the role played by black feminist critics in bridging the two schools is controversial. While black and white feminists have objected to the sexism of black literary history, black women have also challenged the racism of feminist literary history. Black male writers have protested against the representation of black men in the fiction of Afro-American women novelists, and Ishmael Reed's latest novel, *Reckless Eyeballing* (1986), imagines a violent vengeance on feminists in general and black feminist writers in particular.

Yet this record of misunderstanding obscures what I think are the strong and important connections between the two kinds of cultural criticism; we have much to gain by a dialogue.[5] Both feminist and Afro-American criticism have brought together personal, intellectual, and political issues in our confrontations with the Western literary tradition. We have both followed traditional patterns in the institutionalization of critical movements, from our beginnings in a separatist cultural aesthetics, born out of participation in a protest movement; to a middle stage of professionalized focus on a specific text-milieu in an alliance with academic literary theory; to an expanded and pluralistic critical field of expertise on sexual or racial difference. Along with gay and post–Colonial critics, we share many critical metaphors, theories, and dilemmas, such as the notion of a double-voiced discourse, the imagery of the veil, the mask, or the closet; and the problem of autonomy versus mimicry and civil disobedience.

In abandoning marginal territories of our own for places in the poststructuralist critical wilderness, do black and feminist critics also risk exchanging authenticity for imitation, and self-generated critical models for what Lisa Jardine calls Designer Theory? If we oppose the idea that women should have the exclusive franchise on "gender" or blacks the franchise on "race," what can be the distinguishing idiom or role of the black or feminist critic, and how do we identify the place from which we speak? Can we make the compromises necessary for acceptance by the mainstream, and still work for a criticism of our own? Or is the dream of an alternative criticism which is "simultaneously subversive and self-authenticating" the most utopian of all sub-cultural fantasies?[6]

THE BLACK CRITICAL REVOLUTION

In a splendidly argued essay called "Generational Shifts and the Recent Criticism of Afro-American Literature," Houston Baker has drawn on the work of Thomas Kuhn and Lewis Feuer to account for the transformations within Afro-American criticism from the 1950s to the early 1980s. He suggests that intergenerational conflict and the pressures of ascendant class interests can explain the movement towards alliance with the mainstream.[7] While Baker's essay is the most important and coherent account we have of the black critical revolution, his concept of the "generational shift" still raises a number of problems. First of all, critics cannot be assigned to generations with any precision, since, as David Riesman reminds us, people "are not born in batches, as are pancakes, but are born continuously."[8] The shifts within the critical fields, moreover, cannot be seen simply in generational terms, since in the humanities, intelligent people often transform and revise their theoretical positions in the light of new ideas, rather than stubbornly clinging to their original paradigms unto death. Within feminist criticism, indeed, the tendency of such writers as Toril Moi to construct rigid binary oppositions of feminist thought without regard for the complex permutations and exchanges within feminist discourse today, ignores the historical contexts in which ideas began, and the process of self-criticism and revision which has kept them sharp.[9]

A second problem with Baker's essay, and with Afro-American critical history in general, is that it does not take sufficient account of gender, and of the role of black women in shaping both literary and critical discourse. In using a number of his categories, then, I have tried to rethink them as well in the light of black feminist writing.

Before the Civil Rights Movement, criticism of Afro-American literature was dominated by "integrationist poetics"—skepticism about a unified black consciousness, and the ambition to have black writers merge with the mainstream of the American literary tradition. This view was articulated in the 1940s and 1950s by such male writers and scholars as Richard Wright, Arthur P. David, and Sterling Brown, who denied any specificity to "Negro writing" and insisted that black literature should measure up to and be judged by the standards of the dominant critical community. As Davis wrote in an introduction to *The Negro Caravan* in 1941, "the Negro writes in the forms evolved in English and American literature. . . . The editors considered Negro writing to be American writing, and literature by American Negroes to be a segment of American literature." [10] Since black Americans were promised equal rights under such legislation as the 1954 Supreme Court decision, so too, integrationist critics hoped, "Negro writing" would win an equal place in American literary culture. Meanwhile, they argued, black writers "must demand a single standard of criticism," and reject any special consideration on the basis of race. The occasional success of a writer like Ralph Ellison was taken to prove that a serious black artist would be recognized.

Yet integrationist poetics rested on the optimistic and deluded belief that a "single standard of criticism" could respond equitably and intelligently to Afro-American writing, that the "single" standard could be universal, rather than a cultural straitjacket based on the limited and exclusive literary values of an elite. [11] In practice, black writing was often viewed by white critics using the excuse of integrationist poetics as inferior or flawed. Moreover, even when black male writers won recognition, novels by black women such as Ann Petry's *The Street* (1946) and Gwendolyn Brooks's *Maud Martha* (1953) were marginalized by the black and white male literary communities. As Mary Helen Washington has argued, the "real 'invisible man' of the 1950s was the black woman." [12]

Integrationist poetics, however, was challenged in the 1960s by the new political ideology which Stokely Carmichael christened "Black Power." Calling for racial leadership and identity, and for a rejection of the racist standards masked as equality offered by white society, Black Power generated the cultural forms of the Black Arts movement, led by Afro-American writers, artists, and intellectuals such as Amiri Baraka (LeRoi Jones), Larry Neal, Addison Gayle, Jr., and Stephen Henderson. These leaders of the black male intelligentsia insisted on the uniqueness and authenticity of black expression, especially in folk forms and music, and rejected the idea that a uniform standard of criticism derived from white culture could be adequate to the interpretation and evaluation of Black Art. Indeed, Black Art proposed "a radical reordering of the Western cultural aesthetic . . . a separate symbolism, mythology, critique, and iconology." [13] The term "negritude," originating in Paris, the Caribbean, and Francophone Africa, celebrated the existence of a unique black artistic consciousness transcending nationality. Via the concept of negritude, as Melvin Dixon has explained, a "generation of blacks dispersed through the world reclaimed a part of their identity as members of the African diaspora." [14]

In the United States, the Black Aesthetic attempted to produce "a distinctive code for the creation and evaluation of black art." [15] "Blackness" itself became an ontological and critical category for assessing Afro-American literature. Stephen Henderson, one of the major theorists of the Black Aesthetic, argued that the black poem must not be considered in isolation, as the New Critics had maintained, but as a verbal performance in the fullest contexts of the "Black Experience," the "complex galaxy of personal, social, institutional, historical, religious, and mythical meanings that affect everything we say or do as Black people sharing a common heritage." [16] Its value could be determined only by the black interpretive community which shared the "Soul Field" of Afro-American culture.

Thus the Black Aesthetic offered the possibility of an autonomous and coherent black literary-critical discourse, not merely imitative of or parasitic on the white tradition, but in possession of its own roots, themes, structures, terms, and symbols from Afro-American culture. Moreover, the theoretical privileging of the black interpretive community gave the individual black critic a kind of cultural authority that enabled him or her to rise within the profession. As Baker notes, the predication of blackness as a "distinct and positive category of existence . . . was not only a radical political act designed to effect the liberation struggles of Afro-America, but also a bold critical act designed to break the interpretive monopoly on Afro-American expressive culture that had been held from time immemorial by a white liberal-critical establishment that set 'a single standard of criticism.'" [17]

The importance of the Black Aesthetic in the establishment of Afro-American literature cannot be overestimated. But to many black intellectuals, the Black Aesthetic also appeared narrow, chauvinistic, mystical, and theoretically weak. If only black critics were qualified by virtue of their racial experience to interpret black literature, they feared, it would remain ghettoized forever.

In practice, too, the theoretical privileging of the revolutionary black artist and the black critical imagination was open to charges of sexism; the major texts of the Black Aesthetic ignored or patronized women's imaginative and critical writing, just as the Black Power movement, in Stokely Carmichael's other notorious phrase, defined the position of women as "prone." [18] By 1970, beginning with the publication of Toni Morrison's *The Bluest Eye*, black feminist writers and critics began to make their voices heard within the literary community. Alice Walker was teaching courses on black women writers at Wellesley and the University of Massachusetts in the early 1970s, and leading others such as Toni Cade Bambara in "looking for Zora"—carrying out the quest for Zora Neale Hurston, who had been ignored by male critics of the Black Aesthetic, as the literary and critical foremother of the black female literary tradition. Black feminist critics such as Barbara Smith, Mary Helen Washington, Gloria Hull, and Barbara Christian raised important questions about the place of women within the Afro-American literary canon, and within the decade, some male theorists of the Black Aesthetic, including Stephen Henderson and Amiri Baraka, reconsidered their earlier positions. "When Black women discovered a political context that involved both race and gender," Henderson wrote in the introduction to Mari Evans's *Black Women Writers* (1983), "Our history in this country took a special turn, and our literature made a quantum leap toward maturity and honesty."

Yet even when the question of sexism was addressed, there were blatant theoretical weaknesses in the Black Aesthetic. Their concept of "race" was romantic and ideological; they ignored new developments within literary criticism. As Houston Baker concludes:

> The defensive inwardness of the Black Aesthetic—its manifest appeal to a racially-conditioned, revolutionary, and intuitive standard of critical judgment—made the new paradigm an ideal instrument of vision for those who wished to usher into the world new and *sui generis* Afro-American objects of investigation. Ultimately, though, such introspection could not answer the kinds of theoretical questions occasioned by the entry of these objects into the world. In a sense, the Afro-American literary-critical investigator had been given—through a bold act of the critical imagination—a unique literary tradition but no distinctive theoretical vocabulary with which to discuss this tradition.[19]

The political collapse of the Black Power movement, the advent of women's liberation, and the impact of European literary theory in the United States, all led to the demise of the Black Aesthetic. It was succeeded in the late 1970s by a new wave of young black intellectuals, benefitting from the academic prestige the Black Aesthetic had won for black writing, yet skeptical of the cultural claims of the Black Arts movement, and opposed to its separatist policies and poetics. Trained in such deconstructionist centers as Cornell and Yale, these critics sought to establish a "sound theoretical framework for the study of Afro-American literature," by situating it within the discourse of poststructuralist literary theory. Instead of seeing themselves primarily as spokesmen for art in the black community, with the mission of helping to create a revolutionary black literary consciousness in American society, they defined themselves as Afro-American specialists in the theoretical community, with the goal of rendering "major contributions to contemporary theory's quest to 'save the text.'"[20]

Among the central critical texts of the generation Houston Baker calls the "reconstructionists" are two major anthologies, *Afro-American Literature: The Reconstruction of Instruction* (1979), edited by Robert B. Stepto and Dexter Fisher; and *Black Literature and Literary Theory* (1984), edited by Henry Louis Gates, Jr. Stepto's "Introduction" to *Afro-American Literature* argues for a mixture of formal and cultural approaches to the black literary text, which is still seen as the object of a black critical practice, and as the primary subject of a sophisticated and formalized Afro-American pedagogy. *Afro-American Literature*, published by the Modern Language Association, represented the intersection of Afro-American studies and the English department. It suggested ways that black or white teachers of American literature could learn to be competent readers of Afro-American writing.

Gates's anthology goes considerably further, and could easily be subtitled "the reconstruction of deconstruction." Dedicated to the memories of Charles Davis and Paul de Man, *Black Literature and Literary Theory* presents itself in its structure, themes, and rhetoric, as a "two-toned" critical discourse, poised between black studies and the Yale School. Gates defines his textual territory as African, Caribbean, and Afro-American literatures, and his purpose as the application of contemporary literary theory to black literature. The anthology begins with

Gates's own dazzling manifesto of black deconstruction, "Criticism in the Jungle." Like Ishmael Reed's *Mumbo Jumbo* (1972), a central novel in Gates's canon of black literature, which provides the epigraph to the essay, the title itself is double-voiced. Gates parodies or signifies upon Geoffrey Hartman's manifesto of rhetorical criticism, *Criticism in the Wilderness*, published in 1980; he alludes ironically to a stereotyped image of primitive and exotic African origins (cf. Vachel Lindsay's "The Congo") and thus literalizes the "sacred jungle" of Hartman's text; and he slyly suggests that black theory must make its way not only in the indeterminate heart of darkness and in the pan-African cultural jungle (the home of the "signifying monkey" and the Tar Baby), but also in the far more dangerous blackboard jungle of professional critical debate.

Gates sees his mission as one of saving the black text from the political and ideological contexts which have repressed its signifying systems, in treating it more as sociology, anthropology, or a document of the black experience, than as art. If the black tradition is to move "into the mainstream of critical debate in the profession," it must free itself from polemic and apply the lessons of formalism, structuralism, and poststructuralism. Gates is a bold and confident spokesman for this new program:

> The black literary tradition now demands, for sustenance and for growth, the sorts of reading which it is the especial province of the literary critic to render; and these sorts of reading will all share a fundamental concern with the nature and functions of figurative language as manifested in specific texts. No matter to what ends we put our readings, we can never lose sight of the fact that a text is not a fixed "thing" but a rhetorical structure which functions in response to a complex set of rules. It can never be related satisfactorily to a reality outside itself merely in a one-to-one relation.[21]

Two major problems came to the fore, however, in the reconstructionist project. First, who is qualified to be a critic of black literature? Second, can black criticism appropriate white or Western literary theory without sacrificing its hard-won independence and individuality? In the earlier phases of black criticism, black critics were first the reluctant or de facto partisans of "Negro writing" and then the passionate advocates of "black literature." During the phase of the Black Aesthetic, black artists and intellectuals who had become frustrated by the condescension or indifference of the white literary establishment toward Afro-American writing staked their own claim to a privileged critical authority within the black cultural tradition. With the early reconstructionist phase, however, the emphasis on the blackness of the ideal critic was abandoned in the interests of establishing black literature in the canon, and replaced by a focus on professional expertise. For Stepto and Fisher in 1979, the teacher of Afro-American literature need no longer be black, and blackness is no guarantee of authority in deciphering the text. Rather, the teacher must be trained to read the "ingrained cultural metaphors," "coded structures," and "poetic rhetoric" of the Afro-American text.[22]

By 1984, as Gates asserts, the "critic of black literature" no longer needs to have a special relationship to Afro-American culture, or a commitment to social change, obligations which saddle the critical project of reading black literature well with an impossible sociological burden. Instead the critic of black literature is an intellectual specialist who writes "primarily for other critics of literature." [23] Moreover, the critic of black literature can no longer be a mere amateur, either an ordinary reader, a practicing artist, or an untheoretical teacher, but must come from the professional community of poststructuralist literary critics, trained in the difficult new methodologies and theories of reading, and fluent in their terms.

The retreat from the populism of the Black Aesthetic could scarcely be more emphatic. Houston Baker, himself a critic who has tried to mediate between the cultural anthropology of the Black Aesthetic and poststructuralism, and whose essay on Ralph Ellison is included in *Black Literature and Literary Theory*, links the rise of black poststructuralism to the rise of black professionals in academia "whose class status . . . and privileges are . . . contingent upon their adherence to accepted (i.e., white) standards. . . ." With the decline of a mass black audience for critical or political discourse in the aftermath of the 1960s, Baker argues, a "class-oriented professionalism among Afro-American literary critics" has led to a "sometimes uncritical imposition upon Afro-American culture of literary theories borrowed from prominent white scholars." [24] While Baker maintains that reconstructionist critics impose such theories without a rigorous analysis of their ethnocentrism, Gates, as we have seen, believes that the black literary tradition itself "demands" to be read in these sophisticated theoretical ways, for "sustenance and growth"—that is, in order to maintain a critical growth curve within academia that gives it parity with the dominant tradition of Dante, Milton, Hölderlin, and Rousseau.

In a more telling critique than these sociological objections, however, Baker further protests that Gates simplifies and distorts the theories of the Black Aestheticians, and that he creates a semiotic circle around literature that cuts literary language off from the verbal behavior of Afro-American culture and that isolates the black text from the complex cultural systems that give meaning to its words. Gates's response is to challenge the idea of a unified black subject in terms taken from poststructuralism. Both in his introduction and in his own essay on Ellison and Reed, Gates emphasizes this critique of the "transcendent black subject, integral and whole, self-sufficient and plentiful, the 'always already' black signified, available for literary representation in received Western forms as would be the water dippered from a deep and dark well." [25]

Yet despite his critical rhetoric, Gates is not completely prepared to abandon either the politics of black presence or a vividly particularized sense of Afro-American culture and the black vernacular; and there are a number of contradictions and tensions in his essay pointing towards a different, if repressed, desire. He refers frequently to a "signifying black difference" produced by the process of applying literary theory to the black text, as if the black text were so powerful a catalyst that its combination with deconstruction explosively "changes both the received theory and received ideas about the text." [26] Moreover, his anonymous expert, the "critic of black literature," sometimes merges with a more personal and specific black critic struggling to represent a "black self" in ethnocentric Western languages that makes blackness a figure of absence and negation. This black critic speaks in the Afro-American idiom "which makes the black tradition our very own," as well as in the professional idiom of Ithaca or New Haven. [27]

These conflicts between academic centrality and a black tradition and "criticism of our own" became even more pronounced with the newest critical wave. Most recently, the black critic and the critic of black literature have been joined by the Third-World critic and the critic of Third-World literature, whose subject is "the curious dialectic between formal language use and the inscription of metaphorical racial differences."[28] Metaphorical? Yes, according to the leading figure and theorist in this group, once again Henry Louis Gates, Jr., who edited a special issue of the journal *Critical Inquiry* called "'Race,' Writing, and Difference" in autumn 1985: "Race, as a meaningful criterion within the biological sciences, has long been recognized to be a fiction. When we speak of 'the white race' or 'the black race,' 'the Jewish race' or 'the Aryan race,' we speak in biological misnomers, and more generally, in metaphors."[29] As Anthony Appiah points out, "apart from the visible morphological characteristics of skin, hair, and bone, by which we are inclined to assign people to the broadest racial categories— black, white, yellow—," current genetic research proves that there are few biological characteristics of "race."[30] Apart from these unimportant "gross differences," the kind of positive black racial identity advocated by W. E. B. DuBois, involving a common language, history, and tradition, is thus wholly unscientific, and "must go" (p. 27). At the mitochondrial or cellular level, according to Appiah, race has little to do with biological differences between people. What we are talking about, then, is a linguistic construct.

While some black critics, like Houston Baker, might observe that "the shift to the common ground of subtle academic discourse is . . . ultimately unhelpful in a world where New York taxi drivers scarcely ever think of mitochondria before refusing to pick me up,"[31] the move to "race" as a fundamental rhetorical category in the study of writing and the shaping of critical theory would seem to be the manifest destiny of black criticism, giving it an unlimited access to Third World, colonial, and Western literature, and granting it a primary term like class in Marxist criticism. One of the major advantages of the category of "race" is that it problematizes the dominant as well as the Other, and provides a way of talking about "Western" or "white" genres and forms. Moreover, the emphasis on "race" is a brilliant solution to the problem of establishment indifference to the black literary tradition. If black criticism requires expertise in the black text, there will be a lot of important "other critics of literature" who will never qualify. There is no way to compel Jacques Derrida to read Toni Morrison or Ishmael Reed. But when the subject is the rhetorical inscription of "race," Derrida can legitimately be brought inside the hermeneutic circle of Third-World criticism, with a political essay on South Africa, while it would be very hard to include him in the reconstructionist project except as a mentor.

From another perspective, however, the shift to "race" also marks an obvious swerve away from Afro-American criticism. The quotation marks around "race" signal not only the questioning of racial essentialism, but also the effacement of black identity and an Afro-American literary canon. The very small number of Afro-American literary critics in the volume itself is striking. In a follow-up issue, which became part of the book version published by the University of Chicago Press, there were additional pieces by Jane Tompkins, Christopher Miller, and Tzvetan Todorov, and a debate between two South African critical activists and Derrida. Most of these essays are extremely good, and several are even brilliant;

what is disturbing about the issue is not the quality of the criticism, but the implications of the fact that the first issue of *Critical Inquiry* edited by a black critic and devoted to the question of race and writing has a list of contributors virtually indistinguishable from any other issue of *Critical Inquiry*. The most unusual part of the issue is the ad section at the back, where books by Trudier Harris, Sunday Anozie, and Hortense Spillers, among others, are featured. The reader of the volume must wonder whether the installation of "race" will displace the study of black literature, and reinstitute a familiar canon, now seen from the perspective of the racial trope. It's troubling, too that while gender is given some rhetorical attention as a fundamental category of critical analysis in Gates's introduction, and has been a central concern of both his and Houston Baker's recent work, in this volume the responsibility for dealing with gender is almost entirely delegated to the female contributors.[32] And finally, it's revealing that after a vigorous critique and rebuttal of Tzvetan Todorov's contribution to the debate, Gates still believes that the counter-cultural critic must use the language of the dominant since it is the only one Todorov will even pay mild attention to: "Todorov can't even hear us, Houston, when we talk his academic talk; how he gonna hear us if we 'talk *that* talk,' the talk of the black idiom?"[33] In the female vernacular of my own past, or as my mother used to say, why talk to the wall? Why does it still matter so much to be heard by the tone-deaf masters of European theory when other and larger audiences want to listen?

These aspects of the volume are particularly disturbing since in his introductory essay, Gates announces a significant shift in his own thinking, away from his defiant reconstructionist stance to a recognition of the dangers of assimilation, and a renewed emphasis on the cultural grounding of black literature: "I once thought it our most important gesture to *master* the canon of criticism, to *imitate* and *apply* it, but I now believe that we must turn to the black tradition itself to develop theories of criticism indigenous to our literatures." Gates now warns of the dangers in black poststructuralism and the need for Third-World critics to "analyze the language of contemporary criticism itself, recognizing especially that hermeneutic systems are not universal, color-blind, apolitical, or neutral. . . . To attempt to appropriate our own discourses by using Western theory uncritically is to substitute one mode of neocolonialism for another."[34]

THE FEMINIST CRITICAL REVOLUTION

The debates within Afro-American criticism and theory have many parallels within the feminist critical community, and indeed the genealogies of black and feminist criticism are strikingly similar in many respects. For the sake of emphasizing these parallels, and for convenience of reference, I have given names to the various phases and modes which make up the complex totality of feminist literary criticism; but it should be understood that none of these approaches has the exact historical and political specificity that may be claimed by some of the stages of Afro-American criticism. None of these overlapping phases has been superseded or discredited, and in general each has undergone considerable change through a vigorous internal debate.

Before the Women's Liberation Movement, criticism of women's writing took the form of an *androgynist poetics*, denying the uniqueness of a female literary consciousness, and advocating a single or universal standard of critical judgment which women writers had to meet. The women's movement of the late 1960s initiated both a *feminist critique* of male culture and a *Female Aesthetic* celebrating women's culture. By the mid-1970s, academic feminist criticism, in league with interdisciplinary work in women's studies, entered a new phase of *gynocritics*, or the study of women's writing. With the impact of European literary and feminist theory in the late 1970s, *gynesic* or poststructuralist feminist criticism, dealing with "the feminine" in philosophy, language, and psychoanalysis, became an important influence on the field as a whole. And in the late 1980s, we are seeing the rise of *gender theory*, the comparative study of sexual difference.

In contrast to black criticism, where integrationist poetics is at least currently unacceptable, androgynist poetics continues to have many partisans among women writers, creating an apparent conflict between writers and critics that the media have relished. It disturbed many feminist critics, including myself, when Gail Godwin and Cynthia Ozick attacked the *Norton Anthology of Literature by Women* on the grounds that the creative imagination is sexless and that the concept of a female literary tradition was insulting to women who (like Godwin) regard themselves as disciples of Joseph Conrad. I think it unlikely that black writers will raise similar objections to the forthcoming *Norton Anthology of Black Literature*, edited by the indefatigable and phenomenal Skip Gates.

Nevertheless, androgynist poetics, which can be an unexamined misogyny that demands a spurious "universality" from women's writing, as integrationist poetics did from black writers, as well as a form of feminine self-hatred, also speaks for genuinely serious and permanent concerns within feminist criticism. The androgynist position was articulated early on by Mary Ellmann in *Thinking About Women* (1969), which wittily deconstructed the pernicious effects of thinking by sexual analogy; and by Carolyn Heilbrun in *Toward a Recognition of Androgyny* (1973), which argued that "our future salvation lies in a movement away from sexual polarization and the prison of gender."[35] Among contemporary American writers, Joyce Carol Oates is probably the most persuasive representative of this position. In an essay entitled "(Woman) Writer: Theory and Practice" (1986), Oates protests the category of "woman" or "gender" in art: "Subject-matter is culture-determined, not gender-determined. And the imagination, in itself genderless, allows us all things."

Since the 1970s, however, while acknowledging the writer's need to feel free of labels, most feminist critics have rejected the concept of the genderless "imagination," and have argued from a variety of perspectives that the imagination cannot escape from the unconscious structures and strictures of gender identity. These arguments may emphasize the impossibility of separating the imagination from a socially, sexually, and historically positioned self, as in Sandra Gilbert's sensible insistence that "what is finally written is, whether consciously or not, written by the whole person. . . . If the writer is a woman who has been raised as a woman—and I daresay only a very few biologically anomalous human females have *not* been raised as women—how can her sexual identity be split off from her literary energy? Even a denial of her femininity . . . would surely be significant to an understanding of the dynamics of her aesthetic creativity."[36] A more systematic feminist critique of the woman writer's unified and sexless "imagination" comes from Lacanian psychoanalysis, which describes the split in the female subject within language. In a psycholinguistic world structured by father-son resemblance and by the primacy of male logic, woman is a gap or a silence, the invisible and unheard sex. In contrast to the "writer only" problems of androgynist poetics, therefore, most feminist critics insist that the way to contend with patriarchal bias against women is not to deny sexual difference but to dismantle gender hierarchies. Not sexual difference itself, but rather its meaning within patriarchal ideology—"division, oppression, inequality, interiorized inferiority for women"—must be attacked.[37]

The first break with androgynist poetics was the affirmation of womanhood as a positive factor in literary experience. As in the development of a Black Aesthetic, the Female Aesthetic evolved during the early years of the women's liberation movement as a radical response to a past in which the assumed goal for women's literature had been a smooth passage into a neuter and "universal" aesthetic realm. Instead the Female Aesthetic maintained that women's writing expressed a distinct female consciousness, that it constituted a unique and coherent literary tradition, and that the woman writer who denied her female identity restricted or even crippled her art. At the same time, a feminist critique of androcentric literature and criticism examined the "misogyny of literary practice: the stereotyped images of women in literature as angels or monsters, the . . . textual harassment of women in classic and popular male literature, and the exclusion of women from literary history."[38]

Virtually all of the romantic and invigorating images of independence that characterized the Black Aesthetic have their counterpart in the Female Aesthetic as well. In contrast to the hegemony of what it characterized as the arid and elitist "methodolatry" of patriarchal criticism, the Female Aesthetic proposed the empowerment of the common woman reader (indeed we could also see here a conjunction of Women's Liberation with what Terry Eagleton has called the Reader's Liberation Movement), and the celebration of an intuitive female critical consciousness in the interpretation of women's texts. In striking parallels to the Black Aesthetic, the Female Aesthetic also spoke of a vanished nation, a lost motherland; of the female vernacular or Mother Tongue; and of a powerful but neglected women's culture. In her introduction to an anthology of international women's poetry, for example, Adrienne Rich put forth the compelling hypothesis of a female diaspora:

> The idea of a common female culture—splintered and diasporized among the male cultures under and within which women have survived—has been a haunting though tentative theme of feminist thought over the past few years. Divided from each other through our dependencies on men—domestically, tribally, and in the world of patronage and institutions—our first need has been to recognize and reject these divisions, the second to begin exploring all that we share in common as women on this planet.[39]

This phase of intellectual rebellion, gynocentrism, and critical separatism was a crucial period in the experience of women who had always played subordinate roles as dutiful academic daughters, research assistants, second readers, and faculty wives. Via the Female Aesthetic, women experimented with efforts to inscribe a female idiom in critical discourse and to define a feminist critical stylistics based on women's experience. In "Toward a Feminist Aesthetic" (1978), Julia Penelope Stanley and Susan J. Wolfe (Robbins) proposed that "the unique perceptions and interpretations of women require a literary style that reflects, captures, and embodies the quality of our thought," a "discursive, conjunctive style instead of the complex, subordinating, linear style of classification and distinction."[40]

French feminist writing of the same period, although it came out of radically different intellectual sources, also produced the concept of *écriture féminine*, analyzing women's style as a writing-effect of rupture and subversion in avant-garde literature, available to both men and women, but connected or analogous to female sexual morphology. The French feminist project of "writing the body" is a particularly strong and revolutionary effort to provide women's writing with an authority based in women's genital and libidinal difference from men. While the French critique of phallocentrism takes very different paths in the work of Hélène Cixous, Luce Irigaray, and Julia Kristeva, all explore the possibility of a concentric feminine discourse. Whether clitoral, vulval, vaginal, or uterine; whether centered on semiotic pulsions, childbearing, or jouissance, the feminist theorization of female sexuality/textuality, and its funky audacity in violating patriarchal taboos by unveiling the Medusa, is an exhilarating challenge to phallic discourse.

Yet the Female Aesthetic also had serious weaknesses. As many feminist critics sharply noted, its emphasis on the importance of female biological experience came dangerously close to sexist essentialism. Its efforts to establish a specificity of female writing through the hypothesis of a women's language, a lost motherland, or a cultural enclave, could not be supported by scholarship. The initial identification with the Amazon as a figure of female autonomy and creativity (in the work of Monique Wittig and Ti-Grace Atkinson, among others), and with lesbian separatism as the correct political form for feminist commitment, was both too radical and too narrow for a broadly based critical movement. The concepts of female style or *écriture féminine* described only one avant-garde mode of women's writing, and many feminists felt excluded by a prescriptive stylistics that seemed to privilege the non-linear, experimental, and surreal. Insofar as the Female Aesthetic suggested that only women were qualified to read women's texts, feminist criticism ran the risk of ghettoization. Finally, the essentialism of the universal female subject and the female imagination was open to charges of racism, especially since black women's texts were rarely cited as examples. As black women and others within the women's movement protested against the inattention to racial and class differences between women, the idea of a common women's culture had to be re-examined.

Gynocritics, which developed alongside the Female Aesthetic in the 1970s, has been an effort to resolve some of these problems. It identified women's writing as a central subject of feminist criticism, but rejected the concept of an essential female identity and style. In an essay called "Feminist Criticism in the Wilderness" (1981), a response to Geoffrey Hartman whose title now seems feeble compared to the brilliant riposte of Skip Gates, I argued against feminist fantasies of a wild zone of female consciousness or culture outside of patriarchy, declaring instead that "there can be no writing or criticism outside of the dominant culture." Thus both women's writing and feminist criticism were of necessity "a double-voiced discourse embodying both the muted and the dominant, speaking inside of both feminism and criticism."[41]

Instead gynocriticism has focused on the multiple signifying systems of female literary traditions and intertextualities. In studying women's writing, feminist critics have challenged and revised the prevailing styles of critical discourse, and asked whether theories of female creativity could be developed instead from within the female literary tradition itself. Influenced by the interdisciplinary field of women's studies, they have brought to their reading of women's texts theories and terms generated by the work of such feminist scholars as the historian Carroll Smith-Rosenberg, the psychologist Carol Gilligan, and the sociologist Nancy Chodorow, whose enormously influential study *The Reproduction of Mothering* (1978), revised Freudian psychoanalysis and British object-relations psychology to emphasize the pre-Oedipal phase as the key factor in the construction of gender identity.

The work of Smith-Rosenberg, Chodorow, and Gilligan has led to a wide range of studies in philosophy, social history, and religion endorsing what are called "matriarchal values" of nurturance, caring, nonviolence, and connectedness, and urging their adoption by society as a whole. Feminist critics have used metaphors of this idealized maternity both in the quest for a strong literary matrilineage, and in the rejection of the adversary method in critical discourse. In a famous and moving essay, Alice Walker has described black women writers' "search for our mother's gardens," tracing the suppressed creativity of black women under slavery and poverty to non-verbal art forms.[42] In sharp contrast to the Oedipal poetics of aggression, competition, and defense put forth by Harold Bloom, some American feminist critics have postulated a pre-Oedipal "female poetics of affiliation," dependent on the daughter's bond with the mother, in which intergenerational conflict is replaced by female literary intimacy, generosity, and continuity. Joan Lidoff, Judith Kegan Gardiner, and Elizabeth Abel are among the feminist critics who see women's fluid ego boundaries affecting plot and genre conventions, blurring the lines between lyric and narrative, between realism and romance. Here the Female Aesthetic and postmodernism join in a celebration of heterogeneity, dissolving boundaries, and *différence*.

Although I can hardly claim to be an innocent bystander on the subject of gynocriticism, I would argue that over the past decade it has been sufficiently large, undogmatic, and flexible to have accommodated many theoretical revisions and criticisms, and it has been enormously productive. In a relatively short period of time, gynocritics has generated a vast critical literature on individual women writers, persuasive studies of the female literary tradition from the Middle Ages to the present in virtually every national literature, and important books on what is called "gender and genre": the significance of gender in shaping generic conventions in forms ranging from the hymn to the Bildungsroman. Nevertheless, many of the original gynocritical theories of women's writing were based primarily on nineteenth-century English women's texts, so that a black feminist critic such as Hortense Spillers sees "the gynocritical themes of recent feminist inquiry" as separate from a "black women's writing community."[43] Only in recent years has attention to black women's writing begun to address and redress this issue.

A pivotal text of gynocritics is Sandra Gilbert and Susan Gubar's monumental study *The Madwoman in the Attic* (1979). Gilbert and Gubar offer a detailed revisionist reading of Harold Bloom's theory of the anxiety of influence, transforming his Freudian paradigm of Oedipal struggle between literary fathers and sons into a feminist theory of influence which describes the nineteenth-century woman writer's anxieties within a patriarchal literary culture. Strongly influenced by the work of Gilbert and Gubar, the theoretical program of gynocritics by the 1980s has been marked by increasing attention to "the analysis of female talent grappling with a male tradition," both in literature and criticism, a project that defined both the female literary text and the feminist critical text as the sum of its "acts of revision, appropriation, and subversion," and its differences of "genre, structure, voice, and plot."[44] Gynocritics had derived much of its strength from its self-reflexive properties as a double-voiced mode of women's writing; the anxieties of the nineteenth-century woman writer were much like those of the modern Feminist critic attempting to penetrate literary theory, the most defended bastion of patriarchal prose. Now, as Feminist critics began to profit from their labors and to enjoy some prestige and authority within the profession of literary studies, questions of the complicity between the feminist critical talent and the male critical tradition became acute, and the acts of theoretical revision, appropriation, and subversion in gynocritics itself became the source of a troubling, sometimes obsessive and guilty, self-consciousness.

About this time, too, as reports on the French feminists began to appear in women's studies journals, and as their work became available to American readers through translation, a new group of feminist critics entered the field, primarily through departments of French and Comparative Literature. They saw post-Saussurean linguistics, psychoanalysis, semiotics, and deconstruction as the most powerful means to understanding the production of sexual difference in language, reading, and writing, and they wrote in a language accessible chiefly to other literary critics, rather than to a wider audience. Following the work of Jacques Derrida, Jacques Lacan, Hélène Cixous, Luce Irigaray, and Julia Kristeva, Franco-American feminist critics focused on what Alice Jardine calls "gynesis": the exploration of the textual consequences and representations of "the feminine" in Western thought. Deconstruction has paid little attention to women writers individually or as a group; "for Derrida and his disciples," Jardine notes, "the question of how women might accede to subjecthood, write texts or acquire their own signatures, are *phallogocentric* questions."[45] Some poststructuralist feminist critics thus maintain that "feminist criticism should avoid 'the women's literature ghetto' . . . and return to confrontation with 'the' canon."[46] While gynocritics looks at the patrilineage and matrilineage of the female literary *work*, poststructuralist feminist criticism views the literary *text* as fatherless and motherless; its feminist subjectivity is a product of the reading process. From a gynesic perspective, moreover, disruptions in discourse constitute disruptions of the patriarchal system.

Gynesic criticism has been a major intellectual force within feminist discourse, but the gynesic project has also raised a number of problems. First of all, as black poststructuralism has questioned the transcendent black self, however, so poststructuralist feminist criticism has had to wrestle with the paradox of fundamental theoretical affiliations that undermine the very notion of female subjectivity.

Other modes of feminist criticism have had the empowerment of the female subject as a specific goal. Within the Female Aesthetic, female consciousness was
celebrated as an interpretive guide; within gynocritics, the woman critic could
use her own confrontation with the male critical tradition and her own experience of writing as a guide to understanding the situation of the woman writer.
But if women are the silenced and repressed Other of Western discourse, how
can a Feminist theorist speak *as* a woman about women or anything else? As
Shoshana Felman asks, "If 'the woman' is precisely the Other of any conceivable
Western theoretical focus of speech, how can the woman as such be speaking in
this book? Who is speaking here, and who is asserting the otherness of the
woman?"[47] Kaja Silverman also admits that "the relationship of the female subject to semiotic theory is . . . necessarily an ambivalent one. The theory offers
her a sophisticated understanding of her present cultural condition, but it also
seems to confine her forever to the status of one who is to be seen, spoken, and
analyzed."[48] The rhetorical problems of expressing a black male self to which
Gates briefly alludes in "Criticism in the Jungle" are much less disabling than
the burden, inherent in a gynesic feminist criticism heavily and necessarily dependent on psychoanalytic theory, of speaking from the feminine position of absence, silence, and lack.

Furthermore, while poststructuralist feminists have played a significant role
within poststructuralism as translators and advocates, as well as critics, of the European male theorists, the male feminists who have participated in gynesis, with
some outstanding exceptions (such as Neil Hertz, Stephen Heath, and Andrew
Ross) have tended to present themselves as metacritical masters of the feminine
rather than as students of women's writing, or critics of masculinity. When the
Australian critic Ken Ruthven (sometimes called the Crocodile Dundee of male
feminism) observes in his book *Feminist Literary Studies: An Introduction*, that "the
female 'problematic' is too important to be left in the hands of anti-intellectual
feminists," and could be subjected to much more rigorous metacritical inspec-
tion by impartial men like himself, it's difficult not to be suspicious. Since, when
you come right down to it, Ruthven argues, feminist criticism is "just another
way of talking about books," and he is a guy who "makes a living talking about
books," it would be churlish (or girlish) to try to keep him out of the conversation.[49] In other cases, as I have learned from sad experience, "male feminists" do
not even bother to read the feminist critical texts they are allegedly responding
to, since they always already know what women think. Poststructuralism and
feminism are a familiar and almost obligatory critical couple in the 1980s, but
they are still having to work at their relationship.

Finally, some recent discussions of what they call "Anglo-American" feminist
criticism by poststructuralist feminists have been startlingly *ad feminam* and
harsh, introducing a tone of acrimony into what we had hoped was a mutual, if
pluralistic, enterprise, and eliciting equally intemperate attacks on "theory" in
defensive response. Certainly there are real issues at stake in the theoretical debates, as well as struggles for what Evelyn Fox Keller has called epistemic power
in the feminist critical arena. But the polarization of feminist discourse along dualistic lines seems particularly unfortunate at a moment when there is such a
lively exchange of ideas. While *The Madwoman in the Attic* has yet to be translated
into French, gynesic criticism has been widely read by American feminist critics;

it has modified American work in gynocritics, and vice-versa. It's not exceptional that Sandra Gilbert, for example, should have edited the first English translation of Cixous and Catherine Clément's *La Jeune Née,* or on the other hand, that Barbara Johnson is currently working on black women writers. The complex heterogeneities of contemporary feminist discourse cannot be reduced to hierarchal oppositions.

The latest and most rapidly growing mode of feminist criticism is gender theory, corresponding to the Third-World critic's focus on "race." Within American feminist scholarship, the term "gender" is used to mean the social, cultural, and psychological constructs imposed upon biological sexual difference. Like "race" or "class," "gender" is a fundamental or organic social variable in all human experience. Within gender theory, the object of feminist criticism undergoes another transformation; unlike the emphasis on women's writing that informs gynocritics, or on the signification of "the feminine" within gynesis, gender theory explores ideological inscription and the literary effects of the sex/gender system: "that set of arrangements by which the biological raw material of human sex and procreation is shaped by human social intervention." [50]

The interest in gender theory is not confined to feminist criticism, but has also appeared in feminist thought in the fields of history, anthropology, philosophy, psychology, and science. In "Anthropology and the Study of Gender," Judith Shapiro argues that the goal of feminist research is not to focus on "women," and thus to reify female marginalization, but rather "to integrate the study of gender differences into the central pursuits of the social sciences." [51] In the natural sciences, the path-breaking work of Evelyn Fox Keller, Ruth Bleier, and Donna Haraway has analyzed "the critical role of gender ideology in mediating between science and social forms." [52] The most searching analysis of gender as a historical concept has been carried out by Joan W. Scott; in an essay called "Gender: A Useful Category of Historical Analysis," Scott outlines three goals of gender theory: to substitute the analysis of social constructs for biological determinism in the discussion of sexual difference; to introduce comparative studies of women and men into the specific disciplinary field; and to transform disciplinary paradigms by adding gender as an analytic category. [53]

What are the advantages of gender theory for feminist criticism? Most significantly, gender theory insists that all writing, not just writing by women, is gendered. To define the objective of feminist criticism as an analysis of gender in literary discourse completely opens the textual field. It also provides a way of uncovering the implicit assumptions about gender in literary theory that pretends to be neutral or gender-free. Secondly, the term "gender," like race, problematizes the dominant. Gender theory promises to introduce the subject of masculinity into feminist criticism, and to bring men into the field as students, scholars, theorists, and critics. It has already opened feminist criticism to include the consideration of male homosexuality, both through the pioneering work of Eve Kosofsky Sedgwick and through writing by gay men. Third, the addition of gender as a fundamental analytic category within literary criticism moves feminist criticism from the margin to the center, and has revolutionary transformative potential for the ways that we read, think, and write. Thinking in terms of gender is a constant reminder of the other categories of difference that structure our lives and texts, just as theorizing gender emphasizes the connections between feminist criticism and other minority critical revolutions.

As with Third-World criticism, however, it is too soon to be certain how these possibilities will work out. One danger is that men will continue to read "gender" as a synonym for "femininity," and pontificate about the representation of women without accepting the risks and opportunities of investigating masculinity, or analyzing the gender subtexts of their own critical practice. Another danger, seemingly paradoxical but actually related, is that gender will become a postfeminist term that declares the study of women, and women's writing, obsolete, or what Ruthven denounces as "separatist." The most troubling risk is that gender studies will depoliticize feminist criticism, that men will declare an interest in what one of my colleagues recently called "gender and power," while refusing to call themselves feminists. Even Ronald Reagan and Sylvester Stallone, after all, are interested in gender and power; in some respects, as Joan Scott acknowledges, the term "gender" seems to transcend the politics of feminism, and to promise a "more neutral and objective" scholarly perspective, certainly one more acceptable to men, than the focus on "women."[54] Despite the risks, however, none of these outcomes is inevitable. Gender can be an important expansion of our work, rather than a displacement or depoliticization, if it is defined within a feminist framework that remains committed to the continuing struggle against sexism, racism, and homophobia.

REPETITION AND DIFFERENCE

Where do we go from here? The parallels between Afro-American and feminist criticism show how problematic the idea of a unified "black" or "female" self has become. Whether it is the linguistic skepticism of poststructuralism, or our acknowledgment of the differences between women that stops us, Feminist critics today can no longer speak as and about women with the unselfconscious authority of the past. The female subject, we are told, is dead, a position instead of a person. Our dilemma has even reached the pages of the *New Yorker;* in Tama Janowitz's short story "Engagements," a graduate student in feminist criticism at Yale takes notes as her distraught professor tells of being severely attacked for trying to talk about "women" and "female identity" at a Poetics of Gender conference.[55] Without a claim to subjectivity or group identity, how can we have a feminist criticism of our own?

Black and Third-World critics haunted by the messages of poststructuralism are now facing the same dilemma. Is there a critic-position as well as a subject-position? Gates asks whether "the critic of black literature acquires his or her identity parodically, as it were, in the manner of the parrot," but hopefully concludes that "we are able to achieve difference through repetition" by looking at a different critical object.[56] Homi Bhabha addresses the issue in the contexts of colonialist discourse, citing "mimicry" as a form of "civil disobedience within the discipline of civility: signs of spectacular resistance."[57] In *Ce Sexe qui n'en est pas un*, Luce Irigaray too locates the subversive force of Feminist discourse in a playful mimesis, a mimicry both of phallocentric discourse which exceeds its logic, and of the feminine position within that system. Yet playing with mimesis cannot offer us authority except in individual star turns, especially if the dominant culture wants to play with your mesis too. And in mimicking the language of the dominant, how can we guarantee that mimicry is *understood* as ironic—as civil disobedience, camp, or feminist difference rather than as merely derivative?

Feminist criticism can't afford to settle for mimicry, or to give up the idea of female subjectivity, even if we accept it as a constructed or metaphysical one. To paraphrase Baker, men's clubs hardly ever think of metaphysics before they keep women out; we need what Gayatri Spivak calls a "strategic essentialism" to combat patriarchy.[58] Neither can we abandon our investigation of women's literary history, or give up the belief that through careful reading of women's texts we will develop a criticism of our own that is both theoretical and feminist. This is a task worth pursuing for its intellectual challenge and for its contribution to a truly inclusive theory of literature, rather than for its "defense" of women's creative gifts. The goal Virginia Woolf envisioned for feminist writers and critics in 1928, to labor in poverty and obscurity for the coming of Shakespeare's sister, no longer seems meaningful or necessary. Our enterprise does not stand or fall by proving some kind of parity with male literary or critical "genius"; even assuming that a female Shakespeare or a female Derrida would be recognized, to question the very idea of "genius" is part of Woolf's legacy to us.

Despite our awareness of diversity and deconstruction, feminist critics cannot depend on gynesic ruptures in discourse to bring about social change. During a period when many of the meager gains of the civil rights and women's movements are being threatened or undone by Reaganism and the New Right, when, indeed, there is a backlash against what the Bennetts and Blooms see as too *much* black and female power in the university, there is an urgent necessity to affirm the importance of black and female thinkers, speakers, readers, and writers. The Other Woman may be transparent or invisible to some; but she is still very vivid, important, and necessary to us.

NOTES

Thanks for helpful suggestions on drafts of this paper to members of the School for Criticism and Theory at Dartmouth College, and also to Skip Gates, Houston Baker, Brenda Silver, Marianne Hirsch, Evelyn Fox Keller, Valerie Smith, Daryl Dance, and English Showalter.

1. Mary Ann Caws, "The Conception of Engendering, the Erotics of Editing," in *The Poetics of Gender*, ed. Nancy K. Miller (New York: Columbia U. P., 1986), pp. 42–63. This episode is all the more ironic in the light of the successful protest in spring 1988 by deaf students of Gallaudet College in Washington.

2. Jane Gallop, *The Daughter's Seduction: Feminism and Psychoanalysis* (Ithaca: Cornell U. P., 1982), pp. 126–27.

3. In this paper I need to make distinctions between a generic feminist criticism, practiced by a feminist critic of either sex; "Feminist" criticism practiced by women; and male feminist criticism, practiced by men.

4. Gayatri Chakravorty Spivak, "French Feminism in an International Frame," *Yale French Studies* 62 (1981): 184. See also Jane Gallop, "Annie Leclerc Writing a Letter, with Vermeer," *The Poetics of Gender*, p. 154.

5. For a stimulating example of how such critical cross-fertilization might take place, see Craig Werner, "New Democratic Vistas: Toward a Pluralistic Genealogy," in *Studies in Black American Literature*, II, ed. Joe Weixlmann and Chester Fontenot (Florida: Penkevill Press, 1986), pp. 47–83.

6. See Jonathan Dollimore, "Shakespeare, Cultural Materialism and the New Historicism," *Political Shakespeare: New Essays in Cultural Materialism*, ed. Jonathan Dollimore and Alan Sinfield (Ithaca: Cornell U. P., 1985), p. 15.

7. Houston A. Baker, Jr., "Generational Shifts and the Recent Criticism of Afro-American Literature," *Black American Literature Forum* 15 (Spring 1981): 3–21. My discussion of Afro-American literary theory is profoundly indebted to Baker's essay, and to my discussions with him about parallels to feminist criticism.

8. Quoted in Werner Sollers, *Beyond Ethnicity* (Cambridge: Harvard U. P., 1986), p. 209.

9. See Toril Moi, *Sexual/Textual Politics* (London and New York: Methuen, 1985).

10. Arthur P. Davis, Ulysses Lee, and Sterling Brown, eds., *The Negro Caravan* (New York: Dryden Press, 1941). Through the 1950s, Davis and other Afro-American critics envisioned the eventual disappearance of the social conditions that produced identifiably "Negro" literature.

11. See Baker, "Generational Shifts," pp. 3–4. The term "integrationist poetics" comes from his essay.

12. Mary Helen Washington, "Rage and Silence in *Maud Martha*," in *Black Literature and Literary Theory*, ed. Henry Louis Gates, Jr. (New York and London: Methuen, 1984), p. 258.

13. Larry Neal, "The Black Arts Movement," in *The Black Aesthetic*, ed. Addison Gayle, Jr. (New York: Doubleday, 1971), p. 272.

14. Melvin Dixon, "Rivers Remembering Their Source," in *The Reconstruction of Instruction*, ed. Robert Stepto and Dexter Fisher (New York: MLA, 1979), pp. 25–26.

15. Baker, "Generational Shifts," p. 6.

16. Stephen Henderson, "The Forms of Things Unknown," in his book *Understanding the New Black Poetry* (New York: Morrow, 1973), p. 41.

17. Baker, "Generational Shifts," p. 9.

18. See Barbara Smith, "Toward a Black Feminist Criticism," in *The New Feminist Criticism*, ed. Elaine Showalter (New York: Pantheon, 1985), pp. 168–87; Deborah McDowell, "New Directions for Black Feminist Criticism," in *The New Feminist Criticism*, pp. 186–99; and Mary Helen Washington, "New Lives and New Letters: Black Women Writers at the End of the Seventies," *College English* 43 (Jan. 1981): 1–11.

19. Baker, "Generational Shifts," p. 10.

20. Baker, "Generational Shifts," p. 12; and Henry Louis Gates, Jr., "Criticism in the Jungle," *Black Literature and Literary Theory*, p. 9.

21. Gates, "Jungle," pp. 5, 8.

22. Robert B. Stepto, quoted in Baker, "Generational Shifts," p. 12.

23. Gates, "Jungle," p. 8. By 1987, Gates had drastically changed this formulation: "No matter what theories we seem to embrace, we have more in common with each other than we do with any other critic of any other literature. We write for each other and for our own contemporary writers." (*Figures in Black*, New York: Oxford U. P., 1987, xxii).

24. Baker, "Generational Shifts," p. 11.

25. Henry Louis Gates, Jr., "The Blackness of Blackness: A Critique of the Sign and the Signifying Monkey," *Black Literature and Literary Theory*, p. 297.

26. Gates, "Jungle," p. 9.

27. Gates, "Jungle," p. 8.

28. Gates, "Introduction," *Critical Inquiry*, vol. 12, no. 1 (Autumn 1985): 6.

29. Gates, "Writing, 'Race,' and the Difference It Makes," *Critical Inquiry*, vol. 12, no. 1 (Autumn 1985): 5, 6.

30. Anthony Appiah, "The Uncompleted Argument: Du Bois and the Illusion of Race," *Critical Inquiry*, vol. 12, no. 1 (Autumn 1985): 21–22.

31. Houston A. Baker, Jr., "Caliban's Triple Play," *Critical Inquiry*, vol. 13, no. 1 (Autumn 1986): 186.

32. The exception is Sander L. Gilman, who contributed a controversial essay on race and female sexuality.

33. Henry Louis Gates, Jr., "Talkin' That Talk," *Critical Inquiry*, vol. 13, no. 1 (Autumn 1986): 210.

34. Gates, "Introduction," pp. 13, 15.

35. Carolyn G. Heilbrun, *Toward a Recognition of Androgyny* (New York: Harper Colophon Books, 1973), p. ix.

36. Sandra Gilbert, "Feminist Criticism in the University," in *Criticism in the University*, ed. Gerald Graff and Reginald Gibbons (Evanston: Northwestern U. P., 1985), p. 117.

37. Michèle Barrett, *Women's Oppression Today: Problems in Marxist Feminist Analysis* (London: Villiers, 1980), pp. 112–13.

38. Elaine Showalter, "The Feminist Critical Revolution," in *The New Feminist Criticism*, p. 5.

39. *The Other Voice* (New York: Morrow, 1975), p. xvii.

40. Adrienne Rich, "Toward a Feminist Aesthetic," *Chrysalis* 6 (1978): 59, 67.

41. Showalter, "Feminist Criticism in the Wilderness," in *The New Feminist Criticism*.

42. Alice Walker, *In Search of Our Mothers' Gardens* (San Diego: Harcourt, Brace, Jovanovich, 1983).

43. Hortense Spillers, *Conjuring*, ed. Spillers and Marjorie Pryse (Bloomington: Indiana U. P., 1985), p. 261.

44. Elizabeth Abel, "Introduction," *Writing and Sexual Difference* (Chicago: U. of Chicago Press, 1982), p. 2.

45. Alice Jardine, "Pre-Texts for the Transatlantic Feminist," *Yale French Studies* 62 (1981): 225; and *Gynesis: Configurations of Women and Modernity* (Ithaca: Cornell U. P., 1985), pp. 61–63.

46. Gayle Greene and Coppélia Kahn, "Feminist Scholarship and the Social Construction of Woman," in Green and Kahn, eds., *Making a Difference: Feminist Literary Criticism* (London: Methuen, 1985), pp. 24–27.

47. Shoshana Felman, "Woman and Madness: The Critical Phallacy," *Diacritics* 5 (1975): 10.

48. Kaja Silverman, *The Subject of Semiotics* (New York: Oxford U. P., 1983), p. viii.

49. Ken Ruthven, *Feminist Literary Studies: An Introduction* (Cambridge: Cambridge U. P., 1985), p. 6.

50. Gayle Rubin, "The Traffic in Women," in Rayna Rapp Reiter, ed., *Toward an Anthropology of Women* (New York: Monthly Review Press, 1975), p. 165.

51. Judith Shapiro, "Anthropology and the Study of Gender," in *A Feminist Perspective in the Academy*, ed. Elizabeth Langland and Walter Gove (Chicago: U. of Chicago Press, 1983), p. 112.

52. Evelyn Fox Keller, *Reflections on Gender and Science* (New Haven: Yale U. P., 1985), p. 3.

53. Joan W. Scott, "Gender: A Useful Category of Historical Analysis," *American Historical Review* 5 (November, 1986).

54. Scott, "Gender," p. 1065.

55. Reprinted in Tama Janowitz, *Slaves of New York* (New York: Crown, 1986).

56. Gates, "Jungle," p. 10.

57. Homi Bhabha, "Signs Taken for Words," *Critical Inquiry*, vol. 12, no. 1 (Autumn 1985): 162.

58. See Gayatri Chakravorty Spivak, *In Other Worlds: Essays in Cultural Politics* (London and New York: Routledge, 1987).

canon

~~~~~~

One of the axioms of traditional literary study has been that "great literature" represents "universal" experiences. But as more women and people of diverse ethnic and class backgrounds have begun to study literature, that notion has come into question. What had appeared "universal" to the once-homogeneous group that studied literature and defined what was "great" as well as what was "universal"—a group almost entirely composed of white upper- and upper-middle-class males—does not seem so to the now heterogeneous group. What had once been taken for purely "aesthetic" choices about the literary texts that would be included on course syllabi, in anthologies, and on graduate and undergraduate examinations have begun to be questioned as political and social choices.

The "canon" of literature—those literary works recognized as "great" or at least recognized as worthy to be read and studied in an academic setting—was never as codified as its religious namesake. There was never an official council set up to determine what books would and would not be read; as Lillian Robinson points out in her essay "Treason Our Text," the canon's lack of definition is part of the difficulty in challenging it. There are, nonetheless, many complex mechanisms for creating a "canon" of "authentic" literature (authenticity being one of the standard rubrics of canonicity): individual professors, faculty examination and editorial committees, publishing houses and scholarly journals. The nebulousness of these mechanisms was for many years taken to be proof of the choices' merit—surely, since so many readers *independently* determined a work's merit or lack of it, that judgment was accurate, right?

Feminist critics began exploring just how connected, in fact, those apparently independent groups were: the individual professor read the journals, received the catalogues of the publishing houses and sat on those faculty committees; the faculty committees were the advisory boards to the journals and to the publishing houses; the publishing houses kept in print the books that the individual professors kept ordering for their courses. And most of those individuals making judgments were white upper- and upper-middle-class men. "Independent" judgments, indeed.

Judgment, of course, is at the center of the question of canonicity. What makes literature "great"? What makes it worth studying in a university? What makes it worth reading at all? Early feminist critics found that their answers to these questions were not the same answers that they had been taught in graduate school. Is the purpose of literature to examine "universal" or individual, diverse experiences? Should we value "representative" or "aesthetic" language? What makes an experience "universal"? What guides our choice of what is "aesthetic"? As women readers found supposedly "minor" women writers whose work was more moving, exciting, and representative of *their* experience than that of "major" writers, they began to question the standards of literary taste and to question the grounds on which those standards were based.

As Joanna Russ argues in her 1983 book *How to Suppress Women's Writing*, many judgments of taste are based on an exclusion of difference. As Russ sees it, people are profoundly threatened by difference and are apt to characterize it as inferiority; the threat offered by women's writing, she shows, was effectively suppressed for decades. Russ delineates the variety of critical positions which seem to be arguments about quality but which are in fact arguments about difference. Such arguments are sometimes a matter of ignorance, but sometimes a matter of genuine bad faith; the "Glotologs" who make them often do not even recognize what they are doing ("Glotologs" are the creatures she describes in a science-fiction–inspired prologue who revel in exclusion). In the chapters reprinted here, "Anomalousness" and "Aesthetics," she examines how the lack of literary context for women's writing can be self-perpetuating, because it can continue to make women's writings seem too "different" to include in the canon of literature. In other chapters, she reveals how critical issues of quality have been used to question the validity of writings by women, from the authenticity of their authorship ("She didn't write it" or "She had help"), to the validity of what they write about and what they produce ("She wrote it, but look at what she wrote about"; "She isn't really an artist, and it isn't really art"). Russ argues that we must dispel the notion of absolute values when it comes to judging literary value; as she puts it, "when we all live in the same culture, then it will be time for one literature."

Lillian S. Robinson identifies the task of denying absolute values as both the opportunity and the challenge of feminist criticism in "Treason Our Text: Feminist Challenges to the Literary Canon" (1983). Although challenges to the canon frequently proceed on a case-by-case basis, arguing that this or that woman author deserves to be read because she is "as good as" currently accepted writers, many feminist critics nonetheless advocate opening the whole question of literary value itself. Robinson recognizes the dilemma that the conflict between these two kinds of challenges creates: "What is involved here is more like the *agony* of feminist criticism, for it is the champions of women's literature who are torn between defending the quality of their discoveries and radically redefining quality itself." Robinson goes on to argue that in undertaking such a complicated and conflicted project, feminist critics must examine their own politics, lest they make the exclusionary mistakes they criticize in others; a vague "pluralism" or "populism without the politics of populism" is not enough. Feminist critics must, she argues, undertake a thorough study of aesthetics to avoid a "reverse discrimination" when putting together their own anthologies and syllabi.

Paul Lauter examines precisely these politics of feminist criticism in "Caste, Class, and Canon" (a revised version of his 1987 essay of the same name). After questioning the use of New Critical technique in some feminist criticism, he asks, "Is the *form* of criticism value-free? . . . How is canon—that is, selection—related to, indeed a function of, critical technique?" To answer these questions, Lauter examines first a body of literature not often studied—working-class writing. What he finds is that it is unlikely to be studied because it does not conform to the criteria validated by New Critical technique—innovative or complex language and form, an individual creator—but must be explored in terms of its function or use. Lauter moves from this analysis to a question of why some feminist critics still employ New Critical techniques when the political implications of New Criticism are so antithetical to a feminist undertaking. He argues that since, in the feminist revision of the canon, "the work of criticism and of political action most fully converge," feminist critics cannot rely on solely "literary" criteria, because such criteria are never value-free, and can never be innocently used. Instead, feminist criticism calls for an evaluation of culture, the role literature plays in that culture, and the role that criticism plays in making the world better and our lives fuller.

Nellie McKay's "Reflections of Black Women Writers: Revising the Literary Canon" (1987) stands as a case study of the questions raised by Russ, Robinson, and Lauter. In this essay, she reviews the history of African-American women writers to show how they "have consistently provided for themselves and others . . . a rendering of the black woman's place in the world in which she lives, as she shapes and defines that from her own impulses and actions." These writers, almost all of whom were neglected for decades or even centuries, reveal a very different "American experience" and a different literary tradition from that encountered in anthologies of American literature, and different even from that revealed in writings by African-American men. McKay provides the context in which contemporary African-American writers like Alice Walker or Toni Morrison do not have to appear "anomalous" and sets out the political and social bases for their aesthetics. The inclusion of these writers in the American canon, she argues, "makes more complete the reality of the multifaceted American experience." Along with Russ, Robinson, and Lauter, McKay provides a critique of the notion of "universality" and the myth of "purely aesthetic" judgments of literature.

—DPH

ANOMALOUSNESS

She didn't write it.
She wrote it, but she shouldn't have.
She wrote it, but look what she wrote about.
She wrote it, but "she" isn't really an artist and "it" isn't really serious, of the right genre—i.e., really art.
She wrote it, but she wrote only one of it.
She wrote it, but it's only interesting/included in the canon for one, limited reason.
She wrote it, but there are very few of her.

Here are some anthologies and academic lists, chosen at random, which may aid in seeing how few of her there are.

The Golden Treasury, edited by F. T. Palgrave in 1861, was reedited by Oscar Williams in 1961.[1] Palgrave declares his intention to include only lyrics by writers not living in 1855, "lyric" being defined as "some single thought, feeling, or situation." Williams, who has both added poets to the periods Palgrave covers and brought the anthology up to 1955, says that Palgrave's "own definition of the lyrical as unity of feeling or thought" has been kept as a "determinant of choice," although both standards are flexible enough to include, for Palgrave, Shelley's "To a Skylark" and Keats' "Ode to Autumn"; and for Williams, Eliot's "The Journey of the Magi," Auden's "In Memory of W. B. Yeats," and Lindsay's "The Congo." Palgrave includes four women: Anna Letitia Barbauld, Jane Elliott, Lady Anne Lindsay, and Lady Carolina Nairne, all active mainly in the eighteenth century; the latter three were Scotswomen. Each is represented by one selection. Palgrave did not include either Aphra Behn or Anne Finch, Countess of Winchilsea, although some of their works certainly fall within his definition of the lyric. Nor, in his introduction, does he mention the then-famous Elizabeth Barrett Browning as one of the living poets who "will no doubt claim and obtain their place among the best." Emily Brontë (died 1848) is neither mentioned nor included. Palgrave also omitted Donne, Blake, and Traherne, all added by Williams.

In order to count the percentage of women included in this anthology, I have omitted all poets dead before 1650. The assumption that no women dead before

1650 wrote anything at all is questionable (see Epilogue), but since it's very probably an assumption Palgrave and Williams would make (as would other anthologists) there's no need to load the figures. It's probably fair to assume that Williams would not include Palgrave's female lyricists but impossible to tell which of the male poets he would likewise delete; I will therefore give both sets of figures: Williams' female choices are 8 percent of the total number of poets in the anthology; the addition of Palgrave's choices raises the total to 11 percent.

Of Williams' fourteen women additions, six are nineteenth-century poets: Emily Brontë, Christina Rossetti, Emily Dickinson, Alice Meynell, Elizabeth Barrett Browning, and (surprisingly) George Eliot. There are no seventeenth- or eighteenth-century additions to Palgrave's four. The remaining eight are twentieth-century figures: Leonie Adams, Elizabeth Bishop, Ruth Herschberger, Esther Matthews, Edna St. Vincent Millay, Marianne Moore, Elinor Wylie, and Gene Derwood. The only women represented by more than two selections apiece are Gene Derwood (seven), Emily Dickinson (eight), and Edna Millay (eleven). Elizabeth Barrett Browning is represented by two of the *Sonnets from the Portuguese,* and Christina Rossetti and Dante Gabriel Rossetti each by two poems. If we compare female poets represented by more than two selections with male poets similarly represented, there are three women out of a total of sixty, or 5 percent. (Only one of these women is not a twentieth-century poet.) To recall Van Gerven, "Since . . . only contemporary women poets are represented in any number, it becomes clear that a woman must be extraordinary to outlive her generation—And that a man need not." [2]

In *A Treasury of Great Poems,* Louis Untermeyer includes Aphra Behn and Anne Finch, Countess of Winchilsea (whom Williams excludes). Untermeyer's twentieth-century choices (except for Millay) differ entirely from Williams', yet he ends up with much the same percentage of women poets as Williams does (if we subtract Palgrave's choices): 8.6 percent of the total. This figure holds, by the way, either with or without the inclusion of both editors' twentieth-century male and female choices.

In Auden and Pearson's far less idiosyncratic *Poets of the English Language* (which ends with Yeats), 5 percent of the authors listed are women. (Again I have considered 1650 as a rough beginning date.) Anne Bradstreet is present, but Aphra Behn and Elizabeth Barrett Browning are absent, although in evidence are such male figures as John Byrom, Henry Alabaster, and John Wolcot. In all three anthologies there are sections of anonymous ballads, but no speculation that the authorship of some of these may have been female, although an Elizabethan scholar, Frederick O. Waage, notes "the strong tendency of all social ballads to vindicate covertly their women." [3] I would certainly hesitate to attribute a later ballad like "Once I wore my apron low" to male authorship, and even among the earlier ones there are some which suggest not only female authorship but female revenge—for example, "May Colvin." (Here the false young man who has drowned six women attempts to drown a seventh, but wants her to take off her clothes, which are too costly to rot in the sea. Pretending modesty, she bids him to turn his back and when he does, throws *him* into the sea, triumphantly telling him to keep company with the women he's drowned.)

To turn again to the graduate reading list of the University of Washington's

Department of English (for August 1977), we find no women from 1660 to 1780, four female novelists (but no poets) in nineteenth-century England, and in the United States (up to 1900) four women. The twentieth-century list includes one female novelist, Virginia Woolf, and, out of an elective selection of seven novelists, one black man (Ralph Ellison) and one white woman (Doris Lessing). Out of a similar elective selection of eight poets, two are (white) women: Larkin and Rich. Counting again from about 1660, the number of women is about 6 percent. In an earlier list (1968), Chopin, Chesnutt, and Bradstreet do not appear, but Edith Wharton (invisible in 1977) does. In both lists, Cotton Mather appears but not Margaret Fuller; in 1977 Rochester, William Cowper, and William Collins but not Mary Wollstonecraft. Missing also are Aphra Behn, Fanny Burney, Elizabeth Barrett, and Christina Rossetti; and to give my own very partial list of twentieth-century omissions: Willa Cather (Ernest Hemingway is represented by three selections), Dorothy Richardson, Djuna Barnes, Katherine Mansfield, Carson McCullers, Isak Dinesen, Marianne Moore, Zora Neale Hurston, Elizabeth Bishop, and so on and so on.

What is so striking about these examples is that although the percentage of women included remains somewhere between 5 percent and 8 percent, the personnel change rather strikingly from book to book; Aphra Behn appears and vanishes, Anne Bradstreet is existent or nonexistent according to whom you read, Elizabeth Barrett Browning and Emily Brontë bob up and down like corks, Edith Wharton is part of English literature in 1968 and banished to the outer darkness in 1977—and yet there are always enough women for that 5 percent and never quite enough to get much past 8 percent. It recalls the proportion of female entries (about 7 percent) in those freshman textbooks, chosen not as selections of great literature but in order to teach freshmen to read and write: "the ratio of women writers . . . was fairly constant: about 7%." [4]

In a study of courses given by the Department of English of the women's college she once attended, Elaine Showalter finds (of the writers listed in courses past the freshman year) 17 women out of 313, or just about 5 percent. But which 5 percent? Showalter writes:

> In the twenty-one courses beyond the freshman level . . . there were . . . such [male] luminaries as William Shenstone, James Barrie, and Dion Boucicault; and . . . Lady Mary Wortley Montagu, Anne Bradstreet, Mrs. Centlivre, Fanny Burney, Jane Austen, Charlotte and Emily Brontë, George Eliot, Margaret Fuller, Emily Dickinson, Sarah Orne Jewett, Lady Gregory, Virginia Woolf, Dorothy Richardson, Marianne Moore, Gertrude Stein, and Djuna Barnes.

She adds: "The *Norton Anthology* . . . includes 169 men and 6 women," [5] 3½ percent and 11.6 percent. Average: 7 percent.

Showalter talks of imbalance, but what bothers me is the constancy of the imbalance despite the changes in personnel. For example, Showalter's English Department includes many more women than the University of Washington list; yet in the former case the percentage of women is lower, not higher, than in the latter. It seems that when women are brought into a reading list, a curriculum, or an anthology, men arrive, too—let the number of men drop and the women mysteriously disappear.

Nonetheless, as Van Gerven says:

> the inclusion of only the most extraordinary women [but not only the most extraordinary men] . . . distorts the relevance of those few women . . . who remain. Since women are so often thus isolated in anthologies . . . they seem odd, unconventional, and therefore, a little trivial.

She adds:

> When Dickinson, or any woman poet for that matter, is isolated from all writing in her own and succeeding generations, she appears bizarre, extraneous. . . . Since women writers are thus isolated, they often do not fit into the literary historian's "coherent view of the total literary culture." . . . As each succeeding generation of women . . . is excluded from the literary record, the connections between women . . . writers become more and more obscure, which in turn simply justifies the exclusion of more and more women on the grounds that they are anomalous—they just don't fit in.[6]

Pollution of quality via anomalousness is similar to *pollution of agency via abnormality*. Thus R. P. Blackmur, writing of Emily Dickinson, can speak of:

> [her] private and eccentric . . . relation to the business of poetry. She was neither a professional poet nor an amateur; she was a private poet who wrote indefatigably as other women cook or knit . . . [driven] to poetry instead of antimacassars. Neither her personal education nor the habit of her society . . . gave her the least inkling that poetry is a rational and objective art.[7]

Thus Dickinson's *anomalousness* as a poet, in part referable to her lack of proper education, leads to an assertion of her personal eccentricity (pollution of agency via abnormality) which along with a re-categorizing of Dickinson as not-a-poet and her work as equivalent to antimacassars, converges on the final judgment; her poetry is not what poetry ought to be. Blackmur wrote in 1937, but what he said is not far from the *Commercial Advertiser* review of 1891:

> Extreme hunger often causes strange visions. That this hermitess never satisfied, perhaps never could satisfy, her craving for human companionship, may have first brought her into her strangely visionary state. Upon the theme of human love she becomes absurdly, if not blasphemously, intemperate.[8]

Again pollution of agency is given as the reason for the defects in Dickinson's work, nor are the defects very different: she is "driven" and "hungry," *therefore* not "rational" or temperate. In both accounts she appears as totally isolated, a "private" poet or a "hermitess" whose talent came from nowhere and bore no relation to anything. Yet according to other sources this anomalous being can be placed squarely in a public literary tradition, influenced by it and influencing it in turn. Moers writes:

> Dickinson had been reading about Mrs. Browning in Kate Field's memorial tribute . . . in the September 1861 *Atlantic Monthly* just as, earlier that year, she had read of Julia Ward Howe's . . . abridgment of George Sand's autobiography . . . hundreds of phrases of Dickinson's . . . suggest she had the whole of *Aurora Leigh* almost by heart. . . . Dickinson named Mrs. Browning as mentor; she referred often in her letters to her poems, and to the portraits that friends had sent her.

Moers adds: "Browning scholars do not mention it." And, "Among . . . [some] Dickinsonians . . . the literary relationship is treated with shocked prurience." (She is referring to John Evangelist Walsh's *The Hidden Life of Emily Dickinson*, published in 1971.) According to Moers, Dickinson read little, despite her "single year . . . at Mount Holyoke." She knew Emerson "well . . . perhaps a little Thoreau and Hawthorne; but she pretended, at least, not to have read a line of Whitman, no Melville, no Poe, no Irving. . . ." But she read:

> and re-read . . . Helen Hunt Jackson and Lydia Maria Child, and Harriet Beecher Stowe, and Lady Georgina Fullerton, and Dinah Maria Craik, and Elizabeth Stuart Phelps, and Rebecca Harding Davis, and Harriet Prescott Spofford, and Francesca Alexander, and Mathilda Mackarness and everything that George Eliot . . . ever wrote.

Helen Hunt Jackson "correctly valued Emily Dickinson's poetry and urged her to publish."[9]

As for those whom Dickinson influenced, Amy Lowell wrote "Sisters" in 1925, affirming Dickinson as an "older sister."[10] Rich's "I Am in Danger—Sir" calls Dickinson her ancestor.[11] Juhasz, herself a poet, calls Dickinson "the great woman poet to serve as foremother" and goes on to quote from Lowell's "Sisters," Lynn Strongin's "Emily Dickinson Postage Stamp" (1972), and her own "The Poems of Women" (1973).[12] Van Gerven speculates about Dickinson's possible influence on other women poets.[13]

As for other connections between literary women, Moers' *Literary Women* is a mine of cross-references: if Dickinson read Elizabeth Barrett Browning, the latter "had read it all" [fiction by women] and once said that on her tombstone should be written "*Ci-gît* the greatest novel reader in the world" (p. 61). She corresponded with Harriet Beecher Stowe. Charlotte Brontë went to London, exhibiting "an awkwardness and timidity in literary society that have become legendary"—except with Harriet Martineau (p. 64). George Eliot corresponded with Stowe. Jane Austen read Sarah Harriet Burney, Mrs. Jane West, Anna Maria Porter, Mrs. Anne Grant, Elizabeth Hamilton, Laetitia Matilda Hawkins, Helen Maria Williams "and the rest of the women writers of her day." She studied Maria Edgeworth and Fanny Burney (pp. 66–67). Nor were all the associations literary. George Eliot knew Barbara Leigh Smith (founder of the Association for Promoting the Employment of Women) (p. 28); Charlotte Brontë knew the feminist Mary Taylor; Mrs. Gaskell knew Bessie Parks and read Mrs. Tonna; Harriet Beecher Stowe wrote the introduction to the 1844 edition of Mrs. Tonna's *Works* (p. 39). George Sand reviewed *Uncle Tom's Cabin* with "All honor and respect to you, Madame Stowe" (p. 55), while George Eliot's famous letter about *Daniel*

Deronda and anti-Semitism in England was addressed to Stowe, "whom she honored as her predecessor" (p. 59). Pairings of student with literary mentor are cited by Moers: Willa Cather and Sarah Orne Jewett, Jean Rhys and Charlotte Brontë, Carson McCullers and Isak Dinesen, Nathalie Sarraute, and Ivy Compton-Burnett (p. 68). Elizabeth Barrett and Miss Mitford were correspondents (Flush was a gift from Mitford to her friend), and both wished to send their books, "tied together in a parcel for courage to the great Madame Sand." Miss Barrett wrote, "I would give anything to have a letter from her, though it smelt of cigar. And it would, of course!" (pp. 82–83). Mrs. Browning later visited Mme. Sand twice, despite her husband's objections. There are other surprising influences Moers finds; George Eliot on Gertrude Stein, for example (pp. 98–99). As for single novels, *Consuelo* was read by Charlotte Brontë, Mary Taylor said it was worth learning French to read it, and Willa Cather kept Sand's portrait over her mantelpiece into the 1930s (p. 289). (Moers does not mention along with George Eliot's *Armgart* Isak Dinesen's Pellegrina Leoni, but there may be a connection there, too.) Moers also traces the enormous influence of Mrs. Radcliffe (her books turn up, among other places, in *Shirley*—pp. 192–193) and the even greater influence of *Corinne* (which turns up everywhere). She also finds, in women's works, repeated themes which a synopsis could only travesty.

In some other places studies are beginning to be made of the connections between women artists. For example, Virginia Woolf knew that Geraldine Jewsbury knew Jane Carlyle, but her essay on the two of them gives the impression that Jewsbury was otherwise isolated.[14] A recent issue of *Heresies*, however, links as "intimates" Geraldine Jewsbury, Charlotte Cushman, Fanny Kemble, Harriet Hosmer, and several other women artists. There is the circle around Natalie Barney in the twenties. (Barney complains vigorously of the "artificial Renée [Vivien] whom Colette presents in *Ces Plaisirs!*")[15] Nor are all these networks among artists; Blanche Weisen Cook documents the female support groups surrounding the married Crystal Eastman (who, "surrounded by men who shared her work" had "a feminist support group as well") and the homosexual Jane Addams and Lillian Wald, "involved almost exclusively with women." She also describes the extent to which these relationships between women, whether sexual or not, have been ignored by historians. When the relationships are homosexual (as in the case of Mount Holyoke president, Mary E. Woolley, who lived for years with her lover, the chairwoman of the English Department), it is understandable that "the historical evidence was juggled." Cook provides some examples of the astounding lengths to which historians will go to explain away the obvious.[16] But surely Emily Dickinson's admiration for Elizabeth Barrett is not socially tabooed. Yet Moers can observe, "Among most Dickinsonians the literary relationship is treated with embarrassment" and "Browning scholars . . . do not mention it." And elsewhere:

> Scholarship has averted its refined and weary eyes from the female fiction that Austen's letters inform us was her daily sustenance in the years she became one of the greatest writers in the language.

And again Moers complains that the "stability and integrity" of Mrs. Radcliffe's Gothic heroines have been made to vanish from modern view by:

what was done with the figure by the male writers who followed Mrs. Radcliffe. For most of them . . . the Gothic heroine was quintessentially a defenseless victim, a weakling . . . whose sufferings are the source of her erotic fascination. [Moers suggests elsewhere that the proper model for Emily in *The Mysteries of Udolpho* is not de Sade's female victims but Katharine Hepburn in *The African Queen*.][17]

From Dolores Palomo I find also that the refined eyes of scholarship condemn "one half to two thirds of the fiction printed in the eighteenth century" as minor, mediocre, or salacious—that is, the fiction written by women.[18]

Thus the female tradition in literature has been either ignored, derided, or even (as with Mrs. Radcliffe's property-minded heroines) taken over and replaced. Why? Here is one possible answer, not aesthetic but political (by Judith Long Laws, a psychologist):

> Tokenism is . . . found whenever a dominant group is under pressure to share privilege, power, or other desirable commodities with a group which is excluded. . . . tokenism advertises a promise of mobility which is severely restricted in quantity. . . . the Token does not become assimilated into the dominant group, but is destined for permanent marginality.[19]

Here is another: Novelist Samuel Delany has argued that outside of specifically social situations (like cocktail parties), Americans are trained to "see" a group in which men predominate to the extent of 65 percent to 75 percent as half male and half female. In business and on the street, groups in which women actually number 50 percent tend to be seen as being *more* than 50 percent female.[20] It is not impossible that some similar, unconscious mechanism controls the number of female writers which looks "proper" or "enough" to anthologists and editors. (I am reminded of the folk wisdom of female academics, one of whom whispered to me before a meeting at which we were the only women present, "Don't sit next to me or they'll say we're taking over.")

There are three elements here: a promise, numerical restrictions, and permanent marginality. We have seen the restrictions on the quantity of visibility allowed women writers: that 5 to 8 percent representation. Quality can be controlled by denial of agency, pollution of agency, and false categorizing. I believe that the *anomalousness* of the women writer—produced by the double standard of content and the writer's isolation from the female tradition—is the final means of ensuring permanent marginality. In order to have her "belong" fully to English literature, the tradition to which she belongs must also be admitted. Other writers must be admitted along with their tradition, written and unwritten. Speech must be admitted. Canons of excellence and conceptions of excellence must change, perhaps beyond recognition. In short, we have a complete collapse of the original solution to the problem of the "wrong" people creating the "right" values. When this happens, the very idea that some people *are* "wrong" begins to fade. And that makes it necessary to recognize what has been done to the "wrong" people and why. And that means recognizing one's own complicity in an appalling situation. It means anger, horror, helplessness, fear for one's own privilege, a conviction of personal guilt, and what for professional intellectuals may be even worse, a conviction of one's own profound stupidity. It may mean fear of retaliation. It means knowing that *they* are watching *you*. Imagine a middle-aged, white, male professor (the typical sort in the profession) asked to let into the Sacred Canon of Literature the following:

> call me
> roach and presumptuous
> nightmare on your white pillow. . . .

Audre Lorde, "The Brown Menace or Poem to the
Survival of Roaches"[21]

Anger is hard to take. But there are worse things. Imagine our professor confronted with a long, elegant, comic poem about impotence, masturbation, and premature ejaculation. Here is Canto 9:

> In vain th' inraged Youth essay'd
> To call its [his penis'] fleeting vigor back.
> No motion 'twill from Motion take;
> Excess of Love his Love betray'd:
> In vain he Toils, in vain Commands;
> The Insensible fell weeping in his Hand.[22]

The above is from Aphra Behn's "The Disappointment." Of those who are not ignored completely, dismissed as writing about the "wrong" things, condemned for (whatever passes for) impropriety (that year), described as of merely technical interest (on the basis of a carefully selected few worst works), falsely categorized as other than artists, condemned for writing in the wrong genre, or out of genre, or simply joked about, or blamed for what has, in fact, been deleted from or misinterpreted out of their work by others, it is still possible to say, quite sincerely:

She wrote it, but she doesn't fit in.

Or, more generously: *She's wonderful, but where on earth did she come from?*

NOTES

1. *F. T. Palgrave's The Golden Treasury of the Best Songs and Lyrical Poems: Centennial Edition*, ed. Oscar Williams (New York: New American Library, 1961), pp. viii, ix, xi.

2. Claudia Ven Gerven, "Lost Literary Traditions: A Matter of Influence," MS., p. 2.

3. Frederick O. Waage, "Urban Broadsides of Renaissance England," *Journal of Popular Culture* 11, no. 3 (Winter 1977): 736.

4. Jean S. Mullen, "Freshman Textbooks," *College English* 34 (1972): 79.

5. Elaine Showalter, "Women and the Literary Curriculum," *College English* 32, no. 8 (May 1971): 856.

6. Van Gerven, "Lost Literary Traditions," pp. 2–3, 5–6.

7. Cited by Suzanne Juhasz, *Naked and Fiery Forms: Modern American Poetry by Women: A New Tradition* (New York: Harper & Row, 1976), p. 11.

8. *Ibid.*, p. 9.

9. Moers, *Literary Women*, pp. 83, 85–86, 87, 91–92.

10. Juhasz, *Naked and Fiery Forms*, p. 7.

11. Van Gerven, "Lost Literary Traditions," p. 4.

12. Juhasz, *Naked and Fiery Forms*, pp. 7–9.

13. Van Gerven, "Lost Literary Traditions," p. 5.

14. Virginia Woolf, "Geraldine and Jane," in *The Second Common Reader*, pp. 167–81.

15. Natalie Barney, "Natalie Barney on Renée Vivien," trans. Margaret Porter, *Heresies* 3 (Fall 1977): 71.

16. Blanche Weisen Cook, "Female Support Networks and Political Activism," *Crysalis* 3 (1977): 45–46.

17. Moers, *Literary Women*, pp. 87, 66, 208, 211.

18. Personal interview with Dolores Palomo, summer 1978.

19. Judith Long Laws, "The Psychology of Tokenism: An Analysis," *Sex Roles*, I:1 (1975): 51.

20. Samuel Delany, "To Read the Dispossessed," in *The Jewel-hinged Jaw* (New York: Berkley, 1978), p. 261.

21. Audre Lorde, *The New York Head Shop and Museum* (Detroit: Broadside, 1974), p. 48.

22. In *By a Woman Writt*, ed. Joan Goulianos (Baltimore: Penguin, 1974), p. 92.

AESTHETICS

The re-evaluation and rediscovery of minority art (including the cultural minority of women) is often conceived as a matter of remedying injustice and exclusiveness through doing justice to individual artists by allowing their work into the canon, which will thereby be more complete, but fundamentally unchanged. Sometimes it's also stressed that the erasing of previous injustice will encourage new artists of the hitherto "wrong" groups and thus provide art with more artists who will provide new (or different) material—and that all of this activity will enrich, but not change, the canon of art itself.

But in the case of women, what has been left out? "Merely," says Carolyn Kizer, "the private lives of one half of humanity."[1]

These lives are not lived in isolation from the private and public lives of the other half. Here is Jean Baker Miller describing what happens when the lives of half a community are omitted from the consciousness of the other half:

> Some of the areas of life denied by the dominant group are . . . projected on to all subordinate groups. . . . But other parts of experience are so necessary that they cannot be projected very far away. One must *have* them nearby, even if one can still deny *owning* them. These are the special areas delegated to women.

She adds:

> . . . when . . . women move out of their restricted place, they threaten men in a very profound sense with the need to reintegrate many of the essentials of human development. . . . These things have been warded off and become doubly fearful because they look as if they will entrap men in "emotions," weakness, sexuality, vulnerability, helplessness, the need for care, and other unsolved areas.

And:

> Inevitably the dominant group is the model for "normal human relationships." It then becomes normal to treat others destructively and to derogate

them, to obscure the truth of what you are doing by creating false explanations . . . to keep on doing these things, one need only behave "normally."[2]

A mode of understanding life which wilfully ignores so much can do so only at
the peril of thoroughly distorting the rest. A mode of understanding literature
which can ignore the private lives of half the human race is not "incomplete"; it
is distorted through and through. Feminist criticism of the early 1970s began by
pointing out the simplest of these distortions, that is, that the female characters
of even our greatest realistic "classics" by male writers are often not individ-
ualized portraits of possible women, but creations of fear and desire. At best,
according to Lillian Robinson:

> . . . the problem is . . . [whether] the author, in showing what goes on in a
> heroine's mind, is showing us anything like the mind of an actual human fe-
> male. . . . I am amazed at how many writers have chosen to evade it by ex-
> ternalizing the psychological situation, using "objective" images that convey
> the pattern or content of a woman's thought without actually entering into
> it. . . . Emma Bovary and Anna Karenina, to name two eminently successful
> literary creations, are realized for us in this way.[3]

Some literary creations are not so successful or so innocuous, from Dickens'
incapacity to portray women alone or in solely female society to Hemingway's
misogynistic daydreams. I am thinking especially of Dickens' Bella Wilfer in *Our
Mutual Friend*, vain and pretty, who flirts (quite reasonably) with her father, then
applies the same manner to her younger sister (which is not reasonable) and
then—alone—flirts (impossibly) with her mirror. Women speaking of mirrors
and prettiness make it all too clear that even for pretty women, mirrors are the
foci of anxious, not gratified, narcissism. The woman who knows beyond a doubt
that she is beautiful exists aplenty in male novelists' imaginations; I have yet to
find her in women's books or women's memoirs or in life. Women spend a lot of
time looking in mirrors, but the "compulsion to visualize the self" is a phrase
Moers uses of women in her chapter on Gothic freaks and horrors; the compulsion is a constant check on one's (possible) beauty, not an enjoyment of it.
Dickens' error is simple; how could he have observed the Bellas of his world
alone or heard their thoughts? So he simply extends public behavior into a private
situation. Here is Annis Pratt, on that incarnation of the eternal feminine, Molly
Bloom:

> It is difficult not to feel about Molly Bloom on her chamberpot what Eldridge
> Cleaver must feel about Jack Benny's Rochester, but a good critic will not
> withdraw her attention from a work which is resonant and craftsmanlike even
> if it is chauvinistic.[4]

Robinson, answering Pratt in the same issue of the same journal, refuses to take
so mild a position:

> sexual stereotypes serve *somebody's* interest. . . . I believe only a feminist
> knows what Molly Bloom is really about and can ask the questions that will
> demonstrate the real functioning of sexual myth in Joyce's novel.[5]

In the same issue, Dolores Barracano Schmidt performs this investigation in an essay on "The Great American Bitch," calling this twentieth-century character who appears in men's novels:

> more myth than reality, a fabrication used to maintain the *status quo*. She is a figure about whom a whole cluster of values and taboos clings: women's fight for equality was a mistake . . . women are not equipped for civilization. . . . by being so thoroughly hateful the Great American Bitch of fiction reinforces the sexist view.[6]

Another feminist critic, Cynthia Griffin Wolff, generalizes:

> The definition [in literature] of women's most serious problems and the proposed solutions . . . are . . . covertly tailored to meet the needs of fundamentally *masculine* problems. . . . women appear in literature . . . as conveniences to the resolution of masculine dilemmas.

One of Wolff's examples is the opposition of "virtuous" to "sensuous" woman, a projection of a male split in feeling and value which "relieves . . . [the man] from the difficulties of trying to unite two forces of love." (The "sensuous" woman, as Wolff points out, is not one who desires men but one who is desired by them.) She goes on:

> men may appear stereotypically . . . but the stereotype [e.g., the Warrior] is usually a fantasied solution to an essentially masculine problem. . . . Moreover, there is a . . . significant body of literature which recognizes the limitations of some of these masculine stereotypes [e.g., *The Red Badge of Courage*]. There is no comparable body of anti-stereotype literature about women. . . . Even women writers . . . seem to adopt them.[7]

Judith Fetterley offers even more telling examples:

> . . . when I look at a poem like "The Solitary Reaper" . . . I do not find my experience in it at all. Rather I find that the drama of the poem depends upon a contrast between the male subject as conscious, creative knower and the unknowing female object of his contemplation; it is my wordless, artless, natural and utterly unself-conscious song which has provided the male speaker/poet with the opportunity to define himself as knower. . . . [in "To His Coy Mistress"] the complexity of the speaker's situation, which is the subject of the poem, is modest compared to the complexity of the mistress's position . . . [which is] the essence of *my* relation to the poem.

Elsewhere she states one of the central problems of feminist criticism:

> What happens to one's definition of aesthetic criteria . . . when one is confronted by a literature which does not support the self but assaults it[?][8]

Vonda McIntyre answers:

> Right now a lot of literary and film "classics" are unbearable . . . because of the underlying [sexist] assumptions. In a few generations I think they will be either incomprehensible or so ridiculous as to be funny.[9]

And Ellen Cantarow, looking into her college textbook, finds that next to Pope's line, "Most women have no Characters at all," she once wrote: "SPEAKER TONE DEFINE." She asks:

> Where in my notes was that other girl, the girl who once raged at being taken for "a typical Wellesley *girl*?" . . . [there was] intense self-hatred. . . . education at Wellesley . . . didn't just belie our life experience as girls . . . it nullified that experience, rendered it invisible. . . . we lived in a state of schizophrenia that we took to be normal.[10]

A more explicit, systematic rejection of the canon and the standards that support it can be found in the field of art—a rejection I believe parallel to that going on in a more piecemeal fashion in literature. For example, Mary Garrard asks:

> Why is our art history . . . full of virtuous reversals in which a virile, heroic, or austere style suddenly and dramatically replaces a feminine, lyrical, or luxurious one—David over Fragonard, Caravaggio over Salviati, clean international Modern Gropius over wickedly ornamental Sullivan or Tiffany?[11]

Valerie Jaudon and Joyce Kozloff answer:

> The prejudice against the decorative has a long art history and is based on hierarchies: fine art above decorative art, Western art above non-Western art, men's art above women's art . . . "high art" [means] man, mankind, the individual man, individuality, humans, humanity, the human figure, humanism, civilization, culture, the Greeks, the Romans, the English, Christianity, spiritual transcendence, religion, nature, true form, science, logic, creativity, action, war, virility, violence, brutality, dynamism, power, and greatness.
>
> In the same texts other words are used repeatedly in connection with . . . "low art": Africans, Orientals, Persians, Slovaks, peasants, the lower classes, women, children, savages, pagans, sensuality, pleasure, decadence, chaos, anarchy, impotence, exotica, eroticism, artifice, tattoos, cosmetics, ornaments, decoration, carpets, weaving, patterns, domesticity, wallpaper, fabrics, and furniture.

The rest of Jaudon and Kozloff's essay consists of quotations from artists and art historians arranged under such headings as "War and Virility," "Purity in Art as a Holy Cause," and a particularly damning section expressing "the desire for unlimited personal power," which the authors call "Autocracy."[12]

Such associations of art with virility, quality with size, and authenticity with self-aggrandizement appear in literature, too. (One of the strangest conversations I ever had was with a male colleague who stated that Chekhov could not be a "great" artist because he never wrote anything "full-length." In some confusion—apparently short stories and novellas didn't count—I mentioned the plays. These, it seemed, didn't count either; "They're much shorter than novels," said my colleague.) Here is Adrienne Rich, pointing out that the "masterpieces" we have been taught to admire are not merely flawed, but that they may not even mean what we have been taught they mean. In "The Ninth Symphony of Beethoven Understood at Last as a Sexual Message" Rich begins with "A man in terror of impotence," goes on to describe the music as:

music of the entirely
isolated soul
yelling at Joy from the tunnel of the ego
music without the ghost
of another person in it. . . .

What is the man trying to say? Something he would keep back if he could, "bound and flogged" with "chords of Joy." The real situation behind all this pounding?

. . . everything is silence and the
beating of a bloody fist upon
a splintered table.[13]

If the canon is an attempt to shore up the *status quo*, if the masterpieces don't mean what they pretend to mean, then artists must throw away the rules altogether in favor of something else. "Their musty rules of unity, and God knows what besides, if they meant anything," says Aphra Behn, but she goes no further.[14] Rich does, stating:

in pretending to stand for "the human," masculine subjectivity tries to force us to name our truths in an alien language, to dilute them; we are constantly told that the "real" problems . . . are those men have defined, that the problems we need to examine are trivial, unscholarly, nonexistent. . . .

Any woman who has moved from the playing-fields of male discourse into the realm where women are developing our own descriptions of the world, knows the extraordinary sense of shedding . . . someone else's baggage, of ceasing to translate. It is not that thinking becomes easy, but that the difficulties are intrinsic to the work itself, rather than to the environment. . . .[15]

In "ceasing to translate," the "wrong" people begin to make not only good, but genuinely experimental art. Several contemporary women's theater groups have thrown away not only the unities but the lights, the proscenium, the elaborate impressiveness, the "primitivism," and the assault-on-the-audience that marked the theatrical "experiments" of the 1960s. Contemporaneously with the reappearance of feminism, these women's groups have instead created a version of Epic Theater (though nobody's noticed): much narrative, constantly changing characters, many incidents (personal and historical), direct (and sympathetic) commentary to the audience, and the reenactment, sometimes in mime, rather than the here-and-now "hot" acting, of important scenes. These performances are, to my mind, more genuinely experimental than what passed for experimental theater in the 1960s, just as Baldwin's non-fiction is not only beautiful but genuinely experimental in comparison (for example) with much Joyce- or Nabokov-derived modern work. We have been trained to regard certain kinds of art (especially the violent, the arcane, and the assaultive) as "experimental." But there's all the difference in the world between studying oxidation and producing loud noises with gunpowder. The former leads somewhere; the latter (analogous to rock groups' raising the ante with decibelage, luridness, and violence) does not.

There are genuine experiments happening in women's writing. According to Suzanne Juhasz, "In the late sixties and early seventies an explosion of poetry by women occurred. . . ." She goes on, concluding that women are being forced to create new poetic forms, since:

> If the woman poet wants . . . to link her particular experiences with larger universals . . . she can call upon only a percentage of her own experiences. Much of what she knows does not link up to universals because the universals presently in existence are based upon masculine experience, masculine norms.

One way of dealing with the norms of what is or is not universal is to ignore them and relate particulars to particulars. This leads to writing (as Juhasz puts it) in the vernacular and not in Latin. It also leads to rejection slips as she finds out:

> Recently I received a rejection slip from a well-meaning editor who, while admitting the "necessary" nature of my poems, took issue with the fact that my poems "said it all." "Try more denotation, synecdoche, metonymy, suggestion," he said. Yet I and many feminist poets do not want to treat poetry as a metalanguage that needs to be decoded.[16]

Julia Penelope, also, notes the critics' annoyance when "works . . . make the function of the critic obsolete. The . . . work . . . (is) immediately available to the reader, and there is no need for the . . . intervention of the critic as guide or explicator."[17] Noting that the epigram is, by tradition, inferior to the epic, Johasz quotes with delight some of Alta's short poems, for example:

> if you won't make love to me, at least
> get out of my dreams!

Here's another, by black poet Pat Parker, to white women:

> SISTER! your foot's smaller
> but it's still on my neck.

Juhasz finally abandons the idea of the canon altogether:

> a poem works if it lives up to itself. Such a definition contains no built-in ranking system.[18]

And here is Woolf's opinion of the canon:

> They [the children] knew what he liked best—to be forever walking up and down, up and down, with Mr. Ramsay, and saying who had won this, who had won that, who was a "first-rate man" . . . who was "brilliant but . . . fundamentally unsound," who was "undoubtedly the ablest fellow in Bailliol." . . . That was what they talked about.[19]

But if we throw out the linear hierarchy, are we to do without standards altogether? Here is Juhasz again:

> Yet a poem can work and not be good. It can be dull or ordinary, or super-
> ficial. A *good* poem works *powerfully* and *accurately* to communicate between
> poet and reader or listener.[20] [Italics mine]

But which reader? Which listener? The techniques for mystifying women's
lives and belittling women's writing that I have described work by suppressing
context: writing is separated from experience, women writers are separated from
their tradition and each other, public is separated from private, political from
personal—all to enforce a supposed set of absolute standards. What is frightening about black art or women's art or Chicago art—and so on—is that it calls into
question the very idea of objectivity and absolute standards:

This is a good novel.

Good *for what*?

Good *for whom*?

One side of the nightmare is that the privileged group will not recognize that
"other" art, will not be able to judge it, that the superiority of taste and training
possessed by the privileged critic and the privileged artist will suddenly vanish.

The other side of the nightmare is not that what is found in the "other" art
will be incomprehensible, but that it will be all too familiar. That is:

Women's lives are the buried truth about men's lives.

The lives of people of color are the buried truth about white lives.

The buried truth about the rich is who they take their money from and how.

The buried truth about "normal" sexuality is how one kind of sexual expression has been made privileged, and what kinds of unearned virtue and terrors
about identity this distinction serves.

There are other questions: why is "greatness" in art so often aggressive? Why
does "great" literature have to be long? Is "regionalism" only another instance of
down-grading the vernacular? Why is "great" architecture supposed to knock
your eye out at first view, unlike "indigenous" architecture, which must be appreciated slowly and with knowledge of the climate in which it exists? Why is the
design of clothing—those grotesque and sometimes perilously fantastic anatomical–social-role–characterological ideas of the person—a "minor" art? Because it
has a use? In admiring "pure" (i.e., useless) art, are we not merely admiring
Veblenian conspicuous consumption, like the Mandarin fingernail? In Eve Merriam's recent play *The Club* it became clear that masculine and feminine body-
language are very different; gestures socially recognizable as "male" lay claim to
as much space as possible, while comparable "female" gestures are self-protective, self-referential, and take up as little space as possible.

Male reviewers, astonished at a play in which the members of a nineteenth-
century men's club *and* the club's black waiter *and* its boy in buttons *and* its
piano player were all played by women, praised the actresses for their success in
imitating men without making any attempt to hide their own female anatomy. In
her autobiography Judy Chicago comments:

> when the women "acted out" walking down the street and being accosted by
> men, everyone seemed able to "take on" the characteristics of the tough
> swagger, of men "coming on." It was as if they knew the words so well.[21]

Male reviewers understood the point of hearing sexist jokes and songs of the period performed by women, but it took a female reviewer (in *Harper's Bazaar*, I think) to see that the final effect of seeing women in the habiliments of power was utter confusion as to what roles belonged to whom. She called this disappearance of the link between gender and sexual physiology the labels washing off the bottles; I came out of the theater saying, "But what *is* 'women'?" Perhaps this isn't the effect the play had on men, or perhaps male reviewers were not being honest. I think it would be unlikely if a play like this had an identical effect on women and on men.

In art, are we (in fact) trained to admire body language? An obviously aggressive or forceful technique? Loudness? These questions are being asked and dealt with. But they cannot be (and are not being) dealt with by assuming one absolute center of value.

In everybody's present historical situation, there can be, I believe, no single center of value and hence no absolute standards. That does not mean that assignment of values must be arbitrary or self-serving (like my students, whose defense of their poetry is "I felt it"). It does mean that for the linear hierarchy of good and bad it becomes necessary to substitute a multitude of centers of value, each with its own periphery, some closer to each other, some farther apart. The centers have been constructed by the historical facts of what it is to be female or black or working class or what-have-you; when we all live in the same culture, then it will be time for one literature. But that is not the case now. Nor is there one proper "style." There are many kinds of English (including Anglo-Indian) and before determining whether (for example) Virginia Woolf "writes better than" Zora Neale Hurston, it might be a good idea to decide who is addressing the mind's ear and who the mind's eye, in short, *what* English we're talking about. One is a kind of Latin, sculptured, solid, and distinct, into which comes the vernacular from time to time; the other is literary-as-vernacular: fluid, tone-shifting, visually fleeting, with the (impossible) cadences of the mind's ear constantly overriding the memory of the physical ear. (Woolf often writes sentences too long for any but the most experienced actor to speak as a single breath-unit.) If the one kind of English is too slow and too eternally set, is not the other kind too facile, too quick, always a little too thin?

There used to be an odd, popular, and erroneous idea that the sun revolved around the earth.

This has been replaced by an even odder, equally popular, and equally erroneous idea that the earth goes around the sun.

In fact, the moon and the earth revolve around a common center, and this commonly-centered pair revolves with the sun around another common center, except that you must figure in all the solar planets here, so things get complicated. Then there is the motion of the solar system with regard to a great many other objects, e.g., the galaxy, and if at this point you ask *what does the motion of the earth really look like from the center of the entire universe,* say (and where are the Glotolog?), the only answer is:

that it doesn't.

Because there isn't.

NOTES

1. Carolyn Kizer, "Pro Femina," in *No More Masks,* ed. Ellen Bass and Florence Howe (Garden City: Doubleday, 1973), p. 175.

2. Jean Baker Miller, *Toward a New Psychology of Women* (Boston: Beacon Press, 1975), pp. 47, 120, 8.

3. Lillian S. Robinson, "Who's Afraid of a Room of One's Own?" in *The Politics of Literature: Dissenting Essays on the Teaching of English,* ed. Louis Kampf and Paul Lauter (New York: Random House, 1973), pp. 376–77.

4. Annis Pratt, "The New Feminist Criticism," *College English* 32, no. 8 (May 1971): 877.

5. Lillian S. Robinson, "Dwelling in Decencies: Radical Criticism and the Feminist Perspective," *College English* 32, no. 8 (May 1971): 884–87.

6. Dolores Barracano Schmidt, "The Great American Bitch," *College English* 32, no. 8 (May 1971): 904.

7. Cynthia Griffin Wolff, "A Mirror for Men: Stereotypes of Women in Literature," in *Woman: An Issue,* ed. Edwards, et al., pp. 207–8, 217.

8. Judith Fetterley, MLA convention, December 1975, pp. 8–9.

9. McIntyre, *Khatru,* p. 119.

10. Ellen Cantarow, "Why Teach Literature?" in *The Politics of Literature,* ed. Kampf and Lauter, pp. 57–61.

11. Mary D. Garrard, "Feminism: Has It Changed Art History?" *Heresies* 4 (1978): 60.

12. Valerie Jaudon and Joyce Kozloff, "Art Hysterical Notions of Progress and Culture," *Heresies* 4 (1978): 38–42.

13. Adrienne Rich, *Poems Selected and New: 1950–1974* (New York: W. W. Norton, 1975), pp. 205–6.

14. In *By a Woman Writt,* ed. Goulianos, p. 99.

15. Adrienne Rich, "Conditions for Work: The Common World of Women," *Heresies* 3 (1977): 53–54.

16. Juhasz, *Naked and Fiery Forms,* pp. 139, 178–79.

17. Julia Penelope (Stanley), "Fear of *Flying?*", *Sinister Wisdom* 2 (1976): 59.

18. Juhasz, *Naked and Fiery Forms,* pp. 185, 201.

19. Virginia Woolf, *To the Lighthouse* (New York: Harcourt, Brace & World, 1927), p. 15.

20. Juhasz, *Naked and Fiery Forms,* p. 201.

21. Judy Chicago, *Through the Flower: My Life as a Woman Artist* (Garden City: Doubleday, 1975), p. 127.

TREASON OUR TEXT

feminist challenges to the literary canon

~~~~~~

> Successful plots have often had gunpowder in them. Feminist critics have gone so far as to take treason to the canon as our text.[1]
>
> JANE MARCUS

THE LOFTY SEAT OF CANONIZED BARDS (POLLOK, 1827)

As with many other restrictive institutions, we are hardly aware of it until we come into conflict with it; the elements of the literary canon are simply absorbed by the apprentice scholar and critic in the normal course of graduate education, without anyone's ever seeming to inculcate or defend them. Appeal, were any necessary, would be to the other meaning of "canon," that is, to established standards of judgment and of taste. Not that either definition is presented as rigid and immutable—far from it, for lectures in literary history are full of wry references to a benighted though hardly distant past when, say, the metaphysical poets were insufficiently appreciated or Vachel Lindsay was the most modern poet recognized in American literature. Whence the acknowledgment of a subjective dimension, sometimes generalized as "sensibility," to the category of taste. Sweeping modifications in the canon are said to occur because of changes in collective sensibility, but individual admissions and elevations from "minor" to "major" status tend to be achieved by successful critical promotion, which is to say, demonstration that a particular author does meet generally accepted criteria of excellence.

The results, moreover, are nowhere codified: they are neither set down in a single place, nor are they absolutely uniform. In the visual arts and in music, the cold realities of patronage, purchase, presentation in private and public collections, or performance on concert programs create the conditions for a work's canonical status or lack of it. No equivalent set of institutional arrangements exists for literature, however. The fact of publication and even the feat of remaining in print for generations, which are at least analogous to the ways in which pictures and music are displayed, are not the same sort of indicators; they represent less of an investment and hence less general acceptance of their canonicity. In the circumstances, it may seem somewhat of an exaggeration to speak of "the" literary canon, almost paranoid to call it an institution, downright hysterical to characterize that institution as restrictive. The whole business is so much more informal, after all, than any of these terms implies, the concomitant processes so much more gentlemanly. Surely, it is more like a gentlemen's agreement than a repressive instrument—isn't it?

But a gentleman is inescapably—that is, by definition—a member of a privileged class and of the male sex. From this perspective, it is probably quite accurate to think of the canon as an entirely gentlemanly artifact, considering how few works by non-members of that class and sex make it into the informal agglomeration of course syllabi, anthologies, and widely commented-upon "standard authors" that constitutes the canon as it is generally understood. For, beyond their availability on bookshelves, it is through the teaching and study— one might even say the habitual teaching and study—of certain works that they become institutionalized as canonical literature. Within that broad canon, moreover, those admitted but read only in advanced courses, commented upon only by more or less narrow specialists, are subjected to the further tyranny of "major" versus "minor."

For more than a decade now, feminist scholars have been protesting the apparently systematic neglect of women's experience in the literary canon, neglect that takes the form of distorting and misreading the few recognized female writers and excluding the others. Moreover, the argument runs, the predominantly male authors in the canon show us the female character and relations between the sexes in a way that both reflects and contributes to sexist ideology—an aspect of these classic works about which the critical tradition remained silent for generations. The feminist challenge, although intrinsically (and, to my mind, refreshingly) polemical, has not been simply a reiterated attack, but a series of suggested alternatives to the male-dominated membership and attitudes of the accepted canon. In this essay, I propose to examine these feminist alternatives, assess their impact on the standard canon, and propose some directions for further work. Although my emphasis in each section is on the substance of the challenge, the underlying polemic is, I believe, abundantly clear.

THE PRESENCE OF CANONIZED FOREFATHERS (BURKE, 1790)

Start with the Great Books, the traditional desert-island ones, the foundation of courses in the Western humanistic tradition. No women authors, of course, at all, but within the works thus canonized, certain monumental female images: Helen, Penelope, and Clytemnestra, Beatrice and the Dark Lady of the Sonnets, Bérénice, Cunégonde, and Margarete. The list of interesting female characters is enlarged if we shift to the Survey of English Literature and its classic texts; here, moreover, there is the possible inclusion of a female author or even several, at least as the course's implicit "historical background" ticks through and past the Industrial Revolution. It is a possibility that is not always honored in the observance. "*Beowulf* to Virginia Woolf" is a pleasant enough joke, but though lots of surveys begin with the Anglo-Saxon epic, not all that many conclude with *Mrs. Dalloway*. Even in the nineteenth century, the pace and the necessity of mass omissions may mean leaving out Austen, one of the Brontës, or Eliot. The analogous overview of American literary masterpieces, despite the relative brevity and modernity of the period considered, is likely to yield a similarly all-male pantheon; Emily Dickinson may be admitted—but not necessarily—and no one else even comes close.[2] Here again, the male-authored canon contributes to the body of information, stereotype, inference, and surmise about the female sex that is generally in the culture.

Once this state of affairs has been exposed, there are two possible approaches for feminist criticism. It can emphasize alternative readings of the tradition, readings that reinterpret women's character, motivations, and actions and that identify and challenge sexist ideology. Or it can concentrate on gaining admission to the canon for literature by women writers. Both sorts of work are being pursued, although, to the extent that feminist criticism has defined itself as a subfield of literary studies—as distinguished from an approach or method—it has tended to concentrate on writing by women.

In fact, however, the current wave of feminist theory began as criticism of certain key texts, both literary and paraliterary, in the dominant culture. Kate Millett, Eva Figes, Elizabeth Janeway, Germaine Greer, and Carolyn Heilbrun all use the techniques of essentially literary analysis on the social forms and forces surrounding those texts.[3] The texts themselves may be regarded as "canonical" in the sense that all have had significant impact on the culture as a whole, although the target being addressed is not literature or its canon.

In criticism that is more strictly literary in its scope, much attention has been concentrated on male writers in the American tradition. Books like Annette Kolodny's *The Lay of the Land* and Judith Fetterley's *The Resisting Reader* have no systematic, comprehensive equivalent in the criticism of British or European literature.[4] Both of these studies identify masculine values and imagery in a wide range of writings, as well as the alienation that is their consequence for women, men, and society as a whole. In a similar vein, Mary Ellmann's *Thinking About Women* examines ramifications of the tradition of "phallic criticism" as applied to writers of both sexes.[5] These books have in common with one another and with overarching theoretical manifestos like *Sexual Politics* a sense of having been betrayed by a culture that was supposed to be elevating, liberating, and one's own.

By contrast, feminist work devoted to that part of the Western tradition which is neither American nor contemporary is likelier to be more even-handed. "Feminist critics," declare Lenz, Greene, and Neely in introducing their collection of essays on Shakespeare, "recognize that the greatest artists do not necessarily duplicate in their art the orthodoxies of their culture; they may exploit them to create character or intensify conflict, they may struggle with, criticize, or transcend them."[6] From this perspective, Milton may come in for some censure, Shakespeare and Chaucer for both praise and blame, but the clear intention of a feminist approach to these classic authors is to enrich our understanding of what is going on in the texts, as well as how—for better, for worse, or for both—they have shaped our own literary and social ideas.[7] At its angriest, none of this reinterpretation offers a fundamental challenge to the canon as *canon;* although it posits new values, it never suggests that, in the light of those values, we ought to reconsider whether the great monuments are really so great, after all.

SUCH IS ALL THE WORLDE HATHE CONFIRMED AND AGREED UPON, THAT IT IS AUTHENTIQUE AND CANONICAL (T. WILSON, 1553)

In an evolutionary model of feminist studies in literature, work on male authors is often characterized as "early," implicitly primitive, whereas scholarship on female authors is the later development, enabling us to see women—the writers themselves and the women they write about—as active agents rather than passive images or victims. This implicit characterization of studies addressed to male writers is as inaccurate as the notion of an inexorable evolution. In fact, as the very definition of feminist criticism has come increasingly to mean scholarship and criticism devoted to women writers, work on the male tradition has continued. By this point, there has been a study of the female characters or the views on the woman question of every major—perhaps every known—author in Anglo-American, French, Russian, Spanish, Italian, German, and Scandinavian literature.[8]

Nonetheless, it is an undeniable fact that most feminist criticism focuses on women writers, so that the feminist efforts to humanize the canon have usually meant bringing a woman's point of view to bear by incorporating works by women into the established canon. The least threatening way to do so is to follow the accustomed pattern of making the case for individual writers one by one. The case here consists in showing that an already recognized woman author has been denied her rightful place, presumably because of the general devaluation of female efforts and subjects. More often than not, such work involves showing that a woman already securely established in the canon belongs in the first rather than the second rank. The biographical and critical efforts of R. W. B. Lewis and Cynthia Griffin Wolff, for example, have attempted to enhance Edith Wharton's reputation in this way.[9] Obviously, no challenge is presented to the particular notions of literary quality, timelessness, universality, and other qualities that constitute the rationale for canonicity. The underlying argument, rather, is that consistency, fidelity to those values, requires recognition of at least the few best and best-known women writers. Equally obviously, this approach does not call the notion of the canon itself into question.

WE ACKNOWLEDGE IT CANONLIKE, BUT NOT CANONICALL (BISHOP BARLOW, 1601)

Many feminist critics reject the method of case-by-case demonstration. The wholesale consignment of women's concerns and productions to a grim area bounded by triviality and obscurity cannot be compensated for by tokenism. True equity can be attained, they argue, only by opening up the canon to a much larger number of female voices. This is an endeavor that eventually brings basic aesthetic questions to the fore.

Initially, however, the demand for wider representation of female authors is substantiated by an extraordinary effort of intellectual reappropriation. The emergence of feminist literary study has been characterized, at the base, by scholarship devoted to the discovery, republication, and reappraisal of "lost" or undervalued writers and their work. From Rebecca Harding Davis and Kate Chopin through Zora Neale Hurston and Mina Loy to Meridel LeSueur and Rebecca West, reputations have been reborn or remade and a female counter-canon has come into being, out of components that were largely unavailable even a dozen years ago.[10]

In addition to constituting a feminist alternative to the male-dominated tradition, these authors also have a claim to representation in "the" canon. From this perspective, the work of recovery itself makes one sort of *prima facie* case, giving the lie to the assumption, where it has existed, that aside from a few names that are household words—differentially appreciated, but certainly well known— there simply has not been much serious literature by women. Before any aesthetic arguments have been advanced either for or against the admission of such works to the general canon, the new literary scholarship on women has demonstrated that the pool of potential applicants is far larger than anyone has hitherto suspected.

WOULD AUGUSTINE, IF HE HELD ALL THE BOOKS TO HAVE AN EQUAL RIGHT TO CANONICITY . . . HAVE PREFERRED SOME TO OTHERS? (W. FITZGERALD, TRANS. WHITAKER, 1849)

But the aesthetic issues cannot be forestalled for very long. We need to understand whether the claim is being made that many of the newly recovered or validated texts by women meet existing criteria or, on the other hand, that those criteria themselves intrinsically exclude or tend to exclude women and hence should be modified or replaced. If this polarity is not, in fact, applicable to the process, what are the grounds for presenting a large number of new female candidates for (as it were) canonization?

The problem is epitomized in Nina Baym's introduction to her study of American women's fiction between 1820 and 1870:

> Reexamination of this fiction may well show it to lack the esthetic, intellectual and moral complexity and artistry that we demand of great literature. I confess frankly that, although I have found much to interest me in these books, I have not unearthed a forgotten Jane Austen or George Eliot or hit upon the one novel that I would propose to set alongside *The Scarlet Letter*. Yet I cannot avoid the belief that "purely" literary criteria, as they have been employed to identify the best American works, have inevitably had a bias in favor of things male—in favor of, say, a whaling ship, rather than a sewing circle as a symbol of the human community. . . . While not claiming any lit-

erary greatness for any of the novels . . . in this study, I would like at least to begin to correct such a bias by taking their content seriously. And it is time, perhaps—though this task lies outside my scope here—to reexamine the grounds upon which certain hallowed American classics have been called great.[11]

Now, if students of literature may be allowed to confess to one Great Unreadable among the Great Books, my own *bête noire* has always been the white whale; I have always felt I was missing something in *Moby Dick* that is clearly there for many readers and that is there for me when I read, say, Aeschylus or Austen. So I find Baym's strictures congenial, at first reading. Yet the contradictory nature of the position is also evident on the face of it. Am I or am I not being invited to construct a (feminist) aesthetic rationale for my impatience with *Moby Dick*? Do Baym and the current of thought she represents accept "esthetic, intellectual and moral complexity and artistry" as the grounds of greatness, or are they challenging those values as well?

As Myra Jehlen points out most lucidly, this attractive position will not bear close analysis: "[Baym] is having it both ways, admitting the artistic limitations of the women's fiction . . . and at the same time denying the validity of the rulers that measure these limitations, disdaining any ambition to reorder the literary canon and, on second thought, challenging the canon after all, or rather challenging not the canon itself but the grounds for its selection."[12] Jehlen understates the case, however, in calling the duality a paradox, which is, after all, an intentionally created and essentially rhetorical phenomenon. What is involved here is more like the *agony* of feminist criticism, for it is the champions of women's literature who are torn between defending the quality of their discoveries and radically redefining literary quality itself.

Those who are concerned with the canon as a pragmatic instrument rather than a powerful abstraction—the compilers of more equitable anthologies or course syllabi, for example—have opted for an uneasy compromise. The literature by women that they seek—as well as that by members of excluded racial and ethnic groups and by working people in general—conforms as closely as possible to the traditional canons of taste and judgment. Not that it reads like such literature as far as content and viewpoint are concerned, but the same words about artistic intent and achievement may be applied without absurdity. At the same time, the rationale for a new syllabus or anthology relies on a very different criterion: that of truth to the culture being represented, the *whole* culture and not the creation of an almost entirely male white elite. Again, no one seems to be proposing—aloud—the elimination of *Moby Dick* or *The Scarlet Letter*, just squeezing them over somewhat to make room for another literary reality, which, joined with the existing canon, will come closer to telling the (poetic) truth.

The effect is *pluralist, at best,* and the epistemological assumptions underlying the search for a more fully representative literature are strictly empiricist: by including the perspective of women (who are, after all, half-the-population), we will know more about the culture as it actually was. No one suggests that there might be something in this literature itself that challenges the values and even the validity of the previously all-male tradition. There is no reason why the canon need speak with one voice or as one man on the fundamental questions of human experience. Indeed, even as an elite white male voice, it can hardly be said to do so. Yet a commentator like Baym has only to say "it is time, perhaps . . . to reexamine the grounds," *while not proceeding to do so*, for feminists to be accused of wishing to throw out the entire received culture. The argument could be more usefully joined, perhaps, if there *were* a current within feminist criticism that went beyond insistence on representation to consideration of precisely how inclusion of women's writing alters our view of the tradition. Or even one that suggested some radical surgery on the list of male authors usually represented.

After all, when we turn from the construction of pantheons, which have no *prescribed* number of places, to the construction of course syllabi, then something does have to be eliminated each time something else is added, and here ideologies, aesthetic and extra-aesthetic, do necessarily come into play. Is the canon and hence the syllabus based on it to be regarded as the compendium of excellence or as the record of cultural history? For there comes a point when the proponent of making the canon recognize the achievement of both sexes has to put up or shut up; either a given woman writer is good enough to replace some male writer on the prescribed reading list or she is not. If she is not, then either she should replace him anyway, in the name of telling the truth about the culture, or she should not, in the (unexamined) name of excellence. This is the debate that will have to be engaged and that has so far been broached only in the most "inclusionary" of terms. It is ironic that in American literature, where attacks on the male tradition have been most bitter and the reclamation of women writers so spectacular, the appeal has still been only to pluralism, generosity, and guilt. It is populism without the politics of populism.

TO CANONIZE YOUR OWNE WRITERS (POLIMANTERIA, 1595)

Although I referred earlier to a feminist counter-canon, it is only in certain rather restricted contexts that literature by women has in fact been explicitly placed "counter" to the dominant canon. Generally speaking, feminist scholars have been more concerned with establishing the existence, power, and significance of a specially female tradition. Such a possibility is adumbrated in the title of Patricia Meyer Spacks's *The Female Imagination;* however, this book's overview of selected themes and stages in the female life-cycle as treated by some women writers neither broaches nor (obviously) suggests an answer to the question whether there is a female imagination and what characterizes it.[13]

Somewhat earlier, in her anthology of British and American women poets, Louise Bernikow had made a more positive assertion of a continuity and connection subsisting among them.[14] She leaves it to the poems, however, to forge their own links, and, in a collection that boldly and incisively crosses boundaries between published and unpublished writing, literary and anonymous authorship, "high" art, folk art, and music, it is not easy for the reader to identify what the editor believes it is that makes women's poetry specifically "*women's*."

Ellen Moers centers her argument for a (trans-historical) female tradition upon the concept of "heroinism," a quality shared by women writers over time with the female characters they created.[15] Moers also points out another kind of continuity, documenting the way that women writers have read, commented on, and been influenced by the writings of other women who were their predecessors or contemporaries. There is also an unacknowledged continuity between the writer and her female reader. Elaine Showalter conceives the female tradition, embodied particularly in the domestic and sensational fiction of the nineteenth century, as being carried out through a kind of subversive conspiracy between author and audience.[16] Showalter is at her best in discussing this minor "women's fiction." Indeed, without ever making a case for popular genres as serious literature, she bases her arguments about a tradition more solidly on them than on acknowledged major figures like Virginia Woolf. By contrast, Sandra Gilbert and Susan Gubar focus almost exclusively on key literary figures, bringing women writers and their subjects together through the theme of perceived female aberration—in the act of literary creation itself, as well as in the behavior of the created persons or personae.[17]

Moers's vision of a continuity based on "heroinism" finds an echo in later feminist criticism that posits a discrete, perhaps even autonomous "women's culture." The idea of such a culture has been developed by social historians studying the "homosocial" world of nineteenth-century women.[18] It is a view that underlies, for example, Nina Auerbach's study of relationships among women in selected novels, where strong, supportive ties among mothers, daughters, sisters, and female friends not only constitute the real history in which certain women are conceived as living but function as a normative element as well.[19] That is, fiction in which positive relations subsist to nourish the heroine comes off much better, from Auerbach's point of view, than fiction in which such relations do not exist.

In contrast, Judith Lowder Newton sees the heroines of women's fiction as active, rather than passive, precisely because they do live in a man's world, not an autonomous female one.[20] Defining their power as "ability" rather than "control," she perceives "both a preoccupation with power and subtle power strategies" being exercised by the women in novels by Fanny Burney, Jane Austen, Charlotte Brontë, and George Eliot. Understood in this way, the female tradition, whether or not it in fact reflects and fosters a "culture" of its own, provides an alternative complex of possibilities for women, to be set beside the pits and pedestals offered by all too much of the Great Tradition.

CANONIZE SUCH A MULTIFARIOUS GENEALOGIE OF COMMENTS (NASHE, 1593)

Historians like Smith-Rosenberg and Cott are careful to specify that their generalizations extend only to white middle- and upper-class women of the nineteenth century. Although literary scholars are equally scrupulous about the national and temporal boundaries of their subject, they tend to use the gender term comprehensively. In this way, conclusions about "women's fiction" or "female consciousness" have been drawn or jumped to from considering a body of work whose authors are all white and comparatively privileged. Of the critical studies I have mentioned, only Bernikow's anthology, *The World Split Open*, brings labor songs, black women's blues lyrics, and anonymous ballads into conjunction with poems that were written for publication by professional writers, both black and white. The other books, which build an extensive case for a female tradition that Bernikow only suggests, delineate their subject in such a way as to exclude not only black and working-class authors but any notion that race and class might be relevant categories in the definition and apprehension of "women's literature." Similarly, even for discussions of writers who were known to be lesbians, this aspect of the female tradition often remains unacknowledged; worse yet, some of the books that develop the idea of a female tradition are openly homophobic, employing the word "lesbian" only pejoratively.[21]

Black and lesbian scholars, however, have directed much less energy to polemics against the feminist "mainstream" than to concrete, positive work on the literature itself. Recovery and reinterpretation of a wealth of unknown or undervalued texts has suggested the existence of both a black women's tradition and a lesbian tradition. In a clear parallel with the relationship between women's literature in general and the male-dominated tradition, both are by definition part of women's literature, but they are also distinct from and independent of it.

There are important differences, however, between these two traditions and the critical effort surrounding them. Black feminist criticism has the task of demonstrating that, in the face of all the obstacles a racist and sexist society has been able to erect, there is a continuity of black women who have written and written well. It is a matter of gaining recognition for the quality of the writing itself and respect for its principal subject, the lives and consciousness of black women. Black women's literature is also an element of black literature as a whole, where the recognized voices have usually been male. A triple imperative is therefore at work: establishing a discrete and significant black female tradition, then situating it within black literature and (along with the rest of that literature) within the common American literary heritage.[22] So far, unfortunately, each step toward integration has met with continuing exclusion. A black women's tradition has been recovered and revaluated chiefly through the efforts of black feminist scholars. Only some of that work has been accepted as part of either a racially mixed women's literature or a two-sex black literature. As for the gatekeepers of American literature in general, how many of them are willing to swing open the portals even for Zora Neale Hurston or Paule Marshall? How many have heard of them?

The issue of "inclusion," moreover, brings up questions that echo those raised by opening the male-dominated canon to women. How do generalizations about women's literature "as a whole" change when the work of black women is not merely added to but fully incorporated into that tradition? How does our sense of black literary history change? And what implications do these changes have for reconsideration of the American canon?

Whereas many white literary scholars continue to behave as if there were no major black woman writers, most are prepared to admit that certain well-known white writers were lesbians for all or part of their lives. The problem is getting beyond a position that says either "so *that's* what was wrong with her!" or, alternatively, "it doesn't matter who she slept with—we're talking about literature." Much lesbian feminist criticism has addressed theoretical questions about *which* literature is actually part of the lesbian tradition, all writing by lesbians, for example, or all writing by women about women's relations with one another. Questions of class and race enter here as well, both in their own guise and in the by now familiar form of "aesthetic standards." Who speaks for the lesbian community: the highly educated experimentalist with an unearned income or the naturalistic working-class autobiographer? Or are both the *same kind* of foremother, reflecting the community's range of cultural identities and resistance?[23]

A CHEAPER WAY OF CANON-MAKING IN A CORNER (BAXTER, 1639)

It is not only members of included social groups, however, who have challenged the fundamentally elite nature of the existing canon. "Elite" is a literary as well as a social category. It is possible to argue for taking all texts seriously as texts without arguments based on social oppression or cultural exclusion, and popular genres have therefore been studied as part of the female literary tradition. Feminists are not in agreement as to whether domestic and sentimental fiction, the female Gothic, the women's sensational novel functioned as instruments of expression, repression, or subversion, but they have successfully revived interest in the question as a legitimate cultural issue.[24] It is no longer automatically assumed that literature addressed to the mass female audience is necessarily bad because it is sentimental, or for that matter, sentimental because it is addressed to that audience. Feminist criticism has examined without embarrassment an entire literature that was previously dismissed solely because it was popular with women and affirmed standards and values associated with femininity. And proponents of the "continuous tradition" and "women's culture" positions have insisted that this material be placed beside women's "high" art as part of the articulated and organic female tradition.

This point of view remains controversial within the orbit of women's studies, but the real problems start when it comes into contact with the universe of canon formation. Permission may have been given the contemporary critic to approach a wide range of texts, transcending and even ignoring the traditional canon. But in a context where the ground of struggle—highly contested, moreover—concerns Edith Wharton's advancement to somewhat more major status, fundamental assumptions have changed very little. Can Hawthorne's "d——d mob of scribbling women" *really* be invading the realms so long sanctified by Hawthorne himself and his brother geniuses? Is this what feminist criticism or even feminist cultural history means? Is it—to apply some outmoded and deceptively simple categories—a good development or a bad one? If these questions have not been raised, it is because women's literature and the female tradition tend to be evoked as an autonomous cultural experience, not impinging on the rest of literary history.

WISDOME UNDER A RAGGED COATE IS SELDOME CANONICALL (CROSSE, 1603)

Whether dealing with popular genres or high art, commentary on the female tradition usually has been based on work that was published at some time and was produced by professional writers. But feminist scholarship has also pushed back the boundaries of literature in other directions, considering a wide range of forms and styles in which women's writing—especially that of women who did not perceive themselves as writers—appears. In this way, women's letters, diaries, journals, autobiographies, oral histories, and private poetry have come under critical scrutiny as evidence of women's consciousness *and expression.*

Generally speaking, feminist criticism has been quite open to such material, recognizing that the very conditions that gave many women the impetus to write made it impossible for their culture to define them as writers. This acceptance has expanded our sense of possible forms and voices, but it has challenged our received sense of appropriate style. What it amounts to is that if a woman writing in isolation and with no public audience in view nonetheless had "good"—that is, canonical—models, we are impressed with the strength of her text when she applies what she has assimilated about writing to her own experiences as a woman. If, however, her literary models were chosen from the same popular literature that some critics are now beginning to recognize as part of the female tradition, then she has not got hold of an expressive instrument that empowers her.

At the Modern Language Association meeting in 1976, I included in my paper the entire two-page autobiography of a participant in the Summer Schools for Women Workers held at Bryn Mawr in the first decades of the century. It is a circumstantial narrative in which events from the melancholy to the melodramatic are accumulated in a serviceable, somewhat hackneyed style. The anonymous "Seamer on Men's Underwear" had a unique sense of herself both as an individual and as a member of the working class. But was she a writer? Part of the audience was as moved as I was by the narrative, but the majority was outraged at the piece's failure to meet the criteria—particularly, the "complexity" criteria—of good art.

When I developed my remarks for publication, I wrote about the problems of dealing with an author who is trying too hard to write elegantly, and attempted to make the case that clichés or sentimentality need not be signals of meretricious prose and that ultimately it is honest writing for which criticism should be looking.[25] Nowadays, I would also address the question of the female tradition, the role of popular fiction within it, and the influence of that fiction on its audience. It seems to me that, if we accept the work of the professional "scribbling woman," we have also to accept its literary consequences, not drawing the lines at the place where that literature may have been the force that enabled an otherwise inarticulate segment of the population to grasp a means of expression and communication.

Once again, the arena is the female tradition itself. If we are thinking in terms of canon formation, it is the alternative canon. Until the aesthetic arguments can be fully worked out in the feminist context, it will be impossible to argue, in the general marketplace of literary ideas, that the novels of Henry James ought to give place—a *little* place, even—to the diaries of his sister Alice. At this point, I suspect most of our male colleagues would consider such a request, even in the name of Alice James, much less the Seamer on Men's Underwear, little more than a form of "reverse discrimination"—a concept to which some of them are already overly attached. It is up to feminist scholars, when we determine that this is indeed the right course to pursue, to demonstrate that such an inclusion would constitute a genuinely affirmative action for all of us.

The development of feminist literary criticism and scholarship has already proceeded through a number of identifiable stages. Its pace is more reminiscent of the survey course than of the slow processes of canon formation and revision, and it has been more successful in defining and sticking to its own intellectual turf, the female counter-canon, than in gaining general canonical recognition for Edith Wharton, Fanny Fern, or the female diarists of the Westward Expansion. In one sense, the more coherent our sense of the female tradition is, the stronger will be our eventual case. Yet the longer we wait, the more comfortable the women's literature ghetto—separate, apparently autonomous, and far from equal— may begin to feel.

At the same time, I believe the challenge cannot come only by means of the patent value of the work of women. We must pursue the questions certain of us have raised and retreated from as to the eternal verity of the received standards of greatness or even goodness. And, while not abandoning our new-found female tradition, we have to return to confrontation with "the" canon, examining it as a source of ideas, themes, motifs, and myths about the two sexes. The point in so doing is not to label and hence dismiss even the most sexist literary classics, but to enable all of us to apprehend them, finally, in all their human dimensions.

NOTES

1. Jane Marcus, "Gunpowder Treason and Plot," talk delivered at the School of Criticism and Theory, Northwestern University, colloquium "The Challenge of Feminist Criticism," November 1981. Seeking authority for the sort of creature a literary canon might be, I turned, like many another, to the *Oxford English Dictionary*. The tags that head up the several sections of this essay are a by-product of that effort rather than of any more exact and laborious scholarship.

2. In a survey of 50 introductory courses in American literature offered at 25 U.S. colleges and universities, Emily Dickinson's name appeared more often than that of any other woman writer: 20 times. This frequency puts her in a fairly respectable twelfth place. Among the 61 most frequently taught authors, only 7 others are women; Edith Wharton and Kate Chopin are each mentioned 8 times, Sarah Orne Jewett and Anne Bradstreet 6 each, Flannery O'Connor 4 times, Willa Cather and Mary Wilkins Freeman each 3 times. The same list includes 5 black authors, all of them male. Responses from other institutions received too late for compilation only confirmed these findings. See Paul Lauter, "A Small Survey of Introductory Courses in American Literature," *Women's Studies Quarterly* 9 (Winter 1981): 12. In another study, 99 professors of English responded to a survey asking which works of American literature published since 1941 they thought should be considered classics and which books should be taught to college students. The work mentioned

by the most respondents (59 citations) was Ralph Ellison's *Invisible Man*. No other work by a black appears among the top 20 that constitute the published list of results. Number 19, *The Complete Stories of Flannery O'Connor*, is the only work on this list by a woman. (*Chronicle of Higher Education*, September 29, 1982). For British literature, the feminist claim is not that Austen, the Brontës, Eliot, and Woolf are habitually omitted, but rather that they are by no means always included in courses that, like the survey I taught at Columbia some years ago, had room for a single nineteenth-century novel. I know, however, of no systematic study of course offerings in this area more recent than Elaine Showalter's "Women in the Literary Curriculum," *College English* 32 (May 1971): 855–62.

3. Kate Millett, *Sexual Politics* (Garden City, N.Y.: Doubleday, 1970); Eva Figes, *Patriarchal Attitudes* (New York: Stein & Day, 1970); Elizabeth Janeway, *Man's World, Woman's Place: A Study in Social Mythology* (New York: William Morrow, 1971); Germaine Greer, *The Female Eunuch* (New York: McGraw-Hill, 1971); Carolyn G. Heilbrun, *Toward a Recognition of Androgyny* (New York: Harper & Row, 1974). The phenomenon these studies represent is discussed at greater length in a study of which I am a co-author; see Ellen Carol DuBois, Gail Paradise Kelly, Elizabeth Lapovsky Kennedy, Carolyn W. Korsmeyer, and Lillian S. Robinson, *Feminist Scholarship: Kindling in the Groves of Academe* (Urbana: University of Illinois Press, 1985).

4. Annette Kolodny, *The Lay of the Land: Metaphor as Experience and History in American Life and Letters* (Chapel Hill: University of North Carolina Press, 1975); Judith Fetterley, *The Resisting Reader: A Feminist Approach to American Fiction* (Bloomington: Indiana University Press, 1978).

5. Mary Ellmann, *Thinking about Women* (New York: Harcourt, Brace & World, 1968).

6. Carolyn Ruth Swift Lenz, Gayle Greene, and Carol Thomas Neely, eds. *The Woman's Part: Feminist Criticism of Shakespeare* (Urbana: University of Illinois Press, 1980), p. 4. In this vein, see also Juliet Dusinberre, *Shakespeare and the Nature of Woman* (London: Macmillan, 1975); Irene G. Dash, *Wooing, Wedding, and Power: Women in Shakespeare's Plays* (New York: Columbia University Press, 1981).

7. Sandra M. Gilbert, "Patriarchal Poetics and the Woman Reader: Reflections on Milton's Bogey," *PMLA* 93 (May 1978): 368–82. The articles on Chaucer and Shakespeare in *The Authority of Experience: Essays in Feminist Criticism*, ed. Arlyn Diamond and Lee R. Edwards (Amherst: University of Massachusetts Press, 1977), reflect the complementary tendency.

8. As I learned when surveying fifteen years' worth of *Dissertation Abstracts* and MLA programs, much of this work has taken the form of theses or conference papers rather than books and journal articles.

9. See R. W. B. Lewis, *Edith Wharton: A Biography* (New York: Harper & Row, 1975); Cynthias Griffin Woolf, *A Feast of Words: The Triumph of Edith Wharton* (New York: Oxford University Press, 1977); see also Marlene Springer, *Edith Wharton and Kate Chopin: A Reference Guide* (Boston: G. K. Hall, 1976).

10. See, for instance, Rebecca Harding Davis, *Life in the Iron Mills* (Old Westbury, N.Y.: Feminist Press, 1972), with a biographical and critical Afterword by Tillie Olsen; Kate Chopin, *The Complete Works*, ed. Per Seyersted (Baton Rouge: Louisiana State University Press, 1969); Alice Walker, "In Search of Zora Neale Hurston," *Ms.*, March 1975, pp. 74–75; Robert Hemenway, *Zora Neale Hurston* (Urbana: University of Illinois Press, 1978): Zora Neale Hurston, *I Love Myself When I Am Laughing and Also When I Am Looking Mean and Impressive* (Old Westbury: Feminist Press, 1979), with introductory material by Alice Walker and Mary Helen Washington; Carolyn G. Burke, "Becoming Mina Loy," *Women's Studies* 7 (1979): 136–50; Meridel LeSueur, *Ripening* (Old Westbury: Feminist Press, 1981); on LeSueur, see also Mary McAnally, ed., *We Sing Our Struggle: A Tribute to Us All* (Tulsa, Okla.: Cardinal Press, 1982); *The Young Rebecca: Writings of Rebecca West, 1911–1917*, selected and introduced by Jane Marcus (New York: Viking Press, 1982).

The examples cited are all from the nineteenth and twentieth centuries. Valuable work has also been done on women writers before the Industrial Revolution. See Joan Goulianos, ed., *By a Woman Writt: Literature from Six Centuries by and About Women* (Indianapolis: Bobbs-Merrill, 1973); Mary R. Mahl and Helene Koon, eds., *The Female Spectator: English Women Writers before 1800* (Bloomington: Indiana University Press, 1977).

11. Nina Brown, *Women's Fiction: A Guide to Novels By and About Women in America, 1820–70* (Ithaca: Cornell University Press, 1978), pp. 14–15.

12. Myra Jehlen, "Archimedes and the Paradox of Feminist Criticism," *Signs* 6 (Summer 1981): 592.

13. Patricia Meyer Spacks, *The Female Imagination* (New York: Alfred A. Knopf, 1975).

14. *The World Split Open: Four Centuries of Women Poets In England and America, 1552–1950*, ed. and intro. Louise Bernikow (New York: Vintage Books, 1974).

15. Ellen Moers, *Literary Women: The Great Writers* (Garden City, N.Y.: Doubleday, 1976).

16. Elaine Showalter, *A Literature of Their Own: British Women Novelists from Brontë to Lessing* (Princeton, N.J.: Princeton University Press, 1977).

17. Sandra M. Gilbert and Susan Gubar, *Madwoman in the Attic: The Woman Writer and the Nineteenth-Century Literary Imagination* (New Haven, Conn.: Yale University Press, 1979).

18. Carroll Smith-Rosenberg, "The Female World of Love and Ritual: Relations Between Women in Nineteenth-Century America," *Signs* (Fall 1975): 1–30; Nancy F. Cott, *The Bonds of Womanhood: "Woman's Sphere" in New England, 1780–1830* (New Haven, Conn.: Yale University Press, 1977).

19. Nina Auerbach, *Communities of Women: An Idea in Fiction* (Cambridge, Mass.: Harvard University Press, 1979). See also Janet M. Todd, *Women's Friendship in Literature* (New York: Columbia University Press, 1980); Louise Bernikow, *Among Women* (New York: Crown, 1980).

20. Judith Lowder Newton, *Women, Power, and Subversion: Social Strategies in British Fiction* (Athens: University of Georgia Press, 1981).

21. On the failings of feminist criticism with respect to black and lesbian writers, see Barbara Smith, "Toward a Black Feminist Criticism," *The New Feminist Criticism*, ed. Elaine Showalter (New York: Pantheon, 1985), pp. 168–85; Mary Helen Washington, "New Lives and New Letters: Black Women Writers at the End of the Seventies," *College English* 43 (January 1981): 1–11; Bonnie Zimmerman, "What Has Never Been: An Overview of Lesbian Feminist Literary Criticism," in this volume, pp. 117–37.

22. See, e.g., Smith, "Toward a Black Feminist Criticism"; Barbara Christian, *Black Women Novelists: The Development of a Tradition, 1892–1976* (Westport, Conn.: Greenwood Press, 1980); Erlene Stetson, ed., *Black Sister: Poetry by Black American Women, 1764–1980* (Bloomington: Indiana University Press, 1981) and its forthcoming sequel; Gloria Hull, "Black Women Poets from Wheatley to Walker," in *Sturdy Black Bridges: Visions of Black Women in Literature*, ed. Roseann P. Bell et al. (Garden City, N.Y.: Anchor Books, 1979); Mary Helen Washington, "Introduction: In Pursuit of Our Own History," *Midnight Birds: Stories of Contemporary Black Women Writers* (Garden City, N.Y.: Anchor Books, 1980); the essays and bibliographies in *But Some of Us Are Brave: Black Women's Studies*, ed. Gloria Hull, Patricia Bell Scott, and Barbara Smith (Old Westbury: Feminist Press, 1982).

23. See Zimmerman, "What Has Never Been"; Adrienne Rich, "Jane Eyre: Trials of a Motherless Girl," *Lies, Secrets, and Silence: Selected prose, 1966–1978* (New York: W. W. Norton, 1979); Lillian Faderman, *Surpassing the Love of Men: Romantic Friendship and Love Between Women from the Renaissance to the Present* (New York: William Morrow, 1981); the literary essays in *Lesbian Studies*, ed. Margaret Cruikshank (Old Westbury, N.Y.: Feminist Press, 1982).

24. Some examples on different sides of the question are: Ann Douglas, *The Feminiza-*

tion of American Culture (New York: Alfred A. Knopf, 1976); Elaine Showalter, *A Literature of Their Own* and her article "Dinah Mulock Craik and the Tactics of Sentiment: A Case Study in Victorian Female Authorship," *Feminist Studies* 2 (May 1975): 5–23; Katherine Ellis, "Paradise Lost: The Limits of Domesticity in the Nineteenth-Century Novel," *Feminist Studies* 2 (May 1975): 55–65.

25. Lillian S. Robinson, "Working/Women/Writing," *Sex, Class, and Culture* (Bloomington: Indiana University Press, 1978), p. 252.

CASTE, CLASS, AND CANON

~~~~~~

I

I want to consider two problems in this essay, problems which—as I shall try to show—are closely related, although they may not at first glimpse appear to be. One problem, as my title suggests, involves the "canon" of literature—that is, the works from the past that we continue to read, teach, and write about. I am less concerned here with describing the history or features of a canon, or proposing alternatives to the canons we have inherited, than in exploring some of the factors that have continued to shape it. In particular, I want to consider how "class" and "caste," especially as they emerge in the work of literary analysis, shape canon. Examining the relationships of class, caste, and canon will, I believe, aid in understanding what we might mean by "feminist criticism," the second problem I wish to address. To frame that problem somewhat differently, how does—does?—the project of feminist criticism differ from other forms of literary analysis, and especially the formalisms rooted in the work of the New Critics? Can the question of the canon serve as a lens to help focus the project of feminist criticism?

I want to begin with an experience I had at the 1980 National Women's Studies Association convention during a session on the practice of feminist literary criticism. A group of young critics, all women, described to the audience how they met regularly at a library centrally located in their city, how they prepared and discussed various texts, and how they aided each other in developing their critical skills and range. They then handed out a poem and read it aloud, each one taking one section, and began discussing it by having each member of the group present a short statement about it. Then the audience was invited to join in the discussion. It seems like a reasonable process, and I am sure that—especially for those living in relatively isolated areas—it felt like the rushing of falls in the desert. But as the session wore on I found myself getting more and more restive, indeed rather irritated.

I tried to trace my growing anger. It seemed to derive from the dynamic of the panel itself; it had, I thought, to do with the *form* of criticism, almost all close analysis of text. I found myself, reluctantly, painfully, being drawn back into the tortured style of graduate-school competition: "can you top this?" As much macho as mind filled the room. Was this feminist criticism? I began to wonder: is the *form* of criticism value-free? Is critical technique simply a tool, like trigonometry? Well, is trigonometry value-free?

There was a second problem, the poem under consideration. As might be guessed, the poem was one from Adrienne Rich's *The Dream of a Common Language*. I want to be very clear about my comment here: I respect Adrienne Rich's poetry very much, and I particularly like that book. I think the poem that was under discussion quite a good poem indeed. But I remembered Deborah Hilty's questioning such a focus in a paper she prepared for a Midwest Modern Language Association conference. Why was it, she asked, that such panels always seem to take up poems by Adrienne Rich? Why not Judy Grahn or Susan Griffin? Or Vera Hall? or Malvina Reynolds? Or Gwendolyn Brooks? Adrienne Rich, by the way, was among the first to ask precisely that question.

Those two questions—about the technique of criticism and the subject for analysis—led, in turn, to a third question: what connection existed between the selection of the poem and the kind of criticism, really the kind of response, being undertaken? Or, to put it another way, how is *canon*—that is, selection—related to, indeed a *function of*, critical technique? That is the fundamental question I want to consider here—the relationship of style in criticism to the canon of literature. But before I address that question specifically, I want simply to outline the nest of questions implicit in the central one:

—Can the canon significantly change if we retain essentially the same critical techniques and priorities?
—Where do the techniques of criticism come from? Do they fall from the sky? Or do they arise out of social practice? And if the latter, from what social practice?
—Out of what social practice, from what values, did close analysis of complex texts arise?
—Do we perpetuate those values in pursuing the critical practice derived from them?
—Does such critical practice effectively screen from our appreciation, even our scrutiny, other worlds of creativity, of art?
—Are there other worlds of art out there whose nature, dynamics, values we fail to appreciate because we ask the wrong questions, or don't know what questions to ask? Or maybe shouldn't simply be asking questions?

Such questions clearly enough reveal the drift of my argument. But to summarize it: I think the literary canon as we have known it is a product in significant measure of our training in a male, white, bourgeois cultural tradition, including in particular the formal techniques of literary analysis. And further, that other cultural traditions provide alternate views about the nature and function of art, and of approaches to it. Indeed, if our concern is to change the canon "radically"—that is, at its roots—as distinct from grafting on to it a few odd branches, we must look at the full range of these alternate traditions. This argument holds, I believe, whether one is concerned with working-class art, the art of minority groups, or much of the art of women. For in significant ways, all "marginalized" groups have experiences and traditions distinct from those of the dominant majority. In this paper I focus initially on working-class and black traditions, both for their inherent interest and also because they provide us with revealing perspectives on women's art as well as on feminist criticism.

II

Raymond Williams' distinction between "working-class" and "bourgeois" culture provides a useful starting point:

> . . . a culture is not only a body of intellectual and imaginative work; it is also and essentially a whole way of life. The basis of a distinction between bourgeois and working-class culture is only secondarily in the field of intellectual and imaginative work. . . . The crucial distinguishing element in English life since the Industrial Revolution is not language, not dress, not leisure—for these indeed will tend to uniformity. The crucial distinction is between alternative ideas of the nature of social relationship.
>
> "Bourgeois" is a significant term because it marks that version of social relationship which we usually call individualism: that is to say, an idea of society as a neutral area within which each individual is free to pursue his own development and his own advantage as a natural right. . . . [Both] this idea [of service] and the individualistic idea can be sharply contrasted with the idea that we properly associate with the working class: an idea which, whether it is called communism, socialism, or cooperation regards society neither as neutral nor as protective, but as the positive means for all kinds of development, including individual development.[1]

Writing from a British perspective, Williams perhaps underestimates the significance of works of imagination in defining "working-class culture": "It is not proletarian art, or council houses, or a particular use of languages; it is, rather, the basic collective idea, and the institutions, manners, habits of thought and intentions which proceed from this."[2] But his fundamental point is critical to understand: while broad areas of the culture are common to the working class and the bourgeoisie, there remains a "crucial distinction . . . between alternative ideas of the nature of social relationship." This distinction significantly explains differing "institutions, manners, habits of thought and intentions." Distinct cultures also help shape ideas about the nature of art, its functions, the processes of its creation, the nature of the artist and of the artist's social role.

There is nothing very mysterious about this: people whose experiences of the world significantly differ, whose material conditions of life, whose formal and informal training, whose traditions, sometimes even whose language, differ—and especially people whose understanding of their own life-chances and opportunities, their "place"—differ will think about things differently, will talk about things differently, will value at least some things differently, will express themselves *to* different people *in* different ways and *about* different experiences, at least in some measure.

But that is all very abstract. We need to be somewhat more specific about differences between working-class and bourgeois art and literature. Unfortunately, there are relatively few cultural, and particularly literary, analyses of working-class materials (at least in Western practice). Martha Vicinus' *The Industrial Muse*[3] is a unique full-length study, but confined to Great Britain; Dan Tannacito examines the poetry of Colorado miners around the turn of this century;[4] an article of mine provides bibliographical and some theoretical approaches to working-class women's literature;[5] Lawrence Levine brilliantly explores the historical relationships between black culture and consciousness.[6] Even from this limited number of analyses certain features of working-class or "popular"[7] art emerge clearly. First, working-class art often is produced in group situations, rather than in the privacy of a study—or garret—and it is similarly experienced in the hall, the church, the work-site, the quilting bee, the picket line. It thus emerges from the experiences of a particular group of people facing particular problems in a particular time. Much of it is therefore not conceived as timeless and transcendent; rather, it might be called "instrumental." As Tannacito puts it, "the value of the Colorado miners' poetry derived exclusively from the use made of the poems by their audience. The audience was an immediate one. The objective [in writing] was inseparable from those goals" toward which the workers' lives directed them. Vicinus points out that working-class artists, themselves persuaded of the power of literature to "influence people's behavior," aimed to "persuade readers to adopt particular beliefs." Some recommended the bourgeois values embodied in the culture of what they thought of as their "betters." Others, despairing of social and political change, devoted their work to reassuring readers that their lives, debased as they might have become, still had value, and to providing at least some entertainment and consolation in an oppressive world. Many wrote to help change the status quo. Their work, Vicinus says, aimed "to arouse and focus social tension in order to channel it toward specific political actions." By "clarifying" or making vivid economic, social, and political relationships between working people and those who held power, they helped to "shape individual and class consciousness" and to "imbue a sense of class solidarity that encouraged working people to fight for social and political equality."

Tannacito provides a number of instances of the ways in which the miner poets tried to accomplish such goals. Poems of "praise," for example, explicitly tried to link heroic deeds of the past with the contemporary workers' community. Other poems sought to inspire specific forms of struggle, job actions, voting, boycotts. Miner poets, like working-class artists generally, wrote about the world they and their readers shared: the job, oppression by bosses, the militia and the scabs, a heritage of common struggle. They saw art not as a means for removing people from the world in which they lived—however desirable that might seem— nor as a device for producing "catharsis" or "stasis." Rather, art aimed to inspire consciousness about and actions within the world, to make living in that world more bearable, to extend experiences of that world, indeed to enlarge the world working people could experience. Thus, even as sophisticated an example of working-class fiction as Tillie Olsen's "Tell Me a Riddle" centrally concerns the problem of inspiring a new generation with the values, hopes, and images that directed the actions and aspirations of an earlier generation and that lie buried under the grit produced by forty years of daily life. Or consider how Morris Rosenfeld renders the experience of time-discipline in his work as a pants presser:

The Clock in the workshop,—it rests not a moment;
It points on, and ticks on: eternity—time;
Once someone told me the clock had a meaning,—
In pointing and ticking had reason and rhyme. . . .
At times, when I listen, I hear the clock plainly;—
The reason of old—the old meaning—is gone!
The maddening pendulum urges me forward
To labor and still labor on.
The tick of the clock is the boss in his anger.
The face of the clock has the eyes of the foe.
The clock—I shudder—Dost hear how it draws me?
It calls me "Machine" and it cries [to] me "Sew"![8]

Rosenfeld is concerned to capture, and to mourn, the passing in a particular historical moment of an older, less time-disciplined order of work, as well as the degradation of the worker to the status of machine. The poem gives names and pictures to the experiences that Rosenfeld and his fellow-workers encountered in moving from the shtetl to the sweatshops of the new world.

Working-class art thus functions to focus consciousness and to develop ideology, but it can also play a variety of other roles. Songs were used, especially by black slaves and nominally free laborers, to set the pace of work in a group and, at the same time, to relieve the tension and pent-up feelings born of oppressive labor. Leaders lined out a rhythm for hoeing, chopping, lifting bales, for rowing boats. At the same time, the songs spoke realistically about the shared labor, and more covertly, perhaps, about those exacting it.[9] Similarly, sorrow songs or spirituals served not only to express grief and to sustain hope in slavery, but they were also used as signals to prepare for escapes from it (see Levine, pp. 30–31). Similarly, during the Civil Rights movement of the 1950s and 1960s, what were originally church hymns underwent conversion to marching songs and sometimes means for triumphing over one's jailers.

Clearly, the conception of the functions of art are here very different from those propounded, say, by Aristotle, or Milton, or Coleridge—or formalist criticism, as I shall indicate in a moment. It is not, however, only conception or function which differ, but also form and technique, and even the manner of creation of much working-class art. In characterizing the distinctive qualities of the song styles of black slaves, Levine emphasizes "its overriding antiphony, its group nature, its pervasive functionality, its improvisational character, its strong relationship in performance to dance and bodily movements and expression. . . ." (p. 6). Some of these qualities are peculiar to styles derived from West African roots, but some are characteristic of other working-class cultures. New songs are often based upon old ones, and there is less concern with the unique qualities of art than with building variations upon tunes, themes, and texts well known in the community. For example, songs like "Hold the Fort" and "We Are Building a Strong Union," which began as gospel hymns, went through a series of metamorphoses in order to serve the needs of a diverse sequence of worker's organizations—in the case of the former, including the British transport workers, the Knights of Labor, and the Industrial Workers of the World. The Wobbly poet Joe Hill constructed some of his best-known songs as take-offs on Salvation Army hymns. The spiritual "Oh, Freedom" became one of the most popular songs of the Civil Rights movement; as the movement's militance increased, many singers changed the song's refrain from "Before I be a slave/ I be buried in my grave/ and go home to my Lord/ And be free" to "Before . . . grave/ And I'll fight for my right/ To be free."

In many ways, working-class art, like other elements in working-class life, is highly traditional; certainly innovative form is not a primary consideration and "make it new" a slogan which would be viewed with some suspicion. Similarly, working-class poetry and song, especially, but also tales and stories are often built around repeated elements—refrains, formulae, commonly-accepted assumptions about characters. Language, too, is often simpler, sometimes commonplace, certainly less "heightened" than that of "high-culture" verse. Many of these characteristics are common to literary forms rooted in oral art—made necessary by the exigencies of memory and improvisation. Some may arise from the artist's desire to avoid a fancy vocabulary unfamiliar to the audience, or esoteric images and allusions. Thus a poem like Rosenfeld's carefully works with materials as familiar to his readers as gaberdine was to him.

In some respects, as well, these characteristics are derived from the communal character of the creation of certain working-class art forms. One old former slave describes the creation of a "spiritual" in a pre-Civil War religious meeting in these words:

> I'd jump up dar and den and hollar and shout and sing and pat, and dey would all cotch de words and I'd sing it to some old shout song I'd heard 'em sing from Africa, and dey'd all take it up and keep at it, and keep a-addin' to it, and den it would be a spiritual.[10]

In such situations, the individual creator is generally less significant than the group; or, rather, to the extent that individuals are creators, they shape a common stock to new group purposes without diminishing or expropriating that common stock. The song leader in church is not asked to provide new hymns (much less copyright old ones) and would be looked at with suspicion if she did so. She is asked to reinvigorate a hymn that is known, perhaps to add something especially appropriate for the occasion.[11] The jazz musician may be admired for a new melody, but probably more important—at least until recently—is the ability to ring variations on melodies the listeners know and follow. I am emphasizing here the "folk," communal elements of working-class art, in some degree at the expense of art produced by self-conscious individual working-class artists. I do so because an approach through people's culture helps to focus certain distinctive qualities of working-class art, certain "centers of gravity," not so easily seen if one concentrates on the productions of separate artists. Yet, obviously, a continuum exists between songs, poems, and tales which are, so to speak, common property and works created primarily by individual imaginations.

But what is critical here is precisely the relationship between individual and community. Levine, for example, directly connects the *form* of the spiritual with the underlying social reality of black slave life:

> Just as the process by which the spirituals were created allowed for simultaneous individual and communal creativity, so their very structure provided

simultaneous outlets for individual and communal expression. The overriding antiphonal structure of the spirituals—the call and response pattern which Negroes brought with them from Africa and which was reinforced in America by the practice of lining out hymns—placed the individual in continual dialogue with his community, allowing him at one and the same time to preserve his voice as a distinct entity and to blend it with those of his fellows.[12]

I would carry the argument in a slightly different direction by suggesting that one center of gravity of working-class art is its high level of integration of creator and audience. Works often have their origin, as well as their being, in situations which do not absolutely distinguish active performer/artist from passive audience. Or when the distinction is relatively clearer, the artist's "product" is offered *not* primarily for its *exchange* value (money for that song or painting), but for its *use* in the lives of the people to whom it is directed. A moving example is provided by the Kentucky mountain songs sung at the funeral of "Jock" Yablonski and recorded with great majesty in the film *Harlan County, U.S.A.*

In a larger sense, all working-class art (perhaps all art[13]) must be explored precisely in terms of its *use*. Partly that is a function of marginality itself: the struggle for existence and dignity necessarily involves all available resources, including art. But partly, I think, this phenomenon is explained by the fundamental character of working-class culture, what Williams called "solidarity." It is not simply a slogan or an abstraction that happens to appeal to many people who work. It is, rather, a way of describing the culture of people who have been pushed together into workplaces and communities where survival and growth enforce interdependence. In this context, the work of the artist—while it may in some respects be expressive and private—remains overwhelmingly functional in his or her community. And an approach to it cannot strip it of this context without ripping away its substance.

My argument began from the premise that the conditions of life of working-class people have produced ideas about social relationships crucially distinct from those of the bourgeoisie. This distinction shaped differing institutions, manners, and ideas about culture and art. In order to approach working-class culture, then, we must begin not with presuppositions about what literature *is* and is *not*, or what is valuable in it or not, but rather by asking in what forms, on what themes, in what circumstances, and to what *ends* do working people speak and sing and write and signify to each other. We must, in other words, discover the distinctive rules and measures of working-class art and thus the critical strategies and tools appropriate to them.

"Are you saying," someone might object, "that the rules and measures—the critical tools—we now possess are invalid, somehow biased or irrelevant?" Here, indeed, is the nub of the matter. For we do approach culture with certain presuppositions, frameworks, touchstones which we learn and which we learn to valorize. I have tried here to state as neutrally as I can certain of the qualities and origins of working-class art. I have not tried to lay a spiritual like "Roll, Jordan" or a poem like Rosenfeld's alongside, say, Donne's "A Valediction: forbidding mourning" in order to evaluate one in relation to another, or all against some "universal" standard of measurement. For the central issue is not which is "better," but what we mean by "better." And I am sure it is clear by now that I believe such standards of judgment, which shape the canon, to be rooted in assumptions derived from class and caste about the techniques, qualities, and especially the functions of art.

I do not want to be misleading here: I do not believe that somewhere out there is a working-class poet, ignored through bourgeois prejudice, who actually wrote better metaphysical poems than Donne or more singular odes than Shelley. No more do I think that a factory organized along truly socialist lines will be more "efficient" and "productive" than a capitalist factory; capitalists often find means to do rather well what it is they want to do—in this case to squeeze as much profit from workers as they can. But that does not necessarily make for a humane, safe, creative, or socially responsible workplace. The goals are different; the values and thus the priorities different. On the other hand, it has been demonstrated that there are forgotten black and white women writers who wrote fiction as good in traditional terms as that of many of the white men with whom we are familiar. As Williams pointed out, there are vast shared areas of culture. My main point, however, is that if there probably are no working-class metaphysical poets, neither did Donne write verses for "Roll, Jordan." And if "Roll, Jordan" does not demonstrate the fine elaboration of complex language to be found in "A Valediction," it is also the fact that none of Donne's poems—not all of them together I dare say—has served to sustain and inspire so many thousands of oppressed people. What, finally, is art about?

III

Mr. Allen Tate had an answer for us. "Good poetry," he writes in "Tension in Poetry," "is a unity of all the meanings from the furthest extremes of intension and extension. . . . the meaning of poetry is its 'tension,' the full organized body of all the extension and intension that we can find in it." [15] In the same essay he attacks Edna St. Vincent Millay's "Justice Denied in Massachusetts," a poem written in gloomy reaction to the execution of Sacco and Vanzetti.

> Let us abandon then our gardens and go home
> And sit in the sitting-room.
> Shall the larkspur blossom or the corn grow under this cloud?
> Sour to the fruitful seed
> Is the cold earth under this cloud,
> Fostering quack and weed, we have marched upon but cannot conquer;
> We have bent the blades of our hoes against the stalks of them.
>
> Let us go home, and sit in the sitting-room.
> Not in our day
> Shall the cloud go over and the sun rise as before,
> Beneficent upon us
> Out of the glittering bay,
> And the warm winds be blown inward from the sea
> Moving the blades of cord
> With a peaceful sound.

"These lines," Tate claims, "are mass language: they arouse an affective state in one set of terms, and suddenly an object quite unrelated to those terms gets the benefit of it." The Millay poem, he continues,

> is no doubt still admired, by persons to whom it communicates certain feelings about social justice, by persons for whom the lines are the occasion of feelings shared by them and the poet. But if you do not share those feelings, as I happen not to share them in the images of desiccated nature, the lines and even the entire poem are impenetrably obscure.[16]

It once occurred to me that Tate might be using "obscure" in a Pickwickian sense, for whatever one might think of the Millay poem it seems rather less obscure than Tate's critique. But then, from his point of view, "communication in poetry" is a fallacy. The poet is "not responsible to society for a version of what it thinks it is or what it wants." The poet is responsible to his conscience. And he (the pronoun remains Tate's) is responsible "for the virtue proper to him as poet, for his special *arête:* for the mastery of a disciplined language which will not shun the full report of reality conveyed to him by his awareness: he must hold, in Yeats' great phrase, 'reality and justice in a single thought.'"[17] Elsewhere Tate approvingly quotes I. A. Richards to the effect that poetry is "complete knowledge": "The order of completeness that it achieves in the great works of the imagination is not the order of experimental completeness aimed at by the positivist sciences. . . . For the completeness of *Hamlet* is not of the experimental order, but of the experienced order; it is, in short, of the mythical order."[18]

Given this self-contained idea of poetry, it is not surprising that formalist critics like Tate should develop techniques emphasizing intense analysis of a poem's language and its "tensions." Or that they should conceive the primary task of the "man of letters" as preserving "the integrity, the purity, and the reality of language wherever and for whatever purpose it may be used." "He must," Tate goes on to explain, approach this task "through the letter—the letter of the poem, the letter of the politician's speech, the letter of the law; for the use of the letter is in the long run our one indispensible test of the actuality of our experience."[19] How different this conservative, monitory role from that staked out for the American Scholar by Emerson. Besides, is it really necessary to talk about the taste of rotting fruit to test its actuality? However that might be, Tate's ultimate vision of the "man of letters" asserts an even weightier function:

> . . . the duty of the man of letters is to supervise the culture of language, to which the rest of culture is subordinate, and to warn us when our language is ceasing to forward the ends proper to man. The end of social man is communion in time through love, which is beyond time.[20]

The man of letters thus stands a priest of language, linking society and culture with the transcendent.

But why devote such attention to these ideas, or once again pillory an often-abused guru of the New Criticism? Has not criticism passed beyond the exegetical stage? In theory, it has. In practice, however, and especially in the common practice of the *classroom*, the dominant mode of procedure remains exploring the "furthest extremes of intension and extension" we may find in a text. And the texts we prefer are, on the whole, those which invite such *explication*. One or another version of formalism remains, in short, the meat and potatoes of what men—and women—of letters stir up for our students and readers. And while Tate's ecclesiastical trappings may have been doffed as rather too quaint and burdensome, something of the incense lingers in the justification for what we do. Thus it seems to me important to ask what social and political values generate the forms of criticism and its justifications we find in Tate and his fellows.

There is a second, perhaps more fundamental reason for examining Tate's ideas. He and his New Critical peers were the first generation to pose what became, and still is, the dominant paradigm of academic criticism. I want to suggest that, regardless of form, academic criticism in the past half century has retained a common set of social and political roots and a consistent function. An image may help flesh this assertion. In *Invisible Man* Ellison pictures a statue of the "Founder," his hands holding the edges of a veil, which covers the face of the black youth kneeling before him. The speaker of the book comments that it is never clear whether the Founder is lifting the veil from the boy's face, or holding it ever more firmly in its place. That ambiguous image may stand for the academic critic; is he (I want to retain the overwhelmingly appropriate pronoun) offering enlightenment by lifting the veil or holding the student in a kind of darkness?

In feminist pedagogy a distinction has developed between two forms of teaching: one, which often involves the display of a specialized vocabulary, has the tendency to overwhelm students, paralyzing them before the erudition of the teacher; another, seen as developing from the equalitarian ideals of feminism, tries to legitimize the student's own responses to a text, to history, to experience as the starting points for analysis and thus understanding. To be sure, it has often been easy to overstate this distinction between—in crude shorthand—lecturer as authority and discussion leader as participant, to convert pedagogical tendencies into behavioral absolutes; indeed, to elevate difference in style into fiercely-held educational principles. For all that rhetoric has burdened us with inflation of difference, the differences remain, more perhaps as foci or what I have called "centers of gravity" than as differences in kind. Analogous "centers of gravity" can, I think, be charted in criticism. Is the objective result of criticism to help readers formulate, understand, and develop their own responses? To open a text to a common reader? Or is it to make the reader feel excluded from the critical enterprise, sense his or her own responses to a work as essentially irrelevant to the process of its exploration? The latter result has, it seems to me, the concomitant effect—or, perhaps I should say, underlying motive—of confirming the position, the cultural power, of the critic himself—even while, as was historically the case in the 1920s and 1930s, the real social authority of the class from which "men of letters" were drawn was being eroded. In fact, I want to argue, the major project of criticism as it developed from patriarchs like Tate was the confirmation of the authoritative position, at least with respect to culture, of the Man of Letters and his caste. And while the *forms* of criticism have changed—from New Criticism to structuralism to poststructuralism—the *functions* of academic criticism seem to me to have remained constant, related primarily to the status, power, and careers of critics.[21]

There is, furthermore, an awful logic to the changes in form that derives precisely from the persistence of function. At the beginning, formal analysis did—as it still can—help illuminate texts. And as differing kinds of analyses developed, these too added to the illumination, albeit with increasing marginality. But a law of diminishing returns necessarily begins to operate with the thirtieth explication of "A Valediction," or the eighteenth lick of ice-cream, and the eye of the beholder starts to shift from the qualities of the text to the qualities of the comment, from the poet to the critic; with the exhaustion of the ways of looking at a pigeon, we begin to observe the antics of the pigeon-watchers. And thus emerges a speculative criticism claiming equality with the literary texts, once the objects to be illuminated, and framed in a language increasingly impenetrable to the common reader. The project of such criticism *is* its politics.

This is not to say that academic critics are by character and inclination conscious elitists; my point is not, in any case, characterological. The very momentum, not to say corpulence, of academic criticism hides its political origins. But in sad fact, cultural institutions move in the directions established by their initial political impetus unless or until they are redirected by the intervention of a new political force—like the social and cultural movements of the 1960s and 1970s. Thus, to understand contemporary academic criticism we must examine its roots and its values as these appear in their rudimentary form.

These values emerge into severe profile from Tate's account of the limitations of southern literature:

> But the abolition of slavery did not make for a distinctively Southern literature. We must seek the cause of our limitations elsewhere. It is worth remarking, for the sake of argument, that chattel slavery is not demonstrably a worse form of slavery than any other upon which an aristocracy may base its power and wealth. That *African* chattel slavery was the worst groundwork conceivable for the growth of a great culture of European pattern, is scarcely at this day arguable. . . . The distance between white master and black slave was unalterably greater than that between white master and white serf after the destruction of feudalism. The peasant *is* the soil. The Negro slave was a barrier between the ruling class and the soil. If we look at aristocracies in Europe, say in eighteenth-century England, we find at least genuine social classes, each carrying on a different level of the common culture. But in the Old South, and under the worse form of slavery that afflicts both races today, genuine social classes do not exist. The enormous "difference" of the Negro doomed him from the beginning to an economic status purely: he has had much the same thinning influence upon the class above him as the anonymous city proletariat has had upon the culture of industrial capitalism. . . .
>
> The white man got nothing from the Negro, no profound image of himself in terms of the soil. . . . But the Negro, who has long been described as a responsibility, got everything from the white man. The history of French culture, I suppose, has been quite different. The high arts have been grafted upon the peasant stock. We could graft no new life upon the Negro; he was too different, too alien.[22]

It is not my intent to comment upon the less than genteel racism, the abysmal cultural chauvinism, or even the simple historical ignorance of this passage. But it does make amply clear the elitist soil in which Tate's formalist ideas of poetry and the "man of letters" are rooted. The New Criticism is the fruit—strange fruit—of such plants. But that metaphor is rather too easy. In plain fact, criticism which makes all-important the special languages that specially-trained critics share with specially-cultivated poets is finally a means for defending special privilege. It is a version of what Raymond Williams calls the "dominative" use of language.

Meridel LeSueur, who studied with Tate and others at the University of Minnesota, has a different way of drawing the connection between the politics and the critical style of these men of letters:

> It was just like being bitten every morning by a black spider—paralysis set in. They taught the structure of the short story this way: you run around Robin Hood's barn, have two or three conclusions, and then come to a kind of paralysis. Ambiguity is a very seductive idea.[23]

The paralysis of ambiguity in a world crying for change fits well with "Reactionary Essays on Poetry and Ideas."

I am not suggesting that formalist critics are necessarily racists or political reactionaries in their personal outlooks. Or that every formalist move necessarily builds higher the bulwarks of bourgeois culture. But it seems to me natural to suspect a project with such roots. And thus (returning at last to the nest of questions I raised many pages back) to propose that, indeed, critical tactics carry with them rather more ideological baggage than we might at first have suspected.

In the opening section of *Stealing the Language: The Emergence of Women's Poetry in America* (1986), Alicia Ostriker has analyzed how that ideology operated to marginalize women poets. She cites, among other documents, John Crowe Ransom's essay on Millay,[24] which nicely illustrates how the formalist aesthetic principles Ransom shared with Tate worked in practice. Ransom writes:

> Man distinguishes himself from woman by intellect, but he should keep it feminized. He knows he should not abandon sensibility and tenderness, though perhaps he has generally done so. . . . But the problem does not arise for a woman. Less pliant, safer as a biological organism, she remains fixed in her famous attitudes, and is indifferent to intellectuality. I mean, of course, comparatively indifferent; more so than a man. (p. 78)

Thus, from Ransom's point of view, Millay's is a lesser "vein of poetry," "spontaneous, straightforward in diction," with "transparently simple" structures and "immediate" effects (pp. 103–5). Indeed, a good deal of Ransom's essay is devoted to showing how, in effect, Millay's "excitingly womanlike" poems display little analyzable "intention" or "extension," and thus are not intellectually challenging. It seems to me clear how in these works patriarchy and racism emerge into critical categories and a methodology that helped place the work of most white women and black writers behind the veil.

Perhaps the final step in the elevation of this critical tradition into orthodoxy was that taken by Lionel Trilling. Tate and Ransom were in some sense defensive, protecting what remained of the privilege of the "man of letters" and his class against the incursions of the crowd, and often cloaking their political sentiments with the mantle of cultural appraisal. Trilling, by contrast, mounts an offensive by situating matters of critical opinion precisely at "the dark and bloody crossroads where literature and politics meet." By so doing, he converts the question of canon into a question of political judgment and moral values. He is thus able to train on that already "bloody crossroads" the devastating weapons of Cold-War rhetoric. His method is perhaps best illustrated in his two-part essay "Reality in America."[25]

Between the writing of the first section of the essay (*Partisan Review,* January-February, 1940) and the second (*The Nation,* April 20, 1946) intruded, among other things, the Second World War, the Holocaust, the first A-bombs, and—perhaps most important to its point—the emergence of the Cold War and the beginnings of anticommunist hysteria in the United States. Part I is primarily an attack on the literary taste and cultural values of V. L. Parrington. Nina Baym has complained that in his search for the "essence" of American culture Trilling offers no *aesthetic* basis for his literary preferences; nor does he present any "notion of culture more valid than Parrington's."[26] While it is true that in this part of the essay Trilling does not develop his aesthetic standards, he displays a clear preference for artists who, in his view, "contain a large part of the dialectic [of cultural struggle or debate] within themselves, their meaning and power lying in their contradictions. . . ." Indeed, Trilling goes on, in the freighted, redundant language of thirties' political debate, "they contain within themselves . . . the very essence of the culture, and the sign of this is that they do not submit to serve the ends of any one ideological group or tendency" (p. 20). The non-partisanship of artists, their refusal to "submit" to any "group," to "serve" any ideology, here becomes the flag of their cultural significance, an idea which certainly held sway for much of the quarter century following Trilling's presentation of it in, can we say "ironically," *Partisan.* How artists differ from the rest of us in embodying the contradictions of our culture, Trilling does not say; in any case, as later becomes clear, his point is to mark out, like Tate, the difference between how "true" artists and critics think and how "the modern crowd thinks when it decides to think" (p. 28).

To be sure, as Baym points out, Trilling's rhetoric masks the real partisanship of a writer like Hawthorne, even while it provides one basis for devaluing the work, say, of Harriet Beecher Stowe. To detach ourselves from Trilling's judgments, his canon, it has not proved sufficient to demonstrate that Hawthorne and Stowe were both, in their differing ways, partisan; rather, I think, we have had to bring into question his idea that detachment from ideology or "tendency" is a necessary artistic virtue, much less a philosophically credible notion.

But non-partisanship is finally rather a negative criterion of value in art. In part II of the essay, as Bruce Spear has shown, Trilling does indeed present a crucial line of aesthetic defense for his canon, symbolized by Henry James, whom he poses against Theodore Dreiser and his defenders.[27] James, he claims, "was devoted to an extraordinary moral perceptiveness," powerfully aware of "tragedy, irony, and multitudinous distinctions"; but above all, James' work shows "electric qualities of mind, through a complex and rapid imagination and with a kind of authoritative immediacy" (pp. 22, 25). By contrast, Trilling tells us, even Dreiser's defenders acknowledge that his ideas are often unformed, his moral perceptions crude, and his style, above all his style, clumsy. It is in style, finally, that Trilling locates quality: "The great novelists have usually written very good prose, and what comes through even a bad translation is exactly the power of mind that made the well-hung sentence of the original text. In literature style is so little the mere clothing of thought—need it be insisted on at this late date?— that we may say that from the earth of the novelist's prose spring his characters, his ideas, and even his story itself" (p. 27). The failure of Dreiser's liberal defenders—Charles Beard, Granville Hicks, Edward Berry Burgum, and above all F. O. Matthiessen—at least according to Trilling, derives precisely from that form of "progressive" politics which places a concern for "realism" and usefulness above "electric qualities of mind." Or, rather,

> The liberal judgment of Dreiser and James goes back of politics, goes back to the cultural assumptions that make politics. We are still haunted by a kind of political fear of the intellect which Tocqueville observed in us more than a century ago. American intellectuals, when they are being consciously American or political, are remarkably quick to suggest that an art which is marked by perception and knowledge, although all very well in its way, can never get us through gross dangers and difficulties. And their misgivings become the more intense when intellect works in art as it ideally should, when its processes are vivacious and interesting and brilliant. (p. 23)

With his sliding "we"s and "us"s, his use of "political" and "American" as disparagements, his erection of James upon a mound of melioratives, Trilling is attempting to obliterate the fundamental distinction between, on the one hand, suspicion of art that is predominantly artful, precious, self-enclosed, and, on the other, gross anti-intellectualism. But for us, what his argument comes to is this: intellect displayed in brilliance of style displaces whatever other criteria might be posed for the evaluation of art.

With this argument we have returned to our central issue: the relationship of canon and critical practice, the "crossroads" of literature and politics. What Trilling is about in this essay is hanging round the necks of Dreiser's defenders (and James' doubters) not only his crudities of style, but his presumably consequent anti-Semitism, his late religiosity, his later conversion to communism. In short, as Spear convincingly documents, Trilling is deeply engaged in a struggle over cultural politics, in particular with Matthiessen. The stake was not merely one's preference for the style, the subjects, or even the values of James or Dreiser— even if that constituted the universe of choice. At stake was whether there would be room in the canon, in legitimate critical discourse, in the American university or, indeed, polity for the kinds of political commitments Matthiessen and other progressives tried to maintain, and which they recognized, along with his many failings, in Dreiser. Trilling's victory, and it was that, at least then, placed at the center of literary value, and thus of literary study, those figures like James who best exemplified his ideas of complexity of imagination and brilliance of surface, who displayed in their prose the cultural "tensions" Trilling took to exemplify American intellectual history. What he accomplished, or rather what his accomplishment represents, was at once the legitimation of textual analysis by critics sensitive to the electric qualities of the Jameses as the correct form of literary study and the exiling of those forms of cultural analysis used by "progressives"

from Parrington to Matthiessen to the outskirts of literary, indeed political, respectability. To think like them, to write like Dreiser, to acknowledge one's ideology, to be partisan was not merely vulgar; it had become by 1946 a sign that you
were a cultural risk, unsafe to be determining the texts from which tomorrow's
intellectual leaders would draw their images of the world.

IV

By this long and perhaps burdensome route we return to that room in Lawrence,
Kansas, that panel on feminist criticism, and maybe even my growing anger. For
I came to that panel with the more or less the ideas I've outlined. It seemed to
me that while there are broad shared areas, the social experiences and the cultures of women and men diverge at significant points. I do not have ready terms,
like "individualism" and "solidarity," to characterize the distinct organizing
principles, but it seemed quite plain that significantly diverse experiences will
produce significantly diverse cultural forms, among men and women, just as
among blacks and whites, working people and bourgeoisie. And that, therefore,
the application to women's art of principles and standards derived almost exclusively from the study of men's art will tend to obscure, even hide, and certainly
undervalue what women have created. Indeed, the application of critical standards and tactics derived from white, male—not to say racist and elitist—culture
not only obscures female accomplishment, on the one side, but reinforces the
validity of those critical standards and what they represent, on the other. Thus I
thought that panel's project was grafting Adrienne Rich's poem onto Allen Tate's
stock—to borrow a Tate metaphor—rather than joining the dialogue in which
The Dream of a Common Language and *The Common Woman* poems both participate.
It is not that the panelists shared Tate's and Ransom's values; rather, in pursuing
their techniques, the panel seemed to me to reinforce the structures of academic
elitism.

I hope this will not be misconstrued into an odd shorthand report like "Lauter
says there's a peculiar female sensibility and that criticism is male, so feminists
should be doing something else, as yet unspecified." I do *not* know if there is
such a thing as a female sensibility. "Sensibility" is a psychological category and
is approachable, I think, only through individuals. I am talking not of sensibility
but of *culture,* which is a social category. It cannot be used to predict individual
behavior, but it is critical to understanding how we perceive, indeed what we
look at, as well as how we conceive the structures of language we call works
of art.

Formalist critics, I am suggesting, are trapped within their culture, restricted
in what they look at and by who looks. Why? First, because they have derived
much of their cultural data from a narrow base, largely art composed by white
Western men (as Tate's comment on southern culture reveals). They have not
adequately considered art from outside that tradition, except, as it were, after
the fact, after they had donned their theoretical spectacles. Also these spectacles
have been ground by the social and economic pressures which characteristically
mold the residents of academe. For criticism is not solely a pure activity of mind,
an expression of altruism directed toward revealing truth, or even the play of in-

tellect upon the surfaces of language. It may upon occasion be these. It will also in some measure be an ideology constructed in order to insure and enhance the social and economic position of the critic and his class—even occasionally, now, "her" class. To put it another way, the connection we have seen of New Critical methodology with reactionary politics is no accident, nor is the obscurity of, say, *Diacritics*. An adequate theory of criticism can only be developed by fully considering the art produced by women, by working people, and by national minorities; further, such art needs to be understood in light of its own principles, not simply in terms and categories derived from so-called "high culture," or on the basis of the imperatives imposed by careerism or reigning institutional priorities.

Thus the first task in the project of feminist criticism seems to me the recovery of lost works by women, and the restoration of the value of disdained genres. In part a restorative literary history is required simply for the sake of intellectual honesty. But more important, as I have suggested, is the imperative for broadening the "text milieu" from which we derive critical and historical propositions. Now this task has considerably been advanced in the last decade, as witness, on the one hand, the publications of feminist and university presses and, on the other, the recent issuance of Gilbert and Gubar's *Norton Anthology of Literature by Women* and the new *Heath Anthology of American Literature* (two volumes). But the work is by no means complete nor, for a number of reasons, is it likely soon to be. For example, women writers of early and mid-nineteenth-century America are known to most readers, even most academics, mainly secondhand, through such useful studies as Nina Baym's.[28] In fact, writers of substance like Caroline Kirkland, Lydia Maria Child, and Alice Cary are seldom read, in part because their books have not until recently been reissued for over a hundred years,[29] in part because they have not been given the legitimation of academic study even to the degree that someone as marginal as William Gilmore Simms has been. Most important, the modern outlook, and particularly modern criticism, has been out of sympathy with the sensibilities displayed in the work of such authors. I shall have more to say about that in a moment. Suffice it here to say it is unlikely that the deep obscurity in which women writers from Sherwood Bonner to Zitkala-Sa are hidden is peculiarly an American phenomenon, thus I doubt whether we are close to the end of the process of rediscovery.

More certainly, even, we are far from establishing the distinctive qualities of the art of these and many better known women writers. This seems to me the second major task of feminist criticism. Studies like those by Baym, Barbara Christian, Elaine Showalter, and Sandra Gilbert and Susan Gubar[30] are only among some of the better-known works devoted to establishing thematic and formal connections among women writers. A parallel task is defining the distinctive thematic and formal characteristics of particular women writers. Elizabeth Ammon's examination of the structure of Jewett's *The Country of the Pointed Firs*[31] provides an especially useful example because it implicitly questions received norms about the structure of short fictions and suggests that Jewett used a distinct, and perhaps gender-linked form.

There is, of course, a certain dialectic between the rediscovery of works and an adequate account of characteristics that link them to other texts. In reevaluating the work of Caroline Kirkland, Judith Fetterley has suggested that *A New Home, Who'll Follow* is in essence a series of elaborated letters and that the letter form represented for women a halfway house between the privacy of correspondence and the public act of authorship, an act seen by many in the early nineteenth century as unseemly for women. That suggestion took on for me powerful implications as I reread Sarah Grimké's *Letters on the Equality of the Sexes* and Lydia Maria Child's *Letters from New-York*, thought about the letter form adopted by Margaret Fuler in the last years of her life, and finally focused (thanks particularly to two of my students, Ellen Louise Hart and Katie King) on the implications of such precedents on the major form of Emily Dickinson's (self-)"publication"—letters:

> This is my letter to the World
> That never wrote to Me . . .

It would at this point claim too much to propose correspondence as constituting a fundamental model for many American nineteenth-century women of letters, but as we come to know more about these writers that may, indeed, be one conclusion. I mention this hypothesis as one illustration of how the dialectic between rediscovery of texts and definition of characteristic themes and forms operates. It also leads us toward two additional objectives in the project of feminist criticism.

These I would describe as decentering male texts, on the one hand, and moving female texts from the margins of culture to the core. Decentering male texts (including phallocentric criticism) was in many respects the initial concern of the earliest feminist critics. It took two forms: first, studies of the images of women, often absurd or vile, projected in widely-respected work by male writers. Second, and in these days of theoretical sophistication too often condescended to, were works like Kate Millett's pioneering and courageous *Sexual Politics* (1970). It need hardly be said that the work of decentering male-centered culture as it is expressed in language, syntax, form, and institutional configuration remains a major concern of current feminist criticism. Indeed, the major contribution of contemporary French feminist writing may be in this area. What is surprising, perhaps, is how persistent phallocentric historical models have remained despite the accumulated weight of contrary evidence.

A vivid illustration of how male-centered literary history continues to obscure the work of women writers was provided by Leslie Fiedler in an essay called "Literature and Lucre," featured in the *New York Times Book Review* (May 31, 1981), and reprinted in one of Fiedler's recent books. Fiedler pictures the history of the novel in America as a struggle between "high Art and low," between "those writers among us who aspire to critical acclaim and an eternal place in libraries" and "the authors of 'best sellers.'" The former, "sophisticated novelists," include Charles Brockden Brown, Poe, Hawthorne, and Melville, all male, as Fiedler points out. The latter tradition, "a series of deeply moving though stylistically undistinguished fictions . . . begins with Susanna Rowson's *Charlotte Temple*, reaches a nineteenth-century high point with Harriet Beecher Stowe's *Uncle Tom's Cabin* and a twentieth-century climax with Margaret Mitchell's *Gone With the Wind*."

This spurious battle of the sexes, and the image of the failed artist which supposedly emerges from it, can be sustained only by ignoring huge parts of American literary history. For example, Fiedler proclaims that "only in the last decade of this century did it become possible, first in fact, then in fiction, for a novelist highly regarded by critics (Norman Mailer is an example) to become wealthy long before his death. . . ." This is patrifocal history with a vengeance, since it altogether ignores Edith Wharton, Willa Cather, and Ellen Glasgow, not to speak of Stowe, E.D.E.N. Southworth (who was much praised by contemporary critics), Jewett, Mary Austin, and even William Dean Howells. Most of these women novelists, among others, were and still are "highly regarded by critics," and did very well from their writing. But more to the point, bringing them up altogether explodes the theory, or perhaps myth, Fiedler wishes to float, that in America writers have either been (until our generation) successful *or* artistic:

> . . . both primary and secondary literature in the United States, the novels and poems of which we are most proud and the critical autobiographical [sic] works written on them, reflect the myth of the "serious" writer as an alienated male, condemned to neglect and poverty by a culture simultaneously commercialized and feminized.

Since the women novelists don't fit this nice theory, "we" need to ignore them. And also ignore the fact that writers like Melville and Hawthorne indeed aspired to popularity and were enraged by what they took to be the failure of their audience to appreciate them.

Nor is it at all clear as Fiedler makes out that Stowe, for example, was not artistic as well as successful. On the contrary, recent studies have documented her artistry. In linking her to Rowson and Mitchell, Fiedler is trying to stigmatize her with the unstated labels, familiar from critics like Tate, of "sentimental" and "mass market." "Sentimental" and "mass" are terms, like "regional," "popular," "minor," which have been undergoing reexamination[32] since it became clear they were used to bury much of value on specious assumptions, like the proposition that the suppression of feelings, even tears, is a more legitimate basis for fiction than their display.[33] In short, the problem with Fiedler's theory is that it begins with a truncated set of data, examines them from a dazzlingly parochial angle of vision, and, not surprisingly, concludes by reenforcing the artistic centrality of the traditional male texts which have constituted the canon.

Moreover, the myth of the unappreciated artist itself requires a differing analysis. Myths constitute metaphorical ideologies. Here, the problem for American male writers is construed as the frailty of his audience. It might equally well be posed as the obstinate refusal of many male novelists to take that dominantly female audience seriously. In concluding her second series of stories entitled *Clovernook* (1853), Alice Cary deftly questions the motives of those who, as Fiedler puts it, aspire to "an eternal place in libraries":

> In our country, though all men are not "created equal," such is the influence of the sentiment of liberty and political equality, that:
>
> > "All thoughts, all passions, all delights,
> > Whatever stirs this mortal frame,"

may with as much probability be supposed to affect conduct and expectation in the log cabin as in the marble mansion; and to illustrate this truth, to dispel that erroneous belief of the necessary baseness of the "common people" which the great masters in literature have in all ages labored to create, is a purpose and an object in our nationality to which the finest and highest genius may wisely be devoted; but which may be effected in a degree by writings as unpretending as these reminiscences of what occurred in and about the little village where I from childhood watched the pulsations of surrounding hearts.[34]

Cary's comment not only raises questions about the values of the literary "masters," but suggests the importance of an alternative standard embodied in the "unpretending . . . reminiscences" of her village which she—and, indeed, many American women writers—presents.

And that comment brings me to the last part of the project of feminist criticism upon which I wish to touch: the effort to move the work of women from the margins toward the center of culture. Here, the work of criticism and of political action most fully converge. For in the first instance, it was not the work of critics that refocused attention on the distinctive concerns of women writers, any more than black aestheticians initially established the conditions for recognizing the traditions of African-American composition. On the contrary, it was the movements for social, economic, and political change of the 1960s and 1970s that challenged long-held assumptions about what was significant as subject matter for literary art by challenging the assumptions about what was significant for people. Meridel LeSueur once described how her story "Annunciation," which deals with pregnancy, was turned down by editors demanding fighting and fornicating. That may stand as a symbol of my point here: it will *not* be on the basis solely of "literary" criteria that the days and works of women—any more than of other marginalized groups—will be established at the center of cultural concern.

In California, the school system in cooperation with certain universities has launched an ambitious "Literature Project" designed to reinvigorate the teaching of English at the secondary level. Part of that effort has involved the creation of model curricula, including what are called "core" and "extended" readings. One model thematic unit is titled "Journey to Personal Fulfillment." The "core" readings are these: Dickens, *Great Expectations;* Twain, *Huckleberry Finn* and *Life on the Mississippi;* Shaw, *Pygmalion;* Cather, "Paul's Case"; Kafka, "The Hunger Artist"; Auden, "The Unknown Citizen"; Eliot, "The Hollow Men"; and Whitman, "The Ox-Tamer." These selections suggest that an old canard still lives: "Choose works that interest the boys; the girls will read anything." That reflection is reenforced by considering that among the "extended readings" are *Jane Eyre, Wuthering Heights*, E. B. Browning's *Sonnets from the Portuguese*, the autobiographies of Mme. Curie and Helen Keller, and Alice Walker's "African Images." Further, one might wonder, in a state in which Latinos, Asian-Americans, American Indians, and Blacks will shortly constitute a majority, whether all of these works together constitute any adequate portrait of journeys to "personal fulfillment." I do not cite this instance to mock the very concerned people working in this important project. On the contrary, I think we need to admire and support their efforts, even as we criticize them. But it will not be critical practice alone that will shift what is perceived and treated as "core." To be sure, as literary people we need to reexamine hierarchies of taste as expressed in subject matter, genre, language and imagery, as well as in conceptions of literary function and audience.[35] Still, there is little more than can be done to establish the *literary* equality of the work of the Brontës and Twain. It will be our work as political people, rather, as citizens of real communities, that will be critical to achieving the axial transformation to which we aspire. Revolution is not, finally, in and of the word alone.

Nor should this come as a surprise. It is a commonplace of scholarship informed by a working-class perspective—often honored, I must admit, in the breach—that the point is not to describe the world, but to change it. So it must be, I think, with feminist criticism: it cannot be neutral, simply analytic, formal. It need always to be asking how its project is changing the world, reconstructing history as well as consciousness, so that the accomplishments of women can be fully valued and, more important, so that the lives of women and men can more fully be lived.

NOTES

This essay originally appeared, in somewhat different form, in *A Gift of Tongues: Critical Challenges in Contemporary American Poetry*, ed. Marie Harris and Kathleen Aguero (Athens: University of Georgia Press, 1987), pp. 57–82. I want to express my appreciation for the creativity and support of the editors. Portions of the essay also appear in my own Canons and Contexts (Oxford).

1. Raymond Williams, *Culture and Society, 1780–1950* (New York: Harper Torchbooks, 1966), pp. 325–326.

2. *Ibid.*, p. 327.

3. Martha Vicinus, *The Industrial Muse* (New York: Barnes and Noble, 1974); see, especially, pp. 1–3.

4. Dan Tannacito, "Poetry of the Colorado Miners: 1903–1906," *Radical Teacher*, #15 (March, 1980), pp. 1–8. Appended to Tannacito's article is a small anthology of miners' poetry.

5. Paul Lauter, "Working-Class Women's Literature—An Introduction to Study," *Women in Print, I*, ed. Ellen Messer-Davidow and Joan Hartman (New York: Modern Language Association, 1982), pp. 109–34.

6. Lawrence Levine, *Black Culture and Black Consciousness: Afro-American Folk Thought from Slavery to Freedom* (New York: Oxford University Press, 1977). See also Anthony Heilbut, *The Gospel Sound* and Peter Guralnick, *Sweet Soul Music* (New York: Harper and Row, 1986).

7. I am distinguishing between "working-class," "folk," or "popular" (peoples') culture and what Dwight MacDonald characterized as "mass culture." Popular culture, what people who share class (or ethnicity and race) produce in communicating with one another, can be separated from what is produced as a commodity, generally at the lowest common denominator, for consumption by masses of people. To be sure, the distinction is not always clear-cut, but it is worth seeking.

8. Quoted by Herbert G. Gutman, *Work, Culture, and Society in Industrializing America* (New York: Knopf, 1976), pp. 23–24, from Melech Epstein, *Jewish Labor in the United States* (New York, 1950), pp. 290–291.

9. See John W. Blassingame, *The Slave Community* (New York: Oxford, 1972), pp. 49–59.

10. Jeanette R. Murphy, "The Survival of African Music in America," *Popular Science Monthly*, LV (Sept. 1899), 662; quoted by Blassingame, op. cit., pp. 27–28.

11. See "The Burning Struggle: The Civil Rights Movement," an interview with Bernice Johnson Reagon, *Radical America*, 12 (11-12/78), 18–20.

12. *Black Culture and Black Consciousness*, p. 33; cf. p. 207.

13. The usual distinctions between "poetry" and "propaganda," or between "fine arts" and "crafts" hinge on the issue of function. Modern critics have, in one form or another, generally assumed that "poetry is its own excuse for being" and that a poem should "not mean, but be." This is not the place to argue such claims. I don't find them particularly convincing, though it is obvious enough that art can have differing functions in different cultures. Let it suffice here to assert that viewing working-class culture from the standpoint of such assumptions will fatally mislead the critic.

15. Allen Tate, "Tension in Poetry," *Essays of Four Decades* (Chicago: The Swallow Press, 1968), p. 64.

16. *Ibid.*, p. 58.

17. "To Whom is the Poet Responsible?" *Essays of Four Decades*, p. 27.

18. "Literature as Knowledge," *Essays of Four Decades*, p. 104.

19. "The Man of Letters in the Modern World," *Essays of Four Decades*, p. 14.

20. *Ibid.*, p. 16.

21. In rereading this, it seems to me that I have made it sound like all academic critics are centers of independent power. Clearly, people in academe respond to institutional priorities, corporate definitions of appropriate career tracks. Indeed, most teachers and literary scholars are the victims of established modes of performance rather than their creators. It is not my intention to blame the victims but rather to make clear the source of that victimization. Cf. my article "The Two Criticisms: Structure, Lingo and Power in the Discourse of Academic Humanists," in *Canons and Contexts* (New York: Oxford, 1991).

22. *Reactionary Essays on Poetry and Ideas* (Freeport, NY: Books for Libraries, 1968), pp. 154–157.

23. The comment was quoted in a press release connected with the publication of her collection *Ripening* (Old Westbury, NY: The Feminist Press, 1982).

24. "The Poet as Woman," *The World's Body* (New York: Scribner's 1938).

25. The essay was printed as a single unit in *The Liberal Imagination* (New York: Viking Press, 1950). I shall be quoting from the Anchor Books edition (Garden City: Doubleday, 1954), pp. 15–32.

26. "Melodramas of Beset Manhood: How Theories of American Fiction Exclude Women Authors," *The New Feminist Criticism*, ed. Elaine Showalter (New York: Pantheon, 1985), p. 68.

27. In the following paragraphs I am deeply indebted to two fine essays by Bruce Spear of the University of California, Santa Cruz. They are "Cold War Aesthetics: Edmund Wilson, Lionel Trilling, and F. O. Matthiessen" and "The Late Work of F. O. Matthiessen: Criticism, Politics, and Spirit."

28. *Women's Fiction: A Guide to Novels by and About Women in America, 1820–1870* (Ithaca: Cornell University Press, 1978).

29. Steps toward changing the absolute unavailability of texts were taken when Indiana University Press issued Judith Fetterley's collection of early- and mid-nineteenth-century American women writers, Rutgers University Press began to issue its excellent series of reprints of the work of writers like Child, Rose Terry Cooke, and Cary, and Oxford University Press began to issue the Schomburg series of works by black women writers. Still, little of Child, Fanny Fern, or Sarah Josepha Hale is accessible. Only one work by Rebecca Harding Davis is available, "Life in the Iron Mills," first restored in an edition

from The Feminist Press and now enshrined in some anthologies of American literature. Only within the last few years have works by Elizabeth Stuart Phelps become available; and even some of H. B. Stowe's texts are unavailable in paperback. Nor is there any edition of the work of the most widely published black woman writer of the nineteenth century, Frances Ellen Watkins Harper, though Frances Foster is attempting to remedy that. Still, other minority works, by men as well as by women, remain to be reprinted—or, as in the case of nineteenth-century autobiographies in Spanish, printed for the first time.

30.   Barbara Christian, *Black Women Novelists: The Development of a Tradition, 1892–1976* (Westport, CT: Greenwood Press, 1980); Elaine Showalter, *A Literature of Their Own: British Women Novelists from Bronte to Lessing* (Princeton: Princeton University Press, 1977); Sandra M. Gilbert and Susan Gubar, *The Madwoman in the Attic: The Woman Writer and the Nineteenth-Century Literary Imagination* (New Haven: Yale University Press, 1979).

31.   "Going in Circles: The Female Geography of Jewett's *Country of the Pointed Firs, Studies in the Literary Imagination,* 16 (Fall, 1983), esp. 85–89.

32.   See, for example, Jane Tompkins, *Sensational Designs* (New York: Oxford, 1988).

33.   See, for example, Baym, *Woman's Fiction,* pp. 25, 144.

34.   Alice Cary, *Clovernook, or Recollections of Our Neighborhood in the West, Second Series* (New York: Redfield, 1853), pp. 363–364.

35.   My own effort in this direction is represented by "The Literatures of America—A Comparative Discipline," prepared for a Soviet-American conference on minority literatures in the United States, University of Pennsylvania, July, 1985, and printed in *Canons and Contexts* (1991).

REFLECTIONS ON BLACK WOMEN WRITERS
revising the literary canon

There is no doubt that black women as writers have made drastic inroads into the American literary consciousness since the beginning of the 1970s, and the film success of Alice Walker's *The Color Purple* has indeed placed the entire group within a new dimension in the national consciousness. Aside from its merits (or demerits) as book and/or movie, *The Color Purple* is important for what its popularity means in terms of the recognition it compels for the works of black women. Thousands, perhaps millions, of people who had not, until now, ever heard the name of Alice Walker, and countless others who had, but who were able to ignore her (although she had been publishing fiction and poetry since the late 1960s), have seen and will see the film—learn her name, and respond to her work, whether they acknowledge its richness, or see it as a misrepresentation of the black experience. Above the din of the controversy that *The Color Purple* has sparked inside and outside of the black community, many will discover something new about the experiences of black women in America. For what black women as writers have consistently provided for themselves and others has been a rendering of the black woman's place in the world in which she lives, as she shapes and defines that from her own impulses and actions.

Before *The Color Purple* the only comparable achievement for a black woman writer was made by Lorraine Hansberry's *A Raisin in the Sun*, which was first staged in 1959. This play, for which Hansberry won the New York Drama Critics Circle Award of "Best Play of the Year," over Tennessee William's *Sweet Bird of Youth*, Archibald MacLeish's *JB*, and Eugene O'Neill's *A Touch of the Poet*, made her not only the youngest American, the first woman, and the first black person to achieve that honor, but also the first black woman to have her work produced on Broadway. *A Raisin the Sun*, seen by millions of Americans on stage, screen, and television, has been translated into more than thirty languages and produced on all continents of the globe. It foreshadowed the emergence of a new movement in black theater, a new place in letters for black women writers, and opened one artistic door onto the large stage of the Civil Rights Movement of the 1960s and 1970s.

A Raisin in the Sun is not autobiographical. Lorraine Hansberry came from a black middle-class family which had long overcome the problems faced by the characters in her play. But if Hansberry was economically removed from the dilemma of the Youngers, the family she writes about, she was nevertheless emotionally attached to the issues she explored through them, issues that remained at the core of the lives of the majority of black people in America in the 1950s. The experiences of her dramaturgical family were part of the collective three-hundred-year-old consciousness of what it meant to be born black in America. In giving several of the key roles in her play to women, she had also followed in the footsteps of her less well-known earlier sisters who had sought to write out of their black female awareness and point of view on that reality.

At the center of *Raisin* is that most memorable Mama: Lena Younger, whose grandeur takes vengeance for all the black mammies previously presented in American literature. For black women in American literature, from the beginning, have been depicted as either sexually loose and therefore tempters of men, or obedient and subservient mammies, loving and tender to the white children they raised and forever faithful to the owners they served. Lena Younger defies more than two hundred years of such stereotyping of black women, and turns black female strength, too often maligned by everyone else, into the means by which her son Walter shapes his emerging manhood. Lorraine Hansberry was not the first black woman who gave us such a positive image of black women, but she was the first in her own time whose voice reached as wide an audience as hers did. Her achievement opened a wider way for the black women writers who came after her.

What is significant in the Lena Younger image in *Raisin* for the purposes of this paper is that she is the central force that holds her family together, that she has no ambivalences regarding the inherent human worth and dignity of herself and those whom she loves, and that speaking from inside of her own experiences, she demonstrates that the black struggle to transcend dwarfs the victimization that would otherwise have destroyed black people a long time ago. And while Mama Younger stands as the force at the center of her family, there are also the other women in that drama whose roles are fully as important as her own: daughter Beneatha, who wants to be a doctor so that she will be able to heal sick and broken black bodies, but whose sophisticated cynicism meets with the stern rebuke of her mother; and Ruth, Walter's wife, whose concerns for the welfare and well-being of her children precipitates a family controversy over abortion that belies the notion that poor and/or black people produce babies without consideration for what happens after they arrive. Years later, when Ruth will tell Travis and his siblings stories about their grandmother, or when Beneatha recalls her young adulthood and the conflicts she had with her mother, the scripts to those narratives will bear no resemblances to the majority of those concerning black mothers and/or women that appear in the literature written by black men or white men or women.

Since the success of *A Raisin in the Sun* the names of an impressive number of black women writers have become fairly well known to large numbers of Americans, and at the same time new and different images of black women have emerged from their pens. But while it is accurate to give credit to Hansberry's success as foreshadowing the contemporary wider recognition of black women writers and critics, the momentum it signaled had its beginnings more than two hundred years earlier. The history of the creative efforts of black women in

America began with the beginnings of literacy, in 1746 with Lucy Terry's "Bars Fight," a poem about an Indian raid on the white settlement of Deerfield, Massachusetts, and continued with Phillis Wheatley's *Poems on Various Subjects, Religious and Moral* in 1773. Terry's and Wheatley's extant works confirm that black women in the eighteenth century had literary voices which they made bold to use, while black women of the nineteenth century, building on what preceded them, authenticated their voices by speaking to local and national issues that had direct impact on the lives of black people. From Sojourner Truth, abolitionist and feminist, who could neither read nor write but whose words were recorded by others, to Jarena Lee, evangelist, who documented the hundreds of miles she logged across the country preaching and teaching and saving souls, to Maria Stewart, the first woman in the country to make a profession of the public lecture circuit, and Anna Julia Cooper and Frances Watkins Harper, whose feminist, antiracist writings are as contemporary as today, we know that these women spoke loud and clear in celebration of the positive characteristics of human life, and in strong criticism of racial and gender oppression. This history assures us that black women have not ever been artistically or critically silent, even though for most of the past their voices went largely ignored by those who did not wish to hear them. In their own voices, black women have always confirmed and authenticated the complexity of the black American female experience, and in so doing have debunked the negative stereotypes that others created of them while denying them audience for their words. Now, finally admitted to a larger hearing than they ever previously enjoyed, both past and present black female literary voices combine to alter the historical nature of the discourse and to play a prominent role in revising the canon from which they were long excluded.

There is no need here to again recite the history of the stereotyping of black women in American literature by others than themselves. That has been adequately done by several critics.[1] It is important, however, to note that the efforts to reverse the negative images of black women in literature began as early as these women began to find an opportunity to write: with the slave narratives, fiction, poetry, and nonfiction prose of the nineteenth century. The spoken words of women like Sojourner Truth, and the writings of other women like Stewart, Cooper, and Watkins Harper, among others, were primary in the struggle against slavery and the abuses of women, especially of black women. Their boldness and assertiveness define these women as a highly intelligent, morally outraged group in a struggle against white injustice to blacks and male dominance of women.

In the earliest known novel by a black woman, *Our Nig or Sketches from the Life of a Free Black* (1859), by Harriet Wilson, the abused heroine, Frado, is a hardworking, honest child of mixed racial parentage who is caught in a web of white hatred and cruelty. Frado is neither an immoral woman nor a mammy, the most frequent of the stereotypes of black women in that time, and Wilson uses her characterization of the helpless child to emphasize the unfairness of a social structure that permitted individuals to treat black people in a less-than-human fashion. In writing this novel, Wilson, of whom not a great deal is known, was the flesh-and-blood example of the rebel against the treatment she outlined in her book. As such, she provided another concrete example of black women's estimation of their self-worth. For one thing, she explicitly wrote her narrative as a means of earning money to take care of herself and her ailing son. Wilson, who lived in Boston and other areas of New England, and who sets her work in that geographical location, took advantage of the tradition of the sentimental female novel, which at that time enjoyed enormous popularity. The form of her book—the epigraphs, style, and structure of the narrative—shows that she was well aware of many of the conventions of novel writing at the time, and that she considered them valuable to plead the case, not of the poor white heroine who eventually achieves a good marriage and a happy home, as they did in the white female novels, but of an abused black child and woman who was unable to realize the goals of white protagonists. Wilson, deserted by her husband, was sufficiently self-assured to imagine that writing held the possibilities of a vocation for her.

But the slave narrative, not fiction, was the mode that dominated the earliest Afro-American attempts at literature, which through its existence revised the nature of the American "Self." Until recently, most of the attention to this body of work has focused on the writings of men, with *The Narrative of Frederick Douglass, An American Slave, Written by Himself* receiving the majority of the plaudits. It is now recognized that the female slave narrative deserves attention for its own sake—for its unique contributions to the genre. The narrative of Harriet Jacobs, in particular, *Incidents in the Life of a Slave Girl*, published in 1861 under the name of Linda Brent, is a stunning literary success, equal in every way to the preeminent male slave narrative. Jacobs, a South Carolina slave who became a fugitive at age twenty-seven, told a story that brilliantly deconstructs the meaning of the female slave experience in relationship to that of her male counterpart and the white world around her. The literary prowess she displayed in her careful delineation of the sexual harassment she suffered from her owner, her masterly circumvention of his intentions toward her, her patience and determination to free herself and her children, and her understanding of the differences between psychological and physical freedom make her tale a female classic. As an early narrative by a black woman, one of the most significant contributions that *Incidents* makes to the history is its identification of the existence of and effectiveness of a woman's community in which black and white, slave and free women sometimes joined forces to thwart the brutal plans of masters against helpless slave women. In Harriet Wilson's *Our Nig*, the cruel stepmother of the fairy-tale convention is replaced by the cruel mistress and her equally cruel daughter, while the men in the story, sympathetic to Frado, are ineffective against the wickedness of the female members of their family. On the contrary, Jacobs, who hides in the crawl space of her grandmother's house for seven years in real life, is assisted in this effort by a number of women until she can safely escape. Similarly, other black women's slave narratives pay tribute to the roles that women play as models and inspiration in their struggle to rise above oppression. The "sisterhood" of black women and the peculiarity of relations between black and white women that appears in later black women's literature were already well documented in the black female slave narrative tradition.

If the slave narrative as a genre revised the concept of the American self, then, as a separate body of work, the narratives written by slave women are especially important for their revisionist elements in relationship to the narratives of ex-slave men and the American female experience in the autobiographical accounts of white women. We are indebted to Frances Foster's study, "'In Respect to Females . . .': Differences in the Portrayals of Women by Male and Female Narrators," for alerting us to the implications of gender in slave narratives a few years ago.[2] Of necessity, the experiences of white women in the age of the "cult of true womanhood" were very separate from those of black slave women, but slave men and women also had different perceptions of their common condition. In the narratives of ex-slave men, for instance, slave women appear completely helpless and fully exploited. Much of this is identified as the result of their sexual vulnerability, and the women are pictured as victims without recourse to means of protecting or of defending themselves. Images of these women on auction blocks, stripped to their waists, their children having been sold away from them—all because of the licentiousness of their masters—are among those that abound in the literature. In Douglass's narrative for instance, he is painstaking in his descriptions of the beatings slave women were often given. His accounts of the sounds of the whips against their flesh and the flow of the blood from their backs are graphic. On the other hand, in telling their own stories, ex-slave women did not concentrate on the sexual exploitation they suffered. They did not deny it, but they made it clear that there were other elements in their lives which were important to them as well. In short, they saw themselves as more than victims of rape and seduction. As Foster points out, when they wrote, they not only wanted to witness to the atrocities of slavery, but also to celebrate their hard-won escapes. Their stories show them to be strong, courageous, dignified, and spirited in spite of the world in which they were forced to live. They depicted themselves as complex human beings with a desire to engage in discourse that took the breadth of their experiences into consideration. In writing, they were no longer secondary characters in someone else's script, but heroines in their own creations. As noted earlier, these black women writers focused less on individual performance and more on the positive roles that engaged women. They allotted time to the value of family relationships, not only to beatings and mutilations by slave masters. As they related their stories, ex-slave women took control of their narratives in much the same way as they took control of the circumstances that enabled them to survive and escape captivity.

Jacob's narrative provides a good example of this mode. While she tells us of her dilemma with her master, the focus of *Incidents* is largely on her attempts to become free and to free her children. She demonstrates that she had power over her master while she was concealed in her grandmother's house, and she used this power to lead him to believe that she had left the state. She further tells us of her success in finding employment after her escape, and of the happy union she had with her children in the North. Her self-confidence was never destroyed by the abuses of slavery, and her self-esteem remained strong through the difficulties of her escape. Taking up where Foster left off, other critics have noted, from textual evidence in *Incidents*, how well Jacobs understood the meaning of freedom in her dealings with northern whites, especially in her contacts with women. Associated with both the feminist and abolitionist movements, she analyzed her situation and wrote perceptively of the racism of white feminists. Like Wilson, she made use of the sentimental tradition in women's fiction, but skillfully subverted that tradition for her own purposes. It is interesting that both Wilson and Jacobs rejected the convention of marriage and the happy ending of popular white female fiction. There are several less fully developed ex-slave women narratives, but all are equally confirming in their assertion of the positive identity of their authors. Among them we have Elizabeth Keckley, a seamstress who later made a successful living by tending the wardrobes of presidential first ladies in Washington; Susie King Taylor, a woman of many talents, from laundress to schoolteacher; and Amanda Berry Smith, a preacher. All wrote, not only to expose the evils that had been done to them, but also to demonstrate their abilities to gain physical and psychological liberty by transcending those evils.

The poetry, fiction, and nonfiction prose of black women to come out of the latter part of the nineteenth century wage open warfare against racism and gender oppression, on one hand, and on the other, encourage and castigate blacks in an effort to promote the "uplift" of the race. As other critics have often noted, the novels by black men and women with the mulatto heroine were often an appeal to whites for the elimination of atrocities, based on racial prejudices, against blacks, especially in the face of the evidences of the extent of blood co-mingling between the races. Barbara Christian has done an excellent exploration of the range of the intentions of Frances Watkins Harper, for instance, who was responsible for the publication of some eleven volumes of poetry, religious in tone and mainly directed toward the less fortunate, in her effort to "make songs for the people," who spoke out and wrote overtly scathing essays against white racism and sexism. She wrote a novel as well, *Iola LeRoy, Shadows Uplifted* (1892), with a mulatta heroine who revises this type of protagonist as she appears in novels such as William Wells Brown's *Clotel; or The President's Daughter* (1853). Unlike the tragic character whom Brown and others portray, Harper's heroine, given a chance to escape from her race, chooses to marry an Afro-American and dedicate her life to helping unfortunate black people. Anna Julia Cooper, who wrote no fiction, used didactic prose in *A Voice from the South: By a Black Women of the South*, not only to admonish white Americans for their injustices against other Americans, but to celebrate the achievements of black women and to sternly reproach the shortcomings of black men, particularly when those failings diminished the value of what black women strove to achieve.

A much neglected black female voice that spans the period between the end of the nineteenth century and the activities of the Harlem Renaissance of the 1920s is that of Alice Dunbar Nelson, who for a short time was married to the famous Paul Laurence Dunbar. Her importance to the history of Afro-American letters continues to be eclipsed by his. But the recent publication of Dunbar Nelson's diary, *Give Us Each Day, The Diary of Alice Dunbar-Nelson*, edited by Gloria Hull, has added an important work to the corpus of black women's writings. While twentieth-century black women's autobiographies have often proved to be frustrating documents because of their lack of openness, and the tendency of the authors to avoid private disclosures, this diary reveals the side of Dunbar Nelson that would otherwise remain unknown to the world. Dunbar Nelson, who was born in 1875 and died in 1935, like many of the writers of that era, was middle-class, educated, and highly sophisticated, a journalist as well as short-story writer, dramatist, and poet. In the ease with which she handled more than one literary form, she belongs to a group that includes women like Georgia Johnson and Angelina Grimké, both poets and dramatists, whose pens made known that black women were not only involved with the practical problems of education and economics for black people, but also with the creation of art and literature. Most of these women earned a living by teaching, the only respectable profession that was open to them, but one that was also in line with their ideas of service to others. Especially as dramatists, Dunbar Nelson, Johnson, and Grimké addressed many of the social problems facing the black community, and agitated for changes to alter them. Racism of all kinds, including lynching, were topics of their plays, and these women went as far as to take up the issue of poor women and the need for birth control education in the struggle against poverty and ignorance.

On the opposite side of the coin of achievement, from Dunbar Nelson's diary we learn some details of how women of her standing coped with many of the problems that confronted them in their private lives, away from the long days and busy schedules which make their histories as impressive as they are. Space does not permit an accounting of the financial difficulties which she faced for almost all of her life, or the strength and creativity she put into protecting her public image from the chaos of her private world. Suffice it to say that she worried a great deal over an accumulation of debts; that a fear of bouncing checks is one of the themes in the book; and that she was a woman who could pawn her jewelry to pay her water bill, and go immediately from that second task to address a meeting of wives of professional white men, dressed like a "certified check." From the diary too, there is further confirmation of the strength of the women's community which female slave narrators introduced into the literature. Not only did Dunbar Nelson live in a family in which women were pre-eminent, regardless of the men who entered their lives at different times, but her world outside of her family was peopled by women like Mary McLeod Bethune and Nannine Burroughs, famous educators, in addition to the Club Women and the writers and artists of her time.

Dunbar Nelson and the women who appear in her diary are complex figures who do not fit the stereotypes of black women of their day in the literature of others. They were exciting and strong, but they were also very human in the ways in which they responded to experience. They worked, laughed, loved, cried, and survived because they were tough-minded and respected themselves and others. They transgressed the boundaries of the expectations of women in that day, and created themselves in their own images. In respect to what she discloses of their private lives, Dunbar Nelson's diary is extremely important in the process of the revision of the literary images of ambitious upwardly mobile black women of the early part of the century.

The 1920s were the years in which black culture flourished as it has not done before in America, and the center of the activity was in Harlem, New York City. Following on the heels of the large black migration from a rural to an urban environment that began early in the century, and an increase in the West Indian and African populations in the country, the artistic and scholarly communities, as a group, set themselves to the task of defining the black experience in as positive a way as they could. It is now common knowledge that Jessie Fauset, black woman poet and novelist, in her role as W.E.B. Du Bois's assistant at the *Crisis* (one of the most important journals of the time), was instrumental in bringing all of the important writers of the period into public view. In addition, Fauset was the only member of the group to publish three novels between the early 1920s and early 1930s. She, along with Nella Larsen, author of two novels in the late 1920s, have received less attention as writers than their male counterparts because of a perception that their works belong the genteel tradition of the novel of manners. That condition is moving toward rapid change, however, as contemporary black women critics re-evaluate the writings of women before the 1960s; as cooperative publishers make out-of-print texts available for classroom use; and teachers and professors in Women's Studies and Afro-American and other literature courses make use of them.

Not all the women who came of age in the 1920s or who were associated with the Harlem Renaissance emerged then or did their best work in that period. Dorothy West, novelist, short fiction writer, and journalist, and Pauli Murray, family chronicler, poet, and civil rights activist, were young women attracted to the verve of the cultural movement, but whose work appeared later in the 1930s and 1940s. The most illustrious of the women in the later-blooming group to have had an association with the Renaissance was Zora Neale Hurston. In the early 1970s, her work was rediscovered, and it did more than any single writer's work to mobilize the energy of contemporary black women critics. Hurston arrived in New York from Florida by way of Baltimore and Washington, D.C., in 1925, after having won a prize for short fiction published in *Opportunity* magazine. Before her mature work in the 1930s and 1940s she continued to write short stories, earned herself a degree in anthropology from Columbia University, did fieldwork in the South and the West Indies, and was a colorful figure among the Harlem literati. In her time she received only minor praise for her work, and long before her death in 1960 she was forgotten by most of the literary world and derided by those who remembered her. In the early 1970s, her now-acclaimed novel, *Their Eyes Were Watching God* (1937), retrieved her name from oblivion and set the wheels rolling for the new black feminist criticism of the 1970s and 1980s. In relationship to black literature until then, this novel turned aside from the literature of protest against racism and racial discrimination to explore the inner dynamics of black culture, and to introduce, as heroine, the ordinary, uneducated black woman in search of a self-defined identity. Taking place almost entirely within the black community, *Their Eyes* explores primal relations between black men and women as they had never been done before. Here are rural people without concern for "social uplift," but whose lives are rich with a heritage that has fostered black survival for generations. Janie, her central character, is the first black feminist heroine in the fictional canon. At the same time, the folklore in all of her books makes Hurston's work an important source of information far beyond the boundaries of literature. Unfortunately, her other works have often been adjudged "lesser" than *Their Eyes*, even by her most ardent supporters. This too is a judgment that may well be revised in the near future, as at least one other novel of hers, *Moses, Man of the Mountain* (1939), a black folk rendition of the biblical myth, has finally begun to attract critical attention. Her autobiography, *Dust Tracks on a Road*, is a problematical text from the point of view of its concealments and evasions. But again, new studies in black women's autobiographies suggest that such concealments are a prominent convention in the tradition. As black women's autobiography stands, Hurston may not be the exception most people now think she is. However, had she written nothing of importance other than *Their Eyes Were Watching God*, her place in history would still be fully assured. She did indeed change the nature of the black female heroine in American literature.

From the end of the nineteenth century through the conclusion of the 1940s, the women mentioned above were among those who produced works that were representative of the kinds of writings that black women were engaged in for the first part of the century. Although, except for rare exceptions, they never received the public recognition they deserved, they wrote. They were ambitious, versatile in what they could do, and very productive. As nineteenth-century black women writers had done before them, they continued to explore racism and gender oppression in their writings, especially in fiction and autobiography. Because they were working within the black tradition of protest against white racism, they handled this issue more overtly than they tended to do with gender oppression, especially as that existed within the black community. Since most of these writers were members of the intellectual middle class as well, they also gave a good deal of attention to the "progress" of black people as a whole, an idea that tended to place white middle-class values in a position of superiority in relationship to values inherent in Afro-American culture. In the autobiographical literature of the period the emphasis was on the level of achievement women had made in education and economic independence, although many narratives focused on the ways in which these women worked to "elevate" young women and children, mainly by rescuing them from lives of poverty and immorality and leading them to paths of industry and morality. Hurston, as noted above, unlike many of the writers in her time, deviated from popular black trends and looked backwards to the black folk culture for the materials of her art. As a result, she often incurred the anger of her peers, who felt that her stance in applauding the inner vitality of that culture and her lack of attention to the deprivations of racism worked at cross purposes to their goals. They felt that her position undermined their efforts to force social change since it diluted their efforts to present a united front in confronting the white world.

Between 1940 and the beginning of the 1960s there was a good deal of creative activity on the part of black women writers. In 1949 Gwendolyn Brooks received the Pulitzer Prize for poetry, and became the first black American to be so honored. Brooks, whose work began appearing in 1945, continues to be a poet with enormous energy. Her excursions away from poetry produced a novel, *Maud Martha*, in 1953, and an autobiographical narrative that resembles a prose poem, *Report from Part One*, in 1972. Brooks's work, until 1970, though highly stylized, turned to face the plight of urban blacks in her home city of Chicago. Life on the segregated South Side, with its many disadvantages, was the subject of her prize-winning poetry. Her poetry did for blacks in this urban ghetto what Langston Hughes had earlier done for their counterparts in Harlem. In her novel she examined the inner thoughts of a young woman who is not pretty by conventional standards, or dynamic, or specially gifted, but who has the confidence in herself to seek her happiness. Since 1970, Brooks's work has taken on a decided black militant posture.

A number of other writers made important contributions to the literature of black women during these decades. Particularly deserving of special mention are Margaret Alexander Walker, another prize-winning novelist and poet; Adrienne Kennedy, playwright; Alice Childress, playwright and fiction writer; and Ann Petry, journalist, short-story writer, and author of three novels. After some years of neglect, Petry is experiencing a return to acclaim with the 1985 re-publication of her most well-known work, *The Street*, originally issued in 1943. In this novel, written in the naturalistic mode, the heroine, Lutie Johnson, bright, beautiful, ambitious, hard-working, and a single mother, is defeated by the hostile environment of the ghetto, repersented by a Harlem street. In choosing to use the conventions that she did, Petry creates a character who, unlike most black women's heroines, is alienated from all the support systems available to poor black people; the church, extended family, and a network of friends. Other works of the period emphasize the distressing results of racism on black life, but most demonstrate that survival is possible when their protagonists make use of black support institutions. Especially missing in this novel is the community of women that had for so long been a mainstay in the conventions of black women's fiction.

The 1950s ended on a note of great promise for black American women writers, and in spite of the politics of white racism and of gender, and the sexism of many black men, the rising tide of the Civil Rights Movement was helpful to many of these writers. While Lorraine Hansberry's play received the most outstanding acclaim of all in 1959, there were other women who came to public view with less fanfare, but who were of no less importance to the tradition. One such was Paule Marshall, whose novel *Brown Girl, Brownstones*, was the first black narrative to probe the sensibilities of an American-born adolescent girl of West Indian parents. Marshall, since then, has built her literary career around the interconnections blacks of West Indian heritage feel with white western civilization in the United States. For although most of the Islands were colonized by different European countries, African residuals remained stronger in them than among American blacks, largely because the populations in the islands contained a majority of African descendants. In her second novel, *The Chosen Place, The Timeless People*, published a decade after *Brown Girl*, Marshall's heroine is a West Indian woman who, after several years of living in England, returns to her island home to battle the ills of imperialism there. In *Praise Song For the Widow*, her 1983 work, she examines the recovery of "roots" by a middle-aged West Indian American woman on a journey back to her West Indian past. This is a theme that Marshall, a first-generation American with a West Indian background, seems to find fruitful to pursue. Between her novels she has produced a number of short stories as well, most of them with some "island" flavor.

Writers like Gwendolyn Brooks, Margaret Walker, Alice Childress, Paule Marshall, and Ann Petry continue to be productive in the 1980s. Within the last three decades, however, a remarkable number of new writers have joined their company, many of whom have produced an astonishing volume of writings. Those of us who have been privileged to follow the careers of writers Toni Morrison, whose first novel was *The Bluest Eye* (1970), Alice Walker, since her novel *The Third Life of Grange Copeland* (1970), and Maya Angelou, whose first volume of autobiography was called *I Know Why the Caged Bird Sings* (1970), are aware of how large the output has been in a short time. All of these women have produced multiple volumes of fiction, poetry, autobiography, and essays. Even the newest writers to emerge, like Ntozake Shange and Gloria Naylor, who did not publish until the beginning of the 1980s, have been prolific.

The literature of black women of the 1960s, 1970s, and 1980s follows in the tradition of the earlier times, but is also very different from what went before. Previously, in the slave narrative tradition and the fiction, autobiography, and drama, black women worked hard to debunk the negative stereotypes that other writers had imposed on them. In some instances what they produced were counterstereotypes that depicted black women as strong, and always overcoming hardships. The writers of the present generation see no need to perpetuate only those images, and are now exploring all aspects of black women's experiences—their weaknesses and failings, as well as their strengths and ability to transcend race and gender oppression. Writing from inside of their own experiences, and the knowledge of the experiences of black women for more than three hundred years in America, they examine the innate humanity of the characters they portray—characters who embody qualities that make them neither flawless heroines, immoral individuals, or helpless victims. A good example of this reconciliation of human traits shows up in Toni Morrison's first novel, in which a young black girl, driven insane in her quest for the white western ideal of female beauty—blue eyes—is balanced by the second black girl who understood and rejected the self-destructiveness inherent in a black woman's identifying with such an ideal. In like manner, the conflicts between black men and women that Alice Walker exposes in *Grange Copeland* and other novels are more than an accounting of how brutal some black men can be to their women, but rather a search for the roots of that brutality as a means toward reconciliation between the embattled sexes. Morrison, Walker, and dozens of other new black women writers are "prophets for a new day," in which black American women writers are demanding honor in their own country.

The hallmark of contemporary black women's writings is the impulse toward an honest, complicated, and varied expression of the meaning of the black woman's experiences in America. There is little effort to conceal the pain, and just as little to create the ideal, but a great deal to reveal how black women incorporate the negative and positive aspects of self and external reality into an identity that enables them to meet the challenges of the world in which they must live. Not all black women are strong and enduring, yet a core of resistance to emotional and physical oppression, and a will to discover the path to survival and beyond resides even in those works in which these women do not transcend. As I noted earlier, a long history of black women and the art-of-words exists, and the literature of black America, in its oral and written contexts, has been within the province of its women from the beginning of the American experience. The work of the writers has been ongoing, and has included every branch of the literary family. From the perceived utility of the slave narrative of antebellum days to the more highly crafted and sophisticated forms of the present time, black women have told their own stories both as a way of self-confirmation and a means of correcting the erroneous white and male record of their inner reality. Black women writers project a dynamic "I" into the canon, one that makes more complete the reality of the multi-faceted American experience.

NOTES

1. For a detailed but concise history of this stereotyping see Barbara Christian, *Black Women Novelists* (Westwood: Greenwood Press, 1980), 3–34.

2. Frances Foster, "'In Respect to Females . . .': Differences in the Portrayals of Women by Male and Female Narrators," *Black American Literature Forum* 15, no. 2 (Summer 1981), 66–70.

WORKS CITED

Bambara, Toni Cade. *Gorilla, My Love*. New York: Vintage, 1972.

——. *The Salt Eaters*. New York: Vintage, 1980.

——. *The Sea Birds Are Still Alive*. New York: Vintage, 1977.

Brooks, Gwendolyn. *Maud Martha*. New York: Popular Library, 1953.

Butler, Octavia. *Clay's Ark*. New York: St. Martin's Press, 1984.

——. *Kindred*. New York: Simon & Schuster, 1979.

——. *Mind of My Mind*. New York: Doubleday, 1977.

——. *Patternmaster*. New York: Doubleday, 1976.

——. *Survivor*. New York: Doubleday, 1978.

——. *Wild Seed*. New York: Doubleday, 1980.

Chase-Ribound, Barbara. *Sally Hemings*. New York: Viking Perss, 1979.

Childress, Alice. *Like One of the Family: Conversations from a Domestic's Life*. Brooklyn: Independence, 1956.

——. *A Short Walk*. New York: Coward, McCann & Geoghegan, 1979.

Cliffe, Michele. *Abeng*. New York: The Crossing Press, 1984.

Fauset, Jessie Redmond. *The Chinaberry Tree*. New York: Frederick A. Stokes Co., 1931.

——. *Comedy, American Style*. New York: Frederick A. Stokes Co., 1932.

——. *Plum Bun*. New York: Frederick A Stokes Co., 1927.

——. *There is Confusion*. New York: Boni & Liveright, 1924.

Guy, Rosa, *Bird at My Window*. Philadelphia: Lippincott, 1966.

——. *A Measure of Time*. New York: Holt, Rinehart, & Winston, 1983.

——. *Ruby*. New York: Viking Press, 1976.

Harper, Frances E. W. *Iola Leroy, or Shadows Uplifted*. Philadelphia: Garrigues Brothers, 1892.

Hopkins, Pauline Elizabeth. *Contending Forces: A Romance Illustrative of Negro Life, North and South*. Boston: Colored Co-Operative Publishing Co., 1900.

Hunter, Kristin. *God Bless the Child*. New York: Scribner's, 1964. Reprint, New York: Bantam, 1970.

——. *The Lakestown Rebellion*. New York: Scribner's, 1978.

——. *The Landlord*. New York: Scribner's 1966. Reprint, New York: Avon, 1970.

——. *The Survivors*. New York: Scribner's, 1975.

Hurston, Zora Neale. *Jonah's Gourd Vine*. Philadelphia: Lippincott, 1934.

——. *Moses, Man of the Mountain*. Philadelphia: Lippincott, 1939.

——. *Mules and Men*. Philadelphia: J. P. Lippincott, 1935.

——. *Seraph on the Suwanee*. New York: Scribner's Sons, 1948.

——. *Tell My Horse*. 1938. Reprint, Berkeley: Turtle Island, 1981.

——. *Their Eyes Were Watching God*. Philadelphia: Lippincott, 1937.

Jones, Gayl. *Corregidora*. New York: Random House, 1975.

——. *Eva's Man*. New York: Random House, 1976.

——. *White Rat*. New York: Random House, 1977.

Kincaid, Jamaica. *Annie John*. New York: Farrar, Straus & Giroux, 1985.

——. *At the Bottom of the River*. New York: Farrar, Straus & Giroux, 1978.

Larsen, Nella. *Passing*. New York: A. Knopf, 1929.

——. *Quicksand*. New York: A. Knopf, 1928.

Lee, Andrea. *Sarah Phillips*. New York: Random House, 1984.

Marshall, Paule. *Brown Girl, Brownstones*. New York: Random House, 1959.

———. *The Chosen Place, The Timeless People*. New York: Harcourt Brace Jovanovich, 1969.

———. *Praise Song For the Widow*. New York: Putnam, 1983.

Meriwether, Louise M. *Daddy Was a Number Runner*. Englewood Cliffs, N.J.: Prentice-Hall, 1970. New York: Pyramid, 1971.

Morrison, Toni. *The Bluest Eye*. New York: Holt, Rinehart, & Winston, 1970. Reprint, New York: Pocket Books, 1972.

———. *Song of Solomon*. New York: Knopf, 1977.

———. *Sula*. New York: Knopf, 1973.

———. *Tar Baby*. New York: Knopf, 1981.

Naylor, Gloria. *Linden Hills*. New York: Ticknor & Fields, 1985.

———. *The Women of Brewster Place*. Penguin Books, 1982.

Petry, Ann. *Country Place*. Boston: Houghton Mifflin Co., 1947.

———. *The Narrows*. Boston: Houghton Mifflin Co., 1953.

———. *The Street*. Boston: Houghton Mifflin Co., 1946.

Shange, Ntozake. *Betsy Brown*. New York: St. Martin's Press, 1985.

———. *Sassafrass, Cypress and Indigo*. New York: St. Martin's Press, 1982.

Shockley, Ann Allen. *The Black and the White of It*. Florida: Naiad Press, 1980.

———. *Loving Her*. New York: Avon, 1974.

———. *Say Jesus and Come to Me*. Avon, 1982.

Sutherland, Ellease. *Let the Lion Eat Straw*. New York: New American Library, 1979.

Walker, Alice. *The Color Purple*. New York: Harcourt Brace Jovanovich, 1982.

———. *In Love and Trouble*. New York: Harcourt Brace Jovanovich, 1973.

———. *Meridian*. New York: Harcourt Brace Jovanovich, 1976.

———. *The Third Life of Grange Copeland*. New York: Harcourt Brace Jovanovich, 1970.

———. *You Can't Keep a Good Woman Down*. New York: Harcourt Brace Jovanovich, 1981.

Walker, Margaret. *Jubilee*. Boston: Houghton Mifflin, 1966. Reprint, New York: Bantam, 1975.

West, Dorothy. *The Living is Easy*. Boston: Houghton Mifflin Co., 1948.

Wilson, Harriet H. *Our Nig; or, Sketches from the Life of a Free Black in a Two-Story White House, North, Showing that Slavery's Shadows Fall Even There*. Boston: George C. Rand & Avery, 1859; 2nd edition, New York: Vintage Books, 1983.

Wright, Sarah. *This Child's Gonna Live*. New York: Delacorte, 1969. New York: Dell, 1971.

tradition

The late 1970s and early 1980s saw the beginning of the enterprise of mapping out the "tradition" of women's writing. The impulse to tell the story of women authors' relation to their predecessors is part of what Elaine Showalter (in "Feminist Criticism in the Wilderness") named "gynocriticism," the study of female writers in a context of their own, not in relation to the "Great Tradition" that had included a few of them but had rejected so many more. Theories of women's traditions resemble androcentric literary history in that they conceive of literary development in terms of "phases," "modes," or "moments," and they typically see change as evidence of progress. Sometimes, too, they borrow the terminology of mainstream literary movements to describe phases in a tradition, as does Catharine Stimpson when she speaks of "lesbian romanticism" and "lesbian realism," below. Such terms are used, however, without specific reference to their historical links to men's writing.

Because gynocriticism limits its purview to texts written by women, it has become vulnerable to charges of a biologically based essentialism. Critics have become suspicious of assertions about women's writing that seem to suggest universal or ahistorical stereotyping of women, or that seem to point to the physical fact of femaleness as a determinant of how people write. As early as 1977, however, Elaine Showalter's *A Literature of Their Own* anticipated that objection. Showalter—like the other essayists in this section—is very careful to explain that the women's tradition she charts is "the product of a delicate network of influences operating in time," and that it "comes from the still-evolving relationships between women writers and their society." She concentrates on British women writers who published novels after 1840, and she finds in their work "an imaginative continuum, the recurrence of certain patterns, themes, problems, and images from generation to generation." She attributes this to "the female subculture" which, in Victorian England especially, ensured that women's experience of living and of writing would be pointedly distinct from that of men.

Showalter, whose partiality to phases is also evident in her contribution to our "Methodologies" section, helpfully enumerates three moments in the women's tradition she charts: Feminine, Feminist, and Female. Though nonfeminist commentators sometimes unfortunately treat these terms as interchangeable, Showalter painstakingly distinguishes among them, showing how the attitudes novels evince toward women's roles and female authorship are tied in to their cultural contexts in Victorian and modern England. *A Literature of Their Own* does not raise questions about the comparative value of "major" and "minor" novelists' output: Showalter remarks matter-of-factly that "the feminist writers [of the later nineteenth century] were not important artists," without going into the basis for the definition of "important" or "artist" as she does in later work, or as other theorists do here in "Institutions" and "Canon." The purpose of this early moment in finding a tradition was not so much to reclaim lost treasures among obscure women writers, as to "fill in the terrain among . . . literary landmarks," namely, "the Austen peaks, the Brontë cliffs, the Eliot range, and the Woolf hills," as Showalter explains elsewhere in her book. The goal is a new literary history, whose narrative could account for the achievement of women writers everyone accepts as "great."

Sandra M. Gilbert and Susan Gubar are primarily focused in *The Madwoman in the Attic* (1979) upon canonical women writers, though their concentration on the nineteenth century lets them include poets and novelists, British and American, in their tradition. The fragment of the second chapter of *Madwoman* reproduced here, from "Infection in the Sentence: The Woman Writer and the Anxiety of Authorship," can give only a faint indication of the entire work's scale. Over seven hundred pages long, the collaboratively written study elaborates a model of a women's tradition through scores of readings of texts by women authors who have been more or less accepted as "great" writers, ranging from works as obscure as Jane Austen's juvenilia to such generally acknowledged masterpieces as *Middlemarch*. As our sample indicates, the authors allude to points established in previous chapters (here, the mentions of Snow White refer back to a close reading performed in chapter 1) to build their theory of the links among nineteenth-century women writers' texts. Like Showalter, they analyze women writers' relation to their literary foremothers in order to "reveal the extraordinary strength of women's literary accomplishments" against daunting odds.

The first section of the chapter outlines Gilbert and Gubar's enormously influential revision of Harold Bloom's Freudian theory of "the anxiety of influence" among authors. Gilbert and Gubar are quick to point out that Bloom's examples—like Freud's—are all male, and that his theory can neither be adopted nor reversed to account for authors working in the female subculture (which is, for Gilbert and Gubar as for Showalter, a historical given). Women authors, they argue, experience "the anxiety of authorship," doubly explicable as a feminine version of Bloom's theory and as women authors' individual and collective response to the pervasive Western metaphor of "literary paternity," that is, the idea that the author stands in a fatherly relation to the text. "Based on the woman's socially determined sense of her own biology," this anxiety makes its way into women's texts in recurring patterns of themes, forms, and motifs. The excerpt from the chapter places women's anxiety about disease and about their bodies in historical context, links it to authorial anxiety, and begins sketching out strategies some nineteenth-century writers use to express and to overcome their sense of "infection in the sentence," as Emily Dickinson called it. The balance of the chapter, with typical Gilbert-and-Gubar scope, brings the theory to bear upon authors from Aphra Behn to H.D., from Jane Austen to Virginia Woolf, from George Eliot to Charlotte Perkins Gilman.

While Showalter's and Gilbert and Gubar's traditions revise literary history to better account for the place of canonized women writers in it, other theorists have sketched out alternate traditions, parallel to but not dependent upon the developments in writing by white, heterosexual, middle-class women authors. Here we have selected two accounts of such traditions—the lesbian novel and the African–American women's novel—to suggest the diversity of traditions that have been perceived in women's writing, but by no means to exhaust the possibilities. Both Catharine R. Stimpson and Barbara Christian are working here to write literary histories of traditions that had been entirely excluded from conventional studies of "great literature" and that hold only a peripheral place in traditions based on "great women writers." Each conceives of the tradition she sketches out as independent and free-standing, though each also marks the ways her tradition has developed in response to and in reaction against the dominant culture's conception of lesbians and of black women.

Catharine R. Stimpson's "Zero Degree Deviancy: The Lesbian Novel in English" (1981) depends for its thesis on this model of response and reaction. The idea of "writing degree zero" (borrowed from Roland Barthes) begins with the assumption that all texts are written and read in a context, and that all writing and reading will be marked by influences coming from that context: a "zero-degree" text, free of such markings, is a theoretical near-impossibility. In the case of the lesbian novel, Stimpson explains, the relevant context is homophobia: "Because the violent yoking of homosexuality and deviancy has been so pervasive in the modern period, little or no writing about it can ignore that conjunction." Stimpson sees most lesbian novels as confronting that conjunction according to one of two narrative patterns, "the dying fall," where the lesbian protagonist is defeated (epitomized in Radclyffe Hall's *The Well of Loneliness*) and "the enabling escape," where she prevails. ("Enabling," in this usage, carries none of the negative connotations it has recently acquired in the language of pop-psychology; it means something like what "empowering" means now.) Stimpson's use of "lesbian" is, she says, "severely literal"; she is making this choice of definition in the context of the debate outlined in Bonnie Zimmerman's essay in the "Methodologies" section. Stimpson surveys the image and the fate of the lesbian protagonist in fiction from Hall's formerly obscure novel, through Mary McCarthy's popular success, *The Group*, to Bertha Harris's highly experimental *Lover*. She traces a distinct pattern of progress in the tradition, observing that "a far less tormented lesbian has surfaced" in fiction since the 1960s, and holding that "the lesbian novel has offered up Hall's [dark] vision, but it has also sheltered and released the rejection of that vision, offering an alternative process of affirmation of the lesbian body and transcendence of a culturally traced, scarring stigma." The tradition of the lesbian novel, then, can be seen as contributing to the formation of a positive identity among lesbians.

The positive formation of black women's identity is the issue in Barbara Christian's "Trajectories of Self-Definition: Placing Contemporary Afro-American Women's Fiction" (1983). Just as Stimpson focuses on textual strategies for confronting homophobia, Christian looks at the ways black women's novels respond to the conjunction of racism and sexism in America. Christian sees the tradition of black women writers as a continuous struggle to achieve self-expression, "to be able to use the range of one's voice, to attempt to express the totality of self" in the face of the culture's negative stereotyping of black women. Like the other cartographers of traditions, Christian perceives a shift: whereas early black women novelists addressed a primarily white audience, either conforming to the dominant notion of the "feminine ideal" in their portraits of black heroines or struggling against that ideal, novelists since Gwendolyn Brooks are "putting more emphasis on reflecting the process of self-definition . . . that women have always had to be engaged in, rather than refuting the general society's definition of them." This movement, which Christian breaks down chronologically into phases, coincides—not accidentally—with the novelists' move toward addressing a black audience first, and a mainstream audience only incidentally.

Christian, like Stimpson, sees ground for hope in the most recent developments of the tradition. She affirms the broader variety of social class and geographical placement that emerged among black women's protagonists in the early 1980s, and lauds the arrival of the black lesbian heroine in recent works. For Christian as for Stimpson, an appreciation of the black women novelists' tradition has consequences extending beyond academic circles. As Christian puts it, "the fiction of the early eighties communicates the sense that women of color can no longer be perceived as marginal to the empowerment of all America women and that an understanding of their reality and imagination is essential to the process of change that the entire society must undergo in order to transform itself." Whether the tradition in question embraces primarily canonical authors, lesbian novelists, black women writers, or another group of female authors, the pupose of telling the story of the tradition is always the same, always the social transformation Christian envisions.

—RRW

THE FEMALE TRADITION

The advent of female literature promises woman's view of life, woman's experience: in other words, a new element. Make what distinctions you please in the social world, it still remains true that men and women have different organizations, consequently different experiences. . . . But hitherto . . . the literature of women has fallen short of its functions owing to a very natural and a very explicable weakness—it has been too much a literature of imitation. To write as men write is the aim and besetting sin of women; to write as women is the real task they have to perform.

—G. H. LEWES, "THE LADY NOVELISTS," 1852

English women writers have never suffered from the lack of a reading audience, nor have they wanted for attention from scholars and critics. Yet we have never been sure what unites them as women, or, indeed, whether they share a common heritage connected to their womanhood at all. Writing about female creativity in *The Subjection of Women* (1869), John Stuart Mill argued that women would have a hard struggle to overcome the influence of male literary tradition, and to create an original, primary, and independent art. "If women lived in a different country from men," Mill thought, "and had never read any of their writings, they would have a literature of their own." Instead, he reasoned, they would always be imitators and never innovators. Paradoxically, Mill would never have raised this point had women not already claimed a very important literary place. To many of his contemporaries (and to many of ours), it seemed that the nineteenth century was the Age of the Female Novelist. With such stellar examples as Jane Austen, Charlotte Brontë, and George Eliot, the question of women's aptitude for fiction, at any rate, had been answered. But a larger question was whether women, excluded by custom and education from achieving distinction in poetry, history, or drama, had, in defining their literary culture in the novel, simply appropriated another masculine genre. Both George Henry Lewes and Mill, spokesmen for women's rights and Victorian liberalism in general, felt that, like the Romans in the shadow of Greece, women were overshadowed by male cultural imperialism: "If women's literature is destined to have a different collective character from that of men," wrote Mill, "much longer time is necessary than has yet elapsed before it can emancipate itself from the influence of accepted models, and guide itself by its own impulses."[1]

There is clearly a difference between books that happen to have been written by women, and a "female literature," as Lewes tried to define it, which purposefully and collectively concerns itself with the articulation of women's experience, and which guides itself "by its own impulses" to autonomous self-expression. As novelists, women have always been self-conscious, but only rarely self-defining. While they have been deeply and perennially aware of their individual identities and experiences, women writers have very infrequently considered whether these experiences might transcend the personal and local, assume a collective form in art, and reveal a history. During the intensely feminist period from 1880 to 1910, both British and American women writers explored the theme of an Amazon utopia, a country entirely populated by women and completely isolated from the male world. Yet even in these fantasies of autonomous female communities, there is no theory of female art. Feminist utopias were not visions of primary womanhood, free to define its own nature and culture, but flights from the male world to a culture defined in opposition to the male tradition. Typically the feminist utopias are pastoral sanctuaries, where a population of prelapsarian Eves cultivate their organic gardens, cure water pollution, and run exemplary child care centers, but do not write books.

In contradiction to Mill, and in the absence, until very recently, of any feminist literary manifestoes, many readers of the novel over the past two centuries have nonetheless had the indistinct but persistent impression of a unifying voice in women's literature. In *The History of the English Novel*, Ernest Baker devotes a separate chapter to the women novelists, commenting that "the woman of letters has peculiarities that mark her off from the other sex as distinctly as peculiarities of race or of ancestral traditions. Whatever variety of talent, outlook or personal disposition may be discernible among any dozen women writers taken at random, it will be matched and probably outweighed by resemblances distinctively feminine."[2] Baker wisely does not attempt to present a taxonomy of these feminine "peculiarities"; most critics who have attempted to do so have quickly found themselves expressing their own cultural biases rather than explicating sexual structures. In 1852, Lewes thought he could identify the feminine literary traits as Sentiment and Observation; in 1904, William L. Courtney found that "the female author is at once self-conscious and didactic"; in 1965, Bernard Bergonzi explained that "women novelists . . . like to keep their focus narrow."[3] Women reading each other's books have also had difficulties in explaining their potential for what George Eliot called a "precious specialty, lying quite apart from masculine aptitudes and experience." Eliot herself tried to locate the female specialty in the maternal affections.[4]

Statements about the personal and psychological qualities of the woman novelist have also flourished, and have been equally impressionist and unreliable. The "lady novelist" is a composite of many stereotypes: to J. M. Ludlow, she is a creature with ink halfway up her fingers, dirty shawls, and frowsy hair; and to W. S. Gilbert, a "singular anomaly" who never would be missed.[5] To critics of the twentieth century, she is childless and, by implication, neurotic: "We remind ourselves," writes Carolyn Heilbrun, "that of the great women writers, most have been unmarried, and those who have written in the state of wedlock have done so in peaceful kingdoms guarded by devoted husbands. Few have had children."[6] Nancy Milford asks whether there were any women "who married in their youth and bore children and continued to write . . . think of the women who have written: the unmarried, the married and childless, the very few with a single child and that one observed as if it were a rock to be stubbed against."[7]

There are many reasons why discussion of women writers has been so inaccurate, fragmented, and partisan. First, women's literary history has suffered from an extreme form of what John Gross calls "residual Great Traditionalism,"[8] which has reduced and condensed the extraordinary range and diversity of English women novelists to a tiny band of the "great," and derived all theories from them. In practice, the concept of greatness for women novelists often turns out to mean four or five writers—Jane Austen, the Brontës, George Eliot, and Virginia Woolf—and even theoretical studies of "the woman novelist" turn out to be endless recyclings and recombinations of insights about "indispensable Jane and George."[9] Criticism of women novelists, while focusing on these happy few, has ignored those who are not "great," and left them out of anthologies, histories, textbooks, and theories. Having lost sight of the minor novelists, who were the links in the chain that bound one generation to the next, we have not had a very clear understanding of the continuities in women's writing, nor any reliable information about the relationships between the writers' lives and the changes in the legal, economic, and social status of women.

Second, it has been difficult for critics to consider women novelists and women's literature theoretically because of their tendency to project and expand their own culture-bound stereotypes of femininity, and to see in women's writing an eternal opposition of biological and aesthetic creativity. The Victorians expected women's novels to reflect the feminine values they exalted, although obviously the woman novelist herself had outgrown the constraining feminine role. "Come what will," Charlotte Brontë wrote to Lewes, "I cannot, when I write, think always of myself and what is elegant and charming in femininity; it is not on these terms, or with such ideas, that I ever took pen in hand."[10] Even if we ignore the excesses of what Mary Ellmann calls "phallic criticism" and what Cynthia Ozick calls the "ovarian theory of literature," much contemporary criticism of women writers is still prescriptive and circumscribed.[11] Given the difficulties of steering a precarious course between the Scylla of insufficient information and the Charybdis of abundant prejudice, it is not surprising that formalist-structuralist critics have evaded the issue of sexual identity entirely, or dismissed it as irrelevant and subjective. Finding it difficult to think intelligently about women writers, academic criticism has often overcompensated by desexing them.

Yet since the 1960s, and especially since the reemergence of a Women's Liberation Movement in England and in America around 1968, there has been renewed enthusiasm for the idea that "a special female self-awareness emerges through literature in every period."[12] The interest in establishing a more reliable critical vocabulary and a more accurate and systematic literary history for women writers is part of a larger interdisciplinary effort by psychologists, sociologists, social historians, and art historians to reconstruct the political, social, and cultural experience of women.

Scholarship generated by the contemporary feminist movement has increased our sensitivity to the problems of sexual bias or projection in literary history, and has also begun to provide us with the information we need to understand the evolution of a female literary tradition. One of the most significant contributions has been the unearthing and reinterpretation of "lost" works by women writers, and the documentation of their lives and careers.

In the past, investigations have been distorted by the emphasis on an elite group, not only because it has excluded from our attention great stretches of literary activity between, for example, George Eliot and Virginia Woolf, but also because it has rendered invisible the daily lives, the physical experiences, the personal strategies and conflicts of ordinary women. If we want to define the ways in which "female self-awareness" has expressed itself in the English novel, we need to see the woman novelist against the backdrop of the women of her time, as well as in relation to other writers in history. Virginia Woolf recognized that need:

> The extraordinary woman depends on the ordinary woman. It is only when we know what were the conditions of the average woman's life—the number of her children, whether she had money of her own, if she had a room to herself, whether she had help in bringing up her family, if she had servants, whether part of the housework was her task—it is only when we can measure the way of life and the experience of life made possible to the ordinary woman that we can account for the success or failure of the extraordinary woman as writer.[13]

As scholars have been persuaded that women's experience is important, they have begun to see it for the first time. With a new perceptual framework, material hitherto assumed to be nonexistent has suddenly leaped into focus. Interdisciplinary studies of Victorian women have opened up new areas of investigation in medicine, psychology, economics, political science, labor history, and art.[14] Questions of the "female imagination" have taken on intellectual weight in the contexts of theories of Karen Horney about feminine psychology, Erik Erikson about womanhood and the inner space, and R. D. Laing about the divided self. Investigation of female iconography and imagery has been stimulated by the work of art historians like Linda Nochlin, Lise Vogel, and Helene Roberts.[15]

As the works of dozens of women writers have been rescued from what E. P. Thompson calls "the enormous condescension of posterity,"[16] and considered in relation to each other, the lost continent of the female tradition has risen like Atlantis from the sea of English literature. It is now becoming clear that, contrary to Mill's theory, women have had a literature of their own all along. The woman novelist, according to Vineta Colby, was "really neither single nor anomalous," but she was also more than a "register and a spokesman for her age."[17] She was part of a tradition that had its origins before her age, and has carried on through our own.

Many literary historians have begun to reinterpret and revise the study of women writers. Ellen Moers sees women's literature as an international movement, "apart from, but hardly subordinate to the mainstream: an undercurrent, rapid and powerful. This 'movement' began in the late eighteenth century, was multinational, and produced some of the greatest literary works of two centuries, as well as most of the lucrative pot-boilers."[18] Patricia Meyer Spacks, in *The Fe-*

male Imagination, finds that "for readily discernible historical reasons women have characteristically concerned themselves with matters more or less peripheral to male concerns, or at least slightly skewed from them. The differences between traditional female preoccupations and roles and male ones make a difference in female writing."[19] Many other critics are beginning to agree that when we look at women writers collectively we can see an imaginative continuum, the recurrence of certain patterns, themes, problems, and images from generation to generation.

This book is an effort to describe the female literary tradition in the English novel from the generation of the Brontës to the present day, and to show how the development of this tradition is similar to the development of any literary subculture. Women have generally been regarded as "sociological chameleons," taking on the class, life-style, and culture of their male relatives. It can, however, be argued that women themselves have constituted a subculture within the framework of a larger society, and have been unified by values, conventions, experiences, and behaviors impinging on each individual. It is important to see the female literary tradition in these broad terms, in relation to the wider evolution of women's self-awareness and to the ways in which any minority group finds its direction of self-expression relative to a dominant society, because we cannot show a pattern of deliberate progress and accumulation. It is true, as Ellen Moers writes, that "women studied with a special closeness the works written by their own sex";[20] in terms of influences, borrowings, and affinities, the tradition is strongly marked. But it is also full of holes and hiatuses, because of what Germaine Greer calls the "phenomenon of the transience of female literary fame"; "almost uninterruptedly since the Interregnum, a small group of women have enjoyed dazzling literary prestige during their own lifetimes, only to vanish without trace from the records of posterity."[21] Thus each generation of women writers has found itself, in a sense, without a history, forced to rediscover the past anew, forging again and again the consciousness of their sex. Given this perpetual disruption, and also the self-hatred that has alienated women writers from a sense of collective identity, it does not seem possible to speak of a "movement."

I am also uncomfortable with the notion of a "female imagination." The theory of a female sensibility revealing itself in an imagery and form specific to women always runs dangerously close to reiterating the familiar stereotypes. It also suggests permanence, a deep, basic, and inevitable difference between male and female ways of perceiving the world. I think that, instead, the female literary tradition comes from the still-evolving relationships between women writers and their society. Moreover, the "female imagination" cannot be treated by literary historians as a romantic or Freudian abstraction. It is the product of a delicate network of influences operating in time, and it must be analyzed as it expresses itself, in language and in a fixed arrangement of words on a page, a form that itself is subject to a network of influences and conventions, including the operations of the marketplace. In this investigation of the English novel, I am intentionally looking, not at an innate sexual attitude, but at the ways in which the self-awareness of the woman writer has translated itself into a literary form in a specific place and time-span, how this self-awareness has changed and developed, and where it might lead.

I am therefore concerned with the professional writer who wants pay and publication, not with the diarist or letter-writer. This emphasis has required careful consideration of the novelists, as well as the novels, chosen for discussion. When we turn from the overview of the literary tradition to look at the individuals who composed it, a different but interrelated set of motives, drives, and sources becomes prominent. I have needed to ask why women began to write for money and how they negotiated the activity of writing within their families. What was their professional self-image? How was their work received, and what effects did criticism have upon them? What were their experiences as women, and how were these reflected in their books? What was their understanding of womanhood? What were their relationships to other women, to men, and to their readers? How did changes in women's status affect their lives and careers? And how did the vocation of writing itself change the women who committed themselves to it? In looking at literary subcultures, such as black, Jewish, Canadian, Anglo-Indian, or even American, we can see that they all go through three major phases. First, there is a prolonged phase of *imitation* of the prevailing modes of the dominant tradition, and *internalization* of its standards of art and its views on social roles. Second, there is a phase of *protest* against these standards and values, and *advocacy* of minority rights and values, including a demand for autonomy. Finally, there is a phase of *self-discovery*, a turning inward freed from some of the dependency of opposition, a search for identity.[22] An appropriate terminology for women writers is to call these stages, *Feminine, Feminist*, and *Female*. These are obviously not rigid categories, distinctly separable in time, to which individual writers can be assigned with perfect assurance. The phases overlap; there are feminist elements in feminine writing, and vice versa. One might also find all three phases in the career of a single novelist. Nonetheless, it seems useful to point to periods of crisis when a shift of literary values occurred. In this book I identify the Feminine phase as the period from the appearance of the male pseudonym in the 1840s to the death of George Eliot in 1880; the Feminist phase as 1880 to 1920, or the winning of the vote; and the Female phase as 1920 to the present, but entering a new stage of self-awareness about 1960.

It is important to understand the female subculture not only as what Cynthia Ozick calls "custodial"[23]—a set of opinions, prejudices, tastes, and values prescribed for a subordinate group to perpetuate its subordination—but also as a thriving and positive entity. Most discussions of women as a subculture have come from historians describing Jacksonian America, but they apply equally well to the situation of early Victorian England. According to Nancy Cott, "we can view women's group consciousness as a subculture uniquely divided against itself by ties to the dominant culture. While the ties to the dominant culture are the informing and restricting ones, they provoke within the subculture certain strengths as well as weaknesses, enduring values as well as accommodations."[24] The middle-class ideology of the proper sphere of womanhood, which developed in post-industrial England and America, prescribed a woman who would be a Perfect Lady, an Angel in the House, contentedly submissive to men, but strong in her inner purity and religiosity, queen in her own realm of the Home.[25] Many observers have pointed out that the first professional activities of Victorian women, as social reformers, nurses, governesses, and novelists, either were based in the home or were extensions of the feminine role as teacher, helper, and mother of mankind. In describing the American situation, two historians have seen a subculture emerging from the doctrine of sexual spheres:

> By "subculture" we mean simply "a habit of living" . . . of a minority group which is self-consciously distinct from the dominant activities, expectations, and values of a society. Historians have seen female church groups, reform associations, and philanthropic activity as expressions of this subculture in actual behavior, while a large and rich body of writing by and for women articulated the subculture impulses on the ideational level. Both behavior and thought point to child-rearing, religious activity, education, home life, associationism, and female communality as components of women's subculture. Female friendships, strikingly intimate and deep in this period, formed the actual bonds.[26]

For women in England, the female subculture came first through a shared and increasingly secretive and ritualized physical experience. Puberty, menstruation, sexual initiation, pregnancy, childbirth, and menopause—the entire female sexual life cycle—constituted a habit of living that had to be concealed. Although these episodes could not be openly discussed or acknowledged, they were accompanied by elaborate rituals and lore, by external codes of fashion and etiquette, and by intense feelings of female solidarity.[27] Women writers were united by their roles as daughters, wives, and mothers; by the internalized doctrines of evangelicalism, with its suspicion of the imagination and its emphasis on duty; and by legal and economic constraints on their mobility. Sometimes they were united in a more immediate way, around a political cause. On the whole these are the implied unities of culture, rather than the active unities of consciousness.

From the beginning, however, women novelists' awareness of each other and of their female audience showed a kind of covert solidarity that sometimes amounted to a genteel conspiracy. Advocating sisterhood, Sarah Ellis, one of the most conservative writers of the first Victorian generation, asked: "What should we think of a community of slaves, who betrayed each other's interests? of a little band of shipwrecked mariners upon a friendless shore who were false to each other? of the inhabitants of a defenceless nation, who would not unite together in earnestness and good faith against a common enemy?"[28] Mrs. Ellis felt the binding force of the minority experience for women strongly enough to hint, in the prefaces to her widely read treatises on English womanhood, that her female audience would both read the messages between her lines and refrain from betraying what they deciphered. As another conservative novelist, Dinah Mulock Craik, wrote, "The intricacies of female nature are incomprehensible except to a woman; and any biographer of real womanly feeling, if ever she discovered, would never dream of publishing them."[29] Few English women writers openly advocated the use of fiction as revenge against a patriarchal society (as did the American novelist Fanny Fern, for example), but many confessed to sentiments of "maternal feeling, sisterly affection, *esprit de corps*"[30] for their readers. Thus the clergyman's daughter, going to Mudie's for her three-decker novel by another clergyman's daughter, participated in a cultural exchange that had a special personal significance.

It is impossible to say when women began to write fiction. From about 1750 on, English women made steady inroads into the literary marketplace, mainly as novelists. As early as 1773, the *Monthly Review* noticed that "that branch of the literary trade" seemed "almost entirely engrossed by the ladies." J.M.S. Tompkins finds that most eighteenth-century epistolary novels were written by women; the Minerva Press published twice as many novels by women as by men; and Ian Watt simply says that the majority of all eighteenth-century novels came from the female pen.[31] At the same time, men were able to imitate, and even usurp, female experience. Oliver Goldsmith suspected that men were writing sentimental novels under female pseudonyms, and men did write books on childcare, midwifery, housekeeping, and cooking.[32]

Early women writers' relationship to their professional role was uneasy. Eighteenth-century women novelists exploited a stereotype of helpless femininity to win chivalrous protection from male reviewers and to minimize their unwomanly self-assertion. In 1791 Elizabeth Inchbald prefaced *A Simple Story* with the lie that she was a poor invalid who had written a novel despite "the utmost detestation to the fatigue of inventing."[33] At the turn of the century, women evaded the issue of professional identity by publishing anonymously. In 1810 Mary Brunton explained in a letter to a friend why she preferred anonymity to taking credit for her novels:

> I would rather, as you well know, glide through the world unknown, than have (I will not call it *enjoy*) fame, however brilliant, to be pointed at,—to be noticed and commented upon—to be suspected of literary airs—to be shunned, as literary women are, by the more unpretending of my own sex; and abhorred as literary women are, by the pretending of the other!—my dear, I would sooner exhibit as a rope-dancer.[34]

Here again we need to remember the distinction between the novel as a form, and the professional role of the novelist. Many of the most consistent themes and images of the feminine novel, from the mysterious interiors of Gothic romance to the balancing of duty and self-fulfillment in domestic fiction, can be traced back to the late eighteenth century. Certainly nineteenth-century women novelists had some familiarity with Burney, Edgeworth, Radcliffe, and Austen, as well as with scores of lesser writers such as Inchbald and Hofland. But almost no sense of communality and self-awareness is apparent among women writers before the 1840s, which Kathleen Tillotson sees as the decade in which the novel became the dominant form. Tillotson points out that, despite the respectful attention paid by mid-Victorian critics to Jane Austen (attention that had some negative impact on Victorian women novelists), there appears to have been relatively little direct influence by Austen on Mrs. Gaskell, Harriet Martineau, the Brontës, and several minor writers.[35] Even George Eliot's debt to Austen has been much exaggerated by the concept of the Great Tradition.[36] The works of Mary Wollstonecraft were not widely read by the Victorians due to the scandals surrounding her life.

More important than the question of direct literary influence, however, is the difference between the social and professional worlds inhabited by the eighteenth- and nineteenth-century women. The early women writers refused to deal with a professional role, or had a negative orientation toward it. "What is my life?" lamented the poet Laetitia Landon. "One day of drudgery after another; difficulties incurred for others, which have ever pressed upon me beyond health, which every year, in one severe illness after another, is taxed beyond its strength; envy, malice, and all uncharitableness—these are the fruits of a successful literary career for a woman."[37] These women may have been less than sincere in their insistence that literary success brought them only suffering, but they were not able to see themselves as involved in a vocation that brought responsibilities as well as conflicts, and opportunities as well as burdens. Moreover, they did not see their writing as an aspect of their female experience, or as an expression of it.

Thus, in talking about the situation of the feminine novelists, I have begun with the women born after 1800, who began to publish fiction during the 1840s when the job of the novelist was becoming a recognizable profession. One of the many indications that this generation saw the will to write as a vocation in direct conflict with their status as women is the appearance of the male pseudonym. Like Eve's fig leaf, the male pseudonym signals the loss of innocence. In its radical understanding of the role-playing required by women's effort to participate in the mainstream of literary culture, the pseudonym is a strong marker of the historical shift.

There were three generations of nineteenth-century feminine novelists. The first, born between 1800 and 1820, included all the women who are identified with the Golden Age of the Victorian authoress: the Brontës, Mrs. Gaskell, Elizabeth Barrett Browning, Harriet Martineau, and George Eliot. The members of this group, whose coevals were Florence Nightingale, Mary Carpenter, Angela Burdett, and other pioneer professionals, were what sociologists call "female role innovators"; they were breaking new ground and creating new possibilities. The second generation, born between 1820 and 1840, included Charlotte Yonge, Dinah Mulock Craik, Margaret Oliphant, and Elizabeth Lynn Linton; these women followed in the footsteps of the great, consolidating their gains, but were less dedicated and original. The third generation, born between 1840 and 1860, included sensation novelists and children's book writers. They seemed to cope effortlessly with the double roles of woman and professional, and to enjoy sexual fulfillment as well as literary success. Businesslike, unconventional, efficient, and productive, they moved into editorial and publishing positions as well as writing.

By the time the women of the first generation had entered upon their careers, there was already a sense of what the "feminine" novel meant in terms of genres. By the 1840s women writers had adopted a variety of popular genres, and were specializing in novels of fashionable life, education, religion, and community, which Vineta Colby subsumes under the heading "domestic realism." In all these novels, according to Inga-Stina Ewbank, "the central preoccupation . . . is with the woman as an influence on others within her domestic and social circle. It was in this preoccupation that the typical woman novelist of the 1840s found her proper sphere: in using the novel to demonstrate (by assumption rather than exploration of standards of womanliness) *woman's* proper sphere."[38] A double standard of literary criticism had also developed, as I show in chapter 3, with a special set of terms and requirements for fiction by women.

There was a place for such fiction, but even the most conservative and devout women novelists, such as Charlotte Yonge and Dinah Craik, were aware that the "feminine" novel also stood for feebleness, ignorance, prudery, refinement, propriety, and sentimentality, while the feminine novelist was portrayed as vain, publicity-seeking, and self-assertive. At the time that Victorian reviewers assumed that women readers and women writers were dictating the content of fiction, they deplored the pettiness and narrowness implied by a feminine value system. "Surely it is very questionable," wrote Fitzjames Stephen, "whether it is desirable that no novels should be written except those fit for young ladies to read."[39]

Victorian feminine novelists thus found themselves in a double bind. They felt humiliated by the condescension of male critics and spoke intensely of their desire to avoid special treatment and achieve genuine excellence, but they were deeply anxious about the possibility of appearing unwomanly. Part of the conflict came from the fact that, rather than confronting the values of their society, these women novelists were competing for its rewards. For women, as for other subcultures, literature became a symbol of achievement.

In the face of this dilemma, women novelists developed several strategies, both personal and artistic. Among the personal reactions was a persistent self-deprecation of themselves as women, sometimes expressed as humility, sometimes as coy assurance-seeking, and sometimes as the purest self-hatred. In a letter to John Blackwood, Mrs. Oliphant expressed doubt about "whether in your most manly and masculine of magazines a womanish story-teller like myself may not become wearisome."[40] The novelists publicly proclaimed, and sincerely believed, their antifeminism. By working in the home, by preaching submission and self-sacrifice, and by denouncing female self-assertiveness, they worked to atone for their own will to write.

Vocation—the will to write—nonetheless required a genuine transcendence of female identity. Victorian women were not accustomed to *choosing* a vocation; womanhood was a vocation in itself. The evangelically inspired creed of work did affect women, even though it had not been primarily directed toward them. Like men, women were urged to "bear their part in the *work* of life."[41] Yet for men, the gospel of work satisfied both self-interest and the public interest. In pursuing their ambitions, they fulfilled social expectations.

For women, however, work meant labor for *others*. Work, in the sense of self-development, was in direct conflict with the subordination and repression inherent in the feminine ideal. The self-centeredness implicit in the act of writing made this career an especially threatening one; it required an engagement with feeling and a cultivation of the ego rather than its negation. The widely circulated treatises of Hannah More and Sarah Ellis translated the abstractions of "women's mission" into concrete programs of activity, which made writing appear selfish, unwomanly, and unchristian. "'What shall I do to gratify myself—to be admired—or to vary the tenor of my existence?'" are not, according to Mrs. Ellis, "questions which a woman of right feelings asks on first awakening to the avocations of the day." Instead she recommends visiting the sick, fixing breakfast for anyone setting on a journey in order to spare the servant, or general "devotion to the good of the whole family." "Who can believe," she asks fervently, "that days, months, and years spent in a continual course of thought and action similar to this, will not produce a powerful effect upon the character?"[42] Of course it did; one notices first of all that feminine writers like Elizabeth Barrett Browning, "Charlotte Elizabeth," Elizabeth M. Sewell, and Mrs. Ellis herself had to overcome deep-seated guilt about authorship. Many found it necessary to justify their work by recourse to some external stimulus or ideology. In their novels, the heroine's aspirations for a full, independent life are undermined, punished, or replaced by marriage.

Elizabeth Barrett Browning's *Aurora Leigh* (1857) is one of the few autobiographical discussions of feminine role conflict. Aurora's struggle to become an artist is complicated by the self-hatred in which she has been educated, by her internalized convictions of her weakness and narcissism, and by the gentle scorn of her suitor Romney. She defies him, however, and invokes divine authority to reject his proposal that she become his helpmeet:

> You misconceive the question like a man
> Who sees the woman as the complement
> Of his sex merely. You forget too much
> That every creature, female as the male,
> Stands single in responsible act and thought . . .
> I too have my vocation,—work to do,
> The heavens and earth have set me.
>
> (Book II, 460–466)

Aurora succeeds as a poet. But she marries Romney in the end, having learned that as a woman she cannot cope with the guilt of self-centered ambition. It is significant that Romney has been blinded in an accident before she marries him, not only because he has thereby received firsthand knowledge of being handicapped and can empathize with her, but also because he then needs her help and can provide her with suitably feminine work. When Aurora tells Romney that "No perfect artist is developed here/ From any imperfect woman" (Book IX, 648–649) she means more than the perfection of love and motherhood; she means also the perfection of self-sacrifice. This conflict remains a significant one for English novelists up to the present; it is a major theme for women novelists from Charlotte Brontë to Penelope Mortimer. Male novelists like Thackeray, who came from an elite class, also felt uncomfortable with the aggressive self-promotion of the novelist's career. As Donald Stone points out:

> Thackeray's ambivalent feelings towards Becky Sharp indicate the degree to which he attempted to suppress or make light of his own literary talents. The energies which make her (for a time) a social success are akin to those which made him a creative artist. In the hands of a major woman novelist, like Jane Austen or George Eliot, the destructive moral and social implications of Becky's behavior would have been defined more clearly and more urgently. Jane Austen's dissection of Lydia Bennet, and George Eliot's demolition of Rosamond Vincy, for example, indicate both how and why the defense of the status quo—insofar as women of the nineteenth century were concerned— was most earnestly and elaborately performed by women writers. Their heroines are hardly concerned with self-fulfillment in the modern sense of the term, and if they have severely limited possibilities in life it is because their authors saw great danger in, plus a higher alternative to, the practice of self-assertiveness.[43]

The dilemma is stated by George Eliot in *Romola* as the question of where "the duty of obedience ends and the duty of resistance begins."[44] Yet this was the question any Victorian woman with the will to write would have had to ask herself: what did God intend her to do with her life? Where did obedience to her father and husband end, and the responsibility of self-fulfillment become paramount? The problem of obedience and resistance that women had to solve in their own lives before they could begin to write crops up in their novels as the heroine's moral crisis. The forms that the crisis takes in feminine fiction are realistically mundane—should Margaret, in Mrs. Gaskell's *North and South,* lie to protect her brother? should Ethel May, in Charlotte Younge's *Daisy Chain,* give up studying Greek to nurse her father?—but the sources were profound, and were connected to the women novelists' sense of epic life. At the same time that they recognized the modesty of their own struggles, women writers recognized their heroism. "A new Theresa will hardly have the opportunity of reforming a conventual life," wrote George Eliot in *Middlemarch,* "any more than a new Antigone will spend her heroic piety in daring all for a brother's burial: the medium in which their ardent deeds took shape is forever gone. But we insignificant people with our daily words and acts are preparing the lives of many Dorotheas, some of which may present a far sadder sacrifice than that of the Dorothea whose story we know." [45]

The training of Victorian girls in repression, concealment, and self-censorship was deeply inhibiting, especially for those who wanted to write. As one novelist commented in 1860, "Women are greater dissemblers than men when they wish to conceal their own emotions. By habit, moral training, and modern education, they are obliged to do so. The very first lessons of infancy teach them to repress their feelings, control their very thoughts." [46] The verbal range permitted to English gentlewomen amounted almost to a special language. The verbal inhibitions that were part of the upbringing of a lady were reinforced by the critics' vigilance. "It is an immense loss," lamented Alice James, "to have all robust and sustaining expletives refined away from one." [47] "Coarseness" was the term Victorian readers used to rebuke unconventional language in women's literature. It could refer to the "damns" in *Jane Eyre,* the dialect in *Wuthering Heights,* the slang of Rhoda Broughton's heroines, the colloquialisms in *Aurora Leigh,* or more generally to the moral tone of a work, such as the "vein of perilous voluptuousness" one alert critic detected in *Adam Bede.* [48] John Keble censored Charlotte Yonge's fiction, taking the greatest care "that no hint of 'coarseness' should sully the purity of Charlotte's writings. Thus he would not allow Theodora in *Heartsease* to say that 'really she had a heart, though some people thought it was only a machine for pumping blood.' He also transformed the 'circle' of the setting sun into an 'orb' and a 'coxcomb' into a 'jackanapes'." [49] While verbal force, wit, and originality in women was criticized, a bland and gelatinous prose won applause. "She writes as an English gentlewoman should write," the *North British Review* complimented Anne Marsh in 1849; "her pages are absolutely like green pastures." [50] Reduced to a pastoral flatness, deprived of a language in which to describe their bodies or the events of their bodies, denied the expression of pain as well as the expression of pleasure, women writers appeared deficient in passion.

It is easy to understand why many readers took the absence of expression for the absence of feeling. In "The False Morality of Lady Novelists," W. R. Greg argued that woman's sexual innocence would prevent her ever writing a great novel:

Many of the saddest and deepest truths in the strange science of sexual affection are to her mysteriously and mercifully veiled and can only be purchased at such a fearful cost that we cannot wish it otherwise. The inevitable consequence however is that in treating of that science she labours under all the disadvantages of partial study and superficial insight. She is describing a country of which she knows only the more frequented and the safer roads, with a few of the sweeter scenes and the prettier by-paths and more picturesque detours which be not far from the broad and beaten thoroughfares; while the rockier and loftier mountains, and more rugged tracts, the more sombre valleys, and the darker and more dangerous chasms, are never trodden by her feet, and scarcely ever dreamed of by her fancy.[51]

The results of restrictive education and intensive conditioning were taken as innate evidence of natural preference. In an ironic twist, many reviewers who had paternally barred the way to the sombre valleys, the darker chasms, and the more rugged tracts also blamed women for the emasculation of male prose, finding, like the *Prospective Review*, that the "writing of men is in danger of being marked" by "the delicacy and even fastidiousness of expression which is *natural* to educated women" [my italics].[52] When G. H. Lewes complained in 1852 that the literature of women was "too much a literature of imitation" and demanded that women should express "what they have really known, felt and suffered,"[53] he was asking for something that Victorian society had made impossible. Feminine novelists had been deprived of the language and the consciousness for such an enterprise, and obviously their deprivation extended beyond Victoria's reign and into the twentieth century. The delicacy and verbal fastidiousness of Virginia Woolf is an extension of this feminized language.

Florence Nightingale thought the effort of repression itself drained off women's creative energy. "Give us back our suffering," she demanded in *Cassandra* (1852), "for out of nothing comes nothing. But out of suffering may come the cure. Better have pain than paralysis."[54] It does sometimes seem as if feminine writers are metaphorically paralyzed, as Alice James was literally paralyzed, by refinement and restraint, but the repression in which the feminine novel was situated also forced women to find innovative and covert ways to dramatize the inner life, and led to a fiction that was intense, compact, symbolic, and profound. There is Charlotte Brontë's extraordinary subversion of the Gothic in *Jane Eyre*, in which the mad wife locked in the attic symbolizes the passionate and sexual side of Jane's personality, an alter ego that her upbringing, her religion, and her society have commanded her to incarcerate. There is the crippled artist heroine of Dinah Craik's *Olive* (1850), who identifies with Byron, and whose deformity represents her very womanhood. There are the murderous little wives of Mary Braddon's sensation novels, golden-haired killers whose actions are a sardonic commentary on the real feelings of the Angel in the House.

Many of the fantasies of feminine novels are related to money, mobility, and power. Although feminine novelists punished assertive heroines, they dealt with personal ambition by projecting the ideology of success onto male characters, whose initiative, thrift, industry, and perseverance came straight from the woman author's experience. The "woman's man," discussed in chapter 4, was often a more effective outlet for the "deviant" aspects of the author's personality than were her heroines, and thus male role-playing extended beyond the pseudonym to imaginative content.

Protest fiction represented another projection of female experience onto another group; it translated the felt pain and oppression of women into the championship of millworkers, child laborers, prostitutes, and slaves. Women were aware that protest fiction converted anger and frustration into an acceptable form of feminine and Christian expression. In the social novels of the 1840s and 1850s, and the problem novels of the 1860s and 1870s, women writers were pushing back the boundaries of their sphere, and presenting their profession as one that required not only freedom of language and thought, but also mobility and activity in the world. The sensation novelists of the 1870s, including Mary Braddon, Rhoda Broughton, and Florence Marryat, used this new freedom in a transitional literature that explored genuinely radical female protest against marriage and women's economic oppression, although still in the framework of feminine conventions that demanded the erring heroine's destruction.

From Jane Austen to George Eliot, the woman's novel had moved, despite its restrictions, in the direction of an all-inclusive female realism, a broad, socially informed exploration of the daily lives and values of women within the family and the community. By 1880, the three-decker had become flexible enough to accommodate many of the formerly unprintable aspects of female experience. Yet with the death of George Eliot and the appearance of a new generation of writers, the woman's novel moved into a Feminist phase, a confrontation with male society that elevated Victorian sexual stereotypes into a cult. The feminists challenged many of the restrictions on women's self-expression, denounced the gospel of self-sacrifice, attacked patriarchal religion, and constructed a theoretical model of female oppression, but their anger with society and their need for self-justification often led them away from realism into oversimplification, emotionalism, and fantasy. Making their fiction the vehicle for a dramatization of wronged womanhood, they demanded changes in the social and political systems that would grant women male privileges and require chastity and fidelity from men. The profound sense of injustice that the feminine novelists had represented as class struggle in their novels of factory life becomes an all-out war of the sexes in the novels of the feminists. Even their pseudonyms show their sense of feminist pride and of matriarchal mission to their sisters; one representative feminist called herself "Sarah Grand." In its extreme form, feminist literature advocated the sexual separatism of Amazon utopias and suffragette sisterhoods.

In the lives of the feminists, the bonds of the female subculture were particularly strong. The feminists were intensely devoted to each other and needed the support of close, emotional friendships with other women as well as the loving adulation of a female audience. In this generation, which mainly comprises women born between 1860 and 1880, one finds sympathetically attuned women writing in teams; Edith Somerville and Violet Martin were even said to have continued the collaboration beyond the grave.[55] Although they preached individualism, their need for association led to a staggering number of clubs, activities, and causes, culminating in the militant groups and the almost terrifying collectivity of the suffrage movement. They glorified and idealized the womanly values of chastity and maternal love, and believed that those values must be forced upon a degenerate male society.

In their lives and in their books, most feminist writers expressed both an awareness of, and a revulsion from, sexuality. Like the feminine novelists, they projected many of their own experiences onto male characters, creating, for example, the Scarlet Pimpernels, "effeminate" fops by day and fearless heroes by night, semi-androgynous symbols of a generation in uneasy transition. To some degree these tactics were typical of the period in which they wrote; male novelists were creating "masculine" independent women who, as Donald Stone puts it, "could be used as a cover for those men who, for one reason or another, were anxious to proclaim their own standards and follow their own instincts."[56]

As the feminists themselves often seem neurotic and divided in their roles, less productive than earlier generations, and subject to paralyzing psychosomatic illnesses, so their fiction seems to break down in its form. In the 1890s the three-decker novel abruptly disappeared due to changes in its marketability, and women turned to short stories and fragments, which they called "dreams," "keynotes," and "fantasias." At the turn of the century came the purest examples of feminist literature, the novels, poems, and plays written as suffragette propaganda and distributed by the efficient and well-financed suffrage presses.

The feminist writers were not important artists. Yet in their insistence on exploring and defining womanhood, in their rejection of self-sacrifice, and even in their outspoken hostility to men, the feminist writers represented an important stage, a declaration of independence, in the female tradition. They did produce some interesting and original work, and they opened new subjects for other novelists. Sarah Grand's powerful studies of female psychology, George Egerton's bitter short stories, and Olive Schreiner's existential socialism were all best sellers in their own day and still hold attention. Through political campaigns for prostitutes and working women, and in the suffrage crusades, the feminists insisted on their right to use the male sexual vocabulary, and to use it forcefully and openly. The feminists also challenged the monopoly of male publishers and rebelled against the dictatorship of the male establishment. Men—John Chapman, John Blackwood, Henry Blackett, George Smith—had published the works of feminine novelists and had exerted direct and enormous power over their contents. Sarah Grand parodied the masculine critical hegemony by describing a literary journal she called the *Patriarch,* and feminist journalists, writing in their own magazines, argued against the judgments of the men of letters. In the 1860s the sensation novelists had begun to retain their copyrights, work with printers on a commission basis, and edit their own magazines. The feminists continued to expand this economic control of publishing outlets. Virginia Woolf, printing her own novels at the Hogarth Press, owed much of her independence to the feminists' insistence on the need for women writers to be free of patriarchal commercialism.

In its early stages feminist analysis was naive and incoherent, but by the turn of the century Mona Caird, Elizabeth Robins, and Olive Schreiner were producing cogent theories of women's relationship to work and production, to class structure, and to marriage and the family.[57] Robins and other members of the Women Writers Suffrage League were beginning to work out a theory of women's literature, making connections between the demands of the male publishing industry, the socialization of women, and the heroines, plots, conventions, and images of women's fiction. Finally, the militant suffrage movement forced women writers to confront their own beliefs about women's rights, and in the process to reexamine their own self-hatred and inhibition.

English women (or at least those women who were over thirty, householders, the wives of householders, occupiers of property of £5 or more annual value, or university graduates) were given the franchise in 1918 by a government grateful for their patriotism during World War I.[58] Ironically, the death of many young male writers and poets during the war left English women writers with a poignant sense of carrying on a national literary tradition that had, at its heart, excluded them. Women felt a responsibility to continue, to take the men's place, but they also felt a pitiful lack of confidence. Alice Meynell's poem "A Father of Women" conveys some of the anxiety, as well as the guilt, of the survivors:

> Our father works in us,
> The daughters of his manhood. Not undone
> Is he, not wasted, through transmuted thus,
>   and though he left no son.

Meynell calls upon her father's spirit in the poem to arm her "delicate mind," give her "courage to die," and to crush in her nature "the ungenerous art of the inferior."

The literature of the last generation of Victorian women writers, born between 1880 and 1900, moved beyond feminism to a Female phase of courageous self-exploration, but it carried with it the double legacy of feminine self-hatred and feminist withdrawal. In their rejection of male society and masculine culture, feminist writers had retreated more and more toward a separatist literature of inner space. Psychologically rather than socially focussed, this literature sought refuge from the harsh realities and vicious practices of the male world. Its favorite symbol, the enclosed and secret room, had been a potent image in women's novels since *Jane Eyre*, but by the end of the century it came to be identified with the womb and with female conflict. In children's books, such as Mrs. Molesworth's *The Tapestry Room* (1879) and Dinah Craik's *The Little Lame Prince* (1886), women writers had explored and extended these fantasies of enclosure. After 1900, in dozens of novels from Frances Hodgson Burnett's *A Secret Garden* (1911) to May Sinclair's *The Tree of Heaven* (1917), the secret room, the attic hideaway, the suffragette cell came to stand for a separate world, a flight from men and from adult sexuality.

The fiction of Dorothy Richardson, Katherine Mansfield, and Virginia Woolf created a deliberate female aesthetic, which transformed the feminine code of self-sacrifice into an annihilation of the narrative self, and applied the cultural analysis of the feminists to words, sentences, and structures of language in the novel. Their version of modernism was a determined response to the material culture of male Edwardian novelists like Arnold Bennett and H. G. Wells, but, like D. H. Lawrence, the female aestheticists saw the world as mystically and totally polarized by sex. For them, female sensibility took on a sacred quality, and its exercise became a holy, exhausting, and ultimately self-destructive rite, since woman's receptivity led inevitably to suicidal vulnerability.

Paradoxically, the more female this literature became in the formal and theoretical sense, the farther it moved from exploring the physical experience of women. Sexuality hovers on the fringes of the aestheticists' novels and stories, disguised, veiled, and denied. Androgyny, the sexual ethic of Bloomsbury and an important concept of the period, provided an escape from the confrontation with the body. Erotically charged and drenched with sexual symbolism, female aestheticism is nonetheless oddly sexless in its content. Again, "a room of one's own," with its insistence on artistic autonomy and its implied disengagement from social and sexual involvement, was a favorite image.

After the death of Virginia Woolf in 1941, the English women's novel seemed adrift. The harsh criticism of Bloomsbury, of female aestheticism, and especially of Virginia Woolf by writers for *Scrutiny* in the 1930s had pointed out the problems of disengagement. In her late writings, *The Years* (1937) and *Three Guineas* (1938), Woolf herself had tried to move in the direction of social realism. During the 1940s and 1950s, however, women writers, many of an older generation, continued to work in conservative modes untouched by either modernism or a sense of personal experiment. The works of such novelists as Rose Macaulay and Ivy Compton-Burnett are closely connected to a female tradition in their themes and awareness, but they seem to represent a passive rather than an active continuity. This passivity is one aspect of the larger situation of the postwar English novel. Adrian Mitchell describes "the disease of the British artist since 1945" as "a compulsion to stay small, to create perfect miniatures, to take no major risks."[59]

In the 1960s the female novel entered a new and dynamic phase, which has been strongly influenced in the past ten years by the energy of the international women's movement. The contemporary women's novel observes the traditional forms of nineteenth-century realism, but it also operates in the contexts of twentieth-century Freudian and Marxist analysis. In the fiction of Iris Murdoch, Muriel Spark, and Doris Lessing, and the younger writers Margaret Drabble, A. S. Byatt, and Beryl Bainbridge, we are beginning to see a renaissance in women's writing that responds to the demands of Lewes and Mill for an authentically female literature, providing "woman's view of life, woman's experience." In drawing upon two centuries of the female tradition, these novelists have been able to incorporate many of the strengths of the past with a new range of language and experience. Like the feminine novelists, they are concerned with the conflicts between art and and love, between self-fulfillment and duty. They have insisted upon the right to use vocabularies previously reserved for male writers and to describe formerly taboo areas of female experience. For the first time anger and sexuality are accepted not only as attributes of realistic characters but also, as in Murdoch's *The Severed Head*, Lessing's *The Golden Notebook*, and A. S. Byatt's *The Game*, as sources of female creative power. Like the feminist novelists, contemporary writers are aware of their place in a political system and their connectedness to other women. Like the novelists of the female aesthetic, women novelists today, Lessing and Drabble particularly, see themselves as trying to unify the fragments of female experience through artistic vision, and they are concerned with the definition of autonomy for the woman writer. As the women's movement takes on cohesive force, and as feminist critics examine their literary tradition, contemporary women novelists will have to face the problems that black, ethnic, and Marxist writers have faced in the past: whether to devote themselves to the forging of female mythologies and epics, or to move beyond the female tradition into a seamless participation in the literary mainstream that might be regarded either as equality or assimilation.

Feminine, feminist, or female, the woman's novel has always had to struggle against the cultural and historical forces that relegated women's experience to the second rank. In trying to outline the female tradition, I have looked beyond the famous novelists who have been found worthy, to the lives and works of many women who have long been excluded from literary history. I have tried to discover how they felt about themselves and their books, what choices and sacrifices they made, and how their relationship to their profession and their tradition evolved. "What is commonly called literary history," writes Louise Bernikow, "is actually a record of choices. Which writers have survived their time and which have not depends upon who noticed them and chose to record the notice.[60] If some of the writers I notice seem to us to be Teresas and Antigones, struggling with their overwhelming sense of vocation and repression, many more will seem only Dorotheas, prim, mistaken, irreparably minor. And yet it is only by considering them all—Millicent Grogan as well as Virginia Woolf—that we can begin to record new choices in a new literary history, and to understand why, despite prejudice, despite guilt, despite inhibition, women began to write.

NOTES

1. "The Subjection of Women," in John Stuart Mill and Harriet Taylor Mill, *Essays on Sex Equality*, ed. Alice S. Rossi, Chicago, 1970, ch. III, p. 207.

2. Some Women Novelists," *History of the English Novel*, x, London, 1939, p. 194.

3. G. H. Lewes, "The Lady Novelists," *Westminster Review*, n.s. II (1852): 137; W. L. Courtney, *The Feminine Note in Fiction*, London, 1904, p. xiii; Bernard Bergonzi, *New York Review of Books*, June 3, 1965. In a review of Beryl Bainbridge's *The Bottle Factory Outing*, Anatole Broyard comments "that quite a few extremely attractive women write rather despairing books" (*New York Times*, May 26, 1975, p. 13).

4. "Silly Novels by Lady Novelists," *Westminster Review* LXVI (1856); reprinted in *Essays of George Eliot*, ed. Thomas Pinney, New York, 1963, p. 324.

5. "Ruth," *North British Review* XIX (1853): 90–91; and "Ko-Ko's Song" in *The Mikado*. The stereotype of the woman novelist that emerges in the early nineteenth century conflates the popular images of the old maid and the bluestocking; see Vineta Colby, *Yesterday's Woman: Domestic Realism in the English Novel*, Princeton, 1974, pp. 115–116, and Katharine M. Rogers, *The Troublesome Helpmate: A History of Misogyny in Literature*, Seattle, 1966, pp. 201–207.

6. Introduction to May Sarton, *Mrs. Stevens Hears the Mermaids Singing*, New York, 1974, p. xvi.

7. "This Woman's Movement" in *Adrienne Rich's Poetry*, ed. Barbara Charlesworth Gelpi and Albert Gelpi, New York, 1975, p. 189.

8. *The Rise and Fall of the Man of Letters*, London, 1969, p. 304.

9. Cynthia Ozick, "Women and Creativity," in *Woman in Sexist Society*, ed. Vivian Gornick and Barbara K. Moran, New York, 1971, p. 436.

10. Letter of November 1849, in Clement Shorter, *The Brontës: Life and Letters*, II, London, 1908, p. 80.

11. Mary Ellmann, *Thinking About Women*, New York, 1968, pp. 28–54; and Ozick, "Women and Creativity," p. 436.

12. Patricia Meyer Spacks, *The Female Imagination*, New York, 1975, p. 3.

13. "Women and Fiction," *Collected Essays*, London, 1967, p. 142.

14. See, for example, Sheila Rowbotham, *Hidden from History*, London, 1973; Martha Vicinus, ed., *Suffer and Be Still: Women in the Victorian Age*, Bloomington, Indiana, 1972; Mary S. Hartman and Lois N. Banner, eds., *Clio's Consciousness Raised: New Perspectives on*

the History of Women, New York, 1974, and Françoise Basch, *Relative Creatures: Victorian Women in Society and the Novel*, New York, 1974.

15. Linda Nochlin, "Why Are There No Great Women Artists?" in *Woman in Sexist Society;* Lise Vogel, "Fine Arts and Feminism: The Awakening Consciousness," *Feminist Studies* II (1974): 3–37; Helene Roberts, "The Inside, the Surface, the Mass: Some Recurring Images of Women," *Women's Studies* II (1974): 289–308.

16. *The Making of the English Working Class*, New York, 1973, p. 12.

17. Vineta Colby, *The Singular Anomaly: Women Novelists of the Nineteenth Century*, New York, 1970, p. 11.

18. "Women's Lit: Profession and Tradition," *Columbia Forum* I (Fall 1972): 27.

19. Spacks, p. 7.

20. Moers, "Women's Lit," 28.

21. "Flying Pigs and Double Standards," *Times Literary Supplement*, (July 26, 1974): 784.

22. For helpful studies of literary subcultures, see Robert A. Bone, *The Negro Novel in America*, New York, 1958; and Northrop Frye, "Conclusion to *A Literary History of Canada*," in *The Stubborn Structure: Essays on Criticism and Society*, Ithaca, 1970, pp. 278–312.

23. "Women and Creativity," p. 442.

24. Nancy F. Cott, introduction to *Root of Bitterness*, New York, 1972, pp. 3–4.

25. For the best discussions of the Victorian feminine ideal, see Françoise Basch, "Contemporary Ideologies," in *Relative Creatures*, pp. 3–15; Walter E. Houghton, *The Victorian Frame of Mind*, New Haven, 1957, pp. 341–343; and Alexander Welsh's theory of the Angel in the House in *The City of Dickens*, London, 1971, pp. 164–195.

26. Christine Stansell and Johnny Faragher, "Women and Their Families on the Overland Trail, 1842–1867," *Feminist Studies* II (1975): 152–153. For an overview of recent historical scholarship on the "two cultures," see Barbara Sicherman, "Review: American History," *Signs: Journal of Women in Culture and Society* I (Winter 1975): 470–484.

27. For a sociological account of patterns of behavior for Victorian women, see Leonore Davidoff, *The Best Circles: Society, Etiquette and the Season*, London, 1973, esp. pp. 48–58, 85–100.

28. Sarah Ellis, *The Daughters of England*, New York, 1844, ch. IX, p. 90.

29. Dinah M. Craik, "Literary Ghouls," *Studies from Life*, New York, n.d., p. 13.

30. Letter of October 6, 1851, in *Letters of E. Jewsbury to Jane Welsh Carlyle*, ed. Mrs. Alex Ireland, London, 1892, p. 426. For Fanny Fern, see Ann Douglas Wood, "The 'Scribbling Women' and Fanny Fern: Why Women Wrote," *American Quarterly* XXIII (Spring 1971): 1–24.

31. J.M.S. Tompkins, *The Popular Novel in England 1770–1800*, London, 1932, pp. 119–121; Dorothy Blakey, *The Minerva Press 1790–1820*, London, 1939; and Ian Watt, *The Rise of the Novel*, London, 1963, pp. 298–299.

32. Myra Reynolds, *The Learned Lady in England 1650–1760*, New York, 1920, pp. 89–91.

33. William McKee, *Elizabeth Inchbald, Novelist*, Washington, D.C., 1935, p. 20.

34. "Memoirs of the Life of Mrs. Mary Brunton by Her Husband," preface to *Emmeline*, Edinburgh, 1819, p. xxxvi.

35. Kathleen Tillotson, *Novels of the Eighteen-Forties*, London, 1956, pp. 142–145.

36. For a refutation of Leavis's view of Austen and Eliot, see Gross, *Rise and Fall of the Man of Letters*, pp. 302–303.

37. Quoted in S. C. Hall, *A Book of Memories of Great Men and Women of the Age*, London, 1877, p. 266.

38. Inga-Stina Ewbank, *Their Proper Sphere: A Study of the Brontë Sisters as Early-Victorian Female Novelists*, London, 1966, p. 41.

39. *Saturday Review*, IV (July 11, 1857): 40–41. See also David Masson, *British Novelists and Their Styles*, Cambridge, 1859, p. 134.

40. *Autobiography and Letters of Mrs. M.O.W. Oliphant,* ed., Mrs. Harry Cogshill, New York, 1899, p. 160.

41. "An Enquiry into the State of Girls' Fashionable Schools," *Fraser's* XXXI (1845): 703.

42. Sarah Ellis, *The Women of England,* New York, 1844, p. 9.

43. "Victorian Feminism and the Nineteenth-Century Novel," *Women's Studies* I (1972): 69.

44. *Romola,* New York, 1898, II, ch. XXIII, p. 157.

45. *Middlemarch,* ed., Gordon S. Haight, Boston, 1956, "Finale," p. 612.

46. Jane Vaughan Pinckney, *Tacita Tacit,* II, p. 276; quoted in Myron Brightfield, *Victorian England in Its Novels,* IV, Los Angeles, 1968, p. 27.

47. *The Diary of Alice James,* ed., Leon Edel, New York, 1934, p. 66.

48. *British Quarterly Review* XLV (1867): 164. On the term "coarseness," see Ewbank, *Their Proper Sphere,* pp. 46–47.

49. Margaret Mare and Alicia C. Percival, *Victorian Best-Seller: The World of Charlotte Yonge,* London: 1947, p. 133.

50. James Lorimer, "Noteworthy Novels," XI (1849): 257.

51. "The False Morality of Lady Novelists," *National Review,* VII, (1859): 149.

52. "Puseyite Novels," VI (1850): 498.

53. "The Lady Novelists," 132.

54. "Cassandra," in *The Cause,* ed. Ray Strachey, Port Washington, N.Y., 1969, p. 398.

55. See Maurice Collis, *Somerville and Ross,* London, 1968, for an account of the careers of Edith Somerville and Violet Martin. After Martin's death in 1915, the "collaboration" continued through psychic communications. Katherine Bradley and Edith Cooper wrote under the name of "Michael Field;" the sisters Emily and Dorothea Gerard used the name "E. D. Gerard" for such joint efforts as *Beggar My Neighbor* (1882).

56. "Victorian Feminism and the Nineteenth-Century Novel," 79.

57. Mona Caird, *The Morality of Marriage,* London, 1897; Elizabeth Robins, *Way Stations,* London, 1913; Olive Schreiner, *Women and Labour,* London, 1911.

58. See Andrew Rosen, *Rise Up, Women!* London, 1974, p. 266.

59. Quoted in Bernard Bergonzi, *The Situation of the Novel,* London, 1972, p. 79.

60. *The World Split Open: Four Centuries of Women Poets in England and America, 1552–1950,* New York, 1974, p. 3.

SANDRA M. GILBERT AND SUSAN GUBAR

INFECTION IN THE SENTENCE
the woman writer and the anxiety of authorship

> The man who does not know sick women does not know women.
> —S. WEIR MITCHELL

> I try to describe this long limitation, hoping that with such power as is now mine, and such use of language as is within that power, this will convince any one who cares about it that this "living" of mine had been done under a heavy handicap. . . .
> —CHARLOTTE PERKINS GILMAN

> A Word dropped careless on a Page
> May stimulate an eye
> When folded in perpetual seam
> The Wrinkled Maker lie
> Infection in the sentence breeds
> We may inhale Despair
> At distances of Centuries
> From the Malaria—
> —EMILY DICKINSON

> I stand in the ring
> in the dead city
> and tie on the red shoes
> . . . .
> They are not mine,
> they are my mother's,
> her mother's before,
> handed down like an heirloom
> but hidden like shameful letters.
> —ANNE SEXTON

What does it mean to be a woman writer in a culture whose fundamental definitions of literary authority are, as we have seen, both overtly and covertly patriarchal? If the vexed and vexing polarities of angel and monster, sweet dumb Snow White and fierce mad Queen, are major images literary tradition offers women, how does such imagery influence the ways in which women attempt the pen? If the Queen's looking glass speaks with the King's voice, how do its per-petual kingly admonitions affect the Queen's own voice? Since his is the chief voice she hears, does the Queen try to sound like the King, imitating his tone, his inflections, his phrasing, his point of view? Or does she "talk back" to him in her own vocabulary, her own timbre, insisting on her own viewpoint? We believe these are basic questions feminist literary criticism—both theoretical and prac-tical—must answer, and consequently they are questions to which we shall turn again and again, not only in this chapter but in all our readings of nineteenth-century literature by women.

That writers assimilate and then consciously or unconsciously affirm or deny the achievements of their predecessors is, of course, a central fact of literary his-tory, a fact whose aesthetic and metaphysical implications have been discussed in detail by theorists as diverse as T. S. Eliot, M. H. Abrams, Erich Auerbach, and Frank Kermode.[1] More recently, some literary theorists have begun to explore what we might call the psychology of literary history—the tensions and anxieties, hostilities and inadequacies writers feel when they confront not only the achievements of their predecessors but the traditions of genre, style, and metaphor that they inherit from such "forefathers." Increasingly, these critics study the ways in which, as J. Hillis Miller has put it, a literary text "is in-habited . . . by a long chain of parasitical presences, echoes, allusions, guests, ghosts of previous texts."[2]

As Miller himself also notes, the first and foremost student of such literary psychohistory has been Harold Bloom. Applying Freudian structures to literary genealogies, Bloom has postulated that the dynamics of literary history arise from the artist's "anxiety of influence," his fear that he is not his own creator and that the works of his predecessors, existing before and beyond him, assume es-sential priority over his own writings. In fact, as we pointed out in our discussion of the metaphor of literary paternity, Bloom's paradigm of the sequential histori-cal relationship between literary artists is the relationship of father to son, specif-ically that relationship as it was defined by Freud. Thus Bloom explains that a "strong poet" must engage in heroic warfare with his "precursor," for, involved as he is in a literary Oedipal struggle, a man can only become a poet by somehow invalidating his poetic father.

Bloom's model of literary history is intensely (even exclusively) male, and nec-essarily patriarchal. For this reason it has seemed, and no doubt will continue to seem, offensively sexist to some feminist critics. Not only, after all, does Bloom describe literary history as the crucial warfare of fathers and sons, he sees Milton's fiercely masculine fallen Satan as *the* type of the poet in our culture, and he metaphorically defines the poetic process as a sexual encounter between a male poet and his female muse. Where, then, does the female poet fit in? Does she want to annihilate a "forefather" or a "foremother"? What if she can find no models, no precursors? Does she have a muse, and what is its sex? Such ques-tions are inevitable in any female consideration of Bloomian poetics.[3] And yet, from a feminist perspective, their inevitability may be just the point; it may, that is, call our attention not to what is wrong about Bloom's conceptualization of the dynamics of Western literary history, but to what is right (or at least suggestive) about his theory.

For Western literary history *is* overwhelmingly male—or, more accurately, patriarchal—and Bloom analyzes and explains this fact, while other theorists have ignored it, precisely, one supposes, because they assumed literature had to be male. Like Freud, whose psychoanalytic postulates permeate Bloom's literary psychoanalyses of the "anxiety of influence," Bloom has defined processes of interaction that his predecessors did not bother to consider because, among other reasons, they were themselves so caught up in such processes. Like Freud, too, Bloom has insisted on bringing to consciousness assumptions readers and writers do not ordinarily examine. In doing so, he has clarified the implications of the psychosexual and sociosexual contexts by which every literary text is surrounded, and thus the meanings of the "guests" and "ghosts" which inhabit texts themselves. Speaking of Freud, the feminist theorist Juliet Mitchell has remarked that "psychoanalysis is not a recommendation *for* a patriarchal society, but an analysis of one."[4] The same sort of statement could be made about Bloom's model of literary history, which is not a recommendation for but an analysis of the patriarchal poetics (and attendant anxieties) which underlie our culture's chief literary movements.

For our purposes here, however, Bloom's historical construction is useful not only because it helps identify and define the patriarchal psychosexual context in which so much Western literature was authored, but also because it can help us distinguish the anxieties and achievements of female writers from those of male writers. If we return to the question we asked earlier—where does a woman writer "fit in" to the overwhelmingly and essentially male literary history Bloom describes?—we find we have to answer that a woman writer does *not* "fit in." At first glance, indeed, she seems to be anomalous, indefinable, alienated, a freakish outsider. Just as in Freud's theories of male and female psychosexual development there is no symmetry between a boy's growth and a girl's (with, say, the male "Oedipus complex" balanced by a female "Electra complex") so Bloom's male-oriented theory of the "anxiety of influence" cannot be simply reversed or inverted in order to account for the situation of the woman writer.

Certainly if we acquiesce in the patriarchal Bloomian model, we can be sure that the female poet does not experience the "anxiety of influence" in the same way that her male counterpart would, for the simple reason that she must confront precursors who are almost exclusively male, and therefore significantly different from her. Not only do these precursors incarnate patriarchal authority (as our discussion of the metaphor of literary paternity argued), they attempt to enclose her in definitions of her person and her potential which, by reducing her to extreme stereotypes (angel, monster) drastically conflict with her own sense of her self—that is, of her subjectivity, her autonomy, her creativity. On the one hand, therefore, the woman writer's male precursors symbolize authority; on the other hand, despite their authority, they fail to define the ways in which she experiences her own identity as a writer. More, the masculine authority with which they construct their literary personae, as well as the fierce power struggles in which they engage in their efforts of self-creating, seem to the woman writer directly to contradict the terms of her own gender definition. Thus the "anxiety of influence" that a male poet experiences is felt by a female poet as an even more primary "anxiety of authorship"—a radical fear that she cannot create, that because she can never become a "precursor" the act of writing will isolate or destroy her.

This anxiety is, of course, exacerbated by her fear that not only can she not fight a male precursor on "his" terms and win, she cannot "beget" art upon the (female) body of the muse. As Juliet Mitchell notes, in a concise summary of the implications Freud's theory of psychosexual development has for women, both a boy and a girl, "as they learn to speak and live within society, want to take the father's [in Bloom's terminology the precursor's] place, and *only the boy will one day be allowed to do so.* Furthermore both sexes are born into the desire of the mother, and as, through cultural heritage, what the mother desires is the phallus-turned-baby, *both* children desire to be the phallus for the mother. Again, *only the boy can fully recognize himself in his mother's desire.* Thus *both* sexes repudiate the implications of femininity," but the girl learns (in relation to her father) "that her subjugation to the law of the father entails her becoming the representative of 'nature' and 'sexuality,' a chaos of spontaneous, intuitive creativity."[5]

Unlike her male counterpart, then, the female artist must first struggle against the effects of socialization which makes conflict with the will of her (male) precursors seem inexpressibly absurd, futile, or even—as in the case of the Queen in "Little Snow White"—self-annihilating. And just as the male artist's struggle against his precursor takes the form of what Bloom calls revisionary swerves, flights, misreadings, so the female writer's battle for self-creation involves her in a revisionary process. Her battle, however, is not against her (male) precursor's reading of the world but against his reading of *her.* In order to define herself as an author she must redefine the terms of her socialization. Her revisionary struggle, therefore, often becomes a struggle for what Adrienne Rich has called "Re-vision—the act of looking back, of seeing with fresh eyes, of entering an old text from a new critical direction . . . an act of survival."[6] Frequently, moreover, she can begin such a struggle only by actively seeking a *female* precursor who, far from representing a threatening force to be denied or killed, proves by example that a revolt against patriarchal literary authority is possible.

For this reason, as well as for the sound psychoanalytic reasons Mitchell and others give, it would be foolish to lock the woman artist into an Electra pattern matching the Oedipal structure Bloom proposes for male writers. The woman writer—and we shall see women doing this over and over again—searches for a female model not because she wants dutifully to comply with male definitions of her "femininity" but because she must legitimize her own rebellious endeavors. At the same time, like most women in patriarchal society, the woman writer does experience her gender as a painful obstacle, or even a debilitating inadequacy; like most patriarchally conditioned women, in other words, she is victimized by what Mitchell calls "the inferiorized and 'alternative' (second sex) psychology of women under patriarchy."[7] Thus the loneliness of the female artist, her feelings of alienation from male predecessors coupled with her need for sisterly precursors and successors, her urgent sense of her need for a female audience together with her fear of the antagonism of male readers, her culturally conditioned timidity about self-dramatization, her dread of the patriarchal authority of art, her anxiety about the impropriety of female invention—all these phenomena of "inferiorization" mark the woman writer's struggle for artistic self-definition and differentiate her efforts at self-creating from those of her male counterpart.

As we shall see, such sociosexual differentiation means that, as Elaine Showalter has suggested, women writers participate in a quite different literary subculture from that inhabited by male writers, a subculture which has its own distinctive literary traditions, even—though it defines itself *in relation to* the "main," male-dominated, literary culture—a distinctive history.[8] At best, the separateness of this female subculture has been exhilarating for women. In recent years, for instance, while male writers seem increasingly to have felt exhausted by the need for revisionism which Bloom's theory of the "anxiety of influence" accurately describes, women writers have seen themselves as pioneers in a creativity so intense that their male counterparts have probably not experienced its analog since the Renaissance, or at least since the Romantic era. The son of many fathers, today's male writer feels hopelessly belated; the daughter of too few mothers, today's female writer feels that she is helping to create a viable tradition which is at last definitively emerging.

There is a darker side of this female literary subculture, however, especially when women's struggles for literary self-creation are seen in the psychosexual context described by Bloom's Freudian theories of patrilineal literary inheritance. As we noted above, for an "anxiety of influence" the woman writer substitutes what we have called an "anxiety of authorship," an anxiety built from complex and often only barely conscious fears of that authority which seems to the female artist to be by definition inappropriate to her sex. Because it is based on the woman's socially determined sense of her own biology, this anxiety of authorship is quite distinct from the anxiety about creativity that could be traced in such male writers as Hawthorne or Dostoevsky. Indeed, to the extent that it forms one of the unique bonds that link women in what we might call the secret sisterhood of their literary subculture, such anxiety in itself constitutes a crucial mark of that subculture.

In comparison to the "male" tradition of strong, father-son combat, however, this female anxiety of authorship is profoundly debilitating. Handed down not from one woman to another but from the stern literary "fathers" of patriarchy to all their "inferiorized" female descendants, it is in many ways the germ of a disease or, at any rate, a disaffection, a disturbance, a distrust, that spreads like a stain throughout the style and structure of much literature by women, especially—as we shall see in this study—throughout literature by women before the twentieth century. For if contemporary women do now attempt the pen with energy and authority, they are able to do so only because their eighteenth- and nineteenth-century foremothers struggled in isolation that felt like illness, alienation that felt like madness, obscurity that felt like paralysis to overcome the anxiety of authorship that was endemic to their literary subculture. Thus, while the recent feminist emphasis on positive role models has undoubtedly helped many women, it should not keep us from realizing the terrible odds against which a creative female subculture was established. Far from reinforcing socially oppressive sexual stereotyping, only a full consideration of such problems can reveal the extraordinary strength of women's literary accomplishments in the eighteenth and nineteenth centuries.

Emily Dickinson's acute observations about "infection in the sentence," quoted in our epigraphs, resonate in a number of different ways, then, for women writers, given the literary woman's special concept of her place in literary psychohistory. To begin with, the words seem to indicate Dickinson's keen consciousness that, in the purest Bloomian or Millerian sense, pernicious "guests" and "ghosts" inhabit all literary texts. For any reader, but especially for a reader who is also a writer, every text can become a "sentence" or weapon in a kind of metaphorical germ warfare. Beyond this, however, the fact that "infection in the sentence *breeds*" suggests Dickinson's recognition that literary texts are coercive, imprisoning, fever-inducing; that, since literature usurps a reader's interiority, it is an invasion of privacy. Moreover, given Dickinson's own gender definition, the sexual ambiguity of her poem's "Wrinkled Maker" is significant. For while, on the one hand, "we" (meaning especially women writers) "may inhale Despair" from all those patriarchal texts which seek to deny female autonomy and authority, on the other hand "we" (meaning especially women writers) "may inhale Despair" from all those "foremothers" who have both overtly and covertly conveyed their traditional authorship anxiety to their bewildered female descendants. Finally, such traditional, metaphorically matrilineal anxiety ensures that even the maker of a text, when she is a woman, may feel imprisoned within texts—folded and "wrinkled" by their pages and thus trapped in their "perpetual seam[s]" which perpetually tell her how she *seems*.

Although contemporary women writers are relatively free of the infection of this "Despair" Dickinson defines (at least in comparison to their nineteenth-century precursors), an anecdote recently related by the American poet and essayist Annie Gottlieb summarizes our point about the ways in which, for all women, "Infection in the sentence breeds":

> When I began to enjoy my powers as a writer, I dreamt that my mother had me sterilized! (Even in dreams we still blame our mothers for the punitive choices our culture forces on us.) I went after the mother-figure in my dream, brandishing a large knife; on its blade was writing. I cried, "Do you know what you are doing? You are destroying my femaleness, my *female power*, which is important to me *because of you!*" [9]

Seeking motherly precursors, says Gottlieb, as if echoing Dickinson, the woman writer may find only infection, debilitation. Yet still she must seek, not seek to subvert, her "*female power*, which is important" to her because of her lost literary matrilineage. In this connection, Dickinson's own words about mothers are revealing, for she alternately claimed that "I never had a mother," that "I always ran Home to Awe as a child. . . . He was an awful Mother but I liked him better than none," and that "a mother [was] a miracle." [10] Yet, as we shall see, her own anxiety of authorship was a "Despair" inhaled not only from the infections suffered by her own ailing physical mother, and her many tormented literary mothers, but from the literary fathers who spoke to her—even "lied" to her—sometimes near at hand, sometimes "at distances of Centuries," from the censorious looking glasses of literary texts.

It is debilitating to by *any* woman in a society where women are warned that if they do not behave like angels they must be monsters. Recently, in fact, social scientists and social historians like Jessie Bernard, Phyllis Chesler, Naomi Weisstein, and Pauline Bart have begun to study the ways in which patriarchal socialization literally makes women sick, both physically and mentally. [11] Hysteria, the disease with which Freud so famously began his investigations into the dynamic connections between *psyche* and *soma*, is by definition a "female disease," not so much because it takes its name from the Greek word for womb, *hyster* (the organ which was in the nineteenth century supposed to "cause" this emotional disturbance), but because hysteria did occur mainly among women in turn-of-the-century Vienna, and because throughout the nineteenth century this mental illness, like many other nervous disorders, was thought to be caused by the female reproductive system, as if to elaborate upon Aristotle's notion that femaleness was in and of itself a deformity.[12] And, indeed, such diseases of maladjustment to the physical and social environment as anorexia and agoraphobia did and do strike a disproportionate number of women. Sufferers from anorexia—loss of appetite, self-starvation—are primarily adolescent girls. Sufferers from agoraphobia—fear of open or "public" places—are usually female, most frequently middle-aged housewives, as are sufferers from crippling rheumatoid arthritis.[13]

Such diseases are caused by patriarchal socialization in several ways. Most obviously, of course, any young girl, but especially a lively or imaginative one, is likely to experience her education in docility, submissiveness, self-lessness as in some sense sickening. To be trained in renunciation is almost necessarily to be trained to ill health, since the human animal's first and strongest urge is to his/her *own* survival, pleasure, assertion. In addition, each of the "subjects" in which a young girl is educated may be sickening in a specific way. Learning to become a beautiful object, the girl learns anxiety about—perhaps even loathing of—her own flesh. Peering obsessively into the real as well as metaphoric looking glasses that surround her, she desires literally to "reduce" her own body. In the nineteenth century, as we noted earlier, this desire to be beautiful and "frail" led to tight-lacing and vinegar-drinking. In our own era it has spawned innumerable diets and "controlled" fasts, as well as the extraordinary phenomenon of teenage anorexia.[14] Similarly, it seems inevitable that women reared for, and conditioned to, lives of privacy, reticence, domesticity, might develop pathological fears of public places and unconfined spaces. Like the comb, stay-laces, and apple which the Queen in "Little Snow White" uses as weapons against her hated step-daughter, such afflictions as anorexia and agoraphobia simply carry patriarchal definitions of "femininity" to absurd extremes, and thus function as essential or at least inescapable parodies of social prescriptions.

In the nineteenth century, however, the complex of social prescriptions these diseases parody did not merely urge women to act in ways which would cause them to become ill; nineteenth-century culture seems to have actually admonished women to *be* ill. In other words, the "female diseases" from which Victorian women suffered were not always byproducts of their training in femininity; they were the goals of such training. As Barbara Ehrenreich and Deirdre English have shown, throughout much of the nineteenth century "Upper- and upper-middle-class women were [defined as] 'sick' [frail, ill]; working-class women were [defined as] 'sickening' [infectious, diseased]." Speaking of the "lady," they go on to point out that "Society agreed that she was frail and sickly," and consequently a "cult of female invalidism" developed in England and America. For the products of such a cult, it was, as Dr. Mary Putnam Jacobi wrote in 1895, "considered natural and almost laudable to break down under all conceivable varieties of strain—a winter dissipation, a houseful of servants, a quarrel with a female friend, not to speak of more legitimate reasons. . . . Constantly considering their nerves, urged to consider them by well-intentioned but short-sighted advisors, [women] pretty soon become nothing but a bundle of nerves."[15]

Given this socially conditioned epidemic of female illness, it is not surprising to find that the angel in the house of literature frequently suffered not just from fear and trembling but from literal and figurative sicknesses unto death. Although her hyperactive stepmother dances herself into the grave, after all, beautiful Snow White has just barely recovered from a catatonic trance in her glass coffin. And if we return to Goethe's Makarie, the "good" woman of *Wilhelm Meister's Travels* whom Hans Eichner has described as incarnating her author's ideal of "contemplative purity," we find that this "model of selflessness and of purity of heart . . . this embodiment of *das Ewig-Weibliche,* suffers from migraine headaches."[16] Implying ruthless self-suppression, does the "eternal feminine" necessarily imply illness? If so, we have found yet another meaning for Dickinson's assertion that "Infection in the sentence breeds." The despair we "inhale" even "at distances of centuries" may be the despair of a life like Makarie's, a life that *"has no story."*

At the same time, however, the despair of the monster-woman is also real, undeniable, and infectious. The Queen's mad tarantella is plainly unhealthy and metaphorically the result of too much storytelling. As the Romantic poets feared, too much imagination may be dangerous to anyone, male or female, but for women in particular patriarchal culture has always assumed mental exercises would have dire consequences. In 1645 John Winthrop, the governor of the Massachusetts Bay Colony, noted in his journal that Anne Hopkins "has fallen into a sad infirmity, the loss of her understanding and reason, which had been growing upon her divers years, by occasion of her giving herself wholly to reading and writing, and had written many books," adding that "if she had attended her household affairs, and such things as belong to women . . . she had kept her wits."[17] And as Wendy Martin has noted:

> in the nineteenth century this fear of the intellectual woman became so intense that the phenomenon . . . was recorded in medical annals. A thinking woman was considered such a breach of nature that a Harvard doctor reported during his autopsy on a Radcliffe graduate he discovered that her uterus had shrivelled to the size of a pea.[18]

If, then, as Anne Sexton suggests (in a poem parts of which we have also used here as an epigraph), the red shoes passed furtively down from woman to woman are the shoes of art, the Queen's dancing shoes, it is as sickening to be a Queen who wears them as it is to be an angelic Makarie who repudiates them. Several passages in Sexton's verse express what we have defined as "anxiety of authorship" in the form of a feverish dread of the suicidal tarantella of female creativity:

> All those girls
> who wore red shoes,
> each boarded a train that would not stop.
> . . . .
> They tore off their ears like safety pins.
> Their arms fell off them and became hats.

Their heads rolled off and sang down the street.
And their feet—oh God, their feet in the market place—
. . . the feet went on.
The feet could not stop.
. . . .
They could not listen.
They could not stop.
What they did was the death dance.

What they did would do them in.

Certainly infection breeds in these sentences, and despair: female art, Sexton suggests, has a "hidden" but crucial tradition of uncontrollable madness. Perhaps it was her semi-conscious perception of this tradition that gave Sexton herself "a secret fear" of being "a reincarnation" of Edna Millay, whose reputation seemed based on romance. In a letter to DeWitt Snodgrass she confessed that she had "a fear of writing as a woman writes," adding, "I wish I were a man—I would rather write the way a man writes."[19] After all, dancing the death dance, "all those girls/ who wore the red shoes" dismantle their own bodies, like anorexics renouncing the guilty weight of their female flesh. But if their arms, ears, and heads fall off, perhaps their wombs, too, will "shrivel" to "the size of a pea"?

In this connection, a passage from Margaret Atwood's *Lady Oracle* acts almost as a gloss on the conflict between creativity and "femininity" which Sexton's violent imagery embodies (or dis-embodies). Significantly, the protagonist of Atwood's novel is a writer of the sort of fiction that has recently been called "female gothic," and even more significantly she too projects her anxieties of authorship into the fairy-tale metaphor of the red shoes. Stepping in glass, she sees blood on her feet, and suddenly feels that she has discovered:

> The real red shoes, the feet punished for dancing. You could dance, or you could have the love a good man. But you were afraid to dance, because you had this unnatural fear that if you danced they'd cut your feet off so you wouldn't be able to dance. . . . Finally you overcame your fear and danced, and they cut your feet off. The good man went away too, because you wanted to dance.[20]

Whether she is a passive angel or an active monster, in other words, the woman writer feels herself to be literally or figuratively crippled by the debilitating alternatives her culture offers her, and the crippling effects of her conditioning sometimes seem to "breed" like sentences of death in the bloody shoes she inherits from her literary foremothers.

Surrounded as she is by images of disease, traditions of disease, and invitations both to disease and to dis-ease, it is no wonder that the woman writer has held many mirrors up to the discomforts of her own nature. As we shall see, the notion that "Infection in the sentence breeds" has been so central a truth for literary women that the great artistic achievements of nineteenth-century novelists and poets from Austen and Shelly to Dickinson and Barrett Browning are often both literally and figuratively concerned with disease, as if to emphasize the effort with which health and wholeness were won from the infectious "vapors" of despair and fragmentation. Rejecting the poisoned apples her culture offers her, the woman writer often becomes in some sense anorexic, resolutely closing her mouth on silence (since—in the words of Jane Austen's Henry Tilney—"a woman's only power is the power of refusal"[21]), even while she complains of starvation. Thus both Charlotte and Emily Brontë depict the travails of starved or starving anorexic heroines, while Emily Dickinson declares in one breath that she "had been hungry, all the Years," and in another opts for "Sumptuous Destitution." Similarly, Christina Rossetti represents her own anxiety of authorship in the split between one heroine who longs to "suck and suck" on goblin fruit and another who locks her lips fiercely together in a gesture of silent and passionate renunciation. In addition, many of these literary women become in one way or another agoraphobic. Trained to reticence, they fear the vertiginous openness of the literary marketplace and rationalize with Emily Dickinson that "Publication—is the Auction/ Of the Mind of Man" or, worse, punningly confess that "Creation seemed a mighty Crack—/ To make me visible."[22]

As we shall also see, other diseases and dis-eases accompany the two classic symptoms of anorexia and agoraphobia. Claustrophobia, for instance, agoraphobia's parallel and complementary opposite, is a disturbance we shall encounter again and again in women's writing throughout the nineteenth century. Eye "troubles," moreover, seem to abound in the lives and works of literary women, with Dickinson matter-of-factly noting that her eye got "put out," George Eliot describing patriarchal Rome as "a disease of the retina," Jane Eyre and Aurora Leigh marrying blind men, Charlotte Brontë deliberately writing with her eyes closed, and Mary Elizabeth Coleridge writing about "Blindness" that came because "Absolute and bright,/ The Sun's rays smote me till they masked the Sun."[23] Finally, aphasia and amnesia—two illnesses which symbolically represent (and parody) the sort of intellectual incapacity patriarchal culture has traditionally required of women—appear and reappear in women's writings in frankly stated or disguised forms. "Foolish" women characters in Jane Austen's novels (Miss Bates in *Emma*, for instance) express Malapropish confusion about language, while Mary Shelley's monster has to learn language from scratch and Emily Dickinson herself childishly questions the meanings of the most basic English words: "Will there really be a 'Morning'?/ Is there such a thing as 'Day'?"[24] At the same time, many women writers manage to imply that the reason for such ignorance of language—as well as the reason for their deep sense of alienation and inescapable feeling of anomie—is that they have *forgotten* something. Deprived of the power that even their pens don't seem to confer, these women resemble Doris Lessing's heroines, who have to fight their internalization of patriarchal strictures for even a faint trace memory of what they might have become.

"Where are the songs I used to know,/ Where are the notes I used to sing?" writes Christina Rossetti in "The Key-Note," a poem whose title indicates its significance for her. "I have forgotten everything/ I used to know so long ago."[25] As if to make the same point, Charlotte Brontë's Lucy Snowe conveniently "forgets" her own history and even, so it seems, the Christian name of one of the central characters in her story, while Brontë's orphaned Jane Eyre seems to have lost (or symbolically "forgotten") her family heritage. Similarly, too, Emily Brontë's Heathcliff "forgets" or is made to forget who and what he was; Mary

Shelley's monster is "born" without either a memory or a family history; and Elizabeth Barrett Browining's Aurora Leigh is early separated from—and thus induced to "forget"—her "mother land" of Italy. As this last example suggests, however, what all these characters and their authors really fear they have forgotten is precisely that aspect of their lives which has been kept from them by patriarchal poetics: their matrilineal heritage of literary strength, their "female power" which, as Annie Gottlieb wrote, is important to them *because of* (not in spite of) their mothers. In order, then, not only to understand the ways in which "Infection in the sentence breeds" for women but also to learn how women have won through disease to artistic health we must begin by redefining Bloom's seminal definitions of the revisionary "anxiety of influence." In doing so, we will have to trace the difficult paths by which nineteenth-century women overçame their "anxiety of authorship," repudiated debilitating patriarchal prescriptions, and recovered or remembered the lost foremothers who could help them find their distinctive female power. . . .

NOTES

Epigraphs: *Doctor on Patient* (Philadelphia: Lippincott, 1888), quoted in Ilza Veith, *Hysteria: The History of a Disease* (Chicago: University of Chicago Press, 1965), pp. 219–20; *The Living of Charlotte Perkins Gilman* (New York: Harper / Row, 1975; first published 1935), p. 104; J. 1261 in *The Poems of Emily Dickinson*, ed. Thomas Johnson, 3 vols. (Cambridge, Mass.: The Belknap Press of Harvard University Press, 1955: all subsequent references are to this edition); "The Red Shoes," *The Book of Folly* (Boston: Houghton Mifflin, 1972), pp. 28–29.

1. In "Tradition and the Individual Talent," Eliot of course considers these matters; in *Mimesis* Auerbach traces the ways in which the realist includes what has been previously excluded from art; and in *The Sense of an Ending* Frank Kermode shows how poets and novelists lay bare the literariness of their predecessors' forms in order to explore the dissonance between fiction and reality.

3. J. Hillis Miller, "The Limits of Pluralism, III: The Critic as Host," *Critical Inquiry* (Spring 1977):446.

3. For a discussion of the woman writer and her place in Bloomian literary history, see Joanne Feit Diehl, "'Come Slowly—Eden': An Exploration of Women Poets and their Muse," *Signs* 3, no. 3 (Spring 1978): 572–87. See also the responses to Diehl in *Signs* 4, no. 1 (Autumn 1978): 188–96.

4. Juliet Mitchell, *Psychoanalysis and Feminism* (New York: Vintage, 1975), p. xiii.

5. Ibid., pp. 404–05.

6. Adrienne Rich, "When We Dead Awaken: Writing as Re-Vision," in *Adrienne Rich's Poetry*, ed. Barbara Charlesworth Gelpi and Albert Gelpi (New York: Norton, 1975), p. 90.

7. Mitchell, *Psychoanalysis and Feminism*, p. 402.

8. See Elaine Showalter, *A Literature of Their Own* (Princeton: Princeton University Press, 1977).

9. Annie Gottlieb, "Feminists Look at Motherhood," *Mother Jones* (November 1976):53.

10. *The Letters of Emily Dickinson*, ed. Thomas Johnson, 3 vols. (Cambridge, Mass.: The Belknap Press of Harvard University Press, 1958), 2:475; 2:518.

11. See Jessie Bernard, "The Paradox of the Happy Marriage," Pauline B. Bart, "Depression in Middle-Aged Women," and Naomi Weisstein, "Psychology Constructs the Female," all in Vivian Gornick and Barbara K. Moran, ed., *Woman in Sexist Society* (New York:

Basic Books, 1971). See also Phyllis Chesler, *Women and Madness* (New York: Doubleday, 1972), and—for a summary of all these matters—Barbara Ehrenreich and Deidre English, *Complaints and Disorders: The Sexual Politics of Sickness* (Old Westbury: The Feminist Press, 1973).

12. In *Hints on Insanity* (1861) John Millar wrote that "Mental derangement frequently occurs in young females from Amenorrhoea, especially in those who have any strong hereditary predisposition to insanity," adding that "an occasional warm hipbath or leeches to the pubis will . . . be followed by complete mental recovery." In 1873, Henry Mauldsey wrote in *Body and Mind* that "the monthly activity of the ovaries . . . has a notable effect upon the mind and body; wherefore it may become an important cause of mental and physical derangement." See especially the medical opinions of John Millar, Henry Maudsley, and Andrew Wynter in *Madness and Morals: Ideas on Insanity in the Nineteenth Century*, ed. Vieda Skultans (London and Boston: Routledge / Kegan Paul, 1975), pp. 230–35.

13. See Marlene Boskind-Lodahl, "Cinderella's Stepsisters: A Feminist Perspective on Anorexia Nervosa and Bulimia," *Signs* 2, no. 2 (Winter 1976): 342–56; Walter Blum, "The Thirteenth Guest," (on agoraphobia), in *California Living, The San Francisco Sunday Examiner and Chronicle* (17 April 1977): 8–12; Joan Archart-Treichel, "Can Your Personality Kill You?" (on female rheumatoid arthritis, among other diseases), *New York* 10, no. 48 (28 November 1977): 45: "According to studies conducted in recent years, four out of five rheumatoid victims are women, and for good reason: The disease appears to arise in those unhappy with the traditional female-sex role."

14. More recent discussions of the etiology and treatment of anorexia are offered in Hilde Bruch, M.D., *The Golden Cage: The Enigma of Anorexia Nervosa* (Cambridge, Mass.: Harvard University Press, 1978), and in Salvador Minuchin, Bernice L. Rosman, and Lester Baker, *Psychosomatic Families: Anorexia Nervosa in Context* (Cambridge: Harvard University Press, 1978).

15. Quoted by Ehrenreich and English, *Complaints and Disorders*, p. 19.

16. Eichner, "The Eternal Feminine," Norton Critical Edition of *Faust*, p. 620.

17. John Winthrop, *The History of New England from 1630 to 1649*, ed. James Savage (Boston, 1826), 2:216.

18. Wendy Martin, "Anne Bradstreet's Poetry: A Study of Subversive Piety," *Shakespeare's Sisters*, ed. Gilbert and Gubar, pp. 19–31.

19. "The Uncensored Poet: Letters of Anne Sexton," *Ms.* 6, no. 5 (November 1977): 53.

20. Margaret Atwood, *Lady Oracle* (New York: Simon and Schuster, 1976), p. 335.

21. See *Northanger Abbey*, chapter 10: "You will allow, that in both [matrimony and dancing], man has the advantage of choice, woman only the power of refusal."

22. See Dickinson, *Poems*, J. 579 ("I had been hungry, all the Years"), J. 709 ("Publication—is the Auction"), and J. 891 ("To my quick ear the Leaves—conferred"); see also Christina Rossetti, "Goblin Market."

23. See Dickinson, *Poems*, J. 327 ("Before I got my eye put out"), George Eliot, *Middlemarch*, book 2, chapter 20, and M. E. Coleridge, "Doubt," in *Poems by Mary E. Coleridge*, p. 40.

24. See Dickinson, *Poems*, J. 101.

25. *The Poetical works of Christina G. Rossetti*, 2 vols. (Boston: Little Brown, 1909), 2:11.

CATHARINE R. STIMPSON

ZERO DEGREE DEVIANCY

the lesbian novel in english

In her poem "Diving into the Wreck" (1972), Adrienne Rich imagined a descent into the sea of history that might see the damage that was done and the treasures that prevail. The poem has been a mandate for feminist critics as they measure the damage patriarchal cultures have inflicted and the treasures that a female tradition has nevertheless accumulated. We have yet to survey fully, however, the lesbian writers who worked under the double burden of a patriarchal culture and a strain in the female tradition that accepted and valued heterosexuality.[1] It is these writers whom I want to ground more securely in the domain of feminist criticism.[2]

My definition of the lesbian—as writer, as character, and as reader—will be conservative and severely literal. She is a woman who finds other women erotically attractive and gratifying. Of course a lesbian is more than her body, more than her flesh, but lesbianism partakes of the body, partakes of the flesh. That carnality distinguishes it from gestures of political sympathy with homosexuals and from affectionate friendships in which women enjoy each other, support each other, and commingle a sense of identity and well-being. Lesbianism represents a commitment of skin, blood, breast and bone. If female and male gay writings have their differences, it is not only because one takes Sappho and the other Walt Whitman as its great precursor. They simply do not spring from the same physical presence in the world.

To my lexicographical rigidity I will add an argument that is often grim. Because the violent yoking of homosexuality and deviancy has been so pervasive in the modern period, little or no writing about it can ignore that conjunction. A text may support it, leeringly or ruefully. It may reject it, fiercely or ebulliently. Moral or emotional indifference is improbable. Few, if any, homosexual texts can exemplify writing at the zero degree, that degree at which writing, according to Roland Barthes, is " . . . basically in the indicative mood, or . . . amodal . . . [a] new neutral writing . . . [that] takes its place in the midst of . . . ejaculation and judgements; without becoming involved in any of them; [that] . . . consists precisely in their absence."[3] Lesbian novels in English have responded judgmentally to the perversion that has made homosexuality perverse by developing two repetitive patterns: the dying fall, a narrative of damnation, of the lesbian's suffering as a lonely outcast attracted to a psychological lower caste; and the enabling escape, a narrative of the reversal of such descending trajectories, of the lesbian's rebellion against social stigma and self-contempt. Because the first has been dominant during the twentieth century, the second has had to flee from the imaginative grip of that tradition as well.

If the narratives of damnation reflect larger social attitudes about homosexuality, they can also extend an error of discourse about it: false universalizing, tyrannical univocalizing. Often ahistorical, as if pain erased the processes of time, they can fail to reveal the inseparability of the twentieth-century lesbian novel and the twentieth century: " . . . in the nineteenth century . . . homosexuality assumed its modern form," which the next century was to exhibit.[4] One symptom of modernization, of the refusal to exempt the lesbian from the lurching logic of change, was a new sexual vocabulary. Before the end of the nineteenth century, homosexuality might have been subsumed under such a term as "masturbation."[5] Then lesbians became "lesbians." The first citation for lesbianism as a female passion in *The Shorter Oxford English Dictionary* is 1908, for "sapphism" 1890.

The public used its new language with pity, hostility, and disdain.[6] The growing tolerance of an optionally nonprocreative heterosexuality failed to dilute the abhorrence of a necessarily nonprocreative homosexuality, especially if practicing it threatened to mean social as well as sexual self-sufficiency. In her study of birth control, Linda Gordon states: "We must notice that the sexual revolution was not a general loosening of sexual taboos but only of those on nonmarital heterosexual activity. Indeed, so specifically heterosexual was this change that it tended to intensify taboos on homosexual activity and did much to break patterns of emotional dependency and intensity among women."[7] Both female and male writers absorbed such strong cultural signals. If "guilt and anxiety rarely appear in homosexual literature until the late nineteenth century, . . . [they] become the major theme of *Angst* . . . after 1914."[8] Evidently, freedom in one place may serve as an innoculation against its permissible appearance elsewhere. The more autonomy women claim in one sphere, the more they may enter into an obscure balancing act that may lead to tighter restrictions upon them in another.

Such an environment nurtured external and internal censorship. During a century in which the woman writer as such became less of a freak, the lesbian writer had to inhibit her use of material she knew intimately but which her culture might hold to be, at best, freakish. She learned that being quiet, in literature and life, would enable her to "pass." Silence could be a passport into the territory of the dominant world. In a quick-witted recent novel, June Arnold's *Sister Gin*, an aging mother responds to her middle-aged daughter's attempt to talk to her about her lesbianism: "But she shouldn't say that word. It isn't a nice word. 'People don't care what you do as long as you don't tell them about it. I know that.'"[9] Such silence signifies a subterranean belief in the magical power of language. If the lesbian were to name herself, her utterance might carry a taint from speaker to listener, from mouth to ear. Silence is also a shrewd refusal to provoke punitive powers—be they of the family, workplace, law, or church. Obviously this survival tactic makes literature impossible. Culture, then, becomes the legatee of linguistic zeros, of blank pages encrypted in tombs critics will never excavate.

If the lesbian writer wished to name her experience but still feared plain speech, she could encrypt her text in another sense and use codes.[10] In the fall-out of history, the words "code" and "zero" lie together. The Arabs translated the Hindu for "zero" as *sifr* ("empty space"), in English "cipher." As the Arabic grew in meanings, *sifr* came to represent a number system forbidden in several places but still secretly deployed, and cipher became "code." In some lesbian fiction, the encoding is allegorical, a straightforward shift from one set of terms to another, from a clitoris to a cow. Other acts are more resistant to any reading that might wholly reveal, or wholly deny, lesbian eroticism.

Take for example "the kiss," a staple of lesbian fiction. Because it has shared with women's writing in general a reticence about explicitly representing sexual activity, the kiss has had vast metonymic responsibilities. Simultaneously, its exact significance has been deliberately opaque. Look at three famous kiss scenes:

> It was a very real oblivion. Adele was roused from it by a kiss that seemed to scale the very walls of chastity. She flung away on the instant filled with battle and revulsion. [Gertrude Stein, Q.E.D.]

> Julia blazed. Julia kindled. Out of the night she burnt like a dead white star. Julia opened her arms. Julia kissed her on the lips. Julia possessed it. [Virginia Woolf, "Slater's Pins Have No Points"]

> Then came the most exquisite moment of her whole life passing a stone urn with flowers in it. Sally stopped; picked a flower; kissed her on the lips. The whole world might have turned upside down! . . . she felt that she had been given a present, wrapped up, and told just to keep it, not to look at it—a diamond, something infinitely precious, wrapped up . . . she uncovered, or the radiance burnt through the revelation, the religious feeling! [Woolf, *Mrs. Dalloway*]

Does the kiss encode transgression or permissibility? Singularity or repeatability? Impossibility or possibility? The same character, "O," can stand for both the zero of impossibility and for the possibilities of female sexuality.[11] Does the kiss predict the beginning of the end, or the end of the beginning, or a lesbian erotic enterprise? Or is it the event that literally embraces contradictions?

Still, the overt will out. As if making an implicit, perhaps unconscious pact with her culture, the lesbian writer who rejects both silence and excessive coding can claim the right to write for the public in exchange for adopting the narrative of damnation. The paradigm of this narrative is Radclyffe Hall's *The Well of Loneliness*—published, banned in England, and quickly issued elsewhere in 1928, by which time scorn for lesbianism had hardened into orthodoxy.[12] Novelist as well as novel have entered minor mythology. Hall represents the lesbian as scandal and the lesbian as woman-who-is-man, who proves "her" masculinity through taking a feminine woman-who-is-woman as "her" lover. In a baroque and savage satire published after *The Well of Loneliness*, Wyndham Lewis excoriates a den of dykes in which a woman artist in "a stiff Radcliffe-Hall collar, of antique masculine cut" torments a heterosexual fellow and dabbles with a voluptuous mate.[13] He is too jealous and enraged to recognize either the sadness of costume and role reversal (the stigmatized seeking to erase the mark through aping the stigmatizers) or the courage of the masquerade (the emblazoning of defiance and jaunty play).[14] Be it mimicry or bravery, the woman who would be man reaches for status and for freedom. The man who would be woman, because of the devaluation of the female and feminine, participates, in part, in a ritual of degradation.

Comparing *The Well of Loneliness* to Hall's life reveals a discrepancy between the pleasures she seems to have found with her lover, Una Taylor, Lady Troubridge, and the sorrows of her hero, Stephen Gordon. Hall offers a parallel to the phenomenon of the woman novelist who creates women characters less accomplished and successful than she. In addition, the novel is more pessimistic about the threat of homosexuality *as such* to happiness than Hall's earlier novel, *The Unlit Lamp* (1924). Set in roughly the same time period as *The Well of Loneliness*, *The Unlit Lamp* dramatizes a triangle of mother, daughter, and governess. The daughter and governess have a long, unconsummated, ultimately ruptured lesbian relationship. Their grief is less the result of a vile passion and the reactions to it than of the daughter's failure of nerve, her father's patriarchal crassness, her mother's possessive manipulations, and the constrictions provincial England places on the New Woman.

In brief, *The Well of Loneliness* tends to ignore the more benign possibilities of lesbianism. Hall projects homosexuality as a sickness. To deepen the horror, the abnormal illness is inescapable, preordained; an ascribed, not an achieved, status. For Stephen is a "congenital invert," the term John Addington Symonds probably coined around 1883 and Havelock Ellis later refined: "Sexual inversion, as here understood, means sexual instinct turned by inborn constitutional abnormality towards persons of the same sex. It is thus a narrower term than homosexuality, which includes all sexual attractions between persons of the same sex." The congenital female invert has male physical traits—narrow hips, wide shoulders—as "part of an organic instinct."[15] Stephen also has a livid scar on her cheek. Literally, it is a war wound; socially, a mark of the stigmatized individual who may blame the self for a lack of acceptability;[16] mythically, the mark of Cain. *The Well of Loneliness* stresses the morbidity of a stigma that the politics of heaven, not of earth, must first relieve.

Yet Hall planned an explicit protest against that morbidity. Indeed, having Stephen Gordon be a congenital invert who has no choice about her condition strengthens Hall's argument about the unfairness of equating homosexuality with punishable deviancy. The novel claims that God created homosexuals. If they are good enough for Him, they ought to be good enough for us. Hall cries out for sacred and social toleration, for an end to the cruelties of alienation. In the novel's famous last paragraph, Stephen gasps, "God . . . we believe; we have told You we believe. . . . We have not denied You, then rise up and defend us. Acknowledge us, oh God, before the whole world. Give us the right to our existence."[17] Ironically, the very explicitness of that cry in a climate increasingly harsh for lesbians, combined with the vividness of Hall's description of homosexual subworlds, propelled *The Well of Loneliness* into scandal while the far more subversive, if subtle, *Unlit Lamp* was a success. To double the irony, Hall's strategies of protest against damnation so entangle her in damnation that they intensify the sense of its inevitability and power. The novel's attack on homophobia becomes particularly self-defeating. The text is, then, like a Janus with one face looming larger than the other. It gives the heterosexual a voyeuristic tour and the vicarious comfort of reading about an enforced stigma—in greater measure than it provokes guilt. It gives the homosexual, particularly the lesbian, riddling images of pity, self-pity, and terror—in greater measure than it consoles.

The Well of Loneliness lacks the intricacies of Djuna Barnes' Nightwood, another parable of damnation, published eight years later. Its lack of intricacy, plus its notoriety and the way in which it inscribes damnation, helped to transform its status from that of subject of an obscenity trial to that of an immensely influential, token lesbian text. As one historian writes, "most of us lesbians in the 1950s grew up knowing nothing about lesbianism except Stephen Gordon." [18] Despite, or perhaps because of, its reputation, critics have ignored its structural logic, an error I want to remedy now.

Each of the novel's five sections (or acts) ends unhappily, the parts replicating and reinforcing the movement of the whole. Book 1 begins with Stephen's birth to a loving, rich couple. [19] The happiness of their legitimate, heterosexual union is the positive term that opposes the woe lurking in wait for illegitimate, homosexual ones. Although Sir Philip Gordon had wanted a son, he loves his daughter. Wise, courageous, kind, honorable, attentive, athletic, he embodies a fantasy of the perfect father Hall never had, the perfect man she could never become. Lady Anna, however, who had simply wanted a baby, instinctively repudiates her "unnatural" daughter. Though mother and child are of the same sex, they share neither gender nor love. Hall's idealization of Sir Philip and her regrets about Lady Anna are early markers of a refusal to link a protest against homophobia with one against patriarchal values.

During her late adolescence, Stephen meets a visiting Canadian, Martin Hallam. They become the best of brotherly friends—until Martin falls in love with Stephen. His emotions shock her; her shock stuns him; he leaves the neighborhood. Stephen's introduction to heterosexual passion, to her a form of homosexual incest, confirms her inability to pass even the most benign of initiation rites for girls. The loss of her "brother," however, is far less painful than the accidental death of her father, which ends book 1: it deprives her of "companionship of mind, . . . a stalwart barrier between her and the world, . . . and above all of love" (p. 121).

So bereft, Stephen behaves blindly. She falls in love with Angela Crosby, fickle, shallow, and married. As Angela strings Stephen along with a few of those conventional kisses, she sets her up as a rival of two men: husband Ralph and lover Roger. The masculinized lesbian has few advantages in competition with natural males. To keep Ralph from finding out about Roger, Angela shows him a love letter from Stephen and claims to be the innocent victim of odd affections. Ralph takes the letter to Lady Anna, who gives Stephen the choice of leaving her beloved ancestral estate or watching Lady Anna leave it. Finding her "manhood," Stephen accepts exile. With a loyal governess, a favorite horse, and a private income, she abandons Eden for London. Hall concludes book 2 with the punishment of expulsion, proving that even the aristocratic homosexual must suffer.

In the city, Stephen completes the rites of maturity for inverts. She finds a home: Paris, the center of literary lesbianism in the first part of the twentieth century. She finds work: literature itself. She writes a wonderful and famous novel. As Cain's mark was from God, so both Ellis and Hall give their inverts some compensations: intelligence and talent. If the body is negatively deviant, the mind is positively so. Hall demands that the invert use that intelligence and talent. Hard work will be a weapon against the hostile world; cultural production an answer to the society that repudiates a Stephen because she has been forced to repudiate reproduction. Finally, serving a larger cause, Stephen becomes a valiant member of a World War I women's ambulance corps. (Hall here explores, if peripherally, that standard setting of the lesbian text: a community of women.) But despite the personal bravery of both female and male warriors, the war is a wasteland. Stephen's personal anguish and confusion over her sexuality, then, find a larger, historical correlative in the trenches, as Hall ends book 3 with a lament for the dead.

During the war, however, Stephen has met a poorer, younger, Welsh woman, Mary Llewellyn, whom she takes to a Mediterranean villa. For a while they suppress their physical longing. In Stephen's fears that sex will destroy love, ecstasy intimacy, Hall is suggesting that the stigma of homosexuality is tolerable as long as the erotic desire that distinguishes the lesbian remains repressed. The conclusion—that a released eros will provoke the destructive potential of the stigma—places Hall in that Western tradition that links sex and death. In addition, she is attributing to lesbianism a conventional belief about female sexuality in general: that women prefer love and romance to physical consummation. Ultimately Mary's needs overwhelm Stephen's chivalrous hope to protect her from them. Though their bodies, like those of any homosexual couple, are anatomically similar, their relationship embodies a number of dyadic roles. Into their closed and exclusive world they structure multiple polarized differences, primarily that between female and male. Hall exults:

> Stephen as she held the girl in her arms, would feel that indeed she was all things to Mary; father, mother, friend and lover, all things; and Mary all things to her—the child, the friend, the beloved, all things. But Mary, because she was perfect woman, would rest without thought, without exultation, without question; finding no need to question since for her there was now only one thing—Stephen. [p. 134]

Seeking metaphors for their passion, Hall, like many lesbian novelists, turns to nature, both tamed and untamed: to vineyards, fruit trees, flowers, the four elements, the moon. Such standard tropes carry the implicit burden of dissolving the taint of "unnatural" actions through the cleansing power of natural language.[20]

Most idylls, even those of refound Edens, must end. Hall concludes book 4 with the ominous "And thus in a cloud of illusion and glory, sped the last enchanted days at Orotava" (p. 317). Stephen and Mary return to Paris. There, with their loving dog, they are happy—for a while; but Mary, restless, begins to seek diversion with other lesbians and in the homosexual underworld, particularly in the bars that modern cities nurture. Bars can serve as a source of warm, egalitarian *communitas* for the marginal homosexual who must also aspire to the far more prestigious heterosexual world that is a structural reference group.[21] But the fearful, puritanical Stephen despises them; like many fictive lesbians, she finds security in a sanctified domesticity. Though a friend reasonably tells Stephen that Mary has too little to do, especially when Stephen is obsessively writing, Hall just as reasonably locates the primary source of strain between the lovers in the tension between their little world and the larger world of society and family that fears them.

Whatever the cause, Mary mopes and hardens. Then, a secular *deus ex machina*, Martin Hallam returns. Stephen's alter ego, he, too, has been wounded in the war. He, too, falls in love with Mary. The two fight it out for her. Though Stephen wins, the price is too high: where she once had Mary's soul but feared possession of the body, she may now possess the body but not the soul. For God's scheme includes congenital heterosexuals as well as congenital inverts. Mary has, somewhat belatedly, realized that she is one of them. Martyring herself in the religion of love, Stephen pretends to be having an affair with a woman friend, Valerie Seymour. She stays out for two nights. When she returns, her mock confession of infidelity drives the distraught Mary into the night and the arms of the waiting Martin, whom Stephen has posted in the street below.

Throughout book 5, Hall's religiosity has become more and more omnipresent: her attraction to Catholic theology, architecture, and liturgy; her anxious queries about God's real allegiance in the war between Stephen's little world and that which would damn it. As Stephen renounces Mary, she has a compensatory vision, at once hallucination, inspiration, and conversion experience. She will become the voice of the voiceless stigmatized; she will help them break through to a new, sympathetic recognition. So willing, Stephen finds that "her barren womb became fruitful—it ached with its fearful and sterile burden " (p. 437).

That juxtaposition of fruitfulness and aching burdens is a final bit of information about the unevenly balanced duality of Hall's text. Yet she does create the figure of Valerie Seymour, a charismatic teetotaler who keeps a famous Parisian salon. Amidst the volatile gloom of Stephen's histrionics, she is serenely sunny. She, too, finds homosexuality congenital, but she lyrically interprets fate as a friendly boon: "Nature was trying to do her bit; inverts were being born in increasing numbers, and after a while their numbers would tell, even with the fools who still ignored Nature" (p. 406). Though Hall does little with Valerie, she signifies the presence of a second consciousness about lesbianism that *The Well of Loneliness* and the forces surrounding it helped to submerge, screen, and render secondary during the mid-twentieth century. This consciousness, aware of the labelling of lesbianism as a pollutant, nevertheless chose to defy it.

The "Kinsey Report" suggests the existence of such a mentality. Of 142 women with much homosexual experience, 70 percent reported no regrets.[22] This consciousness has manifested itself in literature in two ways. First, in lesbian romanticism: fusions of life and death, happiness and woe, natural imagery and supernatural strivings, neoclassical paganism with a ritualistic cult of Sappho, and modern beliefs in evolutionary progress with a cult of the rebel. At its worst an inadvertent parody of *fin-de-siècle* decadence, at its best lesbian romanticism ruthlessly rejects a stifling dominant culture and asserts the value of psychological autonomy, women, art, and a European cultivation of the sensuous, sensual, and voluptuous. Woolf's *Orlando* is its most elegant and inventive text, but its symbol is probably the career of Natalie Barney, the cosmopolitan American who was the prototype of Valerie Seymour.[23]

The second mode is lesbian realism: the adaption of the conventions of the social and psychological novel to appraise bonds between women and demonstrate that such relationships are potentially of psychic and moral value. The slyest realistic text is Stein's *Autobiography of Alice B. Toklas*, but less tricky examples include *The Unlit Lamp* and another ignored novel,Helen R. Hull's *Labyrinth* (1923). There one sister marries an ambitious, egocentric man. A second sister lives with an ambitious, generous woman. The first sister is unhappy and confined; the second happy and productive.[24] What *Labyrinth* implies, other realistic texts state explicitly: even though the lesbian may have children whom she loves, she must reject the patriarchal family, which the stigma against her helps to maintain, if she is to reject repression as well. The tension between the role of mother, which the lesbian may desire, and the traditional family structure, in which women are subordinate, is obviously far more characteristic of lesbian than gay-male writing. A man may have both paternity and power, but a woman must too often choose between maternity and comparative powerlessness.

In 1963 Mary McCarthy's *The Group* brought that submerged, screened, secondary consciousness to public prominence. Second on the fiction best-seller list for its year, selling well over 3,000,000 copies by 1977, *The Group* showed that lesbianism could be an acceptable, even admirable, subject—particularly if a writer of unquestioned heterosexuality served as the gatekeeper. Moreover, McCarthy was tactfully judicious about the erotic details of lesbian sexuality. Cleverly, if perhaps inadvertently, McCarthy fused lesbian romanticism and lesbian realism. In characterization, setting, style, and some of its assumptions, *The Group* was realistic, but its heroine was wonderfully romantic. For Lakey is self-assured, intelligent, beautiful, charitable, and anti-Fascist; she wears violet suits; she has lived in Europe; she has an affair with a baroness. In brief, she personifies the most glamorous of enabling escapes from stigma and self-contempt. The members of The Group, all Vassar graduates, also prefigure the possible response of liberal readers of this novel to the claims of this secondary consciousness to primary status. Lakey, after she returns from Europe, cannot be damned; indeed, she must be respected. Yet The Group finds encounters with her awkwardly enigmatic and strange; strangely and enigmatically awkward.

Since *The Group*, a far less tormented lesbian has surfaced—to supplement, if not wholly supplant, the Stephens and Marys. In some texts by nonlesbians, she is little more than a romp, a sexual interlude and caper. Like masturbation and the orgy, homosexuality has become a counter in the game of erotic writing. Trade fiction has claimed the provinces of pornography and sexology. Other texts, however, primarily by lesbians and sympathetic feminists, damn the lesbian's damnation. Their appearance in strength is the result of a confluence of forces. Certainly a material cause was the founding of several journals, magazines, and presses that could publish the products of a more audacious sexual ideology and practice. Among the most substantial, for the lesbian novel, was the small trade house, Daughters, Inc. Its subtitle, "Publishers of Books by Women," reflects its founders' theory that feminism would create new genres. Existing in that climate, which might have a certain early crudity, would be a "freer lesbian novel, and Daughters would be a medium that lesbian novelists could count on."[25] Among the social causes of the reappearance of a submerged consciousness and its narrative of the enabling escape have been the women's movement, more flexible attitudes toward marriage (so often contrasted favorably to the putative anarchy of homosexual relations), the "modernization of sex," which encourages a rational, tolerant approach to the complexities of eros,[26] and the growing entrance of more women into the public labor force, which gives a financial autonomy inseparable from genuine sexual independence.

The new texts are hopeful about homosexuality and confident about the lesbian's power to name her experience and experiment with literary form.[27] These novels invert the application of the label of deviant: the lesbian calls those who would call her sinful or sick themselves sinful or sick; she claims for herself the language of respectability. In a sweet novel of the 1960s, Elana Nachman's *River-finger Woman*, the protagonist fantasizes about enlightening some benighted heterosexuals. She and her lover will make a movie "so that people would see that lesbians are beautiful, there is nothing, nothing at all unnatural about them, they too can have weddings and be in the movies."[28] Mingling fiction, journalism, autobiography, and polemic, Jill Johnston declares in her book *Lesbian Nation* that "that awful life of having to choose between being a criminal or going straight was over. We were going to legitimatize ourselves as criminals."[29] Obviously these dreams and manifestos are still enmeshed in older vocabularies of value. A few books approach indifference. Less attracted to acts of reversal, they hint at a Barthian writing degree zero.[30]

Among the first of the more hopeful lesbian novels was *A Place for Us,* which its author (using the name Isabel Miller) published privately in 1969 and which a commercial press reissued as *Patience and Sarah* in 1972. That was the year of the Stonewall Resistance, the defense of a New York gay bar against a police raid that symbolizes the beginning of the Gay Liberation movement. The history of *A Place for Us*—the pseudonym, the dual publication—shows both the presence and the dissolution of a fear of lesbian material. Its author's comments about *The Well of Loneliness* reveal both the influence of and a resistance to Hall's earlier gesticulations: "I think Radclyffe Hall was antihomosexual. . . . I first read *The Well of Loneliness* when I was about seventeen. . . . I was very excited. But I didn't like the characters, I didn't like the arrogance of the heroine."[31] Gentle, kindly, *A Place for Us* tells of two nineteenth-century women who run away together from patriarchal brutalities to build their farm in New York State. Almost immediately after *A Place for Us*, the most successful of the new texts appeared, Rita Mae Brown's *Rubyfruit Jungle* (1973), which during the 1970s replaced *The Well of Loneliness* as the one lesbian novel someone might have read. In *Rubyfruit Jungle* (the title alludes to the female genitals), Molly Bolt (a name that alludes to freedom and flight) escapes from a seedy provincial background to triumph over mean men, shallow women, bad schools, menial jobs, and lesbian-baiting.

If *A Place for Us* adapts the narrative of the enabling escape to the pastoral domestic idyll, *Rubyfruit Jungle* integrates it with the picaresque and the *Bildungs-*

roman. Together these novels dramatize two contradictory attitudes about sex and gender that preface the contemporary lesbian novel. The first of these attitudes is a bristling contempt for sexual role playing (*A Place for Us* is an exception here). The protagonist in *Riverfinger Woman* asserts: "we were too modern already to believe that one of us was the man and the other . . . the woman. We felt like neither men nor women. We were females, we were queers. . . . We knew we had the right to love whomever we loved." [32] Under the influence of an existential ethic that praises the freely forged self and of a feminist ideology that negates patriarchal practices, such novels abandon the customs of a Radclyffe Hall. Yet they are simultaneously conscious of sex. Males, particularly traditional ones, are in disrepute. Some novels, such as Arnold's *Sister Gin*, articulate punitive fantasies—some violent, some playful—which they justify as catharsis or self-defense. The female and the female world are honorable, as structural reference and source of *communitas*. Women ask not only for equality but for self-celebration; less for rehabilitation of men than for independence from them.

Lesbian novels thus map out the boundaries of female worlds. [33] Some of the bonds within these boundaries are erotic, a proud isosexuality that separates the lesbian novel from other, more guarded explorations, such as Charlotte Perkins Gilman's *Herland*. Characters also search, however, for alter egos, moral and psychological equivalents, which the term "sister" signifies. Poignantly, painfully, they seek the mother as well. [34] A mother waits at the heart of the labyrinth of some lesbian texts. There she unites past, present, and future. Finding her, in herself and through a surrogate, the lesbian reenacts a daughter's desire for the woman to whom she was once so linked, from whom she was then so severed. Because the mother was once a daughter, a woman approaching her can serve as the mother's mother even as she plays out the drama of a daughter. In such complex mother/daughter exchanges and interchanges, the women explore both narcissistic and anaclitic love. Of course lesbianism is far more than a matter of mother/daughter affairs, but the new texts suggest that one of its satisfactions is a return to primal origins, to primal loves, when female/female, not male/female, relationships structured the world. A lesbian's jealousy, then, spurs like blood from the cut of terror at the possibility of losing again the intimacy that has at last been regained.

To focus on mothers and daughters—or on any personal bonds—is too narrow; psychology hardly defines the totality of our lives. In several texts the world of women is also a political center of solidarity and resistance. As such it can perform social experiments that the larger culture might regard attentively. To name such communities, the lesbian writer calls on myth: prehistorical matriarchies; the Amazons; Sappho and her school. The myths, also current in contemporary feminist ideology, were popular in stylish lesbian circles in the earlier part of the twentieth century. Part of their value is their ability to evoke atemporal resonances within narratives that are separate from such patriarchal religious structures as the Catholic church before which Hall knelt. When novelists grant myths the status of history (easier to do with Sappho than with Amazons and primeval matriarchs), their error, because it occurs in the freewheeling context of fiction, is more palatable than in the stricter context of programmatic ideology, political theory, and "herstory."

The most ambitious and the cleverest of the new novels in English is perhaps

Bertha Harris' *Lover* (1976). The lesbian novel has tended to be, and remains, formally staid, a conventionality that has served both a homosexual and heterosexual audience. The lesbian, as she struggles against the hostilities of the larger world, can find comfort in the ease of reading. Between text and self she may also establish a sense of community. The heterosexual, as she or he nears unfamiliar and despised material, can find safety in the same ease of reading. The continued strength of literary form can stand for the continued strength of the larger community's norms. However, Harris, an American equivalent of Monique Wittig, experiments with narrative pattern as a possible coefficient of her vision of sexuality. A modernist, she fragments and collapses characters, settings, chronology, and states of mind. Her central presence appears as Veronica (also the name of the second wife of Veronica's bigamist grandfather); as Flynn; as Bertha; and as "I." In each guise the voice is both fiction and the author in the act of writing fiction. In brief, *Lover* is another book about becoming a book.

Harris is ingenious, sardonic, parodic—an economical comic intelligence. Another cultural consequence of the stigma against the lesbian is that it deforms comedy. Those who support the stigma, such as Wyndham Lewis, may freely assault the homosexual with hostile satire and burlesque. Those who internalize the stigma use the same weapons as a form of self-assault. Only when the stigma is simultaneously comprehended and despised can the comedy of a Harris, or of a Barnes before her, emerge.[35] It is a satire, often elaborate, even grotesque and baroque, that ultimately adorns rather than mutilates its subject. Barnes' enigmatic and rich prose has deeply influenced Harris, but more immediately, so has Nabokov's, his "tricking and fooling and punning and literary joking."

Some people in the feminist and lesbian press have criticized Harris and others for these adventures. Harris has been called inaccessible, as if modernism were itself an indecipherable code. She is, therefore, supposedly ideologically unsound, stopping that illusory creature, the average lesbian, from using literature to articulate her experience and urge rebellion against its nastier aspects. Harris has explanations for such prescriptive reviews. She believes that the feminist and lesbian press still lacks an informed criticism to mediate between texts and a large audience, and she finds too few "well-read reviewers, conscious of literary traditions." The press must learn to do what modern art has done: to create a self-explanatory body of criticism. Furthermore, "the lesbian readership" wants a "positive image" in its novels. Part of the huge popularity of *Rubyfruit Jungle* is due to its ebullient self-admiration. Such easy hedonism and heroism is, of course, didactically helpful and politically worthwhile, but it also "prevents a deeper look into the nature of things and the nature of lesbianism."

The baffled response to *Lover* is ironic, for few writers have given the lesbian a more lyrical identity. Harris explores the various roles women have played: grandmother, mother, daughter, sister, wife and second wife, businesswoman in man's clothing, prostitute, factory worker, movie star, muse and tutelary spirit, warrior, artist, fake saint, martyr. She codifies difference of role in order to assess similarities of the players and to find a common basis for a community of women. There the primary difference will be between lover and beloved—though lovers can be loved and the beloved lovers. The phallus may not be unwelcome, especially if necessary for breeding, but the nonphallic lesbian has a privileged status. In loving women she exalts both self and other. Harris also anoints this paradigm and paramour as an omnipotent cosmic spirit. Capable of anything and every-thing, she is polymorphic, amorphic, transmorphic, and orphic. She both pic-tures margins and escapes them. She is the principle of creativity, of a fertility of both mind and body. As such she incarnates the genesis of the world itself, once suppressed, which might be reappearing now. In an essay about Barnes and les-bian literature, Harris might be talking about *Lover* itself:

> There is not a literature that is not based on the pervasive sexuality of its time; and as that which is male disappears (sinks slowly in the west) and as the originally all-female world reasserts itself by making love to itself, the primary gesture toward the making at last of a decent literature out of the experience of a decent world might simply be a woman like myself following a woman like Djuna Barnes, and all she might represent down a single street on a particular afternoon.[36]

Not everyone will accept Harris' only partially ironic apocalyptic fantasy. Her picture of the damned does, however, reverse that of *The Well of Loneliness*. The lesbian novel has offered up Hall's vision, but it has also sheltered and released the rejection of that vision, offering an alternative process of affirmation of the lesbian body and transcendence of a culturally traced, scarring stigma. It has been a deviant voice that has both submitted to deviancy and yearned to nullify that judgment. Feminist critics, zeroing in on that voice, can serve as its acous-tical engineers. We can listen for its variations, fluctuations, blurrings, coded sig-nals, and lapses into mimicry or a void. As we do, we must also try to hear, in wonder and in rage, words and phrases that might explain what is now a mystery: why people wish to stigmatize, to dominate, to outlaw, and to erase a particular longing for passion and for love.

NOTES

Early versions of this paper were read at Brown University, Hampshire College, the Columbia University Seminar on Women in Society, and the Modern Language Associa-tion. I am grateful to Adrienne Rich, Elizabeth Wood, and Elizabeth Abel for their comments.

1. The number of texts about lesbians, by lesbians and nonlesbians, is unclear. There are about twenty-three hundred entries in Gene Damon and Lee Stuart's *The Lesbian in Literature: A Bibliography* (San Francisco, 1967) and about nineteen hundred entries in the revised edition by Damon, Jan Watson, and Robin Jordan (Reno, Nev., 1975). While this second edition has more nonfiction entries and has been updated, the compilers have also cut over a thousand entries from the first edition because they referred to "trash" men had written for male readers (p. 26). The pioneering survey of the figure of the lesbian in Western literature remains Jeannette H. Foster's *Sex Variant Women in Literature: A Histori-cal and Quantitative Survey* (London, 1958), but adding to it now is Lillian Faderman's valu-able *Surpassing the Love of Men* (New York, 1981).

2. For a study of the French literary tradition, see Elaine Marks, "Lesbian Intertex-tuality," in *Homosexualities and French Literature*, ed. George Stambolian and Marks (Ithaca, N.Y., 1979), pp. 353–77. Several of the articles on female sexuality which were collected in *Women—Sex and Sexuality*, ed. Stimpson and Ethel Spector Person (Chicago, 1980), have insights into modern lesbianism.

3. Roland Barthes, *Writing Degree Zero*, trans. Annette Lavers and Colin Smith (Boston, 1970), pp. 76–77. Barthes has claimed that a recent novel, Renaud Camus' *Tricks* (trans. Richard Howard [New York, 1981]), which I read in manuscript, exemplifies homosexual writing at the degree zero. In his preface, Barthes says that homosexuality is " . . . still at the stage of excitation where it provokes what might be called feats of discourse," but "Camus' narratives are neutral, they do not participate in the game of interpretation." I suggest that *Tricks* does interpret a pattern of male homosexual activity as a fascinating, intense, limited, and only apparently permissible form of experience.

4. Gayle Rubin, introduction to Renée Vivien's *A Woman Appeared to Me*, trans. Jeannette H. Foster (Reno, Nev., 1976), p. v.

5. see Vern L. Bullough and Martha Voght, "Homosexuality and Its Confusion with the 'Secret Sin' in Pre-Freudian America," *Journal of the History of Medicine and Allied Sciences* (Spring 1973):143–55; rpt. in Bullough, *Sex, Society, and History* (New York, 1976), pp. 112–24. My thanks to Mari Jo Buhle for bringing this article to my attention.

6. See Bullough, *Sexual Variance in Society and History* (New York, 1976), p. 605.

7. Linda Gordon, *Woman's Body, Woman's Right: A Social History of Birth Control in America* (New York, 1976), p. 164.

8. Rictor Norton, "The Homosexual Literary Tradition," *College English* 35, no. 6 (March 1974):677; see also *College English* 36, no. 3 (November 1974), "The Homosexual Imagination," ed. Norton and Louis Crew. For an enthusiastic survey of lesbian writing, see *Margins* 23 (August 1975), "Focus: Lesbian Feminist Writing and Publishing," ed. Beth Hodges, esp. Julia P. Stanley, "Uninhabited Angels: Metaphors for Love" (pp. 7–10), which makes several points similar to mine here. For critical studies of the literature about male homosexuals, see Roger Austen, *Playing the Game: The Homosexual Novel in America* (Indianapolis, 1977), and Robert K. Martin, *The Homosexual Tradition in American Poetry* (Austin, Tex., 1979).

9. June Arnold, *Sister Gin* (Plainfield, Vt., 1975), p. 82. For an account of a facade that a lesbian community kept up, see Vern and Bonnie Bullough, "Lesbianism in the 1920s and 1930s: A Newfound Study," *Signs* 2, no. 4 (Summer 1977):895–904.

10. I have written about coding by those who consider themselves sexual anomalies in "The Mind, the Body, and Gertrude Stein," *Critical Inquiry* 3, no. 3 (Spring 1977): 489–506. Detailed work on Stein's codes includes: Richard Bridgman, *Gertrude Stein in Pieces* (New York, 1970); Linda Simon, *Biography of Alice B. Toklas* (Garden City, N.Y., 1977); William Gass, *World within the Word* (New York, 1978), pp. 63–123; and Elizabeth Fifer, "Is Flesh Advisable: The Interior Theater of Gertrude Stein," *Signs* 4, no. 3 (Spring 1979):472–83.

11. See Nina Auerbach, *Communities of Women: An Idea in Fiction* (Cambridge, Mass., 1978), pp. 186–87, for more comment on the "O."

12. See Blanche Wiesen Cook, "'Women Alone Stir My Imagination': Lesbianism and the Cultural Tradition," *Signs* 4, no. 4 (Summer 1979):718, and Lillian Faderman, "Love between Women in 1928" (paper delivered at the Berkshire Conference, Vassar College, Poughkeepsie, N.Y., 18 June 1981).

13. Wyndham Lewis, *The Apes of God* (New York, 1932), p. 222.

14. My comments footnote Sandra M. Gilbert's "Costumes of the Mind: Transvestism as Metaphor in Modern Literature," *Critical Inquiry* 7, no. 2 (Winter 1980):391–417.

15. Havelock Ellis, "Sexual Inversion," *Studies in the Psychology of Sex*, 2 vols. (1901; New York, 1936), 1:1, 122.

16. Erving Goffman's *Stigma: Notes on the Management of Spoiled Identity* (Englewood Cliffs, N.J., 1963), pp. 8–9, has influenced my analysis here.

17. Radclyffe Hall, *The Well of Loneliness* (1928; New York, 1950), p. 437; all further references to this work will be included in the text.

18. Cook, "Women Alone," p. 719.

19. Though Hall's father deserted her mother around the time of Hall's birth, he left the child a generous inheritance. She was one of several aesthetic lesbians whose incomes permitted them to do more or less as they pleased. Class cannot abolish the stigma of homosexuality, but it can mitigate some of the more painful impressions.

20. As late as 1974, when the American Psychoanalytic Association voted to declassify homosexuality as a mental illness, lesbian writers were still dipping into the reservoir of such romantic tropes, as in Kate Millett's *Flying* (New York, 1974): "Taste of salt. Catching it in my mouth. A thirst to suckle it. . . . Very small thing. Pain of tenderness. . . . Fire. The vulva a sun setting behind trees" (p. 536).

21. I am gratefully adapting these terms from Victor Turner's "Passages, Margins, and Poverty," *Dramas, Fields, and Metaphors: Symbolic Action in Human Society* (Ithica, N.Y., 1974), p. 233.

22. Alfred C. Kinsey et al., *Sexual Behavior in the Human Female* (1953; New York, 1965), p. 477. I am sure that this secondary consciousness will appear in autobiographical texts that scholars have previously ignored or been ignorant of. See, e.g., Elsa Gidlow, "Memoirs," *Feminist Studies* 6, no. 1 (Spring 1980):103–27.

23. See Rubin, introduction to Vivien's *A Woman Appeared to Me*, and George Wickes, *The Amazon of Letters: The Life and Loves of Natalie Barney* (New York, 1976).

24. A more ironic and subtle English equivalent is Elizabeth Bowen's *The Hotel* (New York, 1928). Patricia Highsmith's ("Claire Morgan") *The Prince of Salt* (New York, 1952), like *Labyrinth*, is about the family and the lesbian's need to leave it even if she is a mother.

25. Bertha Harris (personal interview, New York, 3 August 1977); unless otherwise indicated, all further quotations from Harris are from this interview. See also Lois Gould, "Creating a Women's World," *New York Times Magazine*, 2 January 1977, pp. 34, 36–38.

26. I am indebted for this concept to Paul Robinson's *The Modernization of Sex* (New York, 1976). I have written in more detail about the relationship of the women's movement to American culture in "Women and American Culture," *Dissent* 27, no. 3 (Summer 1980): 299–307.

27. Ann Allen Shockley has suggested that the taboo on such a lesbian voice has been stronger in the black community than in the white, but even there the gags have loosened; see Shockley, "The Black Lesbian in American Literature: An Overview," in *Conditions Five, The Black Women's Issue*, ed. Lorraine Bethel and Barbara Smith (1979):133–42. The entire issue is courageous and important. See also J. R. Roberts, *Black Lesbians: An Annotated Bibliography* (Tallahassee, 1981), with a foreword by Smith.

28. Elana Nachman, *Riverfinger Woman* (Plainfield, Vt., 1974), p. 13.

29. Jill Johnston, *Lesbian Nation: The Feminist Solution* (New York, 1973), p. 97.

30. For example, in Linda Crawford's *A Class by Herself* (New York, 1976), pills and booze compel a far greater renunciatory attention than does the stigma of lesbianism.

31. Alma Routsong ("Isabel Miller"), interview in Jonathan Katz, *Gay American History: Lesbians and Gay Men in the U.S.A.* (New York, 1976), p. 442. The career of one professional novelist replicates the historical shift from a stress on the stigmatized text to its rejection. As "Ann Aldrich," Marijane Meaker wrote widely read novels about the romances and difficulties of the lesbian subculture. Then under her own name she published *Shockproof Sydney Skate* (New York, 1972). Profitable, well received, it is about a triangle consisting of a woman, the younger woman with whom she has an affair, and her son, who is in love with the younger woman as well. The lesbian circles are little more absurd than any other subject of a comedy of manners.

32. Nachman, *Riverfinger Woman*, p. 13.

33. For a scrupulous exploration of lesbianism and women's worlds in the poetry of the 1960s and 1970s, see Mary Carruthers, "Imaging Women: Notes Towards a Feminist Poetic," *Massachusetts Review* 20, no. 2 (Summer 1979):281–407.

34. See, e.g., Joan Winthrop, *Underwater* (New York, 1974), p. 256. Winthrop has her

central character indulge in a good deal of masculine role playing, which occurs with a certain *esprit* but is only one aspect of personality, not a controlling force as it is in *The Well of Loneliness*. That the role playing takes place after a radical mastectomy is a point Winthrop does not explore. She does, however, say that her heroine's fantasies of being male were the product of years of her own "repression" (personal interview, Sag Harbor, N.Y., 28 July 1976).

35.   A notable example is Barnes' *Ladies Almanack: Written and Illustrated by a Lady of Fashion* (1928; New York, 1972). A dazzling analysis of this work is Susan Snaider Lanser's "Speaking in Tongues: *Ladies Almanack* and the Language of Celebration," *Frontiers* 4, no. 3 (Fall 1979): 39–46. The issue devotes itself to lesbian history and culture.

36.   Harris, "The More Profound Nationality of Their Lesbianism: Lesbian Society in Paris in the 1920s," in *Amazon Expedition: A Lesbian Feminist Anthology*, ed. Harris et al. (Washington, N.J., 1973), p. 88; see also "What We Mean to Say: Notes Toward Defining the Nature of Lesbian Literature," *Heresies* 3 (Fall 1977): 5–8, an issue of exceptional interest.

TRAJECTORIES OF SELF-DEFINITION
placing contemporary afro-american women's fiction

In many ways, this essay is the culmination of the work I'd been doing on Afro-American women writers since 1980. In it I use the historical analysis I'd done in papers such as "The Uses of History," the insights I'd gained from doing analysis of individual writers, and my growing interest in African women writers. What pulled all these insights together for an overview of the literature was the short piece I'd done for *KPFA Folio* and the responses I'd received from the longer paper that grew out of that article. At the same time, Hortense Spillers and Marjorie Pryse were planning a volume of Afro-American women writers. Their comments on my original paper certainly sharpened my focus.

The centrality of Afro-American women's literature to a world view that we must assert in order to change our societies sent me on a search for the development of the self in that literature. In conducting that search, certain new patterns in the literature began to emerge. One of these, the lesbian theme, resulted in my writing another essay; another, the influence of Afro-American women and African women on each other, affected the essay on Buchi Emecheta and Alice Walker that I'd been struggling with. "Trajectories" both summarizes and projects some of my own findings about the vitality and significance of Afro-American women's fiction.

I

> I see a greater and greater commitment among black women writers to understand self, multiplied in terms of the community, the community multiplied in terms of the nation, and the nation multiplied in terms of the world. You have to understand what your place as an individual is and the place of the person who is close to you. You have to understand the space between you before you can understand more complex or larger groups.[1]
> —Alexis DeVeau

In this straightforward statement, Alexis DeVeau alludes to a dominant theme in Afro-American women's fiction of the last decade, as well as to the historical tension from which that theme has emerged. Of course, many literate persons might say that the commitment to self-understanding and how that self is related to the world within which it is situated is at the core of good fiction and that this statement is hardly a dramatic one. Yet, for Afro-American women writers, such an overtly self-centered point of view has been difficult to maintain because of the way they have been conceptualized by black as well as white society. The extent to which Afro-American women writers in the seventies and eighties have been able to make a commitment to an exploration of self, as central rather than marginal, is a tribute to the insights they have culled in a century or so of literary activity. For Afro-American women writers today are no longer marginal to literature in this country; some of them are its finest practitioners.

But in order to really understand the remarkable achievement of a Toni Morrison, an Alice Walker, a Paule Marshall, or the budding creativity of a Gloria Naylor or an Alexis DeVeau, one must appreciate the tradition from which they have come and the conflict of images with which their foremothers have had to contend. For what Afro-American women have been permitted to express, in fact to contemplate, as part of the self, is gravely affected by other complex issues. The development of Afro-American women's fiction is, in many instances, a mirror image of the intensity of the relationship between sexism and racism in this country. And while many of us may grasp this fact in terms of economics or social status, we often forget the toll it takes in terms of self-expression and therefore self-empowerment. To be able to use the range of one's voice, to attempt to express the totality of self, is a recurring struggle in the tradition of these writers from the nineteenth century to the present. Although this essay could hardly survey the scope of such an inquiry, I am interested in showing some measure of the extent to which the tradition has developed to the point where Alexis DeVeau can make the claim she does, and how that claim has resulted in the range of expression that marks the fiction of the seventies and eighties.

Early Afro-American women novelists indicate, through their stated intentions, their primary reasons for writing their works. Frances Harper, for example in her preface to *Iola LeRoy*, made clear her purpose when she wrote that "her story's mission would not be in vain if it awaken in the hearts of our countrymen a stronger sense of justice and a more Christian-like humanity."[2] Harper was pleading for the justice due Afro-Americans who in the 1890s were being lynched, burned out, raped, and deprived of their rights as citizens in the wake of the failure of Reconstruction. Iola LeRoy, Haper's major character, does not attempt to understand either herself as an individual or black women as a group. Rather, Iola LeRoy is a version of the "lady" Americans were expected to respect and honor, even though she is black. By creating a respectable ideal heroine, according to the norms of the time, Harper was addressing not herself, black women, or black people, but her white countrymen.

Audience was a consideration, as well, for Jessie Fauset, the most published Afro-American woman novelist of the Harlem Renaissance. She, together with Nella Larsen, wanted to correct the impression most white people had that all black people lived in Harlem dives or in picturesque, abject poverty.[3] She tells us why she chose to create the heroines she did in her preface to *The Chinaberry Tree* (1931). Beginning with the disclaimer that she does not write to establish a thesis, she goes on to point out that the novel is about "those breathing spells in-between spaces where colored men and women work and live and go their ways with no thought of the problem. What are they like then? So few of the other

Americans know."[4] And she concludes her preface by identifying the class to which her characters belong: the Negro who speaks of "his old Boston families, old Philadelphians, old Charlestonians."[5]

Both Harper and Fauset were certainly aware of the images, primarily negative, of black people that predominated in the minds of white Americans. They constructed their heroines to refute those images, as their way of contributing to the struggle of black people for full citizenship in this country. Of necessity their language was outer-directed rather than inwardly searching, for their characters were addressed to "the other Americans" who blocked the collective development of blacks. To white American readers, self-understanding for black characters might have seemed a luxury. To the extent that these writers emphasized the gender as well as the race of their heroines they were appealing to a white female audience that understood the universal trials of womanhood. These writers' creations, then, were conditioned by the need to establish "positive" images of black people; hence, the exploration of self, in all its complexity, could hardly be attempted.

To a large extent, and necessarily so until the 1940s, most black women fiction writers directed their conscious intention toward a refutation of the negative images imposed upon all black women, images decidedly "masculine" according to the norm of the times.[6] Nonetheless, from *Iola LeRoy* (1892) to Dorothy West's *The Living is Easy* (1948), there is an incredible tension between the "femininity" of the heroines and their actual behavior. On the one hand, the writers try to prove that black women *are* women, that they achieve the ideal of other American women of their time, that is, that they are beautiful (fair), pure, upper class, and would be nonaggressive, dependent beings, if only racism did not exist. At the same time, they appear to believe that if Afro-American women were to achieve the norm, they would lose important aspects of themselves. The novels, especially those about passing, embody this tension. But even in the novels that do not focus on this theme, the writers emphasize the self-directedness of their heroines, as well as their light-skinned beauty and Christian morality. Thus, Iola LeRoy believes that women should work; Pauline Hopkins's heroine in *Contending Forces* (1900) wants to advance the race; Fauset's characters, though class-bound, have ambition to an unfeminine degree; Larsen's heroine Helga Crane in *Quicksand* (1928), though restricted by conventional morality, senses the power of her sensuality and the lie the image of the lady represents.

The tension between the femininity of these heroines and their "contrary instincts"[7] has its roots, in part, in the fact that Afro-American women, contrary to the norm, could not survive unless they generated some measure of self-definition. If they tried to live by the female version of The American Dream, as pure, refined, protected, and well-provided for, they were often destroyed, as is Lutie Johnson, Ann Petry's heroine in *The Street* (1946). And even if they secured a measure of the Dream, some, like Cleo in West's *The Living is Easy*, become destructive, frustrated, alienated from self.

One notable exception to this trend in early Afro-American women writers' works is Zora Neale Hurston's *Their Eyes Were Watching God* (1937). In this work Hurston portrays the development of Janie Stark as a black woman who achieves self-fulfillment and understanding. It is interesting to note, however, that Hurston was obviously aware that the literature of that time focused on the black woman's drive toward economic stability and "feminine" ideals. She constructs the novel so that Janie moves through three stages that embody different views of black women: In her relationship with her first husband, Logan Killicks, Janie is treated like a mule; she is rescued from that state by marrying Jody Starks, who wants her to become a lady, "The Queen of the Porch."[8] But Hurston critiques the achievement of economic stability through feminine submission in marriage as *the* desirable goal for the black woman. She portrays the disastrous consequences of this goal on Janie—that she becomes, in this situation, a piece of desirable property, cut off from her community and languishing in the repression of her natural desire to be herself. Though Janie's relationship with Tea Cake is not ideal, Hurston does present us with a vision of possibility in terms of some parity in a relationship between a woman and a man, based not on material gain or ownership of property but on their desire to know one another.

It is significant, I believe, that Hurston characterizes this relationship as play, pleasure, sensuality, which is for her the essential nature of nature itself, as symbolized by the image of the pear tree that pervades the novel. It is also critical to an appreciation of Hurston's radical effect on the tradition of Afro-American women's fiction that her language is so different from the language of the "conventional" novel of the times. Rooted in black English, Hurston used metaphors derived from nature's play to emphasize the connection between the natural world and the possibilities of a harmonious social order. And in keeping with her choice of language, she structures her novel as a circle, in which the returning Janie explores her own development by telling her story to Phoeby, whose name means the moon, and who is her best friend and the symbolic representative of the community.

In its radical envisioning of the self as central and its use of language as a means of exploring the self as female and black, *Their Eyes Were Watching God* is a forerunner of the fiction of the seventies and eighties. In general, though, most novels published before the 1950s embodied the tension between writers' apparent acceptance of an ideal of woman derived from white upper-class society and the reality with which their protagonists had to contend. And most seemed to be written for an audience that excluded even the writers themselves.

But the attempt to present "positive" images of the black woman, to restrict her characterization to a prescribed ideal, did not result in any improvement in her image or her condition. Rather, the refutation of negative images created a series of contradictions between the image that black women could not attain, though they sometimes internalized, and the reality of their existence. That tension increased throughout the first half of the century, until the 1940s, when the destruction it created becomes apparent in the fiction written by black women. The heroines of this period, Lutie Johnson in *The Street* and Cleo Judson in *The Living is Easy*, are defeated both by social reality and by their lack of self-knowledge. Self-knowledge was critical if black women were to develop the inner resources they would need in order to cope with larger social forces.

II

Beginning with Gwendolyn Brooks's *Maud Martha* (1953), we can observe a definite shift in the fiction of Afro-American women, a shift in point of view and intention that still characterizes the novels written today. Afro-American women writers are, as Alexis DeVeau noted, putting more emphasis on reflecting the process of self-definition and understanding that women have always had to be engaged in, rather than refuting the general society's definition of them. The shift is, of course, not a sudden or totally complete one; there are many phases in the process.

The first phase focused on portraying what the early literature tended to omit, namely, the complex existence of the ordinary, dark-skinned woman, who is nei-ther an upper-class matron committed to an ideal of woman that few could attain, as in the novels of the Harlem Renaissance, nor a downtrodden victim, totally at the mercy of a hostile society, as in Ann Petry's *The Street*.

Gwendolyn Brooks claims that her intention in writing *Maud Martha* was to paint a portrait of an ordinary black woman, first as daughter, then as mother, and to show what she makes of her "little life."[9] What Brooks emphasizes in the novel is Maud Martha's *awareness* that she is seen as common (and therefore as unimportant), and that there is so much more in her than her "little life" will allow her to be. Yet, because Maud Martha constructs her own standards, she manages to transform that "little life" into so much more despite the limits set on her by her family, her husband, her race, her class, whites, and American so-ciety. Maud Martha emerges neither crushed nor triumphant. She manages, though barely, to be her own creator. Her sense of her own integrity is rooted mostly in her own imagination—in her internal language as metaphors derived from women's experience, metaphors that society usually trivializes but which Brooks presents as the vehicles of insight. Though Maud Martha certainly does not articulate a language (or life) of overt resistance, she does prepare the way for such language in that she sees the contradiction between her real value as a black woman and how she is valued by those around her.

Perhaps because *Maud Martha* was such a departure from the usual characteri-zations of Afro-American women in previous fiction, the novel went out of print almost immediately after it appeared. Nonetheless, it was to influence Paule Marshall, whose *Browngirl, Brownstones* (1959) is a definite touchstone in con-temporary Afro-American women's fiction. In a lecture she gave in 1968 Marshall pointed to *Maud Martha* as "the finest portrayal of an Afro-American woman in the novel"[10] to date and as a decided influence on her work. And in characteriz-ing Brooks's protagonist, Marshall notes Maud Martha functions as an artist; in that way, this novel carries on the African tradition that the ordinary rituals of daily life are what must be made into art."[11] The elements Marshall noted in *Maud Martha*—a focus on the complexity of women characters who are central rather than marginal to the world and the significance of daily rituals through which these women situate themselves in the context of their specific commu-nity and culture—are dominant characteristics of her own novels.

Like *Maud Martha*, the emphasis in *Browngirl, Brownstones* is on the black-woman as mother and daughter. In an interview with Alexis DeVeau in 1980, Marshall recalls that she wrote her first novel in the late 1950s as a relief from a tedious job. She wrote the novel not primarily for publication but as a process of understanding, critiquing, and celebrating her own personal history.[12] In under-standing "the talking women," who were the most vivid memories of her youth, Marshall also demonstrates through her portrayal of Silla Boyce how the role of *mother* for this black woman is in conflict with her role as *wife* because of the racism that embattles her and her community. Marshall's novel, as well as

Brooks's, was certainly affected by society's attitude that black women were matriarchs, domineering mothers who distorted their children who in turn disrupted society—a vortex of attitudes that culminated in the Moynihan Report. In attempting to understand her maternal ancestors, then, Marshall had to penetrate the social stereotypes that distorted their lives.

Few early Afro-American women's novels focused on the black woman's role as mother because of the negative stereotype of the black woman as mammy that pervaded American society. But instead of de-emphasizing the black woman's role as mother, Marshall probes its complexity. She portrays Silla Boyce as an embittered woman caught between her own personality and desires and the life imposed on her as a mother who must destroy her unorthodox husband in order to have a stable family (as symbolized by the brownstone). This analysis of the black mother prefigures other analyses of this theme in the 1970s, especially Toni Morrison's *Sula* and Alice Walker's *Meridian*. And Marshall shows that racist and sexist ideology is intertwined, for Silla's and Deighton Boyce's internalization of the American definition of woman and man runs counter to their own beings and to their situation as black people in American society and precipitates the tragedy that their relationship becomes.

Silla, however, is not an internal being like Maud Martha. She fights, supported by her women friends who use their own language to penetrate illusion and verbally construct their own definitions in order to wage their battle. As a result, Selina, Silla's daughter, will, by the end of the novel, have some basis for the journey to self-knowledge upon which she embarks, fully appreciating the dilemma that her mother and father could not solve.

Like Brooks's novel, *Browngirl, Brownstones* emphasizes how the black community, its customs and mores, affects the process of the black woman's exploration of self. But Marshall's novel also stresses the importance of culture and language as contexts for understanding *society's* definitions of man and woman, veering sharply away from much of the preceding literature, which emphasized advancement for black women in terms of white American values. She portrays the Barbadian-American community both as a rock her characters can stand on and as the obstacle against which they must struggle in order to understand and develop their own individuality. Finally, though, Selina's decision to return to the Caribbean is her attempt to claim her own history as a means of acquiring self-consciousness. In *Browngirl, Brownstones*, an appreciation of one's ethnic and racial community becomes necessary for black women in their commitment to self-development.

The emphasis on community and culture in *Maud Martha* and *Browngirl, Brownstones* as a prerequisite for self-understanding reflected a growing sense among Afro-Americans in the late 1950s and 1960s of their own unique cultural identity. But by 1970, when Toni Morrison's *The Bluest Eye* and Alice Walker's *The Third Life of Grange Copeland* were published, black women writers' stance toward their communities had begun to change. The ideology of the sixties had stressed the necessity for Afro-Americans to rediscover their blackness, their unity in their blackness. As positive as that position was to the group's attempt to empower itself, one side effect was the tendency to idealize the relationship between black men and women, to blame sexism in the black community solely on racism or to justify a position that black men were superior to women.

During the sixties few novels by Afro-American women were published;

rather, poetry and drama dominated the literature, perhaps because of the immediacy of these forms and the conviction that literature should be as accessible as possible to black communities. The result of that change in perception about audience was that Afro-American writers consciously began to view their communities as the group to which they were writing. Black communities are clearly one of the many audiences to which Morrison and Walker addressed their first novels, for both works critique those communities and insist that they have deeply internalized racist stereotypes that radically affect their definitions of woman and man. In both novels, the community is directly responsible for the tragedies of the major characters—for the madness of Pecola Breedlove, for the suicide of Margaret Copeland, and for the murder of Mem Copeland by her husband. In *The Bluest Eye*, Morrison emphasizes the women's view of themselves. In *Grange Copeland*, Walker stresses the men's view. In these novels it is not only that an individual heroine accepts the sexist and racist definitions of herself, but that the entire black community, men and women, accept this construct—resulting in the destruction of many black women.

This fiction in the early 1970s represents a second phase, one in which the black community itself becomes a major threat to the survival and empowerment of women, one in which women must struggle against the definitions of gender. The language of this fiction therefore becomes a language of protest, as Afro-American women writers vividly depict the victimization of their protagonists. Morrison, Walker, Gayl Jones, and Toni Cade Bambara all expose sexism and sexist violence in their own communities. But it is not so much that they depict an altered consciousness in their protagonists; rather, it is that their attitudes toward their material and the audience to which they address their protest have changed since the novels of the 1940s with their emphasis on oppression from outside the black community. In the novels of the early 1970s, there is always someone who learns not only that white society must change, but also that the black communities' attitudes toward women must be revealed and revised. Interestingly, in *The Bluest Eye* it is Claudia McTeer, Pecola's peer and friend, who undergoes this education, while in *The Third Life* it is the grandfather, Grange, who must kill his son, the fruit of his initial self-hatred, in order to save his granddaughter Ruth. Both Claudia and Ruth possess the possibility of constructing their own self-definitions and affecting the direction of their communities because they have witnessed the destruction of women in the wake of prevailing attitudes.

By the mid-1970s, the fiction makes a visionary leap. In novels like *Sula* and *Meridian*, the woman is not thrust outside her community. To one degree or another, she chooses to stand outside it, to define herself as in revolt against it. In some ways, Sula is the most radical of the characters of 1970s fiction, for she overturns the conventional definition of good and evil in relation to women by insisting that she exists primarily as and for herself—not to be a mother or to be the lover of men. In other ways, Meridian is more radical in that she takes a revolutionary stance by joining a social movement, the Civil Rights Movement, which might have redefined American definitions of both race *and* gender. Sula stands alone as a rebel; Meridian gradually creates a community of support. It is important that both of these women claim their heritage. Sula and Meridian are who they are because of their *maternal* ancestry and their knowledge of that ancestry;

it is from their mothers that they acquire their language. This is also true of Merle Kimbona in Marshall's second novel, *The Chosen Place, The Timeless People*. Though published in 1969, this novel depicts a black woman as both outside and inside the black world, as both outside and inside the West. As such, Merle becomes a spokesperson for her people, both female and male, who do not always understand their own dilemmas.

The heroines of the mid-1970s are sociopolitical actors in the world. Their stance is rebellious; their consciousness has been altered, precisely because of the supposed crimes they are perceived as having committed against Motherhood, and beyond the constraints society imposes on female sexuality. Yet they are wounded heroines, partly because their communities are deeply entrenched in their view of woman as essentially a mother or as the lover of a man. But although these characters are critical of their own communities, they come back to them and work out their resistance in that territory. Marshall and Walker both extend their analyses to the ways in which white women are also affected by definitions of sex and race. Essentially, though, it is within the context of black communities, rather than in the world of women, that they struggle.

By the mid-seventies, Afro-American women fiction writers like Paule Marshall, Toni Morrison, Alice Walker, Toni Cade Bambara, and Gayl Jones had not only defined their cultural context as a distinctly Afro-American one, but they had also probed many facets of the interrelationship of sexism and racism in their society. Not only had they demonstrated the fact that sexism existed in black communities, but they had also challenged the prevailing definition of woman in American society, especially in relation to motherhood and sexuality. And they had insisted not only on the centrality of black women in Afro-American history, but also on their pivotal significance to present-day social political developments in America.

III

The novels of the eighties continue to explore these themes—that sexism must be struggled against in black communities and that sexism is integrally connected to racism. The fiction of this period—Morrison's *Song of Solomon* (1978) and *Tar Baby* (1980), Gloria Naylor's *The Women of Brewster Place* (1980), Toni Cade Bambara's *The Salt Eaters* (1980), Alice Walker's *You Can't Keep a Good Woman Down* (1981) and *The Color Purple* (1982), Joyce Carol Thomas's *Marked by Fire* (1982), Ntozake Shange's *Sassafras, Cypress and Indigo* (1982), Audre Lorde's *Zami* (1982), and Paule Marshall's *Praisesong for the Widow* (1983)—cannot be treated collectively, for each reflects a great deal of difference. Yet all of these novels look at ways in which the quality of black women's lives is affected by the interrelationship of sexism and racism. And many of them go a step further. The pose the question concerning what community black women must belong to in order to understand themselves most effectively in their totality as blacks *and* women.

Morrison's novels, of those of the major writers, have moved farthest away from the rebellious woman stance of the mid-seventies, for she has focused, in her last two books, on men as much as women. Still, she makes an attempt in both novels to figure out the possibilities of healing and community for her women characters. In *Song of Solomon*, Pilate is such a character, although she derives her accumulated wisdom from her father and primarily benefits Milkman, her nephew, rather than any other woman in the novel. Jadine in *Tar Baby* is portrayed as the woman who has taken a position so far removed from her community that she becomes a part of the West. In her search for self, she becomes selfish; in her desire for power, she loses essential parts of herself. Thus, Morrison has moved full circle from Pecola, who is destroyed by her community, to Jadine, who destroys any relationship to community in herself.

On the other end of the spectrum, Walker's Celie comes close to liberating herself through the community of her black sisters, Nettie, Sofia, and Shug, and is able to positively affect the men of her world. The motif of liberation through one's sisters is repeated in Shange's *Sassafras* in which the healing circle is that of black women: three sisters and their mother. In contrast to the novels of the early 1970s, because of the presence of a strong woman's community, the major protagonists do survive, some with the possibility of wholeness. Ironically, the lush *Tar Baby* is the most pessimistic; the spare *Color Purple* the most optimistic. Morrison sees no practical way out of the morass of sexism, racism, and class privilege in the western world, as it is presently constructed, for anyone, black, white, female, or male. Walker, however, sees the possibility of empowerment for black women if they create a community of sisters that can alter the present-day unnatural definitions of woman and man.

Between these two ends of the spectrum, other novelists propose paths to empowerment. In Marshall's most recent novel, *Praisesong for the Widow* (1983), Avey Johnson must discard her American value of obsessive materialism, must return to her source, must remember the ancient wisdom of African culture—that the body and spirit are one, that harmony cannot be achieved unless there is a reciprocal relationship between the individual and the community—if she is to define herself as a black woman. Her journey through myth and ritual, precipitated by the dream of her old great aunt, takes her back in time and space as she prepares to move forward in consciousness. So, too, with Audre Lorde's *Zami* (1982), in that she probes the cosmology of her black maternal ancestors in order to place herself. Lorde focuses more specifically than Marshall on a community of women who live, love, and work together as the basis for the creation of a community that might effect the empowerment of Afro-American women. These fictional works are similar, however, in that the search for a unity of self takes these women to the Caribbean and ultimately to Africa.

In fact, in many of these novels, Africa and African women become important motifs for trying out different standards of new womanhood. In *Tar Baby*, Toni Morrison uses the image of the African woman in the yellow dress as a symbol for authenticity that the jaded Jadine lacks. It is this woman's inner strength, beauty, and pride, manifested in the defiant stance of her body, that haunts Jadine's dreams and throws her into such a state of confusion that she flees her Parisian husband-to-be and retreats to the Isle de Chevaliers in the Caribbean. In contrast, Alice Walker reminds us in *The Color Purple*, one third of which is set in Africa, that "black women have been the mule of the world there, and the mule of the world here," [13] and that sexism flourishes in Africa. Audre Lorde begins *Zami* by describing her foremothers in Grenada: "There is a softer edge of African sharpness upon these women, and they swing through the rain-warm streets with an arrogant gentleness that I remember in strength and vulnerability."[14] Like Lorde, Marshall recalls in *Praisesong for the Widow* the uniquely African quality of the women she encounters in her Caribbean sojourn on Carriacou, an African-ness that reminds her of her Great Aunt Cuney who lived in Tatum, South Carolina. The recurring motif of *Praisesong,* itself a distinctly African form, is "her body she always usta say might be in Tatum but her mind, her mind was long gone into the Ibo's."[15] Marshall concentrates more than any of the other novelists of this period on delineating the essential African wisdom still alive in New World black communities. Ntozake Shange, too, uses African motifs in *Sassafras,* focusing on their centrality in U.S. southern culture and especially on the development of sensuality in her three sister protagonists. She quite consciously links African rhythms, dance, and style to a uniquely Afro-American woman culture, which is at the core of this book's intentions and connects it to the style and rhythms of other Third-World American women.

What is particularly interesting about these novelists' use of African elements in relation to the concept of woman is their sense of concreteness rather than abstraction. All of the major characters in the books I've just mentioned have moved from one place to another and have encountered other worlds distinctly different from their own. Mobility of black women is a new quality in these books of the early eighties, for black women, in much of the previous literature, were restricted in space by their condition. This mobility is not cosmetic. It means that there is increased interaction between black women from the U.S., the Caribbean, and Africa, as well as other women of color. And often it is the movement of the major characters from one place to another (*Tar Baby*'s Jadine from Paris to the Caribbean to the U.S.; *Praisesong*'s Avey Johnson from White Plains to Grenada; *Sassafras*'s Cypress from San Francisco to New York; *Color Purple*'s Nettie from the U.S. South to Africa) that enlarges and sharpens their vision.

Not only is mobility through space a quality of present-day fiction; so also is mobility from one class to another. In contrast to the novels of the twenties, which focused on upper middle-class black women, novels of the forties, which tended to emphasize proletarian women, or novels of the seventies, which featured lower middle-class women, many of the novels of this period present the development of black women who have moved from one class to another as a major theme of work. Thus, Jadine in *Tar Baby,* Celie in *Color Purple,* and Avey Johnson in *Praisesong* have all known poverty and have moved to a point where they have more material security. Still there are many variations in these authors' analyses of such a movement.

In *Tar Baby,* Jadine is able to reap the material benefits of her aunt's and uncle's relationship to Valerian, their white wealthy employer, and becomes, in some ways, an Afro-American Princess. Morrison's analysis of Jadine's focus on security and comfort emphasizes the danger that obsession with material things might have for the ambitious black woman. In pursuing her own desire to "make it," Jadine forgets how to nurture those who have made it possible for her to be successful. She forgets her "ancient properties"[16] as Therese, the Caribbean sage, points out, and succumbs to the decadent western view of woman. Paule Marshall also focuses on the dangers of materialism, on how the fear of poverty and failure has affected Avey and Jay Johnson's marriage and their sense of themseles as black, to such an extent that they do not even recognize their own faces. *Praisesong* has, as one of its major themes, middle-aged, middle-class Avey Johnson's journey back to herself, an essential part of which is the African wisdom still alive in the rituals of black societies in the West. While Morrison warns us that our ancient properties can be easily eroded by the materialism of the West, Marshall emphasizes the seemingly irrational ways in which the collective memory of black people has a hold even on the Avey Johnsons of America. Alice Walker approaches the element of class mobility in another way. Celie does not lose her sense of community or her spiritual center as she moves from dire poverty and deprivation to a more humane way of living, perhaps because she comes to that improvement in her life through inner growth and through the support of her sisters.

One effect of such a variety of themes and characters in the fiction of the early eighties is not only black women writers' analysis of the intersection of class, race, and gender, but also their presentation of many styles of life, many different ways of approaching the issues that confront them as blacks, as women, as individual selves.

This expression of a range of experience is nowhere more apparent than in these authors' treatment of their characters' sexuality. One radical change in the fiction of the 1980s is the overt explorations of lesbian relationships among black women and how these relationships are viewed by black communities. This exploration is not, I believe, to be confused with the emphasis on friendship among black women that is a major theme in earlier literature. This new development may have a profound effect on present-day attitudes about the relationship between sex and race and about the nature of women. The beginning of this exploration has already shown that lesbianism is a complex subject, for sexual relationships between women are treated differently in *The Color Purple, The Women of Brewster Place, Sassafras,* and *Zami.*

In *The Color Purple,* the love/sex relationship between Celie and Shug is at the center of the novel and is presented as a natural, strengthening process through which both women, as well as the people around them, grow. Walker also seems to be influenced by Zora Neale Hurston's use of language in *Their Eyes Were Watching God,* a book that she greatly admires, for the lesbian relationship between Celie and Shug is expressed through the metaphors of nature and in the form of black English. In a sense, Walker in *The Color Purple* does for the sexual relationships between black women what Hurston in *Their Eyes Were Watching God* did for sexual relationships between black women and men. In contrast, Gloria Naylor, in *The Women of Brewster Place,* places more emphasis on the reactions of the small community to which the lovers belong, as well as their own internalization of social views about lesbianism. There is more concentration in this novel on the oppression that black lesbians experience. Appropriately Naylor uses metaphors of endurance rooted in Afro-American folk speech. In Shange's *Sassafras,* the sexual relationship between Cypress and her lover is a part of a community of lesbian women who, while affirming themselves, are also sometimes hostile to one another as the outer world might be. The lesbian community in *Sassafras* is an imperfect one, and Cypress's sexual love for another woman is but part of a continuum of sexual love that includes her involvement with men.

In *Zami*, however, the definition of a lesbian relationship is extended, since Lorde beautifully demonstrates how the heritage of her Grenadian mother is integrally connected to her development as a woman-identified woman. In using the word *Zami* as a title, a word that means "women who live, love and work together,"[17] Lorde searches for the connections between myth, poetry, and history that might shift the focus of the definition of humankind, particularly black humankind, from one that is predominantly male. One question that these novels leave unanswered is whether the bond between women might be so strong that it might transcend the racial and class divisions among women in America and make possible a powerful women's community that might effect significant change.

The emphasis on the culture of women as a means to self-understanding and growth is not only treated thematically in this new fiction, but it is also organic to the writers' forms. Increasingly, the language and forms of black women's fiction are derived from women's experiences as well as from Afro-American culture. The most revolutionary transformation of the novel's form is Alice Walker's *The Color Purple*. It is written entirely in letters, a form that (along with diaries) was the only one allowed women to record their everyday lives and feelings, their "herstory." And of equal importance, Walker explores the richness and clarity of black folk English in such a way that the reader understands that the inner core of a person cannot be truly known except through her own language. Like Walker, Ntozake Shange consciously uses a potpourri of forms primarily associated with women: recipes, potions, letters, as well as poetry and dance rhythms, to construct her novel. In *Song of Solomon* and *Tar Baby*, Morrison continues to explore Afro-American folktales and folklore, the oral tradition of black people, which as Marshall reminds us in *Praisesong for the Widow* is often passed on from one generation to the next by women. Marshall also uses dream, ritual, hallucination, and the metaphors of women's experience in composing the ritualistic process of *Praisesong*. This exploration of new forms based on the black woman's culture and her story has, from my perspective, revitalized the American novel and opened up new avenues of expression, indelibly altering our sense of the novelistic process.

Thematically and stylistically, the tone of the fiction of the early eighties communicates the sense that women of color can no longer be perceived as marginal to the empowerment of all American women and that an understanding of their reality and imagination is essential to the process of change that the entire society must undergo in order to transform itself. Most importantly, black women writers project the belief, as Alexis DeVeau pointed out, that commitment to an understanding of self is as wide as the world is wide. This new fiction explores in a multiplicity of ways Alice Walker's statement in a recent interview:

> Writing to me is not about audience exactly. It's about living. It's about expanding myself as much as I can and seeing myself in as many roles and situations as possible. Let me put it this way. If I could live as a tree, as a

river, as the moon, as the sun, as a star, as the earth, as a rock, I would. Writing permits me to be more than I am. Writing permits me to experience life as any number of strange creations.[18]

NOTES

1. Claudia Tate, ed., *Black Women Writers At Work* (New York: Continuum Publishing, 1983), p. 55.
2. Francis Harper, *Iola LeRoy, Shadows Uplifted*, 3rd ed. (Boston: James H. Earle, 1895), p. 281.
3. Hiroko Sato, "Under that Harlem Shadow: A Study of Jessie Fauset and Nella Larsen," in *The Harlem Renaissance Remembered*, ed. Arna Bontemps (New York: Dodd Mead, 1972), p. 67.
4. Jessie Redmon Fauset, Foreword to *The Chinaberry Tree* (New York: Frederick A. Stokes Co., 1931).
5. Ibid.
6. For a discussion of this question see Barbara T. Christian, *Black Women Novelists: The Development of a Tradition 1892–1976*, (Westport, Conn.: Greenwood Press, 1980).
7. Alice Walker uses this phrase most effectively in her essay "In Our Mothers' Gardens," *Ms.*, 2 #11 (May 1974), p. 71.
8. Zora Neale Hurston, *Their Eyes Were Watching God* (New York: Fawcett Publishing, 1965 edition; first printed by Lippincott, Co., 1937), p. 42.
9. Gwendolyn Brooks, *Report from Part I* (Detroit: Broadside Press, 1972), p. 162.
10. Paule Marshall, "The Negro Woman Writer," tape of lecture at conference, Howard University, 1968.
11. Mary Helen Washington, "Book Review of Barabara Christian's *Black Women Novelists*," *Signs: Journal of Women in Culture and Society*, 8, no. 1 (August 1982): p. 179.
12. Alexis DeVeau, "Paule Marshall—In Celebration of Our Triumph," *Essence*, X, no. 1 (May 1980): 96.
13. Gloria Steinem, "Do You Know This Woman? She Knows You—A Profile of Alice Walker," *Ms.*, X, no. 12 (June 1982).
14. Audre Lorde, *Zami, A New Spelling of My Name* (Watertown, MA.: Persephone Press, 1982), p. 9.
15. Paule Marshall, *Praisesong for the Widow* (New York: G. P. Putnam's Sons, 1983), p. 39.
16. Toni Morrison, *Tar Baby* (New York: Knopf, 1981), p. 305.
17. Lorde, *Zami*, p. 255.
18. Tate, *Black Women at Work*, p. 185.

body

━━━

"**W**rite yourself. Your body must be heard." Since Hélène Cixous first issued this call in 1974, there have been continual attempts to sort out just what it means, what a discourse that "let the body be heard" would look like, and whether it is even possible. What would it mean for the body to have a language? What would the body say?

Of course, one could take these questions literally, but their real import is to raise the issue of sexual difference, to suggest that perhaps difference extends into the realm of language. Indeed, the essays here raise the possible existence of *l'écriture féminine*, "feminine writing," which is different from the kind of writing usually valued in Western culture, and which is specifically gendered. Although not restricted to writers who are biologically sexed female (Cixous offers Jean Genet as one of her examples), feminine writing, nonetheless, is seen here to vary along gender lines, to correspond to culturally determined gender codes: *his* language is rational, logical, hierarchical, and linear; *her* language is a-rational (if not irrational), contra-logical (if not illogical), resistant to hierarchies, and circular.

At the heart of the movement which is called *l'écriture féminine* (founded in France by several women writers, including Cixous and Irigaray, in the mid-1970s) is a refusal to accept the traditional Western separation of mind and body. As in so many other kinds of oppositional definitions, one term has historically been privileged at the expense of the other, and one has been linked with the male, one with the female (for an elaboration of the implications of these oppositions for feminism, see Shoshana Felman's essay in "Institutions"). Woman, linked with body rather than mind, was supposed to be antithetical to writing, an activity said to be restricted to the intellect. The authors associated with *l'écriture féminine* have challenged these traditional notions in two ways: first, by celebrating woman's association with the body, thereby refusing the subordination of body to mind; and second, by refusing to accept the separation between the two. "Writing the body" or "letting the body be heard" are clearly attempts at refuting the sense of writing as a strictly mental thing.

The field which has, to date, most thoroughly explored the connections between mind, body and language is psychoanalysis, so the writings of Sigmund Freud and French psychoanalyst Jacques Lacan serve as important subtexts to both Cixous's and Irigaray's essays (readers who are not familiar with Lacanian theory or terminology may want to read the introduction to "Desire" before reading the essays here). Questions of the relation between being biologically sexed female and culturally gendered feminine are central to all four of the essays. Unlike Freud, who saw female sexuality as a "dark continent" yet to be explored, these authors see female sexuality as something which is likely to be apparent in a woman's written text. Although the four would not necessarily agree with Freud's postulate that "biology is destiny," they do raise the possibility that biology makes itself heard in literary discourse.

Hélène Cixous's influential and often-cited essay, "The Laugh of the Medusa" (published in French in 1975; revised and translated into English in 1976), is impossible to summarize, and for good reasons. Simultaneously, this essay *is about* and *is* "feminine writing." Here, Cixous both discusses and illustrates her theories of women's writing: it is not linear, logical, or progressive, which means that it is not constrained by traditional (masculine? patriarchal?) notions of argumentation and development. The movement of the essay is more fluid than direct, more experimental than argumentative. Cixous aims for her reader to understand the nature of women's writing as much from the way in which she writes, as from what she writes about.

Cixous's essay is highly quotable and challenging. Her claim that women writers always retain a bit of the mother in them ("There is always within her at least a little of that good mother's milk. She writes in white ink.") provides a richness of evocation and metaphor that has spoken to a large number of feminist writers and critics. But such claims also remain troubling to feminists who have resisted a sense of being tied to the biological. Cixous's writing provides a central focus for questions of separatism, biological determinism, and bodily metaphors—how far should we take our insistence upon difference? "The Laugh of the Medusa," as its title might suggest, ultimately celebrates that which in women has been denigrated for centuries, and urges us to embrace "difference" and to use it.

In "This Sex Which Is Not One" (published in French 1977; translated into English 1985), Luce Irigaray carries on Cixous's celebration of the difference of the female body, and develops issues she raises in *Speculum of the Other Woman* (part of which is reprinted in "Desire"). Rejecting traditional psychoanalytic notions, which take male sexuality as the norm and model, Irigaray suggests that female sexuality is not marked by "lack" (the lack of a penis, of a singular sex organ), but by multiplicity and abundance. Working by analogy, then, Irigaray argues that femininity—and the language of femininity—is not singular (not "one") either, but multiple. Therefore, woman's pleasure in language, like her pleasure in sexuality, is not direct, linear, or singular: "'she' sets off in all directions leaving 'him' unable to discern the coherence of any meaning." Being forced into masculine language, on the other hand, leaves woman always missing pieces of herself and makes her experience herself as fragmented. Irigaray suggests that the realization of this language would not result in women's "wholeness," if by that we mean "unicity" and singularity, nor in "ownership" (she finds property and ownership to be foreign to femininity), but that its realization would allow for woman's "nearness" to herself.

"This Sex Which Is Not One" closes with an analysis of the oppression of women, an oppression which Irigaray sees in terms set out by Marx and by French anthropologist Claude Lévi-Strauss; women are turned into property, into objects of exchange between men, a transaction which denies their subjectivity and turns them into objects. Irigaray urges women to use their nearness to themselves to develop a closeness to each other, to work together to resist the oppression which denies them their pleasure and their language.

Ann Rosalind Jones summarizes and critiques the work of four French feminist writers (Julia Kristeva, Luce Irigaray, Hélène Cixous, and Monique Wittig) in "Writing the Body: Toward an Understanding of *l'Écriture Féminine*" (1981). She explains at what points these writers differ from and agree with one another, noting that while Irigaray, Cixous, and Wittig envision a separate language for women metaphorically based on women's physical experience of sexuality, Kristeva sees women's role in language primarily as providing oppositional force within traditional discourses. Jones offers several cautions about *l'écriture féminine*, though. She warns against the notion of an "essential" female sexuality, noting that all psychoanalytic models of sexuality (from which Irigaray and Cixous work) recognize sexuality as culturally constructed. To accept these cultural constructs as "natural," she argues, could be dangerous. She further cautions against the political effects of taking "women" as too generalized a category, since race, class, and national origin may account for more differences than would gender. Finally, Jones questions whether "writing from the body" is possible (given many women's difficulties with using language) or desirable (given the richness of our historical connections to cultural and linguistic traditions). Despite these reservations, Jones urges American feminists to take the critique offered by *l'écriture féminine* seriously, and to put its hopeful offer of real possibilities into play.

Susan Stanford Friedman addresses the differences between women's and men's writing directly in "Creativity and the Childbirth Metaphor: Gender Difference and Literary Discourse" (1989). Stanford Friedman does not attempt to resolve the disagreement between writers (like Cixous) who insist on the connection between women's writing and their bodies and the reservations of others (like Simone de Beauvoir, Nina Auerbach, and Elaine Showalter) who are suspicious of "essentialism" that would tie creativity too much to procreativity. Instead, she offers three other ways to understand women's difference as writers, taking the childbirth metaphor as her example.

Stanford Friedman approaches the use of this metaphor from three directions: First, she looks at how the childbirth metaphor—which links the production of a literary text to the (re)production of a child—is at odds with itself, at least within patriarchal Western culture's sexual division of labor. Second, she looks at the experience of *reading* the metaphor, arguing that, since readers almost always know the author's biological sex, reading a male-authored text is a different experience from reading a female-authored one. Finally, she turns to the difference gender makes for writers using childbirth as a metaphor, arguing that women who have actually borne children have a different relation to the metaphor than do men and childless women; she delineates a continuum against which to read women's uses of the metaphor, where childbirth and literary creativity are not sundered, as they are in Western culture, but reunited. She explicitly links this language to "feminine writing": "Long before Cixous's utopian essay about the *future* inscription of femininity, women have subverted the regressive birth metaphor and transformed it into a sign representing their own delivery into speech through (pro)creativity." Standford Friedman points to a way that literary language can avoid the oppositional thinking of Western culture, a way that women's bodies can influence—and have influenced—their language.

—DPH

THE LAUGH OF THE MEDUSA

I shall speak about women's writing: about *what it will do*. Woman must write her self: must write about women and bring women to writing, from which they have been driven away as violently as from their bodies—for the same reasons, by the same law, with the same fatal goal. Woman must put herself into the text—as into the world and into history—by her own movement.

The future must no longer be determined by the past. I do not deny that the effects of the past are still with us. But I refuse to strengthen them by repeating them, to confer upon them an irremovability the equivalent of destiny, to confuse the biological and the cultural. Anticipation is imperative.

Since these reflections are taking shape in an area just on the point of being discovered, they necessarily bear the mark of our time—a time during which the new breaks away from the old, and, more precisely, the (feminine) new from the old (*la nouvelle de l'ancien*). Thus, as there are no grounds for establishing a discourse, but rather an arid millennial ground to break, what I say has at least two sides and two aims: to break up, to destroy; and to foresee the unforeseeable, to project.

I write this as a woman, toward women. When I say "woman," I'm speaking of woman in her inevitable struggle against conventional man; and of a universal woman subject who must bring women to their senses and to their meaning in history. But first it must be said that in spite of the enormity of the repression that has kept them in the "dark"—that dark which people have been trying to make them accept as their attribute—there is, at this time, no general woman, no one typical woman. What they have *in common* I will say. But what strikes me is the infinite richness of their individual constitutions: you can't talk about *a* female sexuality, uniform, homogeneous, classifiable into codes—any more than you can talk about one unconscious resembling another. Women's imaginary is inexhaustible, like music, painting, writing: their stream of phantasms is incredible.

I have been amazed more than once by a description a woman gave me of a world all her own which she had been secretly haunting since early childhood. A world of searching, the elaboration of knowledge, on the basis of a systematic experimentation with the bodily functions, a passionate and precise interrogation of her erotogeneity. This practice, extraordinarily rich and inventive, in particular as concerns masturbation, is prolonged or accompanied by a production of forms, a veritable aesthetic activity, each stage of rapture inscribing a resonant vision, a composition, something beautiful. Beauty will no longer be forbidden.

I wished that that woman would write and proclaim this unique empire so that other women, other unacknowledged sovereigns, might exclaim: I, too, overflow; my desires have invented new desires, my body knows unheard-of songs. Time and again I, too, have felt so full of luminous torrents that I could burst—burst with forms much more beautiful than those which are put up in frames and sold for a stinking fortune. And I, too, said nothing, showed nothing; I didn't open my mouth, I didn't repaint my half of the world. I was ashamed. I was afraid, and I swallowed my shame and my fear. I said to myself: You are mad! What's the meaning of these waves, these floods, these outbursts? Where is the ebullient, infinite woman who, immersed as she was in her naïveté, kept in the dark about herself, led into self-disdain by the great arm of parental-conjugal phallocentrism, hasn't been ashamed of her strength? Who, surprised and horrified by the fantastic tumult of her drives (for she was made to believe that a well-adjusted normal woman has a . . . divine composure), hasn't accused herself of being a monster? Who, feeling a funny desire stirring inside her (to sing, to write, to dare to speak, in short, to bring out something new), hasn't thought she was sick? Well, her shameful sickness is that she resists death, that she makes trouble.

And why don't you write? Write! Writing is for you, you are for you; your body is yours, take it. I know why you haven't written. (And why I didn't write before the age of twenty-seven.) Because writing is at once too high, too great for you, it's reserved for the great—that is for "great men"; and it's "silly." Besides, you've written a little, but in secret. And it wasn't good, because it was in secret, and because you punished yourself for writing, because you didn't go all the way, or because you wrote, irresistibly, as when we would masturbate in secret, not to go further, but to attenuate the tension a bit, just enough to take the edge off. And then as soon as we come, we go and make ourselves feel guilty—so as to be forgiven; or to forget, to bury it until next time.

Write, let no one hold you back, let nothing stop you: not man; not the imbecilic capitalist machinery, in which publishing houses are the crafty, obsequious relayers of imperatives handed down by an economy that works against us and off our backs; and not *yourself*. Smug-faced readers, managing editors, and big bosses don't like the true texts of women—female-sexed texts. That kind scares them.

I write woman: woman must write woman. And man, man. So only an oblique consideration will be found here of man; it's up to him to say where his masculinity and femininity are at: this will concern us once men have opened their eyes and seen themselves clearly.[1]

Now women return from afar, from always: from "without,' from the heath where witches are kept alive; from below, from beyond "culture"; from their childhood which men have been trying desperately to make them forget, condemning it to "eternal rest." The little girls and their "ill-mannered" bodies immured, well-preserved, intact unto themselves, in the mirror. Frigidified. But are they ever seething underneath! What an effort it takes—there's no end to it—for the sex cops to bar their threatening return. Such a display of forces on both sides that the struggle has for centuries been immobilized in the trembling equilibrium of a deadlock.

Here they are, returning, arriving over and again, because the unconscious is impregnable. They have wandered around in circles, confined to the narrow room in which they've been given a deadly brainwashing. You can incarcerate them, slow them down, get away with the old Apartheid routine, but for a time only. As soon as they begin to speak, at the same time as they're taught their name, they can be taught that their territory is black: because you are Africa, you are black. Your continent is dark. Dark is dangerous. You can't see anything in the dark, you're afraid. Don't move, you might fall. Most of all, don't go into the forest. And so we have internalized this horror of the dark.

Men have committed the greatest crime against women. Insidiously, violently, they have led them to hate women, to be their own enemies, to mobilize their immense strength against themselves, to be the executants of their virile needs. They have made for women an antinarcissism! A narcissism which loves itself only to be loved for what women haven't got! They have constructed the infamous logic of antilove.

We the precocious, we the repressed of culture, our lovely mouths gagged with pollen, our wind knocked out of us, we the labyrinths, the ladders, the trampled spaces, the bevies—we are black and we are beautiful.

We're stormy, and that which is ours breaks loose from us without our fearing any debilitation. Our glances, our smiles, are spent; laughs exude from all our mouths; our blood flows and we extend ourselves without ever reaching an end; we never hold back our thoughts, our signs, our writing; and we're not afraid of lacking.

What happiness for us who are omitted, brushed aside at the scene of inheritances; we inspire ourselves and we expire without running out of breath, we are everywhere!

From now on, who, if we say so, can say no to us? We've come back from always.

It is time to liberate the New Woman from the Old by coming to know her— by loving her for getting by, for getting beyond the Old without delay, by going out ahead of what the New Woman will be, as an arrow quits the bow with a movement that gathers and separates the vibrations musically, in order to be more than her self.

I say that we must, for, with a few rare exceptions, there has not yet been any writing that inscribes femininity; exceptions so rare, in fact, that, after plowing through literature across languages, cultures, and ages,[2] one can only be startled at this vain scouting mission. It is well known that the number of women writers (while having increased very slightly from the nineteenth century on) has always been ridiculously small. This is a useless and deceptive fact unless from their species of female writers we do not first deduct the immense majority whose workmanship is in no way different from male writing, and which either obscures women or reproduces the classic representations of women (as sensitive—intuitive—dreamy, etc.)[3]

Let me insert here a parenthetical remark. I mean it when I speak of male writing. I maintain unequivocally that there is such a thing as *marked* writing; that, until now, far more extensively and repressively than is ever suspected or admitted, writing has been run by a libidinal and cultural—hence political, typically masculine—economy; that this is a locus where the repression of women has been perpetuated, over and over, more or less consciously, and in a manner that's frightening since it's often hidden or adorned with the mystifying charms of fiction; that this locus has grossly exaggerated all the signs of sexual opposition (and not sexual difference), where woman has never *her* turn to speak—this being all the more serious and unpardonable in that writing is precisely *the very possibility of change*, the space that can serve as a springboard for subversive thought, the precursory movement of a transformation of social and cultural structures.

Nearly the entire history of writing is confounded with the history of reason, of which it is at once the effect, the support, and one of the privileged alibis. It has been one with the phallocentric tradition. It is indeed that same self-admiring, self-stimulating, self-congratulatory phallocentrism.

With some exceptions, for there have been failures—and if it weren't for them, I wouldn't be writing (I-woman, escapee)—in that enormous machine that has been operating and turning out its "truth" for centuries. There have been poets who would go to any lengths to slip something by at odds with tradition—men capable of loving love and hence capable of loving others and of wanting them, of imagining the woman who would hold out against oppression and constitute herself as a superb, equal, hence "impossible" subject, untenable in a real social framework. Such a woman the poet could desire only by breaking the codes that negate her. Her appearance would necessarily bring on, if not revolution—for the bastion was supposed to be immutable—at least harrowing explosions. At times it is in the fissure caused by an earthquake, through that radical mutation of things brought on by a material upheaval when every structure is for a moment thrown off balance and an ephemeral wildness sweeps order away, that the poet slips something by, for a brief span, of woman. Thus did Kliest expend himself in his yearning for the existence of sister-lovers, maternal daughters, mother-sisters, who never hung their heads in shame. Once the palace of magistrates is restored, it's time to pay: immediate bloody death to the uncontrollable elements.

But only the poets—not the novelists, allies of representationalism. Because poetry involves gaining strength through the unconscious and because the unconscious, that other limitless country, is the place where the repressed manage to survive: women, or as Hoffman would say, fairies.

She must write her self, because this is the invention of a *new insurgent* writing which, when the moment of her liberation has come, will allow her to carry out the indispensable ruptures and transformations in her history, first at two levels that cannot be separated.

a) Individually. By writing her self, woman will return to the body which has been more than confiscated from her, which has been turned into the uncanny stranger on display—the ailing or dead figure, which so often turns out to be the nasty companion, the cause and location of inhibitions. Censor the body and you censor breath and speech at the same time.

Write your self. Your body must be heard. Only then will the immense resources of the unconscious spring forth. Our naphtha will spread, throughout the world, without dollars—black or gold—nonassessed values that will change the rules of the old game.

To write. An act which will not only "realize" the decensored relation of woman to her sexuality, to her womanly being, giving her access to her native strength; it will give her back her goods, her pleasures, her organs, her immense bodily territories which have been kept under seal; it will tear her away from the superegoized structure in which she has always occupied the place reserved for the guilty (guilty of everything, guilty at every turn: for having desires, for not having any; for being frigid, for being "too hot"; for not being both at once; for being too motherly and not enough; for having children and for not having any; for nursing and for not nursing . . .)—tear her away by means of this research, this job of analysis and illumination, this emancipation of the marvelous text of her self that she must urgently learn to speak. A woman without a body, dumb, blind, can't possibly be a good fighter. She is reduced to being the servant of the militant male, his shadow. We must kill the false woman who is preventing the live one from breathing. Inscribe the breath of the whole woman.

b) An act that will also be marked by woman's *seizing* the occasion to *speak*, hence her shattering entry into history, which has always been based *on her suppression*. To write and thus to forge for herself the antilogos weapon. To become *at will* the taker and initiator, for her own right, in every symbolic system, in every political process.

It is time for women to start scoring their feats in written and oral language.

Every woman has known the torment of getting up to speak. Her heart racing, at times entirely lost for words, ground and language slipping away—that's how daring a feat, how great a transgression it is for a woman to speak—even just open her mouth—in public. A double distress, for even if she transgresses, her words fall almost always upon the deaf male ear, which hears in language only that which speaks in the masculine.

It is by writing, from and toward women, and by taking up the challenge of speech which has been governed by the phallus, that women will confirm women in a place other than that which is reserved in and by the symbolic, that is, in a place other than silence. Women should break out of the snare of silence. They shouldn't be conned into accepting a domain which is the margin or the harem.

Listen to a woman speak at a public gathering (if she hasn't painfully lost her wind). She doesn't "speak," she throws her trembling body forward; she lets go of herself, she flies; all of her passes into her voice, and it's with her body that she vitally supports the "logic" of her speech. Her flesh speaks true. She lays herself bare. In fact, she physically materializes what she's thinking; she signifies it with her body. In a certain way she *inscribes* what she's saying, because she doesn't deny her drives the intractable and impassioned part they have in speaking. Her speech, even when "theoretical" or political, is never simple or linear or "objectified," generalized: she draws her story into history.

There is not that scission, that division made by the common man between the logic of oral speech and the logic of the text, bound as he is by his antiquated relation—servile, calculating—to mastery. From which proceeds the niggardly lip service which engages only the tiniest part of the body, plus the mask.

In women's speech, as in their writing, that element which never stops resonating, which, once we've been permeated by it, profoundly and imperceptibly touched by it, retains the power of moving us—that element is the song: first music from the first voice of love which is alive in every woman. Why this privileged relationship with the voice? Because no woman stockpiles as many defenses for countering the drives as does a man. You don't build walls around yourself, you don't forego pleasure as "wisely" as he. Even if phallic mystification has generally contaminated good relationships, a woman is never far from "mother" (I mean outside her role functions: the "mother" as nonname and as source of goods). There is always within her at least a little of that good mother's milk. She writes in white ink.

Woman for women.—There always remains in woman that force which produces/is produced by the other—in particular, the other woman. *In* her, matrix, cradler; herself giver as her mother and child; she is her own sister-daughter. You might object, "What about she who is the hysterical offspring of a bad mother?" Everything will be changed once woman gives woman to the other woman. There is hidden and always ready in woman the source; the locus for the other. The mother, too, is a metaphor. It is necessary and sufficient that the best of herself be given to woman by another woman for her to be able to love herself and return in love the body that was "born" to her. Touch me, caress me, you the living no-name, give me my self as myself. The relation to the "mother," in terms of intense pleasure and violence, is curtailed no more than the relation to childhood (the child that she was, that she is, that she makes, remakes, undoes, there at the point where, the same, she mothers herself). Text: my body—shot through with streams of song; I don't mean the overbearing, clutchy "mother" but, rather, what touches you, the equivoice that affects you, fills your breast with an urge to come to language and launches your force; the rhythm that laughs you; the intimate recipient who makes all metaphors possible and desirable; body (body? bodies?), no more describable than god, the soul, or the Other; that part of you that leaves a space between yourself and urges you to inscribe in language your woman's style. In women there is always more or less of the mother who makes everything all right, who nourishes, and who stands up against separation; a force that will not be cut off but will knock the wind out of the codes. We will rethink womankind beginning with every form and every period of her body. The Americans remind us, "We are all Lesbians"; that is, don't denigrate woman, don't make of her what men have made of you.

Because the "economy" of her drives is prodigious, she cannot fail, in seizing the occasion to speak, to transform directly and indirectly *all* systems of exchange based on masculine thrift. Her libido will produce far more radical effects of political and social change than some might like to think.

Because she arrives, vibrant, over and again, we are at the beginning of a new history, or rather of a process of becoming in which several histories intersect with one another. As subject for history, woman always occurs simultaneously in several places. Woman un-thinks[4] the unifying, regulating history that homogenizes and channels forces, herding contradictions into a single battlefield. In woman, personal history blends together with the history of all women, as well as national and world history. As a militant, she is an integral part of all liberations. She must be farsighted, not limited to blow-by-blow interaction. She foresees that her liberation will do more than modify power relations or toss the ball over to the other camp; she will bring about a mutation in human relations, in thought, in all praxis: hers is not simply a class struggle, which she carries forward into a much vaster movement. Not that in order to be a woman-in-struggle(s) you have to leave the class struggle or repudiate it; but you have to split it open, spread it out, push it forward, fill it with the fundamental struggle so as to prevent the class struggle, or any other struggle for the liberation of a class of people, from operating as a form of repression, pretext for postponing the inevitable, the staggering alteration in power relations and in the production of individuals. This alteration is already upon us—in the United States, for example, where millions of night crawlers are in the process of undermining the family and disintegrating the whole of American sociality.

The new history is coming; it's not a dream, though it does extend beyond men's imagination, and for good reason. It's going to deprive them of their conceptual orthopedics, beginning with the destruction of their enticement machine.

It is impossible to *define* a feminine practice of writing, and this is an impossibility that will remain, for this practice can never be theorized, enclosed, coded—which doesn't mean that it doesn't exist. But it will always surpass the discourse that regulates the phallocentric system; it does and will take place in areas other than those subordinated to philosophico-theoretical domination. It will be conceived of only by subjects who are breakers of automatisms, by peripheral figures that no authority can ever subjugate.

Hence the necessity to affirm the flourishes of this writing, to give form to its movement, its near and distant byways. Bear in mind to begin with (1) that sexual opposition, which has always worked for man's profit to the point of reducing writing, too, to his laws, is only a historico-cultural limit. There is, there will be more and more rapidly pervasive now, a fiction that produces irreducible effects of femininity. (2) That it is through ignorance that most readers, critics, and writers of both sexes hesitate to admit or deny outright the possibility or the pertinence of a distinction between feminine and masculine writing. It will usually be said, thus disposing of sexual difference: either that all writing, to the extent that it materializes, is feminine; or, inversely—but it comes to the same thing—that the act of writing is equivalent to masculine masturbation (and so the woman who writes cuts herself out a paper penis); or that writing is bisexual, hence neuter, which again does away with differentiation. To admit that writing is precisely working (in) the in-between, inspecting the process of the same and of the other without which nothing can live, undoing the work of death—to admit this is first to want the two, as well as both, the ensemble of the one and the other, not fixed in sequences of struggle and expulsion or some other form of death but infinitely dynamized by an incessant process of exchange from one subject to another. A process of different subjects knowing one another and beginning one another anew only from the living boundaries of the other: a multiple and inexhaustible course with millions of encounters and transformations of the same into the other and into the in-between, from which woman takes her forms (and man, in his turn; but that's his other history).

In saying "bisexual, hence neuter," I am referring to the classic conception of bisexuality, which, squashed under the emblem of castration fear and along with the fantasy of a "total" being (though composed of two halves), would do away with the difference experienced as an operation incurring loss, as the mark of dreaded sectility.

To this self-effacing, merger-type bisexuality, which would conjure away castration (the writer who puts up his sign: "bisexual written here, come and see," when the odds are good that it's neither one nor the other), I oppose the *other bisexuality* on which every subject not enclosed in the false theater of phallocentric representationalism has founded his/her erotic universe. Bisexuality: that is, each one's location in self (*repérage en soi*) of the presence—variously manifest and insistent according to each person, male or female—of both sexes, nonexclusion either of the difference or of one sex, and, from this "self-permission," multiplication of the effects of the inscription of desire, over all parts of my body and the other body.

Now it happens that at present, for historico-cultural reasons, it is women who are opening up to and benefiting from this vatic bisexuality which doesn't annul differences but stirs them up, pursues them, increases their number. In a certain way, "woman is bisexual"; man—it's a secret to no one—being poised to keep glorious phallic monosexuality in view. By virtue of affirming the primacy of the phallus and of bringing it into play, phallocratic ideology has claimed more than one victim. As a woman, I've been clouded over by the great shadow of the scepter and been told: idolize it, that which you cannot brandish. But at the same time, man has been handed that grotesque and scarcely enviable destiny (just imagine) of being reduced to a single idol with clay balls. And consumed, as Freud and his followers note, by a fear of being a woman! For, if psychoanalysis was constituted from woman, to repress femininity (and not so successful a repression at that—men have made it clear), its account of masculine sexuality is now hardly refutable: as with all the "human" sciences, it reproduces the masculine view, of which it is one of the effects.

Here we encounter the inevitable man-with-rock, standing erect in his old Freudian realm, in the way that, to take the figure back to the point where linguistics is conceptualizing it "anew," Lacan preserves it in the sanctuary of the phallos (ϕ) "sheltered" from *castration's lack!* Their "symbolic" exists, it holds power—we, the sowers of disorder, know it only too well. But we are in no way obliged to deposit our lives in their banks of lack, to consider the constitution of the subject in terms of a drama manglingly restaged, to reinstate again and again the religion of the father. Because we don't want that. We don't fawn around the supreme hole. We have no womanly reason to pledge allegiance to the negative. The feminine (as the poets suspected) affirms: " . . . And yes," says Molly, carrying *Ulysses* off beyond any book and toward the new writing: "I said yes, I will Yes."

The Dark Continent is neither dark nor unexplorable.—It is still unexplored only because we've been made to believe that it was too dark to be explorable. And because they want to make us believe that what interests us is the white continent, with its monuments to Lack. And we believed. They riveted us between two horrifying myths: between the Medusa and the abyss. That would be enough to set half the world laughing, except that it's still going on. For the phallologocentric sublation[5] is with us, and it's militant, regenerating the old patterns, anchored in the dogma of castration. They haven't changed a thing: they've theorized their desire for reality! Let the priests tremble, we're going to show them our sexts!

Too bad for them if they fall apart upon discovering that women aren't men, or that the mother doesn't have one. But isn't this fear convenient for them? Wouldn't the worst be, isn't the worst, in truth, that women aren't castrated, that they have only to stop listening to the Sirens (for the Sirens were men) for history to change its meaning? You only have to look at the Medusa straight on to see her. And she's not deadly. She's beautiful and she's laughing.

Men say that there are two unrepresentable things: death and the feminine sex. That's because they need femininity to be associated with death; it's the jitters that give them a hard-on! for themselves! They need to be afraid of us. Look at the trembling Perseuses moving backward toward us, clad in apotropes. What lovely backs! Not another minute to lose. Let's get out of here.

Let's hurry: the continent is not impenetrably dark. I've been there often. I was overjoyed one day to run into Jean Genet. It was in *Pompes funèbres*. [6] He had come there led by his Jean. There are some men (all too few) who aren't afraid of femininity.

Almost everything is yet to be written by women about femininity: about their sexuality, that is, its infinite and mobile complexity, about their eroticization, sudden turn-ons of a certain miniscule-immense area of their bodies; not about destiny, but about the adventure of such and such a drive, about trips, crossings, trudges, abrupt and gradual awakenings, discoveries of a zone at one time timorous and soon to be forthright. A woman's body, with its thousand and one thresholds of ardor—once, by smashing yokes and censors, she lets it articulate the profusion of meanings that run through it in every direction—will make the old single-grooved mother tongue reverberate with more than one language.

We've been turned away from our bodies, shamefully taught to ignore them, to strike them with that stupid sexual modesty; we've been made victims of the old fool's game: each one will love the other sex. I'll give you your body and you'll give me mine. But who are the men who give women the body that women blindly yield to them? Why so few texts? Because so few women have as yet won back their body. Women must write through their bodies, they must invent the impregnable language that will wreck partitions, classes, and rhetorics, regulations and codes, they must submerge, cut through, get beyond the ultimate reserve-discourse, including the one that laughs at the very idea of pronouncing the word "silence," the one that, aiming for the impossible, stops short before the word "impossible" and writes it as "the end."

Such is the strength of women that, sweeping away syntax, breaking that famous thread (just a tiny little thread, they say) which acts for men as a surrogate umbilical cord, assuring them—otherwise they couldn't come—that the old lady is always right behind them, watching them make phallus, women will go right up to the impossible.

When the "repressed" of their culture and their society returns, it's an explosive, *utterly* destructive, staggering return, with a force never yet unleashed and equal to the most forbidding of suppressions. For when the Phallic period comes to an end, women will have been either annihilated or borne up to the highest and most violent incandescence. Muffled throughout their history, they have lived in dreams, in bodies (though muted), in silences, in aphonic revolts.

And with such force in their fragility; a fragility, a vulnerability, equal to their incomparable intensity. Fortunately, they haven't sublimated; they've saved their skin, their energy. They haven't worked at liquidating the impasse of lives without futures. They have furiously inhabited these sumptuous bodies: admirable hysterics who made Freud succumb to many voluptuous moments impossible to confess, bombarding his Mosaic statue with their carnal and passionate body words, haunting him with their inaudible and thundering denunciations, dazzling, more than naked underneath the seven veils of modesty. Those who, with a single word of the body, have inscribed the vertiginous immensity of a history which is sprung like an arrow from the whole history of men and from biblico-capitalist society, are the women, the supplicants of yesterday, who come as forebears of the new women, after whom no intersubjective relation will ever be the same. You, Dora, you the indomitable, the poetic body, you are the true "mistress" of the Signifier. Before long your efficacity will be seen at work when your speech is no longer suppressed, its point turned in against your breast, but written out over against the other.

In body.—More so than men who are coaxed toward social success, toward sublimation, women are body. More body, hence more writing. For a long time it has been in body that women have responded to persecution, to the familial-conjugal enterprise of domestication, to the repeated attempts at castrating them. Those who have turned their tongues 10,000 times seven times before not speaking are either dead from it or more familiar with their tongues and their mouths than anyone else. No, I-woman am going to blow up the Law: an explosion henceforth possible and ineluctable; let it be done, right now, *in* language.

Let us not be trapped by an analysis still encumbered with the old automatisms. It's not to be feared that language conceals an invincible adversary, because it's the language of men and their grammar. We mustn't leave them a single place that's any more theirs alone than we are.

If woman has always functioned "within" the discourse of man, a signifier that has always referred back to the opposite signifier which annihilates its specific energy and diminishes or stifles its very different sounds, it is time for her to dislocate this "within," to explode it, turn it around, and seize it; to make it hers, containing it, taking it in her own mouth, biting that tongue with her very own teeth to invent for herself a language to get inside of. And you'll see with what ease she will spring forth from that "within"—the "within" where once she so drowsily crouched—to overflow at the lips she will cover the foam.

Nor is the point to appropriate their instruments, their concepts, their places, or to begrudge them their position of mastery. Just because there's a risk of identification doesn't mean that we'll succumb. Let's leave it to the worriers, to masculine anxiety and its obsession with how to dominate the way things work—knowing "how it works" in order to "make it work." For us the point is not to take possession in order to internalize or manipulate, but rather to dash through and to "fly."[7]

Flying is woman's gesture—flying in language and making it fly. We have all learned the art of flying and its numerous techniques; for centuries we've been able to possess anything only by flying; we've lived in flight, stealing away, finding, when desired, narrow passageways, hidden crossovers. It's no accident that *voler* has a double meaning, that it plays on each of them and thus throws off the agents of sense. It's no accident: women take after birds and robbers just as robbers take after women and birds. They (*illes*)[8] go by, fly the coop, take pleasure in jumbling the order of space, in disorienting it, in changing around the furniture, dislocating things and values, breaking them all up, emptying structures, and turning propriety upside down.

What woman hasn't flown/stolen? Who hasn't felt, dreamt, performed the gesture that jams sociality? Who hasn't crumbled, held up to ridicule, the bar of separation? Who hasn't inscribed with her body the differential, punctured the system of couples and opposition? Who, by some act of transgression, hasn't overthrown successiveness, connection, the wall of circumfusion?

A feminine text cannot fail to be more than subversive. It is volcanic; as it is written it brings about an upheaval of the old property crust, carrier of masculine investments; there's no other way. There's no room for her if she's not a he. If she's a her-she, it's in order to smash everything, to shatter the framework of institutions, to blow up the law, to break up the "truth" with laughter.

For once she blazes *her* trail in the symbolic, she cannot fail to make of it the chaosmos of the "personal"—in her pronouns, her nouns, and her clique of referents. And for good reason. There will have been the long history of gynocide. This is known by the colonized peoples of yesterday, the workers, the nations, the species off whose backs the history of men has made its gold; those who have known the ignominy of persecution derive from it an obstinate future desire for grandeur; those who are locked up know better than their jailers the taste of free air. Thanks to their history, women today know (how to do and want) what men will be able to conceive of only much later. I say woman overturns the "personal," for if, by means of laws, lies, blackmail, and marriage, her right to herself has been extorted at the same time as her name, she has been able, through the very movement of mortal alienation, to see more closely the inanity of "propriety," the reductive stinginess of the masculine-conjugal subjective economy, which she doubly resists. On the one hand she has constituted herself necessarily as that "person" capable of losing a part of herself without losing her integrity. But secretly, silently, deep down inside, she grows and multiplies, for, on the other hand, she knows far more about living and about the relation between the economy of the drives and the management of the ego than any man. Unlike man, who holds so dearly to his title and his titles, his pouches of value, his cap, crown, and everything connected with his head, woman couldn't care less about the fear of decapitation (or castration), adventuring, without the masculine temerity, into anonymity, which she can merge with, without annihilating herself: because she's a giver.

I shall have a great deal to say about the whole deceptive problematic of the gift. Woman is obviously not that woman Nietzsche dreamed of who gives only in order to.[9] Who could ever think of the gift as a gift-that-takes? Who else but man, precisely the one who would like to take everything?

If there is a "propriety of woman," it is paradoxically her capacity to depropriate unselfishly, body without end, without appendage, without principle "parts." If she is a whole, it's a whole composed of parts that are wholes, not simple partial objects but a moving, limitlessly changing ensemble, a cosmos tirelessly traversed by Eros, an immense astral space not organized around any one sun that's any more of a star than the others.

This doesn't mean that she's an undifferentiated magma, but that she doesn't lord it over her body or her desire. Though masculine sexuality gravitates around the penis, engendering that centralized body (in political anatomy) under the dictatorship of its parts, woman does not bring about the same regionalization which serves the couple head/genitals and which is inscribed only within boundaries. Her libido is cosmic, just as her unconscious is worldwide. Her writing can only keep going, without ever inscribing or discerning contours, daring to make these vertiginous crossings of the other(s) ephemeral and passionate sojourns in him, her, them, whom she inhabits long enough to look at from the point closest to their unconscious from the moment they awaken, to love them at the point closest to their drives; and then further, impregnated through and through with these brief, identificatory embraces, she goes and passes into infinity. She alone dares and wishes to know from within, where she, the outcast, has never ceased to hear the resonance of fore-language. She lets the other language speak—the language of 1,000 tongues which knows neither enclosure nor death. To life she refuses nothing. Her language does not contain, it carries; it does not hold back, it makes possible. When id is ambiguously uttered—the wonder of being several—she doesn't defend herself against these unknown women whom she's surprised at becoming, but derives pleasure from this gift of alterability. I am spacious, singing flesh, on which is grafted no one knows which I, more or less human, but alive because of transformation.

Write! and your self-seeking text will know itself better than flesh and blood, rising, insurrectionary dough kneading itself, with sonorous, perfumed ingredients, a lively combination of flying colors, leaves, and rivers plunging into the sea we feed. "Ah, there's her sea," he will say as he holds out to me a basin full of water from the little phallic mother from whom he's inseparable. But look, our seas are what we make of them, full of fish or not, opaque or transparent, red or black, high or smooth, narrow or bankless; and we are ourselves sea, sand, coral, seaweed, beaches, tides, swimmers, children, waves. . . . More or less wavily sea, earth, sky—what matter would rebuff us? We know how to speak them all.

Heterogeneous, yes. For her joyous benefits she is erogenous; she is the erotogeneity of the heterogeneous: airborne swimmer, in flight, she does not cling to herself; she is dispersible, prodigious, stunning, desirous and capable of others, of the other woman that she will be, of the other woman she isn't, of him, of you.

Woman, be unafraid of any other place, of any same, or any other. My eyes, my tongue, my ears, my nose, my skin, my mouth, my body-for-(the)-other—not that I long for it in order to fill up a hole, to provide against some defect of mine, or because, as fate would have it, I'm spurred on by feminine "jealousy"; not because I've been dragged into the whole chain of substitutions that brings that which is substituted back to its ultimate object. That sort of thing you would expect to come straight out of "Tom Thumb," out of the *Penisneid* whispered to us by old grandmother ogresses, servants to their father-sons. If they believe, in order to muster up some self-importance, if they really need to believe that we're dying of desire, that we are this hole fringed with desire for their penis—that's their immemorial business. Undeniably (we verify it at our own expenses—but also to our amusement), it's their business to let us know they're getting a hard-on, so that we'll assure them (we the maternal mistresses of their little pocket signifier) that they still can, that it's still there—that men structure themselves only by being fitted with a feather. In the child it's not the penis that the woman desires, it's not that famous bit of skin around which every man gravitates. Pregnancy cannot be traced back, except within the historical limits of the ancients, to some form of fate, to those mechanical substitutions brought about by the unconscious of some eternal "jealous woman"; not to penis envies; and not to narcissism or to some sort of homosexuality linked to the ever-present mother! Begetting a child doesn't mean that the woman or the man must fall ineluctably into patterns or must recharge the circuit of reproduction. If there's a risk there's not an inevitable trap: may women be spared the pressure, under the guise of consciousness-raising, of a supplement of interdictions. Either you want a kid or you don't—*that's your business*. Let nobody threaten you; in satisfying your desire, let not the fear of becoming the accomplice to a sociality succeed the old-time fear of being "taken." And man, are you still going to bank on everyone's blindness and passivity, afraid lest the child make a father and, consequently, that in having a kid the woman land herself more than one bad deal by engendering all at once child—mother—father—family? No; it's up to you to break the old circuits. It will be up to man and woman to render obsolete the former relationship and all its consequences, to consider the launching of a brand-new subject, alive, with defamilialization. Let us demater-paternalize rather than deny woman, in an effort to avoid the cooptation of procreation, a thrilling era of the body. Let us defetishize. Let's get away from the dialectic which has it that the only good father is a dead one, or that the child is the death of his parents. The child is the other, but the other without violence, bypassing loss, struggle. We're fed up with the reuniting of bonds forever to be severed, with the litany of castration that's handed down and genealogized. We won't advance backward anymore; we're not going to repress something so simple as the desire for life. Oral drive, anal drive, vocal drive—all these drives are our strengths, and among them is the gestation drive—just like the desire to write: a desire to live self from within, a desire for the swollen belly, for language, for blood. We are not going to refuse, if it should happen to strike our fancy, the unsurpassed pleasures of pregnancy which have actually been always exaggerated or conjured away—or cursed—in the classic texts. For if there's one thing that's been repressed, here's just the place to find it: in the taboo of the pregnant woman. This says a lot about the power she seems invested with at the time, because it has always been suspected, that, when pregnant, the woman not only doubles her market value, but—what's more important—takes on intrinsic value as a woman in her own eyes and, undeniably, acquires body and sex.

There are thousands of ways of living one's pregnancy; to have or not to have with that still invisible other a relationship of another intensity. And if you don't have that particular yearning, it doesn't mean that you're in any way lacking. Each body distributes in its own special way, without model or norm, the nonfinite and changing totality of its desires. Decide for yourself on your position in the arena of contradictions, where pleasure and reality embrace. Bring the other to life. Women know how to live detachment; giving birth is neither losing nor increasing. It's adding to life an other. Am I dreaming? Am I misrecognizing?

You, the defenders of "theory," the sacrosanct yes-men of Concept, enthroners of the phallus (but not the penis):

Once more you'll say that all this smacks of "idealism," or what's worse, you'll splutter that I'm a "mystic."

And what about the libido? Haven't I read the "Signification of the Phallus"? And what about separation, what about that bit of self for which, to be born, you undergo an ablation—an ablation, so they say, to be forever commemorated by your desire?

Besides, isn't it evident that the penis gets around in my texts, that I give it a place and appeal? Of course I do. I want all. I want all of me with all of him. Why should I deprive myself of a part of us? I want all of us. Woman of course has a desire for a "loving desire" and not a jealous one. But not because she is gelded; not because she's deprived and needs to be filled out, like some wounded person who wants to console herself or seek vengeance. I don't want a penis to decorate my body with. But I do desire the other for the other, whole and entire, male or female; because living means wanting everything that is, everything that lives, and wanting it alive. Castration? Let others toy with it. What's a desire originating from a lack? A pretty meager desire.

The woman who still allows herself to be threatened by the big dick, who's still impressed by the commotion of the phallic stance, who still leads a loyal master to the beat of the drum: that's the woman of yesterday. They still exist, easy and numerous victims of the oldest of farces: either they're cast in the original silent versions in which, as titanesses lying under the mountains they make with their quivering, they never see erected that theoretic monument to the golden phallus looming, in the old manner, over their bodies. Or, coming today out of their *infans* period and into the second, "enlightened" version of their virtuous debasement, they see themselves suddenly assaulted by the builders of the analytic empire and, as soon as they've begun to formulate the new desire, naked, nameless, so happy at making an appearance, they're taken in their bath by the new old men, and then, whoops! Luring them with flashy signifiers, the demon of interpretation—oblique, decked out in modernity—sells them the same old handcuffs, baubles, and chains. Which castration do you prefer? Whose degrading do you like better, the father's or the mother's? Oh, what pwetty eyes, you pwetty little girl. Here, buy my glasses and you'll see the Truth-Me-Myself tell you everything you should know. Put them on your nose and take a fetishist's look (you are me, the other analyst—that's what I'm telling you) at your body and the body of the other. You see? No? Wait, you'll have everything explained to you, and you'll know at last which sort of neurosis you're related to. Hold still, we're going to do your portrait, so that you can begin looking like it right away.

Yes, the naïves to the first and second degree are still legion. If the New Women, arriving now, dare to create outside the theoretical, they're called in by the cops of the signifier, fingerprinted, remonstrated, and brought into the line of order that they are supposed to know; assigned by force of trickery to a precise place in the chain that's always formed for the benefit of a privileged signifier. We are pieced back to the string which leads back, if not to the Name-of-the-Father, then, for a new twist, to the place of the phallic-mother.

Beware, my friend, of the signifier that would take you back to the authority of a signified! Beware of diagnosis that would reduce your generative powers.

"Common" nouns are also proper nouns that disparage your singularity by classifying it into species. Break out of the circles; don't remain within the psychoanalytic closure. Take a look around, then cut through!

And if we are legion, it's because the war of liberation has only made as yet a tiny breakthrough. But women are thronging to it. I've seen them, those who will be neither dupe nor domestic, those who will not fear the risk of being a woman; will not fear any risk, any desire, any space still unexplored in themselves, among themselves and others or anywhere else. They do not fetishize, they do not deny, they do not hate. They observe, they approach, they try to see the other woman, the child, the lover—not to strengthen their own narcissim or verify the solidity or weakness of the master, but to make love better, to invent.

Other love.—In the beginning are our differences. The new love dares for the other, wants the other, makes dizzying, precipitous flights between knowledge and invention. The woman arriving over and over again does not stand still; she's everywhere, she exchanges, she is the desire-that-gives. (Not enclosed in the paradox of the gift that takes nor under the illusion of unitary fusion. We're past that.) She comes in, comes-in-between herself me and you, between the other me where one is always infinitely more than one and more than me, without the fear of ever reaching a limit; she thrills in our becoming. And we'll keep on becoming! She cuts through defensive loves, motherages, and devourations: beyond selfish narcissism, in the moving, open, transitional space, she runs her risks. Beyond the struggle-to-the-death that's been removed to the bed, beyond the love-battle that claims to represent exchange, she scorns at an Eros dynamic that would be fed by hatred. Hatred: a heritage, again, a reminder, a duping subservience to the phallus. To love, to watch-think-seek the other in the other, to despecularize, to unhoard. Does this seem difficult? It's not impossible, and this is what nourishes life—a love that has no commerce with the apprehensive desire that provides against the lack and stultifies the strange; a love that rejoices in the exchange that multiplies. Wherever history still unfolds as the history of death, she does not tread. Opposition, hierarchizing exchange, the struggle for mastery which can end only in at least one death (one master—one slave, or two nonmasters ≠ two dead)—all that comes from a period in time governed by phallocentric values. The fact that this period extends into the present doesn't prevent woman from starting the history of life somewhere else. Elsewhere, she gives. She doesn't "know" what she's giving, she doesn't measure it; she gives, though, neither a counterfeit impression nor something she hasn't got. She gives more, with no assurance that she'll get back even some unexpected profit from what she puts out. She gives that there may be life, thought, transformation. This is an "economy" that can no longer be put in economic terms. Wherever she loves, all the old concepts of management are left behind. At the end of a more or less conscious computation, she finds not her sum but her differences. I am for you what you want me to be at the moment you look at me in a way you've never seen me before: at every instant. When I write, it's everything that we don't know we can be that is written out of me, without exclusions, without stipulation, and everything we will be calls us to the unflagging, intoxicating, unappeasable search for love. In one another we will never be lacking.

TRANSLATED BY KEITH COHEN AND PAULA COHEN

NOTES

1. Men still have everything to say about their sexuality, and everything to write. For what they have said so far, for the most part, stems from the opposition activity/passivity from the power relation between a fantasized obligatory virility meant to invade, to colonize, and the consequential phantasm of woman as a "dark continent" to penetrate and to "pacify." (We know what "pacify" means in terms of scotomizing the other and misrecognizing the self.) Conquering her, they've made haste to depart from her borders, to get out of sight, out of body. The way man has of getting out of himself and into her whom he takes not for the other but for his own, deprives him, he knows, of his own bodily territory. One can understand how man, confusing himself with his penis and rushing in for the attack, might feel resentment and fear of being "taken" by the woman, of being lost in her, absorbed or alone.

2. I am speaking here only of the place "reserved" for women by the Western world.

3. Which works, then, might be called feminine? I'll just point out some examples: one would have to give them full readings to bring out what is pervasively feminine in their significance. Which I shall do elsewhere. In France (have you noted our infinite poverty in this field?—the Anglo-Saxon countries have shown resources of distinctly greater consequence), leafing through what's come out of the twentieth century—and it's not much—the only inscriptions of femininity that I have seen were by Colette, Marguerite Duras, . . . and Jean Genet.

4. *Dé-pense,* a neologism formed on the verb *penser,* hence "unthinks," but also "spends" (from *dépenser*).—Tr.

5. Standard English term for the Hegelian *Aufhebung,* the French *la relève.*

6. Jean Genet, *Pompes funèbres* (Paris, 1948), p. 185 [privately published].

7. Also, "to steal." Both meanings of the verb *voler* are played on, as the text itself explains in the following paragraph.—Tr.

8. *Illes* is a fusion of the masculine pronoun *ils,* which refers back to birds and robbers, with the feminine pronoun *elles,* which refers to women.—Tr.

9 Reread Derrida's text, "Le style de la femme," in *Nietzsche aujourd'hui* (Union Générale d'Editions, Coll. 10/18), where the philosopher can be seen operating an *Aufhebung* of all philosophy in its systematic reducing of woman to the place of seduction: she appears as the one who is taken for; the bait in person, all veils unfurled, the one who doesn't give but who gives only in order to (take).

THIS SEX WHICH IS NOT ONE

Female sexuality has always been conceptualized on the basis of masculine parameters. Thus the opposition between "masculine" clitoral activity and "feminine" vaginal passivity, an opposition which Freud—and many others—saw as stages, or alternatives in the development of a sexually "normal" woman, seems rather too clearly required by the practice of male sexuality. For the clitoris is conceived as a little penis pleasant to masturbate so long as castration anxiety does not exist (for the boy child), and the vagina is valued for the "lodging" it offers the male organ when the forbidden hand has to find a replacement for pleasure-giving.

In these terms, woman's erogenous zones never amount to anything but a clitoris-sex that is not comparable to the noble phallic organ, or a hole-envelope that serves to sheathe and massage the penis in intercourse: a non-sex, or a masculine organ turned back upon itself, self-embracing.

About woman and her pleasure, this view of the sexual relation has nothing to say. Her lot is that of "lack," "atrophy" (of the sexual organ), and "penis envy," the penis being the only sexual organ of recognized value. Thus she attempts by every means available to appropriate that organ for herself: through her somewhat servile love of the father-husband capable of giving her one, through her desire for a child-penis, preferably a boy, through access to the cultural values still reserved by right to males alone and therefore always masculine, and so on. Woman lives her own desire only as the expectation that she may at least come to possess an equivalent of the male organ.

Yet all this appears quite foreign to her own pleasure, unless it remains within the dominant phallic economy. Thus, for example, woman's autoeroticism is very different from man's. In order to touch himself, man needs an instrument: his hand, a woman's body, language. . . . And this self-caressing requires at least a minimum of activity. As for woman, she touches herself in and of herself without any need for mediation, and before there is any way to distinguish activity from passivity. Woman "touches herself" all the time, and moreover no one can forbid her to do so, for her genitals are formed of two lips in continuous contact.

Thus, with herself, she is already two—but not divisible into one(s)—that caress each other.

This autoeroticism is disrupted by a violent break-in: the brutal separation of the two lips by a violating penis, an intrusion that distracts and deflects the woman from this "self-caressing" she needs if she is not to incur the disappearance of her own pleasure in sexual relations. If the vagina is to serve *also*, but *not only*, to take over the little boy's hand in order to assure an articulation between auto-eroticism and heteroeroticism in intercourse (the encounter with the totally other always signifying death), how, in the classic representation of sexuality, can the perpetuation of autoeroticism for woman be managed? Will woman not be left with the impossible alternative between a defensive virginity, fiercely turned in upon itself, and a body open to penetration that no longer knows, in this "hole" that constitutes its sex, the pleasure of its own touch? The more or less exclusive—and highly anxious—attention paid to erection in Western sexuality proves to what extent the imaginary that governs it is foreign to the feminine. For the most part, this sexuality offers nothing but imperatives dictated by male rivalry: the "strongest" being the one who has the best "hard-on," the longest, the biggest, the stiffest penis, or even the one who "pees the farthest" (as in little boys' contests). Or else one finds imperatives dictated by the enactment of sadomasochistic fantasies, these in turn governed by man's relation to his mother: the desire to force entry, to penetrate, to appropriate for himself the mystery of this womb where he has been conceived, the secret of his begetting, of his "origin." Desire/need, also to make blood flow again in order to revive a very old relationship—intrauterine, to be sure, but also prehistoric—to the maternal.

Woman, in this sexual imaginary, is only a more or less obliging prop for the enactment of man's fantasies. That she may find pleasure there in that role, by proxy, is possible, even certain. But such pleasure is above all a masochistic prostitution of her body to a desire that is not her own, and it leaves her in a familiar state of dependency upon man. Not knowing what she wants, ready for anything, even asking for more, so long as he will "take" her as his "object" when he seeks his own pleasure. Thus she will not say what she herself wants; moreover, she does not know, or no longer knows, what she wants. As Freud admits, the beginnings of the sexual life of a girl child are so "obscure," so "faded with time," that one would have to dig down very deep indeed to discover beneath the traces of this civilization, of this history, the vestiges of a more archaic civilization that might give some clue to woman's sexuality. That extremely ancient civilization would undoubtedly have a different alphabet, a different language. . . . Woman's desire would not be expected to speak the same language as man's; woman's desire has doubtless been submerged by the logic that has dominated the West since the time of the Greeks.

Within this logic, the predominance of the visual, and of the discrimination and individualization of form, is particularly foreign to female eroticism. Woman takes pleasure more from touching than from looking, and her entry into a dominant scopic economy signifies, again, her consignment to passivity: she is to be the beautiful object of contemplation. While her body finds itself thus eroticized, and called to a double movement of exhibition and of chaste retreat in order to stimulate the drives of the "subject," her sexual organ represents *the horror of nothing to see*. A defect in this systematics of representation and desire. A "hole" in its scoptophilic lens. It is already evident in Greek statuary that this nothing-to-see has to be excluded, rejected, from such a scene of representation. Woman's genitals are simply absent, masked, sewn back up inside their "crack."

This organ which has nothing to show for itself also lacks a form of its own. And if woman takes pleasure precisely from this incompleteness of form which allows her organ to touch itself over and over again, indefinitely, by itself, that pleasure is denied by a civilization that privileges phallomorphism. The value granted to the only definable form excludes the one that is in play in female autoeroticism. The *one* of form, of the individual, of the (male) sexual organ, of the proper name, of the proper meaning . . . supplants, while separating and dividing, that contact of *at least two* (lips) which keeps woman in touch with herself, but without any possibility of distinguishing what is touching from what is touched.

Whence the mystery that woman represents in a culture claiming to count everything, to number everything by units, to inventory everything as individualities. *She is neither one nor two*. Rigorously speaking, she cannot be identified either as one person, or as two. She resists all adequate definition. Further, she has no "proper" name. And her sexual organ, which is not *one* organ, is counted as *none*. The negative, the underside, the reverse of the only visible and morphologically designatable organ (even in the passage from erection to detumescence does pose some problems): the penis.

But the "thickness" of that "form," the layering of its volume, its expansions and contractions and even the spacing of the moments in which it produces itself as form—all this the feminine keeps secret. Without knowing it. And if woman is asked to sustain, to revive, man's desire, the request neglects to spell out what it implies as to the value of her own desire. A desire of which she is not aware, moreover, at least not explicitly. But one whose force and continuity are capable of nurturing repeatedly and at length all the masquerades of "femininity" that are expected from her.

It is true that she still has the child, in relation to whom her appetite for touch, for contact, has free rein, unless it is already lost, alienated by the taboo against touching of a highly obsessive civilization. Otherwise her pleasure will find, in the child, compensations for and diversion from the frustrations that she too often encounters in sexual relations per se. Thus maternity fills the gaps in a repressed female sexuality. Perhaps man and woman no longer caress each other except through that mediation between them that the child—preferably a boy—represents? Man, identified with his son, rediscovers the pleasure of maternal fondling; woman touches herself again by caressing that part of her body: her baby-penis-clitoris.

What this entails for the amorous trio is well known. But the Oedipal interdiction seems to be a somewhat categorical and factitious law—although it does provide the means for perpetuating the authoritarian discourse of fathers—when it is promulgated in a culture in which sexual relations are impracticable because man's desire and woman's are strangers to each other. And in which the two desires have to try to meet through indirect means, whether the archaic one of a sense-relation to the mother's body, or the present one of active or passive extension of the law of the father. These are regressive emotional behaviors, exchanges of words too detached from the sexual arena not to constitute an exile with respect to it: "mother" and "father" dominate the interactions of the couple, but as social roles. The division of labor prevents them from making love. They produce or reproduce. Without quite knowing how to use their leisure. Such little as they have, such little indeed as they wish to have. For what are they to do with leisure? What substitute for amorous resource are they to invent? Still . . .

Perhaps it is time to return to that repressed entity, the female imaginary. So woman does not have a sex organ? She has at least two of them, but they are not identifiable as ones. Indeed, she has many more. Her sexuality, always at least double, goes even further: it is *plural*. Is this the way culture is seeking to characterize itself now? Is this the way texts write themselves/are written now? Without quite knowing what censorship they are evading? Indeed, woman's pleasure does not have to choose between clitoral activity and vaginal passivity, for example. The pleasure of the vaginal caress does not have to be substituted for that of the clitoral caress. They each contribute, irreplaceably, to woman's pleasure. Among other caresses. . . . Fondling the breasts, touching the vulva, spreading lips, stroking the posterior wall of the vagina, brushing against the mouth of the uterus, and so on. To evoke only a few of the most specifically female pleasures. Pleasures which are somewhat misunderstood in sexual difference as it is imagined—or not imagined, the other sex being only the indispensable complement to the only sex.

But *woman has sex organs more or less everywhere*. She finds pleasure almost anywhere. Even if we refrain from invoking the hystericization of her entire body, the geography of her pleasure is far more diversified, more multiple in its differences, more complex, more subtle, than is commonly imagined—in an imaginary rather too narrowly focused on sameness.

"She" is indefinitely other in herself. This is doubtless why she is said to be whimsical, incomprehensible, agitated, capricious . . . not to mention her language, in which "she" sets off in all directions leaving "him" unable to discern the coherence of any meaning. Hers are contradictory words, somewhat mad from the standpoint of reason, inaudible for whoever listens to them with ready-made grids, with a fully elaborated code in hand. For in what she says, too, at least when she dares, woman is constantly touching herself. She steps ever so slightly aside from herself with a murmur, an exclamation, a whisper, a sentence left unfinished. . . . When she returns, it is to set off again from elsewhere. From another point of pleasure, or of pain. One would have to listen with another ear, as if hearing *an "other meaning" always in the process of weaving itself, of embracing itself with words, but also of getting rid of words in order not to become fixed, congealed in them.* For if "she" says something, it is not, it is already no longer, identical with what she means. What she says is never identical with anything, moreover; rather, it is contiguous. *It touches (upon).* And when it strays too far from that proximity, she breaks off and starts over at "zero": her body-sex.

It is useless, then, to trap women in the exact definition of what they mean, to make them repeat (themselves) so that it will be clear; they are already elsewhere in that discursive machinery where you expected to surprise them. They have returned within themselves. Which must not be understood in the same way as within yourself. They do not have the interiority that you have, the one you perhaps suppose they have. Within themselves means *within the intimacy of that silent, multiple, diffuse touch.* And if you ask them insistently what they are thinking about, they can only reply: Nothing. Everything.

Thus what they desire is precisely nothing, and at the same time everything. Always something more and something else besides that *one*—sexual organ, for example—that you give them, attribute to them. Their desire is often interpreted, and feared, as a sort of insatiable hunger, a voracity that will swallow you whole. Whereas it really involves a different economy more than anything else, one that upsets the linearity of a project, undermines the goal-object of desire, diffuses the polarization toward a single pleasure, disconcerts fidelity to a single discourse. . . .

Must this multiplicity of female desire and female language be understood as shards, scattered remnants of a violated sexuality? A sexuality denied? The question has no simple answer. The rejection, the exclusion of a female imaginary certainly puts woman in the position of experiencing herself only fragmentarily, in the little-structured margins of a dominant ideology, as waste, or excess, what is left of a mirror invested by the (masculine) "subject" to reflect himself, to copy himself. Moreover, the role of "femininity" is prescribed by this masculine specula(riza)tion and corresponds scarcely at all to woman's desire, which may be recovered only in secret, in hiding, with anxiety and guilt.

But if the female imaginary were to deploy itself, if it could bring itself into play otherwise than as scraps, uncollected debris, would it represent itself, even so, in the form of *one* universe? Would it even be volume instead of surface? No. Not unless it were understood, yet again, as a privileging of the maternal over the feminine. Of a phallic maternal, at that. Closed in upon the jealous possession of its valued product. Rivaling man in his esteem for productive excess. In such a race for power, woman loses the uniqueness of her pleasure. By closing herself off as volume, she renounces the pleasure that she gets from the *nonsuture of her lips:* she is undoubtedly a mother, but a virgin mother; the role was assigned to her by mythologies long ago. Granting her a certain social power to the extent that she is reduced, with her own complicity, to sexual impotence.

(Re-)discovering herself, for a woman, thus could only signify the possibility of sacrificing no one of her pleasures to another, of identifying herself with none of them in particular, *of never being simply one.* A sort of expanding universe to which no limits could be fixed and which would not be incoherence nonetheless—nor that polymorphous perversion of the child in which the erogenous zones would lie waiting to be regrouped under the primacy of the phallus.

Woman always remains several, but she is kept from dispersion because the other is already within her and is autoerotically familiar to her. Which is not to say that she appropriates the other for herself, that she reduces it to her own property. Ownership and property are doubtless quite foreign to the feminine. At least sexually. But not *nearness*. Nearness so pronounced that it makes all discrimination of identity, and thus all forms of property, impossible. Woman derives pleasure from what is *so near that she cannot have it, nor have herself*. She herself enters into a ceaseless exchange of herself with the other without any possibility of identifying either. This puts into question all prevailing economies: their calculations are irremediably stymied by woman's pleasure, as it increases indefinitely from its passage in and through the other.

However, in order for woman to reach the place where she takes pleasure as a woman, a long detour by way of the analysis of the various systems of oppression brought to bear upon her is assuredly necessary. And claiming to fall back on the single solution of pleasure risks making her miss the process of going back through a social practice that *her* enjoyment requires.

For woman is traditionally a use-value for man, an exchange value among men; in other words, a commodity. As such, she remains the guardian of material substance, whose price will be established, in terms of the standard of their work and of their need/desire, by "subjects": workers, merchants, consumers. Women are marked phallicly by their fathers, husbands, procurers. And this branding determines their value in sexual commerce. Woman is never anything but the locus of a more or less competitive exchange between two men, including the competition for the possession of mother earth.

How can this object of transaction claim a right to pleasure without removing her/itself from established commerce? With respect to other merchandise in the marketplace, how could this commodity maintain a relationship other than one of aggressive jealousy? How could material substance enjoy her/itself without provoking the consumer's anxiety over the disappearance of his nurturing ground? How could that exchange—which can in no way be defined in terms "proper" to woman's desire—appear as anything but a pure mirage, more foolishness, all too readily obscured by a more sensible discourse and by a system of apparently more tangible values?

A woman's development, however radical it may seek to be, would thus not suffice to liberate woman's desire. And to date no political theory or political practice has resolved, or sufficiently taken into consideration this historical problem, even though Marxism has proclaimed its importance. But women do not constitute, strictly speaking, a class, and their dispersion among several classes makes their political struggle complex, their demands sometimes contradictory.

There remains, however, the condition of underdevelopment arising from women's submission by and to a culture that oppresses them, uses them, makes of them a medium of exchange, with very little profit to them. Except in the quasi-monopolies of masochistic pleasure, the domestic labor force, and reproduction. The power of slaves? Which are not negligible powers, moreover. For where pleasure is concerned, the master is not necessarily well served. Thus to reverse the relation, especially in the economy of sexuality, does not seem a desirable objective.

But if women are to preserve and expand their autoeroticism, their homosexuality, might not the renunciation of heterosexual pleasure correspond once again to the disconnection from power that is traditionally theirs? Would it not involve a new prison, a new cloister, built of their own accord? For women to undertake tactical strikes, to keep themselves apart from men long enough to learn to defend their desire, especially through speech, to discover the love of other women while sheltered from men's imperious choices that put them in the position of rival commodities, to forge for themselves a social status that compels recognition, to earn their living in order to escape from the condition of prostitute . . . these are certainly indispensable stages in the escape from their proletarization on the exchange market. But if their aim were simply to reverse the order of things, even supposing this to be possible, history would repeat itself in the long run, would revert to sameness: to phallocratism. It would leave room neither for women's sexuality, nor for women's imaginary, nor for women's language to take (their) place.

NOTE

This text was originally published as "Ce Sexe qui n'en est pas un," in *Cahiers du Grif*, no. 5. English translation: "This Sex Which Is Not One," trans. Claudia Reeder, in *New French Feminisms*, ed. Elaine Marks and Isabelle de Courtivron (New York, 1981), pp. 99–106.

ANN ROSALIND JONES

WRITING THE BODY

toward an understanding
of l'écriture féminine

France is today the scene of feminisms. The Mouvement de Libération des femmes (MLF) grows every year, but so do the factions within it: feminist journals carry on bitter debates, a group of women writers boycotts a feminist publishing house, French women at conferences in the United States contradict each other's positions at top volume (Monique Wittig to Hélène Cixous: "Ceci est un scandale!"). But in the realm of theory, the French share a deep critique of the modes through which the West has claimed to discern evidence—or reality—and a suspicion concerning efforts to change the position of women that fail to address the forces in the body, in the unconscious, in the basic structures of culture that are invisible to the empirical eye. Briefly, French feminists in general believe that Western thought has been based on a systematic repression of women's experience. Thus their assertion of a bedrock female nature makes sense as a point from which to deconstruct language, philosophy, psychoanalysis, the social practices, and direction of patriarchal culture as we live in and resist it.

This position, the turn to *féminité* as a challenge to male-centered thinking, has stirred up curiosity and set off resonances among American feminists, who are increasingly open to theory, to philosophical, psychoanalytic, and Marxist critiques of masculinist ways of seeing the world. (Speakers at recent U.S. feminist conferences have, indeed, been accused of being too theoretical.) And it seems to me that it is precisely through theory that some of the positions of the French feminists need to be questioned—as they have been in France since the beginnings of the MLF. My intention, then, is to pose some questions about theoretical consistency and (yes, they can't be repressed!) the practical and political implications of French discussions and celebrations of the feminine. For if one posits that female subjectivity is derived from women's physiology and bodily instincts as they affect sexual experience and the unconscious, both theoretical and practical problems can and do arise.

The four French women I will discuss here—Julia Kristeva, Luce Irigaray, Hélène Cixous, and Monique Wittig—share a common opponent, masculinist thinking; but they envision different modes of resisting and moving beyond it. Their common ground is an analysis of Western culture as fundamentally oppressive, as phallogocentric. "I am the unified, self-controlled center of the universe," man (white, European, and ruling class) has claimed. "The rest of the world, which I define as the Other, has meaning only in relation to me, as man/ father, possessor of the phallus."[1] This claim to centrality has been supported not only by religion and philosophy, but also by language. To speak and especially to write from such a position is to appropriate the world, to dominate it through verbal mastery. Symbolic discourse (language, in various contexts) is another means through which man objectifies the world, reduces it to his terms, speaks in place of everything and everyone else—including women.

How, then, are the institutions and signifying practices (speech, writing, images, myths, and rituals) of such a culture to be resisted? These French women agree that resistance does take place in the form of *jouissance*, that is, in the direct reexperience of the physical pleasures of infancy and of later sexuality, repressed but not obliterated by the Law of the Father.[2] Kristeva stops here; but Irigaray and Cixous go on to emphasize that women, historically limited to being sexual objects for men (virgins or prostitutes, wives or mothers), have been prevented from expressing their sexuality in itself or for themselves. If they can do this, and if they can speak about it in the new languages it calls for, they will establish a point of view (a site of *différence*) from which phallogocentric concepts and controls can be seen through and taken apart, not only in theory, but also in practice. Like Cixous, Wittig has produced a number of *textes féminins*, but she insists that the theory and practice of *féminité* must be focused on women among themselves, rather than on their divergence from men or from men's views of them. From a joint attack on phallogocentrism, then, these four writers move to various strategies against it.

Julia Kristeva, a founding member of the semiotic-Marxist journal *Tel Quel*, and the writer of several books on avant-garde writers, language, and philosophy, finds in psychoanalysis the concept of the bodily drives that survive cultural pressures toward sublimation and surface in what she calls "semiotic discourse": the gestural, rhythmic, preferential language of such writers as Joyce, Mallarmé, and Artaud.[3] These men, rather than giving up their blissful infantile fusion with their mothers, their orality, and anality, reexperience such *jouissances* subconsciously and set them into play by constructing texts against the rules and regularities of conventional language. How do women fit into this scheme of semiotic liberation? Indirectly, as mothers, because they are the first love objects from which the child is typically separated and turned away in the course of his initiation into society. In fact, Kristeva sees semiotic discourse as an incestuous challenge to the symbolic order, asserting as it does the writer's return to the pleasures of his preverbal identification with his mother and his refusal to identify with his father and the logic of paternal discourse. Women, for Kristeva, also speak and write as "hysterics," as outsiders to male-dominated discourse, for two reasons: the predominance in them of drives related to anality and childbirth, and their marginal position vis-à-vis masculine culture. Their semiotic style is likely to involve repetitive, spasmodic separations from the dominating discourse, which, more often, they are forced to imitate.[4]

Kristeva doubts, however, whether women should aim to work out alternative discourses. She sees certain liberatory potentials in their marginal position, which is (admirably) unlikely to produce a fixed, authority-claiming subject/ speaker or language: "In social, sexual and symbolic experiences, being a woman has always provided a means to another end, to becoming something else: a subject-in-the-making, a subject on trial." Rather than formulating a new discourse, women should persist in challenging the discourses that stand: "If women have a role to play, . . . it is only in assuming a *negative* function: reject everything finite, definite, structured, loaded with meaning, in the existing state of society. Such an attitude places women on the side of the explosion of social codes: with revolutionary movements."[5] In fact, "woman" to Kristeva represents not so much a sex as an attitude, any resistance to conventional culture and language; men, too, have access to the *jouissance* that opposes phallogocentrism:

> A feminist practice can only be . . . at odds with what already exists so that we may say "that's not it" and "that's still not it." By "woman" I mean that which cannot be represented, what is not said, what remains above and beyond nomenclatures and ideologies. There are certain "men" who are familiar with this phenomenon.[6]

For Luce Irigaray, on the contrary, women have a specificity that distinguishes them sharply from men. A psychoanalyst and former member of l'Ecole freudienne at the University of Paris (Vincennes), she was fired from her teaching position in the fall of 1974, three weeks after the publication of her study of the phallocentric bias in Freud. *Speculum de l'autre femme* is this study, a profound and wittily sarcastic demonstration of the ways in which Plato and Freud define woman: as irrational and invisible, as imperfect (castrated) man. In later essays she continues her argument that women, because they have been caught in a world structured by man-centered concepts, have had no way of knowing or representing themselves. But she offers as the starting point for a female self-consciousness the facts of women's bodies and women's sexual pleasure, precisely because they have been so absent or so misrepresented in male discourse. Women, she says, experience a diffuse sexuality arising, for example, from the "two lips" of the vulva, and a multiplicity of libidinal energies that cannot be expressed or understood within the identity-claiming assumptions of phallocentric discourse ("I am a unified, coherent being, and what is significant in the world reflects my male image").[7] Irigaray argues further that female sexuality explains women's problematic relationship to (masculine) logic and language:

> . . . *woman has sex organs just about everywhere.* She experiences pleasure almost everywhere. . . . The geography of her pleasure is much more diversified, more multiple in its differences, more complex, more subtle, than is imagined—in an imaginary [system] centered a bit too much on one and the same.
>
> "She" is infinitely other in herself. That is undoubtedly the reason she is called temperamental, incomprehensible, perturbed, capricious—not to mention her language in which "she" goes off in all directions and in which "he" is unable to discern the coherence of any meaning. Contradictory words seem a little crazy to the logic of reason, and inaudible for him who listens with ready-made grids, a code prepared in advance. In her statements—at least when she dares to speak out—woman retouches herself constantly.[8]

Irigaray concedes that women's discovery of their autoeroticism will not, by itself, arrive automatically or enable them to transform the existing order: "For a woman to arrive at the point where she can enjoy her pleasure as a woman, a long detour by the analysis of the various systems that oppress her is certainly necessary."[9] Irigaray herself writes essays using Marxist categories to analyze men's use and exchange of women, and in others she uses female physiology as a source of critical metaphors and counterconcepts (against physics, pornography, Nietzsche's misogyny, myth),[10] rather than literally. Yet her focus on the physical bases for the difference between male and physical sexuality remains the same: women must recognize and assert their *jouissance* if they are to subvert phallocentric oppression at its deepest levels.

Since 1975, when she founded women's studies at Vincennes, Hélène Cixous has been a spokeswoman for a group Psychanalyse et Politique and a prolific writer of texts for their publishing house, des femmes. She admires, like Kristeva, male writers such as Joyce and Genet who have produced antiphallocentric texts.[11] But she is convinced that women's unconscious is totally different from men's, and that it is their psychosexual specificity that will empower women to overthrow masculinist ideologies and to create new female discourses. Of her own writing she says, "Je suis là où ça parle" ("I am there where the it/id/the female unconscious speaks.").[12] She has produced a series of analyses of women's suffering under the laws of male sexuality (the first-person narrative *Angst*, the play *Portrait de Dora*, the libretto for the opera *Le Nom d'Oedipe*) and a growing collection of demonstrations of what id-liberated female discourse might be: *La, Ananké, and Illa.* In her recent *Vivre l'orange* (des femmes, 1979), she celebrates the Brazilian writer Clarice Lispector for what she sees as a peculiarly female attentiveness to objects, the ability to perceive and represent them in a nurturing rather than dominating way. She believes that this empathetic attentiveness and the literary modes to which it gives rise, arise from libidinal rather than social-cultural sources: the "typically feminine gesture, not culturally but libidinally, [is] to produce in order to bring about life, pleasure, not in order to accumulate."[13]

Cixous criticizes psychoanalysis for its "thesis of a 'natural' anatomical determination of sexual difference-opposition," focusing on physical drives rather than body parts for her definition of male female contrasts: "It is at the level of sexual pleasure in my opinion that the difference makes itself most clearly apparent in as far as woman's libidinal economy is neither identifiable by a man nor referable to the masculine economy."[14] In her manifesto for *l'écriture féminine*, "The Laugh of the Medusa" (1975), her comparisons and lyricism suggest that she admires in women a sexuality that is remarkably constant and almost mystically superior to the phallic single-mindedness it transcends:

> Though masculine sexuality gravitates around the penis, engendering that centralized body (in political anatomy) under the dictatorship of its parts, woman does not bring about the same regionalization which serves the couple head/genitals and which is inscribed only within boundaries. Her libido is cosmic, just as her unconscious is worldwide.

She goes on immediately, in terms close to Irigaray's, to link women's diffuse sexuality to women's language—written language, in this case:

> Her writing can only keep going, without ever inscribing or discerning contours. . . . She lets the other language speak—the language of 1,000 tongues

> which knows neither enclosure nor death. . . . Her language does not contain, it carries; it does not hold back, it makes possible.[15]

The passage ends with her invocation of other bodily drives (*pulsions* in French) in a continuum with women's self-expression:

> Oral drive, anal drive, vocal drive—all these drives are our strengths, and among them is the gestation drive—just like the desire to write: a desire to live self from within, a desire for the swollen belly, for language, for blood.

In her theoretical and imaginative writing alike (*La Jéune née*, 1975, typically combines the two) Cixous insists on the primacy of multiple, specifically female libidinal impulses, in women's unconscious and in the writing of the liberatory female discourses of the future.

What Kristeva, Irigaray, and Cixous do in common, then, is to oppose women's bodily experience (or, in Kristeva's case, women's bodily effect as mothers) to the phallic/symbolic patterns embedded in Western thought. Although Kristeva does not privilege women as the only possessors of prephallocentric discourse, Irigaray and Cixous go further: if women are to discover and express who they are, to bring to the surface what masculine history has repressed in them, they must begin with their sexuality. And their sexuality begins with their bodies, with their genital and libidinal difference from men.

For various reasons, this is a powerful argument. We have seen versions of it in the radical feminism of the United States, too. In the French context, it offers an island of hope in the void left by the deconstruction of humanism, which has been revealed as an ideologically suspect invention by men. If men are responsible for the reigning binary system of meaning—identity/other, man/nature, reason/chaos, man/woman—women, relegated to the negative and passive pole of this hierarchy, are not implicated in the creation of its myths. (Certainly, they are no longer impressed by them!) And the immediacy with which the body, the id, *jouissance*, are supposedly experienced promises a clarity of perception and a vitality that can bring down mountains of phallocentric delusion. Finally, to the extent that the female body is seen as a direct source of female writing, a powerful alternative discourse seems possible: to write from the body is to recreate the world.

But *féminité* and *écriture féminine* are problematic as well as powerful concepts. They have been criticized as idealist and essentialist, bound up in the very system they claim to undermine; they have been attacked as theoretically fuzzy and as fatal to constructive political action.[16] I think all these objections are worth making. What's more, they must be made if American women are to sift out and use the positive elements in French thinking about *féminité*.

First off, the basic theoretical question: can the body be a source of self-knowledge? Does female sexuality exist prior to or in spite of social experience? Do women in fact experience their bodies purely or essentially, outside the damaging acculturation so sharply analyzed by women in France and elsewhere? The answer is no, even in terms of the psychoanalytic theory on which many elements in the concept of *féminité* depend. Feminists rereading Freud and Jacques Lacan, and feminists doing new research on the construction of sexuality all agree that sexuality is not an innate quality in women or in men; it is developed through the individual's encounters with the nuclear family and with the symbolic systems set in motion by the mother-father pair as the parents themselves carry out socially imposed roles toward the child. Freud, Juliet Mitchell has shown, describes the process through which girls in our society shift their first love for their mothers to a compensatory love for their fathers and develop a sense of their own anatomy as less valued socially than that of boys.[17] Nancy Chodorow has documented and theorized the difficulty of this shift and used it to account for the complex affective needs of girls and women.[18] To the analysis of the process through which sexual identity is formed Lacan adds the role of the father as bearer of language and culture; he identifies the symbolic value attributed to the phallus as the basis for contrasts and contrasting values that the child incorporates as she attempts to make sense of and fit herself into the phallocentric world. So if early gender identity comes into being in response to patriarchal structures—as, for example, Chodorow, Lacan, and Dorothy Dinnerstein argue[19]—and if even the unconscious is sexed in accordance with the nuclear family, then there seems to be no essential stratum of sexuality unsaturated with social arrangements and symbolic systems. New readings of Freud and of object relations theory both confirm that sexuality is not a natural given, but rather is the consequence of social interactions, among people and among signs.

Theoretical work and practical evidence strongly suggest that sexual identity ("I am a woman, I experience my body as sexual in this way") never takes shape in isolation or in a simply physical context. The child becomes male or female in response to the females and males she encounters in her family and to the male and female images she constructs according to her experience—especially her loss of direct access to either parent.[20] The desires of the child and of the adult who grows out of the child finally result not from the isolated erotic sensitivities of the child's body; these sensitivities are interpreted through the meanings the child attaches to her body through early experience in a sexed world. To take from psychoanalysis the concepts of drive and libido without talking about what happens later to the child's systems of self-perception is to drop out the deepest level at which phallocentric society asserts its power: the sexed family as it imprints itself on the child's sense of herself as a sexed being.

Psychoanalytic theory is not feminist dogma, and feminists have also analyzed the sexist ideologies that confront women past the age of childhood in the family. Not surprisingly, these ideologies make their way into many women's day-to-day experience of their bodies, even in situations that we have designed to be free of male domination. For instance, liberatory practices such as masturbation, lesbianism, and woman-centered medicine coexist with thoroughly phallocentric habits of thought and feeling; they are not liberatory simply because they aspire to be. Some women discover, for example, that their masturbation is accompanied by puzzlingly unenlightened fantasies; contrary to the claims of *féminité*, women's autoeroticism, at least in these decades, is shot through with images from a phallically dominated world. Similarly, many lesbians recognize their need to resist roles of domination and submission that bear a grim, even parodic resemblance to heterosexual relationships. Women giving birth may wonder whether the optimistic, even heroic terminology of natural childbirth is not related to the suspect ideal of "taking it like a man." Even in the self-help clinics set up to spare women the sexist bias of the male gynecological establishment, a phallo-centric *magasin des images* may prevail. A counselor at such a clinic, showing a friend of mine her cervix for the first time in a mirror, made a remark (uninten-tionally; that's the point) that struck us both as far less liberating than it was in-tended to be: "Big, isn't it? Doesn't it look powerful? As good as a penis any day." All in all, at this point in history, most of us perceive our bodies through a jumpy, contradictory mesh of hoary sexual symbolization and political counter-response. It is possible to argue that the French feminists make of the female body too unproblematic pleasurable and totalized an entity.

Certainly, women's physiology has important meanings for women in various cultures, and it is essential for us to express those meanings rather than to submit to male definitions—that is, appropriations—of our sexuality. But the female body hardly seems the best site to launch an attack on the forces that have alien-ated us from what our sexuality might become. For if we argue for an innate, precultural femininity, where does that position (though in *content* it obviously diverges from masculinist dogma) leave us in relation to earlier theories about women's "nature"? I myself feel highly flattered by Cixous's praise for the nur-turant perceptions of women, but when she speaks of a drive toward gestation, I begin to hear echoes of the coercive glorification of motherhood that has plagued women for centuries. If we define female subjectivity through universal biologi-cal/libidinal given, what happens to the project of changing the world in feminist directions? Further, is women's sexuality so monolithic that a notion of a shared, typical femininity does justice to it? What about variations in class, in race, and in culture among women? What about changes over time in *one* woman's sexu-ality (with men, with women, by herself)? How can one libidinal voice—or the two vulval lips so startlingly presented by Irigaray—speak for all women?

The psychoanalytic critique of *féminité* as a concept that overlooks important psychosocial realities is not the only critique that can be brought against posi-tions like Irigaray's and Cixous's. Other French women have made a strong, ma-terialist attack on what they call *néo-féminité*, objecting to it as an ideal bound up through symmetrical opposition in the very ideological system feminists want to destroy. (*Questions féministes*, the journal founded in 1977 with Simone de Beau-voir as titular editor, is a central source for this kind of thinking in France.) Mate-rialist feminists such as Christine Delphy and Colette Guillaumin are suspicious of the logic through which *féminité* defines men as phallic—solipsistic, aggres-sive, excessively rational—and then praises women, who, by nature of their con-trasting sexuality, are other-oriented, empathetic, multiimaginative. Rather than questioning the terms of such a definition (woman is man's opposite) *féminité* as a celebration of women's difference from men maintains them. It reverses the values assigned to each side of the polarity, but it still leaves man as the de-termining referent, not departing from the opposition male/female, but par-ticipating in it.

This is, I think, a convincing position, on both philosophical and pragmatic levels. What we need to do is to move outside that male-centered, binary logic altogether. We need to ask not how Woman is different from Man (though the question of how women differ from what men *think* they are is important). We need to know how women have come to be who they are through history, which is the history of their oppression by men and male-designed institutions. Only through an analysis of the power relationships between men and women, and practices based on that analysis, will we put an end to our oppression—and only then will we discover what women are or can be. More strategically, we need to know whether the assertion of a shared female nature made by *féminité* can help us in feminist action toward a variety of goals: the possibility of working, or working in marginal or newly defined ways, or of not working in the public world at all; the freedom for a diversity of sexual practices; the right to motherhood, childlessness, or some as yet untheorized participation in reproduction; the affirmation of historically conditioned female values (nurturance, communal rather than individualistic ambitions, insistence on improving the quality of private life); *and* the exploration of new ones. If we concentrate our energies on opposing a counterview of Woman to the view held by men in the past and the present, what happens to our ability to support the multiplicity of women and the various life possibilities they are fighting for in the future?

In a critique of *féminité* as praise of women's difference from men, the name of Monique Wittig must be mentioned. Active in the early seventies in the Féministes révolutionnaires and a contributor from the beginning to *Questions féministes*, Wittig has written four quite different books, which are nonetheless related through her focus on women among themselves: the schoolgirls of *L'Opoponax*, the tribal sisterhood of *Les Guérrillères*, the passionate couple of *Le Corps lesbien*, the users of the postphallocentric vocabulary laid out in *Brouillon pour un dictionnaire des amantes*. Wittig writes her novels, her monologues, and histories to explore what social relationships among women-identified women are or might be.[21] She rewrites traditional culture in mocking takeovers: one entry in *Brouillon pour un dictionnaire* is "Ainsi parlait Frederika, conte pour enfants" ("Thus Spake Frederika, children's story"), surely one of the least reverent allusions to Friedrich Nietzsche to come out of French critiques of culture. She also invents new settings, such as the ceremonies and festivals of *Les Guérrillères* and *Le Corps lesbien*, and new modes, such as the feminized epic of *Les Guérrillères* and the lyric dialogue of *Le Corps lesbien*, to represent what a female/female life— separatist but not isolationist—might be.

As Wittig's talks at recent conferences in the United States show, she is suspicious both of the oppositional thinking that defines woman in terms of man and of the mythical/idealist strain in certain formulations of *féminité*.[22] In her argument for a more politically centered understanding of women at the Second Sex Conference in New York (September 1979), she used a Marxist vocabulary which may be more familiar to U.S. feminists than the philosophical and psychoanalytic frameworks in which Irigaray and Cixous work:

> It remains . . . for us to define our oppression in materialist terms, to say that women are a class, which is to say that the category "woman," as well as "man," is a political and economic category, not an eternal one. . . . Our first task . . . is thoroughly to dissociate "women" (the class within which we fight) and "woman," the myth. For "woman" does not exist for us; it is only an imaginary formation, while "women" is the product of a social relationship.[23]

Colette Guillaumin, arguing along similar lines in *Questions féministes*, points out that the psychic characteristics praised by advocates of *féminité* have in fact been determined by the familial and economic roles imposed on women by men. There is nothing liberatory, she insists, in women's claiming as virtues qualities that men have always found convenient. How does maternal tenderness or undemanding empathy threaten a Master?[24] The liberating stance is, rather, the determination to analyze and put an end to the patriarchal structures that have produced those qualities without reference to the needs to women.

I have another political objection to the concept of *féminité* as a bundle of Everywoman's psychosexual characteristics: it flattens out the lived differences among women. To the extent that each of us responds to a particular tribal, national, racial, or class situation vis-a-vis men, we are in fact separated from one another. As the painful and counterproductive splits along class and racial lines in the American women's movement have shown, we need to understand and respect the diversity in our concrete social situations. A monolithic vision of shared female sexuality, rather than defeating phallocentrism as doctrine and practice, is more likely to blind us to our varied and immediate needs and to the specific struggles we must coordinate in order to meet them. What is the meaning of "two lips" to heterosexual women who want men to recognize their clitoral pleasure—or to African or Middle-Eastern women who, as a result of pharaonic clitoridectomies, have neither lips nor clitoris through which to *jouir?* Does a celebration of the Maternal versus the Patriarchal make the same kind of sense, or any sense, to white, middle-class women who are fighting to maintain the right to abortion, to black and Third-World women resisting enforced sterilization, to women in subsistence-farming economies where the livelihood of the family depends on the work of every child who is born and survives? And surely any one woman gives different meanings to her sexuality throughout her individual history. Freedom from sexual expectations and activity may well be what girls in the Western world most need because they are typically sexualized all too soon by the media, advertising, peer pressures, and child pornography; women of various ages undergo radical changes in sexual identity and response as they enter relationships with men, with women, or choose celibacy and friendship as alternatives. And it is hard to see how the situations of old women, consigned to sexual inactivity because of their age or, if they are widowed, to unpaid work in others' families or to isolated poverty, can be understood or changed through a concept of *jouissance.* I wonder again whether one libidinal voice, however non-phallocentrically defined, can speak to the economic and cultural problems of all women.

Hence, I would argue that we need the theoretical depth and polemical energy of *féminité* as an alternative idea. But a historically responsive and powerful unity among women will come from our ongoing, shared practice, our experience in and against the material world. As a lens and a partial strategy, *féminité* and *ecriture féminine* are vital. Certainly, women need to shake off the mistaken and contemptuous attitudes toward their sexuality that permeate Western (and other) cultures and languages at their deepest levels, and working out self-representations that challenge phallocentric discourses is an important part of that ideological struggle. Women have already begun to transform not only the subject matter, but also the ways of producing meaning in poetry, fiction, film, and visual arts. (Indeed, feminist research suggests that the French may have been too hasty in their claim that women are only now beginning to challenge the symbolic order.) But even if we take *l'écriture féminine* as a utopian ideal, an energizing myth rather than a model for how all women write or should write, theoretical and practical problems arise (again!) from an ideal defined in this way. Can the body be the source of a new discourse? Is it possible, assuming an unmediated and *jouissant* (or, more likely, a positively reconstructed) sense of one's body, to move from that state of unconscious excitation directly to a written female text?

Madeleine Gagnon says yes, in *La Venue à l'écriture*, written with Cixous in 1977. Her view is that women, free from the self-limiting economy of male libido ("I will come once and once only, through one organ alone; once it's up and over, that's it; so I must beware, save up, avoid premature overflow"), have a greater spontaneity and abundance in body and language both.

> We have never been masters of others or of ourselves. We don't have to confront ourselves in order to free ourselves. We don't have to keep watch on ourselves, or to set up some other erected self in order to understand ourselves. All we have to do is let the body flow, from the inside; all we have to do is erase . . . whatever may hinder or harm the new forms of writing; we retain whatever fits, whatever suits us. Whereas man confronts himself constantly. He pits himself against and stumbles over his erected self.[25]

But psychoanalytic theory and social experience both suggest that the leap from body to language is especially difficult for women.[26] Lacanian theory holds that a girl's introduction into language (the symbolic order represented by the father and built on phallic/nonphallic oppositions) is complex, because she cannot identify directly with the positive poles of that order. And in many preliterate and postliterate cultures, taboos against female speech are enforced: injunctions to silence, mockery of women's chatter or "women's books" abound. The turn taking in early consciousness-raising groups in the United States was meant precisely to overcome the verbal hesitancy induced in women by a society in which men have had the first and the last word. Moreover, for women with jobs, husbands or lovers, children, activist political commitments, finding the time and justification to write at all presents an enormous practical and ideological problem.[27] We are more likely to write, and to read each other's writing, if we begin by working against the concrete difficulties and the prejudices surrounding women's writing than if we simplify and idealize the process by locating writing as a spontaneous outpouring from the body.

Calls for a verbal return to nature seem especially surprising coming from women who are otherwise (and rightly!) suspicious of language as penetrated by phallocentric dogma. True, conventional narrative techniques, as well as grammar and syntax, imply the unified viewpoint and mastery of outer reality that men have claimed for themselves. But literary modes and language itself cannot be the only targets for transformation; the *context* for women's discourses needs to be thought through and broadened out. A woman may experience *jouissance* in a private relationship to her own body, but she writes for others. Who writes? Who reads? Who makes women's texts available to women? What do women want to read about other women's experience? To take a stance as a woman poet or novelist is to enter into a role crisscrossed with questions of authority, of audience, of the modes of publication and distribution. I believe that we are more indebted to the "body" of earlier women writers and to feminist publishers and booksellers than to any woman writer's libidinal/body flow. The novelist Christiane Roche-fort sums up with amusing directness the conflicting public forces and voices that create the dilemma of the French woman who wants to write:

> Well. So here you are now, sitting at your writing table, alone, not allowing anybody anymore to interfere. Are you free?
>
> First, after this long quest, you are swimming in a terrible soup of val-ues—for, to be safe, you had to refuse the so-called female values, which are not female but a social scheme, and to identify with male values, which are not male but an appropriation by men—or an attribution to men—of all human values, mixed up with the anti-values of domination-violence-oppression and the like. In this mixture, where is your real identity?
>
> Second, you are supposed to write in certain forms, preferably: I mean you feel that in certain forms you are not too much seen as a usurper. Novels. Minor poetry, in which case you will be stigmatized in French by the name of "poetesse": not everybody can afford it. . . .
>
> You are supposed, too, to write *about* certain things: house, children, love. Until recently there was in France a so-called *littérature féminine*.
>
> Maybe you don't want to write *about*, but to write, period. And of course, you don't want to obey this social order. So, you tend to react against it. It is not easy to be genuine.[28]

Whatever the difficulties, women are inventing new kinds of writing. But as Irigaray's erudition and plays with the speaking voice show (as do Cixous's mis-chievous puns and citations of languages from Greek though German to Portu-guese, and Wittig's fantastic neologisms and revision of conventional genres), they are doing so deliberately, on a level of feminist theory and literary self-consciousness that goes far beyond the body and the unconscious. That is also how they need to be read. It takes a thorough-going familiarity with *male* figure-heads of Western culture to recognize the intertextual games played by all these writers; their work shows that a resistance to culture is always built, at first, of bits and pieces of that culture, however they are disassembled, criticized, and transcended. Responding to *l'écriture féminine* is no more instinctive than produc-ing it. Women's writing will be more accessible to writers and readers alike if we recognize it as a conscious response to socioliterary realities, rather than accept it as an overflow of one woman's unmediated communication with her body. Even-tually, certainly, the practice of women writers will transform what we can see and understand in a literary text; but even a woman setting out to write about her body will do so against and through her socioliterary mothers, midwives, and sisters. We need to recognize, too, that there is nothing universal about French versions of *écriture féminine*. The speaking, singing, tale telling, and writing of women in cultures besides that of the Ile de France need to be looked at and understood in their social context if we are to fill in an adequate and genuinely empowering picture of women's creativity.

But I risk, after all this, overstating the case against *féminité* and *l'écriture fémi-nine*, and that would mean a real loss. American feminists can appropriate two important elements, at least, from the French position: the critique of phallo-centrism in all the material and ideological forms it has taken, and the call for new representations of women's consciousness. It is not enough to uncover old heroines or to imagine new ones. Like the French, we need to examine the words, the syntax, the genres, the archaic and elitist attitudes toward language and representation that have limited women's self-knowledge and expression during the long centuries of patriarchy. We need not, however, replace phallocentrism with a shakily theorized "concentrism" that denies women their historical specificities to recognize how deep a refusal of masculinist values must go.[29] If we remember that what women really share is an oppression on all levels, although it affects us each in different ways—if we can translate *féminité* into a concerted attack not only on language, but also directly upon the sociosexual arrangements that keep us from our own potentials and from each other—then we are on our way to becoming "les jeunes nées" envisioned by French feminisms at their best.

NOTES

1. For a summary of the intellectual background of French feminism, see Elaine Marks, "Women and Literature in France," *Signs* 3, no. 4 (Summer 1978): 832–42. Phallogocentrism at work is powerfully analyzed by Shoshana Felman in her study of the characters and critics of a short story by Balzac, "Women and Madness: the Critical Phallacy," *Diacritics* 5, no. 4 (Winter 1975): 2–10, and in this volume.

2. *Jouissance* is a word rich in connotations. "Pleasure" is the simplest translation. The noun comes from the verb *jouir,* meaning to enjoy, to revel in without fear of the cost; also,to have an orgasm. See Stephen Heath's Translator's Note in Roland Barthes's *Image-Music-Text* (New York: Hill and Wang, 1978), p. 9. A note to Introduction 3 in *New French Feminisms: An Anthology,* ed. Elaine Marks and Isabelle de Courtivron (Amherst: University of Massachusetts Press, 1980), explains feminist connotations of *jouissance* as follows:

> This pleasure, when attributed to a woman, is considered to be of a different order from the pleasure that is represented within the male libidinal economy often described in terms of the capitalist gain and profit motive. Women's *jouissance* carries with it the notion of fluidity, diffusion, duration. It is a kind of potlatch in the world of orgasms, a giving, expending, dispensing of pleasure without concern about ends or closure. [p. 36, n. 8]

The Law of the Father is Lacan's formulation for language as the medium through which human beings are placed in culture, a medium represented and enforced by the figure of the father in the family. See Anika Lemaire, *Jacques Lacan,* trans. David Macey (London: Routledge and Kegan Paul, 1977), especially Part 7, "The Role of the Oedipus in accession to the symbolic."

3. Julia Kristeva's books include *Semiotike: Recherches pour une semanalyse* (Paris: Tel Quel, 1969); *Le Texte du roman* (The Hague: Mouton, 1970); *Des Chinoises* (Paris: des femmes, 1974); *La Révolution du langage poétique* (Paris: Seuil, 1974); *Polylogue* (Paris: Seuil, 1977); and *Pouvoirs de l'horreur: essai sur l'abjection* (Paris: Seuil, 1980). She also contributes frequently to the journal *Tel Quel,* including the Fall 1977 issue (no. 74) on women and women's writing. For her criticism of certain notions of *féminité,* see her interview with Françoise van Rossum-Guyon, "A Partier de *Polylogue,*" in *Revue des sciences humaines* 168, no. 4 (December 1977): 495–501.

4. Kristeva, "Le Sujet en procès," in *Polylogue,* p. 77. See, in the same volume, her

discussion of maternity as an experience that breaks down the categories of masculinist thought, in "Maternité selon Giovanni Bellini," pp. 409–38. She expands her argument about the meanings of maternity for women's creativity, in "Un nouveau type d'intellectuel: le dissident" and "Héréthique de l'amour," *Tel Quel*, no. 74 (Fall 1977): 3–8, 30–49. For an explanation of her theory of the semiotic and of Irigaray's concepts of *l'écriture féminine*, see Josette Féral, "Antigone, or the Irony of the Tribe," *Diacritics* 8, no. 2 (Fall 1978): 2–14.

5. "Oscillation du 'pouvoir' au 'refus,'" an interview by Xavière Gauthier in *Tel Quel*, no. 58 (Summer 1974), translated in *New French Feminisms*, pp. 166–67. This collection of translated excerpts from French feminist writers is likely to be very useful to English-language readers.

6. Kristeva, "La femme, ce n'est jamais ça," an interview in *Tel Quel*, no. 59 (Fall 1974), translated in *New French Feminisms*, pp. 134–38. Kristeva has written mainly about male writers, but see her comments on some typically feminine themes in a dozen recent French women writers in "Oscillation," *Tel Quel*, no. 48 (Summer 1974): 100–102. She comments on certain elements of women's style in her interview with van Rossum-Guyon (see n.3), although she derives them from social rather than libidinal sources.

7. Luce Irigaray, an interview, "Women's Exile," in *Ideology & Consciousness*, no. 1 (1977): 62–67, translated and introduced by Diana Adlam and Couze Venn.

8. Irigaray, "Ce Sexe qui n'en est pas un," in *Ce Sexe qui n'en est pas un* (Paris: Minuit, 1977), translated in *New French Feminisms*, p. 103, and in this volume. Irigaray's books since *Ce Sexe* are *Et l'Une ne bouge sans l'autre* (Paris: Minuit, 1979) and *Amante marine* (Paris: Minuit, 1980). Her first book was a clinical study, *Le Langage des déments* (The Hague: Mouton, 1973).

9. *New French Feminisms*, p. 105.

10. Irigaray discusses the historical position of women in Marxist terms in "Le Marché aux femmes," in *Ce Sexe*. Her responses to Nietzsche are in *Amante marine*.

11. Hélène Cixous's studies of male writers include her doctoral thesis, *L'Exil de Joyce ou l'art du remplacement* (Paris: Grasset, 1968); *Prénoms de personne (sur Hoffman, Kleist, Poe, Joyce)* (Paris: Seuil, 1974); and introductions to James Joyce and Lewis Carroll for Aubier. Since 1975, all her books have been published by des femmes.

12. Cixous, "Entretien avec Françoise van Rossum-Guyon," *RSH* 168 (December 1977): 488. "Ça parle" is a Lacanian formula, but elsewhere (in her fiction/essay *Partie* [Paris: des femmes, 1976], for example) she mocks what she sees as the Father/phallus obsession of recent psychoanalysis.

13. Cixous, "Entretien," p. 487; and *Vivre l'orange* [includes an English version by Cixous with Ann Liddle and Sarah Cornell] (Paris: des femmes, 1980), pp. 9, 105–107.

14. Cixous, "Sorties," in *La Jeune née* (Paris: Bibliotheque 10/18, 1975).

15. *New French Feminism*, pp. 259–60.

16. The opening manifesto of *Questions féministes* is a long and persuasive critique of *néo-féminité*, translated in *New French Feminisms* as "Variations on Common Themes," pp. 212–30. See also the appraisal by Beverly Brown and Parveen Adama, "The Feminine Body and Feminist Politics," *m/f* 3 (1979): 33–37.

17. Juliet Mitchell, *Psychoanalysis and Feminism* (New York: Vintage, 1975). See especially "The Holy Family, Part 4: The Different Self, the Phallus and the Father," pp. 382–98.

18. Nancy Chodorow, *The Reproduction of Mothering* (Berkeley: University of California Press. 1978).

19. Dorothy Dinnerstein, *The Mermaid and the Minotaur: Sexual Arrangements and Human Malaise* (New York: Harper and Row, 1977).

20. Jacqueline Rose, in an article on Freud's analysis of the hysteric Dora, emphasizes that the male/female roles internalized by the child enter the unconscious at such a deep

level that they govern the production of dreams. Dora, who desires a woman, represents herself as a man—a striking example of the socialized image of desire, "'Dora'—Fragment of an Analysis," *m/f* [1979]: 5–21.

21. Wittig's books have all been translated into English: *L'Opopanox* by Helen Weaver (Plainfield, Vt.: Daugter's Press Reprint, 1976); *Les Guérillères* by David Le Vay (New York: Avon, 1973); *The Lesbian Body* by David Le Vay (New York: Avon 1976); *Lesbian Peoples: Material for a Dictionary* (with substantial revisions) by Wittig and Sande Zeig (New York: Avon, 1979).

22. Wittig, "The Straight Mind," speech given at the Feminist as Scholar Conference in May 1979 at Barnard College, New York, N.Y.

23. Wittig, "One Is Not Born a Woman," text of the speech given at the City University of New York Graduate Center, September 1979.

24. Colette Guillaumin, "Question de différence," *Questions féministes* 6 (September 1979): 3–21. Guillaumin points out that the claim to "difference" comes from other oppressed groups as well (Third World and U.S. blacks, for example), who have not yet succeeded in putting their desire for political self-determination into effect. To assert their difference against the ruling class strengthens their group solidarity, but at the expense of an analysis of the political sources of that difference.

25. Madeleine Gagnon, "Corps I," *New French Feminisms*, p. 180. See Changal Chawaf for a similar statement, in "La Chair linguistique," *New French Feminisms*, pp. 177–78.

26. Cora Kaplan combines psychoanalytic and anthropological accounts of women's hesitations to speak, in "Language and Gender," *Papers on Patriarchy* (Brighton, England: Women's Publishing Collective, 1976). Similarly, Sandra M. Gilbert and Susan Gubar demonstrate how socially derived ambivalence toward the role of writer has acted upon women's writing in English, in *The Madwoman in the Attic: The Woman Writer and the Nineteenth-Century Literary Imagination* (New Haven: Yale University Press, 1979).

27. See Tillie Olsen's *Silences* (New York: Delacorte, 1979) for a discussion of the practical demands and self-doubts that have hindered women's writing, especially "The Writer-Woman: One out of Twelve," pp. 177–258.

28. Christiane Rochefort, "Are Women Writers Still Monsters?" a speech given at the University of Wisconsin, Madison, Wis., February 1975, translated in *New French Feminisms*, pp. 185–86.

29. "Concentrism" is Elaine Showalter's term, used in a speech, "Feminist Literary Theory and Other Impossibilities," given at the Smith College Conference on Feminist Literary Criticism, Northampton, Mass., October 25, 1980.

SUSAN STANFORD FRIEDMAN

CREATIVITY AND THE CHILDBIRTH METAPHOR
gender difference in literary discourse

> Thus, great with child to speak, and helpless in my throes,
> Biting my trewand pen, beating myself for spite,
> "Fool," said my muse to me, "look in thy heart and write."
>
> PHILIP SIDNEY (1591)

> The poet is in labor. She has been told that it will not hurt but it has hurt
> so much that pain and struggle seem, just now, the only reality. But at the
> very moment when she feels she will die, or that she is already in hell,
> she hears the doctor saying, "Those are the shoulders you are feeling
> now"—and she knows the head is out then, and the child is pushing and
> sliding out of her, insistent, a poem.
>
> DENISE LEVERTOV (1967)

The childbirth metaphor has yoked artistic creativity and human procreativity for centuries in writers as disparate as Philip Sidney and Erica Jong, William Shakespeare and Mary Shelley, Alexander Pope and Denise Levertov. Men as well as women have used the metaphor extensively, taking female anatomy as a model for human creativity in sharp contrast with the equally common phallic analogy, which uses male anatomy for its paradigm.[1] As Sandra Gilbert and Susan Gubar have shown, the association of the pen and paintbrush with the phallus in metaphors of creativity has resulted in an "anxiety of authorship" for aspiring women writers: to wield a pen is a masculine act that puts the woman writer at war with her body and her culture.[2] In contrast to the phallic analogy that implicitly excludes women from creativity, the childbirth metaphor validates women's artistic effort by unifying their mental and physical labor into (pro)-creativity.

The childbirth metaphor is a controversial one that has been both celebrated and rejected by contemporary feminist theorists, critics, and writers. On the one hand, French theorists who promote the concept of *l'écriture féminine* insist on a poetic of the female body. As Hélène Cixous writes, "women must write through their bodies." Women, "never far from 'mother,'" write "in white ink." Using the birth metaphor itself, Cixous describes "the gestation drive" as "just like the desire to write: a desire to live self from within, a desire for a swollen belly, for language, for blood."[3] Similarly, American poet Stephanie Mines seeks "a language structued like my body," and Sharon Olds describes both the birth of her child and her poem as "this giving birth, this glistening verb" in a "language of blood."[4] On the other hand, many feminists oppose modes of thought they consider biologically deterministic, essentialist, and regressive. Mary Ellmann's witty critique of all analogical thinking based on the body, whether phallic or ovarian, anticipates the more recent concerns of others.[5] Simone de Beauvoir warns that this concept of writing from the body establishes a "counter-penis," and Elaine Showalter and Nina Auerbach fear that it represents the development of a regressive biologism. Showalter asks "if to write is metaphorically to give birth, from what organ can males generate texts?" "Anatomy is textuality" within a biological paradigm, Showalter argues. Biological analogies ultimately exclude one sex from the creative process, and in a patriarchal society it is women's creativity that is marginalized. Ann Rosalind Jones further suggests that the concept of *l'écriture féminine* posits an essential female sexuality that lies outside culture, an ahistorical assumption that particularly ignores the differences among women across cultures and through time. Poet Erica Jong states flatly that the comparison of "human gestation to human creativity" is "thoroughly inexact."[6]

Without attempting to resolve this debate, this essay will contribute to it by examining the ways in which women and men have encoded different concepts of creativity and procreativity into the metaphor itself. Highlighting how, in Elizabeth Abel's words, "gender informs and complicates both the writing and the reading of texts," the childbirth metaphor provides a concrete instance of genuine gender difference in literary discourse as constituted both by the readers and the writers of a given text.[7] I will explore three aspects of the childbirth metaphor: first, the cultural resonance of the childbirth metaphor; second, gender difference in the metaphor's meaning as constructed in the process of *reading;* and third, gender difference as reflected in the process of *writing.* Examination of these aspects will reveal that women writers have often risked the metaphor's dangerous biologism in order to challenge fundamental binary oppositions of patriarchal ideology between word and flesh, creativity and procreativity, mind and body. Cixous's utopian call for women's writing from the body may lament that "with a few rare exceptions, there has not yet been any writing that inscribes femininity."[8] But women's use of the childbirth metaphor demonstrates not only a "marked" discourse distinct from phallogocentric male use of the same metaphor but also a subversive inscription of women's (pro)creativity that has existed for centuries.

CULTURAL RESONANCE OF THE CHILDBIRTH METAPHOR

Contextual reverbations of the childbirth metaphor ensure that it can never be "dead," merely what Max Black calls "an expression that no longer has a pregnant metaphorical use."[9] The childbirth metaphor has always been "pregnant" with resonance because childbirth itself is not neutral in literary discourse. Whether it appears as subject or vehicle of expression, childbirth has never achieved what Roland Barthes calls "writing degree zero," the language of "innocence," "freed from responsibility in relation to all possible context."[10] The context of the childbirth metaphor is the institution of motherhood in the culture at large. Consequently, the meaning of the childbirth metaphor is overdetermined by psychological and ideological resonances evoked by, but independent of, the text. No doubt, there is variation in the intensity and kind of conscious and unconscious charge that any reader or writer brings to the metaphor. But because it relies on an event fundamental to the organization of culture and psyche, the birth metaphor remains "pregnant" with significance.

The paradox of the childbirth metaphor is that its contextual resonance is fundamentally at odds with the very comparison it makes. While the metaphor draws together mind and body, word and womb, it also evokes the sexual division of labor upon which Western patriarchy is founded. The vehicle of the metaphor (procreation) acts in opposition to the tenor it serves (creation) because it inevitably reminds the reader of the historical realities that contradict the comparison being made. Facing constant challenges to their creativity, women writers often find their dilemma expressed in terms of the opposition between books and babies. Ellen Glasgow, for example, recalled the advice of a literary man: "The best advice I can give you is to stop writing and go back to the South and have some babies. The greatest woman is not the woman who has written the finest book, but the woman who has had the finest babies." [11] Male paternity of texts has not precluded their paternity of children. But for both material and ideological reasons, maternity and creativity have appeared to be mutually exclusive to women writers. [12]

The historical separation evoked by the childbirth metaphor is so entangled with the language of creation and procreation that the metaphor's very words establish their own linguistic reverberation. Words about the production of babies and books abound with puns, common etymologies, and echoing sounds that simultaneously yoke and separate creativity and procreativity. This wordplay reveals not only currents of unconscious thought as Sigmund Freud has described but also the structures of patriarchy that have divided *labor* into men's *production* and women's *reproduction*. Underlying these words is the familiar dualism of mind and body, a key component of Western patriarchal ideology. *Creation* is the act of the mind that brings something new into existence. *Procreation* is the act of the body that reproduces the species. A man *conceives* an idea in his brain, while a woman *conceives* a baby in her womb, a difference highlighted by the post-industrial designation of the public sphere as man's domain and the private sphere as woman's place. The *pregnant* body is necessarily female; the *pregnant* mind is the mental province of genius, most frequently understood to be inherently masculine. [13] *Confinement* of men suggests imprisonment—indignities to, not the fulfillment of manhood. *Delivery* from confinement suggests the restoration of men's autonomy, not its death. *Confinement* of women, in contrast, alludes to the final stages of pregnancy before *delivery* into the bonds of maternity, the very joy of which has suppressed their individuality in patriarchy.

These linguistically inscribed separations echo religious ones, which in turn resonate through the childbirth metaphor. God's punishment of Adam and Eve in Genesis has provided divine authority for the sexual division of labor. Adam's *labor* is to produce the goods of society by the "sweat of his brow," an idiom that collapses man's muscular and mental work. Eve's *labor* is to reproduce the species in pain and subservience to Adam. More importantly, the Christian tradition built on the masculine monotheism of Judaism by appropriating the power of the Word for a masculine diety and his son. In the worship of ancient near-Eastern goddesses such as Inanna, Isis, and Demeter, woman's physical capacity to give birth served as the paradigm of all origins. But where God the Father supplanted the Goddess as Mother, the mind became the symbolic womb of the universe. According to the gospel of John, "In the beginning was the Word, and the Word was with God, and the Word was God. The same was in the beginning with God. All things were made by Him; and without Him was not any thing made that was made." The power of the Word became the paradigm of male creativity, indeed the foundation of Western patriarchal ideology.[14]

This masculine appropriation of the creative Word attempts to reduce women to the processes of their body. As Friedrich Nietzsche's Zarathustra pronounces: "Everything concerning woman is a puzzle, and everything concerning woman has one solution: it is named pregnancy."[15] This "solution" projects the concept of woman as being without thought, without speech, in the creation of culture. Before the discovery of the ovum, woman's womb was represented as the mere material vessel into which man dropped his divine seed. But even after women's active part in conception became understood, cultural representations of woman based in the mind-body split continued to separate the creation of man's mind from the procreation of woman's body. According to patriarchal definition, de Beauvoir writes, woman "has ovaries, a uterus; these peculiarities imprison her in her subjectivity, circumscribe her within the limits of her own nature. It is often said that she thinks with her glands."[16] Julia Kristeva argues that phallogo-centric hegemony makes woman "a specialist in the unconscious, a witch, a bac-chanalian. . . . . A *marginal speech,* with . . . regard to science, religion, and philosophy of the *polis* (witch, child, underdeveloped, not even a poet, at best a poet's accomplice). A *pregnancy.*"[17]

The linguistic, religious, and historical resonance of the childbirth metaphor contradicts the fundamental comparison the metaphor makes. Although its basic analogy validates women's participation in literary creativity, its contextual refer-ence calls that participation into question. Because contextual resonance comes alive in a given text through the agency of the reader, the reader has a key role to play in the constitution of the metaphor's meaning.

GENDER DIFFERENCE: READING THE CHILDBIRTH METAPHOR

Reader response theories emphasize the role of the reader to the construction meaning in any text.[18] Situated differently in relationship to the issue of moth-erhood, female and male readers are most likely to hear the contextual resonance of the childbirth metaphor from their gendered perspectives. But I would like to focus on the presence of "the reader in the text" as it is established by the specific nature of metaphor. Contradiction is inherent in metaphor, which presents "an insight into likeness" seen "in spite of, and through, the different."[19] The interac-tion of a metaphor's component parts—that is, the similar and the dissimilar—requires a reader to complete the process of reconciliation. Paradoxically, a literal falsehood becomes a figurative truth in the mind of the reader. The reader "con-ceives" the new truth by seeing the dynamic interaction between contradictory elements that move toward resolution. Karsten Harries identifies this interaction as a "semantic collision" that leads to "semantic collusion" as the reader becomes aware of the grounds of comparison.[20] Paul Ricoeur describes this process as a "transition from literal incongruence to metaphorical congruence," that nonetheless retains a "split reference." From this "semantic clash" a new meaning emerges, but it continues to evoke the "previous incompatibility and the new compatibility."[21] For Paul de Man, this clash represents the inherently subversive nature of metaphor, which disrupts the logical discourse of the rational mind.[22] Metaphor's dependence on the reader for an awareness of contradiction and resolution represents a linguistic "cultivation of intimacy," according to Ted Cohen. Like a joke, a metaphor presents a puzzle to the reader, one which results in a "sense of close community" and "shared awareness" once it has been resolved.[23]

Levertov's extended narrative metaphor (see epigraph), which invites the reader to feel the exultant pain of giving birth to a poem, provides a good example for the role of the reader in the creation of meaning. The tension that gives this metaphor its potency is built upon the reader's awareness of both "incompatibility" and "compatibility." The first collision that the reader must overcome is the metaphor's literal falsehood: the equation of poem and baby. The poet's extreme effort to birth the head, the momentary hesitation at the baby's shoulders, and the final insistence of delivery are details so precisely tied to the last moments of childbirth that they heighten the dissimilarity of creativities at the same time that they intensify the comparison. The second collision exists specifically in the reader's mind as a result of the metaphor's historical resonance. Levertov's metaphor defies the cultural separation of creation and procreation by joining the functions and feelings of mind and body. To move this collision toward collusion, the reader must follow Levertov's subversion of historical forces.

The reader's sex and perspective on childbirth no doubt affect the resolution of Levertov's metaphor, a variation that I will not address in this essay. Instead, the gender difference in the reading of the metaphor that I will explore is the alteration of meaning that results from the reader's awareness of the sex of the metaphor's author. We seldom read any text without knowledge of the author's sex. The title page itself initiates a series of expectations that influence our reading throughout, expectations intensified by the overdetermined childbirth metaphor. The reader's knowledge that Levertov is a woman, potentially a mother, "informs and complicates" the reading of her metaphor. This knowledge changes the interaction process of the metaphor—its incongruity, its movement toward congruity, and its implied "community" of author and reader. Change the pronoun to "he" and the reader's construction of meaning would alter profoundly: "The poet is in labor. He has been told that it will not hurt but it has hurt so much. . . . The child is pushing out of him, insistent, a poem." This change introduces a new collision, one present to some degree in *all* metaphors featuring a parturient father. Confined to "headbirths," men *cannot* literally conceive and birth babies.[24] The reader's awareness of this biological collision contributes to a perpetual tension in the metaphor, one that threatens to overwhelm the movement toward resolution.

Levertov herself appears to have been sensitive to the impact of gender on the reader's completion of the metaphor's meaning. Immediately following her metaphor of the mother-poet is a metaphor of a father-poet who must watch from a distance the birth of the poem he begat. Levertov deliberately avoids making the two metaphors precisely parallel: "The poet is a father. Into the air, into the fictional landscape of the delivery room, wholly man-made. . . . emerges . . . the remote consequence of a dream of his, acted out nine months before, the rhythm that became words." [25] Levertov's refusal to envision male creation of a poem in the concrete terms of female physiological delivery underlines the significance of the actor's biological capacity to the reading of the metaphor. Her evocative description of the impersonal, scrubbed delivery rooms of the fifties and sixties heightens the reader's awareness of historical context. The similar, yet dissimilar analogies further clarify the multilayered complexities of reading the birth metaphor. As a woman writer, Levertov has used the birth metaphor to describe both a female and a male act of creativity. In reading these metaphors, we are not only aware of her perspective as a woman, but also of how the shift in the actor's biological sex subtly alters the dynamics and meaning of the metaphor.

By focusing on the reader's awareness of the author's (or actor's) sex, we can pinpoint the gender difference in male- and female-authored metaphors. A male childbirth metaphor has three collisions for the reader to overcome: the literally false equation of books and babies, the biological impossibility of men birthing both books and babies, and the cultural separation of creation and procreation. These collisions do more than provide effective tension for the metaphor. The metaphor's incongruity overshadows congruity; collision drowns out collusion. The metaphor's tenor (creativity) and vehicle (procreativity) are kept perpetually distinct. More than an interaction of sameness and difference, the male metaphor is an analogy at war with itself. History and biology combine to make it a form of literary *couvade*, male appropriation of procreative labor to which women have been confined. Man's womblike mind and phallic pen are undeniably contrasting images of creativity, but underlying both metaphors are resonating allusions to a brotherhood of artists. The "close community" to which Cohen refers is established through a "shared awareness" of male birthright and female confinement.

The impact on the reader of these heightened collisions in the male childbirth metaphor is evident in an eighteenth-century mock-heroic conceit about a self-indulgent poet: "He produced a couplet. When our friend is delivered of a couplet, with infinite labour, and pain, he takes to his bed, has straw laid down, the knocker tied up, and expects his friends to call and make inquiries." [26] The irony of this extended metaphor depends upon the reader's continuing awareness of the comparison's biological impossibility. The speaker, Reverend Sidney Smith, maintains the separation of tenor and vehicle in order to diminish the poet *manqué* for acting ridiculously like what he is not and could never be—a postpartum mother. Fusion of creation and procreation in the mind of the reader would destroy the metaphor's humor.

The way in which cultural as well as biological resonances intensify the contradictory core of the male birth metaphor is evident in James Joyce's more recent variations of the analogy in his letters and *Ulysses*. In a letter to his wife Nora on 21 August 1912, Joyce writes: "I went then into the backroom of the office and sitting at the table, thinking of the book I have written, the child which I have carried for years and years in the womb of the imagination as you carried in your womb the children you love, and of how I had fed it day after day out of my brain and my memory."[27] Joyce's metaphor compares his mental production with Nora's pregnancies, an analogy that draws together the labor of women and men. But at the same time, Joyce evokes the distinctions between the mind and the body, between his wife's procreativity and his own creativity. His comparison replicates the sexual division of labor and reinforces the mind-body split permeating the patristic tradition that influenced his own Jesuit background. Joyce carried his childbirth metaphor to elaborate lengths in the planning and execution of "Oxen in the Sun," the episode in *Ulysses* in which Bloom visits the lying-in hospital where Mrs. Purefoy has been in labor for three days. As the tired woman labors to birth a baby, the exhausted narrator moves through the gestation of literary style from the earliest English alliterative poetics up to the "frightful jumble" of modern dialects. Mind and body, word and deed, man and woman, are simultaneously drawn together in analogy but separated irrevocably in function. Joyce's extensive plans for the chapter highlight this continuing separation. He charted the gestation of styles according to the nine months of pregnancy and assigned to each style images and motifs appropriate to the corresponding stages of fetal development. Like Nora, Mrs. Purefoy is delivered of a baby. Like Joyce himself, the narrator is delivered of the Word. The fact that Joyce partly envies the fecundity of female flesh and despairs at the sterility of male minds does not alter the fundamental sexual dualism of his complex birth metaphors: Joyce's women produce infants through the channel of flesh, while his men produce a brainchild through the agency of language.[28]

Paradoxically, the childbirth metaphor that reinforces the separation of creation and procreation in a male text becomes its own opposite in a female text. Instead of contributing to the reification of Western culture, the female metaphor expresses a fundamental rebellion against it. It represents a defiance of historical realities and a symbolic reunion of mind and body, creation and procreation. The female metaphor establishes a matrix of creativities based on woman's double-birthing potential. As Amy Lowell asks in "The Sisters," her poem about the female poetic tradition: "Why are we/ Already mother-creatures, double bearing/ With matrices in body and brain?"[29] Within the matrices of body and brain, *both* creation and procreation become multifaceted events—physical and mental, rational and emotional, conscious and unconscious, public and private, personal and political.

The different meaning of the female childbirth metaphor results from the way the reader alters the interaction of incongruity and congruity in a woman's analogy. The metaphor's literal falsehood remains the same as it does in a male comparison. Babies are never books. But the reader's awareness that the metaphor features a woman changes how the biological and historical resonances work. First, the reader knows that the author has the biological capacity men lack to birth both books and babies. Second, the reader recognizes that the author's analogy defies the cultural prescription of separated creativities. The metaphor's historical resonance does not emphasize the division of creativity and procreativity, as it does in a male text. Rather, it makes the reader aware that the woman's reclamation of the pregnant Word is itself a transcendence of historical prescription, one that perfectly conjoins form and content. Consequently, the woman's authorship of the birth metaphor enhances the metaphor's movement toward a reconciliation of contradictory parts. The intensification of collusion and congruity in the female metaphor allows the tenor and vehicle to mingle and fuse, while the same elements in the male metaphor remain irrevocably distinct. This resolution, which relies on the reader's awareness of the author's sex, not only completes the metaphor but more fundamentally affirms woman's special access to creativity. In so doing, the woman's metaphor is genuinely subversive or "disruptive." [30] Rather than covertly excluding women from the community of artists as the male metaphor does, the woman's birth metaphor suggests that her procreative powers make her specially suited to her creative labors. God the Father is no longer the implicit model of creativity. Instead, the Goddess as Mother provides the paradigm for the (re)production of woman's speech.

A seventeenth-century poem by Katherine Philips, well-known in her day as "The Matchless Orinda," illustrates how the poet's double-birthing potential reduces the childbirth metaphor's collision and moves its contradiction swiftly toward resolution. The poem is an elegy for her infant who died forty days after birth.

> Tears are my Muse and sorrow all my art,
> So piercing groans must be thy elegy.
> . . . .
> An off'ring too for thy sad tomb I have,
> Too just a tribute to thy early hearse,
> Receive these gasping numbers to thy grave,
> The last of thy unhappy mother's verse. [31]

Elegies conventionally move from the poet's grief to a consolation based on immortality achieved through art. Orinda's "tribute" to her baby is no exception. What makes her elegy different is the presence of the childbirth metaphor to affirm this immortality. The "piercing groans" of grief that produce the elegy recall the pain of childbirth. The poet's "gasping" labor with her verse, motivated by a new mother's grief, echoes her own labor in delivery forty days ago. Both labors result in a poem that (re)births her son in the permanent domain of literature. Tenor and vehicle reverberate back and forth, each describing the experience of the other in a poem whose subject is simultaneously the pains of creativity and procreativity saddened by death. The reader's awareness of Orinda's biological and artistic motherhood makes this fusion of creation and procreation into (pro)creation possible.

Anne Bradstreet's poem "The Author to Her Book," not only demonstrates the significance of biology, but it also illustrates how the reader's knowledge of female authorship changes the metaphor's historical resonance. Bradstreet's poem, found among her papers after her death, served as the preface to the posthumous second edition of her poems. Her brother-in-law had published the first edition without her knowledge. In a prefatory poem, he called the anonymous volume her "infant" and imagined how she would "complain 't is too unkind/ To force a woman's birth, provoke her pain,/ Expose her labors to the world's disdain." [32] Like Orinda's birth metaphor, his comparison depends heavily on Bradstreet's biological maternity. Bradstreet answers and extends this childbirth metaphor for the entire twenty-five lines of poem, addressing her book as "Thou ill-formed offspring of my feeble brain,/ Who after birth didst by my side remain/ Till snatched from thence by friends, less wise than true."[33] The self-deprecation of her metaphor may reflect the insecurity of the woman writer in the public domain of letters. But it also exhibits an entirely conventional modesty characteristic of seventeenth-century male tropes which frequently beg mercy from the critics for their brainchildren.[34]

What makes Bradstreet's metaphor different from the birth metaphors of her time is the reader's awareness that her analogy defies the cultural prescription to procreativity. Like the male metaphor, her comparison of motherhood and authorship reminds the reader of their historical separation. But unlike the male metaphor, her analogy subverts that contextual resonance instead of reinforcing it. This defiance of history strengthens the comparison and promotes the resolution toward which all metaphors move. Where Joyce's tenor and vehicle remain distinct in "Oxen in the Sun," Bradstreet's metaphor unites motherhood and authorship into a new whole. Tenor and vehicle become indistinguishable as the poem becomes a definition of mothering children as well as books. Pride and modesty, joy and irritation, love and hate, represent the feelings she has as both mother and author toward the intertwined labors that fill her with ambivalence:

> At thy return my blushing was not small,
> My rambling brat (in print) should mother call,
> I cast thee by as one unfit for light,
> Thy visage was so irksome in my sight;
> Yet being mine own, at length affection would
> Thy blemishes amend, if so I could:
> I washed thy face, but more defects I saw,
> And rubbing off a spot still made a flaw.
> I stretched thy joints to make thee even feet,
> Yet still thou run'st more hobbling than is meet;
> In better dress to trim thee was my mind,
> But nought save homespun cloth i'th'house I find.
> In this array 'mongst vulgars may'st thou roam.
> In critic's hands beware thou dost not come.[35]

The role of the reader in completing the birth metaphors of Reverend Smith and Philips, Joyce and Bradstreet, is crucial, so imporant, in fact, that it suggests a possible methodology for the broader attempt to identify gender difference or a feminine aesthetic in literary discourse or the visual arts. Such attempts usually posit gendered qualities independent of the reader residing in a given text's words, images, style, or technique. Virginia Woolf, for example, describes a feminine sentence, and Judy Chicago identifies circular forms in the visual arts as female imagery.[36] However useful in identifying gender-related tendencies, this approach is often imprecise at best and implicitly prescriptive at worst. Attempts to identify the sex of a writer or an artist without external clues often fail. Exceptions for either sex are problematic. How, for example, should we describe a male painter who uses core imagery or a woman who favors pointed shapes? The terms "feminine" and "masculine" as descriptions of qualities inherent in the image suggest that the man who uses "feminine" imagery and the woman who uses "masculine" imagery are not painting "through the body."

The case of the childbirth metaphor highlights such theoretical and method-ological problems and illustrates the usefulness of a reader response approach to the identification of gender difference.[37] The distinction between female and male discourse lies not in the metaphor itself but rather in the way its final mean-ing is constituted in the process of reading. Without external contexts, it is often impossible to identify the sex of an author using a childbirth metaphor, espe-cially because male use has been at least as common as female use. Take, for example, the extended metaphor of nineteenth-century writer:

> To pass from conception to execution, to produce, to bring the idea to birth, to raise the child laboriously from infancy, to put it nightly to sleep surfeited, to kiss it in the mornings with the hungry heart of a mother, to clean it, to clothe it fifty times over in new garments which it tears and casts away, and yet not revolt against the trials of this agitated life—this unwearying mater-nal love, this habit of creation—this execution and its toil.

This loving description of literary parentage is less ambivalent and more senti-mental than Bradstreet's, but it presents a similar emphasis on birth leading to a lifetime of maternal nurturance. A theoretical approach that identifies male or female discourse as a quality solely in the text would have difficulty explaining that this metaphor is Honoré de Balzac's description of the creative process.[38] An approach that focuses on the *reader* in the identification of gendered discourse is better equipped to deal with the revelation of authorship. The meaning of Bal-zac's metaphor changes with the reader's awareness of its generator's sex. As a male metaphor, this nineteenth-century passage expresses a biologically impos-sible and historically unlikely embrace of motherhood. As a female metaphor, this passage would express a defiant reunion of what patriarchal culture has kept mutually exclusive—"this unwearying maternal love, this habit of creation." This difference of meaning in the very same words exists in the mind of the reader because of how gender generates alternative readings of the childbirth metaphor.

GENDER DIFFERENCE: WRITING THE CHILDBIRTH METAPHOR

The significance of "the reader in the text" does not preclude a corresponding analysis of the writer in the text. Gender "informs and complicates" the *writing* as well as the *reading* of the childbirth metaphor. Any given birth metaphor exists within the artist's individual vision and specific formulation—the function it serves within the larger text and project of the artist. Sidney's metaphor (see epi-graph), for example, serves the larger purpose of implicating poetic inspiration with desire and initiating the Renaissance love plot: Astrophel's love for Stella makes "great with child to speak." Balzac identifies with woman's lifetime labor and Joyce separates himself from it. Levertov's mother- and father-poets exist to make her point that the poet is "in the world," not separate from it. T. S. Eliot takes recourse to the metaphor to express the opposite, his theory of the text's autonomy: "he is oppressed by a burden which he must bring to birth in order to obtain relief. . . . And then he can say to the poem: 'Go away! Find a place for yourself in a book—and don't expect *me* to take any further interest in you.'" [39] Jean Rhys uses the metaphor to decide when to let go of *Wide Sargasso Sea*. Her publisher reported that "she wrote to tell me that she had been having a recurring dream in which, to her dismay, she was pregnant. Then it came again, only this time the baby had been born and she was looking at it in its cradle—'such a puny weak thing. So the book must be finished, and that must be what I think about it really. I don't dream about it any more.'" [40] The pervasive use of the birth metaphor at Los Alamos to describe the creation of the first atomic bomb (known as "Oppenheimer's baby," christened informally as "Little Boy," and dropped from a plane named Enola Gay, after the pilot's mother) serves to obscure the bomb's destructiveness and implicate women in its birth. [41] At first glance, individual variation appears more significant than the author's sex to the full meaning of the childbirth metaphor.

Nonetheless, without denying exceptions to generalization, we can broadly cluster formulations of the birth metaphor along gender lines. These gender differences in the *writing* of the metaphor originate in the contrasting perspectives toward childbirth that women and men bring to their individual formulations. For biological and historical reasons, childbirth is an event whose meaning is constituted differently by women and men. This difference informs why they use it and what they use it for. Men's use of the metaphor begins in distance from and attraction to the Other. Karen Horney, for example, asks if men's "impulse to create" is "due to their feeling of playing a relatively small part in the creation of living beings, which constantly impels them to an overcompensation in achievement." Gershon Legman applies this theory specifically to the male birth metaphor, which he calls "a male motherhood of authorship," an archetypal fantasy of great power and persistence determined by largely unconscious fear and envy of woman's sexual and reproductive powers. Elizabeth Sacks expands on this "womb envy" to say that the male metaphor serves as "an essential outlet for unconscious or repressed feminine elements in the masculine psyche." [42] Its use reflects the attempt to reabsorb into consciousness those repressed elements in themselves that culture has projected onto woman. Because of these psychological determinants, then, the male metaphor might be a covert, indeed, largely unconscious, tribute to woman's special generative power, a vestige from the worship of the primal goddess as paradigm of (pro)creativity. This "tribute" is deceptive, however. The male comparison of creativity with woman's procreativity equates the two as if both were valued equally, whereas they are not. This elevation of procreativity seemingly idealizes woman and thereby obscures woman's real lack of authority to create art as well as babies. As an appropriation of women's (pro)creativity, the male metaphor subtly helps to perpetuate the confinement of women to procreation.

On the whole, the function of male birth metaphors within the context of the writer's larger vision tends to reflect the dominant cultural representations of woman's nature current in a given historical era. Throughout the evolution of Judeo-Christian patriarchy, women have served as the symbol for qualities men desire and reject, revere and fear, envy and hate. Defined and controlled within an androcentric system of representation, the ideological concepts of women's sexual and reproductive powers have been the backbone of these ambivalent perspectives. This general representation stands behind the evolution of meaning in the male birth metaphor described by Terry Castle. She notes, for example, that male birth metaphors were abundant both during the Enlightenment and the Romantic era—but with opposite meanings. Satirists like Pope and Dryden associated the human birth process with "deformed poetic productivity" and regularly deflected in onto the enemy poet. The bad poet was above all a "begetter" who breeds out of his own distempered fancy repulsive "offspring" because his lack of reason makes him like "the one who gives birth, who conceives and brings forth, [who] is nowhere in control, but rather is subject to a purely spontaneous animal function." Castle argues that the equally abundant, but overwhelmingly positive uses of the birth metaphor in the Romantic period resulted from a fundamental change in poetics. The Romantics repeatedly used the metaphor not to condemn their enemies but to define the production of art as "a spontaneous process independent of intention, precept, or even consciousness.[43] Women's lack of control over pregnancy attracted the Romantics, who affirmed the "organic nature of poetic genius" that produces a poem effortlessly, without the painful struggle of the intellect. As Percy Shelley wrote in his *Defense of Poetry*, "a great statue or picture grows under the power of the artist as a child in the mother's womb."[44]

What Castle did not note is that this shift from repulsion to idealization parallels a historical evolution in the representation of women. In both periods, the organic processes of human body were symbolically associated with women, along with emotion and intuition. However, the Enlightenment celebration of Reason incorporated a definition of the body as the inferior, "animal" aspect of human nature. Although the eighteenth century saw the dramatic rise of writing by and for women, disgust for sheer physicality or emotionalism often represented by woman was common among the Augustan satirists.[45] Consequently, eighteenth-century male birth metaphors embodied this intertwined disgust for woman and the human body she represented. In his *Essay Concerning Human Understanding,* John Locke's attack on all metaphor as a mode of knowledge illustrates this matrix of meaning. He calls metaphor a "monstrous birth," a dangerous "changeling" of the rational mind, and further denounces it by likening it to woman, whose seductive power enslaves the masculine mind. As woman seduces man, so metaphor traps reason, and procreativity inhibits creativity.[46] Within such a gynophobic ethos, the childbirth metaphor becomes the ultimate insult to a male artist's creativity.

The Romantic period's embrace of intuition, emotion, organicism—all qualities associated with the feminine—transformed the birth metaphor into something positive. But whether rejected as repulsive or celebrated as creative, woman's procreativity in both the Enlightenment and the Romantic periods was perceived through an androcentric lens as a mindless, unconscious, uncontrolled act of the body. Both the positive and negative manifestations of the male metaphor perpetuate the mind–body split it attempts to transcend through analogy. Both therefore reaffirm creativity as the province of men and procreativity as the primary destiny of women.

For women, as for men, use of the childbirth metaphor is psychologically charged and overdetermined. But while men's use of the metaphor begins in a fascination for the Other, women's use originates in conflict with themselves as Other. Unlike men, women using the metaphor necessarily confront the patriarchally imposed, essential dilemma of their artistic identity: the binary system that conceives woman and writer, motherhood and authorhood, babies and books, as mutually exclusive. Women writers have faced childbirth with an ambivalence born of its association with their status in society. Consequently, their birth metaphors variously encode the very issues of their authorship as women and their womanhood as authors.

The childbirth metaphors of women and men differ not only in their psychological charge but also in their function within the larger work. While men's metaphors often reflect the ethos of their times, women's metaphors tend to be deeply personal statements about how they try to resolve their conflict with cultural prescription. Because of its affirmation of a unified (pro)creation, Levertov's birth metaphor is more like the birth metaphors of Bradstreet and Philips than it is like the ambivalent birth metaphors of some contemporary women writers. Not so predictably in tune with the times as male metaphors, female metaphors are often figurative expressions of the strategies by which their authors confront the double bind of the woman writer: how to be a woman and a writer within a discourse that has steadfastly separated the two. Consequently, where men's metaphors tend to perpetuate the separation of creativities, women's metaphors tend to deconstruct it.

In general, women's birth metaphors cover a wide spectrum of personal statement, reproducing the central debates over the relationship between poetics and the body. At one end of the continuum, women's birth metaphors express a fundamental acceptance of a masculinist aesthetic that separates creativity and procreativity. At the other end of the continuum is a defiant celebration of (pro)creation, a gynocentric aesthetic based on the body. At points along the spectrum are expressions of fear, ambivalence, and a dialectical search for transcendence of the binary system of creativity. Although any one of these metaphoric expressions might be found at different historical periods, the more widespread feminism has been at any given point in time, the more likely it has been for birth metaphors to cluster at the subversive end of the spectrum. In the twentieth century, the spread of feminism has combined with the greater freedom for discourses on sexuality to break the relative silence about the childbirth in literary discourse. Although childbirth has been central to women's experience, it has been at the periphery of literary representation until the last fifty years. As Muriel Rukeyser notes, "one is on the edge of the absurd the minute one tries to relate the experience of birth to the silence about it in poetry."[47] For a long time women have indirectly addressed this largely ignored, trivialized, distorted, or taboo subject by introducing their versions of the birth metaphor into literary discourse. Concurrent with the second wave of feminism from about 1965 to the present, there has been an explosion of women's writing about pregnancy, childbirth, nursing, and motherhood. Birth imagery to describe the self-creation of both woman and artist permeates contemporary women's writing. Nonetheless, women's birth metaphors still retain an individual stamp encoding each woman's negotiation of the conflict between creation and procreation. An exploration of women's writing at different points along the continuum will illustrate representative resolutions of this conflict, as well as the basic contrast with male birth metaphors.

The first point on the continuum of women's birth metaphors is the use of the metaphor to confirm the patriarchal separation of creativities. Fanny Appleton Longfellow, for example, relies on the metaphor to explain her resignation from creative work to engage in procreative labor. She stopped writing her journal after the birth of her first baby and notes in her final entry: "With this day my journal ends, for I have now a living one to keep faithfully, more faithfully than this." Less Victorian than Mrs. Longfellow, Elinor Wylie nonetheless uses the metaphor to express her sense of failure as a woman after repeated miscarriages. She thinks of her poems as substitute children, born of a mother *manqué*. Margaret Mead, a writer, mother, and feminist, projects her anxiety about this rebellious combination onto her statement that "something very special happens to women when they know that they will not have a child—or any more children. . . . Suddenly, their whole creativity is released—they paint or write as never before." [48] These women from different historical periods nonetheless write into their analogies a belief that procreation and creation are mutually exclusive.

The next point along the continuum is birth metaphors encoding a fear of combining creation and procreation. Given that the underside of fear is often desire, such metaphors contain a matrix of forbidden wish and guilt for trespass. Mary Shelley, daughter of feminist Mary Wollstonecraft, did not have her mother's intrepid belief that women could fulfill the desire for both writing and mothering. [49] In *Frankenstein*, she relies on an elaborate narrative of the birth metaphor to express her essential fear that the patriarchal separation of creativities is necessary. The novel is a macabre reversal of the male Romantic metaphors of organic creativity. Shelley uses the metaphor negatively in both the narrative and her 1831 preface to a later edition. She refers to her book as "my hideous progeny," an "offspring" about a scientist who seeks to discover "the deepest mysteries of creation" by procreating life. Frankenstein's quest takes the form of doing with his brain what women do with their bodies, a point Shelley emphasizes with her pervasive analogies between his work and the stages of woman's "confinement" throughout the preface and the narrative. [50] The life he creates from the womb of his brain, however, is not the beautiful child of woman's production, but a hideous-looking monster who terrifies his "father" and "creator." Frankenstein rejects his creation, denies the monster's repeated requests for love, and thereby sets in motion the monster's revengeful destruction of Frankenstein's family. One approach to this multifaceted tale is to read it as an exploration of creativity ridden with anxiety and anger about gender, motherhood, and artistic creation. Look at what happens, Shelley seems to say, when men try to procreate. And what will happen when I try to create like a man? [51]

Mary Shelley's encoded ambivalence is not far on the spectrum from women's use of the metaphor to explore more directly their desire for and fear of possible fusion of literary and literal motherhood. Sylvia Plath's fascination with pregnancy and childbirth is evident in a number of pathbreaking poems about women's amabivalence toward the changes in their bodies and identity that pregnancy brings, works such as "Three Women: A Poem for Three Voices," "Metaphors," "Morning Song," "You're," "Heavy Women," and "Nick and the Candlestick." "I'm a riddle in nine syllables/ . . . / I've eaten a bag of green apples,/ Boarded the train there's no getting off," she writes in "Metaphors." [52] Delighted with her experience of natural childbirth, what Adrienne Rich has called unalienated labor, Plath could write playfully about procreation as well. [53]

But first as a "riddle in nine syllables" and later, a mother-poet who, in the last year of her life, had to write at four A.M. before her babies awoke, Plath's child-birth metaphors for creativity are ridden with self-loathing and fear of motherhood as biological entrapment. The "childless woman" in "Childless Woman" is a poet whose "womb/ Rattles its pod/ . . . / Uttering nothing but blood." After the birth of her second child, she wrote a terrifying poem called "Barren Woman," in which her womb's emptiness is a metaphor for the emptiness of her creative mind.[54] In "Stillborn," the union of creation and procreation presages the silence of death.

> These poems do not live: it's a sad diagnosis.
> They grew their toes and fingers well enough
>
> . . . .
>
> They sit so nicely in the pickling fluid!
> They smile and smile and smile and smile at me.
>
> . . . .
>
> But they are dead, and their mother near dead with distraction,
> And they stupidly stare, and do not speak of her.[55]

In contrast to Plath, Erica Jong lives in a time and place where feminism has made the combination of motherhood and authorship more acceptable. Reflecting this historical change, her birth metaphors are less fearful than Plath's. Nonetheless, Jong's ambivalence leads her to embrace and then reject the metaphor, a wavering that suggests her awareness of the metaphor's double potential for regression and liberation. Poetry written before her own pregnancy uses metaphors of menstruation, pregnancy, and birth to test out the relationship between her body and her art. In "Dear Marys, Dear Mother, Dear Daughter," she recognizes that "Doctor Frankenstein/ was punished/ for his pride:/ the hubris of a man/ creating life."[56] In "Menstruation in May," Jong attempts to unite mind and body, creation and procreation.

> I squeeze my breast
> for the invisible ink of milk.
> I bear down hard—
> no baby's head appears.
> The poems keep flowing monthly
> like my blood.
> The word is flesh, I say
> still unconvinced.
> The Flesh is flesh.
> The word is on its own.[57]

Jesus was the incarnate God, the Word made flesh. Can woman, Jong asks, unite her word with her flesh? She tries out the same metaphoric equation of milk and ink that Cixous uses, but her attempt to posit a single (pro)creative process leaves her "still unconvinced." In "Playing with the Boys," Jong expresses more confidence in a body-based aesthetic as she links her pen, menstruation, and potential to birth babies in the definition of her art.

> I am not part of their game.
> I have no penis.
> I have a pen, two eyes
> & I bleed monthly.
>
> When the moon shines on the sea
> I see the babies
> riding on moonwaves
> asking to be born.[58]

When Jong became pregnant, however, this wavering turned into outright hostility to the birth metaphor in her essay "Creativity vs. Generativity." "Only a man (or a woman who had never been pregnant)," she writes, "would compare creativity to maternity, pregnancy to the creation of a poem or novel."[59] Underlying her resistance to the metaphor is both anger and fear. She quotes Joyce's letter to his wife and hears a territorial hostility to women writers in the male metaphor: "Men have the feeling that women can create life in their bodies, therefore, how dare they create art?"[60] Even more deeply, she fears that pregnancy will sabotage her creative drive: "I have dreaded pregnancy as a loss of control over my destiny, my body and my life. I had fantasies of death in childbirth, the death of my creativity during pregnancy, the alteration of my body into something monstrous, the loss of my intelligence through mysterious hormonal sabotage."[61]

While Jong oscillates between inviting, then banishing, the association of creation and procreation, H. D. used the birth metaphor to explore the process of moving from ambivalence toward motherhood to a celebration of its connection to authorship. She represents a further point on the continuum, the move to use the metaphor as a poetic for women's writing. In her *roman à clef, Asphodel*, for example, H. D. expresses the fear she felt during her first pregnancy that the attempt to combine speech and childbirth was a form of madness:

> When her flaming mind beat up and she found she was caught, her mind not taking her as usual like a wild bird but her mind-wings beating, beating and her feet caught, her feet caught, glued like a wildbird in a bird lime. . . . No one had known this. No one would ever know it for there were no words to tell it in. . . . Women can't speak and clever women don't have children. So if a clever woman does speak, she must be mad. She is mad. She wouldn't have had a baby, if she hadn't been.[62]

The image of a wild bird caught in bird lime is a metaphor for the tie between creation and procreation against which the poet struggles in fear. This pregnancy ends traumatically in stillbirth. But later in the novel, H. D. transforms that bondage into a powerful bond. With the flight of a wild swallow as omen, she decides not to abort her second pregnancy but to take the birth of her child as a symbol of a regenerated poetic identity. The experience of pregnancy itself doesn't hinder, but rather releases, her creative drive.[63] H. D. later encodes this resolution into the mythos of her complex epics of the forties and fifties. Incarnating the birth metaphor, the Lady in *Trilogy* and Isis in *Hermetic Definition* are goddesses whose procreative power can regenerate human life and inspire the poet. The Lady is the pregnant Word, but she appears to the poet without the Child, bearing instead the empty book of life which the poet must complete. Isis inspires the aging poet who feels silenced by men, either in their capacity as lovers or as fellow poets. The lover's double rejection of her writing and woman-hood has been particularly devastating. The poet frees herself from his negative influence by writing a poem about him, a poem whose progress she charts as the trimesters of pregnancy. Her poem is the child; its birth signals her freedom from obsession. The poet-as-procreator fuses with the mother-as-poet in the meta-phoric world of the poem.[64] H. D.'s Isis and Lady serve as Mother-Muses whose (pro)creative message implies an aesthetic based on the female body.

Like H. D., the experience of childbirth itself altered Muriel Rukeyser's poetics and led her to use the childbirth metaphor in "The Poem as Mask" to articulate her new sense of poetic identity and direction. Recalling the dismem-berment of the archetypal poet Orpheus, the poet regards her earlier Orpheus poems as false masks that testify to her alienation. They were "myself, split open, unable to speak, in exile from myself." Childbirth, however, functions as her literal "dismemberment," one which allows her poet-self to incarnate the real Orpheus: "There is memory/ of my torn life, myself split open in sleep, the rescued child/ beside me among the doctors." No more are her poems "masks": "Now, for the first time, the god lifts his hand,/ the fragments join in me with their own music."[65] Attesting to the inspirational power of her new (pro)creative aesthetic, "Nine Poems for the Unborn Child" and *Body of Waking* weave media-tions on pregnancy and art that insistently relate authorship and motherhood.

"Split open" in the stillbirth of her premature baby, Anaïs Nin similarly expe-riences a transformation, one that leads her to embrace (pro)creation as a self-conscious, prescriptive aesthetic. As the next point on the continuum, Nin uses the birth metaphor to advocate a feminine form of writing, one that proceeds from the body. Otto Rank, her analyst, sharply posed the tradition of separated creativities for her: "Perhaps," he told her, "you may discover now what you want—to be a woman or an artist." Later, he added that "to create it is necessary to destroy. Woman cannot destroy . . . that may be why she has rarely been a great artist."[66] While pregnant, Nin struggled to finish *Winter of Artifice* and re-peatedly used the birth metaphor in her diary to describe her labor: "Writing now shows the pains of childbearing. . . . I yearn to be delivered of this book. It is devouring me."[67] Writing about the stillbirth in her diary and the short story "Birth" led Nin to counter Rank's phallic aesthetic with a body-based aesthetic of her own. "The art of woman," she writes, "must be torn in the womb-cells of the mind. . . . woman's creation far from being like man's must be exactly like her creation of children, that is it must come out of her own blood, englobed by her womb, nourished with her own milk."[68] As she pursues the meaning of a womb-based art, however, Nin becomes entangled in the regressive biologisms that concern Showlater, Auerbach, and de Beauvoir. "Woman does not forget she needs the fecundator," Nin muses, "she does not forget that everything that is born of her is planted in her. If she forgets this she is lost . . . a woman alone creating is not a beautiful spectacle. . . . The woman was born mother, mistress, wife, sister, she was born to represent union, communion, communication. . . . Woman was born to *be* the connecting link between man and his human self. . . . Woman's role in creation should be parallel to her role in life."[69] Nin's difficulty in separating the womb from woman's traditional role as man's support led her to create a birth metaphor that was itself a trap. Its determinism prescribed what women should write and how they must direct their creative energies toward the support of men, who are the necessary fecundators of women's writing.

Not all self-consciously formulated poetics of the female body have led women into prescriptive or deterministic entrapment, however. Representing the next point along the spectrum, Ntozake Shange uses the birth metaphor to chart the evolution of her poetics from the "universality" of male discourse to the specificity of female discourse. In "wow . . . yr just like a man," she tells of how she sought the approval of male poets by suppressing "alla this foolishness bout . . . bodies & blood & kids & what's really goin on at home/ well & that ain't poetry/ that's goo-ey gaw/ female stuff/ & she wasn't like that/ this woman they callt a poet." The birth metaphor is sign and symptom of her transformation:

> as a woman & a poet/ i've decided to wear my ovaries on my sleeve/ raise my poems on milk/ & count my days by the flow of my mensis/ the men who were poets were aghast/ they fled the scene in fear of becoming unclean . . . and she waz left with an arena of her own . . . where music & mensis/ are considered very personal/ & language a tool for exploring space.[70]

Shange's recent volume of poetry celebrates this female poetic in an uproarious poem entitled "Oh, I'm 10 Months Pregnant," in which a weary, pregnant poet complains to her doctor about how "the baby was confused/ the baby doesn't know/ she's not another poem":

> this baby wants to jump out of my mouth
> at a reading someplace/
> the baby's refusing to come out/down
> she wants to come out a spoken word
> & i have no way to reach her/she is
> no mere choice of words/how can i convince her
> to drop her head & take on the world like the
> rest of us[71]

Shange's new female poetic, fed by her own disruptively "unclean" body, is written in black English, a linguistic act that implicitly characterizes her aesthetic not only as female but also as Afro-American. In her essay "One Child of One's Own," Alice Walker uses the childbirth metaphor to define even more directly the fusion of her womanhood and blackness in her writing. She makes black women's double-birthing powers the foundation of a (pro)creativity that defies both sexism and racism. White feminists, she writes, have ignored black women's motherhood of both books and babies—by leaving black women's writing out of their anthologies and critical books; by keeping black women's sexuality and mothering invisible, as in the nonvaginal design of the Sojourner Truth plate in Judy Chicago's *Dinner Party*. Walker's completion of her first novel three days before her daughter's birth reconstitutes the (pro)creativity that racism and sexism have suppressed: "I had changed forever. From a woman whose 'womb' had been in a sense, her head—that is to say, certain small seeds had gone in, rather different if not larger or better 'creations' had come out—to a woman who

. . . had two wombs! No. To a woman who had written books, conceived in her head, and who had also engendered at least one human being in her body." [72]

Lesbian writers have faced an even more severe cultural denial of their procreative womanhood in the homophobic belief that lesbianism and motherhood are mutually exclusive categories. Lesbians, many of whom are themselves mothers, use the childbirth metaphor to define a poetic of the body and affirm a vision of regenerated womanhood and world. In "Metamorphosis," Pat Parker describes how her love for a woman impregnated her with the vision central to her poetry: "fill me with you/ & I become/pregnant with love/ give birth/ to revolution." [73] Like Paula Gunn Allen's celebration of the Spider Creatix of Southwest Indian religion in "Prologue" and in "Grandmother," Judy Grahn's hymn "She Who" envisions a multidimensioned birth that reenacts the primal power of woman's (pro)creativity.

> the labor of She Who carries and bears is the first
> labor all over the world
> the waters are breaking everywhere
> everywhere the waters are breaking
> the labor of She Who carries and bears
> and raises and rears is the first labor,
> there is no other first labor. [74]

Lucille Clifton's sequence of Kali poems serves as a fitting conclusion to the wide spectrum of uses to which women writers of all periods have put the birth metaphor. In brilliantly condensed form, Clifton fuses literary and biological childbirth in a way that incorporates experience and aesthetic, terror and joy, ambivalence and celebration, separation and transcendence, body and spirit, animal and divine, pain and exultation. "She Understands Me" is a central poem in the sequence about her muse, the terrifying force of creativity she names after the black Hindu Goddess Kali:

> it is all blood and breaking
> blood and breaking.the thing
> drops out of its box squalling
> into the light.they are both squalling,
> animal and cage.her bars lie wet, open
> and empty and she has made herself again
> out of flesh out of dictionaries,
> she is always emptying and it is all
> the same wound the same blood the same breaking. [75]

The line "out of flesh out of dictionaries" is key, invoking the familiar birth metaphor linking babies and words. But where the male poet's conceit necessarily reinforces the division of mind and body, Clifton creates an ambiguity of subject highlighted by the absence of space between sentences and the lack of capitalization. The poem is simultaneously about the birth of a child and a poem. It is a visceral, raw view of childbirth, one that stresses the animal-like power of a transrational force but not in the negative mode of the Enlightenment metaphors. Clifton forthrightly names the process of (pro)creativity: the pregnant mind-body empties herself, squalling and bloody. The title, which suggests that the muse and mother understand each other, unifies the two subjects of the poem so that creativity and procreativity are inseparably joined. Indeed, the poem suggests ultimately that the poet's pregnancy produces multiple births. "She has made herself again": she is her own mother as well as mother to squalling babies and poems. She is both word and flesh, by divine and poetic authority.

CONCLUSION

The childbirth metaphor for creativity illustrates how gender "informs and complicates the reading and writing of texts." The basic analogy of creation and procreation remains the same for both women and men. However, female and male metaphors mean differently and mean something different, indeed something opposite. Male metaphors intensify difference and collision, while female metaphors enhance sameness and collusion. In spite of individual variation, male metaphors often covertly affirm the traditional separation of creativity and procreativity. Female metaphors, in contrast, tend to defy those divisions and reconstitute woman's fragmented self into a (pro)creative whole uniting word and flesh, body and mind.

These gender differences in childbirth metaphors project contrasting concepts of creativity. The male childbirth metaphor paradoxically beckons woman toward the community of creative artists by focusing on what she alone can create, but then subtly excludes her as the historically resonant associations of the metaphor reinforce the separation of creativities into mind and body, man and woman. The female childbirth metaphor challenges this covert concept of creativity by proposing a genuine bond between creation and procreation and by suggesting a subversive community of artists who can literally and literarily (pro)create. This biologic poetic does indeed run the risk of biological determinism, as de Beauvoir and others have feared. It theoreticlly privileges motherhood as the basis of all creativity, a position that symbolically excludes women without children and all men. It also tends toward a prescriptive poetic that potentially narrows the range of language and experience open to women writers. But women's childbirth metaphors have also served for centuries as a linguistic reunion of what culture has sundered, a linguistic defense against confinement. Long before Cixous's utopian essay about the *future* inscription of femininity, women have subverted the regressive birth metaphor and transformed it into a sign representing their own delivery into speech through (pro)creativity. Emerging like women themselves from the confinement of patriarchal literary tradition, birth metaphors have celebrated women's birthright to creativity. Women's oppression begins with the control of the body, the fruits of labor. Consequently, many women writers have gone directly to the source of powerlessness to reclaim that control through the labor of the mind pregnant with the word.

NOTES

An earlier version of this essay was delivered at the Symposium on Childbirth at the University of Wisconsin in Madison in May 1981. I am greatly indebted to Elizabeth Black, whose bibliographic work for me was supported by a grant from the Women's Studies Research Center at the University of Wisconsin at Madison. For their criticisms and encouragements, I would also like to thank Judith Walzer Leavitt, Nellie McKay, Cyrena N. Pondrom, Alicia Ostriker, Phillip Herring, Eric Rothstein, and Jocelyn Moody. For permission to quote from H. D.'s manuscript, I am grateful to Perdita Schaffner and the Beinecke Rare Book and Manuscript Library, Yale University. Quotations are from Philip Sidney, *Astrophel and Stella* (1591, 1598), in *The Renaissance in England*, ed. Hyder E. Rollins and Herschel Baker (Boston: Heath, 1954), 323; and Denise Levertov, *The Poet in the World* (New York: New Direction, 1973), 107.

1. For discussions of male childbirth metaphors, see Terry J. Castle, "La'bring Bards: Birth *Topoi* and English Poetics," *Journal of English and Germanic Philosophy* 78 (April 1979): 193–208; Mary Ellmann, *Thinking about Women* (New York: Harcourt Brace Jovanovich, 1968), 2–27; Elizabeth Sacks, *Shakespeare's Images of Pregnancy* (New York: St. Martin's Press, 1980); Ernst Robert Curtius, *European Literature and the Latin Middle Ages*, trans. Willard R. Trask (New York: Putnam, 1953), 131–34; Gershon Legman, *Rationale of the Dirty Joke: An Analysis of Sexual Humor* (New York: Grove Press, 1968), 592–96; John H. Smith's "Dialogic Midwifery in Kleist's *Marquise von O* and the Hermeneutics of Telling the Untold in Kant and Plato," *PMLA* 100 (March 1985): 203–18; and Patricia Yaeger's letter to Smith in *PMLA* 100 (October 1985): 812–13. For discussions of female birth metaphors, see Susan Gubar, "The Birth of the Artist as Heroine: (Re)production, the *Kunstlerroman* Tradition, and the Fiction of Katherine Mansfield," in *The Representation of Women in Fiction*, ed. Carolyn G. Heilbrun and Margaret R. Higonnet (Baltimore: Johns Hopkins University Press, 1983), 19–59; Susan Gubar, "'The Blank Page' and the Issues of Female Creativity," *Critical Inquiry* 8 (Winter 1981): 243–64; and Sandra M. Gilbert, *Mother-Rites: Studies in Literature and Maternity*, a work in progress.

2. See Sandra M. Gilbert and Susan Gubar, *The Madwoman in the Attic: The Woman Writer and the Nineteenth-Century Literary Imagination* (New Haven: Yale University Press), 2–106, esp. 2–16; see also Ellmann, 2–27.

3. Hélène Cixous, "The Laugh of the Medusa," trans. Keith Cohen and Paula Cohen, in this volume and in *New French Feminisms: An Anthology*, ed. Elaine Marks and Isabelle de Courtivron (Amherst: University of Massachusetts Press, 1980), 251, 256, 261. See also Luce Irigaray, *This Sex Which Is Not One*, trans. Catherine Porter (Ithaca: Cornell University Press, 1985), 23–33, 205–18; Carolyn Greenstein Burke, "Report from Paris: Women's Writing and the Women's Movement," *Signs* 3 (Summer 1978): 843–55; Ann Rosalind Jones, "Writing the Body: Toward and Understanding of *L'Ecriture féminine*," in this volume and in *Feminist Studies* 7 (Summer 1981): 247–63; and Susan Rubin Suleiman, "(Re)Writing the Body: The Politics and Poetics of Female Eroticism," in *The Female Body in Western Culture: Contemporary Perspectives*, ed. Susan Rubin Suleiman (Cambridge: Harvard University Press, 1986): 7–29.

4. Stephanie Mines, "My Own Impression," in *Networks: An Anthology of San Francisco Bay Area Women Poets*, ed. Carol A. Simone (Palo Alto: Vortext, 1979), 118; Sharon Olds, "The Language of the Brag," *Ms. Magazine* (August 1980): 38.

5. Ellmann, *Thinking about Women*, 2–27.

6. Simone de Beauvoir, "Interview with Alice Schwarzer," *Der Spiegel* (April 1976): quoted in Silvia Bovenschen, "Is There a Feminine Aesthetic? *New German Critique* 10 (Winter 1977): 122; Elaine Showalter, "Feminist Criticism in the Wilderness," *Critical Inquiry* 8 (Winter 1981): 187–88; Nina Auerbach, "Artists and Mothers: A False Alliance," *Women and Literature* 9 (Spring 1978): 3–5, and her review of *The Madwoman in the Attic*, by Gilbert and Gubar, *Victorian Studies* 23 (Summer 1980): 506; Jones, 61–63; Erica Jong, "Creativity vs. Generativity: The Unexamined Lie," *The New Republic* 180 (13 Jan. 1979): 27.

7. Elizabeth Abel, Editor's Introduction, *Critical Inquiry* 8 (Winter 1981): 173.

8. Cixous, 248. This view may do more to dismiss and trivialize the subversive achievement and survival of women writers against a hostile culture than the patriarchal

canon itself. See Alicia Ostriker, "Comment on Margaret Homan's 'Her Very Own Howl': The Ambiguities of Representation in Recent Women's Fiction," *Signs* 10 (Spring 1985): 597–600.

9.   Max Black, "More about Metaphor," in *Metaphor and Thought*, ed. Andrew Ortony (New York: Cambridge University Press, 1979), 26.

10.   Roland Barthes, *Writing Degree Zero*, trans. Annette Lavers and Colin Smith (New York: HIll & Wang, 1976), 75–77. See also Catharine R. Stimpson's discussion of Barthes in "Zero Degree Deviancy: The Lesbian Novel in English," in this volume and in *Critical Inquiry* 8 (Winter 1981): 363–80. For discussions of contextual analysis of metaphors, see George Whalley, "Metaphor," in *Princeton Encyclopedia of Poetry and Poetics* (Princeton: Princeton University Press, 1974), 494; and Wayne C. Booth, "Ten Literal 'Theses,'" in *On Metaphor,* ed. Sheldon Sacks (Chicago: University of Chicago Press, 1978), 173–74.

11.   Quoted in Tillie Olsen, *Silences* (New York: Delta, 1972), 199–200.

12.   For discussions of the incompatibility of motherhood and authorship, see, for example, Virginia Woolf, *A Room of One's Own* (1929; reprint, New York: Harcourt Brace & World, 1957), 20–24, 69–70; Olsen, 6–21; Lola Ridge, "Woman and the Creative Will" (1919), in *Michigan Occasional Papers* 18 (Spring 1981): 1–23; Catharine R. Stimpson, "Power, Presentations, and the Presentable," in *Issues in Feminism: A First Course in Women's Studies*, ed. Sheila Ruth (Boston: Houghton Mifflin, 1980), 426–40; Adrienne Rich, *Of Woman Born: Motherhood as Experience and Institution* (New York: Norton, 1976), 156–62; and the sharp exchange between George Sand and a male writer in Bovenschen, 114–15.

13.   See, for example, the theories of female inferiority of intellect and creative genius by men such as Aristotle, Aquinas, Rousseau, Kant, Darwin, and Schopenhauer, excerpted in *History of Ideas on Women: A Source Book,* ed. Rosemary Agonito (New York: Putnam, 1977). See also critiques of scientific theories of female inferiority in Ruth Bleier, *Science and Gender: A Critique of Biology and Its Theories on Women* (New York: Pergamon Press, 1984); and James Hillman, *The Myth of Analysis: Three Essays in Archetypal Psychology* (Evanston: Northwestern University Press, 1972), 215–99.

14.   Gen. 3: 16–19, John, 1: 1–4. See also Mary Daly, *Beyond God the Father: Toward a Philosophy of Women's Liberation* (Boston: Beacon, 1973); Gilbert; Diane Wolkstein and Samuel Noah Kramer, *Inanna: Queen of Heaven and Earth, Her Stories and Hymns for Sumer* (New York: Harper, 1983); J. A. Phillips, *Eve: The History of an Idea* (New York: Harper & Row, 1984); Merlin Stone, *When God Was a Woman* (New York: Harcourt Brace Jovanovich, 1978).

15.   Friedrich Nietzche, *Thus Spake Zarathustra* (1883), trans. and selected by Agonito in her *History of Ideas on Women,* 268.

16.   Simone de Beauvoir, *The Second Sex*, trans. H. M. Parshley (1949: reprint, New York: Bantam, 1968), xv.

17.   Julia Kristeva, *About Chinese Women*, trans. Anita Barrows (New York: Urizen Books, 1974), 35–36.

18.   See, for example, Susan R. Suleiman and Inge Crossman, eds., *The Reader in the Text: Essays on Audience and Interpretation* (Princeton: Princeton University Press, 1980).

19.   Paul Ricoeur, "The Metaphorical Process as Cognition, Imagination, and Feeling," in *On Metaphor,* 146. For recent theoretical debates on metaphor, see, in addition to *On Metaphor,* Whalley; Ortony; and *Philosophical Perspectives on Metaphor*, ed. Mark Johnson (Minneapolis: University of Minnesota Press, 1981). For a discussion of metaphor and speech act theory, see Ted Cohen, "Figurative Speech and Figurative Acts," in *Philosophical Perspectives on Metaphor,* 182–99.

20.   Karsten Harries, "Metaphor and Transcendence," in *On Metaphor,* 71.

21.   Ricoeur, in *On Metaphor,* 145–47, 151–54.

22.   Paul de Man, "The Epistemology of Metaphor," in *On Metaphor,* 11–14, 28.

23. Ted Cohen, "Metaphor and the Cultivation of Intimacy," in *On Metaphor*, 6, 7.

24. The term "headbirth," a variation on the more comon "brainchild," is featured in Günter Grass's novel *Headbirths, or the Germans Are Dying Out*, trans. Ralph Mannheim (New York: Harcourt Brace Jovanovich, 1982). Advertisements for the novel show an embryo emerging from a male head, still attached to the brain by a twisting umbilical cord, a visual form that highlights the biological incongruity of the male birth metaphor.

25. Levertov, 107.

26. Lady Holland, *Memoir*, quoted in Legman, 593. Like Levertov's father-poet, this metaphor features a female author and male actor, a dissonance that contributes to the metaphor's wit as much as the actor's biological incapacity to give birth.

27. Richard Ellman, ed. *Selected Letters of James Joyce* (New York: Viking, 1975), 202–3. See also his *James Joyce: A Biography* (London: Oxford University Press, 1959), 306–9.

28. James Joyce, *Ulysses* (1922; rev. ed., New York: Random House, 1961), 383–428. See also Ellmann, ed., *Selected Letters*, 230, 251–52; and the discussion of "Oxen in the Sun" in Phillip F. Herring, *Joyce's Ulysses Notesheets in the British Museum* (Charlottesville: University of Virginia Press, 1972), 30–37, 162–264. Joyce's envy of female procreation is evident in Bloom's hallucination of giving birth in the "Circe" episode of *Ulysses* (429–609) and in the irony that perpetually undercuts the products of men's minds in his works (such as the narrator's increasingly jumbled words in "Oxen in the Sun" and Stephen's sterility in both *Ulysses* and *Portrait of the Artist as a Young Man*).

29. Amy Lowell, "The Sisters," in *No More Masks! An Anthology of Poems by Women*, ed. Florence Howe and Ellen Bass (New York: Anchor, 1973), 40.

30. As Paul de Man describes all metaphors in *On Metaphor*, 11–14, 28.

31. Katherine Philips, "Upon the Death of Hector Philips," in *The World Split Open: Four Centuries of Women Poets*, ed. Louise Bernikow (New York: Random House, 1974), 59–60. For a discussion of women poet's re-vision of conventional elegy, see Celeste M. Schenck, "Feminism and Deconstruction: Re-Constructing the Elegy," *Tulsa Studies in Women's Literature* 5 (Spring 1986): 13–28.

32. John Woodbridge, "To My Dear Sister, The Author of These Poems," in *The Poems of Mrs. Anne Bradstreet*, with Introduction by Charles Eliot Norton (New York: The Duodecimos, 1897), 8.

33. Jeannine Hensley, ed., *The Works of Anne Bradstreet* (Cambridge: Harvard University Press, 1967), 221.

34. See, for example, James Smith, "Epistle Dedicatory, to the Reader" (1658), in which he writes: "Curteous Reader, I had not gone my full time when by a sudden fright, occasioned by the Beare and Wheel-barrow on the Bank-side, I fell in travaile, and therefore cannot call this a timely issue, but a Mischance, which I must put out to the world to nurse; hoping it will be fostered with the greater care, because of its own innocency," quoted in Sacks, *Shakespeare's Images of Pregnancy*, 6–7.

35. See *Works of Anne Bradstreet*, 221.

36. Woolf, 156–62. Judy Chicago, *Through the Flower: My Struggle As a Woman Artist* (1975; rev. ed. New York: Anchor Books, 1982), 141–44. See also Judy Chicago and Miriam Schapiro, "Female Imagery," *Womanspace Journal* 1 (Summer 1973): 11–14; Lucy R. Lippard, *From the Center: Feminist Essays on Women's Art* (New York: Dutton, 1978), 80–95; and Bovenschen.

37. Although beyond the scope of this essay, it would be fruitful to extend a reader response approach beyond the issue of the reader's awareness of the author's sex to the sex and perspective of the reader. A female reader, for example, might be more likely to hear the collisions in the male metaphor than a male reader. A woman who has experienced childbirth may be more likely to feel the reunion of creation and procreation in a female metaphor than a woman who cannot have or chooses not to have children. Women who resent the privilege that mothers in patriarchy have in relationship to women without chil-

dren may find the childbirth metaphor oppressive rather than subversive. Any discourse charged with gender issues will be differently understood by women and men and by individuals whose perspectives on those issues differ.

38. Quoted in Olsen, 12.

39. T. S. Eliot, *The Three Voices of Poetry* (New York: Cambridge University Press, 1954), 29–30.

40. Diana Athill, *Smile Please: An Unfinished Biography* (New York: Harper & Row, 1979), 8–9.

41. I am indebted to Evelyn Fox Keller for sending her "Exposing Secrets," a Paper delivered at the conference "Feminist Studies: Reconstituting Knowledge," Milwaukee, April 1985, in which she quotes selected birth metaphors for the bomb collected by Brian Easlea in *Fathering the Unthinkable: Masculinity, Scientists, and the Nuclear Arms Race* (London: Pluto Press, 1983).

42. Karen Horney, *Feminine Psychology* (New York: Norton, 1967), 61; Legman, 592–96. Elizabeth Sacks, *Shakespeare's Images of Pregnancy*, 5.

43. Castle, 201–2, 205.

44. Percy Shelley, *Defence of Poetry*, in *Critical Theory Since Plato*, ed. Hazard Adams (New York: Harcourt Brace Jovanovich, 1971), 511. See Brewster Ghiselin's discussion of this organicism and the birth metaphor in his Introduction to *The Creative Process: A Symposium* (New Yokr: Mentor, 1952), 21, and the examples of the birth metaphor in his selections from Thomas Wolfe, Allen Tate, Stephen Spender, Paul Valery, A. E. Houseman, and Amy Lowell. See also the repeated organic birth metaphors in Cary Nelson, *The Incarnate Word: Literature as Verbal Space* (Urbana: University of Illinois Press. 1973), 6, 22–23, 50–51, 126–27, 129–43, 161, 182–83, 196–97, 242.

45. See, for example, Susan Gubar, "The Female Monster in Augustan Satire," *Signs* 3 (Winter 1977): 380–94.

46. John Locke, *An Essay Concerning Human Understanding*, ed. John W. Yolton (New York, 1961), 2: 105–6, 115, 175. See de Man's discussion of Locke's fear of metaphor's disruptive discourse in *On Metaphor*, 11–28. See also Arthur O. Lovejoy, *The Great Chain of Being* (Cambridge: Harvard University Press, 1957).

47. Muriel Rukeyser, "A Simple Theme," *Poetry* 74 (July 1949): 237. For a similar complaint, see E. M. Forster, *Aspects of the Novel* (1927; reprint, New York: Harcourt Brace & World, 1974), 75. Women's private writings before the twentieth century are a much richer source for women's perspectives on childbirth than public discourse. See Judith Walzer Leavitt and Whitney Walton, "'Down to Death's Door': Women's Perceptions of Childbirth," in *Women and Health in America: Historical Essays*, ed. Judith Walzer Leavitt (Madison: University of Wisconsin Press, 1984), 155–65. For criticism on representations of childbirth in literature, see Gubar, "The Birch"; Rich, 164–67; Carol H. Poston, "Childbirth in Literature," *Feminist Studies* 4 (June 1978): 18–31; Madeleine Riley, *Brought to Bed* (New York: A. S. Barnes, 1968); Loralee MacPike, "The Social Values of Childbirth in the Nineteenth-Century Novel," *International Journal of Women's Studies* 3 (March–April 1980): 117–30; John Hawkins Miller, "'Temple and Sewer': Childbirth, Prudery, and Victoria Regina," in *The Victorian Family: Structure and Stresses*, ed. Anthony S. Wohl (New York: St. Martin's Press, 1978); Irene Dash, "The Literature of Birth Abortion," *Regionalism and the Female Imagination* 3 (Spring 1977): 8–13; Rachel Blau DuPlessis, "Washing Blood," *Feminist Studies* 4 (June 1978): 1–12; Alicia Ostriker, "Body Language: Imagery of the Body in Women's Poetry," in *The State of Language*, ed. Leonard Michaels and Christopher Ricks (Berkeley: University of California Press, 1980), 247–63.

48. Fanny Appleton Longfellow, *Mrs. Longfellow*, ed. Edward Wagenknecht (New York: Longmans, Green, 1956); Cheryl Walker, "The Experienced Woman Poet" (Paper delivered at the Modern Language Association Convention, December 1981); Margaret Mead, *Blackberry Winter: My Earlier Years* (New York: William Morrow, 1972), 246–47.

49. See Mary Poovey, "'My Hidous Progeny': Mary Shelley and the Feminization of Romanticism," *PMLA* 95 (May 1980): 332–47.

50. Mary Shelley, *Frankenstein; or The Modern Prometheus* (1818; reprint, London: Oxford University Press, 1969), 10, 41, 48, 51–57, 99–109, 160, 222.

51. For different readings of Shelley's anxiety about motherhood, see Ellen Moers, *Literary Women: The Great Writers* (New York: Anchor, 1977), 138–51; Gilbert and Gubar, 213–47; Poovey; and Paul Sherwin, *"Frankenstein:* Creation or Catastrophe," *PMLA* 96 (October 1981): 883–903.

52. Sylvia Plath, *The Collected Poems*, ed. Ted Hughes (New York: Harper & Row, 1981), 116. For Plath's poems on pregnancy and birth as experience and/or metaphor, see 141–42, 157–58, 176–87, 240–42, 259, 272–73.

53. See, for example, "Metaphors," "You're," and "Heavy Women" in *Collected Poems*, 116, 141, 158. According to Ted Hughes, the birth of her first child was an exhilarating experience that contributed to the beginning of Plath's genuine poetic voice. See "Notes on the Chronological Order of Sylvia Plath's Poems," in *The Art of Sylvia Plath: A Symposium*, ed. Charles Newman (Bloomington: University of Indiana Press, 1970), 193. For a discussion of the alienated and unalienated labors of childbirth, see Rich, 157–85.

54. Plath's *Collected Poems* 259, 157. See also Ostriker's discussion of Plath's negative body imagery in "Baby Language," 250–52.

55. Plath's *Collected Poems*, 142. Plath's friend Anne Sexton also used the metaphor of aborted birth to describe her feeling of artistic failure in "The Silence," in which "the words from my pen . . . leak out of it like a miscarriage." See *The Book of Folly* (Boston: Houghton Mifflin, 1972), 32–33.

56. Erica Jong, *Loveroot* (New York: Holt, Rinehart, & Winston, 1975), 16–18.

57. Jong, *Loveroot*, 72–73.

58. Jong, *Loveroot*, 58–59.

59. Jong, "Creativity vs. Generativity," 27.

60. Jong, "Creativity vs. Generativity," 27, and Erica Jong, *Here Comes and Other Poems* (New York: Signet, 1975), 9.

61. Jong, "Creativity vs. Generativity," 28. See also "Penis Envy," in *Loveroot*, 81–82, and "Mother," in *Tangled Vines: A Collection of Mother & Daughter Poems*, ed. Lyn Lifson (Boston: Beacon Press, 1978), 52. Since the birth of her child, Jong once again relates procreation and creation. See her letter in the *New York Times Book Review* (18 Dec. 1983): 30, which lists recent women's writing about childbirth, including her most recent volumes. *At the Edge of the Body*, published about the time of her child's birth, includes birth metaphors (New York: Holt, Rinehard & Winston, 1979), 7–9, 24, 63.

62. H. D. (Hilda Doolittle), *Asphodel* (1921–22), 12. The unpublished manuscript is at Beinecke Rare Book and Manuscript Library, Yale University. I am indebeted to Beinecke Library and Perdita Schaffner (H. D.'s daughter and literary executor) for permission to quote from the manuscript.

63. For H. D.'s discussion of the creative "womb-brain," see her *Notes on Thought and Vision*, an essay on poetics written in 1919 shortly after the birth of her daughter (San Francisco: City Lights Books, 1982), 19–22. For other accounts of childbirth reinforcing artistic creativity for women in the visual arts, see Tania Mourand in Lucy Lippard, "The Pains and Pleasures of Rebirth: Women's Body Art," *Art in America* 64 (May/June 1976): 79; Sandra Donaldson, "'Suddenly you've become somebody else': A Study of Pregnancy and the Creative Woman," an unpublished paper; Joelynn Snyder-Ott, *Women and Creativity* (Millbrace, Calif.: Les Femmes, 1978).

64. H. D., *Trilogy* (New York: New Directions, 1973), 89–105. H. D., *Hermetic Definition* (New York: New Directions, 1972). For related discussions of H. D., see Susan Stanford Friedman, *Psyche Reborn: The Emergence of H. D.* (Bloomington: Indiana University

Press, 1981), 45–55; Deborah Kelley Kloepfer, "Flesh Made Word: Maternal Inscription in H. D.," *Sagetrieb* 3 (Spring 1984):27–48; Vincent Quinn, "H. D.'s 'Hermetic Definition': The Poet as Archetypal Mother," *Contemporary Literature* 18 (Winter 1977):51–61.

65. Muriel Rukeyser, "The Poem as Mask," *The Collected Poems* (New York: McGraw-Hill, 1978), 435. See also 148, 283–91, 303–10, 397–434.

66. Anaïs Nin, *The Diary, Volume One, 1931–1934*, ed. Gunther Stuhlmann (New York: Harcourt Brace Jovanovich, 1966), 309. See also 280–83, 290–94. Anaïs Nin, *The Diary, Volume Two, 1934–1939*, ed. Gunther Stuhlmann (New York: Harcourt Brace Jovanovich, 1967), 31. For a defense of Rank's treatment of Nin, see Sharon Spencer, "Delivering the Woman Artist from the Silence of the Womb: Otto Rank's Influence on Anaïs Nin," *The Psychoanalytic Review* 69 (Spring 1982):111–29.

67. Nin, *Diary, Volume One*, 314–15.

68. Nin, *Diary, Volume Two*, 233, 234. Anaïs Nin, "Birth," in *Under a Glass Bell* (Chicago: Swallow Press, 1948), 96–101.

69. Nin, *Diary, Volume Two*, 233–34.

70. Ntozake Shange, *Nappy Edges* (New York: Bantam, 1978), 17.

71. Ntozake Shange, *A Daughter's Geography* (New York: St. Martin's Press, 1983), 31. See also "We Need a God Who Bleeds Now," 51.

72. Alice Walker, *In Search of Our Mother's Gardens: Womanist Prose* (New York: Harcourt Brace Jovanovich, 1983), 361–83. Birth metaphors in the work of women of color and other minorities are especially common among contemporary writers. See also Audre Lorde, "Paperweight" and "Now That I Am Forever with Child" in *Networks*, 112–17; Sonia Sanchez, "Rebirth," in *A Blues Book for Blue Black Magical Women* (Detroit: Broadside Press, 1974), 47; E. M. Broner, *Her Mothers* (Berkeley: Berkeley Medallion, 1975).

73. Pat Parker, *Movement in Black* (Oakland, Calif.: Diana Press, 1978), 132.

74. Paula Gunn Allen, "Prologue," in *The Woman Who Owned the Shadows* (San Francisco: Spinsters, Ink, 1983), 1–2, and "Grandmother," in *The Third Woman: Minority Women Writers of the United States*, ed. Dexter Fisher (Boston: Houghton Mifflin, 1982), 126. See "She Who," in *The Work of a Common Woman: The Collected Poetry of Judy Grahn, 1964–77* (Trumansburg, N.Y.: Crossing Press, 1978), 76–109. See also Radclyffe Hall's central birth metaphor at the end of *The Well of Loneliness* (1928; reprint, New York: Pocket Books, 1950), 437.

75. Lucille Clifton, *An Ordinary Woman* (New York: Random House, 1974), 50. For the Kali sequence, see 47–62. Clifton writes extensively about motherhood in this volume and in her *Two-Headed Woman* (Amherst: University of Massachusetts Press, 1980).

desire

~~~~~~

In a late essay, Sigmund Freud asked his now famous question: "What does the woman [the little girl] want?" The essays in this section take up that question of wanting—of desire—from a number of different points of view, asking not only what the woman wants, but what is wanted of/from her. Freud's own answer, that the little girl wanted a penis, has been heatedly debated ever since (as is evident from the essays in "The Body," which probably should be read in conjunction with this section). The essayists here return to that debate to explore whether there is a more positive term available to describe women's longings than "envy" and whether or not female desire must always be subordinate to male desire. In different ways, they ask whether woman's desire must necessarily spring from a "lack" and be related to acquisition, or whether her desire could be more positive: a wish for the chance to do something with what she already has.

The term "desire" is dense with inter-textual connections. It is usually understood here as it was used by the French psychoanalyst and re-reader of Freud, Jacques Lacan. According to Lacan, each peson encounters a deep split when s/he begins to use language; his own contention that we "enter language" suggests his sense of the exteriority of linguistic experience. He argued that language is a force which utterly changes the being who uses it and which creates and structures the unconscious. Because language is always metaphorical (it always *stands for* something else and can never *be* that thing), there is always a gap between expressing a wish and receiving its answer, since language can never fully express exactly what we want. That gap is desire. For Lacan, our desire is always for *jouissance*, a term that refers both to orgasm and to a state of blissful, ecstatic union which would complete us, would heal the "split" that occurred when we entered language. This desire is unrealizable. Its impossibility does not, however, keep us from continually seeking its fulfillment.

"Desire" becomes an issue for feminists because of the precarious relation women have to it. "The Woman" is understood, by Lacan, to be desirable to man because of the (false) beliefs that she will be able to complete him, that she is his Other (all that he is not), and that union with her is a union with all he is not. Lacan's famous assertion, "~~The~~ Woman does not exist," does not refer to real women, but to this imaginary woman who could complete man. Desire is also important to women because of how their own desires are defined—and thereby limited—within psychoanalytic discourse; as Luce Irigaray warns, such restrictions within the realm of discourse may well limit the possibilities open to women in the world of lived experience.

The symbol most central to desire, for Lacan, is the phallus. Although it bears a connection to the physical penis, Lacan argued (in the essay "The Signification of the Phallus" in *Ecrits*) that it did not represent the physical organ itself, but came, metaphorically, to stand for all that was desirable. The origin of this signification is, for Lacan as it was for Freud, the castration complex; the male fears the loss of the penis, the female feels the anxiety of never having had one, and therefore the penis comes to represent that which is desirable. But Lacan insists that its symbolic force always exceeds its reference to the physical organ. Not surprisingly, though, this is one point which has troubled feminist writers deeply; the line separating phallus and penis is very fine. The "phallocentrism" (centering on the phallus) of Lacan's reliance on a male metaphor irrevocably marks his work as male-dominated and male-privileging, and therefore raises serious questions for its applicability to feminist thought.

Feminists have nonetheless used psychoanalysis in their critique of gender, despite misgivings about its phallocentrism. Psychoanalysis provides a framework for understanding how gender is defined, how it comes into being. Further, one of Freud's chief contributions, as Dianne Hunter points out in "Hysteria, Psychoanalysis and Feminism: The Case of Anna O.," was the idea of listening to what hysterical women had to say; for literary critics, the model of listening to (or reading) previously uninterpretable texts is a powerful one. Finally, feminists have recognized that psychoanalysis has been (with Marxism) a discourse that has shaped the twentieth century. To ignore it, to refuse to participate in it and change it, would be to be concede this important ground to other, and often hostile, forces. (See Cora Kaplan's "Pandora's Box: Subjectivity, Class and Sexuality in Socialist Feminist Criticism," in "Class" and Mary Jacobus's "Reading Woman (Reading)," in "Men," for further arguments in favor of including psychoanalysis in feminism.)

Two other Lacanian terms will be useful in reading the following essays: "the symbolic" and "the imaginary." For Lacan, language exists in "the order of the symbolic," because language symbolizes things in the world. "The symbolic" refers to the connection between signifier (a word) and signified (what it stands for) which is always arbitrarily established; we could just as easily call a dog "un chien" since there is no essential connection between the four-footed hairy creature and the word "dog." The system in which these symbols work is always outside the subject who uses it and that subject is never in control of the system. Lacan calls this arbitrary system the "Law of the Father," because of its structural similarity to the establishment of paternity and its chronological connection to the Oedipal complex. "The imaginary," on the other hand, is the realm of the image. Unlike symbols, whose connection to what they signify is arbitrary, images have a visual relation to the signified. The imaginary is typified, for Lacan, in the relation of the subject to his/her mirror image: that image both is and is not the subject. Whereas the symbolic is triadic—signifier, signified, and signifying system—the imaginary is dyadic—image and signified.

Desire has become an issue for literary critics because it exists within the field of language; as Lacan understood it, desire was the motivation for all language. As one of the most intense involvements with language, literature can be understood as a playing out of desire. Desire is its origin and root. The essays here explore the ways literature can be shaped by and can be a vehicle for desire. They also explore how literary critical techniques, when applied to nonliterary texts like Freud's own lectures, can reveal unspoken desire.

The writers here are concerned with how desire shapes some issues that are crucial to feminist criticism: Are desire and its forms specific to each gender? Does desire shape our understanding of sameness and difference? How is desire related to political power? The central question about desire for literary critics is perhaps best reflected in Eve Kosofsky Sedgwick's contribution at the end of this section: How is sexual/political desire expressed in literary representations? (For other essays which explore how desire can be a feminist/literary issue, see also Linda Kauffman's "Devious Channels of Decorous Ordering: Rosa Coldfield in

Absalom, Absalom!," in "Discourse" and Nancy Armstrong's "The Rise of the Domestic Woman," in "Class.")

In "Another 'Cause'—Castration" (French edition, 1974; English translation, 1985), Luce Irigaray directly confronts Freud's troublesome notion of "penis envy." This selection is part of a longer essay, "The Blind Spot of An Old Dream of Symmetry," from *Speculum of the Other Woman*, and is Irigaray's interrogation of Freud's essay "On Femininity" (in *New Introductory Lectures*), probably the most influential essay ever written on female sexuality. Irigaray begins by questioning several concepts central to Freud's theory of penis envy: She asks why the little girl should necessarily recognize the penis as a valuable, enviable organ at all; why she should experience a sense of "lack" of sexual organs when she clearly *has* not only one but several; and, finally, how it benefits *Freud* to believe that he has the thing which women envy. Working from these contradictions in Freud's essay, Irigaray shows that women's desire is defined in psychoanalytic discourse by male desire, that woman functions for Freud as a mirror that reflects back what the man wants to see.

The whole issue of *visibility* becomes central to Irigaray's questioning here. As Jane Gallop and Laura Mulvey explain, the field of vision has a central place in Lacanian psychoanalytic thought. Lacan describes the original experience of the split in the subject as an experience before a mirror, and has described "the gaze" as itself a source of pleasure (see Mulvey's essay and Lacan's *Four Fundamental Concepts of Psychoanalysis* for a fully elaborated theory of the gaze). For Irigaray, the privilege accorded to visibility in Freud's thought—the penis is more highly valued because it can be seen, and therefore desired—results in a fundamental misrepresentation, or nonrepresentation, of woman's desire. When she confronts the question of why women continue to go along with this mis-/non-representation, Irigaray concludes that it is because woman is defined within it, and is neither given nor allowed any other representation. Because her desire is never represented as such, it is never accorded status as desire.

Part explanation, part analysis, and part interrogation, Jane Gallop's "The Father's Seduction" (1982) follows Irigaray's own technique in its analysis of Irigaray's "Blind Spot in an Old Dream of Symmetry." Gallop points to contradictions, and pursues issues of the writer's own desires as apparent in her text. In particular, Gallop examines Irigaray's own position as herself an analyst: If Freud is the "father" of psychoanalysis, is Irigaray the (hysterical?) daughter? And if she is, how does her desire (as daughter) for the father mark her text? Questions of sameness and difference, of *symmetry* and *asymmetry*, are at issue here: Irigaray uses Freud's technique to analyze Freud; Gallop uses Irigaray's technique to analyze Irigaray; and throughout, the question of the analyst's desire remains problematic.

If, as Irigaray argues elsewhere in *Speculum of the Other Woman*, any theory is always masculine, where does that leave Irigaray's own theorizing? Gallop explores the difficulties Irigaray faces in trying to represent female desire without recourse to a patriarchal system of representation. Irigaray's project, as we see in the portion of her essay reprinted here, is to raise the possibility of a sexuality— and a system of representation—not governed by the phallus, not guided by the principle of sameness, "univocity" and oneness. But, Gallop asks, how can

Irigaray offer a *different* version of femininity without being seduced by the *same?* If she solves the problem, and offers an answer, she risks coming to completion and closure—the mark of phallic "unicity." To avoid this problematic closure, Irigaray offers only questions—but how does one offer new options with only questions? Gallop marks these attempts to avoid authority, to avoid the artificial precision of phallocentrism, but points to the occasion when even Irigaray insists on precision—her statement that she doesn't advocate a daughter's having sex with her father—as evidence of the difficulty of escaping the "law of the father" and of Irigaray's own desire for/seduction by the father.

In "Visual Pleasure and Narrative Cinema" (1975), Laura Mulvey, an avante-garde filmmaker herself, turns her attention toward the representation of women as *objects* of desire in traditional Hollywood films. How do we get pleasure from cinema? Is that pleasure oppressive to women? Mulvey argues that the classic narrative film of the thirties and forties exploits women by using male desire to code the erotic into the dominant patriarchal order. In these films, the camera is used to display women as the objects of fetishistic or voyeuristic gazes (sexually "abnormal" ways of looking), which make them concurrently alluring and threatening. To allay that threat—which Mulvey links, through the use of psychoanalytic theory, to the castration complex—traditional cinema uses three techniques: women are punished at the end of films, their bodies are fragmented by camera shots, or they are made into sexual icons. Mulvey urges new techniques of filmmaking that will end this oppressive use of women as nothing more than objects of desire and that will make film-viewing a more self-conscious, and egalitarian, experience.

Julia Kristeva, author of the influential work *Desire in Language* (1980), links questions of desire to large issues of linguistic, political, and historical change in "Women's Time" (first published in French in 1979; translated into English in 1981). Using both psychoanalytic and socialist frames of reference, Kristeva casts doubt on the whole notion that women's desire is fundamentally different from men's, and pursues what the ramifications of that desire would be if it *were* different. To do this, she sets out a history of the women's movement and links it to women's desire: initially, women wanted political, economic, and reproductive equality, but, more recently, "second generation" feminists have wanted to explore their own difference and the specificity of women's experiences and language. Kristeva is troubled by what she sees as an uncritical acceptance of women's difference; she questions whether the writings published as *l'écriture féminine* (see "The Body" for an elaboration and explanation of this term) are any closer to women's desire than were other forms of writing. She also casts doubt on the notion that women would wield power more positively than men do, citing the recent history of women who have come to power as evidence that there is no difference; she warns that if women's desire *is* really different, those differences may actually make them more, not less, prone to terrorism.

In a move which may strike some as antifeminist, Kristeva provides a model of desire in which gender is not particularly an issue; as she sees it, both men and women suffer from a sense of being unfulfilled and lacking. Both men and women suffer the psychic split which Freud called the *Spaltung* and which Lacan located at the entry into language. Kristeva therefore hopes for a third generation of feminist thinkers who will develop a "space" where "sexual identity" (because it preserves the fiction of an "identity," rather than a fundamental split, in the subject) would disappear. She closes her essay with thoughts about ethics and aesthetics (especially of women's writing) within this new space, wondering if the time to explicitly reintroduce a notion of morality into feminist thought has come.

Like Kristeva, Eve Kosofsky Sedgwick uses both psychoanalytic and socialist theories in her discussion of desire; like Kristeva, she explores the connection between desire and the political. In the introduction and first chapter of *Between Men: English Literature and Male Homosocial Desire* (1985), Sedgwick traces the links between male homosocial desire (which she carefully delineates as not homosexual, but blatantly homophobic) and patriarchal culture. Here she sets out the theoretical groundwork on which the rest of her book is built, questioning how far the connections between radical feminism—which sees gender as *the* fundamental issue—and Marxist theory—which sees power-relations and economics as fundamental—can be drawn.

Sedgwick concludes that one can trace the relations of sexual desire and political power through an examination of the "exchange of women," a theory that women are used to cement relations between men, an idea which has been developed and refined by Freud and by anthropologists Claude Lévi-Strauss and Gayle Rubin, and has been applied to women's psychic lives by Irigaray (see her essay "This Sex Which Is Not One," in "The Body"). Warning that sexual desire and political power cannot be simply equated, Sedgwick seeks to examine the historical relation between the two through representations, questioning what *counts* as sexual as well as the effect that the sexual has on political power. Like each of the other writers in this section, Sedgwick explores the relationship between desire and gender oppression; like the others, she examines how desire is played out in representations.

—DPH

ANOTHER "CAUSE"—CASTRATION

~~~~~~

AS MIGHT BE EXPECTED

The little girl's hostility toward her mother finds other justifications. Such as: the impossibility of satisfying the child's sexual desires; the mother inciting the child to masturbate and then forbidding it to do so; the fact that the bond to the mother is supposedly destined to disappear as a result of its primitive character, since early object cathexes are always highly ambivalent; "it is the special nature of the mother–child relation that leads, with equal inevitability, to the destruc- tion of the child's love; for even the mildest upbringing cannot avoid using com- pulsion and introducing restrictions, and any such intervention in the child's liberty must provoke as a reaction an inclination to rebelliousness and aggressive- ness." But "all these factors . . . are, after all, also in operation in the relation of the *boy* [Freud's italics] to his mother and are yet unable to alienate him from the maternal object." So some specific factor must intervene in the mother–daughter relation and in the development of that relation which would explain "the termi- nation of the attachment of girls to their mother" (p. 124).

> "I *believe* we have found this specific factor, and indeed *where we expected to find it*, even though in a surprising form. *Where we expected to find it*, I say, for it lies in the castration complex. After all, the *anatomical* distinction [between the sexes] *must* express itself in *psychical* consequences. *It was, however, a surprise to learn from analyses that girls hold their mother responsible* for their lack of a penis and do not forgive her for their being thus put at a disadvantage." (p. 124)

One might cite or even recite Freud at length, the Freud of "female sexuality" at least, on the basis of these "I believes," these "where we expected to find its," these "castration complexes"; and also relate them to his failure to be "sur- prised" at the "psychical consequences" of an "anatomical distinction," or to his rather univocal appeal to anatomy to explain a psychical economy—which would supposedly know no other mimesis than that of "nature" according to this interpretation?—and to all those expressions of surprise which, perhaps, mask the upsurge of an *unheimlich* that is much more uncanny, blinding. . . .

THE GAZE, ALWAYS AT STAKE

So the little girl does not forgive her mother for not giving her a penis. At the "*sight* of the genitals of the other sex," girls "*notice the* [sexual?] *difference* and, it must be admitted, its significance too. They feel seriously *wronged*, often declare that they want to '*have something like it too*' . . . and fall victim to '*envy for the penis*', which will leave ineradicable traces on their development and the formation of their character" (p. 125).

The dramatization is quite good, and one can imagine, or dream up, recognition scenes along these lines in the consulting room of psychoanalyst Freud. By rights, though, the question should still be raised of the respective relationships between the gaze and sexual difference, since, he tells us, you have to see it to believe it. And therefore, one must lose sight of something to see it anew? Admittedly. But all the same. . . . Unless all the potency, and the difference (?) were displaced into the gaze(s)? So Freud will see, without being seen? Without being seen seeing? Without even being questioned about the potency of his gaze? Which leads to envy of the omnipotence of gazing, knowing? About sex/ about the penis. To envy and jealousy of the eye-penis, of the phallic gaze? He will be able to see that I don't have one, will realize it in the twinkling of an eye. I shall not see if he has one. More than me? But he will inform me of it. Displaced castration? *The gaze is at stake from the outset.* Don't forget, in fact, what "castration," or the knowledge of castration, owes to the gaze, at least for Freud, The gaze has always been involved.

Now the little girl, the woman, supposedly has *nothing* you can see. She exposes, exhibits the possibility of a *nothing to see*. Or at any rate she shows nothing that is penis-shaped or could substitute for a penis. This is the odd, the uncanny thing, as far as the eye can see, this nothing around which lingers in horror, now and forever, an overcathexis of the eye, of appropriation by the gaze, and of the *phallomorphic* sexual metaphors, its reassuring accomplices.[1]

This nothing, which actually cannot well be mastered in the twinkling of an eye, might equally well have acted as an inducement to perform castration upon an age-old oculocentrism. It might have been interpreted as the intervention of a difference, of a deferent, as a challenge to an imaginary whose functions are often improperly regulated in terms of sight. Or yet again as the "symptom," the "signifier," of the possibility of an *other* libidinal economy, of a heterogeneity unknown in the practice of and discourse about the (designated) libido. Now the "castration complex" in becoming a woman will merely close off, repress? or censure? such possible interpretations. Woman's castration is defined as her having nothing you can see, as her *having* nothing. In her having nothing penile, in seeing that she has No Thing. Nothing *like* man. That is to say, *no sex/organ* that can be seen in a *form* capable of founding its reality, reproducing its truth. *Nothing to be seen is equivalent to having no thing. No being and no truth.*[2] The contract, the collusion, between *one* sex/organ and the victory won by visual dominance therefore leaves woman with her sexual void, with an "actual castration" carried out in actual fact. She has the option of a "neutral" libido or of sustaining herself by "penis envy."

ANATOMY IS "DESTINY"

This "neuter" is hard for Freud to account for in his theory of the difference of the sexes, as we can see from his repeated admissions that the subject of woman's sexuality is still very "obscure." As for what he will have to say about it, what has become "apparent" to him about it, female sexuality can be graphed along the axes of visibility of (so-called) masculine sexuality. For such a demonstration to hold up, the little girl must immediately become a little boy. In the beginning . . . the little girl was (only) a little boy. In other words THERE NEVER IS (OR WILL BE) A LITTLE GIRL. All that remains is to assign her sexual function to this "little boy" with no penis, or at least no penis of any recognized value. Inevitably, the trial of "castration" must be undergone. This "little boy," who was, in all innocence and ignorance of sexual difference, *phallic*, notices how ridiculous "his" sex organ looks. "He" *sees* the disadvantage for which "he" is *anatomically destined:* "he" has only a tiny little sex organ, no sex organ at all, really, an almost invisible sex organ. The almost imperceptible clitoris. The humiliation of being so badly equipped, of cutting such a poor figure, in *comparison* with the penis, with *the* sex organ can only lead to a desire to "have something like it too," and Freud claims that this desire will form the basis for "normal womanhood." In the course of the girl's discovery of her castration, her dominant feelings are of envy, jealousy, and hatred toward the mother—or in fact any woman—who has no penis and could not give one. She desires to be a man or at any rate "like" a man since she cannot actually become one.[3] The little girl does not submit to the "facts" easily, she keeps waiting for "it to grow," and "believes in that possibility for improbably long years." Which means that no attempt will be made by the little girl—nor by the mother? nor by the woman?—to find symbols for the state of "this nothing to be seen," to defend its goals, or to lay claim to its rewards. *Here again no economy would be possible whereby sexual reality can be represented by/for woman.* She remains forsaken and abandoned in her lack, default, absence, envy, etc. and is led to submit, to follow the dictates issued univocally by the sexual desire, discourse, and law of man. Of the father, in the first instance.

WHAT THE FATHER'S DISCOURSE COVERS UP

So, borrowing Freud's own terms, let us question him for example, about his relationship to the parental function. That is, to the exercise of the law—notably the psychoanalytic law—of castration. Why this fear, horror, phobia . . . felt when there is nothing to be seen, why does having nothing that can be seen threaten *his* libidinal economy? And remember in this regard that in the castration scenario Freud has just outlined, it is the boy who looks and is horrified first, and that the little girl merely doubles and confirms by reduplication what he is supposed to have seen. Or not seen. "In [boys] the castration complex arises after they have learnt *from the sight of the female genitals* that the organ which they value so highly need not necessarily accompany the body. At this the boy calls to mind the threats he brought on himself by his doings with that organ, he begins to give credence to them and falls under the influence of *fear of castration*, [Freud's italics] which will be the most powerful motive force in his subsequent development" (p. 125). After which, Freud goes on: "The castration complex of girls is *also* started by the *sight* of the genitals of the other sex. Etc."

Here again the little girl will have to act *like* the little boy, feel the same urge to see, look in the same way, and her resentment at not having a penis must follow and corroborate the horrified astonishment the little boy feels when faced with the strangeness of the nonidentical, the nonidentifiable. The "reality" of the girl's castration could be summed up as follows: you men can see nothing, can know nothing of this; can neither discover nor recognize yourselves in this. All that remains, therefore, is for me, for her (or them), to accept this fact. As a biological fact! The girl thus "enters" into the castration complex in the same way as the boy, like a boy. She "comes out"of it feminized by a decision, which she is duty bound to ratify, that there cannot be a nothing to be seen. The idea that a "nothing to be seen," a something not subject to the rule of visibility or of specula(riza)tion, might yet have some reality, would indeed be intolerable to man. It would serve to threaten the theory and practice of the representation by which he aims to sublimate, or avoid the ban on, masturbation. Auto-erotism has been permitted, authorized, encouraged insofar as it is deferred, exhibited in sublated ways. All this is endangered (caught in the act, one might say) by a *nothing*—that is, a nothing the same, identical, identifiable. By a fault, a flaw, a lack, an absence, outside the system of representations and auto-representations. Which are man's. By a *hole* in men's signifying economy. A nothing that might cause the ultimate destruction, the splintering, the break in their systems of "presence," of "re-presentation" and "representation." A nothing threatening the process of production, reproduction, mastery, and profitability, of meaning, dominated by the phallus—that *master signifier* whose law of functioning erases, rejects, denies the surging up, the resurgence, the recall of a *heterogeneity* capable of reworking the principle of its authority. That authority is minted in concepts, representations and formalizations of language which prescribe, even today, the prevailing theory and practice of "castration." And what weak instruments these are, products of the very system they pretend to challenge. Such collusion with phallocentrism serves only to confirm its power.

THE NEGATIVE IN PHALLOCENTRIC DIALECTIC

Thus the matter before us leads us to ask ourselves, and to ask them:

(1) Does the little girl, the woman, really have "penis envy" in the sense Freud gives to that expression; that is, of wanting "to have something like it too"? This assumption, in fact, governs everything said now and later about female sexuality. For this "envy" programs all of woman's instinctual economy, even, though she does not realize it, *before* the discovery of her castration, at the point when, supposedly, she only was, and wanted to be, a boy.

(2) What is the relationship of that "envy" to man's "desire"? In other words, is it possible that the phobia aroused in man, and notably in Freud, by the uncanny strangeness of the "nothing to be seen" cannot tolerate *her* not having this "envy"? *Her* having other desires, of a different nature from *his* representation of the sexual and from his representations of sexual desire. From his projected, reflected *auto-representations*, shall we say? If woman had desires other than "penis envy," this would call into question the unity, the uniqueness, the simplicity of the mirror charged with sending man's image back to him—albeit inverted. Call into question its flatness. The specularization, and speculation, of the purpose of (*his*) desire could no longer be two-dimensional. Or again: the "penis envy" attributed to woman soothes the anguish man feels, Freud feels, about the coherence of his narcissistic construction and reassures him against what he calls castration anxiety. For if his desire can be signified only as "penis envy," it is a good thing that he has it (one). And that what he has should represent the only goods acceptable for sexual trading.

(3) Why does the term "envy" occur to Freud? Why does Freud choose it? Envy, jealousy, greed are all correlated to lack, default, absence. All these terms describe female sexuality as merely the *other side* or even the *wrong side* of a male sexualism. It could be admitted that the little girl accords a special status to the penis as the instrument of her sexual pleasure and that she displays a centrifugal-centripetal tropism for it. But "penis envy," in the Freudian and indeed psychoanalytic sense, means nothing less than that the little girl, the woman, must despise *her own* pleasure in order to procure a—doubtless ambiguous—remedy for man's castration anxiety. The possibility of losing his penis, of having it cut off, would find a real basis in the *biological* fact of woman's castration. The fear of not having it, of losing it, would be re-presented in the anatomical amputation of woman, in her resentment at lacking a sex organ and in her correlative "envious" urge to gain possession of it. The castration anxiety of not having it, or losing it, would thus be supported by the representation of the female sex, whereas *the desire to have it* would confirm man in the assurance that he has it, still, while reminding him at the same time—in one of the essential rules of the game—that he risks having her take it away from him. The fact remains that "penis envy" must above all be interpreted as a symptomatic index—laid down as a law of the economy of woman's sexuality—of the pregnancy of the desire for the same, whose guarantee, and transcendental signifier or signified, will be the phallus. The Phallus. If it were not so, why not *also* analyze the "envy" for the vagina? Or the uterus? Or the vulva? Etc. The "desire" felt by each pole of sexual difference "to have something like it too"? The resentment at being faulty, lacking, with respect to a heterogene, to an other? The "disadvantage" mother nature puts you to by providing only *one* sex organ? All of this would require, entail, demand an other sex, a different sex—a sex that shared in the same while remaining different[4]—for sexual pleasure to be possible. But finally, in Freud, sexual pleasure boils down to being plus or minus one sex organ: the penis. And sexual "otherness" comes down to "not having it." Thus, woman's lack of penis and her envy of the penis *ensure the function of the negative*, serve as representatives of the negative, in what could be called a *phallocentric*—or phallotropic—dialectic.[5] And if "sexual function" demands that the little boy should turn away

from his—real—mother whom convention forbids he should get with child, if what is indicated by the "castration complex" forces him to "sublimate" his instincts toward his mother, let us say that, as far as he is concerned, man will *lose nothing* thereby, and that the loss will amount only to a risk, a fear, a "fantasy" of loss. And that the *nothing* of sex, the *not* of sex, will be borne by woman.

But, ipso facto, "castration" cannot be what makes the relation between the sexes practicable or assures the possibility for both repetition and "displacement" of the relation *between two sexes*. It must serve as a reminder of the negative which is attributed to woman, to the female sex—in *reality* too, for more verisimilitude—an attribution that would guarantee its "sublation" [6] in the sublimation of the penis. With sex and sexualness being sublated into representations, ideas, laws, dominated by the Phallus. The relationship to the negative, for man, will always have been imaginary—imagined, imaginable—, hence the impetus it gives to fictive, mythic, or ideal productions that are only afterward defined as laws assuring the permanence and circularity of this system. The legislation reestablishes, then, the castration complex, notably of woman, which will serve, along with other edicts, to transform into a historical program the fables relating to men's sexual practices.

(4) As for woman, one may wonder why she submits so readily to this makebelieve, why she "mimics" so perfectly as to forget she is acting out man's contraphobic projects, projections, and productions of her desire. Specifically, why does she accept that her desire only amounts to "penis envy"? What fault, deficiency, theft, rape, rejection, repression, censorship, of representations of her sexuality bring about such a subjection to man's desire-discourse-law about her sex? Such an atrophy of her libido? Which will never be admissible, envisionable, except insofar as it props up male desire. For the "penis envy" alleged against woman is—let us repeat—a remedy for man's fear of losing one. If *she* envies it, then *he* must have it. If *she* envies what *he* has, then it must be valuable. The only thing valuable enough to be envied? The very standard of all value. Woman's fetishization of the male organ must indeed be an indispensable support of its price on the sexual market.

IS WORKING OUT THE DEATH DRIVES LIMITED TO MEN ONLY?

So let us speculate that things happen this way because, in psychoanalytic parlance, *the death drives can be worked out only by man*,[7] never, under any circumstances, by woman. She merely "services" the work of the death instincts. Of man.

Thus, by suppressing her drives, by pacifying and making them passive, she will function as pledge and reward for the "total reduction of tension." By the "free flow of energy" in coitus, she will function as a promise of the libido's evanescence, just as in her role as "wife" she will be assigned to maintain coital homeostasis, "constancy." To guarantee that the drives are "bound" in/by marriage. She will also be the place referred to as "maternal" where the automatism of repetition, the reestablishment of an earlier economy, the infinite regression of pleasure, can occur. Back to the sleep of Lethe, to lethargy. Except that she is charged at the same time with preserving, regenerating, and rejuvenating the organism, notably through sexual reproduction. She is wholly devoted to giving life, then, source and re-source of life. To being still the restoring, nourishing mother who prolongs the work of death by sustaining it; death makes a detour through the revitalizing female-maternal.

You will have realized that the "sexual function" also requires aggressiveness from the male, and that this authorizes an economy of death drives whereby the "subject" disengages and protects himself by diverting his energies to the "object." And, by maintaining the subject–object polarity in sexual activity, woman will provide man with an outlet for that "primary masochism" which is dangerous and even life-threatening for the "psychic" as well as the "organic" self. Now, Freud states that this "primary" or "erogenous" masochism will be reserved to woman and that both her "constitution" and "social rules" will forbid her any sadistic way to work out these masochistic death drives. She can only "turn them around" or "turn them inward." The sadism of the anal–sadistic stage is also transformed, at a secondary level, into masochism: activity is turned into passivity, sadism is "turned back" from the "object" onto the "subject." Secondary masochism added to primary masochism—this is apparently the "destiny" of the death drives in woman, and they survive only because of their unalterably sexuate nature, through the erotization of this "masochism."

But further, in order to trans-form his death drives and the whole instinctual dualism, in order to use his life to ward off death for as long as it takes to choose a death, man will have to work on building up his ego. On raising his own tomb, if you like. The new detour along the road to death, through/for the construction of narcissistic monuments, involves pulling the libido back from the object onto the self and desexualizing it so it can carry out more sublimated activities. Now, if this ego is to be valuable, some "mirror"[8] is needed to reassure it and re-insure it of its value. Woman will be the foundation for this specular duplication, giving man back "his" image and repeating it as the "same." If an *other* image, an *other* mirror were to intervene, this inevitably would entail the risk of mortal crisis. Woman will therefore be this sameness—or at least its mirror image—and, in her role of mother, she will facilitate the repetition of the same, in contempt for her difference. Her own sexual difference. Moreover, through her "penis envy," she will supply anything that might be lacking in this specula(riza)tion. Calling back, now and forever, that *remainder* that melts into the depths of the mirror, that sexual energy necessary to carry out the work. The work of death.

So "woman" can function as place—evanescent beyond, point of discharge—as well as time—eternal return, temporal detour—for the sublimation and, if possible, mastery of the work of death. She will also be the representative-representation (*Vorstellung-Repräsentanz*), in other words, of the death drives that cannot (or theoretically could not) be perceived without horror, that the eye (of) consciousness refuses to recognize. In a protective misprision that cannot be put aside without the failure of a certain gaze: which is the whole point of castration. Up to this point, *the main concepts of psychoanalysis, its theory, will have taken no account of woman's desire*, not even of "her" castration. For their ways are too narrowly derived from the history and the historicization of (so-called) male sexuality. From that process by which consciousness comes into being and woman remains the place for the inscription of repressions. All of which demands that, without knowing it, she should provide a basis for such fantasies as the amputation of her sex organ, and that the "anatomy" of her body should put up the security for reality. She provides irrefutable, because natural, proof that this is not a matter of the silent action of the death drives. She will therefore be despoiled, without recourse, of all valid, valuable images of her sex/organs, her body. She is condemned to "psychosis," or at best "hysteria," for lack—censorship? foreclusion? repression?—of a valid signifier for her "first" desire and for her sex/organs.

This doesn't mean that the question of castration isn't raised for woman but rather that it refers back in reality to the father's castration, including the father of psychoanalysis—to his fear, his refusal, his rejection, of an *other* sex. For if to castrate woman is to inscribe her in the law of the same desire, *of the desire for the same*, what exactly is "castration"? And what is the relationship of the agent of castration to the concept and its practice?

NOTES

1. Cf. the relationship Freud establishes between castration anxiety, the fear of losing one's sight, and the fear of one's father's death (in "The Uncanny," *SE*, XVII: 219–52). Or again this: "It often happens that neurotic men declare that they feel there is something uncanny about the female genital organs. This *unheimlich* place, however, is the entrance to the former *Heim* (home) of all human beings, to the place where each one of us lived once upon a time and in the beginning. . . . In this case, too, then, the *unheimlich* is what was once *heimisch*, familiar; the prefix 'un' is the token of repression" ("The Uncanny," p. 245). For the moment let us concentrate on the strange disquiet felt about the female genitals. The woman-mother would be *unheimlich* not only by reason of a repression of a primitive relationship to the maternal but also because her sex/organs are strange, yet close; while "heimisch" as a mother, woman would remain "un" as a woman. Since woman's sexuality is no doubt the most basic form of the *unheimlich*.

2. This echoes Leibniz's question in *Principles of Nature and of Grace Founded on Reason:* "Why is there something rather than nothing?" Or again: "That which is truly not *one* entity, is not truly one *entity* either": Leibniz, letter to Arnauld, April 30, 1687. (Leibniz, *Philosophical Writings*, ed. G. H. R. Parkinson, trans. Mary Morris and G. H. R. Parkinson [London: Dent, 1934 and 1973], pp. 199 and 67.)

3. In other words, the "fact of castration" will leave woman with only one option—the semblance, the mummery of femininity, which will always already have been to "act like" the value recognized by/for the male. The fact that certain men want to "act like" women thus raises the question whether they thereby take back for themselves that "femininity" which was assigned to woman as an inferior copy of their relation to the origin.

4. Of course this will initially imply bisexuality, but here it would evoke instead the "brilliance" of the mirror which explodes into sexual pleasure, like and unlike according to each sex.

5. This might be understood as a tautology, unless the word "a" is re-marked. In other words, if dialectic has *the* one, *the* same as the horizon of its process, then it is necessarily phallocentric.

6. Translation of *Aufhebung*.

7. For the following section, the reader should refer to *Beyond the Pleasure Principle*, "Instincts and their Vicissitudes," *SE*, XIV, and "The Economic Problem of Masochism," *SE*, XIX.

8. A certain flat mirror would thus serve to desexualize drives and thereby work out funeral monuments for the "subject's" ego.

THE FATHER'S SEDUCTION

The first third of Luce Irigaray's *Speculum de l'autre femme* is called 'The Blind Spot of an Old Dream of Symmetry.' It is a close reading of 'Femininity,' one of Freud's *New Introductory Lectures on Psycho-Analysis* (1933). This encounter between Irigaray's feminist critique and Freud's final text on woman is an important training ground for a new kind of battle, a feminine seduction/disarming/unsettling of the positions of phallocratic ideology. Irigaray's tactic is a kind of reading: close reading, which separates the text into fragments of varying size, quotes it and then comments with various questions and associations. She never sums up the meaning of Freud's text, nor binds all her commentaries, questions, associations into a unified representation, a coherent interpretation. Her commentaries are full of loose ends and unanswered questions. As a result, the reader does not so easily lose sight of the incoherency and inconsistency of the text.

That could be seen as a victory for feminism. The Man's order is disturbed by the woman with the impertinent questions and the incisive comments. But as with all seductions, the question of complicity poses itself. The dichotomy active/passive is always equivocal in seduction, that is what distinguishes it from rape. So Freud might have been encouraging Irigaray all along, 'asking for it.' By exhibiting this "symptom," this crisis-point in metaphysics where the sexual "indifference" which assured metaphysics its coherence and "closure" finally exposes itself, Freud proposes it to analysis: his text asking to be heard, to be read' (*Speculum*, p. 29).

Freud might have seduced Irigaray. It might be psychoanalysis that has won over feminism. The very strategy of reading with which Irigaray works Freud over is presented by Freud himself earlier in these *New Introductory Lectures* where he writes, 'we ask the dreamer, too, to free himself from the impression of the manifest dream, to divert his attention from the dream as a whole on to the separate portions of its content and to report to us in succession everything that occurs to him in relation to each of these portions—what associations present themselves to him if he focuses on each of them separately.'[1]

Freud's text asks for analysis. Not just any analysis, but the peculiar technique developed in psychoanalysis for dealing with dreams and other 'symptoms.' Freud proposed the model of the rebus for understanding dreams. According to the dictionary, a rebus is 'a riddle composed of words or syllables depicted by symbols or pictures that suggest the sound of the words or syllables they represent.' As a total picture, a unified representation, the rebus makes no sense. It is only by separating the picture into its elements, dealing with them one at a time, making all possible associations, that one can get anywhere. So psychoanalysis in its technique if not its theory offers an alternative to coherent, unified representation.

The rebus-text shatters the manifest unity so as to produce a wealth of associations which must necessarily be reduced if the goal of interpretation is to reach a final, definitive meaning, the 'latent dream-thoughts.' The unconscious is reappropriated to the model of consciousness—a circumscription analogous to the reappropriation of otherness, femininity to sameness, masculinity. Whereas Freud proposes the rebus as merely a path to the 'latent thoughts,' Irigaray radicalizes Freud's rebus. Irigaray's dream-analysis ('The Blind Spot of an Old *Dream* of Symmetry') does not offer a final latent thought, but merely presents the abundance of associations, not editing those that 'lead nowhere.'

Yet Irigaray's encounter with Freud is not a psychoanalysis. Freud is not there to associate. Irigaray both asks questions (the analyst's role) and supplies associations (the dreamer's role). And since many questions go unanswered they appear directed to the reader, who thus becomes the dreamer. She does not aim to decipher Freud's peculiar psyche, but rather to unravel 'an old dream,' everyone's dream, even Irigaray's dream. The dream is everyone's inasmuch as everyone is within 'the metaphysical closure,' inasmuch as any reader is a 'subject,' which is to say has been philosophically reduced to a unified, stable, sexually indifferent subject, trapped in the old dream of symmetry.

('Symmetry' from the Greek *summetros*—'of like measure'; from *sun*—'like, same,' and *metron*—'measure.' Symmetry is appropriating two things to like measure, measure by the same standard: for example the feminine judged by masculine standards. Judged by masculine measures, woman is inadequate, castrated.)

On the first page of *Speculum*, Irigaray interrupts Freud's text with the attributive indicator: 'he says, they [masculine plural] say.' She repeatedly does that, attributing Freud's words to both a masculine singular and a masculine plural subject pronoun. The old dream belongs to any subject, to anyone speaking and therefore in the position of subject. 'Every theory of the "subject" [Every theory about the subject as well as every theory produced by a subject] will always have been appropriate(d) to the "masculine"' (*Speculum*, p. 165). The neutral 'subject' is actually a desexualized, sublimated guise for the masculine sexed being. Woman can be subject by fitting male standards which are not appropriate to, cannot measure any specificity of femininity, any difference. Sexual indifference is not lack of sexuality, but lack of any different sexuality, the old dream of symmetry, the other, woman, circumscribed into woman as man's complementary other, his appropriate opposite sex.

But what of '*the blind spot* of an old dream of symmetry'? What is the blind spot? What cannot be seen, what is excluded from the light? According to Freud, the sight of woman's genitalia horrifies the young boy because he sees an absence. Mark that he does not see what is there, he sees the absence of a phallus.

Nothing to see, nothing that looks like a phallus, nothing of like measure (*summetros*), no coherent visual representation in a familiar form. Nothing to see becomes nothing of worth. The privilege of sight over other senses, oculocentrism, supports and unifies phallocentric, sexual theory (theory—from the Greek *theoria*, from *theoros*, 'spectator,' from *thea*, 'a viewing'). *Speculum* (from *specere*, 'to look at') makes repeated reference to the oculocentrism of theory. 'Every theory of the "subject" will always have been appropriate(d) to the "masculine."' Every *theoria*, every viewing of the subject will have always been according to phallomorphic standards. Hence there is no valid representation of woman; but only a lack.

The female sex organs are the blind spot. Freud's theory must occult female sexuality, in order to manifest symmetry. But a blind spot can also be thought as the locus of greatest resistance in a dream, the least easily interpretable point and thus the most tantalizing. To call a text a dream in a Freudian context is not like calling it an illusion. To point to the blind spot of a dream is *not a moral condemnation*. For it to be a moral condemnation, it would be grounded in an ethic of absolute *luc*idity and en*light*enment. The etymology of such words implies the morality of oculocentrism. Dreams are the 'royal road to the unconscious' and ask for reading destructive of unified 'phallomorphic' representation, the very reading Irigaray gives. The locus of greatest resistance, 'the blind spot' is the heart of the dream, the crisis-point crying, begging for analysis.

Blind also like Oedipus is blinded. Freud is assimilated by Irigaray to Oedipus. Freud, man, is never really out of the Oedipus complex, never resolves his Oedipal phase. According to Freud, the end of the Oedipus complex marks the end of the boy's phallic phase. The phallic phase is characterized by the opposition phallic/castrated. In that phase there is no representation of an other sex— the vagina, for example, is 'unknown.' Supposedly, the difference between the phallic phase and adult sexuality is that the dichotomy phallic/castrated gives way to the opposition masculine/feminine. But if, as Irigaray finds in her reading of Freud, the boy, the man, never resolves his Oedipal complex, then he never leaves the phallic phase, and the opposition masculine/feminine merely masks the opposition phallic/castrated. 'A boy's mother is the first object of his love, and she remains so too during the formation of his Oedipus complex and, *in essence, all through his life*' (*NIL*, p. 118, my italics). Woman's destiny is to become her husband's mother: 'A marriage is not made secure until the wife has succeeded in making her husband her child as well and in acting as a mother to him' (*NIL*, pp. 133–4). The blind spot is the price of man's inability to escape his Oedipal destiny. Theory cannot see woman, but can only represent, re-present, make present again endlessly, 'all through his life,' Mother, the masculine subject's *own* original complementary other.

Oedipus/Freud is an old riddle-solver. Oedipus solved the riddle of the sphinx; Freud learned to read the rebus of dreams. In the Freud text that Irigaray analyzes there is another riddle at stake: 'Throughout history people have knocked their heads against the riddle of the nature of femininity.' Yet Irigaray never quotes or comments on this sentence. It occurs on the second page of 'Femininity' and is followed by four lines of poetry—the only poetry in this text. Irigaray only begins her reading of 'Femininity' after the poetry, in fact immediately after the poetry, thus ignoring the first two pages of text. Reading *Speculum*, one would never notice she does not begin at the beginning, for the paragraph she does start with 'makes sense' as an opening for Freud's lecture.

What are we to make of this exclusion of a large section of the text? Although here and there a few words or even a short sentence are omitted from Irigaray's reinscription of Freud, this is the only exclusion of such major proportion. Perhaps we must read this as another blind spot of an old dream of symmetry.

The section omitted is introductory and diverse, speaking of many things and not just on the topic of femininity. So one of the effects of Irigaray's omission is to give a more consistent, more unified representation of the text. In the same way, omitting the poetry homogenizes the discourse. The heterogeneous must be ignored by phallocentrism. Irigaray's forgetting renders Freud's text more phallocentric. Perhaps, then, the 'forgetting' is a tactical decision. Does she choose to ignore the materiality of the text in order to delineate and condemn the 'phallocentric theory'? She does not consistently use this tactic. At other moments in *Speculum* she emphasizes the crisis-points of confusion and contradiction, signalling the workings of the unconscious and the 'feminine' in Freud's text. Is it the inconsistency of her strategy, the lack of unity to her reading, that makes it most effective as an unsettling of phallocentric discourse?

Whatever the foundation for it, her omission, like Freud's 'blind spot,' has the effect of begging for analysis, implicating her reader in the kind of reading she is doing. In this addendum to Irigaray's dream-work, this investigation of her 'blind spot,' I would like to spend some time on the lines of poetry, as the least homogenized part of Freud's discourse, most resistant to an economy of the same. In this I am following the lead of another feminist, Lacanian reader, Shoshana Felman, who has written: '*Literature . . . is the unconscious of psychoanalysis; . . .* the unthought out shadow in psychoanalytic *theory* is precisely its own involvement with literature; . . . literature *in* psychoanalysis functions precisely as its "*unthought*": as the condition of possibility *and* the self-subversive *blind spot* of psychoanalytic *thought*.'[2] Felman's terms are resonant with those at play in Irigaray. The 'shadow in *theory*' calls to the oculocentric etymology of theory, and the appearance of the 'blind spot,' also in that visual register, implicates this quotation in our present investigation. 'Literature' in Felman's discussion plays the same role (support and blind spot) in relation to psychoanalytic theory as 'the feminine' in Irigaray's reading. It might be appropriate to look at the effect of this poetry on Freud's 'Femininity.'

Freud has just said: 'Throughout history people have knocked their heads against the riddle of the nature of femininity' and then he quotes: 'Heads in hieroglyphic bonnets/ Heads in turbans and black birettas/ Heads in wigs and thousand other/ Wretched, sweating heads of humans.' A puzzling inclusion, in many ways. Why quote poetry about heads instead of about woman? The poem has the effect of emphasizing the marginal word 'heads,' which is used in Freud's sentence in a figurative sense and ought to efface itself. Yet the poetry, repeating the word four times, makes 'heads' the dominant word in the sentence. The 'riddle of femininity' is eclipsed by an obsession with heads.

Irigaray suggests (*Speculum*, p. 39) that in Freud's theory the materiality of sex is obliterated by 'the Idea of sex' (she capitalizes to recall Plato and metaphysics). In other words, the riddle of sex, of sexual difference, the puzzling otherness there in its unresolved materiality is occulted, leaving in its place metaphysics, the Idea, in other words, 'heads . . . heads . . . heads.'

The enigmatic 'hieroglyphic bonnet' suggests Egypt and in this riddle context reminds us of the riddle of the Sphinx. We think of Oedipus and the way solving riddles leads to blindness. A 'solved' riddle is the reduction of heterogeneous material to logic, to the homogeneity of logical thought, which produces a blind spot, the inability to see the otherness that gets lost in the reduction. Only the unsolved riddle, the process of riddle-work before its final completion, is a confrontation with otherness.

Hieroglyphs themselves are a sort of riddle. Indeed, like a rebus, they present pictures which as a whole are not unified, and can only be read if one distinguishes the elements. 'Hieroglyphic' has the figurative sense of 'having a hidden meaning' and also 'hard to read, undecipherable.' As if the mysterious 'hieroglyphic bonnet' were itself a hieroglyph, this reader cannot determine if it is undecipherable or has a hidden meaning she cannot uncover. Such is also the puzzle of this entire poetic interruption. Why did Freud put it here? Why did Irigaray forget it?

The four lines are from Heinrich Heine's *Nordsee* (The Baltic), from a section of the poem entitled 'Fragen' (Questions). As an intrusion into Freud's lecture the poem indeed poses many questions: Why a poem about heads? Why a poem here and nowhere else? What is a hieroglyphic bonnet? Perhaps this hieroglyphic intrusion is not unlike Irigaray's interruptions. She often inserts a parenthetic question mark into Freud's or her own text, not altering the statement, but merely calling it into question. Much of her commentary consists in merely asking questions. And the largest section of her next book *Ce Sexe qui n'en est pas un* is, like Heine's poem, entitled 'Questions,'[3] Of course, unlike Irigaray's questions, Heine's are well buried. Freud's text only attributes the lines to *Nordsee*, not mentioning the title 'Fragen.' (Although it appears in a footnote to the English translation, the title 'Fragen' is in neither the German nor the French versions.) And there are no questions in the four lines of poetry quoted. Simply the reader's question: Why are these lines here?

None the less, might not Irigaray's impertinent questions already be implicit in the disruption to Freud's lecture, the interruption of his discourse, the distraction from his main point, wrought by Heine's poetry, Heine's 'Fragen'? After all, it can be construed to make her point about the sublimation of sex into 'heads.' Does she forget the poem so as to forget her already inscribed place in Freud's text? her own complicity in the dream symmetry she decries? Is she not reducing Freud to a single discourse, thus making his text more phallic, more centred? Perhaps any text can be read as either body (site of contradictory drives and heterogeneous matter) or Law? The exclusion of the Heine poem serves to place Freud more firmly on the side of the Law, which enables Irigaray to be more firm, more certain of her position against him. To be against the Law is to be outside the Law. But to be against a body is a more ambiguous, unsettling position.

In Heine's 'Questions' a youth asks the sea to answer 'life's hidden riddle, the riddle primeval and painful.' He asks specifically: 'Tell me, what signifies man? From whence doth he come? And where doth he go?' There is no answer, only the murmuring of the sea. The poem then ends with the line: 'And a fool is awaiting the answer.'[4]

At the beginning of the section called 'Questions' in *Ce Sexe*, Irigaray writes: 'Since the writing and publication of *Speculum*, many questions have been asked. And this book is, in a way, a collection of questions. It does not "really" answer them. It pursues their questioning. It continues to interrogate' (p. 119). The fool waits for an answer. Irigaray is not interested in the answer. She pursues a ceaseless questioning which has not time and is not foolish enough to wait for an answer.

The first part of Irigaray's 'Questions' takes place in a philosophy seminar, where, in response to *Speculum*, she has been invited as 'authority on women,' for the students to ask her questions. The situation is somewhat analogous to that of 'Femininity,' in which Freud is lecturing on women, professing about women, allowing the audience to learn from his expertise. Tied up in this dialectic of questions and answers is the problematic of 'authority on women.' To have a theory of woman is already to reduce the plurality of woman to the coherent and thus phallocentric representations of theory. Irigaray, as professor of woman, is in the role of 'subject of theory,' subject theorizing, a role appropriate to the masculine. She is in Freud's role, dreaming his dream. How can she avoid it without simply giving up speaking, leaving authority to men and phallocentrism?

She begins the transcribed seminar with this introduction: 'There are questions that I don't really see how I could answer. In any case "simply"' (*Ce Sexe*, p. 120). She can respond to a question, give associations, keep talking, hopefully continue to interrogate. But she 'doesn't see,' has a blind spot which she exposes: her inability to give a 'simple' answer, a unified, definitive answer, the kind valorized by an ideology of well-framed representation. She is inadequate to a phallomorphic answer. The phallus is singular ('simple'), represents a unified self, as opposed to the indefinite plurality of female genitalia (clitoris, vagina, lips—how many?, cervix, breasts—Irigaray is fond of making the list, which never has quite the same elements, never is 'simply' finished).

'In other words,' she continues, 'I don't know how to conduct here some *renversement* [overthrow/reversal] of the pedagogic relation in which, holding a truth about woman, a theory of woman, I could answer your questions: answer for woman in front of you.' The pedagogic relation expects her as 'authority' to have a 'truth,' a 'theory' which would allow her to 'simply' answer. She would then 'answer for woman,' speak for her not as her. Woman would be the subject-matter, the material of her discourse. She would trade woman, just as women have always been 'merchandise' in a commerce between men. Woman is passed from the hands of the father to the husband, from the pimp to the john, from the professor to the student who asks questions about the riddle of femininity.

There is a certain pederasty implicit in pedagogy. A greater man penetrates a lesser man with his knowledge. The *homo*sexuality means that both are measurable by the same standards, by which measure one is greater than the other. Irigaray uncovers a sublimated male homosexuality structuring all our institutions: pedagogy, marriage, commerce, even Freud's theory of so-called heterosexuality. Those structures necessarily exclude women, but are unquestioned because sublimated—raised from suspect homo*sexuality* to secure homo*logy*, to the sexually indifferent *logos*, science, logic.

But what of Irigaray's phrase: 'I don't know how to conduct here some *renverse-*

ment of the pedagogic relaton'? Again she is admitting, from the position of supposed knowledge, her inadequacy—'I don't know.' That already is a reversal of
the pedagogic relation. The teacher 'knows,' the student does not. But what
Irigaray does not know is how to reverse the relation, how to get out of the position of authority. Her lack of knowledge is specifically her inability to speak her
lack of knowledge, her inability to make a non-phallic representation. Of course
there is also the sense that a woman in the role of authority is already a reversal.
But she cannot carry off that reversal, cannot profess about women, cannot
'simply' theorize. 'Renversement' means both 'reversal' and 'overthrow.' The
pedagogic relation ought to be overthrown, but this subversion tends to be a reversal, which would bring us back to the same. If men and women, teachers and
students switched places, there would still be an economy of symmetry, in which
the knowledge of the one, the theory of the one, was the gauge for measuring
the worth of the other, still no dialogue between two different sexes, knowl-
edges, only a homologue with one side lacking what the other has.

'I will thus not bring definitions into a questioned discourse.' She does not
know what to do to bring about an upset of the pedagogic, pederastic relation,
but she can decide what not to do. She refuses definitions, definiteness which
fixes plurality into unified representations. She will not bring definitions from
outside into a 'questioned discourse.' The process of questioning is a specific
dialectic shattering stable assumptions and producing contextual associations. To
bring in ready-made definitions as answer to questions is not really to allow one's
discourse or authority to be called into question. Such prepared answers are not
part of a specific dialogue, but simply immutable truth that is unaffected by dialogue. That sort of relation—the mocked-up, artificial, Socratic dialogue of pedagogy with the 'answer' prior to and independent of the question and the
questioning—denies any possibility of an unsettling contact with the questioner's otherness, one that might affect definition. Good pedagogic definition
remains aloof from the situation, free from the desires of student and teacher,
free from desire, sexually indifferent. Irigaray's uncertain, indeterminate attempt
to respond to questions without giving definitive answers thus attempts really to
engage the questions, to dialogue with something *hetero* (other) rather than being
trapped in the *homo* (same).

Compare Irigaray's seminar to Freud's situation in the 'lecture' on femininity.
First, there is the difference between lecture and seminar, the seminar supposedly implying a plurality of contribution, whereas the lecture divides into
speaker presumed to have knowledge and listeners presumed to learn—to be
lacking in knowledge.[5] But as Irigaray reminds us in the first footnote of *Speculum*, 'Femininity' is a fictive lecture. In the preface to the *New Introductory Lectures*, Freud writes: 'These new lectures . . . have never been delivered. . . . If,
therefore, I once more take my place in the lecture room, it is only by an artifice
of the imagination; it may help me not to forget to bear the reader in mind as I
enter more deeply into my subject.'

As he 'enters more deeply into his subject,' in this case as he 'enters more
deeply' into woman, he needs an 'artifice of the imagination,' a fantasy that he
is really communicating not just trapped in his own sameness. Freud fantasizes
the lecture hall so as to conjure up the comforting pederastic relation as he
penetrates into femininity. Whereas Irigaray will not give answers, and publishes

the questions posed by others, Freud, with the exception of the Heine fragment and its hidden questions, writes from an imaginary dialogue in which otherness is simply a fantasy, an artificial projection. Such is, according to Irigaray, the so-called heterosexual encounter: man's relation is only to his imaginary other; femininity is no more encountered as otherness and difference than in Freud's audience.

Irigaray takes Freud's fictive lecture and forces it into a dialogic context. She becomes the reader, not Freud's imagined reader, but an impertinent questioner. Although Freud begins his lecture 'Ladies and Gentlemen,' a few pages later (right after the Heine poem and its shift of emphasis from woman to man), he says: 'Nor will *you* have escaped worrying over this problem, because *you* are men; as for the *women among you* this will not apply, *they* are themselves this riddle' (my italics). When he explicitly addresses the audience as sexed beings, he reserves the second person pronoun for men, and refers to women with the third person pronoun. Freud talks *to* men *about* women. I have provided my own translation because Strachey's translation (*NIL*, p. 113) covers over this telling inequity in Freud's text, using the second person pronoun for both sexes. Irigaray's 'impertinence' is her assumption of the place of Freud's interlocutor, an exclusively male position. As a woman, this lecture does not speak to her, only about her. But she speaks up, responds, breaking the homosexual symmetry.

Irigaray impertinently asks a few questions, as if the student, the women, the reader were not merely a lack waiting to be filled with Freud's knowledge, but a real interlocutor, a second viewpoint. And in her questions a certain desire comes through, not a desire for a 'simple answer,' but for an encounter, a hetero-sexual dialogue. Not in the customary way we think heterosexual—the dream of symmetry, two opposite sexes complementing each other. In that dream the woman/student/reader ends up functioning as mirror, giving back a coherent, framed representation to the appropriately masculine subject. There is no real sexuality of the *heteros*. 'Will there ever be any relation between the sexes?'—asks Irigaray (*Speculum*, p. 33).

Irigaray's reading of Freud seeks that 'relation between the sexes.' Her aggression is not merely some man-hating, penis-envying urge to destroy the phallocentric oppressor. She lays fiery siege to the Phallus, out of a yearning to get beyond its prohibitiveness and touch some masculine body. It is the rule of the Phallus as standard for any sexuality which denigrates women, and makes any relation between the sexes impossible, any relation between two modalities of desire, between two desires unthinkable. The rule of the Phallus is the reign of the One, of Unicity. In the 'phallic phase,' according to Freud, 'only one kind of genital organ comes into account—the male.'[6] Freud, man, is arrested in the phallic phase, caught in the reign of the One, obsessively trying to tame otherness in a mirror-image of sameness.

In the transcribed seminar, Irigaray says: 'What I desire and what I am waiting for, is what men will do and say if their sexuality gets loose from the empire of phallocratism' (*Ce Sexe*, pp. 133–4). The masculine exists no more than does the feminine. The specificity of both is suppressed by the reign of the Idea, the Phallus. Freud is not without a certain awareness of this. Something like the trace of a non-phallic masculinity can be read in a footnote that appears a few sentences after his statement about 'one kind of genital organ': 'It is remarkable, by the way, what a small degree of interest the other part of the male genitals, the little sac with its contents, arouses in the child. From all one hears in analyses one could not guess that the male genitals consist of anything more than the penis.' 'By the way,' in a remark marginal to the central thrust of his argument can be found that which must be left aside by phallocentrism. Yet it is precisely because of the anatomical discrepancies in 'all one hears in analysis' that analysis can be the place where the untenable reductions that constitute the reign of the phallus are most noticeable.

The difference, of course, between the phallic suppression of masculinity and the phallic suppression of femininity is that the phallic represents (even if inaccurately) the masculine and not the feminine. By giving up their bodies, men gain power—the power to theorize, to represent themselves, to exchange women, to reproduce themselves and mark their offspring with their name. All these activities ignore bodily pleasure in pursuit of representation, reproduction, production. 'In this "phallocratic" power, man is not without loss: notably in regard to the enjoyment of his body' (*Ce Sexe*, p. 140).

Irigaray's reading of Freud's theory continually discovers an ignoring of pleasure. The theory of sexuality is a theory of the sexual function (ultimately the reproductive function) and questions of pleasure are excluded, because they have no place in an economy of production. Commenting on Freud's discussion of breast-feeding, Irigaray remarks: 'Every consideration of pleasure in nursing appears here to be excluded, unrecognized, prohibited. That, certainly, would introduce some nuances in such statements' (*Speculum*, p. 13). A consideration of pleasure would introduce a few nuances into the theory ('nuance,' from *nue*, cloud). A consideration of pleasure might cloud the theory, cloud the view, reduce its ability to penetrate with clarity, to appropriate. The distinction of active and passive roles becomes more ambiguous when it is a question of pleasure. And it is the distintion active/passive which is in question in Freud's discussion of nursing.

Freud writes: 'A mother is active in every sense towards the child; the act of nursing itself may equally be described as the mother suckling the baby or as her being sucked by it' (*NIL*, p. 115). The sentence seems contradictory. If a mother is so clearly 'active in every sense,' why is the only example chosen so easily interpretable as either active or passive? The difficulty is symptomatic of one of the most insistent problems for Freud—the relation of the dichotomies active/passive and masculine/feminine. According to Freud, the opposition active/passive characterizes the anal phase, whereas masculine/feminine is the logic of adult sexuality. In this discussion of the mother Freud is trying to show how improper it is to identify feminine with passive, masculine with active, since a mother is clearly feminine and clearly active. Again and again in different books and articles over a span of twenty years,[7] Freud will try to differentiate and articulate the anal dichotomy and the adult sexual opposition. Without much success.

In 'Femininity' Freud refers to the confusion of these two oppositions as 'the error of superimposition.' The footnote to the English translation indicates that such an error consists in 'mistaking two different things for a single one' (*NIL*, p. 115). Thus 'the error of superimposition' is emblematic of what Irigaray finds as the general 'error' of Freud's sexual theory—mistaking two different sexes for a single one.

In the French translation of the text,[8] 'Überdeckungsfehler' ('the error of su-perimposition') becomes 'l'erreur de raisonnement analogique,' 'the error of analogical reasoning.' The specific superimposition in this text is both analogical and anal-logical. Anal logic organizes everything according to the opposition ac-tive/passive. The phrase 'analogical reasoning' ties the whole problematic of de-fining sexual difference in a non-anal logic to another persistent embarrassment. For Freud, analogy is dangerously seductive. In 1905 he writes: 'Shall we not *yield to the temptation* to construct [the formation of a joke] on the analogy of the formation of a dream?' In 1937: 'I have not been able to *resist the seduction* of an analogy.'[9] Is not the guilty compulsion to analogy symptomatic of Freud's in-ability to escape anal logic?

Irigaray suggests that Freud's model of sexuality has a strong anal erotic bias. The faeces become other products (a baby, a penis, a representation, a theory)[10] but the emphasis is on the product. Why else would the ambiguous nursing (de-scribable in either active or passive terms) be so clearly an 'activity'? Indeed breast-feeding constitutes the model of the Freudian oral phase, which is defined as prior to the opposition active/passive. Freud's anal logic thus even intrudes into the very stage defined as pre-anal. In this case, the inconsistency cannot be explained as a legacy in a later stage from the earlier anal period. We are faced with the anal fixation of the theory itself.

An accusation of contradiction could be levelled at this point. Earlier in the present text Freud has been deemed 'arrested in the phallic phase.' Now he is judged 'arrested' in the anal phase. It is not a question of resolving this contradic-tion, of fixing the diagnosis of Freud's personal pathology. Freud himself ac-knowleged that the stages of development are not clearly separate and distinct. The attempt to isolate each stage could be considered an effect to reduce sex-uality to only one modality at any given moment, symptomatic of the rule of the One.

The investment in unicity, in one sexuality, shows itself in Freud's description of the little girl 'in the phallic phase.' (Of course, the very assimilation of the girl into a *phallic* phase is already a sign of 'an error of superimposition,' analogical reasoning.) Freud insists that, in the phallic phase, little girls only get pleasure from their clitoris and are unfamiliar with the rest of their genitalia. (Remember the phallic phase is characterized as recognizing only one kind of sexual organ.) Yet others have found girls at this stage aware of vaginal sensations, and Freud dismisses this peremptorily as well as somewhat contradictorily: 'It is true that there are a few isolated reports of early vaginal sensations as well, but it could not be easy to distinguish these from sensations in the anus or vestibulum; *in any case they cannot play a great part.* We are *entitled to keep our view* that in the phallic phase of girls the clitoris is the leading erotogenic zone' (*NIL*, p. 118, italics mine). Why 'can they not play a great part'? Because then 'we' would not be 'entitled to keep our *view*,' keep our *theoria*. Entitled by what or whom? The blind spot is ob-vious; what must be protected is 'our view,' appropriate to the masculine.

Freud insists on reducing the little girl's genitalia to her clitoris because that organ fits 'our view,' is phallomorphic, can be measured by the same standard (*summetros*). 'We are now obliged to recognize that the little girl is a little man' (*NIL*, p. 118), declares Freud, making the phallocentric pederastic economy clear. The girl is assimilated to a male model, male history and, 'naturally,' found lacking. The condition of that assimilation is the reduction of any possible complexity, plural sexuality, to the one, the simple, in this case to the phallomorphic clitoris.

Once reduced to phallomorphic measures, woman is defined as 'really castrated,' by Freud/man. As such she is the guarantee against man's castration anxiety. She has no desires that don't complement his, so she can mirror him, provide him with a representation of himself which calms his fears and phobias about (his own potential) otherness and difference, about some 'other view' which might not support his narcissistic overinvestment in his penis. 'As for woman, *on peut se demander* [one could wonder, ask oneself] why she submits so easily . . . to the counter-phobic projects, projections, productions of man relative to his desire' (*Speculum*, p. 61).

The expression for wondering, for speculation, which Irigaray uses above, is the reflexive verb 'se demander,' literally 'to ask oneself.' Most of the 'impertinent questions' in *Speculum* seem to be addressed to Freud, or men, or the reader. But this question of woman's easy submission she must ask herself. And the answer is not so obvious. A little later, she attempts to continue this line of questioning: 'And why does she lend herself to it so easily? Because she's suggestible? Hysterical? But one can catch sight of the vicious circle' (*Speculum*, p. 69). This question of the complicity, the suggestibility of the hysteric who 'finally says in analysis [what is not] foreign to what she is expected to say there' (*Speculum*, p. 64) leads us to the contemplation of another vicious circle—the (hysterical) daughter's relationship to the father (of psychoanalysis).

The daughter's desire for her father is desperate: 'the only redemption of her value as a girl would be to seduce the father, to draw from him the mark if not the admission of some interest' (*Speculum*, p. 106). If the phallus is the standard of value, then the Father, possessor of the phallus, must desire the daughter in order to give her value. But the Father is a man (a little boy in the anal, the phallic phase) and cannot afford to desire otherness, an other sex, because that opens up his castration anxiety. The father's refusal to seduce the daughter, to be seduced by her (seduction wreaking havoc with anal logic and its active/passive distribution), gains him another kind of seduction (this one more one-sided, more like violation), a veiled seduction in the form of the law. The daughter submits to the father's rule, which prohibits the father's desire, the father's penis, out of the desire to seduce the father by doing his bidding and thus pleasing him.

That is the vicious circle. The daughter desires a heterosexual encounter with the father, and is rebuffed by the rule of the homo-logical, raising the homo over the hetero, the logical over the sexual, decreeing neither the hetero nor the sexual worthy of the father. Irigaray would like really to respond to Freud, provoke him into a real dialogue. But the only way to seduce the father, to avoid scaring him away, is to please him, and to please him one must submit to his law which proscribes any sexual relation.

Patriarchal law, the law of the father, decrees that the 'product' of sexual union, the child, shall belong exclusively to the father, be marked with his name. Also that the womb which bears that child should be a passive receptacle with no claims on the product, the womb 'itself possessed as a means of (re)production' (*Speculum*, p. 16). Irigaray understands woman's exclusion from production via a reading of Marx and Engels which she brings in as a long association near the end of her reading of Freud's dream. That exclusion of the woman is inscribed in her relation to the father. Any feminist upheaval, which would change woman's definition, identity, name as well as the foundations of her economic status, must undo the vicious circle by which the desire for the father's desire (for his penis) causes her to submit to the father's law, which denies his desire/penis, but operates in its place, and according to Irigaray, even procures for him a surplus of pleasure.

The question of why woman complies must be asked. To ask that question is to ask what woman must not do anymore, what feminist strategy ought to be. Only a fool would wait for an answer, deferring the struggle against phallocentrism until a definitive explanation were found. In lieu of that 'answer,' I would like slowly to trace a reading of a section of *Speculum* which concerns the father and the daughter, in this case specifically the father of psychoanalysis and his hysterics, but also the father of psychoanalytic theory and his daughter Irigaray.

Irigaray reads in Freud an account of an episode from the beginnings of psychoanalysis which '*caused [him] many distressing hours*' (Irigaray's italics): 'In the period in which the main interest was directed to discovering infantile sexual traumas, almost all my woman patients told me that they had been seduced by their father. I was driven to recognize in the end, that these reports were untrue and so came to understand that hysterical symptoms are derived from phantasies and not from real occurrences' (*NIL*, p. 120; *Speculum*, p. 40). Irigaray suggests that the reader 'imagine that x, of the masculine gender, of a ripe age, uses the following language, how would you interpret it: "it caused me many distressing hours," "almost all *my* woman patients told *me* that they had been seduced by their *father*."' Irigaray invites her reader to interpret Freud. She does not offer a definitive reading, closing the text, making it her property, but only notes those phrases which seem interpretable, drawing the rebus but not giving the solution, so as to induce her reader to play analyst.

'And let us leave the interpretation to the discretion of each analyst, be she/he improvised for the occasion. It would even be desirable if she/he were, otherwise he/she would risk having already been seduced, whatever her/his sex, or her/his gender, by the *father* of psychoanalysis' (pp. 40–1, Irigaray's italics). The reader is considered an analyst and capable of his/her own interpretation. But Irigaray recognizes that 'the analyst' in question may not 'really' be a psychoanalyst, but rather be the recipient of a sort of battlefield promotion, prepared only by the experience of reading Freud with Irigaray. *Speculum* becomes a 'training analysis,' the reading of it preparing the reader to make her/his own interpretations. And the analyst trained by *Speculum* is likely to be a better analyst of Freud than a proper psychoanalyst, for any analyst—male or female, masculine or feminine, *Irigaray herself*— is likely to have been seduced by Freud, seduced by his theory.

There is a contrast here between two different kinds of analyst. The one privileged by Irigaray is an amateur, a 'wild analyst,'[11] not 'entitled' to analyze, but simply a reader, who can catch symptoms and make her/his own interpretations. The other sort of analyst is a professional, which is to say has investments in analysis as an identity and an economically productive system, and a transference onto Freud, that is, a belief in Freud's knowledge. The analyst is likely to 'see' according to Freud's theory, having been seduced into sharing 'our view,' giving a predictable 'Freudian' interpretation, one that always hears according to the same standards, returning every text to pre-existent Freudian models, 'bringing definitions into a discourse from outside.' Irigaray as an analyst is perhaps not as likely to give an attentive, specific interpretation as is her reader. So that, once again, as in the *Ce Sexe* seminar, she proceeds to some sort of overthrow of a certain hierarchy between theoretical writer as distributor of knowledge and reader as passive, lacking consumer.

But certain questions pose themselves to this reader at this point. Can Irigaray really overthrow the pedagogic relation, or is this merely a ruse to flatter the reader into less resistance, a ploy to seduce her reader? For she *does* go on to interpret, simply having deferred it for a few sentences. As in an artificial, Socratic (pederastic) dialogue, if she asks the reader to think for him/her self, that reader will produce an answer which the teacher expected all along, the right answer. Like Freud in the *New Introductory Lectures*, Irigaray is fantasizing a reader, one who would make the same associations as she does, one created in her own image.

It is thus interesting that at this point Irigaray is reasoning by analogy—Freud: hysteric :: father : daughter :: Freud : any other psychoanalyst. Analogy, as Irigaray has said, is one of the 'eternal operations which support the defining of difference in function of the a priori of the same' (*Speculum*, p. 28). The analogy of analyst to father is the analytic analogy *par excellence*, the fact of transference. Transference is the repetition of infantile prototype relations, of unconscious desires in the analytic relation. Without transference, psychoanalysis is simply literary criticism, by an unimplicated, discriminating reader, lacking either affect or effect.

The example of *the* analytic analogy suggests a way of overturning the phallocentric effects of analogy. Analogy cannot simply be avoided, it is radically tempting. Transference occurs everywhere, not just in psychoanalysis but in any relation where the other is 'presumed to know,' relations to teachers, loved ones, doctors. But psychoanalysis provides the opportunity to analyze the transference, take cognizance of it as such and work it through. Likewise Irigaray's use of analogy in a context where analogy has been analyzed provides a way of making the economic function of analogy evident. The phallocentric effect of analogy would be explicit, and thus less powerful.

Her use of analogy as well as her projection of a reader in her own image, a narcissistic mirror, means she has acceded to a certain economy of the homo . . . and the auto . . . , the economy which men have and women are excluded from. Of course, the 'answer' is not to set up another homosexual economy, but that may be necessary as one step to some hetero-sexuality. 'Of course, it is not a question, in the final analysis, of demanding the *same* attributions. Still it is necessary that women arrive at the same so that consideration be made, be imposed of the differences that they would elicit there' (*Speculum*, pp. 148–9). Women need to reach 'the same': that is, be 'like men,' able to represent themselves. But they also need to reach 'the same,' 'the homo': their own homosexual economy, a female homosexuality that ratifies and glorifies female standards. The two 'sames' are inextricably linked. Female homosexuality, when raised to an ideology, tends to be either masculine (women that are 'like men') or essentialistic (based on some ascertainable female identity). The latter is as phallic as the former for it reduces heterogeneity to a unified, rigid representation. But without a female homosexual economy, a female narcissistic ego, a way to represent herself, a woman in a heterosexual encounter will always be engulfed by the male homosexual economy, will not be able to represent her difference. Woman must demand 'the same,' 'the homo' and then not settle for it, not fall into the trap of thinking a female 'homo' is necessarily any closer to a representation of otherness, an opening for the other.

Yet having posed these questions of Irigaray's own imaginary economy, I might also say she was right about her reader. Her fantasized reader would be the impertinent questioner she is. I am asking Irigaray Irigarayan questions, reopening the interrogation when Luce becomes too tight, when she seems to settle on an answer. I have been seduced into a transference onto her, into following her suggestion, into saying 'what is not foreign to what I am expected to say,' into playing 'wild analysis.'

'This seduction', she continues, 'is covered of course, in practice or theory, by a normative statement, by a *law*, which denies it.' A new element is introduced by Irigaray and emphasized: the law. This term, foreign to the Freud passage she is reading, not suggested by him, is Irigaray's own association, her remaining in excess of the Freudian seduction. 'Law' is a political term, refers to patriarchy, the law of the father, and here will refer to Freud's legislative control of his theory, his normative prescriptions.

Her text continues with another sentence from Freud: 'It was only later that I was able to recognize in the phantasy of being seduced by the father *the expression of the typical Oedipus complex* in women' (*NIL,* p. 120; *Speculum,* p. 41, Irigaray's italics). The seduction by the father is not only a mere fantasy, but is the manifestation of a typical complex, one that is supposed to be universal, and therefore a law of Freudian theory. Given Irigaray's introduction to this passage, we read that the Oedipus complex, the incest taboo, the law forbidding intercourse between father and daughter, covers over a seduction, masks it so it goes unrecognized. Also covered over is a seduction in the theory, whereby psychoanalysts through their transference onto Freud (their unfulfillable desire for his love and approval) accept his immutable theoretical laws.

'It would be too risky, it seems, to admit that the father could be a seducer, and even eventually that he desires to have a daughter *in order* to seduce her. That he wishes to become an analyst in order to exercise by hypnosis, suggestion, transference, interpretation bearing on the sexual economy, on the proscribed, prohibited sexual representations, a *lasting seduction upon the hysteric*' (Irigaray's italics) (p. 41). Freud as a father must deny the possibility of being seductive. Patriarchy is grounded in the uprightness of the father. If he were devious and unreliable, he could not have the power to legislate. The law is supposed to be just—that is, impartial, indifferent, free from desire.

'It is necessary to endure the law which exculpates the operation. But, of course, if under cover of the law the seduction can now be practised at leisure, it appears just as urgent to interrogate *the seductive function of the law itself* (Irigaray's italics) (p. 41). For example, the law which prohibits sexual intercourse between analyst and patient actually makes the seduction last forever. The sexually actualized seduction would be complicitous, nuanced, impossible to delineate into active and passive roles, into the anal logic so necessary for a traditional distribution of wealth and power. But the 'lasting seduction' of the law is never consummated and as such maintains the power of the prohibited analyst. The seduction which the daughter desires would give her contact with the father as masculine sexed body. The seduction which the father of psychoanalysis exercises refuses her his body, his penis, and asks her to embrace his law, his indifference, his phallic uprightness.

Psychoanalysis works because of the tranference, which is to say because the hysteric transfers her desire to seduce her father, to be seduced by him, onto her analyst. But since the fantasy of seducing the father is produced in analysis, it is produced for the analyst. In order to please him, in order to seduce him, in order to give him what he wants. The installation of the law in psychoanalysis, the prohibition of the analyst's penis by the Doctor in a position to validate the hysteric, to announce her as healthy, sets up the desperate situation outlined by Irigaray: 'the only redemption of her value as a girl would be to seduce the father' (*Speculum*, p. 106).

'Thus is it not simply true, nor on the other hand completely false, to claim that the little girl fantasizes being seduced by her father, because it is just as pertinent to admit that *the father seduces his daughter* but that, refusing to recognize and realize his desire—not always it is true—, *he legislates to defend himself from it*' (*Speculum*, p. 41, Irigaray's italics). The father's law is a counterphobic mechanism. He must protect himself from his desire for the daughter. His desire for the feminine threatens his narcissistic overvaluation of his penis. It is so necessary to deny his attraction for the little girl that Freud denies her existence: 'We must admit that the little girl is a little man.' If the father were to desire his daughter he could no longer exchange her, no longer possess her in the economy by which true, masterful possession is the right to exchange. If you cannot give something up for something of like value, if you consider it nonsubstitutable, then you do not possess it any more than it possesses you. So the father must not desire the daughter for that threatens to remove him from the homosexual commerce in which women are exchanged between men, in the service of power relations and community for the men.

Also: if the father desires his daughter as daughter he will be outside his Oedipal desire for his mother, which is to say also beyond 'the phallic phase.' So the law of the father protects him and patriarchy from the potential havoc of the daughter's desirability. Were she recognized as desirable in her specificity as daughter, not as son ('little man') nor as mother, there would be a second sexual economy besides the one between 'phallic little boy' and 'phallic mother.' An economy in which the stake might not be a reflection of the phallus, the phallus's desire for itself.

'In place of the desire for the sexed body of the father there thus comes *to be proposed, to be imposed, his law*, that is to say an institutionalizing and institutionalized discourse. In part, defensive (Think of those "distressing hours." . . .)' (pp. 41–2, Irigaray's italics). The father gives his daughter his law and protects himself from her desire for his body, protects himself from his body. For it is only the law—and not the body—which constitutes him as patriarch. Paternity is corporeally uncertain, without evidence. But patriarchy compensates for that with the law which marks each child with the father's name as his exclusive property.

'That is not to say that the father *should* make love with his daughter—from time to time it is better to state things precisely—but that it would be good to call into question this mantle of the law with which he drapes his desire, and his sex (organ)' (p. 42, Irigaray's italics). The strategic difference between a prescriptive 'should' and a suggestive 'it would be good' is emphasized by this sentence. But suggestion may have always been a more devious, more powerful mode of prescription.

'It would be good' to question the law's appearance of indifference, as Irigaray questions it, and find the phallic stake behind it. 'It would be good' to lift 'the mantle of the law' so that the father's desire and his penis are exposed. But that does not mean the 'answer' is for the father to make love to his daughter. Irigaray, above all, avoids giving an answer, a prescription such as 'the father *should* make love with his daughter.' Not that he might not, not that it might not be a way to lift the law and expose the sexed body. The 'should' is underlined, because that is what Irigaray will not say. She will not lay down a law about how to lift the law.

If she did lay down such a law—'the father should make love with his daughter'—it would, like all laws, mask and support a desire. The negated appearance of this law suggests the mechanism Freud called *Verneinung*—'Procedure whereby the subject, while formulating one of his wishes, thoughts or feelings which has been repressed hitherto, contrives, by disowning it, to continue to defend himself against it.'[12] What surfaces that Irigaray needs to disown is her desire to impose the law upon the father, her desire for a simple reversal rather than an overthrow of patriarchy.

This sentence is marked as symptomatic, asking for analysis, by the parenthetical remark, 'from time to time it is better to state things precisely.' 'From time to time' pretends this is a random moment; it just happens to fall at this moment that she will be precise. But this is the only such remark in all of her reading of Freud; this is the point where she is most afraid of a misunderstanding. Her desire to be precise is in direct contradiction to something she says later in *Speculum* about feminist strategies of language: 'No clear nor univocal statement can, in fact, dissolve this mortgage, this obstacle, all of them being caught, trapped, in the same reign of credit. It is as yet better to speak only through equivocations, allusions, innuendos, parables. . . . Even if you are asked for some *précisions* [precise details]' (*Speculum*, p. 178). All clear statements are trapped in the same economy of values, in which clarity (oculocentrism) and univocity (the One) reign. Precision must be avoided, if the economy of the One is to be unsettled. Equivocations, allusions, etc. are all flirtatious; they induce the interlocutor to listen, to encounter, to interpret, but defer the moment of assimilation back into a familiar model. Even if someone asks for *précisions*, even if that someone is oneself, it is better for women to avoid stating things precisely.

Yet on one point Luce Irigaray tightens up, prefers to be precise, to return to an economy of clarity and univocity. The locus of her conservatism, her caution, her need to defend herself, is the question of making love with the father. It is terrifying to lift the mantle of the law and encounter the father's desire. What if in making love the father still remained the law, and the daughter were just passive, denied? The father's law has so restructured the daughter and her desires that it is hard, well nigh impossible, to differentiate the Father (that is to say, the Law) from the male sexed body. What if making love with the father were merely a ruse to get the impertinent daughter to give up her resistance to the law?

Irigaray clutches for something stable, something precise, because she too is a 'subject,' with a stake in identity. And the law of the father gives her an identity, even if it is not her own, even if it blots out her feminine specificity. To give it up is not a 'simple' matter. It must be done over and over.

Later she will say of her method in *Speculum*, 'what was left for me to do was to *have an orgy with the philosophers*' (*Ce Sexe*, p. 147, Irigaray's italics). Intercourse with the philosophers, the father of psychoanalysis included, is her method of insinuation into their system, of inducing them to reveal the phallocentrism, the desire cloaked in their sexual indifference. Perhaps these are merely two different moments in her inconsistency: a brave, new, loose moment—'have an orgy with the philosophers'—and a defensive, cautious moment—refusal to make love with the father.

But perhaps these are not merely two moments. The two situations are *analogous, but not the same*. Some terms may be more frightening, more sensitive than others. 'Father' may be more threatening than 'philosophers.' She writes in *Ce Sexe:* 'As far as the family is concerned, *my answer will be simple* and clear: the family has always been the privileged locus of the exploitation of women. Thus, as far as familialism is concerned, there is no ambiguity!' (pp. 139–40, my italics). Yet earlier in the same text she says she cannot give a 'simple answer.' Also: 'faire l'amour' (make love) may be more threatening than 'faire la noce' (have an orgy). Maybe what frightens her is not seduction of the father or by the father but 'making love.' 'Love' has always been sublimated, idealized desire, away from the bodily specificity and towards dreams of complementarity, and the union of opposites, difference resolved into the One. 'Love' is entangled with the question of woman's complicity; it may be the bribe which has persuaded her to agree to her own exclusion. It may be historically necessary to be momentarily blind to father-love; it may be politically effective to defend—tightly, unlucidly—against its inducements, in order for a 'relation between the sexes,' in order to rediscover some feminine desire, some desire for a masculine body that does not respect the Father's law.

NOTES

1. Sigmund Freud, *New Introductory Lectures on Psycho-Analysis, Standard Edition*, vol. XXII, pp. 10–11. Hereafter referred to as *NIL*.

2. Shoshana Felman. 'To Open the Question,' *Literature and Psychoanalysis: The Question of Reading: Otherwise, Yale French Studies*, 55–6 (1977) p. 10. All italics Felman's except 'blind spot.'

3. Luce Irigaray, *Ce Sexe qui n'en est pas un* (Editions de Minuit, 1977). In this context of questions it is interesting to notice Felman's titles: 'The Question of Reading,' 'To Open the Question.'

4. *The Poems of Heine, Complete*, trans. Edgar Alfred Bowring (G. Bell and Sons, 1916) p. 260.

5. Is then the ironic lesson of Jacques Lacan's 'Seminars,' which are enormous lectures, in which he functions as the only and ultimate 'subject presumed to know,' that a

seminar is always merely a disguised lecture, that one does not know how to overthrow the pedagogic relation?

6. Freud, 'The Infantile Genital Organization,' *Standard Edition*, vol. XIX, p. 142.

7. The most glaring of these symptomatic attempts to disengage the anal definitions from the genital can be found in a 1915 footnote to the third of Freud's *Three Essays on the Theory of Sexuality;* a footnote to Chapter 4 of *Civilization and its Discontents* (1930); and here in 'Femininity' (1933).

8. *Nouvelles Conférences sur la psychanalyse* (Gallimard, Collection Idées). This is the edition Irigaray uses.

9. The first quotation is from *Jokes and their Relation to the Unconscious*, the second from 'Constructions in Analysis.' The italics in both are mine.

10. Freud provides the model for metaphorization of faeces in 'On Transformations of Instinct as Exemplified in Anal Erotism' (1917), *Standard Edition* vol. XVII.

11. The term is Freud's from his article on '"Wild" Psychoanalysis,' *Standard Edition*, vol. XI.

12. J. Laplanche and J. B. Pontalis, *The Language of Psycho-analysis*, p. 201.

WORKS CITED

Felman, Shoshana, 'To Open the Question,' *Yale French Studies* 55–6 (1978/79).

Freud, Sigmund, *Civilization and its Discontents, The Standard Edition of the Complete Psychological Works* (Hogarth Press, 1953–74) vol. XXI.

———, 'Constructions in Analysis,' *Standard Edition*, vol. XXIII.

———, 'Female Sexuality,' *Standard Edition*, vol. XXI.

———, 'The Infantile Genital Organization,' *Standard Edition*, vol. XIX.

———, *Jokes and Their Relation to the Unconscious, Standard Edition*, vol. VIII.

———, *New Introductory Lectures on Psycho-Analysis, Standard Edition*, vol. XXII.

———, '"Wild" Psychoanalysis,' *Standard Edition*, vol. XI.

———, 'On Transformations of Instinct as Exemplified in Anal Erotism,' *Standard Edition*, vol. XVII.

Heine, Heinrich, *The Poems, Complete*, trans. Edgar Alfred Bowring (G. Bell and Sons, 1916).

Irigaray, Luce, *Ce Sexe qui n'en est pas un* (Éditions de Minuit, 1977).

———, *Speculum de l'autre femme* (Éditions de Minuit, 1974).

Lacan, Jacques, 'A la mémoire d'Ernest Jones: Sur sa théorie du symbolisme,' *Écrits* (Éditions du Seuil, 1966).

———, 'The Agency of the Letter in the Unconscious,' *Écrits: A Selection*, trans. Alan Sheridan (Tavistock and Norton, 1977).

———, 'La Chose freudienne,' *Écrits*.

———, 'The Freudian Thing,' *Écrits: A Selection*.

———, *The Four Fundamental Concepts of Psycho-Analysis*, trans. Alan Sheridan (Hogarth and Norton, 1976).

———, 'The Insistence of the Letter in the Unconscious,' trans. Jan Miel, *Structuralism* (Anchor Books, 1970).

———, 'L'Instance de la lettre dans l'inconscient,' *Écrits*.

———, 'Intervention sur le transfert,' *Écrits*.

———, 'Kant avec Sade,' *Écrits*.

———, 'The Mirror Stage,' *Écrits: A Selection*.

———, 'Position de l'inconscient,' *Écrits*.

———, 'Propos directifs pour un congrès sur la sexualité féminine,' *Écrits*.

————, *Le Séminaire livre XI: les quatre concepts fondamentaux de la psychanalyse* (Editions du Seuil, 1973).

————, *Le Séminaire livre XX: Encore* (Éditions du Seuil, 1975).

————, 'Séminaire sur "La Lettre volée,"' *Écrits*.

————, 'Seminar on the Purloined Letter,' trans. Jeffrey Mehlman, *Yale French Studies*, 48 (1972).

————, 'La Signification du phallus,' *Écrits*.

————, 'The Signification of the Phallus,' *Écrits: A Selection*.

————, 'Le Stade du miroir,' *Écrits*.

————, 'La Subversion du sujet et la dialectique du désir,' *Écrits*.

————, 'The Subversion of the Subject and the Dialectic of Desire,' *Écrits: A Selection*.

————, *Télévision* (Éditions du Seuil, 1973).

Laplanche, Jean and Pontalis, Jean-Baptiste, *The Language of Psycho-Analysis*, trans. Donald Nicholson-Smith (Hogarth Press, 1973).

LAURA MULVEY

VISUAL PLEASURE AND NARRATIVE CINEMA

I INTRODUCTION

(a) A Political Use of Psychoanalysis

This paper intends to use psychoanalysis to discover where and how the fascination of film is reinforced by pre-existing patterns of fascination already at work within the individual subject and the social formations that have moulded him. It takes as its starting-point the way film reflects, reveals and even plays on the straight, socially established interpretation of sexual difference which controls images, erotic ways of looking and spectacle. It is helpful to understand what the cinema has been, how its magic has worked in the past, while attempting a theory and a practice which will challenge this cinema of the past. Psychoanalytic theory is thus appropriated here as a political weapon, demonstrating the way the unconscious of patriarchal society has structured film form.

The paradox of phallocentrism in all its manifestations is that it depends on the image of the castrated women to give order and meaning to its world. An idea of woman stands as linchpin to the system: it is her lack that produces the phallus as a symbolic presence, it is her desire to make good the lack that the phallus signifies. Recent writing in *Screen* about psychoanalysis and the cinema has not sufficiently brought out the importance of the representation of the female form in a symbolic order in which, in the last resort, it speaks castration and nothing else. To summarise briefly: the function of woman in forming the patriarchal unconscious is twofold: she firstly symbolises the castration threat by her real lack of a penis and secondly thereby raises her child into the symbolic. Once this has been achieved, her meaning in the process is at an end. It does not last into the world of law and language except as a memory, which oscillates between memory of maternal plentitude and memory of lack. Both are posited on nature (or on anatomy in Freud's famous phrase). Woman's desire is subjugated to her image as bearer of the bleeding wound; she can exist only in relation to castration and cannot transcend it. She turns her child into the signifier of her own desire to possess a penis (the condition, she imagines, of entry into the symbolic). Either she must gracefully give way to the word, the name of the father and the law, or else struggle to keep her child down with her in the half-light of the imaginary. Woman then stands in patriarchal culture as a signifier for the male other, bound by a symbolic order in which man can live out his fantasies and obsessions through linguistic command by imposing them on the silent image of woman still tied to her place as bearer, not maker, of meaning.

There is an obvious interest in this analysis for feminists, a beauty in its exact rendering of the frustration experienced under the phallocentric order. It gets us nearer to the roots of our oppression, it brings closer an articulation of the problem, it faces us with the ultimate challenge: how to fight the unconscious structured like a language (formed critically at the moment of arrival of language) while still caught within the language of the patriarchy? There is no way in which we can produce an alternative out of the blue, but we can begin to make a break by examining patriarchy with the tools it provides, of which psychoanalysis is not the only but an important one. We are still separated by a great gap from important issues for the female unconscious which are scarcely relevant to phallocentric theory: the sexing of the female infant and her relationship to the symbolic, the sexually mature woman as non-mother, maternity outside the signification of the phallus, the vagina. But, at this point, psychoanalytic theory as it now stands can at least advance our understanding of the *status quo*, of the patriarchal order in which we are caught.

(b) Destruction of Pleasure as a Radical Weapon

As an advanced representation system, the cinema poses questions about the ways the unconscious (formed by the dominant order) structures ways of seeing and pleasure in looking. Cinema has changed over the last few decades. It is no longer the monolithic system based on large capital investment exemplified at its best by Hollywood in the 1930s, 1940s and 1950s. Technological advances (16mm and so on) have changed the economic conditions of cinematic production, which can now be artisanal as well as capitalist. Thus it has been possible for an alternative cinema to develop. However self-conscious and ironic Hollywood managed to be, it always restricted itself to a formal *mise en scène* reflecting the dominant ideological concept of the cinema. The alternative cinema provides a space for the birth of a cinema which is radical in both a political and an aesthetic sense and challenges the basic assumptions of the mainstream film. This is not to reject the latter moralistically, but to highlight the ways in which its formal preoccupations reflect the psychical obsessions of the society which produced it and, further, to stress that the alternative cinema must start specifically by reacting against these obsessions and assumptions. A politically and aesthetically avant-garde cinema is now possible, but it can still only exist as a counterpoint.

The magic of the Hollywood style at its best (and of all the cinema which fell within its sphere of influence) arose, not exclusively, but in one important aspect, from its skilled and satisfying manipulation of visual pleasure. Unchallenged, mainstream film coded the erotic into the language of the dominant patriarchal order. In the highly developed Hollywood cinema it was only through these codes that the alienated subject, torn in his imaginary memory by a sense of loss, by the terror of potential lack in fantasy, came near to finding a glimpse of satisfaction: through its formal beauty and its play on his own formative obsessions. This article will discuss the interweaving of that erotic pleasure in film, its meaning and, in particular, the central place of the image of woman. It is said that analysing pleasure, or beauty, destroys it. That is the intention of this article. The satisfaction and reinforcement of the ego that represent the high point of film history hitherto must be attacked. Not in favour of a reconstructed new pleasure, which cannot exist in the abstract, nor of intellectualised unpleasure, but to make way for a total negation of the ease and plenitude of the narrative fiction film. The alternative is the thrill that comes from leaving the past behind without simply rejecting it, transcending outworn or oppressive forms, and daring to break with normal pleasurable expectations in order to conceive a new language of desire.

II PLEASURE IN LOOKING/FASCINATION WITH THE HUMAN FORM

A   The cinema offers a number of possible pleasures. One is scopophilia (pleasure in looking). There are circumstances in which looking itself is a source of pleasure, just as, in the reverse formation, there is pleasure in being looked at. Originally, in his *Three Essays on Sexuality*, Freud isolated scopophilia as one of the component instincts of sexuality which exist as drives quite independently of the erotogenic zones. At this point he associated scopophilia with taking other people as objects, subjecting them to a controlling and curious gaze. His particular examples centre on the voyeuristic activities of children, their desire to see and make sure of the private and forbidden (curiosity about other people's genital and bodily functions, about the presence or absence of the penis and, retrospectively, about the primal scene). In this analysis scopophilia is essentially active. (Later, in 'Instincts and Their Vicissitudes,' Freud developed his theory of scopophilia further, attaching it initially to pregenital auto-eroticism, after which, by analogy, the pleasure of the look is transferred to others. There is a close working here of the relationship between the active instinct and its further development in a narcissistic form.) Although the instinct is modified by other factors, in particular the constitution of the ego, it continues to exist as the erotic basis for pleasure in looking at another person as object. At the extreme, it can become fixated into a perversion, producing obsessive voyeurs and Peeping Toms whose only sexual satisfaction can come from watching, in an active controlling sense, an objectified other.

At first glance, the cinema would seem to be remote from the undercover world of the surreptitious observation of an unknowing and unwilling victim. What is seen on the screen is so manifestly shown. But the mass of mainstream film, and the conventions within which it has consciously evolved, portray a hermetically sealed world which unwinds magically, indifferent to the presence of the audience, producing for them a sense of separation and playing on their voyeuristic fantasy. Moreover the extreme contrast between the darkness in the auditorium (which also isolates the spectators from one another) and the brilliance of the shifting patterns of light and shade on the screen helps to promote the illusion of voyeuristic separation. Although the film is really being shown, is there to be seen, conditions of screening and narrative conventions give the spectator an illusion of looking in on a private world. Among other things, the position of the spectators in the cinema is blatantly one of repression of their exhibitionism and projection of the repressed desire onto the performer.

B   The cinema satisfies a primordial wish for pleasurable looking, but it also goes further, developing scopophilia in its narcissistic aspect. The conventions of mainstream film focus attention on the human form. Scale, space, stories are all anthropomorphic. Here, curiosity and the wish to look intermingle with a fascination with likeness and recognition: the human face, the human body, the relationship between the human form and its surroundings, the visible presence of the person in the world. Jacques Lacan has described how the moment when a child recognises its own image in the mirror is crucial for the constitution of the ego. Several aspects of this analysis are relevant here. The mirror phase occurs at a time when children's physical ambitions outstrip their motor capacity, with the result that their recognition of themselves is joyous in that they imagine their mirror image to be more complete, more perfect than they experience in their own body. Recognition is thus overlaid with misrecognition: the image recognised is conceived as the reflected body of the self, but its misrecognition as superior projects this body outside itself as an ideal ego, the alienated subject which, reintrojected as an ego ideal, prepares the way for identification with others in the future. This mirror moment predates language for the child.

Important for this article is the fact that it is an image that constitutes the matrix of the imaginary, of recognition/misrecognition and identification, and hence of the first articulation of the I, of subjectivity. This is a moment when an older fascination with looking (at the mother's face, for an obvious example) collides with the initial inklings of self-awareness. Hence it is the birth of the long love affair/despair between image and self-image which has found such intensity of expression in film and such joyous recognition in the cinema audience. Quite apart from the extraneous similarities between screen and mirror (the framing of the human form in its surroundings, for instance), the cinema has structures of fascination strong enough to allow temporary loss of ego while simultaneously reinforcing it. The sense of forgetting the world as the ego has come to perceive it (I forgot who I am and where I was) is nostalgically reminiscent of that pre-subjective moment of image recognition. While at the same time, the cinema has distinguished itself in the production of ego ideals, through the star system for instance. Stars provide a focus or centre both to screen space and screen story where they act out a complex process of likeness and difference (the glamorous impersonates the ordinary).

C   Sections A and B have set out two contradictory aspects of the pleasurable structures of looking in the conventional cinematic situation. The first, scopophilic, arises from pleasure in using another person as an object of sexual stimulation through sight. The second, developed through narcissism and the constitution of the ego, comes from identification with the image seen. Thus, in film terms, one implies a separation of the erotic identity of the subject from the object on the screen (active scopophilia), the other demands identification of the ego with the object on the screen through the spectator's fascination with and recognition of his like. The first is a function of the sexual instincts, the second of ego libido. This dichotomy was crucial for Freud. Although he saw the two as interacting and overlaying each other, the tension between instinctual drives and

self-preservation polarises in terms of pleasure. But both are formative structures, mechanisms without intrinsic meaning. In themselves they have no signification, unless attached to an idealisation. Both pursue aims in indifference to
perceptual reality, and motivate eroticised phantasmagoria that affect the subject's perception of the world to make a mockery of empirical objectivity.

During its history, the cinema seems to have evolved a particular illusion of
reality in which this contradiction between libido and ego has found a beautifully
complementary fantasy world. In *reality* the fantasy world of the screen is subject
to the law which produces it. Sexual instincts and identification processes have a
meaning within the symbolic order which articulates desire. Desire, born with
language, allows the possibility of transcending the instinctual and the imaginary, but its point of reference continually returns to the traumatic moment of
its birth: the castration complex. Hence the look, pleasurable in form, can be
threatening in content, and it is woman as representation/image that crystallises
this paradox.

III WOMAN AS IMAGE, MAN AS BEARER OF THE LOOK

A   In a world ordered by sexual imbalance, pleasure in looking has been split
between active/male and passive/female. The determining male gaze projects its
fantasy onto the female figure, which is styled accordingly. In their traditional
exhibitionist role women are simultaneously looked at and displayed, with their
appearance coded for strong visual and erotic impact so that they can be said to
connote *to-be-looked-at-ness*. Woman displayed as sexual object is the *leitmotif* of
erotic spectacle: from pin-ups to strip-tease, from Ziegfeld to Busby Berkeley,
she holds the look, and plays to and signifies male desire. Mainstream film neatly
combines spectacle and narrative. (Note, however, how in the musical song-and-
dance numbers interrupt the flow of the diegesis.) The presence of woman is an
indispensable element of spectacle in normal narrative film, yet her visual presence tends to work against the development of a story-line, to freeze the flow of
action in moments of erotic contemplation. This alien presence then has to be
integrated into cohesion with the narrative. As Budd Boetticher has put it:

> What counts is what the heroine provokes, or rather what she represents. She
> is the one, or rather the love or fear she inspires in the hero, or else the con-
> cern he feels for her, who makes him act the way he does. In herself the
> woman has not the slightest importance.

(A recent tendency in narrative film has been to dispense with this problem altogether; hence the development of what Molly Haskell has called the 'buddy
movie,' in which the active homosexual eroticism of the central male figures can
carry the story without distraction.) Traditionally, the woman displayed has
functioned on two levels: as erotic object for the characters within the screen
story, and as erotic object for the spectator within the auditorium, with a shifting
tension between the looks on either side of the screen. For instance, the device
of the show-girl allows the two looks to be unified technically without any apparent break in the diegesis. A woman performs within the narrative; the gaze of the
spectator and that of the male characters in the film are neatly combined without

breaking narrative verisimilitude. For a moment the sexual impact of the performing woman takes the film into a no man's land outside its own time and space. Thus Marilyn Monroe's first appearance in *The River of No Return* and Lauren Bacall's songs in *To Have and Have Not*. Similarly, conventional close-ups of legs (Dietrich, for instance) or a face (Garbo) integrate into the narrative a different mode of eroticism. One part of a fragmented body destroys the Renaissance space, the illusion of depth demanded by the narrative; it gives flatness, the quality of a cut-out or icon, rather than verisimilitude, to the screen.

B   An active/passive heterosexual division of labour has similarly controlled narrative structure. According to the principles of the ruling ideology and the psychical structures that back it up, the male figure cannot bear the burden of sexual objectification. Man is reluctant to gaze at his exhibitionist like. Hence the split between spectacle and narrative supports the man's role as the active one of advancing the story, making things happen. The man controls the film fantasy and also emerges as the representative of power in a further sense: as the bearer of the look of the spectator, transferring it behind the screen to neutralise the extra-diegetic tendencies represented by woman as spectacle. This is made possible through the processes set in motion by structuring the film around a main controlling figure with whom the spectator can identify. As the spectator identifies with the main male protagonist, he projects his look onto that of his like, his screen surrogate, so that the power of the male protagonist as he controls events coincides with the active power of the erotic look, both giving a satisfying sense of omnipotence. A male movie star's glamorous characteristics are thus not those of the erotic object of the gaze, but those of the more perfect, more complete, more powerful ideal ego conceived in the original moment of recognition in front of the mirror. The character in the story can make things happen and control events better than the subject/spectator, just as the image in the mirror was more in control of motor co-ordination.

In contrast to woman as icon, the active male figure (the ego ideal of the identification process) demands a three-dimensional space corresponding to that of the mirror recognition, in which the alienated subject internalised his own representation of his imaginary existence. He is a figure in a landscape. Here the function of film is to reproduce as accurately as possible the so-called natural conditions of human perception. Camera technology (as exemplified by deep focus in particular) and camera movements (determined by the action of the protagonist), combined with invisible editing (demanded by realism), all tend to blur the limits of screen space. The male protagonist is free to command the stage, a stage of spatial illusion in which he articulates the look and creates the action. (There are films with a woman as main protagonist, of course. To analyse this phenomenon seriously here would take me too far afield. Pam Cook and Claire Johnston's study of *The Revolt of Mamie Stover* in Phil Hardy [ed.], *Raoul Walsh* [Edinburgh, 1974], shows in a striking case how the strength of this female protagonist is more apparent than real.)

C1   Sections III A and B have set out a tension between a mode of representation of woman in film and conventions surrounding the diegesis. Each is associated with a look: that of the spectator in direct scopophilic contact with the female form displayed for his enjoyment (connoting male fantasy) and that of the spectator fascinated with the image of his like set in an illusion of natural space, and through him gaining control and possession of the woman within the di-egesis. (This tension and the shift from one pole to the other can structure a single text. Thus both in *Only Angels Have Wings* and in *To Have and Have Not*, the film opens with the woman as object of the combined gaze of spectator and all the male protagonists in the film. She is isolated, glamorous, on display, sex-ualised. But as the narrative progresses she falls in love with the main male pro-tagonist and becomes his property, losing her outward glamorous characteristics, her generalised sexuality, her show-girl connotations; her eroticism is subjected to the male star alone. By means of identification with him, through participation in his power, the spectator can indirectly possess her too.)

But in psychoanalytic terms, the female figure poses a deeper problem. She also connotes something that the look continually circles around but disavows: her lack of a penis, implying a threat of castration and hence unpleasure. Ulti-mately, the meaning of woman is sexual difference, the visually ascertainable absence of the penis, the material evidence on which is based the castration com-plex essential for the organisation of entrance to the symbolic order and the law of the father. Thus the woman as icon, displayed for the gaze and enjoyment of men, the active controllers of the look, always threatens to evoke the anxiety it originally signified. The male unconscious has two avenues of escape from this castration anxiety: preoccupation with the re-enactment of the original trauma (investigating the woman, demystifying her mystery), counterbalanced by the devaluation, punishment or saving of the guilty object (an avenue typified by the concerns of the *film noir*); or else complete disavowal of castration by the sub-stitution of a fetish object or turning the represented figure itself into a fetish so that it becomes reassuring rather than dangerous (hence overvaluation, the cult of the female star).

This second avenue, fetishistic scopophilia, builds up the physical beauty of the object, transforming it into something satisfying in itself. The first avenue, voyeurism, on the contrary, has associations with sadism: pleasure lies in ascer-taining guilt (immediately associated with castration), asserting control and sub-jugating the guilty person through punishment or forgiveness. This sadistic side fits in well with narrative. Sadism demands a story, depends on making some-thing happen, forcing a change in another person, a battle of will and strength, victory/defeat, all occurring in a linear time with a beginning and an end. Fetishistic scopophilia, on the other hand, can exist outside linear time as the erotic instinct is focused on the look alone. These contradictions and ambiguities can be illustrated more simply by using works by Hitchcock and Sternberg, both of whom take the look almost as the content or subject matter of many of their films. Hitchcock is the more complex, as he uses both mechanisms. Sternberg's work, on the other hand, provides many pure examples of fetishistic scopophilia.

C2   Sternberg once said he would welcome his films being projected upside-down so that story and character involvement would not interfere with the spec-tator's undiluted appreciation of the screen image. This statement is revealing but ingenuous: ingenuous in that his films do demand that the figure of the woman (Dietrich, in the cycle of films with her, as the ultimate example) should be identifiable; but revealing in that it emphasises the fact that for him the pictorial space enclosed by the frame is paramount, rather than narrative or identification processes. While Hitchcock goes into the investigative side of voyeurism, Sternberg produces the ultimate fetish, taking it to the point where the powerful look of the male protagonist (characteristic of traditional narrative film) is broken in favour of the image in direct erotic rapport with the spectator. The beauty of the woman as object and the screen space coalesce; she is no longer the bearer of guilt but a perfect product, whose body, stylised and fragmented by close-ups, is the content of the film and the direct recipient of the spectator's look.

Sternberg plays down the illusion of screen depth; his screen tends to be one-dimensional, as light and shade, lace, steam, foliage, net, streamers and so on reduce the visual field. There is little or no mediation of the look through the eyes of the main male protagonist. On the contrary, shadowy presences like La Bessière in *Morocco* act as surrogates for the director, detached as they are from audience identification. Despite Sternberg's insistence that his stories are irrelevant, it is significant that they are concerned with situation, not suspense, and cyclical rather than linear time, while plot complications revolve around misunderstanding rather than conflict. The most important absence is that of the controlling male gaze within the screen scene. The high point of emotional drama in the most typical Dietrich films, her supreme moments of erotic meaning, take place in the absence of the man she loves in the fiction. There are other witnesses, other spectators watching her on the screen, their gaze is one with, not standing in for, that of the audience. At the end of *Morocco*, Tom Brown has already disappeared into the desert when Amy Jolly kicks off her gold sandals and walks after him. At the end of *Dishonoured*, Kranau is indifferent to the fate of Magda. In both cases, the erotic impact, sanctified by death, is displayed as a spectacle for the audience. The male hero misunderstands and, above all, does not see.

In Hitchcock, by contrast, the male hero does see precisely what the audience sees. However, although fascination with an image through scopophilic eroticism can be the subject of the film, it is the role of the hero to portray the contradictions and tensions experienced by the spectator. In *Vertigo* in particular, but also in *Marnie* and *Rear Window*, the look is central to the plot, oscillating between voyeurism and fetishistic fascination. Hitchcock has never concealed his interest in voyeurism, cinematic and non-cinematic. His heroes are exemplary of the symbolic order and the law—a policeman (*Vertigo*), a dominant male possessing money and power (*Marnie*)—but their erotic drives lead them into compromised situations. The power to subject another person to the will sadistically or to the gaze voyeuristically is turned onto the woman as the object of both. Power is backed by a certainty of legal right and the established guilt of the woman (evoking castration, psychoanalytically speaking). True perversion is barely concealed under a shallow mask of ideological correctness—the man is on the right side of the law, the woman on the wrong. Hitchcock's skilful use of identification processes and liberal use of subjective camera from the point of view of the male protagonist draw the spectators deeply into his position, making them share his uneasy gaze. The spectator is absorbed into a voyeuristic situation within the screen scene and diegesis, which parodies his own in the cinema.

In an analysis of *Rear Window*, Douchet takes the film as a metaphor for the cinema. Jeffries is the audience, the events in the apartment block opposite correspond to the screen. As he watches, an erotic dimension is added to his look, a central image to the drama. His girlfriend Lisa had been of little sexual interest to him, more or less a drag, so long as she remained on the spectator side. When she crosses the barrier between his room and the block opposite, their relationship is reborn erotically. He does not merely watch her through his lens, as a distant meaningful image, he also sees her as a guilty intruder exposed by a dangerous man threatening her with punishment, and thus finally giving him the opportunity to save her. Lisa's exhibitionism has already been established by her obsessive interest in dress and style, in being a passive image of visual perfection; Jeffries's voyeurism and activity have also been established through his work as a photo-journalist, a maker of stories and captor of images. However, his enforced inactivity, binding him to his seat as a spectator, puts him squarely in the fantasy position of the cinema audience.

In *Vertigo*, subjective camera predominates. Apart from one flashback from Judy's point of view, the narrative is woven around what Scottie sees or fails to see. The audience follows the growth of his erotic obsession and subsequent despair precisely from his point of view. Scottie's voyeurism is blatant: he falls in love with a woman he follows and spies on without speaking to. Its sadistic side is equally blatant: he has chosen (and freely chosen, for he had been a successful lawyer) to be a policeman, with all the attendant possibilities of pursuit and investigation. As a result, he follows, watches and falls in love with a perfect image of female beauty and mystery. Once he actually confronts her, his erotic drive is to break her down and force her *to tell* by persistent cross-questioning.

In the second part of the film, he re-enacts his obsessive involvement with the image he loved to watch secretly. He reconstructs Judy as Madeleine, forces her to conform in every detail to the actual physical appearance of his fetish. Her exhibitionism, her masochism, make her an ideal passive counterpart to Scottie's active sadistic voyeurism. She knows her part is to perform, and only by playing it through and then replaying it can she keep Scottie's erotic interest. But in the repetition he does break her down and succeeds in exposing her guilt. His curiosity wins through; she is punished.

Thus, in *Vertigo*, erotic involvement with the look boomerangs: the spectator's own fascination is revealed as illicit voyeurism as the narrative content enacts the processes and pleasures that he is himself exercising and enjoying. The Hitchcock hero here is firmly placed within the symbolic order, in narrative terms. He has all the attributes of the patriarchal superego. Hence the spectator, lulled into a false sense of security by the apparent legality of his surrogate, sees through his look and finds himself exposed as complicit, caught in the moral ambiguity of looking. Far from being simply an aside on the perversion of the police, *Vertigo* focuses on the implications of the active/looking, passive/looked-at split in terms of sexual difference and the power of the male symbolic encapsulated in the hero. Marnie, too, performs for Mark Rutland's gaze and masquerades as the perfect to-be-looked-at image. He, too, is on the side of the law until, drawn in by obsession with her guilt, her secret, he longs to see her in the act of committing a crime, make her confess and thus save her. So he, too, becomes complicit as he acts out the implications of his power. He controls money and words; he can have his cake and eat it.

IV SUMMARY

The psychoanalytic background that has been discussed in this article is relevant to the pleasure and unpleasure offered by traditional narrative film. The scopophilic instinct (pleasure in looking at another person as an erotic object) and, in contradistinction, ego libido (forming identification processes) act as formations, mechanisms, which mould this cinema's formal attributes. The actual image of woman as (passive) raw material for the (active) gaze of man takes the argument a step further into the content and structure of representation, adding a further layer of ideological significance demanded by the patriarchal order in its favourite cinematic form—illusionistic narrative film. The argument must return again to the psychoanalytic background: women in representation can signify castration, and activate voyeuristic or fetishistic mechanisms to circumvent this threat. Although none of these interacting layers is intrinsic to film, it is only in the film form that they can reach a perfect and beautiful contradiction, thanks to the possibility in the cinema of shifting the emphasis of the look. The place of the look defines cinema, the possibility of varying it and exposing it. This is what makes cinema quite different in its voyeuristic potential from, say, strip-tease, theatre, shows and so on. Going far beyond highlighting a woman's to-be-looked-at-ness, cinema builds the way she is to be looked at into the spectacle itself. Playing on the tension between film as controlling the dimension of time (editing, narrative) and film as controlling the dimension of space (changes in distance, editing), cinematic codes create a gaze, a world and an object, thereby producing an illusion cut to the measure of desire. It is these cinematic codes and their relationship to formative external structures that must be broken down before mainstream film and the pleasure it provides can be challenged.

To begin with (as an ending), the voyeuristic–scopophilic look that is a crucial part of traditional filmic pleasure can itself be broken down. There are three different looks associated with cinema: that of the camera as it records the pro-filmic event, that of the audience as it watches the final product, and that of the characters at each other within the screen illusion. The conventions of narrative film deny the first two and subordinate them to the third, the conscious aim being always to eliminate intrusive camera presence and prevent a distancing awareness in the audience. Without these two absences (the material existence of the recording process, the critical reading of the spectator), fictional drama cannot achieve reality, obviousness and truth. Nevertheless, as this article has argued, the structure of looking in narrative fiction film contains a contradiction in its own premises: the female image as a castration threat constantly endangers the unity of the diegesis and bursts through the world of illusion as an intrusive, static, one-dimentional fetish. Thus the two looks materially present in time and space are obsessively subordinated to the neurotic needs of the male ego. The camera becomes the mechanism for producing an illusion of Renaissance space, flowing movements compatible with the human eye, an ideology of representation that revolves around the perception of the subject; the camera's look is disavowed in order to create a convincing world in which the spectator's surrogate can perform with verisimilitude. Simultaneously, the look of the audience is denied an intrinsic force: as soon as fetishistic representation of the female image threatens to break the spell of illusion, and the erotic image on the screen appears directly (without mediation) to the spectator, the fact of fetishisation, concealing as it does castration fear, freezes the look, fixates the spectator and prevents him from achieving any distance from the image in front of him.

This complex interaction of looks is specific to film. The first blow against the monolithic accumulation of traditional film conventions (already undertaken by radical film-makers) is to free the look of the camera into its materiality in time and space and the look of the audience into dialectics and passionate detachment. There is no doubt that this destroys the satisfaction, pleasure and privilege of the 'invisible guest,' and highlights the way film has depended on voyeuristic active/passive mechanisms. Women, whose image has continually been stolen and used for this end, cannot view the decline of the traditional film form with anything much more than sentimental regret.

WOMEN'S TIME

The nation—dream and reality of the nineteenth century—seems to have reached both its apogee and its limits when the 1929 crash and the National-Socialist apocalypse demolished the pillars that, according to Marx, were its essence: economic homogeneity, historical tradition, and linguistic unity.[1] It could indeed be demonstrated that World War II, though fought in the name of national values (in the above sense of the term), brought an end to the nation as a reality: It was turned into a mere illusion which, from that point forward, would be preserved only for ideological or strictly political purposes, its social and philosophical coherence having collapsed. To move quickly toward the specific problematic that will occupy us in this article, let us say that the chimera of economic *homogeneity* gave way to *interdependence* (when not submission to the economic superpowers), while *historical* tradition and *linguistic* unity were recast as a broader and deeper determinant: what might be called a *symbolic denominator*, defined as the cultural and religious memory forged by the interweaving of history and geography. The variants of this memory produce social territories which then redistribute the cutting up into political parties which is still in use but losing strength. At the same time, this memory or symbolic denominator, common to them all, reveals beyond economic globalization and/or uniformization certain characteristics transcending the nation that sometimes embrace an entire continent. A new social ensemble superior to the nation has thus been constituted, within which the nation, far from losing its own traits, rediscovers and accentuates them in a strange temporality, in a kind of "future perfect," where the most deeply repressed past gives a distinctive character to a logical and sociological distribution of the most modern type. For this memory or symbolic common denominator concerns the response that human groupings, united in space and time, have given not to the problems of the *production* of material goods (i.e., the domain of the economy and of the human relationships it implies, politics, etc.) but, rather, to those of *reproduction*, survival of the species, life and death, the body, sex, and symbol. If it is true, for example, that Europe is representative of such a sociocultural ensemble, it seems to me that its existence is based more on this "symbolic denominator," which its art, philosophy, and religions manifest, than on its economic profile, which is certainly interwoven with collective memory but whose traits change rather rapidly under pressure from its partners.

It is clear that a social ensemble thus constituted possesses both a *solidity* rooted in a particular mode of reproduction and its representations through which the biological species is connected to its humanity, which is a tributary of time; as well as a certain *fragility* as a result of the fact that, through its universality, the symbolic common denominator is necessarily echoed in the corresponding symbolic denominator of another sociocultural ensemble. Thus, barely constituted as such, Europe finds itself being asked to compare itself with, or even to recognize itself in, the cultural, artistic, philosophical, and religious constructions belonging to other supranational sociocultural ensembles. This seems natural when the entities involved were linked by history (e.g., Europe and North America, or Europe and Latin America), but the phenomenon also occurs when the universality of this denominator we have called symbolic juxtaposes modes of production and reproduction apparently opposed in both the past and the present (e.g., Europe and India, or Europe and China). In short, with sociocultural ensembles of the European type, we are constantly faced with a double problematic: that of their *identity* constituted by historical sedimentation, and that of their *loss of identity* which is produced by this connection of memories which escape from history only to encounter anthropology. In other words, we confront two temporal dimensions: the time of linear history, of *cursive time* (as Nietzsche called it), and the time of another history, thus another time, *monumental time* (again according to Nietzsche), which englobes these supranational, sociocultural ensembles within even larger entities.

I should like to draw attention to certain formations which seem to me to summarize the dynamics of a sociocultural organism of this type. The question is one of sociocultural groups, that is, groups defined according to their place in production, but especially according to their role in the mode of reproduction and its representations, which, while bearing the specific sociocultural traits of the formation in question, are *diagonal* to it and connect it to other sociocultural formations. I am thinking in particular of sociocultural groups which are usually defined as age groups (e.g., "young people in Europe"), as sexual divisions (e.g., "European women"), and so forth. While it is obvious that "young people" or "women" in Europe have their own particularity, it is nonetheless just as obvious that what defines them as "young people" or as "women" places them in a diagonal relationship to their European "origin" and links them to similar categories in North America or in China, among others. That is, insofar as they also belong to "monumental history," they will not be only European "young people" or "women" of Europe but will echo in a most specific way the universal traits of their structural place in reproduction and its representations.

Consequently, the reader will find in the following pages, first, an attempt to situate the problematic of women in Europe within an inquiry on time: that time which the feminist movement both inherits and modifies. Second, I will attempt to distinguish two phases or two generations of women which, while immediately universalist and cosmopolitan in their demands, can nonetheless be differentiated by the fact that the first generation is more determined by the implications of a national problematic (in the sense suggested above), while the second, more determined by its place within the "symbolic denominator," is European *and* trans-European. Finally, I will try, both through the problems approached and through the type of analysis I propose, to present what I consider a viable stance for a European—or at least a European woman—within a domain which is henceforth worldwide in scope.

WHICH TIME?

"Father's time, mother's species," as Joyce put it; and, indeed, when evoking the name and destiny of women, one thinks more of the *space* generating and forming the human species than of *time*, becoming, or history. The modern sciences of subjectivity, of its genealogy and accidents, confirm in their own way this intuition, which is perhaps itself the result of a sociohistorical conjuncture. Freud, listening to the dreams and fantasies of his patients, thought that "hysteria was linked to place."[2] Subsequent studies on the acquistion of the symbolic function by children show that the permanence and quality of maternal love condition the appearance of the first spatial references which induce the child's laugh and then induce the entire range of symbolic manifestations which lead eventually to sign and syntax.[3] Moreover, antipsychiatry and psychoanalysis as applied to the treatment of psychoses, before attributing the capacity for transference and communication to the patient, proceed to the arrangement of new places, gratifying substitutes that repair old deficiencies in the maternal space. I could go on giving examples. But they all converge on the problematic of space, which innumerable religions of matriarchal (re)appearance attribute to "woman," and which Plato, recapitulating in his own system the atomists of antiquity, designated by the aporia of the *chora,* matrix space, nourishing, unnameable, anterior to the One, to God and, consequently, defying metaphysics.[4]

As for time, female[5] subjectivity would seem to provide a specific measure that essentially retains *repetition* and *eternity* from among the multiple modalities of time known through the history of civilizations. On the one hand, there are cycles, gestation, the eternal recurrence of a biological rhythm which conforms to that of nature and imposes a temporality whose stereotyping may shock, but whose regularity and unison with what is experienced as extrasubjective time, cosmic time, occasion vertiginous visions and unnameable *jouissance.*[6] On the other hand, and perhaps as a consequence, there is the massive presence of a monumental temporality, without cleavage or escape, which has so little to do with linear time (which passes) that the very word "temporality" hardly fits: All-encompassing and infinite like imaginary space, this temporality reminds one of Kronos in Hesiod's mythology, the incestuous son whose massive presence covered all of Gea in order to separate her from Ouranos, the father.[7] Or one is reminded of the various myths of resurrection which, in all religious beliefs, perpetuate the vestige of an anterior or concomitant maternal cult, right up to its most recent elaboration, Christianity, in which the body of the Virgin Mother does not die but moves from one spatiality to another within the same time via dormition (according to the Orthodox faith) or via assumption (the Catholic faith).[8]

The fact that these two types of temporality (cyclical and monumental) are traditionally linked to female subjectivity insofar as the latter is thought of as necessarily maternal should not make us forget that this repetition and this eternity are found to be the fundamental, if not the sole, conceptions of time in numerous civilizations and experiences, particularly mystical ones.[9] The fact that certain currents of modern feminism recognize themselves here does not render them fundamentally incompatible with "masculine" values.

In return, female subjectivity as it gives itself up to intuition becomes a problem with respect to a certain conception of time: time as project, teleology, linear and prospective unfolding; time as departure, progression, and arrival—in other words, the time of history.[10] It has already been abundantly demonstrated that this kind of temporality is inherent in the logical and ontological values of any given civilization, that this temporality renders explicit a rupture, an expectation, or an anguish which other temporalities work to conceal. It might also be added that this linear time is that of language considered as the enunciation of sentences (noun + verb; topic–comment; beginning–ending), and that this time rests on its own stumbling block, which is also the stumbling block of that enunciation—death. A psychoanalyst would call this "obsessional time," recognizing in the mastery of time the true structure of the slave. The hysteric (either male or female) who suffers from reminiscences would, rather, recognize his or her self in the anterior temporal modalities: cyclical or monumental. This antinomy, one perhaps embedded in psychic structures, becomes, nonetheless, within a given civilization, an antinomy among social groups and ideologies in which the radical positions of certain feminists would rejoin the discourse of marginal groups of spiritual or mystical inspiration and, strangely enough, rejoin recent scientific preoccupations. Is it not true that the problematic of a time indissociable from space, of a space-time in infinite expansion, or rhythmed by accidents or catastrophes, preoccupies both space science and genetics? And, at another level, is it not true that the contemporary media revolution, which is manifest in the storage and reproduction of information, implies an idea of time as frozen or exploding according to the vagaries of demand, returning to its source but uncontrollable, utterly bypassing its subject and leaving only two preoccupations to those who approve of it: Who is to have power over the origin (the programming) and over the end (the use)?

It is for two precise reasons, within the framework of this article, that I have allowed myself this rapid excursion into a problematic of unheard of complexity. The reader will undoubtedly have been struck by a fluctuation in the term of reference: mother, woman, hysteric. . . . I think that the apparent coherence which the term "woman" assumes in contemporary ideology, apart from its "mass" or "shock" effect for activist purposes, essentially has the negative effect of effacing the differences among the diverse functions or structures which operate beneath this word. Indeed, the time has perhaps come to emphasize the multiplicity of female expressions and preoccupations so that from the intersection of these differences there might arise, more precisely, less commercially, and more truthfully, the real *fundamental difference* between the two sexes: a difference that feminism has had the enormous merit of rendering painful, that is, productive of surprises and of symbolic life in a civilization which, outside the stock exchange and wars, is bored to death.

It is obvious, moreover, that one cannot speak of Europe or of "women in Europe" without suggesting the time in which this sociocultural distribution is situated. If it is true that a female sensibility emerged a century ago, the chances are great that by introducing *its own* notion of time, this sensibility is not in agreement with the idea of an "eternal Europe" and perhaps not even with that of a "modern Europe." Rather, through and with the European past and present, as through and with the ensemble of "Europe," which is the repository of memory, this sensibility seeks its own trans-European temporality. There are, in any case, three attitudes on the part of European feminist movements toward this conception of linear temporality, which is readily labeled masculine and which is at once both civilizational and obessional.

TWO GENERATIONS

In its beginnings, the women's movement, as the struggle of suffragists and of existential feminists, aspired to gain a place in linear time as the time of project and history. In this sense, the movement, while immediately universalist, is also deeply rooted in the sociopolitical life of nations. The political demands of women; the struggles for equal pay for equal work, for taking power in social institutions on an equal footing with men; the rejection, when necessary, of the attributes traditionally considered feminine or maternal insofar as they are deemed incompatible with insertion in that history—all are part of the *logic of identification*[11] with certain values: not with the ideological (these are combated, and rightly so, as reactionary) but, rather, with the logical and ontological values of a rationality dominant in the nation-state. Here it is unnecessary to enumerate the benefits which this logic of identification and the ensuing struggle have achieved and continue to achieve for women (abortion, contraception, equal pay, professional recognition, etc.); these have already had or will soon have effects even more important than those of the Industrial Revolution. Univeralist in its approach, this current in feminism *globalizes* the problems of women of different milieux, ages, civilizations, or simply of varying psychic structures, under the label "Universal Woman." A consideration of *generations* of women can only be conceived of in this global way as a succession, as a progression in the accomplishment of the initial program mapped out by its founders.

In a second phase, linked, on the one hand, to the younger women who came to feminism after May 1968 and, on the other, to women who had an aesthetic or psychoanalytic experience, linear temporality has been almost totally refused, and as a consequence there has arisen an exacerbated distrust of the entire political dimension. If it is true that this more recent current of feminism refers to its predecessors and that the struggle for sociocultural recognition of women is necessarily its main concern, this current seems to think of itself as belonging to another generation—qualitatively different from the first one—in its conception of its own identity and, consequently, of temporality as such. Essentially interested in the specificity of female psychology and its symbolic realizations, these women seek to give a language to the intrasubjective and corporeal experiences left mute by culture in the past. Either as artists or writers, they have undertaken a veritable exploration of the *dynamic of signs*, an exploration which relates this tendency, at least at the level of its aspirations, to all major projects of aesthetic and religious upheaval. Ascribing this experience to a new generation does not only mean that other, more subtle problems have been added to the demands for sociopolitical identification made in the beginning. It also means that, by demanding recognition of an irreducible identity, without equal in the opposite sex and, as such, exploded, plural, fluid, in a certain way nonidentical, this feminism situates itself outside the linear time of identities which communicate through projection and revindication. Such a feminism rejoins, on the one hand, the archaic (mythical) memory and, on the other, the cyclical or monumental temporality of marginal movements. It is certainly not by chance that the European and trans-European problematic has been posited as such at the same time as this new phase of feminism.

Finally, it is the mixture of the two attitudes—*insertion* into history and the radical *refusal* of the subjective limitations imposed by this history's time on an experiment carried out in the name of the irreducible difference—that seems to have broken loose over the past few years in European feminist movements, particularly in France and in Italy.

If we accept this meaning of the expression "a new generation of women," two kinds of questions might then be posed. What sociopolitical processes or events have provoked this mutation? What are its problems: its contributions as well as dangers?

SOCIALISM AND FREUDIANISM

One could hypothesize that if this new generation of women shows itself to be more diffuse and perhaps less conscious in the United States and more massive in Western Europe, this is because of a veritable split in social relations and mentalities, a split produced by socialism and Freudianism. I mean by *socialism* that egalitarian doctrine which is increasingly broadly disseminated and accepted as based on common sense, as well as that social practice adopted by governments and political parties in democratic regimes which are forced to extend the zone of egalitarianism to include the distribution of goods as well as access to culture. By *Freudianism* I mean that lever, inside this egalitarian and socializing field, which once again poses the question of sexual difference and of the difference among subjects who themselves are not reducible one to the other.

Western socialism, shaken in its very beginnings by the egalitarian or differential demands of its women (e.g., Flora Tristan), quickly got rid of those women who aspired to recognition of a specificity of the female role in society and culture, only retaining from them in the egalitarian and universalistic spirit of Enlightenment Humanism, the idea of a necessary identification between the two sexes as the only and unique means for liberating the "second sex." I shall not develop here the fact that this "ideal" is far from being applied in practice by these socialist-inspired movements and parties and that it was in part from the revolt against this situation that the new generation of women in Western Europe was born after May 1968. Let us just say that in theory, and as put into practice in Eastern Europe, socialist ideology, based on a conception of the human being as determined by its place in *production* and the *relations of production*, did not take into consideration this same human being according to its place in *reproduction*, on the one hand, or in the *symbolic order*, on the other. Consequently, the specific character of women could only appear as nonessential or even nonexistent to the totalizing and even totalitarian spirit of this ideology.[12] We begin to see that this same egalitarian and in fact censuring treatment has been imposed, from Enlightenment Humanism through socialism, on religious specificities and, in particular, on Jews.[13]

What has been achieved by this attitude remains nonetheless of capital importance for women, and I shall take as an example the change in the destiny of women in the socialist countries of Eastern Europe. It could be said, with only slight exaggeration, that the demands of the suffragists and existential feminists have, to a great extent, been met in these countries, since three of the main egalitarian demands of early feminism have been or are now being implemented despite vagaries and blunders: economic, political, and professional equality. The fourth, sexual equality, which implies permissiveness in sexual relations (including homosexual relations), abortion, and contraception, remains stricken by taboo in Marxian ethics as well as for reasons of state. It is, then, this fourth equality which is the problem and which therefore appears *essential* in the struggle of a new generation. But simultaneoously and as a consequence of these socialist accomplishments—which are in fact a total deception—the struggle is no longer concerned with the quest for equality but, rather, with difference and specificity. It is precisely at this point that the new generation encounters what might be called the *symbolic* question.[14] Sexual difference—which is at once biological, physiological, and relative to reproduction—is translated by and translates a difference in the relationship of subjects to the symbolic contract which *is* the social contract: a difference, then, in the relationship to power, language, and meaning. The sharpest and most subtle point of feminist subversion brought about by the new generation will henceforth be situated on the terrain of the inseparable conjunction of the sexual and the symbolic, in order to try to discover, first, the specificity of the female, and then, in the end, that of each individual woman.

A certain saturation of socialist ideology, a certain exhaustion of its potential as a program for a new social contract (it is obvious that the effective realization of this program is far from being accomplished, and I am here treating only its system of thought) makes way for . . . Freudianism. I am, of course, aware that this term and this practice are somewhat shocking to the American intellectual consciousness (which rightly reacts to a muddled and normatizing form of psychoanalysis) and, above all, to the feminist consciousness. To restrict my remarks to the latter: Is it not true that Freud has been seen only as a denigrator or even an exploiter of women? as an irritating phallocrat in a Vienna which was at once Puritan and decadent—a man who fantasized women as sub-men, castrated men?

CASTRATED AND/OR SUBJECT TO LANGUAGE

Before going beyond Freud to propose a more just or more modern vision of women, let us try, first, to understand his notion of castration. It is, first of all, a question of an *anguish* or *fear* of castration, or of correlative penis *envy;* a question, therefore, of *imaginary* formations readily perceivable in the *discourse* of neurotics of both sexes, men and women. But, above all, a careful reading of Freud, going beyond his biologism and his mechanism, both characteristic of his time, brings out two things. First, a presupposition for the "primal scene," the castration fantasy and its correlative (penis envy) are hypotheses, a priori suppositions intrinsic to the theory itself, in the sense that these are not the ideological fantasies of their inventor but, rather, logical necessities to be placed at the "origin" in order to explain what unceasingly functions in neurotic discourse. In other words, neurotic discourse, in man and woman, can only be understood in terms of its own logic when its fundamental causes are admitted as the fantasies of the primal scene and castration, even if (as may be the case) nothing renders them present in reality itself. Stated in still other terms, the reality of castration is no more real than the hypothesis of an explosion which, according to modern astrophysics, is at the origin of the universe: Nothing proves it, in a sense it is an article of faith, the only difference being that numerous phenomena of life in this "big-bang" universe are explicable only through this initial hypothesis. But one is infinitely more jolted when this kind of intellectual method concerns inanimate matter than when it is applied to our own subjectivity and thus, perhaps, to the fundamental mechanism of our epistemophilic thought.

Moreover, certain texts written by Freud (*The Interpretation of Dreams*, but especially those of the second topic, in particular the *Metapsychology*) and the recent extensions (notably by Lacan),[15] imply that castration is, in sum, the imaginary construction of a radical operation which constitutes the symbolic field and all beings inscribed therein. This operation constitutes signs and syntax; that is, language, as a *separation* from a presumed state of nature, of pleasure fused with nature so that the introduction of an articulated network of differences, which refers to objects henceforth and only in this way separated from a subject, may constitute *meaning*. This logical operation of separation (confirmed by all psycholinguistic and child psychology) which preconditions the binding of language which is already syntactical, is therefore the common destiny of the two sexes, men and women. That certain biofamilial conditions and relationships cause women (and notably hysterics) to deny this separation and the language which ensues from it, whereas men (notably obsessionals) magnify both and, terrified, attempt to master them—this is what Freud's discovery has to tell us on this issue.

The analytic situation indeed shows that it is the penis which, becoming the major referent in this operation of separation, gives full meaning to the *lack* or to the *desire* which constitutes the subject during his or her insertion into the order of language. I should only like to indicate here that, in order for this operation constitutive of the symbolic and the social to appear in its full truth and for it to be understood by both sexes, it would be just to emphasize its extension to all that is privation of fullfillment and of totality; exclusion of a pleasing, natural, and sound state: in short, the break indispensable to the advent of the symbolic.

It can now be seen how women, starting with this theoretical apparatus, might try to understand their sexual and symbolic difference in the framework of social, cultural, and professional realization, in order to try, by seeing their position therein, either to fulfill their own experience to a maximum or—but always starting from this point—to go further and call into question the very apparatus itself.

LIVING THE SACRIFICE

In any case, and for women in Europe today, whether or not they are conscious of the various mutations (socialist and Freudian) which have produced or simply accompanied their coming into their own, the urgent question on our agenda might be formulated as follows: *What can be our place in the symbolic contract?* If the social contract, far from being that of equal men, is based on an essentially sacrificial relationship of separation and articulation of differences which in this way produces communicable meaning, what is our place in this order of sacrifice and/or of language? No longer wishing to be excluded or no longer content with the function which has always been demanded of us (to maintain, arrange, and perpetuate this sociosymbolic contract as mothers, wives, nurses, doctors, teachers . . .), how can we reveal our place, first as it is bequeathed to us by tradition, and then as we want to transform it?

It is difficult to evaluate what in the relationship of women to the symbolic as it reveals itself now arises from a sociohistorical conjuncture (patriarchal ideology, whether Christian, humanist, socialist or so forth), and what arises from a structure. We can speak only about a structure observed in a sociohistorical context, which is that of Christian, Western civilization and its lay ramifications. In this sense of psychosymbolic structure, women, "we" (is it necessary to recall the warnings we issued at the beginning of this article concerning the totalizing use of this plural?) seem to feel that they are the casualties, that they have been left out of the sociosymbolic contract, of language as the fundamental social bond. They find no affect there, no more than they find the fluid and infinitesimal significations of their relationships with the nature of their own bodies, that of the child, another woman, or a man. This frustration, which to a certain extent belongs to men also, is being voiced today principally by women, to the point of becoming the essence of the new feminist ideology. A therefore difficult, if not impossible, identification with the sacrificial logic of separation and syntactical sequence at the foundation of language and the social code leads to the rejection of the symbolic—lived as the rejection of the paternal function and ultimately generating psychoses.

But this limit, rarely reached as such, produces two types of counterinvestment of what we have termed the sociosymbolic contract. On the one hand, there are attempts to take hold of this contract, to possess it in order to enjoy it as such or to subvert it. How? The answer remains difficult to formulate (since, precisely, any formulation is deemed frustrating, mutilating, sacrificial) or else is in fact formulated using stereotypes taken from extremist and often deadly ideologies. On the other hand, another attitude is more lucid from the beginning, more self-analytical which—without refusing or sidestepping this sociosymbolic order—consists in trying to explore the constitution and functioning of this contract, starting less from the knowledge accumulated about it (anthropology, psychoanalysis, linguistics) than from the very personal affect experienced when facing it as subject and as a woman. This leads to the active research,[16] still rare, undoubtedly hesitant but always dissident, being carried out by women in the human sciences; particularly those attempts, in the wake of contemporary art, to break the code, to shatter language, to find a specific discourse closer to the body and emotions, to the unnameable repressed by the social contract. I am not speaking here of a "woman's language," whose (at least syntactical) existence is highly problematical and whose apparent lexical specificity is perhaps more the product of a social marginality than of a sexual-symbolic difference.[17]

Nor am I speaking of the aesthetic quality of productions by women, most of which—with a few exceptions (but has this not always been the case with both sexes?)—are a reiteration of a more or less euphoric or depressed romanticism and always an explosion of an ego lacking narcissistic gratification.[18] What I should like to retain, nonetheless, as a mark of collective aspiration, as an undoubtedly vague and unimplemented intention, but one which is intense and which has been deeply revealing these past few years, is this: The new generation of women is showing that its major social concern has become the sociosymbolic contract as a sacrificial contract. If anthropologists and psychologists, for at least a century, have not stopped insisting on this in their attention to "savage thought," wars, the discourse of dreams, or writers, women are today affirming—and we consequently face a mass phenomenon—that they are forced to experience this sacrificial contract against their will.[19] Based on this, they are attempting a revolt which they see as a resurrection but which society as a whole understands as murder. This attempt can lead us to a not less and sometimes more deadly violence. Or to a cultural innovation. Probably to both at once. But that is precisely where the stakes are, and they are of epochal significance.

THE TERROR OF POWER OR THE POWER OF TERRORISM

First in socialist countries (such as the U.S.S.R. and China) and increasingly in Western democracies, under pressure from feminist movements, women are being promoted to leadership positions in government, industry, and culture. Inequalities, devalorizations, underestimations, even persecution of women at this level continue to hold sway in vain. The struggle against them is a struggle against archaisms. The cause has nonetheless been understood, the principle has been accepted.[20] What remains is to break down the resistance to change. In this sense, this struggle, while still one of the main concerns of the new generation, is not, strictly speaking, *its* problem. In relationship to *power*, its problem might rather be summarized as follows: What happens when women come into power and identify with it? What happens when, on the contrary, they refuse power and create a parallel society, a counter-power which then takes on aspects ranging from a club of ideas to a group of terrorist commandos?[21]

The assumption by women of executive, industrial, and cultural power has not, up to the present time, radically changed the nature of this power. This can be clearly seen in the East, where women promoted to decision-making positions suddenly obtain the economic as well as the narcissistic advantages refused them for thousands of years and become the pillars of the existing governments, guardians of the status quo, the most zealous protectors of the established order.[22] This identification by women with the very power structures previously considered as frustrating, oppressive, or inaccessible has often been used in modern times by totalitarian regimes: the German National-Socialists and the Chilean junta are examples of this.[23] The fact that this is a paranoid type of counterinvestment in an initially denied symbolic order can perhaps explain this troubling phenomenon; but an explanation does not prevent its massive propagation around the globe, perhaps in less dramatic forms than the totalitarian ones mentioned above, but all moving toward leveling, stabilization, conformism, at the cost of crushing exceptions, experiments, chance occurrences.

Some will regret that the rise of a libertarian movement such as feminism ends, in some of its aspects, in the consolidation of conformism; others will rejoice and profit from this fact. Electoral campaigns, the very life of political parties, continue to bet on this latter tendency. Experience proves that too quickly even the protest or innovative initiatives on the part of women inhaled by power systems (when they do not submit to them right off) are soon credited to the system's account; and that the long-awaited democratization of institutions as a result of the entry of women most often comes down to fabricating a few "chiefs" among them. The difficulty presented by this logic of integrating the second sex into a value system experienced as foreign and therefore counterinvested is how to avoid the centralization of power, how to detach women from it, and how then to proceed, through their critical, differential, and autonomous interventions, to render decision-making institutions more flexible.

Then there are the more radical feminist currents which, refusing homologation to any role of identification with existing power no matter what the power may be, make of the second sex a *countersociety*. A "female society" is then constituted as a sort of alter ego of the official society, in which all real or fantasized possibilities for *jouissance* take refuge. Against the sociosymbolic contract, both sacrificial and frustrating, this countersociety is imagined as harmonious, without prohibitions, free and fulfilling. In our modern societies which have no hereafter or, at least, which are caught up in a transcendency either reduced to this side of the world (Protestantism) or crumbling (Catholicism and its current challenges), the countersociety remains the only refuge for fulfillment since it is precisely an a-topia, a place outside the law, utopia's floodgate.

As with any society, the countersociety is based on the expulsion of an excluded element, a scapegoat charged with the evil of which the community duly constituted can then purge itself;[24] a purge which will finally exonerate that community of any future criticism. Modern protest movements have often reiterated this logic, locating the guilty one—in order to fend off criticism—in the foreign, in capital alone, in the other religion, in the other sex. Does not feminism become a kind of inverted sexism when this logic is followed to its conclusion? The various forms of marginalism—according to sex, age, religion, or ideology—represent in the modern world this refuge for *jouissance*, a sort of laicized transcendence. But with women, and insofar as the number of those feeling concerned by this problem has increased, although in less spectacular forms than a few years ago, the problem of the countersociety is becoming massive: It occupies no more and no less than "half of the sky."

It has, therefore, become clear, because of the particular radicalization of the second generation, that these protest movements, including feminism, are not "initially libertarian" movements which only later, through internal deviations or external chance manipulations, fall back into the old ruts of the initially combated archetypes. Rather, the very logic of counterpower and of countersociety necessarily generates, by its very structure, its essence as a simulacrum of the combated society or of power. In this sense and from a viewpoint undoubtedly too Hegelian, modern feminism has only been but a moment in the interminable process of coming to consciousness about the implacable violence (separation, castration, etc.) which constitutes any symbolic contract.

Thus the identification with power in order to consolidate it or the constitution of a fetishist counterpower—restorer of the crises of the self and provider of a *jouissance* which is always already a transgression—seem to be the two social forms which the face-off between the new generation of women and the social contract can take. That one also finds the problem of terrorism there is structurally related.

The large number of women in terrorist groups (Palestinian commandos, the Baader-Meinhoff Gang, Red Brigades, etc.) has already been pointed out, either violently or prudently according to the source of information. The exploitation of women is still too great and the traditional prejudices against them too violent for one to be able to envision this phenomenon with sufficient distance. It can, however, be said from now on that this is the inevitable product of what we have called a denial of the sociosymbolic contract and its counterinvestment as the only means of self-defense in the struggle to safeguard an identity. This paranoid-type mechanism is at the base of any political involvement. It may produce different civilizing attitudes in the sense that these attitudes allow a more or less flexible reabsorption of violence and death. But when a subject is too brutally excluded from this sociosymbolic stratum; when, for example, a woman feels her affective life as a woman or her condition as a social being too brutally ignored by existing discourse or power (from her family to social institutions); she may, by counterinvesting the violence she has endured, make of herself a "possessed" agent of this violence in order to combat what was experienced as frustration— with arms which may seem disproportional, but which are not so in comparison with the subjective or more precisely narcissistic suffering from which they originate. Necessarily opposed to the bourgeois democratic regimes in power, this terrorist violence offers as a program of liberation an order which is even more oppressive, more sacrificial than those it combats. Strangely enough, it is not against totalitarian regimes that these terrorist groups with women participants unleash themselves but, rather, against liberal systems, whose essence is, of course, exploitative, but whose expanding democratic legality guarantees relative tolerance. Each time, the mobilization takes place in the name of a nation, of an oppressed group, of a human essence imagined as good and sound; in the name, then, of a kind of fantasy of archaic fulfillment which an arbitrary, abstract, and thus even bad and ultimately discriminatory order has come to disrupt. While that order is accused of being oppressive, is it not actually being reproached with being too weak, with not measuring up to this pure and good, but henceforth lost, substance? Anthropology has shown that the social order is sacrificial, but sacrifice orders violence, binds it, tames it. Refusal of the social order exposes one to the risk that the so-called good substance, once it is unchained, will explode, without curbs, without law or right, to become an absolute arbitrariness.

Following the crisis of monotheism, the revolutions of the past two centuries, and more recently fascism and Stalinism, have tragically set in action this logic of the oppressed goodwill which leads to massacres. Are women more apt than other social categories, notably the exploited classes, to invest in this implacable machine of terrorism? No categorical response, either positive or negative, can currently be given to this question. It must be pointed out, however, that since the dawn of feminism, and certainly before, the political activity of exceptional women, and thus in a certain sense of liberated women, has taken the form of murder, conspiracy, and crime. Finally, there is also the connivance of the young girl with her mother, her greater difficulty than the boy in detaching herself from the mother in order to accede to the order of signs as invested by the absence and separation constitutive of the paternal function. A girl will never be able to re-establish this contact with her mother—a contact which the boy may possibly rediscover through his relationship with the opposite sex—except by becoming a mother herself, through a child, or through a homosexuality which is in itself extremely difficult and judged as suspect by society; and, what is more, why and in the name of what dubious symbolic benefit would she want to make this de-tachment so as to conform to a symbolic system which remains foreign to her? In sum, all of these considerations—her eternal debt to the woman-mother—make a woman more vulnerable within the symbolic order, more fragile when she suf-fers within it, more virulent when she protects herself from it. If the archetype of the belief in a good and pure substance, that of utopias, is the belief in the om-nipotence of an archaic, full, total, englobing mother with no frustration, no sep-aration, with no break-producing symbolism (with no castration, in other words), then it becomes evident that we will never be able to defuse the violences mobi-lized through the counterinvestment necessary to carrying out this phantasm, unless one challenges precisely this myth of the archaic mother. It is in this way that we can understand the warnings against the recent invasion of the women's movements by paranoia,[25] as in Lacan's scandalous sentence "There is no such thing as Woman."[26] Indeed, she does *not* exist with a capital "W," possessor of some mythical unity—a supreme power, on which is based the terror of power and terrorism as the desire for power. But what an unbelievable force for subver-sion in the modern world! And, at the same time, what playing with fire!

CREATURES AND CREATRESSES

The desire to be a mother, considered alienating and even reactionary by the preceding generation of feminists, has obviously not become a standard for the present generation. But we have seen in the past few years an increasing number of women who do not only consider their maternity compatible with their profes-sional life or their feminist involvement (certain improvements in the quality of life are also at the origin of this: an increase in the number of day-care centers and nursery schools, more active participation of men in child care and domestic life, etc.) but also find it indispensable to their discovery, not of the plenitude, but of the complexity of the female experience, with all that this complexity comprises in joy and pain. This tendency has its extreme: in the refusal of the paternal function by lesbian and single mothers can be seen one of the most vio-lent forms taken by the rejection of the symbolic outlied above, as well as one of the most fervent divinizations of maternal power—all of which cannot help but trouble an entire legal and moral order without, however, proposing an alternative to it. Let us remember here that Hegel distinguished between female right (familial and religious) and male law (civil and political). If our societies know well the uses and abuses of male law, it must also be recognized that female right is designated, for the moment, by a blank. And if these practices of maternity, among others, were to be generalized, women themselves would be responsible for elaborating the appropriate legislation to check the violence to which, otherwise, both their children and men would be subject. But are they capable of doing so? This is one of the important questions that the new generation of women encounters, especially when the members of this new generation refuse to ask those questions, seized by the same rage with which the dominant order originally victimized them.

Faced with this situation, it seems obvious—and feminist groups become more aware of this when they attempt to broaden their audience—that the refusal of maternity cannot be a mass policy and that the majority of women today see the possibility for fulfillment, if not entirely at least to a large degree, in bringing a child into the world. What does this desire for motherhood correspond to? This is one of the new questions for the new generation, a question the preceding generation had foreclosed. For want of an answer to this question, feminist ideology leaves the door open to the return of religion, whose discourse, tried and proved over thousands of years, provides the necessary ingredients for satisfying the anguish, the suffering, and the hopes of mothers. If Freud's affirmation—that the desire for a child is the desire for a penis and, in this sense, a substitute for phallic and symbolic dominion—can be only partially accepted, what modern women have to say about this experience should nonetheless be listened to attentively. Pregnancy seems to be experienced as the radical ordeal of the splitting of the subject:[27] redoubling up of the body, separation and coexistence of the self and of an other, of nature and consciousness, of physiology and speech. This fundamental challenge to identity is then accompanied by a fantasy of totality—narcissistic completeness—a sort of instituted, socialized, natural psychosis. The arrival of the child, on the other hand, leads the mother into the labyrinths of an experience that, without the child, she would only rarely encounter: love for an other. Not for herself, nor for an identical being, and still less for another person with whom "I" fuse (love or sexual passion). But the slow, difficult, and delightful apprenticeship in attentiveness, gentleness, forgetting oneself. The ability to succeed in this path without masochism and without annihilating one's affective, intellectual, and professional personality—such would seem to be the stakes to be won through guiltless maternity. It then becomes a creation in the strong sense of the term. For this moment, utopian?

On the other hand, it is in the aspiration toward artistic and, in particular, literary creation that woman's desire for affirmation now manifests itself. Why literature?

Is it because, faced with social norms, literature reveals a certain knowledge and sometimes the truth itself about an otherwise repressed, nocturnal, secret, and unconscious universe? Because it thus redoubles the social contract by exposing the unsaid, the uncanny? And because it makes a game, a space of fantasy and pleasure, out of the abstract and frustrating order of social signs, the words of everyday communication? Flaubert said, "Madame Bovary, c'est moi." Today many women imagine, "Flaubert, c'est moi." This identification with the potency of the imaginary is not only an identification, an imaginary potency (a fetish, a belief in the maternal penis maintained at all costs), as a far too normative view of the social and symbolic relationship would have it. This identification also bears witness to women's desire to lift the weight of what is sacrificial in the social contract from their shoulders, to nourish our societies with a more flexible and free discourse, one able to name what has thus far never been an object of circulation in the community: the enigmas of the body, the dreams, secret joys, shames, hatreds of the second sex.

It is understandable from this that women's writing has lately attracted the maximum attention of both "specialists" and the media.[28] The pitfalls encountered along the way, however, are not to be minimized: For example, does one not read there a relentless belittling of male writers whose books, nevertheless, often serve as "models" for countless productions by women? Thanks to the feminist label, does one not sell numerous works whose naïve whining or market-place romanticism would otherwise have been rejected as anachronistic? And does one not find the pen of many a female writer being devoted to phantasmic attacks against Language and Sign as the ultimate supports of phallocratic power, in the name of a semi-aphonic corporality whose truth can only be found in that which is "gestural" or "tonal"?

And yet, no matter how dubious the results of these recent productions by women, the symptom is there—women are writing, and the air is heavy with expectation: What will they write that is new?

IN THE NAME OF THE FATHER, THE SON . . . AND THE WOMAN?

These few elements of the manifestations by the new generation of women in Europe seem to me to demonstrate that, beyond the sociopolitical level where it is generally inscribed (or insribes itself), the women's movement—in its present stage, less aggressive but more artful—is situated within the very framework of the religious crisis of our civilization.

I call "religion" this phantasmic necessity on the part of speaking beings to provide themselves with a *representation* (animal, female, male, parental, etc.) in place of what constitutes them as such, in other words, symbolization—the double articulation and syntactic sequence of language, as well as its preconditions or substitutes (thoughts, affects, etc.). The elements of the current practice of feminism that we have just brought to light seem precisely to constitute such a representation which makes up for the frustrations imposed on women by the anterior code (Christianity or its lay humanist variant). The fact that this new ideology has affinities, often revindicated by its creators, with so-called matriarchal beliefs (in other words, those beliefs characterizing matrilinear societies) should not overshadow its radical novelty. This ideology seems to me to be part of the broader antisacrificial current which in animating our culture and which, in its protest against the constraints of the sociosymbolic contract, is no less exposed to the risks of violence and terrorism. At this level of radicalism, it is the very principle of sociality which is challenged.

Certain contemporary thinkers consider, as is well known, that modernity is characterized as the first epoch in human history in which human beings attempt to live without religion. In its present form, is not feminism in the process of becoming one?

Or is it, on the contrary and as avant-garde feminists hope, that having started with the idea of difference, feminism will be able to break free of its belief in Woman, Her power, Her writing, so as to channel this demand for difference into each and every element of the female whole, and, finally, to bring out the singularity of each woman, and beyond this, her multiplicities, her plural languages, beyond the horizon, beyond sight, beyond faith itself?

A factor for ultimate mobilization? Or a factor for analysis?

Imaginary support in a technocratic era where all narcissism is frustrated? Or instruments fitted to these times in which the cosmos, atoms, and cells—our true contemporaries—call for the constitution of a fluid and free subjectivity?

The question has been posed. Is to pose it already to answer it?

ANOTHER GENERATION IS ANOTHER SPACE

If the preceding can be *said*—the question whether all this is *true* belongs to a different register—it is undoubtedly because it is now possible to gain some distance on these two preceding generations of women. This implies, of course, that a *third* generation is now forming, at least in Europe. I am not speaking of a new group of young women (though its importance should not be underestimated) or of another "mass feminist movement" taking the torch passed on from the second generation. My usage of the word "generation" implies less a chronology than a *signifying space*, a both corporeal and desiring mental space. So it can be argued that as of now a third attitude is possible, thus a third generation, which does not exclude—quite to the contrary—the *parallel* existence of all three in the same historical time, or even that they be interwoven one with the other.

In this third attitude, which I strongly advocate—which I imagine?—the very dichotomy man/woman as an opposition between two rival entities may be understood as belonging to *metaphysics*. What can "identity," even "sexual identity," mean in a new theoretical and scientific space where the very notion of identity is challenged?[29] I am not simply suggesting a very hypothetical bisexuality which, even if it existed, would only, in fact, be the aspiration toward the totality of one of the sexes and thus an effacing of difference. What I mean is, first of all, the demassification of the problematic of *difference*, which would imply, in a first phase, an apparent de-dramatization of the "fight to the death" between rival groups and thus between the sexes. And this not in the name of some reconciliation—feminism has at least had the merit of showing what is irreducible and even deadly in the social contract—but in order that the struggle, the implacable difference, the violence be conceived in the very place where it operates with the maximum intransigence, in other words, in personal and sexual identity itself, so as to make it disintegrate in its very nucleus.

It necessarily follows that this involves risks not only for what we understand today as "personal equilibrium" but also for social equilibrium itself, made up as it now is of the counterbalancing of aggressive and murderous forces massed in social, national, religious, and political groups. But is it not the insupportable situation of tension and explosive risk that the existing "equilibrium" presupposes which leads some of those who suffer from it to divest it of its economy, to detach themselves from it, and to seek another means of regulating difference?

To restrict myself here to a personal level, as related to the question of women, I see arising, under the cover of a relative indifference toward the militance of the first and second generations, an attitude of retreat from sexism (male as well as female) and, gradually, from any kind of anthropomorphism. The fact that this might quickly become another form of spiritualism turning its back on social problems, or else a form of repression[30] ready to support all status quos, should not hide the radicalness of the process. This process could be summarized as an *interiorization of the founding separation of the sociosymbolic contract*, as an introduction of its cutting edge into the very interior of every identity whether subjective, sexual, ideological, or so forth. This in such a way that the habitual and increasingly explicit attempt to fabricate a scapegoat victim as foundress of a society or a countersociety may be replaced by the analysis of the potentialities of *victim/executioner* which characterize each identity, each subject, each sex.

What discourse, if not that of a religion, would be able to support this adventure which surfaces as a real possibility, after both the achievements and the impasses of the present ideological reworkings, in which feminism has participated? It seems to me that the role of what is usually called "aesthetic practices" must increase not only to counterbalance the storage and uniformity of information by present-day mass media, data-bank systems, and, in particular, modern communications technology, but also to demystify the identity of the symbolic bond itself, to demystify, therefore, the *community* of language as a universal and unifying tool, one which totalizes and equalizes. In order to bring out—along with the *singularity* of each person and, even more, along with the multiplicity of every person's possible identifications (with atoms, e.g., stretching from the family to the stars)—the *relativity of his/her symbolic as well as biological existence*, according to the variation in his/her specific symbolic capacities. And in order to emphasize the *responsibility* which all will immediately face of putting this fluidity into play against the threats of death which are unavoidable whenever an inside and an outside, a self and an other, one group and another, are constituted. At this level of interiorization with its social as well as individual stakes, what I have called "aesthetic practices" are undoubtedly nothing other than the modern reply to the eternal question of morality. At least, this is how we might understand an ethics which, conscious of the fact that its order is sacrificial, reserves part of the burden for each of its adherents, therefore declaring them guilty while immediately affording them the possibility for *jouissance*, for various productions, for a life made up of both challenges and differences.

Spinoza's question can be taken up again here: Are women subject to ethics? If not to that ethics defined by classical philosophy—in relationship to which the ups and downs of feminist generations seem dangerously precarious—are women not already participating in the rapid dismantling that our age is experiencing at various levels (from wars to drugs to artificial insemination) and which poses the *demand* for a new ethics? The answer to Spinoza's question can be affirmative only at the cost of considering feminism as but a *moment* in the thought of that anthropomorphic identity which currently blocks the horizon of the discursive and scientific adventure of our species.

Translated by Alice Jardine and Harry Blake

NOTES

1. The following discussion emphasizes Europe in a way which may seem superfluous to some American readers given the overall emphasis on deterritorialization. It is, however, essential to the movement of an article that is above all devoted to the necessity of paying attention to the place from which we speak.—AJ.

2. Sigmund Freud and Carl G. Jung, *Correspondence* (Paris: Gallimard, 1975), 1:87.

3. R. Spitz, *La Première Année de la vie de l'enfant* [First year of life: a psychoanalytic study of normal and deviant development of object relations] (Paris: PUF, 1958); D. Winnicott, *Jeu et réalité [Playing and reality] (Paris: Gallimard, 1975); Julia Kristeva, "Noms de lieu" in Polylogue* (Paris: Editions du Seüil, 1977), translated as "Place Names" in Julia Kristeva, *Desire in Language: A Semiotic Approach to Literature and Art,* ed. Leon S. Roudiez, trans. Thomas Gora, Alice Jardine, and Leon Roudiez (New York: Columbia University Press, 1980) (hereafter cited as *Desire in Language*).

4. Plato *Timeus* 52: "Indefinitely a place; it cannot be destroyed, but provides a ground for all that can come into being; itself being perceptible, outside of all sensation, by means of a sort of bastard reasoning; barely assuming credibility, it is precisely that which makes us dream when we perceive it, and affirm that all that exists must be somewhere, in a determined place. . . ." (author's translation).

5. As most readers of recent French theory in translation know, *la féminin* does not have the same pejorative connotations it has come to have in English. It is a term used to speak about women in general, but, as used most often in this article, it probably comes closest to our "female" as defined by Elaine Showalter in *A Literature of Their Own* (Princeton, N.J.: Princeton University Press, 1977). I have therefore used either "women" or "female" according to the context (cf. also n. 9 in "Introduction to Julia Kristeva's 'Women's Time'" [*Signs* 7 (1981): 5–12; herafter cited as "Introduction"]). "Subjectivity" here refers to the state of being "a thinking, speaking, acting, doing or writing agent" and never, e.g., as opposed to "objectivity" (see the glossary in *Desire in Language*).—AJ.

6. I have retained *jouissance*—that word for pleasure which defies translation—as it is rapidly becoming a "believable neologism" in English (see the glossary in *Desire in Language*).—AJ.

7. This particular mythology has important implications—equal only to those of the oedipal myth—for current French thought.—AJ.

8. See Julia Kristeva, "Hérétique de l'amour," *Tel quel,* no. 74 (1977), pp. 30–49.

9. See H. C. Puech, *La Gnose et la temps* (Paris: Gallimard, 1977).

10. See Alice Jardine, "Introduction to Julia Kristeva's 'Women's Time,'" *Signs* vol. 7 no. 1 (1981): 5–12.

11. The term "identification" belongs to a wide semantic field ranging from everyday language to philosophy and psychoanalysis. While Kristeva is certainly referring in principle to its elaboration in Freudian and Lacanian psychoanalysis, it can be understood here, as a logic, in its most general sense (see the entry on "identification" in Jean LaPlanche and J. B. Pontalis, *Vocabulaire de la psychanalyse* [The language of psychoanalysis] [Paris: Presses Universitaires de France, 1967; rev. ed., 1976]).—AJ.

12. See D. Desanti, "L'Autre Sexe des bolcheviks," *Tel quel,* no. 76 (1978); Julia Kristeva, *Des Chinoises* (Paris: Editions des femmes, 1975), translated as *On Chinese Women,* trans. Anita Barrows (New York: Urizen Press, 1977).

13. See Arthur Hertzberg, *The French Enlightenment and the Jews* (New York: Columbia University Press, 1968); *Les Juifs et la révolution française,* ed. B. Blumenkranz and A. Seboul (Paris: Edition Privat, 1976).

14. Here, "symbolic" is being more strictly used in terms of that function defined by Kristeva in opposition to the semiotic: "it involves the thetic phase, the identification of

subject and its distinction from objects, and the establishment of a sign system" (see the glossary in *Desire in Language*, and Alice Jardine, "Theories of the Feminine: Kristeva," *Enclitic*, in press).—AJ.

15. See, in general, Jacques Lacan, *Ecrits* (Paris: Editions du Seuil, 1966) and in particular, Jacques Lacan, *Le Séminaire XX: Encore* (Paris: Editions du Seuil, 1975).—AJ.

16. This work is periodically published in various academic women's journals, one of the most prestigious being *Signs: Journal of Women in Culture and Society*, University of Chicago Press. Also of note are the special issues: "Ecriture, féminité, féminisme," *La Revue des sciences humaines* (Lillie III), no. 4 (1977); and "Les Femmes et la philosophie," *Le Doctrinal de sapience* (Editions Solin), no. 3 (1977).

17. See linguistic research on "female language": Robin Lakoff, *Language and Women's Place* (new York: Harper & Row, 1974); Mary R. Key, *Male/Female Language* (Metuchen, N.J.: Scarecrow Press, 1973); A. M. Houdebine, "Les Femmes et la langue," *Tel quel*, no. 74 (1977), pp. 84–95. The contrast between these "empirical" investigations of women's "speech acts" and much of the research in France on the conceptual bases for a "female language" must be emphasized here. It is somewhat helpful, if ultimately inaccurate, to think of the former as an "external" study of language and the latter as an "internal" exploration of the process of signification. For further contrast, see, e.g., "Part II: Contemporary Feminist Thought in France: Translating Difference" in *The Future of Difference*, ed. Hester Eisenstein and Alice Jardine (Boston: G. K. Hall & Co., 1980); the "Introductions" to *New French Feminisms*, ed. Elaine Marks and Isabelle de Courtivron (Amherst: University of Massachusetts Press, 1980); and for a very helpful overview of the problem of "difference and language" in France, see Stephen Heath, "Difference" in *Screen* 19 no. 3 (Autumn 1978): 51–112.—AJ.

18. This is one of the more explicit references to the mass marketing of "écriture féminine" in Paris over the last ten years.—AJ.

19. The expression *à leur corps défendant* translates as "against their will," but here the emphasis is on women's bodies: literally, "against their bodies." I have retained the former expression in English, partly because of its obvious intertextuality with Susan Brownmiller's *Against Our Will* (New York: Simon & Schuster, 1975). Women are increasingly describing their experience of the violence of the symbolic contract as a form of rape.—AJ.

20. Many women in the West who are once again finding all doors closed to them above a certain level of employment, especially in the current economic chaos, may find this statement, even qualified, troubling, to say the least. It is accurate, however, *in principle:* whether that of infinite capitalist recuperation or increasing socialist expansion— within both economies, our integration functions as a kind of *operative* illusion.—AJ.

21. The very real existence and autonomous activities of both of these versions of women's groups in Europe may seem a less urgent problem in the United States where feminist groups are often absorbed by the academy and/or are forced to remain financially dependent on para-academic/governmental agencies.—AJ.

22. See *Des Chinoises*.

23. See M. A. Macciocchi, *Eléments pour une analyse du fascisme* (Paris: 10/18, 1976); Michèle Mattelart, "Le Coup d'état au féminin," *Les Temps modernes* (January 1975).

24. The principles of a "sacrificial anthropology" are developed by René Girard in *La Violence et la sacré* [Violence and the sacred] (Paris: Grasset, 1972) and esp. in *Des Choses cachées depuis la fondation du monde* (Paris: Grasset, 1978).

25. Cf. Micheline Enriquez, "Fantasmes paranoiaques: différences des sexes, homosexualité, loi du père," *Topiques*, no. 13 (1974).

26. See Jacques Lacan, "Dieu et la jouissance de la femme" in *Encore* (Paris: Editions du Seuil, 1975), pp. 61–71, esp. p. 68. This seminar has remained a primary critical and polemical focus for multiple tendencies in the French women's movement. For a brief discussion of the seminar in English, see Heath (n. 17 above).—AJ.

27. The "split subject" (from *Spaltung* as both "splitting" and "cleavage"), as used in Freudian psychoanalysis, here refers directly to Kristeva's "subject in process/in question/on trial" as opposed to the unity of the transcendental ego (see n. 14 in "Introduction").—AJ.

28. Again a reference to *écriture féminine* as generically labeled in France over the past few years and not to women's writing in general.—AJ.

29. See Seminar on *Identity* directed by Lévi-Strauss (Paris: Grasset & Fasquelle, 1977).

30. Repression (*le refoulement* or *Verdrangung*) as distinguished from the foreclosure (*la foreclusion* or *Verwerfung*) evoked earlier in the article (see LaPlanche and Pontalis).—AJ.

INTRODUCTION FROM *BETWEEN MEN*

I. HOMOSOCIAL DESIRE

The subject of this book is a relatively short, recent, and accessible passage of English culture, chiefly as embodied in the mid-eighteenth- to mid-nineteenth-century novel. The attraction of the period to theorists of many disciplines is obvious: condensed, self-reflective, and widely influential change in economic, ideological, and gender arrangements. I will be arguing that concomitant changes in the structure of the continuum of male "homosocial desire" were tightly, often causally bound up with the other more visible changes; that the emerging pattern of male friendship, mentorship, entitlement, rivalry, and hetero- and homosexuality was in an intimate and shifting relation to class; and that no element of that pattern can be understood outside of its relation to women and the gender system as a whole.

"Male homosocial desire": the phrase in the title of this study is intended to mark both discriminations and paradoxes. "Homosocial desire," to begin with, is a kind of oxymoron. "Homosocial" is a word occasionally used in history and the social sciences, where it describes social bonds between persons of the same sex; it is a neologism, obviously formed by analogy with "homosexual," and just as obviously meant to be distinguished from "homosexual." In fact, it is applied to such activities as "male bonding," which may, as in our society, be characterized by intense homophobia, fear and hatred of homosexual.[1] To draw the "homosocial" back into the orbit of "desire," of the potentially erotic, then, is to hypothesize the potential unbrokenness of a continuum between homosocial and homosexual—a continuum whose visibility, for men, in our society, is radically disrupted. It will become clear, in the course of my argument, that my hypothesis of the unbrokenness of this continuum is not a *genetic* one—I do not mean to discuss genital homosexual desire as "at the root of" other forms of male homosociality—but rather a strategy for making generalizations about, and marking historical differences in, the *structure* of men's relations with other men. "Male homosocial desire" is the name this book will give to the entire continuum.

I have chosen the word "desire" rather than "love" to mark the erotic emphasis because, in literary critical and related discourse, "love" is more easily used to name a particular emotion, and "desire" to name a structure; in this study, a series of arguments about the structural permutations of social impulses fuels the critical dialectic. For the most part, I will be using "desire" in a way analogous to the psychoanalytic use of "libido"—not for a particular affective state or emotion, but for the affective or social force, the glue, even when its manifestation is hostility or hatred or something less emotively charged, that shapes an important relationship. How far this force is properly sexual (what, historically, it means for something to be "sexual") will be an active question.

The title is specific about *male* homosocial desire partly in order to acknowledge from the beginning (and stress the seriousness of) a limitation of my subject; but there is a more positive and substantial reason, as well. It is one of the main projects of this study to explore the ways in which the shapes of sexuality, and what *counts* as sexuality, both depend on and affect historical power relationships.[2] A corollary is that in a society where men and women differ in their access to power, there will be important gender differences, as well, in the structure and constitution of sexuality.

For instance, the diacritical opposition between the "homosocial" and the "homosexual" seems to be much less thorough and dichotomous for women, in our society, than for men. At this particular historical moment, an intelligible continuum of aims, emotions, and valuations links lesbianism with the other forms of women's attention to women: the bond of mother and daughter, for instance, the bond of sister and sister, women's friendship, "networking," and the active struggles of feminism.[3] The continuum is crisscrossed with deep discontinuities—with much homophobia, with conflicts of race and class—but its intelligibility seems now a matter of simple common sense. However agonistic the politics, however conflicted the feelings, it seems at this moment to make an obvious kind of sense to say that women in our society who love women, women who teach, study, nurture, suckle, write about, march for, vote for, give jobs to, or otherwise promote the interests of other women, are pursuing congruent and closely related activities. Thus the adjective "homosocial" as applied to women's bonds (by, for example, historian Carroll Smith-Rosenberg)[4] need not be pointedly dichotomized as against "homosexual"; it can intelligibly denominate the entire continuum.

The apparent simplicity—the unity—of the continuum between "women loving women" and "women promoting the interests of women," extending over the erotic, social, familial, economic, and political realms, would not be so striking if it were not in strong contrast to the arrangement among males. When Ronald Reagan and Jesse Helms get down to serious logrolling on "family policy," they are men promoting men's interests. (In fact, they embody Heidi Hartmann's definition of patriarchy: "relations between men, which have a material base, and which, though hierarchical, establish or create interdependence and solidarity among men that enable them to dominate women.")[5] Is their bond in any way congruent with the bond of a loving gay male couple? Reagan and Helms would say no—disgustedly. Most gay couples would say no—disgustedly. But why not? Doesn't the continuum between "men-loving-men" and "men-promoting-the-interests-of-men" have the same intuitive force that it has for women?

Quite the contrary: much of the most useful recent writing about patriarchal structures suggests that "obligatory heterosexuality" is built into male-dominated kinship systems, or that homophobia is a *necessary* consequence of such patriarchal instutitions as heterosexual marriage.[6] Clearly, however convenient it might be to group together all the bonds that link males to males, and by which males enhance the status of males—usefully symmetrical as it would be, that grouping meets with a prohibitive structural obstacle. From the vantage point of our own society, at any rate, it has apparently been impossible to imagine a form of patriarchy that was not homophobic. Gayle Rubin writes, for instance, "The suppression of the homosexual component of human sexuality, and by corollary, the oppression of homosexuals, is . . . a product of the same system whose rules and relations oppress women."[7]

The historical manifestations of this patriarchal oppression of homosexuals have been savage and nearly endless. Louis Crompton makes a detailed case for describing the history as genocidal.[8] Our own society is brutally homophobic; and the homophobia directed against both males and females is not arbitrary or gratuitous, but tightly knit into the texture of family, gender, age, class, and race relations. Our society could not cease to be homophobic and have its economic and political structures remain unchanged.

Nevertheless, it has yet to be demonstrated that, because most patriarchies structurally include homophobia, therefore patriarchy structurally *requires* homophobia. K. J. Dover's recent study, *Greek Homosexuality*, seems to give a strong counterexample in classical Greece. Male homosexuality, according to Dover's evidence, was a widespread, licit, and very influential part of the culture. Highly structured along lines of class, and within the citizen class along lines of age, the pursuit of the adolescent boy by the older man was described by stereotypes that we associate with romantic heterosexual love (conquest, surrender, the "cruel fair," the absence of desire in the love object), with the passive part going to the boy. At the same time, however, because the boy was destined in turn to grow into manhood, the assignment of roles was not permanent.[9] Thus the love relationship, while temporarily oppressive to the object, had a strongly educational function; Dover quotes Pausanias in Plato's *Symposium* as saying "that it would be right for him [the boy] to perform any service for one who improves him in mind and character."[10] Along with its erotic component, then, this was a bond of mentorship; the boys were apprentices in the ways and virtues of Athenian citizenship, whose privileges they inherited. These privileges included the power to command the labor of slaves of both sexes, and of women of any class including their own. "Women and slaves belonged and lived together," Hannah Arendt writes. The system of sharp class and gender subordination was a necessary part of what the male culture valued most in itself: "Contempt for laboring originally [arose] out of a passionate striving for freedom from necessity and a no less passionate impatience with every effort that left no trace, no monument, no great work worthy to remembrance";[11] so the contemptible labor was left to women and slaves.

The example of the Greeks demonstrates, I think, that while heterosexuality is necessary for the maintenance of any patriarchy, homophobia, against males at any rate, is not. In fact, for the Greeks, the continuum between "men loving men" and "men promoting the interests of men" appears to have been quite seamless. It is as if, in our terms, there were no perceived discontiniuty between the male bonds at the Continental Baths and the male bonds at the Bohemian Grove[12] or in the boardroom or Senate cloakroom.

It is clear, then, that there is an asymmetry in our present society between, on the one hand, the relatively continuous relation of female homosocial and homo-sexual bonds, and, on the other hand, the radically discontinuous relation of male homosocial and homosexual bonds. The example of the Greeks (and of other, tribal cultures, such as the New Guinea "Sambia" studies by G. H. Herdt) shows, in addition, that the structure of homosocial continuums is cultur-ally contingent, not an innate feature of either "maleness" or "femaleness." In-deed, closely tied though it obviously is to questions of male vs. female power, the explanation will require a more exact mode of historical categorization than "patriarchy," as well, since patriarchal power structures (in Hartmann's sense) characterize both Athenian and American societies. Nevertheless, we may take as an explicit axiom that the historically differential shapes of male and female homosociality—much as they themselves may vary over time—will always be articulations and mechanisms of the enduring inequality of power between women and men.

Why should the different shapes of the homosocial continuum be an interest-ing question? Why should it be a *literary* question? Its importance for the prac-tical politics of the gay movement as a minority rights movement is already obvious from the recent history of strategic and philosophical differences be-tween lesbians and gay men. In addition, it is theoretically interesting partly as a way of approaching a larger question of "sexual politics": What does it mean—what difference does it make—when a social or political relationship is sex-ualized? If the relation of homosocial to homosexual bonds is so shifty, then what theoretical framework do we have for drawing any links between sexual and power relationships?

II. SEXUAL POLITICS AND SEXUAL MEANING

This question, in a variety of forms, is being posed importantly by and for the different gender-politics movements right now. Feminist along with gay male theorists, for instance, are disagreeing actively about how direct the relation is between power domination and sexual sadomasochism. Start with two arrest-ing images: the naked, beefy motorcyclist on the front cover, or the shockingly battered nude male corpse on the back cover, of the recent so-called "Polysex-uality" issue of *Semiotext(e)* (4, no. 1 [1981])—which, for all the women in it, ought to have been called the semisexuality issue of *Polytext*. It seemed to be a purpose of that issue to insist, and possibly not only for reasons of radical-chic titillation, that the violence imaged in sadomasochism is not mainly theatrical, but is fully continuous with violence in the real world. Women Against Pornograhy and the framers of the 1980 NOW Resolution on Lesbian and Gay Rights share the same view, but without the celebratory glamor: to them too it seems intuitively clear that to sexualize violence or an image of violence is simply to extend, un-changed, its reach and force.[13] But, as other feminist writers have reminded us, another view is possible. For example: is a woman's masochistic sexual fantasy really only an internalization and endorsement, if not a cause, of her more gen-eral powerlessness and sense of worthlessness? Or may not the sexual drama stand in some more oblique, or even oppositional, relation to her political experi-ence of oppression?[14]

The debate in the gay male community and elsewhere over "man–boy love" asks a cognate question: can an adult's sexual relationship with a child be simply a continuous part of a more general relationship of education and nurturance? Or must the inclusion of sex quantatively alter the relationship, for instance in the direction of exploitiveness? In this case, the same NOW communiqué that had assumed an unbroken continuity between sexualized violence and real, social violence, came to the opposite conclusion on pedophilia: that the injection of the sexual charge *would* alter (would corrupt) the very substance of the relationship. Thus, in moving from the question of sadomasochism to the question of pedophilia, the "permissive" argument and the "puritanical" argument have essentially exchanged their assumptions about how the sexual relates to the social.

So the answer to the question "what difference does the inclusion of sex make" to a social or political relationship, is—it varies: just as, for different groups in different political circumstances, homosexual activity can be either supportive of or oppositional to homosocial bonding. From this and the other examples I have mentioned, it is clear that there is not some ahistorical *Stoff* of sexuality, some sexual charge that can be simply added to a social relationship to "sexualize" it in a constant and predictable direction, or that splits off from it unchanged. Nor does it make sense to *assume* that the sexualized form epitomizes or simply condenses a broader relationship. (As, for instance, Kathleeen Barry, in *Female Sexual Slavery*, places the Marquis de Sade at the very center of all forms of female oppression, including traditional genital mutilation, incest, and the economic as well as the sexual exploitation of prostitutes.)

Instead, an examination of the relation of sexual desire to political power must move along two axes. First, of course, it needs to make use of whatever forms of analysis are most potent for describing historically variable power asymmetries, such as those of class and race, as well as gender. But in conjunction with that, an analysis of representation itself is necessary. Only the model of representation will let us do justice to the (broad but not infinite or random) range of ways in which sexuality functions as a signifier for power relations. The importance of the rhetorical model in this case is not to make the problems of sexuality or of violence or oppression sound less immediate and urgent; it is to help us analyze and use the really very disparate intuitions of political immediacy that come to us from the sexual realm.

For instance, a dazzling recent article by Catharine MacKinnon, attempting to go carefully over and clear out the grounds of disagreement between different streams of feminist thought, arrives at the following summary of the centrality of sexuality per se for every issue of gender:

> Each element of the female *gender* stereotype is revealed as, in fact, *sexual*. Vulnerability means the appearance/reality of easy sexual access; passivity means receptivity and disabled resistance. . . ; softness means pregnability by something hard. . . . Woman's infantilization evokes pedophilia; fixation on dismembered body parts . . . evokes fetishism; idolization of vapidity, necrophilia. Narcissism insures that woman identifies with that image of herself that man holds up. . . . Masochism means that pleasure in violation becomes her sensuality.

And MacKinnon sums up this part of her argument: "Socially, femaleness means femininity, which means attractiveness to men, which means sexual attractiveness, which means sexual availability on male terms."[15]

There's a whole lot of "mean"-ing going on. MacKinnon manages to make every manifestation of sexuality mean the same thing, by making every instance of "meaning" mean something different. A trait can "mean" as an element in a semiotic system such as fashion ("softness means pregnability"); or anaclitically, it can "mean" its complementary opposite ("Woman's infantilization evokes pedophilia"); or across time, it can "mean" the consequence that it enforces ("Narcissism insures that woman identifies. . . . Masochism means that pleasure in violation becomes her sensuality"). MacKinnon concludes, "What defines woman as such is what turns men on." But what defines "defines"? That every node of sexual experience is in *some* signifying relation to the whole fabric of gender oppression, and vice versa, is true and important, but insufficiently exact to be of analytic use on specific political issues. The danger lies, of course, in the illusion that we do know from such a totalistic analysis where to look for our sexuality and how to protect it from expropriation when we find it.

On the other hand, one value of MacKinnon's piece was as a contribution to the increasing deftness with which, over the last twenty years, the question has been posed, "Who or what is the subject of the sexuality we (as women) enact?" It has been posed in terms more or less antic or frontal, phallic or gyno-, angry or frantic—in short, perhaps, Anglic or Franco-. But in different terms it is this same question that has animated the complaint of the American "sex object" of the 1960s, the claim since the 70s for "women's control of our own bodies," and the recently imported "critique of the subject" as it was used by French feminists.

Let me take an example from the great ideological blockbuster of white bourgeois feminism, its apotheosis, the fictional work that has most resonantly thematized for successive generations of American women the constraints of the "feminine" role, the obstacles to and the ravenous urgency of female ambition, the importance of the economic motive, the compulsiveness and destructiveness of romantic love, and (what MacKinnon would underline) the centrality and the total alienation of female sexuality. Of couse, I am referring to *Gone With the Wind*. As MacKinnon's paradigm would predict, in the life of Scarlett O'Hara, it is expressly clear that to be born female is to be defined entirely in relation to the role of "lady," a role that does take its shape and meaning from a sexuality of which she is not the subject but the object. For Scarlett, to survive as a woman does mean learning to see sexuality, male power domination, and her traditional gender role as all meaning the same dangerous thing. To absent herself silently from each of them alike, and learn to manipulate them from behind this screen as objects or pure signifiers, as men do, is the numbing but effective lesson of her life.

However, it is *only* a white bourgeois feminism that this view apotheosizes. As in one of those trick rooms where water appears to run uphill and little children look taller than their parents, it is only when viewed from one fixed vantage in any society that sexuality, gender roles, and power domination can seem to line up in this perfect chain of echoic meaning. From an even slightly more ec-centric or disempowered perspective, the *dis*placements and *dis*continuities of the signifying chain come to seem increasingly definitive. For instance, if it is true in this novel that all the women characters exist in some meaning-ful relation to the role of "lady," the signifying relation grows more tortuous—though at the same time, in the novel's white bourgeois view, more totally determining—as the women's social and racial distance from that role grows. Melanie is a woman as

she is a lady; Scarlett is a woman as she is required to be and pretends to be a
lady; but Belle Watling, the Atlanta prostitute, is a woman not in relation to her
own role of "lady," which is exiguous, but only negatively, in a compensatory
and at the same time parodic relation to Melanie's and Scarlett's. And as for
Mammy, her mind and life, in this view, are *totally* in thrall to the ideal of the
"lady," but in a relation that excludes herself entirely: she is the template, the
support, the enforcement, of Scarlett's "lady" role, to the degree that her personal femaleness loses any meaning whatever that is not in relation to Scarlett's
role. Whose mother is Mammy?

At the precise intersection of domination and sexuality is the issue of rape.
Gone With the Wind—both book and movie—leaves in the memory a most graphic
image of rape:

> As the negro came running to the buggy, his black face twisted in a leering
> grin, she fired point-blank at him. . . . The negro was beside her, so close
> that she could smell the rank odor of him as he tried to drag her over the
> buggy side. With her own free hand she fought madly, clawing at his face,
> and then she felt his big hand at her throat and, with a ripping noise, her
> basque was torn open from breast to waist. Then the black hand fumbled
> between her breasts, and terror and revulsion such as she had never known
> came over her and she screamed like an insane woman.[16]

In the wake of this attack, the entire machinery by which "rape" is signified in
this culture rolls into action. Scarlett's menfolk and their friends in the Ku Klux
Klan set out after dark to kill the assailants and "wipe out that whole Shantytown
settlement," with the predictable carnage on both sides. The question of how
much Scarlett is to blame for the deaths of the white men is widely mooted, with
Belle Watling speaking for the "lady" role—"She caused it all, prancin' bout
Atlanta by herself, enticin' niggers and trash"—and Rhett Butler, as so often,
speaking from the central vision of the novel's bourgeois feminism, assuring her
that her desperate sense of guilt is purely superstitious (chs. 46, 47). In preparation for this central incident, the novel had even raised the issue of the legal
treatment of rape victims (ch. 42). And the effect of that earlier case, the classic
effect of rape, had already been to abridge Scarlett's own mobility and, hence,
personal and economic power: it was to expedite her business that she had
needed to ride by Shantytown in the first place.

The attack on Scarlett, in short, fully means rape, both *to her* and to all the
forces in her culture that produce and circulate powerful meanings. It makes no
difference at all that one constituent element of rape is missing; but the missing
constituent is simply sex. The attack on Scarlett had been for money; the black
hands had fumbled between the white breasts because the man had been told
that was where she kept her money; Scarlett knew that; there is no mention of
any other motive; but it does not matter in the least, the absent sexuality leaves
no gap in the character's, the novel's, or the society's discourse of rape.

Nevertheless, *Gone With the Wind* is not a novel that omits enforced sexuality.
We are shown one actual rape in fairly graphic detail; but when it is white hands
that scrabble on white skin, its ideological name is "blissful marriage." "[Rhett]
had humbled her, used her brutally through a wild mad night and she had gloried

in it" (ch. 54). The sexual predations of white men on Black women are also a presence in the novel, but the issue of force vs. content is never raised there; the white male alienation of a Black woman's sexuality is shaped differently from the alienation of the white woman's, to the degree that rape ceases to be a meaningful term at all. And if forcible sex ever did occur between a Black male and female character in this world, the sexual event itself would have no signifying power, since Black sexuality "means" here only as a grammatic transformation of a sentence whose true implicit subject and object are white.

We have in this protofeminist novel, then, in this ideological microcosm, a symbolic economy in which both the meaning of rape and rape itself are insistently circulated. Because of the racial fracture of the society, however, *rape and its meaning circulate in precisely opposite directions*. It is an extreme case; the racial fracture is, in America, more sharply dichotomized than others except perhaps for gender. Still, other symbolic fractures such as class (and by fractures I mean the lines along which the quantitative differentials of power may in a given society be read as qualitative differentials with some other name) are abundant and actively disruptive in every social constitution. The signifying relation of sex to power, of sexual alienation to political oppression, is not the most stable, but precisely the most volatile of social nodes, under this pressure.

Thus, it is of serious political importance that our tools for examining the signifying relation be subtle and discriminate ones, and that our literary knowledge of the most crabbed or oblique paths of meaning not be oversimplified in the face of panic-inducing images of real violence, especially the violence of, around, and to sexuality. To assume that sex signifies power in a flat, unvarying relation of metaphor or synecdoche will always entail a blindness, not to the rhetorical and pyrotechnic, but to such historical categories as class and race. Before we can fully achieve and use our intuitive grasp of the leverage that sexual relations seem to offer on the relations of oppression, we need more—more different, more complicated, more diachronically apt, more off-centered—more daring and prehensile applications of our present understanding of what it may mean for one thing to signify another.

III. SEX OR HISTORY?

It will be clear by this point that the centrality of sexual questions in this study is important to its methodological ambitions, as well. I am going to be recurring to the subject of sex as an especially charged leverage-point, or point for the exchange of meanings, *between* gender and class (and in many societies, race), the sets of categories by which we ordinarily try to describe the divisions of human labor. And methodologically, I want to situate these readings as a contribution to a dialectic within femininst theory between more and less historicizing views of the oppression of women.

In a rough way, we can label the extremes on this theoretical spectrum "Marxist feminism" for the most historicizing analysis, "radical feminism" for the least. Of course, "radical feminism" is so called not because it occupies the farthest "left" space on a conventional political map, but because it takes gender itself, gender alone, to be the most radical division of human experience, and a relatively unchanging one.

For the purposes of the present argument, in addition, and for reasons that I will explain more fully later, I am going to be assimilating "French" feminism—deconstructive and/or Lacanian-oriented feminism—to the radical-feminist end of this spectrum. "French" and "radical" feminism differ on very many very important issues, such as how much respect they give to the brute fact that everyone gets categorized as either female or male; but they are alike in seeing all human culture, language, and life as structured in the first place—structured radically, transhistorically, and essentially *similarly*, however coarsely or finely—by a drama of gender difference. (Chapter 1 discusses more fully the particular terms by which this structuralist motive will be represented in the present study.) French-feminist and radical-feminist prose tend to share the same vatic, and perhaps imperialistic, uses of the present tense. In a sense, the polemical energy behind my arguments will be a desire, through the rhetorically volatile subject of sex, to recruit the representational finesse of deconstructive feminism in the service of a more historically discriminate mode of analysis.

The choice of sexuality as a thematic emphasis of this study makes salient and problematical a division of thematic emphasis between Marxist-feminist and radical-feminist theory as they are now practiced. Specifically, Marxist feminism, the study of the deep interconnections between on the one hand historical and economic change, and on the other hand the vicissitudes of gender division, has typically proceeded in the absence of a theory of sexuality and without much interest in the meaning or experience of sexuality. Or more accurately, it has held implicitly to a view of female sexuality as something that is essentially of a piece with reproduction, and hence appropriately studied with the tools of demography; or else essentially of a piece with a simple, prescriptive hegemonic ideology, and hence appropriately studied through intellectual or legal history. Where important advances have been made by Marxist-feminist–oriented research into sexuality, it has been in areas that were already explicitly distinguished as deviant by the society's legal discourse: signally, homosexuality for men and prostitution for women. Marxist feminism has been of little help in unpacking the historical meanings of women's experience of heterosexuality, or even, until it becomes legally and medically visible in this century, of lesbianism.[17]

Radical feminism, on the other hand, in the many different forms I am classing under that head, has been relatively successful in placing sexuality in a prominent and interrogative position, one that often allows scope for the decentered and the contradictory. Kathleen Barry's *Female Sexual Slavery*, Susan Griffin's *Pornography and Silence*, Gilbert and Gubar's *The Madwoman in the Attic*, Jane Gallop's *The Daughter's Seduction*, and Andrea Dworkin's *Pornography: Men Possessing Women* make up an exceedingly heterogeneous group of texts in many respects—in style, in urgency, in explicit feminist identification, in French or Amerian affiliation, in "brow"-elevation level. They have in common, however, a view that sexuality is centrally problematical in the formation of women's experience. And in more or less sophisticated formulations, the subject as well as the ultimate object of female heterosexuality within what is called patriarchal culture are seen as male. Whether in literal interpersonal terms or in internalized psychological and linguistic terms, this approach privileges sexuality and often sees it within the context of the structure that Lévi-Strauss analyzes as "the male traffic in women."

This family of approaches has, however, shared with other forms of structuralism a difficulty in dealing with the diachronic. It is the essence of structures viewed as such to reproduce themselves; and historical change from this point of view appears as something outside of structure and threatening—or worse, *not* threatening—to it, rather than in a formative and dialectical relation with it. History tends thus to be either invisible or viewed in an impoverishingly glaring and contrastive light.[18] Implicitly or explicitly, radical feminism tends to deny that the meaning of gender or sexuality has ever significantly changed; and more damagingly, it can make future change appear impossible, or necessarily apocalyptic, even though desirable. Alternatively, it can radically oversimplify the prerequisites for significant change. In addition, history even in the residual, synchronic form of class or racial difference and conflict becomes invisible or excessively coarsened and dichotomized in the universalizing structuralist view.

As feminist readers, then, we seem poised for the moment between reading sex and reading history, at a choice that appears (though, it must be, wrongly) to be between the synchronic and the diachronic. We know that it must be wrongly viewed in this way, not only because in the abstract the synchronic and the diachronic must ultimately be considered in relation to one another, but because specifically in the disciplines we are considering they are so mutually inscribed: the narrative of Marxist history is so graphic, and the schematics of structuralist sexuality so narrative.

I will be trying in this study to activate and use some of the potential congruences of the two approaches. Part of the underpinning of this attempt will be a continuing meditation of ways in which the category *ideology* can be used as part of an analysis of *sexuality*. The two categories seem comparable in several important ways: each mediates between the material and the representational, for instance; ideology, like sexuality as we have discussed it, *both* epitomizes *and* itself influences broader social relations of power; and each, I shall be arguing, mediates similarly between diachronic, narrative structures of social experience and synchronic, graphic ones. If commonsense suggests that we can roughly group historicizing, "Marxist" feminism with the diachronic and the narrative, and "radical," structuralist, deconstructive, and "French" feminisms with the synchronic and the graphic, then the methodological promise of these two mediating categories will be understandable.

In *The German Ideology*, Marx suggests that the function of ideology is to conceal contradictions in the status quo by, for instance, recasting them into a diachronic narrative of origins. Corresponding to that function, one important structure of ideology is an idealizing appeal to the outdated values of an earlier system, in defense of a later system that in practice undermines the material basis of those values.[19]

For instance, Juliet Mitchell analyzes the importance of the family in ideologically justifying the shift to capitalism, in these terms:

> The peasant masses of feudal society had individual private property; their ideal was simply more of it. Capitalist society seemed to offer more because it stressed the *idea* of individual private property in a new context (or in a context of new ideas). Thus it offered individualism (an old value) plus the apparently new means for its greater realization—freedom and equality (val-

ues that are conspicuously absent from feudalism). However, the only place where this ideal could be given an apparently concrete base was in the maintenance of an old institution: the family. Thus the family changed from being the economic basis of individual private property under feudalism to being the focal point of the *idea* of individual private property under a system that banished such an economic form from its central mode of production—capitalism. . . . The working class work socially in production for the private property of a few capitalists *in the hope of* individual private property for themselves and their families.[20]

The phrase "A man's home is his castle" offers a nicely condensed example of ideological construction in this sense. It reaches *back* to an emptied-out image of mastery and integration under feudalism in order to propel the male wage-worker *forward* to further feats of alienated labor, in the service of a now atomized and embattled, but all the more intensively idealized home. The man who has this home is a different person from the lord who has a castle; and the forms of property implied in the two possessives (his [mortgaged] home/his [inherited] castle) are not only different but, as Mitchell points out, mutually contradictory. The contradiction is assuaged and filled in by transferring the lord's political and economic control over the *environs* of his castle to an image of the father's personal control over the *inmates* of his house. The ideological formulation thus permits a criss-crossing of agency, temporality, and space. It is important that ideology in this sense, even when its form is flatly declarative ("A man's home is his castle"), is always at least implicitly narrative, and that, in order for the re-weaving of ideology to be truly invisible, the narrative is necessarily chiasmic in structure: that is, that the subject of the beginning of the narrative is different from the subject at the end, and that the two subjects cross each other in a rhetorical figure that conceals their discontinuity.

It is also important that the sutures of contradiction in these ideological narratives become most visible under the disassembling eye of an alternative narrative, ideological as that narrative may itself be. In addition, the diachronic opening-out of contradictions within the status quo, even when the project of that diachronic recasting is to conceal those very contradictions, can have just the opposite effect of making them newly visible, offering a new leverage for critique. For these reasons, distinguishing between the construction and the critique of ideological narrative is not always even a theoretical possibility, even with relatively flat texts; with the fat rich texts that we are taking for examples in this project, no such attempt will be made.

Sexuality, like ideology, depends on the mutual redefinition and occlusion of synchronic and diachronic formulations. The developmental fact that, as Freud among others has shown, even the naming of sexuality as such is always retroactive in relation to most of the sensations and emotions that constitute it,[21] is *historically* important. What *counts* as the sexual is, as we shall see, variable and itself political. The exact, contingent space of indeterminacy—the place of shifting over time—of the mutual boundaries between the political and the sexual is, in fact, the most fertile space of ideological formation. This is true because ideological formation, like sexuality, depends on retroactive change in the naming or labelling of the subject.[22]

The two sides, the political and the erotic, necessarily obscure and misrepresent each other—but in ways that offer important and shifting affordances to all parties in historical gender and class struggle.

IV. WHAT THIS BOOK DOES

The difficult but potentially productive tension between historical and structuralist forms of feminism, in the theoretical grounding of this book, is echoed by a tension in the book between historical and more properly literary organization, methodologies, and emphases. Necessarily because of my particular aptitudes and training, if for no better reason, the historical argument almost throughout is embodied in and guided by the readings of the literary texts. For better and for worse, the large historical narrative has an off-centering effect on the discrete readings, as the introversive techniques of literary analysis have in turn on the historical argument. The resulting structure represents a continuing negotiation between the book's historicizing and dehistoricizing motives. The two ways in which I have described to myself the purpose of this book express a similar tension: first, to make it easier for readers to focus intelligently on male homosocial bonds throughout the heterosexual European erotic ethos; but secondly, to use the subject of sexuality to show the usefulness of certain Marxist-feminist historical categories for literary criticism, where they have so far had relatively little impact.

Chapter 1 of the book, "Gender Asymmetry and Erotic Triangles," locates the book's focus on male homosocial desire within the structural context of triangular, heterosexual desire. René Girard, Freud, and Lévi-Strauss, especially as he is interpreted by Gayle Rubin, offer the basic paradigm of "male traffic in women" that will underlie the entire book. In the next three chapters a historically deracinated reading of Shakespeare's Sonnets, a partially historical reading of Wycherley's *The Country Wife*, and a reading of Sterne's *A Sentimental Journey* in relation to the inextricable gender, class, and national anxieties of mid-eighteenth-century English men both establish some persistent paradigms for discussion, and begin to locate them specifically in the terms of modern England.

Chapters 5 and 6, on homophobia and the Romantic Gothic, discuss the paranoid Gothic tradition in the novel as an exploration of the changing meaning and importance of homophobia in England during and after the eighteenth century. A reading of James Hogg's *Confessions of a Justified Sinner* treats homophobia not most immediately as an oppression of homosexual men, but as a tool for manipulating the entire spectrum of male bonds, and hence the gender system as a whole.

Chapters 7 and 8 focus on more "mainstream," public Victorian ideological fictions, and on the fate of the women who are caught up in male homosocial exchange. This section treats three Victorian texts, historical or mock-historical, that claim to offer accounts of changes in women's relation to male bonds: Tennyson's *The Princess*, Thackeray's *Henry Esmond*, and Eliot's *Adam Bede;* it approaches most explicitly the different explanatory claims of structuralist and historical approaches to sex and gender.

Chapters 9 and 10, on Dickens' Victorian Gothic, show how Dickens' last two novels delineate the interactions of homophobia with nineteenth-century class and racial as well as gender division.

Finally, a Coda, "Toward the Twentieth Century: English Readers of Whitman," uses an account of some influential English (mis-)understandings of Whitman's poetry, to sketch in the links between mid-Victorian English sexual politics and the familiar modern Anglo-American landscape of male homosexuality, heterosexuality, and homophobia as (we think) we know them.

The choices I have made of texts through which to embody the argument of the book are specifically *not* meant to begin to delineate a separate male-homosocial literary canon. In fact, it will be essential to my argument to claim that the European canon as it exists is already such a canon, and most so when it is most heterosexual. In this sense, it would perhaps be easiest to describe this book (as will be done more explicitly in chapter 1) as a recasting of, and a refocusing on, René Girard's triangular schematization of the existing European canon in *Deceit, Desire, and the Novel*. In fact, I have simply chosen texts at pleasure from within or alongside the English canon that represented particularly interesting interpretive problems, or particularly symptomatic historical and ideological nodes, for understanding the politics of male homosociality.

I hope it is obvious by this point that I mean to situate this book in a dialectically usable, rather than an authoritative, relation to the rapidly developing discourse of feminist theory. Of course, the readings and interpretations are as careful in their own terms as I have known how to make them; but at the same time I am aware of having privileged certain arresting (and hence achronic) or potentially generalizable formulations, in the hope of making interpretations like these dialectically available to readers of other texts, as well. The formal models I have had in mind for this book are two very different books, Girard's *Deceit, Desire, and the Novel* and Dorothy Dinnerstein's *The Mermaid and the Minotaur:* not in this instance because of an agreement with the substance of their arguments, but because each in a relatively short study with an apparently idiosyncratic focus nevertheless conveys a complex of ideas forcefully enough—even, repetitiously enough—to make it a usable part of any reader's repertoire of approaches to her or his personal experience and future reading. *From* that position in the repertoire each can be—must be—criticized and changed. To take such a position has been my ambition for this book. Among the directions of critique and alteration that seem to me most called for, but which I have been unable so far to incorporate properly in the argument itself, are the following:

First, the violence done by my historicizing narrative to the literary readings proper shows perhaps most glaringly in the overriding of distinctions and structural considerations of genre. And in general, the number and the *different*ness of the many different mechanisms of mediation between history and text—mechanisms with names like, for instance, "literary convention," "literary history"— need to be reasserted in newly applicable formulations.

At the same time, the violences done to a historical argument by embodying it in a series of readings of works of literature are probably even more numerous and damaging. Aside from issues of ideological condensation and displacement that will be discussed in chapters 7 and 8, the form of violence most obvious to me is simply the limitation of my argument *to* the "book-writing classes"—a group that is distinctive in more than merely socioeconomic terms, but importantly in those terms as well.

Next, the isolation, not to mention the absolute subordination, of women, in the structural paradigm on which this study is based (see chapter 1 for more on this) is a distortion that necessarily fails to do justice to women's own powers, bonds, and struggles.[23] The absence of lesbianism from the book was an early and, I think, necessary decision, since my argument is structured around the distinctive relation of the male homosocial spectrum to the transmission of unequally distributed power. Nevertheless, the exclusively heterosexual perspective of the book's attention to women is seriously impoverishing in itself, and also an index of the larger distortion. The reading of *Henry Esmond* is the only one that explicitly considers the bond of woman with woman in the context of male homosocial exchange; but much better analyses are needed of the relations between female-homosocial and male-homosocial structures.

The book's almost exclusive focus on male authors is, I think, similarly justified for this early stage of this particular inquiry; but it has a similar effect of impoverishing our sense of women's own cultural resources of resistance, adaptation, revision, and survival. My reluctance to distinguish between "ideologizing" and "de-ideologizing" narratives may have had, paradoxically, a similar effect of presenting the "canonical" cultural discourse in an excessively protean and inescapable (*because* internally contradictory) form. In addition, the relation between the traffic-in-women paradigm used here and hypotheses, such as Dinnerstein's, Chodorow's, and Kristeva's in *Powers of Horror*, of a primary fear in men and women of the maternal power of women, is yet to be analyzed.

Again, the lack of entirely usable paradigms, at this early moment in feminist theory, for the complicated relations among violence, sexual violence, and the sadomasochistic sexualization of violence,[24] has led me in this book to a perhaps inappropriately gentle emphasis on modes of gender oppression that could be (more or less metaphorically) described in economic terms.

At the same time, the erotic and individualistic bias of literature itself, and the relative ease—not to mention the genuine pleasure—of using feminist theoretical paradigms to write about eros and sex, have led to a relative deemphasis of the many, crucially important male homosocial bonds that are less glamorous to talk about—such as the institutional, bureaucratic, and military.

Finally, and I think most importantly, the focus of this study on specifically English social structures, combined with the hegemonic claim for "universality" that has historically been implicit in the entire discourse of European social and psychological analysis, leave the relation of my discussion to non-European cultures and people entirely unspecified, and at present, perhaps, to some extent unspecifiable. A running subtext of comparisons between English sexual ideology and some ideologies of American racism is not a token attempt to conceal that gap in the book's coverage, but an attempt to make clear to other American readers some of the points of reference in white America that I have used in thinking about English ideology. Perhaps what one can most appropriately ask of readers who find this book's formulations useful is simply to remember that, important as it is that they be criticized at every step of even European applications, any attempt to treat them as cross-cultural or (far more) as universal ought to involve the most searching and particular analysis.

As a woman and a feminist writing (in part) about male homosexuality, I feel I must be especially explicit about the political groundings, assumptions, and ambitions of this study in that regard, as well. My intention throughout has been to conduct an antihomophobic as well as feminist inquiry. However, most of the (little) published analysis up to now of the relation between women and male homosexuality has been at a lower level of sophistication and care than either feminist or gay male analysis separately. In the absence of workable formulations about the male homosocial spectrum, this literature has, with only a few recent exceptions,[25] subscribed to one of two assumptions: either that gay men and all women share a "natural," transhistorical alliance and an essential identity of interests (e.g., in breaking down gender stereotypes);[26] or else that male homosexuality is an epitome, a personification, an effect, or perhaps a primary cause of woman-hating.[27] I do not believe either of these assumptions to be true. Especially because this study discusses a continuum, a potential structural congruence, and a (shifting) relation of meaning between male homosexual relationships and the male patriarchal relations by which women are oppressed, it is important to emphasize that I am not assuming or arguing either that patriarchal power is primarily or necessarily homosexual (as distinct from homosocial), or that male homosexual desire has a primary or necessary relationship to misogyny. Either of those arguments would be homophobic and, I believe, inaccurate. I will, however, be arguing that homophobia directed by men against men is misogynistic, and perhaps transhistorically so. (By "misogynistic" I mean not only that it is oppressive of the so-called feminine in men, but that it is oppressive of women.) The greatest potential for misinterpretation lies here. Because "homosexuality" and "homophobia" are, in any of their avatars, historical constructions, because they are likely to concern themselves intensely with each other and to assume interlocking or mirroring shapes, because the theater of their struggle is likely to be intrapsychic or intra-institutional as well as public, it is not always easy (sometimes barely possible) to distinguish them from each other. Thus, for instance, Freud's study of Dr. Schreber shows clearly that *the repression of homosexual desire* in a man who by any commonsense standard was heterosexual, occasioned paranoid psychosis; the psychoanalytic use that has been made of this perception, however, has been, not against *homophobia* and its schizogenic force, but against *homosexuality*—against homosexuals—on account of an association between "homosexuality" and mental illness.[28] Similar confusions have marked discussions of the relation between "homosexuality" and fascism. As the historically constructed nature of "homosexuality" as an institution becomes more fully understood, it should become possible to understand these distinctions in a more exact and less prejudicious theoretical context.

Thus, profound and intuitable as the bonds between feminism and antihomophobia often are in our society, the two forces are not the same. As the alliance between them is not automatic or transhistorical, it will be most fruitful if it is analytic and unpresuming. To shed light on the grounds and implications of that alliance, as well as, through these issues, on formative literary texts, is an aim of the readings that follow.

GENDER ASYMMETRY AND EROTIC TRIANGLES

The graphic schema on which I am going to be drawing most heavily in the readings that follow is the triangle. The triangle is useful as a figure by which the "commonsense" of our intellectual tradition schematizes erotic relations, and because it allows us to condense into a juxtaposition with that folk-perception several somewhat different streams of recent thought.

René Girard's early book, *Deceit, Desire, and the Novel,* was itself something of a schematization of the folk-wisdom of erotic triangles. Through readings of major European fictions, Girard traced a calculus of power that was structured by the relation of rivalry between the two active members of an erotic triangle. What is most interesting for our purposes in his study is its insistence that, in any erotic rivalry, the bond that links the two rivals is as intense and potent as the bond that links either of the rivals to the beloved: that the bonds of "rivalry" and "love," differently as they are experienced, are equally powerful and in many senses equivalent. For instance, Girard finds many examples in which the choice of the beloved is determined in the first place, not by the qualities of the beloved, but by the beloved's already being the choice of the person who has been chosen as a rival. In fact, Girard seems to see the bond between rivals in an erotic triangle as being even stronger, more heavily determinant of actions and choices, than anything in the bond between either of the lovers and the beloved. And within the male-centered novelistic tradition of European high culture, the triangles Girard traces are most often those in which two males are rivals for a female; it is the bond between males that he most assiduously uncovers.

The index to Girard's book gives only two citations for "homosexuality" per se, and it is one of the strengths of his formulation not to depend on how homosexuality as an entity was perceived or experienced—indeed, on what was or was not considered sexual—at any given historical moment. As a matter of fact, the symmetry of his formulation always depends on *suppressing* the subjective, historically determined account of which feelings are or are not part of the body of "sexuality." The transhistorical clarity gained by this organizing move naturally has a cost, however. Psychoanalysis, the recent work of Foucault, and feminist historical scholarship all suggest that the place of drawing the boundary between the sexual and the not-sexual, like the place of drawing the boundary between the realms of the two genders, *is* variable, but is *not* arbitrary. That is (as the example of *Gone With the Wind* suggests), the placement of the boundaries in a particular society affects not merely the definitions of those terms themselves— sexual/nonsexual, masculine/feminine—but also the apportionment of forms of power that are not obviously sexual. These include control over the means of production and reproduction of goods, persons, and meanings. So that Girard's account, which thinks it is describing a dialectic of power abstracted from either the male/female or the sexual/nonsexual dichotomies, is leaving out of consideration categories that in fact preside over the distribution of power in every known society. And because the distribution of power according to these dichotomies is not and possibly cannot be symmetrical, the hidden symmetries that Girard's triangle helps us discover will always in turn discover hidden obliquities. At the same time, even to bear in mind the lurking possibility of the Girardian symmetry is to be possessed of a graphic tool for historical measure. It will make it easier for us to perceive and discuss the mutual inscription in these texts of male homosocial and heterosocial desire, and the resistances to them.

Girard's argument is of course heavily dependent, not only on a brilliant intuition for taking seriously the received wisdom of sexual folklore, but also on a schematization from Freud: the Oedipal triangle, the situation of the young child that is attempting to situate itself with respect to a powerful father and a beloved mother. Freud's discussions of the etiology of "homosexuality" (which current research seems to be rendering questionable as a set of generalizations about personal histories of "homosexuals")[1] suggest homo- and heterosexual outcomes in adults to be the result of a complicated play of desire for and identification with the parent of each gender: the child routes its desire/identification through the mother to arrive at a role like the father's, or vice versa. Richard Klein summarizes this argument as follows:

> In the normal development of the little boy's progress towards heterosexuality, he must pass, as Freud says with increasing insistence in late essays like "Terminable and Interminable Analysis," through the stage of the "positive" Oedipus, a homoerotic identification with his father, a position of effeminized subordination to the father, as a condition of finding a model for his own heterosexual role. Conversely, in this theory, the development of the male homosexual requires the postulation of the father's absence or distance and an abnormally strong identification by the child with the mother, in which the child takes the place of the father. There results from this scheme a surprising neutralization of polarities: heterosexuality in the male . . . presupposes a homosexual neutralization phase as the condition of its normal possibility: homosexuality, obversely, requires that the child experience a powerful heterosexual identification.[2]

I have mentioned that Girard's reading presents itself as one whose symmetry is undisturbed by such differences as gender; although the triangles that most shape his view tend, in the European tradition, to involve bonds of "rivalry" between males "over" a woman, in his view *any* relation of rivalry is structured by the same play of emulation and identification, whether the entities occupying the corners of the triangle be heroes, heroines, gods, books, or whatever. In describing the Oedipal drama, Freud notoriously tended to place a male in the generic position of "child" and treat the case of the female as being more or less the same, "mutatis mutandis"; at any rate, as Freud is interpreted by conventional American psychoanalysis, the enormous difference in the degree and kind of female and male power enters psychoanalytic view, when at all, as a result rather than as an active determinant of familial and intrapsychic structures of development. Thus, both Girard and Freud (or at least the Freud of this interpretive tradition) treat the erotic triangle as symmetrical—in the sense that its structure would be relatively unaffected by the power difference that would be introduced by a change in the gender of one of the participants.

In addition, the asymmetry I spoke of in section 1 of the Introduction—the radically disrupted continuum, in our society, between sexual and nonsexual male bonds, as against the relatively smooth and palpable continuum of female homosocial desire—might be expected to alter the structure of erotic triangles in ways that depended on gender, and for which neither Freud nor Girard would offer an account. Both Freud and Girard, in other words, treat erotic triangles under the Platonic light that perceives no discontinuity in the homosocial continuum—none, at any rate, that makes much difference—even in modern Western society. There is a kind of bravery about the proceeding of each in this respect, but a historical blindness, as well.

Recent readings and reinterpretations of Freud have gone much farther in taking into account the asymmetries of gender. In France, recent psychoanalytic discourse impelled by Jacques Lacan identifies power, language, and the Law itself with the phallus and the "name of the father." It goes without saying that such a discourse has the potential for setting in motion both feminist and virulently misogynistic analyses; it does, at any rate, offer tools, though not (so far) historically sensitive ones, for describing the mechanisms of patriarchal power in terms that are at once intrapsychic (Oedipal conflict) and public (language and the Law). Moreover, by distinguishing (however incompletely) the phallus, the locus of power, from the actual anatomical penis,[3] Lacan's account creates a space in which anatomic sex and cultural gender may be distinguished from one another and in which the different paths of *men's* relations to male power might be explored (e.g. in terms of class). In addition, it suggests ways of talking about the relation between the individual male and the cultural institutions of masculine domination that fall usefully under the rubric of representation.

A further contribution of Lacanian psychoanalysis that will be important for our investigation is the subtlety with which it articulates the slippery relation—already adumbrated in Freud—between desire and identification. The schematic elegance with which Richard Klein, in the passage I have quoted, is able to summarize the feminizing potential of desire for a woman and the masculine potential of subordination to a man, owes at least something to a Lacanian grinding of the lenses through which Freud is being viewed. In Lacan and those who have learned from him, an elaborate meditation on introjection and incorporation forms the link between the apparently dissimilar processes of desire and identification.

Recent American feminist work by Dorothy Dinnerstein and Nancy Chodorow also revises Freud in the direction of greater attention to gender/power difference. Coppélia Kahn summarizes the common theme of their argument (which she applies to Shakespeare) as follows:

Most children, male or female, in Shakespeare's time, Freud's, or ours, are not only borne but raised by women. And thus arises a crucial difference between the girl's developing sense of identity and the boy's. For though she follows the same sequence of symbiotic union, separation and individuation, identification, and object love as the boy, her femininity arises in relation to a person of the *same* sex, while his masculinity arises in relation to a person of the *opposite* sex. Her femininity is reinforced by her original symbiotic union with her mother and by the identification with her that must precede identity, while his masculinity is threatened by the same union and the same identification. While the boy's sense of *self* begins in union with the feminine, his sense of *masculinity* arises against it.[4]

It should be clear, then, from what has gone before, on the one hand that there are many and thorough asymmetries between the sexual continuums of women and men, between female and male sexuality and homosociality, and most pointedly between homosocial and heterosocial object choices for males; and on the other hand that the status of women and the whole question of arrangements between genders, is deeply and inescapably inscribed in the structure even of relationships that seem to exclude women—even in male homosocial/homosexual relationships. Heidi Hartmann's definition of patriarchy in terms of "relationships between men" (see introduction 1), in making the power relationships between men and women appear to be dependent on the power relationships between men and men, suggests that large-scale social structures are congruent with the male–male–female erotic triangles described most forcefully by Girard and articulated most thoughtfully by others. We can go further than that, to say that in any male-dominated society, there is a special relationship between male homosocial (*including* homosexual) desire and the structures for maintaining and transmitting patriarchal power: a relationship founded on an inherent and potentially active structural congruence. For historical reasons, this special relationship may take the form of ideological homophobia, ideological homosexuality, or some highly conflicted but intensively structured combination of the two. (Lesbianism also must always be in a special relation to patriarchy, but on different [sometimes opposite] grounds and working through different mechanisms.)

Perhaps the most powerful recent argument through (and against) a traditional discipline that bears on these issues has occurred within anthropology. Based on readings and critiques of Lévi-Strauss and Engels, in addition to Freud and Lacan, Gayle Rubin has argued in an influential essay that patriarchal heterosexuality can best be discussed in terms of one or another form of the traffic in women: it is the use of women as exchangeable, perhaps symbolic, property for the primary purpose of cementing the bonds of men with men. For example, Lévi-Strauss writes, "The total relationship of exchange which constitutes marriage is not established between a man and a woman, but between two groups of men, and the woman figures only as one of the objects in the exchange, not as one of the partners."[5] Thus, like Freud's "heterosexual" in Richard Klein's account, Lévi-Strauss's normative man uses a woman as a "conduit of a relationship" in which the true *partner* is a man.[6] Rejecting Lévi-Strauss's celebratory treatment of this relegation of women, Rubin offers, instead, an array of tools for specifying and analyzing it.

Luce Irigaray has used the Lévi-Straussian description of the traffic in women to make a resounding though expensive leap of register in her discussion of the relation of heterosexual to male homosocial bonds. In the reflections translated into English as "When the Goods Get Together," she concludes: "[Male] homosexuality is the law that regulates the sociocultural order. Heterosexuality amounts to the assignment of roles in the economy."[7] To begin to describe this relation as having the asymmetry of (to put it roughly) *parole* to *langue* is wonderfully pregnant; if her use of it here is not a historically responsive one, still it has potential for increasing our ability to register historical difference.

The expensiveness of Irigaray's vision of male homosexuality is, oddly, in a sacrifice of sex itself: the male "homosexuality" discussed here turns out to represent anything but actual sex between men, which—although it is also, importantly, called "homosexuality"—has something like the same invariable, tabooed status for her larger, "real" "homosexuality" that incest has in principle for Lévi-Straussian kinship in general. Even Irigaray's supple machinery of meaning has the effect of transfixing, then sublimating, the quicksilver of sex itself.

The loss of the diachronic in a formulation like Irigaray's is, again, most significant, as well. Recent anthropology, as well as historical work by Foucault, Sheila Rowbotham, Jeffrey Weeks, Alan Bray, K. J. Dover, John Boswell, David Fernbach, and others, suggests that among the things that have changed radically in Western culture over the centuries, and vary across cultures, about men's genital activity with men are its frequency, its exclusivity, its class associations, its relation to the dominant culture, its ethical status, the degree to which it is seen as defining nongenital aspects of the lives of those who practice it, and, perhaps most radically, its association with femininity or masculinity in societies where gender is a profound determinant of power. The virility of the homosexual orientation of male desire seemed as self-evident to the ancient Spartans, and perhaps to Whitman, as its effeminacy seems in contemporary popular culture. The importance of women (not merely of "the feminine," but of actual women as well) in the etiology and the continuing experience of male homosexuality seems to be historically volatile (across time, across class) to a similar degree. Its changes are inextricable from the changing shapes of the institutions by which gender and class inequality are structured.

Thus, Lacan, Chodorow and Dinnerstein, Rubin, Irigaray, and others, making critiques from within their multiple traditions, offer analytical tools for treating the erotic triangle not as an ahistorical, Platonic form, a deadly symmetry from which the historical accidents of gender, language, class, and power detract, but as a sensitive register precisely for delineating relationships of power and meaning, and for making graphically intelligible the play of desire and identification by which individuals negotiate with their societies for empowerment.

NOTES

Introduction

1. The notion of "homophobia" is itself fraught with difficulties. To begin with, the word is etymologically nonsensical. A more serious problem is that the linking of fear and

hatred in the "-phobia" suffix, and in the word's usage, does tend to prejudge the question of the cause of homosexual oppression: it is attributed to fear, as opposed to (for example) a desire for power, privilege, or material goods. An alternative term that is more suggestive of collective, structurally inscribed, perhaps materially based oppression is "heterosexism." This study will, however, continue to use "homophobia," for three reasons. First, it will be an important concern here to question, rather than to reinforce, the presumptively symmetrical opposition between homo- and heterosexuality, which seems to be implicit in the term "heterosexism." Second, the etiology of individual people's attitudes toward male homosexuality will not be a focus of discussion. And third, the ideological and thematic treatments of male homosexuality to be discussed from the late eighteenth century onward do combine fear and hatred in a way that is appropriately called phobic. For a good summary of social science research on the concept of homophobia, see Morin and Garfinkle, "Male Homophobia."

2. For a good survey of the background to this assertion, see Weeks, *Sex*, pp. 1–18.

3. Adrienne Rich describes these bonds as forming a "lesbian continuum," in her essay, "Compulsory Heterosexuality and Lesbian Existence," in Stimpson and Person, *Women*, pp. 62–91, especially pp. 79–82.

4. "The Female World of Love and Ritual," in Cott and Pleck, *Heritage*, pp. 311–42; usage appears on, e.g., pp. 316, 317.

5. "The Unhappy Marriage of Marxism and Feminism: Towards a More Progressive Union," in Sargent, *Women and Revolution*, pp. 1–41; quotation is from p. 14.

6. See, for example, Rubin, "Traffic," pp. 182–83.

7. Rubin, "Traffic," p. 180.

8. Crompton, "Gay Genocide"; but see chapter 5 for a discussion of the limitations of "genocide" as an understanding of the fate of homosexual men.

9. On this, see Miller, *New Psychology*, ch. 1.

10. Dover, *Greek Homosexuality*, p. 91.

11. Arendt, *Human Condition*, p. 83, quoted in Rich, *On Lies*, p. 206.

12. On the Bohemian Grove, an all-male summer camp for American ruling-class men, see Domhoff, *Bohemian Grove;* and a more vivid, although homophobic, account, van der Zee, *Men's Party*.

13. The NOW resolution, for instance, explicitly defines sadomasochism, pornography, and "pederasty" (meaning pedophilia) as issues of "exploitation and violence," *as opposed to* "affectional/sexual preference/orientation." Quoted in *Heresies 12*, vol. 3, no. 4 (1981), p. 92.

14. For explorations of these viewpoints, see *Heresies, ibid.;* Snitow et al., *Powers;* and Samois, *Coming*.

15. MacKinnon, "Feminism," pp. 530–31.

16. Mitchell, *Gone*, p. 780. Further citations will be incorporated within the text and designated by chapter number.

17. For a discussion of these limitations, see Vicinus, "Sexuality." The variety of useful work that is possible within these boundaries is exemplified by the essays in Newton et al., *Sex and Class*.

18. On this, see McKeon, "Marxism."

19. Juliet Mitchell discusses this aspect of *The German Ideology* in *Women's Estate*, pp. 152–58.

20. Mitchell, *Woman's Estate*, p. 154.

21. The best and clearest discussion of this aspect of Freud is Laplanche, *Life and Death*, especially pp. 25–47.

22. On this, see ch. 8 of *Between Men*.

23. For an especially useful discussion of the absence of women from the work of Girard, see Moi, "Missing Mother."

24. On this see (in addition to Snitow et al., *Powers*) Breines and Gordon, "Family Violence."

25. The following books are, to a greater or lesser extent, among the exceptions: Fernbach, *Spiral Path;* Mieli, *Homosexuality;* Rowbotham and Weeks, *Socialism;* Dworkin, *Pornography.*

26. The most influential recent statement of this position is Heilbrun, *Androgyny.*

27. See Irigaray, "Goods"; and Frye, *Politics*, pp. 128–51. Jane Marcus's work on Virginia Woolf makes use of Maria-Antonietta Macciocchi's homophobic formulation, "the Nazi community is made by homosexual brothers who exclude the woman and valorize the mother." Marcus says, "The Cambridge Apostles' notions of fraternity surely appeared to Woolf analogous to certain fascist notions of fraternity." Macciocchi's formulation is quoted in Jane Caplan, "Introduction to Female Sexuality in Fascist Ideology," *Feminist Review* 1 (1979), p. 62. Marcus's essay is "Liberty, Sorority, Misogyny," in Heilbrun and Higonnet, *Representation*, pp. 60–97; quotation is from p. 67.

28. On this see Hocquenghem, *Homosexual Desire*, pp. 42–67.

Gender Asymmetry and Erotic Triangles

1. On this, see Bell et al., *Sexual Preferences.*
2. Review of *Homosexualities*, p. 1077.
3. On this see Gallop, *Daughter's Seduction*, pp. 15–32.
4. Kahn, *Man's Estate*, pp. 9–10.
5. *The Elementary Structures of Kinship* (Boston: Beacon, 1969), p. 115; quoted in Rubin, "Traffic," p. 174.
6. Rubin, *ibid.*
7. Irigaray, "Goods," pp. 107–10.

WORKS CITED

Arendt, Hannah. *The Human Condition.* Chicago: University of Chicago Press, 1958.

Barry, Kathleen. *Female Sexual Slavery.* New York: Prentice-Hall, 1979.

Bell, Alan P., Martin S. Weinberg, and Sue Kiefer Hammersmith. *Sexual Preference: Its Development in Men and Women.* Bloomington: Indiana University Press, 1981.

Bray, Alan. *Homosexuality in Renaissance England.* London: Gay Men's Press, 1982.

Breines, Wini, and Linda Gordon. "The New Scholarship on Family Violence." *Signs* 8, no. 3 (Spring 1983), pp. 490–531.

Chodorow, Nancy. "Mothering, Male Dominance, and Capitalism." In *Capitalist Patriarchy and the Case for Socialist Feminism.* Ed. Zillah Eisenstein. New York: Monthly Review, 1979, pp. 83–106.

——— *The Reproduction of Mothering: Psychoanalysis and the Sociology of Gender.* Berkeley: University of California Press, 1978.

Cott, Nancy F., and Elizabeth H. Pleck, eds. *A Heritage of Her Own: Toward a New Social History of American Women.* New York: Simon and Schuster, 1979.

Crompton, Louis. "Gay Genocide: From Leviticus to Hitler." In *The Gay Academic.* Ed. Louie Crew. Palm Springs, Calif.: ETC Publications, 1978, pp. 67–91.

Dickens, Charles. *David Copperfield.* Ed. Trevor Blount. Harmondsworth, Sussex: Penguin, 1966.

——— *The Mystery of Edwin Drood.* Ed. Margaret Cardwell. Oxford: Oxford University Press, 1972.

——— *Our Mutual Friend.* Ed. Stephen Gill. Harmondsworth: Penguin, 1971.

Dinnerstein, Dorothy. *The Mermaid and the Minotaur: Sexual Arrangements and Human Malaise.* New York: Harper & Row–Colophon, 1976.

Domhoff, G. William. *The Bohemian Grove and Other Retreats: A Study in Ruling-Class Co-hesiveness*. New York: Harper & Row, 1974.

Dover, K. J. *Greek Homosexuality*. New York: Random House–Vintage, 1980.

Dworkin, Andrea. *Pornography: Men Possessing Women*. New York: G. P. Putnam's Sons–Perigee Books, 1981.

Eliot, George. *Adam Bede*. Illustrated Cabinet Edition. 2 vols. Boston: Dana Estes, n.d.

Fernbach, David. *The Spiral Path: A Gay Contribution to Human Survival*. Alyson Press, 1981.

Foucault, Michel. *The History of Sexuality: Volume I. An Introduction*. Tr. Robert Hurley. New York: Pantheon, 1978.

Frye, Marilyn. *The Politics of Reality: Essays in Feminist Theroy*. Trumansburg, N.Y.: The Crossing Press, 1983.

Gallop, Jane. *The Daughter's Seduction: Feminism and Psychoanalysis*. Ithaca: Cornell University Press, 1982.

Gilbert, Sandra, and Susan Gubar, *The Madwoman in the Attic: The Woman Writer and the Nineteenth-Century Literary Imagination*. New Haven: Yale University Press, 1979.

Girard, René. *Deceit, Desire, and the Novel: Self and Other in Literary Structure*. Tr. Yvonne Freccero. Baltimore: Johns Hopkins University Press, 1972.

Griffin, Susan. *Pornography and Silence: Culture's Revenge Against Nature*. New York: Harper & Row, 1981.

Heilbrun, Carolyn G. *Toward a Recognition of Androgyny*. New York: Harper & Row–Colophon, 1973.

Heilbrun, Carolyn G., and Margaret Higonnet, eds. *The Representation of Women in Fiction: Selected Papers from the English Institute, 1981*. New series, no. 7. Baltimore: Johns Hopkins University Press, 1978.

Herdt, G. H. *Guardians of the Flutes: Idioms of Masculinity: A Study of Ritualized Homosexual Behavior*. New York: McGraw-Hill, 1981.

Hocquenghem, Guy. *Homosexual Desire*. Tr. Daniella Dangoor. London: Allison & Busby, 1978.

Hogg, James. *The Private Memoirs and Confessions of a Justified Sinner*. New York: Norton, 1970.

Irigaray, Luce. "When the Good Get Together." In *New French Feminisms*, ed. Elaine Marks and Isabelle de Courtivron. New York: Schocken, 1981, pp. 107–11.

Kahn, Coppélia. *Man's Estate: Masculine Identity in Shakespeare*. Berkeley: University of California Press, 1981.

Klein, Richard. Review of *Homosexualities in French Literature*. *MLN* 95, no. 4 (May 1980), pp. 1070–80.

Kristeva, Julia. *Powers of Horror: An Essay on Abjection*. Tr. S. Roudiez. New York: Columbia University Press, 1982.

Laplanche, Jean. *Life and Death in Psychoanalysis*. Tr. Jeffrey Mehlman. Baltimore: Johns Hopkins University Press, 1976.

Lévi-Strauss, Claude. *The Elementary Structures of Kinship*. Boston: Beacon Press, 1969.

MacKinnon, Catharine A.. "Feminism, Marxism, Method, and the State: An Agenda for Theory." *Signs* 7, no. 3 (Spring 1982), pp. 515–44.

McKeon, Michael. "The 'Marxism' of Claude Lévi-Strauss." *Dialectical Anthropology* 6 (1981), pp. 123–50.

Mieli, Mario. *Homosexuality and Liberation: Elements of a Gay Critique*. London: Gay Men's Press, 1977.

Miller, Jean Baker. *Toward a New Psychology of Women*. Boston: Beacon Press, 1976.

Mitchell, Juliet. *Women's Estate*. New York: Random House–Vintage, 1973.

Mitchell, Margaret. *Gone With the Wind*. New York: Avon, 1973.

Moi, Toril. "The Missing Mother: The Oedipal Rivalries of René Girard." *Diacritics* 12, no. 2 (Summer 1982), pp. 21–31.

Morin, Stephen M., and Ellen M. Garfinkle. "Male Homophobia." In *Gayspeak: Gay Male and Lesbian Communication*. Ed. James W. Chesebro. New York: Pilgrim Press, 1981, pp. 117–29.

Rowbotham, Sheila, and Jeffrey Weeks. *Socialism and the New Life: The Personal and Sexual Politics of Edward Carpenter and Havelock Ellis*. London: Pluto Press, 1977.

Rubin, Gayle. "The Traffic in Women: Notes Toward a Political Economy of Sex." In *Toward an Anthropology of Women*. Ed. Rayna Reiter. New York: Monthly Review Press, 1975, pp. 157–210.

Samois, ed. *Coming to Power: Writing and Graphics on Lesbian S/M*. Boston: Alyson, 1982.

Sargent, Lydia, ed. *Women and Revolution: A Discussion of the Unhappy Marriage of Marxism and Feminism*. Boston: South End Press, 1981.

Snitow, Ann, Christine Stansell, and Sharon Thompson, eds. *Powers of Desire: The Politics of Sexuality*. New York: Monthly Review Press–New Feminist Library, 1983.

Sterne, Laurence. *A Sentimental Journey Through France and Italy*. Ed. Graham Petrie. Hammondsworth: Penguin, 1967.

Stimpson, Catharine R., and Ethel Spector Person, eds. *Women: Sex and Sexuality*. Chicago: University of Chicago Press, 1980.

Tennyson, Alfred, Lord. *The Princess: A Medley*. In *The Poems of Tennyson*, ed. Christopher Ricks. London: Longmans, 1969, pp. 743–844.

Thackeray, William Makepeace. *The History of Henry Esmond, Esq. Written By Himself*. Biographical Edition. New York: Harper, 1903.

van der Zee, John. *The Greatest Men's Party on Earth: Inside the Bohemian Grove*. New York: Harcourt Brace Jovanovich, 1974.

Vicinus, Martha. "Sexuality and Power: A Review of Current Work in the History of Sexuality." *Feminist Studies* 8, no. I (Spring 1982), pp. 133–56.

Weeks, Jeffrey. *Coming Out: Homosexual Politics in Britain from the Nineteenth Century to the Present*. London: Quartet Books, 1977.

———— *Sex, Politics, and Society: The Regulation of Sexuality Since 1800*. London: Longman, 1981.

Wycherley, William. *The Country Wife*. Ed. Thomas H. Fujimura. Regents Restoration Drama Series. Lincoln, Neb.: University of Nebraska Press, 1965.

reading

In literary terms, "reading" can mean two distinct things; the first meaning centers on texts, the second on receivers of texts. First, "a reading" is an interpretation, one critic's version of what a piece of writing has to say. "A feminist reading," in this usage, would be an interpretation of a text assuming gender's centrality to what the text means. In "a feminist reading" of a text, gender can come into play as something represented in the text (as in "images-of-woman" criticism); as something shaping the experience, and therefore the writing, of the author; or as a significant influence in the life—and, therefore, the interior experience—of the particular reader who is trying to understand what the text says.

"Reading," in its second literary sense, refers directly to that interior experience of readers, understood as an activity or a process. Rarely do theorists or critics make empirical studies of what actual readers do when they peruse books, although a few do apply psychoanalytic or ethnographic principles to their observations of real readers reading. More often, reader-response theorists hypothesize a universalized abstraction called "the reader," and they descirbe what "he" feels, thinks, or does when confronted with a given text. For such critics, "reading" is something conceptual, based—one assumes—on their own personal experiences with texts. In the theoretical work of such reader-response specialists as Peter Brooks, Norman Holland, David Bleich, and Wolfgang Iser, gender seldom surfaces as a potential influence upon "the reader's" experience. "Feminist reading," then, would be the reception and processing of texts by a reader who is conceived of not only as possibly female, but also as conscious of the tradition of women's oppression in patriarchal culture. The feminist reader—whether in fact male or female—is committed to breaking the pattern of that oppression by calling attention to the ways some texts can perpetuate it.

Judith Fetterley's *The Resisting Reader* (1977) is one of the first attempts to conceptualize feminist reading, a process that Fetterley says occurs when a female reader confronts an androcentric (male-centered) or even a misogynist (anti-woman) text. Explaining that "great" American literature treats male experience as universal, Fetterley argues that reading the American canon requires one to "identify as male," to sympathize with masculine heroes whose troubles are overtly or covertly associated with the women in their stories. This has led, Fetterley says, to the "immasculation" of the woman reader, who must identify "against herself" as she reads, thus becoming a "divided self." The "resisting reader" would work to "exorcise" the male-imposed part of that self, to be conscious of the way American classics exclude and alienate her. Fetterley's book fills out the readings of novels she sketches in the introductory chapter reprinted here; we have included her treatment of "Rip Van Winkle" to illustrate her method for describing what happens when her female reader confronts an androcentric text.

Fetterley takes gender as a biological given; within her argument, a person's sex is the primary determinant of the identification process he or she undergoes while reading. Jonathan Culler, in "Reading as a Woman" (1982, part of a chapter in *On Deconstruction* about reader-centered theories in general) quotes Shoshana Felman's "Critical Phallacy" essay (reprinted here in "Institutions") to ask whether "woman" is to be defined by anatomy or by culture. Drawing upon Fetterley as well as upon other feminist scholars, Culler breaks the recent history of feminist reading into "three moments" which bring forward some assumptions Fetterley leaves implicit. Culler's "first moment" is feminist criticism's assertion that gendered experience carries over from one's personal/social life into one's reading, and its confrontation of "the problem of women as consumers of male-produced literature." The "second moment" Culler describes as the effect achieved by the "postulate" of a woman reader, which served to make male and female readers begin questioning the assumptions about gender on which their reading had traditionally been based. Culler locates Fetterley's work in this second moment, for she calls into question the traditional assumption that a male reading perspective is "gendered neutral." The "third moment" for Culler has less to do specifically with reading than with a critique of all Western culture: in it, feminists (who here use "woman" in neither a biological nor even a social sense, but rather to mean *any* radical force subverting patriarchal discourse) question whether "rational" literary criticism might be culpably "in complicity with the preservation of male authority," and explore alternative, nonrational ways to read literature.

Culler's account is, of course, nothing if not rational, but—as a man constructing a history of feminist reading—he is scrupulous in taking seriously the projects he describes. Never directly arguing that a man might "read as a woman," Culler only implies that the idea of "hypothesizing" a woman reader might allow all readers—male and female—to construct the gender of their reading positions for themselves. Culler cites no examples of men "reading as women," and—since his own project holds no place for interpretations of literary texts—he performs no readings of his own. While that distinguishes his piece from the others in this section, perhaps the most significant difference between Culler's account of reading and those by Rich, Fetterley, and Schwieckart is that Culler's essay contains no "I"—the personal presence of the critic/reader is not an issue in his piece as it is in the others'.

Culler writes of reading-as-a-woman in the context of deconstruction and of the difficulties poststructuralist theory poses for every kind of reading. Patrocinio P. Schweickart—whose essay "Reading Ourselves" (1986) seems, at first glance, to reproduce many points in Culler's—tells the history of reader-centered feminist criticism for a more directly polemical purpose. Her "I" is strongly present, and her "we" speaks for feminist critics; her agenda is explicitly "to *change the world*." Arguing that reader-centered criticism must attend to "difference" if it is to be taken seriously, Schweickart begins by supplying three parables of reading, leading to a fourth. Schweickart retells Wayne Booth's story of his life as a reader, in which he compares himself to Malcolm X and suppresses crucial differences arising from racial experience; she juxtaposes Booth's story with Malcolm X's own version of how he became a reader, a story which—Schweickart asserts—speaks only for and to men, suppressing the differences gender can make. Schweickart answers the two men's stories with two versions of feminist reading. The first—a woman's angry encounter with texts written by misogynist men—is from Virginia Woolf's *A Room of One's Own;* the second—a woman's confrontation of Emily Dickinson's poems, texts by another woman whose interior experience is nevertheless pointedly *not* identical to the reader's own—is from Adrienne Rich's "Vesuvius at Home."

Schweickart's essay pulls together the others in this section by pointing out that *how* feminists read depends on *what* they read (that is, whether the literary text was written from a male or a female perspective). Largely indebted to Culler for her survey of reader-centered theory, Schweickart tackles his question about whether feminist reading must be specific to female readers by appealing to female psychology: she cites the suggestion of feminist psychoanalysts that women's identities (their "ego boundaries") are less strictly delineated than those of men. In the end, Schweickart sees reading theory as a potentially powerful tool for "building and maintaining connections among women."

Moving abruptly from the conceptual community of women envisioned by reader-centered theorists to a flesh-and-blood community of readers in the American midwest, Janice Radway's chapter from *Reading the Romance* (1984) takes us into the empirical study of how some real women say they actually read. Working from interviews, conversations, and questionnaires inquiring into the reading practice of a group of suburban white women in the pseudonymous "Smithton," Radway takes an anthropological approach to try to explain how and why the women love to read commercially produced romances. She provides statistics to support her descriptions of the kinds of setting, action, characters, and closure that appeal most strongly to her sample group. Following the principles of anthropologist Clifford Geertz and psychoanalyst Nancy Chodorow, Radway also speculates about the basic needs these women seem to satisfy with their romance reading. Although she is careful in the beginning of her chapter to limit her generalizations to the race and class, the regional and educational background of "the Smithton women," her project raises broader questions about the "therapeutic value" of romance reading for women living in "a culture that creates needs in [them] that it cannot fulfill." In Radway's work, "reading" is more than a process: it is a way of life, a means of coping with the troublesome gender politics of ordinary middle-class experience.

—RRW

INTRODUCTION

on the politics of literature

I

Literature is political. It is painful to have to insist on this fact, but the necessity of such insistence indicates the dimensions of the problem. John Keats once objected to poetry "that has a palpable design upon us." The major works of American fiction constitute a series of designs on the female reader, all the more potent in their effect because they are "impalpable." One of the main things that keeps the design of our literature unavailable to the consciousness of the woman reader, and hence impalpable, is the very posture of the apolitical, the pretense that literature speaks universal truths through forms from which all the merely personal, the purely subjective, has been burned away or at least transformed through the medium of art into the representative. When only one reality is encouraged, legitimized, and transmitted and when that limited vision endlessly insists on its comprehensiveness, then we have the conditions necessary for that confusion of consciousness in which impalpability flourishes. It is the purpose of this book to give voice to a different reality and different vision, to bring a different subjectivity to bear on the old "universality." To examine American fictions in light of how attitudes toward women shape their form and content is to make available to consciousness that which has been largely left unconscious and thus to change our understanding of these fictions, our relation to them, and their effect on us. It is to make palpable their designs.

American literature is male. To read the canon of what is currently considered classic American literature is perforce to identify as male. Though exceptions to this generalization can be found here and there—a Dickinson poem, a Wharton novel—these exceptions usually function to obscure the argument and confuse the issue: American literature is male. Our literature neither leaves women alone nor allows them to participate. It insists on its universality at the same time that it defines that universality in specifically male terms. "Rip Van Winkle" is paradigmatic of this phenomenon. While the desire to avoid work, escape authority, and sleep through the major decisions of one's life is obviously applicable to both men and women, in Irving's story this "universal" desire is made specifically male. Work, authority, and decisionmaking are symbolized by Dame Van

Winkle, and the longing for flight is defined against her. She is what one must escape from, and the "one" is necessarily male. In Mailer's *An American Dream*, the fantasy of eliminating all one's ills through the ritual of scapegoating is equally male: the sacrificial scapegoat is the woman/wife and the cleansed survivor is the husband/male. In such fictions the female reader is co-opted into participation in an experience from which she is explicitly excluded; she is asked to identify with a selfhood that defines itself in opposition to her; she is required to identify against herself.

The woman reader's relation to American literature is made even more problematic by the fact that our literature is frequently dedicated to defining what is peculiarly American about experience and identity. Given the pervasive male bias of this literature, it is not surprising that in it the experience of being American is equated with the experience of being male. In Fitzgerald's *The Great Gatsby*, the background for the experience of disillusionment and betrayal revealed in the novel is the discovery of America, and Daisy's failure of Gatsby is symbolic of the failure of America to live up to the expectations in the imagination of the men who "discovered" it. America is female; to be American is male; and the quintessential American experience is betrayal by woman. Henry James certainly defined our literature, if not our culture, when he picked the situation of women as the subject of *The Bostonians*, his very American tale.

Power is the issue in the politics of literature, as it is in the politics of anything else. To be excluded from a literature that claims to define one's identity is to experience a peculiar form of powerlessness—not simply the powerlessness which derives from not seeing one's experience articulated, clarified, and legitimized in art, but more significantly the powerlessness which results from the endless division of self against self, the consequence of the invocation to identify as male while being reminded that to be male—to be universal, to be American—is to be *not female*. Not only does powerlessness characterize woman's experience of reading, it also describes the content of what is read. Each of the works chosen for this study presents a version and an enactment of the drama of men's power over women. The final irony, and indignity of the woman reader's relation to American literature, then, is that she is required to dissociate herself from the very experience the literature engenders. Powerlessness is the subject and powerlessness the experience, and the design insists that Rip Van Winkle/Frederic Henry/Nick Carraway/Stephen Rojack speak for us all.

The drama of power in our literature is often disguised. In "Rip Van Winkle," Rip poses as powerless, the henpecked husband cowering before his termagant Dame. Yet, when Rip returns from the mountains, armed by the drama of female deposition witnessed there, to discover that his wife is dead and he is free to enjoy what he has always wanted, the "Shucks, M'am, I don't mean no harm" posture dissolves. In Sherwood Anderson's "I Want to Know Why," the issue of power is refracted through the trauma of a young boy's discovery of what it means to be male in a culture that gives white men power over women, horses, and niggers. More sympathetic and honest than "Rip," Anderson's story nevertheless exposes both the imaginative limits of our literature and the reasons for those limits. Storytelling and art can do no more than lament the inevitable—boys must grow up to be men; it can provide no alternative vision of being male. Bathed in nostalgia, "I Want to Know Why" is infused with the perspective it abhors, because finally to disavow that perspective would be to relinquish power. The lament is self-indulgent; it offers the luxury of feeling bad without the responsibility of change. And it is completely male-centered, registering the tragedy of sexism through its cost to men. At the end we cry for the boy and not for the whores he will eventually make use of.

In Hawthorne's "The Birthmark," the subject of power is more explicit. The fact of men's power over women and the full implications of that fact are the crux of the story. Aylmer is free to experiment on Georgiana, to the point of death, because she is both woman and wife. Hawthorne indicates the attractiveness of the power that marriage puts in the hands of men through his description of Aylmer's reluctance to leave his laboratory and through his portrayal of Aylmer's inherent discomfort with women and sex. And why does Aylmer want this power badly enough to overcome his initial reluctance and resistance? Hitherto Aylmer has failed in all his efforts to achieve a power equal to that of "Mother" nature. Georgiana provides an opportunity for him to outdo nature by remaking her creation. And if he fails, he still will have won because he will have destroyed the earthly embodiment and representative of his adversary. Hawthorne intends his character to be seen as duplicitous, and he maneuvers Aylmer through the poses of lover, husband, and scientist to show us how Aylmer attempts to gain power and to use that power to salve his sense of inadequacy. But even so, Hawthorne, like Anderson, is unwilling to do more with the sickness than call it sick. He obscures the issue of sexual politics behind a haze of "universals" and clothes the murder of wife by husband in the language of idealism.

Though the grotesque may serve Faulkner as a disguise in the same way that the ideal serves Hawthorne, "A Rose for Emily" goes farther than "The Birthmark" in making the power of men over women an overt subject. Emily's life is shaped by her father's absolute control over her; her murder of Homer Barron is *re*action, not action. Though Emily exercises the power the myths of sexism make available to her, that power is minimal; her retaliation is no alternative to the patriarchy which oppresses her. Yet Faulkner, like Anderson and Hawthorne, ultimately protects himself and short-circuits the implications of his analysis, not simply through the use of the grotesque, which makes Emily eccentric rather than central, but also through his choice of her victim. In having Emily murder Homer Barron, a northern day-laborer, rather than Judge Stevens, the southern patriarch, Faulkner indicates how far he is willing to go in imagining even the minimal reversal of power involved in retaliation. The elimination of Homer Barron is no real threat to the system Judge Stevens represents. Indeed, a few day-laborers may have to be sacrificed here and there to keep that system going.

In *A Farewell to Arms*, the issue of power is thoroughly obscured by the mythology, language, and structure of romantic love and by the invocation of an abstract, though spiteful, "they" whose goal it is to break the good, the beautiful, and the brave. Yet the brave who is broken is Catherine; at the end of the novel Catherine is dead, Frederic is alive and the resemblance to "Rip Van Winkle" and "The Birthmark" is unmistakable. Though the scene in the hospital is reminiscent of Aylmer's last visit to Georgiana in her chambers, Hemingway, unlike Hawthorne, separates his protagonist from the source of his heroine's death, locating the agency of Catherine's demise not simply in "them" but in her biology. Frederic survives several years of war, massive injuries, the dangers of a desperate retreat, and the threat of execution by his own army; Catherine dies in her first pregnancy. Clearly, biology is destiny. Yet, Catherine is as much a scapegoat as Dame Van Winkle, Georgiana, Daisy Fay, and Deborah Rojack. For Frederic to survive, free of the intolerable burdens of marriage, family, and fatherhood, yet with his vision of himself as the heroic victim of cosmic antagonism intact, Catherine must die. Frederic's necessities determine Catherine's fate. He is, indeed, the agent of her death.

In its passionate attraction to the phenomenon of wealth, *The Great Gatsby* reveals its author's consuming interest in the issue of power. In the quintessentially male drama of poor boy's becoming rich boy, ownership of women is invoked as the index of power: he who possesses Daisy Fay is the most powerful boy. But when the rich boy, fearing finally for his territory, repossesses the girl and, by asking "Who is he," strips the poor boy of his presumed power, the resultant animus is directed not against the rich boy but against the girl, whose rejection of him exposes the poor boy's powerlessness. The struggle for power between men is deflected into safer and more certain channels, and the consequence is the familiar demonstration of male power over women. This demonstration, however, is not simply the result of a greater safety in directing anger at women than at men. It derives as well from the fact that even the poorest male gains something from a system in which all women are at some level his subjects. Rather than attack the men who represent and manifest that system, he identifies with them and acquires his sense of power through superiority to women. It is not surprising, therefore, that the drama of *The Great Gatsby* involves an attack on Daisy, whose systematic reduction from the glamorous object of Gatsby's romantic longings to the casual killer of Myrtle Wilson provides an accurate measure of the power available to the most "powerless" male.

By his choice of scene, context and situation, Henry James in *The Bostonians* directly confronts the hostile nature of the relations between men and women and sees in that war the defining characteristics of American culture. His honesty provides the opportunity for a clarification rather than a confusion of consciousness and offers a welcome relief from the deceptions of other writers. Yet the drama, while correctly labeled, is still the same. *The Bostonians* is an unrelenting demonstration of the extent, and an incisive analysis of the sources, of the power of men as a class over women as a class. Yet, though James laments women's oppression, and laments it because of its effects *on women*, he nevertheless sees it as inevitable. *The Bostonians* represents a kind of end point in the literary exploration of sex/class power; it would be impossible to see more clearly and feel more deeply and still remain convinced that patriarchy is inevitable. Indeed, there is revolution latent in James's novel, and, while he would be the last to endorse it, being far more interested in articulating and romanticizing the tragic elements in women's powerlessness, *The Bostonians* provides the material for that analysis of American social reality which is the beginning of change.

Norman Mailer's *An American Dream* represents another kind of end point. Mailer is thoroughly enthralled by the possibility of power that sexism makes available to men, absolutely convinced that he is in danger of losing it, and completely dedicated to maintaining it, at whatever cost. It is impossible to imagine a more frenzied commitment to the maintenance of male power than Mailer's. In *An American Dream* all content has been reduced to the enactment of men's power over women, and to the development and legitimization of that act Mailer brings every strategy he can muster, not the least of which is an extended elaboration of the mythology of female power. In Mailer's work the effort to obscure the issue, disguise reality, and confuse consciousness is so frantic that the antitheses he provides to protect his thesis become in fact his message and his confusions shed a lurid illumination. If *The Bostonians* induces one to rearrange James's conceptual framework and so to make evitable his inevitable, *An American Dream* induces a desire to eliminate Mailer's conceptual framework altogether and start over. Beyond his frenzy is only utter nausea and weariness of spirit and a profound willingness to give up an exhausted, sick, and sickening struggle. In Mailer, the drama of power comes full circle; at once the most sexist writer, he is also the most freeing, and out of him it may be possible to create anew.

II

But what have I to say of *Sexual Politics* itself? Millett has undertaken a task which I find particularly worthwhile: the consideration of certain events or works of literature from an unexpected, even startling point of view. Millett never suggests that hers is a sufficient analysis of any of the works she discusses. Her aim is to wrench the reader from the vantage point he has long occupied, and force him to look at life and letters from a new coign. Hers is not meant to be the last word on any writer, but a wholly new word, little heard before and strange. For the first time we have been asked to look at literature as women; we, men, women and Ph.D.s, have always read it as men. Who cannot point to a certain over-emphasis in the way Millett reads Lawrence or Stalin or Euripides. What matter? We are rooted in our vantage points and require transplanting which, always dangerous, involves violence and the possibility of death.
　　—Carolyn Heilbrun[1]

The method that is required is not one of correlation but of *liberation*. Even the term "method" must be reinterpreted and in fact wrenched out of its usual semantic field, for the emerging creativity in women is by no means a merely cerebral process. In order to understand the implications of this process it is necessary to grasp the fundamental fact that women have had the power of *naming* stolen from us. We have not been free to use our own powr to name ourselves, the world, or God. The old naming was not the product of dialogue—a fact inadvertently admitted in the Genesis story of Adam's naming the animals and the woman. Women are now realizing that the universal imposing of names by men has been false because partial. That is, inadequate words have been taken as adequate.
　　—Mary Daly[2]

Re-vision—the act of looking back, of seeing with fresh eyes, of entering an old text from a new critical direction—is for us more than a chapter in cultural history: it is an act of survival. Until we can understand the assumptions in which we are drenched we cannot know ourselves. And this drive to self-knowledge, for woman, is more than a search for identity: it is part of her refusal of the self-destructiveness of male-dominated society. A radical critique of literature, feminist in its impulse, would take the work first of all as a clue to how we live, how we have been living, how we have been led to imag-

ine ourselves, how our language has trapped as well as liberated us; and how
we can begin to see—and therefore live—afresh.
—Adrienne Rich[3]

A culture which does not allow itself to look clearly at the obvious through
the universal accessibility of art is a culture of tragic delusion, hardly viable.
—Cynthia Ozick[4]

When a system of power is thoroughly in command, it has scarcely need to
speak itself aloud; when its workings are exposed and questioned, it becomes not only subject to discussion, but even to change.
—Kate Millett[5]

Consciousness is power. To create a new understanding of our literature is to
make possible a new effect of that literature on us. And to make possible a new
effect is in turn to provide the conditions for changing the culture that the literature reflects. To expose and question that complex of ideas and mythologies
about women and men which exist in our society and are confirmed in our literature is to make the system of power embodied in the literature open not only to
discussion but even to change. Such questioning and exposure can, of course, be
carried on only by a consciousness radically different from the one that informs
the literature. Such a closed system cannot be opened up from within but only
from without. It must be entered into from a point of view which questions its
values and assumptions and which has its investment in making available to consciousness precisely that which the literature wishes to keep hidden. Feminist
criticism provides that point of view and embodies that consciousness.

In "A Woman's Map of Lyric Poetry," Elizabeth Hampsten, after quoting in
full Thomas Campion's "My Sweetest Lesbia," asks, "And Lesbia, what's in it
for her?"[6] The answer to this question is the subject of Hampsten's essay and the
answer is, of course, nothing. But implicit in her question is another answer—a
great deal, for someone. As Lillian Robinson reminds us, "and, always, *cui
bono*—who profits?"[7] The questions of who profits, and how, are crucial because
the attempt to answer them leads directly to an understanding of the function of
literary sexual politics. Function is often best known by effect. Though one of
the most persistent of literary stereotypes is the castrating bitch, the cultural reality is not the emasculation of men by women but the *immasculation* of women
by men. As readers and teachers and scholars, women are taught to think as men,
to identify with a male point of view, and to accept as normal and legitimate a
male system of values, one of whose central principles is misogyny.

One of the earliest statements of the phenomenon of immasculation, serving
indeed as a position paper, is Elaine Showalter's "Women and the Literary Curriculum." In the opening part of her article, Showalter imaginatively recreates
the literary curriculum the average young woman entering college confronts:

> In her freshman year she would probably study literature and composition,
> and the texts in her course would be selected for their timeliness, or their
> relevance, or their power to involve the reader, rather than for their absolute
> standing in the literary canon. Thus she might be assigned any one of the
> texts which have recently been advertised for Freshman English: an an-

thology of essays, perhaps such as *The Responsible Man*, "for the student who wants literature relevant to the world in which he lives," or *Conditions of Men*, or *Man in Crisis: Perspectives on The Individual and His World*, or again, *Representative Men: Cult Heroes of Our Time*, in which thirty-three men represent such categories of heroism as the writer, the poet, the dramatist, the artist, and the guru, and the only two women included are the Actress Elizabeth Taylor and The Existential Heroine Jacqueline Onassis. . . . By the end of her freshman year, a woman student would have learned something about intellectual neutrality; she would be learning, in fact, how to think like a man.[8]

Showalter's analysis of the process of immasculation raises a central question: "What are the effects of this long apprenticeship in negative capability on the self-image and the self-confidence of women students?" And the answer is self-hatred and self-doubt: "Women are estranged from their own experience and unable to perceive its shape and authenticity. . . . they are expected to identify as readers with a masculine experience and perspective, which is presented as the human one. . . . Since they have no faith in the validity of their own perceptions and experiences, rarely seeing them confirmed in literature, or accepted in criticism, can we wonder that women students are so often timid, cautious, and insecure when we exhort them to 'think for themselves.'?"[9]

The experience of immasculation is also the focus of Lee Edwards's article, "Women, Energy, and *Middlemarch*." Summarizing her experience, Edwards concludes:

> Thus, like most women, I have gone through my entire education—as both student and teacher—as a schizophrenic, and I do not use this term lightly, for madness is the bizarre but logical conclusion of our education. Imagining myself male, I attempted to create myself male. Although I knew the case was otherwise, it seemed I could do nothing to make this other critically real.

Edwards extends her analysis by linking this condition to the effects of the stereotypical presentation of women in literature:

> I said simply, and for the most part silently that, since neither those women nor any women whose acquaintances I had made in fiction had much to do with the life I led or wanted to lead, I was not female. Alien from the women I saw most frequently imagined, I mentally arranged them in rows labelled respectively insipid heroines, sexy survivors, and demonic destroyers. As organizer I stood somewhere else, alone perhaps, but hopefully above them.[10]

Intellectually male, sexually female, one is in effect no one, nowhere, immasculated.

Clearly, then, the first act of the feminist critic must be to become a resisting rather than an assenting reader and, by this refusal to assent, to begin the process of exorcizing the male mind that has been implanted in us. The consequence of this exorcism is the capacity for what Adrienne Rich describes as re-vision—"the act of looking back, of seeing with fresh eyes, of entering an old text from a new critical direction." And the consequence, in turn, of this re-vision is that books will no longer be read as they have been read and thus will lose their power to bind us unknowingly to their designs. While women obviously cannot rewrite literary works so that they become ours by virtue of reflecting our reality, we can accurately name the reality they do reflect and so change literary criticism from a closed conversation to an active dialogue.

In making available to women this power of naming reality, feminist criticism is revolutionary. The significance of such power is evident if one considers the strength of the taboos against it:

> I permit no woman to teach . . . she is to keep silent.
> —St. Paul

> By Talmudic law a man could divorce a wife whose voice could be heard next door. From there to Shakespeare: "Her voice was ever soft, / Gentle, and low—an excellent thing in woman." And to Yeats: "The women that I picked spoke sweet and low / And yet gave tongue." And to Samuel Beckett, guessing at the last torture, The Worst: "a woman's voice perhaps, I hadn't thought of that, they might engage a soprano."
> —Mary Ellmann[11]

> The experience of the class in which I voiced my discontent still haunts my nightmares. Until my face froze and my brain congealed, I was called prude and, worse yet, insensitive, since I willfully misread the play in the interest of proving a point false both to the work and in itself.
> —Lee Edwards[12]

The experience Edwards describes of attempting to communicate her reading of the character of Shakespeare's Cleopatra is a common memory for most of us who have become feminist critics. Many of us never spoke; those of us who did speak were usually quickly silenced. The need to keep certain things from being thought and said reveals to us their importance. Feminist criticism represents the discovery/recovery of a voice, a unique and uniquely powerful voice capable of canceling out those other voices, so movingly described in Sylvia Plath's *The Bell Jar*, which spoke about us and to us and at us but never for us.

III

The eight works analyzed in this book were chosen for their individual significance, their representative value, and their collective potential. They are interconnected in the ways that they comment on and illuminate each other, and they form a dramatic whole whose meaning transcends the mere sum of the parts. These eight are meant to stand for a much larger body of literature; their individual and collective designs can be found elsewhere repeatedly.

The four short stories form a unit, as do the four novels. These units are subdivided into pairs. "Rip Van Winkle" and "I Want to Know Why" are companion pieces whose focus is the fear of and resistance to growing up. The value of Anderson's story lies mainly in the light it sheds on Irving's, making explicit the fear of sexuality only implied in "Rip" and focusing attention on the strategy of deflecting hostility away from men and onto women. "The Birthmark" and "A

Rose for Emily" are richly related studies of the consequences of growing up and, by implication, of the reasons for the resistance to it. In both stories sexual desire leads to death. More significantly, they are brilliant companion analyses of that sex/class hostility that is the essence of patriarchal culture and that underlies the adult identity Anderson's boy recoils from assuming. "The Birthmark" is the story of how to murder your wife and get away with it; "A Rose for Emily" is the story of how the system which allows you to murder your wife makes it possible for your wife to murder you.

Both *A Farewell to Arms* and *The Great Gatsby* are love stories; together they demonstrate the multiple uses of the mythology of romantic love in the maintenance of male power. In addition they elaborate on the function of scapegoating evident in "Rip Van Winkle" and "The Birthmark." In its more obvious connection of the themes of love and power *The Great Gatsby* brings closer to consciousness the hostility which *A Farewell to Arms* seeks to disguise and bury. *The Bostonians* and *An American Dream* form the most unlikely and perhaps the most fascinating of the pairs. In both, the obfuscation of romantic love has been cleared away and the issue of power directly joined. James's novel describes a social reality—male power, female powerlessness—which Mailer's denies by creating a social mythology—female power, male powerlessness—that inverts that reality. Yet finally, the intention of Mailer's mythology is to maintain the reality it denies. *The Bostonians* forces the strategies of *An American Dream* into the open by its massive documentation of women's oppression, and *An American Dream* provides the political answer to *The Bostonians*'s inevitability by its massive, though unintended, demonstration of the fact that women's oppression grows not out of biology but out of men's need to oppress.

The sequence of both the stories and the novels is generated by a scale of increasing complexity, increasing consciousness, and increasing "feminist" sympathy and insight. Thus, the movement of the stories is from the black and white of "Rip Van Winkle," with its postulation of good guy and villain and its formulation in terms of innocent fable, to the complexity of "A Rose for Emily," whose action forces sexual violence into consciousness and demands understanding for the erstwhile villain. The movement of the novels is similar. *A Farewell to Arms* is as simplistic and disguised and hostile as "Rip Van Winkle"; indeed, the two have many affinities, not the least of which is the similarity of their sleep-centered protagonists who believe that women are a bad dream that will go away if you just stay in bed long enough. The sympathy and complexity of consciousness in *The Bostonians* is even larger than that in "A Rose for Emily," and is exceeded only by the imagination of *An American Dream*, which is "feminist" not by design but by default. Yet the decision to end with *An American Dream* comes not simply from its position on the incremental scale. *An American Dream* is "Rip Van Winkle" one hundred and fifty years later, intensified to be sure, but *exactly the same story*. Thus, the complete trajectory of the immasculating imagination of American literature is described by the movement from "Rip Van Winkle" to *An American Dream*, and that movement is finally circular. This juxtaposition of beginning and end provides the sharpest possible exposure of that circular quality in the design of our literature, apparent in the movements within and between works, which defines its imaginative limits. Like the race horse so loved by

Anderson's boy, the imagination which informs our "classic" American literature runs endlessly round a single track, unable because unwilling to get out of
the race.

NOTES

1. Carolyn Heilbrun, "Millett's *Sexual Politics:* A Year Later," *Aphra* 2 (Summer 1971), 39.

2. Mary Daly, *Beyond God the Father: Toward a Philosophy of Women's Liberation* (Boston:
Beacon, 1973), p. 8.

3. Adrienne Rich, "When We Dead Awaken: Writing as Re-Vision," *College English* 34
(1972), 18.

4. Cynthia Ozick, "Women and Creativity: The Demise of the Dancing Dog," *Motive*
29 (1969); reprinted in *Woman in Sexist Society*, eds. Vivian Gornick and Barbara Moran
(New York: Signet–New American Library, 1972), p. 450.

5. Kate Millett, *Sexual Politics* (Garden City: Doubleday, 1970), p. 58.

6. *College English* 34 (1973), 1075.

7. "Dwelling in Decencies: Radical Criticism and the Feminist Perspective," *College
English* 32 (1971), 887; reprinted in *Sex, Class, and Culture* (Bloomington: Indiana University Press, 1978), p. 16.

8. *College English* 32 (1971), 855.

9. Ibid., 856–57.

10. *Massachusetts Review* 13 (1972), 226, 227.

11. *Thinking About Women* (New York: Harcourt Brace Jovanovich, 1968), pp. 149–50.

12. Edwards, p. 230.

PALPABLE DESIGNS

an american dream: "rip van winkle"

Washington Irving is reported to have spent a June evening in 1818 talking with his brother-in-law about the old days in Sleepy Hollow. Melancholy of late, the writer was pleased to find himself laughing. Suddenly he got up and went to his room. By morning he had the manuscript of the first and most famous American short story, and his best single claim to a permanent reputation.[1]

The figure of Rip Van Winkle presides over the birth of the American imagination; and it is fitting that our first successful homegrown legend should memorialize, however playfully, the flight of the dreamer from the shrew—into the mountains and out of time, away from the drab duties of home and town toward the good companions and the magic keg of beer. Ever since, the typical male protagonist of our fiction has been a man on the run, harried into the forest and out to sea, down the river or into combat—anywhere to avoid "civilization," which is to say, the confrontation of a man and woman which leads to the fall to sex, marriage, and responsibility.[2]

Engendered in melancholy, released through nostalgia, and interchanged with sleep—what better place to begin than with Washington Irving's "Rip Van Winkle," the story which marked the emergence of American literature at home and abroad, which began the long dream of our fiction, and which has become an inherent part of our national mythology. In writing "Rip Van Winkle," Irving adapted to the American scene, setting, and psyche the elements of a German folktale, itself a version of a time-honored legend. In making this translation he produced a classic statement of character and theme in American literature. As Rip is a protagonist whom one will encounter again and again in the pages of our fiction, so his story presents the fantasy woven by our writers on the underside of our national consciousness, in subconscious counterpoint to the official voice of our public rhetoric.

"Rip Van Winkle" is the dreamwork of the persona created by Benjamin Franklin in his *Autobiography*, the inevitable consequence of the massive suppressions required by Franklin's code of success. The voice to which Rip gives ear is the exact opposite of the voice embodied in the *Autobiography*, with its imperatives for self-improvement and for constant and regulated activity, for a day neatly parceled out in preplanned units, goal- and future-oriented, built on a commitment to accumulation and an investment in the notion of progress. "Early to bed and early to rise makes a man healthy, wealthy and wise," cried Franklin, to which Rip responds with an infinite desire for sleep. If Franklin's *Autobiography* represents one kind of American success story, "Rip Van Winkle" represents another, for what his story records is the successful evasion of the demands and values that speak through Franklin. And if Franklin's book is a testament to how lucky it is to be an American, "Rip Van Winkle" is perhaps the first registering of a disillusionment with America as idea and fact which Mark Twain was later to articulate in the voice of another famous villager, Pudd'nhead Wilson: "It was wonderful to find America, but it would have been more wonderful to miss it."

Central in Irving's formulation of his classic American story is the role he gives to women. The German tale on which he based "Rip" has no equivalent for Dame Van Winkle; she is Irving's creation and addition. Irving's tale is distinguished from its source by his elaboration of the psychology behind the experience of protracted sleep, and this elaboration is in turn distinguished by women's involvement in it. What drives Rip away from the village and up into the mountains and what makes him likely partaker of the sleep-inducing liquor is his wife; all the ills from which Rip seeks escape are symbolically located in the person of the offending Dame Van Winkle. Thus, an essential part of the Americanness of Irving's story is the creation of woman as villain: as obstacle to the achievement of the dream of pleasure; as mouthpiece for the values of work, responsibility, adulthood—the imperatives of Benjamin Franklin. Significantly, Irving's tale connects the image of woman with the birth of America as a nation and with the theme of growing up.

Rip is the first in a long line of American heroes as "nice guys." He is a "great favorite" and is possessed of "universal popularity." Everybody in the village loves him; children shout with joy at his appearance and not a dog will bark at him. He is kind, simple, good-natured, and meek. He is never too busy to join the children at their sports or to run errands for the women or to assist the men in their projects. Having no concerns of his own, he responds to the needs of others. In a Benjamin Franklin world, where everyone else is busy pursuing goals, Rip represents that *summum bonum*, a person with nothing to do. His popularity derives from his availability and from a concomitant self-effacement and meekness of spirit.

There is one person with whom Rip is not popular, whom he will not serve, and whose demands go unanswered; that is, of course, his wife. The source of Rip's resistance to Dame Van Winkle is not laziness, for he will fish and hunt all day, tramping through miles of forest and swamp, up hill and down. Nor is the source of his resistance a distaste for work, since he is glad to assist in the roughest toil of the community, whether husking Indian corn or building stone fences. Rather, Rip resists Dame Van Winkle because she represents what he ought to do. What Rip rejects is the belief that the end of work is the accumulation of profit; what he resists is the imperative "thou shalt make money." Inverting Franklin's pattern of increment, the saga of the poor boy who begins with only two loaves of bread and ends as one of the richest men in the city of Philadelphia, Rip refuses to touch his patrimonial estate and has let it dwindle until it is nothing more than a poor parched acre. Yet Rip's resistance is not simply to work as a way to profit; it is equally to work as a moral imperative—that which one ought to do as opposed to that which one wants to do. Rip is willing to do everything *except* what he ought to; his commitment is to pleasure and play. Like his more famous successor, Huckleberry Finn, Rip wages a subterranean and passive revolt against the superego and its imperatives.

Rip's refusal to do what he ought is in effect a refusal to be what he ought. He rejects the role of master, preferring instead to be servant; no father to his children, he is instead the playmate of others' children; his concept of political responsibility consists of listening to the contents of months-old newspapers drawled out by the village schoolmaster and commented on by the puffs from Nicholas Vedder's pipe. Although a descendant of the Van Winkles, "who figured so gallantly in the chivalrous days of Peter Stuyvesant," Rip has inherited little of the martial character of his worthy ancestors. His pleasure in hunting lies not in killing but rather in being outside, free, roaming through woods and hills at will. Indeed, his essential lack of aggression is reflected in the way he refuses the imperatives to be otherwise. Rip's idea of fighting is the passive resistance of evasion. And what he evades, of course, is conflict: the war between the sexes, the war between the colonies and the mother country. Rip rejects the conventional image of masculinity and the behavior traditionally expected of an adult male and identifies himself with characteristics and behaviors assumed to be feminine and assigned to women. Thus, the figure who "presides over the birth of the American imagination" is in effect a female-identified woman-hater. Here is a conflict whose evasion requires all of Irving's art—and gets it; for Irving is as dedicated to avoiding conflict as his hero, sinking the history of colonial conflict in the confusion of Dutch Hendrik with English Henry, converting the tombstone connotations of R.I.P. and the death wish behind it to the fantasy of endless rebirth.

Dame Van Winkle is the unsympathetic thorn in Rip's exceedingly sympathetic side. She is the embodiment of all the values he rejects, the would-be enforcer of all the imperatives he is fleeing, the spoiler of his holiday, the enemy. "Rip Van Winkle" is one of the first American books in which man, nature, and beast (who is always male too—Rip would not go into the woods with a "bitch") are sacrosanctly linked and woman is seen as the agent of civilization that seeks to repress this holy trinity. In opposition to Rip's pleasure principle, Dame Van Winkle is voluble on the subject of work and on the value of practicality. The opposition of Rip and Dame is extended to women and men in general. In the opening paragraph Irving notes that the "good wives" of the village regard the Catskills as "perfect barometers," enabling them to forecast the weather with accuracy. How marked a contrast to the web of fancy cast over these same mountains by the narrator, Diedrich Knickerbocker. Dream states, imagination, and play in "Rip Van Winkle" are clearly the prerogatives of men. The fantasy figures from the dream past who play in the Catskills are all male. Rip's "perpetual club of the sages, philosophers, and other idle personages of the village" is all male too and is dedicated to the pure pleasure of sitting long afternoons in the shade and telling "endless sleepy stories about nothing."

Dame Van Winkle is linked to civilization and to the institutions which it is composed of in another way. She is connected to politics through the somewhat elaborated metaphor of "petticoat government" and to America's coming of age as a separate political entity by virtue of the similarity between her behavior and that of the politicos Rip encounters on his return to the village; their shrill and disputatious tones are the very echo of the voice of the termagant Dame. If women are bad because they are portrayed as governmental, government is bad because it is portrayed as female. It is not hard—there are lots of pointers along the way—to get from Irving's Dame to Ken Kesey's Big Nurse, who is bad because she represents a system whose illegitimacy is underscored by the fact that *she*, a woman, represents it.

In its simplest terms, the basic fantasy "Rip Van Winkle" embodies is that of being able to sleep long enough to avoid at once the American Revolution and the wife. The story imagines and enacts a successful evasion of civilization and of the imperatives of adulthood. Rip sleeps through those years when one is expected to be politically, personally, and sexually mature and thus moves from the boyhood of youth to the boyhood of an old age that promises to go on forever. In addition, he accomplishes something else: access to life in an all-male world, a world without women, the ideal American territory. Like Melville a half-century later, Irving invokes as playground a world which is perforce exclusively male—the world of men on ships exploring new territories. Rip encounters in the mountains the classic elements of American male culture: sport invested with utter seriousness; highly ritualized nonverbal communication; liquor as communion; and the mystique of male companionship. In an act of camaraderie, based on a sure and shared instinct as to the life-expectancy of termagants, the little men provide Rip with the opportunity and instrument of escape.

The experience in the mountains, however, is not simply an act of evasion, culminating in the perfect communion of males; it is equally an act of invasion, carrying out on a larger scale the pattern of Rip's "femininity" and suggesting that the secret source of his fantasy lies in a fear and envy of women. What Rip sees in the mountains is a reversal of the pattern that prevails in the village, for here it is men who invade female territory and dominate it and drive the women out. The material appended as postscript to the story gains its significance in light of this reversal. The postscript contains Indian legends, the first of which concerns the old squaw spirit who ruled the Catskills and "influenced the weather, spreading sunshine or clouds over the landscape, and sending good or bad hunting seasons." Rip's vision in the mountains displaces this legend, making men the gods of weather and relegating women to the position of mere interpreters of their thunder. "Rip Van Winkle" constitutes a patriarchal revolution in miniature in which men assume the powers previously accorded to women and female-centered myths are replaced by male-centered myths. Emblematic of this displacement, the legend of the old squaw spirit is appended as postscript, while the epigraph of the story is an invocation to Woden, God of Saxons, whose son and sometimes other self was Thor, god of thunder.

When Rip awakens from his sleep in the mountains, his first concern is his wife—what excuse can he make to her for his "overnight" absence from home. This concern, however, soon gives way to a larger sense of unease. His clean, well-oiled gun has been replaced by a rusty old firelock with a worm-eaten stock;

his dog is nowhere to be found; there is no sign anywhere of the men he encountered in the mountains or of the place where they played. Metaphorically as well
as literally Rip, upon awakening, is out of joint. Unease moves toward terror as
Rip returns to the village and it becomes clearer and clearer to him that the world
he left is not the world he has returned to. Like the Catskills, with which he has
such an affinity, Rip seems "dismembered," something left behind on a great
drive forward, onward, westward. With each succeeding encounter his sense of
himself becomes more and more confused until at last, when forced to identify
himself, he can only cry, "I'm not myself—I'm somebody else—that's me
yonder—no—that's somebody else got into my shoes—I was myself last night,
but I fell asleep on the mountain, and they've changed my gun, and everything's
changed, and I'm changed, and I can't tell what's my name, or who I am."

"Rip Van Winkle" is a fantasy tinged with terror, a dreamwork with hints of
nightmare. Yet its tone is finally one of reconciliation and incorporation. In "Rip
Van Winkle" one can go home again. Rip's village eventually believes his statement that he means no harm, dismisses its view of him as lunatic or spy, and
accords him the identity of returning hero. He is embraced as one who is connected by his age to what is now perceived as that more pleasant past before the
Revolution and by his experience in the mountains to that still more pleasant
past before America ever was, to that time when it was still an idea in the mind of
Europe. He is the one who has rejected the identities handed to him, the "per-
fumes" of "houses and rooms" which Whitman resists at the opening of "Song
of Myself"; who has experienced the fears attendant upon such a rejection,
and who has nevertheless emerged as living proof that it can be done. He has indulged the communal dream of escape from all forms of responsibility and all the
forces which threaten the life of pleasure. Having slept through those years when
adulthood is expected, he is allowed to remain now and forever a boy. Perceiving
as he does that all that has happened in his absence is the exchange of one
George for another, Rip inevitably suggests that the most meaningful relationship one can have to the Revolution is to have slept through it. His experience in
the mountains at once displaces the events of the Revolution and presents itself
as the logical substitute for them. The real act of rebellion in Irving's tale is
Rip's, and it is he who has enacted the real American Revolution. Thus, it is
proper that he is recognized by the little men as one fit to join that long line of
heroes who have disappeared into mountains where they sleep and wait until
their time and world is ready.[3]

But what is a woman to do with "Rip Van Winkle"? How is she to read our
"first and most famous" story in which the American imagination is born if
the defining act of that imagination is to identify the real American Revolution
with the avoidance of adulthood, which means the avoidance of women, which
means the avoidance of one's wife? What is the impact of this American dream on
her? The answer is obvious: disastrous. What is an essentially simple act of identification when the reader of the story is male becomes a tangle of contradictions
when the reader is female. Where in this story is the female reader to locate herself? Certainly she is not Rip, for the fantasy he embodies is thoroughly male and
is defined precisely by its opposition to woman. Nor is she Dame Van Winkle, for
Dame is not a person: she is a scapegoat, the enemy, the OTHER. Without name
or identity other than that of Rip's Dame, she is summarized, explained, and

dismissed through the convention of stereotypes as a "termagant wife," a shrew, a virago. Because she is abstracted and reduced to a stereotype whose mechanism she endlessly repeats, her death is presented as a joke on that mechanism and is viewed as a great relief. Dame Van Winkle is a male mechanism, not a woman. What, then, of her daughter, Judith, who takes Rip in where Dame threw him out and who appears to be a pleasant alternative to her mother? Yet, what is Judith really except her mother married to someone other than her father? Marry her to her brother and, sure enough, you would have a daughter as like the mother as the son is like the father.

The woman who reads "Rip Van Winkle" finds herself excluded from the experience of the story. She is no part of the act of resistance, nor does she recognize herself in that which is being resisted. Indeed, the full extent of her exclusion can be seen in the fact that those qualities which are potentially admirable aspects of the female role are assigned to Rip and made positive because they are part of *his* character, while what is negative about the male role is accorded to Dame Van Winkle, who is made a masculine authority figure and damned for it.

It would be nice if the female reader, upon realizing the dimensions of her exclusion from the story, could dismiss "Rip Van Winkle" as having nothing to do with her. Unfortunately, however, the story enforces a certain experience on her. While not identifying with Dame Van Winkle, she nevertheless cannot fully escape the sense of being somehow implicated in the indictment of her sex that Dame Van Winkle represents. She cannot read the story without being assaulted by the negative images of women it presents. Primary among them is that view, as pervasive in American literature as it is in Western culture, of women as each other's natural and instinctive enemies: "Certain it is that he was a great favorite among the good wives of the village, who, as usual with the amiable sex, took his part in all family squabbles and never failed, whenever they talked those matters over in their evening gossipings, to lay all the blame on Dame Van Winkle." Surely this is one of Irving's nastier ironies, an example of what Philip Young calls his "whimsical antifeminism."[4] And the real rub is the fact that the story forces the female reader to enact its definition of her sex. A woman reading "Rip Van Winkle" becomes perforce one of Irving's "good wives," taking Rip's side and laying all the blame on Dame Van Winkle; that is the way the story is written. The consequence for the female reader is a divided self. She is asked to identify with Rip and against herself, to scorn the amiable sex and act just like it, to laugh to Dame Van Winkle and accept that she represents "woman," to be at once both repressor and repressed, and ultimately to realize that she is neither. Rip's words upon returning home after his twenty-year evasion are ironically appropriate to her: "I'm not myself—I'm somebody else—that's me yonder—no—that's somebody else . . . I can't tell what's my name, or who I am."

The somewhat ironic tone Irving adopts toward his material might be adduced as evidence of a certain complexity to his immasculating imagination. He puts the story in the mouth of Diedrich Knickerbocker, who has already been established as a figure of fun in *Knickerbocker's History of New York*. The frame of the story makes us aware that there is more than one teller of this tale, and we would be wrong to miss the ironic Irving behind the dreamy Knickerbocker. The difficulty, however, is that Irving's irony seems finally a gesture, a sop thrown to the critical faculties of his readers so that he may the more successfully float his fantasy. Irving is still committed to his dream and to the antifeminism underlying it, despite the fact that he casts it as a joke. For however much he may mock Rip and protest that his tale is but a fantasy, Dame Van Winkle is still stuck with the stigmata of her shrewhood and the effect of Irving's story is still to make escaping her a national good, an American dream.

NOTES

1. Philip Young, "Fallen from Time: The Mythic Rip Van Winkle," *Kenyon Review* 22 (1960); reprinted in *Psychoanalysis and American Fiction*, ed. Irving Malin (New York: Dutton, 1965), p. 23.

2. Leslie Fiedler, *Love and Death in the American Novel* (1960; rpt. New York: Meridian-World, 1962), xx–xxi.

3. Both Young, op. cit., and Henry Pochmann, "Irving's German Sources in *The Sketch Book*," *Studies in Philology* 27 (1930), 489–94, discuss at some length the heroic context of Rip's experience, which includes such figures as King Arthur, Charlemagne, and Frederick Rothbart.

4. Young, p. 29n.

READING AS A WOMAN

Suppose the informed reader of a work of literature is a woman. Might this not make a difference, for example, to "the reader's experience" of the opening chapter of *The Mayor of Casterbridge*, where the drunken Michael Henchard sells his wife and infant daughter to a sailor for five guineas at a country fair? Citing this example, Elaine Showalter quotes Irving Howe's celebration of Hardy's opening:

> To shake loose from one's wife; to discard that drooping rag of a woman, with her mute complaints and maddening passivity; to escape not by slinking abandonment but through the public sale of her body to a stranger, as horses are sold at a fair; and thus to wrest, through sheer amoral wilfulness, a second chance out of life—it is with this stroke, so insidiously attractive to male fantasy, that *The Mayor of Casterbridge* begins.

The male fantasy that finds this scene attractive may also be at work transforming Susan Henchard into a "drooping rag," passive and complaining—a portrait scarcely sustained by the text. Howe goes on to argue that in appealing to "the depths of common fantasy," the scene draws us into complicity with Henchard. Showalter comments:

> In speaking of "our common fantasies," he quietly transforms the novel into a male document. A woman's experience of this scene must be very different; indeed, there were many sensation novels of the 1870s and 1880s which presented the sale of women into marriage from the point of view of the bought wife. In Howe's reading, Hardy's novel becomes a kind of sensation-fiction, playing on the suppressed longings of its male audience, evoking sympathy for Henchard because of his crime, not in spite of it. ["The Unmanning of the Mayor of Casterbridge," pp. 102–3]

Howe is certainly not alone in assuming that "the reader" is male. "Much reading," writes Geoffrey Hartman in *The Fate of Reading*, "is indeed like girl-watching, a simple expense of spirit" (p. 248). The experience of reading seems to be that of a man (a heart-man?) for whom girl-watching is the model of an expense of spirit in a waste of shame.[1] When we posit a woman reader, the result is an analogous appeal to experience: not to the experience of girl-watching but to the experience of being watched, seen as a "girl," restricted, marginalized. A recent anthology that stresses the continuity between women's experience and the experience of women reading is appropriately entitled *The Authority of Experience: Essays in Feminist Criticism*. One contributor, Maurianne Adams, explains:

> Now that the burden of trying to pretend to a totally objective and value-free perspective has finally been lifted from our shoulders, we can all admit, in the simplest possible terms, that our literary insights and perceptions come, in part at least, from our sensitivity to the nuances of our own lives and our observations of other people's lives. Every time we rethink and reassimilate *Jane Eyre*, we bring to it a new orientation. For women critics, this orientation is likely not to focus particular attention upon the dilemmas of the male, to whom male critics have already shown themselves understandably sensitive, but rather on Jane herself and her particular circumstances. ["*Jane Eyre:* Woman's Estate," pp. 140–41]

"Rereading *Jane Eyre*," she notes, "I am led inevitably to feminist issues, by which I mean the status and economics of female dependence in marriage, the limited options available to Jane as an outlet for her education and energies, her need to love and to be loved, to be of service and to be needed. These aspirations, the ambivalence expressed by the narrator toward them, and the conflicts among them, are all issues raised by the novel itself" (p. 140).

An unusual version of this appeal to women's experience is an essay in the same collection by Dawn Lander that explores the literary commonplace that "the frontier is no place for a woman," that women hate the primitive conditions, the absence of civilization, but most stoically endure them. Lander reports that her own experience as a woman living in the desert made her question this cliché and seek out what frontier women had written about their lives, only to discover that her "own feelings about the wilderness were duplicated in the experience of historic and contemporary women" ("Eve among the Indians," p. 197). Appealing to the authority first of her own experience and then of others' experiences, she reads the myth of women's hatred of the frontier as an attempt by men to make the frontier an escape from everything women represent to them, an escape from renunciation to a paradise of male camaraderie where sexuality can be an aggressive, forbidden commerce with nonwhite women. Here the experience of women provides leverage for exposing this literary topos as a self-serving male view of the female view.

Women's experience, many feminist critics claim, will lead them to value works differently from their male counterparts, who may regard the problems women characteristically encounter as of limited interest. An eminent male critic, commenting on *The Bostonians*, observes that "the doctrinaire demand for equality of the sexes may well seem to promise but a wry and constricted story, a tale of mere eccentricity" (Lionel Trilling, *The Opposing Self*, p. 109). This is no doubt what Virginia Woolf calls "the difference of view, the difference of standard" (*Collected Essays*, vol. 1, p. 204). Responding to a male critic who had patronizingly reproached her for trying to "aggrandize [Charlotte] Gilman's interesting but minor story" of incarceration and madness, "The Yellow Wallpaper," by comparing it with Poe's "The Pit and the Pendulum," Annette Kolodny notes that while she finds it as skillfully crafted and tightly composed as anything in Poe, other considerations doubtless take precedence when judging whether it is "minor" or not: "what may be entering into *my* responses is the fact that, as a female reader, I find the story a chillingly symbolic evocation of realities which women daily encounter even in our own time" ("Reply to Commentaries," p. 589). Conviction that their experience as women is a source of authority for their responses as readers has encouraged feminist critics in their revaluation of celebrated and neglected works.

In this first moment of feminist criticism, the concept of a woman reader leads to the assertion of continuity between women's experience of social and familial structures and their experience as readers. Criticism founded on this postulate of continuity takes considerable interest in the situations and psychology of female characters, investigating attitudes to women or the "images of women" in the works of an author, a genre, or a period. In attending to female characters in Shakespeare, the editors of a critical anthology observe, feminist critics are "compensating for the bias in a critical tradition that has tended to emphasize male characters, male themes, and male fantasies" and drawing attention instead to the complexity of women characters and their place in the order of male values represented in the plays (Lenz et al., *The Woman's Part*, p. 4). Such criticism is resolutely thematic—focused on woman as a theme in literary works—and resolute too in its appeal to the literary and nonliterary experience of readers.

> Feminist criticism of Shakespeare begins with an individual reader, usually, although not necessarily, a female reader—a student, teacher, actor—who brings to the plays her own experience, concerns, questions. Such readers trust their responses to Shakespeare even when they raise questions that challenge prevailing critical assumptions. Conclusions derived from these questions are then tested rigorously against the text, its myriad contexts, and the explorations of other critics. [p. 3]

Criticism based on the presumption of continuity between the reader's experience and a woman's experience and on a concern with images of women is likely to become most forceful as a critique of the phallocentric assumptions that govern literary works. This feminist critique is by now a familiar genre, authoritatively established by such works as Simone de Beauvoir's *The Second Sex*, which, while indicating familiar ways of thinking about women, provides readings of the myths of women in Montherlant, Lawrence, Claudel, Breton, and Stendhal. A similar enterprise, in which a woman reader responds critically to the visions embodied in the literature celebrated by her culture, is Kate Millett's *Sexual Politics*, which analyzes the sexual visions or ideologies of Lawrence, Miller, Mailer, and Genet. If these discussions seem exaggerated or crude, as they have seemed to male critics who find it hard to defend the sexual politics of the writers they may have admired, it is because by posing the question of the relation between sex and power and assembling relevant passages from Lawrence, Miller, and Mailer, one displays in all their crudity the aggressive phallic visions of three "counterrevolutionary sexual politicians" (p. 233). (Genet, by contrast, subjects the code of male and female roles to withering scrutiny.)

Millett's strategy in reading as a woman is "to take an author's ideas seriously when, like the novelists covered in this study, they wish to be taken seriously," and to confront them directly. "Critics who disagree with Lawrence, for example, about any issue are fond of saying that his prose is awkward. . . . It strikes me as better to make a radical investigation which can demonstrate why Lawrence's analysis of a situation is inadequate, or biased, or his influence pernicious, without ever needing to imply that he is less than a great and original artist" (p. xii).

Instead of playing down, as critics are wont to do, those works whose sexual vision is most elaborately developed, Millett pursues Lawrence's sexual religion to an apotheosis where sexuality is separated from sex: the priests of "The Women Who Rode Away" are "supernatural males, who are 'beyond sex' in a pious fervor of male supremacy that disdains any genital contact with woman, preferring instead to deal with her by means of a knife." This pure or ultimate maleness is, Lawrence says, "something primevally male and cruel" (p. 290). Miller's sexual ethos is much more conventional: "his most original contribution to sexual attitudes is confined to giving the first full expression to an ancient sentiment of contempt": he has "given voice to certain sentiments which masculine culture had long experienced but always rather carefully suppressed" (pp. 309, 313). As for Mailer, his defense of Miller against Millett's critique confirms Millett's analysis of Mailer himself, as "a prisoner of the virility cult . . . whose powerful intellectual comprehension of what is most dangerous in the masculine sensibility is exceeded only by his attachment to the malaise" (p. 314). Here is Mailer restating, in Miller's defense, their male ideology:

> For he captured something in the sexuality of men as it had never been seen before, precisely that it was man's sense of awe before woman, his dread of her position one step closer to eternity (for in that step were her powers) which made men detest women, revile them, humiliate them, defecate symbolically on them, do everything to reduce them so one might dare to enter them and take pleasure of them. . . . Men look to destroy every quality in a woman which will give her the powers of a male, for she is in their eyes already armed with the power that she brought them forth, and that is a power beyond measure—the earliest etchings of memory go back to that woman between whose legs they were conceived, nurtured, and near strangled in the hours of birth [*The Prisoner of Sex*, p. 116]

How does a woman read such authors? A feminist criticism confronts the problem of women as the consumer of male-produced literature.

Millett also offers, in an earlier chapter, brief discussions of other works: *Jude the Obscure, The Egoist, Villette,* and Wilde's *Salomé.* Analyzing these reactions to the sexual revolution of the nineteenth century, she establishes a feminist response that has served as a point of departure for debates within feminist criticism—disagreements about whether, for example, despite his sensitive portrait of Sue Bridehead, Hardy is ultimately "troubled and confused" when it comes to the sexual revolution.[2] But the possibility of quarreling with Millett to develop more subtle feminist readings should not obscure the main point. As Carolyn Heilbrun puts it,

> Millett has undertaken a task which I find particularly worthwhile: the consideration of certain events or works or literature from an unexpected, even startling point of view. . . . Her aim is to wrench the reader from the vantage point he has long occupied, and force him to look at life and letters from a new coign. Hers is not meant to be the last word on any writer, but a wholly new word, little heard before and strange. For the first time we have been asked to look at literature as women; we, men, women and Ph.Ds, have always read it as men. Who cannot point to a certain overemphasis in the way Millett reads Lawrence or Stalin or Euripides. What matter? We are rooted in our vantage point and require transplanting. ["Millett's *Sexual Politics:* A Year Later," p. 39]

As Heilbrun suggests, reading as a woman is not necessarily what occurs when a woman reads: women can read, and have read, as men. Feminist readings are not produced by recording what happens in the mental life of a female reader as she encounters the words of *The Mayor of Casterbridge*, though they do rely heavily on the notion of the experience of the woman reader. Shoshana Felman asks, "Is it enough to be a woman in order to speak as a woman? Is 'speaking as a woman' determined by some biological condition or by a strategic, theoretical position, by anatomy or by culture?" ("Women and Madness: The Critical Phallacy," p. 3). The same question applies to "reading as a woman."

To ask a woman to read as a woman is in fact a double or divided request. It appeals to the condition of being a woman as if it were a given and simultaneously urges that this condition be created or achieved. Reading as a woman is not simply, as Felman's disjunctions might seem to imply, a theoretical position, for it appeals to a sexual identity defined as essential and privileges experiences associated with that identity. Even the most sophisticated theorists make this appeal—to a condition or experience deemed more basic than the theoretical position it is used to justify. "As a female reader, I am haunted rather by another question," writes Gayatri Spivak, adducing her sex as the ground for a question ("Finding Feminist Readings," p. 82). Even the most radical French theorists, who would deny any positive or distinctive identity to woman and see *le féminin* as any force that disrupts the symbolic structures of Western thought, always have moments, in developing a theoretical position, when they speak as women, when they rely on the fact that they *are* women. Feminist critics are fond of quoting Virginia Woolf's remark that women's "inheritance," what they are given, is "the difference of view, the difference of standard"; but the question then becomes, what is the difference? It is never given as such but must be produced. Difference is produced by differing. Despite the decisive and necessary appeal to the authority of women's experience and of a female reader's experience, feminist criticism is in fact concerned, as Elaine Showalter astutely puts it, "with the way in which the *hypothesis* of a female reader changes our apprehension of a given text, awakening us to the significance of its sexual codes" ("Towards a Feminist Poetics," p. 25, my italics).[3]

Showalter's notion of the *hypothesis* of a female reader marks the double or divided structure of "experience" in reader-oriented criticism. Much male response criticism conceals this structure—in which experience is posited as a given yet deferred as something to be achieved—by asserting that readers simply do in fact have a certain experience. This structure emerges explicitly in a good deal of feminist criticism which takes up the problem that women do not always read or have not always read as women: they have been alienated from an experience appropriate to their condition as women.[4] With the shift to the hypothesis of a female reader, we move to a second moment or level of feminist criticism's dealing with the reader. In the first moment, criticism appeals to experience as a given that can ground or justify a reading. At the second level the problem is precisely that women have not been reading as women. "What is crucial here," writes Kolodny, "is that reading is a *learned* activity which, like many other learned interpretive strategies in our society, is inevitably sex-coded and gender-inflected" ("Reply to Commentaries," p. 588). Women "are expected to identify," writes Showalter, "with a masculine experience and perspective, which is presented as the human one" ("Women and the Literary Curriculum," p. 856). They have been constituted as subjects by discourses that have not identified or promoted the possibility of reading "as a woman." In its second moment, feminist criticism undertakes, through the postulate of a woman reader, to bring about a new experience of reading and to make readers—men and women—question the literary and political assumptions on which their reading has been based.

In feminist criticism of the first sort, women readers identify with the concerns of women characters; in the second case, the problem is precisely that women are led to identify with male characters, against their own interests as women. Judith Fetterley, in a book on the woman reader and American fiction, argues that "the major works of American fiction constitute a series of designs upon the female reader." Most of this literature "insists on its universality at the same time that it defines that universality in specifically male terms" (*The Resisting Reader*, p. xii). One of the founding works of American literature, for instance, is "The Legend of Sleepy Hollow." The figure of Rip Van Winkle, writes Leslie Fiedler, "presides over the birth of the American imagination; and it is fitting that our first successful homegrown legend should memorialize, however playfully, the flight of the dreamer from the shrew" (*Love and Death in the American Novel*, p. xx). It is fitting because, ever since then, novels seen as archetypally American—investigating or articulating a distinctively American experience—have rung the changes on this basic schema, in which the protagonist struggles against constricting, civilizing, oppressive forces embodied by woman. The typical protagonist, continues Fiedler, the protagonist seen as embodying the universal American dream, has been "a man on the run, harried into the forest and out to sea, down the river or into combat—anywhere to avoid 'civilization,' which is to say, the confrontation of a man and a woman which leads to the fall to sex, marriage, and responsibility."

Confronting such plots, the woman reader, like other readers, is powerfully impelled by the structure of the novel to identify with a hero who makes woman the enemy. In "The Legend of Sleepy Hollow," where Dame Van Winkle represents everything one might wish to escape and Rip the success of a fantasy, Fetterley argues that "what is essentially a simple act of identification when the reader of the story is male becomes a tangle of contradictions when the reader is female" (*The Resisting Reader*, p. 9). "In such fictions the female reader is co-opted into participation in an experience from which she is explicitly excluded; she is asked to identify with a selfhood that defines itself in opposition to her; she is required to identify against herself" (p. xii).

One should emphasize that Fetterley is not objecting to unflattering literary representations of women but to the way in which the dramatic structure of these stories induces women to participate in a vision of woman as the obstacle to freedom. Catherine in *A Farewell to Arms* is an appealing character, but her role is clear: her death prevents Frederic Henry from coming to feel the burdens she fears she imposes, while consolidating his investment in an idyllic love and in his vision of himself as a "victim of cosmic antagonism" (p. xvi). "If we weep at the end of the book," Fetterley concludes, "it is not for Catherine but for Frederic Henry. All our tears are ultimately for men, because in the world of *A Farewell to Arms* male life is what counts. And the message to women reading this classic love story and experiencing its image of the female ideal is clear and simple: the only good woman is a dead one, and even then there are questions" (p. 71). Whether or not the message is quite this simple, it is certainly true that the reader must adopt the perspective of Frederic Henry to enjoy the pathos of the ending.

Fetterley's account of the predicament of the woman reader—seduced and betrayed by devious male texts—is an attempt to change reading: "Feminist criticism is a political act whose aim is not simply to interpret the world but to change it by changing the consciousness of those who read and their relation to what they read" (p. viii). The first act of a feminist critic is "to become a resisting rather than an assenting reader and, by this refusal to assent, to begin the process of exorcizing the male mind that has been implanted in us" (p. xxii).

This is part of a broader struggle. Fetterley's account of the woman reader's predicament is powerfully confirmed by Dorothy Dinnerstein's analysis of the effects, on women as well as men, of human nurturing arrangements. "Woman, who introduced us to the human situation and who at the beginning seemed to us responsible for every drawback of that situation, carries for all of us a pre-rational onus of ultimately culpable responsibility forever after" (*The Mermaid and the Minotaur*, p. 234). Babies of both sexes are generally nurtured at first by the mother, on whom they are completely dependent. "The initial experience of dependence on a largely uncontrollable outside source of good is focused on a woman, and so is the earliest experience of vulnerability to disappointment and pain" (p. 28). The result is a powerful resentment of this dependency and a compensatory tendency to identify with male figures, who are perceived as distinct and independent. "Even to the daughter, the mother may may never come to seem so completely an 'I' as the father, who was an 'I' when first encountered" (p. 107). This perception of the mother affects her perception of all women, including herself, and encourages her "to preserve her 'I' ness by thinking of men, not women, as her real fellow creatures"—and to become engaged as a reader in plots of escape from women and domination of women (p. 107). What feminists ignore or deny at their peril, warns Dinnerstein, "is that women share men's anti-female feelings—usually in a mitigated form, but deeply nevertheless. This fact stems partly, to be sure, from causes that other writers have already quite adequately spelled out: that we have been steeped in self-derogatory societal stereotypes, pitted against each other for the favors of the reigning sex, and so on. But it stems largely from another cause, whose effects are much harder to undo: that we, like men, had female mothers" (p. 90). Without a change in nurturing arrangements, fear and loathing of women will not disappear, but some measure of progress might come with an understanding of what women want: "What women want is to stop serving as scapegoats (their own scapegoats as well as men's and children's scapegoats) for human resentment of the human condition. They want this so painfully, and so pervasively, and until quite recently it was such a hopeless thing to want, that they have not yet been able to say out loud that they want it" (p. 234).

This passage illustrates the structure at work in the second moment of feminist criticism and shows something of its power and necessity. This persuasive writing appeals to a fundamental desire or experience of women—what women want, what women feel—but an experience posited to displace the self-mutilating experiences Dinnerstein has described. The experience appealed to is nowhere present as indubitable evidence or *point d'appui*, but the appeal to it is not factitious: what more fundamental appeal could there be than to such a possibility? This postulate empowers an attempt to alter conditions so that women will not be led to cooperate in making women scapegoats for the problems of the human condition.

The most impressive works in this struggle are doubtless books like Dinnerstein's, which analyzes our predicament in terms that make comprehensible a whole range of phenomena, from the self-estrangement of women readers to the particular cast of Mailer's sexism. In literary criticism, a powerful strategy is to produce readings that identify and situate male misreadings. Though it is difficult to work out in positive, independent terms what it might mean to read as a woman, one may confidently propose a purely differential definition: to read as a woman is to avoid reading as a man, to identify the specific defenses and distortions of male readings and provide correctives.

By these lights, feminist criticism is a critique of what Mary Ellmann, in her witty and erudite *Thinking about Women*, calls "phallic criticism." Fetterley's most impressive and effective chapter, for example, may well be her discussion of *The Bostonians*, where she documents the striking tendency of male critics to band together and take the part of Basil Ransom in his determination to win Verena away from her feminist friend, Olive Chancellor. Treating the relation between the women as perverse and unnatural, critics identify with Ransom's fear that female solidarity threatens male dominance and the male character: "The whole generation is womanized; the masculine tone is passing out of the world; . . . The masculine character . . . that is what I want to preserve, or rather, as I may say, to recover; and I must tell you that I don't in the least care what becomes of you ladies while I make the attempt."

Rescuing Verena from Olive is part of this project, for which the critics show considerable enthusiasm. Some recognize Ransom's failings and James's precise delineation of them (others regard this complexity as an artistic error on James's part), but all seem to agree that when Ransom carries Verena off, this is a consummation devoutly to be wished. The narrator tells us in the concluding sentence of the book that Verena will have cause to shed more tears: "It is to be feared that with the union, so far from brilliant, into which she was about to enter, these were not to be the last she was destined to shed." But critics generally regard this, as one of them observes, as "a small price to pay for achieving a normal relationship." Faced with a threat to what they regard as normalcy, male critics become caught up in Ransom's crusade and outdo one another in finding reasons to disparage Olive, the character in whom James shows the greatest interest, as well as the feminist movements James criticizes. The result is a male chorus. "The criticism of *The Bostonians* is remarkable for its relentless sameness, its reliance on values outside the novel, and its cavalier dismissal of the need for textual support" (*The Resisting Reader*, p. 113).

The hypothesis of a female reader is an attempt to rectify this situation: by providing a different point of departure it brings into focus the identification of male critics with one character and permits the analysis of male misreadings. But what it does above all is to reverse the usual situation in which the perspective of a male critic is assumed to be sexually neutral, while a feminist reading is seen as a case of special pleading and an attempt to force the text into a predetermined mold. By confronting male readings with the elements of the text they neglect and showing them to be a continuation of Ransom's position rather than judicious commentary on the novel as a whole, feminist criticism puts itself in the position that phallic criticism usually attempts to occupy. The more convincing its critique of phallic criticism, the more feminist criticism comes to provide the broad and comprehensive vision, analyzing and situating the limited and interested interpretations of male critics. Indeed, at this level one can say that feminist criticism is the name that should be applied to all criticism alert to the critical ramifications of sexual oppression, just as in politics "women's issues" is the name now applied to many fundamental questions of personal freedom and social justice.

A different way of going beyond phallic criticism is Jane Tompkins's discussion of *Uncle Tom's Cabin*, a novel relegated to the trash heap of literary history by male critics and fellow travelers such as Ann Douglas, in her influential book *The Feminization of American Culture*. "The attitude Douglas expresses toward the vast quantity of literature written by women in this country between 1820 and 1870 is the one that the male-dominated scholarly tradition has always expressed—contempt. The query one hears behind every page of her indictment of feminization is: why can't a woman be more like a man?" (*"Sentimental Power,"* p. 81). Though in some respects the most important book of the century, *Uncle Tom's Cabin* is placed in a genre—the sentimental novel—written by, about, and for women, and therefore seen as trash, or at least as unworthy of serious critical consideration. If one does take this book seriously, one discovers, Tompkins argues, that it displays in exemplary fashion the features of a major American genre defined by Sacvan Bercovitch, "the American Jeremaid": "a mode of public exhortation . . . designed to join social criticism to spiritual renewal, public to private identity, the shifting 'signs of the times' to certain traditional metaphors, themes, and symbols," especially those of typological narrative (p. 93). Bercovitch's book, notes Tompkins, "provides a striking instance of how totally academic criticism has foreclosed on sentimental fiction; since, even when a sentimental novel fulfills a man's theory to perfection, he cannot see it. For him the work doesn't even exist. Despite the fact that his study takes no note of the most obvious and compelling instance of the jeremiad since the Great Awakening, Bercovitch's description in fact provides an excellent account of the combination of elements that made Stowe's novel work" (p. 93). Rewriting the Bible as the story of a Negro slave, "*Uncle Tom's Cabin* retells the culture's central myth—the story of the crucifixion—in terms of the nation's greatest political conflict—slavery—and of its most cherished social beliefs—the sanctity of motherhood and the family" (p. 89).

Here the hypothesis of a woman reader helps to identify male exclusions that forestall serious analysis, but once that analysis is undertaken it becomes possible to argue

> that the popular domestic novel of the nineteenth century represents a monumental effort to reorganize culture from the woman's point of view, that this body of work is remarkable for its intellectual complexity, ambition, and resourcefulness, and that, in certain cases, it offers a critique of American society far more devastating than any delivered by better-known critics such as Hawthorne and Melville. . . . Out of the ideological materials they had at their disposal, the sentimental novelists elaborated a myth that gave women the central position of power and authority in the culture; and of these efforts *Uncle Tom's Cabin* is the most dazzling exemplar. [pp. 81–82]

In addition to the devastating attack on slavery, reputed to have "changed the hearts" of many of its readers, the novel attempts to bring on, through the same sort of change of heart, a new social order. In the new society, envisioned in a chapter called "The Quaker Settlement," man-made institutions fade into irrelevance, and the home guided by the Christian woman becomes, not a refuge from the real order of the world, but the center of meaningful activity (p. 95). "The removal of the male from the center to the periphery of the human sphere is the most radical component of this millenarian scheme which is rooted so solidly in the most traditional values—religion, motherhood, home, and family. [In the details of this chapter,] Stowe reconceives the role of men in human history: while Negroes, children, mothers, and grandmothers do the world's primary work, men groom themselves contentedly in a corner" (p. 98).

In this sort of analysis, feminist criticism does not rely on the experience of the woman reader as it does at the first level but employs the hypothesis of a woman reader to provide leverage for displacing the dominant male critical vision and revealing its misprisions. "By 'feminist,'" suggests Peggy Kamuf, "one understands a way of reading texts that points to the masks of truth with which phallocentrism hides its fictions" ("Writing like a Woman," p. 286). The task at this level is not to establish a woman's reading that would parallel a male reading but rather, through argument and an attempt to account for textual evidence, to produce a comprehensive perspective, a compelling reading. The conclusions reached in feminist criticism of this sort are not specific to women in the sense that one can sympathize, comprehend, and agree only if one has had certain experiences which are women's. On the contrary, these readings demonstrate the limitations of male critical interpretations in terms that male critics would purport to accept, and they seek, like all ambitious acts of criticism, to attain a generally convincing understanding—an understanding that is feminist because it is a critique of male chauvinism.

In this second moment of feminist criticism there is an appeal to the potential experience of a woman reader (which would escape the limitations of male readings) and then the attempt to make such an experience possible by developing questions and perspectives that would enable a woman to read as a woman—that is, not "as a man." Men have aligned the opposition male/female with rational/emotional, serious/frivolous, or reflective/spontaneous; and feminist cricitism of the second moment works to prove itself more rational, serious, and reflective than male readings that omit and distort. But there is a third moment in which, instead of contesting the association of the male with the rational, feminist theory investigates the way our notions of the rational are tied to or in complicity with the interests of the male. One of the most striking analyses of this kind is Luce Irigaray's *Speculum de l'autre femme*, which takes Plato's parable of the cave, with its contrast between a maternal womb and a divine paternal *logos*, as the point of departure for a demonstration that philosophical categories have been developed to relegate the feminine to a position of subordination and to reduce the radical Otherness of woman to a specular relation: woman is either ignored or seen as man's opposite. Rather than attempt to reproduce Irigaray's complex argument, one might take a single striking example adduced by Dorothy Dinnerstein, Peggy Kamuf, and others: the connection between patriarchy and the privileging of the rational, the abstract, or the intellectual.

In *Moses and Monotheism*, Freud establishes a relation between three "processes of the same character": the Mosaic prohibition against making a sensible image of God (thus, "the compulsion to worship a God whom one cannot see"), the development of speech ("the new realm of intellectuality was opened up, in which ideas, memories, and inferences became decisive in contrast to the lower psychical activity which had direct perceptions by the sense-organs as its content"), and finally, the replacement of a matriarchal social order by a patriarchal one. The last involves more than a change in juridical conventions. "This turning from the mother to the father points in addition to a victory of intellectuality over sensuality—that is, an advance of civilization, since maternity is proved by the evidence of the senses while paternity is a hypothesis, based on an inference and a premise. Taking sides in this way with a thought-process in preference to a sense perception has proved to be a momentous step" (vol. 23, pp. 113–14). Several pages further on, Freud explains the common character of these processes:

> An advance in intellectuality consists in deciding against direct sense-perception in favour of what are known as the higher intellectual processes—that is, memories, reflections, and inferences. It consists, for instance, in deciding that paternity is more important than maternity, although it cannot, like the latter, be established by the evidence of the senses, and that for that reason the child should bear his father's name and be his heir. Or it declares that our God is the greatest and mightiest, although he is invisible like a gale of wind or like the soul. [Pp. 117–18]

Freud appears to suggest that the establishment of patriarchal power is merely an instance of the general advance of intellectuality and that the preference for an invisible God is another effect of the same cause. But when we consider that the invisible, omnipotent God is God the Father, not to say God of the Patriarchs, we may well wonder whether, on the contrary, the promotion of the invisible over the visible and of thought and inference over sense perception is not a consequence or effect of the establishment of paternal authority: a consequence of the fact that the paternal relation is invisible.

If one wished to argue that the promotion of the intelligible over the sensible, meaning over form, and the invisible over the visible was an elevation of the paternal principle and paternal power over the maternal, one could draw support from the character of Freud's arguments elsewhere, since he shows that numerous enterprises are determined by unconscious interests of a sexual character. Dorothy Dinnerstein's discussions would also support the view that the intangibility and uncertainty of the paternal relation have considerable consequences. She notes that fathers, because of their lack of direct physical connection with babies, have a powerful urge to assert a relation, giving the child their name to establish genealogical links, engaging in various "initiation rites through which they symbolically and passionately affirm that it is they who have themselves created human beings, as compared with the mere flesh spawned by woman. Think also of the anxious concern that men have so widely shown for immortality through heirs, and their efforts to control the sexual life of women to make sure that the children they sponsor really do come from their own seed: the tenuousness of their physical tie to the young clearly pains men in a way that it could not pain bulls or stallions" (*The Mermaid and the Minotaur*, p. 80).

Men's powerful "impulse to affirm and tighten by cultural inventions their unsatisfactorily loose mammalian connection with children" leads them to value highly cultural inventions of a symbolic nature (pp. 80–81). One might predict an inclination to value what are generally termed metaphorical relations—relations of resemblance between separate items that can be substituted for one another, such as obtain between the father and the miniature replica with the same name, the child—over metonymical, maternal relationships based on contiguity.

Indeed, if one tried to imagine the literary criticism of a patriarchal culture, one might predict several likely concerns: (1) that the role of the author would be conceived as a paternal one and any maternal functions deemed valuable would be assimilated to paternity;[5] (2) that much would be invested in paternal authors, to whose credit everything in their textual progeny would redound; (3) that there would be great concern about which meanings were legitimate and which illegitimate (since the paternal author's role in the generation of meanings can only be inferred); and that criticism would expend great efforts to develop principles for, on the one hand, determining which meanings were truly the author's own progeny, and on the other hand, controlling intercourse with texts so as to prevent the proliferation of illegitimate interpretations. Numerous aspects of criticism, including the preference for metaphor over metonymy, the conception of the author, and the concern to distinguish legitimate from illegitimate meanings, can be seen as part of the promotion of the paternal. Phallogocentrism unites an interest in patriarchal authority, unity of meaning, and certainty of origin.

The task of feminist criticism in this third moment is to investigate whether the procedures, assumptions, and goals of current criticism are in complicity with the preservation of male authority, and to explore alternatives. It is not a question of rejecting the rational in favor of the irrational, of concentrating on metonymical relations to the exclusion of the metaphorical, or on the signifier to the exclusion of the signified, but of attempting to develop critical modes in which the concepts that are products of male authority are inscribed within a larger textual system. Feminists will try various strategies—in recent French writing "woman" has come to stand for any radical force that subverts the concepts, assumptions, and structures of traditional male discourse.[6] One might suspect, however, that attempts to produce a new feminine language will prove less effective at this stage than critiques of phallocentric criticism, which are by no means limited to the strategies of feminist criticism's second moment. There, feminist readings identify male bias by using concepts and categories that male critics purport to accept. In this third moment or mode, many of these concepts and theoretical categories—notions of realism, of rationality, of mastery, of explanation—are themselves shown to belong to phallocentric criticism.

Consider, for instance, Shoshana Felman's discussion of the text and readings of Balzac's short story "Adieu," a tale of a woman's madness, its origin in an episode of the Napoleonic wars, and her former lover's attempt to cure it. Feminist perspectives of the first and second moment bring out what was previously ignored or taken for granted, as male critics set aside women and madness to praise the "realism" of Balzac's description of war. Felman shows that critics' dealings with the text repeat the male protagonist's dealings with his former mistress, Stéphanie. "It is quite striking to observe to what extent the logic of the unsuspecting 'realistic' critic can reproduce, one after the other, all of Philippe's delusions" ("Women and Madness: The Critical Phallacy," p. 10).

Philippe thinks he can cure Stéphanie by making her recognize and name him. To restore her reason is to obliterate her otherness, which he finds so unacceptable that he is willing to kill both her and himself if he should fail in his cure. She must recognize him and recognize herself as "his Stéphanie" again. When she finally does so, as a result of Philippe's elaborate realistic reconstruction of the scene of wartime suffering where she lost her reason, she dies. The drama played out in the story reflects back on the attempt by male critics to make the story a recognizable instance of realism, and thus questions their notions of "realism" or reality, of reason, and of interpretive mastery, as instances of a male passion analogous to Philippe's. "On the critical as well as on the literary stage, the same attempt is played out to appropriate the signifier and to reduce its differential repetition; we see the same endeavor to do away with difference, the same policing of identities, the same design of mastery, of *sense-control*. . . . Along with the illusions of Philippe, the realistic critic thus repeats, in turn, his allegorical act of murder, his obliteration of the Other: the critic also, in his own way, *kills the woman*, while killing, at the same time, the question of the text and the text as question" (p. 10).

Balzac's story helps to identify notions critics have employed with the male stratagems of its protagonist and thus to make possible a feminist reading that situates these concepts and describes their limitations. Insofar as the structure and details of Balzac's story provide a critical description of its male critics, exploration and exploitation of its textuality is a feminist way of reading, but a way of reading that poses rather than solves the question of how to get around or to go beyond the concepts and categories of male criticism. Felman concludes, "from this confrontation in which Balzac's text itself seems to be an ironic reading of its own future reading, the question arises: how *should* we read?" (p. 10).

This is also the question posed in feminist criticism's second moment—how should we read? what kind of reading experience can we imagine or produce? what would it be to read "as a woman"? Felman's critical mode thus leads back to the second level at which political choices are debated and where notions of what one wants animate critical practice. In this sense, the third level, which questions the framework of choice and the affiliations of critical and theoretical categories, is not more radical than the second; nor does it escape the question of "experience."

From these varied writings, a general structure emerges. In the first moment or mode, where woman's experience is treated as a firm ground for interpretation, one swiftly discovers that this experience is not the sequence of thoughts present to the reader's consciousness as she moves through the text but a reading or interpretation of "woman's experience"—her own and others'—which can be set in a vital and productive relation to the text. In the second mode, the problem is how to make it possible to read as a woman: the possibility of this fundamental experience induces an attempt to produce it. In the third mode, the appeal to experience is veiled but still there, as a reference to maternal rather than paternal relations or to woman's situation and experience of marginality, which may give rise to an altered mode of reading. The appeal to the experience of the reader provides leverage for displacing or undoing the system of concepts or procedures of male criticism, but "experience" always has this divided, duplicitous character: it has always already occurred and yet is still to be produced—an indispensable point of reference, yet never simply there.

Peggy Kamuf provides a vivid way of understanding this situation of deferral if we transpose what she says about writing as a woman to reading as a woman:

> —"a woman [reading] as a woman"—the repetition of the "identical" term splits that identity, making room for a slight shift, spacing out the differential meaning which has always been at work in the single term. And the repetition has no reason to stop there, no finite number of times it can be repeated until it closes itself off logically, with the original identity recuperated in a final term. Likewise, one can find only arbitrary beginnings for the series, and no term which is not already a repetition: " . . . a woman [reading] as a woman [reading] as a . . . " ["Writing like a Woman," p. 298]

For a woman to read as a woman is not to repeat an identity or an experience that is given but to play a role she constructs with reference to her identity as a woman, which is also a construct, so that the series can continue: a woman reading as a woman reading as a woman. The noncoincidence reveals an interval, a division within woman or within any reading subject and the "experience" of that subject.

NOTES

1. This alerts one to the remarkable scenario of Hartman's recent criticism. *The Fate of Reading* offers this prognostic: most reading is like girl-watching, doubtless "perjur'd, murderous, bloody, full of blame." The cure is a period of *Criticism in the Wilderness*, after which, chastened and purified, criticism can turn to *Saving the Text*—saving it, it turns out, from a frivolous, seductive, and "self-involved" deconstruction that ignores the sacred.

2. See, for example, an early rejoinder by Mary Jacobus, who argues that what Millett calls Hardy's "confusion" is in fact "careful non-alignment": "through Sue's obscurity he probes the relationship between character and idea in such a way as to leave one's mind engaged with her as it is engaged with few women in fiction" ("Sue the Obscure," pp. 305, 325).

3. Feminist criticism is, of course, concerned with other issues as well, particularly the distinctiveness of women's writing and the achievements of women writers. The problems of reading as a woman and of writing as a woman are in many respects similar, but con-

centration on the latter leads feminist criticism into areas that do not concern me here, such as the establishment of a criticism focused on women writers that parallels criticism focused on male writers. Gynocriticism, says Showalter, who has been one of the principal advocates of this activity, is concerned "with woman as the producer of textual meaning, with the history, themes, genres, and structures of literature by women. Its subjects include the psychodynamics of female creativity; linguistics and the problem of a female language; the trajectory of the individual or collective female literary career; literary history; and, of course, studies of particular writers and works" ("Towards a Feminist Poetics," p. 25). For work of this kind, see Sandra Gilbert and Susan Gubar, *The Madwoman in the Attic,* and the collection edited by Sally McConnell-Ginet, Ruth Borker, and Nelly Furman, *Women and Language in Literature and Society* (New York: Praeger, 1980).

4. The analogy with social class is instructive: progressive political writing appeals to the proletariat's experience of oppression, but usually the problem for a political movement is precisely that the members of a class do not have the experience their situation would warrant. The most insidious oppression alienates a group from its own interests as a group and encourages it to identify with the interests of the oppressors, so that political struggles must first awaken a group to its interest and its "experience."

5. See Gilbert and Gubar, *The Madwoman in the Attic,* pp. 3–92. Feminist critics have shown considerable interest in Harold Bloom's model of poetic creation because it makes explicit the sexual connotations of authorship and authority. This oedipal scenario, in which one becomes a poet by struggling with a poetic father for possession of the muse, indicates the problematical situation of a woman who would be a poet. What relation can she have to the tradition?

6. The articles in Elaine Marks and Isabelle de Courtivron's *New French Feminisms* provide an excellent conspectus of recent strategies. See also the discussions in *Yale French Studies* 62 (1981), "Feminist Readings: French Texts/American Contexts." The relation between feminism and deconstruction is a complicated question. For some brief indications, see chapter 2, section 4, of Jonathan Culler, *On Deconstruction* (Ithaca: Cornell University Press, 1982). Derrida's *Eperons,* on Nietzsche and the concept of woman, is a relevant but in many ways unsatisfying document in this case.

WORKS CITED

Adams, Maurianne. "*Jane Eyre:* Woman's Estate." In *The Authority of Experience,* ed. Lee Edwards and Arlyn Diamond. Amherst: University of Massachusetts Press, 1977, pp. 137–59.

Beauvoir, Simone de. *The Second Sex.* New York: Knopf, 1953. A classic of women's liberation and feminist criticism.

Dinnerstein, Dorothy. *The Mermaid and the Minotaur: Sexual Arrangements and Human Malaise.* New York: Harper, 1976. The psychological effects of nurturing arrangements.

Douglas, Ann. *The Feminization of American Culture.* New York: Knopf, 1977.

Ellmann, Mary. *Thinking about Women.* New York: Harcourt Brace, 1968. An early exposure of phallic criticism.

Felman, Shoshana. "Women and Madness: The Critical Phallacy." *Diacritics,* 5.4 (1975), 2–10. A feminist reading of Balzac.

Fetterley, Judith. *The Resisting Reader: A Feminist Approach to American Fiction.* Bloomington: Indiana University Press, 1978. A critique of major novels and a call to resistance.

Fiedler, Leslie. *Love and Death in the American Novel.* New York: Criterion, 1960.

Freud, Sigmund. *Complete Psychological Works,* ed. James Strachey. London: Hogarth, 1953–74. 24 vols.

Gilbert, Sandra M., and Susan Gubar. *The Madwoman in the Attic: The Woman Writer and the Nineteenth-Century Literary Imagination*. New Haven: Yale University Press, 1979.

Hartman, Geoffrey. *The Fate of Reading and Other Essays*. Chicago: University of Chicago Press, 1975.

Heilbrun, Carolyn. "Millett's *Sexual Politics:* A Year Later." *Aphra*, 2 (1971), 38–47.

Jacobus, Mary. "Sue the Obscure." *Essays in Criticism*, 25 (1975): 304–28.

Kamuf, Peggy. "Writing like a Woman." In *Women and Language in Literature and Society*, ed. S. McConnell-Ginet et al. New York: Praeger, 1980, pp. 284–99. A feminist essay focused on *Les Lettres portugaises*.

Kolodny, Annette. "Reply to Commentaries: Women Writers, Literary Historians, and Martian Readers." *New Literary History*, 11 (1980), 587–92. A defense of feminist views on literary history and literary value.

Lander, Dawn. "Eve among the Indians." In *The Authority of Experience*, ed. Lee Edwards and Arlyn Diamond. Amherst: University of Massachusetts Press, 1977, pp. 194–211. On the image and the reality of frontier women.

Lenz, Carolyn, et al., eds. *The Woman's Part: Feminist Criticism of Shakespeare*. Urbana: University of Illinois Press, 1980.

Mailer, Norman. *The Prisoner of Sex*. Boston: Little, Brown, 1971. A defense of sexism.

Millett, Kate. *Sexual Politics*. New York: Doubleday, 1970. A critique of domination in sexual relations and in their literary representations.

Showalter, Elaine. "Towards a Feminist Poetics." In *Women Writing and Writing About Women*, ed. M. Jacobus. London: Croom Helm, 1979, pp. 22—41.

———. "The Unmanning of the Mayor of Casterbridge." In *Critical Approaches to the Fiction of Thomas Hardy*, ed. Dale Kramer. London: Macmillan, 1979, pp. 99–115. A feminist reading of the novel.

———. "Women and the Literary Curriculum." *College English*, 32 (1971), 855–62.

Spivak, Gayatri Chakravorty. "Finding Feminist Readings: Dante-Yeats." *Social Text*, 3 (1980), 73–87.

Tompkins, Jane. "Sentimental Power: *Uncle Tom's Cabin* and the Politics of Literary History." *Glyph*, 8 (1981), 79–102. A feminist critique of the ideology of literary history and a new perspective on "sentimental" fiction.

Trilling, Lionel. *The Opposing Self*. New York: Viking, 1955.

Woolf, Virginia. *Collected Essays*. London: Hogarth, 1966. 4 vols.

PATROCINIO P. SCHWEICKART

READING OURSELVES
toward a feminist theory of reading

~~~~~~

THREE STORIES OF READING

A.   Wayne Booth begins his Presidential Address to the 1982 MLA Convention by considering and rejecting several plausible myths that might enable us "to dramatize not just our inescapable plurality but the validity of our sense that [as teachers and scholars of literature and composition] we belong together, some-how working on common ground." At last he settles on one story that is "perhaps close enough to our shared experience to justify the telling."[1]

Once upon a time there was a boy who fell in love with books. When he was very young he heard over and over the legend of his great-grandfather, a hard-working weaver who so desired knowledge that he figured out a way of working the loom with one hand, his legs, and his feet, leaving the other hand free to hold a book, and worked so steadily in that crooked position that he became per-manently crippled. The boy heard other stories about the importance of reading. Salvation, he came to believe, was to be found in books. When he was six years old, he read *The Wizard of Oz*—his first *real* book—and was rewarded by his Great-Aunt Manda with a dollar.

When the boy grew up, he decided to become a teacher of "litcomp." His initiation into the profession was rigorous, and there were moments when he nearly gave up. But gradually, "there emerged from the trudging a new and sur-prising love, a love that with all my previous reading I had not dreamed of: the love of skill, of craft, of getting clear in my mind and then in my writing what a great writer had got right in his work" (Booth, p. 315). Eventually, the boy, now grown, got his doctorate, and after teaching for thirteen years in small colleges, he returned to his graduate institution to become one of its eminent professors.

Booth caps his narration by quoting from *The Autobiography of Malcolm X*. It was in prison that Malcolm learned to read:

> For the first time I could pick up a book and now begin to understand what the book was saying. Anyone who has read a great deal can imagine the new world that opened. Let me tell you something: from then until I left that prison, in every free moment I had, if I was not reading in the library, I was

> reading on my bunk. . . . [M]onths passed without my even thinking about
> being imprisoned. In fact, up to then, I never had been so truly free in my
> life. (As quoted by Booth, p. 317)

"Perhaps," says Booth, "when you think back now on my family's story about
Great-grandfather Booth, you will understand why reading about Malcolm X's
awakening speaks to the question of where I got my 'insane love' [for books]"
(p. 317).

B.   When I read the Malcolm X passage quoted in Booth's address, the ellipsis roused my curiosity. What, exactly, I wondered, had been deleted? What in
the original exceeded the requirements of a Presidential Address to the MLA?
Checking, I found the complete sentence to read: "Between Mr. Muhammad's
teachings, my correspondence, my visitors—usually Ella and Reginald—and my
reading, months passed without my even thinking about being imprisoned."[2]
Clearly, the first phrase is the dissonant one. The reference to the leader of the
notorious Black Muslims suggests a story of reading very different from Booth's.
Here is how Malcolm X tells it. While serving time in the Norfolk Prison Colony,
he hit on the idea of teaching himself to read by copying the dictionary.

> In my slow, painstaking, ragged handwriting, I copied into my tablet every
> thing on that first page, down to the punctuation marks. . . . Then, aloud, to
> myself, I read back everything I'd written on the tablet. . . . I woke up the
> next morning thinking about these words—immensely proud to realize that
> not only had I written so much at one time, but I'd written words that I never
> knew were in the world. . . . That was the way I started copying what even-
> tually became the entire dictionary. (p. 172)

After copying the dictionary, Malcolm X began reading the books in the prison
library. "No university would ask any student to devour literature as I did when
this new world opened to me, of being able to read and *understand*" (p. 173).
Reading had changed the course of his life. Years later, he would reflect on how
"the ability to read awoke inside me some long dormant craving to be mentally
alive" (p. 179).

What did he read? What did he understand? He read Gregor Mendel's *Findings
in Genetics* and it helped him to understand "that if you started with a black man,
a white man could be produced; but starting with a white man, you never could
produce a black man—because the white chromosome is recessive. And since no
one disputes that there was but one Original Man, the conclusion is clear"
(p. 175). He read histories, books by Will Durant and Arnold Toynbee, by
W. E. B. Du Bois and Carter G. Woodson, and he saw how "the glorious history of the black man" had been "bleached" out of the history books written by
white men.

> [His] eyes opened gradually, then wider and wider, to how the world's white
> men had indeed acted like devils, pillaging and raping and bleeding and
> draining the whole world's non-white people. . . . I will never forget how
> shocked I was when I began reading about slavery's total horror. . . . The
> world's most monstrous crime, the sin and the blood on the white man's
> hands, are almost impossible to believe. (p. 175)

He read philosophy—the works of Schopenhauer, Kant, Nietzsche, and Spinoza—and he concluded that the "whole stream of Western Philosophy was now wound up in a cul-de-sac" as a result of the white man's "elaborate, neurotic necessity to hide the black man's true role in history" (p. 180). Malcolm X read voraciously, and book after book confirmed the truth of Elijah Muhammad's teachings. "It's a crime, the lie that has been told to generations of black men and white both. . . . Innocent black children growing up, living out their lives, dying of old age—and all of their lives ashamed of being black. But the truth is pouring out of the bag now" (p. 181).

Wayne Booth's story leads to the Crystal Ballroom of the Biltmore Hotel in Los Angeles, where we attend the protagonist as he delivers his Presidential Address to the members of the Modern Language Association. Malcolm X's love of books took him in a different direction, to the stage of the Audubon Ballroom in Harlem, where, as he was about to address a mass meeting of the Organization of Afro-American Unity, he was murdered.

C.   As we have seen, an ellipsis links Wayne Booth's story of reading to Malcolm X's. Another ellipsis, this time not graphically marked, signals the existence of a third story. Malcolm X's startling reading of Mendel's genetics overlooks the most rudimentary fact of human reproduction: whether you start with a black man or a white man, without a woman, you get *nothing*. An excerpt from Virginia Woolf's *A Room of One's Own* restores this deleted perspective.[3]

The heroine, call her Mary, says Woolf, goes to the British Museum in search of information about women. There she discovers to her chagrin that woman is, "perhaps, the most discussed animal in the universe?"

> Why does Samuel Butler say, "Wise men never say what they think of women"? Wise men never say anything else apparently. . . . Are they capable of education? Napoleon thought them incapable. Dr. Johnson thought the opposite. Have they souls or have they not souls? Some savages say they have none. Others, on the contrary, say women are half divine and worship them on that account. Some sages hold that they are shallower in the brain; others that they are deeper in consciousness. Goethe honoured them; Mussolini despises them. Wherever one looked men thought about women and thought differently. (pp. 29–30)

Distressed and confused, Mary notices that she has unconsciously drawn a picture in her notebook, the face and figure of Professor von X. engaged in writing his monumental work, *The Mental, Moral, and Physical Inferiority of the Female Sex*. "His expression suggested that he was labouring under some emotion that made him jab his pen on the paper as if he were killing some noxious insect as he wrote, but even when he had killed it that did not satisfy him; he must go on killing it. . . . A very elementary excercise in psychology . . . showed me . . . that the sketch had been made in anger" (pp. 31–32).

Nothing remarkable in that, she reflects, given the provocation. But "How explain the anger of the professor? . . . For when it came to analysing the impression left by these books, . . . there was [an] element which was often present and could not be immediately identified. Anger, I called it. . . . To judge from its effects, it was anger disguised and complex, not anger simple and open" (p. 32).

Disappointed with essayists and professors, Mary turns to historians. But apparently women played no significant role in history. What little information Mary finds is disturbing: "Wife-beating, I read, was a recognized right of a man, and was practiced without shame by high as well as low" (p. 44). Oddly enough, literature presents a contradictory picture.

> If women had no existence save in fiction written by men, we would imagine her to be a person of utmost importance; very various; heroic and mean; splendid and sordid; infinitely beautiful and hideous in the extreme; as great as a man, some think even greater. But this is women in fiction. In fact, as Professor Trevelyan points out, she was locked up, beaten and flung about the room. (p. 45)

At last, Mary can draw but one conclusion from her reading. Male professors, male historians, and male poets can not be relied on for the truth about women. Woman herself must undertake the study of woman. Of course, to do so, she must secure enough money to live on and a room of her own.

Booth's story, we recall, is told within the framework of a professional ritual. It is intended to remind us of "the loves and fears that inform our daily work" and of "what we do when we are at our best," to show, if not a unity, then enough of a "center" "to shame us whenever we violate it." The principal motif of the myth is the hero's insane love for books, and the way this develops with education and maturity into "critical understanding," which Booth defines as that synthesis of thought and passion which should replace, "on the one hand, sentimental and uncritical identifications that leave minds undisturbed, and on the other, hypercritical negations that freeze or alienate" (pp. 317–18). Booth is confident that the experience celebrated by the myth is archetypal. "Whatever our terms for it, whatever our theories about how it happens or why it fails to happen more often, can we reasonably doubt the importance of the moment, at any level of study, when any of us—you, me, Malcolm X, my great-grandfather—succeeds in entering other minds, or 'taking them in,' as nourishment for our own?" (p. 318).

Now, while it is certainly true that something one might call "critical understanding" informs the stories told by Malcolm X and Virginia Woolf, these authors fill this term with thoughts and passions that one would never suspect from Booth's definition. From the standpoint of the second and third stories of reading, Booth's story is utopian. The powers and resources of his hero are equal to the challenges he encounters. At each stage he finds suitable mentors. He is assured by the people around him, by the books he reads, by the entire culture, that he is right for the part. His talents and accomplishments are acknowledged and justly rewarded. In short, from the perspective of Malcolm X's and Woolf's stories, Booth's hero is fantastically privileged.

Utopian has a second meaning, one that is by no means pejorative, and Booth's story is utopian in this sense as well. In overlooking the realities highlighted by the stories of Malcolm X and Virginia Woolf, Booth's story anticipates what might be possible, what "critical understanding" might mean for *everyone*, if only we could overcome the pervasive systemic injustices of our time.

READER-RESPONSE THEORY AND FEMINIST CRITICISM

Reader-response criticism, as currently constituted, is utopian in the same two senses. The different accounts of the reading experience that have been put forth overlook the issues of race, class, and sex, and give no hint of the conflicts, sufferings, and passions that attend these realities. The relative tranquility of the tone of these theories testifies to the privileged position of the theorists. Perhaps, someday, when privileges have withered away or at least become more equitably distributed, some of these theories will ring true. Surely we ought to be able to talk about reading without worrying about injustice. But for now, reader-response criticism must confront the disturbing implications of our historical reality. Paradoxically, utopian theories that elide these realities betray the utopian impulses that inform them.

To put the matter plainly, reader-response criticism needs feminist criticism. The two have yet to engage each other in a sustained and serious way, but if the promise of the former is to be fulfilled, such an encounter must soon occur. Interestingly, the obvious question of the significance of gender has already been explicitly raised, and—this testifies to the increasing impact of feminist criticism as well as to the direct ideological bearing of the issue of gender on reader-response criticism—not by a feminist critic, but by Jonathan Culler, a leading theorist of reading: "If the experience of literature depends upon the qualities of a reading self, one can ask what difference it would make to the experience of literature and thus to the meaning of literature if this self were, for example, female rather than male. If the meaning of a work is the experience of a reader, what difference does it make if the reader is a woman?"[4]

Until very recently this question has not occurred to reader-response critics. They have been preoccupied with other issues. Culler's survey of the field is instructive here, for it enables us to anticipate the direction reader-response theory might take when it is shaken from its slumber by feminist criticism. According to Culler, the different models (or "stories") of reading that have been proposed are all organized around three problems. The first is the issue of control: Does the text control the reader, or vice versa? For David Bleich, Norman Holland, and Stanley Fish, the reader holds controlling interest. Readers read the poems they have made. Bleich asserts this point most strongly: the constraints imposed by the words on the page are "trivial," since their meaning can always be altered by "subjective action." To claim that the text supports this or that reading is only to "moralistically claim . . . that one's own objection is more authoritative than someone else's."[5]

At the other pole are Michael Riffaterre, Georges Poulet, and Wolfgang Iser, who acknowledge the creative role of the reader, but ultimately take the text to be the dominant force. To read, from this point of view, is to create the text according to *its* own promptings. As Poulet puts it, a text, when invested with a reader's subjectivity, becomes a "subjectified object," a "second self" that depends on the reader, but is not, strictly speaking, identical with him. Thus, reading "is a way of giving way not only to a host of alien words, images and ideas, but also to the very alien principle which utters and shelters them. . . . I am on loan to another, and this other thinks, feels, suffers and acts within me."[6]

Culler argues persuasively that, regardless of their ostensible theoretical commitments, the prevailing stories of reading generally vacillate between these reader-
dominant and text-dominant poles. In fact, those who stress the subjectivity of
the reader as against the objectivity of the text ultimately portray the text as
determining the responses of the reader. "The more active, projective, or creative the reader is, the more she is manipulated by the sentence or by the author" (p. 71).

   The second question prominent in theories of reading is closely related to the
first. Reading always involves a subject and an object, a reader and a text. But
what constitutes the objectivity of the text? What is "in" the text? What is supplied by the reader? Again, the answers have been equivocal. On the face of it,
the situation seems to call for a dualistic theory that credits the contributions of
both text and reader. However, Culler argues, a dualistic theory eventually gives
way to a monistic theory, in which one or the other pole supplies everything.
One might say, for instance, that Iser's theory ultimately implies the deter-
minacy of the text and the authority of the author: "The author guarantees the
unity of the work, requires the reader's creative participation, and through his
text, prestructures the shape of the aesthetic object to be produced by the
reader."[7] At the same time, one can also argue that the "gaps" that structure the
reader's response are not built into the text, but appear (or not) as a result of
the particular interpretive strategy employed by the reader. Thus, "there is no
distinction between what the text gives and what the reader supplies; he supplies *everything*."[8] Depending on which aspects of the theory one takes seriously,
Iser's theory collapses either into a monism of the text or a monism of the reader.

   The third problem identified by Culler concerns the ending of the story. Most
of the time stories of reading end happily. "Readers may be manipulated and
misled, but when they finish the book their experience turns into knowledge
. . . as though finishing the book took them outside the experience of reading
and gave them mastery of it" (p. 79). However, some critics—Harold Bloom,
Paul de Man, and Culler himself—find these optimistic endings questionable,
and prefer instead stories that stress the impossibility of reading. If, as de Man
says, rhetoric puts "an insurmountable obstacle in the way of any reading or
understanding," then the reader "may be placed in impossible situations where
there is no happy issue, but only the possibility of playing out the roles dramatized in the text" (Culler, p. 81).

   Such have been the predominant preoccupations of reader-response criticism
during the past decade and a half. Before indicating how feminist critics could
affect the conversation, let me consider an objection. A recent and influential
essay by Elaine Showalter suggests that we should not enter the conversation at
all. She observes that during its early phases, the principal mode of feminist criticism was "feminist critique," which was counter-ideological in intent and concerned with the feminist as *reader*. Happily, we have outgrown this necessary but
theoretically unpromising approach. Today, the dominant mode of feminist criticism is "gynocritics," the study of woman as *writer*, of the "history, styles,
themes, genres, and structures of writing by women; the psychodynamics of female creativity; the trajectory of the individual or collective female career; and
the evolution and laws of a female literary tradition." The shift from "feminist
critique" to "gynocritics"—from emphasis on woman as reader to emphasis on

woman as writer—has put us in the position of developing a feminist criticism that is "genuinely woman-centered, independent, and intellectually coherent."

> To see women's writing as our primary subject forces us to make the leap to a new conceptual vantage point and to redefine the nature of the theoretical problem before us. It is no longer the ideological dilemma of reconciling revisionary pluralisms but the essential question of difference. How can we constitute women as a distinct literary group? What is the *difference* of women's writing?[9]

But why should the activity of the woman writer be more conducive to theory than the activity of the woman reader is? If it is possible to formulate a basic conceptual framework for disclosing the "difference" of women's writing, surely it is no less possible to do so for women's reading. The same difference, be it linguistic, biological, psychological, or cultural, should apply in either case. In addition, what Showalter calls "gynocritics" is in fact constituted by feminist *criticism*—that is, *readings*—of female texts. Thus, the relevant distinction is not between woman as reader and woman as writer, but between feminist readings of male texts and feminist readings of female texts, and there is no reason why the former could not be as theoretically coherent (or irreducibly pluralistic) as the latter.

On the other hand, there are good reasons for feminist criticism to engage reader-response criticism. Both dispute the fetishized art object, the "Verbal Icon," of New Criticism, and both seek to dispel the objectivist illusion that buttresses the authority of the dominant critical tradition. Feminist criticism can have considerable impact on reader-response criticism, since, as Culler has noticed, it is but a small step from the thesis that the reader is an active producer of meaning to the recognition that there are many different kinds of readers, and that women—because of their numbers if because of nothing else—constitute an essential class. Reader-response critics cannot take refuge in the objectivity of the text, or even in the idea that a gender-neutral criticism is possible. Today they can continue to ignore the implications of feminist criticism only at the cost of incoherence or intellectual dishonesty.

It is equally true that feminist critics need to question their allegiance to text- and author-centered paradigms of criticism. Feminist criticism, we should remember, is a mode of *praxis*. The point is not merely to interpret literature in various ways; the point is to *change the world*. We cannot afford to ignore the activity of reading, for it is here that literature is realized as *praxis*. Literature acts on the world by acting on its readers.

To return to our earlier question: What will happen to reader-response criticism if feminists enter the conversation? It is useful to recall the contrast between Booth's story and those of Malcolm X and Virginia Woolf. Like Booth's story, the "stories of reading" that currently make up reader-response theory are mythically abstract, and appear, from a different vantage point, to be by and about readers who are fantastically privileged. Booth's story had a happy ending; Malcolm's and Mary's did not. For Mary, reading meant encountering a tissue of lies and silences; for Malcolm it meant the verification of Elijah Muhammad's shocking doctrines.

Two factors—gender and politics—which are suppressed in the dominant models of reading gain prominence with the advent of a feminist perspective. The feminist story will have *at least* two chapters: one concerned with feminist readings of male texts, and another with feminist readings of female texts. In addition, in this story, gender will have a prominent role as the locus of political struggle. The story will speak of the difference between men and women, of the way the experience and perspective of women have been systematically and fall-aciously assimilated into the generic masculine, and of the need to correct this error. Finally, it will identify literature—the activities of reading and writing—as an important arena of political struggle, a crucial component of the project of interpreting the world in order to change it.

Feminist criticism does not approach reader-response criticism without pre-conceptions. Actually, feminist criticism has always included substantial reader-centered interests. In the next two sections of this paper, I will review these interests, first with respect to male texts, then with respect to female texts. In the process, I will uncover some of the issues that might be addressed and clari-fied by a feminist theory of reading.

THE FEMALE READER AND THE LITERARY CANON

Although reader-response critics propose different and often conflicting models, by and large the emphasis is on features of the process of reading that do not vary with the nature of the reading material. The feminist entry into the conversation brings the nature of the text back into the foreground. For feminists, the ques-tion of *how* we read is inextricably linked with the question of *what* we read. More specifically, the feminist inquiry into the activity of reading begins with the realization that the literary canon is androcentric, and that this has a profoundly damaging effect on women readers. The documentation of this realization was one of the earliest tasks undertaken by feminist critics. Elaine Showalter's 1971 critique of the literary curriculum is exemplary of this work.

> [In her freshman year a female student] . . . might be assigned an anthology of essays, perhaps such as *The Responsible Man,* . . . or *Conditions of Man,* or *Man in Crisis,* or again, *Representative Man: Cult Heroes of Our Time,* in which thirty-three men represent such categories of heroism as the writer, the poet, the dramatist, the artist, and the guru, and the only two women included are the actress Elizabeth Taylor, and the existential Heroine Jacqueline Onassis.
>
> Perhaps the student would read a collection of stories like *The Young Man in American Literature: The Initiation Theme,* or sociological literature like *The Black Man and the Promise of America.* In a more orthodox literary program she might study eternally relevant classics, such as *Oedipus;* as a professor re-marked in a recent issue of *College English,* all of us want to kill our fathers and marry our mothers. And whatever else she might read, she would inev-itably arrive at the favorite book of all Freshman English courses, the classic of adolescent rebellion, *The Portrait of the Artist as a Young Man.*
>
> By the end of her freshman year, a woman student would have learned something about intellectual neutrality; she would be learning, in fact, how

to think like a man. And so she would go on, increasingly with male professors to guide her.[10]

The more personal accounts of other critics reinforce Showalter's critique.

> The first result of my reading was a feeling that male characters were at the very least more interesting than women to the authors who invented them. Thus if, reading their books as it seemed their authors intended them, I naively identified with a character, I repeatedly chose men; I would rather have been Hamlet than Ophelia, Tom Jones instead of Sophia Western, and, perhaps, despite Dostoevsky's intention, Raskolnikov not Sonia.
>
> More peculiar perhaps, but sadly unsurprising, were the assessments I accepted about fictional women. For example, I quickly learned that power was unfeminine and powerful women were, quite literally, monstrous. . . . Bitches all, they must be eliminated, reformed, or at the very least, condemned. . . . Those rare women who are shown in fiction as both powerful and, in some sense, admirable are such because their power is based, if not on beauty, then at least on sexuality.[11]

For a woman, then, books do not necessarily spell salvation. In fact, a literary education may very well cause her grave psychic damage: schizophrenia "is the bizarre but logical conclusion of our education. Imagining myself male, I attempted to create myself male. Although I knew the case was otherwise, it seemed I could do nothing to make this other critically real."[12]

To put the matter theoretically, androcentric literature structures the reading experience differently depending on the gender of the reader. For the male reader, the text serves as the meeting ground of the personal and the universal. Whether or not the text approximates the particularities of his own experience, he is invited to validate the equation of maleness with humanity. The male reader feels his affinity with the universal, with the paradigmatic human being, precisely because he is male. Consider the famous scene of Stephen's epiphany in *The Portrait of the Artist as a Young Man.*

> A girl stood before him in midstream, alone and still, gazing out to sea. She seemed like one whom magic had changed into the likeness of a strange and beautiful seabird. Her long slender bare legs were delicate as a crane's and pure save where an emerald trail of seaweed had fashioned itself as a sign upon the flesh. Her thighs, fuller and softhued as ivory, were bared almost to the hips, where the white fringes of her drawers were like feathering of soft white down. Her slateblue skirts were kilted boldly about her waist and dovetailed behind her. Her bosom was a bird's, soft and slight, slight and soft, as the breast of some dark plummaged dove. But her long fair hair was girlish: and touched with the wonder of mortal beauty, her face.[13]

A man reading this passage is invited to identify with Stephen, to feel "the riot in his blood," and, thus, to ratify the alleged universality of the experience. Whether or not the sight of a girl on the beach has ever provoked similar emotions in him, the male reader is invited to feel his *difference* (concretely, *from the girl*) and to equate that with the universal. Relevant here is Lévi-Strauss's theory that woman functions as currency exchanged between men. The woman in the text converts the text into a woman, and the circulation of this text/woman becomes the central ritual that establishes the bond between the author and his male readers.[14]

The same text affects a woman reader differently. Judith Fetterley gives the most explicit theory to date about the dynamics of the woman reader's encounter with androcentric literature. According to Fetterley, notwithstanding the prevalence of the castrating bitch stereotype, "the cultural reality is not the emasculation of men by women, but the *immasculation* of women by men. As readers and teachers and scholars, women are taught to think as men, to identify with a male point of view, and to accept as normal and legitimate a male system of values, one of whose central principles is misogyny."[15]

The process of immasculation does not impart virile power to the woman reader. On the contrary, it doubles her oppression. She suffers "not simply the powerlessness which derives from not seeing one's experience articulated, clarified, and legitimized in art, but more significantly, the powerlessness which results from the endless division of self against self, the consequence of the invocation to identify as male while being reminded that to be male—to be universal— . . . is to be *not female*."[16]

A woman reading Joyce's novel of artistic awakening, and in particular the passage quoted above, will, like her male counterpart, be invited to identify with Stephen and therefore to ratify the equation of maleness with the universal. Androcentric literature is all the more efficient as an instrument of sexual politics because it does not allow the woman reader to seek refuge in her difference. Instead, it draws her into a process that uses her against herself. It solicits her complicity in the elevation of male difference into universality and, accordingly, the denigration of female difference into otherness without reciprocity. To be sure, misogyny is abundant in the literary canon.[17] It is important, however, that Fetterley's argument can stand on a weaker premise. Androcentricity is a sufficient condition for the process of immasculation.

Feminist critics of male texts, from Kate Millett to Judith Fetterley, have worked under the sign of the "Resisting Reader." Their goal is to disrupt the process of immasculation by exposing it to consciousness, by disclosing the androcentricity of what has customarily passed for the universal. However, feminist criticism written under the aegis of the resisting reader leaves certain questions unanswered, questions that are becoming ripe for feminist analysis: Where does the text get its power to draw us into its designs? Why do some (not all) demonstrably sexist texts remain appealing even after they have been subjected to thorough feminist critique? The usual answer—that the power of male texts is the power of the false consciousness into which women as well as men have been socialized—oversimplifies the problem and prevents us from comprehending both the force of literature and the complexity of our responses to it.

Fredric Jameson advances a thesis that seems to me to be a good starting point for the feminist reconsideration of male texts: "The effectively ideological is also at the same time necessarily utopian."[18] This thesis implies that the male text draws its power over the female reader from authentic desires, which it rouses and then harnesses to the process of immasculation.

A concrete example is in order. Consider Lawrence's *Women in Love*, and for the sake of simplicity, concentrate on Birkin and Ursula. Simone de Beauvoir and Kate Millet have convinced me that this novel is sexist. Why does it remain appealing to me? Jameson's thesis prompts me to answer this question by examining how the text plays not only on my false consciousness but also on my authentic liberatory aspirations—that is to say, on the very impulses that drew me to the feminist movement.

The trick of role reversal comes in handy here. If we reverse the roles of Birkin and Ursula, the ideological components (or at least the most egregious of these, e.g., the analogy between women and horses) stand out as absurdities. Now, if we delete these absurd components while keeping the roles reversed, we have left the story of a woman struggling to combine her passionate desire for autonomous conscious being with an equally passionate desire for love and for other human bonds. This residual story is not far from one we would welcome as expressive of a feminist sensibility. Interestingly enough, it also intimates a novel Lawrence might have written, namely, the proper sequel to *The Rainbow*.

My affective response to the novel Lawrence did write is bifurcated. On the one hand, because I am a woman, I am implicated in the representation of Ursula and in the destiny Lawrence has prepared for her: man is the son of god, but woman is the daughter of man. Her vocation is to witness his transcendence in rapt silence. On the other hand, Fetterley is correct that I am also induced to identify with Birkin, and in so doing, I am drawn into complicity with the reduction of Ursula, and therefore of myself, to the role of the other.

However, the process of immasculation is more complicated than Fetterley allows. When I identify with Birkin, I unconsciously perform the two-stage rereading described above. I reverse the roles of Birkin and Ursula and I suppress the obviously ideological components that in the process show up as absurdities. The identification with Birkin is emotionally effective because, stripped of its patriarchal trappings, Birkin's struggle and his utopian vision conform to my own. To the extent that I perform this feminist rereading *unconsciously*, I am captivated by the text. The stronger my desire for autonomous selfhood and for love, the stronger my identification with Birkin, and the more intense the experience of bifurcation characteristic of the process of immasculation.

The full argument is beyond the scope of this essay. My point is that *certain* (not all) male texts merit a dual hermeneutic: a negative hermeneutic that discloses their complicity with patriarchal ideology, and a positive hermeneutic that recuperates the utopian moment—the authentic kernel—from which they draw a significant portion of their emotional power.[19]

READING WOMEN'S WRITING

Showalter is correct that feminist criticism has shifted emphasis in recent years from "critique" (primarily) of male texts to "gynocritics," or the study of women's writing. Of course, it is worth remembering that the latter has always been on the feminist agenda. *Sexual Politics*, for example, contains not only the critique of Lawrence, Miller, and Mailer that won Millett such notoriety, but also her memorable rereading of *Villette*.[20] It is equally true that interest in women's writing has not entirely supplanted the critical study of patriarchal texts. In a sense "critique" has provided the bridge from the study of male texts to the study of female texts. As feminist criticism shifted from the first to the second, "feminist critique" turned its attention from androcentric texts per se to the androcentric critical strategies that pushed women's writing to the margins of the literary canon. The earliest examples of this genre (for instance, Showalter's "The Double Critical Standard," and Carol Ohmann's "Emily Brontë in the Hands of Male Critics") were concerned primarily with describing and documenting the prejudice against women writers that clouded the judgment of well-placed readers, that is, reviewers and critics.[21] Today we have more sophisticated and more comprehensive analyses of the androcentric critical tradition.

One of the most cogent of these is Nina Baym's analysis of American literature.[22] Baym observes that, as late as 1977, the American canon of major writers did not include a single woman novelist. And yet, in terms of numbers and commercial success, women novelists have probably dominated American literature since the middle of the nineteenth century. How to explain this anomaly?

One explanation is simple bias of the sort documented by Showalter, Ohmann, and others. A second is that women writers lived and worked under social conditions that were not particularly conducive to the production of "excellent" literature: "There tended to be a sort of immediacy in the ambitions of literary women leading them to professionalism rather than artistry, by choice as well as by social pressure and opportunity."[23] Baym adduces a third, more subtle, and perhaps more important reason. There are, she argues, "gender-related restrictions that do not arise out of the cultural realities contemporary with the writing woman, but out of later critical theories . . . which impose their concerns anachronistically, after the fact, on an earlier period."[24] If one reads the critics most instrumental in forming the current theories about American literature (Matthiessen, Chase, Feidelson, Trilling, etc.), one finds that the theoretical model for the canonical American novel is the "melodrama of beset manhood." To accept this model is also to accept as a consequence the exclusion from the canon of "melodramas of beset womanhood," as well as virtually all fiction centering on the experience of women.[25]

The deep symbiotic relationship between the androcentric canon and androcentric modes of reading is well summarized by Kolodny.

> *Insofar as we are taught to read, what we engage are not texts, but paradigms.* . . . Insofar as literature is itself a social institution, so, too, reading is a highly socialized—or learned—activity. . . . We read well, and with pleasure, what we already know how to read; and what we know how to read is to a large extent dependent on what we have already read [works from which we have developed our expectations and learned our interpretative strategies]. What we then choose to read—and, by extension, teach and thereby "canonize"— usually follows upon our previous reading.[26]

We are caught, in other words, in a rather vicious circle. An androcentric canon generates androcentric interpretive strategies, which in turn favor the canonization of androcentric texts and the marginalization of gynocentric ones. To break this cycle, feminist critics must fight on two fronts: for the revision of the canon to include a significant body of works by women, and for the development of the reading strategies consonant with the concerns, experiences, and formal devices that constitute these texts. Of course, to succeed, we also need a community of women readers who are qualified by experience, commitment, and training, and who will enlist the personal and institutional resources at their disposal in the struggle.[27]

The critique of androcentric reading strategies is essential, for it opens up some ideological space for the recuperation of women's writing. Turning now to this project, we observe, first, that a large volume of work has been done, and, second, that this endeavor is coming to look even more complicated and more diverse than the criticism of male texts. Certainly, it is impossible in the space of a few pages to do justice to the wide range of concerns, strategies, and positions associated with feminist readings of female texts. Nevertheless, certain things can be said. For the remainder of this section, I focus on an exemplary essay: "Vesuvius at Home: The Power of Emily Dickinson," by Adrienne Rich.[28] My commentary anticipates the articulation of a paradigm that illuminates certain features of feminist readings of women's writing.

I am principally interested in the rhetoric of Rich's essay, for it represents an implicit commentary on the process of reading women's writing. Feminist readings of male texts are, as we have seen, primarily resisting. The reader assumes an adversarial or at least a detached attitude toward the material at hand. In the opening pages of her essay, Rich introduces three metaphors that proclaim a very different attitude toward her subject.

> The methods, the exclusions, of Emily Dickinson's existence could not have been my own; yet more and more, as a woman poet finding my own methods, I have come to understand her necessities, could have served as witness in her defense. (p. 158)

> I am traveling at the speed of time, along the Massachusetts Turnpike. . . . "Home is not where the heart is," she wrote in a letter, "but the house and adjacent buildings." . . . I am traveling at the speed of time, in the direction of the house and buildings. . . . For years, I have been not so much envisioning Emily Dickinson as trying to visit, to enter her mind through her poems and letters, and through my own intimations of what it could have meant to be one of the two mid-nineteenth-century American geniuses, and a woman, living in Amherst, Massachusetts. (pp. 158–59)

> For months, for most of my life, I have been hovering like an insect against the screens of an existence which inhabited Amherst, Massachusetts between 1830 and 1886 (p. 158) . . . Here [in Dickinson's bedroom] I become again, an insect, vibrating at the frames of windows, clinging to the panes of glass, trying to connect (p. 161)

A commentary on the process of reading is carried on silently and unobtrusively through the use of these metaphors. The first is a judicial metaphor: the feminist reader speaks as a witness in defense of the woman writer. Here we see clearly that gender is crucial. The feminist reader takes the part of the woman writer against patriarchal misreadings that trivialize or distort her work.[29] The second metaphor refers to a principal tenet of feminist criticism: a literary work cannot be understood apart from the social, historical, and cultural context within which it was written. As if to acquiesce to the condition Dickinson had imposed on her friends, Rich travels through space and time to visit the poet on her own *premises*. She goes to Amherst, to the house where Dickinson lived. She rings the bell, she goes in, then upstairs, then into the bedroom that had been "freedom" for the poet. Her destination, ultimately, is Dickinson's mind. But it is not enough to read the poet's poems and letters. To reach her heart and mind, one must take a detour through "the house and adjacent buildings."

Why did Dickinson go into seclusion? Why did she write poems she would not publish? What mean these poems about queens, volcanoes, deserts, eternity, passion, suicide, wild beasts, rape, power, madness, the daemon, the grave? For Rich, these are related questions. The revisionary re-reading of Dickinson's work is of a piece with the revisionary re-reading of her life. "I have a notion genius knows itself; that Dickinson chose her seclusion, knowing what she needed. . . . She carefully selected her society and controlled the disposal of her time. . . . Given her vocation, she was neither eccentric nor quaint; she was determined to survive, to use her powers, to practice necessary economies" (p. 160).

> To write [the poetry that she needed to write] she had to enter chambers of the self in which
>> Ourself, concealed—
>> Should startle most—
> and to relinquish control there, to take those risks, she had to create a relationship to the outer world where she could feel in control. (p. 175)

The metaphor of visiting points to another feature of feminist readings of women's writing, namely, the tendency to construe the text not as an object, but as the manifestation of the subjectivity of the absent author—the "voice" of another woman. Rich is not content to revel in the textuality of Dickinson's poems and letters. For her, these are doorways to the "mind" of a "woman of genius." Rich deploys her imagination and her considerable rhetorical skill to evoke "the figure of powerful will" who lives at the heart of the text. To read Dickinson, then, is to try to visit with her, to hear her voice, to make her live *in* oneself, and to feel her impressive "personal dimensions."[30]

At the same time, Rich is keenly aware that visiting with Dickinson is *only* a metaphor for reading her poetry, and an inaccurate one at that. She signals this awareness with the third metaphor. It is no longer possible to visit with Dickinson; one can only enter her mind through her poems and letters as one can enter her house—through the back door out of which her coffin was carried. In reading, one encounters only a text, the trail of an absent author. Upstairs, at last, in the very room where Dickinson exercised her astonishing craft, Rich finds herself again "an insect, vibrating at the frames of windows, clinging to panes of glass, trying to connect." But though "the scent is very powerful," Dickinson herself is absent.

Perhaps the most obvious rhetorical device employed by Rich in this eesay, more obvious even than her striking metaphors, is her use of the personal voice. Her approach to Dickinson is self-consciously and unabashedly subjective. She clearly describes her point of view—what she saw as she drove across the Connecticut Valley toward Amherst (ARCO stations, McDonald's, shopping plazas, as well as "light-green spring softening the hills, dogwood and wild fruit trees blossoming in the hollows"), and what she thought about (the history of the valley, "scene of Indian uprisings, religious revivals, spiritual confrontations, the blazing-up of the lunatic fringe of the Puritan coal," and her memories of college weekends in Amherst). Some elements of her perspective—ARCO and McDonald's—would have been alien to Dickinson; others—the sight of dogwood and wild fruit trees in the spring, and most of all, the experience of being a woman poet in a patriarchal culture—would establish their affinity.

Rich's metaphors together with her use of the personal voice indicate some key issues underlying feminist readings of female texts. On the one hand, reading is necessarily subjective. On the other hand, it must not be wholly so. One must respect the autonomy of the text. The reader is a visitor and, as such, must observe the necessary courtesies. She must avoid unwarranted intrusions—she must be careful not to appropriate what belongs to her host, not to impose herself on the other woman. Furthermore, reading is at once an intersubjective encounter and something less than that. In reading Dickinson, Rich seeks to enter her mind, to feel her presence. But the text is a screen, an inanimate object. Its subjectivity is only a projection of the subjectivity of the reader.

Rich suggests the central motivation, the regulative ideal, that shapes the feminist reader's approach to these issues. If feminist readings of male texts are motivated by the need to disrupt the process of immasculation, feminist readings of female texts are motivated by the need "to connect," to recuperate, or to formulate—they come to the same thing—the context, the tradition, that would link women writers to one another, to women readers and critics, and to the larger community of women. Of course, the recuperation of such a context is a necessary basis for the nonrepressive integration of women's point of view and culture into the study of a Humanities that is worthy of its name.[31]

FEMINIST MODELS OF READING: A SUMMARY

As I noted in the second section, mainstream reader-response theory is preoccupied with two closely related questions: (1) Does the text manipulate the reader, or does the reader manipulate the text to produce the meaning that suits her own interests? and (2) What is "in" the text? How can we distinguish what it supplies from what the reader supplies? Both of these questions refer to the subject–object relation that is established between reader and text during the process of reading. A feminist theory of reading also elaborates this relationship, but for feminists, gender—the gender inscribed in the text as well as the gender of the reader—is crucial. Hence, the feminist story has two chapters, one concerned with male texts and the other with female texts.

The focus of the first chapter is the experience of the woman reader. What do male texts *do* to her? The feminist story takes the subject–object relation of reading through three moments. The phrasing of the basic question signals the first moment. Control is conferred on the text: the woman reader is immasculated by the text. The feminist story fits well at this point in Iser's framework.

Feminists insist that the androcentricity of the text and its damaging effects on women readers are not figments of their imagination. These are implicit in the "schematized aspects" of the text. The second movement, which is similarly consonant with the plot of Iser's story, involves the recognition of the crucial role played by the subjectivity of the woman reader. Without her, the text is *no-thing*. The process of immasculation is latent in the text, but it finds its actualization only through the reader's activity. In effect, the woman reader is the agent of her own immasculation.[32]

Here we seem to have a corroboration of Culler's contention that dualistic models of reading inevitably disintegrate into one of two monisms. Either the text (and, by implication, the author) or the woman reader is responsible for the process of immasculation. The third moment of the subject–object relation— ushered in by the transfiguration of the heroine into a feminist—breaks through this dilemma. The woman reader, now a feminist, embarks on a critical analysis of the reading process, and she realizes that the text has power to structure her experience. Without androcentric texts she will not suffer immasculation. However, her recognition of the power of the text is matched by her awareness of her essential role in the process of reading. Without her, the text is nothing—it is inert and harmless. The advent of feminist consciousness and the accompanying commitment to emancipatory *praxis* reconstitutes the subject–object relationship within a dialectical rather than a dualistic framework, thus averting the impasse described by Culler between the "dualism of narrative" and the "monism of theory." In the feminist story, the breakdown of Iser's dualism does not indicate a mistake or an irreducible impasse, but the necessity of *choosing* between two modes of reading. The reader can submit to the power of the text, or she can take control of the reading experience. The recognition of the existence of a choice suddenly makes visible the normative dimension of the feminist story: She *should* choose the second alternative.

But what does it mean for a reader to take control of the reading experience? First of all, she must do so without forgetting the androcentricity of the text or its power to structure her experience. In addition, the reader taking control of the text is not, as in Iser's model, simply a matter of selecting among the concretizations allowed by the text. Recall that a crucial feature of the process of immasculation is the woman reader's bifurcated response. She reads the text both as a man and as a woman. But in either case, the result is the same: she confirms her position as other. Taking control of the reading experience means reading the text as it was *not* meant to be read, in fact, reading it against itself. Specifically, one must identify the nature of the choices proffered by the text and, equally important, what the text precludes—namely, the possibility of reading as a woman *without* putting one's self in the position of the other, of reading so as to affirm womanhood as another, equally valid, paradigm of human existence.

All this is easier said than done. It is important to realize that reading a male text, no matter how virulently misogynous, could do little damage if it were an isolated event. The problem is that within patriarchal culture, the experience of immasculation is paradigmatic of women's encounters with the dominant literary and critical traditions. A feminist cannot simply refuse to read patriarchal texts, for they are everywhere, and they condition her participation in the literary and critical enterprise. In fact, by the time she becomes a feminist critic, a woman has already read numerous male texts—in particular, the most authoritative texts of the literary and critical canons. She has introjected not only androcentric texts, but also androcentric reading strategies and values. By the time she becomes a feminist, the bifurcated response characteristic of immasculation has become second nature to her. The feminist story stresses that patriarchal constructs have objective as well as subjective reality; they are inside and outside the text, inside and outside the reader.

The pervasiveness of androcentricity drives feminist theory beyond the individualistic models of Iser and of most reader-response critics. The feminist reader agrees with Stanley Fish that the production of the meaning of a text is mediated by the interpretive community in which the activity of reading is situated: the meaning of the text depends on the interpretive strategy one applies to it, and the choice of strategy is regulated (explicitly or implicitly) by the canons of acceptability that govern the interpretive community.[33] However, unlike Fish, the feminist reader is also aware that the ruling interpretive communities are androcentric, and that this androcentricity is deeply etched in the strategies and modes of thought that have been introjected by all readers, women as well as men.

Because patriarchal constructs have psychological correlates, taking control of the reading process means taking control of one's reactions and inclinations. Thus, a feminist reading—actually a re-reading—is a kind of therapeutic analysis. The reader recalls and examines how she would "naturally" read a male text in order to understand and therefore undermine the subjective predispositions that had rendered her vulnerable to its designs. Beyond this, the pervasiveness of immasculation necessitates a collective remedy. The feminist reader hopes that other women will recognize themselves in her story, and join her in her struggle to transform the culture.[34]

"Feminism affirms women's point of view by revealing, criticizing and examining its impossibility."[35] Had we nothing but male texts, this sentence from Catharine MacKinnon's brilliant essay on jurisprudence could serve as the definition of the project of the feminist reader. The significant body of literature written by women presents feminist critics with another, more heartwarming, task: that of recovering, articulating, and elaborating positive expressions of women's point of view, of celebrating the survival of this point of view in spite of the formidable forces that have been ranged against it.

The shift to women's writing brings with it a shift in emphasis from the negative hermeneutic of ideological unmasking to a positive hermeneutic whose aim is the recovery and cultivation of women's culture. As Showalter has noted, feminist criticism of women's writing proposes to articulate woman's difference: What does it mean for a woman to express herself in writing? How does a woman write as a woman? It is a central contention of this essay that feminist criticism should also inquire into the correlative process of *reading:* What does it mean for a woman to read without condemning herself to the position of other? What does it mean for a woman, reading as a woman, to read literature written by a woman writing as a woman?[36]

The Adrienne Rich essay discussed in the preceding section illustrates a contrast between feminist readings of male texts and feminist readings of female

texts. In the former, the object of the critique, whether it is regarded as an enemy or as symptom of a malignant condition, is the text itself, *not* the reputation
or the character of the author.[37] This impersonal approach contrasts sharply with
the strong personal interest in Dickinson exhibited by Rich. Furthermore, it is
not merely a question of friendliness toward the text. Rich's reading aims beyond
"the unfolding of the text as a living event," the goal of aesthetic reading set by
Iser. Much of the rhetorical energy of Rich's essay is directed toward evoking the
personality of Dickinson, toward making *her* live as the substantial, palpable
presence animating her works.

Unlike the first chapter of the feminist story of reading, which is centered
around a single heroine—the woman reader battling her way out of a maze of
patriarchal constructs—the second chapter features two protagonists—the
woman reader and the woman writer—in the context of two settings. The first
setting is judicial: one woman is standing witness in defense of the other; the
second is dialogic: the two women are engaged in intimate conversation. The
judicial setting points to the larger political and cultural dimension of the project
of the feminist reader. Feminist critics may well say with Harold Bloom that
reading always involves the "art of defensive warfare."[38] What they mean by this,
however, would not be Bloom's individualistic, agonistic encounter between
"strong poet" and "strong reader," but something more akin to "class struggle."
Whether concerned with male or female texts, feminist criticism is situated in
the larger struggle against patriarchy.

The importance of this battle cannot be overestimated. However, feminist
readings of women's writing opens up space for another, equally important, critical project, namely, the articulation of a model of reading that is centered on a
female paradigm. While it is still too early to present a full-blown theory, the
dialogic aspect of the relationship between the feminist reader and the woman
writer suggests the direction that such a theory might take. As in all stories of
reading, the drama revolves around the subject–object relationship between text
and reader. The feminist story—exemplified by the Adrienne Rich essay discussed earlier—features an intersubjective construction of this relationship. The
reader encounters not simply a text, but a "subjectified object": the "heart and
mind" of another woman. She comes into close contact with an interiority—a
power, a creativity, a suffering, a vision—that is *not* identical with her own. The
feminist interest in construing readings as an intersubjective encounter suggests
an affinity with Poulet's (rather than Iser's) theory, and, as in Poulet's model, the
subject of the literary work is its author, *not* the reader: "A book is not only a
book; it is a means by which an author actually preserves [her] ideas, [her] feelings, [her] modes of dreaming and living. It is a means of saving [her] identity
from death. . . . To understand a literary work, then, is to let the individual who
wrote it reveal [herself] to us *in* us."[39]

For all this initial agreement, however, the dialogic relationship the feminist
reader establishes with the female subjectivity brought to life in the process of
reading is finally at odds with Poulet's model. For the interiorized author is
"alien" to Poulet's reader. When he reads, he delivers himself "bound hand and
foot, to the omnipotence of fiction." He becomes the "prey" of what he reads.
"There is no escaping this takeover." His consciousness is "invaded," "an-
nexed," "usurped." He is "dispossessed" of his rightful place on the "center
stage" of his own mind. In the final analysis, the process of reading leaves room

for only one subjectivity. The work becomes "a sort of human being" at "the expense of the reader whose life it suspends." [40] It is significant that the metaphors of mastery and submission, of violation and control, so prominent in Poulet's essay, are entirely absent in Rich's essay of Dickinson. In the paradigm of reading implicit in her essay, the dialectic of control (which shapes feminist readings of male texts) gives way to the dialectic of communication. For Rich, reading is a matter of "trying to connect" with the existence behind the text.

The dialectic also has three moments. The first involves the recognition that genuine intersubjective communication demands the duality of reader and author (the subject of the work). Because reading removes the barrier between subject and object, the division takes place *within* the reader. Reading induces a doubling of the reader's subjectivity, so that one can be placed at the disposal of the text while the other remains with the reader. Now, this doubling presents a problem, for in fact there is only one subject present—the reader. The text—the words on the page—has been written by the writer, but meaning is always a matter of interpretation. The subjectivity roused to life by reading, while it may be attributed to the author, is nevertheless not a seperate subjectivity but a projection of the subjectivity of the reader. How can the duality of subjects be maintained in the absence of the author? In an actual conversation, the presence of another person preserves the duality. Because each party must assimilate and interpret the utterances of the other, we still have the introjection of the subject–object division, as well as the possibility of hearing only what one wants to hear. But in a real conversation, the other person can interrupt, object to an erroneous interpretation, provide further explanations, change her mind, change the topic, or cut off conversation altogether. In reading, there are no comparable safeguards against the appropriation of the text by the reader. This is the second moment of the dialectic—the recognition that reading is necessarily subjective. The need to keep it from being *totally* subjective ushers in the third moment of the dialectic.

In the feminist story, the key to the problem is the awareness of the double context of reading and writing. Rich's essay is wonderfully illustrative. To avoid imposing an alien perspective on Dickinson's poetry, Rich informs her reading with the knowledge of the circumstances in which Dickinson lived and worked. She repeatedly reminds herself and her readers that Dickinson must be read in light of her *own* premises, that the "exclusions" and "necessities" she endured, and, therefore, her choices, were conditioned by her own world. At the same time, Rich's sensitivity to the context of writing is matched by her sensitivity to the context of reading. She makes it clear throughout the essay that her reading of Dickinson is necessarily shaped by her experience and interests as a feminist poet living in the twentieth-century United States. The reader also has her own premises. To forget these is to run the risk of imposing them surreptitiously on the author.

To recapitulate, the first moment of the dialectic of reading is marked by the recognition of the necessary duality of subjects; the second, by the realization that this duality is threatened by the author's absence. In the third moment, the duality of subjects is referred to the duality of contexts. Reading becomes a mediation between author and reader, between the context of writings and the context of reading.

Although feminists have always believed that objectivity is an illusion, Rich's essay is the only one, as far as I know, to exhibit through its rhetoric the necessary subjectivity of reading coupled with the equally necessary commitment to reading the text as it was meant to be read.[41] The third moment of the dialectic is apparent in Rich's weaving—not blending—of the context of writing and the context of reading, the perspective of the author and that of the reader. The central rhetorical device effecting this mediation is her use of the personal voice. As in most critical essays, Rich alternates quotes from the texts in question with her own commentary, but her use of the personal voice makes a difference. In her hands, this rhetorical strategy serves two purposes. First, it serves as a reminder that her interpretation is informed by her own perspective. Second, it signifies her tactful approach to Dickinson; the personal voice serves as a gesture warding off any inclination to appropriate the authority of the text as a warrant for the validity of the interpretation. Because the interpretation is presented as an *interpretation*, its claim to validity rests on the cogency of the supporting arguments, *not* on the authorization of the text.

Rich accomplishes even more than this. She reaches out to Dickinson not by identifying with her, but by establishing their affinity. Both are American, both are women poets in a patriarchal culture. By playing this affinity against the differences, she produces a context that incorporates both reader and writer. In turn, this common ground becomes the basis for drawing the connections that, in her view, constitute the proper goal of reading.

One might ask: Is there something distinctively female (rather than "merely feminist") in this dialogic model? While it is difficult to specify what "distinctively female" might mean, there are currently very interesting speculations about differences in the way males and females conceive of themselves and of their relations with others. The works of Jean Baker Miller, Nancy Chodorow, and Carol Gilligan suggest that men define themselves through individuation and separation from others, while women have more flexible ego boundaries and define and experience themselves in terms of their affiliations and relationships with others.[42] Men value autonomy, and they think of their interactions with others principally in terms of procedures for arbitrating conflicts between individual rights. Women, on the other hand, value relationships, and they are most concerned in their dealings with others to negotiate between opposing needs so that the relationship can be maintained. This difference is consistent with the difference between mainstream models of reading and the dialogic model I am proposing for feminist readings of women's writing. Mainstream reader-response theories are preoccupied with issues of control and partition—how to distinguish the contribution of the author/text from the contribution of the reader. In the dialectic of communication informing the relationship between the feminist reader and the female author/text, the central issue is not of control or partition, but of managing the contradictory implications of the desire for relationship (one must maintain a minimal distance from the other) and the desire for intimacy, up to and including a symbiotic merger with the other. The problematic is defined by the drive "to connect," rather than that which is implicit in the mainstream preoccupation with partition and control—namely, the drive to get it right. It could also be argued that Poulet's model represents reading as an intimate, intersubjective encounter. However, it is significant that in his model, the prospect of close rapport with another provokes both excitement and anxiety. Intimacy, while desired, is also viewed as a threat to one's integrity. For Rich, on the other hand, the prospect of merging with another is problematical, but not threatening.

Let me end with a word about endings. Dialectical stories look forward to optimistic endings. Mine is no exception. In the first chapter the woman reader becomes a feminist, and in the end she succeeds in extricating herself from the androcentric logic of the literary and critical canons. In the second chapter the feminist reader succeeds in effecting a mediation between her perspective and that of the writer. These "victories" are part of the project of producing women's culture and literary tradition, which in turn is part of the project of overcoming patriarchy. It is in the nature of people working for revolutionary change to be optimistic about the prospect of redirecting the future.

Culler observes that optimistic endings have been challenged (successfully, he thinks) by deconstruction, a method radically at odds with the dialectic. It is worth noting that there is a deconstructive moment in Rich's reading of Dickinson. Recall her third metaphor: the reader is an insect "vibrating the frames of windows, clinging to the panes of glass, trying to connect." The suggestion of futility is unmistakable. At best, Rich's interpretation of Dickinson might be considered as a "strong misreading" whose value is in its capacity to provoke other misreadings.

We might say this—but must we? To answer this question, we must ask another: What is at stake in the proposition that reading is impossible? For one thing, if reading is impossible, then there is no way of deciding the validity of an interpretation—the very notion of validity becomes problematical. Certainly it is useful to be reminded that the validity of an interpretation cannot be decided by appealing to what the author "intended," to what is "in" the text, or to what is "in" the experience of the reader. However, there is another approach to the problem of validation, one that is consonant with the dialogic model of reading described above. We can think of validity not as a property inherent in an interpretation, but rather as a *claim* implicit in the *act* of propounding an interpretation. An interpretation, then, is not valid or invalid in itself. Its validity is contingent on the agreement of others. In this view, Rich's interpretation of Dickinson, which is frankly acknowledged as conditioned by her own experience as a twentieth-century feminist poet, is not necessarily a misreading. In advancing her interpretation, Rich implicitly claims its validity. That is to say, to read a text and then to write about it is to seek to connect not only with the author of the original text, but also with a community of readers. To the extent that she succeeds and to the extent that the community is potentially all-embracing, her interpretation has that degree of validity.[43]

Feminist reading and writing alike are grounded in the interest of producing a community of feminist readers and writers, and in the hope that ultimately this community will expand to include everyone. Of course, this project may fail. The feminist story may yet end with the recognition of the impossibility of reading. But this remains to be seen. At this stage I think it behooves us to *choose* the dialectical over the deconstructive plot. It is dangerous for feminists to be overly enamored with the theme of impossibility. Instead, we should strive to redeem the claim that it is possible for a woman, reading as a woman, to read literature written by women, for this is essential if we are to make the literary enterprise into a means for building and maintaining connections among women.

NOTES

I would like to acknowledge my debt to David Schweickart for the substantial editorial work he did on this chapter.

1. Wayne Booth, Presidential Address, "Arts and Scandals 1982," *PMLA* 98 (1983): 313. Subsequent references to this essay are cited parenthetically in the text.

2. *The Autobiography of Malcolm X*, written with Alex Haley (New York: Grover Press, 1964), p. 173. (Subsequent references are cited parenthetically in the text.)

3. Virginia Woolf, *A Room of One's Own* (New York: Harcourt Brace Jovanovich, 1981). (Subsequent references are cited parenthetically in the text.)

4. Jonathan D. Culler, *On Deconstruction: Theory and Criticism after Structuralism* (Ithaca: Cornell University Press, 1982), p. 42. (Subsequent references are cited parenthetically in the text.) Wayne Booth's essay "Freedom of Interpretation: Bakhtin and the Challenge of Feminist Criticism," *Critical Inquiry* 9 (1982): 45–76, is another good omen of the impact of feminist thought on literary criticism.

5. David Bleich, *Subjective Criticism* (Baltimore: Johns Hopkins University Press, 1978), p. 112.

6. Georges Poulet, "Criticism and the Experience of Interiority," trans. Catherine and Richard Macksey, in *Reader-Response Criticism: From Formalism to Structuralism*, ed. Jane Tompkins (Baltimore: Johns Hopkins University Press, 1980) p. 43. Poulet's theory is not among those discussed by Culler. However, since he will be useful to us later, I mention him here.

7. This argument was advanced by Samuel Weber in "The Struggle for Control: Wolfgang Iser's Third Dimension," cited by Culler in *On Deconstruction*, p. 75.

8. Stanley E. Fish, "Why No One's Afraid of Wolfgang Iser," *Diacritics* 11 (1981): 7. Quoted by Culler in *On Deconstruction*, p. 75.

9. Elaine Showalter, "Feminist Criticism in the Wilderness," *Critical Inquiry* 8 (1981): 182–85. Showalter argues that if we see feminist critique (focused on the reader) as our primary critical project, we must be content with the "playful pluralism" proposed by Annette Kolodny: first because no single conceptual model can comprehend so eclectic and wide-ranging an enterprise, and second because "in the free play of the interpretive field, feminist critique can only compete with alternative readings, all of which have the built-in obsolescence of Buicks, cast away as newer readings take their place" (p. 182). Although Showalter does not support Wimsatt and Beardsley's proscription of the "affective fallacy," she nevertheless subscribes to the logic of their argument. Kolodny's "playful pluralism" is more benign than Wimsatt and Beardsley's dreaded "relativism," but no less fatal, in Showalter's view, to theoretical coherence.

10. Elaine Showalter, "Women and the Literary Curriculum," *College English* 32 (1971): 855. For an excellent example of recent work following in the spirit of Showalter's critique, see Paul Lauter, *Reconstructing American Literature* (Old Westbury, N.Y.: Feminist Press, 1983).

11. Lee Edwards, "Women, Energy, and *Middlemarch*," *Massachusetts Review* 13 (1972): 226.

12. Ibid.

13. James Joyce, *The Portrait of the Artist as a Young Man* (London: Jonathan Cape, 1916), p. 195.

14. See also Florence Howe's analysis of the same passage, "Feminism and Literature," in *Images of Women in Fiction: Feminist Perspectives*, ed. Susan Koppelman Cornillon (Bowling Green, Ohio: Bowling Green State University Press, 1972), pp. 262–63.

15. Judith Fetterley, *The Resisting Reader: A Feminist Approach to American Fiction* (Bloomington: Indiana University Press, 1978), p. xx. Although Fetterley's remarks refer specifically to American literature, they apply generally to the entire traditional canon.

16. Fetterley, *Resisting Reader*, p. xiii.

17. See Katharine M. Rogers, *The Troublesome Helpmate: A History of Misogyny in Literature* (Seattle: University of Washington Press, 1966).

18. Fredric Jameson, *The Political Unconscious: Narrative as a Socially Symbolic Act* (Ithaca: Cornell University Press, 1981), p. 286.

19. In *Woman and the Demon: The Life of a Victorian Myth* (Cambridge: Harvard University Press, 1982), Nina Auerbach employs a similar—though not identical—positive hermeneutic. She reviews the myths and images of women (as angels, demons, victims, whores, etc.) that feminist critics have "gleefully" unmasked as reflections and instruments of sexist ideology, and discovers in them an "unexpectedly empowering" mythos. Auerbach argues that the "most powerful, if least acknowledged creation [of the Victorian cultural imagination] is an explosively mobile, magic woman, who breaks the boundaries of family within which her society restricts her. The triumph of this overweening creature is a celebration of the corporate imagination that believed in her" (p. 1). See also idem, "Magi and Maidens: The Romance of the Victorian Freud," *Critical Inquiry* 8 (1981): 281–300. The tension between the positive and negative feminists hermeneutics is perhaps most apparent when one is dealing with the "classics." See, for example, Carol Thomas Neely, "Feminist Modes of Shakespeare Criticism: Compensatory, Justificatory, Transformational," *Women's Studies* 9 (1981): 3–15.

20. Kate Millett, *Sexual Politics* (New York: Avon Books, 1970).

21. Elaine Showalter, "The Double Critical Standard and the Feminine Novel," chap. 3 in *A Literature of Their Own: British Women Novelists from Brontë to Lessing* (Princeton: Princeton University Press, 1977), pp. 73–99; Carol Ohmann, "Emily Brontë in the Hands of Male Critics," *College English* 32 (1971): 906–13.

22. Nina Baym, "Melodramas of Beset Manhood: How Theories of American Fiction Exclude Women Authors," *American Quarterly* 33 (1981): 123–39.

23. Ibid., p. 125.

24. Ibid., p. 130. One of the founding works of American literature is "The Legend of Sleepy Hollow," about which Leslie Fiedler writes: "It is fitting that our first successful homegrown legend would memorialize, however playfully, the flight of the dreamer from the shrew" (*Love and Death in the American Novel* [New York: Criterion, 1960] p. xx).

25. Nina Baym's *Women's Fiction: A Guide to Novels by and about Women in America, 1820–1870* (Ithaca: Cornell University Press, 1978) provides a good survey of what has been excluded from the canon.

26. Annette Kolodny, "Dancing through the Minefield: Some Observations on the Theory, Practice, and Politics of a Feminist Literary Criticism," *Feminist Studies* 6 (1980): 10–12. Kolodny elaborates the same theme in "A Map for Rereading: Or, Gender and the Interpretation of Literary Texts," *New Literary History* 11 (1980): 451–67.

27. For an excellent account of the way in which the feminist "interpretive community" has changed literary and critical conventions, see Jean E. Kennard, "Convention Coverage, or How to Read Your Own Life," *New Literary History* 8 (1981): 69–88. The programs of the MLA Convention during the last twenty-five years offer more concrete evidence of the changes in the literary and critical canons, and of the ideological and political struggles effecting these changes.

28. In Adrienne Rich, *On Lies, Secrets, and Silence: Selected Prose, 1966–1978* (New York: W. W. Norton, 1979). (Subsequent references are cited parenthetically in the text.)

29. Susan Glaspell's story "A Jury of Her Peers" revolves around a variation of this judicial metaphor. The parable of reading implicit in this story has not been lost of feminist critics. Annette Kolodny, for example, discusses how it "explores the necessary gender marking which *must* constitute any definition of 'peers' in the complex process of unraveling truth or meaning." Although the story does not exclude male readers, it alerts us to the fact that "symbolic representations depend on a fund of shared recognitions and

potential references," and in general, "female meaning" is inaccessible to "male inter-pretation." "However inadvertently, [the male reader] is a *different kind* of reader and, . . . where women are concerned, he is often an inadequate reader" ("Map for Rereading," pp. 460–63).

30. There is a strong counter-tendency, inspired by French poststructuralism, which privileges the appreciation of textuality over the imaginative recovery of the woman writer as subject of the work. See, for example, Mary Jacobus, "Is There a Woman in This Text?" *New Literary History* 14 (1982): 117–41, especially the concluding paragraph. The last sentence of the essay underscores the controversy: "Perhaps the question that feminist critics should be asking is not 'Is there a woman in this text?' but rather: 'Is there a text in this woman?'"

31. I must stress that although Rich's essay presents a significant paradigm of feminist readings of women's writing, it is not the only such paradigm. An alternative is proposed by Caren Greenberg, "Reading Reading: Echo's Abduction of Language," in *Women and Language in Literature and Society*, ed. Sally McConnell-Ginet, Ruth Borker, and Nelly Fur-man (New York: Praeger, 1980), pp. 304–9.

Furthermore, there are many important issues that have been left out of my discussion. For example:

a. The relationship of her career as reader to the artistic development of the woman writer. In *The Madwoman in the Attic* (New Haven: Yale University Press, 1980) Sandra Gilbert and Susan Gubar show that women writers had to struggle to overcome the "anxi-ety of authorship" which they contracted from the "sentences" of their predecessors, male as well as female. They also argue that the relationship women writers form with their female predecessors does not fit the model of oedipal combat proposed by Bloom. Rich's attitude toward Dickinson (as someone who "has been there," as a "foremother" to be recovered) corroborates Gilbert and Gubar's claim.

b. The relationship between women writers and their readers. We need actual recep-tion studies as well as studies of the way women writers conceived of their readers and the way they inscribed them in their texts.

c. The relationship between the positive and the negative hermeneutic in feminist readings of women's writing. Rich's reading of Dickinson emphasizes the positive her-meneutic. One might ask, however, if this approach is applicable to *all* women's writing. Specifically, is this appropriate to the popular fiction written by women, e.g., Harlequin Romances? To what extent is women's writing itself a bearer of patriarchal ideology? Janice Radway addresses these issues in "Utopian Impulse in Popular Literature: Gothic Ro-mances and 'Feminist Protest,'" *American Quarterly* 33 (1981): 140–62, and "Women Read the Romance: The Interaction of Text and Context," *Feminist Studies* 9 (1983): 53–78. See also Tania Modleski, *Loving with a Vengeance: Mass-Produced Fantasies for Women* (New York: Methuen, 1982).

32. Iser writes:

> Text and reader no longer confront each other as object and subject, but instead the "division" takes place within the reader [herself]. . . . As we read, there occurs an artificial division of our personality, because we take as a theme for ourselves something we are not. Thus, in reading there are two levels—the alien "me" and the real, virtual "me"—which are never com-pletely cut off from each other. Indeed, we can only make someone else's thoughts into an absorbing theme for ourselves provided the virtual back-ground of our personality can adapt to it. ("The Reading Process: A Phe-nomenological Approach," in Tompkins, *Reader-Response Criticism*, p. 67)

Add the stipulation that the alien "me" is a male who has appointed the universal into his maleness, and we have the process of immasculation described in the third section.

33. Stanley E. Fish, *Is There a Text in This Class? The Authority of Interpretive Communities* (Cambridge: Harvard University Press, 1980), especially pt. 2.

34. Although the woman reader is the "star" of the feminist story of reading, this does not mean that men are excluded from the audience. On the contrary, it is hoped that on hearing the feminist story they will be encouraged to revise their own stories to reflect the fact that they, too, are gendered beings, and that, ultimately, they will take control of their inclination to appropriate the universal at the expense of women.

35. Catharine A. MacKinnon, "Feminism, Marxism, Method, and the State: Toward Feminist Jurisprudence," *Signs* 8 (1981): 637.

36. There is lively debate among feminists about whether it is better to emphasize the essential similarity of women and men, or their difference. There is much to be said intellectually and politically for both sides. However, in one sense, the argument centers on a false issue. It assumes that concern about women's "difference" is incompatible with concern about the essential humanity shared by the sexes. Surely, "difference" may be interpreted to refer to what is distinctive in women's lives and works, *including* what makes them essentially human; unless, of course, we remain captivated by the notion that the standard model for humanity is male.

37. Although opponents of feminist criticism often find it convenient to characterize such works as a personal attack on authors, for feminist critics themselves, the primary consideration is the function of the text as a carrier of patriarchal ideology, and its effect as such especially (but not exclusively) on women readers. The personal culpability of the author is a relatively minor issue.

38. Harold Bloom, *Kabbalah and Criticism* (New York: Seabury, 1975), p. 126.

39. Poulet, "Criticism and the Experience of Interiority," p. 46.

40. Ibid., p. 47. As Culler has pointed out, the theme of control is prominent in mainstream reader-response criticism. Poulet's story is no exception. The issue of control is important in another way. Behind the question of whether the text controls the reader or vice versa is the question of how to regulate literary criticism. If the text is controlling, then there is no problem. The text itself will regulate the process of reading. But if the text is not necessarily controlling, then, how do we constrain the activities of readers and critics? How can we rule out "off-the-wall" interpretations? Fish's answer is of interest to feminist critics. The constraints, he says, are exercised not by the text, but by the institutions within which literary criticism is situated. It is but a small step from this idea to the realization of the necessarily political character of literature and criticism.

41. The use of the personal conversational tone has been regarded as a hallmark of feminist criticism. However, as Jean E. Kennard has pointed out ("Personally Speaking: Feminist Critics and the Community of Readers," *College English* 43 [1981]: 140–45), this theoretical commitment is not apparent in the overwhelming majority of feminist critical essays. Kennard found only five articles in which the critic "overtly locates herself on the page." (To the five she found, I would add three works cited in this essay: "Women, Energy, and *Middlemarch*," by Lee Edwards; "Feminism and Literature," by Florence Howe; and "Vesuvius at Home," by Adrienne Rich.) Kennard observes further that, even in the handful of essays she found, the personal tone is confined to a few introductory paragraphs. She asks: "If feminist criticism has on the whole remained faithful to familiar methods and tone, why have the few articles with an overt personal voice loomed so large in our minds?" Kennard suggests that these personal introductions are invitations "to share a critical response which depends upon unstated, shared beliefs and, to a large extent, experience; that of being a female educated in a male tradition in which she is no longer comfortable." Thus, these introductory paragraphs do not indicate a "transformed critical methodology; they are devices for transforming the reader. I read the later portions of these essays—and by extension other feminist criticism—in a different way because I have been invited to participate in the underground. . . . I am part of a community of feminist readers" (pp. 143–44).

I would offer another explanation, one that is not necessarily inconsistent with Kennard's. I think the use of a personal and conversational tone represents an overt gesture indicating the dialogic mode of discourse as the "regulative ideal" for all feminist discourse. The few essays—indeed, the few introductory paragraphs—that assert this regulative ideal are memorable because they strike a chord in a significant segment of the community of feminist critics. To the extent that we have been touched or transformed by this idea, it will be implicit in the way we read the works of others, in particular, the works of other women. Although the ideal must be overtly affirmed periodically, it is not necessary to do so in all of our essays. It remains potent as long as it is assumed by a significant portion of the community. I would argue with Kennard's distinction between indicators of a transformed critical methodology and devices for transforming the reader. To the extent that critical methodology is a function of the conventions implicitly or explicitly operating in an interpretive community—that is, of the way members of the community conceive of their work and of the way they read each other—devices for transforming readers are also devices for transforming critical methodology.

42.   Jean Baker Miller, *Toward a New Psychology of Women* (Boston: Beacon Press, 1976); and Nancy Chodorow, *The Reproduction of Mothering: Psychoanalysis and the Sociology of Gender* (Berkeley and Los Angeles: University of California Press, 1978); and Carol Gilligan, *In a Different Voice: Psychological Theory and Women's Development* (Cambridge: Harvard University Press, 1982).

43.   I am using here Jürgen Habermas's definition of truth or validity as a claim (implicit in the act of making assertions) that is redeemable through discourse—specifically, through the domination-free discourse of an "ideal speech situation." For Habermas, consensus attained through a domination-free discourse is the warrant for truth. See "Wahrheitstheorien," in *Wirklichkeit und Reflexion: Walter Schulz zum 60. Geburtstag* (Pfullingen: Nesge, 1973), pp. 211–65. I am indebted to Alan Soble's unpublished translation of this essay.

THE READERS AND THEIR ROMANCES

Surrounded by corn and hay fields, the midwestern community of Smithton, with its meticulously tended subdivisions of single-family homes, is nearly two thousand miles from the glass-and-steel office towers of New York City where most of the American publishing industry is housed. Despite the distance separating the two communities, many of the books readied for publication in New York by young women with master's degrees in literature are eagerly read in Smithton family rooms by women who find quiet moments to read in days devoted almost wholly to the care of others. Although Smithton's women are not pleased by every romance prepared for them by New York editors, with Dorothy Evans's help they have learned to circumvent the industry's still inexact understanding of what women want from romance fiction. They have managed to do so by learning to decode the iconography of romantic cover art and the jargon of back-cover blurbs and by repeatedly selecting works by authors who have pleased them in the past.

In fact, it is precisely because a fundamental lack of trust initially characterized the relationship between Smithton's romance readers and the New York publishers that Dorothy Evans was able to amass this loyal following of customers. Her willingness to give advice so endeared her to women bewildered by the increasing romance output of the New York houses in the 1970s that they returned again and again to her checkout counter to consult her about the "best buys" of the month. When she began writing her review newsletter for bookstores and editors, she did so because she felt other readers might find her "expert" advice useful in trying to select romance fiction. She was so successful at developing a national reputation that New York editors began to send her galley proofs of their latest titles to guarantee their books a review in her newsletter. She now also obligingly reads manuscripts for several well-known authors who have begun to seek her advice and support. Although her status in the industry does not necessarily guarantee the representivity of her opinions or those of her customers, it does suggest that some writers and editors believe that she is not only closely attuned to the romance audience's desires and needs but is especially able to articulate them. It should not be surprising to note, therefore, that she proved a willing, careful, and consistently perceptive informant.

I first wrote to Dot in December 1979 to ask whether she would be willing to talk about romances and her evaluative criteria. I asked further if she thought some of her customers might discuss their reading with someone who was interested in what they liked and why. In an open and enthusiastic reply, she said she would be glad to host a series of interviews and meetings in her home during her summer vacation. At first taken aback by such generosity, I soon learned that Dot's unconscious magnanimity is a product of a genuine interest in people. When I could not secure a hotel room for the first night of my planned visit to Smithton, she insisted that I stay with her. I would be able to recognize her at the airport, she assured me, because she would be wearing a lavender pants suit.

The trepidation I felt upon embarking for Smithton slowly dissipated on the drive from the airport as Dot talked freely and fluently about the romances that were clearly an important part of her life. When she explained the schedule of discussions and interviews she had established for the next week, it seemed clear that my time in Smithton would prove enjoyable and busy as well as productive. My concern about whether I could persuade Dot's customers to elaborate honestly about their motives for reading was unwarranted, for after an initial period of mutually felt awkwardness, we conversed frankly and with enthusiasm. Dot helped immensely, for when she introduced me to her customers, she announced, "Jan is just people!" Although it became clear that the women were not accustomed to examining their activity in any detail, they conscientiously tried to put their perceptions and judgments into words to help me understand why they find romance fiction enjoyable and useful.

During the first week I conducted two four-hour discussion sessions with a total of sixteen of Dot's most regular customers. After she informed them of my interest, they had all volunteered to participate. About six more wanted to attend but were away on family vacations. These first discussions were open-ended sessions characterized by general questions posed to the group at large. In the beginning, timidity seemed to hamper the responses as each reader took turns answering each question. When everyone relaxed, however, the conversation flowed more naturally as the participants disagreed among themselves, contradicted one another, and delightedly discovered that they still agreed about many things. Both sessions were tape-recorded. I also conducted individual taped interviews with five of Dot's most articulate and enthusiastic romance readers. In addition, I talked informally to Dot alone for hours at odd times during the day and interviewed her more formally on five separate occasions. Along with twenty-five others approached by Dot herself at the bookstore, these sixteen all filled out a pilot questionnaire designed before I had departed from Philadelphia.

Upon returning from my visit to Smithton, I read as many of the specific titles mentioned during the discussions and interviews that I could acquire, transcribed the tapes, and expanded a field-work journal I had kept while away. In reviewing all of the information and evaluations I had been given, it became clear that I had neither anticipated all of the potentially meaningful questions that might be asked; nor had I always included the best potential answers for the directed-response questions. Accordingly, I redesigned the entire questionnaire and mailed fifty copies to Dot in mid-autumn of 1980. I asked her to give the questionnaire to her "regular" customers (those whom she recognized and had advised more than once about romance purchases) and to give no additional directions other than those on the questionnaire and in an attached explanatory letter. She returned forty-two completed questionnaires to me in early February 1981, during my second sojourn in Smithton.

At that time, I stayed with Dot and her family for a week, watched her daily routine, and talked with her constantly. I also spent three full days at the bookstore observing her interactions with her customers and conversing informally with them myself. I reinterviewed the same five readers during this period, checked points about which I was uneasy, and tested the hypotheses I had formulated already. I also talked at length with Maureen, one of Dot's most forthright readers, who had recently begun writing her own romances.

It is clear that the Smithton group cannot be thought of as a scientifically designed random sample. The conclusions drawn from the study, therefore, should be extrapolated only with great caution to apply to other romance readers. In fact, this study's propositions ought to be considered hypotheses that now must be tested systematically by looking at a much broader and unrelated group of romance readers. Despite the obvious limitations of the group, however, I decided initially to conduct the study for two reasons.

The first had to do with Dot's indisputable success and developing reputation on the national romance scene. The second was that the group was already self-selected and stably constituted. Dot's regular customers had continued to return to her for advice *because* they believed her perceptions accorded reasonably well with theirs. They had all learned to trust her judgment and to rely on her for assistance in choosing a varied array of romance reading material. They found this congenial because it freed all of them from the need to rely solely on a single "line" of books like the Harlequins, that had recently begun to offend and irritate them. It also enabled them to take back some measure of control from the publishers by selectively choosing only those books they had reason to suspect would satisfy their desires and needs. Although there are important variations in taste and habit within the Smithton group, all of the women agree that their preferences are adequately codified by Dorothy Evans.

The nature of the group's operation suggests that it is unsatisfactory for an analyst to select a sample of romances currently issued by American publishers, draw conclusions about the meaning of the form by analyzing the plots of the books in the sample, and then make general statements about the cultural significance of the "romance." Despite the industry's growing reliance on the techniques of semiprogrammed issue to reduce the disjunction between readers' desires and publishers' commodities, the production system is still characterized by a fundamental distance between the originators, producers, and consumers of the fantasies embodied in those romances. Consequently, it must be kept in mind that the people who read romance novels are *not* attending to stories they themselves have created to interpret their own experiences. Because the shift to professional production has reduced self-storytelling substantially, there is no sure way to know whether the narratives consumed by an anonymous public are in any way congruent with those they would have created for themselves and their peers had they not been able to buy them.

Although repeated purchase and consumption of a professionally produced and mass-marketed commodity hints that some kind of audience satisfaction has been achieved, this is not a guarantee that each individual text's interpretation of experience is endorsed by all buyers. In fact, what the Smithton group makes clear is that its members continue to possess very particular tastes in romance fiction that are not adequately addressed by publishers. However, because these corporations have designed their products to appeal to a huge audience by meeting the few preferences that all individuals within the group have in common, they have successfully managed to create texts that are minimally acceptable to Dot and her readers. Moreover, because the Smithton women feel an admittedly intense need to indulge in the romantic fantasy and, for the most part, cannot fulfill that need with their own imaginative activity, they often buy and read books they do not really like or fully endorse. As one reader explained, "Sometimes even a bad book is better than nothing." The act of purchase, then, does not always signify approval of the product selected; with a mass-production system it can just as easily testify to the existence of an ongoing, still only partially met, need.

Precisely because romance publishers have not engineered a perfect fit between the product they offer and all of their readers' desires, the Smithton women have discovered that their tastes are better served when the exchange process is mediated by a trusted selector who assembles a more suitable body of texts from which they can safely make their choices. This particular reliance on a mediator to guide the process of selection suggests that to understand what the romance means, it is first essential to characterize the different groups that find it meaningful and then to determine what each group identifies as its "romance" before attempting any assessment of the significance of the form. Despite the overtly formulaic appearance of the category, there are important differences among novels *for those who read them* that prompt individual decisions to reject or to read. We must begin to recognize this fact of selection within the mass-production process, make some effort to comprehend the principles governing such selection, and describe the content that gives rise to those principles.[1] The Smithton women comprise only one small, relatively homogeneous group that happens to read romances in a determinate way. While their preferences may be representative of those held by women similar to them in demographic characteristics and daily routine, it is not fair to assume that they use romance fiction in the same way as do women of different background, education, and social circumstance. Conclusions about the romance's meaning for highly educated women who work in male-dominated professions, for instance, must await further study.

The reading habits and preferences of the Smithton women are complexly tied to their daily routines, which are themselves a function of education, social role, and class position. Most Smithton readers are married mothers of children, living in single-family homes in a sprawling suburb of a central midwestern state's second largest city (population 850,000 in 1970).[2] Its surrounding cornfields notwithstanding, Smithton itself is an urbanized area. Its 1970 population, which was close to 112,000 inhabitants, represented a 70-percent increase over that recorded by the 1960 census. The community is essentially a "bedroom" community in that roughly 90 percent of those employed in 1970 worked outside Smithton itself. Although this has changed slightly in recent years with the building of the mall in which Dot herself works, the city is still largely residential and dominated by single-family homes, which account for 90 to 95 percent of the housing stock.

Dot and her family live on the fringe of one of Smithton's new housing development in a large, split-level home. When I last visited Smithton, Dot, her husband, Dan, her eldest daughter, Kit, and her mother were living in the house, which is decorated with Dot's needlework and crafts, projects she enjoyed when her children were young. Dot's other two children, Dawn, who is nineteen and married, and Joe, who is twenty-one, do not live with the family. Dot herself was forty-eight years old at the time of the study. Dan, a journeyman plumber, seems both bemused by Dot's complete absorption in romances and proud of her success at the bookstore. Although he occasionally reads thrillers and some nonfiction, he spends his leisure time with fellow union members or working about the house.

Although she is now a self-confident and capable woman, Dot believes she was once very different. She claims that she has changed substantially in recent years, a change she attributes to her reading and her work with people in the bookstore. When asked how she first began reading romances, she responded that it was really at her doctor's instigation. Although he did not suggest reading specifically, he advised her about fifteen years ago that she needed to find an enjoyable leisure activity to which she could devote at least an hour a day. He was concerned about her physical and mental exhaustion, apparently brought on by her conscientious and diligent efforts to care for her husband, three small children, and her home. When he asked her what she did for herself all day and she could list *only* the tasks she performed for others, he insisted that she learn to spend some time on herself if she did not want to land in a hospital. Remembering that she loved to read as a child, she decided to try again. Thus began her interest in romance fiction. Dot read many kinds of books at first, but she soon began to concentrate on romances for reasons she cannot now explain. Her reading became so chronic that when she discovered that she could not rely on a single shop to provide all of the latest releases by her favorite authors, she found in necessary to check four different bookstores to get all of the romances she wanted. Most of her customers commented that before they discovered Dot they did the same thing. Some still attend garage sales and flea markets religiously to find out-of-print books by authors whose more recent works they have enjoyed.

Dot would have continued as one of the legion of "silent" readers had not one of her daughters encouraged her to look for a job in a bookstore to make use of her developing expertise. Although hesitant about moving out into the public world, she eventually mustered the courage to try, soon finding employment at the chain outlet where she still works. She discovered that she thoroughly enjoyed the contact with other "readers," and, as she developed more confidence, she began to make suggestions and selections for uncertain buyers. In the first edition of her newsletter, she explained the subsequent events that led to the creation of her romance review:

> Soon it became apparent that the women who were regular customers were searching me out for my opinions on their selections. Also, the Area Super-

> visor of our store had noticed a sharply marked increase in sales of the gen-
> eral category of romances. . . . So the interviews and articles in . . .
> periodicals began and brought more attention to my so-called expertise.

> The idea for a newsletter and rating of new releases every month . . . be-
> longs to my daughter, who felt we could make this available to a much larger
> group of women readers. As most of them know the prices of books are rising
> and the covers are not always a good indicator of the content of the book.[3]

With the help of her daughter, Kit, she planned, executed, and wrote the first edition of "Dorothy's Diary of Romance Reading," in April 1980. Despite reservations about taking up the role of critical mediator, she explained in her inaugural editorial that she was persuaded to such an authoritarian act by the intensity of her customers' needs and by the inability of the production system to meet them. "I know many women," she commented, "who need to read as an escape as I have over the years and I believe this is good therapy and much cheaper than tranquilizers, alcohol or addictive TV serials which most of my readers say bores them." She added that she intended to separate "the best or better books from the less well written, so as to save the reader money and time." "However," she concluded. "I would never want to take from the ladies the right to choose their own reading materials, only to suggest from my own experience."[4]

Still conscious of the hierarchy implicit in the critic–consumer relationship, Dot continues to be careful about offering evaluative suggestions at the store. Her first question to a woman who solicits her advice is calculated to determine the kinds of romances the reader has enjoyed in the past. "If they are in my category," she explained in one of our interviews, "I start saying, 'OK, what was the last good book you read?' And then if they tell me that, I usually can go from there." Her services, like semi-programmed publication techniques, are designed to gauge already formulated but not fully expressed reader preferences, which she subsequently attempts to satisfy by selecting the proper material from a much larger corpus of published works. Dot can be more successful than distant publishing firms attempting the same service through market research because she personalizes selection at the moment of purchase in a way that the absent publishers cannot.

Dot's unusual success is a function of her participant's understanding of the different kinds of romances, acquired as the consequence of her voracious reading, and of her insistence on the individuality of her readers and their preferences. This is especially evident at the stage in her advising process when she finally displays a selection of books for her customers. "Sometimes," she laments, "I have people who say, 'Well, which one do *you* say is the best of these three?'" Her response indicates the depth of her respect for the singularity of readers and romances despite the fact that those readers are usually thought of as category readers and the romances considered formulaic performances:

> I will say, "They are not alike, they are not written by the same author, they
> are totally and completely different settings and I cannot say you will like
> this one better than this one because they are totally and completely differ-
> ent books." [But they always continue with] "Which one did you like best?"
> And I'll say, "Don't try to pin me down like that because it's not right." I

won't go any further. They have to choose from there because otherwise you're getting sheep. See, I like it when some of my women say, "Hey, I didn't care for that book." And I say, "Hey, how come?"[5]

Because Dot is ever mindful of her readers' dissatisfaction with some of the material flowing from the New York publishers and simultaneously aware of their desire to maintain and satisfy their own personal tastes, she has created a role for herself by facilitating a commercial exchange that benefits the reader as much as it does the producer. At the same time, Dot continues to perpetuate generic distinctions within a category that the publishers themselves are trying to rationalize and standardize. Hers is a strategy which, if not consciously calculated to empower readers with a selective ability, at least tends to operate in that way. By carefully identifying a book's particular historical setting, by relating the amount of sexually explicit description it contains, by describing its use of violence and cruelty, and by remarking about its portrayal of the heroine/hero relationship, she alerts the reader to the book's treatment of the essential features that nearly all of her customers focus on in determining the quality of a romance.

In addition to recognizing individual tastes and respecting personal preferences, Dot also performs another essential function for her regular customers. Although I suspect she was not always as effective at this as she is now, she capably defends her readers' preferences for romance fiction *to themselves*. One would think this unnecessary because so many of her customers come to her expressly seeking romances, but Dot finds that many of her women feel guilty about spending money on books that are regularly ridiculed by the media, their husbands, and their children. Dot encourages her customers to feel proud of their regular reading and provides them with a model of indignant response that they can draw upon when challenged by men who claim superior taste. By questioning them rhetorically about whether their romance reading is any different from their husbands' endless attention to televised sports, she demonstrates an effective rejoinder that can be used in the battle to defend the leisure pursuit they enjoy so much but which the larger culture condemns as frivolous and vaguely, if not explicitly, pornographic.

Dot's vociferous defense of her customers' right to please themselves in any way that does not harm others is an expression of her deeply held belief that women are too often the object of others' criticism and the butt of unjustified ridicule. Although she is not a feminist as most would understand that term, she is perfectly aware that women have been dismissed by men for centuries, and she can and does converse eloquently on the subject. During my second stay in Smithton, she admitted to me that she understands very well why women have pushed for liberal abortion laws and remarked that even though her devoutly held religious convictions would prevent her from seeking one herself, she believes all women should have the right to *choose* motherhood and to control their own bodies. She also feels women should have the right to work and certainly should be paid equally with men. Many of our conversations were punctuated by her expressions of anger and resentment at the way women are constantly "put down" as childish, ignorant, and incapable of anything but housework or watching soap operas.

At first glance, Dot's incipient feminism seems deeply at odds with her interest in a literary form whose ultimate message, one astute observer has noted, is that "pleasure for women is men."[6] The traditionalism of romance fiction will not be denied here, but it is essential to point out that Dot and many of the writers and readers of romances interpret these stories as chronicles of female triumph. Although the particular way they do so will be explored later, suffice it to say here that Dot believes a good romance focuses on an intelligent and able heroine who finds a man who recognizes her special qualities and is capable of loving and caring for her as she wants to be loved. Thus Dot understands such an ending to say that female independence and marriage are compatible rather than mutually exclusive. The romances she most values and recommends for her readers are those with "strong," "fiery" heroines who are capable of "defying the hero," softening him, and showing him the value of loving and caring for another.

It is essential to introduce this here in order to take account adequately of Dot's personal influence on her customers and on their preferences in romance fiction. Because she is an exceptionally strong woman convinced of her sex's capabilities, when she expresses her opinions about a woman's right to pleasure, Dot not only supports her customers but confers legitimacy on the preoccupatoin they share with her. I suspect that in providing this much-needed reinforcement Dot also exerts an important influence on them that must be taken into account. She encourages her customers to think well of themselves not only by demonstrating her interest in them and in their desires but also by presenting them with books whose heroines seem out of the ordinary. Therefore, while the members of the Smithton group share attitudes about good and bad romances that are similar to Dot's, it is impossible to say whether these opinions were formed by Dot or whether she is simply their most articulate advocate. Nonetheless, it must be emphasized that this group finds it possible to select and construct romances in such a way that their stories are experienced as a reversal of the oppression and emotional abandonment suffered by women in real life. For Dot and her customers, romances provide a utopian vision in which female individuality and a sense of self are shown to be compatible with nurturance and care by another.

All of the Smithton readers who answered the questionnaire were female. Dot reported that although she suspects some of the men who buy romances "for their wives" are in fact buying them for themselves, all of the people she regularly advises are women. While the few houses that have conducted market-research surveys will not give out exact figures, officials at Harlequin, Silhouette, and Fawcett have all indicated separately that the majority of romance readers are married women between the ages of twenty-five and fifty. Fred Kerner, Harlequin's vice-president for publishing, for instance, recently reported to Barbara Brotman, of the *Chicago Tribune*, that "Harlequin readers are overwhelmingly women of whom 49 percent work at least part-time. They range in age from twenty-four to forty-nine, have average family incomes of $15,000–20,000, and have high school diplomas but haven't completed college."[7] Harlequin will reveal little else about its audience, but a company executive did tell Margaret Jensen that the Harlequin reading population matches the profile of the "North-American English-speaking female population" in age, family income, employment status, and geographical location.[8] For example, he said that 22 percent of the female population and Harlequin readers are between the ages of twenty-five and thirty-four. Carol Reo, publicity director for Silhouette Romances, has also revealed that the romance audience is almost entirely female, but indicates that 65 percent of Silhouette's potential market is under the age of forty and that 45 percent attended college.[9] If these sketchy details are accurate, the Smithton readers may be more representative of the Silhouette audience than they are of Harlequin's.[10] Unfortunately, the lack of detailed information about the total American audience for Harlequins as well as for other kinds of romances makes it exceedingly difficult to judge the representivity of the Smithton group. Still, it appears evident that the Smithton readers are somewhat younger than either Jensen's Harlequin readers or the Mills and Boon audience.

The age differential may account for the fact that neither Dot nor many of her customers are Harlequin fans. Although Dot reviews Harlequins and slightly more than half of her customers (twenty-four) reported reading them, a full eighteen indicated that they *never* read a Harlequin romance. Moreover, only ten of Dot's customers indicated that Harlequins are among the kinds of romances they *most* like to read. The overwhelming preference of the group was for historicals, cited by twenty (48 percent) as their favorite subgenre within the romance category.[11] Because historicals typically include more explicit sex than the Harlequins and also tend to portray more independent and defiant heroines, we might expect that this particular subgenre would draw younger readers who are less offended by changing standards of gender behavior. This would seem to be corroborated by the fact that only two of the women who listed Harlequins as a favorite also listed historicals.

In addition, the Smithton group also seemed to like contemporary mystery romances and contemporary romances, which were cited by another twelve as being among their favorites. Silhouettes are contemporary romances and, like the historicals, are less conventional than the Harlequins. Not only is their sexual description more explicit but it is not unusual for them to include heroines with careers who expect to keep their jobs after marriage. The similarity between Smithton's tastes and the content of the Silhouettes may thus explain why both audiences are younger than that for the relatively staid Harlequins.

Despite the discrepancies in the various reports, romance reading apparently correlates strongly with the years of young adulthood and early middle age. This is further borne out in the present study by the Smithton women's responses to a question about when they first began to read romances. Although fifteen (36 percent) of the women reported that they began in adolescence between the ages of ten and nineteen, sixteen (38 percent) indicated that they picked up the habit between the ages of twenty and twenty-nine. Another ten (24 percent) adopted romance reading after age thirty.[12]

Thirty-two women (76 percent) in the Smithton group were married at the time of the survey, a proportion that compares almost exactly with the 75 percent of married women included in Jensen's group.[13] An additional three (7 percent) of the Smithton women were single, while five (12 percent) were either widowed, separated, or divorced and not remarried.

Moreover, most of the women in the Smithton group were mothers with children *under* age eighteen (70 percent). Indeed, within the group, only five (12 percent) reported having no children at all. Nine (21 percent) of the Smithton women reported only one child, twelve (29 percent) claimed two children, eleven (27 percent) had three children, and three (7 percent) had four children. Interestingly enough, only five (12 percent) reported children under the age of five, while twenty-four of the women indicated that they had at least one child under age eighteen. Eleven (27 percent), however, reported that all of their children were over age eighteen. Fifteen (36 percent) reported children between ten and eighteen, and another fifteen (36 percent) had at least one child over age eighteen. The relatively advanced age of the Smithton readers' children is not surprising if one takes into account the age distribution of the women themselves and the fact that the mean age at first marriage within the group was 19.9 years.

Once again, the limited size of the sample and the lack of corroborating data from other sources suggest caution in the formation of hypotheses. Nonetheless, it appears that within the Smithton group romance reading correlates with motherhood and the care of children *other* than infants and toddlers.[14] This seems logical because the fact of the older children's attendance at school would allow the women greater time to read even as the children themselves continued to make heavy emotional demands on them for nurturance, advice, and attentive care. It will be seen later that it is precisely this emotional drain caused by a woman's duty to nurture and care for her children and husband that is addressed directly by romance reading at least within the minds of the women themselves.

Given the fact that fifteen (36 percent) of the Smithton readers reported children age ten and under, it should not be surprising to note that sixteen of the women (38 percent) reported that in the preceding week they were keeping house and/or caring for children on a full-time basis. Another nine (21 percent) were working part-time, while still another nine (21 percent) were holding down full-time jobs. In addition, two women failed to respond, two stated that they were retired, one listed herself as a student, and three indicated that they were currently unemployed and looking for work. These statistics seem to parallel those of the Mills and Boon study which found that 33 percent of the sample were represented by full-time housewives, while another 30 percent included housewives with full- or part-time jobs. Both studies suggest that romance reading is very often squeezed into busy daily schedules.

Although Fred Kerner's comment about the average $15,000–$20,000 income of the Harlequin audience is not very illuminating, neither is it at odds with the details reported by Dot's customers. Although four (10 percent) did not answer the question, eighteen (43 percent) in the group indicated a family income of somewhere between $15,000 and $24,999. Another fourteen (33 percent) claimed a joint income of $25,000 to $49,999, while four (10 percent) listed family earnings of over $50,000. The greater affluence of the Smithton group is probably accounted for by the fact that Dot's bookstore is located in one of the twelve most affluent counties in a state with 115. The median family income in Smithton, as reported by the 1970 United States census, was almost $11,000, which compares with the state median income of just slightly less than $9,000.

Before turning to the group's reading history and patterns, it should be noted that exactly half of the Smithton readers indicated that they had earned a high school diploma. Ten (24 percent) of the women reported completing less than three years of college; eight (19 percent) claimed at least a college degree or better. Only one person in the group indicated that she had not finished high school, while two failed to answer the question. Once again, as the Smithton readers appear to be more affluent than Harlequin readers, so also do they seem better educated; the Harlequin corporation claims that its readers are educated below even the statistical norm for the North American female population.

One final detail about the personal history of the Smithton women ought to be mentioned here: attendance at religious services was relatively high among Dot's customers. Although eight (19 percent) of the women indicated that they had not been to a service in the last two years, fifteen (36 percent) reported attendance "once a week or more," while another eight (19 percent) indicated attendance "once or a few times a month." Another nine (21 percent) admitted going to services a few times a year, while two (5 percent) did not answer the question. The women reported membership in a wide variety of denominations. Eight (19 percent) of the women indicated that they were Methodists and eight (19 percent) checked "Christian but non-denominational." The next two groups most heavily represented in the sample were Catholics and Baptists, each with five (12 percent) of the Smithton women.

When the reading *histories* of these women are examined, it becomes clear that, for many of them, romance reading is simply a variation in a pattern of leisure activity they began early in life. Indeed, twenty-two of Dot's customers reported that they first began to read for pleasure before age ten. Another twelve (27 percent) adopted the habit between the ages of eleven and twenty. Only seven (17 percent) of the Smithton women indicated that they began pleasure reading after their teen years. These results parallel earlier findings about the adoption of the book habit. Phillip Ennis found in 1965, for instance, that of the 49 percent of the American population who were "current readers," 34 percent consisted of those who started reading early in life and 15 percent consisted of those who began reading at an advanced age.[15]

When *current* reading habits are examined, however, it becomes clear that the women think that it is the romances that are especially necessary to their daily routine. Their intense reliance on these books suggests strongly that they help to fulfill deeply felt psychological needs. Indeed, one of the most striking findings to come out of the Smithton study was that thirty-seven (88 percent) of Dot's readers indicated that they read religiously every day. Only five of her regular customers claimed to read more sporadically. Twenty-two of the women, in fact, reported reading more than sixteen hours per week, and another ten (24 percent) claimed to read between eleven and fifteen hours weekly.[16] When asked to describe their typical reading pattern once they have begun a new romance, eleven (26 percent) selected the statement, "I won't put it down until I've finished it unless it's absolutely necessary." Thirty more indicated reading "as much of it as I can until I'm interrupted or have something else to do." None of Dot's customers reported a systematic reading pattern of "a few pages a day until done," and only one admitted that she reads solely when she is in the mood. These figures suggest that the Smithton women become intensely involved in the stories they are reading and that once immersed in the romantic fantasy, Dot's customers do not like to return to reality without experiencing the resolution of the narrative.

This need to see the story and the emotions aroused by it resolved is so intense that many of the Smithton women have worked out an ingenious strategy to insure a regular and predictable arrival at the anticipated narrative conclusion. Although they categorize romances in several ways, one of the most basic distinctions they make is that between "quick reads" and "fat books." Quick reads contain less than two hundred pages and require no more than two hours of reading time. Harlequins, Silhouettes, and most Regencies are considered quick reads for occasions when they know they will not be able to "make it through" a big book. If, for example, a woman has just finished one romance but still "is not ready to quit," as one of my informants put it, she will "grab a thin one" she knows she can finish before going to sleep. Fat books, on the other hand, tend to be saved for weekends or long evenings that promise to be uninterrupted, once again because the women dislike having to leave a story before it is concluded. This kind of uninterrupted reading is very highly valued within the Smithton group because it is associated with the pleasure of spending time alone.[17] Although a detailed exploration of the importance of this narrative and emotional resolution must be delayed until chapter 4, where the structure of the romance story and its developing effect on the reader will be considered in detail, let it be said here that the Smithton readers' strategies for avoiding disruption or discontinuity in the story betoken a profound need to arrive at the *ending* of the tale and thus to achieve or acquire the emotional gratification they already can anticipate.

The remarkable extent of their familiarity with the genre is attested to by the number of romances these women read each week. Despite the fact that twenty-six (62 percent) of Dot's customers claimed to read somwhere between one and four books *other* than romances every week, more than a third (fifteen) reported reading from five to nine romances weekly. An additional twenty-two (55 percent) completed between one and four romances every week, while four women indicated that they consume anywhere from fifteen to twenty-five romances during that same period of time. This latter figure strikes me as somewhat implausible because it implies a reading rate of one hundred romances a month. I think this is unlikely given the fact that far fewer romances were issued monthly by publishers at the time of the study. Of course, the women could be reading old romances, but the figure still seems exaggerated. Nonetheless, it is evident that Dot's customers read extraordinary amounts of romance fiction.

Although their chronic reading of these books might sound unusual or idiosyncratic, the Yankelovich findings about romance reading, as noted before, indicate that romance readers are generally heavy consumers. Most, however, are probably not as obsessed as the Smithton readers seem to be. Unfortunately, the Yankelovich discovery that the average romance reader had read nine romances in the last six months does not tell us what proportion of the group read an even larger number of novels. Although 40 percent of the heavy readers (those who had read more than twenty-five books in the last six months) reported having read a romance, thus suggesting the possibility of a correlation between high levels of consumption and romance reading, the study gives no indication of how many of the romance readers actually read anywhere near the number the Smithton women report, which ranges from twenty-four to more than six hundred romances every six months.[18] I think it is safe to say that the Smithton group's reliance on romances is not strictly comparable to that of the occasional reader. Rather, Dot's customers are women who spend a significant portion of every day participating vicariously in a fantasy world that they willingly admit bears little resemblance to the one they actually inhabit. Clearly, the experience must provide some form of required pleasure and reconstitution because it seems unlikely that so much time and money would be spent on an activity that functioned merely to fill otherwise unoccupied time.

The women confirmed this in their answers to a directed-response question about their reasons for reading romance fiction. When asked to rank order the three most important motives for romance reading out of a list of eight, nineteen (45 percent) of the women listed "simple relaxation" as the first choice. Another eight (19 percent) of the readers reported that they read romances "because reading is just for me; it is my time." Still another six (14 percent) said they read "to learn about faraway places and time"; while five (12 percent) insisted that their primary reason is "to escape my daily problems." When these first choices are added to the second and third most important reasons for reading, the totals are distributed as in Table 1:

TABLE 1

Question: Which of the Following Best Describes Why You Read Romances?

a. To escape my daily problems	13
b. To learn about faraway places and times	19
c. For simple relaxation	33
d. Because I wish I had a romance like the heroine's	5
e. Because reading is just for me; it is my time	28
f. Because I like to read about the strong, virile heroes	4
g. Because reading is at least better than other forms of escape	5
h. Because romantic stories are never sad or depressing	10

On the basis of these schematic answers alone I think it logical to conclude that romance reading is valued by the Smithton women because the experience itself is *different* from ordinary experience. Not only is it a relaxing release from the tension produced by daily problems and responsibilities, but it creates a time or space within which a woman can be entirely on her own, preoccupied with her personal needs, desires, and pleasure. It is also a means of transportation or escape to the exotic or, again, to that which is different.

It is important to point out here that the responses to the second questionnaire are different in important ways from the answers I received from the women in the face-to-face interviews and in the first survey. At the time of my initial visit in June 1980, our conversations about their reasons for romance reading were dominated by the words "escape" and "education." Similarly, when asked by the first questionnaire to describe briefly what romances do "better" than other books available today, of the thirty-one answering the undirected question, fourteen of the first respondents *volunteered* that they like romance fiction because it allows them to "escape." It should be noted that "relaxation" was given only once as an answer, while no woman mentoined the idea of personal space.

Both answers *c* and *e* on the second form were given initially in the course of the interviews by two unusually articulate readers who elaborated more fully than most of the women on the meaning of the word "escape." They considered these two answers synonymous with it, but they also seemed to prefer the alternate responses because they did not so clearly imply a desire to avoid duties and responsibilities in the "real" world. Although most of the other women settled for the word "escape" on the first questionnaire, they also liked their sister readers' terms better. Once these were introduced in the group interviews, the other women agreed that romance reading functions best as relaxation and as a time for self-indulgence. Because the switch seemed to hint at feelings of guilt, I decided to add the more acceptable choices to the second survey. Although both answers *c* and *e* also imply movement away from something distasteful in the real present to a somehow more satisfying universe, a feature that appears to testify to romance reading's principal function as a therapeutic release and as a provider of vicarious pleasure, the fact of the women's preference for these two terms over their first spontaneous response suggests again that the women harbor complex feelings about the worth and propriety of romance reading.[19]

The women provided additional proof of their reliance on romance reading as a kind of tranquilizer or restorative agent in their responses to questions about preferred reading times and the habit of rereading favorite romances. When asked to choose from among seven statements the one that best described their reading pattern, twenty-four (57 percent) eschewed specification of a particular time of day in order to select the more general assertion, "It's hard to say when I do most of my reading, since I read every chance I get." Another fourteen claimed to read mostly in the evenings, usually because days were occupied with employment outside the home. In the case of either pattern, however, romances are not picked up idly as an old magazine might be merely to fill otherwise unoccupied time. Rather, romance reading is considered so enjoyable and beneficial by the women that they deliberately work it into busy schedules as often and as consistently as they can.

Rereading is not only a widely practiced habit among the Smithton women but tends to occur most frequently during times of stress or depression. Three fourths of Dot's customers reported that they reread favorite books either "sometimes" (twenty-one) or "often" (eleven). They do so, they explained in the interviews, when they feel sad or unhappy because they know exactly how the chosen book will affect their state of mind. Peter Mann similarly discovered that 46 percent of his Mills and Boon readers claimed to reread "very often," while another 38 percent reported repeat reading "now and then."[20] Unfortunately, he has provided no further information about why or when the women do so. Although it is possible that they may reread in order to savor the details of particular plots, it is clear that for the most part the Smithton women do not. For them, rereading is an activity engaged in expressly to lift the spirits. The following comment from one of the first questionnaires illustrates nicely the kind of correlation the Smithton women see between their daily needs and the effects of romance reading: "Romances are not depressing and very seldom leave you feeling sad inside. When I read for enjoyment I want to be entertained and feel lifted out of my daily routine. And romances are the best type of reading for this effect. Romances also revive my usually optimistic outlook which often is very strained in day-to-day living." Although all of Dot's customers know well that most romances end happily, when their own needs seem unusually pressing they often refuse even the relatively safe gamble of beginning a new romance. Instead, they turn to a romance they have completed previously because they already know how its final resolution will affect them. Romance reading, it would seem, can be valued as much for the sameness of the response it evokes as for the variety of the adventures it promises.[21]

Interestingly enough, the Smithton readers hold contradictory opinions about the repetitious or formulaic quality of the fiction they read. On the one hand, they are reluctant to admit that the characters appearing in romances are similar. As Dot's daughter, Kit, explained when asked to describe a typical heroine in the historical romance, "there isn't a typical one, they all have to be different or you'd be reading the same thing over and over." Her sentiments were echoed frequently by her mother's customers, all of whom claim to value the variety and diversity of romance fiction.

On the other hand, these same women exhibit fairly rigid expectations about what is permissible in a romantic tale and express disappointment and outrage when those conventions are violated. In my first interview with Dot, she discussed a particular author who had submitted a historical novel to her publisher. Although the author explained repeatedly that the book was not a romance, the publisher insisted on packaging it with a standard romance cover in the hope of attracting the huge romance market. The author knew this would anger the audience and, as Dot remarked, "she was not surprised when she got irate letters." Clearly, romances may not deviate too significantly if regular readers are to be pleased. They expect and, indeed, rely upon certain events, characters, and progressions to provide the desired experience.

Dot herself often finds it necessary but difficult to overcome her customers' fixed expectations when she discovers a romance she thinks they will enjoy even though it fails to follow the usual pattern. In the case of *The Fulfillment*, for example, which Dot loved and wanted to share with her women, she worked out an entire speech to get them to buy the book and read it through. The following is a verbatim transcription of her recreation of that speech: "Now this is a good book—but please don't think that it is the run of the mill. It isn't. At one point in this book, you're gonna want to put it down—and you're gonna say, 'Dot didn't tell me this'—and I said, 'Don't put it down. You keep reading.' Every one of them came back and said, 'You were right. I thought why did she give me this book?' They said, 'I kept reading like you said and it was great.'" The problem with this particular book was the fact that the hero died three-quarters of the way through the tale. However, because the author had worked out an unusually complex plot involving the heroine simultaneously with another equally attractive man in an acceptable way, the women did not find her sudden remarriage distasteful. Without Dot's skillful encouragement, however, most of the women would never have read the book past the hero's death.

Dot also tries to circumvent set expectations in her newsletter. She occasionally tells booksellers and readers about books classified by their publishers as something other than a romance. Erroneous categorization occurs, she believes, because the publishers really do not understand what a romance is and thus pay too much attention to meaningless, superficial details that lead to mistaken identifications. Because Jacqueline Marten's *Visions of the Damned* suffered this fate, Dot attempted to alert her readers to the problem classification. Her way of doing so provides an essential clue to the proper identification of a romance, which the women rely on despite their claim that all romanctic novels are different. Of Marten's story, she wrote, "This book, because of cover and title, was classed as an occult. What a mistake! *Visions* is one of the best love stories I've read of late. Get it and read it. I loved it." [22] Although *Visions of the Damned* concerns itself with extrasensory perception and reincarnation, Dot believes that the book's proper plot structure is what makes it a romance. It is not the mere use of the romantic subject matter that qualifies Marten's books as a romance, she explained, but rather its manner of developing the loving relationship. As Dot remarked in a later interview, "Not all love stories are romances." Some are simply novels about love.

If the Smithton readers' stipulations are taken seriously, a romance is, first and foremost, a story about a woman. That woman, however, may not figure in a larger plot simply as the hero's prize, as Jenny Cavileri does, for instance in Erich Segal's *Love Story*, which the Smithton readers claim is not a romance. To qualify as a romance, the story must chronicle not merely the events of a courtship but *what it feels like* to be the *object* of one. Dot's customers insist that this need not be accomplished by telling the story solely from the heroine's point of view, although it is usually managed in this way. Although five of the women refuse to read first-person narratives because they want to be privy to the hero's thoughts and another ten indicate that they prefer to see both points of view, twenty-three of Dot's regular customers indicate that they have no preference about the identity of the narrator. However, all of the women I spoke to, regardless of their taste in narratives, admitted that they want to identify with the heroine as she attempts to comprehend, anticipate, and deal with the ambiguous attentions of a man who inevitably cannot understand her feelings at all. The point of the experience is the sense of exquisite tension, anticipation, and excitement created within the reader as she imagines the possible resolutions and consequences for a woman of an encounter with a member of the opposite sex and then observes that once again the heroine in question has avoided the ever-present potential for disaster because the hero has fallen helplessly in love with her.

In all their comments about the nature of the romance, the Smithton women placed heavy emphasis on the importance of *development* in the romance's portrayal of love. The following two definitions were echoed again and again in other remarks:

> Generally there are two people who come together for one reason or another, *grow to love each other* and *work together solving problems* along the way—united for a purpose. They are light easy reading and always have a happy ending which makes one feel more light-hearted.

> I think [a romance] is a man and woman meeting, the growing awareness, the culmination of the love—*whether it's going to jell or if it's going to fall apart*—but they [the heroine and the hero] have recognized that they have fallen in love [emphasis added].

The women usually articulated this insistence on process and development during discussions about the genre's characteristic preoccupation with what is typically termed "a love-hate relationship." Because the middle of every romantic narrative must create some form of conflict to keep the romantic pair apart until the proper moment, many authors settle for misunderstanding or distrust as the cause of the intermediary delay of the couple's happy union. Hero and heroine are shown to despise each other overtly, even though they are "in love," primarily because each is jealous or suspicious of the other's motives and consequently fails to trust the other. Despite the frequency with which this pattern of conflict is suddenly explained away by the couple's mutual recognition that only misunderstanding is thwarting their relationship, the Smithton women are not convinced when a hero decides within two pages of the novel's conclusion that he has been mistaken about the heroine and that his apparent hatred is actually affection. Dot's customers dislike such "about faces"; they prefer to see a hero and heroine gradually overcome distrust and suspicion and grow to love each other.

Although this depiction of love as a gradual process cannot be considered the defining feature of the genre for all of the Smithton women, slightly more than half (twenty-three) believe it one of the "three most important ingredients" in the narrative. As might have been predicted, when responding to a request to rank order narrative features with respect to their importance to the genre, Dot's customers generally agreed that a happy ending is indispensable. Twenty-two of the women selected this as the essential ingredient in romance fiction out of a list of eleven choices, while a total of thirty-two listed it in first, second, or third place. The runner-up in the "most important" category, however, was "a slowly but consistently developing love between hero and heroine," placed by twenty-three of the women in first, second, or third place. Considered almost equally important by Dot's customers was the romance's inclusion of "some detail about the heroine and the hero after they have finally gotten together."[23] Twenty-two of the women thought this one of the three most important ingredients in the genre. Table 2 summarizes the ranking responses of the Smithton women.

The obvious importance of the happy ending lends credence to the suggestion that romances are valued most for their ability to raise the spirits of the reader. They manage to do so, the rankings imply, by involving that reader vicariously in the gradual evolution of a loving relationship whose culmination she is later permitted to enjoy in the best romances through a description of the heroine's and hero's life together after their necessary union. When combined with the relative unimportance of detailed reports about sexual encounters, it seems clear that the Smithton readers are interested in the verbal working out of a romance, that is, in the reinterpretation of misunderstood actions and in declarations of mutual love rather than in the portrayal of sexual contact through visual imagery.

Beatrice Faust has recently argued in *Women, Sex, and Pornography* that female sexuality is "tactile, verbal, intimate, nurturant, process-oriented and somewhat inclined to monogomy," traits she attributes to biological predisposition and social reinforcement through culture.[24] Although there are important problems with Faust's reliance on biology to account for female preferences in sexual encounters as well as with her assertion that such tastes characterize all women, her parallel claim that women are not excited by the kinds of visual displays and explicit description of physical contact that characterize male pornography is at least true of the Smithton readers. Dot and her customers are more interested in the affective responses of hero and heroine to each other than in a detailed account of their physical contact. Interestingly enough, the Smithton women also explained that they do not like explicit description because they prefer to imagine the scene in

TABLE 2

Question: What Are the Three Most Important Ingredients in a Romance?

Response	First Most Important Feature	Second Most Important Feature	Third Most Important Feature	Total Who Checked Response In One of Top Three Positions
a. A happy ending	22	4	6	32
b. Lots of scenes with explicit sexual description	0	0	0	0
c. Lots of details about faraway places and times	0	1	2	3
d. A long conflict between hero and heroine	2	1	1	4
e. Punishment of the villain	0	2	3	5
f. A slowly but consistently developing love between hero and heroine	8	9	6	23
g. A setting in a particular historical period	3	4	3	10
h. Lots of love scenes with some explicit sexual description	3	7	3	13
i. Lots of love scenes without explicit sexual description	0	3	1	4
j. Some detail about heroine and hero after they've gotten together	1	7	14	22
k. A very particular kind of hero and heroine	3	4	3	10

detail by themselves. Their wish to participate in the gradual growth of love and trust and to witness the way in which the heroine is eventually cared for by a man who also confesses that he "needs" her suggests that the Smithton women do indeed want to see a woman attended to sexually in a tender, nurturant, and emotionally open way. It should be added that these preferences also hint at the existence of an equally powerful wish to see a man dependent upon a woman.

Although Dot's customers will not discuss in any detail whether they themselves are sexually excited by the escalation of sexual tension in a romance, they willingly acknowledge that what they enjoy most about romance reading is the opportunity to project themselves into the story, to become the heroine, and thus to share her surprise and slowly awakening pleasure at being so closely watched by someone who finds her valuable and worthy of love. They have elaborated this preference into a carefully articulated distinction between good and bad romances, which differ principally in the way they portray the hero's treatment of the heroine.

A substantial amount of popular and even scholarly writing about mass-produced entertainment makes the often correct assumption that such fare is cynically engineered to appeal to the tastes of the largest possible audience in the interest of maximum profit.[25] However, a certain portion of it is still written by sincere, well-meaning people who are themselves consumers of the form they work in and indeed proponents of the values it embodies. Despite publishers' efforts at rationalization of romance production through the use of carefully calculated "tip sheets to writers," the genre is not yet entirely written by men and women who do it only to make money. Although many of the most successful authors in the field are professional writers, a significant number of them are "amateurs" drawn to the genre by a desire to write the kind of material they love to read. More often than not, it is the work of *these* women that the Smithton readers like best.

In a letter to the readers of Dot's newsletter, for instance, LaVyrle Spencer has explained that her first book "was written because of one very special lady, Kathleen Woodiwiss," whose book, *The Flame and the Flower*, "possessed me to the point where I found I, too, wanted to write a book that would make ladies' hearts throb with anticipation." She continued, "I even got to the point where I told myself I wanted to do it for her, Kathleen, to give her a joyful reading experience like she'd given me."[26] *The Fulfillment* resulted from this inspiration.

Jude Deveraux, another successful author, also commented in Dot's newsletter on Woodiwiss's role in her decision to become a writer. She so enjoyed *The Flame and the Flower* that she dashed out to buy two more romances to re-create the pleasure Woodiwiss's book had provided. "I planned to stay up all night and read them," she explained to Dot's subscribers, but "by ten o'clock I was so disgusted I threw the books across the room. They were nothing but rape sagas." She gave up, turned off the light, and thought, "If I read the perfect romance, what would the plot be?" Deveraux spent the night creating dialogue in her head and when she arose the next morning, she began writing. The book that resulted, *The Enchanted Land*, with its independent heroine and thoughtful hero, was mentioned often by Dot's customers as one of their favorites.[27]

Even the incredibly prolific and very professional Janet Dailey confesses that she too began the career that has made her a millionaire, by some observers' reckoning, because she wanted to write the kinds of books she most enjoyed reading.[28] Convinced by her husband to go ahead and try, she set out to write a romance. Since that day in 1968, millions of readers have informally acknowledged through their repeat purchases of her books that she understands very well what her readers want.

Given the fact that many romance writers were romance readers before they set pen to paper, it seems logical to expect that their views of the romance might parallel those held by their readers. Of course, this is not universally the case because many romances are considered failures by readers. Some otherwise popular books do not please the entire audience, thus bearing witness to the possibility of a discrepancy between writers' and readers' definitions and conceptions. Rosemary Rogers, for example, is universally detested by the Smithton readers who consider her books "trashy," "filthy," and "perverted." Her views of the romance are at least not representative of this group of regular readers.

Despite exceptions like these, it is striking to note that there is a distinct similarity between the Smithton conception of the romance and that implied in comments about the form by writers who are themselves enthusiastic readers. In an article on "Writing the Gothic Novel," for instance, Phyllis Whitney has cautioned aspiring writers, "no feeling, no story—and that's a rule!" [29] She explains that even though explicit sexual description must never appear in a gothic, this prohibition does not mean sexual feeling should not figure in the stories. In fact, she goes on to say, anticipation and excitement *must* "smolder" beneath the surface in scenes that are "underplayed, suggested rather than stated." That way, Whitney elaborates, "the reader's imagination will work for you." [30] She understands that women like the Smithton readers project themselves into the story by identifying with the heroine as she responds to the hero with all of her "strongly passionate nature." Whitney also knows that those women wish to be shown repeatedly that men can attend to a woman in the manner she most desires. To clarify her point she explains finally that "in the true love scenes, there is always an underlying tenderness that, for a woman, can be an exciting factor in sex— James Bond to the contrary." [31] Like Beatrice Faust and the Smithton women, Phyllis Whitney seems to believe that "women want to love and be made love to as they love babies—that is, in a nurturant fashion." [32] Whitney closes with perhaps her most central piece of advice: "I doubt that you can write Gothic novels unless you like reading them. . . . While I am in the process of writing, I am submerged in my heroine and her problems—and having a wonderful time. Me and all those dark-browed heroes! I'm sure this is the first necessary ingredient, though I'm mentioning it last." [33]

Her attitude has been echoed by Jeanne Glass, an editor at Pyramid Publications, a house that attempts to specialize in the kinds of romances that Smithton readers like. She has written that the sex in romances must be "sensual, romantic, breathy—enough to make the pulse race, but not rough-guy, explicit, constantly brutal." She adds that the predominant flavor must be an "understanding of female *emotions:* hesitancy, doubt, anger, confusion, loss of control, exhilaration, etc." [34]

These comments suggest that some romance writers agree with the Smithton group that a romance is a love story whose gradually evolving course must be experienced from the heroine's point of view. These writers understand that the goal and raison d'être of the genre is its actual, though perhaps temporary, effect on readers like the Smithton women. While explicit description of sexual encounters may be included in some of the genre's variations, the writers agree with their readers that the emphasis in the encounters must be on the love that is being conveyed through sexual contact and not on its physical details.

If readers' and writers' interpretations of their own experiences are taken into account, then, the romance cannot be dismissed as a mere pretense for masturbatory titillation. The reading experience is valued for the way it makes the reader feel, but the feeling it creates is interpreted by the women themselves as a general sense of emotional well-being and visceral contentment. Such a feeling is brought on by the opportunity to participate vicariously in a relationship characterized by *mutual* love and by the hero's quite unusual ability to express his devotion gently and with concern for his heroine's pleasure. The question that needs to be asked, therefore, is *why* the readers find it essential and beneficial to seek out this particular kind of vicarious experience. That can perhaps best be answered by comparing good and bad romances. In explaining what they do when they have determined a particular text's quality, the Smithton women provide clues to both the *deprivation* that prompts their activity and the *fears* that are assuaged and managed in the reading experience.

The reactions of the Smithton women to books they are not enjoying are indicative of the intensity of their need to avoid offensive material and the feelings it typically evokes. Indeed, twenty-three (55 percent) reported that when they find themselves in the middle of a bad book, they put it down immediately and refuse to finish it. Some even make the symbolic gesture of discarding the book in the garbage, particularly if it has offended them seriously. This was the universal fate suffered by Lolah Burford's *Alyx* (1977), a book cited repeatedly as a perfect example of the pornographic trash distributed by publishers under the guise of the romance.

Another nine (21 percent) of the women indicated that although they do not read the rest of the book, they at least skip to the ending "to see how it came out." In responding to the question about why she must read the ending of a book even in the face of evidence that the book is insulting, Maureen explained that to cease following a story in the middle is to remain suspended in the heroine's nightmare while she *is* the heroine. Her comments were corroborated by every other woman I spoke to who engaged in this kind of behavior. In elaborating upon the problem, Maureen also mentioned the kind of books that most upset her:

MAUREEN: A lot of your thicker books—it's rape—sometimes gang rape. I could not handle that in my own life. And since I'm living as the heroine, I cannot handle it in a book. And I hate myself for reading them. But if I start it, I have to get myself out of there, so I have to read my way out.

INTERVIEWER: So you must finish a book?

MAUREEN: Yes, I have to finish it. Even if it's only skimming, one word per page—or sometimes I just read the ending. I have to finish it. But it leaves a bad taste in my mouth forever.

Because nearly all romances end in the union of the two principal characters, regardless of the level of violence inflicted on the heroine during the course of the story, by reading that "happy" conclusion Maureen at least formally assures herself that all works out for the heroine as it should. She cannot simply dismiss the story as a badly managed fiction precisely because she becomes so involved in the tale that she lives it emotionally as her own. She and other readers like her feel it necessary to continue the imaginative pretense just long enough to share the heroine's achievement of mutual love that is the goal of all romance-reading experiences.

This need to read one's way out of a bad situation and to resolve or contain all of the unpleasant feelings aroused by it is so strong in some of the Smithton readers that they read the whole book even when they hate it. In fact, ten (24 percent) of Dot's customers indicated that they *always* finish a book no matter what its quality. Nevertheless, this habit does not testify to a wish or even a need to see women abused. Rather, it is the mark of the intensity with which they desire to be told that an ideal love is possible *even in the worst of circumstances* and that a woman can be nurtured and cared for even by a man who appears gruff and indifferent.

It is necessary to raise this issue of the romance readers' attitude toward the violence that undeniably exists in some romances because several commentators, including Ann Douglas, have recently suggested that women enjoy the experience of reading about others of their sex who are mistreated by men. In "Soft-Porn Culture," Douglas asserts that "the women who couldn't thrill to male nudity in *Playgirl* are *enjoying* the titillation of seeing themselves, not necessarily as they are, but as some men would like to see them: illogical, innocent, *magnetized by male sexuality and brutality*." [35] Although it is hard to disagree with her point about traditional male sexuality, which is still treated as compelling, especially in the Harlequins about which Douglas writes, there is good reason to believe that male brutality is a concern in recent romances, not because women are magnetized or drawn to it, but because they find it increasingly prevalent and horribly frightening.

Clifford Geertz maintains that all art forms, like the Balinese cockfight, render "ordinary everyday experience comprehensible by presenting it in terms of acts and objects which have had their practical consequences removed and been reduced . . . to a level of sheer appearance, where the meaning can be more powerfully articulated and more exactly perceived." [36] If Geertz is correct, then it seems likely that the romance's preoccupation with male brutality is an attempt to understand the meaning of an event that has become almost unavoidable in the real world. The romance may express misogynistic attitudes not because women share them but because they increasingly need to know how to deal with them.

The romance also seems to be exploring the consequences of attempts to counter the increased threat of violence with some sort of defiance. While the final effect of such a display may be, as Douglas claims, the formulation of the message—"don't travel alone"; "men can't stand it"; "men won't let you get away with it" [37]—the motive behind the message is less one of total assent than one of resignation born of fear about what might happen if the message was ignored. Romantic violence may also be the product of a continuing inability to imagine any situation in which a woman might acquire and use resources that would enable her to withstand male opposition and coercion.

When the Smithton readers' specific dislikes are examined in conjunction with their preferences in romance fiction, an especially clear view of the genre's function as an artistic "display" of contemporary cultural habits develops. In particular, when the events and features that the readers *most* detest are taken as indicators of their fears, it becomes possible to isolate the crucial characteristics and consequences of gender relations that prove most troubling to the Smithton women. In chapter 4, through an examination of "the ideal romance," I shall demonstrate that the same awful possibilities of violence that dominate bad romances are always evoked as potential threats to female integrity even in good romances, simply because women are trying to *explain* this situation to themselves. Because the explanation finally advanced in the good romance remains a highly conservative one of traditional categories and definitions, when events that occur in reality are displayed in the text, they are always reinterpreted as mere threats. However, in those romances where the potential consequences of male–female relations are too convincingly imagined or permitted to control the tenor of the book by obscuring the developing love story, the art form's role as *safe* display is violated. In that case, the story treads too closely to the terrible real in ordinary existence that it is trying to explain. Then, the romance's role as conservator of the social structure and its legitimizing ideology is unmasked because the contradictions the form usually papers over and minimizes so skillfully render the romantic resolution untenable even for the women who are usually most convinced by it.

Dot first acquainted me with the features of such a "bad" romance during our initial interview when she informed me that her customers can tell the difference between romances written by women and those written by men. She agrees with their dismissal of male-authored romances, she explained, because very few men are "perceptive" or "sensitive" and because most cannot imagine the kind of "gentleness" that is essential to the good romance. When asked to elaborate on the distinction between a good romance and a bad one, she replied that the latter was "kinky, you know, filled with sado-masochism, cruelty, and all sorts of things." She concluded decisively, "I detest that!"

Her readers apparently do too for in response to a question requesting them to select the three things that "should never appear in a romance" from a list of eleven choices, rape was listed by eleven of the women as the most objectionable feature, while a sad ending was selected by an additional ten. The rest of the group divided almost evenly over explicit sex, physical torture of the heroine or hero, and bed-hopping. Despite the apparent range of dislikes, when their rankings are summarized, clear objections emerge. The women generally agree that bed-hopping or promiscuous sex, a sad ending, rape, physical torture, and weak heroes have no place in the romance. Their choices here are entirely consistent with their belief in the therapeutic value of romance reading. The sad ending logically ranks high on their list of objections because its presence would negate the romance's difference and distance from day-to-day existence, dominated as it so often is by small failures, minor catastrophies, and ongoing disappointments. In addition, without its happy ending, the romance could not hold out the utopian promise that male–female relations can be managed successfully.

I suspect bed-hopping is so objectionable in a romance because the genre is exploring the possibilities and consequences for women of the American middle class of adopting what has been dubbed "the new morality." Most students of the romance have observed that after the 1972 appearance of Woodiwiss's unusually explicit *The Flame and the Flower*, romance authors were free to treat their heroines as sexual creatures capable of arousal and carnal desire. Indeed, the extraordinary popularity of Woodiwiss's novel and its rapid imitation by others seem to suggest that large numbers of American women had been affected by feminism and the sexual revolution of the 1960s. The strong reader distaste for bed-hopping or promiscuous sex suggests, however, that this change in sexual mores was and still is tolerable only within very strict limits. Hence, the "good" romance continues to maintain that a woman acknowledge and realize her feelings *only* within traditional, monogamous marriage. When another text portrays a

TABLE 3

Question: Which of the Following Do You Feel Should
Never Be Included in a Romance?

Response	First Most Objectionable	Second Most Objectionable	Third Most Objectionable	Total
a. Rape	11	6	2	19
b. Explicit sex	6	2	1	9
c. Sad ending	10	4	6	20
d. Physical torture	5	6	7	18
e. An ordinary heroine	1	1	1	3
f. Bed-hopping	4	12	6	22
g. Premarital sex	0	0	1	1
h. A cruel hero	1	5	6	12
i. A weak hero	4	5	7	16
j. A hero stronger than the heroine	0	0	0	0
k. A heroine stronger than the hero	0	1	3	4

heroine who is neither harmed nor disturbed by her ability to have sex with several men, I suspect it is classified as "bad" because it makes explicit the threatening implications of an unleashed feminine sexuality capable of satisfying itself outside the structures of patriarchal domination that are still perpetuated most effectively through marriage.[38] Such a portrayal also strays too close to the suggestion that men do not care for women as individuals but, as the saying goes, are interested only in one thing.

In fact, the Smithton women revealed that they suspected as much when they voiced their anger about male promiscuity and repeatedly complained about romances that advance the double standard. "We do not want to be told," one of Dot's customers explained, "that if you love a man you'll forgive him." Neither do they wish to adopt male standards; Dot and her customers would prefer that men learn to adhere to theirs. The Smithton women overwhelmingly believe that sex is a wonderful form of intimate communication that should be explored only by two people who care for each other deeply and intend to formalize their relationship through the contract of marriage. For them, the romance is neither a recommendation for female revolt nor a strictly conservative refusal to acknowledge any change. It is, rather, a cognitive exploration of the possibility of adopting and managing some attitude changes about feminine sexuality by making room for them within traditional institutions and structures that they understand to be protective of a woman's interests.

Rape and physical torture of the heroine and the hero are obviously objectionable because the readers are seeking an opportunity to be shown a happier, more trouble-free version of existence. Such features are probably also distasteful, however, because the romance, which is never simply a love story, is also an exploration of the meaning of patriarchy for women. As a result, it is concerned with the fact that men possess and regularly exercise power over them in all sorts of circumstances. By picturing the heroine in relative positions of weakness, romances are not necessarily endorsing her situation, but examining an all-too-common state of affairs in order to display possible strategies for coping with it. When a romance presents the story of a woman who is misunderstood by the hero, mistreated and manhandled as a consequence of his misreading, and then suddenly loved, protected, and cared for by him because he recognizes that he mistook the meaning of her behavior, the novel is informing its readers that the minor acts of violence they must contend with in their own lives can be similarly reinterpreted as the result of misunderstandings or of jealousy born of "true love." The readers are therefore assured that those acts do not warrant substantial changes or traumatic upheaval in a familiar way of life.[39]

Woodiwiss's handling of what one reader called "a little forceful persuasion" is acceptable to the Smithton women because they are fully convinced by her attempt to show that the hero's sexual sway over the heroine is always the product of his passion and her irresistibility. Indeed, one publishing house understands this quite well, for in its directions to potential writers it states that rape is not recommended but that one will be allowed under specific conditions if the author feels it is necessary to make a point.[40] Should that rape occur "between the heroine and the hero," the directions specify, it must "never be initiated with the violent motivation that exists in reality" because "a woman's fantasy is to lose control" with someone who really cares for her. "A true rape" can be included only if "it moves the story forward" and if it happens to someone other than the heroine.

Vicious or "true" rape upsets the tenuous balance for most of the Smithton readers because they feel they would not be able to forgive or explain away an overtly malicious act. They cannot understand how a heroine finds it within herself to ignore such an event, forgive the man who violated her, and then grow to love him. As Ann, one of Dot's most outspoken customers, put it, "I get tired of it if they [the heroes] keep grabbing and using sex as a weapon for domination because they want to win a struggle of the wills. I'm tending to get quite a few of these in Harlequins and I think they're terrible." Her comment prompted excited discussion among those in the interview group who had read the recent Harlequins. All of the women agreed that they found Harlequin's new, more explicit preoccupation with male violence nauseating, and several even admitted that they stopped buying them to avoid being subjected to this form of male power. The following explanation of several Harlequin plots was given by another of Dot's customers:

> Four of the eight in the last shipment—they're married and separated four to eight years and all of a sudden *he* decides that they should have stayed together and *he* punishes her. They're gonna get together and live happily ever after, after *he* punishes her! Right!

> That sounds terrible.

> Well, they are. He tricks her into coming back or meeting with him or whatever and he has some sort of powerhold over her either emotionally or physi-

cally—either he'll take her child away or ruin her father. He's determined to win her back. She's good enough to have him now.[41]

This reader's scorn for a typical pattern of explanation in romance fiction makes it clear that there are limits to what can be justified by evoking the irrationality of passionate love. Although opinions about acceptability probably vary tremendously within the entire romance audience, Dot's readers at least seem to agree about the conditions that must be met. Violence is acceptable to them only if it is described sparingly, if it is controlled carefully, or if it is *clearly* traceable to the passion or jealousy of the hero. On the other hand, if it is represented as brutal and vicious, if it is extensively detailed and carried out by many men, or if it is depicted as the product of an obvious desire for power, these same women find that violence offensive and objectionable. This curious and artificial distinction that they draw between "forceful persuasion" and "true rape" is a function of the very pressing need to know how to deal with the realities of male power and force in day-to-day existence.

I suspect their willingness to see male force interpreted as passion is also the product of a wish to be seen as so desirable to the "right" man that he will not take "no" for an answer. Because he finds her irresistible, the heroine need not take any responsibility for her own sexual feelings. She avoids the difficulty of choosing whether to act on them or not. Although female sexuality is thus approvingly incorporated into the romantic fantasy, the individual ultimately held responsible for it is not the woman herself, but once again, a man.

If the qualities of a bad romance reveal the fears and concerns that are troubling to the women who read them, the characteristics they identify with good romances point to the existence of important needs and desires that are met and fulfilled by the perfect romantic fantasy. According to Dot and her customers, the relative excellence of a romance is a function of its treatment of three different aspects of the story. These include the personality of the heroine, the character of the hero, and the particular manner in which the hero pursues and wins the affections of the heroine. If these individuals and relationships are not presented properly, not even ingenious plotting will rescue the novel from "the garbage dump."

On first discussing romances with the Smithton readers, I was struck by the fact that individual books were inevitably registered in their memories as the stories of particular *women*. When specific titles were volunteered to illustrate a point, they were always linked with a capsule plot summary beginning with a statement about the heroine and continuing with the principal events of what was, to the speaker, her tale. Because of her perceived centrality in the romance and because of their admitted tendency to project themselves into the heroine's being, the Smithton readers hold particularly exacting expectations about the qualities the heroine should have and the kinds of behavior she should exhibit.

So consistent are their feelings about heroines, in fact, that no discrepancy appears between their orally reported preferences and those acknowledged on the anonymous questionnaires. Dot's customers inevitably responded to my query about the characteristics of a good heroine with the statement that she must have three traits: intelligence, a sense of humor, and independence. On the questionnaire, nineteen (45 percent) of the women selected intelligence from a list of nine other possibilities as the characteristic they *most* liked to see in a heroine, while nine (21 percent) picked a sense of humor. The only other traits to score significantly were femininity and independence. When the group's rankings are totaled, intellligence joins independence and a sense of humor as the three traits that score significantly higher than all of the others. It seems especially important to note that three-fourths of the group selected intelligence (79 percent) and a sense of humor (74 percent) at least once, whereas independence was chosen by almost half (48 percent) of the Smithton women. Femininity, with its connotation of demure deference, was, however, still a choice of fourteen of the Smithton readers.

It may seem curious to insist here on the importance of the heroine's intelligence and independence to the Smithton women when so many "objective" students of the genre have commented on her typical passivity and quivering helplessness.[42] This harsh analytical judgment, however, is often founded on an assessment of the heroine's ultimate success in solving a mystery, making her desires known, or in refusing to be cowed by the hero. The *results* of her actions, in short, are always measured on a scale whose highest value is accorded the autonomous woman capable of accomplishing productive work in a nondomestic sphere. While the romantic heroine understandably compares badly with this ideal woman, it is important to note that neither Dot nor her readers find such an ideal attractive, nor do they strutinize and evaluate the heroine's success in effecting change or in getting others to do what she wants in order to assess her character. The heroine's personality is, instead, inevitably and securely established for them at the beginning of the tale through a series of simple observations about her abilities, talents, and career choice. Because the Smithton women accept those assertions at face value, they search no further for incidents that might comment on or revise her early portrayal. Not only do they believe in the heroine's honest desire to take care of herself, but they also believe in the mimetic accuracy of the extenuating circumstances that always intervene to thwart her intended actions. The Smithton women are, in sum, significantly more inclined than their feminist critics to recognize the inevitability and reality of male power and the force of social convention to circumscribe a woman's ability to act in her own interests. It must also be said that they are comfortable with the belief that a woman should be willing to sacrifice extreme self-interest for a long-term relationship where mutually agreed-upon goals take precedence over selfish desire.

The point I want to make here is that when analysis proceeds from within the belief system actually brought to bear upon a text by its readers, the analytical interpretation of the meaning of a character's behavior is more likely to coincide with that meaning as it is constructed and understood by the readers themselves. Thus the account offered to explain the desire to experience this particular fantasy is also more likely to approximate the motives that actually initiate the readers' decision to pick up a romance. While the romantic heroine may appear foolish, dependent, and even pathetic to a woman who has already accepted as given the equality of male and female abilities, she appears courageous, and even valiant, to another still unsure that such equality is a fact or that she herself might want to assent to it.

The Smithton women seem to be struggling simultaneously with the promise and threat of the women's movement as well as with their culture's now doubled capacity to belittle the intelligence and activities of "the ordinary housewife." Therefore, while they are still very conservative and likely to admit the rightness of traditional relations between men and women, at the same time they are angered by men who continue to make light of "woman's work" as well as by "women's libbers" whom they accuse of dismissing mothers and housewives as ignorant, inactive, and unimportant. Their desire to believe that the romantic heroine is as intelligent and independent as she is asserted to be even though she is also shown to be vulnerable and most interested in being loved is born of their apparently unconscious desire to realize some of the benefits of feminism within traditional institutions and relationships—hence, the high value attached to the simple *assertion* of the heroine's special abilities. With a few simple statements rather than with truly threatening action on the part of the heroine, the romance author demonstrates for the typical reader the compatibility of a changed sense of the female self and an unchanged social arrangement. In the utopia of romance fiction, "independence" and a secure individual "identity" are never compromised by the paternalistic care and protection of the male.

Although chapter 4 will explore the particular strategies employed by Smithton's favorite romance authors to avoid the real contradictions between dependency and self-definition, I would like to quote here from a lengthy and exuberant discussion carried on in one of the interviews when I asked Dot, her daughter, Kit, and Ann to describe the "ideal" romantic heroine. Rather than list a series of abstract traits as others generally did, these women launched into a fifteen-minute, communally produced plot summary of Elsie Lee's *The Diplomatic Lover* (1971). The delight with which they described the heroine and what they perceived to be her constant control of her situation is as good an example as any of the desire they share with feminists to believe in the female sex's strength and capabilities and in themselves as well. When I asked them why they liked the book so much after they told me they had xeroxed the text for their own use (the book is now out of print), the extended reply began in the following way:

DOT: It's just classic.

ANN: She *decides* that she wants to lose her virginity and picks *him*.

KIT: Well, he's really nice looking; he's a movie star and he's . . .

DOT: Well, the thing is, actually, because she is in a modern workaday world. She's in Washington, D.C., in the diplomatic corps.

KIT: And *she* makes the decision, you know.

DOT: And she's the only one [in the diplomatic community] who's a virgin and her name is Nanny.

ANN: Yes.

DOT: And they call her Nanny-No-No because she's always saying no, no, no!

ANN: She knows, she's read all the textbooks; but she's just never found anyone that set her blood to boiling.

DOT: And she's known him for years.

ANN: But he walks into the room at this one party and all of a sudden . . .

KIT: She makes the decision! It's her birthday.

ANN: She mentally licks her chops.

KIT: She's twenty-three. She decides, "Well, this is it!"

ANN: Yes.

DOT: But you know it's not distasteful. There's nothing . . . it was unusual.

KIT: It was very intimate.

DOT: It's not bold.[43]

In the midst of recounting the rest of the tale, they proudly exclaimed that Nanny "spoke six languages," was "a really good artist," and "did not want to marry him even though she was pregnant" because she believed he was an "elegant tomcat" and would not be faithful to her. These untraditional skills and unconventional attitudes are obviously not seen as fulfilling or quite proper by Lee herself because they are legitimated and rendered acceptable at the novel's conclusion when the hero convinces Nanny of his love, refuses to live without her, and promises to take care of her in the future. Here is the group's recitation of this moment:

DOT: He starts stalking her and this is visually . . .

KIT: It's hysterical.

DOT: You can see it.

KIT: She's backin' off.

DOT: She's trying to get to the stairway to get to her room.

KIT: And make a mad dash.

ANN: She's what they call a "petite pocket Venus type."

DOT: Yes, and he's stalking her and she's backing away and saying, "No, I won't marry you!"

ANN: "I ain't going!"

KIT: "No, just forget that!"

DOT: "No, I don't need you!"

ANN: "And he says I'll camp on your doorstep; I'll picket; unfair to, you know . . ."

As in all romances, female defiance is finally rendered ineffectual and childlike as well as unnecessary by Lee's conclusion. Nonetheless, if we are to understand the full meaning of the story for these women, it is essential to recognize that their temporary reveling in her intelligence, independence, self-sufficiency, and initiative is as important to their experiencing of the book as the fact of her final capture by a man who admits that he needs her. Indeed, after recounting the resolution of this tale, Dot, Kit, and Ann relived again her "seduction of him" by marveling over the moment "when she asks him, and he's drinking and he about chokes to death!"

In novels like *The Diplomatic Lover*, which the Smithton women like best, the happy ending restores the status quo in gender relations when the hero enfolds the heroine protectively in his arms. That ending, however, can also be interpreted as an occasion for the vicarious enjoyment of a woman's ultimate triumph. Dot's readers so interpret it because the heroine, they claim, maintains her integrity on her own terms by exacting a formal commitment from the hero and simultaneously provides for her own future in the only way acceptable to her culture.

The Smithton readers' interest in a strong but still traditional heroine is complemented by their desire to see that woman loved by a very special kind of hero. As noted earlier, these women will read many romances they do not especially like, even when the hero mistreats the heroine, because the experience of the happy ending is more important to them than anything else and because it successfully explains away many individual incidents they do not condone. Nevertheless, they prefer to see the heroine desired, needed, and loved by a man who is strong and masculine, but equally capable of unusual tenderness, gentleness, and concern for her pleasure. In fact, when asked to rank ten male personality traits as to desirability, not one of the Smithton readers listed independence in first, second, or third place. Although this might be explained by suggesting that the women felt no need to single this characteristic out because they assumed that men are, by nature, independent, their interview comments suggest otherwise. Throughout their discussions of particular books, they repeatedly insisted that what they remembered and liked most about favorite novels was the skill with which the author described the hero's recognition of his own deep feelings for the heroine and his realization that he could not live without her. While the women want to feel that the heroine will be protected by the hero, they also seem to want to see her dependency balanced by its opposite, that is, by the hero's dependence on her. In this context, the Smithton women's constant emphasis on the importance of mutuality in love makes enormous sense.

I do not want to suggest here that male protectiveness and strength are not important elements in the romantic fantasy; they are. Remember, sixteen (38 percent) of the women indicated that they think a weak hero is one of the three most objectionable features in a romance. In addition, almost 25 percent of Dot's customers agreed that out of nine traits strength is the third most important in a hero. Still, neither strength nor protectiveness is considered as important as intelligence, gentleness, and an ability to laugh at life, all of which were placed significantly more often by the readers in one of the three top positions on the questionnaire. However, because Dot and her customers rarely initiated discussion of the romantic hero and just as seldom volunteered opinions about specific male characters, it has been difficult to develop a complex picture of their ideal or of the motivation prompting its formation. Even when their responses are displayed in a graph, certain mysteries persist.

The principal difficulty involves the marked preference for an "intelligent" hero. Although it is hard to say why intelligence was ranked so high by the Smithton women, it is possible that the choice is consistent with the high value they place on books, learning, and education and their own upward mobility as well as being a way of reaffirming male excellence and agentivity without also automatically implying female inferiority. The word did appear in discussions of the ideal hero, but the women offered little that would explain its prominence in their questionnaire responses. A few oral comments seemed to hint at the existence of an expectation that an "intelligent" man would be more likely to appreciate and encourage the extraordinary abilities of the ideal heroine, but this link was not volunteered consistently enough to warrant its formulation as the motive behind the fantasy. Equally hard to explain is the emphasis on a sense of humor, although I suspect the interest in this trait masks a desire to see a hero who is up to a "verbal duel" with the heroine. Not only does this create the air of "lightness" so important to the Smithton women, but it also helps to show off the heroine's tart-tongued facility to advantage.

This vagueness about the actual content of the hero's personality persisted throughout many commentaries that tended to center instead on his ability to establish the proper relationship with the heroine. The Smithton women are less

TABLE 4

Question: What Qualities Do You Like to See in a Hero?

Response	Most Important	Second Most Important	Third Most Important	Total
a. Intelligence	14	11	5	30
b. Tenderness	11	8	7	26
c. Protectiveness	3	4	7	14
d. Strength	3	3	9	15
e. Bravery	1	4	2	7
f. Sense of humor	8	5	6	19
g. Independence	0	0	0	0
h. Attractiveness	2	5	3	10
i. A good body	0	2	2	4
j. Other	0	0	0	0
Blank			1	1

interested in the particularities of their heroes as individuals than in the roles the most desirable among them perform. Gentleness and tenderness figure often in their accounts of favorite novels not so much as character traits exhibited by particular men but as the distinguishing feature of the attention accorded the heroine by all good heroes in the outstanding novels. The focus never shifts for these readers away from the woman at the center of the romance. Moreover, men are rarely valued for their intrinsic characteristics but become remarkable by virtue of the special position they occupy vis-à-vis the heroine. The romantic fantasy is therefore not a fantasy about discovering a uniquely interesting life partner, but a ritual wish to be cared for, loved, and validated in a particular way.

In distinguishing the ideal romance from Rosemary Rogers's "perversions," one of the five customers I interviewed at length wondered whether her editor had been male because, she reasoned, "it's a man's type book." When pressed to elaborate, she retorted, "because a man likes the sex in it, you know, Matt Helm and all that type." The distinction she sees here between sex and romance was continually employed by the Smithton women to differentiate pornography, which they associate with men, from their own interest in "insightful love," which they wish men could manage. As Joy said of the recent Harlequins, "all they worry about is sex—that's the first thing on their minds. They don't worry about anything else." She continued, "they don't need that; they need humor and love and caring." Similarly, in one of our final discussions, Dot also elaborated on the differences between pornography and romance and between men and women and, in doing so, identified in a wistful tone the particular characteristic she and her customers believe all men should possess:

> I've always thought that women are more insightful into men's psyches than men are into women's. Well, men just don't take the time. They just don't. And it's always been interesting to me that psychiatrists are probably . . . 85

to 90 percent of the psychiatrists in this country are men and I'm sure they
know the book. I'm sure they know the textbook. But as far as insightful, I
think that is one of the most rare commodities that there is . . . is an insightful man. . . . I don't think men look deep. I think they take even a man
at face value. Whatever they see—that's what the man is.

What the Smithton women are looking for in their search for the perfect romantic fantasy is a man who is capable of the same attentive observation and
intuitive "understanding" that they believe women regularly accord to men. We
will see in chapter 4, in a more thorough examination of the Smithton group's
favorite romances, that the fantasy generating the ideal romantic story thus
fulfills two deeply felt needs that have been activated in women by early object-
relations and cultural conditioning in patriarchal society. On the one hand, the
story permits the reader to identify with the heroine at the moment of her greatest success, that is, when she secures the attention and recognition of her culture's most powerful and essential representative, a man. The happy ending is,
at this level, a sign of a woman's attainment of legitimacy and personhood in a
culture that locates both for her in the roles of lover, wife, and mother.

On the other hand, by emphasizing the intensity of the hero's uninterrupted
gaze and the tenderness of his caress at the moment he encompasses his beloved
in his still always "masculine" arms, the fantasy also evokes the memory of a
period in the reader's life when she was the center of a profoundly nurturant individual's attention. Because this imaginative emotional regression is often denied
women in ordinary existence because men have been prompted by the culture's
asymmetrical conditioning to deny their own capacities for gentle nurturance,
it becomes necessary to fulfill this never-ending need in other areas. Nancy
Chodorow has suggested, in *The Reproduction of Mothering*, that one way for
women to provide this essential sustenance for themselves is through the mothering of others. By taking care of a child in this intense emotional way and by
identifying with her child, Chodorow reasons, a woman is able to nurture herself,
albeit vicariously. However, Chodorow does not comment at any length about
whether this vicarious care and attention prove a perfectly adequate substitute.
The ideal romance, at least as it is conceived by the Smithton women, argues
effectively that it is not. Its stress on the emotional bonding between hero and
heroine suggests that women still desire to be loved, cared for, and understood
by an adult who is singularly capable of self-abnegating preoccupation with a
loved one's needs.

In the next chapter we will discover that it is the constant impulse and duty to
mother others that is responsible for the sense of depletion that apparently sends
some women to romance fiction. By immersing themselves in the romantic fantasy, women vicariously fulfill their needs for nurturance by identifying with a
heroine whose principal accomplishment, if it can even be called that, is her success at drawing the hero's attention to herself, at establishing herself as the object
of his concern and the recipient of his care. Because the reader experiences that
care vicariously, her need is assuaged only as long as she can displace it onto a
fictional character. When that character's story is completed, when the book
must be closed, the reader is forced to return to herself and to her real situation.
Although she may feel temporarily revived, she has done nothing to alter her
relations with others. More often than not, those relations remain unchanged and

in returning to them a woman is once again expected and willing to employ her emotional resources for the care of others. If she is then not herself reconstituted by another, romance reading may suggest itself again as a reasonable compensatory solution. Therefore, the romance's short-lived therapeutic value, which is made both possible and necessary by a culture that creates needs in women that it cannot fulfill, is finally the cause of its repetitive consumption.

NOTES

1. In the course of completing this study of the Smithton readers, I have learned of at least five other such groups functioning throughout the country. Most seem to be informal networks of neighbors or co-workers who exchange romances and information about these books on a regular basis. I have also been told of a group similar to Dot's clustered about a Texas bookseller and have received information about the California-based "Friends of the English Regency," which also publishes a review newsletter and holds an annual Regency "Assemblee" at which it confers the "Georgette" award on favorite Regency romances. There is no way to tell how common this "reading club" phenomenon is, but it is worth investigating. If these clubs are widely relied upon to mediate the mass-production publishing process by individualizing selection, then a good deal of speculation about the meaning of mass-produced literature based on the "mass man" [*sic*] hypothesis will have to be reviewed and possibly rewritten.

2. These and all other figures about Smithton were taken from the *Census of the Population, 1970.* I have rounded off the numbers slightly to disguise the identity of Smithton.

3. Evans, "Dorothy's Diary," April 1980, pp. 1–2.

4. Ibid., p. 2.

5. All spoken quotations have been taken directly from taped interviews. Nearly all of the comments were transcribed verbatim, although in a few cases repeated false starts were excised and marked with ellipses. Pauses in a speaker's commentary have been marked with dashes. I have paragraphed lengthy speeches only when the informant clearly seemed to conclude one topic or train of thought in order to open another deliberately. Lack of paragraphing, then, indicates that the speaker's comments continued apace without significant rest or pause.

6. Snitow, "Mass Market Romance," p. 150.

7. Brotman, "Ah, Romance!," p. B1.

8. Jensen, "Women and Romantic Fiction," p. 289.

9. Quoted in Brotman, "Ah, Romance!," p. B1.

10. See also Mann, *A New Survey*, passim.

11. Readers were instructed to identify the particular kind of romance they liked to "read the most" from a list of ten subgenres. The titles had been given to me by Dot during a lengthy discussion about the different kinds of romances. Although I expected the women to check only one subgenre, almost all of them checked several as their favorites. The categories and totals follow: gothics, 6; contemporary mystery romances, 5; historicals, 20; contemporary romances, 7; Harlequins, 10; Regencies, 4; family sagas, 1; plantation series, 3; spy thrillers, 0; transcendental romances, 0; other, 2.

12. It should be pointed out, however, that these findings could also indicate that romances were not heavily advertised or distributed when the majority of women in this sample were teenagers. Thus, the fact that so many have picked up the romance habit may be as much a function of the recent growth of the industry as of any particular need or predisposition on the part of women at a particular stage in their life cycle. Still, as I will make clear in this and subsequent chapters, romances do address needs associated with the role of mothering for *this* particular group of readers.

13. Jensen, "Women and Romantic Fiction," pp. 290–91.

14. Jensen also reports that all of the married women in her sample have children and that three quarters have children still living at home (ibid., p. 291).

15. Cited in Yankelovich, Skelly, and White, *The 1978 Consumer Research Study on Reading,* p. 325.

16. This compares with the eight-hour weekly average claimed by book readers who read fiction for leisure as reported in Yankelovich, Skelly, and White, ibid., p. 126.

17. Although the Smithton women also commented, as did Jensen's informants, on the ease with which "light reading" like Harlequins and Silhouettes can be picked up and put down when other demands intervene, all of Dot's customers with whom I spoke expressed a preference for finishing a romance in one sitting. Jensen does not say whether her readers would have preferred to read in this way, although she does comment rather extensively on the fact that it is the material circumstances of their jobs as housewives and mothers that most often necessitate what she calls "snatch" reading. She refers to an alternate pattern of reading several books, one after the other, as the "binge." This is not exactly equivalent to the Smithton readers' practice with fat books, but some of them did mention engaging in such behavior as a special treat to themselves. See Jensen, "Women and Romantic Fiction," pp. 300–301 and 312–14.

18. Yankelovich, Skelly, and White, *The 1978 Consumer Research Study on Reading,* pp. 141, 144.

19. The Smithton readers' patterns of explanation and justification will be explored in greater detail in chapter 3.

20. Mann, *A New Survey,* p. 17.

21. For further discussion of this curious failure to trust that a new romance will end happily despite extensive prior acquaintance with the genre, see chapter 6 of *Reading the Romance.*

22. Evans, "Dorothy's Diary," April 1980, p. 1.

23. I included this choice on the final questionnaire because in many of the interviews the women had expressed a distaste for romances that end abruptly with the declaration of love between the principal characters.

24. Faust, *Women, Sex, and Pornography,* p. 67.

25. Richard Hoggart is one of the few who disagrees with this argument. See his comments in *The Uses of Literacy,* pp. 171–75. Jensen has also acknowledged that many Harlequin authors "apparently share the backgrounds, attitudes, and fantasies of their women readers" ("Women and Romantic Fiction," pp. 118–19).

26. Quoted in Evans, "Dorothy's Diary," May 1980, p. 2.

27. Quoted in Evans, "Dorothy's Diary," Newsletter 4, 1980, p. 2. (This issue is not dated by month.)

28. Berman, "They Call Us Illegitimate," p. 38.

29. Whitney, "Writing the Gothic Novel," p. 10.

30. Ibid.

31. Ibid., p. 11.

32. Faust, *Women, Sex, and Pornography,* p. 63.

33. Whitney, "Writing the Gothic Novel," p. 43.

34. Quoted by Glass, "Editor's Report," p. 33.

35. Douglas, "Soft-Porn Culture," p. 28 (italics added).

36. Geertz, "Deep Play," p. 443.

37. Douglas, "Soft-Porn Culture," p. 25.

38. On the connection between patriarchy and marriage, see Hartmann, "The Family as Locus of Gender, Class, and Political Struggle," especially pp. 366–76.

39. None of the Smithton women commented on whether they had ever been hit, pushed around, or forced to have sexual relations against their will, although several did tell me that they know this goes on because it happens to their friends. In summarizing current studies on wife abuse, Rohrbaugh has commented in *Women: Psychology's Puzzle*

that "many researchers in this field agree with Judge Stewart Oneglia's estimate that '50 percent of all marriages involve some degree of physical abuse of the woman'" (p. 350). Rohrbaugh also points out that "studies that define wife abuse as anything from an occasional hard slap to repeated, severe beating suggest that there are 26 million to 30 million abused wives in the United States today" (p. 350). If these figures are accurate, it seems clear that a good many romance readers may very well need to be given a model "explanation" for this sort of behavior.

40.   I would like to thank Star Helmer for giving me a copy of Gallen Books' "tipsheet" for contemporary romances.

41.   The italics have been added here to indicate where Ann placed special emphasis and changed her intonation during her remarks. In each case, the emphasis conveyed both sarcasm and utter disbelief. Two of the most difficult tasks in using ethnographic material are those of interpreting meanings clearly implied by a speaker but not actually said and adequately conveying them in written prose.

42.   See, especially, Modleski, "The Disappearing Act," pp. 444–48.

43.   Again, the italics have been added here to indicate where special emphasis was conveyed through intonation. In each case, the emphasis was meant to underscore the distance between this heroine's behavior and that usually expected of women.

WORKS CITED

Berman, Phyllis. "They Call Us Illegitimate." *Forbes* 6 (March 1978): 37–38.

Brotman, Barbara. "Ah, Romance! Harlequin Has an Affair for Its Readers." *Chicago Tribune*, 2 June 1980, p. B1.

Douglas, Ann. "Soft-Porn Culture." *New Republic*, 30 August 1980, pp. 25–29.

Evans, Dorothy. "Dorothy's Diary of Romance Reading." April 1980–September 1981. Mimeographed newsletters.

Faust, Beatrice. *Women, Sex, and Pornography: A Controversial and Unique Study.* New York: Macmillan Publishing Co., 1980.

Geertz, Clifford. "Deep Play: Notes on the Balinese Cockfight." In *The Interpretation of Cultures*, pp. 412–53. New York: Basic Books, 1973.

Glass, Jeanne. "Editor's Report." *Writer* 90 (April 1977): 33.

Hartmann, Heidi I. "The Family as the Locus of Gender, Class, and Political Struggle: The Example of Housework." *Signs* 6 (Spring 1981): 366–94.

Hoggart, Richard. *The Uses of Literacy: Changing Patterns in English Mass Culture.* Fair Lawn, N.J.: Essential Books, 1957.

Jensen, Margaret. "Women and Romantic Fiction: A Case Study of Harlequin Enterprises, Romances, and Readers." Ph.D. dissertation, McMaster University, 1980.

Mann, Peter H. *A New Survey: The Facts about Romantic Fiction.* London: Mills and Boon, 1974.

Modleski, Tania. "The Disappearing Act: A Study of Harlequin Romances." *Signs* 5 (Spring 1980): 435–48.

Rohrbaugh, Joanna Bunker. *Women: Psychology's Puzzle.* New York: Basic Books, 1979.

Snitow, Ann Barr. "Mass Market Romance: Pornography for Women Is Different." *Radical History Review* 20 (Spring/Summer 1979): 141–61.

Whitney, Phyllis. "Writing the Gothic Novel." *Writer* 80 (February 1967): 9–13, 42–43.

Yankelovish, Skelly, and White. *The 1978 Consumer Research Study on Reading and Book Purchasing.* Prepared for the Book Industry Study Group. Darien, Conn.: The Group, 1978.

discourse

Through the 1980s, feminism and literary theory seemed constantly to be arguing, continually returning to the exasperated question, "Can we talk?" Some feminists—having worked through such poststructuralist critical approaches as deconstruction, psychoanalysis, narratology, and dialogism—now repudiate "theory" as a patriarchal device wielded for dominance of the literary field (see, for example, Jane Tompkins's "Me and My Shadow," in "Autobiography" and Nina Baym's "The Madwoman and Her Languages, in "Methodologies"). But for many feminists, mainstream literary theories hold the promise of precise vocabularies, widely circulated premises, and analytic methods that can lend form to feminist observations and can enable feminist critics to engage in conversation with a critical community that does not necessarily take feminist values for granted. As each of the entries in this section illustrates, the (usually) male originators of poststructuralist theory seldom attend to gender in their formulations of such concepts as text, voice, reader, or discourse. The task for these five feminists—among many others, including Alice Jardine, Elizabeth Meese, Nancy K. Miller, Naomi Schor, and Rita Felski, to mention a few who are not represented in this volume—has been to insert gender into the models proposed by androcentric theorists and to ask what impact consideration of "Femininity" or "the female" might have on the ways theories can be formulated and applied.

We call this section "discourse," partly because an original meaning of that word was "to talk": one might interpret the section's heading in that sense, as a conversation among theoretical communities. But "discourse" has come to mean something else in current critical vocabularies. Broadly speaking, "discourse" refers to a particular use of language in a given time and place: novels, television commercials, or political speeches are not themselves "discourses," in this usage, but rather instances of discourse, of ways language gets used on given topics in a particular culture and society. Each of the five essays here uses "discourse" to mean something slightly different, and each usage carries assumptions that are linked to the literary theory the writer has chosen to employ and revise. These five ways of talking about discourse are by no means comprehensive, but they suggest both the variety and the unity among feminisms' dialogues with literary theory.

Catherine Belsey's "Constructing the Subject; Deconstructing the Text" (1985) may be one of the more difficult selections in *Feminisms* for readers uninitiated into literary theory to grasp, but such readers might consider tackling it first and last, as an introduction to and summary of the recent interplay of feminisms and literary theory. Belsey's focus is "literary discourse," and her project is to survey the major assumptions that have dominated critical thinking about what to do with literature in a poststructuralist era. Belsey carefully weaves together the primary concern of feminism—to change the world by eliminating the oppression of women—with the positions of theorists whose approaches seem, on the face of it, to be apolitical, or else to make class struggle, rather than gender inequities, their highest priority. Establishing definitions for such crucial concepts as "subject," "identity," "discourse," and "ideology," Belsey shows how those terms cross boundaries between the linguistically-based theories of Benveniste and de Saussure, the psychoanalysis of Lacan, the Marxism of Althusser and Macherey, and the semiotic cultural critique of Barthes.

For Belsey, the method of analyzing literary discourse that draws upon the most fruitful accumulation of these concepts is deconstruction, an approach she finds particularly helpful to the feminist who wishes to challenge the subject position constructed for readers within "classic realism." Belsey asserts that critics who follow deconstruction's invitation to "find the multiplicity and diversity of . . . possible meanings" rather than the unity of a text will find it "implicitly criticizes its own ideology; it contains within itself the critique of its own values." Placing an overlay of gender on that deconstructive tenet, Belsey looks at some Sherlock Holmes stories to demonstrate that the shadowy, silent, mysterious, and magical presence of sexualized women in those stories undercuts the narratives' overt endorsements of logic, positivism, and science. Deconstruction, then, is one way to uncover the operations of gender in literary discourse.

In Susan S. Lanser's "Toward a Feminist Narratology" (1986), "discourse" takes on a more specific meaning, borrowed from such structuralist narratologists as Gérard Genette. Here, narrative texts are broken down into two components: "story," or "what happens" in a narrative, and "discourse," or how "what happens" gets rendered in language. The study of narrative discourse seeks to describe and classify the various possible ways that stories can be told, with attention to such matters as voice, perspective, temporal organization, and repetition. Observing that feminists typically shun narratology and that narratologists draw almost exclusively on male-written texts to illustrate their models, Lanser suggests that narratives written or spoken by women cannot always be adequately described within narrative theory's androcentric models. In raising this issue, Lanser seeks to extend the purposes of narratology beyond their traditional boundaries: she is interested in feminist narratology's potential for helping to interpret texts, to describe gendered differences in writing, and to be more explicit than structuralism has been about its ideological positioning as a critical practice.

To illustrate her suggestion, Lanser analyzes a text that stretches traditional definitions of narrative, a letter ostensibly written by a woman, which has at least three entirely different meanings, depending on the perspective of its reader. Lanser shows that the "public" or "private" nature of a narrative utterance has an important effect on the way a reader receives it. As she points out, the "public/private" opposition has played a significant role in the tradition of women's writing, which has, in Western culture, so often taken the form of letters. By thinking about the perspectives from which a narrative can be read and interpreted, Lanser extends narratology's reference beyond the limits of the text, into the "rhetorical circumstance" producing it. In this way, feminist narratology can introduce the concerns of the world of lived experience into structuralist-inspired literary theory.

More straightforwardly than the other contributors to this section, Barbara Johnson (in "Apostrophe, Animation, and Abortion," 1986) equates "discourse" with "rhetoric" and asks what its relation to the "real world" might be: as she so powerfully inquires, "Is there any *inherent* connection between figurative language and questions of life and death?" The question of life and death here is about abortion; the discourse under scrutiny is the poetic figure of apostrophe, or the address to an absent entity which paradoxically both animates and silences the addressee. To bring abortion and apostrophe together is to raise the issue of "discursive positions," or the place from which you speak (for example, as the no-longer-pregnant woman? as the aborted fetus?) in a poem. Johnson looks at poems about abortion, pregnancy, childbirth, and the death of children written in various periods by men and by women, and observes that a difficulty for poets seems to be "the attempt to achieve a full elaboration of any discursive position other than that of child." Johnson's deconstruction of apostrophe in those poems points to the "undecidability" of matters of life and death in poetic discourse, and, in bringing this up, she alludes to the controversy over poststructuralism's reputation for uselessness in the face of politics. As Johnson argues, though (and Belsey, for one, would probably agree), undecidability is not an apolitical condition, but rather is what brings politics into being, what gives them birth.

If Johnson's analysis of abortion and rhetoric begins to raise questions about the relation of the body to discourse, Linda Kauffman's *Discourses of Desire* (1986) makes those questions explicit. For Kauffman, the situation is simple, its ramifications complex: "We need because we are in the body; we demand in speech"; but language can never adequately stand in for "the alphabet of the body." Hence arises the "discourse of desire," the mode that Kauffman identifies as primary to epistolary novels that center on heroines. Taking Roland Barthes's *A Lover's Discourse* farther than he does into the realm of gender studies, Kauffman looks at the "genre of amorous epistolary discourses," or the letter-writing of heroines in love.

Most of the examples in Kauffman's book are drawn from novels that are made up entirely of letters; in choosing "Devious Channels of Decorous Ordering: Rosa Coldfield in *Absalom, Absalom!*," we offer a non-representative piece. But Kauffman argues persuasively here that Rosa—the outraged unmarried old woman who narrates to Quentin Compson much of what he knows about the history of the Sutpen family—strongly resembles epistolary heroines in her use of "amatory discourse." Kauffman's reading rescues Rosa from critics who see her as an alien or mad figure, to place her in the tradition of Richardson's Clarissa Harlowe, whose discourse of desire—like Rosa's—is elegaic. Like epistolary heroines, Rosa uses the discourse of doubleness and dissimulation, of the ideal and idolizing lover, and of self-conscious theatricality. Although Rosa's story is dominated by disappointed desires, Kauffman argues that her discourse is itself a critique of the masculine realm of facts and figures, and that it is an affirmation of love, of faith, and of the body. This conclusion places Kauffman's interpretation of *Absalom* in radical opposition to the received version of what the novel (and Rosa's role) are supposed to mean. For Kauffman, Rosa's discourse is "dialogic," in that it offers a position in the novel against the novel's representation of the male world of logic and ledgers.

In Dale Bauer's book *Feminist Dialogics: A Theory of Failed Community* (1986), dialogic discourse takes center stage. More directly than Kauffman, Bauer draws upon the work of Mikhail M. Bakhtin, the Russian theorist of the novel who combined the concerns of formalist discourse analysis with attention to sociology, ideology, and politics. One of Bakhtin's most influential ideas is that literary discourse in novels never proceeds from a single voice, but is always "polyvocal," "dialogic" in the sense that it is implicitly taking part in a dialogue. *Every* utterance, in this view, contains in it the traces of other articulated positions, which it answers, affirms, revises, or contradicts. On a more literal level, too, novels are "dialogic" in that they contain representations of narrators and characters who say things that diverge from one another's stated positions, and from the author's own. A novel is like a playing field or—as Bauer would have it—a battleground where discourses representing the interests of different groups struggle for dominance.

Bakhtin thinks primarily in terms of class struggle, but Bauer transfers his theory to the realm of gender. Her study of novels by Nathaniel Hawthorne, Henry James, Edith Wharton, and Kate Chopin looks at the voice of the heroine of nineteenth-century American literature who plays the Bakhtinian "fool," misreading and incomprehending, hence subverting, the dominant discourses in the text. According to Bauer, even a heroine's silence—not unusual in the selected corpus—takes on meaning from the perspective of feminist dialogics, through the effort of the feminist reader who tries to read the heroine's voice "back into" the text which excludes it. Bauer scrutinizes the struggle for power and authority in the "battle of languages" that emerges among competing voices in fiction. To take one of Bauer's examples, Hawthorne's *The Blithedale Romance* offers the voices of "the pragmatist, the social reformer, the artist, the feminist," and the discourse of each is continually in dialogic engagement with the others. To be sure, dialogue—talk, conversation, speech addressed to an other—is at the center of each of these feminist analyses of discourse and—as Bauer so accurately points out—power and authority are what is always at stake in theory and criticism of literature, as they are in literary discourse itself.

—RRW

CONSTRUCTING THE SUBJECT
deconstructing the text

~~~~~~

THE SUBJECT IN IDEOLOGY

One of the central issues for feminism is the cultural construction of subjectivity. It seems imperative to many feminists to find ways of explaining why women have not simply united to overthrow patriarchy. Why, since all women experience the effects of patriarchal practices, are not all women feminists? And why do those of us who think of ourselves as feminists find ourselves inadvertently colluding, at least from time to time, with the patriarchal values and assumptions prevalent in our society? Since the late seventeenth century feminists have seen subjectivity as itself subject to convention, education, and culture in its broadest sense. Now feminist criticism has allowed that fiction too plays a part in the process of constructing subjectivity. But how?

In his influential essay 'Ideology and ideological state apparatuses,' Louis Althusser includes literature among the ideological apparatuses which contribute to the process of *reproducing* the *relations of production*, the social relationships which are the necessary condition for the existence and perpetuation of the capitalist mode of production. He does not here develop the argument concerning literature, but in the context both of his concept of ideology and also of the work of Roland Barthes on literature and Jacques Lacan on psychoanalysis it is possible to construct an account of some of the implications for feminist theory and practice of Althusser's position. The argument is not only that literature represents the myths and imaginary versions of real social relationships which constitute ideology, but also that classic realist fiction, the dominant literary form of the nineteenth century and arguably of the twentieth, 'interpellates' the reader, addresses itself to him or her directly, offering the reader as the position from which the text is most 'obviously' intelligible, the position of the *subject in (and of) ideology*.

According to Althusser's reading (re-reading) of Marx, ideology is not simply a set of illusions, as *The German Ideology* seems to argue, but a system of representations (discourses, images, myths) concerning the real relations in which people live. But what is represented in ideology is 'not the system of the real relations which govern the existence of individuals, but the imaginary relation of those individuals to the real relations in which they live' (Althusser 1971, p. 155). In other words, ideology is both a real and an imaginary relation to the world—real in that it is the way in which people really live their relationship to the social relations which govern their conditions of existence, but imaginary in that it discourages a full understanding of these conditions of existence and the ways in which people are socially constituted within them. It is not, therefore, to be thought of as a system of ideas in people's heads, nor as the expression at a higher level of real material relationships, but as the necessary condition of action within the social formation. Althusser talks of ideology as a 'material practice' in this sense: it exists in the behaviour of people acting according to their beliefs (ibid., pp. 155–9).

As the necessary condition of action, ideology exists in commonplaces and truisms as well as in philosophical and religious systems. It is apparent in all that is 'obvious' to us, in 'obviousnesses which we cannot *fail to recognise* and before which we have the inevitable and natural reaction of crying out (aloud or in the "still, small voice of conscience"): "That's obvious! That's right! That's true!"' (ibid., p. 161). If it is true, however, it is not the whole truth. It is a set of omissions, gaps rather than lies, smoothing over contradictions, appearing to provide answers to questions which in reality it evades, and masquerading as coherence in the interests of the social relations generated by and necessary to the reproduction of the existing mode of production.

It is important to stress, of course, that ideology is in no sense a set of deliberate distortions foisted upon a helpless working class by a corrupt and cynical bourgeoisie (or upon victimized women by violent and power hungry men). If there are groups of sinister men in shirt-sleeves purveying illusions to the public these are not the real makers of ideology. Ideology has no creators in that sense, since it exists necessarily. But according to Althusser ideological practices are supported and reproduced in the institutions of our society which he calls Ideological State Apparatuses (ISAs). The phrase distinguishes from the Repressive State Apparatus which works by force (the police, the penal system, the army) those institutions whose existence helps to guarantee consent to the existing mode of production. The central ISA in contemporary capitalism is the educational system, which prepares children to act consistently with the values of society by inculcating in them the dominant versions of appropriate behaviour as well as history, social studies and, of course, literature. Among the allies of the educational ISA are the family, the law, the media and the arts, all helping to represent and reproduce the myths and beliefs necessary to enable people to work within the existing social formation.

The destination of all ideology is the subject (the individual in society) and it is the role of ideology to *construct people as subjects*:

> I say: the category of the subject is constitutive of all ideology, but at the same time and immediately I add that *the category of the subject is only constitutive of all ideology in so far as all ideology has the function (which defines it) of 'constituting' concrete individuals as subjects.* (ibid., p. 160)

Within the existing ideology it appears 'obvious' that people are autonomous individuals, possessed of subjectivity or consciousness which is the source of their

beliefs and actions. That people are unique, distinguishable, irreplaceable identities is 'the elementary ideological effect' (ibid., p. 161).

The obviousness of subjectivity has been challenged by the linguistic theory
which has developed on the basis of the work of Saussure. As Emile Benveniste
argues, it is language which provides the possibility of subjectivity because it is
language which enables the speaker to posit himself or herself as 'I,' as the subject of a sentence. It is in language that people constitute themselves as subjects.
Consciousness of self is possible only through contrast, differentiation: 'I' cannot
be conceived without the conception 'non-I,' 'you,' and dialogue, the fundamental condition of language, implies a reversible polarity between 'I' and 'you.'
'Language is possible only because each speaker sets himself up as a *subject* by
referring to himself as *I* in his discourse' (Benveniste 1971, p. 225). But if language is a system of differences with no positive terms, 'I' designates only the
subject of a specific utterance. 'And so it is literally true that the basis of subjectivity is in the exercise of language. If one really thinks about it, one will see that
there is no other objective testimony to the identity of the subject except that
which he himself thus gives about himself' (ibid., p. 226).

Within ideology, of course, it seems 'obvious' that the individual speaker is
the origin of the meaning of his or her utterance. Post-Saussurean linguistics,
however, implies a more complex relationship between the individual and meaning, since it is language itself which, by differentiating between concepts, offers
the possibility of meaning. In reality, it is only by adopting the position of the
subject within language that the individual is able to produce meaning. As Derrida puts it,

> What was it that Saussure in particular reminded us of? That 'language
> [which consists only of differences] is not a function of the speaking subject.'
> This implies that the subject (self-identical or even conscious of self-iden-
> tity, self-conscious) is inscribed in the language, that he is a 'function' of the
> language. He becomes a *speaking* subject only by conforming his speech . . .
> to the system of linguistic prescriptions taken as the system of differences.
> (Derrida 1973, pp. 145–6)

Derrida goes on to raise the question whether, even if we accept that it is only
the signifying system which makes possible the speaking subject, the signifying
subject, we cannot none the less conceive of a non-speaking, non-signifying subjectivity, 'a silent and intuitive consciousness' (ibid., p. 146). The problem here,
he concludes, is to define consciousness-in-itself as distinct from consciousness
of something, and ultimately as distinct from consciousness of self. If consciousness is finally consciousness of self, this in turn implies that consciousness
depends on differentiation, and specifically on Benveniste's differentiation between 'I' and 'you,' a process made possible by language.

The implications of this concept of the primacy of language over subjectivity
have been developed by Jacques Lacan's reading of Freud. Lacan's theory of the
subject as constructed in language confirms the *decentring* of the individual consciousness so that it can no longer be seen as the origin of meaning, knowledge
and action. Instead, Lacan proposes that the infant is initially an 'hommelette'—
'a little man and also like a broken egg spreading without hindrance in all direc-

tions' (Coward and Ellis 1977, p. 101). The child has no sense of identity, no way of conceiving of itself as a unity, distinct from what is 'other,' exterior to it. During the 'mirror-phase' of its development, however, it 'recognizes' itself in the mirror as a unit distinct from the outside world. This 'recognition' is an identifcation with an 'imaginary' (because imaged) unitary and autonomous self. But it is only with its entry into language that the child becomes a full subject. If it is to participate in the society into which it is born, to be able to act deliberately within the social formation, the child must enter into the symbolic order, the set of signifying systems of culture of which the supreme example is language. The child who refuses to learn the language is 'sick,' unable to become a full member of the family and of society.

In order to speak the child is compelled to differentiate; to speak of itself it has to distinguish 'I' from 'you.' In order to formulate its needs the child learns to identify with the first person singular pronoun, and this identification constitutes the basis of subjectivity. Subsequently it learns to recognize itself in a series of subject-positions ('he' or 'she,' 'boy' or 'girl,' and so on) which are the positions from which discourse is intelligible to itself and others. 'Identity,' subjectivity, is thus a matrix of subject-positions, which may be inconsistent or even in contradiction with one another.

Subjectivity, then, is linguistically and discursively constructed and displaced across the range of discourses in which the concrete individual participates. It follows from Saussure's theory of language as a system of differences that the world is intelligible only in discourse: there is no unmediated experience, no access to the raw reality of self and others. Thus:

> As well as being a system of signs related among themselves, language incarnates meaning in the form of the series of positions it offers for the subject from which to grasp itself and its relations with the real. (Nowell-Smith 1976, p. 26)

The subject is constructed in language and in discourse and, since the symbolic order in its discursive use is closely related to ideology, in ideology. It is in this sense that ideology has the effect, as Althusser argues, of constituting individuals as subjects, and it is also in this sense that their subjectivity appears 'obvious.' Ideology suppresses the role of language in the construction of the subject. As a result, people 'recognize' (misrecognize) themselves in the ways in which ideology 'interpellates' them, or in other words, addresses them as subjects, calls them by their names and in turn 'recognizes' their autonomy. As a result, they 'work by themselves' (Althusser 1971, p. 169), they 'willingly' adopt the subject-positions necessary to their participation in the social formation. In capitalism they 'freely' exchange their labour-power for wages, and they 'voluntarily' purchase the commodities produced. In patriarchal society women 'choose' to do the housework, to make sacrifices for their children, not to become engineers. And it is here that we see the full force of Althusser's use of the term 'subject,' originally borrowed, as he says, from law. The subject is not only a grammatical subject, 'a centre of initiatives, author of and responsible for its actions,' but also a *subjected being* who submits to the authority of the social formation represented in ideology as the Absolute Subject (God, the king, the boss, Man, conscience):

'the individual *is interpellated as a (free) subject in order that he shall submit freely to the commandments of the Subject, i.e. in order that he shall (freely) accept his subjection*' (ibid., p. 169).

Ideology interpellates concrete individuals as subjects, and bourgeois ideology in particular emphasizes the fixed identity of the individual. 'I'm just *like* that'—cowardly, perhaps, or aggressive, generous or impulsive. Astrology is only an extreme form of the determinism which attributes to us given essences which cannot change. Popular psychology and popular sociology make individual behaviour a product of these essences. And underlying them all, ultimately unalterable, is 'human nature.' In these circumstances, how is it possible to suppose that, even if we could break in theoretical terms with the concepts of the ruling ideology, we are ourselves capable of change, and therefore capable both of acting to change the social formation and of transforming ourselves to constitute a new kind of society? A possible answer can be found in Lacan's theory of the precariousness of conscious subjectivity, which in turn depends on the Lacanian conception of the unconscious.

In Lacan's theory the individual is not in reality the harmonious and coherent totality of ideological misrecognition. The mirror-phase, in which the infant perceives itself as other, an image, exterior to is own perceiving self, necessitates a splitting between the *I* which is perceived and the *I* which does the perceiving. The entry into language necessitates a secondary division which reinforces the first, a split between the *I* of discourse, the subject of the utterance, and the *I* who speaks, the subject of the enunciation. There is thus a contradiction between the conscious self, the self which appears in its own discourse, and the self which is only partly represented there, the self which speaks. The unconscious comes into being in the gap which is formed by this division. The unconscious is constructed in the moment of entry into the symbolic order, simultaneously with the construction of the subject. The repository of repressed and pre-linguistic signifiers, the unconscious is a constant source of potential disruption of the symbolic order. To summarize very briefly what in Lacan is a complex and elusive theory, entry into the symbolic order liberates the child into the possibility of social relationship; it also reduces its helplessness to the extent that it is now able to articulate its needs in the form of demands. But at the same time a division within the self is constructed. In offering the child the possibility of formulating its desires the symbolic order also betrays them, since it cannot by definition formulate those elements of desire which remain unconscious. Demand is always only a metonymy of desire (Lemaire 1977, p. 64). The subject is thus the site of contradiction, and is consequently perpetually in the process of construction, thrown into crisis by alterations in language and in the social formation, capable of change. And in the fact that the subject is a *process* lies the possibility of transformation.

In addition, the displacement of subjectivity across a range of discourses implies a range of positions from which the subject grasps itself and its relations with the real, and these positions may be incompatible or contradictory. It is these incompatibilities and contradictions within what is taken for granted which exert a pressure on concrete individuals to seek new, non-contradictory subject-positions. Women as a group in our society are both produced and inhibited by contradictory discourses. Very broadly, we participate both in the liberal–

humanist discourse of freedom, self-determination and rationality and at the same time in the specifically feminine discourse offered by society of submission, relative inadequacy and irrational intuition. The attempt to locate a single and coherent subject-position within these contradictory discourses, and in consequence to find a non-contradictory pattern of behaviour, can create intolerable pressures. One way of responding to this situation is to retreat from the contradictions and from discourse itself, to become 'sick'—more women than men are treated for mental illness. Another is to seek a resolution of the contradictions in the discourses of feminism. That the position of women in society has changed so slowly, in spite of such a radical instability in it, may be partly explained in terms of the relative exclusion of women from the discourse of liberal humanism. This relative exclusion, supported in the predominantly masculine institutions of our society, is implicit, for example, in the use of masculine terms as generic ('rational man,' etc.).

Women are not an isolated case. The class structure also produces contradictory subject-positions which precipitate changes in social relations not only between whole classes but between concrete individuals within those classes. Even at the conscious level, although this fact may itself be unconscious, the individual subject is not a unity, and in this lies the possibility of deliberate change.

This does not imply the reinstatement of individual subjects as the agents of change and changing knowledge. On the contrary, it insists on the concept of a dialectical relationship between concrete individuals and the language in which their subjectivity is constructed. In consequence, it also supports the concept of subjectivity as in process.

It is because subjectivity is perpetually in process that literary texts can have an important function. No one, I think, would suggest that literature alone could precipitate a crisis in the social formation. None the less, if we accept Lacan's analysis of the importance of language in the construction of the subject it becomes apparent that literature as one of the most persuasive uses of language may have an important influence on the ways in which people grasp themselves and their relation to the real relations in which they live. The interpellation of the reader in the literary text could be argued to have a role in reinforcing the concepts of the world and of subjectivity which ensure that people 'work by themselves' in the social formation. On the other hand, certain critical modes could be seen to challenge these concepts, and to call in question the particular complex of imaginary relations between individuals and the real conditions of their existence which helps to reproduce the present relations of class, race and gender.

THE SUBJECT AND THE TEXT

Althusser analyses the interpellation of the subject in the context of ideology in general; Benveniste in discussing the relationship between language and subjectivity is concerned with language in general. None the less, it readily becomes apparent that capitalism in particular needs subjects who work by themselves, who freely exchange their labour-power for wages. It is in the epoch of capitalism that ideology emphasizes the value of individual freedom, freedom of conscience and, of course, consumer choice in all the multiplicity of its forms. The ideology of liberal humanism assumes a world of non-contradictory (and therefore fundamentally unalterable) individuals whose unfettered consciousness is the origin of meaning, knowledge and action. It is in the interest of this ideology above all to suppress the role of language in the construction of the subject, and its own role in the interpellation of the subject, and to present the individual as a free, unified, autonomous subjectivity. Classic realism, still the dominant popular mode in literature, film and television drama, roughly coincides chronologically with the epoch of industrial capitalism. It performs, I wish to suggest, the work of ideology, not only in its representation of a world of consistent subjects who are the origin of meaning, knowledge and action, but also in offering the reader, as the position from which the text is most readily intelligible, the position of subject as the origin both of understanding and of action in accordance with that understanding.

It is readily apparent that Romantic and post-Romantic poetry, from Wordsworth through the Victorian period at least to Eliot and Yeats, takes subjectivity as its central theme. The developing self of the poet, his consciousness of himself as poet, his struggle against the constraints of an outer reality, constitute the preoccupations of *The Prelude, In Memoriam* or *Meditations in Time of Civil War.* The 'I' of these poems is a kind of super-subject, experiencing life at a higher level of intensity than ordinary people and absorbed in a world of selfhood which the phenomenal world, perceived as external and antithetical, either nourishes or constrains. This transcendence of the subject in poetry is not presented as unproblematic, but it is entirely overt in the poetry of this period. The 'I' of the poem directly addresses an individual reader who is invited to respond equally directly to this interpellation.

Fiction, however, in this same period, frequently appears to deal rather in social relationships, the interaction between the individual and society, to the increasing exclusion of the subjectivity of the author. Direct intrusion by the author comes to seem an impropriety; impersonal narration, 'showing' (the truth) rather than 'telling' it, is a requirement of prose fiction by the end of the nineteenth century. In drama too the author is apparently absent from the self-contained fictional world on the stage. Even the text effaces its own existence as text: unlike poetry, which clearly announces itself as formal, if only in terms of the shape of the text on the page, the novel seems merely to transcribe a series of events, to report on a palpable world, however fictional. Classic realist drama displays transparently and from the outside how people speak and behave.

Nevertheless, as we know while we read or watch, the author is present as a shadowy authority and as source of the fiction, and the author's presence is substantiated by the name on the cover or the programme: 'a novel by Thomas Hardy,' 'a new play by Ibsen.' And at the same time, as I shall suggest in this section, the *form* of the classic realist text acts in conjunction with the expressive theory and with ideology by interpellating the reader as subject. The reader is invited to perceive and judge the 'truth' of the text, the coherent, non-contradictory interpretation of the world as it is perceived by an author whose autonomy is the source and evidence of the truth of the interpretation. This model of intersubjective communication, of shared understanding of a text which re-presents the world, is the guarantee not only of the truth of the text but of the reader's existence as an autonomous and knowing subject in a world of knowing subjects. In this way classic realism constitutes an ideological practice in addressing itself to readers as subjects, interpellating them in order that they freely accept their subjectivity and their subjection.

It is important to reiterate, of course, that this process is not inevitable, in the sense that texts do not determine like fate the ways in which they *must* be read. I am concerned at this stage primarily with ways in which they are conventionally read: conventionally, since language is conventional, and since modes of writing as well as ways of reading are conventional, but conventionally also in that new conventions of reading are available. In this sense meaning is never a fixed essence inherent in the text but is always constructed by the reader, the result of a 'circulation' between social formation, reader and text (Heath 1977–8, p. 74). In the same way, 'inscribed subject positions are never hermetically sealed into a text, but are always positions in ideologies' (Willemen 1978, p. 63). To argue that classic realism interpellates subjects in certain ways is not to propose that this process is ineluctable; on the contrary it is a matter of choice. But the choice is ideological: certain ranges of meaning (there is always room for debate) are 'obvious' within the currently dominant ideology, and certain subject-positions are equally 'obviously' the positions from which these meanings are apparent.

Classic realism is characterized by 'illusionism,' narrative which leads to 'closure,' and a 'hierarchy of discourses' which establishes the 'truth' of the story. 'Illusionism' is, I hope, self-explanatory. The other two defining characteristics of classic realism need some discussion. Narrative tends to follow certain recurrent patterns. Classic realist narrative, as Barthes demonstrates in *S/Z,* turns on the creation of enigma through the precipitation of disorder which throws into disarray the conventional cultural and signifying systems. Among the commonest sources of disorder at the level of plot in classic realism are murder, war, a journey or love. But the story moves inevitably towards closure which is also disclosure, the dissolution of enigma through the re-establishment of order, recognizable as a reinstatement or a development of the order which is understood to have preceded the events of the story itself.

The moment of closure is the point at which the events of the story become fully intelligible to the reader. The most obvious instance is the detective story where, in the final pages, the murderer is revealed and the motive made plain. But a high degree of intelligibility is sustained throughout the narrative as a result of the hierarchy of discourses in the text. The hierarchy works above all by means of a privileged discourse which places as subordinate all the discourses that are literally or figuratively between inverted commas.

By these means classic realism offers the reader a position of knowingness which is also a position of identification with the narrative voice. To the extent that the story first constructs, and then depends for its intelligibility, on a set of assumptions shared between narrator and reader, it confirms both the transcendent knowingness of the reader-as-subject and the 'obviousness' of the shared truths in question,

DECONSTRUCTING THE TEXT

Ideology, masquerading as coherence and plenitude, is in reality inconsistent, limited, contradictory, and the realist text as a crystallization of ideology participates in this incompleteness even while it diverts attention from the fact in the apparent plenitude of narrative closure. The object of deconstructing the text is to examine the *process of its production*—not the private experience of the individual author, but the mode of production, the materials and their arrangement in the work. The aim is to locate the point of contradiction within the text, the point at which it transgresses the limits within which it is constructed, breaks free of the constraints imposed by its own realist form. Composed of contradictions, the text is no longer restricted to a single, harmonious and authoritative reading. Instead it becomes *plural*, open to rereading, no longer an object for passive consumption but an object of work by the reader to produce meaning.

It is the work of Derrida which has been most influential in promoting deconstruction as a critical strategy. Refusing to identify meaning with authorial intention or with the theme of the work, deconstruction tends to locate meaning in areas which traditional criticism has seen as marginal—in the metaphors, the set of oppositions or the hierarchies of terms which provide the framework of the text. The procedure, very broadly, is to identify in the text the contrary meanings which are the inevitable condition of its existence as a signifying practice, locating the trace of otherness which undermines the overt project.

Derrida, however, says little specifically about literary criticism or about the question of meaning in fiction. Nor is his work directly political. In order to produce a politics of reading we need to draw in addition on the work of Roland Barthes and Pierre Macherey. In *S/Z*, first published in 1970 (English translation 1975), Barthes deconstructs (without using the word) a short story by Balzac. *Sarrasine* is a classic realist text concerning a castrato singer and a fortune. The narrative turns on a series of enigmas (What is the source of the fortune? Who is the little old man? Who is La Zambinella? What is the connection between all three?). Even in summarizing the story in this way it is necessary to 'lie': there are not 'three' but two, since the little old 'man' is 'La' Zambinella. Barthes breaks the text into fragments of varying lengths for analysis, and adds a number of 'divagations,' pieces of more generalized commentary and exploration, to show *Sarrasine* as a 'limit-text,' a text which uses the modes of classic realism in ways which constitute a series of 'transgressions' of classic realism itself. The sense of plenitude, of a full understanding of a coherent text which is the normal result of reading the realist narrative, cannot here be achieved. It is not only that castration cannot be named in a text of this period. The text is compelled to transgress the conventional antithesis between the genders whenever it uses a pronoun to speak of the castrato. The story concerns the scandal of castration and the death of desire which follows its revelation; it concerns the scandalous origin of wealth; and it demonstrates the collapse of language, of antithesis (difference) as a source of meaning, which is involved in the discourse of these scandals.

Each of these elements of the text provides a point of entry into it, none privileged, and these approaches constitute the degree of polyphony, the 'parsimonious plural' of the readable (*lisible*) text. The classic realist text moves inevitably and irreversibly to an end, to the conclusion of an ordered series of events, to the disclosure of what has been concealed. But even in the realist text certain modes of signification within the discourse—the symbolic, the codes of reference and the *semes*—evade the constraints of the narrative sequence. To the extent that these are 'reversible,' free-floating and of indeterminate authority, the text is plural. In the writable (*scriptible*), wholly plural text all statements are of indeterminate origin, no single discourse is privileged, and no consistent and coherent plot constrains the free play of the discourses. The totally writable, plural text does not exist. At the opposite extreme, the readable text is barely plural. The readable text is merchandize to be consumed, while the plural text requires the production of meanings through the identification of its polyphony. Deconstruction in order to reconstruct the text as a newly intelligible, plural object is the work of criticism.

Barthes's own mode of writing demonstrates his contempt for the readable: *S/Z* is itself a polyphonic critical text. It is impossible to summarize adequately, to reduce to systematic accessibility, and it is noticeable that the book contains no summarizing conclusion. Like *Sarrasine*, *S/Z* offers a number of points of entry, critical discourses which generate trains of thought in the reader, but it would be contrary to Barthes's own (anarchist) argument to order all these into a single, coherent methodology, to constitute a new unitary way of reading, however comprehensive, and so to become the (authoritative) author of a new critical orthodoxy. As a result, the experience of reading *S/Z* is at once frustrating and exhilarating. Though it offers a model in one sense—it implies a new kind of critical practice—it would almost certainly not be possible (or useful) to attempt a wholesale imitation of its critical method(s).

It seems clear that one of the most influential precursors of *S/Z*, though Barthes does not allude to it, was Pierre Macherey's (Marxist) *A Theory of Literary Production*, first published in 1966 (English translation 1978). Despite real and important differences between them, there are similarities worth noting. For instance, Macherey anticipates Barthes in demonstrating that contradiction is a condition of narrative. The classic realist text is constructed on the basis of enigma. Information is initially withheld on condition of a 'promise' to the reader that it will finally be revealed. The discourse of this 'truth' brings the story to an end. The movement of narrative is thus both towards discourse—the end of the story—and towards concealment—prolonging itself by delaying the end of the story through a series of 'reticences,' as Barthes calls them, snares for the reader, partial answers to the questions raised, equivocations (Macherey 1978, pp. 28–9; Barthes 1975, pp. 75–6). Further, narrative involves the reader in an experience of the inevitable in the form of the unforeseen (Macherey 1978, p. 43). The hero encounters an obstacle: will he attempt to overcome it or abandon the quest? The answer is already determined, though the reader, who has only to turn the page to discover it, experiences the moment as one of choice for the hero. In fact, of course, if the narrative is to continue the hero must go on (Barthes 1975, p. 135). Thus the author's autonomy is to some degree illusory. In one sense the author determines the nature of the story: he or she decides what happens. In another sense, however, this decision is itself determined by the constraints of the narrative (Macherey 1978, p. 48), or by what Barthes calls the 'interest' (in both the psychological and the economic senses) of the story (Barthes 1975, p. 135).

The formal constraints imposed by literary form on the project of the work in the process of literary production constitute the structural principle of Macherey's analysis. It is a mistake to reduce the text to the product of a single cause, authorial determination *or* the mechanics of the narrative. On the contrary, the literary work 'is composed from a real diversity of elements which give it substance' (Macherey 1978, p. 49). There may be a direct contradiction between the project and the formal constraints, and in the transgression thus created it is possible to locate an important object of the critical quest.

Fiction for Macherey (he deals mainly with classic realist narrative) is intimately related to ideology, but the two are not identical. Literature is a specific and irreducible form of discourse, but the language which constitutes the raw material of the text is the language of ideology. It is thus an inadequate language, incomplete, partial, incapable of concealing the real contradictions it is its purpose to efface. This language, normally in flux, is arrested, 'congealed' by the literary text.

The realist text is a determinate representation, an intelligible structure which claims to convey intelligible relationships between its elements. In its attempt to create a coherent and internally consistent fictive world the text, in spite of itself, exposes incoherences, omissions, absences and transgressions which in turn reveal the inability of the language of ideology to create coherence. This becomes apparent because the contradiction between the diverse elements drawn from different discourses, the ideological project and the literary form, creates an absence at the centre of the work. The text is divided, split as the Lacanian subject is split, and Macherey compares the 'lack' in the consciousness of the work, its silence, what it cannot say, with the unconscious which Freud explored (ibid., p. 85).

The unconscious of the work (*not*, it must be insisted, of the author) is constructed in the moment of its entry into literary form, in the gap between the ideological project and the specifically literary form. Thus the text is no more a transcendent unity than the human subject. The texts of Jules Verne, for instance, whose work Macherey analyses in some detail, indicate that 'if Jules Verne chose to be the spokesman of a certain ideological condition, he could not choose to be what he in fact became' (ibid., p. 94). What Macherey reveals in Verne's *The Secret of the Island* is an unpredicted and contradictory element, disrupting the colonialist ideology which informs the conscious project of the work. Within the narrative, which concerns the willing surrender of nature to improvement by a team of civilized and civilizing colonizers, there *insists* an older and contrary myth which the consciousness of the text rejects. Unexplained events imply another mysterious presence on what is apparently a desert island. Captain Nemo's secret presence, and his influence on the fate of the castaways from a subterranean cave, is the source of the series of enigmas and the final disclosure which constitute the narrative. But his existence in the text has no part in the overt ideological project. On the contrary, it represents the return of the repressed in the form of a re-enacting of the myth of Robinson Crusoe. This myth evokes both a literary ancestor—Defoe's story—on which all subsequent castaway stories are to some degree conditional, and an ancestral relationship to nature—the creation of an economy by Crusoe's solitary struggle to appropriate and transform the island—on which subsequent bourgeois society is also conditional. The Robinson Crusoe story, the antithesis of the conscious project of the narrative, is also the condition of its existence. It returns, as the repressed experience returns to the consciousness of the patient in dreams and slips of the tongue and in doing so it unconsciously draws attention to an origin and a history from which both desert island stories and triumphant bourgeois ideology are unable to cut themselves off, and with which they must settle their account. *The Secret of the Island* thus reveals, through the discord within it between the conscious project and the insistence of the disruptive unconscious, the *limits* of the coherence of nineteenth-century ideology.

The object of the critic, then, is to seek not the unity of the work, but the multiplicity and diversity of its possible meanings, its incompleteness, the omissions which it displays but cannot describe, and above all its contradictions. In its absences, and in the collisions between its divergent meanings, the text implicitly criticizes its own ideology; it contains within itself the critique of its own values, in the sense that it is available for a new process of production of meaning by the reader, and in this process it can provide a knowledge of the limits of ideological representation.

Macherey's way of reading is precisely contrary to traditional Anglo-American critical practice, where the quest is for the unity of the work, its coherence, a way of repairing any deficiencies in consistency by reference to the author's philosophy or the contemporary world picture. In thus smoothing out contradiction, closing the text, criticism becomes the accomplice of ideology. Having created a canon of acceptable texts, criticism then provides them with acceptable interpretations, thus effectively censoring any elements in them which come into collision with the dominant ideology. To deconstruct the text, on the other hand, is to open it, to release the possible positions of its intelligibility, including those which reveal the partiality (in both senses) of the ideology inscribed in the text.

THE CASE OF SHERLOCK HOLMES

In locating the transitions and uncertainties of the text it is important to remember, Macherey insists, sustaining the parallel with psychoanalysis, that the problem of the work is not the same as its *consciousness* of a problem (Macherey 1978, p. 93). In 'Charles Augustus Milverton,' one of the short stories from *The Return of Sherlock Holmes*, Conan Doyle presents the reader with an ethical problem. Milverton is a blackmailer; blackmail is a crime not easily brought to justice since the victims are inevitably unwilling to make the matter public; the text therefore proposes for the reader's consideration that in such a case illegal action may be ethical. Holmes plans to burgle Milverton's house to recover the letters which are at stake, and both Watson and the text appear to conclude, after due consideration, that the action is morally justifiable. The structure of the narrative is symmetrical: one victim initiates the plot, another concludes it. While Holmes and Watson hide in Milverton's study a woman shoots him, protesting that he has ruined her life. Inspector Lestrade asks Holmes to help catch the murderer. Holmes replies that certain crimes justify private revenge, that his sympathies are with the criminal and that he will not handle the case. The reader is left to ponder the ethical implications of his position.

Meanwhile, on the fringes of the text, another narrative is sketched. It too contains problems but these are not foregrounded. Holmes's client is the Lady Eva Blackwell, a beautiful debutante who is to be married to the Earl of Dovercourt. Milverton has secured letters she has written 'to an impecunious young squire in the country.' Lady Eva does not appear in the narrative in person. The content of the letters is not specified, but they are 'imprudent, Watson, nothing worse.' Milverton describes them as 'sprightly.' Holmes's sympathies, and ours, are with the Lady Eva. None the less we, and Holmes, accept without question on the one hand that the marriage with the Earl of Dovercourt is a desirable one and on the other that were he to see the letters he would certainly break off the match. The text's elusiveness on the content of the letters, and the absence of the Lady Eva herself, deflects the reader's attention from the potentially contradictory ideology of marriage which the narrative takes for granted.

This second narrative is also symmetrical. The murderer too is a woman with a past. She is not identified. Milverton has sent her letters to her husband who in consequence 'broke his gallant heart and died.' Again the text is unable to be precise about the content of the letters since to do so would be to risk losing the sympathy of the reader for either the woman or her husband.

In the mean time Holmes has become engaged. By offering to marry Milverton's housemaid he has secured information about the layout of the house he is to burgle. Watson remonstrates about the subsequent fate of the girl, but Holmes replies:

> 'You can't help it, my dear Watson. You must play your cards as best you can when such a stake is on the table. However, I rejoice to say that I have a hated rival who will certainly cut me out the instant that my back is turned. What a splendid night it is.'

The housemaid is not further discussed in the story.

The sexuality of these three shadowy women motivates the narrative and yet is barely present in it. The disclosure which ends the story is thus scarcely a disclosure at all. Symbolically Holmes has burnt the letters, records of women's sexuality. Watson's opening paragraph constitutes an apology for the 'reticence' of the narrative; 'with *due suppression* the story may be told'; 'The reader will excuse me if I conceal the date *or any other fact*' (my italics).

The project of the Sherlock Holmes stories is to dispel magic and mystery, to make everything explicit, accountable, subject to scientific analysis. The phrase most familiar to all readers—'Elementary, my dear Watson'—is in fact a misquotation, but its familiarity is no accident since it precisely captures the central concern of the stories. Holmes and Watson are both men of science. Holmes, the 'genius,' is a scientific conjuror who insists on disclosing how the trick is done. The stories begin in enigma, mystery, the impossible, and conclude with an explanation which makes it clear that logical deduction and scientific method render all mysteries accountable to reason:

> I am afraid that my explanation may disillusionize you, but it has always been my habit to hide none of my methods, either from my friend Watson or from anyone who might take an intelligent interest in them. ('The Reigate Squires,' *The Memoirs of Sherlock Holmes*)

The stories are a plea for science not only in the spheres conventionally associated with detection (footprints, traces of hair or cloth, cigarette ends), where they have been deservedly influential on forensic practice, but in all areas. They reflect the widespread optimism characteristic of their period concerning the comprehensive power of positivist science. Holmes's ability to deduce Watson's train of thought, for instance, is repeatedly displayed, and it owes nothing to the supernatural. Once explained, the reasoning process always appears 'absurdly simple,' open to the commonest of common sense.

The project of the stories themselves, enigma followed by disclosure, echoes precisely the structure of the classic realist text. The narrator himself draws attention to the parallel between them:

> 'Excellent!' I cried.
>
> 'Elementary,' said he. 'It is one of those instances where the reasoner can produce an effect which seems remarkable to his neighbour because the latter has missed the one little point which is the basis of the deduction. The same may be said, my dear fellow, for the effect of some of these little sketches of yours, which is entirely meretricious, depending as it does upon your retaining in your hands some factors in the problem which are never imparted to the reader. Now, at present I am in the position of these same readers, for I hold in this hand several threads of one of the strangest cases which ever perplexed a man's brain, and yet I lack the one or two which are needful to complete my theory. But I'll have them, Watson, I'll have them!' ('The crooked man,' *Memoirs*)

(The passage is quoted by Macherey [1978, p. 35] in his discussion of the characteristic structure of narrative.)

The project also requires the maximum degree of 'realism'—verisimilitude, plausibility. In the interest of science no hint of the fantastic or the implausible is permitted to remain once the disclosure is complete. This is why even their own existence as writing is so frequently discussed within the texts. The stories are alluded to as Watson's 'little sketches,' his 'memoirs.' They resemble fictions because of Watson's unscientific weakness for story-telling:

> 'I must admit, Watson, that you have some power of selection which atones for much which I deplore in your narratives. Your fatal habit of looking at everything from the point of view of a story instead of as a scientific exercise has ruined what might have been an instructive and even classical series of demonstrations.' ('The Abbey Grange,' *The Return of Sherlock Holmes*)

In other words, the fiction itself accounts even for its own fictionality, and the text thus appears wholly transparent. The success with which the Sherlock Holmes stories achieve an illusion of reality is repeatedly demonstrated. In their Foreword to *The Sherlock Holmes Companion* (1962) Michael and Mollie Hardwick comment on their own recurrent illusion 'that we were dealing with a figure of real life rather than of fiction. How vital Holmes appears, compared with many people of one's own acquaintance.'

De Waal's bibliography of Sherlock Holmes lists twenty-five 'Sherlockian' periodicals apparently largely devoted to conjectures, based on the 'evidence' of the stories, concerning matters only hinted at in the texts—Holmes's education, his income and his romantic and sexual adventures. According to *The Times* in

December 1967, letters to Sherlock Holmes were then still commonly addressed to 221B Baker Street, many of them asking for the detective's help.

None the less these stories, whose overt project is total explicitness, total verisimilitude in the interests of a plea for scientificity, are haunted by shadowy, mysterious and often silent women. Their silence repeatedly conceals their sexuality, investing it with a dark and magical quality which is beyond the reach of scientific knowledge. In 'The Greek interpreter' (*Memoirs*) Sophie Kratides has run away with a man. Though she is the pivot of the plot she appears only briefly: 'I could not see her clearly enough to know more than that she was tall and graceful, with black hair, and clad in some sort of loose white gown.' Connotatively the white gown marks her as still virginal and her flight as the result of romance rather than desire. At the same time the dim light surrounds her with shadow, the unknown. 'The crooked man' concerns Mrs. Barclay, whose husband is found dead on the day of her meeting with her lover of many years before. Mrs. Barclay is now insensible, 'temporarily insane' since the night of the murder and therefore unable to speak. In 'The dancing men' (*Return*) Mrs. Elsie Cubitt, once engaged to a criminal, longs to speak but cannot bring herself to break her silence. By the time Holmes arrives she is unconscious, and she remains so for the rest of the story. Ironically the narrative concerns the breaking of the code which enables her former lover to communicate with her. Elsie's only contribution to the correspondence is the word, 'Never.' The precise nature of their relationship is left mysterious, constructed of contrary suggestions. Holmes says she feared and hated him; the lover claims, 'She had been engaged to me, and she would have married me, I believe, if I had taken over another profession.' When her husband moves to shoot the man whose coded messages are the source of a 'terror' which is 'wearing her away,' Elsie restrains him with compulsive strength. On the question of her motives the text is characteristically elusive. Her husband recounts the story:

> 'I was angry with my wife that night for having held me back when I might have caught the skulking rascal. She said that she feared that I might come to harm. For an instant it had crossed my mind that what she really feared was that *he* might come to harm, for I could not doubt that she knew who this man was and what he meant by those strange signals. But there is a tone in my wife's voice, Mr. Holmes, and a look in her eyes which forbid doubt, and I am sure that it was indeed my own safety that was in her mind.'

After her husband's death Elsie remains a widow, faithful to his memory and devoting her life to the care of the poor, apparently expiating something unspecified, perhaps an act or a state of feeling, remote or recent.

'The dancing men' is 'about' Holmes's method of breaking the cipher. Its project is to dispel any magic from the deciphering process. Elsie's silence is in the interest of the story since she knows the code. But she also 'knows' her feelings towards her former lover. Contained in the completed and fully disclosed story of the decipherment is another uncompleted and undisclosed narrative which is more than merely peripheral to the text as a whole. Elsie's past is central and causal. As a result, the text with its project of dispelling mystery is haunted by the mysterious state of mind of a woman who is unable to speak.

The classic realist text had not yet developed a way of signifying women's sexuality except in a metaphoric or symbolic mode whose presence disrupts the realist surface. Joyce and Lawrence were beginning to experiment at this time with modes of sexual signification but in order to do so they largely abandoned the codes of realism. So much is readily apparent. What is more significant, however, is that the presentation of so many women in the Sherlock Holmes stories as shadowy, mysterious and magical figures precisely contradicts the project of explicitness, transgresses the values of the texts, and in doing so throws into relief the poverty of the contemporary concept of science. These stories, pleas for a total explicitness about the world, are unable to explain an area which none the less they cannot ignore. The version of science which the texts present would constitute a clear challenge to ideology: the interpretation of all areas of life, physical, social and psychological, is to be subject to rational scrutiny and the requirements of coherent theorization. Confronted, however, by an area in which ideology itself is uncertain, the Sherlock Holmes stories display the limits of their own project and are compelled to manifest the inadequacy of a bourgeois scientificity which, working within the constraints of ideology, is thus unable to challenge it.

Perhaps the most interesting case, since it introduces an additional area of shadow, is 'The second stain' (*Return*), which concerns two letters. Lady Hilda Trelawney Hope does speak. She has written before her marriage 'an indiscreet letter . . . a foolish letter, a letter of an impulsive, loving girl.' Had her husband read the letter his confidence in her would have been for ever destroyed. Her husband is none the less presented as entirely sympathetic, and here again we encounter the familiar contradiction between a husband's supposed reaction, accepted as just, and the reaction offered to the reader by the text. In return for her original letter Lady Hilda gives her blackmailer a letter from 'a certain foreign potentate' stolen from the dispatch box of her husband, the European Secretary of State. This political letter is symbolically parallel to the first sexual one. Its contents are equally elusive but it too is 'indiscreet,' 'hot-headed'; certain phrases in it are 'provocative.' Its publication would produce 'a most dangerous state of feeling' in the nation. Lady Hilda's innocent folly is the cause of the theft: she knows nothing of politics and was not in a position to understand the consequences of her action. Holmes ensures the restoration of the political letter and both secrets are preserved.

Here the text is symmetrically elusive concerning both sexuality and politics. Watson, as is so often the case where these areas are concerned, begins the story by apologizing for his own reticence and vagueness. In the political instance what becomes clear as a result of the uncertainty of the text is the contradictory nature of the requirements of verisimilitude in fiction. The potentate's identity and the nature of his indiscretion cannot be named without involving on the part of the reader either disbelief (the introduction of a patently fictional country would be dangerous to the project of verisimilitude) or belief (dangerous to the text's status as fiction, entertainment; also quite possibly politically dangerous). The scientific project of the texts require that they deal in 'facts,' but their nature as fiction forbids the introduction of facts.

The classic realist text instills itself in the space between fact and illusion through the presentation of a simulated reality which is plausible but *not real*. In this lies its power as myth. It is because fiction does not normally deal with 'politics' directly, except in the form of history or satire, that it is ostensibly innocent and therefore ideologically effective. But in its evasion of the real also lies its weakness as 'realism.' Through their transgression of their own values of explicitness and verisimilitude, the Sherlock Holmes stories contain within themselves an implicit critique of their limited nature as characteristic examples of classic realism. They thus offer the reader through the process of deconstruction a form of knowledge, not about 'life' or 'the world,' but about the nature of fiction itself.

Thus, in adopting the form of classic realism, the only appropriate literary mode, positivism is compelled to display its own limitations. Offered as science, it reveals itself to a deconstructive reading as ideology at the very moment that classic realism, offered as verisimilitude, reveals itself as fiction. In claiming to make explicit and *understandable* what appears mysterious, these texts offer evidence of the tendency of positivism to push to the margins of experience whatever it cannot explain or understand. In the Sherlock Holmes stories classic realism ironically tells a truth, though not the truth about the world which is the project of classic realism. The truth the stories tell is the truth about ideology, the truth which ideology represses, its own existence as ideology itself.

WORKS CITED

Althusser, Louis (1971) *Lenin and Philosophy and Other Essays*, tr. Ben Brewster (London: New Left Books).

Barthes, Roland (1975) *S/Z*, tr. Richard Miller (London: Cape).

Benveniste, Emile (1971) *Problems in General Linguistics* (Miami: University of Miami Press).

Conan Doyle, Arthur (1950) *The Memoirs of Sherlock Holmes* (Harmondsworth: Penguin).

Conan Doyle, Arthur (1976) *The Return of Sherlock Holmes* (London: Pan).

Coward, Rosalind and John Ellis (1977) *Language and Materialism* (London: Routledge & Kegan Paul).

Derrida, Jacques (1973) *Speech and Phenomena*, tr. David B. Allison (Evanston: Northwestern University Press).

De Waal, Ronald (1972) *The World Bibliography of Sherlock Holmes* (Greenwich, Conn.: New York Graphic Society).

Hardwick, Michael and Mollie (1972) *The Sherlock Holmes Companion* (London: John Murray).

Heath, Stephen (1977–8) "Notes of Suture," *Screen* 18:4, pp. 48–76.

Lemaire, Anika (1977) *Jacques Lacan*, tr. Davic Macey (London: Routledge & Kegan Paul).

Macherey, Pierre (1978) *A Theory of Literary Production*, tr. Geoffrey Wall (London: Routledge & Kegan Paul).

Nowell-Smith, Geoffrey (1976) 'A note on history discourse,' *Edinburgh 76 Magazine* 1, pp. 26–32.

Saussure, Ferdinand de (1974) *Course in General Linguistics*, tr. Wade Baskin (London: Fontana).

Willemen, Paul (1978) 'Notes on subjectivity—on reading "Subjectivity Under Siege,"' *Screen* 19:1, pp. 41–69.

SUSAN S. LANSER

TOWARD A FEMINIST NARRATOLOGY

What you choose and reject theoretically, then, depends upon what you are practically trying to do. This has always been the case with literary criticism: it is simply that it is often very reluctant to realize the fact. In any academic study we select the objects and methods of procedure which we believe the most important, and our assessment of their importance is governed by frames of interest deeply rooted in our practical forms of social life. Radical critics are no different in this respect: it is just that they have a set of social priorities with which most people at present tend to disagree. This is why they are commonly dismissed as 'ideological,' because 'ideology' is always a way of describing other people's interests rather than one's own.

TERRY EAGLETON (211)

Feminist criticism, like narratology and all good theories perhaps, is an optimistic enterprise, eager to account for the whole of its relevant universe. For nearly two decades it has not only offered new ways of seeing a vast range of texts by both women and men, in virtually every genre and language; it has also scrutinized the assumptions, theories, and methods of literary scholarship, from biography and history to deconstruction and psychoanalysis, from archetypal criticism to reader response. Yet in the sometimes sharp debates both within feminist criticism (especially between "American" and "French" approaches[1]) and between feminism and other critical modes, structuralist-formalist methods have been virtually untouched. In consequence, narratology has had little impact on feminist scholarship, and feminist insights about narrative have been similarly overlooked by narratology. The title of this essay may therefore seem startling, as if I am trying to force an intersection of two lines drawn on different planes: the one scientific, descriptive, and non-ideological, the other impressionistic, evaluative, and political (a false opposition that I hope my opening epigraph helps to dissolve).

Although feminism and narratology cannot really be said to have a history, there have been a few gestures of synthesis. While narratological studies are absent from nearly all of the otherwise eclectic and wide-ranging collections of feminist approaches to literature, the excellent volume *Women and Language in*

Literature and Society (1980) does incorporate essays of structuralist bent.[2] The only direct efforts to link feminism and narratology of which I am aware are Mária Minich Brewer's critique of narratology in "A Loosening of Tongues," Mieke Bal's application of it in "Sexuality, Symbiosis and Binarism" and the recent *Femmes imaginaires*[3] my own attempt to forge a feminist poetics of point of view in *The Narrative Act;* and the very recent essay of Robyn Warhol.[4] Even feminist critics who acknowledge considerable debt to their formalist or structuralist training have sharply criticized its limitations. Naomi Schor vows that she could not practice feminist criticism at all in the "subtle oppression exercised [in American departments of French] by structuralism at its least self-critical and doctrinaire" (ix); Josephine Donovan, speaking from an Anglo-American perspective, rejects "the dissection of literature as if it were an aesthetic machine made up of paradoxes, images, symbols, etc., as so many nuts and bolts easily disintegrated from the whole" ("Women's Poetics" 108).[5] It would be safe, I think, to say that no contemporary theory, whether Anglo-American or continental, has exerted so little influence on feminist criticism or been so summarily dismissed as formalist-structuralist narratology.

In part, of course, this coolness toward narratology—both the practice and the word[6]—is characteristic of the profession as a whole. At the end of her excellent book on narrative poetics, Shlomith Rimmon-Kennan feels compelled to ask whether she has written "an introduction . . . or an obituary" to the field (130). Terry Eagleton uses even stronger death imagery when he likens structuralism to "killing a person in order to examine more conveniently the circulation of the blood" (109). To psychoanalytic critics like Peter Brooks, a formalist narratology, however valuable, cannot grasp "our experience of reading narrative as a dynamic operation" (316).[7] And there is perhaps no surer barometer of professional sentiment than David Lodge's brilliant satire, *Small World*, in which Morris Zapp says of a Sorbonne narratologist, "'Hasn't his moment passed? I mean, ten years ago everybody was into that stuff, actants and functions and mythemes and all that jazz. But now . . . '" (134). Those Anglo-American scholars who were never comfortable with structuralism in general or narratology in particular have probably been relieved at its decline, while most critics grounded in Continental thinking have moved on to post-structuralist theories that offer an exhilarating openness against which narratology may seem mechanical, empirical, hardly conducive to the *plaisir du texte*.

Given a literary climate at best indifferent to narratology, my desire to explore the compatibility of feminism and narratology is also a way to think about what narratology can and cannot do, what place it might have in the contemporary critical environment of American departments of literature, and how it might enrich the hermeneutical enterprise for critics who are not themselves theorists of narrative. My immediate task, however, will be more circumscribed: to ask whether feminist criticism, and particularly the study of narratives by women, might benefit from the methods and insights of narratology and whether narratology, in turn, might be altered by the understandings of feminist criticism and the experience of women's texts. It is in the frank desire to say yes to both these questions that this essay has been conceived. It is in the supposition that the readers of this journal are more involved with narratology than with feminism that my emphasis will be on the second question rather than the first.

There are compelling reasons why feminism (or any explicitly political criticism) and narratology (or any largely formal poetics) might seem incompatible. The technical, often neologistic, vocabulary of narratology has alienated critics of many persuasions and may seem particularly counterproductive to critics with political concerns. Feminists also tend to be distrustful of categories and oppositions, of "a conceptual universe organized into the neat paradigms of binary logic" (Schor ix)[8]—a distrust which explains part of the attraction of feminist theory to Derridean deconstruction. But there are (at least) three more crucial issues about which feminism and narratology might differ: the role of gender in the construction of narrative theory, the status of narrative as mimesis or semiosis, and the importance of context for determining meaning in narrative.

The most obvious question feminism would ask of narratology is simply this: upon what body of texts, upon what understandings of the narrative and referential universe, have the insights of narratology been based? It is readily apparent that virtually no work in the field of narratology has taken gender into account, either in designating a canon or in formulating questions and hypotheses. This means, first of all, that the narratives which have provided the foundation for narratology have been either men's texts or texts treated as men's texts. Genette's formulation of a "Discours du récit" on the basis of Proust's *A la Recherche du temps perdu*, Propp's androcentric morphology of a certain kind of folktale, Greimas on Maupassant, Iser on male novelists from Bunyan to Beckett, Barthes on Balzac, Todorov on the *Decameron*—these are but evident examples of the ways in which the masculine text stands for the universal text. In the structuralist quest for "invariant elements among superficial differences" (Lévi-Strauss 8), for (so-called) universals rather than particulars, narratology has avoided questions of gender almost entirely. This is particularly problematic for those feminist critics—in this country, the majority—whose main interest is the "difference or specificity of women's writing" (Showalter, "Women's Time" 38). The recognition of this specificity has led not only to the rereading of individual texts but to the rewriting of literary history; I am suggesting that it also lead to a rewriting of narratology that takes into account the contributions of women as both producers and interpreters of texts.[9]

This challenge does not deny the enormous value of a body of brilliant narrative theory for the study of women's works; indeed, it has been applied fruitfully to such writers as Colette (Bal, "The Narrating and the Focalizing") and Eliot (Costello) and is crucial to my own studies of narrative voice in women's texts. It does mean that until women's writings, questions of gender, and feminist points of view are considered, it will be impossible even to know the deficiencies of narratology. It seems to me likely that the most abstract and grammatical concepts (say, theories of time) will prove to be adequate. On the other hand, as I will argue later in this essay, theories of plot and story may need to change substantially. And I would predict that the major impact of feminism on narratology will be to raise new questions, to add to the narratological distinctions that already exist, as I will be suggesting below in my discussions of narrative level, context, and voice.

A narratology for feminist criticism would also have to reconcile the primarily semiotic approach of narratology with the primarily mimetic orientation of most (Anglo-American) feminist thinking about narrative. This difference reminds us that "literature is at the juncture of two systems"; one can speak about it as

> a representation of life
> an account of reality
> a mimetic document

and as

> a non-referential linguistic system
> an enunciation supposing a narrator and a listener
> primarily a linguistic construct.
> (Furman 64–65)

Traditionally, structuralist narratology has suppressed the representational aspects of fiction and emphasized the semiotic, while feminist criticism has done the opposite. Feminist critics tend to be more concerned with characters than with any other aspect of narrative and to speak of characters largely as if they were persons. Most narratologists, in contrast, treat characters, if at all, as "patterns of recurrence, motifs which are continually recontextualized in other motifs"; as such, they "lose their privilege, their central status, and their definition" (Weinsheimer 195). This conception could seem to threaten one of feminist criticism's deepest premises: that narrative texts, and particularly texts in the novelistic tradition, are profoundly (if never simply) referential—and influential—in their representations of gender relations. The challenge to both feminism and narratology is to recognize the dual nature of narrative, to find categories and terms that are abstract and semiotic enough to be useful, but concrete and mimetic enough to seem relevant for critics whose theories root literature in "the real conditions of our lives" (Newton 125).

The tendency to pure semiosis is both cause and effect of a more general tendency in narratology to isolate texts from the context of their production and reception and hence from what "political" critics think of as literature's ground of being—the "real world." This is partly a result of narratology's desire for a precise, scientific description of discourse, for many of the questions concerning the relationship of literature to the "real world"—questions of why, so what, to what effect—are admittedly speculative. Thus "when narratology does attempt to account for the contextual, it does so in terms of narrative conventions and codes. Yet their capacity to account for social, historical, or contextual differences always remains limited by the original formalist closure within which such codes and conventions are defined" (Brewer 1143). This is why early in the history of formalism, critics like Medvedev and Bakhtin called for a "sociological poetics" that would be dialectically theoretical and historical: "Poetics provides literary history with direction in the specification of the research material and the basic definitions of its forms and types. Literary history amends the definitions of poetics, making them more flexible, dynamic, and adequate to the diversity of the historical material" (30). My insistence on writing women's texts into the historical canon of narratology has precisely this aim of making it more adequate to the diversity of narrative.

Finally, feminist criticism would argue that narratology itself is ideological, indeed in an important sense fictional. One need not agree wholeheartedly with Stanley Fish that "formal units are always a function of the interpretive model one brings to bear (they are not 'in the text')" (13), to recognize that no interpretive system is definitive or inevitable. But as Fish also reminds us, every theory must believe itself the best theory possible (361). Formalist-structuralist narratology may "know" that its categories are not immanent, but it proceeds as if there were "a stable and immediately knowable text, directly available to classificatory operations that are themselves neutral and innocent of interpretive bias" (Chambers 18–19). Feminist criticism has simply not had this luxury: in its critique of masculine bias, it has of necessity taken the view that theory sometimes says more about the reader than about the text.

A narratology for feminist criticism would begin, then, with the recognition that revision of a theory's premises and practices is legitimate and desirable. It would probably be cautious in its construction of systems and favor flexible categories over fixed sets. It would scrutinize its norms to be sure of what they are normative. It would be willing to look afresh at the question of gender and to re-form its theories on the basis of women's texts, as Robyn Warhol's essay on the "engaging narrator," just published in *PMLA*, begins to do. In both its concepts and its terminology, it would reflect the mimetic as well as the semiotic experience that is the reading of literature, and it would study narrative in relation to a referential context that is simultaneously linguistic, literary, historical, biographical, social, and political. Granted, narratology might have to be willing to cede some precision and simplicity for the sake of relevance and accessibility, to develop terminology less confusing, say, than a series like analepsis, prolepsis, paralepsis, and metalepsis. The valuable and impressive work that has been done in the field would be opened to a critique and supplement in which feminist questions were understood to contribute to a richer, more useful, and more complete narratology. For as I have been trying to suggest, a narratology that cannot adequately account for women's narratives is an inadequate narratology for men's texts as well.

A re-formed narratology should be of particular interest to feminist critics because fiction is the dominant genre in the study of women and literature. The necessarily semiotic nature of even a revised narratology will help to balance feminist criticism's necessarily mimetic commitments. The comprehensiveness and care with which narratology makes distinctions can provide invaluable methods for textual analysis. As Mieke Bal argues, "The use of formally adequate and precise tools is not interesting in itself, but it can clarify other, very relevant issues and provides insights which otherwise remain vague" ("Sexuality" 121). Narratology and feminist criticism might profitably join forces, for example, to explore the teleological aspects of narrative, which have concerned narratologists like Ann Jefferson and Marianna Torgovnick and feminist critics like Rachel Blau DuPlessis. I can imagine a rich dialogue between Armine Mortimer Kotin's and Nancy K. Miller's analyses of the plot of *La Princesse de Clèves*. And a major benefit of narratology is that it offers a relatively independent (pre-textual) framework for studying groups of texts. It could, for example, provide a particularly valuable foundation for exploring one of the most complex and troubling questions for feminist criticism: whether there is indeed a "woman's writing" and/or a female tradition, whether men and women do write differently. For given the volatile nature of the question, the precision and abstraction of narratological systems offers the safety for investigation that more impressionistic theories of difference do not. This kind of research would demonstrate the particular responsiveness of narratology to certain problems for which other theories have not been adequate and hence illustrate its unique value for feminist scholarship.

I would like to begin the movement toward a feminist narratology by identifying some of the questions a feminist reading might raise for narratology. I will emphasize here not so much the fruitful applications which narratology could currently offer but the questions that it does not yet seem to have addressed. I have chosen, instead of a typical piece of fiction, a far more anomalous work because it presents many complexities in a short space of text and allows me to examine several aspects of women's writing and writing in general. The text is a letter, allegedly written by a young bride whose husband censored her correspondence. It appeared in *Atkinson's Casket* in April 1832, sandwiched between a discussion of angels and directions for "calisthenic exercises." [10] No indication is given of the letter's source, authenticity, or authorship. I am assuming, but cannot be certain, that it is apocryphal; I make no assumptions about the author's sex. Here is the text as it appears in the *Casket:*

FEMALE INGENUITY

> *Secret Correspondence.*—A young Lady, newly married, being obliged to show her husband, all the letters she wrote, sent the following to an intimate friend.

> I cannot be satisfied, my Dearest Friend!
> blest as I am in the matrimonial state.
> unless I pour into your friendly bosom,
> which has ever been in unison with mine,
> the various deep sensations which swell
> with the liveliest emotions of pleasure
> my almost bursting heart. I tell you my dear
> husband is one of the most amiable of men,
> I have been married seven weeks, and
> have never found the least reason to
> repent the day that joined us, my husband is
> in person and manners far from resembling
> ugly, crass, old, disagreeable, and jealous
> monsters, who think by confining to secure;
> a wife, it is his maxim to treat as a
> bosom-friend and confidant, and not as a
> plaything or menial slave, the woman
> chosen to be his companion. Neither party
> he says ought to obey implicitly;—
> but each yield to the other by turns—
> An ancient maiden aunt, near seventy,
> a cheerful, venerable, and pleasant old lady,
> lives in the house with us—she is the de-
> light of both young and old—she is ci-
> vil to all the neighborhood round,
> generous and charitable to the poor—
> I know my husband loves nothing more

than he does me; he flatters me more
than the glass, and his intoxication
(for so I must call the excess of his love)
often makes me blush for the unworthiness
of its object, and I wish I could be more deserving
of the man whose name I bear. To
say all in one word, my dear, and to
crown the whole, my former gallant lover
is now my indulgent husband, my fondness
is returned, and I might have had
a Prince, without the felicity I find with
him. Adieu! May you be as blest as I am unable to wish that I could be more
happy.

N. B.—The key to the above letter, is to read the first and then every alternate line.

For purposes of easy reference, I reproduce below the decoded subtext that this reading of alternate lines will yield:

I cannot be satisfied, my Dearest Friend!
unless I pour into your friendly bosom,
the various deep sensations which swell
my almost bursting heart. I tell you my dear
I have been married seven weeks, and
repent the day that joined us, my husband is
ugly, crass, old, disagreeable, and jealous[;]
a wife, it is his maxim to treat as a
plaything or menial slave, the woman
he says ought to obey implicitly;—
An ancient maiden aunt, near seventy,
lives in the house with us—she is the devil to all the neighborhood round.
I know my husband loves nothing more
than the glass, and his intoxication
often makes me blush for the unworthiness
of the man whose name I bear. To
crown the whole, my former gallant lover
is returned, and I might have had
him. Adieu! May you be as blest as I am unhappy.

Written for two readers (the prying husband and the intimate friend) this letter is in an unusually obvious sense a double construction, a blatant specimen of writing over and under censorship. The surface text and subtext are strikingly different both in story and narration, and a narrative theory adequate for describing the whole will have to account for both and for the narrative frame that binds them. In particular, such a text raises for discussion questions about narrative voice, narrative situation, and plot.

Perhaps the most obvious difference between the letters, apart from their contrasting stories, is the difference between the two voices. Some linguists have argued that there is a "woman's language" or a discourse of the powerless:[11] speech that is "polite, emotional, enthusiastic, gossipy, talkative, uncertain, dull, and chatty" in contrast to men's speech or powerful speech, which is "capable, direct, rational, illustrating a sense of humor, unfeeling, strong (in tone and word choice) and blunt" (Kramarae 58). The two letters illustrate many of the differences between these two modes of speech. The surface text is virtually a sampler of "women's language": its self-effacing narrator praises the "more deserving" husband and blushes for her own "unworthiness"; her "liveliest emotions" generate a discourse of repetition, hyperbole, convolution, and grammatical anomaly. It is the voice of one who clearly can*not* "say all in one word," who can assert herself only in empty phrases and a syntax of negativity. The voice of the subtext is, by contrast, strikingly simple and direct, in the kind of language that commands (an all-too-ready) authority.[12] This second narrator shows herself angry, strong, decisive, sure of her judgments, acutely aware of her husband's deficiencies and of her own lost opportunities. Her speech acts— "I repent," "I know," "she is the devil," "I am unhappy"—are acts of conviction; such a voice requires enormous confidence and would probably be accorded an immediate credibility. Beneath the "feminine" voice of self-effacement and emotionality, then, lies the "masculine" voice of authority that the writer cannot inscribe openly. The subtext also exposes the surface text, and hence the surface voice, as a subterfuge, revealing the "feminine style" to be a caricature donned to mask a surer voice in the process of communicating to a woman under the watchful eyes of a man. But this also means that the powerless form called "women's language" is revealed as a potentially subversive—hence powerful—tool.

In *The Narrative Act* I called for a poetics that would go beyond formal classifications in order to describe the subtle but crucial differences between voices like these. For in structural terms the two voices are similar: both are first-person/ protagonist (autodiegetic) narrators (though they are addressing different narratees). Most of the qualities that distinguish the two voices have yet to be codified by narratology. One might ask, for example, what kinds of illocutionary acts the narrator undertakes and whether she undertakes them in a discourse of "presence" or "absence," if we take "absence" to encompass such practices as "irony, ellipsis, euphemism, litotes, periphrasis, reticence, pretermission, digression, and so forth" (Hamon 99). This question, in turn, might lead to a (much-needed) theory that would define and describe *tone* in narrative. Tone might be conceived at least in part as a function of the relationship between the deep and superficial structures of an illocutionary act (e.g., the relationship between an act of judgment and the language in which the judgment is expressed).

This double text recalls an even sharper lesson about narrative voice, the lesson formulated by Bakhtin: that in narrative there is no single voice, that in far subtler situations than this one, voice impinges upon voice, yielding a structure in which discourses of and for the other constitute the discourses of self; that, to go as far as Wayne Booth does, "We are constituted in polyphony" (51). The blatant heteroglossia of this letter—and I shall suggest below that it is even more layered than at first appears—is but a sharper version of the polyphony of all voice and, certainly in visible ways, of the female voices in many women's narratives. For the condition of being woman in a male-dominant society may well necessitate the double voice, whether as conscious subterfuge or as tragic dispossession of the self. Thus in a text like Charlotte Perkins Gilman's "The Yellow Wallpaper," the narrator speaks her desires underneath a discourse constructed for her by her husband John; in Susan Glaspell's "A Jury of Her Peers" two women protect a third from a conviction for murder by communicating in "women's language" under the watchful but unseeing eyes of the Law; in novel after novel Jane Austen constitutes a narrative voice that cannot be pinned down, that can be read according to one's own desires; a novel like Marge Piercy's *Small Changes* builds a double structure through which both its author and its protagonist work out the necessity of living in a world of double discourse (Hansen). A narratology adequate to women's texts (and hence to all texts, though polyphony is more pronounced and more consequential in women's narratives and in the narratives of other dominated peoples) would have to acknowledge and account for this polyphony of voice, identifying and disentangling its strands, as recent studies by Graciela Reyes and Michael O'Neal begin to do.

If we return with this understanding of voice to the double-text letter, it is easy to identify those verbal features that distinguish one from the other by examining the forms of "excess" that were pared away in the decoding process. The first and less significant is a combination of repetition and hyperbole that serves as "filler," yielding phrases like "which has ever been in unison with mine" and "with the liveliest emotions of pleasure." The second is more important, for it creates the syntactic hinge that binds and finally transforms the whole: a series of negations that the subtext will reverse:

> I . . . have *never* found the least reason to repent
> my husband is . . . *far from* resembling . . . monsters
> a wife, it is his maxim to treat . . . *not* as a plaything
> *Neither* party, he says ought to obey implicitly
> I am *unable* to wish that I could be more happy—

This negativity is more than the link between two texts; it is the means by which the two letters finally yield a third: a story, a third voice, a third audience. For the negativity makes of the surface text not one narrator's simple proclamation of happiness but the indictment of an entire social system. What indeed, does the surface paint but the very portrait of marriage that it claims to erase? Each negative statement suggests departure from a social norm, a norm in which brides repent their marriages, husbands are monstrous, women are treated as playthings or slaves, and women's desires are unthinkable. In other words, the surface text, by saying what one particular marriage is not, shows the terrible contours of what its narrator expected marriage to be. While the subtext condemns one man and laments one woman's fate, the surface letter condemns an entire society, presenting as typical the conditions which the subtext implies to be individual. The subtext, then, becomes an instance of the surface text rather than its antithesis; the two versions reveal not opposing but related truths. It is fitting, then, that they meet at their point of dissatisfaction, at the single line—the first—that does not change: "I cannot be satisfied, my dearest Friend!"

In the light of this reading, women's language becomes not simply a vehicle for constructing a more legitimate (masculine, powerful) voice but the voice through which the more global judgment of patriarchal practices is exercised. This text differs from the "palimpsestic" discourse feminist criticism frequently describes in which "surface designs" act simply as a cover to "conceal or obscure deeper, less accessible (and less socially acceptable) levels of meaning" (Gilbert and Gubar 73). Here the "surface design" turns out to be a more damning discourse than the text it purports to protect. The text designed for the husband conceals an undertext (the text designed for the confidante), but the undertext, in turn, creates a new reading of the surface text and hence a third text designed, I would argue, for yet another addressee. This third text is the one constituted by the *public* "display-text"[13] that is the letter *as it appeared* in *Atkinson's Casket*. Its addressee is the *literary* reader; she is neither the duped male nor the sister-confidante but the unidentified public narratee of either sex who can see beyond the immediate context of the writer's epistolary circumstance to read the negative discourse as covert cultural analysis. Thus the literary context of this text provides a third and entirely different reading from the readings yielded to the private audiences of husband and friend. At the same time, it is *the knowledge of* the other two texts, the access to the private texts, that opens the third reading, in a version, perhaps, of what Genette calls *hypertextualité* (*Palimpsestes* 11).

The fact that this letter has several narratees suggests the importance of recognizing the narrative levels a text may contain. Gérard Genette has made an extremely important contribution to narratology in distinguishing the multiple diegetic levels possible in a single text because one narrative may enclose or generate another (Genette, *Narrative Discourse* 227–37; *Nouveau Discours* 55–64). Genette speaks of the outermost level as the *extradiegetic*, of a narrative incorporated within this one as *intradiegetic*, and of a third narrative level as *metadiegetic*. Extradiegetic narrators, says Genette, are usually "author-narrators"—Jane Eyre, George Eliot's "third person" voice—and "as such they occupy the same narrative level as their public—that is, as you and me" (*Narrative Discourse* 229). But as Genette also makes clear, there is no *necessary* connection between extradiegetic narration and a public audience; letter-writers and diarists (Pamela, Werther) may also be extradiegetic narrators. Intra-diegetic (and metadiegetic) narrators—Rochester when he is telling Jane Eyre the story of Bertha Mason, the characters in *Middlemarch*—are conventionally able to address only narratees inscribed *within* the text. In *Frankenstein* Walton's letters to his sister constitute an extradiegetic narrative; Frankenstein's story, told to Walton, is intradiegetic, and the monster's history, narrated to Frankenstein and enclosed within the tale he tells Walton, is metadiegetic. Genette's notion of levels provides a precise way of speaking about such embedded narratives and identifying their narratees—and for describing transgressions across narrative levels (called metalepses) like those Diderot's narrator commits in *Jacques le fataliste*.

But Genette himself recognizes that narrative level has been made too much of, and that indeed it does not take us very far. In the *Nouveau Discours* he makes clear just how relative the distinction of levels is by generating an imaginary scene in which three men sit down, one offers to tell the others a story which he warns will be long, and the storyteller begins, "'For a long time I used to go to bed early . . . '" (64). With a frame of only a sentence, says Genette, the entirety of Proust's *A la Recherche* suddenly becomes an intradiegetic narration. If we look at the letter in terms of Genette's levels, we could identify as either an extradiegetic narrator or simply as an editor the voice that presents the letter as a specimen of "Female Ingenuity" and explains both its context and its secret code to the readers of *Atkinson's Casket*.[14] The diegetic level of the letter is then contingent on this initial decision. And both the surface letter and the subtext, being interlinear, exist on the same level, in an unusual case of double diegesis. Genette's notion of levels does not allow us to say much about the narrative situation of this letter because it applies only to internal relations among parts of a text. It does not describe any individual narrative act *per se*, and it closes off the text from considerations external and contextual.

To provide a more complete analysis of narrative level, I would propose as a complement to Genette's system a distinction between public and private narration. By public narration I mean simply narration (implicitly or explicitly) addressed to a narratee who is external (that is, heterodiegetic)[15] to the textual world and who can be equated with a public readership; private narration, in contrast, is addressed to an explicitly designated narratee who exists only within the textual world. Public narration evokes a direct relationship between the reader and the narratee and clearly approximates most closely the nonfictional author–reader relationship, while in private narration the reader's access is indirect, as it were "through" the figure of a textual persona. Such a distinction, combined with Genette's notions of both level and person, would yield the typology shown on the facing page.

I propose this notion of public and private narrative levels as an additional category particularly relevant to the study of women's texts. For women writers, as feminist criticism has long noted, the distinction between private and public contexts is a crucial and a complicated one. Traditionally speaking, the sanctions against women's writing have taken the form not of prohibitions to write at all but of prohibitions to write for a public audience. As Virginia Woolf comments, "Letters did not count": letters were private and did not disturb a male discursive hegemony. Dale Spender takes the distinctions even further, arguing that the notions of public and private concern not only the general context of textual production but its gender context as well: that is, writing publicly becomes synonymous with writing for and to men. Spender comments:

> The dichotomy of male/female, public/private is maintained by permitting women to write . . . for themselves (for example, diaries) and for each other in the form of letters, 'accomplished' pieces, moral treatises, articles of interest for other women—particularly in the domestic area—and even novels for women. . . . There is no contradiction in patriarchal order while women write for women and therefore remain within the limits of the private sphere; the contradiction arises only when women write for men. (192)

The bride's letter both illustrates Spender's formulation and expands it in important ways. The only public level of narration here is the narration that presents the letter in the *Casket* as the "display" of a correspondence. In relation to this level, the letter itself is a private text, designed for a private readership. Yet the surface letter is intended by its narrator to be an eminently *public* text in relation to the subtext, which is the private text she urgently hopes will *not* be available to the "public" who is her husband. In terms of the I-narrator's intentions, the

LEVEL	PERSON	PUBLIC	PRIVATE
extra-diegetic	heterodiegetic (third-person)	narration of *Emma* or *Middlemarch*	moments of "meta-lepse" in *Jacques le fataliste* when narrator consorts with his characters
	homodiegetic (first-person)	Jane Eyre's narration	letters of Walton or Werther
intradiegetic or metadiegetic	heterodiegetic (third-person)	?	tales of the *Heptameron* or *Scheherezade*
	homodiegetic (first-person)	the "found" memoir of Lionel Verney in Mary Shelley's *The Last Man* or Piran-dello's *Six Characters*	narratives of Frankenstein and the Monster

"public" text is indeed designed for the man, the private (indeed secret) text for the female friend. One must already, then, redefine the simple distinction of public and private to create a category in which a narration is private but is designed to be read as well by someone other than its officially designated narratee;[16] I will call this a semi-private narrative act. To the extent that the surface letter is in some sense public, it dramatizes the way in which women's public discourse may be contaminated by internal or external censorship. This, in turn, helps to explain why historically women writers have chosen, more frequently than men, private forms of narration—the letter, the diary, the memoir addressed to a single individual—rather than forms that require them to address a public readership, and why public and private narratives by women employ different narrative strategies.[17] The concept could also be applied fruitfully to texts in which the narrative level is unclear, as in Gilman's "The Yellow Wallpaper" and Craik's *A Life for a Life*, which seem to implicate a public narratee while purporting to write a private diary.

The application of the distinction public/private to literary texts requires us to think in more complex ways about the dichotomy of gender that Spender attaches to private and public discourse. Here again the letter is illustrative. For if my analysis is persuasive in suggesting the existence of a third text available only to one who has read both the second and the first, and read in the light of a particular understanding both of women and of textuality, then the public text— that is, the one which is directed by the extradiegetic narrator or editor to "anyone"—is also the most hidden text, the hardest to see, for nothing really points to its existence except itself, and it requires a reader who brings to it particular kinds of knowledge. Since it is at the public level of narration that the ideal reading becomes possible, the letter *presented as a display text* also *escapes* the gender associations of the original structure of the intradiegetic narrative (in which it seems that public = male and private = female), suggesting a kind of paradigm for reading "as a woman" that encompasses but is not determined by the question of sex. Equally, when women write novels that use private narrative forms, they are nonetheless writing for a public, and a public that cannot entirely be dichotomized in gender terms. How individual writers negotiate this complex context of gender and public-ity constitutes another important area to investigate.

The difference between Genette's formulation of narrative levels and my own illustrates, I hope, the difference between purely formal and contextual approaches to meaning in narrative. Just as speech act theory understood that the minimal unit of discourse was not the sentence but the *production* of the sentence in a specific context, so the kind of narratology I am proposing would understand that the minimal narrative is the narrative as produced. In the case of the letter that appears in the *Casket*, questions of context are closely related to interpretive possibilities. For depending on whether one sees the letter as a historical document or as a text written deliberately for display—and whether, if "display text," an imitation or a parody—different readings of the letter emerge. If the text is an authentic document, a letter actually written by an unhappy wife that somehow came into the hands of the *Casket*, then the text might become important historical evidence of the ways in which women's writing is conditioned by censorship. If the text were constructed as imitation, it stands as evidence of the *perception*, if not the historical fact, of censorship. But the letter may well have been intended as a parody of the "female style." Indeed, the history of this style, and its connection to the epistolary, provides the context for an interesting possibility. Historically, the letter has such overdetermined associations with women that what became thought of as the "female style," a style acclaimed for its artlessness, its sense of immediacy and lack of forethought, was a style tied to the epistolary mode (Donovan, "The Silence is Broken" 212–14). If the letter is in fact a "display text," it may well be a display of "female ingenuity" not only in the obvious sense of a clever composition that finds a "woman's way" around censorship, but in the service of a broader and literary design: to make mockery of the assumptions about women's "artless" epistolary style, to reveal woman as man's equal in intellectual capacity. For "ingenuity," the *OED* tells us, means not only the (oxymoronic) union of straightforward openness with the genius for skillful, inventive design but also the quality or condition of being a free-born man. And if the letter was written by its own editor, it also provided a convenient and safe vehicle for criticizing male dominance, since an editor need take no responsibility for a private "found" text.

The rhetorical complexity of the letter reminds us that narrative meaning is also a function of narrative circumstance. Narratology has not yet provided satisfying language through which to make distinctions of rhetorical context;[18] feminist criticism, in its concern with questions of authenticity and authorship, might find it difficult even to talk about a text this uncertain in origin. A feminist narratology might acknowledge the existence of multiple texts, each constructed by

a (potential) rhetorical circumstance. To the extent that such questions determine the very *meaning* of narrative, they are questions for narratology.

The final element of my discussion of difference between the bride's two
letters—the question of story or plot—I will treat only sketchily here, for it lies
outside my area of expertise. In traditional terms, the surface text—the one written for the husband—can barely be said to have a plot, and one might of course
argue that it is not a narrative at all. There is not a singular verb tense in the text;
every independent predication is cast in the stative or iterative mode. All the
action that the text implies, hence all there is of story, precedes the narrative
moment; by the time of the writing all conflict—the gap between expectations
and reality—has already been resolved (and not by the protagonist's actions at
all). Notions of both plot and character are strained by such a structure in which
the *actant* is really a recipient, in which nothing whatever is predicted of which
the fulfillment would constitute plot as it is narratologically defined. And although one could also see this stasis as the basis for a plot left to the reader's
imagination, to the extent that plot is a function of modalized predication and
hence of desire (Costello, Brooks), the surface text refuses even the possibility of
plot: "I am *unable to wish* that I could be more happy."

Thus the first text creates stasis of both event and character, an idyll of harmony in which the "indulgent husband," as "bosom friend," is a synthesis of the
confidante with her "friendly bosom" and the "gallant lover": all characters but
the protagonist coalesce into one idealized whole. But the subtext does offer the
elements of a possible plot. Here we have a full-blown triangle—husband, lover,
wife—in which the necessity for a confidante becomes logical. The plot of this
subtext is actually highly conventional: drunken husband, sinister maiden aunt,[19]
gallant suitor in the wings. But here too the expectations for story, though more
fully roused, are shunted aside. While there is one singular event—"my former
gallant lover is returned"—the narrator says, "I *might have* had him," suggesting
that there is no real possibility of change.

Can one speak narratologically of plot or even story in these two letters, or is
one condemned simply to negative definitions—plotlessness, or story without
plot? Narratology is rich in its efforts to pin down the nature of plot. The formulations of Propp, Bremond, Todorov, Costello, Pavel, Prince, all offer useful
ways to talk about large numbers of texts, perhaps of most (premodernist) texts.
But in the case of the letter, each schema fails. Although the subtext is a catalogue of acts of villainy, for example, one cannot say of it as Propp says of his
folktales that "each new act of villainy, each new lack creates a new move" (92).
In his canon movement is possible; here it is not.[20] The units of anticipation and
fulfillment or problem and solution that structure plot according to narrative theorists of plot assume that textual actions are based on the (intentional) deeds of
protagonists; they assume a power, a possibility, that may be inconsistent with
what women have experienced both historically and textually, and perhaps inconsistent even with women's desires. A radical critique like Mária Brewer's suggest that plot has been understood as a "discourse of male desire recounting itself
through the narrative of adventure, project, enterprise, and conquest," the "discourse of desire as separation and mastery" (1151, 1153).

If standard narratological notions of plot do not adequately describe (some) women's texts, then what is needed is a radical revision in theories of plot. For one thing, as Katherine Rabuzzi notes (in Donovan, "Jewett's Critical Theory" 218), "'by and large, most women have known a nonstoried existence.'" Women's experience, says Donovan, often seems, when held against the masculine plot, "static, and in a mode of waiting. It is not progressive, or oriented toward events happening sequentially or climactically, as in the traditional masculine story plot" (218–19). This letter, or a novel like Sarah Orne Jewett's *The Country of the Pointed Firs*, can thus only be defined as a "plotless text." (Donovan, "Women's Poetics," 106). Similarly, some of Grace Paley's finest stories (for example, "Friends" and "Ruthy and Edie" in the most recent collection, *Later the Same Day*), which a traditional narratology would describe as "plotless," are constituted by plots of women's attempts to "make sense" of their world.[21] A contemporary popular novel like Meg Wolitzer's *Hidden Pictures*, which sets up negative possibilities that neither occur nor are noted *not* to occur, when measured against plot theories becomes a "flawed" story making worrisome predictions that it does not fulfill. Yet one could also see this plot as a structure of anxiety and (gradual) relief that corresponds to real-world experiences of women in the difficult circumstances of this novel's protagonists, a lesbian couple raising a son in suburbia. If again and again scholars of women's writing must speak in terms of the "plot*less*" (usually in quotation marks, suggesting their dissatisfaction with the term), then perhaps something is wrong with the notions of plot that have followed from Propp's morphology. Perhaps narratology has been mistaken in trying to arrive at a single definition and description of plot. We will learn more about women's narratives—and about scores of twentieth-century texts—if we make ourselves find language for describing their plots in positive rather than negative terms.

There is another level of plot, too, that the bride's letter urges us to think about. There is, in fact, one sequence of anticipation and fulfillment that this text does fully constitute, and it occurs in the act of writing. In the case of both letters, whether the narrator's life is happy or miserable, what she "cannot be satisfied" without is, simply, *the telling*—narrative itself. The act of writing becomes the fulfillment of desire, telling becomes the single predicated act, as if to tell were in itself to resolve, to provide closure. *Récit* and *histoire*, rather than being separate elements, converge, so that telling becomes integral to the working out of story. Communication, understanding, being understood, becomes not only the objective of the narration but the act that can transform (some aspect of) the narrated world. In a universe where waiting, inaction, reception, predominate, and action is only minimally possible, the narrative act itself becomes the source of possibility.

What happens in the letter, then, is that the wish for the other's happiness substitutes for the possibility of change in one's own life; the writer's experience serves as a (positive or negative) stimulus to the reader's own story. The confidante thus becomes an active participant not simply in narration, but in plot itself; the wish for the narratee's happiness transfers the imperatives of plot, so that the possibilities of change and fulfillment are given over to the narratee. The letter thus suggests a plot behind women's "plotless" narrative, the subversive plot of sharing an experience so that the listener's life may complete the speaker's tale. I would be eager for narratology to talk about such a crossing of the plot of narration with the story plot.

My analysis of this coded letter suggests in sketchy ways aspects of narrative that a revised poetics might scrutinize and codify. A comprehensive theory of voice would develop a framework for describing the elements that constitute polyphony and would formulate a linguistically based theory of narrative tone. Attention to the rhetorical context of narrative—its generic status and the public or private level of the narration—would be understood as important determinants of narrative meaning. And theories of plot and story would be reexamined to find alternatives to the notion of plot as active acquisition or solution and to incorporate the plot that may be generated by the relationship between narrator and narratee. Once it is clear that some (women's) texts cannot be adequately described by traditional, formalist narratology, we begin to see that other texts—postmodernist texts, texts by writers of Asia and Africa, perhaps—may be similarly unaccounted for. It is only, I believe, such an expansive narratology that can begin to fulfill the wish Gerald Prince expresses at the end (164) of his *Narratology:* that "ultimately, narratology can help us understand what human beings are."

NOTES

I am grateful to Michael Ragussis, Leona Fisher, Caren Kaplan, and Harold Mosher for invaluable criticism of this essay in successive manuscript stages.

1. A simple distinction between so-called "American" and "French" feminisms is impossible. By "French" feminism is usually meant feminism conceived within the theoretical premises of poststructuralism and hence heavily indebted to the writings of Derrida, Foucault, Lacan, Kristeva, Cixous, and Irigaray. "American" feminism tends to be conceived within the political imperatives of the American women's liberation movement and the historical experience of women in general and women writers in particular. Both modes are practiced in the United States, and the two have become increasingly intertwined. Nonetheless, the debates go on. For further discussion of the differences see, for example, the introduction and bibliography and the essay by Ann Jones in Showalter, *The New Feminist Criticism;* for an example of the new synthesis, see Meese.

2. See especially Furman 45–54.

3. A piece of Bal's book on the Hebrew Bible is available to English-language readers as "Sexuality, Sin and Sorrow."

4. It is revealing that the single sentence in my book most cited by reviewers is the statement that "my training is deeply formalist, and my perspective as deeply feminist"; clearly many scholars consider feminism and narratology an odd pair.

5. I find it ironic that Donovan's rejection of formalist "dissection" is justified by finding it incompatible with what Evelyn Beck and I have called a "women's epistemology" (Lanser and Beck 86).

6. Particularly in the wake of the new psychoanalytic narrative theories the term *narratology* has fallen into disuse, perhaps perceived as too narrowly structuralist. Critics disagree about the differences between *narratology* and *narrative poetics;* see, for example, Rimmon-Kenan's attempt to distinguish the two in *Narrative Fiction* (133 n.1). *By narratology* I mean simply that branch of poetics concerned with defining and describing all aspects of narrative.

I have chosen throughout this essay to use the word *narratology* rather than *narrative poetics* partly to foreground the dissonance between narratology and feminism and partly to identify more precisely the formalist/structuralist practices that I am discussing here. I will, however, be calling in this essay for a study of narrative that is finally less formalist than *narratology* generally connotes. For that reason, and since I am also suggesting a less alienating terminology for the study of narrative, I can also see the advantages of *narrative poetics*, and I would not hesitate to make the change.

7.   While there is a reader-oriented narratology that emphasizes the process of text production, Rimmon-Kenan is right to imply that "the more far-reaching 'revisionism' of some reader-oriented studies . . . is often at odds with the very project of narrative poetics" (118).

8.   Oppositional thinking has, of course, been sharply disadvantageous to women, as to other dominated groups. Binary pairs of the variety P/not-P are precisely the structures that create hierarchy (as in nonwhite, illiterate, un-American). Categories and classifications, while sometimes also used by feminists, are ripe for Procrustean distortions, for premature closures, for stifling rigidities.

9.   In *The Narrative Act* I have in fact worked with women's texts as well as with men's, and I have also included the narrative theories of neglected women like Vernon Lee and Käte Friedemann. But I did not really undertake the radical reevaluation I am now calling for, one which would mean *beginning* with women's writings (both narrative and theoretical) in order not to remarginalize the marginal, in compensation for a training that has been so strongly biased in favor of male discourse.

10.   I discovered this letter quite accidentally. While browsing through the stacks of the University of Wisconsin-Madison library several years ago, I came across an odd compendium titled *The Genteel Female*, edited by Clifton Furness. Its endpapers consist of the page from *Atkinson's Casket* which contains the letter.

11.   There are three controversies embedded in this topic: whether there is in fact a "women's language," whether it is exclusive to women, and whether it is a negative characteristic. In 1975 Robin Lakoff suggested that women use language forms that differ from men's, and that this language reinforces the social and political powerlessness of women. Other critics have argued that "women's language" is a fiction constructed upon sex stereotypes and that women do not actually speak differently from men. Still others agree that there is difference but rather than seeing the difference as negative, they consider "women's language" better oriented to concern for others and to the careful contextualizing of one's beliefs (rather than the "masculine" assertion of universals). For a sense of this controversy see Spender 32–51. A related question is whether it is more accurate to speak of "women's language" or of "powerless language." On the basis of empirical study in a courtroom context, O'Barr and Atkins found far more credibility accorded to female witnesses speaking in the "powerful style" than to those speaking in the "powerless style."

12.   Richard Sennett believes that simple, direct discourse in the active voice bespeaks a confidence that frequently inspires a too-easy and hence dangerous obeisance. See *Authority*, chapter 5.

13.   Mary Louise Pratt uses the term to designate a text or speech act whose relevance lies in its tellability, and which is thus detachable from its immediate circumstances of production. Literary texts and jokes are examples. See Pratt 136–48.

14.   I thank Harold Mosher for the suggestion that this figure is not actually a narrator at all but merely an editor. I had been considering this voice to be similar to the one that introduces, say, the governess's narrative in *The Turn of the Screw*. The problem, I believe, lies at least in part with Genette's own system, which does not distinguish an editor from an extradiegetic narrator. Such a narrator, after all, may appear only briefly to introduce a major intradiegetic narrative and may do so in the guise of an editor.

15.   I am suggesting that not only narrators but also narratees can be heterodiegetic or

homodiegetic—that is, within or outside the fictional world—and that a homodiegetic narrator can address a heterodiegetic narratee (although it would constitute a narrative transgression for a heterodiegetic narrator to address a homodiegetic narratee). I have decided not to use these terms, however, in order to avoid confusion with heterodiegetic and homodiegetic narrators and because of my commitment to simplify narrative terminology.

16. This is somewhat different from the case of a letter that is intercepted by a character for whom it was not destined, as happens frequently, say, in *Clarissa*. The difference is that in this case the narrator *knows* her text will be intercepted and has structured the surface narrative accordingly.

17. The differences between private and public narration in narratives by women are a major focus of the book I am now completing on women writers and narrative voice.

18. As Susan Léger has pointed out to me, a book like Ross Chambers's *Story and Situation* is a healthy exception to this norm.

19. I am aware that my analysis of the letters has omitted any discussion of the maiden aunt and that her "maidenness" makes her a particularly interesting figure in the context of the portraits of marriage in these letters.

20. One could argue that the presence of a lover in the subtext keeps eternally open the possibility of action, even if that action seems to be thwarted by the given text. Such a possibility testifies to the power of the desire for plot.

21. For the example of these Paley stories I am indebted to Alan Wilde, whose book, *Middle Ground: Studies in Contemporary American Fiction* (Philadelphia: University of Pennsylvania Press, 1987), includes a chapter on her work.

WORKS CITED

Bakhtin, M. M. "Discourse in the Novel." *The Dialogic Imagination*. Trans. Caryl Emerson and Michael Holquist. Austin: U of Texas P, 1981. 259–422.

Bal, Mieke. *Femmes imaginaires: l'ancien testament au risque d'une narratologie critique*. Paris: Nizet; Montreal: HMH, 1986.

———. "The Narrating and the Focalizing: A Theory of the Agents in Narrative." *Style* 17 (1983): 234–69.

———. "Sexuality, Semiosis and Binarism: A Narratological Comment on Bergen and Arthur." *Arethusa* 16.1–2 (1983): 117–35.

———. "Sexuality, Sin, and Sorrow: The Emergence of Female Character (A Reading of Genesis 1–3)." *The Female Body in Western Culture*. Ed. Susan Rubin Suleiman. Cambridge: Harvard UP, 1986. 317–38.

Booth, Wayne C. "Freedom of Interpretation: Bakhtin and the Challenge of Feminine Criticism." *Critical Inquiry* 9 (1982): 45–76.

Bremond, Claude. *Logique du récit*. Paris: Seuil, 1973.

Brewer, Mária Minich. "A Loosening of Tongues: From Narrative Economy to Women Writing." *MLN* 99 (1984): 1141–61.

Brooks, Peter. "Narrative Desire." *Style* 18 (1984): 312–27.

———. *Reading for the Plot*. New York: Knopf, 1984.

Chambers, Ross. *Story and Situation: Narrative Seduction and the Power of Fiction*. Minneapolis: U of Minnesota P, 1984.

Costello, Edward. "Modality and Narration: A Linguistic Theory of Plotting." Diss. Wisconsin, 1975.

Donovan, Josephine. "Sarah Orne Jewett's Critical Theory: Notes Toward a Feminine Literary Mode." *Critical Essays on Sarah Orne Jewett*. Ed. Gwen L. Nagel. Boston: Hall, 1984.

————. "The Silence is Broken." *Women and Language in Literature and Society*. Ed. Sally McConnel-Ginet et al. New York: Praeger, 1980. 205–18.

————. "Toward a Women's Poetics." *Tulsa Studies in Women's Literature*. 3.1–2 (1984): 99–110.

DuPlessis, Rachel Blau. *Writing Beyond the Ending: Narrative Strategies of Twentieth-Century Women Writers*. Bloomington: Indiana UP, 1985.

Eagleton, Terry. *Literary Theory: An Introduction*. Minneapolis: U of Minnesota P, 1983.

"Female Ingenuity." *Atkinson's Casket or Gems of Literature, Wit and Sentiment*. No. 4, Philadelphia, April 1832: 186.

Fish, Stanley. *Is There a Text in this Class? The Authority of Interpretive Communities*. Boston: Harvard UP, 1980.

Furman, Nelly. "The politics of language: beyond the gender principle?" *Making a Difference: Feminist Literary Criticism*. Ed. Gayle Greene and Coppelia Kahn. London: Methuen, 1985. 59–79.

————. "Textual Feminism." *Women and Language in Literature and Society*. Ed. Sally McConnell-Ginet et al. New York: Praeger, 1980. 45–54.

Furness, Clifton, ed. *The Genteel Female*. New York: Knopf, 1931.

Genette, Gérard. *Narrative Discourse: An Essay in Method*. Trans. Jane E. Lewin. Ithaca: Cornell UP, 1980. Trans. of "Discours du récit." *Figures III*. Paris: Seuil, 1972.

————. *Nouveau Discours du récit*. Paris: Seuil, 1983.

————. *Palimpsestes: la littérature au second degré*. Paris: Seuil, 1982.

Gilbert, Sandra, and Susan Gubar. *The Madwoman in the Attic: The Woman Writer and the Nineteenth-Century Literary Imagination*. New Haven: Yale UP, 1979.

Hamon, Philip. "Text and Ideology: For a Poetics of the Norm." *Style* 17 (1983): 95–119.

Hansen, Elaine Tuttle. "The Double Narrative Structure of *Small Changes*." *Contemporary American Women Writers: Narrative Strategies*. Ed. Catherine Rainwater and William J. Scheick. Lexington: UP of Kentucky, 1985.

Jefferson, Ann. "*Mise en abyme* and the Prophetic in Narrative." *Style* 17 (1983): 196–208.

Kotin, Armine Mortimer. "Narrative Closure and the Paradigm of Self-Knowledge in *La Princesse de Clèves*." *Style* 17 (1983): 181–95.

Kramarae, Cheris. "Proprietors of Language." *Women and Language in Literature and Society*. Ed. Sally McConnel-Ginet et al. New York: Praeger, 1980. 58–68.

Lakoff, Robin. *Language and Woman's Place*. New York: Harper and Row. 1975.

Lanser, Susan Sniader. *The Narrative Act: Point of View in Prose Fiction*. Princeton: Princeton UP, 1981.

Lanser, Susan Sniader, and Evelyn Torton Beck. "(Why) Are There No Great Women Critics?—And What Difference Does It Make?" *The Prism of Sex: Essays in the Sociology of Knowledge*. Ed. Julia Sherman and Evelyn T. Beck. Madison: U of Wisconsin P, 1979. 79–91.

Lévi-Strauss, Claude. *Myth and Meaning*. New York: Schocken, 1978.

Lodge, David. *Small World*. New York: Macmillan, 1984.

McConnell-Ginet, Sally, Ruth Borker, and Nelly Furman, eds. *Women and Language in Literature and Society*. New York: Praeger, 1980.

Medvedev, P. N., and M. M. Bakhtin. *The Formal Method in Literary Scholarship: A Critical Introduction to Sociological Poetics*. Trans. Albert J. Wehrle. Baltimore: Johns Hopkins UP, 1978.

Meese, Elizabeth A. *Crossing the Double-Cross: The Practice of Feminist Criticism*. Chapel Hill: U of North Carolina P, 1986.

Miller, Nancy K. "Emphasis Added: Plots and Plausibilities in Women's Fiction." *The New Feminist Criticism: Essays on Women, Literature, and Theory*. Ed. Elaine Showalter. New York: Pantheon, 1985. 339–60.

Newton, Judith. "Making—and Remaking—History: Another Look at 'Patriarchy.'" *Tulsa Studies in Women's Literature* 3.1–2 (1984): 125–41.

O'Barr, William M., and Bowman K. Atkins. "'Women's Language' or 'Powerless Language'?" *Women and Language in Literature and Society*. Ed. Sally McConnell-Ginet et al. New York: Praeger, 1980. 93–110.

O'Neal, Michael. "Point of View and Narrative Technique in the Fiction of Edith Wharton." *Style* 17 (1983): 270–89.

Pavel, Thomas G. *The Poetics of Plot: The Case of English Renaissance Drama*. Minneapolis: U of Minnesota P, 1985.

Pratt, Mary Louise. *Toward a Speech Act Theory of Literary Discourse*. Bloomington: Indiana UP, 1977.

Prince, Gerald. *Narratology: The Form and Function of Narrative*. Berlin: Mouton, 1982.

Propp, Vladimir. *Morphology of the Folktale*. Ed. Louis A. Wagner. 2nd ed. Austin: U of Texas P, 1968.

Reyes, Graciela. *Polifonía textual: La citación en el relato literario*. Madrid: Gredos, 1984.

Rimmon-Kennan, Shlomith. *Narrative Fiction: Contemporary Poetics*. London: Methuen, 1983.

Schor, Naomi. *Breaking the Chain: Women, Theory, and French Realist Fiction*. New York: Columbia UP, 1985.

Sennett, Richard. *Authority*. New York: Knopf, 1980.

Showalter, Elaine, ed. *The New Feminist Criticism: Essays on Women, Literature, and Theory*. New York: Pantheon, 1985.

———. "Women's Time, Women's Space; Writing the History of Feminism Criticism." *Tulsa Studies in Women's Literature* 3: 1–2 (1984): 29–43.

Spender, Dale. *Man Made Language*. London: Routledge and Kegan Paul, 1980.

Torgovnick, Marianna. *Closure in the Novel*. Princeton: Princeton UP, 1981.

Warhol, Robyn R. "Toward a Theory of the Engaging Narrator: Earnest Interventions in Gaskell, Stowe, and Eliot." *PMLA* 101 (1986): 811–18.

Weinsheimer, Joel. "Theory of Character: *Emma*." *Poetics Today* 1: 1–2 (1979): 185–211.

APOSTROPHE, ANIMATION, AND ABORTION

> The abortion issue is as alive and controversial in the body politic as it is in the academy and the courtroom.
>
> JAY L. GARFIELD, *ABORTION: MORAL AND LEGAL PERSPECTIVES*

Although rhetoric can be defined as something politicians often accuse each other of using, the political dimensions of the scholarly study of rhetoric have gone largely unexplored by literary critics. What, indeed, could seem more dry and apolitical than a rhetorical treatise? What could seem farther away from budgets and guerrilla warfare than a discussion of anaphora, antithesis, prolepsis, and preterition? Yet the notorious CIA manual[1] on psychological operations in guerrilla warfare ends with just such a rhetorical treatise: an appendix on techniques of oratory which lists definitions and examples for these and many other rhetorical figures. The manual is designed to set up a Machiavellian campaign of propaganda, indoctrination, and infiltration in Nicaragua, underwritten by the visible display and selective use of weapons. Shoot softly, it implies, and carry a big schtick. If rhetoric is defined as language that says one thing and means another, then the manual is in effect attempting to maximize the collusion between deviousness in language and accuracy in violence, again and again implying that targets are most effectively hit when most indirectly aimed at. Rhetoric, clearly, has everything to do with covert operations. But are the politics of violence already encoded in rhetorical figures as such? In other words, can the very essence of a political issue—an issue like, say, abortion—hinge on the structure of a figure? Is there any *inherent* connection between figurative language and questions of life and death, of who will wield and who will receive violence in a given human society?

As a way of approaching this question, I will begin in a more traditional way by discussing a rhetorical device that has come to seem almost synonymous with the lyric voice: the figure of apostrophe. In an essay in *The Pursuit of Signs*, Jonathan Culler indeed sees apostrophe as an embarrassingly explicit emblem of procedures inherent, but usually better hidden, in lyric poetry as such.[2] Apostrophe in the sense in which I will be using it involves the direct address of an absent, dead, or inanimate being by a first-person speaker: "O wild West Wind, thou breath of Autumn's being. . . ." Apostrophe is thus both direct and indirect: based etymologically on the notion of turning aside, of digressing from straight speech, it manipulates the I/Thou structure of *direct* address in an indirect, fictionalized way. The absent, dead, or inanimate entity addressed is thereby made present, animate, and anthropomorphic. Apostrophe is a form of ventriloquism through which the speaker throws voice, life, and human form into the addressee, turning its silence into mute responsiveness.

Baudelaire's poem "Moesta et Errabunda,"[3] whose Latin title means "sad and vagabond," raises questions of rhetorical animation through several different grades of apostrophe. Inanimate objects like trains and ships or abstract entities like perfumed paradises find themselves called upon to attend to the needs of a plaintive and restless lyric speaker. Even the poem's title poses questions of life and death in linguistic terms: the fact that Baudelaire here temporarily resuscitates a dead language prefigures the poem's attempts to function as a finder of lost loves. But in the opening lines of the poem, the direct-address structure seems straightforwardly *un*figurative: "Tell me, Agatha." This could be called a minimally fictionalized apostrophe, although that is of course its fiction. Nothing at first indicates that Agatha is any more dead, absent, or inanimate than the poet himself.

The poem's opening makes explicit the relation between direct address and the desire for the *other's* voice: "Tell me—*you* talk." But something strange soon happens to the face-to-face humanness of this conversation. What Agatha is supposed to talk about starts a process of dismemberment that might have something to do with a kind of reverse anthropomorphism: "Does your heart sometimes take flight?" Instead of conferring a human shape, this question starts to undo one. Then, too, why the name Agatha? Baudelaire scholars have searched in vain for a biographical referent, never identifying one, but always presuming that one exists. In the Pléiade edition of Baudelaire's complete works, a footnote sends the reader to the only other place in Baudelaire's oeuvre where the name Agathe appears—a page in his *Carnets* where he is listing debts and appointments. This would seem to indicate that Agathe was indeed a real person. What do we know about her? A footnote to the *Carnets* tells us she was probably a prostitute. Why? See the poem "Moesta et Errabunda." This is a particularly stark example of the inevitable circularity of biographical criticism.

If Agathe is finally only a proper name written on two different pages in Baudelaire, then the name itself must have a function as a name. The name is a homonym for the word "agate," a semiprecious stone. Is Agathe really a stone? Does the poem express the Orphic hope of getting a stone to talk?

In a poem about wandering, taking flight, getting away from "here," it is surprising to find that, structurally, each stanza acts out not a departure but a return to its starting point, a repetition of its first line. The poem's structure is at odds with its *apparent* theme. But we soon see that the object of the voyage is precisely to return—to return to a prior state, planted in the first stanza as virginity, in the second as motherhood (through the image of the nurse and the pun on *mer/mère*), and finally as childhood love and furtive pleasure. The voyage outward in space is a figure for the voyage backward in time. The poem's structure of address backs up, too, most explicitly in the third stanza. The cry apostrophizing train and ship to carry the speaker off leads to a seeming reprise of the opening line, but by this point the inanimate has entirely taken over: instead of addressing Agatha directly, the poem asks whether Agatha's heart ever speaks the line the poet himself has spoken four lines earlier. Agatha herself now drops out of the poem, and direct address is temporarily lost, too, in the grammar of the sentence ("*Est-il vrai que . . .*"). The poem seems to empty itself of all its human characters and voices, acting out a *loss* of animation—which is in fact its subject: the loss of childhood aliveness brought about by the passage of time. The poem thus enacts in its own temporality the loss of animation it situates in the temporality of the speaker's life.

At this point it launches into a new apostrophe, a new direct address to an abstract, lost state: "How far away you are, sweet paradise." The poem reanimates, addresses an image of fullness and wholeness and perfect correspondence ("what we love is worthy of our loves"). This height of liveliness, however, culminates strangely in an image of death. The heart that formerly kept trying to fly away now drowns in the moment of reaching its destination ["Où dans la volupté pure le coeur se noie!"]. There may be something to gain, therefore, by deferring arrival, as the poem next seems to do by interrupting itself before grammatically completing the fifth stanza. The poem again ceases to employ direct address and ends by asking two drawn-out, self-interrupting questions. Is that paradise now farther away than India or China? Can one call it back and animate it with a silvery voice? This last question—"Peut-on le rappeler avec des cris plaintifs/ Et l'animer encore d'une voix argentine?"—is a perfect description of apostrophe itself: a trope which, by means of the silvery voice of rhetoric, calls up and animates the absent, the lost, and the dead. Apostrophe itself, then, has become not just the poem's mode but also the poem's theme. In other words, what the poem ends up wanting to know is not how far away childhood is, but whether its own rhetorical strategies can be effective. The final question becomes: can this gap be bridged; can this loss be healed, through language alone?

Shelley's "Ode to the West Wind," which is perhaps the ultimate apostrophic poem, makes even more explicit the relation between apostrophe and animation. Shelley spends the first three stanzas demonstrating that the west wind is a figure for the power to animate: it is described as the breath of being, moving everywhere, blowing movement and energy through the world, waking it from its summer dream, parting the waters of the Atlantic, uncontrollable. Yet the wind animates by bringing death, winter, destruction. How do the rhetorical strategies of the poem carry out this program of animation through the giving of death?

The apostrophe structure is immediately foregrounded by the interjections, four times spelled "O" and four times spelled "oh." One of the bridges this poem attempts to build is the bridge between the "O" of the pure vocative, Jakobson's conative function, or the pure presencing of the second person, and the "oh" of pure subjectivity, Jakobson's emotive function, or the pure presencing of the first person.

The first three stanzas are grammatical amplifications of the sentence "O thou, hear, oh, hear!" All the vivid imagery, all the picture painting, come in clauses subordinate to this obsessive direct address. But the poet addresses, gives animation, gives the capacity of responsiveness, to the wind, not in order to make it speak but in order to make it listen to him—in order to make it listen to him doing nothing but address *it*. It takes him three long stanzas to break out of this intense near-tautology. As the fourth stanza begins, the "I" starts to inscribe itself grammatically (but not thematically) where the "thou" has been. A power struggle starts up for control over the poem's grammar, a struggle which mirrors the rivalry named in such lines as: "If I were now what I was then, I would ne'er have *striven as thus with thee* in prayer in my sore need." This rivalry is expressed as a comparison: "less free than thou," but then: "One *too like* thee." What does it mean to be "too like"? Time has created a loss of similarity, a loss of animation that has made the sense of similarity even more hyperbolic. In other words, the poet, in becoming less than—less like the wind—somehow becomes more like the wind in his rebellion against the loss of likeness.

In the final stanza the speaker both inscribes and reverses the structure of apostrophe. In saying "be thou me," he is attempting to restore metaphorical exchange and equality. If apostrophe is the giving of voice, the throwing of voice, the giving of animation, then a poet using it is always in a sense saying to the addressee, "Be thou me." But this implies that a poet has animation to give. And *that* is what this poem is saying is not, or is no longer, the case. Shelley's speaker's own sense of animation is precisely what is in doubt, so that he is in effect saying to the wind, "I will animate you so that you will animate, or reanimate, me." "Make me thy lyre. . . ."

Yet the wind, which is to give animation, is also a giver of death. The opposition between life and death has to undergo another reversal, another transvaluation. If death could somehow become a positive force for animation, then the poet would thereby create hope for his own "dead thoughts." The animator that will blow his words around the world will also instate the power of their deadness, their deadness as power, the place of maximum potential for renewal. This is the burden of the final rhetorical question. Does death necessarily entail rebirth? If winter comes, can spring be far behind? The poem is attempting to appropriate the authority of natural logic—in which spring always does follow winter—in order to clinch the authority of cyclic reversibility for its own prophetic powers. Yet because this clincher is expressed in the form of a rhetorical question, it expresses natural certainty by means of a linguistic device that mimics *no* natural structure and has no stable one-to-one correspondence with a meaning. The rhetorical question, in a sense, leaves the poem in a state of suspended animation. But that, according to the poem, is the state of maximum potential.

Both the Baudelaire and the Shelley, then, end with a rhetorical question that both raises and begs the question of rhetoric. It is as though the apostrophe is ultimately directed toward the reader, to whom the poem is addressing Mayor Koch's question: "How'm I doing?" What is at stake in both poems is, as we have seen, the fate of a lost child—the speaker's own former self—and the possibility of a new birth or a reanimation. In the poems that I will discuss next, these structures of apostrophe, animation, and lost life will take on a very different cast through the foregrounding of the question of motherhood and the premise that the life that is lost may be someone else's.

In Gwendolyn Brooks's poem "The Mother," the structures of address are shifting and complex. In the first line ("Abortions will not let you forget"), there is a "you" but there is no "I." Instead, the subject of the sentence is the word "abortions," which thus assumes a position of grammatical control over the poem.

As entities that disallow forgetting, the abortions are not only controlling but animate and anthropomorphic, capable of treating persons as objects. While Baudelaire and Shelley addressed the anthropomorphized other in order to repossess their lost selves, Brooks is representing the self as eternally addressed and possessed by the lost, anthropomorphized other. Yet the self that is possessed here is itself already a "you," not an "I." The "you" in the opening lines can be seen as an "I" that has become alienated, distanced from itself, and combined with a generalized other, which includes and feminizes the reader of the poem. The grammatical I/Thou starting point of traditional apostrophe has been replaced by a structure in which the speaker is simultaneously eclipsed, alienated, and confused with the addressee. It is already clear that something has happened to the possibility of establishing a clear-cut distinction in this poem between subject and object, agent and victim.

The second section of the poem opens with a change in the structure of address. "I" takes up the positional place of "abortions," and there is temporarily no second person. The first sentence narrates: "I have heard in the voices of the wind the voices of my dim killed children." What is interesting about this line is that the speaker situates the children's voices firmly in a traditional romantic locus of lyric apostrophe—the voices of the wind, Shelley's "West Wind," say, or Wordsworth's "gentle breeze."[4] Gwendolyn Brooks, in other words, is here explicitly rewriting the male lyric tradition, textually placing aborted children in the spot formerly occupied by all the dead, inanimate, or absent entities previously addressed by the lyric. And the question of animation and anthropomorphism is thereby given a new and disturbing twist. For if apostrophe is said to involve language's capacity to give life and human form to something dead or inanimate, what happens when those questions are literalized? What happens when the lyric speaker assumes responsibility for producing the death in the first place, but without being sure of the precise degree of human animation that existed in the entity killed? What is the debate over abortion about, indeed, if not the question of when, precisely, a being assumes a human form?

It is not until line 14 that Brooks's speaker actually addresses the dim killed children. And she does so not directly, but in the form of a self-quotation: "I have said." This embedding of the apostrophe appears to serve two functions here, just as it did in Baudelaire: a self-distancing function, and a foregrounding of the question of the adequacy of language. But whereas in Baudelaire the distance between the speaker and the lost childhood is what is being lamented, and a restoration of vividness and contact is what is desired, in Brooks the vividness of the contact is precisely the source of the pain. While Baudelaire suffers from the dimming of memory, Brooks suffers from an inability to forget. And while Baudelaire's speaker actively seeks a fusion between present self and lost child, Brooks's speaker is attempting to fight her way out of a state of confusion between self and other. This confusion is indicated by the shifts in the poem's structures of address. It is never clear whether the speaker sees herself as an "I" or a "you," an addressor or an addressee. The voices in the wind are not created *by* the lyric apostrophe; they rather initiate the need for one. The initiative of speech seems always to lie in the other. The poem continues to struggle to clarify the relation between "I" and "you," but in the end it only succeeds in expressing the inability of its language to do so. By not closing the quotation in its final line, the poem, which began by confusing the reader with the aborter, ends by implicitly including the reader among those aborted—and loved. The poem can no more distinguish between "I" and "you" than it can come up with a proper definition of life. For all the Yeatsian tripartite aphorisms about life as what is past or passing or to come, Brooks substitutes the impossible middle ground between "You were born, you had body, you died" and "It is just that you never giggled or planned or cried."

In line 28, the poem explicitly asks, "Oh, what shall I say, how is the truth to be said?" Surrounding this question are attempts to make impossible distinctions: got/did not get, deliberate/not deliberate, dead/never made. The uncertainty of the speaker's control as a subject mirrors the uncertainty of the children's status as an object. It is interesting that the status of the human subject here hinges on the word "deliberate." The association of deliberateness with human agency has a long (and very American) history. It is deliberateness, for instance, that underlies that epic of separation and self-reliant autonomy, Thoreau's *Walden*. "I went to the woods," writes Thoreau, "because I wished to live deliberately, to front only the essential facts of life" [66]. Clearly, for Thoreau, pregnancy was not an essential fact of life. Yet for him as well as for every human being that has yet existed, someone else's pregnancy is the very *first* fact of life. How might the plot of human subjectivity be reconceived (so to speak) if pregnancy rather than autonomy is what raises the question of deliberateness?

Much recent feminist work has been devoted to the task of rethinking the relations between subjectivity, autonomy, interconnectedness, responsibility, and gender. Carol Gilligan's book *In a Different Voice* (and this focus on "voice" is not irrelevant here) studies gender differences in patterns of ethical thinking. The central ethical question analyzed by Gilligan is precisely the decision whether to have, or not to have, an abortion. The first time I read the book, this struck me as strange. Why, I wondered, would an investigation of gender *differences* focus on one of the questions about which an even-handed comparison of the male and the female points of view is impossible? Yet this, clearly, turns out to be the point: there is difference *because* it is not always possible to make symmetrical oppositions. As long as there is symmetry, one is not dealing with difference but rather with versions of the same. Gilligan's difference arises out of the impossibility of maintaining a rigorously logical binary model for ethical choices. Female logic, as she defines it, is a way of rethinking the logic of choice in a situation in which none of the choices are good. "Believe that even in my deliberateness I was not deliberate": believe that the agent is not entirely autonomous, believe that I can be subject and object of violence at the same time, believe that I have not chosen the conditions under which I must choose. As Gilligan writes of the abortion decision, "the occurrence of the dilemma itself precludes nonviolent resolution" [94]. The choice is not between violence and nonviolence, but between simple violence to a fetus and complex, less determinate violence to an involuntary mother and/or an unwanted child.

Readers of Brooks's poem have often read it as an argument against abortion. And it is certainly clear that the poem is not saying that abortion is a good thing. But to see it as making a simple case for the embryo's right to life is to assume that a woman who has chosen abortion does not have the right to mourn. It is to assume that no case *for* abortion can take the woman's feelings of guilt and loss into consideration, that to take those feelings into account is to deny the right to choose the act that produced them. Yet the poem makes no such claim: it attempts the impossible task of humanizing both the mother and the aborted children while presenting the inadequacy of language to resolve the dilemma without violence.

What I would like to emphasize is the way in which the poem suggests that the arguments for and against abortion are structured through and through by the rhetorical limits and possibilities of something akin to apostrophe. The fact that apostrophe allows one to animate the inanimate, the dead, or the absent implies that whenever a being is apostrophized, it is thereby automatically animated, anthropomorphized, "person-ified." (By the same token, the rhetoric of calling makes it difficult to tell the difference between the animate and the inanimate, as anyone with a telephone answering machine can attest.) Because of the ineradicable tendency of language to animate whatever it addresses, rhetoric itself can always have already answered "yes" to the question of whether a fetus is a human being. It is no accident that the anti-abortion film most often shown in the United States should be entitled "The Silent Scream." By activating the imagination to believe in the anthropomorphized embryo's mute responsiveness in exactly the same way that apostrophe does, the film (which is of course itself a highly rhetorical entity) is playing on rhetorical possibilities that are inherent in all linguistically-based modes of representation.

Yet the function of apostrophe in the Brooks poem is far from simple. If the fact that the speaker addresses the children at all makes them human, then she must pronounce herself guilty of murder—but only if she discontinues her apostrophe. As long as she addresses the children, she can keep them alive, can keep from finishing with the act of killing them. The speaker's attempt to absolve herself of guilt depends on never forgetting, never breaking the ventriloquism of an apostrophe through which she cannot define her identity otherwise than as the mother eaten alive by the children she has never fed. Who, in the final analysis, exists by addressing whom? The children are a rhetorical extension of the mother, but she, as the poem's title indicates, has no existence apart from her relation to them. It begins to be clear that the speaker has written herself into a poem she cannot get out of without violence. The violence she commits in the end is to her own language: as the poem ends, the vocabulary shrinks away, words are repeated, nothing but "all" rhymes with "all." The speaker has written herself into silence. Yet hers is not the only silence in the poem: earlier she had said, "You will never . . . silence or buy with a sweet." If sweets are for silencing, then by beginning her apostrophe, "Sweets, if I sinned . . ." the speaker is already saying that the poem, which exists to memorialize those whose lack of life makes them eternally alive, is also attempting to silence once and for all the voices of the children in the wind. It becomes impossible to tell whether language is what gives life or what kills.

> Women have said again and again "This body is *my* body!"
> and they have reason to feel angry, reason to feel that it has been
> like shouting into the wind.
> —Judith Jarvis Thomson, "A Defense of Abortion"

It is interesting to note the ways in which legal and moral discussions of abortion tend to employ the same terms as those we have been using to describe the figure of apostrophe. "These disciplines [philosophy, theology, and civil and canon law] variously approached the question in terms of the point at which the embryo or fetus became 'formed' or recognizably human, or in terms of when a 'person' came into being, that is, infused with a 'soul' or 'animated'" [Blackmun, *Roe vs. Wade, Abortion: Moral and Legal Perspectives*, Garfield and Hennessey, Eds. 15]. The issue of "fetal personhood" [Garfield and Hennessey, 55] is of course a way of bringing to a state of explicit uncertainty the fundamental difficulty of defining personhood in general [cf. Luker 6]. Even if the question of defining the nature of "persons" is restricted to the question of understanding what is meant by the word "person" in the United States Constitution (since the Bill of Rights guarantees the rights only of "persons"), there is not at present, and probably will never be, a stable legal definition. Existing discussions of the legality and morality of abortion almost invariably confront, leave unresolved, and detour around the question of the nature and boundaries of human life. As Justice Blackmun puts it in *Roe vs. Wade:* "We need not resolve the difficult question of when life begins. When those trained in the respective disciplines of medicine, philosophy, and theology are unable to arrive at any consensus, the judiciary, at this point in the development of man's knowledge, is not in a position to speculate as to the answer" [27]. In the case of *Roe vs. Wade,* the legality of abortion is derived from the pregnant couple's right to privacy—an argument which, as Catharine MacKinnon argues in "*Roe vs. Wade:* A Study in Male Ideology" [Garfield and Hennessey 45–54], is itself problematic for women, since by protecting "privacy" the courts also protect the injustices of patriarchal sexual arrangements. When the issue is an unwanted pregnancy, some sort of privacy has already, in a sense, been invaded. In order for the personal to avoid being reduced once again to the non-political, privacy, like deliberateness, needs to be rethought in terms of sexual politics. Yet even the attempt to re-gender the issues surrounding abortion is not simple. As Kristin Luker convincingly demonstrates, the debate turns around the claims not only of woman vs. fetus or of woman vs. patriarchal state, but also of woman vs. woman:

> Pro-choice and pro-life activists live in different worlds, and the scope of their lives, as both adults and children, fortifies them in their belief that their views on abortion are the more correct, more moral, and more reasonable. When added to this is the fact that should "the other side" win, one group of women will see the very real devaluation of their lives and life resources, it is not surprising that the abortion debate has generated so much heat and so little light. [Luker 215]
> . . . .
> Are pro-life activists, as they claim, actually reaching their cherished goal of "educating the public to the humanity of the unborn child?" As we begin to seek an answer, we should recall that motherhood is a topic about which people have very complicated feelings, and beause abortion has beome the battleground for different definitions of motherhood, neither the pro-life nor the pro-choice movement has ever been "representative" of how most Americans feel about abortion. More to the point, all our data suggest that

> *neither of these groups will ever be able to be representative.* [224, emphasis in
> original]

It is often said, in literary-theoretical circles, that to focus on undecidability is to be apolitical. Everything I have read about the abortion controversy in its present form in the United states leads me to suspect that, on the contrary, the undecidable *is* the political. There is politics precisely because there is undecidability.

And there is also poetry. There are striking and suggestive parallels between the "different voices" involved in the abortion debate and the shifting address-structures of poems like Gwendolyn Brooks's "The Mother." A glance at several other poems suggests that there tends indeed to be an overdetermined relation between the theme of abortion and the problematization of structures of address. In Anne Sexton's "The Abortion," six 3-line stanzas narrate, in the first person, a trip to Pennsylvania where the "I" has obtained an abortion. Three times the poem is interrupted by the italicized lines:

> *Somebody who should have been born*
> *is gone.*

Like a voice-over narrator taking superegoistic control of the moral bottom line, this refrain (or "burden," to use the archaic term for both "refrain" and "child in the womb") puts the first-person narrator's authority in question without necessarily constituting the voice of a separate entity. Then, in the seventh and final stanza, the poem extends and intensifies this split:

> Yes, woman, such logic will lead
> to loss without death. Or say what you meant,
> you coward . . . this baby that I bleed.

Self-accusing, self-interrupting, the narrating "I" turns on herself (or is it someone else?) as "you," as "woman." The poem's speaker becomes as split as the two senses of the word "bleed." Once again, "saying what one means" can only be done by ellipsis, violence, illogic, transgression, silence. The question of who is addressing whom is once again unresolved.

As we have seen, the question of "when life begins" is complicated partly because of the way in which language blurs the boundary between life and death. In "Menstruation at Forty," Sexton sees menstruation itself as the loss of a child ("two days gone in blood")—a child that exists because it can be called:

> I was thinking of a son. . . .
> You! . . .
> Will you be the David or the Susan?
> . . .
> David! Susan! David! David!
> . . .
> my carrot, my cabbage,
> I would have possessed you before all women,
> calling your name,
> calling you mine.

The political consequences and complexities of addressing—of "calling"—are made even more explicit in a poem by Lucille Clifton entitled "The Lost Baby Poem." By choosing the word "dropped" ("i dropped your almost body down"), Clifton renders it unclear whether the child has been lost through abortion or through miscarriage. What is clear, however, is that that loss is both mourned and rationalized. The rationalization occurs through the description of a life of hardship, flight, and loss: the image of a child born into winter, slipping like ice into the hands of strangers in Canada, conflates the scene of Eliza's escape in *Uncle Tom's Cabin* with the exile of draft resisters during the Vietnam War. The guilt and mourning occur in the form of an imperative in which the notion of "stranger" returns in the following lines:

> if i am ever less than a mountain
> for your definite brothers and sisters. . . .
> . . . let black men call me stranger
> always   for your never named sake.

The act of "calling" here correlates a lack of name with a loss of membership. For the sake of the one that cannot be called, the speaker invites an apostrophe that would expel *her* into otherness. The consequences of the death of a child ramify beyond the mother–child dyad to encompass the fate of an entire community. The world that has created conditions under which the loss of a baby becomes desirable must be resisted, not joined. For a black woman, the loss of a baby can always be perceived as a complicity with genocide. The black mother sees her own choice as one of being either a stranger or a rock. The humanization of the lost baby addressed by the poem is thus carried out at the cost of dehumanizing, even of rendering inanimate, the calling mother.

Yet each of these poems exists, finally, *because* a child does not.[5] In Adrienne Rich's poem "To a Poet," the rivalry between poems and children is made quite explicit. The 'you' in the poem is again aborted, but here it is the mother herself who could be called "dim and killed" by the fact not of abortion but of the institution of motherhood. And again, the structures of address are complex and unstable. The deadness of the "you" cannot be named: not suicide, not murder. The question of the life or death of the addressee is raised in an interesting way through Rich's rewriting of Keats's sonnet on his mortality. While Keats writes, "When I have fears that *I* will cease to be" ["When I Have Fears"], Rich writes "and I have fears that *you* will cease to be." If poetry is at stake in both intimations of mortality, what is the significance of this shift from "I" to "you"? On the one hand, the very existence of the Keats poem indicates that the pen has succeeded in gleaning something before the brain has ceased to be. No such grammatical guarantee exists for the "you." Death in the Keats poem is as much a source as it is a threat to writing. Hence, death, for Keats, could be called the mother of poetry while motherhood, for Rich, is precisely the death of poetry. The Western myth of the conjunction of word and flesh implied by the word "incarnate" is undone by images of language floating and vanishing in the toilet bowl of real-flesh needs. The word is not made flesh; rather, flesh unmakes the mother-poet's word. The difficulty of retrieving the "you" as poet is enacted by the structures of address in the following lines:

> I write this   not for you
> who fight to write your own
> words fighting up the falls
> but for another woman   dumb

In saying "I write this not for you," it is almost as though Rich is excluding as addressee anyone who could conceivably be reading this poem. The poem is setting aside both the "I" and the "you"—the pronouns Benveniste associates with personhood—and reaches instead toward a "she," which belongs in the category of "non-person." The poem is thus attempting the impossible task of directly addressing not a second person but a third person—a person who, if she is reading the poem, cannot be the reader the poem has in mind. The poem is trying to include what is by its own grammar exluded from it—to animate through language the non-person, the "other woman." Therefore, this poem, too, is bursting the limits of its own language, inscribing a logic that it itself reveals to be impossible—but necessary. Even the divorce between writing and childbearing is less absolute than it appears: in comparing the writing of words to the spawning of fish, Rich's poem reveals itself to be trapped between the inability to combine and the inability to separate the woman's various roles.

In each of these poems, then, a kind of competition is implicitly instated between the bearing of children and the writing of poems. Something unsettling has happened to the analogy often drawn by male poets between artistic creation and procreation. For it is not true that literature contains no examples of male pregnancy. Sir Philip Sidney, in the first sonnet from "Astrophel and Stella," describes himself as "great with child to speak," but the poem is ultimately produced at the expense of no literalized child. Sidney's labor pains are smoothed away by a midwifely apostrophe ("'Fool,' said my Muse to me, 'look in thy heart, and write!'") [The Norton Anthology of Poetry, 1:12–14], and by a sort of poetic Caesarian section, out springs the poem we have, in fact, already finished reading. Mallarmé, in "Don du poème," describes himself as an enemy father seeking nourishment for his monstrous poetic child from the woman within apostrophe-shot who is busy nursing a literalized daughter. But since the woman presumably has two breasts, there seems to be enough to go around. As Shakespeare assures the fair young man, "But were some child of yours alive that time,/ You should live twice in it and in my rhyme" [Sonnets, 17:13–14]. Apollinaire, in his play Les Mamelles de Tirésias, depicts woman as a de-maternalized neo-Malthusian leaving the task of childbearing to a surrealistically fertile husband. But again, nothing more disturbing than Tiresian cross-dressing seems to occur. Children are alive and well, and far more numerous than ever. Indeed, in one of the dedicatory poems, Apollinaire indicates that his drama represents a return to health from the literary reign of the poète maudit:

> La féconde raison a jailli de ma fable,
> Plus de femme stérile et non plus d'avortons . . .

> [Fertile reason springs out of my fable,
> No more sterile women, no aborted children]

This dig at Baudelaire, among others, reminds us that in the opening poem to *Les Fleurs du mal* ("Bénédiction"), Baudelaire represents the poet himself as an abortion manqué, cursed by the poisonous words of a rejecting mother. The question of the unnatural seems more closely allied with the bad mother than with the pregnant father.

Even in the seemingly more obvious parallel provided by poems written to dead children by male poets, it is not really surprising to find that the substitution of poem for child lacks the sinister undertones and disturbed address exhibited by the abortion poems we have been discussing. Ben Jonson, in "On My First Son," calls his dead child "his best piece of poetry," while Mallarmé, in an only semi-guilty *Aufhebung*, transfuses the dead Anatole to the level of an idea. More recently, Jon Silkin has written movingly of the death of a handicapped child ("something like a person") as a change of silence, not a splitting of voice. And Michael Harper, in "Nightmare Begins Responsibility," stresses the powerlessness and distrust of a black father leaving his dying son to the care of a "white-doctor-who-breathed-for-him-all-night." But again, whatever the complexity of the voices in that poem, the speaker does not split self-accusingly or infra-symbiotically in the ways we have noted in the abortion/motherhood poems. While one could undoubtedly find counter-examples on both sides, it is not surprising that the substitution of art for children should not be inherently transgressive for the male poet. Men have in a sense always had no choice but to substitute something for the literal process of birth. That, at least, is the belief that has long been encoded into male poetic conventions. It is as though male writing were by nature procreative, while female writing is somehow by nature infanticidal.

It is, of course, as problematic as it is tempting to draw general conclusions about differences between male and female writing on the basis of these somewhat random examples. Yet it is clear that a great many poetic effects may be colored according to *expectations* articulated through the gender of the poetic speaker. Whether or not men and women would "naturally" write differently about dead children, there is something about the connection between motherhood and death that refuses to remain comfortably and conventionally figurative. When a woman speaks about the death of children in any sense other than that of pure loss, a powerful taboo is being violated. The indistinguishability of miscarriage and abortion in the Clifton poem indeed points to the notion that *any* death of a child is perceived as a crime committed by the mother, something a mother ought by definition to be able to prevent. That these questions should be so inextricably connected to the figure of apostrophe, however, deserves further comment. For there may be a deeper link between motherhood and apostrophe than we have hitherto suspected.

The verbal development of the infant, according to Lacan, begins as a demand addressed to the mother, out of which the entire verbal universe is spun. Yet the mother addressed is somehow a personification, not a person—a personification of presence or absence, of Otherness itself.

> Demand in itself bears on something other than the satisfactions it calls for.
> It is demand of a presence or of an absence—which is what is manifested in

the primordial relation to the mother, pregnant with that Other to be situated *within* the needs that it can satisfy. Insofar as [man's] needs are subjected to demand, they return to him alienated. This is not the effect of his real dependence. . . , but rather the turning into signifying form as such, from the fact that it is from the locus of the Other that its message is emitted. [*Ecrits* 286]

If demand is the originary vocative, which assures life even as it inaugurates alienation, then it is not surprising that questions of animation inhere in the rhetorical figure of apostrophe. The reversal of apostrophe we noted in the Shelley poem ("animate me") would be no reversal at all, but a reinstatement of the primal apostrophe in which, despite Lacan's disclaimer, there is precisely a link between demand and animation, between apostrophe and life-and-death dependency.[6] If apostrophe is structured like demand, and if demand articulates the primal relation to the mother as a relation to the Other, then lyric poetry itself— summed up in the figure of apostrophe—comes to look like the fantastically intricate history of endless elaborations and displacements of the single cry, "Mama!" The question these poems are asking, then, is what happens when the poet is speaking as a mother—a mother whose cry arises out of—and is addressed to—a dead child?

It is no wonder that the distinction between addressor and addressee should become so problematic in poems about abortion. It is also no wonder that the debate about abortion should refuse to settle into a single voice. Whether or not one has ever been a mother, everyone participating in the debate has once been a child. Rhetorical, psychoanalytical, and political structures are profoundly implicated in one another. The difficulty in all three would seem to reside in the attempt to achieve a full elaboration of any discursive position other than that of child.

NOTES

1. I would like to thank Tom Keenan of Yale University for bringing this text to my attention. The present essay has in fact benefited greatly from the suggestions of others, among whom I would like particularly to thank Marge Garber, Rachel Jacoff, Carolyn Williams, Helen Vendler, Steven Melville, Ted Morris, Stamos Metzidakis, Steven Ungar, and Richard Yarborough.

2. Cf. also Paul de Man, in "Lyrical Voice in Contemporary Theory": "Now it is certainly beyond question that the figure of address is recurrent in lyric poetry, to the point of constituting the generic definition of, at the very least, the ode (which can, in turn, be seen as paradigmatic for poetry in general)" [61].

3. For complete texts of the poems under discussion, see the appendix to this article in its original form, in *Diacritics* vol. 5, No. 4 (1975): 29–47.

4. It is interesting to note that the "gentle breeze," apostrophized as "Messenger" and "Friend" in the 1805–6 *Prelude* (Book 1, line 5), is, significantly, not directly addressed in the 1850 version. One might ask whether this change stands as a sign of the much-discussed waning of Wordsworth's poetic inspiration, or whether it is, rather, one of a number of strictly rhetorical shifts that *give the impression* of a wane, just as the shift in Gwendolyn Brooks's poetry from her early impersonal poetic narratives to her more recent direct-address poems gives the impression of a politicization.

5. For additional poems dealing with the loss of babies, see the anthology *The Limits of Miracles* collected by Marion Deutsche Cohen. Sharon Dunn, editor of the *Agni Review*, told me recently that she has in fact noticed that such poems have begun to form almost a new genre.

6. An interesting example of a poem in which an apostrophe confers upon the total Other the authority to animate the self is Randall Jarrell's "A Sick Child," which ends: "All that I've never thought of—think of me!"

WORKS CITED

Allison et al., Eds. *The Norton Anthology of Poetry*. New York: W. W. Norton, 1975.

Apollinaire, Guillaume. *Les Mamelles de Tirésias. L'Enchanteur pourrissant*. Paris: Gallimard, 1972.

Baudelaire, Charles. *Oeuvres complètes*. Paris: Pléiade, 1976.

Brooks, Gwendolyn. "The Mother." *Selected Poems*. New York: Harper & Row, 1963.

Clifton, Lucille. "The Lost Baby Poem." *Good News About the Earth*. New York: Random House, 1972.

Cohen, Marion Deutsche, Ed. *The Limits of Miracles*. South Hadley, Eng.: Bergin & Garvey, 1985.

Culler, Jonathan. *The Pursuit of Signs*. Ithaca: Cornell UP, 1981.

de Man, Paul. "Lyrical Voice in Contemporary Theory." *Lyric Poetry: Beyond New Criticism*. Ed. Hosek and Parker. Ithaca: Cornell UP, 1985.

Gilligan, Carol. *In a Different Voice*. Cambridge, MA: Harvard UP, 1982.

Harper, Michael. *Nightmare Begins Responsibility*. Urbana: U of Illinois P, 1975.

Jarrell, Randall. "A Sick Child." *The Voice that is Great within Us*. Ed. Hayden Caruth. New York: Bantam, 1970.

Jonson, Ben. "On My First Son." *The Norton Anthology of Poetry*. Ed. Allison et al. New York: W. W. Norton, 1975.

Keats, John. "When I Have Fears." *The Norton Anthology of Poetry*. Ed. Allison et al. New York: W. W. Norton, 1975.

Lacan, Jacques. *Ecrits*. Trans. Sheridan. New York: W. W. Norton, 1977.

Luker, Kristin. *Abortion and the Politics of Motherhood*. Berkeley: U of California P, 1984.

Mallarmé, Stéphane. *Oeuvres complètes*. Paris: Pléiade, 1961.

———. *Pour un Tombeau d'Anatole*. Ed. Richard. Paris: Seuil, 1961.

Rich, Adrienne. "To a Poet." *The Dream of a Common Language*. New York: W. W. Norton, 1978.

Sexton, Anne. "The Abortion." *The Complete Poems*. Boston: Houghton Mifflin, 1981.

Shakespeare, William. *Sonnets*. Ed. Booth. New Haven: Yale UP, 1977.

Shelley, Percy Bysshe. "Ode to the West Wind." *The Norton Anthology of Poetry*. Ed. Allison et al. New York: W. W. Norton, 1975.

Sidney, Sir Philip. "Astrophel and Stella." *The Norton Anthology of Poetry*. Ed. Allison et al. New York: W. W. Norton, 1975.

Thomson, Judith Jarvis. "A Defense of Abortion." *Rights, Restitution, Risk*. Ed. William Parent. Cambridge, MA: Harvard UP, 1986.

Thoreau, Henry David. *Walden*. New York: Signet, 1960.

Wordsworth, William. *The Prelude*. Ed. de Selincourt. London: Oxford UP, 1959.

DEVIOUS CHANNELS OF DECOROUS ORDERING
rosa coldfield in absalom, absalom!

Language (that meager and fragile thread . . . by which the little surface corners and edges of men's secret and solitary lives may be joined for an instant now and then before sinking back into the darkness where the spirit cried for the first time and was not heard and will cry for the last time and will not be heard then either).

GRANDFATHER COMPSON

There is something in the touch of flesh with flesh which abrogates, cuts sharp and straight across the devious intricate channels of decorous ordering, which enemies as well as lovers know because it makes them both—touch and touch of that which is the citadel of the central I-Am's private own.

ROSA COLDFIELD

ALIEN DISCOURSE

Before language, desire: the spirit, the darkness in which the spirit cries, the need that makes the spirit cry, and the touch that abrogates—all are represented as being prior to language in *Absalom, Absalom!*[1] The novel explores the solipsism of individual consciousness, the magnitude and meagerness of language, the insatiability of desire. Language is a thread, but a touch has the power to cut (like the knives, sabres, and scythes in the novel) through language—to annul the word through the far greater potency of the flesh. Like James's governess in *The Turn of the Screw,* Rosa Coldfield recognizes the aesthetic attractions of language—its intricacy and decorum—but she also sees its devious, evasive, abstract elements, which the governess exploits but never confesses. Rosa recognizes that all the artificial barriers of caste, color, and code that divide humankind are sustained by language; yet she envisions in the touch of flesh with flesh *"the fall of all the eggshell shibboleth of caste and color too."*[2]

Although Rosa does not state it, the context in which she utters these words—when Clytie stops her on the stairs at Sutpen's Hundred—makes it clear that even though the shibboleths may crumble, the touch of Clytie's flesh on her own does not necessarily result in unity, reconciliation, union. Every major character—black and white, lover and beloved, son and father—shares her yearning for that touch. But that desire is thwarted at every turn. Denial, displacement, and repudiation blight the lives in *Absalom, Absalom!* not only of individuals but of entire generations. Faulkner's novel, like *The Turn of the Screw*, is burdened with multiple voices and multiple hauntings, with baffled ghosts and psychic possession. Sutpen is commonly viewed as the most potent figure in the novel, despite—or because of—his death. What hasn't been noticed, however, is that the operative dichotomy that reveals the underlying structure of adversarial antithesis is *dead/alive*, just as day/dream was in *The Turn of the Screw*.[3] Sutpen is more "alive" than Quentin, who is a pale shade, his "very body was an empty hall echoing. . . . he was not a being, an entity, he was a commonwealth" (12). Sutpen, moreover, has been the focus of exhaustive critical analyses of the relation of history to myth in the novel, but the relation of myth to love has been wholly overlooked.[4]

Of all the narratives in the novel then, which one is a discourse of desire? Who exactly is the lover in the text? It is not Quentin, recreating his incestuous desire for his sister in an imaginative reconstruction of the relationship between Henry and Judith Sutpen. It is not Mr. Compson, lingering lovingly on the sensuousness of Charles Bon's octoroon mistress. It is not even Charles himself, writing love letters to Judith while awaiting his destiny. The female lover, who is herself related to myth, for Faulkner compares her to Cassandra, has remained invisible as the lover in the novel because she, like Cassandra, has been dismissed as mad. Rosa Coldfield is the lover in *Absalom, Absalom!*, endlessly reconstructing her desire and deconstructing its object, lamenting her pain and sustaining her passion by weaving her narrative. Her narrative is not epistolary, yet it is an amorous discourse, a long meditation in the absence of the beloved, spoken out loud. The emphasis on her voice is indeed crucial, for she does not merely tell what happened, she shows the effects. Her narrative, indeed, lies at the extremes of showing and telling, so far removed from mere plot that it could simply be called talking, and it is that talking which gives her voice its overwhelming intensity. Her discourse thus disrupts the dichotomies of diegesis and mimesis, of present and past, for what Quentin hears is not a mere story but its repercussions, not a memory but its living presence as trace.[5]

Diegesis signifies a journey already made. Like all the heroines of amorous discourse, Rosa is a haunted woman whose very talking evokes the trace of Sutpen. Sutpen, like Quint and Jessel, is "unhouseled, unaneled"; while Rosa speaks, "the ghost mused with shadowy docility as if it were the voice which he haunted where a more fortunate one would have had a house" (8). Not only does Faulkner underscore the dialogic dimensions of Rosa's discourse in this passage by stressing Rosa's voice, but her dialogue is a soliloquy as well, imagined as a struggle for discourse staged in discourse. Language itself is a struggle; Rosa tries to put her experience into words, but it defies all attempts at articulation and comprehension. This is why she is as haunted and as haggard as her predecessors (both Jessel and the governess) in James's tale: her "wan haggard face" watches Quentin as she speaks in a "grim haggard amazed voice." The very fact that she is still amazed after forty-three years of attempting to understand what happened to her simultaneously highlights the necessity of the attempt and its futility. Even her senses are confounded as she talks: "hearing-sense [would] self-confound and the long-dead object of her impotent yet indomitable frustration would appear, as though by outraged recapitulation evoked, quiet inattentive and harmless, out of the biding and dreamy and victorious dust" (7–8).[6] (*Impotent/indomitable* rephrases the fundamental structural dichotomy of *dead/alive*.) Furthermore, not only is the dead Sutpen excusably inattentive, but so is the live Quentin. His entire perception of Rosa is shaped by a similar dichotomization of youth and age, which prevents him from ever really "attending" her. In speculating about her voice, for instance, his words echo the tragic ones of his grandfather. Quentin thinks: "Maybe it (the voice, the talking, the incredulous and unbearable amazement) had even been a cry aloud once . . . long ago when she was a girl—of young and indomitable unregret, of indictment of blind circumstance and savage event" (14). His attempt at empathetic identification fails, because he cannot recognize that Rosa's talking is a discourse of desire, the cry of a spirit who deserves to be heard. He never succeeds in joining the "surface edge" of his life to hers through language. Nor is he capable of imagining that a young girl's spirit may lie immured in "old flesh," as the repetition of the word *old* reveals when he rejects the possibility that she is crying out now too: "Now now: now only the lonely thwarted old female flesh embattled for forty-three years in the old insult, the old unforgiving outraged and betrayed by the final and complete affront which was Sutpen's death" (14). In my view, Rosa's narrative is a last cry from one who remembers not only her youth, her hopes, and her capacity for love but her sexual desire; who is, moreover, capable of imagining a world of possibility beyond the one that has negated her, as Quentin negates her here.

Most critics, however, find Rosa not a passionate but a pathetic creature. Given the sophistication of the analyses of narrative in the novel, it is remarkable how many critics accept Quentin's evaluation of Rosa without recognizing how much more his negation reveals about himself than about her. Critics who discuss Rosa at all choose to emphasize her grotesqueness, her Gothicism, her bitterness. Why her desire and the rhetoric of amorous discourse has been overlooked is a matter for speculation. The oversight is related, I think, to what Barthes calls the philosophical solitude of the lover, which arises because no modern system of thought accounts for love. Instead, "Christian discourse . . . exhorts [the lover] to repress and to sublimate. Psychoanalytical discourse . . . commits him to give up his [beloved] as lost. As for Marxist discourse, it has nothing to say. If it should occur to me to knock at these doors in order to gain recognition *somewhere* . . . for my 'madness' (my 'truth'), these doors close one after the other; and when they are all shut, there rises around me a wall of language which oppresses and repulses me."[7] The female lover faces even greater oppression and repulsion, for as we have seen, she has been reduced to a few well-worn clichés: the mannish intellectual (Heloise); the seduced virgin (the Portuguese nun); the frigid martyr (Clarissa); the gullible plain Jane (Jane Eyre); the frustrated spinster (the governess in James's tale). The female lover is frequently regarded merely as a madwoman, frigid and furious. No system of discourse seriously considers her suffering, her passion, or the range and resourcefulness of her imaginative powers. Scholarly descriptions of Rosa reveal how quick modern critics have been to dismiss lovers as repressed, disturbed, or mad. Cleanth Brooks desccribes Rosa's language as a "dithyramb of hate . . . [a] shrill, tense voice . . . [of] Norn-like frenzy."[8] As in *The Turn of the Screw*, the clear implication is that female "tension" is sexual, as Albert Guerard reveals: "Her ornate, often sexualized rhetoric and rhythms of almost insane intensity . . . admirably convey a particular disturbed personality. . . . [Her] ranting [is] controlled by exquisitely timed . . . sentences . . . [in a] hysterical narrative . . . of wild rhetoric."[9] Guerard is representative of all those critics whose "systems"—psychoanalytic or otherwise—have failed to recognize Rosa. He is particularly provocative because he senses that there is a language in *Absalom, Absalom!* that he can neither define nor assimilate. He notes that "all the narrators share Faulkner's ironic love of hyperbole and paradox, of absurd oxymoron and analogy drawn from an alien area of discourse."[10] Here again, as in *The Turn of the Screw*, perhaps the limitations of modernist irony obscure one of the fundamental strains of discourse in Faulkner's masterpiece. My aim, by showing the close connection of Rosa's narrative to the genre of amorous epistolary discourse, is to make it a little less alien.

Of all the narratives in the novel, Rosa's has the most personal immediacy. She—not Quentin—is the character who is most passionately engaged in her discourse, yet she is dismissed as readily as James's governess as a "frustrated spinster," as if the words were redundant. This distorted perception of her is wholly shaped by Mr. Compson, Quentin, and Shreve, none of whom ever really see Rosa as anything but a warped, bitter, outraged, pathetic old woman.[11] She is like the enigmatic letter announcing her death, which Quentin cannot decipher.

Here again, the dichotomy *dead/alive* is central, for it is one thing to indulge in imaginative reconstruction of the long-dead Sutpen, Bon, and Judith, but Rosa is not remote. She has personal, immediate relations with the characters who negate her. The Sutpens may be ghosts, but she is not, although both Compsons try to make her one. When Quentin asks his father why he must obey Rosa's summons, he replies, "Years ago we in the South made our women into ladies. Then the War came and made the ladies into ghosts. So what else can we do, being gentlemen, but listen to them being ghosts?" (12). They try to distance themselves from her by thus reducing her complexity—to gain the kind of aesthetic distance that is ordered and arranged into art. But how, one wonders, can they hope to understand the long-dead Sutpens if they cannot even comprehend the woman who is their contemporary, as Shreve implies when he confronts Quentin at the end with the challenge: "You dont even know about the old dame, the Aunt Rosa. . . . You dont even know about her." Rosa resists reduction, however, as Shreve senses when he perceives that "she refused at the last to be a ghost" (362).

Her narrative, then, is no mere diatribe by a mad woman. She refuses to conform to the town's view of "an old lady that died young of outrage." Rosa remarks that touch makes enemies as well as lovers, and she herself is both: the object of her love is Charles Bon; the object of both her desire *and* her enmity is Thomas Sutpen. Her narrative thus reflects the characteristic Ovidian doubleness and dissimulation. Her motives for summoning Quentin are as duplicitous as the duality of her focus on Sutpen and Bon. She wants to set the record straight, but she also has some purpose that she withholds. As in previous discourses, Rosa is torn by a thousand conflicting emotions; she oscillates from love to hate, forgiveness to revenge, pathos to despair. She sounds like the preacher without a pulpit, the judge without power to punish, the prophet without a following, reminding us that the discourse of pathos is always a surrogate for an earlier genre—that of amorous epistolary discourse. Her very name records the doubleness in her rhetoric, her desire, her character; she combines the passion of courtly love (*Le Roman de la rose*) with cold fascination and fury. Although she invests Charles Bon with all the qualities of courtly romance, Sutpen is the focus of her fury. Bon is the absence to which Rosa gives shape, as she herself explains:

> There must have been some seed he left, to cause a child's vacant fairy-tale to come alive. . . . even before I saw the photograph I could have recognized, nay, described, the very face. But I never saw it. I do not even know of my own knowledge that Ellen ever saw it, that Judith ever loved it, that Henry slew it: so who will dispute me when I say, Why did I not invent, create it?—And I know this: if I were God I would invent out of this seething turmoil we call progress something . . . which would adorn the barren mirror altars of every plain girl who breathes with such as this . . . this pictured face. It would not even need a skull behind it; almost anonymous, it would only need vague inference of some walking flesh and blood desired by someone else even if only in some shadow-realm of make-believe. (146–47)

The passage is a remarkable revelation of desire: Bon is the idol who adorns Rosa's mirror altar; he is the sacrifice on the altar of Sutpen's design. Rosa worships someone she never saw, yet she is one of three surviving witnesses to his having lived at all. (The others are Clytie and Henry.) What she worships is an image, framed and frozen in a photograph, as removed from the actual being as language is. That photograph, moreover, is an altar that transforms Rosa from plain girl into devotee. Thus, in contrast to such lover-tyrants as Lovelace and Rochester, Rosa is not narcissistic. She worships not her own "barren" reflection but a photo, which gives her an image—what Barthes would call an "Image-repertoire." Like a face in a mirror, furthermore, language is a mirror not of presence but of the image of presence.[12] The repeated emphasis on vacancy, vagueness, and make-believe reveals that Bon is not only absent in retrospect, that for Rosa he was always absent. She is, actually, acutely aware of the fictiveness of her desire and of her own highly self-conscious literary powers, for what she worships is not Bon but the idea of Bon and his very absence: his footprint obliterated by the rake, the fading sound of his breathing, *"his foot, his passing shape, his face, his speaking voice, his name: Charles Bon, Charles Good, Charles Husband-soon-to-be"* (148). The Keatsian and Shakespearean images with which she endlessly recreates her passion illuminate her attachment to the idol she has built for herself, the receptacle, of all her hopes and illusions. If, as we saw in the previous chapter, the ambiguous beauty of the governess's passion is that she only saw her employer twice, the "beauty" of Rosa's is that she never sees Charles Bon at all. Thus when John Irwin argues that Rosa can never become Bon's lover because Judith never becomes Bon's wife, his approach to Rosa's remarkable imaginative powers is far too literal.[13] My point is just the opposite: Rosa sees herself as a more perfect lover precisely because her emotions are centered on the idol she invents. Just as unheard melodies are sweeter in Keats's "Ode on a Grecian Urn," Rosa's desire is perfect because it is conceived, nurtured, and sustained solely in the imagination. The same code of perfection that makes the governess's desire ambiguous in *The Turn of the Screw* is endorsed by Rosa in relation to Charles Bon.

Unlike James's governess, however, Rosa does not insist on coercing her narrative into one fixed meaning for all time. One sign that she lacks her predecessor's fixity of intention is that she does not even bother to write down her narrative, although she is a skilled and prolific writer of thousands of odes and eulogies. As in James's tale, the question of what the narrative is worth arises; here, as there, it is an object of exchange, of barter. Rosa speculates that Quentin may one day write down her story to buy a gown or a chair for his wife, since the only kind of production left for southerners after the war is literary production about their loss, their despair, their failure (9–10). Quentin's skepticism, however, does not accurately reflect Rosa's real attitude about her story, although the same paradoxical explanation is repeated again and again: "It cant matter . . . and yet it must matter" (127).

Indeed, just as the governess mythologizes the children in *The Turn of the Screw*, Rosa retrospectively mythologizes Sutpen, transforming him from a damn fool into a demon. In both James's text and Faulkner's, the mythologizing tendency belongs in the "province of the antithesis" between angel and demon.[14] We saw in the last chapter how in mythologizing the children, the governess's organizing dichotomy was good/evil; Rosa falls into precisely the same pattern, retrospectively regarding Charles Bon as "Charles Good" and Thomas Sutpen as the devil incarnate. But the distinction between Rosa the *focus* and Rosa the *voice* is crucial here, for at the time the events that she narrates occurred, her views of Sutpen went through three distinct stages; she is raised to regard him as an ogre; when he comes home from the war her attitude softens; and it is not until he repudiates her that she reverts—with some justice—to her initial opinion of his bedevilment.

Thus if Bon is at first the receptacle of Rosa's illusions, Sutpen is the one who shatters them. She never invests Sutpen with the kind of perfection that she attributed to Bon; neither is her hatred uniformly consistent throughout her narrative. Most critics overlook the fact that Sutpen becomes the focus of Rosa's desire because she saw in him the possibility of salvaging something of *"the old lost enchantment of the heart."* He is, in short, as much the epitome of lack as Bon is, astounding as it seems. Sutpen is the very figure of absence, despite the fact that Rosa cannot even say how often she sees Sutpen "for the reason that," according to Mr. Compson, "waking or sleeping, the aunt had taught her to see nothing else" (62).

Like all the other characters in the novel, Sutpen never does "see" Rosa herself. Her experience with him, indeed, consists of repeated nullification. Even after he "proposes," Rosa realizes that *"My presence was to him only the absence of black morass and snarled vine"* (166). Yet once their marriage is planned, she allows herself to hope anew, to believe that he *"was not oblivious of me but only unconscious and receptive"* (167). Unfortunately, as in *Jane Eyre* and *The Turn of the Screw*, a critical moment of rupture comes because the beloved is a destroyer of love. Sutpen suggests that he and Rosa breed first and marry later, if she bears a son who survives. As in the earlier texts, the scene is stricken with death precisely because the heroine realizes that the beloved is incapable of recognizing her humanity:

> [I] *did believe there was that magic in unkin blood which we call by the pallid name of love that would be, might be sun for him. . . . And then one afternoon . . . the death of hope and love, the death of pride and principle, and then the death of everything*

> *save the old outraged and aghast unbelieving . . . . oh I told you he had not thought of*
> *it until that moment, that prolonged moment which contained the distance between the*
> *house and wherever it was he had been standing when he thought of it: and this too*
> *coincident: it was the very day on which he knew definitely and at last exactly how*
> *much of his hundred square miles he would be able to save and keep and call his own*
> *on the day when he would have to die. . . . he stood with the reins over his arm (and*
> *no hand on my head now) and spoke the bald outrageous words exactly as if he*
> *were consulting with Jones or with some other man about a bitch dog or a cow or*
> *mare.* (168)

Significantly, Rosa specifically draws attention to the absence of Sutpen's touch here; this is no more "coincident" than that the death of love coincides with the decimation of Sutpen's Hundred and with Sutpen's own death day. No coincidence, it is the *consequence*, foreshadowed by the allusion to the mare, for it is Sutpen's comparison of Milly to a mare which leads Wash to murder him, Milly, and the newborn. Sutpen is thus a symbol not just of a megalomaniacal male principle, but of the other, inaccessible and unknowable; it is partly because he is unknowable that all the characters in the novel are obsessed with him. For Rosa, too, he is the magical other who holds the keys to the edifice but denies her access.

Rosa the *focus* compares both Bon and Sutpen to fairy-tale figures: Bon "makes a vacant fairy-tale come alive," whereas the child Rosa saw Sutpen as "an ogre, a djinn, a Bluebeard." (The latter, one remembers, hangs his wives in the turret chamber.) Brontë's Rochester, significantly, is also compared to Bluebeard because of his cruel treatment of Bertha Mason. Not only do Bluebeard, Rochester, and Sutpen all stand convicted of inhospitable treatment of their wives, but in Sutpen the enigmatic character of a Rochester is combined with scores of depraved—albeit mysterious—activities, including wrestling with Negroes in the barn. The cumulative mystery of his depravities brings to mind the range of unspecified evils that Henry James leaves to the reader's imagination in *The Turn of the Screw*. Thus, if the heroines who write discourses of desire are Rosa's predecessors, Sutpen's are the lover-tyrants. Rosa, indeed, recognizes her place in the repetitive structure of seduction, betrayal, and abandonment. Like Ovid's heroines, Heloise, Mariane, Clarissa, Jane Eyre, and James's governess, Rosa, too, discovers that she is neither the first to be seduced nor the last be betrayed. Where she draws on Keats, Shakespeare, and romance in her re-creation of Bon, for Sutpen her sources are the Old Testament, Milton, and the Brothers Grimm. In one poetic passage, full of Miltonic cadences, she notes the replication of her rivals while describing Wash Jones as

> *that brute progenitor of brutes whose granddaughter was to supplant me, if not in my*
> *sister's house at least in my sister's bed to which (so they will tell you) I aspired—that*
> *brute who (brute instrument of that justice which presides over human events which,*
> *incept in the individual, runs smooth, less claw than velvet: but which, by man or*
> *woman flouted, drives on like fiery steel and overrides both weakly just and unjust*
> *strong, both vanquisher and innocent victimized, ruthless for appointed right and*
> *truth) brute who was . . . to preside upon the various shapes and avatars of Thomas*
> *Sutpen's devil's fate.* (134)

In the elevation and intensity of her rhetoric, Rosa is unquestionably theatrical here, and such self-conscious theatricality is a distinguishing feature of amorous discourse; the heroine creates roles, plots, dramas, and fictions to occupy herself in the beloved's absence. Rosa, moreover, is acutely aware of her theatricality where both Bon and Sutpen are concerned. Her motive for her frequent forays into Judith's room to look at Bon's picture is *"not to dream . . . but to renew, rehearse, the part as the faulty though eager amateur might steal wingward in some interim of the visible scene to hear the prompter's momentary voice"* (147). This passage illuminates the difference between her desire for Bon and for Sutpen: with Bon she nurtured the illusion of perfection, but her desire was completely imaginative; with Sutpen she was willing to forgo perfection, to accept the vagaries of fortune and the change that the war wrought in him and, instead of remaining a spectator, to take the risk of becoming a principal player in the drama.

Instead, Rosa is devastated to discover that Sutpen's view of her is purely utilitarian. He must have a male heir, and to insure that he gets one, he proposes to beget the heir before signing the contract of marriage. Outrageous as the proposition is, Rosa reacts so vehemently because it reenforces the fundamental trauma of nullification that marks every stage of her existence. Her entire childhood is described in terms of lack. She has only her aunt for mother and father; her sister, she is taught, "vanished, not only out of the family and the house but out of life too" (60); her childhood is marked by the absence of play and is passed in "that aged and ancient and timeless *absence of youth* which consisted of a Cassandralike listening beyond closed doors, of lurking in dim halls" (60, my italics). Sutpen's obliteration of her thus has far more cumulative force than it might otherwise have. Since nullification has been the pattern of her life, she dedicates herself to hating him to break the pattern, combating nullification by mythologizing Sutpen and herself. Ignored by her father, excluded from her cousins' company, ridiculed by her sister when she offers to help Judith, she describes herself as a *"small plain frightened creature whom neither man nor woman had ever looked at twice"* (141). Rosa's narrative, like so many amorous discourses, thus arises from extreme silence and solitude, as she explains: *"Instead of accomplishing the processional and measured milestones of the childhood's time I lurked, unapprehended as though, shod with the very damp and velvet silence of the womb, I displaced no air, gave off no betraying sound, from one closed forbidden door to the next"* (145). That closed forbidden door is a multifaceted metaphor for the deprivation Rosa suffers—of light, of touch, of love, of the entire range of experiences in human development. Indeed, an astonishing number of forbidden doors, gates, and corridors appear in the novel: Goodhue Coldfield nails the attic door shut; Henry stops Bon at the gate; Clytie stops Rosa on the stair; Sutpen forbids Wash entrance; there is a door in Quentin's consciousness through which he cannot pass. All these images contribute to the sense of the novel as a labyrinth and to the narrative line as a thread. Many of the images replicate Sutpen's humiliation at the door of Pettibone's mansion, which in turn is a reenactment of the psychic shock Pip in *Great Expectations* suffers at the door of Satis House. (Satis: desire increases in direct proportion to humiliation and rejection, as in Rosa's narrative.) The connection of humiliation to narration and naming can be seen by comparing the reactions of young Pip and young Thomas Sutpen. Just as Thomas "couldn't get it straight yet. . . . he was seeking among what little he had to call experience for something to measure it by, and he couldn't find anything" (233), Pip describes himself as being "so humiliated, hurt, spurned, offended, angry, sorry—I cannot hit upon the right name for the smart—God knows what its name was. . . . As I cried I kicked the wall . . . so bitter were my feelings, and so sharp was *the smart without a name,* that needed counteraction." [15] Rosa Coldfield's own efforts to find the words to express her pain are similarly related to humiliation and to the frustration of her desire. From abandonment, then, comes the birth of language; loss is the structure. Loss, indeed, is what structures the lives of all the characters in the novel: Sutpen's loss of innocence at Pettibone's door, Eulalia's loss of Sutpen, Charles Bon's search for the lost father, Judith's unmarried widowhood. And looming over all these losses is the loss of the Civil War. Language is a means of exorcism or of enchantment, a ceaseless lament against the underlying structure of loss, lack, absence.

Like previous writing heroines, Rosa is attempting to reorder experience and make it comprehensible, to reconstruct her desire while exorcising its object, Sutpen. Her narrative is an effort to comprehend and, simultaneously, an acknowledgement of the futility of that effort. One source of her frustration, indeed, is that no telling can express the meaning of her tale; it has to be traced and retraced, as Theseus retraces Ariadne's thread in the labyrinth. This, too, is one of the distinguishing characteristics of amorous discourse: "to deplore that words should betray an 'ineffable' emotion which nevertheless demands to be avowed." [16] Amorous discourses are always critiques of language, for the alphabet of the body has to be replaced with what is considered an inadequate system of signs: words. Rosa reveals her awareness both of the inadequacy of language and of her compulsion to repeat when she tells Quentin: *"I will tell you what he did and let you be the judge. (Or try to tell you, because there are some things for which three words are three too many, and three thousand words that many words too less, and this is one of them. It can be told; I could take that many sentences, repeat the bold blank naked and outrageous words just as he spoke them, and . . . leave you only that Why? Why? and Why? that I have asked and listened to for almost fifty years)"* (166–167). Rosa's amorous discourse is thus a self-address as well as an address to the other. As a critique of language, it is a lament at the enormity of the pain and the paucity of the words to describe it. As one critic, writing of Emily Dickinson, puts it, "Pain is the space where words would be, the hole torn out of language." [17] One thinks not only of Rosa's reference to the blank, naked words but of Clarissa's earlier lamentation that, if she had received a kind word from her family before she died, she would have "filled in the blanks" that pain made when she was very weak and very ill. Hatred is a way of filling in the blanks in Sutpen's enigmatic character, but hatred is not Rosa's only response to Sutpen. Quentin is wrong when he reflects: *"Maybe you have to know anybody awful well to love them but when you have hated somebody for forty-three years you will know them awful well so maybe it's better then, maybe it's fine then because after forty-three years they cant any longer surprise you or make you either very contented or very mad"* (14). Quentin exaggerates by formulating solutions to the unsolvable mystery of personality in terms of either/or dichotomies. The fact is that Rosa expresses as much love, pity, and regret for Sutpen as she does hatred, as the opening strophe and antistrophe make clear: Sutpen *"died. Without regret, Miss Rosa Coldfield says—(Save by her) Yes, save by her"* (9). *Save* signifies not only "except" but "salvation." In Shakespeare's Sonnet 12, there is no way to triumph over time, "Save breed, to brave him when he takes thee hence." In *Absalom, Absalom!* the idea that breeding is the braving of time is particularly ironic, since it is Sutpen's view of women as mere breeders which leads Wash, like the Grim Reaper and Father Time, to behead him with the scythe.

Sutpen's proposition to Rosa is most devastating, finally, because he makes no effort to reciprocate. What is outrageous, ultimately, is the utter disparity between how Rosa thought Sutpen saw her—as a source of sunlight and hope—and his actual attitude toward women as brood mares.

His mare's name, incidentally, is Penelope; in the short story, "Wash," the mare is Griselda—ironic allusions to the patient figure of the woman who waits. Now Rosa is not only the one who waits in the novel. All the women whose men go to war are waiting. Judith, moreover, is poignantly contrasted to other women, for she waits not only "not knowing for what, but . . . not even knowing for why" (126) after Henry repudiates his birthright and departs with Charles. But it is Rosa—intractable and unforgetting—who remains to interpret events in the end. It is Rosa who summons Quentin. It is Rosa who conjures up the past and is the catalyst for the entire plot. She embodies the classical figure of absence—its textuality. She is the writing heroine whose predecessors are Penelope, Phaedra, Medea, Ariadne. Indeed, that familiar contrast from Ovid onward between the men at war for their country and the women warring with their passion is reinforced here by Rosa's single-minded obsession with her passion, by her imaginative powers, and by the private theater of her emotions. Rosa's iterative narrative is a vocation. What makes it so memorable is the passionate intensity of her internal battle as she weaves fictions while waiting for the end of war and Sutpen's return, and embroiders them in the long aftermath of solitude and despair.

Her narrative is a defiant effort to break the pattern of nullification that has plagued her entire existence. But no matter what she says, she knows that she will always be called a *"warped bitter orphaned country stick,"* who *"caught a man but couldn't keep him"* (168). No matter how she embroiders and elaborates, she remains trapped in the flesh, in the social system she inherits, in the perceptions of those around her. Barthes's amorous discourse contains a similar lament: "All the solutions I imagine are internal to the amorous system. . . . I order myself to be still in love and to be no longer in love. This kind of identity of the problem and its solution precisely defines the *trap:* I am trapped because it lies outside my reach to change systems: I am 'done for' twice over: inside my own system and because I cannot substitute another system for it. This double noose apparently defines a certain type of madness."[18] Significantly, it is the body that is both trap and release. The needs of the body are made into demands articulated in speech; desire signifies the gap between body and speech, need and demand.[19] For Rosa, the flesh itself is the reminder of what once might have been, of all the potential for fulfillment that is thwarted. Like Clarissa's, her discourse of desire takes the form of an elegy, a testament to all the processes of nature that are stillborn. This stillbirth is what Rosa laments when she describes the trap and the systems that imprison her: *"There are some things which happen to us which the intelligence and the senses refuse just as the stomach sometimes refuses what the palate has accepted but which digestion cannot compass—occurrences which stop us dead as though by some impalpable intervention, like a sheet of glass through which we watch all subsequent events transpire as though in a soundless vacuum, and fade, vanish; are gone, leaving us immobile, impotent, helpless; fixed, until we can die. That was I"* (151–52). Like those of other heroines, Rosa's meditations rely on imagery drawn from the realm of the senses and the body's functions. The lines above are a remarkably acute epiphany about the limits of human comprehension, a vivid contrast between the stasis of Rosa's development and the endlessness of grief, between the intractability of language and the flux of despair. Amorous discourses have no exits; the only way out, as Clarissa demonstrates, is death. In Faulkner's novel, Sutpen escapes his obsession with his grand design by dying; Rosa remains trapped in hers. She rages because she cannot disentangle herself from the threads of memory, frustration, and desire, whereas Sutpen has "kicked himself loose of the earth," like Conrad's Kurtz. This is ultimately what Rosa can never forgive: for Sutpen the rest is silence; for Rosa there is no rest, only recollection, reflection, repetition.

There is thus great poignancy in Mr. Compson's letter to Quentin describing Rosa's death, for he hopes that Rosa gains a bourne where there are actual people to be recipients of her outrage *and* her commiseration, her hatred *and* her pity (377). These words signal once again the doubleness of all lovers' discourses and reveal that reciprocity is the key. Traditionally, as we have seen, the abandoned lover prefers anything, even active hatred, to indifference. Hatred, after all, at least involves engagement. I think this sense of *engagement* is what Faulkner means when Shreve describes Rosa as "irrevocably *husbanded* . . . with the abstract carcass of outrage and revenge" (180, my italics). What moves lovers to rage is the utter lack of involvement or recognition, and this aloofness has far-reaching ramifications in *Absalom, Absalom!* not only in Sutpen's relations with women but in his refusal to recognize Charles Bon as well. Reciprocity is the vital ingredient missing in Sutpen's recipe for morality, in his grand design, and in all his relations.

ANOTHER LOST FATHER, ANOTHER SEARCH

Sutpen denies to each character what each most desires: the touch of flesh with flesh—the only means by which the shibboleths of caste and color are ever even momentarily breached. Like Rosa, Charles Bon yearns for Sutpen's touch beyond all else; he is willing to forsake Henry, Judith, the octoroon, and his son to satisfy this desire:

> There would be that flash, that instant of indisputable recognition between them and he would know for sure and forever—thinking maybe *That's all I want. He need not even acknowledge me; I will let him understand just as quickly that he need not do that, that I do not expect that.* . . . Because he knew exactly what he wanted; it was just the saying of it—the physical touch even though in secret, hidden—the living touch of that flesh warmed before he was born by the same blood which it had bequeathed him to warm his own flesh with, to be bequeathed by him in turn to run hot and loud in veins and limbs after that first flesh and then his own were dead. (319)

The passage reiterates the desire that "the little surface corners and edges of men's secret and solitary lives may be joined for an instant . . . before sinking back into the darkness" (251). What is devastating here is that, even if Sutpen had ever known how little Bon wanted, it is doubtful that he would have given it. One of the many tragedies for Sutpen's descendants is that they ask so little but receive still less. Denied his father's touch, Charles Bon chooses to destroy himself. Since the father who could have touched him "declined to do it, nothing mattered to him now, revenge or love or all, since he knew now that revenge could not compensate him nor love assuage" (343).

Compare these lines from Swinburne's *Anactoria:*

> Alas, that neither moon nor snow nor dew
> Nor all cold things can purge me wholly through,
> Assuage me nor allay me nor appease,
> Till supreme sleep shall bring me bloodless ease.

As Geoffrey Carter points out, *bloodless* here is a pun in which *blood* has, besides its obvious sense, the Shakespearean-Jacobean connotation of "hot blood" (passion) that cannot be allayed or cooled. This observation multiplies Faulkner's allusiveness, since Charles Bon meditates on the warm blood Sutpen bequeathed him. As is well known, Faulkner was a great admirer of Swinburne and imitated him in his own poetry. Faulkner's Swinburnian allusions reinforce the dialogic intertextuality in lovers' discourses, moreover, for it is Sappho who addresses these lines to Anactoria in a lament of unrequited love. Carter goes on to observe that "the violence and suddenness of Sappho's shifts in mood remind us of Pope's 'Eloisa to Abelard,' for Swinburne too is dealing with the ultimate anguish and despair of a lover." [20]

As happened when the governess rejected Miss Jessel, the self denied merely proliferates in *Absalom, Absalom!* The pattern of self-destruction set off by Sutpen's repudiation is reenacted generation after generation. Bon's suicidal passivity; Charles Etienne de St. Velery Bon's masochistic quest for physical contact through beatings he provokes; Jim Bond's bellows—all are motivated by the same psychic trauma of denial of any and all human bonds that should unite this family—indeed, the human family. We need because we are in the body; we demand in speech. While the Sutpen mansion burns, Bond is a mere *thing* howling: "Somewhere something lurked which bellowed, something human since the bellowing was in human speech, even though the reason for it would not have seemed to be" (375). The reason "would not have seemed to be" because to trace the direct relation of Bond's desire back to Sutpen seems to be beyond the capacity of reason. The heart has questions that the mind can't answer; the spirit cries unheard at the beginning and at the end; desire precedes language.

The relation is nonetheless directly traceable to Sutpen's own thwarted desire to speak and to be heard. Central to *Absalom, Absalom!* as to *The Turn of the Screw,* is silence, "the long silence of notpeople, in notlanguage" in which the ordeal of consciousness unfolds. As in *The Turn of the Screw,* the source of the entire tragedy lies in the unsaid—specifically in an undelivered message, for Sutpen's grand design stems from his humiliation at Pettibone's door. He undertakes the mission to deliver the message in "good faith" and finds himself brutally confronted with the distinctions of caste and code, forcibly made to understand that as "white trash," he can be silenced, sent around back by the Negro butler. As Thoreau observed, no one can combat injustice as effectively as someone who has experienced a little of it in his own person. (One thinks of Rochester's redemption, which is achieved when he comes to comprehend powerlessness by experiencing it. He discovers what it feels like to be silenced, as he silenced Bertha Mason.) But Sutpen proceeds to dedicate his life not to combating such injustice but to perpetuating it. Here, the consequence of being "shut up" is Sutpen's entire design. Sutpen, however, utterly dissociates himself from the powerless little boy who stood in front of the mansion. Instead, he resolves to become powerful enough to be one of the oppressors rather than the oppressed. At his hands, Eulalia and Charles Bon suffer the same inexplicable and unspoken rejection he experienced. He repudiates their desire for "the physical touch . . . the living touch." The hot, loud blood, like the spirit crying unheard, is doomed to be denied, cooled, silenced, sepulchered. Words—tranquil and taunting, illuminating and inscrutable, impotent and ineradicable—are the only legacy passed on.

The yearning for the touch of love is what led Faulkner to reflect (speaking of Emily Grierson) that if a natural instinct is repressed, it comes up somewhere else in a tragic form.[21] The form it takes in *Absalom, Absalom!*, as in "A Rose for Emily" and *The Turn of the Screw*, is murder. Furthermore, Faulkner gives his ghost story two turns by doubling the figure of female fury; two women are betrayed by the same man, Sutpen brutally betrays first Eulalia, the mother of his son, then Rosa, the barren spinster doomed to be the chronicler of the age, the critic of language and society. As we have seen, one of the ways in which amorous discourse is dialogic is in its positing of another logic that defies society's view. Rosa therefore counterpoints her own discourse with the refrain from another discourse: the collective voice of the town. She punctuates the story she is telling by revealing her awareness of the story the town tells about her: *"Oh yes, I know"* (of their gossip); *"they will have told you doubtless already how"* (this or that happened); *"doubtless you already know"* (what the gossips have said) (134, 168). The town's voice has reduced Rosa to a bit of doggerel: *"Rosie Coldfield, lose him, weep him; caught a man but couldn't keep him"* (168). Indeed, part of the intensity and tension of Rosa's narrative is the result of the disparity between what she felt and what the gossips report. Their reports, actually, attain the status of truth by sheer volume and ceaseless repetition. The same thing happens to Emily Grierson; the irony of Faulkner's "A Rose for Emily" lies in the disparity between the townspeople's voyeurism, their smug certainty, and the grisly remains of Homer with which Emily surprises them in the end. In view of the ways in which amorous discourse is a reply to and an absorption of other texts, one might say that just as Jane Eyre speaks for Bertha Mason, Rosa Coldfield speaks for Emily Grierson. Just as Rosa's narrative becomes interwoven with others within the novel, the novel itself is interwoven with subsequent tales; Rosa subsequently speaks the silence of the mute woman in "A Rose for Emily"; indeed the very title—particularly the word *rose*—points to the relation between the two women and their desire. Faulkner's characteristic counterpointing of themes and characters in a continuing chronicle also characterizes the dialogic dynamism of amorous discourse from the *Heroides* onward.[22]

Of all the narrators in the novel, it is Rosa who is most aware of the desire for the human touch and of its implications, for she comments on it repeatedly.

When Sutpen returns from the war, she tells us that he touches Judith, speaking, *"four sentences of simple direct words behind beneath above which I felt that same rapport of communal blood which I sensed that day while Clytie held me from the stairs"* (159). In this scene, she is once again the outsider, excluded from the magic circle of the beloved and from the rapport for which she yearns. Later, she seems briefly included in that circle when Sutpen declares their engagement. What she remembers most of all is his touch. As she tries to comprehend her birth, her childhood, her dawning womanhood, her imagery centers on the body: the womb, gestation, the embryo, and desire. Her spirit cried out when she was young, and it cries out in her narrative, but no one hears either the first or the last time. No one ever asks her what she remembers, what memory means to her, what its relation is to the body. But she answers all these questions when she observes how the body goes on remembering long after mind and words evaporate: *"That is the substance of remembering—sense, sight, smell: the muscles with which we see and hear and feel—not mind, not thought: there is no such thing as memory: the brain recalls just what the muscles grope for: no more, no less. . . . Ay, grief goes, fades; we know that—but ask the tear ducts if they have forgotten how to weep"* (143).[23]

Rosa thus restates the fundamental value system of amorous discourse, valorizing the heart as sign, the senses as signifiers, the body as alphabet. She has a great deal to offer Quentin, if he could but hear her, for throughout her narrative she relates body to mind, feeling to thought, words to senses, intuition to intellect. Quentin, however, sees only discontinuities. Quentin's obsession with the Henry–Bon–Judith relationship, for example, mirrors his obsession with Caddy's virginity. Virginity epitomizes all absolutes: either his sister is a virgin or she is a whore. Upon that minute membrane, he constructs all his elaborate abstractions about honor, and—like Abelard, the Portuguese nun's family, and the Harlowes—Quentin conceives of honor as the exclusive property of the male. Rosa, in contrast, describes virginity not as an absolute but as a continuum, a process. She compares herself to the lover *"who spies to watch, taste, touch that maiden revery of solitude which is the first thinning of the veil we call virginity"* (147–48). Of her own sexuality, moreover, she speaks frankly in terms that are not a condemnation but a celebration: she affirms her own potential for love and the urge of her own desire by comparing herself to a *"warped chrysalis of what blind perfect seed: for who shall say what gnarled forgotten root might not bloom yet with some globed concentrate more globed and concentrate and heady-perfect because the neglected root was planted warped and lay not dead but merely slept forgot?"* (144). In the imagery of Keatsian ripeness and ecstasy (heady-perfect), Rosa affirms the potential her sexuality had to be fuller, more vital, more "concentrate," precisely *because* her desires had been so long deferred. Indeed, she continually contrasts the masculine obsession with such abstractions as honor, courage, and glory to the *"indomitable woman-blood* [which] *ignores the man's world in which the blood kinsman shows the courage or cowardice, the folly or lust or fear, for which his fellows praise or crucify him"* (153). Therefore, Mr. Compson errs when he describes women as deluded, determined to live in an air of unreality, to ignore the *"shades and shapes of facts"* (211); women simply affirm values that he and Quentin find alien. Rosa, like all heroines of amorous discourses, demonstrates that the discourse itself is an affirmation, made in the full awareness that it goes against the facts and figures: for as Faulkner was fond of saying, truth is whatever touches the heart. Again and again he contrasts the meagerness of facts with the heart's powers of invention, the paucity of literalism with the richness of infinitely transcribable desire.

THESEUS, DIONYSUS, AND ARIADNE'S THREAD

The same issues of authority, authorship, ownership, and identity that are so central in amorous discourse also dominate Faulkner's novel. Legitimacy, paternity, and lineage are indeed Sutpen's overriding obsessions, and Faulkner uses the thread as a metaphor for the narrative line, reenforcing the motif of doubling and repetition. The relation of Rosa to Ariadne is particularly provocative, for the doubling of Ariadne's relation to Theseus and Dionysus is compressed in the novel into one male figure: Sutpen. Sutpen's traits are frequently specifically associated with threads on a spool, signifying the conflicts in his own character. One thread contains Theseus' characteristics: shrewdness, courage, will, rationality. The other contains Dionysian elements: impulsiveness, unpredictability, instinct.

Sutpen is Thesean when he tries to discover where he made his "mistake"; he explains to Grandfather Compson how eminently rational and judicious he was when he abandoned his first wife and son:

> I was faced with condoning a fact which had been foisted upon me without my knowledge during the process of building toward my design, which meant the absolute and irrevocable negation of the design; or in holding to my original plan for the design in pursuit of which I had incurred this negation. I chose, and I made to the fullest what atonement lay in my power for whatever injury I might have done in choosing, paying even more for the privilege of choosing as I chose than I might have been expected to, or even (by law) required. (273)

Like Rochester, Sutpen abandons a Creole wife from the West Indies whose heritage is tainted by some unspecified hereditary evil; a crucial aspect of the novel is the fact that the allegation of Eulalia Bon's Negro blood is never proven. This demonstrates once again that those who can define are the masters, for those who make the laws and enforce them to do so by a selective manipulation of the facts that they pride themselves on collecting objectively. Sutpen's justification of his actions resembles Rochester's rationalization of bigamy. The writing heroines in amorous discourses invariably address their letters to lovers who themselves have much in common. Sutpen is a lover-tyrant who combines the traits of Ovid's warriors and who exhibits Abelard's tyranny. Lovelace's violence, and Rochester's specious logic. Mr. Compson ironically calls it *"the old logic, the old morality which had never yet failed to fail him"* (279–80). It fails him because there are so many Dionysian forces that cannot be reduced and constrained by intellect and rationality, by a "code of logic and morality, his formula and recipe of fact and deduction" (275). The Dionysian facets of Sutpen's character, moreover, create internal and external pressures. His insulting proposition to Rosa, for instance, is an unpremeditated act—sheer impulse, Rosa insists: *"He had never once thought about what he asked me to do until the moment he asked it because I know that he would not have waited two months or even two days to ask it"* (166). His drunken bouts in the scuppernong arbor with Wash further connect him to the god of wine, who was also known as the sufferer who grieves for his own pain. Since Dionysus is also the vine pruned so severely that it seems incapable of producing again, it is significant that during the battle in the West Indies, one wound "came pretty near leaving [Sutpen] that virgin for the rest of his life" (254). Potency and fertility, of course, are the roots of Sutpen's obsession: *"he was now past sixty and . . . possibly he could get but one more son, had at best but one more son in his loins, as the old cannon might know when it has just one more shot in its corporeality"* (279).

While evoking the images of loom, thread, and spool, Faulkner makes it clear that Sutpen weaves nothing from these threads of Theseus and Dionysus in his character. Instead, the images represent the thwarting of desire and the coming of death: *"The thread of shrewdness and courage and will ran onto the same spool which the thread of his remaining days ran onto and that spool almost near enough for him to reach out his hand and touch it"* (279). Unlike Rosa, Sutpen creates nothing. Instead, like Dionysus, like Lovelace, like Rochester, he is the "ambiguous seducer-rescuer in a family romance involving defeat or death for the father figures, and a complex role for the female figures as murderous mothers, as self-slaying victims, and as transfigured mates for the god." [24] In Faulkner's family romance, one thinks of Eulalia Bon as the murderous mother; Clytie as the self-slayer; and Milly Jones as the mate for Sutpen. Defeated or dead father figures also abound: Goodhue Coldfield, Charles Bon, Wash Jones, and Sutpen himself. Therefore, the multiplication of images of the phallus at the end (Sutpen's horse, his whip, the rusty scythe, the butcher knife) merely inscribes its loss. [25]

Like Persephone, Dionysus dies with the coming of cold, reduced to a gnarled stump. The connection of Sutpen to the god of the vine gives us an added insight into Rosa's preoccupation with wisteria, snarled vines, and roots. Indeed, if Sutpen resembles Dionysus dying of cold, Rosa believes that she *"might be sun for him"* (168), that she can bring him to life again. She describes him as being *"like the swamp-freed pilgrim feeling earth and tasting sun and light again and aware of neither but only of darkness' and morass' lack"* (167–68).

Rosa's responses to Sutpen are thus remarkably varied and complex and Shreve's and Quentin's repeated emphasis on her hatred must not be allowed to overshadow her hope, her pity, her compassion for Sutpen. Clarissa tells Lovelace that if he could be sorry for himself, she could be sorry too; Rosa manages to make a similar imaginative leap from her own suffering to empathetic identification with Sutpen's. She vanquishes her childhood vision of him as an ogre, for when he comes home from the war, she sees him not as *"the ogre; villain true enough, but* [as] *a mortal fallible one less to invoke fear than pity . . . victim . . .* [of] *solitary despair"* (167). Now Rosa knows something about both solitude and despair, but she is less solipsistic and monomaniacal than Sutpen, and she makes a supreme effort to hear and to respond to the last cry of another spirit.

Sutpen, too, is conscious of spirit, but of an entirely different order: he is obsessed with the waste and loss of potency, with "th'expense of spirit in a waste of shame." Like previous lover-tyrants, he views woman metonymically. He merely wants a womb in which to deposit his seed, as one deposits money in the bank. Sutpen equates sexuality with depletion, as he reveals when he notes that he could have reminded Eulalia of "these wasted years, these years which would now leave me behind with my schedule not only the amount of elapsed time which their number represented, but that compensatory amount of time represented by their number which I should now have to spend to advance myself once more to the point I had reached and lost" (264). This fundamental fear leads him to calculate and compute everything: he wars with his flesh, carefully devising strategies for the dispersal of his seed, and tactics for conserving it, remaining a virgin until he marries in order to preserve his potency. Like Lovelace, he is not motivated by love or even lust; instead sex is merely a vehicle for his power, his ambition, his design. Significantly, not one male narrator ever notices or challenges Sutpen's assumptions about the depletion of potency. None of the men ever examines the implications of using economic metaphors of getting, spending, paying, for male sexuality. They overlook the angle of vision that female sexuality may offer; objectively, after all, the female has far more to fear than the male, since the loss of her reproductive powers occurs some twenty years sooner than Sutpen's "last shot." (He is past sixty when he impregnates Milly.) Thus the obsession with impotence is not rooted in biology but is yet another of those imprisoning abstractions that paralyze so many of the male characters in Faulkner's fiction.

If the male vision of sexuality is depletion, the female's is of plenitude. Sexuality is as bountiful as the sun in the comparison Rosa makes repeatedly. It is infinite, inexhaustible, measureless—utterly beyond all boundaries, all male categories of worth and value. Yet male characters see female sexuality as a labyrinth, treacherous and mysterious. As Grandfather Compson asks Sutpen, "Didn't the dread and fear of females which you must have drawn in with the primary mammalian milk teach you better?" (265). If to Rosa, sexuality is a cup overflowing, to the male it is always in danger of being drained. In my view, the male narrators never challenge Sutpen's view because they share it; it is so deeply rooted that they don't even recognize it, and this primary dis-ease with sexuality is a vicious circle, for it makes them sterile and impotent. Where Lovelace's existence is a "cursed still-life," Sutpen is, like Sam Fathers, "himself his own battleground, the scene of his own vanquishment, and the mausoleum of his defeat."[26] Quentin's body, similarly, resembles "a barracks filled with . . . ghosts still recovering . . . from the fever which had cured the disease, waking from the fever without even knowing that it had been the fever itself which they had fought against and not the sickness, looking with stubborn recalcitrance backward beyond the fever and into the disease with actual regret, weak from the fever yet free of the disease and not even aware that the freedom was that of impotence" (12). This fever is the Civil War, which cures them of the disease which is slavery. Slavery made them powerful; so they regret being cured, since the cure leaves them impotent. Apparently, male potency derives from and depends on the oppression of others, sexually and racially. This understanding sheds new light on the obsession with the phallus in the novel, which is a stark contrast to the metaphors from nature (wisteria, the sun, honeysuckle, the earth) that Rosa uses to describe love and sex.

THE LEDGER

I have argued that *dialogism* in discourses of desire signifies not just dialogue, but an entirely different *logic*, one opposed to Aristotelianism and, as the conflict between Ovid and Virgil demonstrates, to all officially endorsed structures and institutions (law, economics, politics) that have their roots in formal logic. Heloise, for example, stands in stark opposition to the master logician Abelard; Clarissa and Jane Eyre both defy the "eminently rational" logic of Lovelace and Rochester. As we have seen, everything conspires to render the heroine's alternative logic invisible, as when the Portuguese nun gets "lost in translation" because of the publisher, Claude Barbin. Among so many male narrators in *Absalom, Absalom!*, Rosa Coldfield gets lost in translation too. In order to appreciate the scope of her affirmation and her rebellion, I must, therefore, digress briefly to delineate the dominant logic that she defies. Because all the male narrators endorse the same logic, which she opposes, and because so many of our judgments of Rosa are filtered through their perceptions, it is doubly important to reveal the specious argument upon which their judgments are based. Theirs is the logic of the phallus, and among the many multiple figures of the phallus in the novel, I shall examine just one: the ledger. Inscribed in the ledger is an entire economy of sexuality that marks the radical difference between Rosa and the males in the novel. The ledger's columns and computations of spending and getting, its list of Negroes bought, bred, and sold—all reveal how fundamental the equation of sex and money is in the false economy of Sutpen's design and, alas, in the entire South. The ledger, moreover, dominates the imagination of every male character in the novel: Goodhue Coldfield, Grandfather Compson, and Wash Jones, as well as the main narrators, all view existence in terms of what is spent and what is saved, in terms of debts owed, bills paid, credits accumulated. Every male who tells even a fraction of the story not only repeats but validates the sterile economy that Sutpen's sexuality encodes. For instance, it is not Rosa but Mr. Compson who insists that Rosa was "born at the price of her mother's life." It is Mr. Compson who (probably quite accurately) describes Goodhue Coldfield as he spent "three days in a mental balancing of his terrestrial accounts, found the result and proved it. . . . Doubtless the only pleasure which he had ever had was not in the meager spartan hoard which he had accumulated . . . —not in the money but in its representation of a balance in whatever spiritual counting-house he believed would some day pay his sight drafts on self-denial and fortitude" (84). In contrast to Rosa, who affirms the possibility that sexual fulfillment might be "more perfect" because it has been so long deferred, who thinks not in terms of numbers or computations, Mr. Compson goes so far as to calculate copulations when he describes the Sutpens as being "integer for integer, larger, more heroic . . . [than we who are] author and victim too of a thousand . . . copulations and divorcements" (89). Shreve and Quentin are equally infected with this niggardly debit-credit mentality. Their imaginations, too, are ruled by the ledger. Shreve imagines that Charles Bon woke up one spring morning and "lay right still in bed and took stock, added the figures and drew the balance" (330). It is Shreve, moreover, who refers to God as a "Creditor" whom Sutpen hopes to fool "by illusion and obfuscation by concealing behind the illusion that time had not elapsed and change occurred the fact that he was now almost sixty years old, until he could get himself a new batch of children to bulwark him" (179–80). Quentin protests that Shreve "sounds just like father," but he too sounds like his father. The very nature of male sexuality, in fact, makes all the male narrators sound alike because they share the fundamental assumptions that Sutpen enacts. Quentin automatically validates Sutpen's sexual economy here, for he proceeds to describe him as

> the old wornout cannon which realizes that it can deliver just one more fierce shot and crumble to dust in its own furious blast and recoil . . . the old demon, the ancient varicose and despairing Faustus fling his final main now with the Creditor's hand already on his shoulder, running his little country store now for his bread and meat, haggling tediously over nickels and dimes with rapacious and poverty-stricken whites and negroes, who at one time could have galloped for ten miles in any direction without crossing his own boundary, uusing out of his meager stock the cheap ribbons and beads . . . with which even an old man can seduce a fifteen-year-old country girl. (181–83)

While Sutpen haggles and hoards, Milly's "increasing belly" grows in mocking juxtaposition to Sutpen's shrunken stature.

The same patriarchal economy that makes sex a commodity devalues the female; this devaluation too remains unchallenged by all the male narrators in the text. Indeed, when Shreve realizes that Milly's infant is not a boy but a girl, his only response is not a protest, but simply, "Oh." Women are chattel whom men price according to a complex system of computation involving the exact fractions of blood, as with Charles Bon's octoroon mistress. Charles justifies this system by first accusing God, then white women of perpetrating it to protect their own chastity; in reality it is yet another indictment of the economics of male sexuality. Woman is viewed metonymically; the octoroon's vagina and the white virgin's hymen are assigned market values correlated to their function: the octoroon serves the white man's lust as the white virgin serves his honor. (Dr. Johnson's declaration that chastity is of the utmost importance because all property depends upon it comes to mind.) Mr. Compson imagines Charles explaining that the octoroon was made by white men,

> created and produced [by] them; we even made the laws which declare that one eighth of a specified kind of blood shall outweigh seven eighths of another kind. . . . we do save that one, who but for us would have been sold to any brute who had the price, not sold to him for the night like a white prostitute, but body and soul for life to him who could have used her with more impunity than he would dare to use an animal, heifer or mare, and then discarded or sold or even murdered when worn out or when her keep and her price no longer balanced. (115–16)

Thus Sutpen's "domain" signifies more than his compulsion to dominate all, more than his compulsion to name (and thus to define) not only all his children ("the entire fecundity of dragon's teeth") but all abstractions, all the "eggshell shibboleth of caste and color." He dominates not just by *defining* such abstractions as Beauty, Woman, Virginity, Honor, and Negro but by assigning a dollar value to those abstractions in the marketplace. When he returns from the war, for instance, Rosa reflects retrospectively that marrying her would have "gained him at the lowest possible price the sole woman available to wive him" (166). Women are synonymous with virgin land, the sole function of which is to turn fertile crops into cash. Thus, whether Rosa is "cold" is debatable, but—in the logic of male sexual economy—she is definitely a *field;* as she discovers in the aftermath of abandonment. Eulalia Bon's lawyer epitomizes the *reductio ad absurdum* of a masculine economy that turns human emotions and sexuality into financial transactions. He is imagined as having a secret drawer or a secret safe with a secret paper in it, which computes Sutpen's success and plots his ruin: *"Today Sutpen finished robbing a drunken Indian of a hundred miles of virgin land, val. $25,000. . . . 7:52 p.m. today married. . . . Say 1 year. . . . Son. Intrinsic val. possible though not probable forced sale of house & land. . . . Emotional val. plus 100% times nil. plus val. crop. . . . Daughter . . . 1859. . . . Query: bigamy threat, Yes or No. Possible No. Incest threat: Credible Yes. . . . Certain"* (301, 310). The lawyer is merely an exaggeration of Sutpen himself, whose obsession with time is as pronounced as it is with money; like sex, time indeed *is* money. A close analysis of the novel's rhetoric would reveal how consistently the use of legal language reveals a debased moral code.[27] Faulkner's theme, however, is not simply that lawyers are corrupt or that legality is diametrically opposed to morality. His characterization of the lawyer reminds us once again of the close connection of amorous discourse to the language of courtrooms and trials. The lawyer is the extreme embodiment of all those—from Goodhue Coldfield to Sutpen and Mr. Compson—who exploit and control, who view life in terms of facts and computations and whose debit-credit mentality makes them obsessed with possession, domination, and settling accounts.

"Bond," as the Negro Luster points out, is "a lawyer word. What day puts you under when de Law ketches you" (215). This law is always a negation, and an unbearable bondage to negativity enslaves all the characters infected with this niggardly economy. Not only is the South's economic system corrupt, not only is Sutpen's morality myopic, but the male equation of sex with money makes the very idea of meaningful bonds savagely ironic. Just as the lawyer is the extreme example of male acquisition, of male "getting," in economic terms, Jim Bond is the epitome in sexual terms. He is the *reductio ad absurdum* of the logic of the phallus, of the law that measures fractions of blood, computes the number of copulations, and counts ejaculations. The phallic ledger looms largest on the last page of the novel, which is devoted to Shreve's final nihilistic vision:

> "So it took Charles Bon and his mother to get rid of old Tom, and Charles Bon and the octoroon to get rid of Judith, and Charles Bon and Clytie to get rid of Henry; and Charles Bon's mother and Charles Bon's grandmother got rid of Charles Bon. So it takes two niggers to get rid of one Sutpen, dont it? . . . Which is all right, it's fine; it clears the whole ledger, you can tear all the pages out and burn them, except for one thing. . . . You've got one nigger left. One nigger Sutpen left. Of course . . . you never will be able to use him. But you've got him there still." (377–78)

Yet even on the last page of the novel, an alternative to Shreve's dark vision opens out, spills over. As with Rosa's analogy of sexuality to sunlight, one might posit an entirely different economy based on giving and loving rather than on hoarding here, for one might argue that instead of lack, there is always something left, something from which human existence can replenish itself, as in a few thousand years we may replenish the human race from the loins of African kings. Faulkner sees time and existence as cyclical, like the sun, not linear, like the ledger. He does not endorse either Shreve's vision or Quentin's, although he gives the last word to Quentin. As in Henry James's tale, what is named and thus given a reality is hatred rather than love. The tragedy (for even if Sutpen is not tragic, his descendants are) is that rather than *do* and *love*, Quentin's final words are *dont* and *hate*. Rather than being able to affirm anything, his final words are a denial and a lie, for he does hate the South, as men hate what they don't understand.

Quentin hates women for the same reason. He confesses that he still hears Jim Bond howling at night, but he hates being haunted and he hates being a ghost. In my view, he hates Rosa too, because all he can see in her is his own eventual fate—to be yet another living ghost. He thus demonstrates that in Rosa he sees not a face but a mirror, a projection of his own deepest doubts and fears. He never does decipher her, although he stares steadily at the letter announcing her death: "It was becoming quite distinct; he would be able to decipher the words soon, in a moment; even almost now, now, now" (377). Her spirit was not heard when it cried for the last time, and *now* never comes.

As in *The Turn of the Screw*, Faulkner's novel is filled with written agreements, contracts, papers, ledgers, and letters that seem to be without origin or end. When the novel opens, Rosa has already sent a written summons to Quentin "out of another world almost—the queer archaic sheet of ancient good notepaper written over with the neat faded cramped script" (10). Sutpen's rise depends on a written agreement involving a bill of lading which gives Goodhue Coldfield cash and Sutpen a wife, as well as a wedding license, a "patent" of respectability. There are, moreover, all sorts of certificates that fail to certify, binding agreements that fail to bind. Sutpen receives a citation for bravery from Lee, but as Wash discovers, it certifies neither his honor nor his humanity. A letter, furthermore, is the focal point of desire in myriad ways: Quentin and Shreve speculate that Charles is hoping for a letter from Sutpen saying *"I am your father. Burn this,"* but the letter never comes. The letters in *Absalom, Absalom!* repeat the pattern so characteristic of amorous epistolary discourse: they have no date, no salutation, no signature, yet the more inscrutable they are, the more they seem to signify. What is astonishing about the passage below is the degree to which Mr. Compson's response to the letter partakes of literature; his many allusions to formulas, proportions, and miscalculations are all revealing. He is describing a love letter that Charles Bon wrote to Judith:

> It's just incredible. It just does not explain. Or perhaps that's it: they dont explain and we are not supposed to know. We have a few old mouth-to-mouth tales; we exhume from old trunks and boxes and drawers letters without salutation or signature, in which men and women who once lived and

breathed are now merely initials or nicknames not of some now incomprehensible affection which sound to us like Sanskrit or Chocktaw; we see dimly
people, the people in whose living blood and seed we ourselves lay dormant
and waiting, in this shadowy attenuation of time possessing now heroic proportions, performing their acts of simple passion and simple violence, impervious to time and inexplicable. . . . They are there, yet something is
missing; they are like a chemical formula exhumed along with the letters
from that forgotten chest, carefully, the paper old and faded and falling to
pieces, the writing faded, almost indecipherable, yet meaningful, familiar in
shape and sense, the name and presence of volatile and sentient forces; you
bring them together in the porportions called for; but nothing happens; you
re-read, tedious and intent, poring, making sure that you have forgotten
nothing, made no miscalculation; you bring them together again and again
nothing happens: just the words, the symbols, the shapes themselves, shadowy inscrutable and serene, against that turgid background of a horrible and
bloody mischancing of human affairs. (100–101)

As Lacan has said, "A cryptogram takes on its full dimension only when it is in a
lost language."[28] The statement is a psychoanalytic version of Keats's "unheard
melodies are sweeter," for Lacan is referring to the agency of the Imaginary in
the unconscious. Rather than freeing one from language, the Imaginary exists in
dynamic interrelations with the realms of the Symbolic and the Real. My interest
in the passage involves Faulkner's representation of lack and loss, and the ways
those representations structure the narratives. As we saw with Clarissa's crypt,
letters in Faulkner's text overflow their bounds, yet remain cryptic. Mr. Compson's reflections shed light on the paradoxes involved in viewing the letter as
literature and literature as a letter, for Faulkner might well be describing the fate
of the reader of the novel. Within the novel, the death of the authors of the
letters, of course, gives birth to reader-narrators like Mr. Compson, readers who
invest the correspondents with the heroic proportions of the past. Rosa Coldfield
is both in and out of this world, "a crucified child," imprisoned in a house that
"like her . . . had been created to fit into and complement a world in all ways a
little smaller than the one in which it found itself" (8, 10). Rosa is isolated from
"general space," from the world at large, by time and space; she lives "parti-
tioned" in a "dim hot airless" office, in the "coffin-smelling gloom . . . as if there
were prisoned in it like in a tomb all the suspiration of slow heat-laden time" (7,
8, 10). Rosa's room resembles the cloisters of Heloise and the Portuguese nun, as
well as Clarissa's crypt. Rosa's eloquent speech issues from this funereal environment; as with all amorous discourses, it is a self-address—internal as well as external. Derrida explores the ambiguities of interiority and exteriority when he
describes a crypt as a kind of forum, "like a closed rostrum or speaker's box, a
safe: sealed, and thus internal to itself, a secret interior within the public
square. . . . The inner forum is (a) safe, an outcast. . . . That is the condition,
and the strategem, of the cryptic enclave's ability to isolate, to protect, to shelter
from any penetration, from anything which can filter in from the outside along
with air, light, or sounds, along with the eye or the ear, the gesture or the spoken
word."[29] Like Clarissa's writing of her last will and testament, Rosa's "office" is
to encrypt desire and inscribe the memory of what might have been. Clarissa is

indeed her closest analogue among the writing heroines in this book, for the discourse of desire once again takes the form of an elegy. Yet it is paradoxically also an affirmation.

THE LOOM

Rosa consciously affirms the existence of something beyond the literal, legalistic language of ledger-books, beyond language itself, indeed. She speaks of her desire as being made of myriad elements that language cannot begin to describe. Desire *"has no words to speak with other than 'This was called light,' that 'smell,' that 'touch,' that other something which has bequeathed not even name for sound of bee or bird or flower's scent or light or sun or love"* (145). What Rosa, like all the heroines of amorous discourses, posits is another logic, one that defies all the calculations and abstractions of all the eggshell shibboleths. She demonstrates once again that amorous discourse is an affirmation, for she maintains that *"there is that might-have-been which is the single rock we cling to above the maelstrom of unbearable reality"* (149–50). Even more remarkable than her affirmation here is her definition of that "might-have-been," for despite the brutality of Sutpen's rejection, despite all the waste and grief and sorrow, she defines it as love and faith. This affirmation is the way to surmount all the imprisoning abstractions that reduce the human spirit to economic matters, that negate truth with mere facts, for Rosa possesses the *"true wisdom which can comprehend that there is a might-have-been which is more true than truth"* (143), which consists of *"love and faith at least above the murdering and the folly, to salvage at least from the humbled indicted dust something anyway of the old lost enchantment of the heart"* (150).

The qualifiers—"at least," "something anyway"—point to the difficulty of finding something, anything, to affirm in the aftermath of devastation. The Civil War reveals the catastrophic results of assigning dollar values to human beings as if they were livestock, of equating sex with money, of reducing human emotions to economic integers. Rosa realizes the folly of trying to balance accounts—emotionally, morally, spiritually—for one can never settle accounts because nothing is ever "settled"; *was is*. Rosa, like Clarissa before her, affirms that *"there is no all, no finish"*; even as the soul leaves the body, the soul contains *"that spark, that dream which, as the globy and complete instant of its freedom mirrors and repeats (repeats? creates . . .) all of space and time and massy earth, relicts the seething and anonymous miasmal mass which in all the years of time has taught itself no boon of death but only how to re-create, renew"* (143).[30] Not only is nothing ever finished, but whatever is left over will be used to renew, to recreate, as Rosa recreates her passion in her narrative. She is the chronicler of the time, the one who records births, deaths, and disasters not only in the family Bible but in the imaginations of a younger generation. Like Ariadne, she is the one who waits, who gives shape to absence and weaves its fictions. Faulkner finally makes Rosa's relation to Ariadne explicit when he juxtaposes Rosa's sewing with the slow unraveling of the South during the war. She steals the cloth from her father's store and spends her days and nights

> sewing tediously and without skill on the garments which she was making for her niece's trousseau and which she had to keep hidden . . . whipping lace out of raveled and hoarded string and thread and sewing it onto garments while news came of Lincoln's election and the fall of Sumpter [*sic*] and she scarce listening, hearing and losing the knell and doom of her native land between two tedious and clumsy stitches on a garment which she would never wear and never remove for a man whom she was not even to see alive. (78)

What Rosa demonstrates here is the opposite of the debit-credit mentality of niggardly economy; she toils to give a gift of love to the woman who will marry the man she loves. Significantly, Judith repeats the same act of generosity for her rival. She not only raises her lover's bastard son but dies while tending his yellow fever. It is the female who weaves and spins, and this creative impulse is closely allied with identity, as Judith reflects: "You are born at the same time with a lot of other people, all mixed up with them, like trying to, having to, move your arms and legs with strings only the same strings are hitched to all the other arms and legs and the others all trying and they dont know why either except that the strings are all in one another's way like five or six people all trying to make a rug on the same loom only each one wants to weave his own pattern into the rug" (127). This vision of interdependence is what Sutpen never manages to achieve or even to comprehend. Therefore, he creates nothing, despite the fact that his design, his very life, and all the lives his touches draw on the imagery of loom, thread, and spool. In contrast, Judith, Clytie, and Rosa form a triumvirate: they are like the three fates who *"spun thread and wove the cloth"* (155). Sex becomes *"some forgotten atrophy like the rudimentary gills we call the tonsils,"* and they cease to be circumscribed by such abstractions as Woman or Negro, for they endure *"amicably, not as two white women and a negress, not as three negroes or three white, not even as three women, but merely as three creatures . . . as though we were one being, interchangeable and indiscriminate"* (155). In my view, the radical proportions of Rosa's vision have been entirely overlooked. The three women can do anything a man can do—chop wood, plow fields, mend fences; the fact that they are indiscriminate highlights the hollowness of the dominant means by which the white man "discriminates" between himself and Negro, between himself and woman. The logic of male sexual economy requires that woman and Negro be reduced to the level of abstraction so the white male can define himself in terms of what he is not; the self/other dichotomy imprisons all others in the vague category of "other-than-himself." The miracle, in my view, is that despite her imprisonment in the rigid structures of male logic and patriarchal discourse, Rosa Coldfield manages to defy those structures and to make an affirmation by embroidering her vision of what might-have-been.[31]

The loom is thus an alternative to the ledger: a collaborative creative endeavor among women, "above the murdering and the folly," "the fine dead sounds" of glory, honor, warfare. One thinks again of the contrast between Socrates' condemnation of Eros as a sophist, and Sappho's celebration of Eros as a weaver of tales, for the loom leads directly back to Sappho, weaving her lyric-webs, and Ariadne, affirming the primacy of the heart's desires. Yet those desires are continually in danger of being effaced by others. In "The Figure in the Carpet," for instance, J. Hillis Miller is fascinated by Ariadne, but he compares his essay to Theseus' impossible attempts at mastery: "the dance of the too rational Theseus . . . marked out ever-changing, winding figures . . . compulsively retracing the labyrinth in an always frustrated desire to master it. . . . The present essay is one more execution of the dance of Theseus." [32] Miller acknowledges the limitations of language, but one wonders why Ariadne—her role, her fate, her desires—seems to have disappeared. As in the case of the *Portuguese Letters*, when critics set about discussing the difficulty of writing or translating, what gets lost in translation is frequently the woman. Barbin, the interpreter who appears to efface himself, instead ends up erasing the nun. Here, similarly, Ariadne's desire gets lost amid the obsession with mastery (and masters) and the labyrinth of narrative. Thus, in charting Theseus' quest, Miller replicates his crime. By focusing on Sutpen's quest, on his obsession with mastery, critics have consistently done the same thing to Rosa Coldfield. When Quentin confronts Henry at the end, he sees Clytie as "the one who owns the terror" (369). But the drama of the telling belongs to Rosa; she is the one who articulates not only the doom, the curse, and the fatality of Sutpen's downfall, but the sorrow and the pity of it as well. Her narrative establishes a pattern that is but one of many woven on the loom, one with a complex texture of hatred *and* love, fury *and* faith. She dedicates herself to what Barthes, in his amorous discourse, calls the Loquela: "The flux of language through which the subject tirelessly rehashes the effects of a wound or the consequences of an action: an emphatic form of the lover's discourse. . . . I spin, unwind and weave the lover's case, and begin all over again (these are the meanings of the verg $\mu\eta\rho\upsilon\omega\mu\alpha\iota$ (*meruomaī*): to spin, to unwind, to weave)." [33] Thus in the absence of the touch of flesh with flesh, Rosa gives shape to lack and elaborates the fictions of loss that structure all the lives around her. She makes her presence felt by transforming passion into art, weaving and reweaving through "devious intricate channels of decorous ordering."

NOTES

1. On the relation of desire to language, see Jacques Lacan, *The Language of the Self*, trans. Anthony Wilden (Baltimore: Johns Hopkins Univ. Press, 1968), and *Ecrits: A Selection*, trans. Alan Sheridan (New York: W. W. Norton, 1977). In Lacanian terms, desire lies in the gap between the demands made in speech and the needs of the body; since those needs are unarticulated, they can be said to precede language, although one never escapes from the web of language. See pages 256, 261n., 272 below.

2. William Faulkner, *Absalom, Absalom!* (New York: Modern Library, 1966), p. 139, hereinafter cited parenthetically in the text by page number.

3. Roland Barthes, *S/Z: An Essay*, trans. Richard Miller (New York: Hill and Wang, 1974), p. 18.

4. On the relation of history to myth, see Melvin Backman, "Sutpen and the South: A Study of *Absalom, Absalom!*," *PMLA* 80 (1965), 596–604; Lennart Bjork, "Ancient Myths and the Moral Framework of Faulkner's *Absalom, Absalom!*," *American Literature* 35 (1963), 196–204; Donald M. Kartiganer, "The Role of Myth in *Absalom, Absalom!*," *Modern Fiction Studies* 9 (1963), 357–69; Michael Millgate, "The Firmament of Man's History: Faulkner's Treatment of the Past," *Mississippi Quarterly* 25 (Spring 1972 supplement),

25–35; Lewis P. Simpson, "Faulkner and the Legend of the Artist," in *Faulkner: Fifty Years after "The Marble Faun,"* ed. George H. Wolfe (Tuscaloosa: Univ. of Alabama Press, 1976).

5. Cf. Gérard Genette, *Narrative Discourse: An Essay in Method*, trans. Jane E. Lewin (Ithaca: Cornell Univ. Press, 1980), pp. 167–68.

6. On diegesis and voice, see Genette, chap. 5. On diegesis as a repetitive journey, see J. Hillis Miller, "Ariachne's Broken Woof," *Georgia Review* 31 (1977), 44–60, and "The Figure in the Carpet," *Poetics Today* 1:3 (1980), 107–18. Homer Barron's corpse in "A Rose for Emily" lies, too, in an "even coating of the patient and biding dust." On the relation of the two texts, see note 22 below.

7. Roland Barthes, *A Lover's Discourse: Fragments*, trans. Richard Howard (New York: Hill and Wang, 1978), p. 211.

8. Cleanth Brooks, "The Poetry of Miss Rosa Canfield [*sic*]," *Shenandoah* 21 (Spring 1970), 199–206.

9. Albert Guerard, *The Triumph of the Novel: Dickens, Dostoevsky, Faulkner* (New York: Oxford Univ. Press, 1976), pp. 323, 329.

10. Ibid., p. 321.

11. See J. Gary Williams, "Quentin Finally Sees Miss Rosa," *Criticism* 21 (Fall 1979), 331–46. Williams maintains, "Quentin really has not heard, in any profound sense, anything Rosa has said in chapter 5" (335).

12. Sharon Cameron, *Lyric Time: Dickinson and the Limits of Genre* (Baltimore: Johns Hopkins Univ. Press, 1979), pp. 198.

13. John T. Irwin, *Doubling and Incest/Repetition and Revenge* (Baltimore: Johns Hopkins Univ. Press, 1975), pp. 74–75.

14. Barthes, *S/Z*, p. 17.

15. Charles Dickens, *Great Expectations* (Baltimore: Penguin Books, 1965), p. 92 (bk. 1, chap. 8), my italics. One thinks as well of Clarissa locked in her room, and of the closed, forbidden doors in Brontë's novel: Jane Eyre is locked behind a massive door to the red room, and Bertha Mason is locked behind another door in the attic. Like the governesses in both *Jane Eyre* and *The Turn of the Screw*, Rosa is a threshold figure, poised between past and present, between the world before and after the Civil War, between the world of Sutpen and that of Quentin Compson. She is, however, not so much poised as cramped: she summons Quentin in a letter "out of another world almost," written on an "archaic" sheet of notepaper in a "cramped script" (10).

16. Denis de Rougemont discusses the ineffable in *Love in the Western World*, trans. Montgomery Belgion (London: Faber and Faber, 1940), p. 159–60. While tracing the "origins" of the ineffable as a motif, de Rougemont overlooks the considerable cunning, duplicity, and evasiveness that may be at play in any lover's exhortation of the ineffable, as is certainly the case in *The Sorrows of Young Werther* and in *The Turn of the Screw*.

17. Cameron, p. 158.

18. Barthes, *A Lover's Discourse*, p. 143.

19. The formulation is Jacques Lacan's, in "The Insistence of the Letter in the Unconscious," *Yale French Studies* 36/37 (1966), 112–47.

20. Geoffrey Carter, "Sexuality and the Victorian Artist: Dickens and Swinburne," in *Sexuality and Victorian Literature*, ed. Don Richard Cox, Tennessee Studies in Literature, vol. 27 (Knoxville: Univ. of Tennessee Press, 1984), p. 153.

21. *Faulkner in the University: Class Conferences at the University of Virginia, 1957–1958*, ed. Frederick L. Gwynn and Joseph L. Blotner (New York: Vintage, 1965), p. 185.

22. Faulkner wrote "A Rose for Emily" in 1929, the same year that *The Sound and the Fury* appeared; *Absalom, Absalom!* was published in 1936. The Faulknerian embroidering of one tale in another also illustrates that no repetition is exactly the same and no telling is univocal, unequivocal, or determinate. Some scholars insist that *The Sound and the Fury*

should be viewed autonomously from *Absalom, Absalom!* (Guerard, p. 311, for example). Although Faulkner is not always reliable, his view is at least worth noting: "Quentin Compson, of the Sound & Fury, tells it, or ties it together; he is the protagonist so that it is not complete apocrypha. I use him because it is just before he is to commit suicide because of his sister, and I use his bitterness which he has projected on the South in the form of hatred of it and its people to get more out of the story itself than a historical novel would be." *Selected Letters of William Faulkner*, ed. Joseph Blotner (New York: Random House, 1977), p. 79. John T. Irwin, *Doubling and Incest? Repetition and Revenge*, and Cleanth Brooks, "The Narrative Structure of *Absalom, Absalom,*" *Georgia Review* 29:2 (Summer 1975), 366–94, are among the critics who stress the interrelation of the two novels.

23.   Over twenty years later, Faulkner mentioned the same contrast between facts and truth, between memory as a mere log or catalogue and memory as a muscle, an instinct, something prior to language, when he described his own memory as being "phenomenal . . . in the sense that the muscle remembers. . . . it's not anything that's really catalogued into the mind, it's catalogued into whatever muscles of the human spirit produce the book" *Faulkner in the University*, p. 203.

24.   Although J. Hillis Miller never mentions Faulkner, I am indebted to his essay "Ariadne's Thread: Repetition and the Narrative Line," *Critical Inquiry* 3 (Autumn 1976), 57–77.

25.   Ibid., p. 76.

26.   Faulkner, *Go Down, Moses* (New York: Modern Library, 1955), p. 168.

27.   See Marvin Singleton, "Personae at Law and in Equity," *Papers on Language and Literature* 3 (Fall 1967), 354–70.

28.   Lacan, "Insistence of the Letter in the Unconscious," p. 129.

29.   Jacques Derrida, "Fors," trans. Barbara Johnson, *Georgia Review* 31 (Spring 1977), 64–116.

30.   Compare the affirmation in *Go Down, Moses*, another novel that contrasts the logic of ledgers and legalities with the myriad ways in which accounts can never be settled nor anything in life ever finished: "You always wear out life long before you have exhausted the possibilities of living. . . . all that could not have been invented and created just to be thrown way. . . . And the earth dont want to just keep things, hoard them: it wants to use them again" (186).

31.   I should note that even when Rosa is not being interpreted by Mr. Compson, Quentin, or Shreve, there are moments when her own voice is clearly Calvinistic. Nevertheless, those passages can be attributed to Rosa as *voice*—looking back after Sutpen injures her—rather than to Rosa as *focus*. As stated earlier, her aunt's Calvinism imbues the child Rosa with the sense of Sutpen's evil; when he returns from the war she views him as mortal, fallible, and despairing; and when he repudiates her, she reverts to her initial opinion of his inherent evil. What I have focused on in this chapter is her second, softer attitude towards Sutpen, since the male narrators so distort this phase by labeling her merely as the Scorned Woman.

32.   Miller, "The Figure in the Carpet," p. 107, n. 1. See also Miller, "Ariadne's Thread," pp. 71–74.

33.   Barthes, *A Lover's Discourse*, p. 160.

GENDER IN BAKHTIN'S CARNIVAL

For Bakhtin, language bequeaths us many social voices, and these voices construct both selves and characters-as-selves. The explicit and implicit interplay of these voices reveals the way a specific historical and cultural context fashions the self. The cultural context also operates in a similar way to fashion the self according to gender differences. With Bakhtin's method, we can work toward a sociological and ideological stylistics of the novel. To add gender considerations, as I want to do here, is to refashion Bakhtin's sociological stylistics into a feminist dialogics.

The main charge against postmodern criticism, as Craig Owens reports it in "The Discourse of Others: Feminists and Postmodernism," is that it is essentially reluctant to engage the "insistent feminist voice": ". . . if one of the most salient aspects of our postmodern culture is the presence of an insistent feminist voice (and I use the terms *presence* and *voice* advisedly), theories of postmodernism have tended either to neglect or to repress that voice. The absence of discussions of sexual difference in writings about postmodernism, as well as the fact that few women have engaged in the modernism/postmodernism debate, suggest that postmodernism may be another masculine invention engineered to exclude women."[1] Thus, Owens attacks decontextualized literary criticism as a no-woman's-land (with exceptions like Gertrude Stein). Feminists, too, have been wont until recently to separate themselves from postmodernism—to read themselves *out* rather than *in* critical dialogue: Myra Jehlen writes in "Archimedes and the Paradox of Feminist Criticism" that feminists have been "too successful in constructing an alternate footing," and Teresa de Lauretis echoes this complaint when she notes that "the contradiction of feminist theory itself [is that it is] at once excluded from discourse and imprisoned within it."[2]

My project is to determine a viable intersection between feminism—my own feminist voice—and modern/postmodern criticism, particularly through Bakhtin. There is no zone which gender does not enter and dispute the territory. Owens questions the primacy of the visual, the same attack French feminists like Luce Irigaray make on all languages of "truth"; Owens claims that what the postmodern critics can't *see* is the feminist *voice*, with Wayne Booth a curious exception.[3] My aim is to show that the feminist voice (rather than the male gaze) can construct and dismantle the exclusive community and patriarchal critical discourse. With voice (and not with the gaze), these heroines can engage in the battle Bakhtin suggests is the basis for community. The opposition between the surveillant gaze and the disruptive (excessive or insistent) voice constitutes the structure of these ambivalent texts. My project in rereading these novels is not to look for a world elsewhere beyond patriarchal language, but to locate in language gendered voices.

Bakhtin opens the way for a feminist dialogic approach to texts by overstepping the "authority" of the text and emphasizing (in "Discourse in Life and Discourse in Art") the triangular relation between reader, text, author. The feminist struggle is not one between a conscious "awakened" or natural voice *and* the voice of patriarchy "out there." Rather, precisely because we all internalize the authoritative voice of patriarchy, we must struggle to refashion inherited social discourses into words which rearticulate intentions (here feminist ones) other than normaltive or disciplinary ones. One of Bakhtin's most crucial statements about reading and the listener's role comes toward the end of "Discourse in Life":

> This constant *coparticipant* [the listener's inherited social and ideological voices] in all our conscious acts determines not only the content of consciousness but also—and this is the main point for us—the very *selection* of the content, the selection of what precisely we become conscious of, and thus determines also those *evaluations* which permeate consciousness and which psychology usually calls the "emotional tone" of consciousness. It is precisely from this constant participant in all our conscious acts that the listener who determines artistic form is engendered.[4]

What the listener selects from the work of art—from the author's and characters' voices in the text—produces the critical orientation, the emotional tone. Power circulates through this participation. But what is more important is that this selection process always involved in reading/listening to the text "engenders" us. The act of reading is one of the modes by which we acquire our social—indeed, gendered—orientations to or identification with the world, as a form of cultural contact. By reading as a feminist—attuned to the exclusions and inclusions of interpretive communities—we foreground the sexual differences involved in our readings of the world, of all social signs. If, in fact, "One never reads except by identification" as Catherine Clément and Hélène Cixous debate in "Exchange," then this identification engenders (reinforces gender difference) at the same time that the act of reading reveals gender.[5]

I am not out to reduce the feminist ambivalence toward language or toward male codes in general, but to thematize that ambivalence. As Laura Mulvey argues about "visual pleasure," woman

> stands in patriarchal culture as signifier for the male other, bound by a symbolic order in which man can live out his fantasies and obsessions through linguistic command, by imposing them on the silent image of woman still tied to her place as bearer of meaning, not maker of meaning.[6]

In the texts that I will examine, the women refuse to be silent bearers of meaning, but have not yet been accepted as makers of meaning. When women step out of their traditional function as sign; when they refuse the imposition of the gaze; when they exchange their sign-status for that of manipulator of signs, they do so through dialogic polemics. And, at that moment of refusal, they become threatening to the disciplinary culture which appears naturalized. This refusal initiates the battle among voices. In these novels, there are no interpretive communities willing to listen to women's alien and threatening discourse.

Out of this contradiction in modes of reading the world, I want to propose a model for reading based on a feminist dialogics, on the translation of the gaze (of the community, of reading) into hearing dialogized voices. My effort, then, is to read the woman's voice—excluded or silenced by dominant linguistic or narrative strategies—back *into* the dialogue in order to reconstruct the process by which she was read out in the first place.[7] The women in these novels refuse to participate in a language which would erase their difference. Rather, by unsettling or displacing the dominant discourse, they reveal the vincibility of the One/Same. The ambivalence toward interpretive community arises from an aggressivity which is often masked by an alteration between a speaking and silenced female subject. Freud argues in *Civilization and Its Discontents* that ambivalence is accompanied by guilt (perhaps making women into Catherine Clément's "guilty ones").[8] Although inclusion in the community might mask this guilt, it would occur at the expense of a defiant voice.

Therefore, to end these novels with suicide or sacrifice is *not* to put an end to the dialogue about sexual difference as the plot traces out that trajectory. In three cases, the novels end ambivalently, with what Margaret Higonnet might call "speaking suicides."[9] If Bakhtin has it right, however, the dialogue never ends. Literary suicide and sacrifice are metaphors for a refusal to be conscripted; suicide forces the internal dialogue into the open, raising questions about sexual difference rather than closing them. Voice can be reconceived as a means of power and activity because it engages dialogue, opening up discourse as fluid. To open another's discourse is to make it vulnerable to change, to exposure, to the carnival. The feminine voices in these novels draw out the others' codes by which their authority is formulated. These resisting voices violate the codes, and with those linguistic impulses, their unconscious wills come into view. The contradiction between these wills and the disciplined wills of the community inform the events of the novel. The characters evade the prison house of language (or struggle against such imprisoning) for what Holquist and Clark term an ecosystem of language.[10] According to Bakhtin in *Problems of Dostoevsky's Poetics* (1929), ". . . the boundaries of the individual will can be in principle exceeded. One could put it this way: the artistic will of polyphony is a will to combine many wills, a will to the event."[11] Thus, the conflicting voices produce the event which draws the reader (as one who identifies) in as one of the many wills called into question by the novel. Identity, then, is always tested and altered. The alienating processes of the interpretive community are revealed through our own (often) alienated feminist identificatory reading. A feminist dialogics is a paradigm which acknowledges individual acts of reading as an experience of otherness and challenges the cultural powers which often force us to contain or restrict the otherness of textual voices.

My first reaction to Bakhtin was to become seduced by his theory of dialogism, since it seemed to offer a utopian ground for all voices to flourish; at least all voices could aspire to internal polemic or dialogism. Yet Bakhtin's blind spot is the battle. He does not work out the contradiction between the promise of utopia or community and the battle which always is waged for control. Within Bakhtin's metaphor of the struggle is a privileging of competition and ascendancy, as well as a privileging of the internally persuasive over the authoritative (even though this is the ground upon which Vološinov attacks Freud), of victors over victims in the battle. While Bakhtin privileges an overthrow of the traditional hierarchy, he also suggests a way to make discourse one's own before it expropriates the self speaking it. On the contrary, in Lacan's scheme, the experience of loss accompanies the acquisition of language.[12] But in Bakhtin's, the loss is a failure to have acquired enough social languages to engage in internal polemic—a battle with the reigning ideology of the culture. Bakhtin's will to dialogism is an empowering model, for it shows how to undermine powerful (authoritative) discourses at the site of the carnivalized body, the self which masquerades in authoritative life.

I want to turn the tables and investigate, instead, the external polemics—the means by which these heroines force the polemic to be a communal property rather than an internal one. The notion of internal polemics is a dangerous one for feminism in that it seems to argue for nonspeech or silence. However, language acquisition—the orchestration of many social languages—becomes cultural capital, a way to work within the dominant, prevailing values by subverting them consciously, by seeing through them and articulating that unveiling.

Because all language is "inherited" and because it is all socially and ideologically charged, the conflict of voices in a novel can reveal power structures and potential resistances to those structures. The dialogue begins when one speaker attempts to insert his or her utterance into a social situation; that is, inserts a voice, of whatever character, into the conversation that marks social relations. And, the listeners' role is to respond with their own perspective on the world. In "Discourse in Life and Discourse in Art," Vološinov/Bakhtin claims that style reveals the inner speech of the author, "which does not lend itself to control" and which is "a product of his entire social life" (Vološinov 114). In addition, style reveals the gap between social authority or what the author says—what is controlled—and the excess—the cultural unconscious—which isn't. As such, style suggests the gap between the inner life of the author, the orchestration of the characters' voice (the "second voice" of the novel), and the listener—"the constant participant in a person's inner and outer speech" (Vološinov 114). This listener, then, articulates the gap between internally persuasive speech and the authoritative discourses with which inner speech may come into conflict. With Bakhtin's dialogics, critics can theorize the process by which alien or rival social languages are excluded and silenced. The novels I examine show the process by which historically divergent voices are made uniform or made to appear uniform, a process which leads to a central, dominant ideological stance—to closure. In this way, the author orchestrates his or her themes, through the interrelation of voices, their contradictions, their juxtapositions, their exclusions.[13]

Characters represent social, ideological, and stratified voices, voices which are not univocally the author's but which compete with and foreground the prevailing codes in the society which the author opens up as topics of discourse. These voices, that is, represent thematized views of a social phenomenon—the dynamic languages from different contexts refashioned, brought into play, and dialogized in the novels. As they are structured in the work, these voices objectify and subvert the systematic power of language. The "feminine" in the novels, I would argue in Luce Irigaray's terms, emerges in a "disruptive excess"; this excess is a language—we might call it the voice of gender—which moves beyond the atomic self or body into the larger discursive corpus and which cannot entirely be accounted for in Bakhtin's dialogic model, thereby making useful a theory of feminist dialogics.[14]

Each character's voice within the dialogized novel represents ways of seeing the world; that voice competes for ascendancy to power or, at least, an intense relationship on the threshold where boundaries between the languages of self and other break down. In "Discourse in the Novel" (1934–35), Bakhtin explains novelization as a dialogizing force: "The novel orchestrates all its themes, the totality of the world of objects and ideas depicted and expressed in it, by means of the social diversity of speech types . . . and by the differing individual voices that flourish under such conditions. Authorial speech, the speeches of narrators, inserted genres, the speech of characters are merely those fundamental compositional unities with whose help heteroglossia . . . can enter the novel; each of them permits a multiplicity of social voices and a wide variety of their links and interrelationships (always more or less dialogized)" (DI 263). As Bakhtin demonstrates in *Problems of Dostoevsky's Poetics*, the author's voice blends with, contradicts, disappears, and reemerges throughout the novel, thereby creating in the characters fully articulated and "autonomous" voices with their "own individual word." Language, then, is no longer merely a carrier of theme, but is a theme itself. By noting the voices "that flourish under such conditions," we can grasp the hierarchy of social speech types—indeed, of social stratification—within the communities represented by fiction (DI 263). Thus, by experiencing the otherness in the text, we can grasp the powers which either restrict or subvert that otherness.

The dialogue leads to contradiction, constituting the battle Bakhtin figures as the locus of the utterance: "Within the arena of almost every utterance an intense interaction and struggle between one's own and another's word is being waged, a process in which they oppose or dialogically interanimate each other" (DI 354).[15] This internal clash of competing voices creates the split between the authoritative and the internally persuasive, between the desire to conform and the desire to resist (for Bakhtin, the centrifugal and centripetal forces of language). This dialogue cannot be reduced to a "final" meaning or intention. In fact, in the following readings of four American fictions, this dispossession of the atomic individual—the self—leads to an ideological conflict and contradiction which, as I argue, animates the dialogue. Bakhtin describes the discourse of the speaking character as an *ideologeme*: "It is precisely as ideologemes that discourse becomes the object of representation in the novel, and it is for the same reason novels are never in danger of becoming mere aimless verbal play . . . [or] susceptible to aestheticism as such, to a purely formalistic playing about with words" (DI 333). These ideologemes are arranged to demonstrate the social conflicts among ways of seeing the world. Although these novels begin with an orchestration of voices, a disciplinary action against the defiant voice occurs as a seemingly necessary outcome of plot—a silencing of the other.

Bakhtin's question is not "what is an author?" but "where is an author?" Once an author "transcribes" language in a novel, the order of the languages becomes a dialogic one, one "which orchestrates the intentional theme of the author" (DI 299). Significantly, society therefore speaks through the authors' (and characters') languages even as they speak. The author "ventriloquating" these voices does not represent his or her own voice; rather, the style—the author's choices and exclusions—articulates the play of gendered voices.

That is, in a feminist dialogics, these textual voices are sexually differentiated in an economy of otherness. If we conceive of the novel as a univocal or monologic presentation of the author's perspective or consciousness, a novel such as Hawthorne's *The Blithedale Romance* merely becomes propaganda for the argument against utopian social experiments or against Zenobia's liberating discourse. Yet, given the competing voices of the pragmatist, the social reformer, the artist, the feminist, we can analyze the novel in order to suggest how structural hierarchies—based on gender, class, power in general—are formulated in a battle of languages.[16] The dialogic structure, then, would reveal the place of the reader's voice within the structure of the novel, for our critical voices, too, respond to the dialogue in the novel. And in this response we are engendered, marked by the readings we construct.[17] We acquire "ourselves" by engaging in our own dialogue with others, and especially with texts that challenge our beliefs. In the act of reading, we divest ourselves of the illusion of monologic selfhood. Finally, we align ourselves with the symbolic order of our own world and test this order against the texts that have already been "spoken." We discover our own multiple identities (multivocality) against the grain of dominant ideology which fixes us as unitary subjects. Carroll Smith-Rosenberg writes that "'Language,' like class, is never static."[18] History keeps consciousness in flux; identity and gender, then, are polyvocal, often contradictory, always multiple.

Feminist criticism, in its earliest phase, addresses and redresses the exclusion, the silence, of the female voice. However, even as a "silenced" zone, the female voice competes and contests for authority. Bakhtin reminds us that "the novel always includes in itself the activity of coming to know another's word, a coming to knowledge whose process is represented in the novel" (DI 353). Coming to know another's words is the first step toward asserting self-consciousness in an interpretive community. Moreover, the operation of self-consciousness acts as a disruptive power of traditional codes:

> Self-consciousness, as the artistic dominant in the construction of the hero's image, is by itself sufficient to break down the monologic unity of an artistic world—but only on condition that the hero, as self-consciousness, is really represented and not merely expressed, that is, does not fuse with the author, does not become the mouthpiece for his voice. . . . If the umbilical cord uniting the hero to his creator is not cut, then what we have is not a work of art but a personal document. (PDP 51)

The metaphor of authoring as a female act—of giving birth and cutting the umbilical cord—is telling and imperative for my revision of Bakhtin: if inscription into language is inherited, the identification Bakhtin makes between mothering/authoring shows that inscription into the symbolic need not always be coopted or repressive. In fact, the transition for both mother and child requires the letting-go between mother–child and author–text (as Dickinson has it, too, in "After Great Pain"). This letting-go encourages dialogism since the child/text speaks for itself and with others, just as the author/mother moves on to another production. To read Bakhtin as a feminist is to see the dialogic structure as an intermediate (or ambivalent) space between the imaginary (the creation of art) and the symbolic (the text)—a spatial rather than a symbolic representation.[19] The reader or listener, in this scheme, is between the two stages, an ambivalent space which privileges neither the imaginary nor the symbolic. It is the space of sexual play, of engendering. Hawthorne, James, Wharton, and Chopin do "cut the umbilical cord" of their creations, allowing their characters to reveal themselves in language. The dialogized novel, then, undermines an ideological unity (be it patriarchal or feminist, liberal or conservative) that the monologic novel erases in favor of ideological closure.

Although the novels of this study end, interestingly, with typically romantic resolutions, the dialogues remain unresolved, always a ground of competition. While the plot resolutions give closure to the novels, the dialogue resists that closure. This dialogue is "forever dying, living, being born," so we see the end as a moment rather than as a "final word" (DI 365). "What is realized in the novel is the process of coming to know one's own language as it is perceived in someone else's language, coming to know one's own belief system in someone else's system" (DI 365). I want to rephrase this notion for my own feminist intentions: this coming to know the other is at the heart of the feminist act of reading the novel, just as it is at the heart of the characters' coming to know themselves as other in a world where patriarchal language aspires to monologism. Gabriele Schwab asks the question this way in "Reader–Response and the Aesthetic Experience of Otherness": "How . . . can we, after the deconstructionist challenge, argue for a recognition of otherness in the act of reading—which also implies the recognition of textual constraints for interpretation—without denying that misreadings, creative as well as uncreative ones, are engendered by the semantic and structural instabilities of language itself?" The other of and within literature—or misreadings thematized to represent the other—can affect and change language itself.[20] For instance, feminists read phallocentric discourse as the other, reading themselves as signs in the margins and the "unsaids" of the text, or "overreading" their own intentions into the text. The women readers in the text assert their otherness not by surrendering, but by forcing their language into the context/contest of the dominant languages. That is, not by erasing but by highlighting their otherness can they do battle with patriarchal codes.

With this imperative in mind, I want to appropriate Bakhtin's explanation of one important stage which is crucial to my study of Hawthorne, James, Wharton, and Chopin. I refer here to the "other" as gendered rather than the "other" as counter-cultural. Bakhtin claims that the image of the Fool carries over into the modern novel from its earlier forms—in the picaresque adventure novel, for one. It is not that fools appear as characters, but that their characteristics of simplicity and naïveté inform the modern novel:

> Even if the image of the fool (and the image of the rogue as well) loses its
> fundamental organizing role in the subsequent development of novelistic

> prose, nevertheless the very aspect of *not grasping* the conventions of society (the degree of society's conventionality), not understanding lofty pathos—charged labels, things and events—such incomprehension remains almost everywhere an essential ingredient of prose style. Either the prose writer represents the world through the words of a *narrator* who does not understand this world, does not acknowledge its poetic, scholarly or otherwise lofty and significant labels; or else the prose writer introduces a *character* who does not understand; or, finally, the direct style of the author himself involves a deliberate (polemical) failure to understand the habitual ways of conceiving the world. (DI 402)

This failure to understand is represented in each of the novels I consider, for the women's misreading of the social conventions results in a dialogue about those very interpretive norms. Zenobia's and Coverdale's, Maggie's, Lily's, and Edna's incomprehensions force them into a dialogic confrontation with the other voices, the other ideologemes represented in the novels. In fact, this failure shapes the styles of these novels. And in this resulting dialogue, the women's own ideologemes are made clear in the process of articulating their values to others and assimilating others' values to their own emerging ones. As women in patriarchal communities, they are essentially other to the norms of their community. As fool—a type I read as a resisting reader *within* the text—these women provide the means of unmasking dominant codes. Mary Russo refers to these women as Female Grotesques in her essay of the same name; they are "repressed and undeveloped."[21] Stupidity (a form of resistance) forces the unspoken repressions into the open, thus making them vulnerable to interpretation, contradiction, and dialogue.

Historically, the fool has not been a woman and has not exercised the freedom of, say, Lear's fool. But the freedom of Shakespeare's fool is that of wisdom and wit; the freedom of Bakhtin's fool is that of incomprehension. All the more important, then, is this variation on a literary topos: the play of speech which is traditionally allowed the male fool is denied these uncomprehending women. Nevertheless, these characters refuse to let their voices be inhabited by the discourse which reduces all bodies to the same voice. Umberto Eco explains the situation of the "comic" or misreading fool as follows: the character is not "at fault. Maybe the frame is wrong."[22] The role of the reader, that is, is to question and restructure the "cultural and intertextual frames" in which the character operates and is made foolish.

Bakhtin explains that "Stupidity (incomprehension) in the novel is always polemical: it interacts dialogically with an intelligence (a lofty pseudo intelligence) with which it polemicizes and whose mask it tears away" (DI 403). In other words, "naive" characters resist understanding the world according to dominant conventions, resist abstract categories of language, and also refuse to (or cannot) accept whole-heartedly the ideology of the other; their naïveté remains and because of this ignorance, not despite it, a struggle emerges. "For this reason stupidity (incomprehension) in the novel is always implicated in language, in the word: at its heart always lies a polemical failure to understand someone else's discourse, someone else's pathos-charged lie that has appropriated the world and aspires to conceptualize it, a polemical failure to understand generally accepted, canonized, inveterately false languages with their lofty labels for things and events. . . ." (DI 403). This polemical misunderstanding or misreading is not a question of what the characters will or will not accept; as fools, most often their polemics is an intentional narrative strategy and crucial to the revealing (and, indeed, unmasking) of dialogue in the novel.

For example, a "multitude of different novelistic-dialogic situations" exist between the heroine fools and others who are fixed in the dominant discourse: between, for example, Zenobia and Hollingsworth (the reformer), Zenobia and Coverdale (the poet-romancer), Maggie and the Jewish shopkeeper (the semiotician), Lily and the hat-makers (the coopted laborers), Edna and Adèle (the perfect mother-woman): all of these situations reveal the ideological structures of language, of institutional controls and discipline. The "fool" serves to defamiliarize the conventions which have been accepted as "natural," as myth:

> Regarding fools or regarding the world through the eyes of a fool, the novelist's eye is taught a sort of prose vision, the vision of a world confused by conventions of pathos and by falsity. A failure to understand languages that are otherwise generally accepted and that have the appearance of being universal teaches the novelist how to perceive them physically as *objects*, to see their relativity, to externalize them, to feel out their boundaries, that is, it teaches him how to expose and structure images of social languages. (DI 404)

"Confused" is the focal term: we are meant to be unsettled by these dialogues between fools and accepted languages, just as we are meant to be unsettled by feminist criticism which seeks to shake up the critical communities which do not acknowledge the excluded margins. What Bakhtin might teach us, then, is to conceive of the discourses within the novel as objects, as ideologemes which require interpretation and revision and which involve us in what Gabriele Schwab calls the "vertiginous undertow" of language.[23] In fact, such a "prose wisdom" allows us to see that no language is universal. Bakhtin calls this study of stupidity and incomprehension "a basic (and extremely interesting) problem in the history of the novel" (DI 404): that problem of misreading is the core of my study of Hawthorne, James, Wharton, and Chopin.

Finally, women "on the threshold" of a social or cultural crisis become powerful in the marginal realm which constitutes the carnival world. By "carnivalization," I mean here, as Bakhtin has it, the "transposition of carnival into the language of literature" which serves to make every voice in the communal performance heard and unrestricted by official or authoritative speech (PDP 122). The fool is able to assert her defiant voice through carnival, the masquerade, the parody of the "official" lives she leads. Bakhtin's carnival hero seeks to resist the essentializing framework "of *other people's* words about [them] that might finalize and deaden [them]" (PDP 59). The carnival is the realm of desire unmasked, taken out of the law of culture, and involved in an economy of difference. While the authoritative discourse demands conformity, the carnivalized discourse renders invalid any codes, conventions, or laws which govern or reduce the individual to an object of control. Contrary to Irigaray, I argue that the carnival (or masquerade) need not reinvest women in the specular economy or in masculine desire, but can take them out of it.[24] This is neither to condemn as Irigaray does nor to celebrate as Bakhtin does the intermediate space; I want to question its informing ambivalence. The carnival reveals the characters as subjects of their own discourse rather than objects of an official line or finalizing word. Because carnival potentially involves everyone, it sets the scene for dialogue, for communal heteroglossia:

> The laws, prohibitions, and restrictions that determine the structure and order of ordinary life, that is noncarnival, life are suspended during carnival: what is suspended first of all is hierarchical structure and all the forms of terror, reverence, piety, and etiquette connected with it—that is, everything resulting from socio-hierarchical inequality or any other form of inequality among people (including age). All *distance* between people is suspended, and a special carnival category goes into effect: *free and familiar contact among people*. (PDP 122–23)

Carnival suspends discipline—the terror, reverence, piety, and etiquette which contribute to the maintenance of the social order. The carnival participants overthrow the hierarchical conventions which exclude them and work out a new mode of relation, one dialogic in nature. Therefore, they resist noncarnival life within community by reinventing relations in the carnival. These Bakhtinian fools resist convention, using the threat of the inconclusive, open-ended possibilities of dialogue to retain subversive force in the social arena. As Bakhtin explains, the carnival, however, cannot last. It is functional, a means of resisting conventions and revising them, without destroying them completely.[25]

I want to end with a claim from Adrienne Rich: "All silence has a meaning."[26] Through Bakhtin's principle of the dialogization of the novel, we can interpret the silenced or suicidal voice of female characters compelling a dialogue with those others who would prefer to think they do not exist. Annette Kolodny writes that we read "not texts but paradigms," not "reality" but instead ways of seeing and making meaning in the world.[27] As old conventions and ways of reading prove untenable, new interpretive communities emerge and transform our literary history and allow for revised interpretations of experience. We cannot think of going beyond these communities, I would agree with Bakhtin, except through subverting them and the opposition between freedom and utopia. Such has been the revolution in the leftist, structuralist poetics and politics of the sixties and seventies, in current versions of reader-response criticism, and now in a feminist dialogics. Like Maggie in James's novel who reads the golden bowl, readers take up the symbolic object—the text—and make sense of it in the context of specific historical, cultural, and social events. We learn to exercise our conventions on the text, but not to find a meaning hidden there. The act of reading, then, as cultural strategy is the first step toward revisioning and rearticulating voice (the "private property" of our internally persuasive language) and our place in the social dialogue. Reading is not "free," but an activity determined by the text and by the ideological discourses one brings to bear on the text. We cannot posit our own readings as acts of disengagement or as acts of critical neu-

trality; rather, the acts of reading prove to engender us, reinforcing sexual difference. Interpretation is an act that is always interanimated with *other* critical
discourses and *other* ideologies, including those of sexual difference.

NOTES

1. Craig Owens, "The Discourse of Others: Feminists and Postmodernism," in *The Anti-Aesthetic*, ed. Hal Foster (Port Townsend, Washington: Bay Press, 1983), p. 61. The debate about what whether the "gaze" is male is informed by Mary Ann Doane's and E. Ann Kaplan's theorizing of the female gaze. Kaplan's essay—"Is the gaze male?" in *Women and Film* (New York: Methuen Press, 1983)—is interesting to me because she claims that feminist film critics "have (rightly) been wary of admitting the degree to which the pleasure [of looking] comes from identification with objectification" (p. 33). The problem of identificatory readings is beyond the scope of my study, but a crucial topic for the discussion of a specific female pleasure.

2. Myra Jehlen, "Archimedes and the Paradox of Literary Criticism," in *The Signs Reader* (Chicago: University of Chicago Press, 1982), p. 71. See also Teresa de Lauretis's *Alice Doesn't*, p. 7.

3. Wayne C. Booth, "Freedom of Interpretation: Bakhtin and the Challenge of Feminist Criticism," in *Critical Inquiry* 9, 1 (September 1982): 45–76. Although Booth takes sides against Bakhtin's reading of Rabelais in order to support his own feminist perspective, he ignores, I think, the potential in Bakhtin's theory for revisioning the silenced voices of women in the dialogue/discourse of social power.

Wayne Booth seems to be the target of the hour for feminist critics, despite his own recent turn to an "ethics of reading" which takes feminist concerns into account. In "Rereading as a Woman: The Body in Practice" (in *The Female Body in Western Culture* [Cambridge: Harvard University Press, 1986]), Nancy K. Miller accuses Booth of reiterating the old joke that "feminists have no sense of humor" (p. 354).

Patrocinio Schweickart also begins her dialogue with postmodernism in "Reading Ourselves: A Feminist Theory of Reading" (in *Gender and Reading: Essays on Readers, Texts, and Contexts* [Baltimore: Johns Hopkins University Press, 1986]) by responding to Wayne Booth's story of reading, a "utopian" fiction in which gender or class or race doesn't matter. In Booth's vision, reading delivers the utopian: "Booth's story [of his own love of reading] anticipates what might be possible, what 'critical understanding' might mean for *everyone*, if only we could overcome the pervasive systemic injustices of our time" (p. 35). Instead of this utopian vision, Schweickart calls for a feminist theory of reading: "While it is still too early to present a full-blown theory, the dialogic aspect of the relationship between the feminist reader and the woman writer suggests the direction that such a theory might take" (p. 52). It is not clear whether she means this "dialogic aspect" in Bakhtin's sense, but this essay will explore what a "feminist dialogism" might mean.

4. V. N. Vološnikov, "Discourse in Life and Discourse in Art," in *Freudianism: A Marxist Critique*, trans. I. R. Titunik (New York: Academic Press, 1976), p. 115.

5. Hélène Cixous and Catherine Clément, *The Newly Born Woman*, trans. Betsy Wing (Minneapolis: University of Minnesota Press, 1986), p. 148.

6. Laura Mulvey, "Visual Pleasure and Narrative Cinema," in *Screen* 16, 3 (Autumn 1975): 7.

7. See Nancy Miller's "Arachnologies," in *The Poetics of Gender* (New York: Columbia University Press, 1986), especially page 292, note 27.

8. Catherine Clément formulates the subversiveness of guilt in her essay which is part of *The Newly Born Woman*.

9. Margaret Higonnet explains "suicide as interpretation" in "Speaking Silences: Women's Suicide" (in *The Female Body in Western Culture*). Women's consciousnesses are not finalized by suicide; as Higonnet argues, suicide is a narrative strategy; the death must be addressed by the other characters: "To take one's life is to force others to read one's death. . . . The act is a self-barred signature; its destructive narcissism seems to some particularly feminine" (pp. 68–69). Not for Higonnet, and I would argue, not for Bakhtin: the suicidal signature is a decision not to let others finalize or deaden one's character by monologism. In Bakhtin's vision, suicide forces the others to enter into a dialogic relation with the one to whom such a relation was denied in life. Higonnet claims, "Language becomes action; action becomes and yet requires language."

10. Michael Holquist and Katerina Clark, *Mikhail Bakhtin* (Cambridge: Belknap Press, 1984), p. 227.

11. Mikhail Bakhtin, *Problems of Dostoevsky's Poetics*, ed. and trans. Caryl Emerson (Minneapolis: University of Minnesota Press, 1984), p. 21. All further references will be made parenthetically throughout the chapters (PDP).

12. In *Figuring Lacan: Criticism and the Cultural Unconscious* (Lincoln: University of Nebraska Press, 1987), Juliet Flower MacCannell argues for Lacan's usefulness for a feminist subversion of language: "The feminist reaction to Lacan has been highly productive. In a mode quite different from the Oedipal rivalry generally assumed to be crucial to cultural creation, Lacan's reading by feminism has unleashed not a series of works designed to dethrone, decentre or deny Lacan but works dedicated to reformulating the imagery, the vocabulary and the network of associations attached to the figure of the woman" (p. 3). Desire and language, for Lacan, is associated with alienation. I see Bakhtin's sociolinguistics as a way to overcome this alienation effect.

13. See Marcelle Marini's "Feminism and Literary Criticism: Reflections on the Disciplinary Approach," in *Women in Culture and Politics: A Century of Change*. Marini points out that this dialogic model lands us "somewhere between the real and the utopic, without ever managing to take shape to the point of becoming society's image for an entire community." Such a context would overstep the "question of *one* feminine language and *one* masculine language; rather, in the end, of a plurality of languages, without definite ownership, in which flexible identities would be in a constant state of becoming. . . ." (p. 154).

14. Luce Irigaray, *This Sex Which Is Not One*, p. 78. Terry Castle's essay on carnivalization in the eighteenth-century novel opens up this topic of disruption for my reading of the carnival and the nineteenth-century didactic purpose. See "The Carnivalization of Eighteenth-Century English Narrative" in *PMLA* 99, 5 (October 1984): 903–916.

15. See Michael Holquist's "Answering as Authoring," in *Critical Inquiry* 10, 2 (December 1983): 307–319. Holquist's claims are important to my own argument: "Human being is acted out in a *logosphere*, a space where meaning occurs as a function of the constant struggle between centrifugal forces that seek to keep things apart and in motion, that increase difference and tend toward the extreme of life and consciousness, and centripetal forces that strive to make things cohere, to stay in place, and which tend toward the extreme of death and brute matter. . . . These forces contend with each other at all levels of existence: in the physical universe, the cells of the body, the processes of mind, as well as in the ideologies of social organization. The constant dialogue between—and among—these partners in the activity of being finds its most comprehensive model in the activity of communication" (p. 309).

16. Lacan writes in "The Mirror Stage," trans. Alan Sheridan (*Ecrits* [New York: W. W. Norton, 1977]) that we need to distrust the altruistic versions of the self: ". . . we place no trust in altruistic feeling, we who lay bare the aggressivity that underlies the activity of the philanthropist, the idealist, the pedagogue, and even the reformer" (p. 7). Without a claim to appropriate Lacanian psychoanalysis as my own method, I do want to suggest that this unmasking of altruism is part of the project of the readings which follow.

17. For a discussion of the dangers of this marking, see Monique Wittig's "The Mark of Gender," in *The Poetics of Gender*, pp. 63–73.

18. Carroll Smith-Rosenberg, "Writing History: Language, Class, and Gender," in *Feminist Studies/Critical Studies*, ed. Teresa de Lauretis (Bloomington: Indiana University Press, 1986), p. 36.

19. See Gabriele Schwab's "The Genesis of the Subject, Imaginary Functions, and Poetic Language," in *New Literary History* 15 (Spring 1984): 453–474. Schwab argues that the imaginary does not lose its importance at the genesis of the subject, but remains influential in the subject's development: "However both anticipation and elimination are also decided by the internalized image of the Other, and thus we always come back to the imaginary." See also Jessica Benjamin's "A Desire of One's Own" in *Feminist Studies/Critical Studies* for her fine discussion of the distinction between spatial and symbolic constitutive models of women's desire, especially page 95.

20. Gabriele Schwab, "Reader-Response and the Aesthetic Experience of Otherness," in *Stanford Literature Review* (Spring 1986), p. 112. See Nancy Miller's formulation of "overreading" in "Arachnologies," in *The Poetics of Gender:* "What I want to propose instead as a counterweight to this story of the deconstructed subject, restless with what he already knows, is a poetics of the *underread* and a practice of 'overreading.' The aim of this practice is double. It aims first to unsettle the interpretive model which thinks that it knows when it is rereading, and what is in the library, confronting its claims with Kolodny's counterclaim that 'what we engage are not texts but paradigms' (8)" (p. 274).

21. Mary Russo, "Female Grotesques," in *Feminist Studies/Critical Studies*, p. 219.

22. Umberto Eco, "The frames of comic 'freedom'" in *Carnival!*, p. 8. Eco's distinction between "comic" and "humor" is one I employ throughout my readings of the Bakhtinian fool: "Humor does not pretend, like carnival, to lead us beyond our own limits. . . . It is never off limits, it undermines limits from inside. . . . Humor does not promise us liberation: on the contrary, it warns us about the impossibility of global liberation, reminding us of the presence of a law that we no longer have reason to obey. In doing so it undermines the law. It makes us feel the uneasiness of living under a law—any law" (p. 8). In this revision of Bakhtin's carnival, Eco demonstrates his hesitancy to adopt carnival as a realm of "*actual* liberation" (p. 3), as I do. What he does claim, and what I would emphasize, is that the comic works on the basis of a rule or law unspoken, but already understood. Humor "casts in doubt other cultural codes. If there is a possibility of transgression, it lies in humor rather than in comic." Michael Andre Bernstein's "When the Carnival Turns Bitter" in *Bakhtin* works through the function of the "wise fool" upon which I draw my own distinction: "Even in English Renaissance drama where the 'wise fool' attached to a court enjoys the liberty to speak freely to his master on a permanent, if precarious, basis, the audience learns very quickly when the fool's words contain a truth which the master ignores only at his own peril and when the quips are merely witty repartee. Lear's fool, for example, seeks, too often in vain, to instruct his vain king" (pp. 106–7).

23. Schwab, "Reader-Response," p. 124.

24. Luce Irigaray, p. 133.

25. See Mary Ann Doane's "Film and the Masquerade: Theorising the Female Spectator," in *Screen* 23, 3–4 (1982): 74–87. Doane's comments on the masquerade are crucial: "To masquerade is to manufacture a lack in the form of a certain distance between oneself and one's image" (p. 82). That is, Doane suggests that the masquerader is in control, since "masquerade is anti-hysterical for it works to effect a separation between the cause of desire and oneself." I would say that the anti-hysterical effects a distance, but not a separation, between the subject and desire. See Mary Russo's essay for a defense of Irigaray, p. 223.

26. Adrienne Rich, "Disloyal to Civilization," in *On Lies, Secrets, and Silence* (New York: W. W. Norton & Company, 1979), p. 308.

27. Annette Kolodny, "Dancing Through the Minefield: Some Observations on Theory, Practice and Politics of a Feminist Literary Criticism," in *Feminist Studies* 6, 1 (Spring 1980): 8.

ethnicity

"From margin to center": bell hooks's famous phrase seems comfortably enough to describe the movement of women's studies as a whole. Feminism has, after all, worked to pull women's voices, experiences, and concerns out of the periphery of official culture, and has insisted upon placing gender-related issues squarely in the middle of all academic fields of inquiry. If women have traditionally occupied the margins, though, women of color have been doubly marginalized. And such women whose sexual preference, class, or nationality differentiate them even further from the heterosexual, middle-class, American "norm" have—until recently—been pushed so far into the margin as to have been almost imperceptible to the academic eye. The essays in this section are working (along with the output of such scholars as hooks, Gloria Anzaldúa, Valerie Smith, Claudia Tate, and Hortense Spillers, among others represented elsewhere in this volume) to redress the marginalization of women of color in mainstream feminisms, as well as in the culture at large.

The argumentative strategies of these essayists closely parallel those of feminists who do not bring race into the foreground of their studies. Like the white feminists represented in the "Methodologies" section, these five authors speak up not to bury difference, but to praise it. In their framework of assumptions, ethnic difference (like gender difference) is culturally constructed. "Ethnicity," as we are using it here, refers to a person's cultural orientation as it has been shaped by the traditions and experiences associated with that person's race, which is itself not a biological matter, but another arbitrarily defined category within culture and society. In these critics' work, a focus on ethnicity requires adjustments in the information and the perspective which a reader brings to the experience of reading. From these critics' point of view, what you know (or, more importantly, don't know) about a literary work's extraliterary context will determine your appreciation of it, and what you have experienced (directly or imaginatively) will shape the perspective you take in evaluating or understanding it.

Experience, therefore, plays a crucial role in feminist criticism that focuses on race. Barbara Smith's "The Truth That Never Hurts: Black Lesbians in Fiction in the 1980s" (1990) is a good example, moving freely as it does among academic observations, personal anecdotes, and literary analysis. Smith is one of the few authors in *Feminisms* to bring up activism, an issue far more central to academic feminisms than its representation in this volume would suggest. As Smith explains, the experience of activism affects not only the information a feminist critic brings to her work, but all her perceptions. In this project, Smith brings to bear what she knows about homophobia (as a scholar, as an activist, and as a black lesbian) upon her examination of the way black lesbians have been portrayed in the fiction of the 1980s.

Taking Gloria Naylor's *The Women of Brewster Place*, Alice Walker's *The Color Purple*, and Audre Lord's *Zami: A New Spelling of My Name* as her examples, Smith analyzes each in terms of its "verisimilitude" (or believability on the level of such formal elements as plot, setting, and characterization) and its "authenticity" (or its plausibility and desirability as a statement of what the experience of black lesbians is like). Smith finds Naylor's portrayal of a black lesbian couple a "nightmare," strong in verisimilitude but—from the perspective of a black lesbian reader especially—lacking authenticity; she calls Walker's buoyant story of love between women an "idyll," a "fable," brimming with authenticity, but short on verisimilitude. Lorde's autobiographical *Zami* splits the difference for Smith, providing "a vision of possibilities for Black Lesbians surviving whole, despite all"—and Smith remarks that it is no surprise that *Zami* was not published by any prominent commercial press.

In Paula Gunn Allen's "Kochinnenako in Academe" (1986), the experience in question is that of native American tribal tradition. Allen reproduces an English-language version of an oral tale about a female character, translated in the early twentieth century by a white man. Allen subjects this Keres tale to three readings, showing how profoundly one's expectations and information will affect one's reading of a minority-culture text. First, subtly applying the tools of structuralist narrative theory, Allen shows how the translator's unselfconscious allegiance to Western patriarchal storylines has caused him to distort the content and form of the tale. From a tribal perspective, she explains, the English rendition is nonsense, as it dismantles the ritual nature of the original to force it into a linear tale of conflict and resolution. Next, Allen considers what an Anglo-American feminist might say about the translated tale, observing that such a reader would have good reason to jump to false conclusions about the oppression of women in the culture supposedly represented by the story. Then Allen proposes a "feminist-tribal interpretation," bringing together her knowledge of the Keres "perception, aesthetics, and social system" with her awareness of what gender signifies in Keres culture.

The "feminist-tribal" perspective allows Allen to reveal "how the interpolations of patriarchal thinking distort all the relationships in the story and, by extension, how such impositions of patriarchy on gynocracy disorder harmonious social and spiritual relationships." As this last remark indicates, Allen—like Smith—is interested in the effect stories have on the world of lived experience; she asserts that the Westernization of native American tales is partly responsible for the problematic relations between the sexes in tribes today. Like Smith's, then, Allen's literary criticism is a form of activism, a way of bringing structuralist-inspired abstractions to life.

As both Smith's and Allen's essays imply, community is a theme frequently recurring in criticism focused on marginalized groups. Just as it figures in their explanations of what is "different" about black lesbian or native American cultures, community takes center stage in Yvonne Yarbro-Bejarano's "Chicana Literature from a Chicana Feminist Perspective" (1987). Yarbro-Bejarano is working here to coalesce a community of Chicana writers, literary and academic, who struggle to appropriate literary authority for themselves.

Yarbro-Bejarano raises an issue central to all feminisms, but especially urgent for the doubly-marginalized woman of color who wants to write. That issue is the woman writer's assertion of her subjectivity in the act of telling stories about herself and others like her. "In telling these stories," she says, "Chicanas refuse the dominant culture's definition of what a Chicana is. In writing, they refuse the objectification imposed by gender roles and racial and economic exploitation." The storytelling community of the Chicana writer is—like that of the native American—an oral one; Yarbro-Bejarano addresses some of the complications that arise for the Chicana who strives for "an authentic language" she can use to commit her stories to paper. The essay's conclusion points to recurrences of the themes of writing and community in Chicana literature, showing how closely related the efforts of the Chicana author and the Chicana feminist critic can be.

Amy Ling's "I'm Here: An Asian American Woman's Response" (1987) seeks more directly than the other four essays to place ethnically-focused criticism in the context of feminist literary theory. This piece (like the Jane Tompkins entry in "Autobiography") is an answer to Ellen Messer-Davidow's essay in *New Literary History*, "The Philosophical Bases of Feminist Literary Criticisms." The plural form of Messer-Davidow's title, and the presence of no fewer than seven responses in that issue of the journal, indicate the growing awareness in the late 1980s of the multiplicity of perspectives that can shape feminist efforts. Indeed, Messer-Davidow's term "perspectivism" works well for Ling, who brings it up from the position of a critic working on Chinese American women's literature written in English, her previously all-but-invisible field of study. Ling's response applies basic feminist principles about literary value and critical practices (like those represented here in "Canon" and "Methodologies") to explain what it means for her to do ethnically-centered criticism of women's writing.

Ling points out that while all minorities are marginalized, some groups are treated as more peripheral to the mainstream than others. And while she acknowledges that "we cannot all be remembered all the time," she expresses the (possibly "utopian") wish that "the result of . . . attention were that everyone would be not merely more tolerant of each other's perspectives but actively interested." Toward sparking that interest, Ling briefly describes the turn-of-the-century novels of "the Eaton sisters, the first writers of Asian ancestry to publish in the United States," and—like all the critics in this section—she emphasizes the importance of understanding something about the Eaton sisters' historical circumstances for an appreciation of their texts.

Equally concerned with historical context is Hazel Carby, in "It Jus' Be's Dat Way Sometime: The Sexual Politics of Women's Blues" (1988). Carby briefly notes the tendency of mainstream feminism to "marginalize non-white women," and quickly turns to her own focus, "the production of a discourse of sexuality by black women." Carby concentrates on the "women-dominated blues" of the 1920s, examining how female writers and singers of blues lyrics represented their sexuality in their songs. This corpus allows Carby to extend her study beyond the middle-class boundaries that have tended, she explains, to erase sexuality from the study of black women writers.

Community again becomes the focus, as Carby considers the role the blues singer played in forming black women's ideas about their lives and opportunities. Performing close readings of some of the blues songs that refer most explicitly to sex, Carby celebrates the "exercise of power and control over sexuality" that women's blues embodied for a time. Alluding once again to the community of writers, artists, readers, and critics that figures so prominently in ethnically-centered feminisms, Carby says of the blues singers, "we hear the 'we' when they say 'I.'" The same conviction holds true for each of these critics committed to recovering the voices and the subjectivity of women of color in American texts of every kind.

—RRW

BARBARA SMITH

THE TRUTH THAT NEVER HURTS

black lesbians in fiction in the 1980s

In 1977, when I wrote *Toward a Black Feminist Criticism*, I wanted to accomplish several goals. The first was simply to point out that Black women writers existed, a fact generally ignored by white male, Black male, and white female readers, teachers, and critics. Another desire was to encourage Black feminist criticism of these writers' work, that is, analyses that acknowledged the reality of sexual oppression in the lives of Black women. Probably most urgently, I wanted to illuminate the existence of Black Lesbian writers and to show how homophobia insured that we were even more likely to be ignored or attacked than Black women writers generally.

In 1985, Black women writers' situation is considerably different than it was in 1977. Relatively speaking, Black women's literature is much more recognized, even at times by the white, male literary establishment. There are a growing number of Black women critics who rely upon various Black feminist critical approaches to studying the literature. There has been a marked increase in the number of Black women who are willing to acknowledge that they are feminists, including some who write literary criticism. Not surprisingly, Black feminist activism and organizing have greatly expanded, a precondition which I cited in 1977 for the growth of Black feminist criticism. More writing by Black Lesbians is available, and there has even been some positive response to this writing from non-Lesbian Black readers and critics. The general conditions under which Black women critics and writers work have improved. The personal isolation we face and the ignorance and hostility with which our work is met have diminished in some quarters but have by no means disappeared.

One of the most positive changes is that a body of consciously Black feminist writing and writing by other feminists of color actually exists. The publication of a number of anthologies has greatly increased the breadth of writing available by feminists of color. These include *Conditions: Five, The Black Women's Issue* (1979); *This Bridge Called My Back: Writings by Radical Women of Color* (1981); *All the Women Are White, All the Blacks Are Men, But Some of Us Are Brave: Black Women's Studies* (1982); *A Gathering of Spirit: North American Indian Women's Issue* (1983); *Cuentos: Stories by Latinas* (1983); *Home Girls: A Black Feminist Anthology* (1983); *Bearing*

Witness/Sobreviviendo: An Anthology of Native American/Latina Art and Literature (1984); and *Gathering Ground: New Writing and Art by Northwest Women of Color* (1984). First books by individual authors have also appeared, such as *Claiming an Identity They Taught Me to Despise* (1980) and *Abeng* (1984) by Michelle Cliff; *Narratives: Poems in the Tradition of Black Women* (1982) by Cheryl Clarke; *For Nights Like This One* (1983) by Becky Birtha; *Loving in the War Years: Lo Que Nunca Pasó por Sus Labios* (1983) by Cherríe Moraga; *The Words of a Woman Who Breathes Fire* (1983) by Kitty Tsui; and *Mohawk Trail* (1985) by Beth Brant (Degonwadonti). Scholarly works provide extremely useful analytical frameworks, for example, *Common Differences: Conflicts in Black and White Feminist Perspectives* by Gloria I. Joseph and Jill Lewis (1981); *Black Women Writers at Work* edited by Claudia Tate (1983); *When and Where I Enter: The Impact of Black Women on Race and Sex in America* by Paula Giddings (1984); and *Black Feminist Criticism: Perspectives on Black Women Writers* by Barbara Christian (1985).

Significantly, however, "small" or independent, primarily women's presses published all but the last four titles cited and almost all the authors and editors of these alternative press books (although not all of the contributors to their anthologies) are Lesbians. In his essay, "The Sexual Mountain and Black Women Writers," critic Calvin Hernton writes:

> The declared and lesbian black feminist writers are pioneering a black feminist criticism. This is not to take away from other writers. All are blazing new trails. But especially the declared feminists and lesbian feminists—Barbara Smith, Ann Shockley, Cheryl Clarke, Wilmette Brown, and the rest— are at the forefront of the critics, scholars, intellectuals, and ideologues of our time.[1]

Yet Hernton points out that these writers are "subpopular," published as they are by nonmainstream presses. In contrast, non-Lesbian Black women writers have been published by trade publishers and are able to reach, as Hernton explains, a "wider popular audience."

In her excellent essay, "No More Buried Lives: The Theme of Lesbianism" on Audre Lorde's *Zami*, Gloria Naylor's *The Women of Brewster Place*, Ntozake Shange's *Sassafras, Cypress and Indigo*, and Alice Walker's *The Color Purple*, critic Barbara Christian makes a similar observation. She writes:

> Lesbian life, characters, language, values are *at present* and *to some extent* becoming respectable in American literature, partly because of the pressure of women-centered communities, partly because publishers are intensely aware of marketing trends. . . . I say, *to some extent*, because despite the fact that Walker received the Pulitzer for *The Color Purple* and Naylor the American Book Award for *The Women of Brewster Place*, I doubt if *Home Girls*, an anthology of black feminist and lesbian writing that was published by Kitchen Table Press, would have been published by a mainstream publishing company.[2]

Significantly, Christian says that "Lesbian life, characters, language, values" are receiving qualified attention and respectability, but Lesbian writers themselves are not. No doubt, this is why she suspects that no trade publisher would publish

Home Girls, which contains work by women who write openly as Lesbians, and which defines Lesbianism politically as well as literarily.

The fact that there is such a clear-cut difference in publishing options for Black Lesbian writers (who are published solely by independent presses) and for non-Lesbian and closeted Black women writers (who have access to both trade and alternative publishers) indicates what has *not* changed since 1977. It also introduces the focus of this essay.[3] I am concerned with exploring the treatment of Black Lesbian writing and Black Lesbian themes in the context of Black feminist writing and criticism.

Today, not only are more works by and about Black women available, but a body of specifically Black feminist writing exists. Although both the general category of Black women's literature and the specific category of Black feminist literature can be appropriately analyzed from a Black feminist critical perspective, explicitly Black feminist literature has a unique set of characteristics and emphases which distinguishes it from other work. Black feminist writing provides an incisive critical perspective on sexual political issues that affect Black women—for example, the issue of sexual violence. It generally depicts the significance of Black women's relationships with each other as a primary source of support. Black feminist writing may also be classified as such because the author identifies herself as a feminist and has a demonstrated commitment to women's issues and related political concerns. An openness in discussing Lesbian subject matter is perhaps the most obvious earmark of Black feminist writing and not because feminism and Lesbianism are interchangeable, which of course they are not.

For historical, political, and ideological reasons, a writer's consciousness about Lesbianism bears a direct relationship to her consciousness about feminism. It was in the context of the second wave of the contemporary feminist movement, influenced by the simultaneous development of an autonomous gay liberation movement, that the political content of Lesbianism and Lesbian oppression began to be analyzed and defined. The women's liberation movement was the political setting in which anti-Lesbian attitudes and actions were initially challenged in the late 1960s and early 1970s and where, at least in theory, but more often in fact, homophobia was designated unacceptable, at least in the movement's more progressive sectors.

Barbara Christian also makes the connection between feminist consciousness and a willingness to address Lesbian themes in literature. She writes:

> Some of the important contributions that the emergence of the lesbian theme has made to Afro-American Women's literature are: the breaking of stereotypes so that black lesbians are clearly seen as *women*, the exposure of homophobia in the black community, and an exploration of how that homophobia is related to the struggle of all women to be all that they can be—in other words to feminism.
>
> That is not to say that Afro-American women's literature has not always included a feminist perspective. The literature of the seventies, for example, certainly explored the relationship between sexism and racism and has been at the forefront of the development of feminist ideas. One natural outcome of this exploration is the lesbian theme, for society's attack on lesbians is the cutting edge of the anti-feminist definition of women.[4]

Black feminist writers, whether Lesbian or non-Lesbian, have been aware of and influenced by the movement's exploring, struggling over, and organizing around Lesbian identity and issues. They would be much more likely to take Black Lesbian experiences seriously and to explore Black Lesbian themes in their writing, in contrast with authors who either have not been involved in the women's movement or who are antifeminist. For example, in her very positive review of *Conditions: Five, The Black Women's Issue*, originally published in *Ms.* magazine in 1980, Alice Walker writes:

> Like black men and women who refused to be the exceptional "pet" Negro for whites, and who instead said they were "niggers" too (the original "crime" of "niggers" and lesbians is that they prefer themselves), perhaps black women writers and nonwriters should say, simply, whenever black lesbians are being put down, held up, messed over, and generally told their lives should not be encouraged, *We are all lesbians*. For surely it is better to be thought a lesbian, and to say and write your life exactly as you experience it, than to be a token "pet" black woman for those whose contempt for our autonomous existence makes them a menace to human life.[5]

Walker's support of her Lesbian sisters in real life is not unrelated to her ability to write fiction about Black women who are lovers, as in *The Color Purple*. Her feminist consciousness undoubtedly influenced the positiveness of her portrayal. In contrast, an author like Gayl Jones, who has not been associated with or seemingly influenced by the feminist movement, has portrayed Lesbians quite negatively.[6]

Just as surely as a Black woman writer's relationship to feminism affects the themes she might choose to write about, a Black woman critic's relationship to feminism determines the kind of criticism she is willing and able to do. The fact that critics are usually also academics, however, has often affected Black women critics' approach to feminist issues. If a Black woman scholar's only connection to women's issues is via women's studies, as presented by white women academics, most of whom are not activists, her access to movement analyses and practice will be limited or nonexistent. I believe that the most accurate and developed theory, including literary theory, comes from practice, from the experience of activism. This relationship between theory and practice is crucial when inherently political subject matter, such as the condition of women as depicted in a writer's work, is being discussed. I do not believe it is possible to arrive at fully developed and useful Black feminist criticism by merely reading about feminism. Of course every Black woman has her own experiences of sexual political dynamics and oppression to draw upon, and referring to these experiences should be an important resource in shaping her analyses of a literary work. However, studying feminist texts and drawing only upon one's *individual* experiences of sexism are insufficient.

I remember the point in my own experience when I no longer was involved on a regular basis in organizations such as the Boston Committee to End Sterilization Abuse and the Abortion Action Coalition. I was very aware that my lack of involvement affected my thinking and writing *overall*. Certain perceptions were simply unavailable to me because I no longer was doing that particular kind of ongoing work. And I am referring to missing something much deeper than access to specific information about sterilization and reproductive rights. Activism has spurred me to write the kinds of theory and criticism I have written and has provided the experiences and insights that have shaped the perceptions in my work. Many examples of this vital relationship between activism and theory exist in the work of thinkers such as Ida B. Wells-Barnett, W. E. B. Du Bois, Lillian Smith, Lorraine Hansberry, Frantz Fanon, Barbara Deming, Paolo Freire, and Angela Davis.

A critic's involvement or lack of involvement in activism, specifically in the context of the feminist movement, is often signally revealed by the approach she takes to Lesbianism. If a woman has worked in organizations where Lesbian issues have been raised, where homophobia was unacceptable and struggled with, and where she had the opportunity to meet and work with a variety of Lesbians, her relationship to Lesbians and to her own homophobia would undoubtedly be affected. The types of political organizations in which such dialogue occurs are not, of course, exclusively Lesbian and may focus upon a range of issues, such as women in prison, sterilization abuse, reproductive freedom, health care, domestic violence, and sexual assault.

Black feminist critics who are Lesbians can usually be counted upon to approach Black women's and Black Lesbian writing nonhomophobically. Non-Lesbian Black feminist critics are not as dependable in this regard. I even question at times designating Black women—critics and noncritics alike—as feminists who are actively homophobic in what they write, say, or do, or who are passively homophobic because they ignore Lesbian existence entirely.[7] Yet such critics are obviously capable of analyzing other sexual and political implications of the literature they scrutinize. Political definitions, particularly of feminism, can be difficult to pin down. The one upon which I generally rely states: "Feminism is the political theory and practice that struggles to free *all* women: women of color, working-class women, poor women, disabled women, lesbians, old women—as well as white, economically privileged, heterosexual women. Anything less than this vision of total freedom is not feminism, but merely female self-aggrandizement."[8]

A Black gay college student recently recounted an incident to me that illustrates the kind of consciousness that is grievously lacking among nonfeminist Black women scholars about Black Lesbian existence. His story indicates why a Black feminist approach to literature, criticism, and research in a variety of disciplines is crucial if one is to recognize and understand Black Lesbian experience. While researching a history project, he contacted the archives at a Black institution that has significant holdings on Black women. He spoke to a Black woman archivist and explained that he was looking for materials on Black Lesbians in the 1940s. Her immediate response was to laugh uproariously and then to say that the collection contained very little on women during that period and nothing at all on Lesbians in any of the periods covered by its holdings.

Not only was her reaction appallingly homophobic, not to mention impolite, but it was also inaccurate. One of the major repositories of archival material on Black women in the country of course contains material by and about Black Lesbians. The material, however, is not identified and defined as such and thus remains invisible. This is a classic case of "invisibility [becoming] an unnatural disaster," as feminist poet Mitsuye Yamada observes.[9]

I suggested a number of possible resources to the student and in the course of our conversation I told him I could not help but think of Cheryl Clarke's classic poem, "Of Althea and Flaxie." It begins:

> In 1943 Althea was a welder
> very dark
> very butch
> and very proud
> loved to cook, sew, and drive a car
> and did not care who knew she kept company with a woman.[10]

The poem depicts a realistic and positive Black Lesbian relationship which survives Flaxie's pregnancy in 1955, Althea's going to jail for writing numbers in 1958, poverty, racism, and, of course, homophobia. If the archivist's vision had not been so blocked by homophobia, she would have been able to direct this student to documents that corroborate the history embodied in Clarke's poem.

Being divorced from the experience of feminist organizing not only makes it more likely that a woman has not been directly challenged to examine her homophobia, but it can also result in erroneous approaches to Black Lesbian literature, if she does decide to talk or write about it. For example, some critics, instead of simply accepting that Black Lesbians and Black Lesbian writers exist, view the depiction of Lesbianism as a dangerous and unacceptable "theme" or "trend" in Black women's writing. Negative discussions of "themes" and "trends," which may in time fade, do not acknowledge that for survival, Black Lesbians, like any oppressed group, need to see our faces reflected in myriad cultural forms, including literature. Some critics go so far as to see the few Black Lesbian books in existence as a kind of conspiracy and bemoan that there is "so much" of this kind of writing available in print; they put forth the supreme untruth that it is actually an advantage to be a Black Lesbian writer.

For each Lesbian of color in print there are undoubtedly five dozen whose work has never been published and may never be. The publication of Lesbians of color is a "new" literary development, made possible by alternative, primarily Lesbian/feminist presses. The political and aesthetic strength of this writing is indicated by its impact having been far greater than its actual availability. At times its content has had revolutionary implications. But the impact of Black Lesbian feminist writing, to which Calvin Hernton refers, should not be confused with easy access to print, to readers, or to the material perks that help a writer survive economically.

Terms like "heterophobia," used to validate the specious notion that "so many" Black women writers are now depicting loving and sexual relationships between women, to the exclusion of focusing on relationships with men, arise in an academic vacuum, uninfluenced by political reality. "Heterophobia" resembles the concept of "reverse racism." Both are thoroughly reactionary and have nothing to do with the actual dominance of a heterosexual white power structure.

Equating Lesbianism with separatism is another error in terminology, which will probably take a number of years to correct. The title of a workshop at a major Black women writers' conference, for example, was "Separatist Voices in the New Canon." The workshop examined the work of Audre Lorde and Alice Walker, neither of whom defines herself as a separatist, either sexually or racially.

In his introduction to *Confirmation: An Anthology of African American Women*, co-editor Imamu Baraka is critical of feminists who are separatists, but he does not mention that any such thing as a Lesbian exists. In his ambiguous yet inherently homophobic usage, the term "separatist" is made to seem like a mistaken political tendency, which correct thinking could alter. If "separatist" equals Lesbian, Baraka is suggesting that we should change our minds and eradicate ourselves. In both these instances the fact that Lesbians do not have sexual relationships with men is thought to be the same as ideological Lesbian "separatism." Such an equation does not take into account that the majority of Lesbians of color have interactions with men and that those who are activists are quite likely to be politically committed to coalition work as well.

Inaccuracy and distortion seem to be particularly frequent pitfalls when non-Lesbians address Black Lesbian experience because of generalized homophobia and because the very nature of our oppression may cause us to be hidden or "closeted," voluntarily or involuntarily isolated from other communities, and as a result unseen and unknown. In her essay, "A Cultural Legacy Denied and Discovered: Black Lesbians in Fiction by Women," Jewelle Gomez asserts the necessity for realistic portrayals of Black Lesbians:

> These Black Lesbian writers . . . have seen into the shadows that hide the existence of Black Lesbians and understand they have to create a universe/home that rings true on all levels. . . . The Black Lesbian writer must throw herself into the arms of her culture by acting as student/teacher/participant/observer, absorbing and synthesizing the meanings of our existence as a people. She must do this despite the fact that both our culture and our sexuality have been severely truncated and distorted.
>
> Nature abhors a vacuum and there is a distinct gap in the picture where the Black Lesbian should be. The Black Lesbian writer must recreate our home, unadulterated, unsanitized, specific and not isolated from the generations that have nurtured us.[11]

This is an excellent statement of what usually has been missing from portrayals of Black Lesbians in fiction. The degree of truthfulness and self-revelation that Gomez calls for encompasses the essential qualities of verisimilitude and authenticity that I look for in depictions of Black Lesbians. By verisimilitude I mean how true to life and realistic a work of literature is. By authenticity I mean something even deeper—a characterization which reflects a relationship to self that is genuine, integrated, and whole. For a Lesbian or a gay man, this kind of emotional and psychological authenticity virtually requires the degree of self-acceptance inherent in being out. This is not a dictum, but an observation. It is not a coincidence, however, that the most vital and useful Black Lesbian feminist writing is being written by Black Lesbians who are not caught in the impossible bind of simultaneously hiding identity yet revealing self through their writing.

Positive and realistic portrayals of Black Lesbians are sorely needed, portraits that are, as Gomez states, "unadulterated, unsanitized, specific." By positive I do not mean characters without problems, contradictions, or flaws, mere uplift literature for Lesbians, but instead, writing that is sufficiently sensitive and complex, which places Black Lesbian experience and struggles squarely within the realm of recognizable human experience and concerns.

As African-Americans, our desire for authentic literary images of Black Lesbians has particular cultural and historical resonance, since a desire for authentic images of ourselves as Black people preceded it long ago. After an initial period of racial uplift literature in the nineteenth and early twentieth centuries, Black artists during the Harlem Renaissance of the 1920s began to assert the validity of fully Black portrayals in all art forms including literature. In his pivotal essay of 1926, "The Negro Artist and the Racial Mountain," Langston Hughes asserted:

> We younger Negro artists who create now intend to express our individual dark-skinned selves without fear or shame. If white people are pleased we are glad. If they are not, it doesn't matter. We know we are beautiful. And ugly too. The tom-tom cries and the tom-tom laughs. If colored people are pleased we are glad. If they are not, their displeasure doesn't matter either. We build our temples for tomorrow, strong as we know how, and we stand on top of the mountain, free within ourselves.[12]

Clearly, it was not always popular or safe with either Black or white audiences to depict Black people as we actually are. It still is not. Too many contemporary Blacks seem to have forgotten the universally debased social-political position Black people have occupied during all the centuries we have been here, up until perhaps the Civil Rights Movement of the 1960s. The most racist definition of Black people has been that we were not human.

Undoubtedly every epithet now hurled at Lesbians and gay men—"sinful," "sexually depraved," "criminal," "emotionally maladjusted," "deviant"—has also been applied to Black People. When W. E. B. Du Bois described life "behind the veil," and Paul Laurence Dunbar wrote,

> We wear the mask that grins and lies,
> It hides our cheeks and shades our eyes,—
> This debt we pay to human guile;
> With torn and bleeding hearts we smile,
> And mouth with myriad subtleties.
>
> Why should the world be overwise,
> In counting all our tears and sighs?
> Nay, let them only see us, while
> We wear the mask.[13]

what were they describing but racial closeting? For those who refuse to see the parallels because they view Blackness as irreproachably normal, but persist in defining same-sex love relationships as unnatural, Black Lesbian feminist poet, Audre Lorde, reminds us: "'Oh,' says a voice from the Black community, 'but being Black is NORMAL!' Well, I and many Black people of my age can remember grimly the days when it didn't used to be!"[14] Lorde is not implying that she believes that there was ever anything wrong with being Black, but points out how distorted "majority" consciousness can cruelly affect an oppressed community's actual treatment and sense of self. The history of slavery, segregation, and racism was based upon the assumption by the powers-that-be that Blackness was decidedly neither acceptable nor normal. Unfortunately, despite legal and social change, large numbers of racist whites still believe the same thing to this day.

The existence of Lesbianism and male homosexuality is normal, too, traceable throughout history and across cultures. It is a society's *response* to the ongoing historical fact of homosexuality that determines whether it goes unremarked as nothing out of the ordinary, as it is in some cultures, or if it is instead greeted with violent repression, as it is in ours. At a time when Acquired Immune Deficiency Syndrome (AIDS), a disease associated with an already despised sexual minority, is occasioning mass hysteria among the heterosexual majority (including calls for firings, evictions, quarantining, imprisonment, and even execution), the way in which sexual orientation is viewed is not of mere academic concern. It is mass political organizing that has wrought the most significant changes in the status of Blacks and other people of color and that has altered society's perceptions about us and our images of ourselves. The Black Lesbian feminist movement simply continues that principled tradition of struggle.

A Black woman author's relationship to the politics of Black Lesbian feminism affects how she portrays Black Lesbian characters in fiction. In 1977, in *Toward a Black Feminist Criticism*, I had to rely upon Toni Morrison's *Sula* (1974), which did not explicitly portray a Lesbian relationship, in order to analyze a Black woman's novel with a woman-identified theme. I sought to demonstrate, however, that because of the emotional primacy of Sula and Nel's love for each other, Sula's fierce independence, and the author's critical portrayal of heterosexuality, the novel could be illuminated by a Lesbian feminist reading. Here I will focus upon three more recent works—*The Women of Brewster Place*, *The Color Purple*, and *Zami: A New Spelling of My Name*—which actually portray Black Lesbians, but which do so with varying degrees of verisimilitude and authenticity, dependent upon the author's relationship to and understanding of the politics of Black Lesbian experience.

Gloria Naylor's *The Women of Brewster Place* (1983) is a novel composed of seven connecting stories. In beautifully resonant language Naylor makes strong sexual political statements about the lives of working poor and working-class Black women and does not hesitate to explore the often problematic nature of their relationships with Black men—lovers, husbands, fathers, sons. Loving and supportive bonds between Black women are central to her characters' survival. However, Naylor's portrayal of a Lesbian relationship in the sixth story, "The Two," runs counter to the positive framework of women bonding she has previously established. In the context of this novel a Lesbian relationship might well embody the culmination of women's capacity to love and be committed to each other. Yet both Lesbian characters are ultimately victims. Although Naylor portrays the community's homophobia toward the lovers as unacceptable, the fate that she designs for the two women is the most brutal and negative of any in the book.

Theresa is a strong-willed individualist, while her lover Lorraine passively yearns for social acceptability. Despite their professional jobs, they have moved to a dead-end slum block because of Lorraine's fears that the residents of their two other middle-class neighborhoods suspected that they were Lesbians. It does not take long for suspicions to arise on Brewster Place, and the two women's differing reactions to the inevitable homophobia they face is a major tension in the work. Theresa accepts the fact that she is an outsider because of her Lesbianism. She does not like being ostracized, but she faces others' opinions with an attitude of defiance. In contrast, Lorraine is obsessed with garnering societal approval and would like nothing more than to blend into the straight world, despite her Lesbianism. Lorraine befriends Ben, the alcoholic building superintendent, because he is the one person on the block who does not reject her. The fact that Ben has lost his daughter and Lorraine has lost her father, because he refused to accept her Lesbianism, cements their friendship. Naylor writes:

> "When I'm with Ben, I don't feel any different from anybody else in the world."
>
> "Then he's doing you an injustice," Theresa snapped, "because we are different. And the sooner you learn that, the better off you'll be."
>
> "See, there you go again. Tee the teacher and Lorraine the student, who just can't get the lesson right. Lorraine who just wants to be a human being—a lousy human being who's somebody's daughter or somebody's friend or even somebody's enemy. But they make me feel like a freak out there, and you try to make me feel like one in here. That only place I've found some peace, Tee, is in that damp ugly basement, where I'm not different."
>
> "Lorraine." Theresa shook her head slowly. "You're a lesbian—do you understand that word?—a butch, a dyke, a lesbo, all those things that kid was shouting. Yes, I heard him! And you can run in all the basements in the world, and it won't change that, so why don't you accept it?"
>
> "I have accepted it!" Lorraine shouted. "I've accepted it all my life, and it's nothing I'm ashamed of. I lost a father because I refused to be ashamed of it—but it doesn't make me any *different* from anyone else in the world."
>
> "It makes you damned different!"
> . . . .
> "That's right! There go your precious 'theys' again. They wouldn't understand—not in Detroit, not on Brewster Place, not anywhere! And as long as they own the whole damn world, it's them and us, Sister—them and us. And that spells different!" [15]

Many a Lesbian relationship has been threatened or destroyed because of how very differently lovers may view their Lesbianism, for example, how out or closeted one or the other is willing to be. Naylor's discussion of difference represents a pressing Lesbian concern. As Lorraine and Theresa's argument shows, there are complicated elements of truth in both their positions. Lesbians and gay men are objectively different in our sexual orientations from heterosexuals. The society raises sanctions against our sexuality that range from inconvenient to violent, and that render our social status and life experiences different. On the other hand we would like to be recognized and treated as human, to have the basic rights enjoyed by heterosexuals, and, if the society cannot manage to support how we love, to at least leave us alone.

In "The Two," however, Naylor sets up the women's response to their identity as an either/or dichotomy. Lorraine's desire for acceptance, although completely comprehensible, is based upon assimilation and denial, while Naylor depicts Theresa's healthier defiance as an individual stance. In the clearest statement of resistance in the story, Theresa thinks: "If they practiced that way with each other, then they could turn back to back and beat the hell out of the world for trying to invade their territory. But she had found no such sparring partner in Lorraine, and the strain of fighting alone was beginning to show on her." (p. 136) A mediating position between complete assimilation or alienation might well evolve from some sense of connection to a Lesbian/gay community. Involvement with other Lesbians and gay men could provide a reference point and support that would help diffuse some of the straight world's power. Naylor mentions that Theresa socializes with gay men and perhaps Lesbians at a bar, but her interactions with them occur outside the action of the story. The author's decision not to portray other Lesbians and gay men, but only to allude to them, is a significant one. The reader is never given an opportunity to view Theresa or Lorraine in a context in which they are the norm. Naylor instead presents them as "the two" exceptions in an entirely heterosexual world. Both women are extremely isolated and although their relationship is loving, it also feels claustrophobic. Naylor writes:

> Lorraine wanted to be liked by the people around her. She couldn't live the way Tee did, with her head stuck in a book all the time. Tee didn't seem to need anyone. Lorraine often wondered if she even needed her. . . .
> . . . She never wanted to bother with anyone except those weirdos at the club she went to, and Lorraine hated them. They were coarse and bitter, and made fun of people who weren't like them. Well, she wasn't like them either. Why should she feel different from the people she lived around? Black people were all in the same boat—she'd come to realize this even more since they had moved to Brewster—and if they didn't row together, they would sink together. (p. 142)

Lorraine's rejection of other Lesbians and gay men is excruciating, as is the self-hatred that obviously prompts it. It is painfully ironic that she considers herself in the same boat with Black people in the story, who are heterosexual, most of whom ostracize her, but not with Black people who are Lesbian and gay. The one time that Lorraine actually decides to go to the club by herself, ignoring Theresa's warning that she won't have a good time without her, is the night that she is literally destroyed.

Perhaps the most positive element in "The Two" is how accurately Naylor depicts and subtly condemns Black homophobia. Sophie, a neighbor who lives across the airshaft from Lorraine and Theresa, is the "willing carrier" of the rumor about them, though not necessarily its initiator. Naylor writes:

> Sophie had plenty to report that day. Ben had said it was terrible in there. No, she didn't know exactly what he had seen, but you can imagine—and they did. Confronted with the difference that had been thrust into their predictable world, they reached into their imaginations and, using an ancient pattern, weaved themselves a reason for its existence. Out of necessity they stitched all of their secret fears and lingering childhood nightmares into this existence, because even though it was deceptive enough to try and look as they looked, talk as they talked, and do as they did, it had to have some hidden stain to invalidate it—it was impossible for them both to be right. So they leaned back, supported by the sheer weight of their numbers and comforted by the woven barrier that kept them protected from the yellow mist that enshrouded the two as they came and went on Brewster Place. (p. 132)

The fact of difference can be particularly volatile among people whose options are severely limited by racial, class, and sexual oppression, people who are already outsiders themselves.

A conversation between Mattie Michaels, an older Black woman who functions as the work's ethical and spiritual center, and her lifelong friend, Etta, further prods readers to examine their own attitudes about loving women. Etta explains:

> "Yeah, but it's different with them."
>
> "Different how?"
>
> "Well . . ." Etta was beginning to feel uncomfortable. "They love each other like you'd love a man or a man would love you—I guess."
>
> "But I've loved some women deeper than I ever loved any man," Mattie was pondering. "And there been some women who loved me more and did more for me than any man ever did."
>
> "Yeah." Etta thought for a moment. "I can second that but it's still different, Mattie. I can't exactly put my finger on it, but . . ."
>
> "Maybe it's not so different," Mattie said, almost to herself. "Maybe that's why some women get so riled up about it, 'cause they know deep down it's not so different after all." She looked at Etta. "It kinda gives you a funny feeling when you think about it that way, though."
>
> "Yeah, it does," Etta said, unable to meet Mattie's eyes. (pp. 140–41)

Whatever their opinions, it is not the women of the neighborhood who are directly responsible for Lorraine's destruction, but six actively homophobic and woman-hating teenage boys. Earlier that day Lorraine and Kiswana Browne had encountered the toughs who unleashed their sexist and homophobic violence on the two young women. Kiswana verbally bests their leader, C. C. Baker, but he is dissuaded from physically retaliating because one of the other boys reminds him: "That's Abshu's woman, and that big dude don't mind kickin' ass" (p. 163). As a Lesbian, Lorraine does not have any kind of "dude" to stand between her and the violence of other men. Although she is completely silent during the encounter, C. C.'s parting words to her are, "I'm gonna remember this, Butch!" That night when Lorraine reurns from the bar alone, she walks into the alley which is the boys' turf. They are waiting for her and gang-rape her in one of the most devastating scenes in literature. Naylor describes the aftermath:

> Lorraine lay pushed up against the wall on the cold ground with her eyes staring straight up into the sky. When the sun began to warm the air and the horizon brightened, she still lay there, her mouth crammed with paper bag, her dress pushed up under her breasts, her bloody pantyhose hanging from her thighs. She would have stayed there forever and have simply died from starvation or exposure if nothing around her had moved. (p. 171)

She glimpses Ben sitting on a garbage can at the other end of the alley sipping wine. In a bizarre twist of an ending Lorraine crawls through the alley and mauls him with a brick she happens to find as she makes her way toward him. Lorraine's supplicating cries of "'Please. Please.' . . . the only word she was fated to utter again and again for the rest of her life" conclude the story (pp. 171, 173).

I began thinking about "The Two" because of a conversation I had with another Black Lesbian who seldom comes in contact with other Lesbians and who has not been active in the feminist movement. Unlike other women with whom I had discussed the work, she was not angry, disappointed, or disturbed by it, but instead thought it was an effective portrayal of Lesbians and homophobia. I was taken aback because I had found Naylor's depiction of our lives so completely demoralizing and not particularly realistic. I thought about another friend who told me she found the story so upsetting she was never able to finish it. And of another who had actually rewritten the ending so that Mattie hears Lorraine's screams before she is raped and saves her. In this "revised version," Theresa is an undercover cop, who also hears her lover's screams, comes into the alley with a gun, and blows the boys away. I was so mystified and intrigued by the first woman's defense of Naylor's perspective that I went back to examine the work.

According to the criteria I have suggested, although the Lesbian characters in "The Two" lack authenticity, the story possesses a certain level of verisimilitude. The generalized homophobia that the women face, which culminates in retaliatory rape and near murderous decimation, is quite true to life. Gay and Lesbian newspapers provide weekly accounts, which sometimes surface in the mainstream media, of the constant violence leveled at members of our communities. What feels disturbing and inauthentic to me is how utterly hopeless Naylor's view of Lesbian existence is. Lorraine and Theresa are classically unhappy homosexuals of the type who populated white literature during a much earlier era, when the only options for the "deviant" were isolation, loneliness, mental illness, suicide, or death.

In her second novel, *Linden Hills* (1985), Naylor indicates that Black gay men's options are equally grim. In a review of the work, Jewelle Gomez writes:

> One character disavows a liaison with his male lover in order to marry the appropriate woman and inherit the coveted Linden Hills home. . . . We receive so little personal information about him that his motivations are obscure. For a middle-class, educated gay man to be blind to alternative lifestyles in 1985 is not inconceivable but it's still hard to accept the melodrama of his arranged marriage without screaming "dump the girl and buy a ticket to Grand Rapids!" Naylor's earlier novel [*The Women of Brewster Place*] presented a similar limitation. While she admirably attempts to portray black gays as integral to the fabric of black life she seems incapable of imagining black gays functioning as healthy, average people. In her fiction, although they are not at fault, gays must still be made to pay. This makes her books sound like a return to the forties, not a chronicle of the eighties.[16]

Gomez's response speaks to the problems that many Lesbian feminists have with Naylor's versions of our lives, her persistent message that survival is hardly possible. I do not think we simply want "happy endings," although some do occur for Lesbians both in literature and in life, but an indication of the spirit of survival and resistance which has made the continuance of Black Lesbian and gay life possible throughout the ages.

In considering the overall impact of "The Two," I realized that because it is critical of homophobia, it is perhaps an effective story for a heterosexual audience. But because its portrayal of Lesbianism is so negative, its message even to heterosexuals is ambiguous. A semi-sympathetic straight reader's response might well be: "It's a shame something like that had to happen, but I guess that's what you get for being queer." The general public does not want to know that it is possible to be a Lesbian of whatever color and not merely survive, but thrive. And neither does a heterosexual publishing industry want to provide them with this information.

The impact of the story upon Lesbian readers is quite another matter. I imagine what might happen if a Black woman who is grappling with defining her sexuality and who has never had the opportunity to read anything else about Lesbians, particularly Black ones, were to read "The Two" as a severely cautionary tale. Justifiably, she might go no further in her exploration, forever denying her feelings. She might eventually have sexual relationships with other women, but remain extremely closeted. Or she might commit suicide. As a Black Lesbian reader, I find Naylor's dire pessimism about our possibilities to be the crux of my problems with "The Two."

Alice Walker's portrayal of a Lesbian relationship in her novel *The Color Purple* (1982) is as optimistic as Naylor's is despairing. Celie and Shug's love, placed at the center of the work and set in a rural southern community between the World Wars, is unique in the history of African-American fiction. The fact that a book with a Black Lesbian theme by a Black woman writer achieved massive critical acclaim, became a bestseller, and was made into a major Hollywood film is unprecedented in the history of the world. It is *The Color Purple* which homophobes and antifeminists undoubtedly refer to when they talk about how "many" books currently have both Black Lesbian subject matter and an unsparing critique of misogyny in the Black community. For Black Lesbians, however, especially writers, the book has been inspirational. Reading it we think it just may be possible to be a Black Lesbian and live to tell about it. It may be possible for us to write it down and actually have somebody read it as well.

When I first read *The Color Purple* in galleys in the spring of 1982, I believed it was a classic. I become more convinced every time I read it. Besides great storytelling, perfect Black language, killingly subtle Black women's humor, and an unequivocal Black feminist stance, it is also a deeply philosophical and spiritual work. It is marvelously gratifying to read discussions of nature, love, beauty, God, good, evil, and the meaning of life in the language of our people. The book is like a jewel. Any way you hold it to the light you will always see something new reflected.

The facet of the novel under consideration here is Walker's approach to Lesbianism, but before going further with that discussion, it is helpful to understand that the work is also a fable. The complex simplicity with which Walker tells her story, the archetypal and timeless Black southern world in which it is set, the clear-cut conflicts between good and evil, the complete transformations undergone by several of the major characters, and the huge capacity of the book to teach are all signs that *The Color Purple* is not merely a novel, but a visionary tale. That it is a fable may account partially for the depiction of a Lesbian relationship unencumbered by homophobia or fear of it and entirely lacking in self-scrutiny about the implications of Lesbian identity.

It may be Walker's conscious decision to deal with her readers' potentially negative reactions by using the disarming strategy of writing as if women falling in love with each other were quite ordinary, an average occurrence which does

not even need to be specifically remarked. In the "real world" the complete ease
with which Celie and Shug move as lovers through a totally heterosexual milieu
would be improbable, not to say amazing. Their total acceptance is one clue that
this is indeed an inspiring fable, a picture of what the world could be if only
human beings were ready to create it. A friend told me about a discussion of the
book in a Black writers' workshop she conducted. An older Black woman in the
class asserted: "When that kind of business happens, like happened between
Shug and Celie, you know there's going to be talk." The woman was not reacting
to *Purple* as a fable or even as fiction, but as a "real" story, applying her knowledge of what would undoubtedly happen in real life where most people just
aren't ready to deal with Lesbianism and don't want to be.

Because the novel is so truthful, particularly in its descriptions of sexual oppression and to a lesser extent racism, the reader understandably might question
those aspects of the fable which are not as plausible. Even within the story itself,
it is conceivable that a creature as mean-spirited as Mr. —— might have something to say about Shug, the love of his life, and Celie, his wife, sleeping together in his own house. For those of us who experience homophobia on a daily
basis and who often live in fear of being discovered by the wrong person(s), like
the teenage thugs in "The Two," we naturally wonder how Celie and Shug, who
do not hide their relationship, get away with it.

Another fabulous aspect of Celie's and Shug's relationship is that there are no
references to how they think about themselves as Lesbian lovers in a situation
where they are the only ones. Although Celie is clearly depicted as a woman who
at the very least is not attracted to men and who is generally repulsed by them, I
am somewhat hesitant to designate her as a Lesbian because it is not a term that
she would likely apply to herself and neither, obviously, would the people
around her. In a conversation with Mr. —— in the latter part of the book Celie
explains how she feels:

> He say, Celie, tell me the truth. You don't like me cause I'm a man?
> I blow my nose. Take off they pants, I say, and men look like frogs to me.
> No matter how you kiss 'em, as far as I'm concern, frogs is what they stay.
> I see, he say.[17]

Shug, on the other hand, is bisexual, another contemporary term that does not
necessarily apply within the cultural and social context Walker has established.
There is the implication that this is among her first, if not only sexual relationship with another woman. The first and only time within the novel when Shug
and Celie make love, Walker writes:

> She say, I love you, Miss Celie. And then she haul off and kiss me on the
> mouth.
> *Um*, she say, like she surprise. I kiss her back, say, *um*, too. Us kiss and
> kiss till us can't hardly kiss no more. Then us touch each other.
> I don't know nothing bout it, I say to Shug.
> I don't know much, she say. (p. 109)

Despite her statement of inexperience, Shug is a wonderfully sensual and attractive woman who takes pleasure in all aspects of living from noticing "the

color purple in a field" to making love with whomever. When Shug tries to explain to Celie why she has taken up with a nineteen-year-old boy, the two women's differing perspectives and sexual orientations are obvious. Walker writes:

> But Celie, she say. I have to make you understand. Look, she say. I'm gitting old. I'm fat. Nobody think I'm good looking no more, but you. Or so I thought. He's nineteen. A baby. How long can it last?
> He's a man. I write on the paper.
> Yah, she say. He is. And I know how you feel about men. But I don't feel that way. I would never be fool enough to take any of them seriously, she say, but some mens can be a lots of fun.
> Spare me, I write. (p. 220)

Eventually Shug comes back to Celie and Walker implies that they will live out their later years together. The recouplings and reunions that occur in the novel might also indicate that the story is more fantasy than fact. But in Celie and Shug's case, the longevity of their relationship is certainly a validation of love between women.

The day Shug returns, Celie shows her her new bedroom. Walker writes:

> She go right to the little purple frog on my mantelpiece.
> What this? she ast.
> Oh, I say, a little something Albert carve for me. (p. 248)

Not only is this wickedly amusing after Celie and Mr. ——'s discussion about "frogs," but Mr. ——'s tolerance at being described as such to the point of his making a joke-gift for Celie seems almost too good to be true. Indeed Mr. ——'s transformation from evil no-count to a sensitive human being is one of the most miraculous one could find anywhere. Those critics and readers who condemn the work because they find the depiction of men so "negative" never seem to focus on how nicely most of them turn out in the end. Perhaps these transformations go unnoticed because in Walker's woman-centered world, in order to change, they must relinquish machismo and violence, the very thought of which would be fundamentally disruptive to the nonfeminist reader's world-view. It is no accident that Walker has Celie, who has become a professional seamstress and designer of pants, teach Mr. —— to sew, an ideal way to symbolize just how far he has come. In the real world, where former husbands of Lesbian mothers take their children away with the support of the patriarchal legal system, and in some cases beat or even murder their former wives, very few men would say what Mr. —— says to Celie about Shug: "I'm real sorry she left you, Celie. I remembered how I felt when she left me" (p. 238). But in the world of *The Color Purple* a great deal is possible.

One of the most beautiful and familiar aspects of the novel is the essential and supportive bonds between Black women. The only other person Celie loves before she meets Shug is her long-lost sister, Nettie. Although neither ever gets an answer, the letters they write to each other for decades and Celie's letters to God before she discovers that Nettie is alive, comprise the entire novel. The work joyously culminates when Nettie, accompanied by Celie's children who were taken away from her in infancy, return home.

Early in the novel Celie "sins against" another woman's spirit and painfully bears the consequences. She tells her stepson, Harpo, to beat his wife Sofia if she doesn't mind him. Soon Celie is so upset about what she has done that she is unable to sleep at night. Sofia, one of the most exquisitely defiant characters in Black women's fiction, fights Harpo right back and when she finds out Celie's part in Harpo's changed behavior comes to confront her. When Celie confesses that she advised Harpo to beat Sofia because she was jealous of Sofia's ability to stand up for herself, the weight is lifted from her soul, the women become fast friends, and she "sleeps like a baby."

When Shug decides that Celie needs to leave Mr. —— and go with her to Memphis, accompanied by Mary Agnes (Squeak), Harpo's lover of many years, they make the announcement at a family dinner. Walker writes:

> You was all rotten children, I say. You made my life a hell on earth. And your daddy here ain't dead horse's shit.
>
> Mr. —— reach over to slap me. I jab my case knife in his hand.
>
> You bitch, he say. What will people say, you running off to Memphis like you don't have a house to look after?
>
> Shug say, Albert. Try to think like you got some sense. Why any woman give a shit what people think is a mystery to me.
>
> Well, say Grady, trying to bring light. A woman can't get a man if peoples talk.
>
> Shug look at me and us giggle. Then us laugh sure nuff. Then Squeak start to laugh. Then Sofia. All us laugh and laugh.
>
> Shug say, Ain't they something? Us say um *hum*, and slap the table, wipe the water from our eyes.
>
> Harpo look at Squeak. Shut up Squeak, he say. It bad luck for women to laugh at men.
>
> She say, Okay. She sit up straight, suck in her breath, try to press her face together.
>
> He look at Sofia. She look at him and laugh in his face. I already had my bad luck, she say. I had enough to keep me laughing the rest of my life. (p. 182)

This marvelously hilarious scene is one of countless examples in the novel of Black women's staunch solidarity. As in *The Women of Brewster Place*, women's caring for each other makes life possible; but in *The Color Purple* Celie and Shug's relationship is accepted as an integral part of the continuum of women loving each other, while in the more realistic work, Lorraine and Theresa are portrayed as social pariahs.

If one accepts that *The Color Purple* is a fable or at the very least has fablelike elements, judgments of verisimilitude and authenticity are necessarily affected. Celie and Shug are undeniably authentic as Black women characters—complex, solid, and whole—but they are not necessarily authentic as Lesbians. Their lack of self-consciousness as Lesbians, the lack of scrutiny their relationship receives from the outside world, and their isolation from other Lesbians make *The Color Purple*'s categorization as a Lesbian novel problematic. It does not appear that it was Walker's intent to create a work that could be definitively or solely categorized as such.

The question of categorization becomes even more interesting when one examines critical responses to the work, particularly in the popular media. Reviews seldom mention that Celie and Shug are lovers. Some critics even go so far as to describe them erroneously as good friends. The fact that their relationship is simply "there" in the novel and not explicitly called attention to as Lesbian might also account for a mass heterosexual audience's capacity to accept the work, although the novel has of course also been homophobically attacked.[18] As a Black Lesbian feminist reader, I have questions about how accurate it is to identify Walker's characters as Lesbians at the same time that I am moved by the vision of a world, unlike this one, where Black women are not forced to lose their families, their community, or their lives, because of whom they love.

A realistic depiction of African American Lesbian experience would neither be a complete idyll nor a total nightmare. Audre Lorde terms *Zami: A New Spelling of My Name* (1982) a "biomythography," a combination of autobiography, history, and myth. I have chosen to discuss it here, because it is the one extended prose work of which I am aware that approaches Black Lesbian experience with *both* verisimilitude and authenticity. *Zami* is an essentially autobiographical work, but the poet's eye, ear, and tongue give the work stylistic richness often associated with well-crafted fiction. At least two other Black women critics, Barbara Christian and Jewelle Gomez, have included *Zami* in their analyses of Black Lesbians in fiction.[19] Because *Zami* spans genres and carves out a unique place in African-American literature as the first full-length autobiographical work by an established Black Lesbian writer, it will undoubtedly continue to be grouped with other creative prose about Black Lesbians.

The fact that *Zami* is autobiographical might be assumed to guarantee its realism. But even when writing autobiographically, an author can pick and choose details, can create a persona that has little or nothing to do with her own particular reality, or she might fabricate an artificial persona with whom the reader cannot possibly identify. A blatant example of this kind of deceptive strategy might be an autobiographical work by a Lesbian that fails to mention that this is indeed who she is; of course there are other less extreme omissions and distortions. Undoubtedly, Lorde has selected the material she includes in the work, and the selectivity of memory is also operative. Yet this work is honest, fully rounded, and authentic. It is not coincidental that of the three works considered here, *Zami* has the most to tell the reader about the texture of Black Lesbian experience and that it is written by an out Black Lesbian feminist. The candor and specificity with which Lorde approaches her life are qualities that would enhance Black Lesbian writing in the future.

Zami is a Carriacou word "for women who work together as friends and lovers."[20] Just as the title implies, *Zami* is woman-identified from the outset and thoroughly suffused with an eroticism focusing on women. Lorde connects her Lesbianism to the model her mother, Linda, provided—her pervasive, often intimidating, strength; her fleeting sensuality when her harsh veneer was lifted—and also to her place of origin, the Grenadian island of Carriacou, where a word already existed to describe who Linda's daughter would become. As in the two novels *The Color Purple* and *The Women of Brewster Place*, in *Zami* relationships between women are at the center of the work. Here they are complex, turbulent, painful, passionate, and essential to the author's survival.

Although Lorde continuously explores the implications of being a Black Lesbian and she has an overt consciousness about her Lesbianism which is missing from Naylor's and Walker's works, she does not define Lesbianism as a problem in and of itself. Despite homophobia, particularly in the left of the McCarthy era; despite isolation from other Black women because she is gay; and despite primal loneliness because of her many levels of difference, Lorde assumes that her Lesbianism, like her Blackness, is a given, a fact of life which she has neither to justify nor explain. This is an extremely strong and open-ended stance from which to write about Black Lesbian experience, since it enables the writer to deal with the complexity of Lesbianism and what being a Black Lesbian means in a specific time and place. Lorde's position allows Black Lesbian experience to be revealed from the inside out. The absence of agonized doubts about her sexual orientation and the revelation of the actual joys of being a Lesbian, including lush and recognizable descriptions of physical passion between women, make *Zami* seem consciously written for a Lesbian reader. This is a significant point because so little is ever written with us in mind, and also because who an author considers her audience to be definitely affects her voice and the levels of authenticity she may be able to achieve. Writing from an avowedly Black Lesbian perspective with Black Lesbian readers in mind does not mean that a work will be inaccessible or inapplicable to non-Black and non-Lesbian readers. Works like *Zami*, which are based in the experiences of writers outside the "mainstream," provide a vitally different perspective on human experience and may even reveal new ways of thinking about supposedly settled questions. Or, as Celie puts it in *The Color Purple:* "If he [God] ever listened to poor colored women the world would be a different place, I can tell you" (p. 175). It would be more different still if "he" also listened to Lesbians.

The fact that *Zami* is written from an unequivocally Black Lesbian and feminist perspective undoubtedly explains why it is the one book of the three under discussion that is published by an alternative press, why it was turned down by at least a dozen trade publishers, including one that specializes in gay titles. The white male editor at that supposedly sympathetic house returned the manuscript saying, "If only you were just one," Black or Lesbian. The combination is obviously too much for the trade publishing establishment to handle. We bring news that others do not want to hear. It is unfortunate that the vast majority of the readers of *The Women of Brewster Place* and *The Color Purple* will never have the opportunity to read *Zami*.

Lorde's description of Black "gay-girl" life in the Greenwich Village of the 1950s is fascinating, if for no other reason than that it reveals a piece of our cultural history. What is even more intriguing is her political activist's sense of how the struggles of women during that era helped shape our contemporary movement and how many of our current issues, especially the desire to build a Black Lesbian community, were very much a concern at that time. The author's search for other Black Lesbians and her lovingly detailed descriptions of the fragments of community she finds give this work an atmosphere of reality missing in "The Two" and *The Color Purple*. Unlike Lorraine and Theresa and Celie and Shug, Lorde is achingly aware of her need for peers. She writes:

> I remember how being young and Black and gay and lonely felt. A lot of it was fine, feeling I had the truth and the light and the key, but a lot if it was purely hell.

> There were no mothers, no sisters, no heroes. We had to do it alone, like our sister Amazons, the riders on the loneliest outposts of the kingdom of Dahomey. . . . There were not enough of us. But we surely tried. (pp. 176–177)

> Every Black Woman I ever met in the Village in those years had some part in my survival, large or small, if only as a figure in the head-count at the Bag on a Friday night.
> Black lesbians in the Bagatelle faced a world only slightly less hostile than the outer world which we had to deal with every day on the outside—that world which defined us as doubly nothing because we were Black and because we were Woman—that world which raised our blood pressures and shaped our furies and our nightmares. . . . All of us who survived those common years have to be a little proud. A lot proud. Keeping ourselves together and on our own tracks, however wobbly, was like trying to play the Dinizulu War Chant or a Beethoven sonata on a tin dog-whistle. (p. 225)

The humor, tenacity, and vulnerability which Lorde brings to her version of being in "the life" are very precious. Here is something to grab hold of, a place to see one's face reflected. Despite the daily grind of racism, homophobia, sexual, and class oppression, compounded by the nonsolutions of alcohol, drugs, suicide, and death at an early age, some women did indeed make it.

Lorde also describes the much more frequent interactions and support available from white Lesbians who were in the numerical majority. Just as they are now, relationships between Black and white women in the 1950s were often undermined by racism, but Lorde documents that some women were at least attempting to deal with their differences. She writes:

> However imperfectly, we tried to build a community of sorts where we could, at the very least, survive within a world we correctly perceived to be hostile to us; we talked endlessly about how best to create that mutual support which twenty years later was being discussed in the women's movement as a brand new concept. Lesbians were probably the only Black and white women in New York City in the fifties who were making any real attempt to communicate with each other; we learned lessons from each other, the values of which were not lessened by what we did not learn. (p. 179)

Lorde approaches the meaning of difference from numerous vantage points in *Zami*. In much of her work prior to *Zami* she has articulated and developed the concept of difference which has gained usage in the women's movement as a whole and in the writing of women of color specifically. From her early childhood, long before she recognizes herself as a Lesbian, the question of difference is *Zami*'s subtext, its ever-present theme. Lorde writes: *"It was in high school that I came to believe that I was different from my white classmates, not because I was Black, but because I was me"* (p. 82). Although Lorde comes of age in an era when little if any tolerance existed for those who did not conform to white male hegemony, her stance and that of her friends is one of rebellion and creative resistance, including political activism, as opposed to conformity and victimization. *Zami* mediates the versions of Lesbianism presented in *The Women of Brewster Place* and

The Color Purple. It is not a horror story, although it reveals the difficulties of Black Lesbian experience. It is not a fable, although it reveals the joys of a life committed to women.

Since much of her quest in *Zami* is to connect with women who recognize and share her differences, particularly other Black Lesbians, it seems fitting that the work closes with her account of a loving relationship with another Black woman, Afrekete. Several years before the two women become lovers, Lorde meets Kitty at a Black Lesbian house party in Queens. Lorde writes:

> One of the women I had met at one of these parties was Kitty.
>
> When I saw Kitty again one night years later in the Swing Rendezvous or the Pony Stable or the Page Three—that tour of second-string gay-girl bars that I had taken to making alone that sad lonely spring of 1957—it was easy to recall the St. Alban's smell of green Queens summer-night and plastic couch-covers and liquor and hair oil and women's bodies at the party where we had first met.
>
> In that brick-faced frame house in Queens, the downstairs pine-paneled recreation room was alive and pulsing with loud music, good food, and beautiful Black women in all different combinations of dress. (p. 241)

The women wear fifties dyke-chic, ranging from "skinny straight skirts" to Bermuda and Jamaica shorts. Just as the clothes, the smells, the song lyrics, and food linger in the author's mind, her fully rendered details of Black Lesbian culture resonate within the reader. I recalled this party scene while attending a dinner party at the home of two Black Lesbians in the deep South earlier this year. One of the hostesses arrived dressed impeccably in white Bermuda shorts, black knee-socks, and loafers. Her hair straightened, 1980s style much like that of the 1950s, completed my sense of déjà vu. Contemporary Black Lesbians are a part of a cultural tradition which we are just beginning to discover through interviews with older women such as Mabel Hampton and the writing of authors like Ann Allen Shockley, Anita Cornwell, Pat Parker, and Lorde.

When she meets Afrekete again, their relationship helps to counteract Lorde's loneliness following the break-up of a long-term relationship with a white woman. The bond between the women is stunningly erotic, enriched by the bond they share as Black women. Lorde writes:

> By the beginning of summer the walls of Afrekete's apartment were always warm to the touch from the heat beating down on the roof, and chance breezes through her windows rustled her plants in the window and brushed over our sweat-smooth bodies, at rest after loving.
>
> We talked sometimes about what it meant to love women, and what a relief it was in the eye of the storm, no matter how often we had to bite our tongues and stay silent. . . .
>
> Once we talked about how Black women had been committed without choice to waging our campaigns in the enemies' strongholds, too much and too often, and how our psychic landscapes had been plundered and wearied by those repeated battles and campaigns.
>
> "And don't I have the scars to prove it," she sighed. "Makes you tough though, babe, if you don't go under. And that's what I like about you; you're like me. We're both going to make it because we're both too tough and crazy

not to!" And we held each other and laughed and cried about what we had paid for that toughness, and how hard it was to explain to anyone who didn't already know it that soft and tough had to be one and the same for either to work at all, like our joy and the tears mingling on the one pillow beneath our heads. (p. 250)

The fact that this conversation occurs in 1957 is both amazing and unremarkable. Black Lesbians have a heritage far older than a few decades, a past that dates back to Africa, as Lorde herself documents in the essay, "Scratching the Surface: Some Notes on Barriers to Women and Loving."[21] Lorde's authentic portrayal of one segment of that history in *Zami* enables us to see both our pasts and futures more clearly. Her work provides a vision of possibility for Black Lesbians surviving whole, despite all, which is the very least we can demand from our literature, our activism, and our lives.

Despite the homophobic exclusion and silencing of Black Lesbian writers, the creation of complex, accurate, and artistically compelling depictions of Black Lesbians in literature has been and will continue to be essential to the development of African-American women's literature as a whole. The assertion of Black women's right to autonomy and freedom, which is inherent in the lives of Black Lesbians and which is made politically explicit in Black Lesbian feminist theory and practice, has crucial implications for all women's potential liberation. Ultimately, the truth that never hurts is that Black Lesbians and specifically Black Lesbian writers are here to stay. In spite of every effort to erase us, we are committed to living visibly with integrity and courage and to telling our Black women's stories for centuries to come.

NOTES

1. Calvin Hernton, "The Sexual Mountain and Black Women Writers," *The Black Scholar* 16, no. 4 (July/August 1985); 7.
2. Barbara Christian, *Black Feminist Criticism: Perspectives on Black Women Writers* (New York: Pergamon, 1986), p. 188.
3. Audre Lorde and Ann Allen Shockley are two exceptions. They have published with both commercial and independent publishers. It should be noted that Lorde's poetry is currently published by a commercial publisher, but that all of her works of prose have been published by independent women's presses. In conversation with Lorde I have learned that *Zami: A New Spelling of My Name* was rejected by at least a dozen commercial publishers.
4. Christian, *Black Feminist Criticism*, pp. 199–200.
5. Alice Walker, "Breaking Chains and Encouraging Life," in *In Search of Our Mothers' Gardens: Womanist Prose* (New York: Harcourt Brace Jovanovich, 1984), pp. 288–289.
6. In her essay "The Black Lesbian in American Literature: An Overview," Ann Allen Shockley summarizes Jones's negative or inadequate treatment of Lesbian themes in her novels *Corregidora* and *Eva's Man* and in two of her short stories. Ann Allen Shockley, "The Black Lesbian in American Literature: An Overview," in *Home Girls: A Black Feminist Anthology*, ed. Barbara Smith (Latham, N.Y.: Kitchen Table Press, 1982), p. 89.
7. In her essay "The Failure to Transform: Homophobia in the Black Community," Cheryl Clark comments: "The black lesbian is not only absent from the pages of black political analysis, her image as a character in literature and her role as a writer are blotted

out from or trivialized in literary criticism written by black women." Clarke also cites examples of such omissions. In *Home Girls*, ed. Smith, pp. 204–205.

8. Barbara Smith, "Racism and Women's Studies," in *All the Women Are White, All the Blacks are Men, But Some of Us Are Brave: Black Women's Studies*, ed. Gloria Hull, Patricia Bell Scott, and Barbara Smith (New York: Feminist Press, 1981), p. 49.

9. Mitsuye Yamada, "Invisibility Is an Unnatural Disaster: Reflections of an Asian American Woman," in *This Bridge Called My Back: Writings by Radical Women of Color*, ed. Cherríe Moraga and Gloria Anzaldua (Latham, N.Y.: Kitchen Table Press, 1984), pp. 35–40.

10. Cheryl Clarke, *Narratives: Poems in the Tradition of Black Women* (Latham, N.Y.: Kitchen Table Press, 1983), p. 15.

11. Jewelle Gomez, in *Home Girls*, ed. Smith, p. 122.

12. Langston Hughes, "The Negro Artist and the Racial Mountain," in *Voices from the Harlem Renaissance*, ed. Nathan Huggins (New York: Oxford, 1976), p. 309. It is interesting to note that recent research has revealed that Hughes and a number of other major figures of the Harlem Renaissance were gay. See Charles Michael Smith, "Bruce Nugent: Bohemian of the Harlem Renaissance," in *In the Life: A Black Gay Anthology*, ed. Joseph F. Beam (Boston: Alyson, 1986), pp. 213–214 and selections by Langston Hughes in *Gay and Lesbian Poetry in Our Time: An Anthology*, ed. Carl Morse and Joan Larkin (New York: St. Martin's, 1988), pp. 204–206.

13. Paul Laurence Dunbar, "We Wear the Mask," in *The Life and Works of Paul Laurence Dunbar*, ed. Wiggins (New York: Kraus, 1971), p. 184.

14. Audre Lorde, "There is No Hierarchy of Oppressions," in *The Council on Interracial Books for Children Bulletin, Homophobia and Education: How to Deal with Name-Calling*, ed. Leonore Gordon, Vol. 14, nos. 3 & 4 (1983), 9.

15. Gloria Naylor, *The Women of Brewster Place* (New York: Penguin, 1983), pp. 165–166. All subsequent references to this work will be cited in the text.

16. Jewelle Gomez, "Naylor's Inferno," *The Women's Review of Books* 2, no. 11 (August 1985), 8.

17. Alice Walker, *The Color Purple* (New York: Washington Square, 1982), p. 224. All subsequent references to this work will be cited in the text.

18. In his essay, "Who's Afraid of Alice Walker?" Calvin Hernton describes the "hordes of . . . black men (and some women)" who condemned both the novel and the film of *The Color Purple* all over the country. He singles out journalist Tony Brown as a highly visible leader of these attacks. Brown both broadcast television shows and wrote columns about a book and movie he admitted neither to have read nor seen. Hernton raises the question, "Can it be that the homophobic, nitpicking screams of denial against *The Color Purple* are motivated out of envy, jealousy and guilt, rather than out of any genuine concern for the well-being of black people?" Calvin Hernton, *The Sexual Mountain and Black Women Writers* (New York: Anchor, 1987), pp. 30–36.

19. Christian, *Black Feminist Criticism*, pp. 187–210. Gomez, in *Home Girls*, ed. Smith, pp. 118–119.

20. Audre Lorde, *Zami: A New Spelling of My Name* (Freedom, Calif.: Crossing, 1983), p. 255. All subsequent references to this work will be cited in the text.

21. Audre Lorde, *Sister Outsider* (Freedom, Calif.: Crossing, 1984), pp. 45–52.

PAULA GUNN ALLEN

KOCHINNENAKO IN ACADEME

three approaches to interpreting a keres indian tale

~~~~~~

I became engaged in studying feminist thought and theory when I was first studying and teaching American Indian literature in the early 1970s. Over the ensuing fifteen years, my own stances toward both feminist and American Indian life and thought have intertwined as they have unfolded. I have always included feminist content and perspectives in my teaching of American Indian subjects, though at first the mating was uneasy at best. My determination that both areas were interdependent and mutually significant to a balanced pedagogy of American Indian studies led me to grow into an approach to both that is best described as tribal-feminism or feminist-tribalism. Both terms are applicable: if I am dealing with feminism, I approach it from a strongly tribal posture, and when I am dealing with American Indian literature, history, culture, or philosophy I approach it from a strongly feminist one.

A feminist approach to the study and teaching of American Indian life and thought is essential because the area has been dominated by paternalistic, male-dominant modes of consciousness since the first writings about American Indians in the fifteenth century. This male bias has seriously skewed our understanding of tribal life and philosophy, distorting it in ways that are sometimes obvious but are most often invisible.

Often what appears to be a misinterpretation caused by racial differences is a distortion based on sexual politics. When the patriarchal paradigm that characterizes western thinking is applied to gynecentric tribal modes, it transforms the ideas, significances, and raw data into something that is not only unrecognizable to the tribes but entirely incongruent with their philosophies and theories. We know that materials and interpretations amassed by the white intellectual establishment are in error, but we have not pinpointed the major sources of that error. I believe that a fundamental source has been male bias and that feminist theory, when judiciously applied to the field, makes the error correctible, freeing the data for reinterpretation that is at least congruent with a tribal perceptual mode.

To demonstrate the interconnections between tribal and feminist approaches as I use them in my work, I have developed an analysis of a traditional Kochinnenako, or Yellow Woman, story of the Laguna-Acoma Keres, as recast by my mother's uncle John M. Gunn in his book *Schat Chen*.[1] My analysis utilizes three approaches and demonstrates the relationship of context to meaning, illuminating three consciousness styles and providing students with a traditionally tribal, nonracist, feminist understanding of traditional and contemporary American Indian life.

SOME THEORETICAL CONSIDERATIONS

Analyzing tribal cultural systems from a mainstream feminist point of view allows an otherwise overlooked insight into the complex interplay of factors that have led to the systematic loosening of tribal ties, the disruption of tribal cohesion and complexity, and the growing disequilibrium of cultures that were anciently based on a belief in balance, relationship, and the centrality of women, particularly elder women. A feminist approach reveals not only the exploitation and oppression of the tribes by whites and white government but also areas of oppression within the tribes and the sources and nature of that oppression. To a large extent, such an analysis can provide strategies for ameliorating the effects of patriarchal colonialism, enabling many of the tribes to reclaim their ancient gynarchical,[2] egalitarian, and sacred traditions.

At the present time, American Indians in general are not comfortable with feminist analysis or action within the reservation or urban Indian enclaves. Many Indian women are uncomfortable with feminism because they perceive it (correctly) as white-dominated. They (not so correctly) believe it is concerned with issues that have little bearing on their own lives. They are also uncomfortable with it because they have been reared in an anglophobic world that views white society with fear and hostility. But because of their fear of and bitterness toward whites and their consequent unwillingness to examine the dynamics of white socialization, American Indian women often overlook the central areas of damage done to tribal tradition by white Christian and secular patriarchal dominance. Militant and "progressive" American Indian men are even more likely to quarrel with feminism; they have benefited in certain ways from white male-centeredness, and while those benefits are of real danger to the tribes, the individual rewards are compelling.

It is within the context of growing violence against women and the concomitant lowering of our status among Native Americans that I teach and write. Certainly I could not locate the mechanisms of colonization that have led to the virulent rise of woman-hating among American Indian men (and, to a certain extent, among many of the women) without a secure and determined feminism. Just as certainly, feminist theory applied to my literary studies clarifies a number of issues for me, including the patriarchal bias that has been systematically imposed on traditional literary materials and the mechanism by which that bias has affected contemporary American Indian life, thought, and culture.

The oral tradition is more than a record of a people's culture. It is the creative source of their collective and individual selves. When that wellspring of identity is tampered with, the sense of self is also tampered with; and when that tampering includes the sexist and classist assumptions of the white world within the body of an Indian tradition, serious consequences necessarily ensue.

The oral tradition is a living body. It is in continuous flux, which enables it to accommodate itself to the real circumstances of a people's lives. That is its strength, but it is also its weakness, for when a people finds itself living within a racist, classist, and sexist reality, the oral tradition will reflect those values and will thus shape the people's consciousness to include and accept racism, classism, and sexism, and they will incorporate that change, hardly noticing the shift. If the oral tradition is altered in certain subtle, fundamental ways, if elements alien to it are introduced so that its internal coherence is disturbed, it becomes the major instrument of colonization and oppression.

Such alterations have occurred and are still occurring. Those who translate or "render" narratives make certain crucial changes, many unconscious. The cultural bias of the translator inevitably shapes his or her perception of the materials being translated, often in ways that he or she is unaware of. Culture is fundamentally a shaper of perception, after all, and perception is shaped by culture in many subtle ways. In short, it's hard to see the forest when you're a tree. To a great extent, changes in materials translated from a tribal to a western language are a result of the vast difference in languages; certain ideas and concepts that are implicit in the structure of an Indian language are not possible in English. Language embodies the unspoken assumptions and orientations of the culture it belongs to. So while the problem is one of translation, it is not simply one of word equivalence. The differences are perceptual and contextual as much as verbal.

Sometimes the shifts are contextual; indeed, both the context and content usually are shifted, sometimes subtly, sometimes blatantly. The net effect is a shifting of the whole axis of the culture. When shifts of language and context are coupled with the almost infinite changes occasioned by Christianization, secularization, economic dislocation from subsistence to industrial modes, destruction of the wilderness and associated damage to the biota, much that is changed goes unnoticed or unremarked by the people being changed. This is not to suggest that Native Americans are unaware of the enormity of the change they have been forced to undergo by the several centuries of white presence, but much of that change is at deep and subtle levels that are not easily noted or resisted.

John Gunn received the story I am using here from a Keres-speaking informant and translated it himself. The story, which he titles "Sh-ah-cock and Miochin or the Battle of the Seasons," is in reality a narrative version of a ritual. The ritual brings about the change of season and of moiety among the Keres. Gunn doesn't mention this, perhaps because he was interested in stories and not in religion or perhaps because his informant did not mention the connection to him.

What is interesting about his rendering is his use of European, classist, conflict-centered patriarchal assumptions as plotting devices. These interpolations dislocate the significance of the tale and subtly alter the ideational context of woman-centered, largely pacifist people whose ritual story this is. I have developed three critiques of the tale as it appears in his book, using feminist and tribal understandings to discuss the various meanings of the story when it is read from three different perspectives.

In the first reading, I apply tribal understanding to the story. In the second, I apply the sort of feminist perspective I applied to traditional stories, historical events, traditional culture, and contemporary literature when I began developing a feminist perspective. The third reading applies what I call a feminist-tribal perspective. Each analysis is somewhat less detailed than it might be; but as I am

interested in describing modes of perception and their impact on our understanding of cultural artifacts (and by extension our understanding of people who
come from different cultural contexts than our own) rather than critiquing a
story, they are adequate.

YELLOW WOMAN STORIES

The Keres of Laguna and Acoma Pueblos in New Mexico have stories that are
called Yellow Woman stories. The themes and to a large extent the motifs of
these stories are always female-centered, always told from Yellow Woman's point
of view. Some older recorded versions of Yellow Woman tales (as in Gunn) make
Yellow Woman the daughter of the hocheni. Gunn translates *hocheni* as "ruler."
But Keres notions of the hocheni's function and position are as cacique or Mother
Chief, which differ greatly from Anglo-European ideas of rulership. However,
for Gunn to render *hocheni* as "ruler" is congruent with the European folktale
tradition.[3]

Kochinnenako, Yellow Woman, is in some sense a name that means Woman-
Woman because among the Keres, yellow is the color for women (as pink and red
are among Anglo-European Americans), and it is the color ascribed to the Northwest. Keres women paint their faces yellow on certain ceremonial occasions and
are so painted at death so that the guardian at the gate of the spirit world, Naiya
Iyatiku (Mother Corn Woman), will recognize that the newly arrived person is a
woman. It is also the name of a particular Irriaku, Corn Mother (sacred corn-ear
bundle), and Yellow Woman stories in their original form detail rituals in which
the Irriaku figures prominently.

Yellow Woman stories are about all sorts of things—abduction, meeting with
happy powerful spirits, birth of twins, getting power from the spirit worlds and
returning it to the people, refusing to marry, weaving, grinding corn, getting
water, outsmarting witches, eluding or escaping from malintentioned spirits, and
more. Yellow Woman's sisters are often in the stories (Blue, White, and Red
Corn) as is Grandmother Spider and her helper Spider Boy, the Sun God or one
of his aspects, Yellow Woman's twin sons, witches, magicians, gamblers, and
mothers-in-law.

Many Yellow Woman tales highlight her alienation from the people: she lives
with her grandmother at the edge of the village, for example, or she is in some
way atypical, maybe a woman who refuses to marry, one who is known for some
particular special talent, or one who is very quick-witted and resourceful. In
many ways Kochinnenako is a role model, though she possesses some behaviors
that are not likely to occur in many of the women who hear her stories. She is,
one might say, the Spirit of Woman.

The stories do not necessarily imply that difference is punishable; on the contrary, it is often her very difference that makes her special adventures possible,
and these adventures often have happy outcomes for Kochinnenako and for her
people. This is significant among a people who value conformity and propriety
above almost anything. It suggests that the behavior of women, at least at certain
times or under certain circumstances, must be improper or nonconformist for the

greater good of the whole. Not that all the stories are graced with a happy ending. Some come to a tragic conclusion, sometimes resulting from someone's inability to follow the rules or perform a ritual in the proper way.

Other Kochinnenako stories are about her centrality to the harmony, balance, and prosperity of the tribe. "Sh-ah-cock and Miochin" is one of these stories. John Gunn prefaces the narrative with the comment that while the story is about a battle, war stories are rarely told by the Keres because they are not "a war like people" and "very rarely refer to their exploits in war."

SH-AH-COCK AND MIOCHIN OR THE BATTLE OF THE SEASONS

In the Kush-kut-ret-u-nah-tit (white village of the north) was once a ruler by the name of Hut-cha-mun Ki-uk (the broken prayer stick), one of whose daughters, Ko-chin-ne-nako, became the bride of Sh-ah-cock (the spirit of winter), a person of very violent temper. He always manifested his presence by blizzards of snow or sleet or by freezing cold, and on account of his alliance with the ruler's daughter, he was most of the time in the vicinity of Kush-kut-ret, and as these manifestations continued from month to month and year to year, the people of Kush-kut-ret found that their crops would not mature, and finally they were compelled to subsist on the leaves of the cactus.

On one occasion Ko-chin-ne-nako had wandered a long way from home in search of the cactus and had gathered quite a bundle and was preparing to carry them home by singeing off the thorns, when on looking up she found herself confronted by a very bold but handsome young man. His attire attracted her gaze at once. He wore a shirt of yellow woven from the silks of corn, a belt made from the broad green blades of the same plant, a tall pointed hat made from the same kind of material and from the top which waved a yellow corn tassel. He wore green leggings woven from kow-e-nuh, the green stringy moss that forms in springs and ponds. His moccasins were beautifully embroidered with flowers and butterflies. In his hand he carried an ear of green corn.

His whole appearance proclaimed him a stranger and as Ko-chin-ne-nako gaped in wonder, he spoke to her in a very pleasing voice asking her what she was doing. She told him that on account of the cold and drouth [*sic*], the people of Kush-kut-ret were forced to eat the leaves of the cactus to keep from starving.

"Here," said the young man, handing her the ear of green corn. "Eat this and I will go and bring more that you may take home with you."

He left her and soon disappeared going towards the south. In a short time he returned bringing with him a big load of green corn. Ko-chin-ne-nako asked him where he had gathered corn and if it grew near by. "No," he replied, "it is from my home far away to the south, where the corn grows and the flowers bloom all the year around. Would you not like to accompany me back to my country?" Ko-chin-ne-nako replied that his home must be very beautiful, but that she could not go with him because she was the wife of Sh-ah-cock. And then she told him of her alliance with the Spirit of Winter, and admitted that her husband was very cold and disagreeable and that she did not love him. The strange young man urged her to go with him to the warm land of the south, saying that he did not fear Sh-ah-cock. But Ko-chin-ne-nako would not consent. So the stranger directed her to return to her home with the corn he had brought and cautioned her not to throw away any of the husks out of the door. Upon leaving he said to her, "you must meet me at this place tomorrow. I will bring more corn for you."

Ko-chin-ne-nako had not proceeded far on her homeward way ere she met her sisters who, having become uneasy because of her long absence, had come in search of her. They were greatly surprised at seeing her with an armful of corn instead of cactus. Ko-chin-ne-nako told them the whole story of how she had obtained it, and thereby only added wonderment to their surprise. They helped her to carry the corn home; and there she again had to tell her story to her father and mother.

When she had described the stranger even from his peaked hat to his butterfly moccasins, and had told them that she was to meet him again on the day following, Hut-cha-mun Ki-uk, the father, exclaimed:

"It is Mi-o-chin!"

"It is Mi-o-chin! It is Mi-o-chin!," echoed the mother. "Tomorrow you must bring him home with you."

The next day Ko-chin-ne-nako went again to the spot where she had met Mi-o-chin, for it was indeed Mi-o-chin, the Spirit of Summer. He was already there, awaiting her coming. With him he had brought a huge bundle of corn.

Ko-chin-ne-nako pressed upon him the invitation of her parents to accompany her home, so together they carried the corn to Kush-kut-ret. When it had been distributed there was sufficient to feed all the people of the city. Amid great rejoicing and thanksgiving, Mi-o-chin was welcomed at the Hotchin's (ruler's) house.

In the evening, as was his custom, Sh-ah-cock, the Spirit of the Winter, returned to his home. He came in a blinding storm of snow and hail and sleet, for he was in a boisterous mood. On approaching the city, he felt within his bones that Mi-o-chin was there, so he called in a loud and blustering voice:

"Ha! Mi-o-chin, are you here?"

For answer, Mi-o-chin advanced to meet him.

Then Sh-ah-cock, beholding him, called again,

"Ha! Mi-o-chin, I will destroy you."

"Ha! Sh-ah-cock, I will destroy you," replied Mi-o-chin, still advancing.

Sh-ah-cock paused, irresolute. He was covered from head to foot with frost (skah). Icycles [*sic*] (ya-pet-tu-ne) draped him round. The fierce, cold wind proceeded from his nostrils.

As Mi-o-chin drew near, the wintry wind changed to a warm summer breeze. The frost and icycles melted and displayed beneath them, the dry, bleached bulrushes (ska-ra-ru-ka) in which Sh-ah-cock was clad.

Seeing that he was doomed to defeat, Sh-ah-cock cried out:

"I will not fight you now, for we cannot try our powers. We will make ready, and in four days from this time, we will meet here and fight for supremacy. The victor shall claim Ko-chin-ne-nako for his wife."

With this, Sh-ah-cock withdrew in rage. The wind again roared and shook the very houses; but the people were warm within them, for Mi-o-chin was with them.

The next day Mi-o-chin left Kush Kutret for his home in the south. Arriving there, he began to make his preparations to meet Sh-ah-cock in battle.

First he sent an eagle as a messenger to his friend, Ya-chun-ne-ne-moot (kind of shaley rock that becomes very hot in the fire), who lived in the west, requesting him to come and help to battle Sh-ah-cock. Then he called together the birds and the four legged animals—all those that live in sunny climes. For his advance guard and shield he selected the bat (pickikke), as its tough skin would best resist the sleet and hail that Sh-ah-cock would hurl at him.

Meantime Sh-ah-cock had gone to his home in the north to make his preparations for battle. To his aid he called all the winter birds and all of the four legged animals of the wintry climates. For his advance guard and shield he selected Shro-ak-ah (a magpie).

When these formidable forces had been mustered by the rivals, they advanced, Mi-o-chin from the south and Sh-ah-cock from the north, in battle array.

Ya-chun-ne-ne-moot kindled his fires and piled great heaps of resinous fuel upon them until volumes of steam and smoke ascended, forming enormous clouds that hurried forward toward Kush-kut-ret and the battle ground. Upon these clouds rode Mi-o-chin, the Spirit of Summer, and his vast army. All the animals of the army, encountering the smoke from Ya-chun-ne-ne-moot's fires, were colored by the smoke so that, from that day, the animals from the south have been black or brown in color.

Sh-ah-cock and his army came out of the north in a howling blizzard and borne forward on black storm clouds driven by a freezing wintry wind. As he came on, the lakes and rivers over which he passed were frozen and the air was filled with blinding sleet.

When the combatants drew near to Kush-kut-ret, they advanced with fearful rapidity. Their arrival upon the field was marked by fierce and terrific strife.

Flashes of lightning darted from Mi-o-chin's clouds. Striking the animals of Sh-ah-cock, they singed the hair upon them, and turned it white, so that, from that day, the animals from the north have worn a covering of white or have white markings upon them.

From the south, the black clouds still rolled upward, the thunder spoke again and again. Clouds of smoke and vapor rushed onward, melting the snow and ice weapons of Sh-ah-cock and compelling him, at length, to retire from the field. Mi-o-chin, assured of victory, pursued him. To save himself from total defeat and destruction, Sh-ah-cock called for armistice.

This being granted on the part of Mi-o-chin, the rivals met at Kush-kut-ret to arrange the terms of the treaty. Sh-ah-cock acknowledged himself defeated. He consented to give up Ko-chin-ne-nako to Mi-o-chin. This concession was received with rejoicing by Ko-chin-ne-nako and all the people of Kush-kut-ret.

It was then agreed between the late combatants that, for all time thereafter, Mi-o-chin was to rule at Kush-kut-ret during one-half of the year, and Sh-ah-cock was to rule during the remaining half, and that neither should molest the other.[4]

John Gunn's version has a formal plot structure that makes the account seem to be a narrative. But had he translated it directly from the Keres, even in "narrative" form, as in a storytelling session, its ritual nature would have been clearer. I can only surmise about how the account might go if it were done that way, basing my ideas on renderings of Keres rituals in narrative forms I am acquainted with. But a direct translation from the Keres would have sounded more like the following than like Gunn's rendition of it:

> Long ago. Eh. There in the North. Yellow Woman. Up northward she went. Then she picked burrs and cactus. Then here went Summer. From the south he came. Above there he arrived. Thus spoke Summer. "Are you here? How is it going?" said Summer. "Did you come here?" thus said Yellow Woman. Then answered Yellow Woman. "I pick these poor things because I am hungry." "Why do you not eat corn and melons?" asked Summer. Then he gave her some corn and melons. "Take it!" Then thus spoke Yellow Woman, "It is good. Let us go. To my house I take you." "Is not your husband there?" "No. He went hunting deer. Today at night he will come back."
>
> Then in the north they arrived. In the west they went down. Arrived then they in the east. "Are you here?" Remembering Prayer Sticks said. "Yes" Summer said. "How is it going?" Summer said. Then he said, "Your daughter Yellow Woman, she brought me here." "Eh. That is good." Thus spoke Remembering Prayer Sticks.

The story would continue, with many of the elements contained in Gunn's version but organized along the axis of directions, movement of the participants, their maternal relationships to each other (daughter, mother, mother chief, etc.), and events sketched in only as they pertained to directions and the division of the year into its ritual/ceremonial segments, one belonging to the Kurena (summer supernaturals or powers who are connected to the summer people or clans) and the other belonging to the Kashare, perhaps in conjunction with the Kopishtaya, the Spirits.

Summer, Miochin, is the Shiwana who lives on the south mountain, and Sh-ah-cock is the Shiwana who lives on the north mountain.[5] It is interesting to note that the Kurena wear three eagle feathers and ctc'otika' feathers (white striped) on their heads, bells, and woman's dress and carry a reed flute, which perhaps is connected with Iyatiku's sister, Istoakoa, Reed Woman.

A Keres Interpretation

When a traditional Keres reads the tale of Kochinnenako, she listens with certain information about her people in mind: she knows, for example, that Hutchamun Kiuk (properly it means Remembering Prayer Sticks, though Gunn translates it as Broken Prayer Sticks)[6] refers to the ritual (sacred) identity of the cacique and that the story is a narrative version of a ceremony related to the planting of corn. She knows that Lagunas and Acomas don't have rulers in the Anglo-European sense of monarchs, lords, and such (though they do, in recent times, have elected governors, but that's another matter), and that a person's social status is determined by her mother's clan and position in it rather than by her relationship to the cacique as his daughter. (Actually, in various accounts, the *cacique* refers to Yellow Woman as his mother, so the designation of her as his daughter is troublesome unless one is aware that relationships in the context of their ritual significance are being delineated here.)

In any case, our hypothetical Keres reader also knows that the story is about a ritual that takes place every year and that the battle imagery refers to events that take place during the ritual; she is also aware that Kochinnenako's will, as expressed in her attraction to Miochin, is a central element of the ritual. She knows further that the ritual is partly about the coming of summer and partly about the ritual relationship and exchange of primacy between the two divisions of the tribe, that the ritual described in the narrative is enacted by men, dressed as Miochin and Sh-ah-cock, and that Yellow Woman in her Corn Mother aspect is the center of this and other sacred rites of the Kurena, though in this ritual she may also be danced by a Kurena mask dancer. (Gunn includes a drawing of this figure, made by a Laguna, and titled "Ko-chin-ne-nako—In the Mask Dances.")

The various birds and animals along with the forces such as warm air, fire, heat, sleet, and ice are represented in the ritual; Hutchamun Kiuk, the time-keeper or officer who keeps track of the ritual calendar (which is intrinsically related to the solstices and equinoxes), plays a central role in the ritual. The presence of Kochinnenako and Hutchamun Kiuk and the Shiwana Miochin and Sh-ah-cock means something sacred is going on for the Keres.

The ritual transfers the focus of power, or the ritual axis, held in turn by two moieties whose constitution reflects the earth's bilateral division between summer and winter, from the winter to the summer people. Each moiety's right to power is confirmed by and reflective of the seasons, as it is reflective of and supported by the equinoxes. The power is achieved through the Iyani (ritual empowerment) of female Power,[7] embodied in Kochinnenako as mask dancer and/or Irriaku. Without her empowering mediatorship among the south and north Shiwana, the cacique, and the village, the season and the moiety cannot change, and balance cannot be maintained.

Unchanging supremacy of one moiety/season over the other is unnatural and therefore undesirable because unilateral dominance of one aspect of existence and of society over another is not reflective of or supported by reality at meteorological or spiritual levels. Sh-ah-cock, is the Winter Spirit or Winter Cloud, a *Shiwana* (one of several categories of supernaturals), and as such is cold and connected to sleet, snow, ice, and hunger. He is not portrayed as cold because he is a source of unmitigated evil (or of evil at all, for that matter).

Half of the people (not numerically but mystically, so to speak) are Winter, and in that sense are Sh-ah-cock; and while this aspect of the group psyche may seem unlovely when its time is over, that same half is lovely indeed in the proper season. Similarly, Miochin will also age—that is, pass his time—and will then give way for his "rival," which is also his complement. Thus balance and harmony are preserved for the village through exchange of dominance, and thus each portion of the community takes responsibility in turn for the prosperity and well-being of the people.

A Keres is of course aware that balance and harmony are two primary assumptions of Keres society and will not approach the narrative wondering whether the handsome Miochin will win the hand of the unhappy wife and triumph over the enemy, thereby heroically saving the people from disaster. The triumph of handsome youth over ugly age or of virile liberality over withered tyranny doesn't make sense in a Keres context because such views contradict central Keres values.

A traditional Keres is satisfied by the story because it reaffirms a Keres sense of rightness, of propriety. It is a tale that affirms ritual understandings, and the Keres reader can visualize the ritual itself when reading Gunn's story. Such a reader is likely to be puzzled by the references to rulers and by the tone of heroic romance but will be reasonably satisfied by the account because in spite of its westernized changes, it still ends happily with the orderly transfer of focality between the moieties and seasons accomplished in seasonal splendor as winter in New Mexico blusters and sleets its way north and summer sings and warms its way home. In the end, the primary Keres values of harmony, balance, and the centrality of woman to maintain them have been validated, and the fundamental Keres principal of proper order is celebrated and affirmed once again.

A Modern Feminist Interpretation

A non-Keres feminist, reading this tale, is likely to wrongly suppose that this narrative is about the importance of men and the use of a passive female figure as a pawn in their bid for power. And, given the way Gunn renders the story, a modern feminist would have good reason to make such an inference. As Gunn recounts it, the story opens in classic patriarchal style and implies certain patriarchal complications: that Kochinnenako has married a man who is violent and destructive. She is the ruler's daughter, which might suggest that the traditional Keres are concerned with the abuses of power of the wealthy. This in turn suggests that the traditional Keres social system, like the traditional Anglo-European ones, suffer from oppressive class structures in which the rich and powerful bring misery to the people, who in the tale are reduced to bare subsistence seemingly as a result of Kochinnenako's unfortunate alliance. A reader making the usual assumptions western readers make when enjoying folktales will think she is reading a sort of Robin Hood story, replete with a lovely maid Marian, an evil Sheriff, and a green-clad agent of social justice with the Indian name Miochin.

Given the usual assumptions that underlie European folktales, the Western romantic view of the Indian, and the usual antipatriarchal bias that characterizes feminist analysis, a feminist reader might assume that Kochinnenako has been compelled to make an unhappy match by her father the ruler, who must be gaining some power from the alliance. Besides, his name is given as Broken Prayer Stick, which might be taken to mean that he is an unholy man, remiss in his religious duties and weak spiritually.

Gunn's tale does not clarify these issues. Instead it proceeds in a way best calculated to confirm a feminist's interpretation of the tale as only another example of the low status of women in tribal cultures. In accordance with this entrenched American myth, Gunn makes it clear that Kochinnenako is not happy in her marriage; she thinks Sh-ah-cock is "cold and disagreeable, and she cannot love him." Certainly, contemporary American women will read that to mean that Sh-ah-cock is an emotionally uncaring, perhaps cruel husband and that Kochinnenako is forced to accept a life bereft of warmth and love. A feminist reader might imagine that Kochinnenako, like many women, has been socialized into submission. So obedient is she, it seems, so lacking in spirit and independence, that she doesn't seize her chance to escape a bad situation, preferring instead to remain obedient to the patriarchal institution of marriage. As it turns out (in Gunn's tale), Kochinnenako is delivered from the clutches of her violent and unwanted mate by the timely intervention of a much more pleasant man, the hero.

A radical feminist is likely to read the story for its content vis à vis racism and resistance to oppression. From a radical perspective, it seems politically significant that Sh-ah-cock is white. That is, winter is white. Snow is white. Blizzards are white. Clearly, while the story does not give much support to concepts of a people's struggles, it could be construed to mean that the oppressor is designated white in the story because the Keres are engaged in serious combat with white colonial power and, given the significance of storytelling in tribal cultures, are chronicling that struggle in this tale. Read this way, it would seem to acknowledge the right and duty of the people in overthrowing the hated white dictator, who by this account possesses the power of life and death over them.

Briefly, in this context, the story can be read as a tale about the nature of white oppression of Indian people, and Kochinnenako then becomes something of a revolutionary fighter through her collusion with the rebel Miochin in the overthrow of the tyrant Sh-ah-cock. In this reading, the tale becomes a cry for liberation and a direct command to women to aid in the people's struggle to overthrow the colonial powers that drain them of life and strength, deprive them of their rightful prosperity, and threaten them with extinction. An activist teacher could use this tale to instruct women in their obligation to the revolutionary struggle. The daughter, her sisters, and the mother are, after all, implicated in the attempt to bring peace and prosperity to the people; indeed, they are central to it. Such a teacher could, by so using the story, appear to be incorporating culturally diverse materials in the classroom while at the same time exploiting the romantic and moral appeal Native Americans have for other Americans.

When read as a battle narrative, the story as Gunn renders it makes clear that the superiority of Miochin rests as much in his commitment to the welfare of the people as in his military prowess and that because his attempt to free the people is backed up by their invitation to him to come and liberate them, he is successful. Because of his success he is entitled to the hand of the ruler's daughter, Kochinnenako, one of the traditional Old World spoils of victory. Similarly, Sh-ah-cock is defeated not only because he is violent and oppressive but because the people, like Kochinnenako, find that they cannot love him.

A radical lesbian separatist might find herself uncomfortable with the story even though it is so clearly correct in identifying the enemy as white and violent. But the overthrow of the tyrant is placed squarely in the hands of another male figure, Miochin. This rescue is likely to be viewed with a jaundiced eye by many feminists (though more romantic women might be satisfied with it, since it's a story about an Indian woman of long ago), as Kochinnenako has to await the coming of a handsome stranger for her salvation, and her fate is decided by her father and the more salutary suitor Miochin. No one asks Kochinnenako what she wants to do; the reader is informed that her marriage is not to her liking when she admits to Miochin that she is unhappy. Nevertheless, Kochinnenako acts like any passive, dependent woman who is exploited by the males in her life, who get what they want regardless of her own needs or desires.

Some readers (like myself) might find themselves wondering hopefully whether Miochin isn't really female, disguised by males as one of them in order to buttress their position of relative power. After all, this figure is dressed in yellow and green, the colors of corn, a plant always associated with Woman. Kochinnenako and her sisters are all Corn Women and her mother is, presumably, the head of the Corn Clan; and the Earth Mother of the Keres, Iyatiku, is Corn Woman herself. Alas, I haven't yet found evidence to support such a wishful notion, except that the mask dancer who impersonates Kochinnenako is male, dressed female, which is sort of the obverse side of the wish.

A Feminist-Tribal Interpretation

The feminist interpretation I have sketched—which is a fair representation of one of my early readings from what I took to be a feminist perspective—proceeds from two unspoken assumptions: that women are essentially powerless and that conflict is basic to human existence. The first is a fundamental feminist position, while the second is basic to Anglo-European thought; neither, however, is characteristic of Keres thought. To a modern feminist, marriage is an institution developed to establish and maintain male supremacy; because she is the ruler's daughter, Kochinnenako's choice of a husband determines which male will hold power over the people and who will inherit the throne.[8]

When Western assumptions are applied to tribal narratives, they become mildly confusing and moderately annoying from any perspective.[9] Western assumptions about the nature of human society (and thus of literature) when contextualizing a tribal story or ritual must necessarily leave certain elements unclear. If the battle between Summer Spirit and Winter Spirit is about the triumph of warmth, generosity, and kindness over coldness, miserliness, and cruelty, supremacy of the good over the bad, why does the hero grant his antagonist rights over the village and Kochinnenako for half of each year?

The contexts of Anglo-European and Keres Indian life differ so greatly in virtually every assumption about the nature of reality, society, ethics, female roles, and the sacred importance of seasonal change that simply telling a Keres tale within an Anglo-European narrative context creates a dizzying series of false impressions and unanswerable (perhaps even unposable) questions.

For instance, marriage among traditional Keres is not particularly related to marriage among Anglo-European Americans. As I explain in greater detail in a later essay, paternity is not an issue among traditional Keres people; a child belongs to its mother's clan, not in the sense that she or he is owned by the clan, but in the sense that she or he belongs within it. Another basic difference is the attitude toward conflict; the Keres can best be described as a conflict-phobic people, while Euro-American culture is conflict-centered. So while the orderly and proper annual transference of power from Winter to Summer people through the agency of the Keres central female figure is the major theme of the narrative from a Keres perspective, the triumph of good over evil becomes its major theme when it is retold by a white man.

Essentially what happens is that Summer (a mask dancer dressed as Miochin) asks Kochinnenako permission, in a ritual manner, to enter the village. She (who is either a mask dancer dressed as Yellow Woman, or a Yellow Corn Irriaku) follows a ritual order of responses and actions that enable Summer to enter. The narrative specifies the acts she must perform, the words she must say, and those that are prohibited, such as the command that she not "throw any of the husks out of the door." This command establishes both the identity of Miochin and constitutes his declaration of his ritual intention and his ritual relationship to Kochinnenako.

Agency is Kochinnenako's ritual role here; it is through her ritual agency that the orderly, harmonious transfer of primacy between the Summer and Winter people is accomplished. This transfer takes place at the time of the year that Winter goes north and Summer comes to the pueblo from the south, the time when the sun moves north along the line it makes with the edge of the sun's house as ascertained by the hocheni calendar keeper who determines the proper solar and astronomical times for various ceremonies. Thus, in the proper time, Kochinnenako empowers Summer to enter the village. Kochinnenako's careful observance of the ritual requirements together with the proper conduct of her sisters, her mother, the priests (symbolized by the title Hutchamun Kiuk, whom Gunn identifies as the ruler and Yellow Woman's father, though he could as properly—more properly, actually—be called her mother), the animals and birds, the weather, and the people at last brings summer to the village, ending the winter and the famine that accompanies winter's end.

A feminist who is conscious of tribal thought and practice will know that the real story of Sh-ah-cock and Miochin underscores the central role that woman plays in the orderly life of the people. Reading Gunn's version, she will be aware of the vast gulf between the Lagunas and John Gunn in their understanding of the role of women in a traditional gynecentric society such as that of the western Keres. Knowing that the central role of woman is harmonizing spiritual relationships between the people and the rest of the universe by empowering ritual activities, she will be able to read the story for its western colonial content, aware that Gunn's version reveals more about American consciousness when it meets tribal thought than it reveals about the tribe. When the story is analyzed within the context to which it rightly belongs, its feminist content becomes clear, as do the various purposes to which industrialized patriarchal people can put a tribal story.

If she is familiar with the ritual color code of this particular group of Native Americans, a feminist will know that white is the color of Shipap, the place where the four rivers of life come together and where our Mother Iyatiku lives. Thus she will know that it is appropriate that the Spirit of Woman's Power/Being (Yellow Woman) be "married" (that is, ritually connected in energy-transferring gestalts) first with Winter who is the power signified by the color white, which informs clouds, the Mountain Tse-pina, Shipap, originating Power, Koshare, the north and northwest, and that half of the year, and then with Summer, whose color powers are yellow and green, which inform Kurena, sunrise, the growing and ripening time of Mother Earth, and whose direction is south and southeast and that portion of the year.

A feminist will know that the story is about how the Mother Corn Iyatiku's "daughter," that is, her essence in one of its aspects, comes to live as Remembering Prayer Sticks' daughter first with the Winter people and then with the Summer people, and so on.

The net effect of Gunn's rendition of the story is the unhappy wedding of the woman-centered tradition of the western Keres to patriarchal Anglo-European tradition and thus the dislocation of the central position of Keres women by their assumption under the rule of the men. When one understands that the hocheni is the person who tells the time and prays for all the people, even the white people, and that the Hutchamun Kiuk is the ruler only in the sense that the Constitution of the United States is the ruler of the citizens and government of the United States, then the Keres organization of women, men, spirit folk, equinoxes, seasons, and clouds into a balanced and integral dynamic will be seen reflected in the narrative. Knowing this, a feminist will also be able to see how the interpolations of patriarchal thinking distort all the relationships in the story and, by extension, how such impositions of patriarchy on gynocracy disorder harmonious social and spiritual relationships.

A careful feminist-tribal analysis of Gunn's rendition of a story that would be better titled "The Transfer of Ianyi (ritual power, sacred power) from Winter to Summer" will provide a tribally conscious feminist with an interesting example of how colonization works, however consciously or unconsciously to misinform both the colonized and the colonizer. She will be able to note the process by which the victim of the translation process, the Keres woman who reads the tale, is misinformed because she reads Gunn's book. Even though she knows that something odd is happening in the tale, she is not likely to apply sophisticated feminist analysis to the rendition; in the absence of real knowledge of the colonizing process of story-changing, she is all too likely to find bits of the Gunn tale sticking in her mind and subtly altering her perception of herself, her role in her society, and her relationship to the larger world.

The hazard to male Keres readers is, of course, equally great. They are likely to imagine that the proper relationship of women to men is subservience. And it is because of such a shockingly untraditional modern interpretation, brought on as much by reading Gunn as by other, perhaps more obvious societal mechanisms, that the relationships between men and women are so severely disordered at Laguna that wife-abuse, rape, and battery of women there has reached frightening levels in recent years.

POLITICAL IMPLICATIONS OF NARRATIVE STRUCTURE

The changes Gunn has made in the narrative are not only changes in content; they are structural as well. One useful social function of traditional tribal literature is its tendency to distribute value evenly among various elements, providing a model or pattern for egalitarian structuring of society as well as literature. However, egalitarian structures in either literature or society are not easily "read" by hierarchically inclined westerners.

Still, the tendency to equal distribution of value among all elements in a field, whether the field is social, spiritual, or aesthetic (and the distinction is moot when tribal materials are under discussion), is an integral part of tribal consciousness and is reflected in tribal social and aesthetic systems all over the Americas. In this structural framework, no single element is foregrounded, leaving the others to supply "background." Thus, properly speaking, there are no heroes, no villains, no chorus, no setting (in the sense of inert ground against which dramas are played out). There are no minor characters, and foreground slips along from one focal point to another until all the pertinent elements in the ritual conversation have had their say.

In tribal literatures, the timing of the foregrounding of various elements is dependent on the purpose the narrative is intended to serve. Tribal art functions something like a forest in which all elements coexist, where each is integral to the being of the others. Depending on the season, the interplay of various life forms, the state of the overall biosphere and psychosphere, and the woman's reason for being there, certain plants will leap into focus on certain occasions. For example, when tribal women on the eastern seaboard went out to gather sassafras, what they noticed, what stood out sharply in their attention, were the sassafras plants. But when they went out to get maple sugar, maples became foregrounded. But the foregrounding of sassafras or maple in no way lessens the value of the other plants or other features of the forest. When a woman goes after maple syrup, she is aware of the other plant forms that are also present.

In the same way, a story that is intended to convey the importance of the Grandmother Spirits will focus on grandmothers in their interaction with grandchildren and will convey little information about uncles. Traditional tales will make a number of points, and a number of elements will be present, all of which will bear some relationship to the subject of the story. Within the time the storyteller has allotted to the story, and depending on the interests and needs of her audience at the time of the storytelling, each of these elements will receive its proper due.

Traditional American Indian stories work dynamically among clusters of loosely interconnected circles. The focus of the action shifts from one character to another as the story unfolds. There is no "point of view" as the term is generally understood, unless the action itself, the story's purpose, can be termed "point of view." But as the old tales are translated and rendered in English, the western notion of proper fictional form takes over the tribal narrative. Soon there appear to be heroes, point of view, conflict, crisis, and resolution, and as western tastes in story crafting are imposed on the narrative structure of the ritual story, the result is a western story with Indian characters. Mournfully, the new form often becomes confused with the archaic form by the very people whose tradition has been re-formed.

The story Gunn calls "Sh-ah-cock and Mi-o-chin or The Battle of the Seasons" might be better termed "How Kochinnenako Balanced the World," though even then the title would be misleading to American readers, for they would see Kochinnenako as the heroine, the foreground of the story. They would see her as the central figure of the action, and of course that would be wrong. There is no central figure in the tale, though there is a central point. The point is concerned with the proper process of a shift in focus, not the resolution of a conflict. Kochinnenako's part in the process is agency, not heroics; even in Gunn's version, she does nothing heroic. A situation presents itself in the proper time, and Yellow Woman acts in accordance with the dictates of timing, using proper ritual as her mode. But the people cannot go from Winter into Summer without conscious acceptance of Miochin, and Yellow Woman's invitation to him, an acceptance that is encouraged and supported by all involved, constitutes a tribal act.

The "battle" between Summer and Winter is an accurate description of seasonal change in central New Mexico during the spring. This comes through in the Gunn rendition, but because the story is focused on conflict rather than on balance, the meteorological facts and their intrinsic relationship to human ritual are obscured. Only a non-Indian mind, accustomed to interpreting events in terms of battle, struggle, and conflict, would assume that the process of transfer had to occur through a battle replete with protagonist, antagonist, a cast of thousands, and a pretty girl as the prize. For who but an industrialized patriarch would think that winter can be vanquished? Winter and Summer enjoy a relationship based on complementarity, mutuality, and this is the moral significance of the tale.

TRIBAL NARRATIVES AND WOMEN'S LIVES

Reading American Indian traditional stories and songs is not an easy task. Adequate comprehension requires that the reader be aware that Indians never think like whites and that any typeset version of traditional materials is distorting.

In many ways, literary conventions, as well as the conventions of literacy, militate against an understanding of traditional tribal materials. Western technological-industrialized minds cannot adequately interpret tribal materials because they are generally trained to perceive their entire world in ways that are alien to tribal understandings.

This problem is not exclusive to tribal literature. It is one that all ethnic writers who write out of a tribal or folk tradition face, and one that is also shared by women writers, who, after all, inhabit a separate folk tradition. Much of women's culture bears marked resemblance to tribal culture. The perceptual modes that women, even those of us who are literate, industrialized, and reared within masculinist academic traditions, habitually engage in more closely resemble inclusive-field perception than excluding foreground-background perceptions.

Women's traditional occupations, their arts and crafts, and their literature and philosophies are more often accretive than linear, more achronological than chronological, and more dependent on harmonious relationships of all elements within a field of perception than western culture in general is thought to be. Indeed, the patchwork quilt is the best material example I can think of to describe the plot and process of a traditional tribal narrative, and quilting is a non-Indian woman's art, one that Indian women have taken to avidly and that they display in their ceremonies, rituals, and social gatherings as well as in their homes.

It is the nature of woman's existence to be and to create background. This fact, viewed with unhappiness by many feminists, is of ultimate importance in a tribal context. Certainly no art object is bereft of background. Certainly the contents and tone of one's background will largely determine the direction and meaning of one's life and, therefore, the meaning and effect of one's performance in any given sphere of activity.

Westerners have for a long time discounted the importance of background. The earth herself, which is our most inclusive background, is dealt with summarily as a source of food, metals, water, and profit, while the fact that she is the fundamental agent of all planetary life is blithely ignored. Similarly, women's activities—cooking, planting, harvesting, preservation, storage, homebuilding, decorating, maintaining, doctoring, nursing, soothing, and healing, along with the bearing, nurturing, and rearing of children—are devalued as blithely. An antibackground bias is bound to have social costs that have so far remained unexplored, but elite attitudes toward workers, nonwhite races, and women are all part of the price we pay for overvaluing the foreground.

In the western mind, shadows highlight the foreground. In contrast, in the tribal view the mutual relationships among shadows and light in all their varying degrees of intensity create a living web of definition and depth, and significance arises from their interplay. Traditional and contemporary tribal arts and crafts testify powerfully to the importance of balance among all elements in tribal perception, aesthetics, and social systems.

Traditional peoples perceive their world in a unified-field fashion that is very different from the single-focus perception that generally characterizes western masculinist, monotheistic modes of perception. Because of this, tribal cultures are consistently misperceived and misrepresented by nontribal folklorists, ethnographers, artists, writers, and social workers. A number of scholars have recently addressed this issue, but they have had little success because the demands of type and of analysis are, after all, linear and fixed, while the requirements of tribal literatures are accretive and fluid. The one is unidimensional, monolithic, excluding, and chronological while the other is multidimensional, achronological, and including.

How one teaches or writes about the one perspective in terms of the other is problematic. This essay itself is a pale representation of a tribal understanding of the Kochinnenako tale. I am acutely aware that much of what I have said is likely to be understood in ways I did not intend, and I am also aware of how much I did not say that probably needed to be said if the real story of the transfer of responsibility from one segment of the tribe to the other is to be made clear.

In the end, the tale I have analyzed is not about Kochinnenako or Sh-ah-cock and Miochin. It is about the change of seasons and it is about the centrality of woman as agent and empowerer of that change. It is about how a people engage themselves as a people within the spiritual cosmos and in an ordered and proper way that bestows the dignity of each upon all with careful respect, folkish humor, and ceremonial delight. It is about how everyone is part of the background that shapes the meaning and value of each person's life. It is about propriety, mutuality, and the dynamics of socioenvironmental change.

NOTES

1. John M. Gunn, *Schat Chen: History, Traditions and Narratives of the Queres Indians of Laguna and Acoma* (Albuquerque, N. Mex.: Albright and Anderson, 1917; reprint, New York: AMS, 1977). Gunn, my mother's uncle, lived among the Lagunas all his adult life. He spoke Laguna (Keres) and gathered information in somewhat informal ways while sitting in the sun visiting with older people. He married Meta Atseye, my great-grandmother, years after her husband (John Gunn's brother) died and may have taken much of his information from her stories or explanations of Laguna ceremonial events. She had a way of "translating" terms and concepts from Keres into English and from a Laguna con-

ceptual framework into an American one, as she understood it. For example, she used to refer to the Navajo people as "gypsies," probably because they traveled in covered wagons and the women wear long, full skirts and head scarves and both men and women wear a great deal of jewelry.

2. In a system where all persons in power are called Mother Chief and where the supreme deity is female, and social organization is matrilocal, matrifocal, and matrilineal, gynarchy is happening. However, it does not imply domination of men by women as patriarchy implies domination by ruling class males of all aspects of a society.

3. His use of the term may reflect the use by his informants, who were often educated in Carlisle or Menaul Indian schools, in their attempt to find an equivalent term that Gunn could understand to signify the deep respect and reverence accorded the hocheni tyi'a'muni. Or he might have selected the term because he was writing a book for an anonymous non-Keres audience, which included himself. Since he spoke Laguna Keres, I think he was doing the translations himself, and his renderings of words (and contexts) was likely influenced by the way Lagunas themselves rendered local terms into English. I doubt, however, that he was conscious of the extent to which his renderings reflected European traditions and simultaneously distorted Laguna-Acoma ones.

Gunn was deeply aware of the importance and intelligence of the Keresan tradition, but he was also unable to grant it independent existence. His major impulse was to link the western Keres with the Sumerians, to in some strange way demonstrate the justice of his assessment of their intelligence. An unpublished manuscript in my possession written by John Gunn after *Schat Chen* is devoted to his researches and speculations into this idea.

4. Gunn, *Schat Chen*, pp. 217–222.

5. Franz Boas, *Keresan Texts*, Publications of the American Ethnological Society, vol. 8, pt. 1 (New York: American Ethnological Society, 1928), writes, "The second and the fourth of the shiwana appear in the tale of summer and winter. . . . Summer wears a shirt of buckskin with squash ornaments, shoes like moss to which parrot feathers are tied. His face is painted with red mica and flowers are tied on to it. . . . Winter wears a shirt of icicles and his shoes are like ice. His shirt is shiny and to its end are tied turkey feathers and eagle feathers" (p. 284).

6. Boas, *Keresan Texts*, p. 288. Boas says he made the same mistake at first, having misheard the word they used.

7. When my sister Carol Lee Sanchez spoke to her university Women's Studies class about the position of centrality women hold in our Keres tradition, one young woman, a self-identified radical feminist, was outraged. She insisted that Sanchez and other Laguna women had been brainwashed into believing that we had power over our lives. After all, she knew that no woman anywhere has ever had that kind of power; her feminist studies had made that fact quite plain to her. The kind of cultural chauvinism that has been promulgated by well-intentioned but culturally entranced feminists can lead to serious misunderstandings such as this and in the process become a new racism based on what becomes the feminist canon. Not that feminists can be faulted entirely on this—they are, after all, reflecting the research and interpretation done in a patriarchal context, by male-biased researchers and scholars, most of whom would avidly support the young radical feminist's strenuous position. It's too bad, though, that feminists fall into the patriarchal trap!

8. For a detailed exposition of what this dynamic consists of, see Adrienne Rich, "Compulsory Heterosexuality and Lesbian Existence," *Signs: Journal of Women in Culture and Society*, vol. 5, no. 4 (Summer 1980). Reprinted in 1982 as a pamphlet with an updated foreward, Antelope Publications, 1612 St. Paul, Denver, CO 80206.

9. Elaine Jahner, a specialist in Lakota language and oral literature, has suggested that the western obsession with western plot in narrative structure led early informant George Sword to construct narratives in the western fashion and tell them as Lakota traditional stories. Research has shown that Sword's stories are not recognized as Lakota traditional

stories by Lakotas themselves; but the tribal narratives that are so recognized are loosely structured and do not exhibit the reliance on central theme or character that is so dear to the hearts of western collectors. As time has gone by, the Sword stories have become a sort of model for later Lakota storytellers who, out of a desire to convey the tribal tales to western collectors have changed the old structures to ones more pleasing to American and European ears. (Personal conversations with Elaine Jahner.)

Education in western schools, exposure to mass media, and the need to function in a white-dominated world have subtly but perhaps permanently altered the narrative structures of the old tales and, with them, the tribal conceptual modes of tribal people. The shift has been away from associative, synchronistic, event-centered narrative and thought to a linear, foreground-centered one. Concurrently, tribal social organization and interpersonal relations have taken a turn toward authoritarian, patriarchal, linear, and misogynist modes—hence the rise of violence against women, an unthinkable event in older, more circular, and tribal times.

YVONNE YARBRO-BEJARANO

CHICANA LITERATURE FROM A CHICANA FEMINIST PERSPECTIVE

What are the implications of a Chicana feminist literary criticism? The existence of a Chicana feminist literary criticism implies the existence, first of all, of a tradition or body of texts by Chicana writers, which in turn implies the existence of a community of Chicanas and ideally of a Chicana feminist political movement. In other words, I do not see the development and application of a Chicana feminist literary criticism as an academic exercise. Like white feminism, Chicana feminism originates in the community and on the streets as political activism to end the oppression of women. This political movement is inseparable from the historical experience of Chicanos in this country since 1848, an experience marked by economic exploitation as a class and systematic racial, social and linguistic discrimination designed to keep Chicanos at the bottom as a reserve pool of cheap labor.

Within this collective experience, the facts and figures concerning Chicanas' education, employment categories and income levels clearly delineate the major areas of struggle for Chicana feminist movement.[1] There have always been Chicanas involved in political activism aimed at the specific situation of Chicanas as working-class women of color, objectified by economic exploitation and discrimination. Lucy González Parsons, the Liga Femenil Mexicanista, Dolores Hernández, Emma Tenayuca, the miners' wives in the strike in Santa Rita, New Mexico in the early 50s, Alicia Escalante and many, many more—these names evoke community, Chicanas who have laid the groundwork for a contemporary movement.

The Chicana feminist critic, then, does not work in isolation, alone with her texts and word processor, typewriter or pad and pencil. She is a Chicana-identified critic, alert to the relationships between her work and the political situation of all Chicanas.[2] The exclusion of Chicanas from literary authority is intimately linked to the exclusion of Chicanas from other kinds of power monopolized by privileged white males. Their struggle to appropriate the "I" of literary discourse relates to their struggle for empowerment in the economic, social and political spheres.

The term "Chicana feminist perspective" also implies certain similarities with and differences from either an exclusively "feminist" or "Chicano" perspective.

While sharing with the feminist perspective an analysis of questions of gender and sexuality, there are important differences between a Chicana perspective and the mainstream feminist one with regard to issues of race, culture, and class. The Chicano perspective, while incorporating these important facets of race, culture and class, has traditionally neglected issues of gender and sexuality. The Chicana feminist is confronted with a dilemma, caught between two perspectives which appeal strongly to different aspects of her experience. In 1981, the publication of *This Bridge Called My Back* documented the rage and frustration of women of color with the white women's movement, not only for the racism, the tokenism, the exclusion and invisibility of women of color, but also for ignoring the issues of working-class women of color (such as forced sterilization).[3] The creative way out of this dilemma is the development of Chicana feminism in coalition with other women of color dedicated to the definition of a feminism which would address the specific situation of working-class women of color who do not belong to the dominant culture. While recognizing her Chicana cultural identity and affirming her solidarity with all Chicanos and other Third-World men and women to combat racial and economic oppression, the Chicana feminist also spearheads a critique of the destructive aspects of her culture's definition of gender roles. This critique targets hterosexist as well as patriarchal prejudice. Above all, Chicana feminism as a political movement depends on the love of Chicanas for themselves and each other as Chicanas.

Perhaps the most important principle of Chicana feminist criticism is the realization that the Chicana's experience as a woman is inextricable from her experience as a member of an oppressed working-class racial minority and a culture which is not the dominant culture. Her task is to show how in works by Chicanas, elements of gender, race, culture and class coalesce. The very term "Chicana" or "mestiza" communicates the multiple connotations of color and femaleness, as well as historical adumbrations of class and cultural membership within the economic structure and dominant culture of the United States. While this may seem painfully obvious, the assertion of this project in Chicana writing is crucial in combatting the tendency in both white feminist and Chicano discourse to see these elements as mutually exclusive. By asserting herself as Chicana or *mestiza*, the Chicana confronts the damaging fragmentation of her identity into component parts at war with each other. In their critique of the "woman's voice" of white feminist theory, Marí C. Lugones and Elizabeth V. Spelman suggest that being invited "to speak about being 'women' . . . in distinction from speaking about being Hispana, Black, Jewish, working-class, etc." is an invitation to silence.[4] The Chicana-identified critic also focuses on texts by Chicanas that involve a dual process of self-definition and building community with other Chicanas. In these works, Chicanas are the subjects of the representations, and often relationships between women form their crucial axes. In the 70s and especially the 80s, their works explore the full spectrum of Chicanas' bonds with Chicanas, including lesbianism. The process of self-definition involves what Black critic bell hooks calls moving from the margin to the center.[5] White male writers take for granted the assumption of the subject role to explore and understand self. The fact that Chicanas may tell stories about themselves and other Chicanas challenges the dominant male concepts of cultural ownership and literary authority. In telling these stories, Chicanas reject the dominant culture's definition of what a Chicana is. In writing, they refuse the objectification imposed by gender roles and racial and economic exploitation.

Chicana writers must overcome external, material obstacles to writing, such as limited access to literacy and the means of literary production, and finding time and leisure to write, given the battle for economic survival. But they must also overcome the internalization of the dominant society's definition of women of color. As Black writer Hattie Gossett phrases it, "who told you anybody wants to hear from you? you aint nothing but a black woman!"[6] In her essay "Speaking in Tongues: A Letter to Third World Women Writers," Gloria Anzaldúa affirms that they must draw power from the very conditions that excluded them from writing in the first place, and write from what she calls the deep core of their identity as working-class women of color who belong to a culture other than the dominant one.[7]

By delving into this deep core, the Chicana writer finds that the self she seeks to define and love is not merely an individual self, but a collective one. In other words, the power, the permission, the authority to tell stories about herself and other Chicanas comes from her cultural, racial/ethnic and linguistic community. This community includes the historical experience of oppression as well as literary tradition. In spite of their material conditions, Chicanas have been writing and telling their stories for over a century. The Chicana writer derives literary authority from the oral tradition of her community, which in turn empowers her to commit her stories to writing.

Since this specific experience has been traditionally excluded from literary representation, it is not surprising that writing that explores the Chicana-as-subject is often accompanied by formal and linguistic innovation. In her essay "Speaking in Tongues," Anzaldúa stresses the need for women of color writers to find their authentic voice, to resist "making it" by becoming less different, to cultivate their differences and their tongues of fire to write about their personal and collective experience as Chicanas (166). The search is for a language that consciously opposes the dominant culture. Poet Cherríe Moraga has written: "I lack language./ The language to clarify/ my resistance to the literate./ Words are a war to me./ They threaten my family." This search for an authentic language may include the fear of incomprehensibility, as the poem goes on to articulate: "To gain the word/ to describe the loss/ I risk losing everything./ I may create a monster . . . / her voice in the distance/ unintelligible illiterate./ These are the monster's words."[8] "Visions of Mexico . . . ," by poet Lorna Dee Cervantes, also speaks of the urgent need to dominate the written word in order to smash stereotypes and rewrite history from the perspective of the oppressed:

> there are songs in my head I could sing to you
> songs that could drone away
> all the mariachi bands you thought you ever heard
> songs that could tell you what I know
> or have learned from my people
> but for that I need words
> simple black nymphs between white sheets of paper
> obedient words obligatory words words I steal
> in the dark when no one can hear me.[9]

As evidenced by the poems quoted above by Moraga and Cervantes, the theme of writing itself may appear as mediator between individual and collective identity in works by Chicanas.

Writing is central in Sandra Cisneros' work of fiction *The House on Mango Street*.[10] *Mango Street* and Helena Marí Viramontes' collection of stories, *Moths*,[11] are innovative in opposite directions—*Moths* characterized by formal experimentation, *Mango Street* by a deceptively simple, accessible style and structure. The short sections that make up this slim novel, *Mango Street*, are marvels of poetic language that capture a young girl's vision of herself and the world she lives in. Though young, Esperanza is painfully aware of the racial and economic oppression her community suffers, but it is the fate of the women in her *barrio* that has the most profound impact on her, especially as she begins to develop sexually and learns that the same fate might be hers. Esperanza gathers strength from the experiences of these women to reject the imposition of rigid gender roles predetermined for her by her culture. Her escape is linked in the text to education and above all to writing. Besides finding her path to self-definition through the women she sees victimized, Esperanza also has positive models who encourage her interest in studying and writing. At the end of the book, Esperanza's journey towards independence merges two central themes, that of writing and a house of her own: "a house as quiet as snow, a space for myself to go, clean as paper before the poem" (100).[12]

Esperanza's rejection of woman's place in the culture involves not only writing but leaving the barrio, raising problematic issues of changing class:

> I put it down on paper and then the ghost does not ache so much. I write it down and Mango says goodbye sometimes. She does not hold me with both arms. She sets me free. One day I will pack my bags of books and paper. One day I will say goodbye to Mango. I am too strong for her to keep me here forever. One day I will go away. Friends and neighbors will say, what happened to Esperanza? Where did she go with all those books and paper? Why did she march so far away? (101–02)

But Esperanza ends the book with the promise to return: "They will not know I have gone away to come back. For the ones I left behind. For the ones who cannot get out" (102).

The House on Mango Street captures the dialectic between self and community in Chicana writing. Esperanza finds her literary voice through her own cultural experience and that of other Chicanas. She seeks self-empowerment through writing, while recognizing her commitment to a community of Chicanas. Writing has been essential in connecting her with the power of women and her promise to pass down that power to other women is fulfilled by the writing and publication of the text itself.

Mango Street is not an isolated example of the importance of writing in Chicana literature. The *teatropoesía* piece *Tongues of Fire*, scripted by Barbara Brinson-Pineda in collaboration with Antonio Curiel (1981), broke new ground in focusing on the Chicana subject as writer, drawing from Anzaldúa's essay which gave the play its title. The text did not privilege one Chicana voice, but created a collective subject through the inclusion of many individual voices speaking to multiple facets of what it means to be Chicana. The tongues of fire of the Chicana writers in the play exposed oppression from without as well as from within the culture, denouncing exploitation and racism but also the subordination of Chicanas through their culture's rigid gender roles and negative attitudes towards female sexuality. Writing emerged as the medium for the definition of the individual subjectivity of the Chicana writer through the articulation of collective experience and identity.

In *The Mixquiahuala Letters*,[13] Ana Castillo plays with the conventions of the epistolary novel, undermining those conventions by inviting the reader to combine and recombine the individual letters in Cortázar fashion. At the same time, the epistolary form calls attention to the role of writing in sifting through and making sense of experience. The narrative voice not only engages in a process of self-exploration through writing, but the form of the writing—letters—foregrounds an explicit exchange with a reader to whom the writing is directed. The novel defines subjectivity in relation to another woman, and the bond between the two women further cemented by the epistolary examination of their relationship is as important as the exploration of self through writing.

In *Giving Up the Ghost*, Cherríe Moraga broke a twenty-year silence in the Chicano theater movement by placing Chicana lesbian sexuality center stage. The text explores the ways in which both lesbian and heterosexual Chicanas' sense of self as sexual beings has been affected by their culture's definitions of masculinity and femininity. The theme of writing emerges at the end of the play. Marisa's writing is both provoked and interrupted by her memories of Amalia and sexual desire, just as the text itself. Marisa's secular "confession" to the audience is the product of her need to exhume and examine her love for this woman and all women. The text presents both the failures and the promises of building community. Just before Marisa speaks of her "daydream[s] with pencil in . . . mouth," she articulates the need for "familia," redefined as women's community: "It's like making familia from scratch/ each time all over again . . . with strangers/ if I must./ If I must, I will."[14]

The love of Chicanas for themselves and each other is at the heart of Chicana writing, for without this love they could never make the courageous move to place Chicana subjectivity in the center of literary representation, or depict pivotal relationships among women past and present, or even obey the first audacious impulse to put pen to paper. Even as that act of necessity distances the Chicana writer from her oral tradition and not so literate sisters, the continuing commitment to the political situation of all Chicanas creates a community in which readers, critics and writers alike participate.[15]

NOTES

1. Elizabeth Waldman, "Profile of the Chicana: A Statistical Fact Sheet," in *Mexican Women in the United States*, Eds. Adelaida del Castillo & Magdalena Mora (Los Angeles: Chicano Studies, U.C.L.A., 1980), 195–204.

2. My understanding of the similarities and differences between Black and Chicana feminist criticism is indebted to Barbara Smith's "Towards Black Feminist Criticism"

(1977), reprinted in *The New Feminist Criticism*, Ed. Elaine Showalter (N.Y.: Pantheon, 1985), 168–85.

3.   *This Bridge Called My Back. Writings by Radical Women of Color*, Eds. Cherríe Moraga & Gloria Anzaldúa (Watertown, Ma.: Persephone Press).

4.   "Have We Got a Theory for You! Feminist Theory, Cultural Imperialism and the Demand for 'the Woman's Voice,'" *Women's Studies International Forum*, 6:6 (1983), 574.

5.   *Feminist Theory: From Margin to Center* (Boston: South End Press, 1984).

6.   *This Bridge Called My Back*, 175–76.

7.   In *This Bridge*, 165–74.

8.   "It's the Poverty," in Anzaldúa, *This Bridge*, 166.

9.   *Emplumada* (Pittsburgh: University of Pittsburgh Press, 1981), 45–46.

10.   *The House on Mango Street* (Houston: Arte Publico Press, 1985).

11.   *Moths and Other Stories* (Houston: Arte Publico Press, 1985).

12.   Sonia Saldívar-Hull includes a discussion of *Mango Street* in "Shattering Silences: The Contemporary Chicana Writer," forthcoming in *Women and Words: Female Voices of Power and Poetry*, Ed. Beverly Stoeltje (University of Illinois Press).

13.   (Binghamton, N.Y.: Bilingual Press, 1986).

14.   (Los Angeles: West End Press, 1986), 58.

15.   The concept of a "Black writing community" is developed by Hortense J. Spillers in "Cross-Currents, Discontinuities: Black Women's Fiction," in *Conjuring. Black Women, Fiction and Literary Tradition*, Eds. Marjorie Pryse and Hortense J. Spillers (Bloomington: Indiana University Press, 1985).

I'M HERE

an asian american woman's response

As one who has been working intensively and almost exclusively in the most basic and practical aspect of feminist scholarship, namely the unearthing and reclaiming of forgotten women writers, I initially felt flattered (They want to know what I think!), then somewhat peeved (They only want to know what I think because they want a token Chinese), and finally sobered (Well, and what *do* I think?) to be invited to comment on Ellen Messer-Davidow's theoretical essay "The Philosophical Bases of Feminist Literary Criticisms." First, I'm grateful to be nudged in this way to lift my head from the part of the garden in which I have been so intently digging—namely, searching for women of Chinese ancestry who have written in English and published in the United States—to see what my sister scholars are doing. I see that they are well aware of and have been debating extensively the same prooblems I have been struggling with, specifically, the dilemmas between politics and aesthetics, between self as central and self as other, between empowering one's self and one's people by retrieving one's past while negotiating with the powerful, and often hostile, outside forces that control our very survival. Or, put another way, how can I write about books that are important to me personally, as a Chinese American woman, and yet maintain a position in a traditional department of English that considers my writers not only third rate but third world and therefore extraneous to the discipline?

It may be true that "*negritude* has analogues with women's aesthetic practices," as Rachel DuPlessis writes in "For the Etruscans,"[1] following a tradition dating back to the mid-nineteenth century when white feminists saw a parallel between their own social situation and that of the black slaves. But white feminists do not have the hurdle of race or nationality between them and acceptance. Granted the hurdle of gender is still in many places very high; nonetheless, the writers white feminists are reclaiming will never be dismissed as "third world." As black women have already pointed out, white women are the grandmothers, mothers, wives, and sisters of white men; thus it would seem natural that granting equality and recognition to their own women would be the first, and a much easier, step for white men than to give respectful attention to descendants of former slaves, prostitutes, and aliens. This, at least, is the perspective from outside the outside. Which is not to say that white feminists do not also perceive themselves as outsiders, and, as such, empathetic allies in the struggle. It is a reminder that, like the descending levels of Dante's *Inferno*, there are many layers of "outside."

As one who has experienced great opposition to the work she is doing—with colleagues making such remarks as "You're a trailblazer, but you're blazing a trail to a place no one wants to go to"—I give a resounding cheer to Messer-Davidow's "perspectivism": "a feminist philosophy that counters objectivism, which privileges objects, and subjectivism, which privileges subjects. Perspectivism would bring together in processes of knowing the personal and cultural, subjective and objective, replacing dichotomies with a systemic understanding of how and what we see. It would explain how we affiliate culturally, acquire a self-centered perspective, experience the perspective of others, and deploy multiple perspectives in inquiry. It would show that perspectivity arises from and defines knowers qualified (in both senses of the word) by their experiences, self-reflection, and contingent standpoints." The open-mindedness of this feminist theory stands in direct contrast to the closed comments of masculinists who dismiss as "trivial" and "insignificant" anything that falls outside their purview. I applaud the philosophical basis that would not only validate the stance I have taken but would require all scholars to be aware of their own perspectives, that would make perspective central and basic to all inquiry instead of seemingly peripheral and irrelevant.

If "perspectivism" were the accepted way and everyone were aware of "agency" and "stance," her own and others', the alienation I initially experienced would be eliminated. For example, when I, a Chinese American woman trained in the traditional classics of Western European and American literature—the "malestream"—first read Maxine Hong Kingston, my overwhelming reaction was discomfort and embarrassment. My self-alienation had been so complete that I experienced my first reading of another Chinese American woman's book as "foreign" and "other" before I relaxed into the realization that I was actually and finally at home as I had been with no other writers I had previously read. My reaction was akin to the child Janie Crawford's experience of not recognizing herself in the photograph in *Their Eyes Were Watching God*. But my later embracing women writers of Chinese ancestry as my central area of research was "to jettison myself off the world," as far as the majority of my male colleagues was concerned. My insistence on the validity of my perspective caused them to wonder about their own, led them to question whether instead of representing a "universal" perspective, they, too, were representing only one perspective: WASP male, Jewish male, black male. This was a disquieting thought; they had grudgingly made room for black and women writers because women are, after all, half the human race, and blacks, well, we do owe them something, don't we? However, the proliferation of perspectives had to be stopped somewhere, for "After all," as one colleague logically explained, "we don't have any Chinese students here, so we don't need a Chinese expert." (When I asked how many sixteenth-century Englishmen we had here, he didn't wish to pursue that line of reasoning.) My perspective challenged the official (white male) canon, and was seen as another threat to the very foundations upon which they had structured their world. I was refusing to believe that only what I had been taught was Good Literature and that everything else—forgotten and ignored—was third rate and deserved to be forgotten and ignored. My stance was a refusal to be "the good little girl," a rejection of what has been called "cultural colonization."[2]

Perspectivism would validate, respect, and encourage every perspective so that WASP males, Jewish males, black males, and white females would need to stretch themselves out of their own skins to understand Maxine Hong Kingston, Lin Taiyi, or Han Suyin, as I have always had to stretch outside of myself to understand James Fenimore Cooper, Bernard Malamud, and Richard Wright. This is what I have always believed reading literature is really all about—getting inside other people's skins and experiencing their lives, regardless of the color of their skin, time period, gender, sexual preference, class, or ethnic background. And yet, at times, it seems a utopian notion.

So I am pleased to be asked to represent Asian American scholars, or more specifically Chinese American women, in this forum. I realize that any forum, even as it includes certain voices, must, of necessity, exclude others. After recently reading Helen Barolini's introduction to an anthology of writings by Italian American women,[3] an introduction that resonates in me in many ways—for Italian American women have suffered similar oppression from the men of their own culture, a similar sense of alienation from the dominant Anglo-American traditions, and the same affinity with black women writers that Chinese American women feel—I fear that the Italian American woman's perspective may have been overlooked, again. It is my guess that, for the present, the more visible minorities have been given the spotlight. As different perspectives develop, not all can be given equal time and space in every forum simply because of physical limitations, but this does not mean we should not encourage their development.

In fact, paradoxically, the more we hear about the experiences of each particular group, the more we learn how much we share as a community of women and how often our commonalities cross cultural and racial barriers. Reading Barolini, like reading Alice Walker's "In Search of our Mother's Gardens" and *The Color Purple*, Audre Lorde's poems and essays, and Virginia Woolf's *A Room of One's Own* is like finding sisters I didn't know I had. How can it be that so many different Others have had experiences and feelings so similar to mine?

And yet, despite our alliance in Outsiderhood, we all must function within the present system while we work for change, and I am a bit uncomfortable about rejecting all male theories simply because they were created by men, as Messer-Davidow seems prone to do. I fear she dismisses too lightly those who would borrow the "useful elements" of the "smorgasbord" of "traditional schools." I have two comments to make on this question. The first is to remind us of the Piaget model of the acquisition of knowledge: "one observes that the subject [in this case, an infant] looks neither at what is too familiar, because he is in a way surfeited with it, nor at what is too new because this does not correspond to anything in his schemata."[4] In other words, we learn by hooking small bits of moderately new knowledge onto old knowledge already in place in our heads. If something new is so radically different that it cannot be hooked onto what is already there, then it remains unattached or unlearned. Thus, if we as feminists can appropriate something useful for our purposes from what is already in the common storehouse, we make our new ideas more accessible to others who are not as far along as we. For example, traditionalists find the idea that women writers of Chinese ancestry are a part of American literature so peculiar that they cannot hear about them unless I link my writers to ones they are familiar with: Chuang Hua's fractured narrative in *Crossings* is akin to Faulkner's *The Sound and the Fury* and parts of Flaubert's *Madame Bovary;* Lin Taiyi's *Dawn Over Chungking* has the poignant power of Anne Frank's diary and her *War Tide* is a tour de force by a seventeen-year-old. In other words, progress is made through little steps, not giant leaps.

Secondly, I find W. E. B. Du Bois's notion of "double consciousness," from *The Souls of Black Folk,* useful in my study of Chinese American women. In fact, Du Bois's elaboration of this double consciousness is applicable to all women: "this sense of always looking at one's self through the eyes of others."[5] John Berger in *Ways of Seeing* noted the same visual and psychological phenomenon: "Men look at women. Women watch themselves being looked at."[6] Elaine Showalter, in "Toward a Feminist Poetics," explains the theoretical impasse in feminist criticism in similar language: "It comes from our own divided consciousness, the split in each of us. We are both the daughters of the male tradition . . . and sisters in a new women's movement."[7] Carol Gilligan notes in *In a Different Voice:* "The difficulty women experience in finding or speaking publicly in their own voices emerges repeatedly in the form of qualification and self-doubt, but also in intimations of a divided judgment, a public assessment and private assessment which are fundamentally at odds."[8] Mikhail Bakhtin's "dialogic imagination" is another useful tool because he too is conscious of "otherness," as experienced aurally, in the many voices in dialogue within one's head.[9] Rachel DuPlessis' essay "For the Etruscans" and Maxine Hong Kingston's *The Woman Warrior* and *China Men* are collages exhibiting the many voices in their heads. Must these theories of double consciousness and dialogic imagination be rejected simply because they were created by men? Though Messer-Davidow is generally against borrowing from male-created systems, she does modify her verb with an adverb: "feminist literary critics who borrow uncritically borrow troubles mainly because our two endeavors are fundamentally incompatible."

In this context, I am reminded of a memorable line by Audre Lorde: "The master's tools will never dismantle the master's house."[10] Much as I enjoy the ring of this line, however, and admire the fierce independence behind it, I find myself finally doubting its veracity. After all, a claw-foot hammer, even if it was made by a man, can both drive nails in and pry them out, depending on your purpose and which side of the head you are using. Tools possess neither memory nor loyalty; they are as effective as the hands wielding them. And, furthermore, why shouldn't women use tools? Annette Kolodny earlier had written, rightly, I believe, "that the many tools needed for our analysis will necessarily be largely inherited and only partly of our own making."[11] Malestream literary critics themselves have been borrowing liberally the tools of anthropology and linguistics. On the other hand, if Lorde was referring to the impossibility of the established system's ability to police itself, then I would, from experience, agree with her.

Messer-Davidow has done a fine intellectual analysis of the problem of women literary scholars in a man's world, and she is bold in arguing for independence, but what about the practical ramifications of secession? I find disquieting her assertion that "the subject of feminist literary criticisms appears to be not literature but the feminist study of ideas about sex and gender that people express in literary and critical media." Trained in literature and hanging on by the skin of my teeth to an English department, I am reluctant to agree that my primary subject is "not literature." I might be in fashion, since, as Elaine Showalter rightly analyzes the present situation in literary criticism, "literary science, in its manic generation of difficult terminology, . . . creates an elite corps of specialists who spend more and more time mastering the theory, less and less time reading the books" (140). However, if I were to agree with Messer-Davidow on this point, I would seem to be siding with a powerful colleague who published an article a number of years ago in which he stated that women's studies has no place in an English department.

If I am a feminist critic, my primary identification is still "literary critic," while "feminist" is the adjective modifying the kind of criticism I do, just as Chinese Americans are primarily Americans with a veneer of Chinese. However, Messer-Davidow is asking us all to be feminists first and then whatever else we are second. Thus we should by her view rightly be called "historical feminists," "literary critical feminists," "scientific feminists," "philosophical feminists," and so on. My proper place would perhaps then be in a women's studies department, but I know only of women's studies programs with part-time faculty borrowed from regular departments. Thus we face a "catch-22" (another borrowing from a male): only if a person is acceptable to a bona fide department will she be able to teach in women's studies, but the bona fide department wants nothing to do with women's studies. What now?

Perhaps what we ought to do is break out of the rigid (male-created) categories and boundaries that separate us. One of the most exciting aspects of Messer-Davidow's article is her pointing out that feminists in many different disciplines are a community all working on the same subject—ideas of sex and gender—though manifested in different "media." The work of feminists in other disciplines—for example, Carol Gilligan in psychology or Alison Jaggar in philosophy—enriches our work in literature and vice versa. Furthermore, in setting forth to discover what women of Chinese ancestry have written and published in the United States, if I find that these women have written what traditional department colleagues would not consider "fine literature," then I must, like Jane Tompkins, redefine "literature" to be broader than the "stylistic intricacy, psychological subtlety, [and] epistemological complexity" that is the current measure of a "good" book, and examine instead "how and why it worked for its readers, in its time." [12] In other words, I do not categorize a writer or her book as "good" or "bad" in the abstract but try to answer the questions: Good for what? For whom? Under what kind of circumstances? And I maintain that I am still studying literature, the written voice of a specific group of people at a specific time.

Take, for example, the Eaton sisters, the first writers of Asian ancestry to publish in the United States. Without knowing the political, social, and immigration history of the turn of the century, there would be no way of understanding why the elder sister, Edith Eaton (1867–1914), used the pseudonym Sui Sin Far (Cantonese for narcissus) and the younger, Winnifred Eaton (1877?–1954), published novels under the Japanese-sounding name Onoto Watanna. We need to be aware of the fact that the Chinese, imported here by the thousands to build the railroads in the late 1860s, were feared and hated as an economic threat while the Japanese, having won a war against China in 1895 and against Russia in 1905, were highly regarded. We must know that Edith felt a sympathy for her Chinese mother and, identifying with her mother's people, resented the injustices they suffered and fought for their rights in articles and stories. Winnifred, seeing her sister go the Chinese route and realizing that Caucasians could not distinguish between Chinese and Japanese, opted to be the favored "Oriental." Without this background information, we would not be aware that Edith's stories are filled with Chinese Americans in situations that emphasize their humanity and lovability because she was intent on opposing the prejudice that Chinese were "heathen" and "unassimilable." Without Edith's work for contrast, we would be less aware that Winnifred's novels, set in Japan and relating stories of romance between charming Japanese or Japanese Eurasian girls and Anglo men, reflected the taste of the day, exploiting stereotypes of the childlike female and the fatherly, powerful male. Not surprisingly, in view of the climate in which they wrote and the directions each chose, Edith produced only one volume of short stories and died relatively young while Winnifred published nearly twenty books and reached the twin pinnacles of popular recognition: Broadway and Hollywood.[13] Were we to use only the formal criteria that Tompkins iterated as the conventional critical standards of our day—"stylistic intricacy, psychological subtlety, epistemological complexity"—the work of the Eaton sisters would not measure up. But why must these be the only measure of the worth of a text? These measures would not reveal the richness of their personal histories or the significance of Edith's work in giving voice to a voiceless people, and of Winnifred's work in revealing the contortions that the prejudices of the day exacted of a woman who wanted to survive. Furthermore, we are anachronistically applying the standards of 1980 to work written in 1880, and many of the writers now considered part of the traditional "canon" would not measure up either.

Messer-Davidow asserts that the ambivalent position that feminist literary critics find themselves in "concerns the way we traditionally structure knowledge" and thus a "way of reconstituting knowledge that evolves from feminist perspectives" is essential. This she ably sets out to do, dissecting the act of criticism into its component parts and offering "perspectivism" as a solution. Her analysis is most impressive, but, being of a practical mind, I find that my problem is not so much one of structuring knowledge as it is my powerlessness versus their power. "Give me one good reason why I should read your writers, other than guilt," a former chairman said to me. How do I answer him? Because they're wonderful writers? Because you'll learn something? The question itself indicates that he is already firmly entrenched in the assumption that these writers are not important to him, except for his guilt in dismissing them unread. If his mind is closed, I can say nothing that will convince him to open it, just as, for example, if someone dislikes tofu, no amount of praise from a tofu-lover can persuade him that tofu is delicious. Perhaps the value of Messer-Davidow's essay may be that this former chair may eventually be persuaded by its theoretical analysis and its abstract language to admit the validity of a variety of perspectives. She at least employs the "discourse" so respected in academia. (Curiously, though she argues for perspectivism, Messer-Davidow reveals little of her own "agency" and "stance," other than her feminism.)

As a Chinese American woman literary scholar, I feel myself at times in the lonely position that Helen Barolini expresses in *The Dream Book* and that Barbara

Smith writes of in "Toward a Black Feminist Criticism." We seem to be the only persons in the world asking the questions: "Where are the writers that are like us?" "Where are our models?" We hope we will not be the only ones to care about the answers. More often than not, we find our particular perspectives ignored. Barolini's introduction contains a myriad of grievances; I have similar complaints. Since the very nature of pioneering research means that no help can be had from those who went before us. I was excited when I received a review copy of Patricia K. Addis's *Through a Woman's I: An Annotated Bibliography of American Women's Autobiographical Writings, 1946–1976*, thinking I had found a research tool at long last. Great was my distress and indignation when I discovered that the "Index of Narratives by Subject Matter" lists "American Indian Woman's Experience" and "Black Woman's Experience" but has no comparable category "Asian American Woman's Experience." And yet Addis's bibliography includes at least five books by Asian American women, including one I had not previously known. Had the indexer realized that "Asian American Woman" is a legitimate category, s/he would have saved me much time and effort. Needless to say, "Italian American Woman's Experience" was also not listed, and in the "Index of Authors by Profession or Salient Characteristic," "Lesbian" is not a category though "Transsexual" is, with one listing under it: "Jorgensen, Christine."[14] This just demonstrates what I've written above—we cannot all be remembered all the time. Even Messer-Davidow herself forgets me. She gives "Hispanic" and "Native American" women the honor of being individually named, but Asian American women, once again, are relegated to the categories of "Third World" and "other."

On the other hand—in DuPlessis's "both/and" fashion (276)—I also feel the excitement of participating in a revolution. The old guard is being shaken, if it has not yet been overthrown. The work I am doing is part of what Adrienne Rich earlier called "re-vision" or "the act of looking back, of seeing with fresh eyes, of entering an old text from a new critical direction,"[15] and also of discovering a female tradition that had been ignored. The feminist perspective that Judith Fetterley applied to her readings of male "classics" in *The Resisting Reader*, for example, was refreshing and exhilarating. The contextual approach and clear-sightedness of Jane Tompkins in *Sensational Designs* is beautiful and breathtaking. The reclamation of forgotten authors by Elaine Showalter, Dale Spender, Catharine Stimpson, Elaine Hedges, Barbara Christian, Mary Helen Washington, Deborah McDowell—all contribute to the feminist rewriting of literary history. Our movement has gained in numbers and in momentum. We may each be working in separate corners of the garden, but we are all working in the same garden. Feminist scholars in different disciplines are all exploring "a common subject, as it is expressed in the particular media they treat," as Messer-Davidow puts it. Our discoveries are answering my father, who once said to me: "What have women ever done in the world? The best in any field—even the 'women's' fields of fashion, cooking, and decorating—have always been men."

The fact that *New Literary History* is highlighting Messer-Davidow's essay and asking for our responses is a recognition of the significance of our work. It would be ideal if the result of this attention were that everyone would be not merely more tolerant of each other's perspectives but actively interested, for only as all the diverse peoples that are Americans find their own voices and sing their individual and communal songs, can we enjoy the full richness and depth in this chorus that is America. Mitsuye Yamada's poem "Mirror, Mirror" expresses it succinctly and well:

> People keep asking me where I come from
>   says my son.
> Trouble is I'm american on the inside
>   and oriental on the outside
>
> No Doug
> Turn that outside in
> THIS is what American looks like.[16]

I may not be able to persuade anyone to like tofu or Asian American writers, but I can tell them, as we're all telling them, we're here.

NOTES

1. Rachel Blau DuPlessis, "For the Etruscans," in *The New Feminist Criticism: Essays on Women, Literature, and Theory*, ed. Elaine Showalter (New York, 1985), p. 285; hereafter cited in text.

2. See, among others, Leslie Marmon Silko's excellent essay on cultural colonization entitled "Language and Literature from a Pueblo Indian Perspective," in *English Literature: Opening Up the Canon*, ed. Leslie A. Fiedler and Houston A. Baker, Jr. (Baltimore, 1981), pp. 54–72.

3. *The Dream Book, An Anthology of Writings by Italian-American Women*, ed. Helen Barolini (New York, 1985), p. 9.

4. Jean Piaget, *The Origins of Intelligence in Children*, tr. Margaret Cook (New York, 1952), p. 68.

5. W. E. Burghardt Du Bois, *The Souls of Black Folk* (New York, 1961), p. 3.

6. John Berger, *Ways of Seeing* (Norwich, England, 1972), p. 47.

7. Elaine Showalter, "Toward a Feminist Poetics," in *The New Feminist Criticism*, ed. Showalter, p. 141; hereafter cited in text.

8. Carol Gilligan, *In a Different Voice: Psychological Theory and Women's Development* (Cambridge, Mass., 1982), p. 16.

9. Mikhail Bakhtin, *The Dialogic Imagination: Four Essays*, ed. Michael Holquist, tr. Caryl Emerson and Michael Holquist (Austin, 1981).

10. Audre Lorde, "The Master's Tools Will Never Dismantle the Master's House," in *Sister Outsider* (Trumansburg, N.Y., 1984), pp. 110–13.

11. Annette Kolodny, "Dancing Through the Minefield," in *The New Feminist Criticism*, ed. Showalter, p. 161.

12. Jane Tompkins, "Sentimental Power: Uncle Tom's Cabin and the Politics of Literary History," in *The New Feminist Criticism*, ed. Showalter, pp. 84, 85.

13. For further information about the Eaton sisters, see my essays "Edith Eaton: Pioneer Chinamerican Writer and Feminist," *American Literary Realism*, 16, No. 2 (1983), 287–98 and "Winnifred Eaton: Ethnic Chameleon," *MELUS*, 11, No. 3 (1984), 5–15.

14. Patricia K. Addis, *Through A Woman's I: An Annotated Bibliography of American Women's Autobiographical Writings, 1946–1976* (Metuchen, N.J., 1983), p. 565.

15. Adrienne Rich, "When We Dead Awaken: Writing as Re-Vision," *College English*, 34 (October 1972), 18.

16. Mitsuye Yamada, *Camp Notes* (San Lorenzo, Cal., 1976), n. pag.; this is the final poem in the chapbook.

IT JUS BE'S DAT WAY SOMETIME
the sexual politics of women's blues

~~~~~~

This essay considers the sexual politics of women's blues in the 1920s. Their story is part of a larger history of the production of Afro-American culture within the North American culture industry. My research has concentrated almost exclusively on those black women intellectuals who were part of the development of an Afro-American literature culture and reflects the privileged place that we accord to writers in Afro-American Studies (Carby, 1987). Within feminist theory, the cultural production of black women writers has been analyzed in isolation from other forms of women's culture and cultural presence and has neglected to relate particular texts and issues to a larger discourse of culture and cultural politics. I want to show how the representation of black female sexuality in black women's fiction and in women's blues is clearly different. I argue that different cultural forms negotiate and resolve very different sets of social contradictions. However, before considering the particularities of black women's sexual representation, we should consider its marginality within a white-dominated feminist discourse.

In 1982, at the Barnard conference on the politics of sexuality, Hortense Spillers condemned the serious absence of consideration of black female sexuality from the various public discourses including white feminist theory. She described black women as "the beached whales of the sexual universe, unvoiced, misseen, not doing, awaiting *their* verb." The sexual experiences of black women, she argued, were rarely depicted by themselves in what she referred to as "empowered texts": discursive feminist texts. Spillers complained of the relative absence of African-American women from the academy and thus from the visionary company of Anglo-American women feminists and their privileged mode of feminist expression.

The collection of the papers from the Barnard conference, the *Pleasure and Danger* (1984) anthology, has become one of these empowered feminist theoretical texts and Spillers' essay continues to stand within it as an important black feminist survey of the ways in which the sexuality of black American women has been unacknowledged in the public/critical discourse of feminist thought (Spillers, 1984). Following Spillers' lead black feminists continued to critique the neglect of issues of black female sexuality within feminist theory and, indeed, I as well as others directed many of our criticisms toward the *Pleasure and Danger* anthology itself (Carby, 1986).

As black women we have provided articulate and politically incisive criticism which is there for the feminist community at large to heed or to ignore—upon that decision lies the future possibility of forging a feminist movement that is not parochial. As the black feminist and educator Anna Julia Cooper stated in 1892, a woman's movement should not be based on the narrow concerns of white middle class women under the name of "women"; neither, she argued, should a woman's movement be formed around the exclusive concerns of either the white woman or the black woman or the red woman but should be able to address the concerns of all the poor and oppressed (Cooper, 1892).

But instead of concentrating upon the domination of a white feminist theoretical discourse which marginalizes non-white women, I focus on the production of a discourse of sexuality by black women. By analyzing the sexual and cultural politics of black women who constructed themselves as sexual subjects through song, in particular the blues, I want to assert an empowered presence. First, I must situate the historical moment of the emergence of women-dominated blues and establish a theoretical framework of interpretation and then I will consider some aspects of the representation of feminism, sexuality, and power in women's blues.

MOVIN' ON

Before World War I the overwhelming majority of black people lived in the South, although the majority of black intellectuals who purported to represent the interests of "the race" lived in the North. At the turn of the century black intellectuals felt they understood and could give voice to the concerns of the black community as a whole. They were able to position themselves as spokespeople for the "race" because they were at a vast physical and metaphorical distance from the majority of those they represented. The mass migration of blacks to urban areas, especially to the cities of the North, forced these traditional intellectuals to question and revise their imaginary vision of "the people" and directly confront the actual displaced rural workers who were, in large numbers, becoming a black working class in front of their eyes. In turn the mass of black workers became aware of the range of possibilities for their representation. No longer were the "Talented Tenth," the practitioners of policies of racial uplift, the undisputed "leaders of the race." Intellectuals and their constituencies fragmented, black union organizers, Marcus Garvey and the Universal Negro Improvement Association, radical black activists, the Sanctified Churches, the National Association of Colored Women, the Harlem creative artists, all offered alternative forms of representation and each strove to establish that the experience of their constituency was representative of the experience of the race.

Within the movement of the Harlem cultural renaissance, black women writers established a variety of alternative possibilities for the fictional representation of black female experience. Zora Neale Hurston chose to represent black people as the rural folk; the folk were represented as being both the source of Afro-American cultural and linguistic forms and the means for its continued existence.

Hurston's exploration of sexual and power relations was embedded in this "folk" experience and avoided the cultural transitions and confrontations of the urban displacement. As Hurston is frequently situated as the foremother of contemporary black women writers, the tendency of feminist literary criticism has been to valorize black women as "folk" heroines at the expense of those texts which explored black female sexuality within the context of urban social relations. Put simply, a line of descent is drawn from *Their Eyes Were Watching God* to *The Color Purple*. But to establish the black "folk" as representative of the black community at large was and still is a convenient method for ignoring the specific contradictions of an urban existence in which most of us live. The culture industry, through its valorization in print and in film of *The Color Purple*, for example, can *appear* to confortably address issues of black female sexuality within a past history and rural context while completely avoiding the crucial issues of black sexual and cultural politics that stem from an urban crisis.

"THERE'S NO EARTHLY USE IN BEIN TOO-GA-THA IF IT DON'T PUT SOME JOY IN YO LIFE." (WILLIAMS, 1981)

However, two other women writers of the Harlem Renaissance, Jessie Fauset and Nella Larsen, did figure an urban class confrontation in their fiction, though in distinctly different ways. Jessie Fauset became an ideologue for a new black bourgeoisie; her novels represented the manners and morals that distinguished the emergent middle class from the working class. She wanted public recognition for the existence of a black elite that was urbane, sophisticated, and civilized but her representation of this elite implicitly defined its manners against the behavior of the new black proletariat. While it must be acknowledged that Fauset did explore the limitations of a middle-class existence for women, ultimately each of her novels depict independent women who surrender their independence to become suitable wives for the new black professional men.

Nella Larsen, on the other hand, offers us a more sophisticated dissection of the rural/urban confrontation. Larsen was extremely critical of the Harlem intellectuals who glorified the values of a black folk culture while being ashamed of and ridiculing the behavior of the new black migrant to the city. Her novel *Quicksand* (1928), contains the first explicitly sexual black heroine in black women's fiction. Larsen explores questions of sexuality and power within both a rural and an urban landscape; in both contexts she condemns the ways in which female sexuality is confined and compromised as the object of male desire. In the city Larsen's heroine, Helga, has to recognize the ways in which her sexuality has an exchange value within capitalist social relations while in the country Helga is trapped by the consequences of woman's reproductive capacity. In the final pages of *Quicksand* Helga echoes the plight of the slave woman who could not escape to freedom and the cities of the North because she could not abandon her children and, at the same time, represents how a woman's life is drained through constant childbirth.

But Larsen also reproduces in her novel the dilemma of a black woman who tries to counter the dominant white cultural definitions of her sexuality: ideologies that define black female sexuality as a primitive and exotic. However the response of Larsen's heroine to such objectification is also the response of many black women writers: the denial of desire and the repression of sexuality. Indeed, *Quicksand* is symbolic of the tension in nineteenth- and early-twentieth-century black women's fiction in which black female sexuality was frequently displaced onto the terrain of the political responsibility of the black woman. The duty of the black heroine toward the black community was made coterminous with her desire as a woman, a desire which was expressed as a dedication to uplift the race. This displacement from female desire to female duty enabled the negotiation of racist constructions of black female sexuality but denied sensuality and in this denial lies the class character of its cultural politics.

It has been a mistake of much black feminist theory to concentrate almost exclusively on the visions of black women as represented by black women writers without indicating the limitations of their middle-class response to black women's sexuality. These writers faced a very real contradiction for they felt that they would publicly compromise themselves if they acknowledged their sexuality and sensuality within a racist sexual discourse thus providing evidence that indeed they were primitive and exotic creatures. But because black feminist theory has concentrated upon the literate forms of black women's intellectual activity the dilemma of the place of sexuality within a literary discourse has appeared as if it were the dilemma of most black women. On the other hand, what a consideration of women's blues allows us to see is an alternative form of representation, an oral and musical women's culture that explicitly addresses the contradictions of feminism, sexuality, and power. What has been called the "Classic Blues," the women's blues of the twenties and early thirties, is a discourse that articulates a cultural and political struggle over sexual relations: a struggle that is directed against the objectification of female sexuality within a patriarchal order but which also tries to reclaim women's bodies as the sexual and sensuous subjects of women's song.

TESTIFYIN'

Within black culture the figure of the female blues singer has been reconstructed in poetry, drama, fiction, and art and used to meditate upon conventional and unconventional sexuality. A variety of narratives, both fictional and biographical, have mythologized the woman blues singer and these mythologies become texts about sexuality. Women blues singers frequently appear as liminal figures that play out and explore the various possibilities of a sexual existence; they are representations of women who attempt to manipulate and control their construction as sexual subjects. In Afro-American fiction and poetry, the blues singer has a strong physical and sensuous presence. Sherley Anne Williams wrote about Bessie Smith:

> the thick triangular
> nose wedged

in the deep brown
face nostrils
flared on a last hummmmmmmmm.

Bessie singing
just behind the beat
that sweet sweet
voice throwing
its light on me

I looked in her face
and seed the woman
I'd become. A big
boned face already
lined and the first line
in her fo'head was
black and the next line
was sex cept I didn't
know to call it that
then and the brackets
round her mouth stood fo
the chi'ren she teared
from out her womb. (Williams, 1982)

Williams has argued that the early blues singers and their songs "helped to solidify community values and heighten community morale in the late nineteenth and early twentieth centuries." The blues singer, she says, uses song to create reflection and creates an atmosphere for analysis to take place. The blues were certainly a communal expression of black experience which had developed out of the call and response patterns of work songs from the nineteenth century and have been described as a "complex interweaving of the general and the specific" and of individual and group experience. John Coltrane has described how the audience heard "we" even if the singer said "I." Of course the singers were entertainers, but the blues was not an entertainment of escape or fantasy and sometimes directly represented historical events (Williams, 1979).

Sterling Brown has testified to the physical presence and power of Ma Rainey who would draw crowds from remote rural areas to see her "smilin' gold-toofed smiles" and to feel like participants in her performance which articulated the conditions of their social existence. Brown in his poem "Ma Rainey" remembers the emotion of her performance of "Back Water Blues" which described the devastation of the Mississippi flood of 1927. Rainey's original performance becomes in Brown's text a vocalization of the popular memory of the flood and Brown's text constructs itself as a part of the popular memory of the "Mother of the Blues" (Brown, 1981).

Ma Rainey never recorded "Backwater Blues" although Bessie Smith did, but local songsters would hear the blues performed in the tent shows or on record and transmit them throughout the community. Ma Rainey and Bessie Smith were among the first women blues singers to be recorded and with Clara Smith, Ethel Waters, Alberta Hunter, Ida Cox, Rosa Henderson, Victoria Spivey, and Lucille Hegamin they dominated the blues-recording industry throughout the twenties.

It has often been asserted that this recording of the blues compromised and adulterated a pure folk form of the blues but the combination of the vaudeville, carnival, and minstrel shows and the phonograph meant that the "folk-blues" and the culture industry product were inextricably mixed in the twenties. By 1928 the blues sung by blacks were only secondarily of folk origin and the primary source for the group transmission of the blues was by phonograph which was then joined by the radio.

Bessie Smith, Ma Rainey, Ethel Waters, and the other women blues singers travelled in carnivals and vaudevilles which included acts with animals, acrobats, and other circus performers. Often the main carnival played principally for white audiences but would have black sideshows with black entertainers for black audiences. In this way black entertainers reached black audiences in even the remotest rural areas. The records of the women blues singers were likewise directed at a black audience through the establishment of "race records," a section of the recording industry which recorded both religious and secular black singers and black musicians and distributed these recordings through stores in black areas: they were rarely available in white neighborhoods.

WHEN A WOMAN GETS THE BLUES . . .

This then is the framework within which I interpret the women blues singers of the twenties. To fully understand the ways in which their performance and their songs were part of a discourse of sexual relations within the black community, it is necessary to consider how the social conditions of black women were dramatically affected by migration, for migration had distinctively different meanings for black men and women. The music and song of the women blues singers embodied the social relations and contradictions of black displacement: of rural migration and the urban flux. In this sense, as singers these women were organic intellectuals; not only were they a part of the community that was the subject of their song but they were also a product of the rural-to-urban movement.

Migration for women often meant being left behind: "Bye Bye Baby" and "Sorry I can't take you" were the common refrains of male blues. In women's blues the response is complex: regret and pain expressed as "My sweet man done gone and left me dead," or "My daddy left me standing in the door," or "The sound of the train fills my heart with misery." There was also an explicit recognition that if the journey were to be made by women it held particular dangers for them. It was not as easy for women as it was for men to hop freight trains and if money was saved for tickets it was men who were usually sent. And yet the women who were singing the songs had made it North and recorded from the "promised land" of Chicago and New York. So, what the women blues singers were able to articulate were the possibilities of movement for the women who "have ramblin on their minds" and who intended to "ease on down the line" for they had made it—the power of movement was theirs. The train, which had symbolized freedom and mobility for men in male blues songs, became a contested symbol. The sound of the train whistle, a mournful signal of imminent desertion and future loneliness, was reclaimed as a sign that women too were on the move. In 1924, both Trixie Smith and Clara Smith recorded "Freight Train Blues." These are the words Clara Smith sang:

> I hate to hear that engine blow, boo hoo.
> I hate to hear that engine blow, boo hoo.
> Everytime I hear it blowin, I feel like ridin too.
>
> That's the freight train blues, I got box cars on my mind.
> I got the freight train blues, I got box cars on my mind.
> Gonna leave this town, cause my man is so unkind.
>
> I'm goin away just to wear you off my mind.
> I'm goin away just to wear you off my mind.
> And I may be gone for a doggone long long time.
>
> I'll ask the brakeman to let me ride the blind.
> I'll ask the brakeman to please let me ride the blind.
> The brakeman say, "Clara, you know this train ain't mine."
>
> When a woman gets the blues she goes to her room and hides.
> When a woman gets the blues she goes to her room and hides.
> When a man gets the blues he catch the freight train and rides.

The music moves from echoing the moaning, mournful sound of the train whistle to the syncopated activity of the sound of the wheels in movement as Clara Smith determines to ride. The final opposition between women hiding and men riding is counterpointed by this musical activity and the determination in Clara Smith's voice. "Freight Train Blues" and then "Chicago Bound Blues," which was recorded by Bessie Smith and Ida Cox, were very popular so Paramount and Victor encouraged more "railroad blues." In 1925 Trixie Smith recorded "Railroad Blues" which directly responded to the line "had the blues for Chicago and I just can't be satisfied" from "Chicago Bound Blues" with "If you ride that train it'll satisfy your mind." "Railroad Blues" encapsulated the ambivalent position of the blues singer caught between the contradictory impulses of needing to migrate North and the need to be able to return for the "Railroad Blues" were headed not for the North but for Alabama. Being able to move both North and South the woman blues singer occupied a privileged space: she could speak the desires of rural women to migrate and voice the nostalgic desires of urban women for home which was both a recognition and a warning that the city was not, in fact, the "promised land."

Men's and women's blues shared the language and experience of the railroad and migration but what that meant was different for each sex. The language of the blues carries this conflict of interests and is the cultural terrain in which these differences were fought over and redefined. Women's blues were the popular cultural embodiment of the way in which the differing interests of black men and women were a struggle of power relations. The sign of the train is one example of the way in which the blues were a struggle within language itself to define the differing material conditions of black women and black men.

BAAAD SISTA

The differing interests of women and men in the domestic sphere were clearly articulated by Bessie Smith in "In House Blues," a popular song from the mid-twenties which she wrote herself but didn't record until 1931. Although the man gets up and leaves, the woman remains, trapped in the house like a caged animal pacing up and down. But at the same time Bessie's voice vibrates with tremendous power which implies the eruption that is to come. The woman in the house is only barely restrained from creating havoc; her capacity for violence has been exercised before and resulted in her arrest. The music, which provides an oppositional counterpoint to Bessie's voice, is a parody of the supposed weakness of women. A vibrating cornet contrasts with the words that ultimately cannot be contained and roll out the front door.

> Sitting in the house with everything on my mind.
> Sitting in the house with everything on my mind.
> Looking at the clock and can't even tell the time.
>
> Walking to my window and looking outa my door.
> Walking to my window and looking outa my door.
> Wishin that my man would come home once more.
>
> Can't eat, can't sleep, so weak I can't walk my floor.
> Can't eat, can't sleep, so weak I can't walk my floor.
> Feel like calling "murder" let the police squad get me once more.
>
> They woke me up before day with trouble on my mind.
> They woke me up before day with trouble on my mind.
> Wringing my hands and screamin, walking the floor hollerin an crying.
>
> Hey, don't let them blues in here.
> Hey, don't let them blues in here.
> They shakes me in my bed and sits down in my chair.
>
> Oh, the blues has got me on the go.
> They've got me on the go.
> They roll around my house, in and out of my front door.

The way in which Bessie growls "so weak" contradicts the supposed weakness and helplessness of the woman in the song and grants authority to her thoughts of "murder."

The rage of women against male infidelity and desertion is evident in many of the blues. Ma Rainey threatened violence when she sang that she was "gonna catch" her man "with his britches down," in the act of infidelity, in "Black Eye Blues." Exacting revenge against mistreatment also appears as taking another lover as in "Oh Papa Blues" or taunting a lover who has been thrown out with "I won't worry when you're gone, another brown has got your water on" in "Titanic Man Blues." But Ma Rainey is perhaps best known for the rejection of a lover

in "Don't Fish in My Sea" which is also a resolution to give up men altogether.
She sang:

> If you don't like my ocean, don't fish in my sea,
> If you don't like my ocean, don't fish in my sea,
> Stay out of my valley, and let my mountain be.
>
> Ain't had no lovin' since God knows when.
> Ain't had no lovin' since God knows when,
> That's the reason I'm through with these no good triflin' men.

The total rejection of men as in this blues and in other songs such as "Trust No
Man" stand in direct contrast to the blues that concentrate upon the bewildered,
often half-crazed and even paralyzed response of women to male violence.

Sandra Leib (1981) has described the masochism of "Sweet Rough Man," in
which a man abuses a helpless and passive woman, and she argues that a distinction must be made between reactions to male violence against women in male
and female authored blues. "Sweet Rough Man," though recorded by Ma
Rainey, was composed by a man and is the most explicit description of sexual
brutality in her repertoire. The articulation of the possibility that women could
leave a condition of sexual and financial dependency, reject male violence, and
end sexual exploitation was embodied in Ma Rainey's recording of "Hustlin
Blues," composed jointly by a man and a woman, which narrates the story of a
prostitute who ends her brutal treatment by turning in her pimp to a judge. Ma
Rainey sang:

> I ain't made no money, and he dared me to go home.
> Judge, I told him he better leave me alone.
>
> He followed me up and he grabbed me for a fight.
> He followed me up and he grabbed me for a fight.
> He said, "Girl, do you know you ain't made no money tonight.
>
> Oh Judge, tell him I'm through.
> Oh Judge, tell him I'm through.
> I'm tired of this life, that's why I brought him to you.

However, Ma Rainey's strongest assertion of female sexual autonomy is a song
she composed herself, "Prove it on Me Blues," which isn't technically a blues
song which she sang accompanied by a Tub Jug Washboard Band. "Prove it on
Me Blues" was an assertion and an affirmation of lesbianism. Though condemned by society for her sexual preference the singer wants the whole world to
know that she chooses women rather than men. The language of "Prove it on Me
Blues" engages directly in defining issues of sexual preference as a contradictory
struggle of social relations. Both Ma Rainey and Bessie Smith had lesbian relationships and "Prove it on Me Blues" vacillates between the subversive hidden
activity of women loving women with a public declaration of lesbianism. The
words express a contempt for a society that rejected lesbians. "They say I do it,
ain't nobody caught me, They sure got to prove it on me." But at the same time

the song is a reclamation of lesbianism as long as the woman publicly names her sexual preference for herself in the repetition of lines about the friends who "must've been women, cause I don't like no men" (Leib, 1981).

But most of the songs that asserted a woman's sexual independence did so in relation to men, not women. One of the most joyous is a recording by Ethel Waters in 1925 called "No Man's Mamma Now." It is the celebration of a divorce that ended a marriage defined as a five year "war." Unlike Bessie Smith, Ethel Waters didn't usually growl, although she could; rather her voice, which is called "sweet-toned," gained authority from its stylistic enunciation and the way in which she almost recited the words. As Waters (1951) said, she tried to be "refined" even when she was being her most outrageous.

You may wonder what's the reason for this crazy smile,
Say I haven't been so happy in a long while
Got a big load off my mind, here's the paper sealed and signed,
And the judge was nice and kind all through the trial.
This ends a five year war, I'm sweet Miss Was once more.

I can come when I please, I can go when I please.
I can flit, fly and flutter like the birds in the trees.
Because, I'm no man's mamma now. Hey, hey.

I can say what I like, I can do what I like.
I'm a girl who is on a matrimonial strike;
Which means, I'm no man's mamma now.

I'm screaming bail
I know how a fella feels getting out of jail
I got twin beds, I take pleasure in announcing one for sale.

Am I making it plain, I will never again,
Drag around another ball and chain.
I'm through, because I'm no man's mamma now.

I can smile, I can wink, I can go take a drink,
And I don't have to worry what my hubby will think.
Because, I'm no man's mamma now.

I can spend if I choose, I can play and sing the blues.
There's nobody messin with my one's and my twos.
Because, I'm no man's mamma now.

You know there was a time,
I used to think that men were grand.
But no more for mine,
I'm gonna label my apartment "No Man's Land. "

I got rid of my cat cause the cat's name was Pat,
Won't even have a male fox in my flat,
Because, I'm no man's mamma now.

Waters' sheer exuberance is infectious. The vitality and energy of the performance celebrates the unfettered sexuality of the singer. The self-conscious and self-referential lines "I can play and sing the blues" situates the singer at the center of a subversive and liberatory activity. Many of the men who were married to blues singers disapproved of their careers, some felt threatened, others, like Edith Johnson's husband, eventually applied enough pressure to force her to stop singing. Most, like Bessie Smith, Ethel Waters, Ma Rainey, and Ida Cox did not stop singing the blues but their public presence, their stardom, their overwhelming popularity, and their insistence on doing what they wanted caused frequent conflict with the men in their personal lives.

FUNKY AND SINFUL STUFF

The figure of the woman blues singer has become a cultural embodiment of social and sexual conflict from Gayl Jones' novel *Corregidora* to Alice Walker's *The Color Purple*. The women blues singers occupied a privileged space; they had broken out of the boundaries of the home and taken their sensuality and sexuality out of the private into the public sphere. For these singers were gorgeous and their physical presence elevated them to being referred to as Goddesses, as the high priestesses of the blues, or like Bessie Smith, as the Empress of the blues. Their physical presence was a crucial aspect of their power; the visual display of spangled dresses, of furs, of gold teeth, of diamonds, of all the sumptuous and desirable aspects of their body reclaimed female sexuality from being an objectification of male desire to a representation of female desire.

Bessie Smith wrote about the social criticism that women faced if they broke social convention. "Young Woman's Blues" threads together many of the issues of power and sexuality that have been addressed so far. "Young Woman's Blues" sought possibilities, possibilities that arose from women being on the move and confidently asserting their own sexual desirability.

> Woke up this morning when chickens were crowing for day.
> Felt on the right side of my pillow, my man had gone away.
> On his pillow he left a note, reading I'm sorry you've got my goat.
> No time to marry, no time to settle down.
>
> I'm a young woman and ain't done running around.
> I'm a young woman and ain't done running around.
> Some people call me a hobo, some call me a bum,
> Nobody know my name, nobody knows what I've done.
> I'm as good as any woman in your town,
> I ain't no high yella, I'm a deep killa brown.
>
> I ain't gonna marry, ain't gonna settle down.
> I'm gonna drink good moonshine and run these browns down.
> See that long lonesome road, cause you know its got a end.
> And I'm a good woman and I can get plenty men.

The women blues singers have become our cultural icons of sexual power but what is often forgotten is that they could be great comic entertainers. In "One

Hour Mama" Ida Cox used comedy to intensify an irreverent attack on male sexual prowess. The comic does not mellow the assertive voice but on the contrary undermines mythologies of phallic power and establishes a series of woman-centered heterosexual demands.

> I've always heard that haste makes waste,
> So, I believe in taking my time
> The highest mountain can't be raced
> Its something you must slowly climb.
>
> I want a slow and easy man,
> He needn't ever take the lead,
> Cause I work on that long time plan
> And I ain't a looking for no speed.
>
> I'm a one hour mama, so no one minute papa
> Ain't the kind of man for me.
> Set your alarm clock papa, one hour that's proper
> Then love me like I like to be.
>
> I don't want no lame excuses bout my lovin being so good,
> That you couldn't wait no longer, now I hope I'm understood.
> I'm a one hour mama, so no one minute papa
> Ain't the kind of man for me.
>
> I can't stand no green horn lover, like a rookie goin to war,
> With a load of big artillery, but don't know what its for.
> He's got to bring me reference with a great long pedigree
> And must prove he's got endurance, or he don't mean snap to me.
>
> I can't stand no crowin rooster, what just likes a hit or two,
> Action is the only booster of just what my man can do.
> I don't want no imitation, my requirements ain't no joke,
> 'Cause I got pure indignation for a guy what's lost his stroke.
>
> I'm a one hour mama, so no one minute papa
> Ain't the kind of man for me.
> Set your alarm clock papa, one hour that's proper,
> Then love me like I like to be.
>
> I may want love for one hour, then decide to make it two.
> Takes an hour 'fore I get started, maybe three before I'm through.
> I'm a one hour mama, so no one minute papa,
> Ain't the kind of man for me.

But this moment of optimism, of the blues as the exercise of power and control over sexuality, was short lived. The space occupied by these blues singers was opened up by race records but race records did not survive the depression. Some of these blues women, like Ethel Waters and Hattie McDaniels, broke through the racial boundaries of Hollywood film and were inserted into a different aspect of the culture industry where they occupied not a privileged but a subordinate space and articulated not the possibilities of black female sexual power but the "Yes, Ma'am"s of the black maid. The power of the blues singer was resurrected in a different moment of black power; re-emerging in Gayl Jones' *Corregidora;* and the woman blues singer remains an important part of our twentieth-century black cultural reconstruction. The blues singers had assertive and demanding voices; they had no respect for sexual taboos or for breaking through the boundaries of respectability and convention, and we hear the "we" when they say "I."

NOTES

This paper was originally a presentation to the conference on "Sexuality, Politics and Power" held at Mount Holyoke College, September 1986. It was reprinted in *Radical America* 20,4 (1986): 9–24. The power of the music can only be fully understood by listening to the songs, which should be played as the essay is read.

WORKS CITED

Brown, S. (1980). "Ma Rainey." *The Collected Poems of Sterling A. Brown*. New York: Harper and Row.

Carby, H. V. (1986). "On the threshold of woman's era: Lynching, empire and sexuality in black feminist theory." In H. L. Gates, Jr. (Ed.), *"Race," Writing and Difference* (pp. 301–316). Chicago: University of Chicago Press.

Carby, H. V. (1987). *Reconstructing Womanhood: The Emergence of the Afro-American Woman Novelist*. New York: Oxford University Press.

Cooper, A. J. (1892). *A Voice from the South*. Xenia, OH: Aldine Publishing House.

Cox, I. (1980). "One hour mama." *Mean Mothers*. Rosetta Records, RR 1300.

Leib, S. (1981). *Mother of the Blues: A Study of Ma Rainey*. Amherst: University of Massachusetts Press.

Rainey, G. (1974). *Ma Rainey*. Milestone Records, M47021.

Smith, B. (n.d.). "In house blues." *The World's Greatest Blues Singer*. Columbia Records, CG33.

Smith, B. (1972). "Young woman's blues." *Nobody's Blues But Mine*. Columbia Records, CG 31093.

Smith, C. (1980). "Freight train blues." *Women's Railroad Blues*. Rosetta Records, RR 1301.

Spillers, H. (1984). "Interstices: A small drama of words." In C. Vance (Ed.), *Pleasure and Danger: Exploring Female Sexuality* (pp. 73–100). London: Routledge and Kegan Paul.

Waters, E. (1951). *His Eye is on the Sparrow*. New York: Doubleday & Co., Inc.

Waters, E. (1982). "No man's mama." *Big Mamas*. Rosetta Records, RR 1306.

Williams, S. A. (1979). "The blues roots of contemporary Afro-American poetry." In M. S. Harper & R. B. Stepto (Eds.), *Chant of Saints* (pp. 123–135). Chicago: University of Illinois Press.

Williams, S. A. (1981). "The house of desire." in E. Stetson (Ed.), *Black Sister: Poetry by Black American Women, 1746–1980*. Bloomington: Indiana University Press.

Williams, S. A. (1982). "Fifteen." *Some One Sweet Angel Chile*. New York: William Morrow and Co., Inc.

history

Great deeds of great men; chronological accounts of battles and borders, treaties and territories: if this is what "history" connoted through much of the twentieth century, the term has recently come to embrace much more. Historiography has departed from diachronic narratives of political and military "events," moving into more synchronic accounts of such matters as conventions for courtship, attitudes toward smell and personal hygiene, and even patterns of weather in the past. The "new history" tries, among other things, to scrutinize the experience of those who have inhabited the margins of culture and society, whose voices had previously been silenced because their race, class, gender, or nationality denied them access to power and self-expression in the world of "events."

In literary studies, "new historicism" (epitomized by such journals as *Representations* and *American Literary History*) holds texts up against nonliterary documents from their own historical period, looking at how a culture's discourse on a topic—be it sexuality, knowledge, madness, punishment (the subjects associated with Michel Foucault, an important influence upon this movement), or something else—affects our interpretation of a work of literature addressing that same topic. New historicism has been very influential in putting literary texts—particularly canonical works of the Renaissance—firmly back into the historical context from which structuralism and its theoretical descendents had tended to alienate them.

Arguably, though, history was already playing a significant role in feminist criticism before new historicism gained its recent popularity. Such feminist commentators as Judith Lowder Newton (in an essay called "History as Usual? Feminism and the 'New Historicism'") and Linda Boose (in "The Family in Shakespeare Studies; or—Studies in the Family of Shakespearians; or—the Politics of Politics") assert that feminists have been bringing history to bear on literary criticism long enough to shake the "new" from "historicism's" usual appellation. To be sure, not all feminist criticism treats "history" in a way that "historicists" would approve. The "images of women" movement of the 1970s, along with certain modes of Freudian and Jungian archetypal criticism (not represented in this volume), tended to locate certain female figures in texts (for example, the "earth mother" or the "bitch goddess") outside of history, pointing to the recurrence of types and of psychological patterns without reference to their specific moments in time. Indeed, in the essay we reprint here, Newton mentions the tendency of gynocriticism (the study of women's literary tradition) "to focus on the presence of unchanging or transhistorical patterns," a focus she identifies as the crucial difference between her project and those of Elaine Showalter, Nina Auerbach, and Sandra M. Gilbert and Susan Gubar. Although these critics arrange their work around historical periods and chronological developments, Newton argues, they do not account for literature's relation to "developing material conditions" or "shifting ideologies." In other words, practitioners of gynocriticism do not usually adopt a Marxist model of explanation for historical change and stasis.

What is perhaps most striking about the five pieces in this section is that they all do make some use of Marxist premises (even though Gayatri Chakravorty Spivak overtly distances herself in her essay from "Marxist critics"), just as they all make explicit their intention to "do history" when reading literary texts. This becomes visible in the writers' focus on questions of class and economics, and in their use of the language of false-consciousness and dominant ideology, capitalism and struggle. As entries in other sections of *Feminisms* (notably "Class," "Discourse," and "Desire") reveal, Marxism has often provided a vocabulary for feminist analysis of women's social and political status. Perhaps one reason for the seeming compatibility of the two modes is Marxism's insistence that there is such a thing as "the material conditions, the real relations" (as Newton calls them) operating in the world. For all our poststructuralist sophistication, our questioning of the truth-status of discourse and texts, all feminists do agree on certain fundamental truths, for example, that the oppression of women is a reality which ought to be eradicated. Marxism's grounding in economic evidence—its belief in the "real"—provides reinforcement for feminism's parallel interests, as well as providing the only popularly operative model for radical or progressive social change. That Marxist history should figure so prominently in historically-centered feminist criticism, then, is no surprise.

The most explicitly Marxist of the selections here, Newton's Introduction to *Women, Power, and Subversion: Social Strategies in British Fiction 1778–1860* (1981) also addresses most directly a central tenet of feminist history, the division in nineteenth-century England and America between the "public sphere"—the world of events, economics, and men—and the "private sphere"—the world of domesticity, morality, and women. The notion of separate spheres grows out of the research of such women's historians as Gerda Lerner, Carroll Smith-Rosenberg, and Mary Ryan, and has provided literary critics with a lens through which to see nineteenth-century women's fiction in the context of the culture (rather than the individual authors) that produced it. Newton's book studies four canonical women's novels, Frances Burney's *Evelina*, Jane Austen's *Pride and Prejudice*, Charlotte Brontë's *Villette*, and George Eliot's *The Mill on the Floss*. Taken outside of historical context, all of these novels could be read as reinforcing a conservative status quo and undermining the potential power of their proto-feminist heroines. Seen within the framework of the ideology of separate spheres, however, the novels take on a subversive aspect.

As Newton explains, nineteenth-century women's conduct manuals promoted the idea that women's "power" consisted not of publicly exercised "ability," but rather of "influence" within the domestic realm. The heroines of these novels, however, possess "ability," and their power—though often covertly manifested—undermines the separate-sphere ideology that was gradually coming to dominate Anglo-American gender relations between Burney's time and Eliot's. A historical approach that looked to women authors' biographies for evidence of feminist rebellion might yield more evidence of "influence" than of "ability" in these writers' extraliterary lives. But, as Newton insists, "To write subversively is more than a means of exercising influence. It is a form of struggle—and a form of power."

The ideology of separate spheres forms the backdrop, too, for Annette Kolodny's chapter from *The Land Before Her: Fantasy and Experience of the American Frontiers, 1630-1860*, "The Domestic Fantasy Goes West" (1984). Like Newton, Kolodny looks at nonliterary texts for evidence of the period's dominant ideology, then reads novels in light of that evidence. Here, the ideology centers on American westward expansion, and particularly upon the role middle-class women—bred to reign in the private, domestic sphere—were supposed to play in that movement. Kolodny begins with the economic realities of the United States's shift from an agrarian to an urban nation during the nineteenth century, and moves from her description of this economic reality to an examination of how pioneer manuals and sentimental novels represented life in the West as a social and cultural antidote. In an era when slavery and industrialization threatened the institution of the family and the traditional middle-class woman's position in it, Kolodny argues, the "pioneer home" became the location for nostalgic fantasies of a life where women could play out a domesticating and civilizing role. Kolodny looks to "historical reality" for the sources of anxiety that prompted this discourse and supported its popularity among readers. Unlike Newton's canonical British novels, the sentimental American novels Kolodny studies here do not operate to subvert the dominant ideology of separate spheres, but rather to reinforce it.

By shifting the focus from the private experience of heroines in novels to the wider arena of empire, and by looking at "first world" texts from an explicitly marginal perspective, Gayatri Chakravorty Spivak adjusts what it means to think about history in connection with feminist criticism. In "Three Women's Texts and a Critique of Imperialism" (1985), Spivak adopts a contentious stance at once: whereas received wisdom would assume that feminism (opposed as it is to the oppression of women) would be "naturally" antithetical to imperialism (the oppression of conquered peoples), Spivak observes that "the emergent perspective of feminist criticism reproduces the axioms of imperialism." She substantiates the charge with reference to feminist readings of *Jane Eyre*, which—Spivak explains—participate in the ideology of individualism that is central to colonializing impulses. To assign a "self" to the "other," to "world" a region or a culture (for example, to designate a group of places as "the third world") by enumerating it in a series where the "first" is "ours," is to participate in imperialism. Spivak shows how *Jane Eyre* supports the ideology of individual uniqueness and "soul making," and reads Jean Rhys's *Wide Sargasso Sea* as a "reinscription" of Brontë's text. Her counterexample is Mary Shelley's *Frankenstein*, which—with its complex playing out of issues of sexual reproduction and self-construction— "deconstructs" the ideology behind a text like *Jane Eyre*.

Spivak asserts that feminist criticism which wants to go beyond the limits established by individualist assumptions must "turn to the archives of imperialist governance"; she also concedes that her essay does not do so, though her later work will. Given the absence of those nonliterary documents from this piece, we can see that Spivak's way of bringing "history" to literary studies is here quite distinct from Newton's, Kolodny's, or Willis's. Spivak does not trace a chronology of women's writing—*Frankenstein*, which deconstructs *Jane Eyre*, was published twenty-nine years before the text whose premises it critiques—nor does she compare a novel's discourse about imperialism with official or nonliterary statements on empire from the period. Instead, Spivak reads the novels with an eye to the history of the long-term, as we can see it from a postcolonial perspective. She is not interested in charting biographies of (or progress through) individual authors; like the Marxist critics from whom she explicitly separates herself, Spivak is more concerned with analyzing the social constitution of the self. "The most I can say," she explains, "is that it is possible to read these texts, within the frame of imperialism and the Kantian ethical moment, in a politically useful way." One of her most politically suggestive conclusions is that "the absolutely Other cannot be selfed," another warning against indulging a Western individualist feminism that would try to name the "Third-World Woman" as a signifier.

Of course, not all feminist-historical scholarship focuses on nineteenth-century literature. Our decision to concentrate *Feminisms* upon criticism of literature written since 1800 precludes our inserting any of the work being done on earlier periods of British literature. For a sample of how a historical approach can inform the study of contemporary writers, we offer the introduction to Susan Willis's *Specifying: Black Women Writing the American Experience* (1987). Like Newton, Willis takes seriously the impact of capitalism upon women's social position; like Kolodny, she traces the effects of urbanization upon women's lives; and like Spivak, she focuses upon the differences that race and culture have made for women who are not white and middle class. More than any of the others, Willis also expresses an interest in individual (black) women, both as authors and characters: she proposes to study the development of any given black heroine "in relation to the historical forces that have shaped the migrations of her race, the struggles of her community, and the relationships that have developed within her community."

Willis proposes to study not just the content of the novels of such writers as Zora Neale Hurston, Toni Morrison, and Alice Walker, but to look at form, at the way history is "embodied in how the novels tell their stories." Willis suggests that her texts, made up as they often are out of "short pieces of writing," are appropriate to the rhythms of agrarian daily life; the texts resemble oral storytelling and, she argues, are reminiscent of "specifying," the black cultural practice of ridiculing opponents and their family members in a raucously public setting ("yo' mama . . ."). Departing as no other contributor to this section does from strictly verbal discourse, Willis also suggests that the forms and rhythms of the black music tradition help to shape black women's fiction. Returning to questions of rhetoric, she argues that her writers use metaphor in a particular way, to collapse historical moments and to suggest affinities between the fictional present and the historical past. "For black women," Willis asserts, "history is a bridge defined along motherlines." For feminist critics—and for some of the new historians—the insertion of gender into inquiries about the past has meant building a similar bridge.

—RRW

POWER AND THE IDEOLOGY OF "WOMAN'S SPHERE"

> . . . women, in their position in life, must be content to be inferior to men; but as their inferiority consists chiefly in their want of power, this deficiency is abundantly made up to them by their capability of exercising influence.
> —SARAH ELLIS, *THE DAUGHTERS OF ENGLAND*, 1845

> . . . as with work on the lower classes, slave populations, and peasants, work on relations between the sexes makes the location of power a trickier business than when one is looking at governments, parties, factions, and clientage systems. Power can lodge in dangerous nooks and crannies.
> —NATALIE ZEMON DAVIS, "'WOMEN'S HISTORY' IN TRANSITION," 1976

> The powers of the weak are, finally, more powerful than we think and can only be ignored by the powerful at their peril.
> —ELIZABETH JANEWAY, "ON THE POWER OF THE WEAK," 1975

In April of 1850, when Elizabeth Gaskell confessed to Tottie Fox that "the discovery of one's exact work in the world is the puzzle: . . . I am sometimes coward enough to wish we were back in the darkness where obedience was the only seen duty of women,"[1] she was finding words for a private and personally troubling experience of a more general ideological crisis, a crisis of confidence over the status, the proper work, and the power of middle-class women. This crisis of confidence, which emerged in the 1830s and 1840s in Great Britain, took the form of a prolonged debate over the "woman question," a debate so extensive that in 1869 Frances Power Cobbe was provoked to remark that "of all theories concerning women, none is more curious than the theory that it is needful to make a theory about them. . . . We are driven to conclude," she continues, that while men grow like trees "women run in moulds, like candles, and we can make them long-threes or short-sixes, whichever we please."[2]

The debate over the "woman question," in addition to its mass production of theories about women's "mission," "kingdom," or "sphere," gave an emphasis to the subject of women's power, and in particular to their influence, which was historically unprecedented. One has only to take manuals addressed to genteel women in the late eighteenth century and lay them alongside those written for middle-class women some sixty to seventy years later to see a deepening tension over women's power begin to manifest itself like footprints in a flower garden. In 1774, for example, in *A Father's Legacy to His Daughters*, John Gregory makes very few allusions to the power or influence of women. Although women are recognized as having been designed to "soften [the] hearts and polish [the] manners" of men, Gregory is less interested in the power women have to redeem men than charmed by the facility with which they please them. Woman's sphere, therefore, is not conceived of as the locus of a particular influence. Genteel women in Gregory's *Legacy* are "companions and equals" of men, rational beings, and their separate world is recommended not because it affords them power but because it lends them scope in which to be rationally human, in which to exercise "good sense and good taste."[3]

Twenty years later, however, James Fordyce makes many references to women's influence. One of his first *Sermons to Young Women* is "on the Importance of the Female Sex, especially the Younger Part," and in it he reassures women that a "principal source of your importance is the very great and extensive influence which you in general have with our sex." Genteel women have more extensive tasks in Fordyce than to polish manners and instill decency: they are to "promote general reformation" among men. And their separate sphere is important less as a realm in which they may demonstrate good taste than as a dominion in which they exercise a specific potency: "There is an influence, there is an empire which belongs to you . . . I mean that which has the heart as its object."[4]

By 1798 Thomas Gisborne, in *An Enquiry into the Duties of the Female Sex*, feels prompted to remind women not only that they have "influence" but that its effects are "various and momentous" and that this influence, like the power of men, extends to society as a whole. Thus, genteel women are urged to consider "the real and deeply interesting effects which the conduct of their sex will always have on the happiness of society." But the insistence upon women's influence reaches a culmination some thirty years later when Sarah Ellis begins *The Women of England* (1839) by declaring both that women's influence is social in nature and that it is in some ways more socially significant than the power of men: "You have deep responsibilities; you have urgent claims; a nation's moral worth is in your keeping."[5]

This same tension and counterinsistence in relation to women's power leave traces on periodical literature addressed to the "woman question." In 1810, for example, an author for the *Edinburgh Review* makes only one reference to women's influence, giving far more emphasis to the dignity, the delightfulness, and the ornamental quality of women's character and to the importance of their personal happiness. But by 1831, in literature of the same kind, power and influence are frequent subjects of concern, and references to both are accompanied by a sharpening distinction between what is appropriate to women and what to men. Most authors—and it is worth noting that much of this literature was written by men—reject the notion that women have power, but they acknowledge and give value to the fact that women possess "enormous," "immense," or "vast" "influence." This influence, of course, is always reassuringly unobtrusive, "secret," "unobserved," an "undercurrent below the surface."[6]

In 1833 a writer for *Fraser's Magazine*, who is actually defending the female character, is still obliged to doubt the existence of amazons, though he admits that there are many instances of "females acting in a body in defence of their homes." In 1841 an author for the *Edinburgh Review* dismisses the proposition that men and women will ever be equal "in power and influence upon the affairs of the world" and warns, rather ill-naturedly, that if women "be made ostensibly powerful . . . the spirit of chivalry . . . will speedily cease." But women do have "immense influence," he concedes, and that influence must "be allowed to flow in its natural channels, namely domestic ones." In the same year a writer for the *Westminster Review* admits that "power" as encoded in laws seems "permanent and transmittable in nature, while influence dies with the possessor," but women, he concludes hopefully, do not *want* power in the first place: " . . . the peculiar duties of women are guarded by instincts and feelings more powerful than the desire for political power."[7]

This valorization of women's influence, it should be clear, was aimed at de-valuing actions and capacities which we can only call other forms of power, and, in this way, the peddling of women's influence, in a sort of ideological market-place, functioned to sustain unequal power relations between middle-class women and middle-class men. Having influence, in fact, having the ability to persuade others to do or to be something that was in *their* own interest, was made contingent upon the renunciation of such self-advancing forms of power as control or self-definition. To have influence, for example, the middle-class woman was urged to relinquish self-definition; she was urged to become identified by her services to others, in particular to men:

> . . . men in general are more apt than women, to act and think as if they were created to exist of, and by, themselves; and this self-sustained existence a wife can only share, in proportion as she is identified in every thing with her husband.

> It is necessary for her to lay aside all her natural caprice, her love of self-indulgence, her vanity, her indolence—in short, her very *self*—and assuming a new nature, which [is] to spend her mental and moral capabilities in devising means for promoting the happiness of others, while her own derives a remote and secondary existence from theirs.[8]

Having influence also required women to lay aside any desire for the power to achieve, especially outside the domestic sphere, for "it is from an ambitious desire to extend the limits of this sphere, that many have brought trouble upon themselves." And even within the home, achievement must be circumscribed. The possession of talent is "the possession of a dangerous heritage—a jewel which cannot with propriety be worn." Most centrally, of course, the power of control must be renounced, and Sarah Ellis apologizes for suggesting that women "preside" even in the home, being "aware that the word *preside*, used as it is here, may produce a startling effect upon the ear of man." To have influence, in effect, meant doing without self-definition, achievement, and control, meant relinquishing power for effacement of the self in love and sacrifice: "All that has been expected to be enjoyed from the indulgence of selfishness, must then of necessity be left out of our calculations, with all that ministers to the pride of superiority, all that gratifies the love of power, all that converts the woman into the heroine."[9]

The preoccupation with women's power that leaves its mark on nineteenth-century manuals and on other literature addressed to the "woman question" reappears like a bold thread in the texture of the works in this study. But it is significant that the heroines of these works, Evelina, Elizabeth Bennet, Lucy Snowe, and Maggie Tulliver, are generally endowed not with power as influence but with power as ability and that Burney, Austen, Brontë, and Eliot give evidence of that "love of power . . . that converts the woman into the heroine." Indeed, it is one of the characteristic strategies of these authors to subvert masculine control and male domination in their novels by quietly giving emphasis to female capability, as if the pattern in the background of an embroidered piece had been subtly worked into relief.

One form of ability, for example, is autonomy, the power of being one's own person, and being one's own person is multiply and often subtly defined. It may mean having one's private opinions—Evelina's letters are full of unflattering observations about men—or it may take the shape of self-defending actions—Evelina refuses a dance partner against the rules; Elizabeth deftly rejects Darcy's proposal. Women are also made powerful in these novels by being endowed with the capacity to achieve, to perform tasks, to act not merely on other individuals but on situations, and although the scope of achievement is more limited in female characters than in male—Madame Beck makes a success of a school for girls but not of being an industrial capitalist—the emphasis given to achievement as power is used in *Villette*, as in other works, to balance or even to outweigh the power of male characters and so to alter what we *feel* in the course of reading the novel about the traditional divisions of power between women and men. Some women writing fiction, it appears, having found it unthinkable, unrealistic, or unhealthy to give their female characters such traditionally masculine power as the power of control, managed to make women *seem* powerful, nevertheless, by giving emphasis and value to power as capacity.

In choosing to focus on female ability, of course, these writers themselves exercised a form of agency, of resistance to dominant values. In their foregrounding of female ability and in their subversive undercutting of male control, they illustrate what Elizabeth Janeway has maintained: even "a withdrawal of attention . . . a concentration on other areas" are "ways in which the weak exercise their power." [10] The ability of female characters and the power strategies of their creators, however, are difficult at first to see, and part of the difficulty at least lies in our own cultural limitations. Our very definitions of power—like our conceptions of "history" or of "art"—have been deformed by traditions which have systematically excluded women. In all fields of women's studies, therefore, our shift in focus from the limitations of women's situation to the reality of their persisting power has raised questions about what power really is. It has committed us both to broadened definitions of power and to a certain openness, to an acknowledgment of the idea that female power "can lodge in dangerous nooks and crannies." [11]

Berenice Carroll, for example, has reminded us that the definition of power primarily as "control, dominance, and influence" is of recent origin and that the primary meaning of power as late as 1933 was "ability, energy, and strength." Power, according to Carroll, has been defined not just as control but also as "ability," as the capacity to assert "one's will over one's body, one's own organs and functions and over the physical environment—a power which is seen as inherently satisfying and not merely as an instrument to other ends, as neither requiring nor leading to the power to command obedience in other persons." [12] Power as ability, that is, has been defined both as achievement and competence and, by implication, as a form of self-definition or self-rule. It is this power of ability or capability that seams together the fiction I am going to explore.

Of course, power in women's fiction may also be difficult to see because power is a subject and a capacity which make women writers ill at ease, and uneasiness breeds disguise or, at the least, obliqueness. In the eighteenth and nineteenth centuries, in particular, the act of writing in itself appeared to lend women a self-assertiveness which seemed out of keeping with properly feminine aspirations. Elaine Showalter suggests that the ambivalence which many women writers felt toward the self-revelation and assertion necessary to writing fiction prompted a whole spectrum of defensive strategies which ranged from the use of male pseudonyms to the punishment of aspiring heroines to the author's insistence in private life on the conventionality of her own womanhood. More recently, Sandra Gilbert and Susan Gubar have isolated a pervasive "anxiety of authorship—a radical fear that she cannot create, that because she can never become a 'precursor' the act of writing will isolate or destroy her" as a crucial mark of women's literary subculture in the nineteenth century. [13] To write at all and then to write of power, perhaps to perform some transforming action in one's fiction upon traditional power divisions, was surely to multiply defensive strategies, and in *Evelina, Pride and Prejudice, Villette,* and *The Mill on the Floss* the ability of female characters and the power strategies of their creators are systematically disguised, offset, or explained into moonshine. Evelina's satirical strictures, for example, are excused by her innocence and by her ignorance of city ways, and Elizabeth Bennet's refreshing self-direction is qualified by her defensive ironies. She may speak her mind to Darcy, may finally change him, and the reader is allowed to enjoy her daring, but at the same time we are continually reminded that Elizabeth is wrong about Wickham and wrong about Darcy and that she is controlled by her desire to please both.

Although each of these novels, moreover, is the story of a quest, the story of entry into the world, of education, and of growth, including growth in power, the heroine's power is sometimes renounced and often diminished at the end of the novel, so that it seems that the work has had nothing to do with power at all. [14] For no matter how much force the heroine is granted at the beginning of her story, ideology, as it governed life and as it governed literary form, required that she should marry, and marriage meant relinquishment of power as surely as it meant the purchase of wedding clothes. Thus, Evelina gives up satire in the third volume of the novel in order to weep, faint, and otherwise prepare herself for the princely Orville, and Elizabeth Bennet, though her own woman to the end, still dwindles by degrees into the moral balance required in Darcy's wife. Even in *Villette* and *The Mill on the Floss,* where marriage plots are more totally resisted, resistance appears ultimately to exhaust authorial resources. The quest of Lucy Snowe ends abruptly with the death of Lucy's fiancé, and in *The Mill on the Floss* the unwed heroine drowns at the end of the novel.

As they wrote about quest and entry into the world these authors, it should be clear, felt the pressure of ideologies which required circumscription of power as rigorously as they required marriage (and more loss of power) as a "happy" ending. These are not difficulties with which male writers have had to wrestle, and it is the experience of these pressures, which are at once acceded to and rebelled against, that gives rise to the peculiar dominance in these novels of tension, disguise, and ultimately disjunctions of form. In any work, of course, it is not only what a text does say but what it does not say that reveals its relation to dominant images, ideas, and values. It is in the "significant *silences* of a text, in its gaps and absences, that the presence of ideology can be most positively felt." [15] But in these novels in particular, the very covertness of power, the nature and degree of its disguise, the very omission of overt reference are of the greatest interest, for subversion, indirection, and disguise are natural tactics of the resisting weak, are social strategies for managing the most intense and the most compelling rebellions.

In these specific novels, finally, the tensions created by each author's struggle with conventions—by her insistence on dealing with female power in the first place, her subversion of traditional power relations, her substitution of ability for influence, and her refusal, for the most part, totally to relinquish the heroine's ability at the end of the story—were surely intensified by the fact that each novel had an unusually direct origin in the author's own experience. Each writer, in fact, appears to be working through some painful personal encounter with culturally imposed patterns of male power and female powerlessness. In Burney this is specifically the shock of being reduced to merchandise in the marriage market. In Austen it is more generally the experience of being without money, without carriages, without options, the enduring experience of suffering restrictions upon her autonomy, and in Brontë and Eliot it is the external and internal limitations imposed on their passionate and half-guilty desire to achieve.

Taken together, then, these novels may be said to register a developing tension over women's power, a tension which appears to have been central to that general crisis of consciousness over the role and status of middle-class women which surfaced in the 1830s and 1840s. What is more significant, however, is that in their subversion of traditional power relations and ultimately in their substitution of female ability for feminine influence these novels delineate a line of covert, ambivalent, but finally radical resistance to the ideology of their day. Taken together, they seem to articulate what Raymond Williams has called an emergent "structure of feeling," a development of consciousness which is as yet embryonic, which is tied to dominant ideology, but which is nevertheless alternative or oppositional to dominant values, suggesting that the alternative to "received and produced fixed forms" is "not silence: not the absence, the unconscious, which bourgeois culture has mythicized. It is a kind of feeling and thinking which is indeed social and material, but each in an embryonic phase before it can become fully articulate and defined exchange." [16]

The line of resistance, moreover, grows bolder as the ideology of women's influence takes hold. Between Burney's *Evelina* in 1778 and Eliot's *The Mill on the Floss* in 1860, conceptions of male power in these novels are expanded so that women's power and the unequal power divisions between women and men become increasingly a matter of overt concern. Men's power in Burney almost always takes the form of force or control in social situations—of assault in ballrooms or ravishment in carriages. Power is the ability to impose one's self on another or to defend one's self from imposition. But in Eliot men's power is the ability not only to dominate others but to define the self and to achieve: " . . . you are a man, Tom, and have power, and can do something in the world."[17] That men have more power than women, therefore, is made more significant in *The Mill on the Floss* than in *Evelina*.

Between Burney and Eliot, too, unequal divisions of power are increasingly perceived or conceived of in these novels as imposed by the community rather than as natural or given. The community as a force, therefore, becomes more and more dominant—although its force may be mystified, as in *Villette*—and that development is accompanied by a growing tendency to portray community values as ideology and as ideology unwittingly internalized by the heroine. At the same time, however, the strategy of giving power to the heroine, the power of ability rather than of influence or control, becomes more and more pronounced and is expressed in the increasing emphasis given to quest—the development of the heroine and especially of her desire for power—at the expense of love. In Burney, for example, an incipient quest plot is simply abandoned to the love plot in the third volume, while in Austen love and quest are forced into an uneasy balance.

Taken together, then, these novels suggest more ways in which women's writing may be both the locus of compensating fantasies and the site of protest, actions expressive of the authors' power, and in this respect the following study develops a line of reading which feminist critics have begun to explore. Patricia Spacks, for example, has written of one woman artist that "her own power was the power to imagine what she wished of others . . . to recreate her experience in a way that made it tolerable." Ellen Moers has written of the gothic and of factory novels as the locus of middle-class women's displaced protest of their lot. Elaine Showalter has suggested several ways in which a subculture of female writers was informed by covert ways of dramatizing the inner life, by fantasies of "money, mobility, and power." Nina Auerbach has explored fictional communities of women as the continuing source of female strength. And most recently Sandra Gilbert and Susan Gubar have posited a whole tradition among female writers of creating "submerged meanings, meanings hidden within or behind the more accessible, 'public' content of their works," so that the works "are in some sense palimpsestic, works whose surface designs conceal or obscure deeper, less accessible (and less socially acceptable) levels of meaning." Each of these critics works helpfully and fertilely within the assumption that "art enables men and women both to order, interpret, mythologize or dispose of their own experience."[18]

But most studies of subversive strategies in women's fiction have tended to focus on the presence of unchanging or transhistorical patterns or have tended to isolate the text not just from developing material conditions but from shifting ideologies as well, and this tendency to universalize has led many of us to claim, rather too easily, that art is a transforming action upon history without our having to say in fact what that history has been. Susan Gubar and Sandra Gilbert, for example, while recognizing the reality of "male-dominated society" and of women's attempts to redefine their society along with their art, have focused their study on women's struggle against "patriarchal literary authority" and patriarchal images and conventions. Nina Auerbach, too, although she makes some striking connections between text and historical context, does not give emphasis

to the changing ideological and material situations in which the evolution of literary myth takes place. My own work differs in that it attempts to trace the shifting
historical situation in which literary redefinitions and evolutions unfolded.

Elaine Showalter, of course, does explore female literary traditions in the context of the "still-evolving relationships between women writers and their society," but where she has given us an overview of a female literary tradition my
own aim has been to lay out paradigms of reading in which the complexities and
ambiguities of the relation between novel and cultural context are central.[19] Indeed, it is one project of this study to suggest how works of women's fiction
might be read in several contexts—in relation to the changing material conditions of women's lives, to the ideological representations and distortions of those
conditions, to an author's particular biographical experience of these, and to the
ideological content and shaping force of such conventions in women's fiction as
the quest and the marriage plot. Following Terry Eagleton (more or less), I have
assumed that a work of fiction presents itself to us less as "historical than as a
sportive flight from history, a reversal and a resistance of history."[20] Although I
make note of the way in which a text might be said to "evoke" historical situations,[21] I have dwelt on the way it relates itself to ideological perceptions or distortions of those situations. I have dwelt, that is, on the way a work of fiction
relates itself to ideas, images, and values which insure that the situation in which
one class has power over another and in which men have power over women is
seen as natural or not seen at all. Specifically, I have asked how these works both
support and resist ideologies which have tied middle-class women to the relative
powerlessness of their lot and which have prevented them from having a true
knowledge of their situation, but I have also tried to consider how ideologies governing middle-class women intersect with and are interdependent upon more
general ideologies which sustain and legitimate the power of the male bourgeoisie in relation to society as a whole.

My aim, in this, has been first to read the text more fully, for to locate threads
of rebellion in a text without articulating rather specifically what is being rebelled
against is to see only part of the pattern in the text itself, and it is not fully to see
the transforming significance—and the limitations—of the subversive themes,
metaphors, or strategies which, with painstaking labor, have been discovered. To
see a text in isolation from its historical conditions is not fully enough to answer
the question "So what?"—a question which Lillian Robinson has posed as the
hardest we can ask ourselves as critics. A second aim has been to understand the
present by coming to better terms with our collective past. Implicit in my focus,
for example, are the assumption that ideology has been central to women's oppression and the assumption that literature gives us a peculiarly revealing access
to the way in which ideology has been experienced. Studying the relation of
literature and ideology allows us to explore one area of what has been called "the
emotional texture of life for individuals in the past . . ." "the existential consequences of occupying a particular social location . . ." "the structure of choices"
which the situation of women afforded them.[22] In examining both the text's subversion of ideology and its adherence to it, moreover, we may come to some
understanding of the degree to which female writers may have acted as agents or
as arbiters of change, for works of fiction practice upon their readers, skew the
angle of vision from which readers experience their relation to the real, the de-

gree of confidence which they feel in traditional social relations. Most important, finally, it is in exploring the ways in which women have experienced ideology in the past that we may come to understand the outlines of its hold upon us in the present and so move closer to our own delivery from illusion.[23]

But to explore the relation of a text to ideology is to do more than examine its relation to ideas, for "it is not the consciousness of [men and women] that determines their being, but on the contrary, their social being that determines their consciousness."[24] To understand the significance of a text's relation of ideology one must also examine the material conditions, the real relations, the contradictions out of which that ideology emerged. Between 1774 and 1845, for example, the particular historical conditions which gave rise to the ideology of woman's sphere are partially and unreflectingly evoked by manuals addressed to genteel women. Between 1774 and 1845, that is, these manuals are informed by the presence of an interesting conjunction. Mounting references to women's influence are accompanied by more and more frequent allusions to a general discontent among genteel women with the limitations of their role and status and by a deepening consciousness of the fact that men of the middle orders are enjoying economic and social mobility. In 1774 Dr. Gregory betrays little consciousness of any troubling insignificance in women's domestic lot. If the handiwork of upper-middle-class women is of no more than "trifling" value, if its significance lies for the most part in its enabling them "to fill up, in a tolerably agreeable way, some of the many solitary hours you must necessarily pass at home," that is a fact which is to be taken for granted. By 1794, however, James Fordyce is far more conscious than Dr. Gregory of married and single women of the middle and upper middle classes who are feeling insignificant or discontent with their sphere. Fordyce, in fact, is apparently surrounded by women with complaints. He hears young women exclaiming that, "though God has given you capacities of intellectual improvement, men have denied you the opportunities of it," and the complaint is "a very common one, and very popular with your sex." Four years later Gisborne begins his *Enquiry* by admitting that the "sphere of domestic life . . . admits far less diversity of action, and consequently of temptation, than is found in the widely differing professions and employments" of men, and he suggests that genteel young women in general complain that "the sphere in which women are destined to move, is so humble and so limited, as neither to require nor reward assiduity." By 1839 dissatisfaction with their lot appears so endemic to ordinary women of the middle class, not just to "masculine" grumblers, that Ellis is moved to begin her manual on a note of sweeping disapproval: "the women of England are . . . less usefull, and less happy than they were." Domestic usefulness particularly is in decline, and the author complains that it is difficult even to praise such "quiet and unobtrusive virtues" as remain "without exciting a desire to forsake the homely household duties of the family circle to practise such as are more conspicuous, and consequently more productive of an immediate harvest of applause."[25]

Significantly, the growing fear—or the increasing evidence—that middle-class women were discontent with the limitations of their sphere is accompanied in these manuals by a deepening awareness of the fact that middle-class men were making money and enjoying a social significance which they had not enjoyed before. In both Fordyce and Gisborne this emphasis on the discontent of women is accompanied by mounting references to the social significance of money among the middle classes, money earned, of course, by males. And in Ellis women's purported discontent with their lack of status is very frequently juxtaposed with a world in which money is everything, in which men are entirely devoted to efforts and calculations relating to their "pecuniary success."

What this unreflecting conjunction of references to female power, female discontent, and economic contradiction evokes is the causal relation between the "woman question" and what came to be perceived at least about the economic value of middle-class women between 1778 and 1860, a period which spans industrial takeoff and the establishment of bourgeois-class society—for the development of industrial capitalism did change the economic situation of middle-class women relative to that of middle-class men. Eric Hobsbawm, for example, notes that the "crucial achievement" of the industrial and French revolutions was that

> they opened careers to talent [the talent of middle-class men], or at any rate to energy, shrewdness, hard work, and greed. Not all careers, and not to the top rungs of the ladder, except perhaps in the USA. And yet, how extraordinary were the opportunities, how remote from the nineteenth century the state hierarchical ideal of the past! . . . in 1750 the son of a book binder would, in all probability, have stuck to his father's trade. Now he no longer had to. Four roads to the stars opened before him: business, education (which in turn led to the three goals of government, service, politics, and the free professions), the arts, and war.[26]

By the mid-nineteenth century the development of industrial capitalism had not led middle-class women along the same four roads. Indeed, although the absence of statistical data makes it difficult to compare women in preindustrial Britain with women of this later time, it has been argued that "industrialization far from emancipating women led to a contraction of some of their traditional functions in the economy—to a degree from which they have yet fully to recover." The nineteenth-century labor force, according to Eric Richards, was increasingly male-dominated, and "apart from domestic service, textiles, stitching, and washing there was little else open to women of any class in England before the final decades of the century."[27] The number of women employed in middle-class occupations, moreover, was even lower, for the trend toward employing women even in such spheres as shops, civil service, and business, all of which were open to men, did not begin until after 1870.[28]

At the same time, the recognized economic status of dependent married middle-class women also suffered a decline relative to the rising economic status of middle-class men, and the causes generally forwarded for what may be seen at least as a *shift in perception* are that, with the development of industrialization, home production of many household products declined; that household industries in which women and children worked alongside husbands and fathers also dwindled;[29] and that, as men's work separated further from the home, new definitions and perceptions of work were further developed, definitions and perceptions which made married women's work in the home less *visible* as work than it had been before.[30]

Literature on the "woman question," for example, makes frequent allusions to a decline in women's domestic labor and economic status, and, without claiming that this literature actually describes the middle-class woman's experience day to day, it is still possible to trace an indication of how women's domestic work was seen.[31] Thus in 1810 an article in the *Edinburgh Review* observes that "the time of women is considered worth nothing at all," and in 1841 the *Westminster Review* remarks that an "attendant effect of luxury and civilization is to procure leisure for the housekeeper as well as everybody else. The greater perfection and division of labor procures for us all the necessities and comforts of life almost ready made."[32] What some literature on the "woman question" also suggests is that this ostensible decline in women's economic activity and the recognized value of their work was linked with a decline in their status as well. In 1869, after remarking that "men have taken away from women the employments which formerly were appropriated to them," such as spinning, sewing, and domestic labors, one author goes on to observe that

> when these and such like avocations were available to women of every rank, they were not only provided with subsistence, but they held that definite place in society and filled those recognized duties which placed them on a footing of substantial dignity, and forbade the raising of any question whether capacities were equal with those of men or not. Not intentionally, but actually, by the progress of science and forms of social existence that position has been taken from women.[33]

Unpaid domestic work lost visibility, then, at a time when it was not yet possible for middle-class women to enter the labor market in any equitable way, and the low status of women's work in the labor market must have enforced the low status of women's work in the home—and vice versa. At the same time, the rising economic and social power of middle-class men gave increasing value to work that was to be done by males, work that was at once public, divorced from the home, and salaried. All this was bound to have an effect on women's status as it also had on their sense of power,[34] and it is largely these economic and social contradictions which gave rise to an ideological crisis in which questions about women's status, power, and influence were central. Indeed, the establishment by the mid-nineteenth century of an ideological emphasis on women's influence was largely an attempt to resolve this economic contradiction and to maintain the subordination of middle-class women to middle-class men, an attempt to keep the lid on middle-class women by assuring them that they *did* have work, power, and status after all.

The ideology of woman's sphere, however, was also established at a time when industrial capitalism was beset both by economic crisis and by working-class unrest. The progress of industrial capitalism, according to Eric Hobsbawm, was far from smooth, and by the 1830s and 1840s it "produced major problems of growth not to mention revolutionary unrest unparalleled in any other period of recent British history." Working-class consciousness, in fact, came into existence between 1815 and 1848, more especially around 1830, shortly before the new ideology of woman's sphere emerged. As in America, the ideology of woman's sphere in Britain may be said to have "enlisted women in their domestic roles to absorb, palliate, and even to redeem the strain of social and economic transformation."[35] Women, in their isolation from competitive economic practices, were to act as the conscience of bourgeois society and through their influence over men mitigate the harshness of an industrial capitalist world. Woman's sphere, therefore, was defined as the "intellectual education of childhood, the moral guidance of youth, the spiritual influence over the home and society, [and] the softening of relations between class and class which bind those together by deeds of love whom the material interests keep apart."[36] In reality, of course, "the canon of domesticity did not directly challenge the modern organization of work and pursuit of wealth. Rather, it accommodated and promised to temper them."[37] The ideology of woman's sphere, that is, served the interests of industrial capitalism by insuring the continuing domination of middle-class women by middle-class men and, through its mitigation of the harshness of economic transition, by insuring the continuing domination of male bourgeoisie in relation to working-class men and women as a whole.

The development of industrial capitalism, then, between *Evelina* and *The Mill on the Floss* empowered middle-class men, economically and socially, while it was *felt* at least to have disempowered middle-class women, and the development of this economic contradiction, of the ideological crisis which it provoked, and the attempts at ideological resolution which accompanied both inform and shape the women's fiction I am going to explore. Indeed, in these novels an emergent and rebellious structure of feeling about inequities of power between women and men is accompanied by a more and more overt evocation—and resentment—of economic inequities as well. Power divisions, for example, are linked with increasing explicitness to differences in economic function. Thus in *Evelina* Burney scorns money consciousness by projecting it onto the vulgar lower classes, but in *Pride and Prejudice* Austen draws attention to a relation between money and power before silently subverting it. In *Villette* access to work that pays is persistently felt to be the most fundamental source of power, although Brontë may be said to present the connection without making it fully articulate, and in *The Mill on the Floss* Eliot analytically evokes what Burney, Austen, and Brontë have either unreflectingly grasped or only partially presented. In *The Mill on the Floss* the division between men's and women's recognized economic functions is the major determinant of their power. And much of the first half of the novel is devoted to analyzing how that relation determines the lives of Tom and Maggie Tulliver.

Protest against power inequities between women and men, moreover, as expressed in the increasing emphasis given to conventional marriage plots, is brought into conjunction with buried protest first against class division and ultimately against capitalist development itself. Indeed the relation of each work to an ideology about women also locates it in relation to general ideologies about class division and ultimately about industrial capitalist relations. Burney, for example, endorses the class power of landed men in order to sustain a courtly ideology about genteel women, while Austen's endorsement of Elizabeth's independence is of a piece with her endorsement of economic individualism in middle-class men. Brontë's bitter resentment of the inequities of money between middle-class women and middle-class men leads to mystified protest on behalf of all those who are "creatures of shadow" rather than "creatures of sunshine," and Eliot's analysis of male and female socialization sees industrial capitalist development as dangerous, if not to the working class, at least to middle-class women.

What might appear at first to be relatively simple resistance to the ideology of woman's sphere therefore takes on, in this larger context, a wider significance; resistance to an ideology governing middle-class women intersects with resistance to ideologies sustaining capitalist relations as a whole, and it is this intersection which helps explain the radical content and finally the radical curtailment of rebellious strategies for women in these novels—an argument if there ever was one for looking at gender in relation to class. For protest of women's powerlessness is disconcerting enough. When it leads—intuitively and half consciously—to resentment of the economic inequities between women and men and to distaste for capitalist ethics and capitalist economic relations as a whole, rebellion becomes far more frightening and much more difficult to sustain, a fact which has its effect on the shape of these novels. What might be seen, that is, as a growth of consciousness that is potentially revolutionary—an emergent feeling on the part of the authors that power divisions are imposed rather than natural and a mounting resistance to those divisions in their fiction—does not in fact find satisfactory expression in their art. In these novels growing resistance produces growing tension, and the tension becomes particularly acute as, historically, the ideology of women's influence and ideologies sustaining industrial capitalism are established. The heroine's, and the author's, rebellion is not abandoned, but it is directed into fantasies of power which are increasingly apparent as fantasies and increasingly difficult to sustain. In Brontë and in Eliot, indeed, the authors themselves seem patently disbelieving.

The thrust of this tension, however, is not toward resignation so much as toward further covertness and further disguise, and this indicates at once the force with which ideology inhibits and the persistence with which women rebelled. Their rebelliousness, moreover, is more than a brand of false consciousness, for if on the one hand subversive writing defuses the desire for power by satisfying the longing for it, on the other subversive writing is itself an action upon one's readers and one's world. It is not only socialist novels which can destroy "conventional illusions" about human relations. Any novel may do so when it "shakes the optimism of the bourgeois world, when it casts doubt on the eternal nature of existing society, even if the author does not propose answers, even though [she] might not openly take sides."[38] To write subversively is more than a means of exercising influence. It is a form of struggle—and a form of power.

NOTES

1. Elizabeth Gaskell, letter to Eliza Fox, [April? 1850], letter 69, in *The Letters of Mrs. Gaskell*, ed. J.A.V. Chapple and Arthur Pollard, p. 109.

2. Frances Power Cobbe, "The Final Cause of Woman," in *Woman's Work and Woman's Culture*, ed. Josephine E. Butler, p. 1.

3. John Gregory, *A Father's Legacy to His Daughters*, pp. 6–7, 52.

4. James Fordyce, *Sermons to Young Women*, 1:24, 26, 213.

5. Thomas Gisborne, *An Enquiry into the Duties of the Female Sex*, pp. 8, 6; Sarah Ellis, *The Women of England*, p. 6.

6. "Advice to Young Ladies on the Improvement of the Mind," *Edinburgh Review* 15

(January 1810): 314; Henry Thomas Buckle, "The Influence of Women on the Progress of Knowledge," *Fraser's Magazine* 57 (April 1858): 396, 397; "Rights and Conditions of Women," *Edinburgh Review* 73 (January 1841): 204; "Spirit of Society in England and France," *Edinburgh Review* 52 (January 1831): 378.

7. "The Female Character," *Fraser's Magazine* 7 (1833): 593; "Rights and Conditions of Women," pp. 192, 204; P.M.Y., "Woman and Her Social Position," *Westminster Review* 35 (January 1841): 22, 25.

8. Sarah Ellis, *The Wives of England*, p. 26; Ellis, *Women of England*, pp. 15–16.

9. Ellis, *Wives of England*, pp. 41, 37, 14, 46.

10. Elizabeth Janeway, "On the Power of the Weak," *Signs* 1 (1975): 105.

11. Natalie Zemon Davis, "'Women's History' in Transition: The European Case," *Feminist Studies* 3 (Spring–Summer 1976): 90.

12. Berenice A. Carroll, "Peace Research: The Cult of Power," *Journal of Conflict Resolution* 16 (December 1972): 585, 588, 589, 591.

13. Showalter, *A Literature of Their Own*, pp. 19, 21, 22, 23; Sandra M. Gilbert and Susan Gubar, *The Madwoman in the Attic*, pp. 49, 51.

14. See Jean E. Kennard, *Victims of Convention*, p. 13. Much of my own thinking about love and quest plots comes from Rachel Blau DuPlessis.

15. Eagleton, *Marxism and Literary Criticism*, p. 35.

16. Raymond Williams, *Marxism and Literature*, pp. 132, 131.

17. George Eliot, *The Mill on the Floss*, ed. Gordon S. Haight, p. 304.

18. Spacks, *The Female Imagination*, p. 219; Showalter, *A Literature of Their Own*, p. 28; Gilbert and Gubar, *The Madwoman in the Attic*, p. 73; Robinson, *Sex, Class, and Culture*, p. 80.

19. Gilbert and Gubar, *The Madwoman in the Attic*, pp. xi, 49; Showalter, *A Literature of Their Own*, p. 12.

20. Terry Eagleton, *Criticism and Ideology*, p. 72.

21. I am perhaps closer here to Pierre Macherey: "The literary work must be studied in a double perspective: in relation to history, and in relation to an ideological version of that history." A text, however, does not "reflect" history for Macherey but "by means of contradictory images . . . represents and evokes the historical contradictions of the period." See *A Theory of Literary Production*, trans. Geoffrey Wall, pp. 115, 126.

22. Charles E. Rosenberg, "Introduction: History and Experience," *The Family in History*, pp. 2, 3.

23. Eagleton, *Criticism and Ideology*, p. 101; Eagleton, *Marxism and Literary Criticism*, p. 18.

24. Karl Marx, "Preface," *A Contribution to the Critique of Political Economy*, quoted in *Dynamics of Social Change*, ed. Howard Selsam, David Goldway, and Harry Martel, p. 52.

25. Gregory, *Legacy*, p. 51; Fordyce, *Sermons*, p. 224; Gisborne, *Enquiry*, pp. 2, 7; Ellis, *Women of England*, pp. 5, 14.

26. Eric J. Hobsbawm, *The Age of Revolution*, pp. 226–227; see also Ivy Pinchbeck, *Women Workers and the Industrial Revolution*, pp. 314–315.

27. Eric Richards, "Women in the British Economy since about 1700: An Interpretation," *History* 59 (October 1974): 337, 349.

28. See Lee Holcombe, *Victorian Ladies at Work*, p. 216.

29. The decline of household industry and the separation of men's work from the home are well documented. See, for example, Alice Clark, *The Working Life of Women in the Seventeenth Century*, p. 269; Pinchbeck, *Women Workers and the Industrial Revolution*, p. 307; Peter Laslett, *The World We Have Lost*, p. 17; Richards, "Women in the British Economy," p. 345; Theresa M. McBride, "The Long Road Home: Women's Work and Industrialization," in *Becoming Visible*, ed. Renate Bridenthal and Claudia Koonz, p. 283.

30. See Lise Vogel, "The Contested Domain: A Note on the Family in the Transition to Capitalism," *Marxist Perspectives* 1 (Spring 1978): 63, 66. See also Nancy F. Cott, *The Bonds of Womanhood*, p. 61.

31. Patricia Branca argues persuasively that middle-class women were not idle, as women's manuals of the period often suggest, but I think it likely that manuals which were, as Branca maintains, "naggingly critical of middle-class women" reflected a general cultural tension about the recognized economic function of such women and about the status of women's work. See *Silent Sisterhood*, p. 16.

32. "Advice to Young Ladies," p. 300; P.M.Y., "Woman and Her Social Position," p. 15.

33. John Boyd-Kinnear, "The Social Position of Women in the Present Age," in *Woman's Work and Woman's Culture*, ed. Butler, pp. 334–335.

34. See Clark, *Working Life of Women*, p. 302; Pinchbeck, *Women Workers and the Industrial Revolution*, p. 312; Heidi Hartmann, "Capitalism, Patriarchy, and Job Segregation by Sex," *Signs* 1 (1976): 152; Margaret George, "From 'Goodwife' to 'Mistress': The Transformation of the Female in Bourgeois Culture," *Science and Society* 37 (1973): 156.

35. Hobsbawm, *Age of Revolution*, pp. 57, 249; Cott, *Bonds of Womanhood*, p. 70.

36. "Female Laboure," *Fraser's Magazine* 61 (March 1860): 371, 370.

37. Cott, *Bonds of Womanhood*, p. 69.

38. Friedrich Engles, quoted in Macherey, *Theory of Literary Production*, p. 119.

WORKS CITED

"Advice to Young Ladies on the Improvement of the Mind." *Edinburgh Review* 15 (January 1810): 299–315.

Auerbach, Nina. *Communities of Women: An Idea in Fiction*. Cambridge, Mass.: Harvard University Press, 1978.

———. "The Power of Hunger: Demonism and Maggie Tulliver. *Nineteenth Century Fiction* 30 (September 1975): 150–171.

Austen, Jane. *Pride and Prejudice*. New York: Holt, Rinehart & Winston, 1949.

Branca, Patricia. *Silent Sisterhood: Middle Class Women in the Victorian Home*. Pittsburgh: Carnegie-Mellon University Press, 1975.

Bridenthal, Renate, and Claudia Koonz, eds. *Becoming Visible: Women in European History*. Boston: Houghton Mifflin, 1977.

Brontë, Charlotte. *Villette*. Ed. Geoffrey Tillotson and Donald Hawes. Boston: Houghton Mifflin, 1971.

Buckle, Henry Thomas. "The Influence of Women on the Progress of Knowledge." *Fraser's Magazine* 57 (April 1858): 395–407.

Burney, Frances. *Evelina: or, The History of a Young Lady's Entrance into the World*. New York: W. W. Norton, 1965.

Carroll, Berenice A. "Peace Research: The Cult of Power." *Journal of Conflict Resolution* 16 (December 1972): 505–616.

Clark, Alice. *The working Life of Women in the Seventeenth Century*. London: Frank Cass, 1968.

Cobbe, Frances Power. *The Duties of Women: A Course of Lectures*. Boston: Geo. H. Ellis, 1882.

———. "The Final Cause of Woman." In *Woman's Work and Woman's Culture: A Series of Essays*, ed. Josephine E. Butler, pp. 1–25. London: Macmillan, 1869.

Cott, Nancy F. *The Bonds of Womanhood: "Woman's Sphere" in New England, 1780–1835*. New Haven: Yale University Press, 1977.

Davis, Natalie Zemon. "'Women's History' in Transition: The European Case." *Feminist Studies* 3 (Spring–Summer 1976): 83–103.

Eagleton, Terry. *Criticism and Ideology: A Study in Marxist Literary Theory*. London: NLB, 1976.

———. *Marxism and Literary Criticism*. Berkeley & Los Angeles: University of California Press, 1976.

Eliot, George. *The Mill on the Floss*. Ed. Gordon S. Haight. Boston: Houghton Mifflin, 1961.

Ellis, Sarah. *The Daughters of England: Their Position in Society, Character, and Responsibilities*, 1845; *The Wives of England: Their Relative Duties, Domestic Influence, and Social Obligations*, 1843; *The Women of England: Their Social Duties, and Domestic Habits*, 1839; rpt. in *The Family Monitor and Domestic Guide*. New York: E. Walker, n.d.

"The Female Character." *Fraser's Magazine* 7 (1833): 591–601.

"Female Labour." *Fraser's Magazine* 61 (March 1860): 359–371.

Fordyce, James. *Sermons to Young Women*. 2 vols. London: A. Millar, W. Law, & R. Cater, 1794.

Gaskell, Elizabeth. *The Letters of Mrs. Gaskell*. Ed. J.A.V. Chapple and Arthur Pollard. Cambridge, Mass.: Harvard University Press, 1967.

George, Margaret. "From 'Goodwife' to 'Mistress': The Transformation of the Female in Bourgeois Culture." *Science and Society* 37 (1973): 152–177.

Gilbert, Sandra, and Susan Gubar. *The Madwoman in the Attic: The Woman Writer and the Nineteenth-Century Literary Imagination*. New Haven: Yale University Press, 1979.

Gisborne, Thomas. *An Enquiry into the Duties of the Female Sex*. Philadelphia: James Humphreys, 1798.

Gregory, John. *A Father's Legacy to His Daughters*. New York: Garland Publishing, 1974.

Hartmann, Heidi. "Capitalism, Patriarchy, and Job Segregation by Sex." *Signs* 1 (1976): 137–169.

Hobsbawm, Eric J. *The Age of Revolution: 1789–1848*. New York: New American Library, 1962.

Holcombe, Lee. *Victorian Ladies at Work: Middle-Class Working Women in England and Wales, 1850–1914*. Newton Abbot: David & Charles, 1973.

Janeway, Elizabeth. "On the Power of the Weak." *Signs* 1 (1975): 103–109.

Kennard, Jean E. *Victims of Convention*. Hamden, Conn.: Archon Books, 1978.

Kinnear, John Boyd. "The Social Position of Women in the Present Age." In *Woman's Work and Woman's Culture: A Series of Essays*, ed. Josephine E. Butler, pp. 332–366. London: Macmillan, 1869.

Laslett, Peter. *The World We Have Lost*. New York: Charles Scribner's Sons, 1965.

Macherey, Pierre. *A Theory of Literary Production*. Trans. Geoffrey Wall. London: Routledge & Kegan Paul, 1978.

Moers, Ellen. *Literary Women*. Garden City, N.Y.: Doubleday, 1976.

Pinchbeck, Ivy. *Women Workers and the Industrial Revolution: 1750–1850*. New York: Augustus M. Kelley, 1969.

P.M.Y. "Woman and Her Social Position." *Westminster Review* 35 (January 1841): 13–27.

Richards, Eric. "Women in the British Economy since about 1700: An Interpretation." *History* 59 (October 1974): 337–357.

"Rights and Conditions of Women." *Edinburgh Review* 73 (January 1841): 189–209.

Robinson, Lillian S. *Sex, Class, and Culture*. Bloomington: Indiana University Press, 1978.

Rosenberg, Charles E. *The Family in History*. Philadelphia: University of Pennsylvania Press, 1975.

Selsam, Howard, David Goldway, and Harry Martel, eds. *Dynamics of Social Change: A Reader in Marxist Social Science*. New York: International Publishers, 1970.

Showalter, Elaine. *A Literature of Their Own: British Women Novelists from Brontë to Lessing*. Princeton: Princeton University Press, 1977.

Spacks, Patricia. *The Female Imagination*. New York: Avon Books, 1972.

"Spirit of Society in England and France." *Edinburgh Review* 42 (January 1831): 374–387.

Vogel, Lise. "The Contested Domain: A Note on the Family in the Transition to Capitalism." *Marxist Perspectives* 1 (Spring 1978): 50–73.

Williams, Raymond. *Marxism and Literature*. Oxford: Oxford University Press, 1977.

ANNETTE KOLODNY

THE DOMESTIC FANTASY GOES WEST

I am lost
near home
—MARIE HARRIS, *INTERSTATE*

In 1852 the Ohio-born writer Alice Carey pictured herself at a window in Cincinnati, looking out across the Ohio river toward the Kentucky shore. "I cannot see the blue green nor the golden green of the oat and wheat fields, that lie beyond these infant cities, nor the dark ridge of woods . . . along their borders," she complained, "for . . . the soaked earth this morning sends up its coal-scented and unwholesome fogs, obscuring the lovely picture that would else present itself."[1] In that image she captured the anxiety of a nation.

By the middle of the nineteenth century, Americans had to struggle to preserve their shared self-image as a nation of independent yeoman farmers. Everywhere there was the inescapable evidence of an increasingly industrial urbanization made possible by a technology forged of steam and iron. Though the collective mind's eye anxiously looked toward an expanding agrarian west, as though in confirmation of the original eighteenth-century dream, contemporary reality betrayed a growing centripetal movement toward the town, the factory, and the city. To be sure, the great bulk of the population remained on the land. Even so, by 1840, the structures of self-subsistence agriculture, organized around commercial towns and household industries, were already yielding before the beginnings of a capitalistic and industrial economy.

Small farmers in the northeast who had been hurt by the financial Panic of 1837 now poured into the cities and factory towns, there joining recent European immigrants to form a new class of urban poor. Fortunes made in manufactures and railroads brought up once productive farmland, converting it into summer homes or grand resorts for the urban rich.[2] And, linking eastern and western markets through a proliferating network of railroads and canals, steam and iron created "infant cities" whose effluvia threatened to obscure even "the oat and wheat fields" of the agricultural west.

Popular resistance to these changes resulted in a wave of antiurbanism that first surfaced at the tail end of the 1830s. James Fenimore Cooper perfectly caught the mood in *Home as Found* (1838) when he pictured Eve Effingham, "with a feeling of delight, . . . escap[ing] from" a New York City that, in her view, "contains so much . . . that is unfit for any place, in order to breathe the pure air, and enjoy the tranquil pleasure of the country."[3] With the 1840s and 1850s that initial response grew into "a sizeable body of journalistic fiction depicting the modern city as a place of lurid sin and crime, economic debasement, and heartless chicanery," while, as Janis Stout points out, the countryside remained, at least imaginatively, "the chief stronghold of sobriety and virtue."[4]

In 1859 Nathaniel Hawthorne incomprehensibly reiterated outdated Jacksonian delusions to declare that the United States was "a country where there is . . . [not] anything but a commonplace prosperity, in broad and simple daylight."[5] In fact, the early statistical data coming out of official commissions and benevolent societies suggested otherwise. A Philadelphia report of 1854 showed 700 professional beggars in that city and 1,800 vagrant children. An official New York State report a year later counted one pauper, living on state charity, for every seventeen persons. In 1853 Massachusetts had 26,000 on relief rolls, one tenth of them under fourteen years of age.[6] And in the cities of the northeast generally, where $1,000 a year represented an average middle-class income, only 1 percent of the population earned over $800.

If these newly emergent signs of industrial growing pains left no perceivable imprint on Hawthorne's fiction, they did nonetheless become the subject matter of that "mob of scribbling women" whom Hawthorne had earlier damned.[7] Ann Sophia Stephens followed the influx of rural people to the city in her 1854 novel, *Fashion and Famine*.[8] A year later, in her most popular work, *The Old Homestead*, she depicted, first, family life eroded by the destructive forces of the city— including official corruption, callous institutions, and the patronage system—and then, in the second part of the novel, she focused on a countryside devastated by the impact of big-city life and wealth, its population absorbed by urban industry and its farms turned into summer playgrounds for vacationing New Yorkers.[9] Novels such as these belied Hawthorne's sanguine optimism.

These novels also contributed to the rabid anti-urbanism by anatomizing the city as a place where the awful realities of class division simply could not be overlooked. Their casts of characters typically included both the very rich and the very poor, with few novels missing the opportunity for scenes of dramatic, intentionally sentimental contrast. In her 1857 novel, *Mabel Vaughan*, for example, Susanna Maria Cummins had her heiress heroine encounter "a little boy, ragged, dirty, and bending beneath the weight of an old basket filled with half-burnt coals," which he accidentally spills onto the cold and wintry New York street.[10] Later that evening, as Mabel Vaughan warms herself before "a brilliant fire" in her elegant mansion, she hears "the cold wind whistle round the corner of the house, [and] she thought again of the little boy and the spilt coals." "Painful visions," we are told, "rose before her of dreary garrets, where half-starved children and despairing mothers crouched beneath scanty coverings, and cried and shivered with the cold" (*MV*, pp. 128, 131).

The frequency of such episodes notwithstanding, it would be a mistake to conclude that the so-called "domestic sentimentalists" of mid-nineteenth-century America were thereby agitating, through their fiction, for radical social change. The manipulation of a reader's sentiments, to be sure, represented a genuine political tool for writers otherwise disenfranchised. Indeed, in some re-spects, mid-nineteenth-century sentimental fiction may be seen as *the* political strategy of the disenfranchised, moving its readers to tears in hopes that the sight of those tears might then move husbands and fathers, sons and brothers, to more public forms of responsiveness. Be that as it may, however, the writers of domestic fictions tended toward amelioration rather than solution. Though they elaborated the evil effects of the transformation from decentralized agrarian to industrial capi-talistic structures—and often with a brutal realism—they did not analyze the transformation itself.

Their focus, instead, was on what they perceived to be the moral challenge to the heart of their fictional vision. The corrupting superfluities of city life or, con-versely, the unremitting poverty of the rural or urban poor seemed to these writ-ers to threaten their vision of the American home that, ideally, was to function as the moral, ethical, and spiritual center of family and nation alike, the nursery of republican virtue, and the haven from the masculine competitiveness of the marketplace. Thus, although 1848 saw the first Paris Commune, the publication of the Communist Manifesto and, in the United States at Seneca Falls, the first women's rights convention, the women who composed the enormously popular domestic fictions of the 1850s, for the most part, continued to concern them-selves with consequences rather than underlying causes. Caroline Kirkland prob-ably voiced the views of most of this sisterhood when she attacked George Sand for being the misguided "flatterer of all who are discontented with their own lot, and who find gratification in shifting the responsibility from themselves to so-ciety and its institutions and abuses." [11]

Because they did not choose to analyze "society and its institutions and abuses," these writers inevitably turned toward the romantic in inventing solu-tions to the difficulties elaborated in their fictions. A young girl's pious patience might, in the end, win some curmudgeonly authority figure to kindness; a reli-gious conversion might salvage a sinking brother and thereby recover the family's farm or business; some other fortuitous reversal of fortune or even the advent of a virtuous hero could move a plot toward happy resolution. But by the 1850s these no longer seemed sufficient solutions where whole communities were being dis-rupted and uprooted. And so a number of novelists began to look toward what Ann Sophia Stephens called "the green west," [12] as though seeking a geographical locale in which the social ills evident in the northeast might forever be evaded.

Removing a heroine to the west was nothing new in women's fiction, of course. As early as 1837, Catharine Maria Sedgwick delivered one young married couple from New York "to the land of promise—the indefinite *West*" in *Live and Let Live; Or, Domestic Service Illustrated.* [13] The fictional removals of the 1850s, however, had about them an urgency that Sedgwick never hinted at; and they portrayed, in vivid detail, as she did not, the idealized "Western home . . . the blessed haven of rest, which afforded . . . a safe and welcome shelter from the storm of adversity and trial" (*MV*, p. 505). During the antebellum decade, the "prairie home," with "its bare white walls, its plain brick hearth, its low-roofed rooms," thus became the emblematic moral counterweight to impoverished country homesteads or city mansions and tenements alike, teaching its inhabi-tants "that happiness is independent of ornament; [and] that contentment brings joy to the humblest fireside" (*MV*, p. 505).

Decades of eager western promotionalism—composed both by women and by men—had had their intended effect. The domestic fictionist who relocated her characters to Illinois or Iowa essentially accepted Charles Fenno Hoffman's earlier assurance of "the ease with which a man can here support a family as a farmer." [14] And not a few of these writers followed Mary Austin Holley in depicting a physical terrain "literally flowing with milk and honey," its bounty generating a social Eden where "there are no poor people . . . and none rich." [15] Indeed, one of the characters in Cummins's *Mabel Vaughan* repeats a favorite refrain from these promotional tracts when she insists of Illinois that "'every effort is sure to find its reward in a land which makes such a rich return for the labor bestowed on it'" (*MV*, p. 355).

It was not only writers dismayed at the increasing industrialization of the northeast who relocated their characters westward, however. The agricultural frontier held an equivalent imaginative appeal for novelists appalled at the dissolution of family bonds (for both blacks and whites) under the chattel slavery system then dominant in the plantation south. Especially following the 1849 formation of the Free-Soil party, pledged to keep slavery out of the territories and newer states, Emma D. E. N. Southworth and Mary Hayden Pike repeatedly showed their native southerners "mak[ing] a new home for themselves in the West." A west that, as Nina Baym notes, stood in their novels "for salvation from the feudal South." [16] Typically, the hero of Southworth's *India: The Pearl of Pearl River* (1856) frees his slaves in Mississippi and then goes west to establish a newspaper called "The True Freeman." [17] The heroine of Pike's *Ida May* (1854) similarly frees her slaves and then heads west with the intention of establishing a center for the training and education of former slaves. [18] In each story, moreover, the free west is credited with making possible what the slaveholding south could not: here the characters' "home is a very happy one" (*I*, p. 401), and loving relationships thrive.

Still, it must be emphasized that, for most of these writers, their commitment to the frontier west derived from an ideology that was inherently nostalgic. At the heart of their western vision was a fantasy of home that, though they did not acknowledge it, harked back to an earlier era. For, as a newly industrializing nation was fast eroding the economic functions of the home and consequently narrowing the scope of women's activity in general, the domestic novel of western relocation still suggested that the home, and particularly women's traditional role within it, held tangible significance. The fact was, by the middle decades of the nineteenth century, the middle-class woman—the main consumer of domestic fiction—was undergoing what Susan Phinney Conrad calls "a status revolution." Her "social status prohibited [the middle-class woman] . . . from wage work in the new cottage industries and sealed her off from that female world of mill and factory," while, at the same time, "the professional training and certification becoming essential for work in medicine, law, and higher education denied her access to these fields." As a result, Conrad concludes, "in direct and ironic contrast to tenets of equality and increased opportunity voiced by Jacksonian America, her opportunities were dwindling." [19]

A number of women spoke out against the shift from the earlier division of labor according to sex to the increasing allotment (or even elimination) of labor according to class. As early as 1835, for example, in her *The History and Condition of Women*, Lydia Maria Child criticized social attitudes that looked down upon middle-class women's gainful employment, insisting that "active industry" implied no "bar to gentility." [20] By 1852, feminist activist Paulina Wright Davis was telling audiences that, where the middle class was concerned, the contemporary woman had no real "function" because "manufactures" had usurped her traditional duties, removing these from home to factory. [21]

Catharine Beecher's solution to the dwindling status of middle-class women was to raise housewifery to "woman's distinctive profession" and to inveigh against an increasing tendency to turn over household chores "to hirelings." [22] Summarizing two decades of speaking and writing on these subjects for an 1865 article in *Harper's New Monthly Magazine*, Beecher defined the new domestic professionalism as "includ[ing] three departments—the training of the mind in childhood, the nursing of infants and of the sick, and all the handicrafts and management of the family state" [23] Beecher's emphases, however, only served to rationalize—and by rationalizing, reinforce—the pervasive *sentimental* domestic ideology of the day.

Addressing a largely comfortable and highly literate middle-class readership, editors of fashionable ladies' magazines and domestic novelists alike suggested that, by eschewing the world of trade and commerce, the home had become something better: a kind of moral and spiritual "beacon-light" in a crass and materialistic world. In one of the more successful novels of 1846, a happy husband writes to a friend that "'when I am absent during the day, and perplexed with the multitudinous cares of an extensive mercantile concern, my home rises before my mind's eye, like a beacon-light to the tempest-tossed mariner. The sweet, consoling thought, that I have such a haven of peace and love soothes and hushes my perturbed spirit.'" [24]

The woman within that home was no less sentimentalized. Catharine Beecher might see her as a "professional," with necessary practical tasks to perform; but the more popular view rendered her the leisured repository for the culture's morals, emotions, and spiritual well-being. Indeed, from the 1830s on, as Americans experienced what Nancy Cott has noted as an accelerated "shift of production and exchange away from the household," [25] middle-class women were simultaneously enjoined to shift their attention away from "money-making." "Our men are sufficiently money-making," announced Sarah Josepha Hale in the Boston *Ladies' Magazine* of 1830. [26] By 1850, now the editor of *Godey's Lady's Book*, Hale continued the theme by asking that her reader forego complaints regarding her diminished economic status and realize that "hers is the empire of the affections." [27] The influential *North American Review* employed a similar vocabulary when it asked women to "leave the rude commerce of camps and the soul-hardening struggling of political power to the harsher spirit of men," while taking up, instead, "the domain of the moral affections [and] the empire of the heart." [28]

Clearly, it was a rhetoric designed to reconcile middle-class and wealthy women to the fact that they had essentially lost their traditional functions and, in their place, been relegated to largely ornamental roles. "If there be any thing likely to banish the fiend *ennui* from the dwellings of women of fortune," recommended Caroline Kirkland in 1854, "it is the habit of assuming a moderate share of the daily cares which go to make home home. To do everything by proxy, . . . deputing our duties and privileges to hirelings," she warned, "is to deprive ourselves of a thousand wholesome, cheerful, innocent interests." [29]

The problem was that the very design of home was also undergoing rapid change. The capacious fireplace traditionally associated with making "home home" and the hearth traditionally associated with women's tasks within the home—these were now disappearing amid the new technology. In an age when popular magazines, even in their titles, continued to link *Hearth and Home,*[30] there was a peculiar distress attached to the fact that the hearth and fireplace were slowly giving way before the gas furnace. Catharine Beecher railed against the change, ostensibly for health reasons, complaining that "as wealth and luxury have increased . . . fire-places have been shut up, and closed stoves and furnaces introduced."[31] The writers of domestic fiction, on the other hand, appreciated the symbolic meanings of household arrangements and so found alternate ways of rejecting the innovation. Associating it with the cold pretensions of excessive wealth, they always made clear that, for them, "a furnace in the cellar" did not a home make.

One of Caroline Kirkland's rare longer fictions, for example, follows a young woman's progress from the happy but simple home of the aunt and uncle who raised her to the elegant mansion of her wealthy and indulgent husband. For her first Christmas as a new wife she insists on inviting her aunt and uncle to dinner, rather than allowing them to orchestrate the festivities, as usual, at "their own board crowned with good cheer." In the end, Kirkland writes, the young bride "prevailed," and the aunt and uncle "exchanged their comfortable dining-room, with sprigs of box stuck in the window-panes, branches of hemlock and wreaths of green forest fringe about the pictures, and a bright, hospitable Christmas fire burning in the grate, for their niece's too magnificent *suite,* curtained with satin and lace till one could not distinguish the snow falling thick through the air without, and warmed by a furnace in the cellar till you felt uncertain whether a fan or a fire were most desirable."[32] In this passage, there is no doubt as to which is the house and which the home; or what pertains to either.

"The story of feminine trials and triumphs," which Nina Baym observes "dominated woman's writing in the 1850s,"[33] must therefore be seen as a literary response born of the anxiety attendant upon rapidly changing role expectations and accelerating technological transitions. In the face of increasingly restricted employment opportunities for middle-class women, "slave wages" for working-class women,[34] quickened industrialization, spreading urbanization, and still carrying with it the memory of the economic upheavals following the Panic of 1837, the domestic fiction of mid-century America sought solace and security in the image of the home "as a moral repository in an immoral society . . . [and] a bastion of stability in a changing, fragmentary world."[35]

The very factors that produced such a fiction also conspired to make the frontier west an attractive setting for its fantasy. To begin with, current wisdom pictured the west—and especially the frontier—as largely agricultural. For most Americans, this implied not only the absence of mills and factories but the absence of those glaring disparities in wealth that had begun to mark the northeast; for novelists like E. D. E. N. Southworth and Mary Hayden Pike, moreover, the small farms of the frontier promised a society untouched by the blot of slavery.[36] In an age that looked with suspicion on the phenomenal fortunes apparently made overnight by factory and mill owners, the west suggested an escape from superfluity, an escape from wealth gained only by investment, and an escape from the exploited labor of the poor. In an era when fewer than 2 percent of the rich were not born rich, the raw frontier could still be fantasized as a realm that might nurture that quintessential American hero, the self-made man.

Above all else, however, the frontier west gave these novelists the chance to displace the gilded mansions and sordid tenements of New York, the dormitory dwellings of the New England mills, and the columned plantation houses of the south with the "very comfortable and pleasant . . . log cabin home." No novel missed the chance to extol its virtues or ignored the opportunity to picture the happy family gathered cozily "about the hearthstone." "Yes, very comfortable and pleasant was that log cabin home," these novels all averred, "and seldom in the splendid parlors of our Atlantic cities does a happier [family] gather about the hearthstone, than that which, after the supper was over, drew around that ample fire-place." In this scene from Caroline Soule's *The Pet of the Settlement* (1860), the daughter of the house is pictured "knitting" clothes that are essential—not merely ornamental—for the family, while her father tends both the fire and a baby, "trotting [the child] on his foot 'to Banbury Cross.'" [37]

It is an image of relaxed domesticity. But it is an image with a point. The domesticity that these novelists pictured in the new west was a domesticity in which women and men alike played important (if different) roles. The father who once spent all his evenings away from home in the counting houses of the city now delights in entertaining children by the hearthside and in taking his family for picnics on the flowering prairies. At the same time, the women in these cabins are given real, but never arduous, work to perform. Theirs is a role that keeps them happily and usefully "busy from early dawn to twilight" (*PS*, p. 196).

Significantly, the "three departments" that Catherine Beecher had entrusted to women are only played out in these novels once the family removes to the west. While the family remains in the east, by contrast, we rarely see the women characters work (unless they are poor), and more often than not, we see them wasting their time in frivolous social pursuits. To the functioning of the log cabin home, however, the woman is essential—as essential as the "ample fire-place" where she does her cooking or boils water for washing, and around which (like herself) the family gathers. Thus, in an age when many middle-class women experienced themselves increasingly displaced from any real responsibility in running a household, the domestic novel of western relocation claimed contemporaneity through the frontier setting, but all the while harked back to patterns symbolic of earlier times—patterns that reestablished women's meaningful centrality in the domestic scene.

No less important, the supposedly unformed frontier settlements offered these novelists a chance to project their idealized notions of community itself. It was, needless to say, a community informed by the domestic ethos in which the values of home and hearth, rather than the market economy, organized the larger social structure. When a small child is found abandoned on the Iowa prairie in Caroline Soule's *The Pet of the Settlement*, for instance, it is not a single household but the settlement as a whole that adopts her, with all the "men, women and children" crying out. "I'll do my part, I'll do my part'" (*PS*, p. 58). Older widows and single men in these novels are similarly adopted by neighboring families who offer them not only a room of their own but the affectionate appellation of "grandmother" or "uncle." Exploiting the familial metaphors inherent in women's promotional writings, novelists like Caroline Soule thus sought to portray communities in which the inhabitants gave palpable meaning to Farnham's description of westerners acting together as "the sons and daughters of this land"; and the characters in these novels repeatedly bear out Holley's description of pioneer Texans as "universally kind and hospitable."[38]

The urgent need for such fantasies, of course, explains these writers' penchant for ignoring what Caroline Kirkland had earlier tried to teach, or what the daily newspapers everywhere declared about the west. Land speculators, absentee landlords, or moneylenders charging anywhere from 30 to 60 percent annual interest do not appear in the westernized domestic fictions.[39] Their representations of the west are never informed by the fact that, as early as 1836, President Andrew Jackson was expressing his alarm at the growing "monopoly of the public lands in the hands of speculators and capitalists, to the injury of the actual settlers in the new States, and of emigrants in search of new homes."[40] Nor did they hint that Jackson's alarm had been well grounded: of the 38,000,000 acres of public lands sold between 1835 and 1837, 29,000,000—that is, almost three-quarters of the whole—were acquired by speculators.[41] Absentee landlords and exploited tenants became the rule, rather than the exception, in places like the prairie counties of central Illinois. And by 1846 an Indiana farmer observed that one-third of the voters in his state were "tenants or day laborers or young men who have acquired no property."[42] In the novels of the domestic fantasists, by contrast, the families relocated westward are universally prosperous, and most characters reap "golden harvests" (*MV*, p. 378).

Refusing also to acknowledge the stark reality of a crude first cabin, constructed of "logs and nothing else, the fire made on the ground, or on a few loose stones, and a hole in the roof for the escape of the smoke,"[43] these writers instead adhered to the further fantasy of the "very comfortable and pleasant . . . log cabin home" (*PS*, p. 102). Lydia Hunt Sigourney captured its essence in her enormously popular, "The Western Home" (a poem which first saw magazine publication at the beginning of the decade and then titled a collection of her poems in 1854). Here, Kirkland's reports of tight quarters and rough puncheon floors are superseded by the prettier picture of a "new home in greenwood fair":

> [The] humble roof was firmly laid,
> Of jointed logs the building made,
> Yet more of space, and comfort too,
> Was there than met the careless view;
> For well these walls the storm could quell,
> And tyrant cold or heat repel.[44]

Discounting Kirkland's descriptions of the sheer drudgery of first settlement, these novelists joined with Sigourney to picture the frontier housewife working "with harmonizing will," finding only "pleasure in her duties." Discounting Kirkland's anger at the dishonest practices of western bankers and land speculators, the novelists asserted, along with Sigourney, that the western home implied "an Eden refuge, sweet and blest." And, like her, they asked their readers to believe that the western "home's secluded bound" (*WH*, p. 31) offered a sure haven from the exploitations of a capitalist economy and the uncertainties of the marketplace. Caroline Soule, for example, portrayed moneylending as a local affair based wholly on benevolence. In *The Pet of the Settlement*, her displaced easterner, Mr. Belden, recoups the fortune earlier lost in the counting-houses of New York by virtue of "patient, honest industry, and not by skin-flint usury," she insists (*PS*, p. 237). In turn, as Soule depicts him, Belden helps others to prosper in Iowa. "'If ye ever happen to get hard up for cash and need a loan to lift ye,'" one of the older pioneers boasts to a prospective newcomer to the settlement, "'there's Belden'll help you along, and won't ask you forty per-cent either, and if he sees ye'r industrious and steady-like, he'll wait till the heavens open before he'll foreclose any mortgage he may have agen ye'" (*PS*, p. 205).

If Soule's portrait of the honorable Belden bore little resemblance to the actuality of eastern-financed moneylending on the western frontier, it nonetheless testified to the underlying motives of her story. In *A New Home*, Kirkland may have aimed at "a veracious history of actual occurrences" (*ANH*, p. 7). The women who followed her lead to western materials, however, wanted only to escape the circumstances that gave rise to what Margaret Fuller had described as "those painful separations, which already desecrate and desolate the Atlantic coast." The domestic fictionists, in short, wanted to believe—as Fuller had wanted to believe—that on the uncrowded and fertile tracts of the western prairies "whole families might live together" in a kind of extended domestic Eden, the sons returning "from their pilgrimages to settle near the parent hearth" and the daughters finding "room near their mother."[45] As a result, though their novels never shied away from depicting the squalor of the urban poor or the mind- and body-numbing labor of an impoverished New England farm,[46] only rarely did these women even approach Kirkland's description of "the tenant of a log-cabin whose family, whatever be its numbers, must burrow in a single room, while a bed or two, a chest, a table, and a wretched handful of cooking utensils, form the chief materials of comfort" (*ANH*, p. 311).

Precisely because these writers were committed to a fantasy and not to any specific geography or agrarian economic organization, moreover, their novels exhibit a particular tension that goes beyond the purposeful masking of historical reality. The reversion to familial configurations from an earlier period, made possible by the isolated border setting, stands side by side in their texts with assertions of development and centrality. For, without ever owning up to the contradiction, the domestic fictionists who turned to western materials generally applaud the change "from a straggling, border village into a populous and central town" (*PS*, p. 235). The point must therefore be made that just because writers like Maria Susanna Cummins and Caroline Soule chose to regenerate their broken and ruined city families in the agricultural west did not mean that they were inveterately opposed to cities, manufacturing, or even to class distinctions. It was only the squalor and corrupting influences of the city, the meaner exploitations of poor laborers by factories, and the vicious disparities of class to which these writers objected. They wanted to evade certain consequences attendant upon an accelerated industrialized urbanization because they saw those consequences ravaging families and destroying the domestic ideals to which they held; but industry and urbanization themselves they did not reject. (Only Mary Hay-

den Pike and E. D. E. N. Southworth actually rejected on ideological and philosophical grounds the plantation society premised on slavery.)

Needless to say, to preserve the fantasy, the domestic fictionists took great
pains to distinguish their fictional western towns from the "crowded, cramped
and choked" environments of the older settlements. *This* town, they assure readers, is "spacious, broad and airy." Caroline Soule declares that the fifteen-year
period of development she catalogues in *The Pet of the Settlement* represents "only
a bright, beautiful change" (*PS*, p. 236). But her language subtly suggests
otherwise:

> Years have come and gone . . . changing [the little Settlement] from a strag-
> gling, border village into a populous and central town; not crowded, cramped
> and choked though, but spacious, broad and airy. The arching trees that line
> each avenue, giving it a picture-look, with their cool and waving shadows,
> while the ample parks, with their green and tasteful hedges, their closely
> shaven lawns, their clustering shrubs, their gorgeous flowers, their sparkling
> fountains, singing birds, tame forest pets, and chattering, dancing little chil-
> dren, are a sweet relief to the dim [*sic:* din] and bustle of its thoroughfares,
> and give to its busiest denizen a taste of that dear country life for which his
> heart is panting. (*PS*, p. 235)

Now so disassociated is the town from its frontier origins that, within its precincts, the busy "denizen" *pants* for even a "taste of that dear country life" that
had gone before. To a genre originally conceived in nostalgia, that sentiment is
here again introduced—though, again, it is never named as such.

The reason such contradictions go unacknowledged is that most of these novelists did not so much want to abandon the east as to offer an idealized alternative
by which it might be regenerated. The west merely provided an appropriate
stage set for elaborating the ideal. Thus, though many a heroine is said to be
"held . . . spell-bound" by "the sudden glory of the extended landscape" (*I*,
p. 194), none of these writers invoked either irony or regret when they pictured
"hundreds of glorious old forest trees falling only to rise again, not as the green
and leafy bowers of singing birds, but . . . as the spacious marts of trade, [or] the
dusty, noisy workshop" (*PS*, p. 191).

The point, after all, was not to suggest that the informing values of hearth and
home could only take hold in the relatively unsophisticated settlements at the
edges of society. The reformist impulse of this fiction needed to demonstrate
that such values could flourish even in the face of accelerating development and
thus serve as a model by which the nation as a whole might be transformed. Displacing the uglier realities of the older regions, the idealized fictional west was to
become central to a new national self-image. And to that end, even the new technology might be useful. As one of the Iowa pioneers in Soule's *The Pet of the Settlement* confidently predicts, in the near future "'there'll come puffin' and blowin'
and snortin' along, that . . . iron horse . . . and then ye see, why we shan't be out
west a bit, but jist in the very centre of creation, with all the world a-coming in to
see how we git along'" (*PS*, p. 205).

Though the bulk of its story line is usually played out on some prairie frontier,
the domestic novel of western relocation was nonetheless a response to eastern—

and not western—concerns. And although the fantasy demands of the genre produced an idealized west onto which women readers might project otherwise threatened visions of home and hearth, writers like Cummins, Southworth, and Soule did not conceive themselves as promotionalists for westward migration. Even so, constrained by the need to make their western idylls persuasive as well as attractive, the domestic fictionists had to offer palliative resolutions to the fears and anxieties that their women readers traditionally associated with westward migration. As a result, following promotionalists like Mary Austin Holley and Eliza Farnham, and adapting many of their happier metaphors as plot structures, the domestic fictionists (even if inadvertently) succeeded in creating a sort of collective "emigrants' guide" that spoke specifically to women.

When Elisabeth Adams wrote from Iowa to her sister in Ohio, in 1846, complaining that "if I could only have mother or a sister here I should be very glad,"[47] she testified to women's general distress at family separations—and to their particular distress at isolation from female relatives. The domestic fictions set in the west, which began to appear just a few years after Adam's arrival in Davenport, responded to this familiar complaint by inventing an ingenious pattern of surrogates. In *Mabel Vaughan*, Cummins provided her heiress heroine with a surrogate sister in the person of a neighboring minister's daughter. And when the Widow Symmes becomes ill in Soule's *The Pet of the Settlement*, the motherless Margaret Belden took her home and "nursed her as a daughter would a mother" (*PS*, p. 244). Upon her recovery, the old woman is urged to remain on in the Belden household and is given a room that, thereafter, all "called . . . affectionately, grandmother's room" (*PS*, p. 245).

Responding to women's reluctance to exchange comfortable household arrangements for primitive conditions—"I miss many of the conveniences of home," Elisabeth Adams admitted in a letter to her sister[48]—the domestic fictionists hinted at a speedy transition from original log cabin to framed house or charming cottage. The fear of geographical isolation to which Elizabeth Adams gave voice soon after her arrival in Iowa—"I am alone tonight, the wind sounds so mournful and the house is so still that I am almost sad"[49]—called forth other devices. To these plaintive chords the domestic fictionists responded with promises of "the iron horse" putting their western settlements, soon enough, "jist in the very centre" of things (*PS*, p. 205). Even the rigors of the journey were minimized, as most of these novelists depicted their characters traveling in relative comfort on steamboats, canalboats, and railroads; and since they generally restricted their settings to frontiers well east of the Missouri River, arduous travel by wagon only rarely figured in their pages.

Perhaps the most tenacious anxiety to which these books responded was the lingering suspicion that women became dessicated or masculinized (or both) on the frontier. Writing from Kansas in 1859, Sarah Everett thanked a sister-in-law in western New York State for sending dress trimmings. She then added: "It was two or three weeks before I could make up my mind to wear anything so gay as that lining and those strings." "I am a very old woman," Sarah explained, "my face is thin sunken and wrinkled, my hands bony withered and hard—I shall look strangely I fear with your nice undersleeves and the coquettish cherry bows."[50] The Sarah Everett who wrote those lines was twenty-nine years old. Whether we take her protests as exaggerations or, more probably, as accurate assessments of the physical toll of pioneering, one crucial fact emerges: Sarah Everett's fear of growing old before her time, of losing the capacity for feminine coquetry, was a fear that most women (and men) associated with westward emigration.

With unerring precision, Cummins directed herself to these fears in *Mabel Vaughan*. To the dread of physical dessication, Cummins offered categorical denials. At twenty-five, now having spent six years in Illinois, Mabel is said to enjoy a "complexion [that] has lost nothing of its fairness; the full brown eye glows with as soft a light; the smile which plays around the mouth is as spontaneous and attractive; and the chestnut hair . . . is as rich and glossy as ever" (*MV*, p. 397). To the fear "that Mabel's manners would lose something of their delicacy . . . [or] her mode of expression, would become masculine and harsh" (*MV*, p. 396), Cummins opposed fully one third of her novel. Portrayed throughout the book as stereotypically patient and passive, though always acutely sensitive to the needs of those around her, Mabel's capacity for "unfailing cheerfulness and sympathy with others' joy" (*MV*, p. 398) is especially emphasized once she removes to Illinois.

These novels exhibited their greatest ingenuity for altering contemporary belief and perception, however, in their strategies for making the prairie landscape seem both inviting and familiar. Only Southworth, in *India*, played upon American women's habitual fear of entrapment within an isolated wooded landscape. She allowed her heroine one fearful night in a log cabin located within an "old primeval forest" (*I*, p. 270), where she is menaced by a pack of hungry wolves. Denominated "'a small, cowardly race'" (*I*, p. 290), though, the wolves are quickly dispatched by the heroine's husband and, thereafter, the young bride is pictured wandering safely and happily in a wilderness garden where, like a latter-day Eve, she gathers "a rich harvest . . . of ripe fruit" (*I*, pp. 294–95). For the most part, however, the landscapes of these novels involve the open spaces of the prairies. And even Southworth describes the prairie stands of trees as "dotted groves" or "like oases in [a] desert" (*I*, p. 294).

In fact, by 1850, the cutting edge of settlement had for so long been identified with the prairie that heavily wooded landscapes no longer figured prominently as emblems of the frontier. Instead, Americans imagined the parklike expanses made famous by Holley and Farnham: unimpeded prospects across rolling and flowered prairies with, here and there, a river and a stand of trees. By the end of the decade, when *The Pet of the Settlement* appeared, the alternations of closed and open spaces had become almost schematic. Soule's characters encounter "on the one side a ten-mile prairie stretching its emerald hues to the golden horizon, . . . on the other, a dense forest" (*PS*, p. 16). And everywhere in these novels, the prairies are said to be carpeted with wild strawberries and "multitudes of roses and pinks" (*PS*, p. 23).

If the prairie frontier was thus made inviting, it was also denuded of its strangeness. "Well, really now," declares a maiden aunt, newly arrived in Illinois, "I don't see such a great difference, after all, between this country and what I've been used to at the East." The domestic novels of western relocation were full of such statements, though none as fully articulated as that of Aunt Sabiah in Cummins's *Mabel Vaughan*:

That 'ere great field, prairie, or whatever you call it, is pretty much like our meadows at home, only it ain't fenced off; and rivers are rivers anywhere, and always will run down hill, and trees are trees, and sky's sky, and as to the people, you say they're most all New England settlers so I don't see there's anything heathenish about the place after all. (*MV*, p. 390)

The comparison of prairies to meadows—a frequent comparison in these novels—without any acknowledgement of the tall prairie grasses unique to the west is trivializing and inadequate, as are the statements about rivers, trees, and sky. But then this was precisely the purpose of the passage: it was intended to trivialize real topographical differences. The closing reference to "New England settlers" then successfully completes the imputation of the customary. And a recognizable social community is thereby transposed to a landscape that has now been reclaimed as familiar.

With strategies such as these, aided by a vocabulary and a symbolic system evocative of Eden, the westernized domestic fictions encouraged women readers to claim the new frontier as a garden of their own—as men had always done—but, at the same time, they followed the promotionalists in redefining what the garden signified. No longer the realm of the isolate Adamic male adventurer, the frontier in these novels came to embrace home, family, and social community informed by their values. If few pioneer women actually encountered such idealized configurations as daily reality, this does not diminish the fact that the novelists' domesticated western fantasy represented a historically important creative act. For it provided prospective female emigrants with a set of images through which to forge some kind of acceptable anticipatory relationship to an unfamiliar landscape.

To fully appreciate the crucial significance of that contribution, we need only recall that it was not simply deteriorating conditions in the east that made the domestic novel turn westward in the 1850s. The nation as a whole had turned its eyes and imagination in that direction. As financial institutions recovered from the Panic of 1837, the two decades preceding the Civil War counted American emigrants and European immigrants, in unprecedented numbers, pushing out to the borderlands along the Missouri River. Beyond the Missouri, lengthening wagon trains began crossing the Great American Desert, heading overland to a fabled Pacific paradise. What made the domestic novel unique in this context was its single-minded insistence upon *women's* participation in the westward movement.

Of course, as the historian Elizabeth Fries Ellet pointed out, women had always been part of these migrations, even if her 1852 *Pioneer Women of the West* was among the first studies devoted to demonstrating that fact.[51] The promotional writings of Mary Austin Holley and Eliza Farnham and Caroline Kirkland's successive volumes on her experience in Michigan notwithstanding, the emigrant's guides upon which most families depended for their dreams and facts about the west still largely continued to ignore women's presence. Almost as an afterthought, following paragraphs of detailed advice concerning clothing and gear for men and boys, one popular overland guide of 1846 commented briefly, "All [women and girls] can do, is to cook for camps . . . nor need they have any wearing apparel, other than their ordinary clothing at home."[52] It was an inaccurate statement of women's many trail duties, and it was bad advice.[53] Worse than that, it all but edited women out of the great westward adventure.

In the face of this kind of repeated refusal to formally prepare women for their role in the westernizing process, the domestic novels of western relocation fulfilled a vital—if unintentional—function. As always in women's fiction, they offered their readers practical advice about housekeeping on a frontier (since some of these authors knew the west firsthand), and they provided symbolic constructs where more conventional sources of information were lacking. These westernized domestic fictions thus represented unique guide-books to uncharted territories and, as such, they offered comforting and familiar image systems that could serve as templates for the organization of experience. Ten years after her arrival in Iowa, for example. Elisabeth Adams still clung to images lifted directly out of the domestic fictionists' pages. "Sometimes," she wrote her husband, "a vision of a pleasant home with a garden and flowers and creeping vines, and children and husband dear all at home, no more to roam, comes over me, and I confess I look forward to its reality with anticipated pleasure."[54]

NOTES

1. Alice Carey [sic], *Clovernook; Or, Recollections of Our Neighborhood in the West*, 2d ser. (New York: Redfield, 1853), p. 13.

2. Caroline Lee Hentz describes "a beautiful valley in New England . . . gradually becoming a favorite summer retreat of some of the metropolitans, who, debilitated or disgusted by the heat and confinement of a city, longed for the chartered air and liberal shade," in *Lovell's Folly. A Novel* (Cincinnati: Hubbard and Edmonds, 1833), pp. 5–6.

3. James Fenimore Cooper, *The Works of James Fenimore Cooper*, 10 vols. (New York: P. F. Collier, 1892), 6:58.

4. Janis P. Stout, *Sodoms in Eden: The City in American Fiction before 1860* (Westport, Conn.: Greenwood Press, 1976), pp. 4, 21.

5. Nathaniel Hawthorne, preface to *The Marble Faun, or The Romance of Monte Beni* (1860), in *The Complete Novels and Selected Tales of Nathaniel Hawthorne*, ed. Norman Holmes Pearson (New York: Random House, 1937), p. 590. Hawthorne, of course, had for some years been residing in Europe when he made this statement.

6. See Russell Blaine Nye, *Society and Culture in America, 1830–1860* (New York: Harper and Row, 1974), p. 43, n. 18.

7. For the context of this incident, see James D. Hart, *The Popular Book: A History of America's Literary Taste* (1950; reprint, Berkeley: University of California Press, 1963), p. 93.

8. Ann Sophia Stephens, *Fashion and Famine* (New York: Bunce and Brother, 1854).

9. Ann Sophia Stephens, *The Old Homestead* (New York: Bunce and Brother, 1855). For a more extensive discussion of this novel, see Nina Baym, *Woman's Fiction: A Guide to Novels by and about Women in America, 1820–1870* (Ithaca: Cornell University Press, 1978), pp. 186–87.

10. [Maria Susanna Cummins], *Mabel Vaughan* (Boston: John P. Jewett and Company; Cleveland: Henry P. B. Jewett, 1857), p. 127 (hereafter cited in the text as *MV*).

11. Kirkland's 1853 remark is quoted in William S. Osborne, *Caroline M. Kirkland* (New York: Twayne Publishers, 1972), p. 123.

12. Ann Sophia Stephens, *Mary Derwent* (Philadelphia: T. B. Peterson and Brothers, 1858), p. 181.

13. [Catharine Maria Sedgwick], *Live and Let Live; Or, Domestic Service Illustrated* (New York: Harper and Brothers, 1837), p. 184.

14. Charles Fenno Hoffman, *A Winter in the West*, 2 vols. (New York: Harper and Brothers, 1835), 1:191.

15. Mary Austin Holley, *Texas. Observations, Historical, Geographical and Descriptive, In a Series of Letters, Written during a Visit to Austin's Colony, with a view to a permanent settlement in that country, in the Autumn of 1831* (Baltimore: Armstrong and Plaskitt, 1833), pp. 14, 127–28.

16. See Baym, p. 122.

17. Emma D. E. N. Southworth's *India: The Pearl of Pearl River* (Philadelphia: T. B. Peterson and Brothers, 1856) was first serialized in 1853 under the title *Mark Sutherland* (hereafter cited in the text as *I*).

18. [Mary Hayden Green Pike], *Ida May: A Story of Things Actual and Possible. By Mary Langdon* [pseud.] (Boston: Phillips, Sampson and Co., 1854). See also Baym, pp. 268–69.

19. Susan Phinney Conrad, *Perish the Thought: Intellectual Women in Romantic America, 1830–1860* (New York: Oxford University Press, 1976), pp. 99–100.

20. Mrs. D. L. Child, *The History and Condition of Women*, 2 vols. (Boston: John Allen and Cox, 1835), 2:260–61.

21. These remarks, first offered at an 1852 Women's Rights Convention, were published by Paulina Wright Davis as "Remarks at the Convention," in *Una* (September 1853): 136–37.

22. Catharine Beecher, "How to Redeem Women's Profession from Dishonor," *Harper's New Monthly Magazine* 31 (November 1865): 710; and Catharine Beecher, *Letters to the People on Health and Happiness* (New York: Harper and Brothers, 1855), p. 183. Of inestimable value to me in this discussion was Kathryn Kish Sklar's *Catharine Beecher: A Study in American Domesticity* (New Haven: Yale University Press, 1973).

23. Beecher, "How to Redeem Women's Profession from Dishonor," p. 710.

24. From Louisa C. Tuthill's *My Wife* (Boston: William Crosby and H. P. Nichols, 1846), quoted in Baym, p. 80.

25. Nancy F. Cott, *The Bonds of Womanhood: "Woman's Sphere" in New England, 1780–1835* (New Haven: Yale University Press, 1977), p. 199.

26. Quoted in ibid., p. 68.

27. Sarah Josepha Hale, "Editor's Table," *Godey's Lady's Book* 40 (January 1850): 76.

28. From "The Social Condition of Woman," *North American Review* 42 (1836): 513, quoted in Conrad, p. 36.

29. Caroline M. Kirkland, "The Island Story," in *Autumn Hours, and Fireside Reading* (New York: Charles Scribner, 1854), p. 196.

30. *Hearth and Home* was published in New York from December 1868 through December 1875; its original editors were Donald G. Mitchell and Harriet Beecher Stowe, although Stowe left the editorial staff after the first year. Under its front-page title, the magazine featured a woodcut of a rustic cottage with children playing around the door.

31. Beecher, *Letters to the People on Health and Happiness*, p. 91.

32. Caroline M. Kirkland, "The Island Story," p. 110.

33. Baym, p. 231.

34. Paulina Wright Davis complained that women who had to earn their own living were forced to enter the "factory and the schoolroom at *slave* wages," in "Remarks at the Convention," p. 136. Catharine Beecher echoed this theme when, after a visit to the much-heralded Lowell, Massachusetts, mills, she wrote that "work of all kinds is got from poor women, at prices that will not keep soul and body together. . . . And then the articles

thus made," she continued, "are sold for prices that give monstrous profits to the capitalist, who thus grows rich on the hard labors of our sex," quoted in Sklar, pp. 172–73.

35. Mary Kelley, "A Woman Alone: Catharine Maria Sedgwick's Spinsterhood in
Nineteenth-Century America," *New England Quarterly* 51, no. 2 (June 1978): 209.

36. Of course, as Henry Nash Smith has pointed out in *Virgin Land: The American West
as Symbol and Myth* (1950; New York: Random House, Vintage Books, 1961), p. 151, "by
1830," there were already "two agrarianisms" contesting "for control of the territories beyond the Mississippi. Each of these new agrarianisms found expression in imaginative and
symbolic terms: that of the South in a pastoral literature of the plantation, that of the
Northwest in the myth of the garden of the world with idealized Western yeoman as its
focal point."

37. Caróline A. Soule, *The Pet of the Settlement. A Story of Prairie-Land* (Boston: A.
Tompkins, 1860), p. 102 (hereafter cited in the text as *PS*).

38. Eliza W. Farnham, *Life in Prairie Land* (New York: Harper and Brothers, 1846),
p. 74; and Holley, p. 127.

39. See Paul W. Gates, *Landlords and Tenants on the Prairie Frontier: Studies in American
Land Policy* (Ithaca: Cornell University Press, 1973), pp. 239, 60.

40. Quoted in ibid., p. 59.

41. See ibid., p. 56.

42. Ibid., p. 240; the entry of March 23, 1846, from the Diary of Calvin Fletcher, is
quoted in Gates, p. 62.

43. Caroline M. Kirkland, *A New Home—Who'll Follow? Or, Glimpses of Western Life*
(1839; reprint, New York: Garrett Press, 1969), p. 48.

44. Lydia H. Sigourney, "The Western Home" in *The Western Home, and Other Poems*
(Philadelphia: Parry and McMillan, 1854), p. 29 (hereafter cited in the text as *WH*).

45. S. M. Fuller, *Summer on the Lakes, in 1843* (Boston: Charles C. Little and James
Brown; New York: Charles S. Francis and Co., 1844), p. 60.

46. See, for example, Julia Caroline Ripley Dorr's *Farmingdale. By Caroline Thomas*
[pseud.] (New York: D. Appleton), 1854); and for a discussion of the novel, see Baym,
pp. 237–38.

47. Elisabeth Adams, Davenport, Iowa, to Emeline M. Robinson, Cleveland, Ohio,
July 14, 1846, in Ephraim Adams Papers, Manuscript Collection, Iowa State Historical
Department.

48. Elisabeth Adams, Davenport, Iowa, to Emeline Robinson, Cleveland, Ohio,
March 17, 1846, in Ephraim Adams Papers.

49. Ibid.

50. "Letters of John and Sarah Everett, 1854–1864: Miami County Pioneers," *Kansas
Historical Quarterly* 3, no. 4 (November 1939): 354. Sarah Everett and her husband immi-
grated to the Kansas Territory in the spring of 1855, along with other eastern "free
staters." She died in 1864.

51. Elizabeth Fries Ellet, *The Pioneer Women of the West* (1852; facsimile reprint, Freeport, N.Y.: Books for Libraries Press, 1973). To be sure, isolated articles, especially in the
literary magazines published in the west, also acknowledged women's participation in the
pioneer experience. The July 1836 issue of the *Western Literary Journal and Monthly Review*,
for example, published an anonymously authored poem entitled, "The Mothers of the
West," which castigated Americans for failing to appreciate women's contribution to the
settlement of the west; and an anonymously authored article, entitled "The Pioneer
Mothers," praised women for going forth as "volunteers to act as hand-maids in rearing a
nation in the wilds of the West . . . with a devotedness and singleness of purpose"
(pp. 106, 101). Unfortunately, isolated pieces like these did not enjoy much cumulative
impact.

52. J. M. Shively, *Route and Distances to Oregon and California, With a Description of*

Watering-Places, Crossings, Dangerous Indians, &c. &c. (Washington, D.C.: William Greer, Printer, 1846) appears as an appendix to Dale Morgan, ed., *Overland in 1846: Diaries and Letters of the California–Oregon Trail*, 2 vols. (Georgetown, Calif.: Talisman Press, 1963), 2:736.

53. For accurate assessments of women's many tasks on the overland trail, see John Mack Faragher, *Women and Men on the Overland Trail* (New Haven: Yale University Press, 1979); Julie Roy Jeffrey, *Frontier Women: The Trans-Mississippi West, 1840–1880* (New York: Hill and Wang, 1979); and Lillian Schlissel, *Women's Diaries of the Westward Journey* (New York: Schocken Books, 1982).

54. Elisabeth Adams, Davenport, Iowa, to Ephraim Adams, Grinnell, Iowa, May 5, 1856, in Ephraim Adams Papers. A native of New Hampshire, Elisabeth Adams had removed to Iowa with her husband who was a Congregationalist minister; his many church-related administrative duties kept him—and his family—constantly on the move in Iowa.

THREE WOMEN'S TEXTS AND A CRITIQUE OF IMPERIALISM

It should not be possible to read nineteenth-century British literature without remembering that imperialism, understood as England's social mission, was a crucial part of the cultural representation of England to the English. The role of literature in the production of cultural representation should not be ignored. These two obvious "facts" continue to be disregarded in the reading of nine-teenth-century British literature. This itself attests to the continuing success of the imperialist project, displaced and dispersed into more modern forms.

If these "facts" were remembered, not only in the study of British literature but in the study of the literatures of the European colonizing cultures of the great age of imperialism, we would produce a narrative, in literary history, of the "worlding" of what is now called "the Third World." To consider the Third World as distant cultures, exploited but with rich intact literary heritages waiting to be recovered, interpreted, and curricularized in English translation fosters the emergence of "the Third World" as a signifier that allows us to forget that "world-ing," even as it expands the empire of the literary discipline.[1]

It seems particularly unfortunate when the emergent perspective of feminist criticism reproduces the axioms of imperialism. A basically isolationist admiration for the literature of the female subject in Europe and Anglo-America establishes the high feminist norm. It is supported and operated by an information-retrieval approach to "Third-World" literature which often employs a deliberately "non-theoretical" methodology with self-conscious rectitude.

In this essay, I will attempt to examine the operation of the "worlding" of what is today "the Third World" by what has become a cult text of feminism: *Jane Eyre*.[2] I plot the novel's reach and grasp, and locate its structural motors. I read *Wide Sargasso Sea* as *Jane Eyre*'s reinscription and *Frankenstein* as an analy-sis—even a deconstruction—of a "worlding" such as *Jane Eyre*'s.[3]

I need hardly mention that the object of my investigation is the printed book, not its "author." To make such a distinction is, of course, to ignore the lessons of deconstruction. A deconstructive critical approach would loosen the binding of the book, undo the opposition between verbal text and the bio-graphy of the named subject "Charlotte Brontë," and see the two as each other's "scene of writing." In such a reading, the life that writes itself as "my life" is as much a production in psychosocial space (other names can be found) as the book that is written by the holder of that named life—a book that is then consigned to what *is* most often recognized as genuinely "social": the world of publication and distribution.[4] To touch Brontë's "life" in such a way, however, would be too risky here. We must rather strategically take shelter in an essentialism which, not wishing to lose the important advantages won by U.S. mainstream feminism, will continue to honor the suspect binary oppositions—book and author, individual and history—and start with an assurance of the following sort: my readings here do not seek to undermine the excellence of the individual artist. If even minimally successful, the readings will incite a degree of rage against the imperialist narrativization of history, that it should produce so abject a script for her. I provide these assurances to allow myself some room to situate feminist individualism in its historical determination rather than simply to canonize it as feminism as such.

Sympathetic U.S. feminists have remarked that I do not do justice to Jane Eyre's subjectivity. A word of explanation is perhaps in order. The broad strokes of my presuppositions are that what is at stake, for feminist individualism in the age of imperialism, is precisely the making of human beings, the constitution and "interpellation" of the subject not only as individual but as "individualist."[5] This stake is represented on two registers: childbearing and soul making. The first is domestic-society-through-sexual-reproduction cathected as "companionate love"; the second is the imperialist project cathected as civil-society-through-social-mission. As the female individualist, not-quite/not-male, articulates herself in shifting relationship to what is at stake, the "native female" as such (*within* discourse, *as* a signifier) is excluded from any share in this emerging norm.[6] If we read this account from an isolationist perspective in a "metropolitan" context, we see nothing there but the psychobiography of the militant female subject. In a reading such as mine, in contrast, the effort is to wrench oneself away from the mesmerizing focus of the "subject-constitution" of the female individualist.

To develop further the notion that my stance need not be an accusing one, I will refer to a passage from Roberto Fernández Retamar's "Caliban."[7] José Enrique Rodó had argued in 1900 that the model for the Latin American intellectual in relationship to Europe could be Shakespeare's Ariel.[8] In 1971 Retamar, denying the possibility of an identifiable "Latin American Culture," recast the model as Caliban. Not surprisingly, this powerful exchange still excludes any specific consideration of the civilizations of the Maya, the Aztecs, the Incas, or the smaller nations of what is now called Latin America. Let us note carefully that, at this stage of my argument, this "conversation" between Europe and Latin America (without a specific consideration of the political economy of the "worlding" of the "native") provides a sufficient thematic description of our attempt to confront the ethnocentric and reverse-ethnocentric benevolent double bind (that is, considering the "native" as object for enthusiastic information-retrieval and thus denying its own "worlding") that I sketched in my opening paragraphs.

In a moving passage in "Caliban," Retamar locates both Caliban and Ariel in the postcolonial intellectual:

> There is no real Ariel–Caliban polarity: both are slaves in the hands of Prospero, the foreign magician. But Caliban is the rude and unconquerable master of the island, while Ariel, a creature of the air, although also a child of the isle, is the intellectual.

> The deformed Caliban—enslaved, robbed of his island, and taught the language by Prospero—rebukes him thus: "You taught me language, and my profit on't/ Is, I know how to curse." ["C," pp. 28, 11]

As we attempt to unlearn our so-called privilege as Ariel and "seek from [a certain] Caliban the honor of a place in his rebellious and glorious ranks," we do not ask that our students and colleagues should emulate us but that they should attend to us ("C," p. 72). If, however, we are driven by a nostalgia for lost origins, we too run the risk of effacing the "native" and stepping forth as "the real Caliban," of forgetting that he is a name in a play, an inaccessible blankness circumscribed by an interpretable text.[9] The stagings of Caliban work alongside the narrativization of history: claiming to *be* Caliban legitimizes the very individualism that we must persistently attempt to undermine from within.

Elizabeth Fox-Genovese, in an article on history and women's history, shows us how to define the historical moment of feminism in the West in terms of female access to individualism.[10] The battle for female individualism plays itself out within the larger theater of the establishment of meritocratic individualism, indexed in the aesthetic field by the ideology of "the creative imagination." Fox-Genovese's presupposition will guide us into the beautifully orchestrated opening of *Jane Eyre*.

It is a scene of the marginalization and privatization of the protagonist: "There was no possibility of taking a walk that day. . . . Out-door exercise was now out of the question. I was glad of it," Brontë writes (*JE*, p. 9). The movement continues as Jane breaks the rules of the appropriate topography of withdrawal. The family at the center withdraws into the sanctioned architectural space of the withdrawing room or drawing room; Jane inserts herself—"I slipped in"—into the margin—"A small breakfast-room *adjoined* the drawing room" (*JE*, p. 9; my emphasis).

The manipulation of the domestic inscription of space within the upwardly mobilizing currents of the eighteenth- and nineteenth-century bourgeoisie in England and France is well known. It seems fitting that the place to which Jane withdraws is not only not the withdrawing room but also not the dining room, the sanctioned place of family meals. Nor is it the library, the appropriate place for reading. The breakfast room "contained a book-case" (*JE*, p. 9). As Rudolph Ackerman wrote in his *Repository* (1823), one of the many manuals of taste in circulation in nineteenth-century England, these low bookcases and stands were designed to "contain all the books that may be desired for a sitting-room without reference to the library."[11] Even in this already triply off-center place, "having drawn the red moreen curtain nearly close, I [Jane] was shrined in double retirement" (*JE*, pp. 9–10).

Here in Jane's self-marginalized uniqueness, the reader becomes her accomplice: the reader and Jane are united—both are reading. Yet Jane still preserves her odd privilege, for she continues never quite doing the proper thing in its proper place. She cares little for reading what is *meant* to be read: the "letterpress." *She* reads the pictures. The power of this singular hermeneutics is precisely that it can make the outside inside. "At intervals, while turning over the leaves of my book, I studied the aspect of that winter afternoon." Under "the clear panes of glass," the rain no longer penetrates, "the drear November day" is rather a one-dimensional "aspect" to be "studied," not decoded like the "letterpress" but, like pictures, deciphered by the unique creative imagination of the marginal individualist (*JE*, p. 10).

Before following the track of this unique imagination, let us consider the suggestion that the progress of *Jane Eyre* can be charted through a sequential arrangement of the family/counter-family dyad. In the novel, we encounter, first, the Reeds as the legal family and Jane, the late Mr. Reed's sister's daughter, as the representative of a near incestuous counter-family; second, the Brocklehursts, who run the school Jane is sent to, as the legal family and Jane, Miss Temple, and Helen Burns as a counter-family that falls short because it is only a community of women; third, Rochester and the mad Mrs. Rochester as the legal family and Jane and Rochester as the illicit counter-family. Other items may be added to the thematic chain in this sequence: Rochester and Céline Varens as structurally functional counter-family; Rochester and Blanche Ingram as dissimulation of legality—and so on. It is during this sequence that Jane is moved from the counter-family to the family-in-law. In the next sequence, it is Jane who restores full family status to the as-yet-incomplete community of siblings, the Riverses. The final sequence of the book is a *community of families*, with Jane, Rochester, and their children at the center.

In terms of the narrative energy of the novel, how is Jane moved from the place of the counter-family to the family-in-law? It is the active ideology of imperialism that provides the discursive field.

(My working definition of "discursive field" must assume the existence of discrete "systems of signs" at hand in the socius, each based on a specific axiomatics. I am identifying these systems as discursive fields. "Imperialism as social mission" generates the possibility of one such axiomatics. How the individual artist taps the discursive field at hand with a sure touch, if not with transhistorical clairvoyance, in order to make the narrative structure move I hope to demonstrate through the following example. It is crucial that we extend our analysis of this example beyond the minimal diagnosis of "racism.")

Let us consider the figure of Bertha Mason, a figure produced by the axiomatics of imperialism. Through Bertha Mason, the white Jamaican Creole, Brontë renders the human/animal frontier as acceptably indeterminate, so that a good greater than the letter of the Law can be broached. Here is the celebrated passage, given in the voice of Jane:

> In the deep shade, at the further end of the room, a figure ran backwards and forwards. What it was, whether beast or human being, one could not . . . tell: it grovelled, seemingly, on all fours; it snatched and growled like some strange wild animal: but it was covered with clothing, and a quantity of dark, grizzled hair, wild as a mane, hid its head and face.[*JE*, p. 295]

In a matching passage, given in the voice of Rochester speaking *to* Jane, Brontë presents the imperative for a shift beyond the Law as divine injunction rather than human motive. In the terms of my essay, we might say that this is the register not of mere marriage or sexual reproduction but of Europe and its not-yet-human Other, of soul making. The field of imperial conquest is here inscribed as Hell:

> "One night I had been awakened by her yells . . . it was a fiery West Indian night. . . .
>
> "'This life,' said I at last, 'is hell!—this is the air—those are the sounds of the bottomless pit! *I have a right* to deliver myself from it if I can. . . . Let me break away, and go home to God!' . . .
>
> "A wind fresh from Europe blew over the ocean and rushed through the open casement: the storm broke, streamed, thundered, blazed, and the air grew pure. . . . It was true Wisdom that consoled me in that hour, and showed me the right path. . . .
>
> "The sweet wind from Europe was still whispering in the refreshed leaves, and the Atlantic was thundering in glorious liberty. . . .
>
> "'Go,' said Hope, 'and live again in Europe. . . . You have done all that God and Humanity require of you.'" [*JE*, pp. 310–11; my emphasis]

It is the unquestioned ideology of imperialist axiomatics, then, that conditions Jane's move from the counter-family set to the set of the family-in-law. Marxist critics such as Terry Eagleton have seen this only in terms of the ambiguous *class* position of the governess.[12] Sandra Gilbert and Susan Gubar, on the other hand, have seen Bertha Mason only in psychological terms, as Jane's dark double.[13]

I will not enter the critical debates that offer themselves here. Instead, I will develop the suggestion that nineteenth-century feminist individualism could conceive of a "greater" project than access to the closed circle of the nuclear family. This is the project of soul making beyond "mere" sexual reproduction. Here the native "subject" is not almost an animal but rather the object of what might be termed the terrorism of the categorical imperative.

I am using "Kant" in this essay as a metonym for the most flexible ethical moment in the European eighteenth century. Kant words the categorical imperative, conceived as the universal moral law given by pure reason, in this way: "In all creation every thing one chooses and over which one has any power, may be used *merely as means;* man alone, and with him every rational creature, is an *end in himself.*" It is thus a moving displacement of Christian ethics from religion to philosophy. As Kant writes: "With this agrees very well the possibility of such a command as: *Love God above everything, and thy neighbor as thyself.* For as a command it requires respect for a law which *commands love* and does not leave it to our own arbitrary choice to make this our principle."[14]

The "categorical" in Kant cannot be adequately represented in determinately grounded action. The dangerous transformative power of philosophy, however, is that its formal subtlety can be travestied in the service of the state. Such a travesty in the case of the categorical imperative can justify the imperialist project by producing the following formula: *make* the heathen into a human so that he can be treated as an end in himself.[15] This project is presented as a sort of tangent in *Jane Eyre*, a tangent that escapes the closed circle of the *narrative* conclusion. The tangent narrative is the story of St. John Rivers, who is granted the important task of concluding the *text*.

At the novel's end, the *allegorical* language of Christian psychobiography—rather than the textually constituted and seemingly *private* grammar of the creative imagination which we noted in the novel's opening—marks the inaccessibility of the imperialist project as such to the nascent "feminist" scenario. The concluding passage of *Jane Eyre* places St. John Rivers within the fold of *Pilgrim's Progress*. Eagleton pays no attention to this but accepts the novel's ideological lexicon, which establishes St. John Rivers' heroism by identifying a life in Calcutta with an unquestioning choice of death. Gilbert and Gubar, by calling *Jane Eyre* "Plain Jane's Progress," see the novel as simply replacing the male protagonist with the female. They do not notice the distance between sexual reproduction and soul making, both actualized by the unquestioned idiom of imperialist presuppositions evident in the last part of *Jane Eyre:*

> Firm, faithful, and devoted, full of energy, and zeal, and truth, [St. John Rivers] labours for his race. . . . His is the sternness of the warrior Greatheart, who guards his pilgrim convoy from the onslaught of Apollyon. . . . His is the ambition of the high master-spirit[s] . . . who stand without fault before the throne of God; who share the last mighty victories of the Lamb; who are called, and chosen, and faithful. [*JE*, p. 455]

Earlier in the novel, St. John Rivers himself justifies the project: "My vocation? My great work? . . . My hopes of being numbered in the band who have merged all ambitions in the glorious one of bettering their race—of carrying knowledge into the realms of ignorance—of substituting peace for war—freedom for bondage—religion for superstition—the hope of heaven for the fear of hell?" (*JE*, p. 376). Imperialism and its territorial and subject-constituting project are a violent deconstruction of these oppositions.

When Jean Rhys, born on the Caribbean island of Dominica, read *Jane Eyre* as a child, she was moved by Bertha Mason: "I thought I'd try to write her a life." [16] *Wide Sargasso sea*, the slim novel published in 1965, at the end of Rhys' long career, is that "life."

I have suggested that Bertha's function in *Jane Eyre* is to render indeterminate the boundary between human and animal and thereby to weaken her entitlement under the spirit if not the letter of the Law. When Rhys rewrites the scene in *Jane Eyre* where Jane hears "a snarling, snatching sound, almost like a dog quarrelling" and then encounters a bleeding Richard Mason (*JE*, p. 210), she keeps Bertha's humanity, indeed her sanity as critic of imperialism, intact. Grace Poole, another character originally in *Jane Eyre*, describes the incident to Bertha in *Wide Sargasso Sea:* "So you don't remember that you attacked this gentleman with a knife? . . . I didn't hear all he said except 'I cannot interfere legally between yourself and your husband.' It was when he said 'legally' that you flew at him'" (*WSS*, p. 150). In Rhys' retelling, it is the dissimulation that Bertha discerns in the word "legally"—not an innate bestiality—that prompts her violent reaction.

In the figure of Antoinette, whom in *Wide Sargasso Sea* Rochester violently renames Bertha, Rhys suggests that so intimate a thing as personal and human identity might be determined by the politics of imperialism. Antoinette, as a white Creole child growing up at the time of emancipation in Jamaica, is caught between the English imperialist and the black native. In recounting Antoinette's development, Rhys reinscribes some thematics of Narcissus.

There are, noticeably, many images of mirroring in the text. I will quote one from the first section. In this passage, Tia is the little black servant girl who is Antoinette's close companion: "We had eaten the same food, slept side by side, bathed in the same river. As I ran, I thought, I will live with Tia and I will be like her. . . . When I was close I saw the jagged stone in her hand but I did not see her throw it. . . . We stared at each other, blood on my face, tears on hers. It was as if I saw myself. Like in a looking glass" (*WSS*, p. 38).

A progressive sequence of dreams reinforces this mirror imagery. In its second occurrence, the dream is partially set in a *hortus conclusus*, or "enclosed garden"—Rhys uses the phrase (*WSS*, p. 50)—a Romance rewriting of the Narcissus topos as the place of encounter with Love.[17] In the enclosed garden, Antoinette encounters not Love but a strange threatening voice that says merely "in here," inviting her into a prison which masquerades as the legalization of love (*WSS*, p. 50).

In Ovid's *Metamorphoses*, Narcissus' madness is disclosed when he recognizes his Other as his self: "Iste ego sum."[18] Rhys makes Antoinette see her *self* as her Other, Brontë's Bertha. In the last section of *Wide Sargasso Sea*, Antoinette acts out *Jane Eyre's* conclusion and recognizes herself as the so-called ghost in Thornfield Hall: "I went into the hall again with the tall candle in my hand. It was then that I saw her—the ghost. The woman with streaming hair. She was surrounded by a gilt frame but I knew her" (*WSS*, p. 154). The gilt frame encloses a mirror: as Narcissus' pool reflects the selfed Other, so this "pool" reflects the Othered self. Here the dream sequence ends, with an invocation of none other than Tia, the Other that could not be selfed, because the fracture of imperialism rather than the Ovidian pool intervened. (I will return to this difficult point.) "That was the third time I had my dream, and it ended. . . . I called 'Tia' and jumped and woke" (*WSS*, p. 155). It is now, at the very end of the book, that Antoinette/Bertha can say: "Now at last I know why I was brought here and what I have to do" (*WSS*, p. 155–56). We can read this as her having been brought into the England of Brontë's novel: "This cardboard house"—a book between cardboard covers—"where I walk at night is not England" (*WSS*, p. 148). In this fictive England, she must play out her role, act out the transformation of her "self" into that fictive Other, set fire to the house and kill herself, so that Jane Eyre can become the feminist individualist heroine of British fiction. I must read this as an allegory of the general epistemic violence of imperialism, the construction of a self-immolating colonial subject for the glorification of the social mission of the colonizer. At least Rhys sees to it that the woman from the colonies is not sacrificed as an insane animal for her sister's consolidation.

Critics have remarked that *Wide Sargasso Sea* treats the Rochester character with understanding and sympathy.[19] Indeed, he narrates the entire middle section of the book. Rhys makes it clear that he is a victim of the patriarchal inheritance law of entailment rather than of a father's natural preference for the firstborn: in *Wide Sargasso Sea*, Rochester's situation is clearly that of a younger son dispatched to the colonies to buy an heiress. If in the case of Antoinette and her identity, Rhys utilizes the thematics of Narcissus, in the case of Rochester and his patrimony, she touches on the thematics of Oedipus. (In this she has her finger on our "historical moment." If, in the nineteenth century, subject-constitution is represented as childbearing and soul making, in the twentieth century psychoanalysis allows the West to plot the itinerary of the subject from Narcissus [the "imaginary"] to Oediupus [the "symbolic"]. This subject, however, is the normative male subject. In Rhys' reinscription of these themes, divided between the female and the male protagonist, feminism and a critique of imperialism become complicit.)

In place of the "wind from Europe" scene, Rhys substitutes the scenario of a suppressed letter to a father, a letter which would be the "correct" explanation of the tragedy of the book.[20] "I thought about the letter which should have been written to England a week ago. Dear Father . . ." (*WSS*, p. 57). This is the first instance: the letter not written. Shortly afterward:

> Dear Father. The thirty thousand pounds have been paid to me without question or condition. No provision made for her (that must be seen to). . . . I will never be a disgrace to you or to my dear brother the son you love. No begging letters, no mean requests. None of the furtive shabby manoeuvres of a younger son. I have sold my soul or you have sold it, and after all is it such a bad bargain? The girl is thought to be beautiful, she is beautiful. And yet . . . [*WSS*, p. 59]

This is the second instance: the letter not sent. The formal letter is uninteresting; I will quote only a part of it:

> Dear Father, we have arrived from Jamaica after an uncomfortable few days. This little estate in the Windward Islands is part of the family property and Antoinette is much attached to it. . . . All is well and has gone according to your plans and wishes. I dealt of course with Richard Mason. . . . He seemed to become attached to me and trusted me completely. This place is very beautiful but my illness has left me too exhausted to appreciate it fully. I will write again in a few days' time. [*WSS*, p. 63]

And so on.

Rhys' version of the Oedipal exchange is ironic, not a closed circle. We cannot know if the letter actually reaches its destination. "I wondered how they got their letters posted," the Rochester figures muses. "I folded mine and put it into a drawer of the desk. . . . There are blanks in my mind that cannot be filled up" (*WSS*, p. 64). It is as if the text presses us to note the analogy between letter and mind.

Rhys denies to Brontë's Rochester the one thing that is supposed to be secured in the Oedipal relay: the Name of the Father, or the patronymic. In *Wide Sargasso Sea*, the character corresponding to Rochester has no name. His writing of the final version of the letter to his father is supervised, in fact, by an image of the *loss* of the patronymic: "There was a crude bookshelf made of three shingles strung together over the desk and I looked at the books, Byron's poems, novels by Sir Walter Scott, *Confessions of an Opium Eater* . . . and on the last shelf, *Life and Letters of* . . . The rest was eaten away" (*WSS*, p. 63).

Wide Sargasso Sea marks with uncanny clarity the limits of its own discourse in Christophine, Antoinette's black nurse. We may perhaps surmise the distance between *Jane Eyre* and *Wide Sargasso Sea* by remarking that Christophine's unfinished story is the tangent to the latter narrative, as St. John Rivers' story is to the former. Christophine is not a native of Jamaica; she is from Martinique. Taxonomically, she belongs to the category of the good servant rather than that of the pure native. But within these borders, Rhys creates a powerfully suggestive figure.

Christophine is the first interpreter and named speaking subject in the text. "The Jamaican ladies had never approved of my mother, 'because she pretty like pretty self' Christophine said," we read in the book's opening paragraph (*WSS*, p. 15). I have taught this book five times, once in France, once to students who had worked on the book with the well-known Caribbean novelist Wilson Harris, and once at a prestigious institute where the majority of the students were faculty from other universities. It is part of the political argument I am making that all these students blithely stepped over this paragraph without asking or knowing what Christophine's patois, so-called incorrect English, might mean.

Christophine is, of course, a commodified person. "She was your father's wedding present to me" explains Antoinette's mother, "one of his presents" (*WSS*, p. 18). Yet Rhys assigns her some crucial functions in the text. It is Christophine who judges that black ritual practices are culture-specific and cannot be used by whites as cheap remedies for social evils, such as Rochester's lack of love for Antoinette. Most important, it is Christophine alone whom Rhys allows to offer a hard analysis of Rochester's actions, to challenge him in a face-to-face encounter. The entire extended passage is worthy of comment. I quote a brief extract:

> "She is Creole girl, and she have the sun in her. Tell the truth now. She don't come to your house in this place England they tell me about, she don't come to your beautiful house to beg you to marry with her. No, it's you come all the long way to her house—it's you beg her to marry. And she love you and she give you all she have. Now you say you don't love her and you break her up. What you do with her money, eh?" [And then Rochester, the white man, comments silently to himself] Her voice was still quiet but with a hiss in it when she said "money." [*WSS*, p. 130]

Her analysis is powerful enough for the white man to be afraid: "I no longer felt dazed, tired, half hypnotized, but alert and wary, ready to defend myself" (*WSS*, p. 130).

Rhys does not, however, romanticize individual heroics on the part of the oppressed. When the Man refers to the forces of Law and Order, Christophine recognizes their power. This exposure of civil inequality is emphasized by the fact that, just before the Man's successful threat, Christophine had invoked the emancipation of slaves in Jamaica by proclaiming: "No chain gang, no tread machine, no dark jail either. This is free country and I am free woman" (*WSS*, p. 131).

As I mentioned above, Christophine is tangential to this narrative. She cannot be contained by a novel which rewrites a canonical English text within the European novelistic tradition in the interest of the white Creole rather than the native. No perspective *critical* of imperialism can turn the Other into a self, because the project of imperialism has always already historically refracted what might have been the absolutely Other into a domesticated Other that consolidates the imperialist self.[21] The Caliban of Retamar, caught between Europe and Latin America, reflects this predicament. We can read Rhys' reinscription of Narcissus as a thematization of the same problematic.

Of course, we cannot know Jean Rhys' feelings in the matter. We can, however, look at the scene of Christophine's inscription in the text. Immediately after the exchange between her and the Man, well before the conclusion, she is simply driven out of the story, with neither narrative nor characterological explanation or justice. "'Read and write I don't know. Other things I know.' She walked away without looking back" (*WSS*, p. 133).

Indeed, if Rhys rewrites the madwoman's attack on the Man by underlining of the misuse of "legality," she cannot deal with the passage that corresponds to St. John Rivers' own justification of his martyrdom, for it has been displaced into the current idiom of modernization and development. Attempts to construct the "Third-World Woman" as a signifier remind us that the hegemonic definition of literature is itself caught within the history of imperialism. A full literary reinscription cannot easily flourish in the imperialist fracture or discontinuity, covered over by an alien legal system masquerading as Law as such, an alien ideology established as only Truth, and a set of human sciences busy establishing the "native" as self-consolidating Other.

In the Indian case at least, it would be difficult to find an ideological clue to the planned epistemic violence of imperialism merely by rearranging curricula or syllabi within existing norms of literary pedagogy. For a later period of imperialism—when the constituted colonial subject has firmly taken hold—straightforward experiments of comparison can be undertaken, say, between the functionally witless India of *Mrs. Dalloway*, on the one hand, and literary texts produced in India in the 1920s, on the other. But the first half of the nineteenth century resists questioning through literature or literary criticism in the narrow sense, because both are implicated in the project of producing Ariel. To reopen the fracture without succumbing to a nostalgia for lost origins, the literary critic must turn to the archives of imperial governance.

In conclusion, I shall look briefly at Mary Shelley's *Frankenstein*, a text of nascent feminism that remains cryptic, I think, simply because it does not speak the language of feminist individualism which we have come to hail as the language of high feminism within English literature. It is interesting that Barbara Johnson's brief study tries to rescue this recalcitrant text for the service of feminist autobiography.[22] Alternatively, George Levine reads *Frankenstein* in the context of the creative imagination and the nature of the hero. He sees the novel as a book about its own writing and about writing itself, a Romantic allegory of reading within which Jane Eyre as unself-conscious critic would fit quite nicely.[23]

I propose to take *Frankenstein* out of this arena and focus on it in terms of that sense of English cultural identity which I invoked at the opening of this essay. Within that focus we are obliged to admit that, although *Frankenstein* is ostensibly about the origin and evolution of man in our society, it does not deploy the axiomatics of imperialism.

Let me say at once that there is plenty of incidental imperialist sentiment in

Frankenstein. My point, within the argument of this essay, is that the discursive field of imperialism does not produce unquestioned ideological correlatives for the narrative structuring of the book. The discourse of imperialism surfaces in a curiously powerful way in Shelley's novel, and I will later discuss the moment at which it emerges.

Frankenstein is not a battleground of male and female individualism articulated in terms of sexual reproduction (family and female) and social subject-production (race and male). That binary opposition is undone in Victor Frankenstein's laboratory—an artificial womb where both projects are undertaken simultaneously, though the terms are never openly spelled out. Frankenstein's apparent antagonist is God himself as Maker of Man, but his real competitor is also woman as the maker of children. It is not just that his dream of the death of mother and bride and the actual death of his bride are associated with the visit of his monstrous homoerotic "son" to his bed. On a much more overt level, the monster is a bodied "corpse," unnatural because bereft of a determinable childhood: "No father had watched my infant days, no mother had blessed me with smiles and caresses; or if they had, all my past was now a blot, a blind vacancy in which I distinguished nothing" (*F,* pp. 57, 115). It is Frankenstein's own ambiguous and miscued understanding of the real motive for the monster's vengefulness that reveals his own competition with woman as maker:

> I created a rational creature and was bound towards him to assure, as far as was in my power, his happiness and well-being. This was my duty, but there was another still paramount to that. My duties towards the beings of my own species had greater claims to my attention because they included a greater proportion of happiness or misery. Urged by this view, I refused, and I did right in refusing, to create a companion for the first creature. [*F,* p. 206]

It is impossible not to notice the accents of transgression inflecting Frankenstein's demolition of his experiment to create the future Eve. Even in the laboratory, the woman-in-the-making is not a bodied corpse but "a human being." The (il)logic of the metaphor bestows on her a prior existence which Frankenstein aborts, rather than an anterior death which he reembodies: "The remains of the half-finished creature, whom I had destroyed, lay scattered on the floor, and I almost felt as if I had mangled the living flesh of a human being" (*F,* p. 163).

In Shelley's view, man's hubris as soul maker both usurps the place of God and attempts—vainly—to sublate woman's physiological prerogative.[24] Indeed, indulging a Freudian fantasy here, I could urge that, if to give and withhold to/ from the mother a phallus is *the* male fetish, then to give and withhold to/from the man a womb might be the female fetish.[25] The icon of the sublimated womb in man is surely his productive brain, the box in the head.

In the judgment of classical psychoanalysis, the phallic mother exists only by virtue of the castration-anxious son; in *Frankenstein*'s judgment, the hysteric father (Victor Frankenstein gifted with his laboratory—the womb of theoretical reason) cannot produce a daughter. Here the language of racism—the dark side of imperialism understood as social mission—combines with the hysteria of masculism into the idiom of (the withdrawal of) sexual reproduction rather than subject-constitution. The roles of masculine and feminine individualists are hence reversed and displaced. Frankenstein cannot produce a "daughter" because "she might become ten thousand times more malignant than her mate . . . [and because] one of the first results of those sympathies for which the demon thirsted would be children, and a race of devils would be propagated upon the earth who might make the very existence of the species of man a condition precarious and full of terror" (*F*, p. 158). This particular narrative strand also launches a thoroughgoing critique of the eighteenth-century European discourses on the origin of society through (Western Christian) man. Should I mention that, much like Jean-Jacques Rousseau's remark in his *Confessions*, Frankenstein declares himself to be "by birth a Genevese" (*F*, p. 31)?

In this overtly didactic text, Shelley's point is that social engineering should not be based on pure, theoretical, or natural-scientific reason alone, which is her implicit critique of the utilitarian vision of an engineered society. To this end, she presents in the first part of her deliberately schematic story three characters, childhood friends, who seem to represent Kant's three-part conception of the human subject: Victor Frankenstein, the forces of theoretical reason or "natural philosophy"; Henry Clerval, the forces of practical reason or "the moral relations of things"; and Elizabeth Lavenza, that aesthetic judgment—"the aerial creation of the poets"—which, according to Kant, is "a suitable mediating link connecting the realm of the concept of nature and that of the concept of freedom . . . (which) promotes . . . *moral* feeling" (*F*, pp. 37, 36).[26]

This three-part subject does not operate harmoniously in *Frankenstein*. That Henry Clerval, associated as he is with practical reason, should have as his "design . . . to visit India, in the belief that he had in his knowledge of its various languages, and in the views he had taken of its society, the means of materially assisting the progress of European colonization and trade" is proof of this, as well as part of the incidental imperialist sentiment that I speak of above (*F*, pp. 151–52). I should perhaps point out that the language here is entrepreneurial rather than missionary:

> He came to the university with the design of making himself complete master of the Oriental languages, as thus he should open a field for the plan of life he had marked out for himself. Resolved to pursue no inglorious career, he turned his eyes towards the East as affording scope for his spirit of enterprise. The Persian, Arabic, and Sanskrit languages engaged his attention. [*F*, pp. 66–67]

But it is of course Victor Frankenstein, with his strange itinerary of obsession with natural philosophy, who offers the strongest demonstration that the multiple perspectives of the three-part Kantian subject cannot cooperate harmoniously. Frankenstein creates a putative human subject out of natural philosophy alone. According to his own miscued summation: "In a fit of enthusiastic madness I created a rational creature" (*F*, p. 206). It is not at all farfetched to say that Kant's categorical imperative can most easily be mistaken for the hypothetical imperative—a command to ground in cognitive comprehension what can be apprehended only by moral will—by putting natural philosophy in the place of practical reason.

I should hasten to add here that just as readings such as this one do not necessarily accuse Charlotte Brontë the named individual of harboring imperialist sentiments, so also they do not necessarily commend Mary Shelley the named individual for writing a successful Kantian allegory. The most I can say is that it is possible to read these texts, within the frame of imperialism and the Kantian ethical moment, in a politically useful way. Such an approach presupposes that a "disinterested" reading attempts to render transparent the interests of the hegemonic readership. (Other "political" readings—for instance, that the monster is the nascent working class—can also be advanced.)

Frankenstein is built in the established epistolary tradition of multiple frames. At the heart of the multiple frames, the narrative of the monster (as reported by Frankenstein to Robert Walton, who then recounts it in a letter to his sister) is of his almost learning, clandestinely, to be human. It is invariably noticed that the monster reads *Paradise Lost* as true history. What is not so often noticed is that he also reads Plutarch's *Lives*, "the histories of the first founders of the ancient republics," which he compares to "the patriarchal lives of my protectors" (*F*, pp. 123, 124). And his *education* comes through "Volney's *Ruins of Empires*," which purported to be a prefiguration of the French Revolution, published after the event and after the author had rounded off his theory with practice (*F*, p. 113). It is an attempt at an enlightened universal secular, rather than a Eurocentric Christian, history, written from the perspective of a narrator "from below," somewhat like the attempts of Eric Wolf or Peter Worsley in our own time.[27]

This Caliban's education in (universal secular) humanity takes place through the monster's eavesdropping on the instruction of an Ariel—Safie, the Christianized "Arabian" to whom "a residence in Turkey was abhorrent" (*F*, p. 121). In depicting Safie, Shelley uses some commonplaces of eighteenth-century liberalism that are shared by many today: Safie's Muslim father was a victim of (bad) Christian religious prejudice and yet was himself a wily and ungrateful man not as morally refined as her (good) Christian mother. Having tasted the emancipation of woman, Safie could not go home. The confusion between "Turk" and "Arab" has its counterpart in present-day confusion about Turkey and Iran as "Middle Eastern" but not "Arab."

Although we are a far cry here from the unexamined and covert axiomatics of imperialism in *Jane Eyre*, we will gain nothing by celebrating the time-bound pieties that Shelley, as the daughter of two antievangelicals, produces. It is more interesting for us that Shelley differentiates the Other, works at the Caliban/Ariel distinction, and *cannot* make the monster identical with the proper recipient of these lessons. Although he had "heard of the discovery of the American hemisphere and *wept with Safie* over the helpless fate of its original inhabitants," Safie cannot reciprocate his attachment. When she first catches sight of him, "Safie, unable to attend to her friend [Agatha], rushed out of the cottage" (*F*, pp. 114, [my emphasis], 129).

In the taxonomy of characters, the Muslim-Christian Safie belongs with Rhys' Antoinette/Bertha. And indeed, like Christophine the good servant, the subject created by the fiat of natural philosophy is the tangential unresolved moment in *Frankenstein*. The simple suggestion that the monster is human inside but monstrous outside and only provoked into vengefulness is clearly not enough to bear the burden of so great a historical dilemma.

At one moment, in fact, Shelley's Frankenstein does try to tame the monster, to humanize him by bringing him within the circuit of the Law. He "repair[s] to a criminal judge in the town and . . . relate[s his] history briefly but with firmness"—the first and disinterested version of the narrative of Frankenstein—"marking the dates with accuracy and never deviating into invective or exclamation. . . . When I had concluded my narration I said, 'This is the being whom I accuse and for whose seizure and punishment I call upon you to exert your whole power. It is your duty as a magistrate" (*F,* pp. 189, 190). The sheer social reasonableness of the mundane voice of Shelley's "Genevan magistrate" reminds us that the absolutely Other cannot be selfed, that the monster has "properties" which will not be contained by "proper" measures:

> "I will exert myself [he says], and if it is in my power to seize the monster, be assured that he shall suffer punishment proportionate to his crimes. But I fear, from what you have yourself described to be his properties, that this will prove impracticable; and thus, while every proper measure is pursued, you should make up your mind to disappointment." [*F,* p. 190]

In the end, as is obvious to most readers, distinctions of human individuality themselves seem to fall away from the novel. Monster, Frankenstein, and Walton seem to become each others' relays. Frankenstein's story comes to an end in death; Walton concludes his own story within the frame of his function as letter writer. In the *narrative* conclusion, he is the natural philosopher who learns from Frankenstein's example. At the end of the *text,* the monster, having confessed his guilt toward his maker and ostensibly intending to immolate himself, is borne away on an ice raft. We do not see the conflagration of his funeral pile—the self-immolation is not consummated in the text: he too cannot be contained by the text. In terms of narrative logic, he is "lost in darkness and distance" (*F,* p. 211)—these are the last words of the novel—into an existential temporality that is coherent with neither the territorializing individual imagination (as in the opening of *Jane Eyre*) nor the authoritative scenario of Christian psychobiography (as at the end of Brontë's work). The very relationship between sexual reproduction and social subject-production—the dynamic nineteenth-century topos of feminism-in-imperialism—remains problematic within the limits of Shelley's text and, paradoxically, constitutes its strength.

Earlier, I offered a reading of woman as womb holder in *Frankenstein.* I would now suggest that there is a framing woman in the book who is neither tangential, nor encircled, nor yet encircling. "Mrs. Saville," "excellent Margaret," "beloved Sister" are her address and kinship inscriptions (*F,* pp. 15, 16, 22). She is the occasion, though not the protagonist, of the novel. She is the feminine *subject* rather than the female individualist: she is the irreducible *recipient*-function of the letters that constitute *Frankenstein.* I have commented on the singular appropriative hermeneutics of the reader reading with Jane in the opening pages of *Jane Eyre.* Here the reader must read with Margaret Saville in the crucial sense that she must *intercept* the recipient-function, read the letters *as* recipient, in order for the novel to exist.[28] Margaret Saville does not respond to close the text as frame. The frame is thus simultaneously not a frame, and the monster can step "beyond the text" and be "lost in darkness." Within the allegory of our reading, the place of both the English lady and the unnamable monster are left open by this great flawed text. It is satisfying for a postcolonial reader to consider this a noble resolution for a nineteenth-century English novel. This is all the more striking because, on the anecdotal level, Shelley herself abundantly "identifies" with Victor Frankenstein.[29]

I must myself close with an idea that I cannot establish within the limits of this essay. Earlier I contended that *Wide Sargasso Sea* is necessarily bound by the reach of the European novel. I suggested that, in contradistinction, to reopen the epistemic fracture of imperialism without succumbing to a nostalgia for lost origins, the critic must turn to the archives of imperialist governance. I have not turned to those archives in these pages. In my current work, by way of a modest and inexpert "reading" of "archives," I try to extend, outside the reach of the European novelistic tradition, the most powerful suggestion in *Wide Sargasso Sea:* that *Jane Eyre* can be read as the orchestration and staging of the self-immolation of Bertha Mason as "good wife." The power of that suggestion remains unclear if we remain insufficiently knowledgeable about the history of the legal manipulation of widow-sacrifice in the entitlement of the British government in India. I would hope that an informed critique of imperialism, granted some attention from readers in the First World, will at least expand the frontiers of the politics of reading.

NOTES

1. My notion of the "worlding of a world" upon what must be assumed to be uninscribed earth is a vulgarization of Martin Heidegger's idea; see "The Origin of the Work of Art," *Poetry, Language, Thought,* trans. Albert Hofstadter (New York, 1977), pp. 17–87.

2. See Charlotte Brontë, *Jane Eyre* (New York, 1960); all further references to this work, abbreviated *JE,* will be included in the text.

3. See Jean Rhys, *Wide Sargasso Sea* (Harmondsworth, 1966); all further references to this work, abbreviated *WSS,* will be included in the text. And see Mary Shelley, *Frankenstein; or, the Modern Prometheus* (New York, 1965); all further references to this work, abbreviated *F,* will be included in the text.

4. I have tried to do this in my essay "Unmaking and Making in *To the Lighthouse,*" in *Women and Language in Literature and Society,* ed. Sally McConnell-Ginet, Ruth Borker, and Nelly Furman (New York, 1980), pp. 310–27.

5. As always, I take my formula from Louis Althusser, "Ideology an Ideological State Apparatuses (Notes towards an Investigation)," *"Lenin and Philosophy and Other Essays,* trans. Ben Brewster (New York, 1971), pp. 127–86. For an acute differentiation between the individual and individualism, see V. N. Vološinov, *Marxism and the Philosophy of Language,* trans. Ladislav Matejka, and I. R. Titunik, Studies in Language, vol. 1 (New York, 1973), pp. 93–94 and 152–53. For a "straight" analysis of the roots and ramifications of English "individualism," see C. B. MacPherson, *The Political Theory of Possessive Individualism: Hobbes to Locke* (Oxford, 1962). I am grateful to Jonathan Rée for bringing this book to my attention and for giving a careful reading of all but the very end of the present essay.

6. I am constructing an analogy with Homi Bhabha's powerful notion of "not-quite/not white" in his "Of Mimicry and Man: The Ambiguity of Colonial Discourse," *October* 28 (Spring 1984): 132. I should also add that I use the word "native" here in reaction to the term "Third-World Woman." It cannot, of course, apply with equal historical justice

to both the West Indian and the Indian contexts nor to contexts of imperialism by transportation.

7. See Roberto Fernández Retamar, "Caliban: Notes towards a Discussion of Culture in Our America," trans. Lynn Garafola, David Arthur McMurray, and Robert Márquez, *Massachusetts Review* 15 (Winter–Spring 1974): 7–72; all further references to this work, abbreviated "C," will be included in the text.

8. See José Enrique Rodó, *Ariel*, ed. Gordon Brotherston (Cambridge, 1967).

9. For an elaboration of "an inaccessible blankness circumscribed by an interpretable text," see my "Can the Subaltern Speak?" *Interpretation of Culture*, eds. Cary Nelson and Lawrence Grossberg (Urbana, Ill., 1988).

10. See Elizabeth Fox-Genovese, "Placing Women's History in History," *New Left Review* 133 (May–June 1982): 5–29.

11. Rudolph Ackerman, *The Repository of Arts, Literature, Commerce, Manufactures, Fashions, and Politics* (London, 1823), p. 310.

12. See Terry Eagleton, *Myths of Power: A Marxist Study of the Brontës* (London, 1975); this is one of the general presuppositions of his book.

13. See Sandra M. Gilbert and Susan Gubar, *The Madwoman in the Attic: The Woman Writer and the Nineteenth-Century Literary Imagination* (New Haven, Conn., 1979), pp. 360–62.

14. Immanuel Kant, *Critique of Practical Reason, The "Critique of Pure Reason," the "Critique of Practical Reason" and Other Ethical Treatises, the "Critique of Judgement,"* trans. J. M. D. Meiklejohn et al. (Chicago, 1952), pp. 328, 326.

15. I have tried to justify the reduction of sociohistorical problems to formulas or propositions in my essay "Can the Subaltern Speak?" The "travesty" I speak of does not befall the Kantian ethic in its purity as an accident but rather exists within its lineaments as a possible supplement. On the register of the human being as child rather than heathen, my formula can be found, for example, in "What Is Enlightenment?" in Kant, *"Foundations of the Metaphysics of Morals," "What Is Enlightenment?" and a Passage from "The Metaphysics of Morals,"* trans. and ed. Lewis White Beck (Chicago, 1950). I have profited from discussing Kant with Johnathan Rée.

16. Jean Rhys, in an interview with Elizabeth Vreeland, quoted in Nancy Harrison, *An Introduction to the Writing Practice of Jean Rhys: The Novel as Women's Text* (Rutherford, N.J., forthcoming). This is an excellent, detailed study of Rhys.

17. See Louise Vinge, *The Narcissus Theme in Western European Literature Up to the Early Nineteenth Century*, trans. Robert Dewsnap et al. (Lund, 1967), chap. 5.

18. For a detailed study of this text, see John Brenkman, "Narcissus in the Text," *Georgia Review* 30 (Summer 1976): 293–327.

19. See, e.g., Thomas F. Staley, *Jean Rhys: A Critical Study* (Austin, Tex. 1979), pp. 108–16; it is interesting to note Staley's masculist discomfort with this and his consequent dissatisfaction with Rhys' novel.

20. I have tried to relate castration and suppressed letters in my "The Letter As Cutting Edge," in *Literature and Psychoanalysis; The Question of Reading: Otherwise*, ed. Shoshana Felman (New Haven, Conn., 1981), pp. 208–26.

21. This is the main argument of my "Can the Subaltern Speak?"

22. See Barbara Johnson, "My Monster/My Self," *Diacritics* 12 (Summer 1982): 2–10.

23. See George Levine, *The Realistic Imagination: English Fiction from Frankenstein to Lady Chatterley* (Chicago, 1981), pp. 23–35.

24. Consult the publications of the Feminist International Network for the best overview of the current debate on reproductive technology.

25. For the male fetish, see Sigmund Freud, "Fetishism," *The Standard Edition of the Complete Psychological Works of Sigmund Freud*, ed. and trans. James Strachey et al., 24 vols.

(London, 1953–74), 21:152–57. For a more "serious" Freudian study of *Frankenstein*, see Mary Jacobus, "Is There a Woman in This Text?" *New Literary History* 14 (Autumn 1982): 117–41. My "fantasy" would of course be disproved by the "fact" that it is more difficult for a woman to assume the position of fetishist than for a man; see Mary Ann Doane, "Film and the Masquerade: Theorising the Female Spectator," *Screen* 23 (Sept./Oct. 1982):74–87.

26. Kant, *Critique of Judgement*, trans. J. H. Bernard (New York, 1951), p. 39.

27. See [Constantin François Chasseboeuf de Volney], *The Ruins; or, Meditations on the Revolutions of Empires*, trans. pub. (London, 1811). Johannes Fabian has shown us the manipulation of time in "new" secular histories of a similar kind; see *Time and the Other: How Anthropology Makes Its Object* (New York, 1983). See also Eric R. Wolf, *Europe and the People without History* (Berkeley and Los Angeles, 1982), and Peter Worsley, *The Third World*, 2d ed. (Chicago, 1973); I am grateful to Dennis Dworkin for bringing the latter book to my attention. The most striking ignoring of the monster's education through Volney is in Gilbert's otherwise brilliant "Horrror's Twin: Mary Shelley's Monstrous Eve," *Feminist Studies* 4 (June 1980): 48–73. Gilbert's essay reflects the absence of race-determinations in a certain sort of feminism. Her present work has most convincingly filled in this gap; see, e.g., her recent piece on H. Rider Haggard's *She* ("Rider Haggard's Heart of Darkness," *Partisan Review* 50, no. 3 [1983]: 444–53.

28. "A letter is always and *a priori* intercepted, . . . the 'subjects' are neither the senders nor the receivers of messages. . . . The letter is constituted . . . by its interception" (Jacques Derrida, "Discussion," after Claude Rabant, "Il n'a aucune chance de l'entendre," in *Affranchissement: Du transfert et de la lettre*, ed. René Major [Paris, 1981], p. 106; my translation). Margaret Saville is not made to appropriate the reader's "subject" into the signature of her own "individuality."

29. The most striking "internal evidence" is the admission in the "Author's Introduction" that, after dreaming of the yet-unnamed Victor Frankenstein figure and being terrified (through, yet not quite through, him) by the monster in a scene she later reproduced in Frankenstein's story, Shelley began her tale "on the morrow . . . with the words 'It was on a dreary night of November'" (*F*, p. xi). Those are the opening words of chapter 5 of the finished book, where Frankenstein begins to recount the actual making of his monster (see *F*, p. 56).

HISTORIES, COMMUNITIES, AND SOMETIMES UTOPIA

History gives topic and substance to black women's writing.[1] No one can read a novel by Toni Morrison or Alice Walker or Paule Marshall without confronting history, feeling its influence and experiencing the changes wrought by history. "They come from Mobile. Aiken. From Newport News. From Marietta. From Meridian."[2] Morrison's litany of place of necessity summons up the past. Culture, too, is synonymous with history. This is a body of writing devoted to the retrieval of Afro-American culture—the language, songs, poems, dance, stories, cuisine, and all the practices that shaped the daily lives of black people, so as to make these newly relevant for Afro-Americans of the eighties. Perhaps Marshall best underscores the function of history in black women's writing when the mother in her novel, *Brown Girl, Brownstones*, angrily asks her daughter, "But who put you so?"[3] All the novels by black women ask the same question. The answer to why Selina is the way she is, or why Sula is Sula, or why Meridian is Meridian involves reconstructing the development of the character's individual personality in relation to the historical forces that have shaped the migrations of her race, the struggles of her community, and the relationships that have developed within her family.

These are the most obvious ways that history enters black women's writing. But I would say the relationship of their work to history is even more essential and significant. The single most important aspect of the history of North America, indeed, one that defines the entire modern history of the Americas and has only reached its most advanced stage in the United States, is the transition from an agrarian to an urban society. It has been estimated that at the turn of the century a third of the labor force in the United States was involved in agrarian production. Today that figure has dwindled to less than 5 percent.[4] Such a change has tremendous implications when measured in economic terms. The effects are all the more profound when we consider the influence on human social relations and the formation of people's sensibilities and desires. This is the historical context and wellspring of American black women writers. I know of no other body of writing that so intimately partakes of the transformation from rural to urban society or so cogently articulates the change in its content as well as its form. Why this is so can be explained once we clarify the historical terms of the transformation as it relates to North America. Most economic theory on the subject has been shaped by the industry of Europe where the movement of land-based workers to the cities had been represented as a transformation in class from peasantry to industrial proletariat. The broad history of Europe is defined by the development of capitalism out of the previous feudal system. The problem with simply sliding the Americas into the European formula is that the post-Columbian world evolved under capitalism.[5] Notwithstanding the manorial architecture and design of the hacienda, notwithstanding the aristocratic demeanor and style of the Southern planter, neither represented feudalism per se nor gave rise to a peasant population analogous to the European model. Agricultural production in the New World was never based on a contract of production for protection, but rather on the dictates of a world market and the need to amass tremendous profits in the metropolis.

The defining instance of agrarian production in America is the plantation—not the freeholding, the slave—not the yeoman farmer. The fact that most Americans believe the reverse, seeing slavery as a purely Southern aberration, not representative of the real America, Midwest America, has a lot to do with the way history is traditionally told from the dominant point of view. In this case, the interests of capitalism are better served if one overlooks the great inequalities of the system, whose primary form of labor control in the New World was slavery, and imagines all workers as free individuals who "sell" their labor power on the open market. As capitalist ideology would have it, the yeoman farmer is the rural equivalent of the industrial proletariat.

The fact is that before the Civil War roughly half of the agrarian labor force was enslaved, and after Emancipation up to the early 1900s much of the agrarian population (both black and white) continued to be bound by the system of debt peonage known as sharecropping. For these reasons, the notion of a rural peasantry does not fit the American reality; so too, for reasons arising out of the marginality of the American rural underclass, it is erroneous to equate migration to the city with a process of proletarianization. Although many forsook the rigors of sharecropping for the hope of a better life up North, not all attained Henry Ford's promise of full employment and five dollars a day. Far more black immigrants than white have discovered that the city is another name for a sporadically employed labor pool. For this reason, urbanization, rather than proletarianization, would be a better way to characterize the history of the transformation from a land-based to an industrial-based economy in North America.

Thus, American history might be better understood from a point of view that has traditionally been seen as a minority position and an economics traditionally defined as marginal or aberrant. But this does not necessarily explain why black women might have a better grasp of history nor why their fiction might better articulate historical change. The black woman's relation to history is first of all a relationship to mother and grandmother. In interviews, Paule Marshall has stressed the influence of her mother's kitchen community on her writing. As a young child growing up in New York, she, like Selena in her novel, would hear her mother and neighbors talk of their Barbadian past while preparing island food. In their accents and conversation they created a cultural context that would later be the source of Marshall's access to the past. Similarly, Alice Walker's book of essays, *In Search of Our Mothers' Gardens*, is devoted to revealing the influence of mothers—both in the flesh and in spirit—on the formation of a black woman's creativity. Recognizing her mother's flower garden as her "art," Walker ponders the subtle (and subversive) ways black women have worked to inspire their daughters and wonders what sort of traces Phyllis Wheatley's mother could have left on her daughter's writing.[6] For black women, history is a bridge defined along motherlines. It begins with a woman's particular genealogy and fans out to include all the female culture heroes, like the folk curers and shamans known as root workers and Obeah women, as well as political activists like Sojourner Truth and Ida B. Wells who have shaped the process and marked the periods of black history. If the present is defined by the city and the North, the past is the South or the more distant Caribbean. Journeying on motherlines gives access to the geography of migration.

While interest in their mothers' and grandmothers' generations gives black women writers access to the past, there are economic and historical reasons why black women are in a better position to grasp history as a concrete experience. The history of black women in this country is the history of a labor force. Almost every black woman living in the United States has as her past the accumulated work of all her female forebears. This is not a generalization. Only recently, with the advent of wage labor, have some black women, the wives of fully employed factory workers, enjoyed interludes of respite from labor. And only now, with the existence of a black bourgeoisie, might it be said that there are some black women in this country who have not worked outside the home for pay. As workers, black women shaped their present and intimately knew the circumstances of their moment in history. Because the mode of labor defines the epochs of history, black women have had firsthand knowledge of slavery, sharecropping, and domestic and wage labor.

But the relationship of black women to history is twofold. As mothers, the reproducers of the labor force, black women have had a keen awareness of history as change. In their hope for their children's future, black women have learned to be attentive to moments of historical transition and many have struggled for social change. In their role as producers, black women have known the present; then, in relation to the economics of reproduction, they have envisioned and strived for the future. As workers, they have sustained their families; as mothers, they have borne the oral histories from their grandmothers to their children. For all these reasons, today's black women writers understand history both as period and as process. Certainly this is the lesson of Alice Walker's great historical novel *The Third Life of Grange Copeland*,[7] whose definition of historical modes and movements defines a conceptualization of history sadly lacking in American schools.

There are many ways that history enters black women's fiction. The most obvious has to do with the way a character's journey enacts the migrations of the race over many generations. This is the case for Grange Copeland, whose journey from South to North embodies the labor migrations for many twentieth-century black Americans to the industrial cities. Journey as metaphor for migration also structures Toni Morrison's *Song of Solomon*, in which Milkman's quest into the South retraces in reverse fashion the migrations of black people from Africa, to the plantations, and then to the Northern cities. Similarly, Paule Marshall's Avey Johnson journeys to the Caribbean to create a bridge to her people's past. In all these novels, the individual's story and experience express the untold histories of black Americans. And in all these cases, geography serves as a means for conceptualizing history either as a specific mode, when it is crystallized in a place such as Morrison's description of Shalimar, or as process, when it is experienced as the duration of journey.

The relationship that obtains in black women's fiction between South and North, or between Caribbean island and Northern metropolis, or between Africa and the United States defines history as economic modes. The portrayal of the South is not backdrop, local color, or nostalgia, but precise delineation of the agrarian mode of production. Similarly, the Northern metropolis is depicted as the site of wage labor and the politics of class. Journey North is felt as the transition between two modes existing simultaneously within capitalism, but the one—the agrarian mode—is destined to pass out of existence.

Black women writers portray the difference between South and North as a difference in economics. Specifically I'll cite Toni Morrison, whose writing is the most metaphorical of today's black women authors and therefore less likely to be apprehended in an economic sense than by comparison to a writer whose references to economics are more explicit, such as Alice Walker. I will also refer to a brief incidental episode in one of Morrison's novels, one not highlighted in the text and certainly not the subject of any critical attention. In this way, I hope to demonstrate just how pervasive economic concerns are and how profound the author's understanding.

The incident occurs in *The Bluest Eye* and takes place in an upstairs apartment occupied by three prostitutes. Here, among the curling irons and bras, the child, Pecola, sits listening to the women's chatter. Out of the banter and gossip, an anecdote begins to emerge, which, for its combination of simplicity and sensuality, cannot help but delight the reader and certainly captures Pecola's attention. A product of the city, the child of a sometimes-employed, alcoholic father and a battered mother whose work as a domestic sustains the family, Pecola will never experience the mode of life she glimpses in Miss Marie's account of eating fried fish with her boyfriend. For Pecola, born in the city's lumpen, and Marie, the urbanized immigrant, the episode depicts a mode of life so different from their present situations as to be the food for utopian fantasy. It is significant that nothing in the anecdote suggests wage labor or even the need for money. This is remarkable since neither Marie nor Pecola are themselves wage earners, but depend for food, clothing, and housing on the fluctuating employment of the men in their lives.

> "Every Saturday we'd get a case of beer and fry up some fish. We'd fry it in meal and egg batter, you know, and when it was all brown and crisp—not hard, though—we'd break open that cold beer . . ." Marie's eyes went soft as the memory of just such a meal sometime, somewhere transfixed her. All her stories were subject to breaking down at descriptions of food. Pecola saw Marie's teeth settling down into the back of crisp sea bass; saw the fat fingers putting back into her mouth tiny flakes of white, hot meat that had escaped from her lips; she heard the "pop" of the beer-bottle cap; smelled the acridness of the first stream of vapor; felt the cold beeriness hit the tongue. (*TBE*, 46)

I want to argue that even though the incident takes place in Chicago, Marie's account of the fish fry is a metaphoric representation of the Southern economy. This is possible because of the economic connotations associated with fish. In the black cultural tradition, "goin' fishin'," fish tales, and fish fries commonly suggest "time off" and the procuring of food by alternative economic means. In fact, throughout American popular culture fishing is often represented as a contestation of private property. Anyone who has grown up on Saturday cartoons and "The Little Rascals" knows that a "NO FISHING" sign is an invitation to hook and line.

The succulent fish, the oil dripping down fingers and mouth, the crunch of fried batter and bone—Morrison's description exemplifies her use of sensual detail to give shape to the opposite of a wage-labor economy that she invariably situates in a residual image of the South. The anecdote offers an alternative to wage labor and industrial alienation; it matters little that the real South was equally oppressive of black people. In fact, the real South has been transcended in the making of a metaphoric memory. The function of the anecdote is to generate the notion of alternative possibilities, not to conjure up a purely nostalgic image of the past and the South. The question at the heart of Morrison's fish tale is: don't we all have a right to experience pleasurable gratification in our daily lives? Given the contradictions and inequalities of capitalism, this is an extremely radical notion.

The South in contemporary black women's fiction is never portrayed as even a partial wage-labor economy, even though many Southerners have worked for a wage, particularly during this century, and a percentage of these have been black. What black women are documenting in the writing is the essential characteristic of the system as a whole as it arose out of slavery. In his book *Blues People*,[8] LeRoi Jones (Amiri Baraka) comments that emancipation signaled the instantaneous need for an entire population of black people to seek a wage. The Southern economy, conditioned by the history of slavery, engendered a number of labor strategies, which, like sharecropping and the labor camps documented in Hurston's *Mules and Men*, bound black people to the land either as farmers or as the primary extractors of raw materials. The pattern of paternalistic domination was continued through a system of debt peonage. This greatly influences the way work is conceptualized. For the laborers in Hurston's portrayal of Florida's turpentine camps, work was clearly something you did because the straw boss (a twentieth-century equivalent of the overseer) told you to do it. An antithetical, although similarly nonwage-labor attitude toward work informs one of Hurston's novels, *Their Eyes Were Watching God*, in which work is depicted as a pleasurable communal experience. One book shows the reality of Southern agrarian labor and the other exemplifies its utopian antithesis, but neither version articulates a sense of work as it is perceived in a wage-labor economy, where the worker trades his or her labor power for the sake of the weekly paycheck. At the heart of wage labor is the notion—no matter how false—of accumulation. If the capitalist turns surplus value back into capital and investments, the laborer ekes out the purchase price of a TV, car, or house. This is the tragic lesson Paule Marshall brings home to the reader in *Brown Girl, Brownstones*, where the transformation from tenant farmer to urban worker is marked by the obsession to "buy house"[9] out of the painfully accumulated nickels and dimes saved from the week's pay. Going North is, then, a metaphor for the transformation from peonage to worker alienation.

I'd like to return to Morrison's fish fry and take up the question Pecola poses to break Miss Marie's spellbinding account of fish and beer:

> "But what about the money?" (*TBE*, 46)

Although Pecola's question is generated out of her recognition of dependency in an economy defined by the possession of money, Morrison is also directing our attention to a very interesting aspect of the Southern agrarian economy and the way it is remembered. As a nonwage-labor economy, the South is very often depicted as a nonmoney economy. This is a typical feature of sharecropping—a whole year's work can be computed in the pages of a book and translated into plow lines and seed in the spring, clothes and supplies in the fall. The ledgers that comprise the secret narrative of Faulkner's story "The Bear" testify to the paucity of exchange involving money and the brisk transaction in human lives and emotions that evolved on the plantation and were handed down to the share-cropping system. Of course, there was real money in the South, tremendous fortunes made and lost, great profits made and squandered. But the money existed at the top, even more so than it has in the industrial North where wage labor allows a pittance to filter into the hands of its employees. In black women's writing about the South, money is never perceived as a fact of life as it is in the proletarian novel where weekly or monthly regularity makes it the worker's vitamin pill. Rather, it very seldom enters people's lives and when it does it comes by way of marginal endeavors like gambling and bootlegging. Hurston's portrayal of Tea Cake, who works in Florida's bean fields but fills his pockets as a gambler, is the Southern antecedent of Miss Marie's Chicago boyfriend. Historically, gambling and bootlegging have afforded black men the opportunity to deal in a money economy without being employed by the economy. In black women's novels these endeavors are transformed out of the grim reality of marginality and dependency and become instead metaphoric statements of alternative economics not incorporated within capitalism.

Perhaps the most fully evolved sense of an alternative economics occurs in *Song of Solomon*.[10] Here, the contrast Morrison develops between Macon Dead and his sister, Pilate, is rooted in real history and demonstrates the development of urban capitalism in relation to its marginal agrarian economy. History follows the trajectory of Macon's life and immigration from the land he remembers farming with his father to Detroit where he rakes in his tenants' rent payments. Macon exemplifies the inception of the black bourgeoisie, whose class status is based, not on big business, but on the professionals and land speculators who are the allies of business. If Macon's development represents the course of real history, his sister's life embodies its utopian tranformation. Although Macon and Pilate derive from the same African progenitor and are nurtured in the same rural economy, Macon, as the male heir, is destined for acceptance into capitalism's history, but Pilate, the woman, is marginal. But what's truly significant about Pilate is that she does not simply represent the rural South as the antithesis of her brother's development. Rather, she embodies the transformation of certain aspects present in the agrarian economy but not allowed to come to fruition in the real history of the South because of its larger economic domination by the industrial economy. Pilate is the realization of the communal and nonaccumulative aspects of the rural economy. Her household is devoted to the pleasurable incorporation of work into daily life. Money enters the household not to be hoarded up but to facilitate giftgiving, wine making, and the balanced flow between economic and human needs. The novel demonstrates just how thoroughly Pilate represents the transcendence of the rural economy when Milkman journeys south to a real agrarian community: Shalimar. Workers in Shalimar assemble before dawn waiting to be shipped to distant farms where they will make a day's substandard wage. The relationships between men and women in Shalimar are more apt to be defined by rivalry than sharing, and anything new or foreign will be viewed with suspicion. In a situation of economic dependency, the lack of accumulation and the economic necessity for communal living are the tangible features of oppression. Pilate lifts these features out of the real economics of the South and brings an alternative economic and social model into being. In her portrayal of Pilate, Morrison asks us to imagine a very different history of the United States, one that might have generated a community much larger than a household. The agrarian system capable of producing such a society could not have evolved under capitalism. If Pilate gives shape to the utopian imagination, she does so in relation to the industrial North and the agrarian South as these have *both* been shaped by capitalism.

I want to move now from considerations of content to form. Clearly, black women writers' sensitivity to history is all the more striking in their development of narrative modes. Just as history is what the novels are about so, too, is it embodied in how the novels tell their stories.

In considering narrative form and its relationship to historical modes, I first of all want to urge the reader to abandon any overly pat notion of history as a chronology. Although rural society might be thought of as being prior to industrial history, both forms have existed simultaneously as halves of capitalism's whole in the New World. Similarly, although a particular writer might be more closely associated with a particular narrative form, the writers are themselves living in two worlds and in touch with both urban and agrarian modes. Early in this century, Zora Neale Hurston already exemplified the dual influence of North and South on her work.

The best way to begin to define the formal characteristics of contemporary black women's writing is to conceive loosely of an overall development from agrarian to urban, but to realize that all the writers as well as the body of their writing embrace the whole of the twentieth century as a period of transition with great variety and inequalities existing side by side. Although a particular narrative mode might predominate in a writer, all the writers will give evidence of all the formal possibilities here defined. For example, I think all of us who have read a number of books by today's black women have noticed what I call the "four-page formula." That is, most of the novels seem to be compiled out of short pieces of writing. This is obviously the case for Morrison's *Sula* and *The Bluest Eye*, in which all the characters and situations seem to be given as pieces lifted out of some much larger narrative continuity. The situation is roughly the same for Walker's *The Color Purple* whose letter-writing format easily conforms with the brief form. Even *Meridian*, which gives an overall impression of narrative totality, is in its opening chapters comprised of short anecdotes. Essentially, the "four-page formula" embodies the storytelling tradition. It shapes Toni Cade Bambara's development of the short story as well as Morrison's version of the novel. The "four-page formula" establishes a teller–listener relationship between author and reader that doesn't necessarily pertain to other examples of contemporary American fiction. In this, black women's writing fundamentally departs from the mainstream of the bourgeois tradition, whose novels presuppose a sustained and leisurely reading; it equally diverges from the postmodern, Robbe-Grillet–type novel, whose narrative bits represent sundering and fragmentation rather than the narrative closure of the four-page anecdote. The "four-page formula," although no longer than most of the Southern folktales related in Hurston's *Mules and Men*, is not so long that it can't make up a bus-stop or telephone conversation. A novel based on the "four-page formula" partakes of the rhythm of daily life as it evolved in an oral agrarian culture.

The strongest influence on the development of black women's narratives derives from the storytelling tradition. As it emerges in Hurston's collection, storytelling in the American South is very different from the tradition that evolved under European feudalism. First of all, there is no storytelling master, no single poet-orator as we might imagine the teller of the *Cantar de Mio Cid*. Such a storyteller would have been chosen for special gifts of memory retention and rhythm. The storyteller and the tale would have to be pleasing to king and commoner alike and the storyteller would have occupied a position of privilege in society. In contrast, everyone in the Southern black community participates in storytelling and story listening. Although certain individuals might give a better rendition of a particular story or might be better endowed as narrators, no one is excluded from telling or denied an audience. Women tell tales equal to men and children as well as the elderly participate. Instead of an individual storyteller occupying a position of privilege, history and the cultural tradition are privileged, as these are the lifeblood and spirit of the community. Furthermore, there is no separation between teller and text. Rather, the speaking subject is at one with the narrative, as are the listeners.

Before demonstrating how the storytelling tradition is felt in contemporary narrative (aside from the "four-page formula"), I'd like to focus on another facet of oral society as it will enhance our understanding of the oral narrative as a formal mode. In *Dust Tracks on a Road*, Hurston draws the striking picture of a woman "specifying" against a fellow camp worker. Her foot up on her neighbor's porch, Big Sweet unleashes every barnyard epithet in her repertoire including the assertion that "his pa was a double-humpted camel and his ma was a grass-gut cow." [11] The practice of "specifying," or name-calling, exemplifies many of the formal features of storytelling as well as some modifications that are important for the development of the narrative. Although name-calling unites the speaking subject and the community, it does so at the expense of the individual being made the object of the abuse. The community is no longer defined as a corpus of teller-listeners, but as witnesses to the textual event. The position of the speaking subject has become marked and, to a degree, isolated. All the terms of the narrative equation have been modified; these modifications begin to suggest the sort of changes produced when the speaking subject becomes an author and the text a novel. Still, "specifying" preserves one aspect of storytelling intact: Just as there is a direct relationship between history and community, just as the meaning of stories includes the meaning of the group, so too does "specifying" insist on a direct relationship between the names and the person being named. The only thing that stands between the signified and the signifier is the name-caller who gives herself as guarantor of the relationship, with the whole community standing witness to the contract. "Specifying" represents a form of narrative integrity. Historically, it speaks for a noncommodified relationship to language, a time when the slippage between words and meaning would not have obtained or been tolerated. Such concerns are important in contemporary black women's writing, as I will show in the discussion of Toni Cade Bambara's "Gorilla, My Love," whose young protagonist rebels precisely against the sort of schism between signified and signifier that not only typifies the narratives and theories generated under late capitalism, but also serves the interests of domination.

Another striking example of how the oral tradition shapes contemporary narrative form occurs in Paule Marshall's *Brown Girl, Brownstones*. As a Barbadian immigrant, Marshall has in her background the tone and rhythm of dialect speech, which she reproduces at certain moments in the book, such as kitchen gatherings and weddings, to give voice and presence to the community. In addition, Marshall has developed a narrative modification of direct dialect in the vocal epithets that introduce many of the novel's chapters. Thus, the voice of the mother echoes through the house:

> "But look at he. Tha's one man don know his own mind. He's always looking for something big and praying hard not to find it." (*BGB*, 21)

Criticizing husband here, neighbor and roomers elsewhere, Silla's condemnations reproduce many aspects of "specifying." However, rather than the figure and voice of Big Sweet, Marshall's narrative adaptation embodies her speaker's voice alone. The community of witnesses, too, has undergone narrative erasure even though the epithets suggest a listening ear—a mute body of household listeners. The difference between "specifying" in Hurston's account and "specifying" as it occurs in Marshall's novel is the difference between a social form and a narrative form. The latter has its origin in the social and recalls for the reader the historical context of its formation, but, as a narrative form, it enjoys a degree of textual independence. These vocal epithets, like the lines from blues tunes and Harlem Renaissance poetry also incorporated into the novel, are recontextualized to give shape to a future tradition and culture whose content is built out of narrative bits.

Much of what I have said so far about storytellers and listeners as the defining mode of agrarian society might also be said with reference to song. Furthermore, it is in the black music tradition that we are best able to see the transition from an agrarian to an urban mode, and at the same time suggest some important parallels with the written narrative. The musical equivalent of storytelling is the plantation work song, which is based on a similar relationship between the singing subject and the body of participants that defines the storytelling community. Although there is very often a lead singer and a body of respondents, the song as text serves to unite the participants as a plural body. The notion of an individual artist is submerged in the music; what's heard is the song. Text and voice are one. All are singers; all are listeners.

As in Africa, where drumming evolved as a system of communication, the Afro-American work song also involves complicated rhythmic patterns. This, combined with the antiphonal singing technique, makes black folk music a multidimensional form. These are the formal features that are further developed in the transition to urban society where the folk form gives way to jazz. And I feel these same formal features suggest links between the muscial text and the development of narrative forms. LeRoi Jones has stated: "Blues playing is the closest imitation of the human voice of any music I've heard."[12] If there is already a close relationship between music and the speaking subject, why not write voices patterned on jazz music? This is precisely what Toni Cade Bambara may have done in composing the many-layered and many-voiced communal conversations that occur in the novel *The Salt Eaters*. Certainly, complicated rhythm and antiphony hold much potential for the modern novel. But more than specific points of contact between jazz music and writing, I feel the development of jazz allows us to grasp larger considerations bearing on narrative and the black novel. As LeRoi Jones defines it, jazz occurs when black music attains a purely instrumentalized form, using, he emphasizes, European instruments. As such, it is the embodiment of the urban. It is the technology of the metropolis welded to the basic formal structure of African and Afro-American music. Jones does not define an evolutionary line from work song to blues to jazz, but like our definition of narrative forms, he sees each representing particular moments in a history in transition, each capable of influencing the other but not becoming the other. Likewise, Hurston's folktales did not become the "four-page formula"; rather, the modern narrative has the same rhythm, desire for closure, and relationship between teller and listener (in this case, writer and reader) as previously existed in the work camps and on the plantation. The "four-page formula," like Marshall's vocal epithets, may suit the format of the modern novel and conform with the technology of book publication, but they embody nonmetropolitan forms as well.

The special relationship between the speaking, or singing, subject and the community of listener-participants has an important bearing on a claim I want to make regarding black women as authors and their novels as texts. Throughout the history of Afro-American music and narrative, one might point to something of a tension between the emergence of individual speakers and the body of listeners or respondents. Various forms and various moments in history have allowed a greater differentiation of the individual: the "specifying" subject, the blues artist, the jazz musician, the author. However, the definition of the subject as an individual occurs only when we see the producer of black culture through the filter of Western bourgeois tradition. From this point of view, we fail to recognize the significance of the text, which is not just a song, story, or novel, not just another commodity to be used up and forgotten, but the embodiment of a community's relationship to history.

There is, however, one very great difference between the narrative forms that pertain to a properly agrarian society and those that evolved in urban conditions. Although folk forms are based on the presence of the speaking subject, which lends the text immediacy and guarantees narrative integrity, the transition to the urban involves the erasure of the speaking subject. Paule Marshall's Silla is a strong and vengefully resourceful woman, but she becomes, in the narrative epithets, a disembodied voice echoing through the house. Finally, with Toni Morrison's novels, we no longer have even the hollowed-out narrative reminders of Hurston's Big Sweet, but the text itself, a plurality of stories, none of them articulated by speaking subjects, but each one seeming to have a concrete reality all its own. It has become fashionable today to define everything as a text: history is a text; daily life is a text. Texts seem to take on a life of their own. I want to make a few critical observations about Toni Morrison's novels as texts because, although it's true these best exemplify the transition to the urban form as manifested by the loss of the speaking subject, they achieve an important, perhaps more profound, understanding of history than might obtain if the personalized agrarian form were simply updated to suit city tastes.

Earlier, I characterized Morrison as the most metaphorical of the black women writers. The narrative form that best expresses the urban as it is produced in relation to a dependent agrarian economy is based on metaphor. In considering metaphor, an essential question arises: if the speaking subject stood as guarantor of the relationship between signified and signifier, what happens to meaning once this relationship is replaced by larger narrative metaphors? Name-calling suggests a direct reciprocity between the name and its object, and the metaphor does have its roots in naming. However, metaphors like Morrison's fish fry substitute extended, sometimes highly condensed, and always multidimensional images for their referents.

The fish fry describes an allegorical relationship to history and suggests the importance of a fuller understanding of allegory in American fiction, one not bound by the rigid relationship between image and hidden meaning usually ascribed, for example, to Hawthorne. George Lamming, a leading artist-intellectual from the Caribbean, once remarked that he felt all his novels were in some way allegorical, and I think he would agree that the great majority of modern Third World writing is allegorical.[13] Indeed, Fredric Jameson has written on the allegorical relationship to history in the work of Sembène Ousmane and Lu Xun.[14] Metaphor and allegory best express the tensions arising out of periods of historical transition that have characterized Third World history from the era of discovery and conquest, through colonization and now more complicated forms of domination.

What's at stake in the use of narrative metaphor is not the particular relationship of a specific signifier to its signified, but the whole of the metaphor to the history whose meaning it allegorically evokes. Once the particularity of signification is no longer in question, the articulation of contradiction emerges as the crux of the narrative. This is true of politically conservative writers as well as the most progressive precisely because meaning is not dependent on a particular speaking subject but arises out of the text itself. This is not to say that the text takes on a life of its own, but rather the text whose mode of articulating history is based on metaphor captures the complex meanings and contradictory relationships generated by capitalism. This is possible because metaphor, based on condensation, delights in defining similarity out of contraries; whereas metonymy, which links contiguous categories, suggests the flow of continuity and cannot produce the distancing necessary for critical scrutiny that is possible in metaphorical relationships.

I am expanding on Freud's definition of condensation as he developed it in the course of his interpretation of dreams and their structure.[15] As Freud saw it, "dream-thoughts" (the images we remember upon awakening) are few by comparison to the great body of meaning these represent. The translation of extensive material into concise images requires "condensation" and produces a metaphoric relation between the body of material and its representative images. Freud found that the analysis of dreams is often complicated by the fact that the remembered images take the place of material that is repressed (the things we really don't want to recognize or remember). As I will subsequently develop these ideas in relation to black women's writing (in particular the chapters on Hurston, Morrison, and Marshall), condensation is what enables metaphorical images to capture history, which for its duration and multiplicity would otherwise require numerous volumes. Metaphor is also what gives expression to aspects of history that the writers themselves may not wholly recognize. The combination of condensation and metaphor defines black women's novels as both modernist and historical. This interpretation may appear to be at odds with the generally accepted notion that literary realism best reflects history. In fact, realism may well reflect history, whereas modernism, by way of condensation, embodies it. This is what makes the writing of black women so thought-provoking and so fraught with contradiction.

In a long article on William Faulkner's "The Bear," I documented how this story by an avowed conservative ideologue articulates the contradictions of race and class in its definition of the characters, their traits, and their relationships.[16] I would like, here, briefly to cite a counterexample from the other end of the political spectrum, Cuba's Nicolas Guillén—whose writing will give another perspective on the Afro-American tradition. I have always been struck by one of Guillén's early poems written before the Revolution and all the more powerful for its great expression of yearning for change. The poem is called, "Casa de la Vecindad" and in it Guillén describes Cuba as "Neighborhood house, patio to the Caribbean."[17] The line is crucial for our understanding of metaphor as the trope best able to embody contradiction. It is as if the phrase were saying two things at once. "Neighborhood house" suggests the squalor of a poorhouse and the familiarity of the barrio—a place where people might languish and die, or conversely, a setting for the warmth of rum and the cadence of a "son" guitar. Similarly, "patio to the Caribbean" also conveys both positive and negative associations: the inferiority of a back porch or stepping-stone to the real, more important world; and the pleasurable seclusion of Latin American architecture and lifestyle. In fact, Guillén's words are saying two things at once and this is precisely how they express larger historical contradictions. Cuba is perceived both as it is: the oppressed preserve of imperialism—and as it might be if one can imagine a postindependence Cuba that did not then come directly under the influence of United States capitalism.

But what Cuba is also includes its future. The contradictions of prerevolutionary Cuba will be the means of its transformation. Thus, the poem ends with images of blood and another set of twofold meanings, bound up and resolved as one:

Here I am with my harsh-"son" guitar
trying to bring out a song.
A song of frenzied dreaming,
a simple song of death and life
with which to greet the future drenched in blood,
red as the sheets, as the thighs,
as the bed
of a woman who's just given birth.[18]

The blood of birth that holds the possibility for death as well as life is the poem's metaphor for its unspoken referent: revolution. Only revolution negates the antithesis between life and death that has haunted all the poem's images. What binds them up is the notion of a future, the "trumpet blast of The First Judgement."[19] Only revolution unites the struggle of all people: the poet whose anguished travail equates that of a woman in labor.

I'd like to return now to black women's fiction to show how Marshall uses metaphor as the trope of contradiction. I'll focus on an episode from *Brown Girl, Brownstones* that depicts Selina trapped in an excruciating interview with an aggressively patronizing white woman. Made to see herself for the first time through the eyes of racist white society, Selina understands the full meaning of alienation. The blackness she grew up in is suddenly, under the white woman's scrutiny, held up in front of her like an object. Horrified, Selina bolts for the door and runs without stopping until she drops from exhaustion:

> The woman's face, voice, touch, fragrance, pursued her as she careened through the maze of traffic and blurred white faces, past spiraling buildings ablaze with light. Car horns bayed behind her, the city's tumid voice mocked her flight. She ran until a stitch pierced her side and her legs cramped. Clutching her leg she limped—like an animal broken by a long hunt—into the deep entranceway of a vacant store and collapsed in the cold shadows there. And like an animal she was conscious only of pain. Long shafts of pain struck true and quivered in each muscle, her lungs wrenched from their sockets with each breath, her heart battered the wall of her chest as if, understanding the truth, it rejected her and wanted to escape. (*BGB*, 200)

In similar fashion to Guillén, it is as if Marshall suddenly started to tell two stories at once: the harrowing flight of the fugitive slave, pursued by the lights, voices, and baying dogs of the bloodthirsty overseers, and Selina's panic-striken flight from white bourgeois persecution. In fact, the metaphor allows Marshall to overlap two historical moments, demonstrating that the contradictions born with capitalism's agrarian mode continue to inform urban society. The metaphor also suggests that if Selina is to overcome alienation and recover her selfhood, she must confront history. Selina's recognition of slavery, her experience of the way it reduced black people to animals, and her union with her race's struggle for freedom are necessary for her self-definition. Only by seeing herself as racist white society sees her—as something sinful, ugly, dark, and fearsome like the night—can Selina transform the manacles of their prejudice into the positive attributes of self. Not to face the reality of blackness as it is perceived in a racist society is to live a lie.

Selina's confrontation with history brings our discussion full circle. The relationship of black women writers to history is enacted in the unfolding of their protagonists' lives. The novels discussed in this volume qualify as historical novels in the fullest sense of the term. Indeed, I know of no other body of writing that brings Lukács' definition of the historical novel to such profound realization. Focusing on the work of Walter Scott and Honoré de Balzac, Lukács demonstrated how these authors broke with the Romantic tradition in the definition of their novel's central characters and in their conceptualization of history as the movement of "popular" forces. Crucial to Lukács' definition of the historical novel is the notion that "world-historical figures" must be shown to arise out of the forces of history. "Scott lets his important figures grow out of the being of the age, he never explains the age from the position of its great representatives, as do the Romantic hero-worshippers."[20] The crux of Lukács' definition of the hero is "typicality"; and he was much impressed that Scott very often demonstrated typicality by "building his novels round a 'middling' merely correct and never heroic 'hero.'"[21]

As we read Lukács' basic tenets today, we are apt to remark how limited he was by his cultural and educational formation in relation to nineteenth-century European history and by his choice of nineteenth-century bourgeois fiction. Nevertheless, his deep understanding of history as class struggle makes possible his radical shift away from elitist concerns and toward a properly Marxian perspective where the "popular" or underclass is revealed as the source of historical definition. Lukács opens the way for us to take his definition of the historical novel and history itself a few steps further and a few steps closer to American history. Although Lukács was much impressed with James Fenimore Cooper, his interest in American writing was restricted to the nineteenth century. If he had ventured into the twentieth and included black women writers like Zora Neale Hurston, then he would have had to rethink his notion of the "typical." Instead of the "middling" character Lukács identifies in the novels of Walter Scott, black women's fiction develops protagonists whose "typicality" (the quality that best allows them to understand and represent a particular era) is their marginality. Lukács found Scott's heroes interesting because they made history visible, but, by their "middling" nature, they really did not participate in history. Rather, the great struggles and contradictions waged around them while they stood on "neutral ground."[22] In contrast, none of the characters in the historical novels written by black women has the luxury of "neutral ground." Rather than casting the "extreme, opposing social forces"[23] in relief, they embody these forces. The story of Sula—Meridian—Selina is the story of contradiction met and made visible in the thoughts and actions of these women who are history and its future.

NOTES

1. I feel that the only way to develop a theoretical approach to the work of contemporary black women writers is to define their writing in relation to a history larger than the personal and literary. Moreover, I suggest that the sense of history that shapes black women's writing is larger and more profound than one specifically determined by race and culture.

2. Toni Morrison, *The Bluest Eye* (New York: Pocket Books, 1972), 67. Hereafter cited as *TBE*.

3. Paule Marshall, *Brown Girl, Brownstones* (Old Westbury, N.Y.: The Feminist Press, 1981), 192. Hereafter cited as *BGB*.

4. See Historical Statistics of the United States Colonial Times to 1970 (Washington, D.C.: US Department of Commerce, Bureau of the Census, 1976), 139.

5. The notion that the conquest of the New World took place in a world economic system already defined by capitalism is one of the basic tenets of dependency economic theory. See Immanuel Wallerstein, *The Modern World System* (New York: Academic Press, 1974).

6. Alice Walker, *In Search of Our Mothers' Gardens* (New York: Harcourt Brace Jovanovich, 1983), 231–43.

7. Alice Walker, *The Third Life of Grange Copeland* (New York: Harcourt Brace Jovanovich, 1977). Hereafter cited as *TLGC*.

8. LeRoi Jones, *Blues People* (New York: William Morrow, 1965).

9. "Buy house" reverberates throughout *Brown Girl, Brownstones*, where it encapsulates the Barbadians' ardent desire for integration into the American system.

10. Toni Morrison, *Song of Solomon* (New York: New American Library, 1977). Hereafter cited as *SOS*.

11. Zora Neale Hurston, *Dust Tracks on the Road* (New York: Arno Press and *New York Times*, 1969), 195. Hereafter cited as *DT*.

12. LeRoi Jones, *Blues People*, 28.

13. George Lamming's remarks come out of a conversation I had with the author at Yale University in the spring of 1981. We were discussing the relationship of his most allegorical novel, *Natives of My Person*, to his other novels.

14. Fredric Jameson developed the significance of allegory at the Robert C. Elliot Memorial Lecture, University of California, San Diego, April 1985.

15. Sigmund Freud, "The Interpretation of Dreams," in *The Standard Edition of the Complete Works of Sigmund Freud*, trans. James Strachey (London: Hogarth Press, 1973), 277–304.

16. See Susan Willis, "Aesthetics of the Rural Slum: Contradictions and Dependency in 'The Bear'" in *Faulkner (New Perspectives)*, ed. Richard Brodhead (Englewood Cliffs, N.J.: Prentice-Hall, 1983), 174–94.

17. Nicolas Guillén, *Man-Making Words* (Amherst: Univ. of Massachusetts Press, 1972), 19.

18. Ibid, 21.

19. Ibid, 19.

20. Georg Lukács, *The Historical Novel* (Boston: Beacon Press, 1962), 39.

21. Ibid, 33.

22. Ibid, 36.

23. Ibid, 36.

class

Difference—the exploration of differences between men and women—has been one of the chief concerns of feminist criticism. Recently, though, feminist theorists have become interested in the differences between women, insisting that to categorize women as just "women" is to reinscribe a sexist ideology that sees all women as just the "same." Differences exist among women in countless aspects, including race, age, sexual preference, and social class. The essays in this section explore not only what the differences of social class might mean, but where they come from, and how they have been—and continue to be—part of the oppression of women. (Other forms of difference are addressed elsewhere in this book; see especially the section on "Ethnicity" for explorations of the differences associated with race; the essays by Catharine R. Stimpson, Bonnie Zimmerman, and Barbara Smith for differences of sexual preference; and the essay by Gayatri Chakravorti Spivak for differences of nationality.)

Many feminists have long felt that not all women share the same struggle, that working women have very different lives and different concerns from those of middle- and upper-class women. Yet when they turn to the most fully theorized analysis of class, Marxist critique, they find that it devotes almost all its attention to men and traditionally male institutions. As Heidi Hartmann asserts in her essay "The Unhappy Marriage of Marxism and Feminism" (quoted as an epigraph to Cora Kaplan's essay below), "The 'Marriage' of marxism and feminism has been like the marriage of husband and wife depicted in English common law: marxism and feminism are one, and that is marxism." Much of the criticism that unites a feminist analysis with attention to issues of social class was born of an uneasiness with feminist and Marxist critiques, a sense that the two had not yet really met on common ground. The essays below attempt to bring analyses of gender and class oppression together in a way that demeans neither.

These essays also try to work through the question of the place in literary studies of what has been traditionally the academic domain of the social sciences. How do gender and class issues become literary questions? Although each essay answers this problem differently, they all share one assumption: Literature has a definite function in society beyond simple aesthetic pleasure. Aesthetic pleasure itself, they argue, is clearly tied to the way literature acts as a social agent (for more on this viewpoint, see the section on "Canon"). Literature does not exist in a realm that is somehow independent of social and political questions, but is intricately involved in our understanding of culture and the shaping of society.

How we study class and gender in literature is the subject of Paul Lauter's "Working-Class Women's Literature: An Introduction to Study" (1979). Lauter argues that we need to first theorize what "working-class women's literature" is before we can study it. Do we define it by the class of the author? the subject? the reader? Do we consider both "folk" literature and "mass" literature? While suggesting that we conceive the term "working-class women" in its widest scope, Lauter argues that we may also need to redefine our sense of what "literature" is. Our emphasis in the past on innovation and individual creativity does not suit a literature born of traditional types and genres which may be communally produced. Literature produced by working people often has taken a very different form than that which has traditionally been studied in English departments. This suggests the excitement of studying working-class women's literature, but also the problematic challenge of it: where does one find such literature? Lauter offers several bibliographies of places to start the search. One of the happy consequences of essays like this one is that more and more of this literature is coming into print. Since this essay was written, two very fine collections of working-women's writings have come into print, *Writing Red: American Women Writers, 1930–40* (from the Feminist Press) and *Calling Home: Working-Class Women's Writings* (from Rutgers University Press).

Cora Kaplan's "Pandora's Box: Subjectivity, Class and Sexuality in Socialist Feminist Criticism" (first published in 1985, reprinted here from *Making a Difference*, and reprinted as well in her book *Sea Changes*) addresses the theoretical problems of a socialist feminist criticism. Too often, she argues, feminism ignores its roots in a liberal humanism that, at its inception in the Romantic period, was sexist and racist (she uses Mary Wollstonecraft's early writings as examples here). The acceptance of the concepts of the "individual self" and the "moral psyche" lead one away from political analysis of the collective. On the other hand, she argues, socialist feminism too often ignores the power of women's psychic lives, treating them as mere products of a social system, indistinguishable from those of men. Kaplan urges that feminist critique avoid such polarization and "come to grips with the relationship between female subjectivity and class identity." Recognizing the difficulty in even defining what we mean by "class" in literary analysis, Kaplan develops a working definition and turns to an analysis of nineteenth-century fiction (here *Jane Eyre*) and our readings of it (represented by Virginia Woolf's reading) to examine the ways that class and sexual identities became "welded together" in the nineteenth century and thereby became "sinister." We need a theory of both class and sexual desire to unpack this complex symbolization, she argues, and to understand the history behind both the literary representation and our own reactions to it.

The other essays in this section begin to show how diverse the possibilities are when considering class in feminist literary study: Leslie W. Rabine looks at "mass" literature and the class of working women who read it, Nancy Armstrong examines the role of one kind of literature—conduct books for women—in establishing the whole idea of a middle class, and Regenia Gagnier discusses how humor works in working-class women's autobiographies. Each author explores not only a different facet of class-relations, but a genre which is different from those which have been typically thought of as "literary" (the romance, conduct book, and autobiography), again upholding Lauter's call for expanding our sense of the literary.

In "Romance in the Age of Electronics: Harlequin Enterprises," Leslie W. Rabine asks how Harlequin romances appeal to the women who read them, usually women who work in clerical positions. Her answer is that these novels appeal to the needs of working women by "focusing on the juncture between their sexual, emotional needs on the one hand and their needs concerning work relations on the other." Noting that more and more Harlequin heroines have jobs, react to a negative work world, and fall in love with their bosses, Rabine suggests that this eroticization of a problematic work world signifies a desire for a "different social structure . . . [where there is] an end to the division between the domestic world of love and sentiment and the public world of work and business." She argues that we cannot isolate the reading of romance novels from the context in which they are read, from the women who read them, or from the production and marketing of the novels (Janice Radway elaborates a similar argument in "The Readers and Their Romances," in "Reading"). The novels represent for these women fantasies of escape from their positions of relative powerlessness in an automated business world, but the form and production of the romances themselves—standardized as they are—neutralize any threat the novels could offer to patriarchal ideology.

Nancy Armstrong also examines how written texts affect readers, but she turns her attention to conduct books written between the late-seventeenth and mid-nineteenth centuries (other chapters in *Desire and Domestic Fiction* examine novels written during this same period). In "The Rise of the Domestic Woman" (1987) she examines how these conduct books laid the groundwork for the sense of the middle class as a class. In setting out the idea of the "domestic woman," who is poised on a continuum between aristocrats and workers, conduct-book writers defined a class-based subjectivity for women that would become the model of subjectivity and individuality for both sexes. Armstrong argues that this new subjectivity fostered a social order through which people of widely varying occupations and incomes could nonetheless recognize a commonality of interest, taste, and class. The rules of conduct, because they seemed to be free of political or ideological bias, came to present readers with "ideology in its most powerful form," that is, an ideology which appears completely natural. In this new social system, the ideal woman becomes domestic woman, she who manages and regulates the household. Following the teachings of these guides, she becomes the means to translate the husband's money into a "home," the controller of domestic economy and, therefore, of domestic desire. Because conduct book writers urge a sense of class identity that is virtually free of material conditions, dependent solely on the ability to control and regulate desire, Armstrong asserts that domestic woman eventually takes on the power to regulate—and thereby to define—the self and subjectivity. Such power, she reveals, allows domestic woman to infinitely transform culture, and marks middle-class subjectivity as ultimately feminine.

Regenia Gagnier's "Between Women: A Cross-Class Analysis of Status and Anarchic Humor" (1988) uses an interdisciplinary approach to investigate the differences between men's and women's humor and between working-class and upper-class women's humor. She opens with a survey of work on humor (in poetics, philosophy, psychology, sociology, and anthropology) and notes that examples from women usually have been ignored by scholars trying to theorize about what people find funny. Classical theories of humor see laughter as an expression of triumph over an inferior, but Gagnier questions whether this model is appropriate for marginal and oppressed groups. For women and people of color, she argues, humor is most often a critique of the system which oppresses them. For both working- and upper-class women, laughter arises from challenges to or transgressions of rules binding women into their gendered roles. Humor arises from making the system (not another group) ludicrous. Women use humor, she argues, as a "prolonged anarchic assault upon the codes constricting them," and they seem to be "exploring difference rather than merely disparaging it." Gagnier examines nineteenth- and early-twentieth-century autobiographical writings by both working-class and upper-class women to find that though there are similarities between them—women of both classes find humor in upsetting the system—working-class women tend to see humor in scenarios of crossing classes while upper-class women evoke laughter by disrupting the rules of their own class. Like the other writers in this section, though, she explores the ways that differences of class reveal themselves in literary texts and how we read them.

—DPH

WORKING-CLASS WOMEN'S LITERATURE
an introduction to study

Writing—and indeed thinking—about working-class literature presents a number of unique problems. To begin with, what do we mean by "working-class literature"? Literature *about* working-class people, literature *by* them, or literature addressed *to* them? If we use the first definition, should we include works that are ignorant of or hostile to the working-class people they write about—like some turn-of-the-century "industrial" novels? If we focus on writing *by* working people, do we include pieces that do not deal with their lives or even with their real concerns, like some "popular" songs? Should we include, say, literature by people of working-class origins, like D. H. Lawrence? To complicate the issue still further, there is the question of audience or, perhaps more accurately, of the differing functions of works with differing audiences. Florence Reece's song "Which Side Are You On?" for example, urges miners to stick together in the union, whereas Edwin Markham's poem "The Man with the Hoe" calls on the "masters, lords and rulers in all lands" to right the wrongs of working people. Since both concern changing the condition of the working class, are both working-class literature? "Life in the Iron Mills," the first significant portrait in American literature of the lives of the industrial workers, clearly addresses a bourgeois audience, while many drugstore novels, like those of Mickey Spillane, attract a substantial working-class readership. Which would one want to retain in a "canon" of working-class fiction? Such questions cannot be answered categorically; we need a more adequate understanding of the techniques, functions, and distinctive qualities of working-class art.

Beyond these issues, there is the question of what defines the working class. Many such definitions exclude more people, especially women, than they include. The traditional image of the American industrial worker, for example, is male, in part because of ignorance about the role of women, historical and current, in United States industry. And the traditional image is also white, reflecting the racially segregated job structure that still persists in some industries.

It seems best to use relatively loose definitions and broad categories, but we must remain sharply aware of the difficulties involved, the manifestations within the culture of efforts to overcome (or to retain) class privilege, patriarchy, and white supremacy. Here I discuss literary works by *and* about working people, written and oral forms, "high," "popular," and "mass" culture. I designate as "working-class people" those who sell their labor for wages; who create in that labor and have taken from them "surplus value," to use Marx's phrase; who have relatively little control over the nature or products of their work; and who are not "professionals" or "managers." I refer to people who, to improve their lot, must either move in *solidarity* with their class or leave it (for example, to become managers).[1] I include those who work in homes, whose labor is sold although not for pay, as surely as is that of those who work in the mills or in the streets. I also include those who work on farms and those whose labor is extorted from them by slavery and peonage. Such categories, though admittedly blurred at the edges, give us at least a reasonable place from which to start.

In dealing with working-class culture, and especially with women's literature, we are confronted by a problem more fundamental than that of definition. It can be seen in a poem by Bertolt Brecht, "A Worker Reads History":

> Who built the seven gates of Thebes?
> The books are filled with names of kings.
> Was it kings who hauled the craggy blocks of stone?
> And Babylon, so many times destroyed,
> Who built the city up each time? In which of Lima's houses,
> That city glittering with gold, lived those who built it?
> In the evening when the Chinese wall was finished
> Where did the masons go? Imperial Rome
> Is full of arcs of triumph. Who reared them up? Over whom
> Did the Caesars triumph? Byzantium lives in some,
> Were all her dwellings palaces? And even in Atlantis of the legend
> The night the sea rushed in,
> The drowning men still bellowed for their slaves.
>
> Young Alexander conquered India.
> He alone?
> Caesar beat the Gauls.
> Was there not even a cook in his army?
> Philip of Spain wept as his fleet
> Was sunk and destroyed. Were there no other tears?
> Frederick the Great triumphed in the Seven Years war. Who
> Triumphed with him?
>
> Each page a victory,
> At whose expense the victory ball?
> Every ten years a great man,
> Who paid the piper?
>
> So many particulars.
> So many questions.

Brecht's poem vividly illustrates that the workers of the world have been hidden from history—omitted from the chronicles, myths, sagas, and fictions that embody it. Less openly, the poem illustrates how much *more* hidden are the women of the working classes, appearing here fleetingly as those who weep for the drowned sailors of Philip's fleet, and, perhaps, as the haulers of stone and the slaves of Atlantis. The chronicles, sagas, fictions, and poems were seldom written by people who labored for their bread. Laborers did not have the leisure or, generally, the literacy to write books (though they did leave us the works of their hands, in materials like stone and wool). And if they were female, still other veils shrouded their lives and limited their creations.

But working people were by no means silent. On the contrary, they have always produced literature. Its forms, however—including the forms of its transmission—its structural elements, and its purposes have been quite different from the dominant written forms of the last twenty-five hundred years or so. To approach working-class culture, therefore, we must lay aside many of our presuppositions about what literature *is* and is *not*.[2] We must begin by asking in what forms, on what themes, in what circumstances, and to what ends working people spoke and sang to one another. How did they gather, examine, transmit, and renew their experiences?

First, we need a broader definition of what we can call "literature." That working-class literature has often taken oral forms is not surprising, since many of its creators, along with their audience, did not read or write. (A theme of working-class art has been the struggle to gain access to the resources of culture and power, including literacy.) The study of working-class art must therefore include works that in the last fifty years have been generally displaced into courses called folklore and the like.[3] Today, when literature departments are more likely than they were a decade ago to include undergraduate folklore courses, as well as women's studies itself, we are better prepared for the interdisciplinary approach required for the study fo folk culture. Similarly, since songs—for reasons I explain below—are one of the forms most widely used by working-class artists, we have to pay attention to their literary elements; many are significant creations of language. In addition, as is true in women's studies generally, we must pay more attention to the "fragmentary" or "incremental" genres—letters, diaries, and documents derived from oral sources.

As we move toward more inclusive definitions of "literature," certain issues that are largely submerged in the study of "high culture" become more critical. For example, it becomes necessary to distinguish between "folk" or "people's" ("popular") culture and what Dwight MacDonald characterized as "mass culture." Popular culture is what people who share class, ethnicity, and/or race produce in communicating with one another, as distinguished from what is produced for consumption by the "masses." There is, obviously, no clear-cut dividing line, and the distinction is particularly difficult for those of us brought up in the bourgeois cultural system, in which the norm is production by artists for consumption by consumers.

The distinction is only in part one of quality, although mass culture, which is often directed by the political imperative of shaping and dominating the consciousness of the masses, generally involves basically simplified ways of appealing to the lowest common denominator—as was illustrated by the sudden flourishing, a few years ago, of TV shows portraying the cop as hero. It is more important here, however, to understand the functions of "popular" art and its patterns of creation. Much working-class culture originates and exists in situations that do not absolutely distinguish between the active "performer/artist" and the passive "audience"; or, if that distinction is made, the artist's "product" is offered not for its *exchange* value (money for the song) but for its *use* in the lives of the people to whom it is directed. A fine example is provided by the Kentucky mountain songs sung with great majesty at the funeral of "Jock" Yablonski and recorded in the film *Harlan County, U.S.A.*

This distinctive quality of popular culture becomes clearer when we consider more fully the processes of creation and the functions of working-class art. The creative process is nowhere better described and analyzed than in Lawrence Levine's *Black Culture and Black Consciousness*,[4] required reading for anyone concerned with this area. Levine has collected a number of vivid, firsthand descriptions of the creation of "sorrow songs," mainly in post–Civil War black churches, and he has examined the common features of these descriptions. One important observation is that new songs were most often based on old ones: a look at most labor songbooks shows that working-class artists were often concerned less with creating a work that would be unique than with building variations on tunes and themes well known in their communities. In many ways, working-class art, like other elements of working-class life, is highly traditional, even "conservative;" innovative form is certainly not a primary consideration. Similarly, working-class poetry and song—and to a lesser extent tales and the like—are often built around repeated elements—refrains, formulas, and commonly accepted assumptions about characters. Language, too, is often simpler, even commonplace, and less "heightened" that that of "high-culture" verse. These characteristics are, of course, common to oral art, made necessary by the exigencies of memory and improvisation.

But they also reflect a certain communal quality, which Levine finds exemplified in the creation of a song—different people chime in, a melody is picked up and carried forward by a new voice, or a chorus swells it spontaneously. In such situations, the individual creator is less important than the group, or rather, if the individual creator shapes a common stock to new group purposes, she or he does so without diminishing or expropriating that common stock. The song leader in church is not asked to provide new hymns (and would be looked at with suspicion for doing so) but is asked to point or enhance a hymn that is known, perhaps to add something especially appropriate to the situation.[5] Early jazz musicians may have been admired for a new melody, but probably more often for their ability to ring variations on melodies the listeners knew and followed. I emphasize the "folk" or communal elements of working-class art at the partial expense of work produced by self-conscious individual working-class artists because this approach helps to bring out distinctive qualities about working-class art that are not seen so easily when one focuses primarily on the production of individual artists. Yet a continuum obviously exists between works created primarily by individual imaginations and the songs, poems, and tales that are, so to speak, common property.[6]

Much working-class art is created and experienced in group situations—not in the privacy of a study, but in the church, the hall, the work site, the meeting hall, the quilting bee, or the picket line. It is thus rooted in the experiences of a particular group of people facing particular problems at a particular time. It is not conceived as timeless and transcendent, nor does it often function in such modes. Understanding this transitoriness is especially important in searching for working-class women's art. Many of the finest men's songs come from the prison chain gang or the work camp, and many women's songs have come from the communal experience of the church—but also from the loneliness of the solitary room often portrayed in the blues. More women's work songs have been located and recorded in recent years and doubtless as we come to understand more about female subcultures, we will discover more about songs and stories exchanged in the markets, mills, quilting rooms, and nurseries.[7]

Understanding the *instrumental* character of working-class art is also important to perceiving the aesthetic theory that informs it, a theory unfamiliar to most of us. Martha Vicinus has discussed the functions of working-class art in *The Industrial Muse* (the only full-length study in English of working-class [British] literature and, with Levine's book, required reading for anyone interested in this area). In a paper on the poetry of the Colorado miners, Dan Tannacito has addressed the same subject. Tannacito suggests that "the real value of the miners' poetry was the immediate use made of it by its local audience of miners and sympathizers" (p. 1). The writers' objectives in writing were inseparable from these goals toward which the lives of the workers directed them. Vicinus points out that working-class artists, themselves persuaded of the power of literature to "influence people's behavior," aimed to "persuade readers to adopt particular beliefs." Some artists recommended middle-class values and the culture of their "betters." Others, believing that social and political change was impossible, reassured readers of the worth of their own culture's values, providing at least entertainment and consolation in a fixed and largely oppressive world. More—certainly most of the poets discussed by Tannacito—aimed to produce change in the status quo. They wrote, Vicinus says, "to arouse and focus social tension in order to channel it toward specific political actions." By "clarifying" economic, social, and political relations between working people and those who held power, these artists helped to "shape individual and class consciousness" and to "imbue a sense of class solidarity that encouraged working people to fight for social and political equality" (Vicinus, pp. 1–3). Tannacito shows how miner poets accomplished such goals: poems of "praise," for example, "commemorate the heroic deeds of model individuals or important past struggles from which the community of workers takes its lessons." Other poems aimed to inspire workers to struggle in particular ways at specific moments. In general, the miner poets and "their allies produced poems for themselves about the realities they shared"—oppression by bosses, common work, the militia, scabs, and a heritage of struggle (Tannacito, pp. 2, 3).

The fundamental points here are that "artists" and "audiences" shared a reality, a similar set of experiences and outlooks on the world. They saw artistic production within the context of that shared experience, the world here and now. Art was not a means of lifting people outside the world in which they lived, or a means of producing "catharsis" and thus achieving "stasis" (if art ever does produce whatever these are). Rather, it was a means of making working people conscious of their world and actions within it, of extending their experiences of that world, indeed of enlarging the world they could experience. Thus, even as sophisticated and artful an example of working-class fiction as Tillie Olsen's "Tell Me a Riddle" is directed to the problem of inspiring a new generation with the values, hopes, and images that directed the actions of an earlier generation and that lie buried under forty years of daily struggle. Theories about the effects of art remain highly problematic, to be sure; I mention them here not to dispute them but to suggest that Aristotelian and other traditional notions will not be helpful in approaching working-class literature. Looking for the timeless and transcendent, for contemplation as an end, for metaphysical complexity of language, and for pastel ironies of tone can only obscure or demean the objectives and excellence of working-class art.

The next step, after developing a theory for an area of art, is to assemble examples and compile bibliographies. This work has begun to some extent for working-class literature in general, but rather little has been done with working-class women's literature. Appendix A lists the bibliographies I have come upon that will be helpful to anyone working in this area. But a word of warning is necessary: searching for examples of *women's* art in most of these bibliographies, like searching in collections, will be frustrating and slow. For example, the massive bibliography of German working-class songs assembled by a collective under the leadership of Inge Lammel lists perhaps a dozen songs by women in over two thousand entries. David Madden's *Proletarian Writers of the Thirties* (Carbondale: Southern Illinois Univ. Press, 1968), while it contains interesting background analyses, includes no woman writer as a subject—or, for that matter, as an author. The important collection *Folklore from the Working Folk of America* (ed. Tristram P. Coffin and Hennig Cohen [Garden City, N.Y.: Anchor-Doubleday, 1973]) focuses on men and presents women primarily as witches, running with wolves, and the like. Even collections from socialist nations provide little help; *Para un mundo amasado por los trabajadores*, selected by Roberto Retamar (La Habana: Editorial de Arte y Literatura, 1973) contains only works by and about men. The compilation of inclusive, annotated bibliographies is thus a priority, as is the writing of descriptive articles. A significant number of works deserve to be reprinted, but there are many, even by individual working-class women writers of the recent past, for which we must first locate copies.

Republication and fresh consideration of a small number of working-class American women fiction writers from the 1920s and 1930s (as well as from more recent times) are, in fact, under way. Harriette Arnow's *The Dollmaker* generally remains in print, and other works by Arnow are becoming available. Arno Press has republished two of Josephine Herbst's novels in the expensive series edited by Elizabeth Hardwick, the Feminist Press has published her novel *Rope of Gold*, and Elinor Langer has written a critical biography of her, *Josephine Herbst* (Boston: Little, Brown, and Co., 1984). Zora Neale Hurston, none of whose major works was available until quite recently, is the subject of a fine biography by Robert Hemenway (Urbana: Univ. of Illinois Press, 1977); and her best novel, *The Eyes Were Watching God*, has also been reprinted (Urbana: Univ. of Illinois Press, 1978), as has her folklore classic, *Mules and Men* (Bloomington: Indiana Univ. Press, 1978). A Zora Neale Hurston reader, *I Love Myself When I Am Laughing*, is available from the Feminist Press (Old Westbury, N.Y., 1979). Edith Summers Kelley's *Weeds* and *The Devil's Hand* were originally reprinted by the Southern Illinois University Press (Carbondale, Ill., 1972, 1974), and the former is being reprinted by the Feminist Press (1982). West End Press has reissued a number of works by Meridel LeSueur, who is still writing; the Feminist Press issued a LeSueur reader,

Ripening, in 1982. Agnes Smedley's *Daughter of Earth* (1927; rpt. Old Westbury, N.Y.: Feminist, 1973) has been in print now for a few years, as are a collection of her writings on Chinese women (Feminist, 1976) and her biography of Chu Teh (*The Great Road* [New York: Monthly Review, 1956]). Also, Jan and Steve Mac-Kinnon have published a biography of Smedley, *Agnes Smedley: The Life and Times of an American Radical* (Berkeley: University of California Press, 1988). Two volumes by Anzia Yezierska, *Bread Givers* (New York: Persea, 1975) and *The Open Cage: An Anzia Yezierska Collection,* ed. Alice Kessler Harns (New York: Persea, 1979), are now in print. And of course, there is Tillie Olsen, the source for much of what we have learned about working-class literature—especially that by women—and the author of classics like *Tell Me a Riddle* (New York: Dell, 1960) and *Yonnondio* (New York: Delacorte, 1974). She remains a fount of inspiration and information.

While a few books by other working-class women fiction writers of the 1920s and 1930s (e.g., Tess Slesinger and Myra Page) are in print here and there, little has been done on most. Such writers include Sarah Henry Atherton, Sanora Bobb, Catherine Brody, Olive Tilford Dargan (Fielding Burke), Lallah S. Davidson, Josephine Johnson, Margerie Latimer, Josephine Lawrence, Grace Lumpkin, Grace McDonald, Ruth McKenney, Page and Slesinger, Anna Louise Strong, Gladys Taber, Mary Heaton Vorse, Clara Weatherwax, Leane Zugsmith; these women were most prominent during the period in which left-wing literature flourished in the United States. Less is known about the women writers of a generation or two earlier who were concerned with the lives of working people, although they themselves seldom had working-class origins. In listing these I cite only a typical book or two for each: Estelle Baker (*The Rose Door,* 1912), Zoë Beckley (*A Chance to Live,* 1918), Helen Campbell (*Miss Melinda's Opportunity,* 1886), Florence Converse (*Children of Light,* 1912), Grace MacGowan Cooke (*The Grapple,* 1905), Amanda Douglas (*Hope Mills,* 1880), Mary Hallock Foote (*Coeur d'Alene,* 1894), Susan Glaspell (*The Visioning,* 1911; Glaspell continued to write fiction and drama well into the 1930s and was a significant figure in the *Masses* and *Liberator* as well as in the Provinceton Playhouse groups), Josephine Conger Kaneko (*A Little Sister of the Poor,* 1909), Myra Kelly (*Little Aliens,* 1910); *Little Citizens,* 1904), Alice Robbins (*Uncle Tom's Tenement,* 1886), Katherine M. Root (*The Stranger at the Hearth,* 1916), Vida Scudder (*A Listener in Babel,* 1903; more of a socialist discussion book than a novel, but fascinating nonetheless); Charlotte Teller (*The Cage,* 1907), and Marie Van Vorst (*Amanda of the Mill,* 1905). Among the interesting books that male authors have written about working-class women—apart from those by Dreiser, Crane, and Sinclair—are Arthur Bullard's *Comrade Yetta* (1913) and Reginald Wright Kauffman's *The House of Bondage* (1910). Not all these books are important works of fiction by any means, nor indeed are all sympathetic to working people, but they do cast light on the lives of workers in the early 1900s and on attitudes toward the working class. Given our inclusive definition of working-class literature, these books need to be reassessed.

Two earlier writers of considerable interest, Rebecca Harding Davis and Elizabeth Stuart Phelps Ward, have recently received attention in articles and dissertations. But only Davis's *Life in the Iron Mills* (1861; rpt. Feminist, 1972), which has an important afterward by Tillie Olsen, and Phelps Ward's *Story of Avis* (1879; rpt. New York: Arno, 1977), concerned with a woman artist not of the working class, are readily available. Phelp's fascinating industrial novel, *The Silent Partner*, remains largely unknown, though it is, as Rideout suggests (App. A), the first American work of fiction after *Life in the Iron Mills* to treat a factory woman's life sympathetically and realistically. *The Silent Partner* is of great historical interest because it antedates most theoreticians in suggesting the importance of cross-class organizing of women; indeed, it implies that working women are organized less by the labor movement as such than by other women. Davis and Phelps are not, to be sure, women of the working class, but they are, as women, distinctively sensitive to working-class lives.

A rich and largely unexplored source of short working-class fiction is provided by the many labor, radical, and immigrant magazines and newspapers, particularly those of the decades immediately before and after the turn of the century. Most such periodicals that were published in English in the United States are listed in Black and Goldwater (see App. A). But there is also much in non–English-language journals and newspapers. Norma Fain Pratt has examined the work of Yiddish women writers (e.g., Celia Drapkin, Anna Margolin, Kadya Molodovski, Ester Schumiatcher, Rachel Holtman, Malcha Lee, Sara Barkin, and Aida Glazer) in periodicals like *Zukunft, Freiheit,* and *Frei arbeter shtime* (Norma Fain Pratt, "Culture and Politics: Yiddish Women Writers, 1900–1940," Jewish Studies Association Convention, Boston, 1978). Similar work could be done for other immigrant groups and with working-class publications from centers like Chicago, Milwaukee, and Minneapolis. (Tannacito provides a useful model, although he deals almost entirely with men.) The working-class world has, after all, never been restricted to "our fathers," however much foremothers have been ignored and submerged.

As one might expect, socialist countries, along with Finland and Sweden, have made more efforts to collect working-class fiction, songs, and poetry than have other countries, although women are not especially well represented in the anthologies I have located. For British working-class fiction, I know of no study equivalent to Martha Vicinus's, which concentrates on ballads, broadsides, music-hall songs, and working-class poetry. But it is likely that in Britain, as in the United States, most such work is issued by feminist and radical journals and publishing houses and has simply not yet found its way into libraries here.

Autobiographies that reflect working-class life are a rich source of information. To be sure, many autobiographies, especially those by white women, were written after the authors had moved into other class circumstances. But taken as a whole, autobiographies constitute a significant body of working-class women's literature. I know of no comprehensive study of such works or even an adequate bibliography that includes both black and white women's autobiographies, much less those by women from other countries or those still in manuscript. Brigane, Fine, and Williams (App. A) provide useful basic bibliographies, which include such categories as slave narratives and immigrant autobiographies. Only a handful of prominent labor and radical organizers—"Mother" Mary Harris Jones, Emma Goldman, and Elizabeth Gurley Flynn—have published autobiographies, but many others probably exist in manuscript. There are at least three collections of interesting short autobiographies of British working-class people: *The Annals of Labor: Autobiographies of British Working-Class People, 1820–1920* (ed. John Burnett [Bloomington: Indiana Univ. Press, 1974],[8] *Life as We Have Known It, by Coopera-*

tive *Working Women* (ed. Margaret L. Davies, intro. Virginia Woolf, 1931; rpt. London: Virago, 1977); *Working Days: Being Personal Records of Sixteen Working Men and Women, Written by Themselves* (ed. Margaret A. Pollock [London: J. Cape, 1926]). A volume called *Women at Work* (Chicago: Quadrangle, 1972) includes both Dorothy Richardson's *The Long Day: The Story of a New York Working Girl* and Elinor Langer's *Inside the New York Telephone Company*. Probably, similar volumes, especially from the 1920s and 1930s, can be found in working-class libraries in English-speaking countries and elsewhere.

No comprehensive book about working-class women's songs and poems exists, nor is there any unified collection of them. I use the words "comprehensive" and "unified" to signify two basic requirement for work in this area. The first has to do with bringing together black and white working-class materials. Almost all writing produced by African-Americans is, by any definitoin, working-class literature: most of the authors have working-class origins, and their subjects and audiences are generally working-class people like themselves. Although some important collections of folk songs—notably those by socialist artists and collectors—do acknowledge that black literature is working-class literature, few secondary works in this area consider songs and poems of black and white working-class women together. The reason, in part, is that the two have different musical traditions: the black folksongs are largely "sorrow songs," or "spirituals," and the blues; the white songs are "country" and British-derived ballads. But separate treatment has obscured the commonalities of female experience as well as the interactions of the two traditions.

The second requirement is to integrate "folk," or "popular," songs with "high-culture" poetry. The two are almost invariably considered distinct. Most collections of women's poetry (with a few exceptions like Louise Bernikow, ed., *The World Split Open* [New York: Vintage, 1974]) ignore blues singers and songwriters like Aunt Molly Jackson. And while serious books on music carefully consider African-American influences on Western composers, starting with Dvořák, few books on formal poetry make even a gesture in that direction. For working-class women's art, such a separation is particularly harmful, whether one is talking of literature or the plastic and visual arts. Women of the past, generally excluded from formal schools and training, created works of art with what one might call "nonacademic" media like quilting, embroidery, and cutouts—works of art that were also useful in their daily lives.[9] Similarly, many women, especially those of working-class origins, were not familiar with academic traditions and academic forms in literature (e.g., the sonnet and blank verse) and used what was familiar or what came readily to hand—like songs that they learned from their grandmothers or in church, on the picket line, at quilting bees, or at other rituals of communal female experience. Such literature, which we generally designate as "song," must be read and studied together with the more academic or high-culture forms for which we usually reserve the term "poetry." And this union should be made *not* simply to show how, for example, Emily Dickinson transcends the banality of consolatory verse and tombstone poetry; rather, we need to become aware of the hierarchy of the categories themselves. Approaching works primarily in terms of their genre may provide the critic with useful, or at least convenient, lines of demarcation. But if we are interested less in literary typology and more in what literature reveals to us about the lives of women, and of working-class women in particular, then this approach is not useful. It implicitly places more value on the kinds of experiences with which "poetry" deals and the kinds of language (and the people who use it) in which it is expressed. Further, the categorization fragments what is continuous and distinctive in female experience, at least in Western societies, regardless of class—for example, labor that is undervalued or trivialized, the ever-threatening union of sexuality and childbearing, the power and limits of "sisterhood," the anger and waste in keeping one's "place." Further, working-class women's literature—by dealing with such concerns as work and especially work for wages, organizing with other women, and the fear of desertion and physical violence—completes the picture of women's lives that most bourgeois forms show only in fragments. Such female experiences, their commonalities and class-based distinctions, come into focus best when we base our work on women's historical reality rather than on the literary distinctions created primarily by male and bourgeois critics.

A "comprehensive" view of working-class women's poetry in the United States thus encompasses songs and more formal verse from both black and white traditions. We specifically need to reexamine the formal, often left-wing working-class poets. The names, though not generally the work, of a few such women, like Genevieve Taggard, are familiar to scholars, but others have been quite lost—for example, Lola Ridge, Hazel Hall, and Sarah N. Cleghorn. The major sources for studying their work are back files of such left-wing periodicals as *Masses, Liberator, Anvil, New Masses,* and *Mainstream* (see, e.g., Jayne Loader's bibliography). With the exception of *May Days,* edited by Taggard, anthologies of women's poetry have not included verse called "Comrade Jesus" (Cleghorn) or "Buttonholes" (Hall). Among the poets of "song" whose writing (or, in a few cases, interpreting) needs serious consideration are "Sis" Cunningham, Aretha Franklin, Sarah Ogan Gunning, Vera Hall, Billie Holliday, Mahalia Jackson, Aunt Molly Jackson, Ma Rainey, Florence Reece, Malvina Reynolds, Jean Ritchie, Bessie Smith, and Ella May Wiggins. For some black singers of the blues and gospel music, reasonably accurate bibliographies—or, more properly, discographies—exist, and often the text of at least one version of a song is in print. It is difficult to know whether even that much attention has been given to the work of women of the labor movement in the United States, although the collection *Hard Hitting Songs for Hard-Hit People* (App. C) does include works by writer-singers like Jackson and Gunning. I have not been able to locate any systematic treatment, like Alan Lomax's book on Vera Hall, of influential artists like the late Malvina Reynolds or "Sis" Cunningham.

I have included as Appendix C a list of sources for working-class women's poetry. This list is by no means definitive. In the first place, many songbooks are quite ephemeral, and the ones I list are those I happened on in the libraries to which I had access; different lists could probably be compiled from the holdings of libraries on the West Coast and in the South and from the personal collections of collector-activists like Mary Elizabeth Barnicle. Second, I have not included books contained in Vicinus' extensive bibliography, many of which I could not check (since they are available only in Britain) to see if they contain women's work. Finally, while extensive collections of working-class poetry and song have been published in Europe, particularly in the socialist countries (and some are included in App. C), these works are only erratically available in American libraries, and, in some cases, the gender of writers cannot be ascertained.

In certain respects, bibliography will be the most useful resource to scholars working in this field. I have therefore included a number of appendixes as a means for sharing with readers what my own research has turned up. I have already mentioned Appendix A (a bibliography of bibliographies) and Appendix C (collections of working-class women's poetry). Appendix B lists collections of both prose and poetry, including some that consist primarily of "documents." Appendix D shows secondary works on working-class women's poetry and song, including a number of biographies of black women artists, a few major analyses of the blues and other expressions of black women's art, as well as the rather rare writings concerned with white working-class songwriters. Appendix E is a very selective list of secondary works that concern or can help inform the study of working-class women's literature. Finally, Appendix F is an even more selective list of magazines that publish, with some regularity, work of interest in this area. Wherever possible, I have examined the books to see whether they include works by or about women.

NOTES

1. A most useful discussion of the distinctions between the working class and the bourgeoisie is that of Raymond Williams in *Culture and Society, 1780–1950* (New York: Harper, 1966), pp. 324–33.

2. See Martha Vicinus, *The Industrial Muse* (New York: Barnes, 1974): "What we call literature, and what we teach, is what the middle class—and not the working class—produced. Our definitions of literature and our canons of taste are class bound; we currently exclude street literature, songs, hymns, dialect and oral storytelling, but they were the most popular forms used by the working class" (p. 1).

3. Note that the study of folk literature was once clearly a part of the literature and language profession; indeed, it was a field considered "appropriate" for female scholars. Louise Pound, the first female president of the Modern Language Association, specialized in the study of songs and ballads, and Mary Elizabeth Barnicle, an early life member of the MLA, was an important folklore collector and political activist.

4. Lawrence W. Levine, *Black Culture and Black Consciousness: Afro-American Folk Thought from Slavery to Freedom* (Oxford: Oxford Univ. Press, 1977), pp. 25–30.

5. See "The Burning Struggle: The Civil Rights Movement," an interview with Bernice Johnson Reagon, *Radical America*, 12 (Nov.–Dec. 1978), 18–20.

6. Dan Tannacito, "Poetry of the Colorado Miners: 1903–1905," *The Radical Teacher*, 15 (1980): "But the historical reality is that workers, like the Colorado miners, wrote poetry in order to share and express their feelings about their experiences as a class. They were creators of their culture as well as creators of their society" (p. 1).

7. Zoltan Kodály, for example, wrote an entire opera, *The Spinning Room*, based on songs exchanged among or sung to women working at their looms and spindles. I have come on pictures of women singing at quilting bees, but I have seen no detailed exposition of what they were singing.

8. In a useful review of this book, Catherine Gallagher discusses stylistic elements used by these and other working-class writers and the problem of an excessive concern, on

the part of professionals, for the work lives of working-class people. See "Workers," *University Publishing*, 5 (Summer 1978), 1, 24.

9. See C. Kurt Dewhurst, Betty MacDowell, and Marsha MacDowell, *Artists in Aprons: Folk Art by American Women* (New York: Dutton, in association with the Museum of American Folk Art, 1979).

APPENDIX A

The following works either constitute or contain bibliographies useful to the study of working-class women's literature. Addresses are given for little-known publishers.

AMS Press, Inc., *Catalogue of the Labor Movement in Fiction and Non-fiction*, c. 1975. A useful publisher's catalog.

Anderson, Eleanor C. *A List of Novels and Stories about Workers*. New York: Woman's Press, 1938. Brief but helpful.

Arno Press. *Books by and about Women*, 1977. Publisher's catalog of several series of reprints. Arno also has a useful catalog of reprints dealing with American labor.

Batchelder, Eleanor, comp. *Plays by Women: A Bibliography*. New York: Womanbooks (201 W. 92nd St., NY 10025), 1977.

Black, Henry. *Radical Periodicals—Their Place in the Library*. Mena, Ark.: Commonwealth Coll., 1937. A brief essay justifying inclusion of such periodicals in library collections; the list of periodicals, with brief descriptions, includes some not listed in Goldwater's later bibliography.

Block, Adrienne Fried, and Carol Neuls-Bates. *A Bibliography of Women's Music*. Westport, Conn.: Greenwood, 1979.

Brignano, Russel C. *Black Americans in Autobiography: An Annotated Bibliography of Autobiographies and Autobiographical Books Written since the Civil War*. Durham, N.C.: Duke Univ. Press, 1974.

Chatham Book Seller (38 Maple St., Chatham, NJ 07928). *Radical Novels: Poetry and Drama in America*, No. 8; *The Political Novel in America*, No. 30; *Black Literature*, Nos. 34, 40; *Radical Novels, etc. in America*, No. 35; *Women's Rights and Liberation*, No. 43; and *Socialism, Communism, Anarchism, Pacifism in the U.S.*, No. 44. These catalogs not only list books for sale but record items not found in major libraries.

Collector's Exchange, comp. Frank Girard. This publication includes a list of periodicals, an index to articles, assorted notes of interest to collectors and anthologists. Write c/o Frank Girard, 4568 Richmond, NW, Grand Rapids, MI 49504.

Daims, Diva, and Janet Grimes. *Towards a Feminist Tradition: An Annotated Bibliography of Novels in English by Women, 1891–1920*. New York: Garland, 1980.

Dellinger, Harold R. "Notes on the Midwestern Literary Rebellion of the Thirties," *West End*, 5 (Summer 1978), 45–48. A genealogical and bibliographical essay, mainly about important left magazines of the 1930s.

Fine, David M. *The City, the Immigrant, and American Fiction, 1880–1920*. Metuchen, N.J.: Scarecrow, 1977. Useful bibliography of novels and stories, a number by forgotten women.

Foner, Philip S. *American Labor Songs of the Nineteenth Century*. Urbana: Univ. of Illinois Press, 1975. The excellent bibliography in this important book includes the locations of rare works.

Franklin, H. Bruce. *The Victim as Criminal and Artist: Literature from the American Prison*. New York: Oxford Univ. Press, 1978. Includes works from slavery life and black life in general as well as works from prison.

George, Zelma. "A Guide to Negro Music: An Annotated Bibliography of Negro Folk and Art Music by Negro Composers. . . ." Diss. New York Univ. 1953. Mainly concerned with music, but helpful nonetheless.

Goldwater, Walter. *Radical Periodicals in America, 1890–1950*. New Haven: Yale Univ. Press, 1964. A list of 321 radical periodicals—dates, places published, editors, etc. Needs to be supplemented with black periodicals.

Greenway, John. *American Folksongs of Protest*. Philadelphia: Univ. of Pennsylvania Press, 1953. Apart from having an important text, the book contains a vital bibliography.

Grimes, Janet, and Diva Daims. *Novels in English by Women, 1891–1920: A Preliminary Checklist*. New York: Garland, 1980.

Guide to Working-Class History. Somerville, Mass.: New England Free Press, c. 1977. Includes novels, oral history, etc.

Humez, Jean. "Women Working in the Arts: A Bibliography and Resource List." Mimeographed, Women's Studies Program, Boston: Univ. of Massachusetts, c. 1976.

Janes, Louis. *Fiction for the Working Man, 1830–1850: A Study of the Literature Produced for the Working Classes in Early Victorian Urban England*. London: Oxford Univ. Press, 1963. Contains a list of penny-issue novels.

Jones, Hettie. *Big Star Fallin' Mama: Five Women in Black Music*. New York: Viking, 1974. Useful brief bibliography and discography and a list of notable women in black music.

Ladyslipper Music (Box 3124, Durham, NC 27705). *Catalogue and Review*, Extensive list of records, tapes, etc., by women singers and some writers.

Lammel, Inge, et al. *Bibliographie der deutschen Arbeiterliedblätter*, 1844–1945. Leipzig: Deutscher Verlag für Musik, 1975. Massive list of 2,000 songs, almost none by women.

Loader, Jayne. *Women on the Left, 1906–1941: A Bibliography of Primary Resources, University of Michigan Papers in Women's Studies*, 2 (Sept. 1975), 9–82. Contains much useful information on journals, reportage, autobiographical writings, poems, and the like.

McBrearty, James G. *American Labor History and Comparative Labor Movements*. Tuscon: Univ. of Arizona Press, 1973. Has a section devoted to a list of novels, which is uneven but helpful.

Michigan Dept. of Education, State Library Services. *Michigan Women: Biographies, Autobiographies and Reminiscences*. Lansing, Mich., 1975. A bibliography.

Ogden, Jean Carter. *Annotated List of Labor Plays*. Rev. ed. New York: American Labor Education Service, 1945.

Porter, Dorothy B. *North American Negro Poets: A Bibliographical Check-List of Their Writing (1760–1944)*. 1945; rpt. New York: Franklin, 1963.

Prestridge, Virginia W. *The Worker in American Fiction*. Champaign: Univ. of Illinois, 1954. Inst. of Labor and Industrial Relations. The most extensive bibliographical work on the subject; describes fiction that, from any point of view, has "authentic working-class problems and conditions as the central theme."

Reuben, Elaine, and Deborah Rosenfelt. "Affirmative Interactions in Literature and Criticism: Some Suggestions for Reading and Research" (Mimeographed). MLA Commission on the Status of Women in the Profession, Dec. 1974. Among other items this contains Tillie Olsen's invaluable reading lists from the *Women's Studies Newsletter* (Vol. 1, No. 1 [1972], Nos. 3, 4 [1973]; Vol. 2, No. 1 [1974]; Sonny San Juan's "Provisional Listing for Third-World Literature/Culture Courses," a bibliography from the *Radical Caucus Newsletter*, 10 (July–August 1973); and the useful (for background) but almost entirely male reading list from an M.A. course—"Literature and Society, 1910–1945" from the same *Radical Caucus Newsletter*.

Rideout, Walter. *The Radical Novel in the U.S., 1900–1945*. New Haven: Yale Univ. Press, 1956. The bibliography, arranged chronologically, is one of the most helpful.

Skowronski, Jo Ann. *Women in American Music: A Bibliography*. Metuchen, N.J.: Scarecrow, 1978. Annotated bibliography of secondary sources—not of collections or anthologies—

covering 1776–1976 and including every possible subject relating to women in American music.

Soltow, Martha Jane, and Mary K. Wery. *American Women and the Labor Movement: An Annotated Bibliography*. Metuchen, N.J.: Scarecrow, 1976. Useful for background and for bibliography of archival sources.

Steiner-Scott, Elizabeth, and Elizabeth Pearce Wagle. *New Jersey Women, 1770–1970: A Bibliography*. Rutherford, N.J.: Fairleigh Dickinson Univ. Press, 1978.

Vicinus, Martha. *The Industrial Muse*. New York: Barnes, 1974. The Bibliography, which, like the text, is extraordinarily rich and comprehensive, may be considered definitive for the British work it covers.

Williams, Ora. *American Black Women in the Arts and Social Sciences: A Bibliographical Survey*. Revised and expanded ed. Metuchen, N.J.: Scarecrow, 1978. The basic bibliography on the subject, with lists of other bibliographies, anthologies, novels, autobiographies, poems, etc.

Women's Soul Publishing, Inc. (Box 11646, Milwaukee, WI 53211). *My Sister's Song: Discography of Women-Made Music*. 1975. Mainly folk and popular, but separate sections on jazz, blues, etc.

APPENDIX B

The following books contain prose (some of it more documentary than imaginative) and/or poetry by working-class women.

Baxandall, Roslyn, Linda Gordon, and Susan Reverby. *American's Working Women: A Documentary History, 1600 to the Present*. New York: Vintage-Random, 1976.

Blassingame, John W., ed. *Slave Testimony*. Baton Rouge: Louisiana State Univ. Press, 1977.

Cole, Josephine, and Grace Silver, comps. *Socialist Dialogues and Recitations*. Chicago: Kerr, 1913.

Conroy, Jack, and Curt Johnson. *Writers in Revolt: The Anvil Anthology, 1933–40*. New York: Lawrence Hill, 1973.

Courlander, Harold. *A Treasury of Afro-American Folklore*. New York: Crown, 1976.

Foner, Philip S., ed. *The Factory Girls*. Urbana: Univ. of Illinois Press, 1977.

Handler, Esther, ed. *The Pavement Trial: A Collection of Poetry and Prose from the Allis-Chalmers Picket Lines*. Foreword by Meridel LeSueur. West Allis, Wisc.: Local 248 United Auto Workers, 1946.

Hicks, Granville, et al., ed. *Proletarian Literature in the United States*. New York: International, 1935.

Hoffman, Nancy, and Florence Howe, eds. *Working Women: An Anthology of Stories and Poems*. Old Westbury, N.Y.: Feminist, 1979.

Keating, P. J. *Working-Class Stories of the 1890's*. London: Routledge and Kegan Paul, 1971. No stories by women but a number about them.

Kornbluh, Joyce. *Rebel Voices: An IWW Anthology*. Ann Arbor: Univ. of Michigan Press, 1964.

Lerner, Gerda. *Black Women in White America*. New York: Pantheon, 1972.

———. *The Female Experience—An American Documentary*. Indianapolis: Bobbs-Merrill, 1977.

Loewenberg, James, and Ruth Bogin, eds. *Black Women in Nineteenth Century American Life*. University Park: Pennsylvania State Univ. Press, 1976.

Münchow, Ursula. *Frühe deutsche Arbeiterautobiographie*. Berlin: Akademie-Verlag, 1973.

North, Joseph, ed. *New Masses: An Anthology of the Rebel Thirties*. New York: International, 1969.

Voigtländer, Annie, ed. *Hierzulande, heutzutage: Lyrik, Prosa, Graphik aus dem werkkreis, "Literatur der Arbeitswelt."* Berlin: Aufbau-Verlag, 1975.

Wenzel, Karl Heinz, Marianne Schmidt, and Konrad Schmidt. *Körnchen Gold: Eine Anthologie Schreibender Arbeiter*. Berlin: Tribüne, 1969.

APPENDIX C

Collections (or articles) containing at least some songs or poems by working-class women writers.

Abelson, Walter. *Songs of Labor*. Newburgh, N.Y.: Paebar, 1947.

Allen, William Francis, Charles Pickard Ware, and Lucy McKim Garrison. *Slave Songs of the United States*. 1867; rpt. Freeport, N.Y.: Books for Libraries, 1971.

Alloy, Evelyn. *Working Women's Music: The Songs and Struggles of Women in the Cotton Mills, Textile Plants, and Needle Trades*. Somerville, Mass.: New England Free Press, 1976.

Althoff, Arneliese, et al. *Für eine andere Deutschstunde, Arbeit und Alltag in neuen Texten*. Ed. Arbeitskreis Progressive Kunst. Oberhausen: Asso Verlag, 1972.

Amalgamated Clothing Workers. *Song Book*. New York, 1940.

Amalgamated Clothing Workers, Local #489. *Picket Line Songs*. Andalusia, Ala., c. 1967.

American Music League. *March and Sing*. New York, 1937.

Arbeiterdichtung: Analysen, Bekenntnisse, Dokumentationen, comp. Öster-reichischen Gessell-schaft für Kulturpolitik. Wuppertal: Hammer, c. 1973.

Arbeiter und Freiheitslieder, No. 1 (1973). Hannover: Arbeiter-Musik-Assoziation.

Bab, Julius. *Arbeiterdichtung*. Berlin: Volksöuhnen-Verlags-und-Vertriebs, 1924.

Balch, Elizabeth. "Songs for Labor," *Survey*, 31 (1914), 408–12, 422–28.

Benet, William Rose, and Norman Cousins. *The Poetry of Freedom*. New York: Random, 1945.

Bogorad, Miriam, et. al., comps. *Songs for America*. New York: Workers Library, 1939.

Bold, Alan. *The Penguin Book of Socialist Verse*. Baltimore: Penguin, 1970.

Busch, Ernst, ed. *Internationale Arbeiterlieder*. Berlin: "Lied der Zeit" Musik-verlag, 1953.

Carpenter, E. *Chants of Labor: A Song-book of the People*. London: 1897; rpt. Allen and Un-win, 1922.

Cheyney, Ralph, ed. *Banners of Brotherhood: An Anthology of Social Vision Verse*. North Montpelier, Vt.: Driftwood, 1933.

Clark, Thomas Curtis, comp. *Poems of Justice*. New York: Willett, Clark and Colby, 1929.

Collinson, Francis. *The Traditional and National Music of Scotland*. London: Routledge and Kegan Paul, 1966.

Commonwealth Labor Songs: A Collection of Old and New Songs for the Use of Labor Unions. Mena, Ark.: Commonwealth Coll., 1938.

Conroy, Jack, and Ralph Cheyney, eds. *Unrest, 1931*. New York: H. Harrison, 1931.

Davis, N. Brian. *The Poetry of the Canadian People, 1720–1920: 200 Years of Hard Work*. Toronto: N C Press, 1976.

Denisoff, R. Serge. *Sing A Song of Social Significance*. Bowling Green, Ohio: Bowling Green Univ. Popular Press, 1972.

Druskin, Mikhail Semenovich. *Russkaia revoliutsionnaia pesnia*. Moscow, 1954.

Every-day Songs for Labour Festivals. London: Labour Party, n.d.

Federal Music Project. *Folk Songs from East Kentucky*. Washington, D.C.: Works Project Administration, c. 1939.

Folksongs of Peggy Seeger. New York: Oak, n.d.

Folk Songs of the Southern Appalachians (as Sung by Jean Ritchie). New York: Oak, 1965.

Foner, Philip S. *American Labor Songs of the Nineteenth Century*. Urbana: Univ. of Illinois Press, 1975.

Fowke, Edith, and Joe Glazer. *Songs of Work and Freedom*. New York: Dover, 1973.

Friedman, Perry, ed. *Hör zu, Mister Bilbo: Lieder aus der Amerikanischen Arbeiterbewegnung, 1860–1950*. Berlin: Rütten und Loening, 1962.

Friedrich, Wolfgang, ed. *Im Klassenkampf: Deutsche revolutionäre Lieder und Gedichte aus der zweiten Hälfte des 19 Jahrhunderts*. Halle: Verlag Sprache und Literatur, 1962.

Glazer, Tom, ed. *Songs of Peace, Freedom and Protest*. New York: David McKay, 1970.

Heisden, Marcel Charles Antoon van der, comp. *Werkmansbrekje*. Utrecht: Het Spectrum, 1971.

Heller, H. *Oesterreichisches Proletarier-Liederbuch*. Wien: Wiener Volksbuch-handlung, c. 1900.

Highlander Folk School. *Songbook*. Monteagle, Tenn.: Highlander Folk School, 1943.

———. *Songs: Labor, Folk, War*. Monteagle, Tenn.: Highlander Folk School, 1944.

Hille, Waldemar, ed. *The People's Song Book*. New York: Oak, various dates.

Industrial Workers of the World. *Songs of the Workers (To Fan the Flames of Discontent)*. Chicago: IWW, many dates and editions.

International Ladies Garment Workers Union. *Dixie Union Songs*. Atlanta, Ga.: ILGWU, n.d.

———. *Everybody Sings*. New York, ILGWU, 1942.

———. *Let's Sing*. New York: ILGWU, 1934.

Kopping, Walter, ed. *Unter Tage, über Tage: Gedichte aus der Arbeitswelt unserer Tage*. Frankfurt a.M.: Europäische Verlags-anstalt, 1966.

Kriselkreisel: Lieder und Texte. Berlin: Arbeitskreis Musik im Klassenkampf, 1974.

Kuhnke, Klaus, comp. *Lieder der Arbeiterklasse, 1919–1933*. Arhensburg: Damokle Verlag, 1971.

Kürbisch, Friedrich G., comp. *Anklage und Botschaft: Die lyrische Aussage der Arbeiter seit 1900*. Hannover: Dietz, 1969.

———. *Arbeiterdichtung: Versuch einer Standortbestimmung*. Wien: Sozialistiche Bildungszentrale, c. 1972.

Lazarus, Emma. *Emma Lazarus: Selections from Her Poetry and Prose*, ed. M. U. Schappes. New York: Book League, Jewish People's Fraternal Order of the International Workers Order, 1947.

Leuchtkugeln: Ernste und heitere Vortragsgedichte für Arbeiterfeste. Berlin: Verlag Vorwärts, 1905.

Levenstein, Adolf, comp. *Arbeiter—Philosophen und Dichter*. Berlin: E. Frowe, 1909.

Lloyd, Albert Lancaster. *Come All Ye Bold Miners: Ballads and Songs of the Coalfields*. London: Lawrence and Wishart, 1952.

Lomax, Alan. *American Ballads and Folk Songs*. New York: Macmillan, 1934.

———. *The Folk Songs of North America*. Garden City, N.Y.: Doubleday, 1960.

———. *Our Singing Country*. New York: Macmillan, 1941.

Lomax, Alan, Woody Guthrie, and Pete Seeger. *Hard Hitting Songs for Hard-Hit People*. New York: Oak, 1967.

Lowenfels, Walter, ed. *For Neruda, for Chile: An International Anthology*. Boston: Beacon, 1975.

MacColl, Ewan, ed. *The Shuttle and the Cage: Industrial Folk Ballads*. London: Workers' Music Association, 1954.

MacColl, Ewan, and Peggy Seeger. *I'm a Freeborn Man and Other Orginal Ballads and Songs*. New York: Oak, 1968.

Marcus, Shmuel, ed. *An Anthology of Revolutionary Poetry*. New York: Active Press, 1929.

Mühle, Hans, ed. *Das Lied der Arbeit, selbstzeugnisse der schaffenden*. Gotha: Leopold Klotz Verlag, 1930.

———. *Das proletarische Schicksal*. Gotha: Leopold Klotz Verlag, 1929.

Münchow, Ursula, ed. *Stimme des Vortrupps: Proletarische Laienlyrik, 1914 bis 1945.* Berlin: Dietz Verlag, 1961.

Nechaev, Egor Efimovich. *U istokov russkoi proletarskoi poezil.* Leningrad, 1965.

Offenburg, Kurt, comp. *Arbeiterdichtung der Gegenwart.* Frankfurt a.M.: Mitteland-Verlag, 1925.

Olivier, Paul. *Les Chansons de Métiers.* Paris: Charpentier et Fasquelle, 1910.

Palmer, Roy, ed. *Poverty Knock: A Picture of Industrial Life in the 19th Century through Songs, Ballads, and Contemporary Accounts.* New Yokr: Cambridge Univ. Press, 1974.

Poslední bitva uzplála: Vybor z veršů a písní dělnických bás níku. Praha: Českozlovenský spisovatel, 1951.

Reynolds, Malvina. *Little Boxes and Other Handmade Songs.* New York: Oak, 1965.

——. *The Malvina Reynolds Songbook.* Berkeley, Calif.: Schroder Music, various editions and dates.

——. *There's Music in the Air.* Berkeley, Calif.: Schroder Music, n.d.

Riddle, Almeda. *A Singer and Her Songs.* Baton Rouge: Louisiana State Univ. Press, 1970.

Salzman, Jack, and Leo Zanderer. *Social Poetry of the 1930's: A Selection.* New York: Burt Franklin, 1978.

Schramm, Godehard, and Bernhard Wenger, comps. *Werkkreis Literatur der Arbetswelt.* Frankfurt a.M.: Fischer-Taschenbuch-Verlag, 1974.

Schwachhofer, Rene, and Wilhelm T. Kaczyk, comps. *Spiegel unseres Werdens: Mensch und Arbeit in der deutschen Dichtung von Goethe bis Brecht.* Berlin: Verlad der Nation, 1969.

Silber, Irwin, ed. *Lift Every Voice! The Second People's Song Book.* New York: People's Artists Publication, c. 1953.

Smith, Lewis Worthington, ed. *Women Poets Today.* New York:: George Sully, 1929.

Songs of the Southern School for Workers. Asheville, N.C.: Southern School for Workers, c. 1940.

Taggard, Genevieve, ed. *May Days: An Anthology of Verse from Masses-Liberator.* New York: Boni and Liveright, 1925.

Trask, Willard R. *The Unwritten Song: Poetry of the Primitive and Traditional Peoples of the World.* 2 vols. New York: Macmillan, 1966–67.

Trent, Lucia, and Ralph Cheyney. *America Arraigned! (Poems on Sacco and Vanzetti).* New York: Dean, 1928.

Vi Viltaende: Ukjente nord-norske arbeiderdikt, 1780–1920. Oslo: Pax, 1975.

Vincent, Leopold. *The Alliance and Labor Songster: A Collection of Labor and Comic Songs.* 1891; rpt. New York: Arno, 1975.

White, Newman I., ed. *American Negro FolkSongs.* Cambridge: Harvard Univ. Press, 1928.

Woolridge, Dorothy, comp. *The Poetry of Toil: An Anthology of Poems.* London: Faber, 1926.

The Worker Looks at the Stars. Vinyard Shore, Mass.: n.p., 1927.

Yearsley, Ann (a milkwoman of Bristol). *Poems, on Several Occasions.* London: T. Cadell, 1785.

——. *Poems, on Various Subjects.* London: Robinson, 1787.

APPENDIX D

Secondary books and articles mainly on working-class women's songs and poetry.

Albertson, Chris. *Bessie.* New York: Stein and Day, 1972.

Armstrong, Toni L., and Sally G. Newbury. "Women's Songbooks: An Introduction and Survey." *Paid My Dues,* 3, No. 1 (1978), 34–36.

Baraka, Imamu Amiri (LeRoi Jones). *Blues People*. New York: Morrow, 1963.

Barry, Phillips. "The Factory Girl's Come-All-Ye." *Bulletin of the Folksong Society of the Northeast*, 2 (1931), 12.

Charters, Samuel. *Poetry of the Blues*. New York: Oak, 1963.

Chilton, John. *Billie's Blues: A Survey of Billie Holiday's Career, 1933–1959*. London: Quartet, 1975.

Cunningham, Agnes "Sis." "Sis Cunningham: Song of Hard Times" (as told to Madelaine Belkin Rose). *Ms.*, 2 (March 1974), 29–32.

Denisoff, R. Serge. *Great Day Coming: Folk Music and the American Left*. Urbana: Univ. of Illinois Press, 1971.

Drew, Caroline. "Remember Ella May!" *Equal Justice (Labor Defender)*, (Sept. 1930), 181.

Feldman, Eugene P. Romayn. "Union Maid Revisited: The Story of Ella Mae Wiggins." *ABC/TV Hootenanny*, 1, No. 3 (1964), 25–26.

Green, Archie, ed. "Aunt Molly Jackson Memorial Issue." *Kentucky Folklore Record*, 7, No. 4 (1961), 129–75.

Greenway, John. *American Folksongs of Protest*. Philadelphia: Univ. of Pennsylvania Press, 1953.

Harrison, Daphne Duval. "Black Women in the Blues Tradition." In *The Afro-American Woman: Struggles and Images*. Ed. Sharon Harley and Rosalyn Terborg-Penn. Port Washington, N.Y.: Kennikat, 1978.

Heath, Colin. "Bessie Smith: Empress of the Blues." *Heritage*, No. 17 (1970), 2–5; No. 18 (1970), 2–5.

Heilbut, Tony. *The Gospel Sound, Good News and Bad Times*. Garden City, N.Y.: Anchor-Doubleday, 1975.

Higginson, Thomas Wentworth. *Army Life in a Black Regiment*. New York: Macmillan, 1962.

Jackson, Aunt Molly. "I Am from Kentucky Born." *Equal Justice (Labor Defender)*, 8 (Jan. 1932), 8.

Japenga, Ann. "Women of the Blues." *Paid My Dues*, No. 5 (1975), 12–14.

Jones, Hettie. *Big Star Fallin' Mama: Five Women in Black Music*. New York: Viking, 1974.

Kahn, Kathy. *Hillbilly Women*. Garden City, N.Y.: Doubleday, 1973.

Korson, George. *Coal Dust on the Fiddle*. Philadelphia: Univ. of Pennslyvania Press, 1943.

Larkin, Margaret. "Ella May's Songs." *Nation*, 9 Oct. 1929, pp. 382–83.

Lomax, Alan. *The Rainbow Sign* (on Vera Hall). New York: Duell, Slaon and Pearce, 1959.

Lovell, John, Jr. *Black Song: The Forge and the Flame*. New York: Macmillan, 1972.

Lynn, Loretta. *Loretta Lynn: Coal Miner's Daughter*. Chicago: Regnery, 1976.

Mitchell, George. *Blow My Blues Away*. Baton Rouge: Louisiana State Univ. Press, 1971.

Monahan, Kathleen. "Women's Songs of the American Labor Movement," Master's thesis Univ. of Pittsburgh, 1975.

———. "Union Maid," *Paid My Dues*. No. 4 (March 1975), 24–26, 36.

Odum, Howard W., and Guy B. Johnson. *Negro Workaday Songs*. 1926; rpt. New York: Negro Univ. Press, 1969.

Oliver, Paul. *Bessie Smith*. New York: Barnes, 1961.

———. *The Meaning of the Blues*. New York: Collier, 1963.

———. *Screening the Blues: Aspects of the Blues Tradition*. London: Cassell, 1968.

———. *The Story of the Blues*. New York: Chilton, 1969.

Ritchie, Jean. *Singing Family of the Cumberlands*. New York: Oxford Univ. Press, 1955.

Rosen, David M. *Protest Songs in America*. Westlake Village, Calif.: Aware, 1972.

Rushing, Andrea Benton. "Images of Black Women in Afro-American Poetry." In *The Afro-American Woman: Struggles and Images*. Ed. Sharon Harley and Rosalyn Terborg-Penn. Port Washington, N.Y.: Kennikat, 1978.

Russell, Michele. "Slave Codes and Liner Notes." *Radical Teacher*, No. 4 (1977), 1–6.

Ryder, Georgia A. "Black Women in Song: Some Sociocultural Images." *Negro History Bulletin*, 39 (May 1976), 60lff.

Seeger, Pete. *The Incompleat Folksinger*. New York: Simon, 1972.

Sing Out! 25 (1976), esp. No. 1: *Songs of the Labor Struggle*, No. 2: *Songs of American Women*, No. 3: *Music of La Raza—Songs of the Puerto Rican Nation*, and No. 5: *Immigrant Traditions in America*.

Southern, Eileen. *The Music of Black Americans: A History*. New York: Norton, 1971.

Southey, Robert. *The Lives and Works of the Uneducated Poets*. Ed. J. S. Childers. 1831; rpt. London: H. Milford, 1925.

Stanford, Ron. "Which Side Are You On? An Interview with Florence Reece," *Sing Out!* 20, No. 6 (1971), 13–15.

Stewart-Baxter, Derrick. *Ma Rainey and the Classic Blues Singers*. New York: Stein and Day, 1970.

"Successful Women Song-Writers." *Literary Digest*, 13 (Oct. 1917), p. 87.

Watson, Edward A. "Bessie's Blues." *New Letters*, 38 (Winter 1971), 64–70.

APPENDIX E

Secondary books and articles especially helpful to the study of working-class women's literature.

Adickes, Sandra. "Mind among the Spindles: An Examination of Some of the Journals, Newspapers and Memoirs of the Lowell Female Operatives." *Women's Studies*, 1 (1973) 279–87.

Dundes, Alan. *Mother Wit from the Laughing Barrel: Readings in the Interpretation of Afro-American Folklore*. Englewood Cliffs, N.J.: Prentice-Hall, 1973.

Farrer, Claire R. Introd. to special issue on women in folklore, *Journal of American Folklore*, 88 (Jan.–March 1975).

Fine, David M. *The City, the Immigrant, and American Fiction*. Metuchen, N.J.: Scarecrow, 1977.

Franklin, H. Bruce. *The Victim as Criminal and Artist: Literature from the American Prison*. New York: Oxford Univ. Press, 1978.

Greiner, Bernhard. *Die Literatru der Arbeitswelt in der DDR*. Heidelberg: Quelle und Meyer, 1974.

Hull, Gloria, Patricia Bell Scott, and Barbara Smith, eds. *But Some of Us Are Brave: Black Women's Studies*. Old Westbury, N.Y.: Feminist, 1982.

Levine, Lawrence W. *Black Culture and Black Consciousness: Afro-American Folk Thought from Slavery to Freedom*. New York: Oxford Univ. Press, 1977.

Lipsitz, George. "Working Peoples' Music," *Cultural Correspondence*, No. 2 (1976), 15–33.

Ragon, Michel. *Les Ecrivains du peuple: Historique, biographies, critique*. Paris: J. Vignau, 1947.

———. *Histoire de la littérature ouvrière du moyen âge à nos jours*. Paris: Éditions Ouvrières, 1953.

———. *Histoire de la littérature proletarienne en France: Littérature ouvrière, littérature paysanne, littérature d'expression populaire*. Paris: A. Michel, 1974.

Randall, Margaret. "Truth Is a Convincing Answer . . . !" (conversations with three Vietnamese women writers). *Left Curve*, No. 3 (1975), 30–35.

Runnquist, Åke. *Arbetarskildare från Hedevind till Fridell*. Stockholm: Bonnier, 1952.

Tannacito, Dan. "Poetry of the Colorado Miners: 1903–1905." *Radical Teacher*, No. 15 (1980), 1–8.

Unwin, Rayner. *The Rural Muse: Studies in the Peasant Poetry of England.* London: Allen and Unwin, 1957.

Vicinus, Martha. *The Industrial Muse.* New York: Barnes, 1974.

Walker, Alice. "In Search of Our Mother's Gardens: The Creativity of Black Women in the South," *Ms.,* 2 (May 1974), 64–70, 105.

Wertheimer, Barbara. *We Were There: The Story of the Working Women in America.* New York: Pantheon, 1977.

APPENDIX F

A very selective list of magazines that regularly run material of interest in the study of working-class women's literature.

Frontiers: A Journal of Women's Studies, esp. 2, No. 2 [Summer 1977], on women's oral history.

Paid My Dues: A Journal of Women and Music.

People's Songs. 4 vols., 1946–49.

Radical Teacher, esp. Nos. 4, 6, 10, 15.

Sing Out! esp. 25, Nos. 1, 2, 3, 5.

West End, esp. 5, No. 1 (1978): *Midwest People's Culture Anthology.*

CORA KAPLAN

PANDORA'S BOX

subjectivity, class and sexuality in socialist feminist criticism

Feminist criticism, as its name implies, is criticism with a Cause, engaged criticism. But the critical model presented to us so far is merely engaged to be married. It is about to contract what can only be a *mésalliance* with bourgeois modes of thought and the critical categories they inform. To be effective, feminist criticism cannot become simply bourgeois criticism in drag. It must be ideological and moral criticism; it must be revolutionary.
LILLIAN ROBINSON, 'DWELLING IN DECENCIES' (1978)

The 'Marriage' of marxism and feminism has been like the marriage of husband and wife depicted in English common law: marxism and feminism are one, and that is marxism . . . we need a healthier marriage or we need a divorce.

HEIDI HARTMANN, 'THE UNHAPPY MARRIAGE
OF MARXISM AND FEMINISM' (1981)

I

In spite of the attraction of matrimonial metaphor, reports of feminist nuptials with either mild-mannered bourgeois criticism or macho mustachioed Marxism have been greatly exaggerated. Neither liberal feminist criticism decorously draped in traditional humanism, nor her red-ragged rebellious sister, socialist feminist criticism, has yet found a place within androcentric literary criticism, which wishes to embrace feminism through a legitimate public alliance. Nor can feminist criticism today be plausibly evoked as a young deb looking for protection or, even more problematically, as a male 'mole' in transvestite masquerade. Feminist criticism now marks out a broad area of literary studies, eclectic, original and provocative. Independent still, through a combination of choice and default, it has come of age without giving up its name. Yet Lillian Robinson's astute pessimistic prediction is worth remembering. With maturity, the most visible, well-defined and extensive tendency within feminist criticism has undoubtedly bought into the white, middle-class, heterosexist values of traditional literary criticism, and threatens to settle down on her own in its cultural suburbs. For, as I see it, the present danger is not that feminist criticism will enter an unequal dependent alliance with any of the varieties of male-centered criticism. It does not need to, for it has produced an all too persuasive autonomous analysis which is in many ways radical in its discussion of gender, but implicitly conservative in its assumptions about social hierarchy and female subjectivity, the Pandora's box for all feminist theory.

This reactionary effect must be interrogated and resisted from within feminism and in relation to the wider socialist feminist project. For, without the class and race perspectives which socialist feminist critics bring to the analysis both of the literary texts and of their conditions of production, liberal feminist criticism, with its emphasis on the unified female subject, will unintentionally reproduce the ideological values of mass-market romance. In that fictional landscape the other structuring relations of society fade and disappear, leaving us with the naked drama of sexual difference as the only scenario that matters. Mass-market romance tends to represent sexual difference as natural and fixed—a constant, transhistorical femininity in libidinized struggle with an equally 'given' universal masculinity. Even where class difference divides lovers, it is there as narrative backdrop or minor stumbling-block to the inevitable heterosexual resolution. Without overstraining the comparison, a feminist literary criticism which privileges gender in isolation from other forms of social determination offers us a similarly partial reading of the role played by sexual difference in literary discourse, a reading bled dry of its most troubling and contradictory meanings.

The appropriation of modern critical theory—semiotic with an emphasis on the psychoanalytic—can be of great use in arguing against concepts of natural, essential and unified identity: against a static femininity and masculinity. But these theories about the production of meaning in culture must engage fully with the effects of other systems of difference than the sexual, or they too will produce no more than an anti-humanist avant-garde version of romance. Masculinity and femininity do not appear in cultural discourse, any more than they do in mental life, as pure binary forms at play. They are always, already, ordered and broken up through other social and cultural terms, other categories of difference. Our fantasies of sexual transgression as much as our obedience to sexual regulation are expressed through these structuring hierarchies. Class and race ideologies are, conversely, steeped in and spoken through the language of sexual differentiation. Class and race meanings are not metaphors for the sexual, or vice versa. It is better though not exact, to see them as reciprocally constituting each other through a kind of narrative invocation, a set of associative terms in a chain of meaning. To understand how gender and class—to take two categories only— are articulated together transforms our analysis of each of them.

The literary text too often figures in feminist criticism as a gripping spectacle in which sexual difference appears somewhat abstracted from the muddy social world in which it is elsewhere embedded. Yet novels, poetry and drama are, on the contrary, peculiarly rich discourses in which the fused languages of class, race and gender are both produced and re-represented through the incorporation of other discourses. The focus of feminist analysis ought to be on that heterogeneity within the literary, on the intimate relation there expressed between all the categories that order social and psychic meaning. This does not imply an attention to content only or primarily, but also entails a consideration of the linguistic processes of the text as they construct and position subjectivity within these terms.

For without doubt literary texts do centre the individual as object and subject of their discourse. Literature has been a traditional space for the exploration of gender relations and sexual difference, and one in which women themselves have been formidably present. The problem for socialist feminists is not the focus on the individual that is special to the literary, but rather the romantic theory of the subject so firmly entrenched within the discourse. Humanist feminist criticism does not object to the idea of an immanent, transcendent subject but only to the exclusion of women from these definitions which it takes as an accurate account of subjectivity rather than as a historically constructed ideology. The repair and reconstitution of female subjectivity through a rereading of literature becomes, therefore, a major part, often unacknowledged, of its critical project. Psychoanalytic and semiotically oriented feminist criticism has argued well against this aspect of feminist humanism, emphasizing the important structural relation between writing and sexuality in the construction of the subject. But both tendencies have been correctly criticized from a socialist feminist position for the neglect of class and race as factors in their analysis. If feminist criticism is to make a central contribution to the understanding of sexual difference, instead of serving as a conservative refuge from its more disturbing social and psychic implications, the inclusion of class and race must transform its terms and objectives.

II

The critque of feminist humanism needs more historical explication than it has so far received. Its sources are complex, and are rooted in that moment almost 200 years ago when modern feminism and Romantic cultural theory emerged as separate but linked responses to the transforming events of the French Revolution. In the heat and light of the revolutionary decade 1790–1800, social, political and aesthetic ideas already maturing underwent a kind of forced ripening. As the progressive British intelligentsia contemplated the immediate possibility of social change, their thoughts turned urgently to the present capacity of subjects to exercise republican freedoms—to rule themselves as well as each other if the corrupt structures of aristocratic privilege were to be suddenly razed. Both feminism as set out in its most influential text, Mary Wollstonecraft's *A Vindication of the Rights of Woman* (1792), and Romanticism as argued most forcefully in Wordsworth's introduction to *Lyrical Ballads* (1800) stood in intimate, dynamic and contradictory relationship to democratic politcs. In all three discourses the social and psychic character of the individual was centred and elaborated. The public and private implications of sexual difference as well as of the imagination and its products were both strongly linked to the optimistic, speculative construction of a virtuous citizen subject for a brave new egalitarian world. Theories of reading and writing—Wollstonecraft's and Jane Austen's as well as those of male Romantic authors—were explicitly related to contemporary politics as expressed in debate by such figures as Tom Paine, Edmund Burke and William Godwin.

The new categories of independent subjectivity, however, were marked from the beginning by exclusions of gender, race and class. Jean-Jacques Rousseau, writing in the 1750s, specifically exempted women for his definition; Thomas

Jefferson, some twenty years later, excluded blacks. Far from being invisible ideological aspects of the new subject, these exclusions occasioned debate and polemic on both sides of the Atlantic. The autonomy of inner life, the dynamic psyche whose moral triumph was to be the foundation of republican government, was considered absolutely essential as an element of progressive political thought.

However, as the concept of the inner self and the moral psyche was used to denigrate whole classes, races and genders, late-nineteenth-century socialism began to de-emphasize the political importance of the psychic self, and redefine political morality and the adequate citizen subject in primarily social terms. Because of this shift in emphasis, a collective moralism has developed in socialist thought which, instead of criticizing the reactionary interpretation of psychic life, stigmatizes sensibility itself, interpreting the excess of feeling as regressive, bourgeois and non-political.

Needless to say, this strand of socialist thought poses a problem for feminism, which has favoured three main strategies to deal with it. In the first, women's psychic life is seen as being essentially identical to men's, but distorted through vicious and systematic patriarchal inscription. In this view, which is effectively Wollstonecraft's, social reform would prevent women from becoming regressively obsessed with sexuality and feeling. The second strategy wholly vindicates women's psyche, but sees it as quite separate from men's, often in direct opposition. This is frequently the terrain on which radical feminism defends female sexuality as independent and virtuous between women, but degrading in a heterosexual context. It is certainly a radical reworking of essentialist sexual ideology, shifting the ground from glib assertions of gender complementarity to the logic of separatism. The third strategy has been to refuse the issue's relevance altogether—to see any focus on psychic difference as itself an ideological one.

Instead of choosing any one of these options, socialist feminist criticism must come to grips with the relationship between female subjectivity and class identity. This project, even in its present early stages, poses major problems for the tendency. While socialist feminists have been deeply concerned with the social construction of femininity and sexual difference, they have been uneasy about integrating social and political determinations with an analysis of the psychic ordering of gender. Within socialist feminism, a fierce and unresolved debate continues about the value of using psychoanalytic theory, because of the supposedly ahistorical character of its paradigms. For those who are hostile to psychoanalysis, the meaning of mental life, fantasy and desire—those obsessive themes of the novel and poetry for the last two centuries—seems particularly intractable to interpretation. They are reluctant to grant much autonomy to the psychic level, and often most attentive to feeling expressed in the work of non-bourgeois writers, which can more easily be read as political statement. Socialist feminism still finds unlocated, unsocialized psychic expression in women's writing hard to discuss in non-moralizing terms.

On the other hand, for liberal humanism, feminist versions included, the possibility of a unified self and an integrated consciousness that can transcend material circumstance is represented as the fulfilment of desire, the happy closure at the end of the story. The psychic fragmentation expressed through female characters in women's writing is seen as the most important sign of their sexual subordination, more interesting and ultimately more meaningful than their social oppression. As a result, the struggle for an integrated female subjectivity in nine-teenth-century texts is never interrogated as ideology or fantasy, but seen as a demand that can actually be met, if not in 1848, then later.

In contrast, socialist feminist criticism tends to foreground the social and eco-nomic elements of the narrative and socialize what it can of its psychic portions. Women's anger and anguish, it is assumed, should be amenable to repair through social change. A positive emphasis on the psychic level is viewed as a valorization of the anarchic and regressive, a way fo returning women to their subordinate ideological place within the dominant culture, as unreasoning social beings. Psy-choanalytic theory, which is by and large morally neutral about the desires ex-pressed by the psyche, is criticized as a confirmation and justification of them.

Thus semiotic or psychoanalytic perspectives have yet to be integrated with social, economic and political analysis. Critics tend to privilege one element or the other, even when they acknowledge the importance of both and the need to relate them. A comparison of two admirable recent essays on Charlotte Brontë's *Villette*, one by Mary Jacobus and the other by Judith Lowder Newton, both in-formed by socialist feminist concerns, can illustrate this difficulty.

Jacobus uses the psychoanalytic and linguistic theory of Jacques Lacan to ex-plore the split representations of subjectivity that haunt *Villette*, and calls atten-tion to its anti-realist gothic elements. She relates Brontë's feminized defence of the imagination, and the novel's unreliable narrator-heroine, to the tension be-tween femininity and feminism that reaches back to the eighteenth-century de-bates of Rousseau and Wollstonecraft. Reading the ruptures and gaps of the text as a psychic narrative, she also places it historically in relationship to nineteenth-century social and political ideas. Yet the social meanings of *Villette* fade and all but disappear before 'the powerful presence of fantasy,' which 'energizes *Villette* and satisfies that part of the reader which also desires constantly to reject reality for the sake of an obedient, controllable, narcissistically pleasurable image of self and its relation to the world' (Jacobus 1979, p. 51). In Jacobus's interpretation, the psyche, desire and fantasy stand for repressed, largely positive elements of a forgotten feminism, while the social stands for a daytime world of Victorian social regulation. These social meanings are referred to rather than explored in the es-say, a strategy which renders them both static and unproblematically unified. It is as if, in order to examine how *Villette* represents psychic reality, the dynamism of social discourses of gender and identity must be repressed, forming the text's new 'unconscious.'

Judith Lowder Newton's chapter on *Villette* in her impressive study of nine-teenth-century British fiction, *Women, Power, and Subversion* (1981), is also con-cerned with conflicts between the novel's feminism and its evocation of female desire. Her interpretation privileges the social meanings of the novel, its search for a possible *détente* between the dominant ideologies of bourgeois femininity and progressive definitions of female autonomy. For Newton, 'the internalized ideology of women's sphere' includes sexual and romantic longings—which for Jacobus are potentially radical and disruptive of mid-Victorian gender ideologies. The psychic level as Newton describes it is mainly the repository for the worst and most regressive elements of female subjectivity: longing for love, depen-dency, the material and emotional comfort of fixed class identity. These desires which have 'got inside' are predictably in conflict with the rebellious, autonomy-seeking feminist impulses, whose source is a rational understanding of class and gender subordination. Her reading centres on the realist text, locating meaning in its critique of class society and the constraints of bourgeois femininity.

The quotations and narrative elements cited and explored by Jacobus and Newton are so different that even a reader familiar with *Villette* may find it hard to believe that each critic is reading the same text. The psychic level exists in Newton's interpretation, to be sure, but as a negative discourse, the dead weight of ideology on the mind. For her, the words 'hidden,' 'private' and 'longing' are stigmatized, just as they are celebrated by Jacobus. For both critics, female subjectivity is the site where the opposing forces of femininity and feminism clash by night, but they locate these elements in different parts of the text's divided selves. Neither Newton nor Jacobus argues for the utopian possibility of a unified subjectivity. But the *longing* to close the splits that characterize femininity—splits between reason and desire, autonomy and dependent security, psychic and social identity—is evident in the way each critic denies the opposing element.

III

My comments on the difficulties of reading *Villette* from a materialist feminist stance are meant to suggest that there is more at issue in the polarization of social and psychic explanation than the problem of articulating two different forms of explanation. Moral and political questions specific to feminism are at stake as well. In order to understand why female subjectivity is so fraught with *Angst* and difficulty for feminism, we must go back to the first full discussion of the psychological expression of femininity, in Mary Wollstonecraft's *A Vindication of the Rights of Woman*. The briefest look will show that an interest in the psychic life of women as a crucial element in their subordination and liberation is not a modern, post-Freudian preoccupation. On the contrary, its long and fascinating history in 'left' feminist writing starts with Wollstonecraft, who set the terms for a debate that is still in progress. Her writing is central for socialist feminism today, because she based her interest in the emancipation of women as individuals in revolutionary politics.

Like so many eighteenth-century revolutionaries, she saw her own class, the rising bourgeoise, as the vanguard of the revolution, and it was to the women of her own class that she directed her arguments. Her explicit focus on the middle class, and her concentration on the nature of female subjectivity, speaks directly to the source of anxiety within socialist feminism today. For it is at the point when women are released from profound social and economic oppression into greater autonomy and potential political choice that their social and psychic expression becomes an issue, and their literary texts become sites of ambivalence. In their pages, for the last 200 years and more, women characters seemingly more confined by social regulation than women readers today speak as desiring subjects. These texts express the politically 'retrogade' desires for comfort, dependence and love as well as more acceptable demands for autonomy and independence.

It is Mary Wollstonecraft who first offered women this fateful choice between the opposed and moralized bastions of reason and feeling, which continues to determine much feminist thinking. The structures through which she developed her ideas, however, were set for her by her mentor Jean-Jacques Rousseau, whose writing influenced the political and social perspectives of many eighteenth-century English radicals. His ideas were fundamental to her thinking about gender as well as about revolutionary politics. In 1792, that highly charged moment of romantic political optimism between the fall of the Bastille and the Terror when *A Vindication* was written, it must have seemed crucial that Rousseau's crippling judgement of female nature be refuted. How else could women freely and equally participate in the new world being made across the Channel? Rousseau's ideas about subjectivity were already immanent in Wollstonecraft's earlier book *Mary: A Fiction* (1788). Now she set out to challenge directly his offensive description of sexual difference which would leave women in post-revolutionary society exactly where they were in unreformed Britain, 'immured in their families, groping in the dark' (Wollstonecraft 1975a, p. 5).

Rousseau had set the terms of the debate in his *Emile* (1762), which describes the growth and education of the new man, progressive and bourgeois, who would be capable of exercising the republican freedoms of a reformed society. In Book V, Rousseau invents 'Sophie' as a mate for his eponymous hero, and here he outlines his theory of sexual asymmetry as it occurs in nature. In all human beings passion was natural and necessary, but in women it was not controlled by reason, an attribute of the male sex only. Women, therefore,

> must be subject all their lives, to the most constant and severe restraint, which is that of decorum; it is therefore necessary to accustom them early to such confinement that it may not afterwards cost them too dear. . . . we should teach them above all things to lay a due restraint on themselves. (Rousseau 1974, p. 332)

To justify this restraint, Rousseau allowed enormous symbolic power to the supposed anarchic, destructive force of untrammelled female desire. As objects of desire Rousseau made women alone responsible for male 'suffering.' If they were free agents of desire, there would be no end to the 'evils' they could cause. Therefore the family, and women's maternal role within it, were, he said, basic to the structure of the new society. Betrayal of the family was thus as subversive as betrayal of the state; adultery in *Emile* is literally equated with treason. Furthermore, in Rousseau's regime of regulation and restraint for bourgeois women, their 'decorum'—the social expression of modesty—would act as an additional safeguard against unbridled, excessive male lust, should its natural guardian, reason, fail. In proscribing the free exercise of female desire, Rousseau disarms a supposed serious threat to the new political as well as social order. To read the fate of a class through the sexual behaviour of its women was not a new political strategy. What is modern in Rousseau's formulation is the harnessing of these sexual ideologies to the fate of a new progressive bourgeoisie, whose individual male members were endowed with radical, autonomous identity.

In many ways, Mary Wollstonecraft, writing thirty years after *Emile*, shared with many others the political vision of her master. Her immediate contemporary Thomas Paine thought Rousseau's work expressed 'a loveliness of sentiment in favour of liberty,' and it is in the spirit of Rousseau's celebration of liberty that Wollstonecraft wrote *A Vindication*. Her strategy was to accept Rousseau's description of adult women as suffused in sensuality, but to ascribe this unhappy state of things to culture rather than nature. It was, she thought, the vicious and damaging result of Rousseau's punitive theories of sexual difference and female education when put into practice. Excessive sensuality was for Wollstonecraft, in 1792 at least, as dangerous if not more so than Rousseau had suggested, but she saw the damage and danger first of all to women themselves, whose potential and independence were intially stifled and broken by an apprenticeship to pleasure, which induced psychic and social dependency. Because Wollstonecraft saw pre-pubescent children in their natural state as mentally and emotionally unsexed as well as untainted by corrupting desire, she bitterly refuted Rousseau's description of innate infantile female sexuality. Rather, the debased femininity she describes is constructed through a set of social practices which by constant reinforcement become internalized parts of the self. Her description of this process is acute:

> Every thing they see or hear serves to fix impressions, call forth emotions, and associate ideas, that give a sexual character to the mind. . . . This cruel association of ideas, which every thing conspires to twist into all their habits of thinking, or, to speak with more precision of feeling, receives new force when they begin to act a little for themselves. (Wollstonecraft 1975a, p. 177)

For Wollstonecraft, female desire was a contagion caught from the projection of male lust, an ensnaring and enslaving infection that made women into dependent and degenerate creatures, who nevertheless had the illusion that they acted independently. An education which changed women from potentially rational autonomous beings into 'significant objects of desire' was, moreover, rarely reversible. Once a corrupt subjectivity was constructed, only a most extraordinary individual could transform it, for 'so ductile is the understanding and yet so stubborn, that the association which depends on adventitious circumstances, during the period that the body takes to arrive at maturity, can seldom be disentangled by reason' (p. 116).

What is disturbingly peculiar to *A Vindication* is the undifferentiated and central place that sexuality as passion plays in the corruption and degradation of the female self. The overlapping Enlightenment and Romantic discourses on psychic economy all posed a major division between the rational and the irrational, between sense and sensibility. But they hold sensibility *in men* to be only in part an antisocial sexual drive. Lust for power and the propensity to physical violence were also, for men, negative components of all that lay on the other side of reason. Thus sensibility in men included a strong positive element too, for the power of the imagination depended on it, and in the 1790s the Romantic aesthetic and the political imagination were closely allied. Sexual passion controlled and mediated by reason, Wordsworth's 'emotion recollected in tranquility,' could also be put to productive use in art—by men. The appropriate egalitarian subjects of Wordsworth's art were 'moral sentiments and animal sensations' as they appeared in everyday life (Wordsworth and Coleridge 1971, p. 261). No woman of the time could offer such an artistic manifesto. In women the irrational, the sensible, even the imaginative are all drenched in an overpowering and subordinating sexuality. And in Wollstonecraft's writing, especially in her last, unfinished novel *Maria, or the Wrongs of Woman* (1798), which is considerably less punitive about women's sexuality in general than *A Vindication*, only maternal feeling survives as a positively realized element of the passionate side of the psyche. By defending women against Rousseau's denial of their reason, Wollstonecraft unwittingly assents to his negative, eroticized sketch of their emotional lives. At various points in *A Vindication* she interjects a wish that 'after some future revolution in time' women might be able to live out a less narcissistic and harmful sexuality. Until then they must demand an education whose central task is to cultivate their neglected 'understanding.'

It is interesting and somewhat tragic that Wollstonecraft's paradigm of women's psychic economy still profoundly shapes modern feminist consciousness. How often are the maternal, romantic-sexual and intellectual capacity of women presented by feminism as in competition for a fixed psychic space. Men seem to have a roomier and more accommodating psychic home, one which can, as Wordsworth and other Romantics insisted, situate all the varieties of passion and reason in creative tension. This gendered eighteenth-century psychic economy has been out of date for a long time, but its ideological inscription still shadows feminist attitudes towards the mental life of women.

The implications of eighteenth-century theories of subjectivity were important for early feminist ideas about women as readers and writers. In the final pages of *A Vindication*, decrying female sentimentality as one more effect of women's psychic degradation, Wollstonecraft criticizes the sentimental fictions increasingly written by and for women, which were often their only education. 'Novels' encouraged in their mainly young, mainly female audience 'a romantic twist of the mind.' Readers would 'only be taught to look for happiness in love, refine on sensual feelings and adopt metaphysical notions respecting that passion.' At their very worst the 'stale tales' and 'meretricious scenes' would by degrees induce more than passive fantasy. The captive, addicted reader might, while the balance of her mind was disturbed by these erotic evocations, turn fiction into fact and 'plump into actual vice' (p. 183). A reciprocal relationship between the patriarchal socialization of women and the literature that supports and incites them to become 'rakes at heart' is developed in this passage. While Wollstonecraft adds that she would rather women read novels than nothing at all, she sets up a peculiarly gendered and sexualized interaction between women and the narrative imaginative text, one in which women become the ultimately receptive readers easily moved into amoral activity by the fictional representation of sexual intrigue.

The political resonance of these questions about reader response was, at the time, highly charged. An enormous expansion of literacy in general, and of the middle-class reading public in particular, swelled by literate women, made the act of reading in the last quarter of the eighteenth century an important practice through which the common sense and innate virtue of a society of autonomous subject-citizens could be reached and moulded. An uncensored press, cheap and available reading matter and a reading public free to engage with the flood of popular literature, from political broadsheets to sensational fiction, was part of the agenda and strategy of British republicanism. 'It is dangerous,' Tom Paine warned the government in the mid-1790s after his own writing had been politically censored, 'to tell a whole people that they should not read.' Reading was a civil right that supported and illustrated the radical vision of personal independence. Political and sexual conservatives, Jane Austen and Hannah More, as well as the republican and feminist left, saw reading as an active, not a passive function of the self, a critical link between the psychic play of reason and passion and its social expression. New social categories of readers, women of all classes, skilled and unskilled working-class males, are described in this period by contemporaries. Depending on their political sympathies, observers saw these actively literate groups as an optimistic symptom of social and intellectual progress or a dire warning of imminent social decay and threatened rebellion.

Wollstonecraft saw sentiment and the sensual as reinforcing an already dominant, approved and enslaving sexual norm, which led women to choose a subordinate social and subjective place in culture. The damage done by 'vice' and 'adultery,' to which sentimental fiction was an incitement, was a blow to women first and to society second. Slavish legitimate sexuality was almost as bad for women in Wollstonecraft's view as unlicensed behaviour. A more liberal regime for women was both the goal and the cure of sentimental and erotic malaise. In *A Vindication* women's subjection is repeatedly compared to all illegitimate hierarchies of power, but especially to existing aristocratic hegemony. At every possible point in her text, Wollstonecraft links the liberation of women from the sensual into the rational literally and symbolically to the egalitarian transformation of the whole society.

'Passionlessness,' as Nancy Cott has suggested (Cott 1978), was a strategy adopted both by feminists and by social conservatives. Through the assertion that women were not innately or excessively sexual, that on the contrary their 'feelings' were largely filial and maternal, the imputation of a degraded subjectivity could be resisted. This alternative psychic organization was represented as both strength and weakness in nineteenth-century debates about sexual difference. In these debates, which were conducted across a wide range of public discourses, the absence of an independent, self-generating female sexuality is used by some men and women to argue for women's right to participate equally in an undifferentiated public sphere. It is used by others to argue for the power and value of the separate sphere allotted to women. And it is used more nakedly to support cruder justifications of patriarchal right. The idea of passionlessness as either a natural or a cultural effect acquires no simple ascendancy in Victorian sexual ideology, even as applied to the ruling bourgeoisie.

As either conservative or radical sexual ideology, asexual femininity was a fragile, unstable concept. It was constructed through a permanently threatened transgression, which fictional narrative obsessively documented and punished. It is a gross historical error to infer from the regulatory sexual discourses in the novel the actual 'fate' of Victorian adulteresses, for novels operated through a set of highly punitive conventions in relation to female sexuality that almost certainly did not correspond to lived social relations. However, novels do call attention to the difficulty of fixing such a sexual ideology, precisely because they construct a world in which there is no alternative to it.

IV

One of the central weaknesses of humanist criticism is that it accepts the idea advanced by classical realism that the function of literature is mimetic or realistic representation. The humanist critic identifies with the author's claim that the text represents reality, and acts as a sympathetic reader who will test the authenticity of the claim through the evidence of the text. The Marxist critic, on the other hand, assumes that author and text speak from a position within ideology—that claims about fictional truth and authenticity are, in themselves, to be understood in relation to a particular historical view of culture and art which evolved in the Romantic period. Semiotic and psychoanalytic theories of representation go even further in rejecting the possibility of authentic mimetic art. They see the literary text as a system of signs that constructs meaning rather than reflecting it, inscribing simultaneously the subjectivity of speaker and reader. Fiction by bourgeois women writers is spoken from the position of a class-specific femininity. It constructs us as readers in relation to that subjectivity through the linguistic strategies and processes of the text. It also takes us on a tour, so to speak, of a waxworks of other subjects-in-process—the characters of the text. These fictional characters are there as figures in a dream, as constituent structures of the narrative of the dreamer, not as correct reflections of the socially real.

It is hard for feminism to accept the implications of this virtual refusal of textual realism, if only because literature was one of the few public discourses in which women were allowed to speak themselves, where they were not the imaginary representations of men. None the less, the subjectivity of women of other classes and races and with different sexual orientations can never be 'objectively' or 'authentically' represented in literary texts by the white, heterosexual, middle-class woman writer, however sympathetically she invents or describes such women in her narrative. The nature of fiction and the eccentric relation of female subjectivity itself both to culture and to psychic identity, as understood from a psychoanalytic perspective, defeats that aim. We can, however, learn a great deal from women's writing about the cultural meanings produced from the splitting of women's subjectivity, especially her sexuality, into class and race categories. But before we say more about this way of reading women's writing we need a more precise working definition of 'class.'

Unlike subjectivity, 'class' has been a central category for socialist feminist criticism, but remains somewhat inert within it, if not within socialist feminist theory as a whole. Socialist critics hesitate to identify their own object of study, the literary text, as a central productive site of class meaning, because it seems too far away from 'real' economic and political determinations. The same worry, conversely, can induce a compensatory claim that *all* the material relations of class can be discovered within the discourse: indeed, that they are most fully represented there, because language is itself material. These positions, which I confess I have parodied a little, remain unresolved in current debate, although efforts at *détente* have been made. They indicate the uneasy relationship between the political and the literary in the Marxist critical project, an unease shared by socialist feminists too.

Among socialist historians in the last few years the understanding of the history of class has undergone vigorous reappraisal in response to debates about the changing composition and politics of the working class in modern capitalist societies. In a recent collection of essays, *The Languages of Class*, the British historian of the nineteenth century, Gareth Stedman Jones, proposes some radical approaches to that history which have an immediate relevance for the analysis of representation. First of all, Stedman Jones asks for a more informed and theoretical attention by historians to the linguistic construction of class. '"Class" is a word embedded in language and should be analysed in terms of its linguistic content,' he states. In the second place, 'class' as a concept needs to be unpacked, and its differential construction in discourse recognized and given a certain autonomy:

> because there are different languages of class, one should not proceed upon the assumption that 'class' as an elementary counter of official social description, 'class' as an effect of theoretical discourse about distribution or productive relations, 'class' as the summary of a cluster of culturally signifying practices or 'class' as a species of political or ideological self-definition, share a single reference point in anterior social reality. (Stedman Jones 1983, pp. 7–8)

While 'anterior social reality' hangs slightly loose in this formulation, the oppressively unitary character of class as a concept is usefully broken down. Class can be seen as defined in different terms at different levels of analysis, as well as being 'made' and 'lived' through a variety of languages at any given point in history.

How can this pulling apart of the languages of class help socialist feminist critics to put class and gender, social and psychic together in a non-reductive way? First of all, these distinctions put a useful space between the economic overview of class—the Marxist or socialist analysis—and the actual rhetoric of class as it appears in a novel. The class language of a nineteenth-century novel is not only or even primarily characterized by reference to the material circumstances of the protagonists, though that may be part of its representation there. The language of class in the novel foregrounds the language of the self, the inner discourse of the subject *as* class language, framing that discourse through the dissonant chorus of class voices that it appropriates and invents. In the novel, class discourse *is* gendered discourse; the positions of 'Emile' and 'Sophie' are given dramatic form. Class is embodied in fiction in a way that it never is either in bourgeois economic discourse or in Marxist economic analysis. In those discourses of class, gender is mystified, presented in ideological form. In fiction, though difference may be presented through sexual ideologies, its immanent, crucial presence in the social relations of class, as well as its psychic effects, is strongly asserted. Fiction refuses the notion of a genderless class subjectivity, and resists any simple reduction of class meaning and class identity to productive forces. This refusal and resistance cannot be written off, or reduced to the humanist ideologies of transcendence which those fictions may also enunciate, for the presence of gendered subjectivity in nineteenth-century fiction is always 'in struggle' with the Romantic ideologies of unified identity.

Within socialist feminist cultural analysis it has been easier to describe the visual or linguistic fusion of class and gender meanings in representation than it has been to assess the role such fusion plays in the construction of either category. Let us assume that in these signifying practices class is powerfully defined through sexual difference, and vice versa, and that these representations are constitutive of certain class meanings, not merely a distorted or mendacious reflection of other languages. 'Class' needs to be read through an ensemble of these languages, often contradictory, as well as in terms of an economic overview. The overpowering presence of gender in some languages of class and its virtual absence in others needs to be related not to a single anterior definition of class reality, but to the heterogeneous and contradictory nature of that reality.

Literature is itself a heterogeneous discourse, which appropriates, contextualizes and comments on other 'languages' of class and gender. This process of intertextuality—the dialogic, as the Russian critic Bakhtin called it (Bakhtin 1981)—undermines the aspirations of the text towards a unifying definition. The language of class in the nineteenth-century novel obsessively inscribes a class system whose divisions and boundaries are at once absolute and impregnable and in constant danger of dissolution. Often in these narratives it is a woman whose class identity is at risk or problematic; the woman and her sexuality are a condensed and displaced representation of the dangerous instabilities of class and gender identity for both sexes. The loss and recuperation of female identity within the story—a favourite lost-and-found theme from *Mansfield Park* to *Tess*—provides an imaginary though temporary solution to the crisis of both femininity and class. Neither category—class or gender—was ever as stable as the ideologies that support them must continually insist. The many-layered, compacted representations of class and gender found in imaginative literature are not generic metaphors, peculiar to fiction, drama and poetry, though in them they are given great scope. They occur in many other nineteenth-century discourses—metonymic, associative tropes which are linked by incomparable similarities, through a threat to identity and status that inheres to both sets of hierarchies, both structures of difference.

The class subjectivity of women and their sexual identity thus became welded together in nineteenth-century discourses and took on new and sinister dimensions of meaning. Ruling groups had traditionally used the sexual and domestic virtue of their women as a way of valorizing their moral authority. By focusing on the issue and image of female sexual conduct, questions about the economic and political integrity of dominant groups could be displaced. When the citizen subject became the crucial integer of political discourse and practice, this type of symbolization, which was always 'about' sexual difference as well as 'about' the political, took on new substantive, material meaning. The moral autonomy of individuals and the moral behaviour of social groups now converged in a political practice and theory—liberal, constitutional and legitimated through an expanding franchise—in which the individual voter was the common denominator of the political. Women, as we have seen, were explicitly excluded from these political practices, but, as we have also seen, attempts to naturalize that exclusion were never wholly successful. Feminism inserted itself into the debate just at the point where theories of innate difference attempted to deny women access to a full political identity. The debate about women's mental life signalled, as I have suggested, a more general anxiety about non-rational, unsocial behaviour. Female subjectivity, or its synecdotal reference, female sexuality, became the displaced and condensed site for the general anxiety about individual behaviour which republican and liberal political philosophy stirred up. It is not too surprising that the morality of the class as a whole was better represented by those who exercised the least political power within it, or that the punishment for female sexual transgression was fictionally represented as the *immediate* loss of social status.

The ways in which class is lived by men and women, like the ways in which sexual difference is lived, are only partly open to voluntary, self-conscious political negotiation. The unconscious processes that construct subjective identity are also the structures through which class is lived and understood, through which political subjection and rebellion are organized. Arguing for the usefulness of psychoanalysis in historical analysis, Sally Alexander emphasizes that its theories do not imply a universal human nature. Rather,

> Subjectivity in this account is neither universal or ahistorical. First structured through relations of absence and loss, pleasure and unpleasure, difference and division, these are simultaneous with the social naming and placing among kin, community, school, class which are always historically specific. (Alexander 1984, p. 134)

Literary texts give these simultaneous inscriptions narrative form, pointing towards and opening up the fragmentary nature of social and psychic identity, drawing out the ways in which social meaning is psychically represented. It is this symbolic shaping of class that we should examine in fiction. Literary texts tell us more about the intersection of class and gender than we can learn from duly noting the material circumstances and social constraints of characters and authors.

However mimetic or realistic the aspirations of fiction, it always tells us less about the purely social rituals of a class society organized around the sexual division of labour than about the powerful symbolic force of class and gender in ordering our social and political imagination. The doubled inscription of sexual and social difference is the most common, characteristic trope of nineteenth-century fictions. In these texts, the difference between women is at least as important an element as the difference between the sexes, as a way of representing both class and gender. This salient fact often goes unnoticed in the emphasis of bourgeois criticism on male/female division and opposition. In turn, this emphasis on heterosexual antagonisms and resolutions effaces the punitive construction of alternative femininities in women's writing. If texts by women reveal a 'hidden' sympathy between women, as radical feminist critics often assert, they equally express positive femininity through hostile and denigrating representations of women. Imperilled bourgeois femininity takes meaning in relation to other female identities, and to the feminized identities of other social groups which the novel constructs and dialogizes. The unfavourable symbiosis of reason and passion ascribed to women is also used to characterize both men and women in the labouring classes and in other races and cultures. The line between the primitive and the degraded feminine is a thin one, habitually elided in dominant discourse and practically used to limit the civil and political rights of all three subordinated categories: blacks, women and the working class.

Through that chain of colonial associations, whole cultures became 'feminized,' 'blackened' and 'impoverished'—each denigrating construction implying and invoking the others. 'True womanhood' had to be protected from this threatened linguistic contamination, not only from the debased subjectivity and dangerous sexuality of the lower-class prostitute, but from all other similarly inscribed subordinate subjectivities. The difference between men and women in the ruling class had to be written so that a slippage into categories reserved for lesser humanities could be averted. These fragmented definitions of female subjectivity were not only a mode through which the moral virtue of the ruling class was represented in the sexual character of its women; they also shaped, and were shaped by, the ways in which women of the middle and upper classes understood and represented their own being. It led them towards projecting and displacing on to women of lower social standing and women of colour, as well as on to the 'traditionally' corrupt aristocracy, all that was deemed vicious and regressive in women as a sex.

It is deeply troubling to find these projected and displaced representations in the writing of sexual and social radicals, and in the work of feminists from Wollstonecraft to Woolf, as well as in conservative sexual and social discourses. They are especially marked in those texts and writers who accept in whole or in part the description of mental life and libidinal economy of the Enlightenment and the moral value attached to it. In *A Vindication*, working-class women are quite unselfconsciously constructed as prostitutes and dirty-minded servants corrupting bourgeois innocence. Turn the page over and you will also find them positioned in a more radical sense as the most brutalized victims of aristocratic and patriarchal despotism. Note the bestial descriptions of the female poor in Elizabeth Barrett Browning's *Aurora Leigh*. Remember the unhappy, ambivalent and contradictory relationship to black subjectivity, male and female, of many mid-nineteenth-century American feminists and abolitionists. Most distressing of all, because nearer to us in time, think about the contrast between Woolf's public polemical support of working-class women and the contempt with which the feelings and interests of her female servants are treated in her diaries, where they exist as lesser beings. These representations are neither natural nor inevitable. They are the historic effects of determinate social divisions and ideologies worked through psychic structures, worked into sexual and social identity. If they are understood they can be changed.

In Ann Radcliffe's *Mysteries of Udolpho*, one of the most popular of the Enlightenment gothic novels of the 1790s, the heroine, Emily, flees from the sinister importunities of her titled foreign host. The scene is rural Italy, as far away as possible from genteel British society. Emily's flight from the castle is precipitous, and in her terror and haste she forgets her hat. Within the world of the text, Emily's bare head threatens her identity as pure woman, as surely as do the violent, lascivious attentions of her pursuer. Both the narrative and her flight are interrupted while Emily restores her identity by purchasing 'a little straw hat' from a peasant girl. A woman without a hat was, in specular terms, a whore; the contemporary readership understood the necessary pause in the story. They understood too that the hat, passed from peasant to lady, securing the class and sexual status of the latter, was not only a fragment of domestic realism set against gothic fantasy. Hat and flight are part of a perfectly coherent psychic narrative in which aristocratic seducer, innocent bourgeois victim, peasant girl and straw hat play out the linked meanings of class and sexuality.

Stories of seduction and betrayal, of orphaned, impoverished heroines of uncertain class origin, provided a narrative structure through which the instabilities of class and gender categories were both stabilized and undermined. Across the body and mind of 'woman' as sign, through her multiple representations, bourgeois anxiety about identity is traced and retraced. A favourite plot, of which *Jane Eyre* is now the best-known example, sets the genteel heroine at sexual risk as semi-servant in a grand patriarchal household. This narrative theme allowed the crisis of middle-class femininity to be mapped on to the structural sexual vulnerability of all working-class servants in bourgeois employment. Such dramas were full of condensed meanings in excess of the representation of sexuality and sexual difference. A doubled scenario, in which the ideological and material difference between working-class and bourgeois women is blurred through condensation, it was popular as a plot for melodrama with both 'genteel' and 'vulgar' audiences.

We do not know very much so far about how that fictional narrative of threatened femininity was understood by working-class women, although it appeared in the cheap fiction written for servant girls as well as in popular theatre. Nineteenth-century bourgeois novels like *Jane Eyre* tell us almost nothing about the self-defined subjectivity of the poor, male or female. For, although they are both rich sources for the construction of dominant definitions *of* the inner lives of the working classes, they cannot tell us anything about how even these ideological inscriptions were lived *by* them. For an analysis of the subjectivity of working-class women we need to turn to non-literary sources, to the discourses in which they themselves spoke. That analysis lies outside the project of this paper but is, of course, related to it.

I want to end this chapter with an example of the kind of interpretative integration that I have been demanding of feminist critics. No text has proved more productive of meaning from the critic's point of view than Charlotte Brontë's *Jane Eyre*. I have referred to the condensation of class meanings through the characterization and narrative of its heroine, but now I want to turn to that disturbing didactic moment in volume I, chapter 12, which immediately precedes the entry of Rochester into the text. It is a passage marked out by Virginia Woolf in *A Room of One's Own*, where it is used to illustrate the negative effect of anger and inequality on the female literary imagination. Prefaced defensively—'Anybody may blame me who likes'—it is a passage about need, demand and desire that exceed social possibility and challenge social prejudice. In Jane's soliloquy, inspired by a view reached through raising the 'trap-door of the attic,' the Romantic aesthetic is reasserted for women, together with a passionate refusal of the terms of feminine difference. Moved by a 'restlessness' in her 'nature' that 'agitated me to pain sometimes,' Jane paces the top floor of Thornfield and allows her 'mind's eye to dwell on whatever bright visions rose before it':

> to let my heart be heaved by the exultant movement which, while it swelled
> it in trouble, expanded it with life; and, best of all, to open my inward ear to
> a tale that was never ended—a tale my imagination created, and narrated
> continuously; quickened with all of incident, life, fire, feeling, that I desired
> and had not in my actual existence. (Brontë 1976, p. 110)

This reverie is only partly quoted by Woolf, who omits the 'visionary' section, moving straight from 'pain . . .' to the paragraph most familiar to us through her citation of it:

> It is in vain to say that human beings ought to be satisfied with tranquillity; they must have action; and they will make it if they cannot find it. Millions are condemned to a stiller doom than mine, and millions are in silent revolt against their lot. Nobody knows how many rebellions besides political rebellions ferment in the masses of life which people earth. Women are supposed to be very calm generally: but women feel just as men feel; they need exercise for their faculties, and a field for their efforts as much as their brothers do; they suffer from too rigid a restraint, too absolute a stagnation, precisely as men would suffer; and it is narrow-minded in their more privileged fellow-creatures to say that they ought to confine themselves to making puddings and knitting stockings, to playing on the piano and embroidering bags. It is thoughtless to condemn them, or laugh at them, if they seek to do more or learn more than custom has pronounced necessary for their sex.
>   When thus alone I not unfrequently heard Grace Poole's laugh. . . .

This shift from feminist polemic to the laugh of Grace Poole is the 'jerk,' the 'awkward break' of 'continuity' that Woolf criticizes. The writer of such a flawed passage

> will never get her genius expressed whole and entire. Her books will be deformed and twisted. She will write in a rage where she should write calmly. She will write foolishly where she should write wisely. She will write of herself when she should write of her characters. She is at war with her lot. How could she help but die young, cramped and thwarted? (Woolf 1973, p. 70)

It is a devastating, controlled, yet somehow uncontrolled indictment. What elements in this digression, hardly a formal innovation in nineteenth-century fiction, can have prompted Woolf to such excess? Elaine Showalter analyses this passage and others as part of Woolf's 'flight into androgyny,' that aesthetic chamber where masculine and feminine minds meet and marry. Showalter's analysis focuses on Woolf's aesthetic as an effect of her inability to come to terms with her sexuality, with sexual difference itself. Showalter's analysis is persuasive in individual terms, but it does not deal with all of the questions thrown up by Brontë's challenge and Woolf's violent response to it. In the sentences that Woolf omits in her own citation, Brontë insists that even the confined and restless state could produce 'many and glowing' visions. Art, the passage maintains, can be produced through the endless narration of the self, through the mixed incoherence of subjectivity spoken from subordinate and rebellious positions within culture. It was this aesthetic that Woolf as critic explicitly rejected.

However, the passage deals with more than sexual difference. In the references to 'human beings' and to unspecified 'millions,' Brontë deliberately and defiantly associates political and sexual rebellion even as she distinguishes between them. In the passage the generic status of 'men' is made truly trans-class and transcultural when linked to 'masses,' 'millions' and 'human beings,' those larger inclusive terms. In 1847, on the eve of the second great wave of modern revolution, it was a dangerous rhetoric to use.

Its meaningful associations were quickly recognized by contemporary reviewers, who deplored the contiguous relationship between revolution and feminism. Lady Eastlake's comments in the *Quarterly Review* of 1849 are those most
often quoted:

> We do not hesitate to say, that the tone of mind and thought which has over-
> thrown authority and violated every code human and divine abroad, and fos-
> tered chartism and rebellion at home is the same which has also written
> *Jane Eyre*.

Yet Charlotte Brontë was no political radical. She is pulled towards the positive
linking of class rebellion and women's revolt in this passage through her anger at
the misrepresentation and suppression of women's identity, not via an already
held sympathy with the other masses and millions. It is a tentative, partial movement in spite of its defiant rhetoric, and it is checked in a moment by the mad,
mocking female laughter, and turned from its course a few pages later by the
introduction of Rochester into the narrative. For Woolf, Jane's soliloquy spoils
the continuity of the narrative with its 'anger and rebellion.' Woolf turns away,
refuses to comprehend the logical sequence of the narration at the symbolic level
of the novel.

Jane's revolutionary manifesto of the subject, which has its own slightly manic
register, invokes that sliding negative signification of women that we have described. At this point in the story the 'low, slow ha'ha!' and the 'eccentric murmurs' which 'thrilled' Jane are ascribed to Grace Poole, the hard-featured
servant. But Grace is only the laugh's minder, and the laugh later becomes 'correctly' ascribed to Rochester's insane wife, Bertha Mason. The uncertain source
of the laughter, the narrator's inability to predict its recurrence—'There were
days when she was quite silent; but there were others when I could not account
for the sounds she made'—both mark out the 'sounds' as the dark side of Romantic female subjectivity.

Retroactively, in the narratives the laughter becomes a threat to all that Jane
had desired and demanded in her roof-top reverie. Mad servant, mad mistress,
foreigner, nymphomaniac, syphilitic, half-breed, aristocrat, Bertha turns violently on keeper, brother, husband and, finally, rival. She and her noises become
the condensed and displaced site of unreason and anarchy as it is metonymically
figured through dangerous femininity in all its class, race and cultural projections. Bertha must be killed off, narratively speaking, so that a moral, Protestant
femininity, licensed sexuality and a qualified, socialized feminism may survive.
Yet the text cannot close off or recuperate that moment of radical association between political rebellion and gender rebellion, cannot shut down the possibility
of a positive alliance between reason, passion and feminism. Nor can it disperse
the terror that speaking those connections immediately stirs up—for Woolf in
any case.

Woolf was at her most vehement and most contradictory about these issues,
which brought together for her, as for many other feminists before and after, a
number of deeply connected anxieties about subjectivity, class, sexuality and
culture. Over and over again in her critical writing, Woolf tries to find ways of
placing the questions inside an aesthetic that disallows anger, unreason and pas-

sion as productive emotions. Like Wollstonecraft before her, she cannot quite shake off the moral and libidinal economies of the Enlightenment. In 'Women and Fiction' (1929) she frames the question another way:

> In *Middlemarch* and in *Jane Eyre* we are conscious not merely of the writer's character, as we are conscious of the character of Charles Dickens, but we are conscious of a woman's presence—of someone resenting the treatment of her sex and pleading for its rights. This brings into women's writing an element which is entirely absent from a man's, unless, indeed, he happens to be a working man, a Negro, or one who for some other reason is conscious of disability. It introduces a distortion and is frequently the cause of weakness. The desire to plead some personal cause or to make a character the mouthpiece of personal discontent or grievance always has a distressing effect, as if the spot at which the reader's attention is directed were suddenly two-fold instead of single. (Woolf 1979, p. 47)

Note how the plea for a sex, a class, a race becomes reduced to individual, personal grievance, how subordinate position in a group becomes immediately pathologized as private disability, weakness. Note too how 'man' in this passage loses its universal connotation, so that it only refers normatively to men of the ruling class. In this passage, as in *Jane Eyre*, the metonymic evocation of degraded subjectivities is expressed as an effect of subordination, not its rationale nor its cause. But the result is still a negative one. For the power to resist through fictional language, the language of sociality and self; the power to move and enlighten, rather than blur and distress through the double focus, is denied. Instead, Woolf announces the death of the feminist text, by proclaiming, somewhat prematurely, the triumph of feminism.

> The woman writer is no longer bitter. She is no longer angry. She is no longer pleading and protesting as she writes. . . . She will be able to concentrate upon her vision without distraction from outside. (Woolf 1979, p. 48)

This too is a cry from the roof-tops of a desire still unmet by social and psychic experience.

Although the meanings attached to race, class and sexuality have undergone fundamental shifts from Wollstonecraft's (and Woolf's) time to our own, we do not live in a post-class society any more than a post-feminist one. Our identities are still constructed through social hierarchy and cultural differentiation, as well as through those processes of division and fragmentation described in psychoanalytic theory. The identities arrived at through these structures will always be precarious and unstable, though *how* they will be so in the future we do not know. For the moment, women still have a problematic place in both social and psychic representation. The problem for women of woman-as-sign has made the self-definition of women a resonant issue within feminism. It has also determined the restless inability of feminism to settle for humanist definitions of the subject, or for materialism's relegation of the problem to determinations of class only. I have emphasized in this chapter some of the more negative ways in which the Enlightenment and Romantic paradigms of subjectivity gave hostage to the making of subordinate identities, of which femininity is the structuring instance. Although psychoanalytic theories of the construction of gendered subjectivity stress difficulty, antagonism and contradiction as necessary parts of the production of identity, the concept of the unconscious and the psychoanalytic view of sexuality dissolve in great part the binary divide between reason and passion that dominates earlier concepts of subjectivity. They break down as well the moralism attached to those libidinal and psychic economies. Seen from this perspective, 'individualism' has a different and more contentious history within feminism than it does in androcentric debates.

It is that history which we must uncover and consider, in both its positive and its negative effects, so that we can argue convincingly for a feminist rehabilitation of the female psyche in non-moralized terms. Perhaps we can come to see it as neither sexual outlaw, social bigot nor dark hiding-place for treasonable regressive femininity waiting to stab progressive feminism in the back. We must redefine the psyche as a structure, not as a content. To do so is not to move away from a feminist politics which takes race and class into account, but to move towards a fuller understanding of how these social divisions and the inscription of gender are mutually secured and given meaning. Through that analysis we can work towards change.

WORKS CITED

Alexander, Sally (1984) 'Women, Class and Sexual Difference,' *History Workshop*, 17, pp. 125–49.

Bakhtin, M. M. (1981) *The Dialogic Imagination: Four Essays*, ed. Michael Holquist. Austin, Texas: University of Texas Press.

Brontë, Charlotte (1976) *Jane Eyre* (1847) ed. Margaret Smith. London: Oxford University Press.

Cott, Nancy F. (1978) 'Passionlessness: An Interpretation of Victorian Sexual Ideology, 1790–1850,' *Signs*, 2, 2, pp. 219–33.

Hartmann, Heidi (1981) 'The Unhappy Marriage of Marxism and Feminism: Towards a More Progressive Union.' In Lydia Sargent (ed.), *The Unhappy Marriage of Marxism and Feminism: A Debate on Class and Patriarchy*, pp. 1–42. London: Pluto Press.

Jacobus, Mary (1979) 'The Buried Letter: Feminism and Romanticism in *Villette*.' In Mary Jacobus (ed.), *Women Writing and Writing about Women*, pp. 42–60. London: Croom Helm.

Marxist-Feminist Literature Collective (1978) 'Women's Writing: *Jane Eyre, Shirley, Villette, Aurora Leigh*.' In *1848: The Sociology of Literature*, proceedings of the Essex conference on the Sociology of Literature (July 1977), pp. 185–206.

Newton, Judith Lowder (1981) *Women, Power, and Subversion: Social Strategies in British Fiction 1778–1860*. Athens, Ga.: University of Georgia Press.

Radcliffe, Ann (1966) *The Mysteries of Udolpho* (1794). London: Oxford University Press.

Robinson, Lillian S. (1978) 'Dwelling in Decencies: Radical Criticism and the Feminist Perspective.' In *Sex, Class and Culture*, pp. 3–21. Bloomington, Ind.: Indiana University Press.

Rousseau, Jean-Jacques (1974) *Emile* (1762). London: Dent.

Said, Edward W. (1978) *Orientalism*. London: Routledge & Kegan Paul.

Stedman Jones, Gareth (1983) *Languages of Class: Studies in English Working Class History 1832–1982*. Cambridge: Cambridge University Press.

Wollstonecraft, Mary (1975a) *A Vindication of the Rights of Woman* (1792). New York: Norton.

Wollstonecraft, Mary (1975b) *Maria, or The Wrongs of Woman* (1798). New York: Norton.

Woolf, Virginia (1973) *A Room of One's Own* (1929). Harmondsworth: Penguin.
Woolf, Virginia (1979) 'Women and Fiction.' In Michèle Barrett (ed.), *Women and Writing*, pp. 44–52. London: Women's Press.
Wordsworth, William, and Coleridge, Samuel Taylor (1971) *Lyrical Ballads* (1798, 1800), ed. R. L. Brett and A. R. Jones. London: Methuen.

ROMANCE IN THE AGE OF ELECTRONICS
harlequin enterprises

Harlequin, as it advertises itself, is the "world's no. 1 publisher of romance fiction!" Like its imitators and rivals, Dell's Candlelight Romances, Bantam's Loveswept, and Simon and Schuster's Silhouette Romances, Harlequin turns out on its giant, computerized printing presses an ever increasing number of uniformly jacketed and uniformly written romantic narratives per month.[1] Formerly a moderately successful Canadian publishing house, in 1971 it hired Lawrence Heisley, a Proctor and Gamble marketing man, as its new president. He turned feminine romantic love into superprofits for his then all-male board of directors by transferring to the sale of books the techniques used to sell detergent to housewives. By turning love into a consumer product, Harlequin increased its net earnings from $110,000 in 1970 to over $21 million by 1980.

But packaging alone cannot account for the loyalty of 14 million readers. The novels' flyleaf assures readers that "no one touches the heart of a woman quite like Harlequin," and marketing statistics—188 million books sold in 1980, sales accounting for 30 percent of all mass market paperbooks in a major bookstore chain—support this claim.[2] What exactly is the secret to a woman's heart that Harlequin and its rivals have learned, and how have they turned this knowledge into profits for themselves?

SECRETS OF A WOMAN'S HEART

Harlequin may owe its dramatic growth in popularity to the fact that the romances now respond to specific needs of working women. Focusing on the juncture between their sexual, emotional needs on the one hand and their needs concerning work relations on the other, it involves both their deepest, most private, most intimate feelings, and at the same time their very broad relations to the process of social history. Impressive analyses by Tania Modleski, Ann Barr Snitow, and Janice A. Radway[3] have explained the popularity of mass market romances by examining how they respond to women's deep yearnings, but have not talked about why these romances have gained their phenomenal popularity just in the last ten to fifteen years. Moreover, in the past couple of years, since

Snitow and Modleski wrote their studies, the romance industry has been undergoing an accelerated process of change. Given the fact that their heroines' stories increasingly join the personal, sexual relations of private life to the work relations of the marketplace, we might ask what in the Harlequin formula responds to new needs of women as a result of recent profound changes in both their domestic and paid labor situations, and how that formula might change in the future.

As Harlequin Romances have become more popular, more and more of their heroines have jobs. Yet these working heroines have more subversive desires than simply to join the labor force: they are reacting to the limits of a sterile, harsh, alienating, fragmented work world itself. In spite of some fairly glamorous jobs, the working Harlequin heroines, melodramatically engaged in defiant struggles with their heroes—who are usually their bosses—demand from them and their world two additional changes in their situation. First, as the heroine struggles against the irresistible power of her hero, she also struggles *for* something, which she calls "love," but beyond that does not define any further. What she wants from the hero is recognition of herself as a unique, exceptional individual. In addition to acknowledging her sexual attraction and her professional competence, he must also recognize her as a subject, or recognize her from her own point of view.

Second, the heroines seek more than simply to succeed in the man's world. An analysis of the romances will show that on an implicit level they seek not so much an improved life within the possibilities of the existing social structure, but a different social structure. The very facts that the hero is both boss and lover, that the world of work and business is romanticized and eroticized, and that in it love flourishes suggest that the Harlequin heroines seek an end to the division between the domestic world of love and sentiment and the public world of work and business.

Since in Harlequin the struggle to gain recognition for a deep feminine self merges with the struggle—however implicit or utopian—to create a new, more integrated world, a reading of these romances uncovers a certain power possessed by even formulaic narratives. Because they cannot help but recount a woman's life all of a piece, they may be able to reveal certain insights about women's lives and women's desires that escape empirical science. These romance narratives show us that an individual woman's need to be recognized in her own sense of self and the need to change a more global social structure are interdependent.

In *Loving with a Vengeance: Mass-Produced Fantasies for Women*, Tania Modleski says that "in Harlequin Romances, the need of women to find meaning and pleasure in activities which are not wholly male-centered such as work or artistic creation is generally scoffed at."[4] But in the past few years that has changed. Although in the mid-seventies, the average Harlequin heroine was either just emerging from home, or was a secretary or nurse who quit her unrewarding job at marriage, by the late seventies, many Harlequin heroines had unusual and interesting, if not bizarre careers. More and more frequently both hero and heroine started taking the heroine's job or creative activity seriously.

Almost never images of passive femininity, the heroines of the late seventies are active, intelligent, and capable of at least economic independence. Nicole, in *Across the Great Divide,* is a dedicated and competent swimming coach; Anna, in *Battle with Desire,* is an internationally known violinist at the age of twenty-two;

Kerry, in *The Dividing Line*, also twenty-two, is on the board of directors of a prestigious department store. Furthermore, the hero often gives moral support to the heroine in her career, and intends to continue supporting her career aspirations after their marriage.[5]

By the early eighties, the heroines' careers go beyond the wildest dreams of the most ardent National Organization for Women member and often become the selling point that distinguishes one romance from another. As one example, Danni in *Race for Revenge* is about to "succeed triumphantly in the male dominated world of motor racing,"[6] and Karla Mortley in Candlelight Romance's *Game Plan* "joins the rugged New York Flyers as a ballet trainer" only to find that "the womanizing quarterback MacGregor proves hard to tackle."[7] In 1984 Harlequin added to its line a new, more sophisticated series, Harlequin Temptations, where the hero worries that the heroine will place her career before him. In the romances of the mid-eighties the careers range from the banal, like movie actresses and famous pop singers, to the unique, like engineering Ph.D. Frankie Warburton in *Love Circuit*, who falls in love with the electronics heir that contracts for her services as a computer consultant. More than one heroine is an advertising executive who falls in love with her client. University editorial assistant Liza Manchester in *Public Affair* is an "outspoken member of Graham University's feminist community" who falls in love with Professor Scott Harburton. And—inevitably—Garbriella Constant in *By Any Other Name* is a best-selling romance writer who falls in love with her publisher.[8]

Although the hero of these romances is not always the heroine's boss, he most often either is the boss or holds a position of economic or professional power over the heroine. More important, as the advertising brochure for the new Harlequin Temptation series demonstrates, the boss figure remains the prototype for the Harlequin hero. Promising to let us experience "The passionate torment of a woman torn between two loves . . . the siren call of a career . . . the magnetic advances of an impetuous employer. . . ," it advertises its flagship novel of the new series, *First Impressions*, by saying: "Tracy Dexter couldn't deny her attraction to her new boss."[9]

Because in Harlequin Romances, plot, characters, style, and erotic scenes have been set by formula, freedom to vary the heroine's job gives an author one of the few avenues for bringing originality, individuality, and creative freedom into a romance. An unusual job offers compositional opportunities for an unusual setting and unusual conflicts between the hero and heroine. But the job situation also serves a deeper purpose. Beyond showing the uncanny ability of mass culture to ingest any kind of social, economic, or cultural historic change in women's lives, these heroines with their fabulous jobs might help to explain why women respond to romance so much more massively than to other mass market reading. New Right how-to books exhort their readers to be "real" women by staying home to protect the family; liberal how-to books, such as *The Cinderella Complex*, urge women to cease wanting to "be *part* of somebody else" and "to get into the driver's seat" of "the man's world";[10] and women's magazines claim to show readers how to excel in each separate segment—sex, work, family, emotion—of their madly disarticulated, schizophrenic lives. Supermarket romances, alone among mass market literature, focus on the conflictive relations among these segments.

WOMEN'S WORK/WOMEN'S CULTURE

The same socioeconomic changes of the 1960s and 1970s, which created a new kind of working woman, also created the conditions for Harlequin's commercial success. These are, according to Harry Braverman in *Labor and Monopoly Capital*, the restructuring of business into huge international conglomerates; the "extraordinary growth of commercial concerns" (like Harlequin) in comparison with production; and along with this the extraordinary explosion of bureaucracy and office work with its systems management, computerization, and assembly-line processing of paper.[11] These conditions include new categories of work, and, occurring around 1960, "the creation of a new class of workers," low-paid clerical workers, overwhelmingly female. According to Roslyn L. Feldbert and Evelyn Nakano Glenn, between 1960 and 1980, employment in clerical and kindred occupations doubled. They cite dramatic growth in work categories created by the new technology, and also by the business expansion that Braverman describes.[12]

The women who work for these huge conglomerates and bureaucracies, in clerical positions, in service positions, and as assemblers of the new electronic machinery, as well as the women whose shopping, banking, education, medical care, and welfare payments have been changed by these new developments, constitute a large part of the readership of Harlequin Romances. And the musicians, painters, poets, coaches, car racers, Olympic athletes, photographers, and female executives of the romances, with their glamorous jobs, are these readers' idealized alter egos. Although readers are well aware that the romances are unreal fantasies, their passionate attachment to the genre could not be explained without an intense identification with the heroine on the level of ego ideal.

Between 40 and 60 percent of the mass market romance readership works outside the home.[13] The assumption has been that these romances contain housewifely fantasies, but if that is so, then why do so many of them revolve around work situations, however glamorized? Among the many possible reasons for this, the most obvious is that as countless statistics show, almost all these readers can expect to work sometime in their lives, moving in and out of the labor market. Moreover, a good number of them can expect to be single mothers, for at least part of their lives. But these fantasies involving work situations suggest that feminists, and especially feminist organizers, might do away with this categorization of women into working women on the one hand and housewives on the other. The content of Harlequins suggests that the readers, like the heroines, do not compartmentalize their lives in this way, becoming different people when they go to work. Although the immediate concerns caused by workplace or home may be different, our deeper abiding concerns remain the same, whether at home or on the job. To draw a strong division between working women and housewives comes perhaps from applying to women a male model. For the average man, work and home really are very different. At work the man must accept the power of his employer, while at home he is master of his family and finds relaxation. The average woman, on the other hand, finds herself contending with a masculine power both at home and at work. By combining the sexual domination of a lover and the economic domination of an employer in the same masculine figure, Harlequins draw attention to the specificity of the contemporary feminine situation.

In a sensitive study that explains the popularity of mass market romances by interviewing a group of readers from one bookstore, Janice Radway says that women report they read the romances for relaxation and escape. "When asked to specify what they are fleeing from," she says, "they invariably mention the 'pressures' and 'tensions' they experience as wives and mothers." [14] A group of working women I spoke to also said they read the romances to escape. But the escape portrayed in the working heroine's romances is somewhat more precise about the pressures and tensions it aims to soothe.

The heroine's fantasy dilemmas compensate exactly for those elements of women's work in the clerical factories—and for that matter in any factories—that critics of job automation find most oppressive. A reading of Harlequin Romances in the context of these critiques yields insights into the heroine's (and perhaps the author's and readers') conflicts; their grievances against their living, working, and sexual situations; and the intensity with which they feel these grievances, but also into the extent to which the romances and their authors have adopted the basic corporate structure of present work relations as the invisible and unchallenged framework of their romantic vision.

Two themes of revolt and fantasy escape that run most strongly through the romances concern the depersonalization of the cybernetic world and the powerlessness of the feminine individual within it. Surprisingly enough, the heroine's lack of power and freedom corresponds rather closely to what sociologists have found out about the worker's lack of power and freedom in the computerized and bureaucritized workplace. According to Braverman, contemporary clerical workers and low-paid factory workers suffer from a lack of control over the work process, over the social use to which products will be put, over their own mental processes, and even over their own bodies. The assmbly line structuring of clerical work, says Braverman, results from applying to office work the techniques of Taylorism, which factory owners began using in the 1920s and 1930s to gain maximum efficiency by breaking down the unity of the labor process into its smallest discrete elements. While Taylorization yields greater productivity, its effects on the worker, whose tasks and bodily movements are also broken down to their smallest elements, are devastating.

With every movement of the office worker or lower paid assembler controlled for maximum efficiency, and every moment of her day accounted for, she has lost all decision-making power not only over the products she is making, but also even over her own bodily movements and minutest scheduling of her own time. Braverman talks about clerical workers feeling "shackled" and quotes a vice-president of an insurance company as saying of a room full of key punchers: "'All they lack is a chain!'" [15] Ida Russakoff Hoos, in *Automation in the Office*, reports interviewing a supervisor who described key punchers keeping supplies of tranquilizers in their desks and feeling "frozen." [16] And Ellen Cantarow cites findings of "appalling rates of coronary heart disease in women clerical workers" [17] as a result of lack of control.

The force of Harlequin comes from its ability to combine, often in the same image, the heroine's fantasy escape from these restraints and her idealized, romanticized, and eroticized compliance with them. It does this through diverse types of story elements, which are remarkably consistent from romance to romance. At first and most simple compensation of the readers' situation is that by contrast to the jobs most working readers have, the jobs of Harlequin heroines, while greatly varied, almost always have in common that the work is meaningful in itself, challenging, has a direct effect on the well-being of other people, is a craft that requires skill or talent, and is one that gains recognition for a job well done. A second, slightly more complex compensatory fantasy is that Harlequin heroines do fight for, and win, control over their jobs and a great deal of freedom.

A central, and one of the most attractive, compensations offered by Harlequin is that the romances respond to the depersonalization of the Harlequin reader's life, not only in her workplace, but also in her shopping, her banking, in her relations to government, to school, and to all the services she now obtains from giant, faceless bureaucracies, which make her feel, as Tessa in *The Enchanted Island* thinks, "like a small, impersonal cog in a machine." [18] The relations between the heroines and their bosses may be love/hate relations, but they are intensely intimate. Although decisions about how the reader spends her time in the corporate workplace are made by real men, she never sees them. In the conglomerate, the real decision makers may be in another state or another country, and in terms of the corporate hierarchy, they are in another universe. They are so removed from the secretary or assembler as to seem disembodied gods. In the world of Harlequin, the god descends from the executive suite and comes to her.

But in addition to this direct compensation for the depersonalized relations of the corporate world, the working heroines also idealize the reader's sense that she herself has been reduced to one more interchangeable part of the office's "integrated systems." In *Battle with Desire* Gareth the hero, who is also violinist Anna's conductor, tells her: "You and I together, Anna, will give them a performance they'll never forget. . . . The music will be a prelude to our love" (p. 157). Yet Anna is hurt and asks herself: "But was it love for herself, or because she had been the instrument of such superb music?" Although Anna's position is a highly idealized fantasy, it raises the same conflict experienced by those women in Hoos's study who feel their bosses regard them (if at all!) as an instrument or a part of the machinery.

A fourth and still more complex compensation concerns directly the theme of power. In the romances, the heroine fights ardently against the power the hero has over her. Because the power figure represents both her lover and her boss, this relation between one man and one woman reverberates on a larger network of social relations, all structured according to inequality of power. Thus the boss-lover can become an analogy for other men in the reader's life, such as her husband. The heroines reject the dependence or submissiveness that is most often forced upon their resisting spirit: Nicole in *Across the Great Divide* finds in her new boss Lang "something too suggestive of a rugged relentlessness . . . that she just couldn't bring herself to suffer meekly and which set her on the offensive." In her own mind, she rejects arrogant hierarchies, and when the board of the swim club threatens to fire her, "she was determined not to submit tamely. If she was going down, she would be going down fighting!" (pp. 30, 165).

In the most complex and contradictory of story elements, the romances combine in one image an escape from the "frozen" feeling of working readers and an eroticized acquiescence to it. The heroine's struggle-filled, stormy relationship with the hero involves a strange combination of tempestuous physical movement and physical restraint by the hero. In one of dozens of examples, Nicole, in *Across the Great Divide*, struggles with Lang.

> "I hate the lot of you!" she sobbed brokenly. "And don't touch me!" trying to jerk out of his hold. "You're all a load of two faced liars, only interested in your own egotistical aims." Then, when he didn't release her, "I said don't *touch* me!" as she began pummelling violently at his broad chest.
>
> "For God's sake, Nicky!" Lange gripped her wrists grimly in one hand and wrenched open the car door with the other. "Get in," he muttered, and bundled her flailing figure on to the back seat. Slamming the door behind them, he pinned her helplessly to his muscular form until she had exhausted her struggles and consented to stay there, crying quietly. (p. 140)

The "shackles" of the office or factory job are on the one hand compensated for by vigorous movement; on the other hand they are romanticized and eroticized. The hero restrains the heroine not out of an impersonal desire for efficiency, but out of a very personal desire to have her respond to him. He restrains her in an attempt to control her anger, to arouse her sexually, to fulfill his burning desire to have her confess her feelings for him, or all three. The heroine's anxiety no longer has its source in the cold, nagging, unpleasant fear that her boss will fire her if she rebels (or that her husband will reject her or worse) but in the warm, seductive, obsessive fear that she will not be able to resist his potent sexual magnetism, especially since he goes to considerable effort to create intimate situations where he can exert it. Transformed by the romances, the heroine's restraint becomes on the one hand intermittent, and on the other hand emotionally and sexually gratifying. Instead of having to take tranquilizers to repress her internalized rage, like the office workers in Hoos's study and Cantarow's article, the Harlequin heroine is privileged to vent it violently and directly against her restrainer, even while this restraint takes an idealized form.

This strange mingling of protest and acquiescence to the situation of many contemporary women makes the Harlequin Romances so seductive and so contradictory. On the one hand, the heroine is empowered to revolt without risking masculine rejection because the hero desires her more the angrier she becomes, but on the other hand, the romances also sexualize her impotence. This particular combination of elements intensifies our emotional involvement with a story that both arouses and nullifies the very subversive impulses that attracted us to it in the first place.

CHANGING TIMES, CHANGING CONFLICT

Harlequin's double message is all the more potent in that the heroine's conflict is also double. At stake for her in the romances that put the work situation at the center of the plot is both her social identity and the deepest core of her feminine self. A surprising number of Harlequins employ the same vocabulary to describe the inner conflict of the heroine as she struggles against the hero on his own grounds where he has all the weapons. His main weapon in this idealized world is his powerful sexual attraction; her main weakness is her susceptibility to that attraction, which quickly becomes total love. Her struggle aims to prevent the hero from exploiting her love for his own sexual desires, and the conflict this struggle awakens in her is described by the key words "humiliation" and "pride." Nicole finds that

> the most galling part of the whole episode had been her unqualified surrender to Lang's lovemaking. That she should have so readily submitted—no, welcomed it was far more honest, she confessed painfully—was something she found impossible to accept. The only thought left to salvage at least some of her *pride* being the knowledge that Lang wasn't aware how deeply her feelings were involved. Her *humiliation* was bad enough now, but it would have known no bounds if she had inadvertently revealed how she really felt about him. (p. 144, italics mine.)

In *Stormy Affair* Amber faces the same problem: "She could not say: 'I would love to live here and marry you but only if you say you love me. . . .' At least she still had sufficient *pride* to avoid the *humiliation* such a statement would cause."[19]

Through the heroine's impossible choice between two painful and destructive alternatives, summed up by the terms "humiliation" and "pride," Harlequin Romances call attention to a feminine character structure that differs from the masculine one. Both Radway and Snitow have discussed this feminine character structure in the Harlequin heroine, and both have relied on Nancy Chodorow's theory to analyze it.[20] According to Chodorow, capitalist-patriarchal family structure and childrearing practices produce in boys more strongly defined and closed-off ego boundaries, and in girls more fluid ego boundaries, so that men tend to define themselves as a separate, self-sufficient entity, while women tend to define themselves in terms of their relation to other people. Unable to adopt a rock-like, closed, thinglike self, such as the one the hero seems to possess, the Harlequin heroine's self alternates until the end of the romance between two forms of destruction: "humiliation," which signals a dissolution of her self into the masculine self, and "pride," a self-control that shrivels up her self by denying its needs and desires. Solution: the hero must recognize and adopt the relational, feminine form of the self.

This difference in character structure between women and men, which Harlequins emphasize as the cause of the heroine's problems, is inherited from the industrial revolution. With the separation of work from home, women were socialized to immerse themselves in the intense emotional world of the domestic sphere. Self-perpetuating family practices made that socialization seem like a "natural" feminine character. Now with the cybernetic revolution, women must also, like men, make their way in the rationalistic world of business, but they take with them the emotional makeup they have inherited from the past. They do not have, and in many cases do not want to have, the harder, more competitive, success-oriented emotional equipment with which men have been socialized in order to succeed, or even simply to survive.

If Harlequin heroines' character structure is inherited from the industrial revolution, their narrative structure is also inherited from one of the most prominent literary genres of the industrial revolution, the romantic novel. Although Sally Mitchell and Tania Modleski have traced the genealogy of Harlequin romances back to forms of nineteenth-century popular fiction, such as seduction novels, historical romances, penny magazine aristocratic romances, and gothic novels,[21] the quest for self-fulfillment carried out by the heroes and heroines of nine-teenth-century high romanticism has also found a twentieth-century refuge in contemporary mass market romances. As writer Louella Nelson told me of her romance *Freedom's Fortune:* "This book is about a woman's quest for courage and self-worth."[22]

The inner conflict of the Harlequin heroines is a more explicitly sexualized version of feminine conflicts analyzed by authors writing during the industrial revolution, such as the Brontë sisters. Problems of sexual difference that beset the Harlequin heroines also confront the heroines of Brontë's *Shirley,* where Caroline Helstone says: "Shirley, men and women are so different: they are in such a different position. Women have so few things to think about—men so many: you may have a friendship with a man while he is almost indifferent to you. Much of what cheers your life may be dependent on him, while not a feel-ing or interest of moment in his eyes may have reference to you." Shirley an-swers: "Caroline . . . don't you wish you had a profession—a trade?"[23]

The Harlequin heroines do have a trade—and a lot of things to think about—but they still resemble the Brontëan heroines in that for them sexual sensation, feelings of love, and rational thought are all intimately connected. They cannot be compartmentalized and sealed off from each other. When these heroines fall in love, they think about love and their lover all the time. The heroes of Harle-quin Romances, like the heroes of *Jane Eyre* and *Shirley,* are emotionally divided between the world of love and the world of business and public affairs, and there-fore fragmented in their psychic structure. For them, or so it seems to the hero-ine, sex is divorced from other feelings, and love from other areas of their life. It seems that whenever he wills it, the hero can simply shut her image off and think about other things.

From this fragmentation, the Harlequin heroes, like their nineteenth-century brothers, M. Emanuel in *Villette* or Robert Moore in *Shirley,* draw their strengths for success in the world. But since the Harlequin heroines must now also survive alone in that world, they can only, as Nicole says, attempt to conceal their feel-ings, try to pretend to be like the hero. But the heroine's wholeness, which is also her weakness, means that her outer appearance and actions cannot but re-flect her inner emotions. The heroines are transparent where the heroes are opaque.

In fact the heroine frequently suspects until the end of the novel that the hero has no tender feelings under his harsh surface, and that therefore he does not have to exhaust all his energy in the fight for self-control the way she does. In *Stormy Affair,* for instance, Amber thinks that "she must pull herself together and not let Hamed Ben Slouma see that he in any way affected her" (p. 25). But "Hamed with his keen perception knew exactly what was going on in her mind. . . .' Perhaps your desires were greater than mine, or do you think it could be that I have more self-control? You're very *transparent,* my charming one'" (p. 100, italics mine). The effect of all these differences between the hero and heroine is to increase the hero's power over this outsider in his world. But even this conflict contains within it wish-fulfilling compensations. If Ben Slouma finds Amber transparent, at least he cares enough to observe her transparency and is interested enough in her to notice what goes on inside her. If the heroine's anger is impotent, at least she has the chance to vent it with great rage at its rightful target, and at least he stays around to listen to it, even, as in the case of Tessa's boss Andrew, "with interest" (*The Enchanted Island,* p. 157).

Utopian and formulaic as they are, in Harlequin Romances the heroine's struggle and conflict serve to overcome something more than a merely psychological passivity or a role that a woman could simply choose to play or not to play. Although its roots in a total social situation are not so clearly shown as in the novels of the Brontës, the Harlequin heroine's conflict is shown to be a very real lack of power to be herself in relations controlled by others. Her very activity and anger are signs of her impotence in the face of the more powerful male. Thus Nicole "seethed impotently" (*Across the Great Divide,* p. 99), and Debra "tried to control the rage and humiliation she was feeling," while Jordan's "composure wasn't disturbed by [Kathleen's] burst of anger."[24]

Like their nineteenth-century predecessors, Jane Eyre, Caroline Helstone, and Lucy Snowe, the Harlequin heroines seek recognition as a subject in their own right from their own point of view. And also like these earlier heroines, Harlequin heroines find that this recognition must take a different form than that sought by romantic heroes. A hero like St. John Rivers in *Jane Eyre* becomes closed in on himself, static, and self-sufficient as an absolute totality when he achieves this recognition. Brontë rejects this form of the self and the narcissistic form of love it demands, and seeks fulfillment for a form of the self which is essentially fluid, essentially changing, and essentially involved in a dynamic, living network of intimate relations with others.

Like the Brontë heroines, although in a less reflective and more narcissistic way,[25] the Harlequin heroines find that women in our soceity are already endowed with this relational form of the self, but that it never achieves recognition or fulfillment. The cause of pain and obscurity rather than success, it in fact tends to get lost altogether in a relation with the hero's harder, closed self, and to merge into his. This is what Anna finds in *Battle with Desire:* "Anna knew she mustn't give in. . . . And it wasn't getting any easier to resist, the urge to fight was melting away, so she made one final attempt at self-respect" (p. 19). What really melts here are the boundaries of the heroine's personhood and her sense of individuality as she loses herself in the other. Harlequins, unlike "real life," provide a solution: the hero adopts the feminine form of the self, recognizes it as valid, and gives the heroine the same tender devotion she gives to him.

The genuis of the Harlequin Romances is to combine the struggle for the recognition of feminine selfhood and the struggle to make the work world a home for that self. As the cover blurb of *The Dividing Line* tells us of Kerry and Ross, who have inherited interests in a department store: "She liked old fashioned friendliness and service. He was all for modern impersonal efficiency. Between them, Sinclairs was becoming a battle ground." Even the idealized form of Kerry's angry struggle against Ross, and violinist Anna's questioning resentment against Gareth, suggest a need to go beyond an analysis like that in *Hearth and Home: Images of Women in the Mass-Media,* edited by Gaye Tuchman, Arlene Kaplan-Daniels, and James Benet. The book criticizes the mass media image of women for implying that "her fate and her happiness rest with a man, not with participation in the labor force,"[26] but it would be impoverishing even the impoverished romances to say that their heroines really want both. They want so much more besides. Not content with Helen Gurley Brown's rationalistic advice to "have it all," they don't want it the way it is now; they want the world of labor to change so that women can find happiness there, and they want men to change so that men will just as much find *their* happiness with women.

Hearth and Home sees hope for equality in "economically productive women who insist on the abandonment of old prejudices and discriminatory behaviors." [27] But Harlequin Romances suggest women who abandon the present structures of economic production because those structures force women to give up their values, their ethos, and even their particular sense of self for success, or, more likely, for mere survival. The vastly popular Harlequin Romances implicitly and potentially pose a demand for profound structural transformations of the total social world we inhabit. And like their romantic forebears, the heroines desire that this new world be not just our same old world improved, but a different, better world. The problem is that Harlequin Enterprises, having learned these secrets to a woman's heart, exploited them by turning them into marketable formulas, which divorced the conflicts from their causes and cut off the path toward reflecting upon any realistic solutions.

ROMANTIC ASPIRATIONS—RATIONALIZED FORM

In her analysis of women readers, Radway has pointed out that "we would do well not to condescend to romance readers as hopeless traditionalists who are recalcitrant in their refusal to acknowledge the emotional costs of patriarchy. We must begin to recognize that romance reading is fueled by dissatisfaction and disaffection." [28] Yet there is a crucial distinction to be made between dismissing the very justifiable fantasies and desires of Harlequin readers or the undoubted achievements of romance writers, and criticizing a multinational publishing corporation that exploits those fantasies and achievements. Modleski is probably closer to the mark when she says of Harlequin that "their enormous and continuing popularity . . . suggests that they speak to very real problems and tensions in women's lives," but that the texts arouse subversive anxieties and desires, and then "work to neutralize them." [29]

The methods of editing, producing, marketing, and distributing Harlequin Romances are part and parcel of the depersonalized, standardized, mechanistic conglomerate system that the Harlequin heroines oppose. Harlequin heroines seek interconnectedness in the social, sexual, and economic world as a whole. Yet their very search is contained in a static, thinglike, literary structure, which denies their quest and turns it into its opposite.

Radway reports that the readers she interviewed understand very well that "the characters and events . . . of the typical romance do not resemble the people and occurrences they must deal with in their lives." [30] At issue in the case of Harlequin, however, is not the illusion that the events in the romances are real, but the illusion that reading a romance constitutes only a relation to a text and to an author. To see the act of reading a romance as simply a relation between the reader and the printed page is to isolate this act from its larger context.

We are used to thinking of a publisher as a mediator between the readers and a book written by an individual author, but Harlequin has changed this. Although Harlequin is studied in few university literary classes, it is referred to in management classes as a sterling example of successful business practices that students should learn to emulate. According to business professor Peter Killing, Harlequin's success is due precisely to its doing away with the reader–text and reader–author relation:

> Harlequin's formula was fundamentally different from that of traditional publishers: content, length, artwork, size, basic formats, and print, were all standardized. Each book was not a new product, but rather an addition to a clearly defined product line. The consequences of this uniformity were significant. The reader was buying a *Harlequin novel*, rather than a book of a certain title by a particular author. . . . There was no need to make decisions about layouts, artwork, or cover design. The standardized size made warehousing and distribution more efficient. Employees hired from mass-marketing companies such as Proctor and Gamble had skills and aptitudes which led them to do well at Harlequin.[31]

Harlequin thought of everything—except the readers, the authors, and the creative freedom which has traditionally been the cornerstone of literature in Western culture. This publishing giant molded romantic aspirations into super-rationalist forms of communication, the very antithesis of the readers' desires.

It is not the idealization of marriage in the romances, nor any specific content, that neutralizes their challenges to patriarchal ideology, but rather the form of the romances, and the form of communication Harlequin sets up between the corporate giant and the readers. Like the Brontëan heroes and heroines, whose desires for sublime sexual communion were a protest against the rationalizing forces of the industrial revolution, the Harlequin romances both protest against and compensate for their readers' dissatisfaction with the Taylorization of their lives as workers and consumers of goods and services. But when Harlequin instituted its new methods, the romantic quest and the sublime sexual communion were themselves Taylorized, so that the apparent escape from a depersonalized, coldly compartmentalized world led the reader right back into it.

Harlequin reduced romantic aspirations to the rational distillation of a formula. The General Editorial Guidelines of 1982 for *Worldwide Library Superromances*, in its directions to writers, broke down the fluid process of the romantic quest into its component set of static categories—"structure," "characters," "plot," "subplots," "romance," "sex," "viewpoint," and "writing style"—and in the past even set forth each step in the plot.

> —Introduction of hero and heroine, their meeting.
> —Initial attraction or conflict between them.
> —Romantic conflicts or heroine's qualms about hero.
> —Counterbalance to developing romance (i.e., sensual scenes, getting to know each other, growth of love vs. conflicts).
> —Hero's role in creating conflict.
> —Resolution of conflicts and happy ending, leading to marriage.
> —The development of the romance should be the primary concern of the author, with other story elements integrated into the romance.[32]

Sex (always of course coupled with "shared feeling rather than pure male domination" [General Editorial Guidelines]) is meted out in measured amounts and in measured doses of "sensuality" at measured intervals of the plot. As a further rationalization, the romantic quest can even be broken down numerically and quantified, so that, as the 1982 Guidelines for Writing Harlequin's *New* American Romances tell us, "parts of the plot can take place anywhere in the world provided that at least 80% of the novel takes place in the United States." [33]

But in 1984, with changes in readers' tastes and the growth of the authors' professional association Romance Writers of America, the Editorial Guidelines deny there is a formula: "Every aspiring Harlequin writer has a very clear picture of what makes these lines so successful, to the extent that some people have even tried to reduce it to a formula." [34]

A CHANGING GENRE: THE AUTHOR AS HEROINE

Yet so much has changed and continues to change since 1980, when growth in the industry led authors to organize Romance Writers of America as a support group, that it is impossible to tell what will happen in the future. Present developments could lead not only to changes in the texts of the romances, but also to changes in the romance industry. Harlequin's very success could open up the potential contradictions inherent in the corporation's methods. The same kinds of struggles against rationalizing power its themes portray could be turned against it. When Romace Writers of America held its first national convention in 1981, the organization saw as its main opponent a literary establishment and vaguely defined public that did not recognize the value of romance as "women's literature." [35] But as conditions governing author–corporate relations change, the industry itself might become another opponent.

Harlequin has responded to declining sales in face of competition by the classic strategy of buying out its major competitor (Silhouette Romances). But authors have had a quite different response to growth in the romance industry. Although Harlequin's monopolizing strategy should work to make even more impersonal the author–publisher relation, authors have been seeking (as if in imitation of their own heroines) more affirming relations with the publisher and greater job satisfaction.

In her study of Harlequin Romances, Margaret Ann Jensen reports that the experience of becoming writers has caused many romance authors to "identify themselves as feminists," to become self-assertive, and to become more aware of themselves as working women who have succeeded in a profession quite difficult to break into. In addition to combating "the negative image of romance in the literary world," romance writers, she says, have two new concerns. They "are attempting to organize to improve the standards within their field"; they are also engaging in "an increasing outspokenness about the romantic fiction industry" and making "critical responses to it." [36] At a Romance Writers of America meeting in South California, one candidate for office in the organization raised these same two issues. She spoke first of the need to "raise the standards of writing" and prevent "mediocre" writing. Then, after mentioning other writers' organizations that are more "militant," she spoke of the need to "increase our clout with publishers" and "improve the deal we're getting on contracts." [37]

Although authors still speak with indignation of the scorn that they face, saying that romances deserve the same respect as mysteries and science fiction, they also raise the above-mentioned other issues concerning the romance industry itself. Authors find themselves disadvantaged by the very marketing practice of Harlequin to which Peter Killing attributes Harlequin's economic success: Harlequin promotes its lines but rarely its authors. And Silhouette has followed suit. In a 1980 interview, Silhouette president P. J. Fennel said: "We're out to get brand name loyalty, so we're not selling individual titles." [38] Because of this practice, and because a romance is on the market for only a month, romance authors have to hustle their own books and find their own markets. They can also, they report, have a difficult time getting royalties from the publisher, with waits of up to two years. [39]

Although this kind of issue is just beginning to be addressed, the issues concerning quality of writing and personal creativity have already begun to be acted upon. Each product line in the romance industry has its own formula, and as the formulas have multiplied, they have also loosened. As a result, an author can pick the line that gives her or him the most freedom. More important, through Romance Writers of America, authors have formed their own critique groups, so that influences on their writing now also come from their peers and not only from the publishing institutions. Romances are beginning to be better and more carefully written, with more variety in the formulas, and with more attention to detail. Although some romances repeat a mechanical version of the formula, other romances like Leigh Roberts's *Love Circuits* are different. Roberts's work, where the hero, tender and loving from the beginning, wears a Charlotte Brontë T-shirt, and where the heroine has a witty sense of humor, brings some surprising transformations to the formula. Like any kind of formula writing—or any kind of writing—romance writing requires skill and talent.

As the corporation follows its destiny of expansion, conglomeration, and product diversification, differences between the mass production needs of the corporation and authors' needs may prove to be potential cracks in the Harlequin machine. The authors' own quest for creative individuality, for economic independence, and for recognition may make them the heroines of their own "real life" romance, with conflicts and adventures outside the text just as gripping as those inside.

NOTES

1. Catering to an exclusively feminine audience, mass market romances are an international phenomenon, with single romances or whole romance series being translated into as many as fourteen languages. Harlequin Enterprises, the best-selling and most successful publisher of this genre, has been imitated by many competitors both in America and in Europe. Harlequin publishes a set number of romances per month, categorized into different series according to a carefully measured degree of explicit sex, known as "sensuality" in the trade. Harlequin publishes Harlequin Romances, Harlequin Presents, and Harlequin Temptations, as well as a mystery-romance series, a gothic romance series, a longer series called Superromances, and an American romance series. Like any corporate consumer product, Harlequin and its competitors are constantly "diversifying" their line, proliferating into a dizzying array of series.

Other publishers now have romance series for more mature and/or divorced women, like Berkeley-Jove's Second Chance at Love, or for adolescent girls, like Simon & Schuster's First Love. This series shares the teen-romance shelves with the Sweet Dream series from Bantam; Young Love from Dell; Caprice from Grosset & Dunlap; and two series from Scholastic, whose Wishing Star and Wild Fire sold 2.25 million copies in 1982.

Information taken from Brett Harvey, "Boy Crazy," *Village Voice* 27 (10–16 Feb. 1982): 48–49; Stanley Meisler, "Harlequins: The Romance of Escapism," *Los Angeles Times*, 15 Nov. 1980, pt. 1, 7–8; Rosemary Nightingale, "True Romances," *Miami Herald*, 5 Jan. 1983; J. D. Reed, "From Bedroom to Boardroom: Romance Novels Court Changing Fancies and Adorable Profits," *Time*, 13 Apr. 1981, 101–4; interview with Jany Saint-Marcoux, editor of Collections sentimentales, Éditions Tallandier; "Romantic Novels Find Receptive Market," *Santa Ana Register*, 26 July 1979, sec. E, 1; *Standard and Poor's Corporation Records* 43, (New York: May 1982), 8475.

2. See Reed. According to Margaret Ann Jensen, the very success of Harlequin has caused these figures to decline drastically. Because so many publishers are now imitating Harlequin and competing with it, Harlequin's "share of the market has dropped to 45 percent. . . . All signs indicate that Harlequin is a financially distressed corporation." See Jensen, *Love's $weet Return: The Harlequin Story* (Toronto: Women's Educational Press, 1984). In order to offset this decline, Harlequin is purchasing Silhouette Romances.

3. Tania Modelski, *Loving with a Vengeance: Mass-Produced Fantasies for Women* (Hamden: Archon Books, 1982); Ann Barr Snitow, "Mass Market Romance: Pornography for Women is Different," *Radical History Review* 20 (Spring–Summer 1979): 141–61, reprinted in *Powers of Desire: The Politics of Sexuality*, ed. Ann Snitow, Christine Stansell, and Sharon Thomas (New York: Monthly Review Press, 1983); Janice A. Radway, "Women Read the Romance: The Interaction of Text and Context," *Feminist Studies* 9 (Spring 1983): 53:78.

4. Modleski, 113.

5. Kerry Allyne, *Across the Great Divide* (1980); Ann Cooper, *Battle with Desire* (1980); Kay Thorpe, *The Dividing Line* (1980). All books published by Harlequin Books, Toronto, London, New York, Amsterdam, Sydney, Hamburg, Paris, Stockholm. Page numbers appear in parentheses in the text.

6. Lynsey Stevens, *Race for Revenge* (Toronto: Harlequin, 1981), Back Cover.

7. Advertisement for Sara Jennings, *Game Plan* (Garden City, N.Y.: Candlelight Ecstasy Romances, 1984), Back Cover.

8. Leigh Roberts, *Love Circuits* (Harlequin Temptations, 1984); Sarah James, *Public Affair* (Harlequin American Romance, 1984); Marion Smith Collins, *By Any Other Name* (Harlequin Temptations, 1984). All books published by Harlequin Enterprises, Toronto. Page numbers appear in parentheses in the text.

9. Advertisement for Harlequin Temptations, found in Harlequin books of July 1984 (Toronto: Harlequin Enterprises, 1984).

10. Colette Dowling, *The Cinderella Complex: Women's Hidden Fear of Independence* (New York: Simon & Schuster Pocket Books, 1981), 2, 54.

11. Harry Braverman, *Labor and Monopoly Capital: The Degradation of Work in the Twentieth Century*, Special Abridged Edition (Special Issue of *Monthly Review*, 26, [July–August 1974]), 50.

According to Braverman, by 1970 in the United States, clerical work was one of the fastest growing occupations and had become one of the lowest paid, its pay "lower than that of every type of so-called blue collar work" (51). Of its 10 million members, by 1978, 79.6 percent were women. In 1970, clerical work included 18 percent of all gainfully employed persons in the United States, a percentage equal to that of production work of all sorts.

12. Roslyn L. Feldberg and Evelyn Nakano Glenn, "Technology and Work Degradation: Effects of Office Automation on Women Clerical Workers," in *Machina ex Dea*, ed. Joan Rothschild (New York: Pergamon Press, 1983), 62.

13. Radway (57) reports that 42 percent of the women in her study work outside the home, and says that Harlequin claims that 49 percent of its audience works outside the home. A 1984 Waldenbooks survey found that 63 percent of its romance readers held jobs outside the home. (Doug Brown, "Research Dissects the Romantic Novel," *L.A. Times*, Sept. 19, 1984, V, 8).

14. Ibid., 60.

15. Braverman, 61.

16. Ida Russakoff Hoos, *Automation in the Office* (Washington, 1961), 53, cited in Braverman.

17. Ellen Cantarow, "Working Can Be Dangerous to Your Health," *Mademoiselle*, August 1982, 114–16.

18. Eleanor Farnes, *The Enchanted Island* (Toronto: Harlequin Enterprises, 1971). Page numbers appear in parentheses in the text.

19. Margaret Mayo, *Stormy Affair* (Toronto: Harlequin Enterprises, 1980). Page numbers appear in parentheses in the text.

20. Radway; Snitow; and Nancy Chodorow, *The Reproduction of Mothering: Psychoanalysis and the Sociology of Gender* (Berkeley: University of California Press, 1978).

21. Sally Mitchell, *The Fallen Angel: Chastity, Class, and Women's Reading, 1835–1880* (Bowling Green, Ohio: Bowling Green University Press, 1981); and Modleski.

22. Personal communication from Louella Nelson, author of *Freedom's Fortune*, Harlequin Superromance (Toronto: Harlequin Books, 1984).

23. Charlotte Brontë, *Shirley* (Baltimore: Penguin Books, 1974), 234–35.

24. Janet Dailey, *The Matchmakers* (Toronto: Harlequin Enterprises, 1978); Elizabeth Graham, *Come Next Spring* (Toronto: Harlequin Enterprises, 1980).

25. For the role of narcissism in the Harlequin Romances, see Modleski.

26. Gaye Tuchman, Arlene Kaplan Daniels, and James Benet, eds., *Hearth and Home: Images of Women in the Mass Media* (New York: Oxford University Press, 1978), 18.

27. Ibid., 4.

28. Radway, 68.

29. Modleski, 14, 30.

30. Radway, 59.

31. Peter Killing, *Harlequin Enterprises Limited: Case Material of the Western School of Business Administration* (London, Ontario: University of Western Ontario, 1978), 3.

32. General Editorial Guidelines, *Worldwide Library Superromances* (Toronto: Harlequin Enterprises, 1982), 2.

33. Guidelines for Writing Harlequin's *New* American Romances (Toronto: Harlequin Enterprises, 1982), 3.

34. *Harlequin Romance and Harlequin Presents Editoral Guidelines* (Ontario: Harlequin Books, 1984), 1.

35. George Christian, "Romance Writers, Going to the Heart of the Matter (and the Market), Call for Recognition," *Publisher's Weekly*, 24 July 1980. The first national conference of Romance Writers of America was held in Houston, in June 1981, with 800 participants, mostly women.

36. Jensen, 73–74.

37. Speech given at a meeting of Romance Writers of America, Orange County Chapter.

38. Vivien Lee Jennings, "The Romance Wars," *Publisher's Weekly*, 24 Aug. 1984, 50–55.

39. Information gathered from conversations with authors at meeting. See note 37.

THE RISE OF THE DOMESTIC WOMAN

> It is only by seeing women in their own homes, among their own set, just as they always are, that you can form any just judgement. Short of that, it is all guess and luck—and will generally be ill-luck. How many a man has committed himself on a short acquaintance, and rued it all the rest of his life!
>
> JANE AUSTEN, *EMMA*

In order to make otherwise undistinguished young women desirable to men of a better social position, conduct books and works of instruction for women specified certain sexual features as those that such men should want in a wife. At the same time, such writing provided people from diverse social groups with a basis for imagining economic interests in common.[1] Thus it was the new domestic woman rather than her counterpart, the new economic man, who first encroached upon aristocratic culture and seized authority from it. This writing assumed that an education ideally made a woman desire to be what a prosperous man desires, which is above all else a female. She therefore had to lack the competitive desires and worldly ambitions that consequently belonged—as if by some natural principle—to the male. For such a man, her desirability hinged upon an education in frugal domestic practices. She was supposed to complement his role as an earner and producer with hers as a wise spender and tasteful consumer. Such an ideal relationship presupposed a woman whose desires were not of necessity attracted to material things. But because a woman's desire could in fact be manipulated by signs of wealth and position, she required an education.

In assuming this, eighteenth-century conduct books and educational treatises for women forced open a contradiction within the existing cultural territory that had been marked out for representing the female. These authors portrayed aristocratic women along with those who harbored aristocratic pretensions as the very embodiments of corrupted desire, namely, desire that sought its gratification in economic and political terms. The books all took care to explain how this form of desire destroyed the very virtues essential to a wife and mother. Narratives of her ideal development would come later. The educational handbooks for women simply mapped out a new field of knowledge as specifically female. In doing so, they declared their intention to recover and preserve a woman's true (sexual) identity in a world run according to other (political and economic) measures of men. With this as its justification, the writing devoted to defining the female wrought an important change in the understanding of power. It severed the language of kinship from that of political relations, producing a culture divided into the respective domains of domestic woman and economic man.

After reading several dozen or more conduct books, one is struck with a sense of their emptiness—a lack of what we today consider "real" information about the female subject and the object world that she is supposed to occupy. Under the sheer force of repetition, however, one does see a figure emerge from the categories that organize these manuals. A figure of female subjectivity, a grammar really, awaited the substance that the novel and its readers, as well as the countless individuals educated according to the model of the new woman, would eventually provide. In such books one can see a culture in the process of rethinking at the most basic level the dominant (aristocratic) rules for sexual exchange. Because they appeared to have no political bias, these rules took on the power of natural law, and as a result, they presented—in actuality, still present—readers with ideology in its most powerful form.

With this in mind, I describe the field of information as represented by eighteenth-century conduct books for women, knowing that the historical importance of the formation of such a field can be understood neither as a psychology nor as a set of rules designed to restrict female behavior. As they revised the sexual contract, authors and readers—men and women both—used the same rules to formulate a new mode of economic thinking, even though they represented that thinking as pertaining only to women. To see the sexual contract once again as an economic contract is the only way, then, to treat modern sexuality as the political language it happens to be. The following discussion argues that, by virtue of its apparent insignificance, a body of writing concerned with devising a special kind of education for women in fact played a crucial role in the rise of the new middle classes in England.

THE BOOK OF CLASS SEXUALITY

Until sometime around the end of the seventeenth century, the great majority of conduct books were devoted mainly to representing the male of the dominant class.[2] For purposes of my argument, it does not really matter whether or not aristocrats were actually the ones to take such instruction seriously. What does matter is what the literate public considered to be the dominant social ideal. Ruth Kelso and Suzanne Hull have shown that during the sixteenth and seventeenth centuries there were relatively few books for instructing women as compared to those available to men. Their research also shows that books addressing a readership with humbler aspirations increased in popularity during the seventeenth century.[3] Although by mid-century they outnumbered conduct books that exalted the attributes of aristocratic women, the distinctively Puritan flavor of some marriage manuals and books on household governance made it quite clear that they were not endorsing the preferred cultural norms.[4] But neither was their advice for women supposed to challenge the aristocratic ideal. Whatever their political attitude toward the aristocracy, these books did not presume to represent a more desirable woman but simply outlined domestic procedures that were practical for people of less means and prestige. An exclusive concern for the practical matters of running a household classified certain handbooks for women as domestic economies, which meant they belonged to an entirely different genre than conduct books that aspired to be courtesy literature. Although some books argued that domestic economy should be part of an ideal gentlewoman's education, they did not come into their own until the last decade of the seventeenth century.[5] Until then, different levels of society held recognizably different ideas about what made a woman marriageable. During the first decades of the eighteenth century, however, categories that had apparently remained fairly constant for centuries underwent rapid transformation.

The distinction between conduct books and domestic economies changed so that each reached out to the other's reader. So popular did these books become that by the second half of the eighteenth century virtually everyone knew the ideal of womanhood they proposed. Joyce Hemlow considers this writing the purest expression of the same interest in manners that one finds in Burney: "the problem of the conduct of the young lady was investigated so thoroughly that the lifetime of Fanny Burney, or more accurately the years 1760–1820, which saw also the rise of the novel of manners, might be called the age of courtesy books for women."[6] To this I would add an important qualification. While the lifetime of Burney—and, one might note, of Austen as well—should indeed be seen as the high point of a tradition of conduct books for women, it would be misleading to suggest that the two kinds of writing—women's courtesy books and novels of manners—sprang into being and passed out of currency together. The production of conduct books long preceded novels of manners and in fact virtually exploded during the period following the failure to renew the licensing act in 1695, thus preceding the novel of manners by several decades.[7] And although today we find authors neither designing curricula to educate young women at home nor writing fiction to demonstrate the proprieties of feminine conduct, the conduct book is still alive and well. Besides all the books and advice columns telling women how to catch and keep a man, and besides numerous magazines imaging the beautiful home, there are also home economics courses that most women must take before graduating from high school. Perhaps because their most basic tenets became social facts with the formation of the national curriculum that included male and female pupils, conduct books have grown more specialized during our own century—concentrating now on thin thighs, on the manners of a business woman, and with equal frequency on such specific domestic skills as French cooking or English gardening, which men are supposed to learn as well as women.

It is safe to say that by the mid-eighteenth century the number of books specifying the qualities of a new kind of woman had well outstripped the number of those devoted to describing the aristocratic male.[8] The growth of this body of writing thus coincided with the rise of the popular press, itself a part of the larger process that Raymond Williams has aptly named "the long revolution."[9] Lord Halifax's *Advice to a Daughter* first appeared in 1688 and ran through two dozen editions, winning great popularity for nearly a century until Dr. Gregory's *A Father's Legacy to his Daughters* and Hester Chapone's *Letters on the Improvement of the Mind* supplanted it. John Mason's study of courtesy literature shows that the number and variety of ladies' conduct books began to increase with the publication of such books as *The Ladies Dictionary* (1694) and *The Whole Duty of Women* (1695).[10] Where men are concerned, his study shows that by mid-century the form gradually mutated into other forms—satire, for example—once the production of the ideal social leader who dominated Renaissance treatises was no longer imagined as its primary goal. Meanwhile, the conduct book for women enjoyed a different fate. Educational literature that addressed a female readership quickly became very popular once it broke free from the aristocratic model, and despite a falling off after the 1820s, many books remained in print well into the nineteenth century.

Throughout this period, countless female conduct books, ladies' magazines, and books of instruction for children all posited a similar feminine ideal and tended toward the same objective of ensuring a happy household. Indeed, the end of the eighteenth century saw not only the publication of proposals for institutions devoted to educating women, but also the development of programs designed to instruct women at home. Erasmus Darwin's *A Plan for the Conduct of Female Education in Boarding Schools* (1798) and the Edgeworths' *Practical Education* (1801) are only two of the more famous efforts at institutionalizing the curriculum proposed by conduct-book literature. In representing the household as a world with its own form of social relations, a distinctively feminine discourse, this body of literature revised the semiotic of culture at its most basic level and enabled a coherent idea of the middle class to take shape. That the relative number of conduct books appeared to decrease as the eighteenth century came to an end was not because the female ideal they represented passed out of vogue. To the contrary, there is every reason to think that by this time the ideal had passed into the domain of common sense where it provided the frame of reference for other kinds of writing, among them the novel. The next chapter will show that Richardson's tediously protracted description of the household in *Pamela* can be supplanted by Austen's minimalist representation precisely because the rules governing sexual relations laid out in the conduct books could be taken for granted. Austen could simply allude where Richardson, in defiance of an earlier notion of sexual relations, had to elaborate for hundreds of pages. More than that, Austen knew perfectly well her readers had identified those rules not only with common sense, if not always with nature, but also with the form of the novel itself.

Conduct books addressed a readership comprising various levels and sources of income and included virtually all people who distinguished themselves from the aristocracy, on the one hand, and from the laboring poor on the other. Although written in various regional, professional, and political voices, each with the specific concerns of a local readership foremost in mind, the conduct books written during the first decades of the eighteenth century nevertheless proposed an ideal that was reappearing with wonderful regularity. Their evident popularity therefore suggests we might detect the presence of a "middle class," as we mean it today, much earlier than other writing from that time in history indicates. Even if we use Hemlow's later dates of 1760–1820 to mark the high point of the writing of manners, we must still confront a historical paradox. Conduct books imply the presence of a unified middle class at a time when other representations of the social world suggest that no such class yet existed. Most other writing in fact suggests that the eighteenth-century Englishman saw himself within a static and hierarchical society, radically different from the dynamic struggle of landlords, capitalists, and laboring poor that would accompany the rise of the middle class during the early decades of the nineteenth century. Harold Perkin provides this encapsulated view of how social relationships were understood in eighteenth-century England: "The old society then was a finely graded hierarchy of great subtlety and discrimination, in which men were acutely aware of their exact relation to those immediately above and below them, but only vaguely conscious except at the very top of their connection with those on their own level."[11] These men apparently felt allegiance only to those immediately above and below them in economic chains, and they probably harbored antagonism toward those who occupied similar positions in other chains of dependency. According to Perkin, the absence of anything resembling a modern middle class is particularly apparent in England, where there was no word for *bourgeoisie* "until the nineteenth century," because "the thing itself did not exist, in the sense of a permanent, self-conscious urban class in opposition to the landed aristocracy" (p. 61). The English view of society proved to be incorrigibly vertical, he continues, for no sooner did one generation of townsmen succeed in business or trade than they sought to raise their social status by becoming country gentlemen.

If conduct books addressed a fairly wide readership with fairly consistent social objectives, then they present us with a historical contradiction of major proportions—a middle class that was not actually there. It was no mystery who occupied the top of the social ladder as well as the bottom, but there are only the most irregular and diverse data concerning those in the middle. Reviewing his information concerning the period from 1688 to 1803, Perkin describes what he calls "the middle ranks" of the "old society":

> The middle ranks were distinguished at the top from the gentry and nobility not so much by lower incomes as by the necessity of earning their living, and at the bottom from the labouring poor not so much by higher incomes as by the property, however small, represented by stock in trade, livestock, tools, or the educational investment of skill or expertise. (p. 23)

We should note that Perkin organizes this field of information negatively in that his description accounts for those people who were neither aristocracy nor laboring poor. Everywhere within this field there were hierarchies—professional and economic—marked by "an infinity of graduated statuses." By the same token, he claims, every occupation was marked "by internal differences of status greater than any which separated it from those outside" (p. 24). This is not to say that Perkin's map of eighteenth-century society is any less a representation than that which can be extrapolated from the conduct books of an earlier time. I am simply suggesting that during the early eighteenth century most authors regarded differences of status as the only accurate way of identifying individuals within the middle ranks of their society. They did not, in other words, perceive what common interests might have united all those at the same social level. That the female conduct book presupposed horizontal affiliations among the literate public where no such affiliations would exist as a matter of practice for another sixty to a hundred years has obvious bearing on social and literary history alike. It marks a basic change in the public understanding of social relations as well as a change in what constituted good taste in reading. But I should hasten to add that the question raised by this body of discourse is not the same one addressed by Ian Watt or Richard Altick in their studies of the novel-reading public. We cannot ask the conduct book to explain what new social elements had been introduced into the readership that so altered its taste.[12] The available data do not allow us to do so. If changes in socioeconomic categories came after similar changes in the categories governing female education, we must ask instead what the new domestic ideal said to a heterogeneous economic group that ensured this ideal would keep on making sense well into the nineteenth century—after political relationships assumed a modern configuration.

During the eighteenth century, the conduct book for women became such a common phenomenon that many different kinds of writers felt compelled to add their wrinkles to the female character. Besides men like Halifax, Rochester, Swift, and Defoe—all of whom tried their hands at writing conduct books for women—there were also pedagogues such as Timothy Rogers, Thomas Gisborne, and T. S. Arthur, clergymen like Rev. Thomas Broadhurst, Dr. Fordyce, and the darling of Austen's generation, Dr. Gregory, as well as a number of women authors such as Sarah Tyler, Miss Catharine E. Beecher, and the Countess Dowager of Carlisle, all of whom have long since faded from cultural memory. Like Hester Chapone, Hannah More, and Maria Edgeworth, some authors made their reputations by writing conduct books, while other conduct-book authors like Mary Wollstonecraft and Erasmus Darwin were known primarily for writing in more prestigious modes. Even when the author's name is obscure, as most of these names indeed are, one can usually infer a social identity from the female virtues to which the writer grants highest priority, for these virtues are inevitably linked to functions which that writer feels are essential to good household management.

Taken together, these local voices comprise a text displaying obvious distinctions between town and country, between old money and new, among income levels and various occupations, and particularly among the different amounts of leisure time people had to occupy. It is the whole purpose of this chapter to show how such points of difference came to be contained within a framework that was remarkably predictable. By dividing the social world on the basis of sex, this body of writing produced a single ideal of the household. But the domestic ideal did not so much speak to middle-class interests as we now understand them. In fact, it is accurate to say that such writing as the conduct books helped to generate the belief that there was such a thing as a middle class with clearly established affiliations before it actually existed. If there is any truth in this, then it is also reasonable to claim that the modern individual was first and foremost a female.

The handbook that gained such immense popularity in England at the end of the seventeenth century was a hybrid form that combined materials from earlier devotional books and books of manners ostensibly written for aristocratic women, with information from books of maternal advice to daughters, as well as with descriptions of the housewife's practical duties as depicted in humbler handbooks of domestic economy, almanacs, and recipe books. Written by Timothy Rogers, an otherwise unremarkable educator with dissenter's sympathies, *The Character of a Good Woman, both in a Single and Married State* provides a particularly useful example of the genre as it appeared at the beginning of the eighteenth century. The book holds true to its subtitle and represents the ideal female as a bipartite character. Among the qualities of the unmarried woman that the author extolls are modesty, humility, and honesty. In earlier writing, these conspicuously passive virtues were considered the antidote to natural deficiencies that had been the female's heritage ever since the Fall of Man. In keeping with Enlightenment strategies, however, the new mode of instruction declares it will cultivate the inherently female qualities that are most likely to ward off the vanity which contemporary social life instills. Published in 1697, *The Character of a Good Woman* does not represent women as more prone to corruption and thus more in need of redemption than men; it exalts female nature because, as the author claims, women are "generally more serious than men. . . , as far beyond in the lessons of Devotion as in the tuneableness and sweetness of your voice."[13] Here passive virtue is both in keeping with female nature and essential to preserving that nature.

The passive virtue of the unmarried woman constitutes only half of the paradigm that rapidly gained currency during the eighteenth century. To the qualities of the innocent maiden, conduct books appended those of the efficient housewife. As if straight from Renaissance handbooks on domestic economy, these books developed categories that defined the ideal woman in her married state. Her representation was as practical and detailed as the maiden's was abstract and homiletic in style. Except for unqualified obedience to her husband, the virtues of the ideal wife appeared to be active. A list of her duties could have included household management, regulation of servants, supervision of children, planning of entertainment, and concern for the sick. It quickly becomes apparent, however, that the main duty of the new housewife was to supervise the servants who were the ones to take care of these matters. The table of contents for *The Young Ladies Companion or, Beauty's Looking-Glass*, which was written in 1740, demonstrates a typical mix of topics drawn from courtesy literature as well as from the practical handbooks: 1. Religion, 2. Husband, 3. House, Family and Children, 4. Behavior and Conversation, 5. Friendships, 6. Censure, 7. Vanity and Affection, 8. Pride, 9. Diversions.[14] At this point in history, the social differences implicit in the different materials that went into conduct books have faded. The features of the devout maiden have been bonded to those of the industrious housewife, forming a new but utterly familiar system of signs.

Contained within the framework of gender rather than status, the earlier meaning of traditionally female features—practical duties and abstract virtues alike—changed even while they seemed to pass into the eighteenth century untouched by the individual imagination. Different categories of female identity, which were drawn from quite diverse traditions of writing and aimed at various social groups, formed a single representation. In their combination, contrary notions of taste transformed one another to form a standard capable of reaching across a broad spectrum of social groups. Once the practical duties of the common housewife had been included within the framework of courtesy literature, they became more and more tightly restricted to those tasks that were performed within and for the household alone. In contrast with earlier domestic economies, the eighteenth-century conduct books ceased to provide advice for the care of livestock or the concoction of medicinal cures. Producing goods to be consumed by the household was apparently no longer their readers' concern. In this respect, even the eighteenth-century instructional literature modeled upon the earlier domestic economies was influenced by courtesy literature. The more practically oriented books still emphasized frugality, for example. But in their instructions for the preparation of food, frugality became a matter of good taste and a way of displaying domestic virtue, not of stretching the resources to meet the needs of the household. In proposing a menu "proper for a frugal as well as a sumptuous table," for example, *The Compleat Housewife or, Accomplished Gentlewoman's Companion* (1734) converted the notion of propriety from an economic norm to a new national standard. A meal commensurate with one's means, in other words, became a meal "suitable to English constitutions and English Palates, wholesome, toothsome, all practical and easy to be performed."[15]

If the female's abstract virtues endowed the duties of the housewife with value, the spiritual virtues honored in earlier courtesy literature became limited in how they might help her perform her practical duties. Once female virtue became so linked to work, conduct books banished from the ideal woman the features that had once seemed desirable because they enhanced the aristocratic woman. In a conduct book of the mid-nineteenth century, T. S. Arthur goes so far as to assault the ideal of cloistered virtue that for centuries had been considered desirable in unmarried aristocratic women. In his view, "What is called the religion of the cloister is no religion at all, but mere selfishness—a retiring from *actual duty in the world,* into an imaginary state of sanctimoniousness" (italics mine).[16] Thomas Broadhurst's *Advice to Young Ladies on the Improvement of the Mind and Conduct of Life* (1810) shows an equally prevalent tendency toward anti-intellectualism directed at women who sought an elite education—once the privilege of well-born women—and the pleasures of intellectual life:

> She who is faithfully employed in discharging the various duties of a wife and daughter, a mother and a friend, is far more usefully occupied than one who, to the culpable neglect of the most important obligations, is daily absorbed by philosophic and literary speculations, or soaring aloft amidst the enchanted regions of fiction and romance.[17]

Such attacks on both religious and intellectual women condemn female virtues associated with the dominant social ideal of earlier culture. In this manner, the conduct books sought to define the practice of secular morality as the woman's natural duty. If certain agrarian and artisan forms of labor were considered unfeminine by virtue of their inclusion in the conduct book, then certain manifestations of aristocratic taste and learning were declared corrupt and opposed to the mental accomplishments of the good wife and mother. In the process, her duties were pared down to those that seem remarkably frivolous but that were—and to some extent still are—considered nonetheless essential to domestic happiness.

I would like to suggest that the peculiar features and extraordinary durability of the domestic ideal had everything to do with its capability to suppress the very conflicts so evident in the bewildering field of dialects comprising this body of writing until the second half of the eighteenth century. The authors of conduct books were acutely sensitive to the subtlest differences in status, and each represented his or her readers' interests in terms of a differential system that opposed country and town, rich and poor, labor and leisure, and no doubt more refined or local socioeconomic interests. Within such a semantic field, the representation of any male role automatically defined a partisan position. In deciding what role a male should ideally fulfill, then, the authors of both fiction and conduct books had to stand on one side or another in a number of these thematic oppositions. And to do so would limit a readership accordingly. The female, in contrast, provided a topic that could bind together precisely those groups who were necessarily divided by other kinds of writing. Virtually no other topic appeared to be so free of bias toward an occupation, political faction, or religious affiliation. In bringing into being a concept of the household on which socially hostile groups felt they could all agree, the domestic ideal helped create the fiction of horizontal affiliations that only a century later could be said to have materialized as an economic reality. As part of an effort to explain how domestic fiction happened to survive and acquire prestige while other forms of writing rose and fell in popularity, the following description demonstrates how formulation of the domestic woman overcame the conflicts and contradictions inherent in most other Enlightenment efforts at rewriting the conditions of history.

A COUNTRY HOUSE THAT IS NOT A COUNTRY HOUSE

It is relatively easy to distinguish those conduct books meant for rural readers from those addressing people in town. Despite these and all the other signs of competing economic interests that presupposed a politically diverse readership, the eighteenth-century books for women nevertheless agreed that the country house should be the site of the ideal household. By this they meant the country house should cease to provide a model of aristocratic culture and should offer instead a model that would be realized in any and all respectable households. This way of representing life in the country house made it possible for competing interest groups to ignore their economic origins and coalesce around a single domestic ideal. The opposition between city and country, which marked a major division between economic and political interests at the time, only enhanced the advantages of the domestic ideal. Urban tradesmen and merchants, for example, ordinarily would have thought they had little in common with independent farmers and grain dealers, and traditional representations of the country house only reinforced this political opposition. The country house of seventeenth-century England had encouraged popular belief that those at the very top of the social hierarchy were the ultimate end of production. In such a hierarchical system of relationships, people who were entitled to a privileged position were expected to display their wealth in certain highly prescribed ways.[18] In its most idealized form, the old society appeared to be governed by a patron who distributed wealth and power down a series of hierarchically organized relationships until virtually every client benefited from this generosity. Such, for example, is the form that social authority assumes in the country-house poems of the seventeenth century.[19]

So important were forms of sumptuary display to maintaining the social order during the sixteenth and seventeenth centuries that a series of royal proclamations detailed the permissible forms of aristocratic display. Using wealth to display the signs of high social status was forbidden to those whose birth and title had not qualified them to do so. In her proclamation of 6 July 1597, Queen Elizabeth voiced concern about the "confusion in all places being great where the meanest are as richly appareled as their betters." [20] By "meanest" she was obviously referring to nonaristocrats whose money could disguise a lack of noble origins. To remedy this situation, she reiterated a national dress code which specified, among other things, that "none shall wear in his apparel cloth of gold or silver tissued, silk of color purple under the degree of an earl, except Knights of the Garter in their purple mantles" (p. 176). Besides listing clothing and materials that must be used according to rank, degree, and proximity to the Queen, the proclamation also limited the total amount one could spend each year on clothing. These restrictions extended to women whose body, like that of the male, was an ornamental body representing the family's place in an intricately precise set of kinship relations determined by the metaphysics of blood. The order extended from viscountesses to barons' daughters and wives of barons' eldest sons, from gentlemen of the privy chamber to those who attended duchesses, countesses, and so forth. The list concluded with an order that "no person under the degrees specified shall wear any guard or welt of silk upon any petticoat, cloak or safeguard" (p. 179).

These attempts to regulate aristocratic display were intended to prevent wealth from obscuring kinship rules that maintained the social hierarchy. This political imperative might well have motivated James I to issue proclamations ordering the nobility out of the city and into the countryside where they were supposed to win popular support by displays of hospitality. Leah S. Marcus has argued that James meant these measures to counter political resistance that was gathering in the city but that also appeared to extend into the countryside in 1616 when attempts by landlords to fence in common land brought about rioting. [21] In a speech to the Star Chamber in that same year, James, like Elizabeth before him, represents the city as a place attracting so many people that "all the countrey is gotten into *London;* so as with time, England will onely be *London,* and the whole countrey be left waste." [22] He claimed that wives and daughters, attracted by foreign fashions, forced their husbands and fathers to abandon the country for London where a woman's virtue would inevitably be tarnished. To correct all these abuses, he issued an injunction to "keepe the old fashion of *England:* For it was wont to be the honour and reputation of the English Nobilitie and Gentry, to liue in the countrey, and keepe hospitalitie" (pp. 343–44). James, in other words, saw the good country life as a means of maintaining popular support for the crown. And with this in mind, he saw to it that the aristocratic practices centered in the country house would represent all that was truly British.

Eighteenth-century conduct books for women therefore contended with two particular powerful traditions, one having to do with the rules for displaying the aristocratic body and the other having to do with the practice of hospitality in the countryside. These symbolic practices authorized aristocratic power—power based on birth and title alone—whose site was the country manor house. It is reasonable to assume that, in opposing these traditions, female conduct books changed the ideal of what English life ought to be when they replaced the lavish displays of aristocratic life with the frugal and private practices of the modern gentleman. This was no doubt the primary political aim of such writing and the main reason why it suddenly attracted so many authors and readers. But the new representation of English country life itself depended on another rhetorical strategy that denigrated the ornamental body of the aristocrat to exalt the retiring and yet ever vigilant domestic woman. In challenging the metaphysics of blood, such a representation would eventually hollow out the material body of the woman in order to fill it with the materials of a gender-based self, or female psychology. Subsequent chapters will trace this process, but my purpose in this chapter is to show how the conduct books' definition of the desirable woman first enabled a substantial number of competing interest groups to identify their economic interests with the same domestic ideal.

This strategy for deflecting the political opposition between country and city can be isolated in any number of handbooks. *The Compleat Housewife or, Accomplished Gentlewoman's Companion* (1734) promises to give its reader a set of "Directions generally for dressing in the best, most natural, and wholesome Manner, such Provisions as are the Products of our Country, and in such a Manner as is most agreeable to English Palates" (p. 2). How the ideal of a table that was fitting and proper for any size purse in the realm actually served agrarian interests becomes apparent when we consider what kind of food the handbook forbids. In claiming it is "to our Disgrace" that Englishmen have "so fondly admired the French Tongue, French *modes,* and French Messes" (p. 2), the author speaks on behalf of agricultural interests. But it is important that he attack the urban taste for things imported by assaulting the "unwholesome" diet which supposedly caters to aristocratic taste. Restricted to domestic matters, his political commentary avoids raising the opposition between agricultural interests and those of an increasing number who were importing goods for urban markets. A few years later, in 1740, *The Young Ladies Companion or, Beauty's Looking-Glass* similarly lashes out against immoderate household expenditures. Using terms that would have been especially meaningful to ambitious townspeople, this author elaborates the economic disaster that ensues from aping aristocratic standards:

> when usual Presents are made, and an expensive Marriage is solemniz'd, gaudy cloaths and Equipage are bought, and perhaps, a London house furnished, a considerable Part of this Portion will be disburs'd and the forlorn Hero of this shewy, noisy farce, will discover too late how much more eligible it had been to have marry'd a LADY well born, of a discreet, modest, and frugal Education, and an agreeable Person with less Money, than a haughty Dame with all her Quality Airs about her. (p. 113)

Despite regional differences, the author who writes for readers in town and the one who addresses a rural readership agree with each other on the components of the ideal domestic life. Both situate the model household in opposition to the excesses of aristocratic behavior, and both contest the prevailing system of status distinctions in order to insist on a discreet and frugal household with a woman educated in the practices of inconspicuous consumption. They maintain that such behavior is a more accurate indication of good breeding than the traditional distinctions of title or wealth. *The Young Ladies Companion or, Beauty's Looking-Glass* also lays out the economic basis for desiring the woman of "discreet, modest, and frugal Education" over and against one of great fortune who is likely to be a "haughty Dame with all her Quality Airs about her." The woman who brings more wealth to the marriage turns out to be a bad investment in this account. She is described as "the dearest purchase now in England, . . . not excepting the *South-Sea Stock*" (p. 115), the notorious financial corporation whose stock rose in several months time from £100 to £1000 in 1720 and then plummeted several months after that. By way of contrast to the woman who brings a large dowry but requires an ostentatious style of living, this gentleman considers the frugal wife a solid investment. "For every thousand Pound" the wealthier woman brings, he calculates, her needs will multiply accordingly: "she spends more than the interest of it; for besides her private expence, the gay furniture, the rich Beds, China-Ware, Tea-Table, visiting rooms, rich coach, etc. must be chiefly placed to her Account" (p. 115). To this way of thinking, the woman who feels so obliged to display signs of status—in the manner of aristocratic women—will soon prove too expensive to keep.

It is important to note that the qualities of the desirable woman—her discretion, modesty, and frugality—described the objectives of an educational program in terms tht spelled out a coherent set of economic policies for the management of the household. The authors of these educational books for women turned the virtues of the new woman into a language resonating with political meaning. These virtues were simultaneously the categories of a pedagogical theory, the form of subjectivity it engendered, the taste that resulted, and the economy that such taste ensured. In arguing for a new set of qualities to desire in a woman, these books therefore made her capable of authorizing a whole new set of economic practices that directly countered what were supposed to be seen as the excesses of a decadent aristocracy. Under the dominion of such a woman, the country house could no longer authorize a political system that made sumptuary display the ultimate aim of production. Instead, it proposed a world where production was an end in itself rather than a means to such an end.

The frugal domestic economy that these conduct books idealize in their educational program for women was one fueled by interest from investments rather than by labor. It differed in this significant respect from the household represented in the sixteenth- and seventeenth-century Puritan handbooks, as well as from the country ideal preferred by James I. This modern household did not identify the source of one's income with a certain craft, trade, region, or family; its economy depended on money earned on investments. Such money made the household into a self-enclosed world whose means of support were elsewhere, invisible, removed from the scene. The few statements quoted above, like those in the discussion to follow, strongly suggest that the good country life so depicted no longer revealed one's origins or political allegiances. The negation of traditional differences between those at the very top and those at the bottom of the social scale cleared the cultural ground for a class sexuality that valued people according to intrinsic personal qualities. A group of people consequently came to understand themselves as part of an educated elite who, in Harry Payne's words, prided themselves on "gentility, science, innovation, . . . and economic realism." [23] Such an ideal representation of the ruling class had the advantage—in theory at least—of making available to many in the middle ranks the good country life that had formerly seemed available only to those of title.

Not only did the pleasures of country life actually crown the success of several generations of English businessmen during the course of the nineteenth century, but apparently the lesser gentry and prosperous farmers also took pains to educate their daughters according to the principles of this conduct-book ideal. By 1825, then, one finds a conduct book modeling the exemplary household on that "of a respectable Country Gentleman, with a young family whose Net Income is from £16,000 to £18,000 a year, and whose expences do not exceed £7000." [24] The author nevertheless described this household in the conventional manner to contrast it sharply with the corrupt and extravagant habits attributed to the old aristocracy. At the same time, one can notice that such criticism of the aristocracy had lost most of its political edge. Sexual differences appear to have become much more important than economic differences in defining an individual's place in the world, and conduct books from the early decades of the nineteenth century had already come to see the country house, not as the center of aristocratic (male) power, but as the perfect realization of the domestic woman's (nonaristocratic) character. During the high Victorian age, this model of middle-class domesticity began to determine the way the aristocracy represented themselves as well. Mark Girouard cites a number of instances that testify to this curious loop in British cultural history:

> In the 1870s Lord and Lady Folkstone chose to be painted singing "Home, Sweet Home" with their eldest son. A portrait of Lord Armstrong, the millionaire arms dealer, shows him reading the newspaper in his dining room inglenook at Cragside, over the fireplace of which is inscribed "East or West, Home is Best." An essential part of the new image cultivated by both new and old families was their domesticity; they were anxious to show that their houses, however grand, were also homes and sheltered a happy family life. [25]

In comparing the domestic ideal as represented in conduct books to its appearance on the English countryside, one discovers a gap of more than a century between these written accounts and their social realization.

I call attention to this discontinuity in order to claim importance for representation itself. I want to suggest that by developing a language strictly for relations within the home, conduct books for women inadvertently provided the terms for rethinking relationships in the political world, for this language enabled authors to articulate both worlds while they appeared to represent only one. To this capability we can probably attribute the persistent sense that the conduct book spoke to male readers even while it addressed itself specifically to women. In so doing, the new domestic ideal succeeded where Defoe's island kingdom had failed. It established a private economy apart from the forms of rivalry and dependency that organized the world of men. The new domestic economy derived power from interest-bearing investments, a form of income that affectively destroyed the old agrarian ideal by effacing the whole system of status signs which lent that ideal its value. At the same time, the new country house harked back to an earlier agrarian world where the household was a largely self-contained social unit. In appearing to be logically prior to ideology in this respect, the new language of the household acquired power akin to that of natural law.

LABOR THAT IS NOT LABOR

Conduct books appear to be as sensitive to the difference between labor and leisure as they are to the tension between town and country or to the line separating the rich from the poor. This distinction was always implicit in the number of idle hours it was assumed a woman had to fill. In figuring out a way to convert this time into an ideal program of education, however, the books took labor and leisure off their separate conceptual planes and placed them in a moral continuum. Here a woman was ranked according to the specifically female virtues she possessed rather than to the value of he family name and social connections. But in order to create such a female system of values in the first place, the conduct books represented the domestic woman in opposition to certain practices attributed to women at both extremes of the social scale. A woman was deficient in female qualities if she, like the aristocratic woman, spent her time in idle amusements. As the conduct books represent them, such activities always aimed at putting the body on display, a carryover from the Renaissance display of aristocratic power. For a woman to display herself in such a manner was the same as saying that she was supposed to be valued for her body and its adornments, not for the virtues she might possess as a woman and wife. By the same token, the conduct books found the laboring woman unfit for domestic duties because she, too, located value in the material body. Conduct books attacked these two traditional notions of the female body in order to suggest that the female had depths far more valuable than her surface. By implying that the essence of the woman lay inside or underneath her surface, the invention of depths in the self entailed making the material body of the woman appear superficial. The invention of depth also provided the rationale for an educational program designed specifically for women, for these programs strove to subordinate the body to a set of mental processes that guaranteed domesticity.

It is important to observe how the conduct books differentiated the new woman from the woman who served as the means of displaying aristocratic power. As if of one mind, they agreed that any woman's value necessarily depreciated as she took up the practice of self-display. "It is true," remarks one book, "that the mere splendour of wealth and title will at all times attract a circle of admirers, as frivolous and uninformed as many of their possessors." Those who aspire to the fashionable world become "low minded satellites of fashion and greatness." They can never equal those whom they endeavor to mirror, the author continues, but "merely flatter themselves that they deserve a brilliancy and consequence from the more dignified body around which they move."[26] Although it appears to speak from an utterly conservative position, one quite in keeping with the ideology that prompted the royal proclamations of Elizabeth and James, this statement is shaped by a revealing contradiction that allows it to serve a set of interests absolutely opposed to those represented by the aristocratic body of Renaissance culture.

According to the logic of this statement, the genuine person of leisure is worth "more" than women who "merely" flatter themselves by virtue of their proximity to aristocratic power, but this is not the distinction that matters most in the author's system of values. While affording a precise way of differentiating members of the fashionable world, "splendour" and "brilliancy" nevertheless fail to provide a reliable way of assessing women. For the author of this conduct book, women who devote themselves to practical matters are less likely to be "frivolous and uninformed" than women who possess "wealth and title." But even though the practical kind "are infinitely to be preferred to that large class of superficial females whose sole ambition it is to be seen and noticed in the circle of gaiety," any outward and visible signs of value, even those of a practical nature, imply some emotional lack in the woman that significantly lowers her value on the marriage market. There is no doubt in the author's mind that "If a woman were only expert in the use of her needle, and properly skilled in domestic economy," she still would not be prepared to meet her domestic obligations.[27] To be completely prepared, she must also have the qualities of mind that ensure her vigilance over the household.

Before abandoning this example, we should take note of the fact that its attack on aristocratic conduct is more than an argument for a certain kind of woman or even for a certain kind of household; it is also an argument against the traditional notion of amusement. What happens to amusement reveals the most characteristic—and indeed powerful—rhetorical strategy of the conduct books. First they negate those practices that had been acceptable or even desirable cultural practices, and then they endow those practices with positive value by placing them within the framework of female subjectivity. It is of equal importance that these books overthrow the tradition going back to the proclamations of Elizabeth and James and, by a second inversion, situate subjectivity prior to the display of the body as the cause of unseemly female behavior. Thus we find the proclivity for self-display among certain woman represented as subjectivity gone awry: "Destitute of all *amusements with herself,* and incapable of perceiving her chief happiness to center at home, in the bosom of her family, a lady of this description daily sallies forth in quest of adventures" (italics mine).[28] The conduct books always use women who pursue amusement as examples to demonstrate why women lacking the conduct-book virtues do not make desirable wives. Such women are "regularly seen in the ballroom or at the card-table, at the opera or in the theatre, among the numberless devotees of dissipation and fashion."[29] That, in a word, is their crime: these women either want to be on display or simply allow themselves to be "seen." It is not that the conduct books disapprove of dancing, enjoying music, playing cards, or even attending theatrical performances when they are enjoyed in the sanctuary of one's parlor. This is a difference that both Austen and Burney scrupulously observe along with conduct-book authors. It is a woman's participation in public spectacle that injures her, for as an object of display, she always loses value as a subject. More than that, these books lump the woman of fashion together with "numberless" others who—in the conduct book's terms—similarly lack the quality of subjectivity that makes a woman desirable; she cannot be "seen" and still be vigilant. As it constitutes the female subject, then, such writing strips the body of the signs of identity that are essential to displaying female value according to aristocratic rules of kinship.

The production of female subjectivity entails the dismantling of the aristocratic body. In fact, the two must be understood as a single rhetorical move. So powerful was the effect of the critique of aristocratic behavior that by the end of the eighteenth century conduct books addressing words of advice to women of noble descent exhibit curious forms of stress and embarrassment. Written in 1806, Elizabeth Hamilton's *Letters: Addressed to the Daughter of a Nobleman on the Formation of Religious and Moral Principle* cannot assume that women of wealth and position also have virtue. She must take pains to argue such virtue back into existence. But even in this she proceeds by defensive strategies as she protests that wealth, beauty, and an elite education do not necessarily cancel out a woman's domestic virtues. On the basis of her familiarity with people of nobility, Mrs. Hamtilon insists "that the consciousness of high descent, and elevated rank, and splendid fortune, does not necessarily give birth to pride; no, not even where, in addition to these advantages, nature has bestowed the most transcendent talents, and the charm of every personal attraction!"[30] In contrast to the ordinary run of conduct books, furthermore, this one must abandon the logic that links outward signs of humility with domestic value. Instead, the author resorts to metaphor. Poetry is apparently the only way she can imagine to counter a logic that pits the brilliant features of aristocratic beauty against the inconspicuous features associated with domesticity (and a woman who wrote poetry could always be accused of indulging in a form of aristocratic display). So thoroughgoing was the condemnation of aristocratic display that Mrs. Hamilton feels compelled to devise figures linking surface to depth so that the brilliance of the surface will not imply an underlying emptiness. "Such persons are to society," she explains, "not only the brightest ornament, but the most estimable blessing. Their influence, like that of the sun, extends not merely to the surface; it penetrates into the dark and hidden places of the earth" (p. 108). By suggesting that a woman could have depth as well as surface, Mrs. Hamilton argues that a woman could excel in both public and private spheres, that she could be the object of the gaze and still possess the subjective qualities required of a good wife and mother. For all her efforts, however, Mrs. Hamilton's metaphors only direct the reader's attention to what could no longer be stated as truth.

It is a curious thing that even though conduct books represented aristocratic behavior as the very antithesis of the domestic woman, they never once exalted labor. They generally found women who worked for their living to be morally bankrupt too. The governess is an obvious case in point. Because her work was restricted to domestic duties, she belonged to the cast of respectable women, and hers was one of the few professions open to women of the gentry who had to support themselves. At the same time, the governess was commonly represented as a threat to the well-being of the household.[31] Whether she was in fact a person of breeding fallen from economic grace or someone of lower rank who hoped to elevate herself through a genteel education, she was marketing her class and education for money. The governess is particularly useful for purposes of my argument because she combines certain features of the aristocracy with those of the working woman. Yet that was clearly not the reason why authors and readers used her for drawing cultural lines. It was by fulfilling the duties of the domestic woman for money that she blurred a distinction on which the very notion of gender appeared to depend. She seemed to call into question an absolutely rigid distinction between domestic duty and labor that was performed for money, a distinction so deeply engraved upon the public mind that the figure of the prostitute could be freely invoked to describe any woman who dared to labor for money. One sweeping condemnation of female servants claimed that "Half the wretched beings of their sex, who live on the deplorable wages of iniquity, for the short time they live at all, are there being discharged out of service to pride." [32] The motivations of any woman who worked out of a desire for money were automatically in doubt, but it must have been particularly disturbing to think of such a woman supervising the young. The governess' transgression of the line distinguishing labor from domestic duty obviously lies behind such common assaults on her character as this: "Nor can we greatly wonder at the false position which governesses hold, when we consider how often they are induced by merely selfish and sordid motives to seek the employment which they ought to engage in only from a conviction of their fitness, mental and moral, for so important a post." [33]

As conduct books differentiated the woman's ideal role from both labor and amusement, they created a new category of labor. One finds that while these books elaborate all of the tasks that can be called domestic duty, they still represent the woman of the house as apparently having nothing to do. Ideally servants would perform most, if not all, of the work specified for maintaining the household. Yet the difference between the excesses that conduct books attributed to country-house life in an aristocratic culture and the domestic economy they envisioned for their readers has everything to do with the presence of the right kind of woman. To solve the enigma of what essential function this woman performed, I must refer back to the distinction between the woman as subject and the woman as the object of display. It is helpful to recall how the domestic woman comes into being as the notion of amusement is redefined within the framework of her subjectivity. In this way, hers appears to be precisely the power to turn behavior into psychological events. More than that, hers is the power to control and evaluate such events. To exercise this power, according to conduct-book logic, requires a passive and retiring woman. In 1798, the notably liberal thinker Erasmus Darwin held forth this kind of woman as the objective of his educational program:

> The female character should possess the mild and retiring virtues rather than the bold and dazzling ones; great eminence in almost anything is sometimes injurious to a young lady; whose temper and disposition should appear to be pliant rather than robust; to be ready to take impressions rather than to be decidedly marked; as great apparent strength of character, however excellent, is liable to alarm both her own and the other sex; and to create admiration rather than affection. [34]

Contrasting attributes shape each sentence, setting the mild-mannered woman of the conduct books against her flashier counterpart, the woman of high social station. Both characterizations are positive, yet one is definitely to be preferred over the other, and in purely semantic terms the domestic woman seems to be the less positive of the two. In other words, this author gives the traditional concept of female beauty its due in order to declare it obsolete. What he calls for is not a woman who attracts the gaze as she did in an earlier culture, but one who fulfills her role by disappearing into the woodwork to watch over the household. And thus Darwin concludes the introduction to his program for female education with this statement:

> Hence if to softness of manners, complacency of countenance, gentle un-
> hurried motion, with a voice clear and yet tender, the charms which enchant
> all hearts can be superadded internal strength and activity of mind, capable
> to transact the business or combat the evils of life, with a due sense of moral
> and religious obligation, all is attained which education can supply; the fe-
> male character becomes compleat, excites our love and commands our admi-
> ration. (p. 4)

In quoting this passage, I simply want to call attention to the shift in diction that locates power in the mental features of the domestic woman, power that was stripped away from the body in the preceding passage. So "compleat," this new woman commands "admiration" as well as "love" whereas before she deserved only "affection." In this comparison between two desirable women, we are witnessing the fact of cultural change from an earlier form of power based on sumptuary display to a modern form that works through the production of subjectivity.

The domestic woman's capacity to supervise was clearly more important than any other factor in determining the victory of this ardently undazzling creature over all her cultural competitors. For this reason, it appears, the peculiar combination of invisibility and vigilance personified in the domestic woman came to represent the principle of domestic economy itself. From *Thoughts in the Form of Maxims Addressed to Young Ladies on their First Establishment in the World* comes the advice, "Do not attempt to destroy his [the male's] innocent pleasures by pretexts of oeconomy; retrench rather your own expences to promote them."[35] The conduct books demonstrate how a woman who sought to enhance her value through forms of self-display would significantly diminish her family's possibilities for happiness, but more than her restraint from such behavior was required in order for the ideal domestic situation to be realized. The simple absence of domestic virtue would eliminate that possibility too. As one author writes:

> Vain are his [her husband's] labours to accumulate, if she cannot, or will not,
> expend with discretion. Vain too are his expectations of happiness if econ-
> omy, order, and regularity, are not to be found at home; and the woman who
> has no feeling and principle sufficient to regulate her conduct in these con-
> cerns, will rarely acquit herself respectable in the more elevated posts of fe-
> male duty.[36]

If "his" aim is "to accumulate," then "hers" is "to regulate," and on "her conduct in these concerns" depends the success of all "his labours." By implication, female "feeling and principle" increase male earning power by freeing up capital even as it is taken in and consumed by the household. The domestic woman executes her role in the household by regulating her own desire. On her "feeling and principle" depends the economic behavior that alone ensures prosperity. So conceived, self-regulation became a form of labor that was superior to labor. Self-regulation alone gave a woman authority over the field of domestic objects and personnel where her supervision constituted a form of value in its own right and was therefore capable of enhancing the value of other people and things.

ECONOMY THAT IS NOT MONEY

Because it suppressed economic differences, particularly concealing the ever-widening gulf between rich and poor, this new form of value made sense to people with widely varying incomes in the old society. Despite its association with wealth and leisure, the country house also carried with it some of the cultural residue of a self-sufficient economy. True to their roots in the domestic economies of an earlier period, conduct books represented such an economy in opposition to one based on money. The conduct books invariably reformulated this opposition as their way of mounting an attack on what they saw as the excesses of a corrupt aristocracy. The recipes comprising the bulk of *The Compleat Housewife or, Accomplished Gentlewoman's Companion* reveal some rather costly ingredients—partridge and venison, for example—that average Englishmen obviously could not afford to enjoy without becoming either gentlemen or poachers. Insisting nonetheless on their suitability "for a frugal as well as for a sumptuous table," the author does not mean to imply that his is a subsistence diet. His intention is that of a reformer: to combat the evils of the aristocratic standard of taste with an alternative standard that is, by implication, better for all but those of the lower rank of society. "There are indeed already in the World various books that treat on the Subject and which bear great Names, as Cooks to Kings, Princes, and Noblemen," his preface declares, but "many of them to us are impracticable, others whimsical, others impalatable, unless to depraved Palates" (p. 2). By representing the more privileged table as an object of disgust, such handbooks invest the frugal table with superior value.

Material differences appear to have little to do with determining the quality of life one can enjoy. As the author of *The Compleat Housewife* situates the ideal table in opposition to meals that display wealth and title, he calls attention to qualities of mind he observes in the objects under his consideration, qualities that include practicality, wholesomeness, steadiness, and concern for health. The frugal table nourishes the social body, just as aristocratic taste corrupts it. Unlike that which enforces hierarchical distinctions, the more moderate standard of living extends to a wide spectrum of individuals within the economy. But if the conduct-book rhetoric did not exclude those at the bottom of the economic ladder from the good life, it never suggested the poor could live life as well as those who had plenty of money. Although relatively few felt compelled to say it in so many words, it was always assumed, as one of the more outspoken authors explains, that "where the blessings of independence and fortune are liberally bestowed, sufficient time may easily be found for all the purposes of mental improvement, without neglecting any of the more important and sacred offices of active vir-tue."[37] Such virtue evidently belonged to the woman who had neither suffered economic scarcity nor indulged in extravagance. As another conduct book ex-plains, one's wife is much more likely to be frugal "if she has always been used to a good style of living in her father's house."[38] This subordination of money to a higher standard of value distinguished the ideal household from family life both at the top and at the bottom of the social ladder where—in each case—people were known for their profligate spending.

All these examples either suggest or openly state that without the domestic woman the entire domestic framework would collapse. From the beginning, her supervisory presence was a necessary component of its cultural logic. The con-sistency with which such terms as "modesty," "frugality," "regularity," and "discretion" recur cannot be ignored. The more practical conduct books address quite different local readerships concerning the constitution of the household, the nature of its objects, the number and kinds of its servants, the manner of its table, the style of its occupants' dress, and the conduct of their leisure activities, often down to the smallest detail in one category or another. But by the time the eighteenth century was well underway, the general categories of a domestic do-main had been established and linked to qualities in the female. She brought these qualities to the sexual contract. At the same time, they were qualities that became demonstrably hers as she ran the household according to the taste that she acquired through a female education. This is to say the female character and that of the home became one and the same as she translated her husband's in-come into the objects and personnel comprising his household. Such an ex-change at once enacted an economic contract and concealed the particular nature of the transaction because it fulfilled the sexual contract.

It must have been a remarkable moment when this way of representing kinship relations took hold. For the first time in history a view was put forth—admittedly a minority view—that appealed to people from radically different backgrounds, with substantially different incomes, and with positions in differ-ent chains of social relations. Any number of people in the middle ranks could thus believe that the same ideal of domestic life was available to them. To imag-ine this was to imagine an order of political relations that was substantially differ-ent from the one in force at that moment of history. To explain why the new mode of political thinking depended on the production of a certain kind of woman, I have chosen *The Compleat Servant*, a handbook from 1825, to demon-strate just how precisely codified—and hence reproducible—the sexual contract had become by the time the new middle classes were beginning to assume cul-tural ascendancy.

Identifying himself as "a servant who had passed time in the homes of the great," the anonymous author of *The Compleat Servant* shows how the principles of domestic economy might be translated into a precise calculus for the good life that could be extended to people of various incomes. Such is the claim of his preface: "As no relations in society are so numerous and universal as those of Masters and Servants—as those of Household Duties and performers of them—so it is proportionately important that they should be well defined and under-stood."[39] His idea of how the domestic economy relates to economy per se is so precise he can graphically represent the conversion of the one into the other:[40]

Net Annual Inc.	Household expense	Servants and equipment	Cloths and extras	Rent and repairs	Reserve
£1000	333	250	250	125	42
£2000	666	500	500	250	84
£3000	1000	750	750	375	375
...	...	...	...	...	...
£10,000	3333	2500	2500	1250	420

Most striking is the way in which this graphic representation translates the economic contract into a sexual one. The first column, or amount of income, represents what the male brings to the exchange. Although this way of designating male value distinguishes one individual from another according to the amount of money each brings to the household, it is important to note that the figure of sexual exchange has already translated the vertical organization of the old society into terms that nearly destroy its heterogeneity. As a result, the figure behaves much like any other representation of the social contract; it creates the very differences it proposes to unify. The chart specifies income as an amount rather than as a form of labor, trade, or service in relation to those whom one serves and who in turn serve him. Value is cut free from its source in human labor, and merely quantitative differences replace the qualitative distinctions of status and rank that held together the old society. In this purely relational system, income alone has come to represent the male party of the sexual exchange.

The transformation of male identity is only one half of an exchange between gender-specific systems of value. The chart cited above records two separate semiotic moves that together implicitly transform the whole organization of British society. The first strips the male of his traditional political identity, which was based on privileges of birth and proximity to the crown. The second converts income (the left-hand column) into the categories of the household. If we have to read vertically to gather the information concerning the male, then the chart requires us to read horizontally for the female. Under her supervision, income is taken into the household where it becomes a field of information organized according to the categories of domestic economy. The female operates in this sexual exchange to transform a given quantity of income into a desirable quality of life. Her powers of supervision ensure the income will be distributed according to certain proportions designed to meet certain domestic criteria, no matter what the amount of the husband's income may be. This double translation of one's social value—from a concept of quality based on birth to a quantity of income, which then materializes as a certain quality of domestic life—creates the economic basis for affiliation among competing interest groups. It creates an ideal exchange in which the female alone can perform the necessary economic transformation. Such a representation implies that people with incomes ranging from £1000 to £10,000 per year could share a world of similar proportions and therefore aspire to the same quality of life. There is also the implication that this world is available to those higher (as indeed the author's exemplary gentleman was) as well as lower on the social ladder, provided they choose to observe the categories comprising the economy of the ideal country life.

But *The Compleat Servant* does not leave it at that. It goes on to elaborate each category of objects, services, and personnel down to the microlevel of the individual item and its value in guineas. So even as this model of good country living has near universal applicability, it also makes quite specific recommendations. To demonstrate how representation can be at once so highly generalized and yet specialized for the individual case, I include the following list, which explains how money should be distributed to personnel: [41]

	Guineas
Housekeeper	24
Female Teacher	30
Lady's Maid	20
Head Nurse	20
Second Ditto	10
Nursery Maid	7
Upper House-Maid	15
Under House-Maid	14
Kitchen Maid	14
Upper Laundry Maid	14
Under Ditto	10
Dairy Maid	8
Second Ditto	7
Still Room Maid	9
Scullion	9
A French Man Cook	80
Butler	50
Coachman	28
Footman	24
Under Ditto	20
Grooms	
Nursery Room Boy	
2 Gameskeepers	
2 Gardeners	

Only a very few of the author's possible readers could hope to meet all the expenses on the list. But in order to create the same household on considerably less, he explains, one need only begin at the top of the list, omit the dittos, and consume in proportion to the amount of one's income. Thus we see why he has included basic housekeepers and childcare personnel at the top of the list, while relegating to the bottom, as least necessary, those servants whom only people of privilege can employ. The vertical system of relationships based on the quantity of the man's income is therefore preserved, but this quantitative standard is also inverted as it is enclosed within a female field of information where qualitative values ideally dominate. The author insists that, even so, anyone can observe the correct proportions and, within proportioning categories, the correct exercise of priorities. In his view, only the exercise of these personal qualities—elsewhere known as "discretion," "modesty," "frugality," and "regularity"—can ensure domestic happiness.

This handbook offers an unusually systematic representation—a grammar, really—of what was by that time in history a common language of objects and domestic personnel. It is fair to say that from the mid-eighteenth century on, every female conduct book presupposed such a grammar just by focusing on one or more of its categories. The principle of translation demonstrated in the above-cited text was at work in most conduct books from the beginning of the eighteenth century. By the early nineteenth century when *The Compleat Servant* appeared, then, this principle had transformed the material surface of social life to the point where such a descriptive grammar could be written. It was not that English homes underwent wholesale redecoration. I think it more likely that the texture of the household changed as people started reading it differently, that is, as people began to regard the household in the terms of a written representation. At least it is quite plausible that domestic life first became an autonomous text when its objects and personnel, which appeared to have little relation to region and the local labor conditions external to them, achieved identity according to an internal force—a psychological principle—that held them all together. By means of this principle of reading, too, the household ceased to display the value of the man's income and instead took on the innermost human qualities of the woman who regulated the domestic economy.

As a world of objects thus invested with meaning, the household could not be invoked and used arbitrarily any more by authors of fiction than by those who wrote conduct books. Domestic fiction proceeded from the assumption that a similar interpretive mechanism could be put in motion merely by representing these objects in language. Such language would be governed by the very same rule that converted material differences into psychological ones, or male values into female norms. Before Richardson wrote *Pamela*, the feminized household was already a familiar field of information, but it had yet to be written as fiction. And by the time Austen's novels appeared, the sophisticated grammar organizing that field evidently had so passed into common knowledge that it could simply be taken for granted. If Austen's writing proceeds with a kind of unprecedented economy and precision, it is at least in part owing to this intertextuality. In her world, one could not only extrapolate a man's net worth from just a few household objects, but could also place his wife on a psychological scale. In *Emma*, for example, Frank Churchill's capricious purchase of a piano for Jane Fairfax represents an intrusion of male values into the exclusively female household of her Aunt Miss Bates. The mere appearance of an object that violates the proportions and priorities of such a household is enough to generate scandalous narratives implying that Jane has given in to seduction. Or Augusta Elton's failure to appreciate Emma's modest style of wedding dress—"Very little white satin, very few lace veils; a most pitiful business!"[42]—is sufficient to brand her own taste as hopelessly bound to materialistic values that contradict the metaphysics of domesticity dominating Austen's ideal community.

Later on, Mrs. Gaskell extended this code of values into the households of the laboring poor. In *Mary Barton*, she describes this scene in order to demonstrate how a woman's devoted application of domestic economy might enhance the value of a man's meager wages:

> In the corner between the window and the fire-side was a cupboard, apparently full of plates and dishes, cups and saucers, and some more nondescript

articles, for which one would have fancied their possessors could find no use—such as triangular pieces of glass to save carving knives and forks from dirtying tablecloths.[43]

The Brontës, on the other hand, would carry the same ideal forth into the Yorkshire countryside where the apportionment of space within a house and the objects that fill it always decribe the coming into being of this object world and the clash between its values and those of the traditional country house. But Dickens would carry the art of this object language to its logical extreme by creating a totally fetishized world. One need not think only of the junk shops that reappear here and there throughout his fiction, nor even of Wemmick's castle in *Great Expectations*, which Lévi-Strauss took as his example par excellence of bricolage, or a second-hand object language.[44] More important even than these curious set pieces are Dickensian representations of the household inhabited by new money. Here one watches objects enter into a demonic exchange with their owners whereby things acquire human qualities and the people who live in a relationship with such things become as objects regulated by the very things they have endowed with human value. As Dorothy Van Ghent has noted, this particular form of exchange between subject and object permeates the Dickensian world and generates its distinctive character, which is that of a world all of surface where individuals convey the absence of depth.[45] There is, for instance, the well-known passage from *Our Mutual Friend* where Dickens allows a piece of the Podsnap plate to pass for commentary on the people assembled around it:

> Hideous solidity was the characteristic of the Podsnap plate. Everything was made to look as heavy as it could, and to take up as much room as possible. Everything said boastfully, "Here you have as much of me in my ugliness as if I were only lead; but I am so many ounces of precious metal worth so much an ounce;—wouldn't you like to melt me down?" A corpulent straggling epergne, blotched all over as if it had broken out in an eruption rather than been ornamented, delivered this address from an unsightly silver platform in the centre of the table.[46]

One should note that this critique of Podsnappery aims not at those who fulfill the conduct-book code, but at those who use objects to display wealth and power. Dickens' affection for cultural inversion leaves unmolested the whole idea of the household as a purely relational system of objects that includes people among them. The appearance of this world of objects that is free of labor distinguishes the home from the world of work and binds individuals together by forms of affection rather than by any need for economic survival. To construct and preserve this world without labor requires unflagging concern and vigilance, however, and this is where the female ideally figures in. She and not the male, as Dickens proves better than anyone else, should endow things with her docile features of character.

THE POWER OF FEMINIZATION

From the beginning of the eighteenth century, conduct books had always presupposed the existence of a gendered self, a self based on the existence of positive female features rather than on the lack or even the inversion of certain qualities of the male. In writing *The Character of a Good Woman, both in a Single and Married State* (1697), for example, the author feels he should defer to a feminine readership on religious matters despite the fact he is speaking as their religious instructor. "To you we are beholden," he says, speaking both as a male and as a member of the clergy, "for the Devotion and Numerousness of our Assemblies, for you are without flattery, generally more serious than Men, and you helpt to make them so."[47] By the end of the eighteenth century, however, such statements of deference not only represented the essential qualities of female nature, but they did so in a way that endowed this representation with the power of behavioral norms. As conduct books transformed the female into the bearer of moral norms and socializer of men, they also changed the qualities once attributed to her nature and turned them into techniques for regulating desire. These techniques aimed at nothing so clearly as producing gender-differentiated forms of economic behavior. Conduct books of the mid-nineteenth century thus completed a circular process that would also change the economic practices considered most natural and desirable in a male.

Written in the United States in 1853, T. S. Arthur's *Advice to Young Ladies on their Duties and Conduct in Life* extends the principle of female virtue into the rationale for a form of economic behavior that became known as the doctrine of enlightened self-interest. This doctrine represented the principle of female education in a way that made it applicable to men as well as to women, as the author's diction implies:

> We are all lovers of ourselves more than lovers of God, and lovers of the world more than lovers of our neighbors; and it is hard for us to conceive how there is any real pleasure to be found in denying our own selfish desires in order to seek the good of another. A very little experience, however, will make us plainly see that the inward delight arising from the consciousness of having done good to another is the sweetest of all delights we have ever known. (p. 13)

This passage first attacks the Christian notion of self-sacrifice on grounds that it violates the facts of human nature over which self-interest holds sway. The Christian ethos is dismissed by the first sentence, however, only to be slipped back in through the second. Once banished, conventional theological doctrine returns in a thoroughly secularized form, as a quality that is considered by the author to be necessary in a woman and that has universal application as well. If conduct books habitually opposed their feminine ethos to aristocratic self-indulgence, then they did so in order to transform man's acquisitive instincts to serve the general good. They did not try to suppress those instincts. Represented as qualities inherent in sexuality, which were then differentiated according to gender, the two forms of desire—acquisitiveness and altruism—posed no contradiction. The sexual exchange converted male acquisitiveness into objects that diffused gratification throughout the household.

The logic of the contract had so thoroughly reorganized sexual relations by the beginning of the nineteenth century that the principle of domestic duty could be extended, then, beyond the middle-class household to form the basis of a general social policy. The reformist platform of Hannah More and her colleagues was founded on this principle. "Even those who admit of the power of female ele-

gance on the manners of men," she argues, "do not always attend to the influence of female principles on their character."[48] If it is given to women to regulate
the desires of men, then domestication constitutes a political force of no meager
consequence, according to More. As she explains in the opening to her *Strictures
on the Modern System of Female Education,*

> The general state of civilized society depends, more than those are aware
> who are not accustomed to scrutinize into the springs of human action, on
> the prevailing sentiments and habits of women, and on the nature of the es-
> timation in which they are held. (p. 313)

Dr. Gregory similarly assures his many readers, "The power of a fine woman
over the hearts of men, of men of the finest parts, is even beyond what she conceives."[49] With a kind of relentlessness, nineteenth-century authors picked up
the language that would identify supervisory skills with a woman's sexual appeal.
Written in 1822, *The New Female Instructor or, Young Woman's Guide to Domestic
Happiness* cites "instances of the ascendancy with which WOMEN OF SENSE have
always gained over men of feeling."[50] Invoking the belief that specific powers
adhered to gender, the author promises to elaborate "all those qualities which
will enable you to attain the much desired art of pleasing, which will entitle you
to the character of a WOMAN OF SENSE, and which will bestow on you all the
power of which I have just spoken" (p. 2).

As such writing turned sexual pleasure into a regulatory power, it also endowed
the power of surveillance with all the characteristics of a benevolent parent. The
new practical curriculum adopted the strategy formulated by conduct-book authors as it set out to produce a self-regulating individual. It would introduce practical mathematics and science into the standard curriculum, to be sure, but
throughout the first half of the nineteenth century and well into the second, the
educational reformers—reformers of all kinds for that matter—concentrated in-
ordinate energy on controlling the peripheral activities of the individual's leisure
rather than on ensuring one's economic survival.[51] Pedagogical concern seemed
to fix upon novels, newspapers, and conversation and not upon the seemingly
more practical areas of knowledge. The next chapter—and indeed the rest of the
book—will focus on this notion of literacy as a form of social control. For now it
need only be said that many conduct-book authors seemed to feel a woman's
education amounted to little more than instilling good reading habits and cultivating conversational skills. They appeared to feel confident that such an education would establish the basis for her effective management of the home.

This notion of women's work as the regulation of information lies behind a
fable included in T. S. Arthur's handbook. It should therefore give us some idea
of how the strategies of domestication would be turned into a broad-reaching—
and inherently colonial—policy in the States. The fable states that its purpose is
to prove that "No matter how many and great may be the disadvantages under
which a young girl may labor, she may yet rise, if she will, very much above the
point, in external condition, from which she started in life."[52] At the same moment when the popularity of self-help philosophy was peaking,[53] the conduct
books declined to show that a working woman could elevate herself socially
through industrious labor. To the contrary, we are told,

> Out of the young girls in the work-room where Ann [the heroine of the fable]
> learned her trade, all with no better advantages than she had possessed,
> seven married men of low minds and vulgar habits, and never rose above
> their original condition. Two were more like Ann, and they were sought by
> young men of a better class. One of them did not marry. (p. 76)

Indeed, the fable shows that as Ann rises above those "of low minds and vulgar habits" through her mastery of the lessons of feminine conduct, she elevates herself socially; she becomes a woman whom "a better class" of men are willing to marry. As far as this story is concerned, all that is necessary for a woman to rise above her "original condition" is to resist the temptations of idleness and become an example of the middle-class norms of femininity. Having established this as the grounds for her sexual appeal to the male, the tale concludes with a description of the reward Ann earns for so nearly embodying the female standard: "And in proportion as she thus rises will she find a higher degree of happiness and be able to do more good than otherwise would have been possible to her" (p. 76). If by internalizing the conduct-book norms, Ann can marry above her station, then altruism is both the reward for this effort of self-regulation and her obligation as the wife of a prosperous man. The tale concludes, in other words, by exalting a form of labor that is no labor at all, but a form of self-regulation that serves as an end in itself.

 This principle would be extrapolated from the household and applied to society at large where it offered a way of displaying aristocratic largesse—or benevolent paternalism, as it is more appropriately called—in relation to those groups who had suffered most from the changes brought about by England's industrialization. The political application of this new idea of labor becomes instantly apparent if one observes how the principle organizing the household was extended outward to provide the liberal rhetoric for representing the relationship between one social group and another. In devising a curriculum for a boarding school run by his two illegitimate daughters, Erasmus Darwin tried to think of a way of instilling in women the idea that their work was its own reward. "There should be a plan in schools to promote the habit as well as the principle of benevolence," as he calls it. With this in mind, he suggests that "each lady might occasionally contribute a small sum, on seeing a needy naked child, to purchase flannel or coarse linen for clothes, which they might learn to cut out, and to make up themselves; and thus the practice of industry might be united with that of liberality."[54] In allowing women to produce goods for charity when it was no longer respectable for them to produce goods for their own kin, much less for purposes of trade, the conduct books fostered a certain form of power relations that would flourish later as the welfare institutions of a modern culture developed.

 It was their acknowledged aptitude for performing acts of charity that first enabled women to move out of the home and into the political arena. As Martha Vicinus has argued, "The public debate about conditions among the urban poor gave reformers the opening they needed."[55] On the basis of a need for charitable work among these newly impoverished social elements, women began carving out territory for domestic work in the larger social arena. Vicinus offers a particularly telling quote from Frances Power Cobbe, an advocate for celibacy among single women, to illustrate this line of argument:

"The private and home duties of *such women as have them* are, beyond all doubt, their first concern, and one which, when fully met, must often engross all their time and energies. But it is an absurdity, peculiar to the treatment of women, to go on assuming that all of them *have* home duties, and tacitly treating those who have none as if they were wrongly placed on God's earth, and had nothing whatever to do in it. There must needs be a purpose for the lives of single women in the social order of Providence . . . she has *not* fewer duties than others, but more extended and perhaps laborious ones. Not selfishness—gross to a proverb—but self-sacrifice more entire than belongs to the double life of marriage, is the true law of celibacy." (pp. 13–14)

Translating Cobbe's statement into the terms of this chapter, one can see the notion of charity was inexorably linked to the female role of household overseer. One can see, too, how the same logic that allowed women to carry the skills they possessed as women into the new world of work would eventually provide the liberal rationale for extending the doctrine of self-regulation and, with it, the subtle techniques of domestic surveillance beyond the middle-class home and into the lives of those much lower down on the economic ladder. It was not uncommon for nineteenth-century conduct books to put forth a rather explicit theory of social control, as exemplified in the following statement:

> Take a mind at the lowest possible grade, the little outcast of the streets, abandoned by parents from whom even nature's humanizing instincts had disappeared, exposed to every influence of evil, and knowing none for good; the first steps to reclaim, to humanize such a mind, would be to place it in a moral atmosphere, to cultivate and raise its intelligence, and to improve its physical condition.[56]

I simply want to take note of how educational theory places all the stress on psychological rehabilitation. The "physical condition" of the "little outcast of the streets" comes as something of an afterthought.

The sexual division of labor may have begun by allowing two different ways of understanding the social reality to coexist side by side, rather like the Puritan model of marriage. But the insertion of a new idea of work into the field of social information would eventually make the sexual division of labor serve as a way of reconceiving the whole. Because they confined themselves strictly to matters of domestic economy, the conduct books may seem less noteworthy in themselves than the other writing characterizing the eighteenth and nineteenth centuries. But what I have been tracing by circling backwards and forwards in time across this relatively ignored yet utterly familiar body of data is the formation of a specialized language of sexuality. In suppressing chronology, my point has been to show how this language—by circulating between the psychological and the economic, as well as between the individual and the state—separated and reconstituted each in relation to the other and so produced a discourse, a new way of packaging cultural information that changed the entire surface of social life. Such a change could not have occurred in a single moment or through the effort of any particular person, even though some kinds of writing clearly enjoyed more currency than others during this period of time. More likely, the change worked through the persistent use of certain terms, oppositions, or figures until sexual differences acquired the status of truth and no longer needed to be written as such. Taking on the power of a metaphysics, then, these categories had the power to influence not only the way people understood work, but also how they viewed, and thus experienced desire for, the world of objects.

Despite noticeable changes in the stress and terminology of the conduct books, which point us outside the household to the vicissitudes of economic life, to social history and the affairs of men, as well as to the sequence of events that have come to comprise literary history, I have for the most part regarded these quite different texts as a single voice and continuous discourse. My purpose in doing so has been to show how I think domestic culture actually worked as a principle of continuity that pervaded the social surface to provide a stable conceptual framework within which these "outside" changes appear as so many variations on the sexual theme. Although a female genre, often written by women and directed at female readers, conduct books of the eighteenth and nineteenth centuries—or for that matter, earlier female conduct books—were attuned to the economic interests that they designated as the domain of the male. By virtue of its apparent detachment from the larger economy of which it was an instrumental part, domestic economy provided the fables in terms of which economic relations would also be rethought. Furthermore, as I have argued, sexual relations could shape this new master narrative precisely because its power seemed to be so restricted.

As conduct books rewrote the female subject for an eighteenth-century audience, they shifted the whole strategic intention of the genre from reproducing the status quo—an aristocratic household—to producing an ever-retreating future. If it preceded the formation of a coherent set of economic policies associated with capitalism, this reformist rhetoric anticipated even the establishment of marriage as a social institution. The conduct books always saw the domestic world as one that ought to be realized. When passage of the Marriage Act of 1754 institutionalized the household and placed it more firmly under state control than ever before, the sense of its futurity did not vanish for authors and readers of conduct books. With the wild demographic shifts of the late eighteenth century and the violent labor disputes of subsequent decades, the sexual division of labor rapidly became a *fait accompli*, but the conduct books preserved their rhetorical edge of a promise yet to be realized. Even today this promise apparently cannot be distinguished from the form itself. Such handbooks still offer the power of self-transformation. The illusion persists that there is a self independent of the material conditions that have produced it and that such a self can transform itself without transforming the social and economic configuration in opposition to which it is constructed. This transformational power still seems to arise from within the self and to affect that self through strategies of self-discipline, the most perfect realization of which is perhaps anorexia nervosa. What we encounter in books of instruction for women, then, is something on the order of Foucault's productive hypothesis that continues to work upon the material body unencumbered by political history because that body is the body of a woman. On grounds that her sexual identity has been suppressed by a class that valued her chiefly for material reasons rather than for herself, the rhetoric of the conduct books produced a subject who in fact had no material body at all. This rhetoric replaced the material body with a metaphysical body made largely of words, albeit words constituting a material form of power in their own right. The modern female body comprised a grammar of subjectivity capable of regulating desire, pleasure, the ordinary care of the body, the conduct of courtship, the division of labor, and the dynamic of family relationships.

As such, the writing of female subjectivity opened a magical space in the culture where ordinary work could find its proper gratification and where the very objects that set men against one another in the competitive marketplace served to bind them together in a community of common domestic values. If the marketplace driven by male labor came to be imagined as a centrifugal force that broke up the vertical chains organizing an earlier notion of society and that scattered individuals willy-nilly across the English landscape, then the household's dynamic was conceived as a centripetal one. The household simultaneously recentered the scattered community at myriad points to form the nuclear family, a social organization with a mother rather than a father as its center. The very fact of its interlocking symmetries suggests that the doubled social world was clearly a myth before it was put into practice, as was indeed the case for almost a century.

NOTES

1. There have been conduct books ever since the Middle Ages. From medieval to modern example, they most always imply a readership who desires self-improvement and for whom self-improvement promises an elevation of social position. For a collection of essays that discuss the wide variety of conduct books from the Middle Ages to the present day, see *The Ideology of Conduct: Essays in Literature and the History of Sexuality*, eds. Nancy Armstrong and Leonard Tennenhouse (New York: Methuen, 1987). For a discussion of conduct books in the Middle Ages, see Kathleen Ashley, "Medieval Courtesy Literature and Dramatic Mirrors for Female Conduct," in *The Ideology of Conduct*. See Ann R. Jones, "Nets and Bridles: Conduct Books for Women 1416–1643," in *The Ideology of Conduct*, for a discussion of conduct literature in Renaissance England and Italy. Also see Suzanne M. Hull, *Chaste Silent & Obedient: English Books for Women 1475–1640* (San Marino, Calif.: Huntington Library, 1982); Ruth Kelso, *The Doctrine for the Lady of the Renaissance* (Urbana, Ill.: University of Illinois Press, 1956); Louis B. Wright, *Middle-Class Culture in Elizabethan England* (Ithaca, N.Y.: Cornell University Press, 1935), pp. 121–227; and John E. Mason, *Gentlefolk in the Making: Studies in the History of English Courtesy Literature and Related Topics from 1531 to 1774* (Philadelphia: University of Pennsylvania Press, 1935). The eighteenth-century conduct book has been discussed by Joyce Hemlow, "Fanny Burney and the Courtesy Books," *PMLA*, 65 (1950), 732–61; Marilyn Butler, *Maria Edgeworth: A Literary Biography* (Oxford: Clarendon, 1972); and Mary Poovey, *The Proper Lady and the Woman Writer: Ideology as Style in the Works of Mary Wollstonecraft, Mary Shelley, and Jane Austen* (Chicago: University of Chicago Press, 1984), pp. 3–47.

2. Frank Whigham, *Ambition and Privilege: The Social Tropes of Elizabethan Courtesy Theory* (Berkeley: University of California Press, 1984); John L. Lievsay, *Stefano Guazzo and the English Renaissance, 1575–1675* (Chapel Hill: University of North Carolina Press, 1961); and Ruth Kelso, *The Doctrine of the English Gentleman in the Sixteenth Century*, Vol. 14, *University of Illinois Studies in Language and Literature* (1929).

3. See, for example, Hull, pp. 31–70.

4. For a discussion of such writing produced by women during the seventeenth century, see Patricia Crawford, "Women's Published Writings 1600–1700," in *Women in English Society 1500–1800*, ed. Mary Prior (New York: Methuen, 1985), pp. 211–81.

5. Bathsua Makin, *An essay to revive the antient education of gentlewomen* (1673), cited by Crawford, p. 229.

6. Hemlow, "Fanny Burney and the Courtesy Books," p. 732.

7. See Crawford's Appendix 2, pp. 265–71.

8. Commenting on a later surge in the publication of conduct books, Mary Poovey claims that "Conduct material of all kinds increased in volume and popularity after the 1740s," p. 15.

9. Raymond Williams notes that the failure to renew the licensing act in 1695 resulted directly in the growth of the press, *The Long Revolution* (London: Chatto and Windus, 1961), pp. 180–81.

10. Mason, *Gentlefolk in the Making*, p. 208. *The Whole Duty of a Woman . . . Written by a Lady* (1695) should not be confused with the later *The Whole Duty of Woman* (1753) written by William Kendrick.

11. Harold Perkin, *The Origins of Modern English Society 1780–1880* (London: Routledge and Kegan Paul, 1969), p. 24. Citations of the text are to this edition. Perkin follows a line of argument similar to Peter Laslett, *The World We Have Lost: England Before the Industrial Age,* 2nd ed. (New York: Charles Scribner's, 1971), pp. 23–54. R. S. Neal has faulted Perkin and Laslett for offering a historical representation of society that does not reveal the makings of a class conflict, *Class in English History 1680–1850* (Totowa, N.J.: Barnes and Noble Books, 1981), pp. 68–99. See as well E. P. Thompson, "Eighteenth-Century English Society: Class Struggle Without Class?" in *Social History*, 3 (1978), 133–65. Perkin responds to Thompson in "The Condescension of Posterity: Middle-Class Intellectuals and the History of the Working Class," in *The Structured Crowd: Essays in English Social History* (Sussex: The Harvester Press, 1981), pp. 168–85. Both Perkin and Laslett rely heavily on the manner in which social relations were represented to formulate histories of those relations. In citing Perkin for certain kinds of information, I am not interested so much in how he says things really were as I am in the representations he uses. I am interested in the struggle among such representations to define a social reality. It is in relation to the data that modern historians consider as history that I position "female" information, which represents, in my opinion, this nascent capitalist thinking.

12. Ian Watt, *The Rise of the Novel* (Berkeley: University of California Press, 1957) and Richard D. Altick, *The English Common Reader: A Social History of the Mass Reading Public 1800–1900* (Chicago: University of Chicago Press, 1957).

13. Timothy Rogers, *The Character of a Good Woman, both in a Single and Married State* (London, 1697), p. 3. Citations of the text are to this edition.

14. *The Young Ladies Companion or, Beauty's Looking-Glass* (London, 1740). Citations of the text are to this edition.

15. E. Smith, *The Compleat Housewife or, Accomplished Gentlewomen's Companion* (London, 1734), p. 2. Citations of the text are to this edition.

16. T. S. Arthur, *Advice to Young Ladies on their Duties and Conduct in Life* (London, 1853), pp. 12. Citations of the text are to this edition. Although this is an American conduct book, its inclusion in the Fawcett Museum collection—whose other holdings in this area are British—suggests that it was among the few that were popular in England as well as abroad. It is possible that the more active duties required of New England women at this time were deemed appropriate for English women of the lower middle classes.

17. Thomas Broadhurst, *Advice to Young Ladies on the Improvement of the Mind and Conduct of Life* (London, 1810), pp. 4–5.

18. Jacques Donzelot writes that "wealth was produced to provide for the munificence of states. It was their [the aristocracy's] sumptuary activity, the multiplication and refinement of the needs of the central authority, that was conducive to production. Hence wealth was in the manifest power that permitted levies by the state for the benefit of a minority." *The Policing of Families*, trans. Robert Hurley (New York: Pantheon, 1979), p. 13.

In this manner, the display of wealth as ornamentation of the body was a sign of social rank that could be read by one and all.

19. For a discussion of the country-house poem, see G. R. Hibbard, "The Country House Poem of the Seventeenth Century," *Journal of the Warburg and Courtauld Institutes*, 19 (1956), 159–74; Charles Molesworth, "Property and Virtue: the Genre of the Country-House Poem in the Seventeenth Century," *Genre*, 1 (1968), 141–57; William Alexander McClung, *The Country House in English Renaissance Poetry* (Berkeley: University of California Press, 1977); Don E. Wayne, *Penshurst: The Semiotics of Place and the Poetics of History* (Madison: University of Wisconsin Press, 1984); and Virginia C. Kinny, *The Country-House Ethos in English Literature 1688–1750: Themes of Personal Retreat and National Expansion* (Sussex: The Harvester Press, 1985). Don E. Wayne argues that it was nostalgia for the ideals of the old but now vanished aristocracy that the new country house was always supposed to summon up; even today the surviving country homes retain, in his words, "a vestige" of "the theater for the enactment of a certain concept of 'home'" (p. 11).

20. *Tudor Royal Proclamations, The Later Tudors: 1588–1603*, vol. III, eds. Paul L. Hughes and James F. Larkin (New Haven: Yale University Press, 1969), p. 175. Citations of the text are to this edition.

21. Leah S. Marcus, " 'Present Occasions' and the Shaping of Ben Jonson's Masques," *ELH*, 45 (1978), 201–25.

22. *The Political Works of James I*, ed. C. H. McIlwain (Cambridge: Harvard University Press, 1918), p. 343. Citations of the text are to this edition.

23. Harry Payne, "Elite *vs* Popular Mentality in the Eighteenth Century," *Studies in Eighteenth Century Culture*, 8 (1979), 110.

24. *The Complete Servant, Being a Practical Guide to the Peculiar Duties and Business of all Descriptions of Servants* (London, 1825), p. 4.

25. Mark Girouard, *Life in the English Country House: A Social and Architectural History* (New Haven: Yale University Press, 1978), p. 270.

26. Broadhurst, p. 8.

27. Broadhurst, pp. 12–13.

28. Broadhurst, p. 18.

29. Broadhurst, p. 18.

30. Elizabeth Hamilton, *Letters: Addressed to the Daughter of a Nobleman on the Formation of Religious and Moral Principle* (London, 1806), p. 109. Citations of the text are to this edition.

31. On this point, see M. Jeanne Peterson, "The Victorian Governess: Status Incongruence in Family and Society," in *Suffer and Be Still: Women in the Victorian Age*, ed. Martha Vicinus (Bloomington: Indiana University Press, 1972), pp. 3–19.

32. *The Young Woman's Companion (Being a Guide to Every Acquirement Essential in Forming the Character of Female Servants, Containing Moral and Religious Letters, Essays and Tales, also Valuable Receipts and Directions, Relating to Domestic Economy)* (London, 1830), p. 32.

33. Mrs. Pullan, *Maternal Counsels to a Daughter: Designed to Aid Her in The Care of Her Health, Improvement of Her Mind, and Cultivation of Her Heart* (London, 1861), p. 227.

34. Erasmus Darwin, *A Plan for the Conduct of Female Education in Boarding Schools* (Dublin, 1798), p. 3. Citations of the text are to this edition.

35. The Countess Dowager of Carlisle, *Thoughts in the Form of Maxims Addressed to Young Ladies on their First Establishment in the World* (London, 1789), p. 4.

36. Mrs. Taylor, *Practical Hints to Young Females on the Duties of a Wife, a Mother, and a Mistress to a Family* (London, 1818), p. 18.

37. Broadhurst, p. 5.

38. T. S. Arthur, p. 191.

39. *The Compleat Servant*, p. 1.

40. *The Compleat Servant*, p. 4.

41. *The Compleat Servant*, p. 270.

42. Jane Austen, *Emma*, ed. Stephen M. Parrish (New York: W. W. Norton, 1972), p. 335.

43. Elizabeth Gaskell, *Mary Barton, A Tale of Manchester Life*, ed. Stephen Gill (Harmondsworth: Penguin, 1970), p. 49.

44. Claude Lévi-Strauss, *The Savage Mind* (Chicago: University of Chicago Press, 1973), p. 150.

45. Dorothy Van Ghent, for example, writes: "This general principle of reciprocal changes, by which things have become as it were daemonically animated and people have been reduced to thing-like characteristics—as if, by a law of conservation of energy, the humanity of which people have become incapable had leaked out into the external environment—may work symbolically in the association of some object with a person so that the object assumes his essence and his meaning. . . . This device of association is a familiar one in fiction; what distinguishes Dickens' use of it is the associated object acts not merely to *illustrate* a person's qualities symbolically—as novelists usually use it—but that it has a necessary metaphysical function in Dickens' universe: in this universe objects actually usurp human essences; beginning as fetishes, they tend to—and sometimes quite literally do—devour and take over the powers of the fetish worshipper." *The English Novel: Form and Function* (New York: Harper and Row, 1961), pp. 130–31.

46. Charles Dickens, *Our Mutual Friend*, ed. Monroe Engel (New York: Random House, 1960), p. 136.

47. Rogers, p. 3.

48. Hannah More, *Strictures on the Modern System of Female Education, The Works of Hannah More*, vol. I (New York, 1848), p. 313.

49. Dr. John Gregory, *A Father's Legacy to his Daughters* (London, 1808), p. 47.

50. *The New Female Instructor or, Young Woman's Guide to Domestic Happiness* (London, 1822), p. 2.

51. I am indebted on this point to Thomas Laqueur's discussion of the Sunday schools as an instrument of social control by virtue of their ability to appropriate leisure time. *Religion and Respectability: Sunday Schools and Working Class Culture 1780–1850* (New Haven: Yale University Press, 1976), pp. 227–39. For a different account of the use of leisure time in the nineteenth century, see Hugh Cunningham, *Leisure in the Industrial Revolution, 1780–1880* (New York: Croom Helm, 1980).

52. Arthur, p. 76.

53. Concerning the popularity of Samuel Smiles' *Self-Help* (1859), a book that represented self-regulation as the key to success in the business world, historian Asa Briggs notes that 20,000 copies were sold within a year of its first appearance. *The Age of Improvement 1783–1867* (London: Longman's, 1959), p. 431.

54. Erasmus Darwin, p. 63.

55. Martha Vicinus, *Independent Women: Work and Community for Single Women 1850–1920* (Chicago: University of Chicago Press, 1985), p. 15. Citations of the text are to this edition.

56. Madame de Walend, *Practical Hints on the Moral, Mental and Physical Training of Girls at School* (London, 1847), p. 64.

BETWEEN WOMEN

*a cross-class analysis of status
and anarchic humor*

In this essay I shall provide an interdisciplinary summary of the current status of
humor theory; inquire into its relationship to humor in women's writing; and in a
cross-class analysis of humor in some Victorian women's autobiographies, examine the relation of status to humor generally.

It is commonly held by paleopsychologists and assumed by humor theorists in
literature, anthropology, linguistics, psychology, and sociology that humor for
humankind originated in the Laugh, generally represented as the primal roar-
of-triumph over the Enemy. From this benign genesis evolved the humorous
practices of ridiculing the Victim and wit at the Victim's expense. From this paleo-
social base, three theories of humor have developed: the cognitive-perceptual,
generally called incongruity theory; the social-behavioral, generally called disparagement theory; and the psychoanalytic, generally called the suppression-
repression, or release, theory (see Raskin, 21–41). Historical proponents of
incongruity theory included Kant in 1790, for whom "laughter is an affection arising from sudden transformations of a strained expectation into nothing" (177);
Schopenhauer in 1819, for whom "the cause of laughter in every case is simply
the sudden perception of incongruity between a concept and the real objects
which have been thought through it" (76); and, in a refined form, Bergson in
1899, for whom "the incongruity gives rise to laughter when the mechanical is
encrusted upon the living" (84). Disparagement theory was perhaps best formulated by Hobbes in 1650 (with his customary generosity): "The passion of laughter is nothing else but the *sudden glory* arising from some . . . *conception* of . . .
eminency in ourselves, by *comparison* with the *infirmity* of others" (46). But as far
back as Plato, malice or envy was thought to be at the root of the Comic (*Philebus*
45–49); and Aristotle subordinates the incongruity of the mechanical, animal-
like Ridiculous to disparagement: "Comedy is an imitation of men worse than
the average; worse . . . as regards one particular kind [of fault], the Ridiculous,
which is a species of the Ugly" ("Poetics" 229). And for Hegel in 1835, laughter
is little more than "an expression of self-satisfied shrewdness" (302). The third,
release, theory was, of course, best stated by Freud: play breaks the bona-fide
communication of earnest, serious information-carriers. The more inhibitions,

for release theory, the better opportunity for humor, which is why so many jokes are about sex, race, and politics.

These three theories are at the base of everything that has followed.[1] Incongruity theory includes the script theory of linguists, in which a text is compatible with two different scripts, one of which is illicit (Raskin, ch. 4); and the frame theory and bisociation of psychologists, in which the collative properties of humor stimuli are relative to the perceiver's knowledge of them, and a situation or idea is perceived in two habitually incompatible frames of reference (McGhee 14 and Suls 40). A refined disparagement theory has by now confined the disparagement to the "unaffiliated" (that is, not self-identified) under the rubric of "disposition" theory, which claims (remarkably) that we are disposed to laugh with our friends at our enemies and we are not disposed to laugh with our enemies at our friends (Zillmann 91–2).[2] But—and this will be significant when we speak of women's humor—such disparagement theories have perplexed sociologists when applied to disempowered groups, as when black people in controlled situations have seemingly perversely laughed at anti-black jokes.[3]

It will come as no surprise that historically theorists of humor have been men, and they have seldom considered the role of gender in humor, although recent discussion of the function of sex in humor should not go unremarked. Some cognitive and neuropsychologists, for example, have viewed the perception of incongruities as an innate capacity of the brain. Thus the holistic processing capacities of the right hemisphere (the "male" side) produce awareness of incongruous relationships, whereas the left (the "female," or analytic, sequential, side) can barely comprehend incongruities, or jokes (McGhee 24–34). Thus neuropsychologists have discovered the "dual process" model, based upon the relative capabilities of the cerebral hemispheres and emotive environment: faced with humorous stimuli, males are "objective" or "field independent," whereas females are "subjective" or "field dependent" (Suls 50, Chapman 146):[4] which means that in public places women look 'round to see who else is laughing and men immediately discern the absolute signification of incongruity and thus the hard core of humor *per se*. Regarding this (until very recently) common topos of behavioral science research, the correlation of "field dependency" with female stereotypes and "field independency" with male stereotypes, a student of mine, Annie Tillery, observed that men are perceived in behavioral science as field insensitive, contextually unaware, and environmentally oblivious.

I pass over the debates over methodology among such physicalist theorists, such as the pros and cons of the Facial Action Coding System (La France 1–12). My point is that although there has been some research on biology and humor, there has in fact been very little in any discipline, on *gender* and humor, that is, little research that analyzes women's humor in a male public domain or that accounts for masculine and feminine humor in the context of their historical power relations. There is some general agreement that male humor has been more aggressive, more akin to the primal roar, than female, and, correlatively, that roaring has been a more acceptable practice for men than women (see Chapman and Foot 361–78). As Nina Auerbach said in an earlier response to this paper, it seems that historically men have preferred women's tears to their more threatening laughter. The anthropologist. Mahadev Apte has concluded from cross-cultural analysis that women's humor in the public realm is constrained by prevalent cultural values of male superiority and dominance and female passivity; that certain social factors like marriage and advanced age remove the constraints and reduce the differences between men's and women's humor; that men fear women's humor for much the same reason that they fear women's sexual freedom—because they encourage women's aggression and promiscuity and thus disrupt the social order; that therefore men desire to control women's humor just as they desire to control women's sexuality—to wit, in the public domain; and finally that women's humor among themselves may not be assimilable to any of these categories (Apte 67–81). If for male theorists humor is functional, promoting group cohesion and intergroup conflict through disparagement, and social control through momentary releases that only serve to reinforce the status quo (see Fine 173), women's humor may do none of the above.

With this female lacuna in the research in mind, I attempted to see what nineteenth- and early-twentieth-century British women—women in a classist and sexist, that is, heavily stratified, society—found funny among themselves. My informants, as it were, are not Jane Austens, not women whose humor has won acclaim in the public arena: they are working-class and educated middle-class women who recorded lives that were either lived or well begun in the nineteenth century and whose expected audience was in most cases other women.[5] It is my thesis that however restricted they were in public, among themselves Victorian women used humor neither for disparagement nor temporary release, but rather as a prolonged anarchic assault upon the codes constricting them. This is to say that their humor primarily lay within the category of incongruity but that their use of incongruity had socio-behavioral implications for exploring difference rather than merely disparaging it and for prolonged critical action rather than momentary release.

In May of 1930 Virginia Woolf responded to Margaret Llewelyn Davies's request that she write the preface for a collection of working women's autobiographies. Woolf responded that books—real books—did not need prefaces, that the collection was not exactly a book, and that therefore she would write not a preface but "the following letter addressed not to the public but to you."[6] In this correspondence between two women about the correspondence of other women Woolf reflects upon the Congress of the Working Women's Co-Operative Guild of June 1913 in Newcastle, where she had first encountered the autobiographers, and registers two instances of humorous incongruity: first, the incongruity of working-class women, who are traditionally "hands" not "heads," giving speeches (an old joke employed by Monty Python, whose charladies discuss Jean-Paul Sartre), and, second, Woolf's incongruous presence among them. Woolf's description reduces the women speaking to automata, in Bergson's term, "mechanical." "A bell struck; a figure rose; a woman took her way from among us; she mounted a platform; she spoke for precisely five minutes; she descended. Directly she sat down another woman rose; mounted the platform; spoke for precisely five minutes and descended; then a third rose, then a fourth—and so it went on, speaker following speaker, one from the right, one from the left, one from the middle, one from the background—each took her way to the stand, said what she had to say, and gave place to her successor" (xvi).

In Aristotle's *Poetics*, humor, as distinguished from comedy—and, importantly, to be so distinguished in the rest of this essay—occurs when one sympathizes with the ridiculous animal-like breaker of rules because one sees the contradiction between it and the frame it cannot comply with. One may even think that the frame is wrong, which leads to criticism of a set of cultural and intertextual frames. In this sense humor is metasemiotic, casting in doubt other cultural codes. In Umberto Eco's terms, humor reminds us of the presence of a law that we no longer have reason to obey.

It is this sympathetic, supportive humor that we see in Woolf and that, I believe, derives from Victorian women's social status. From the distance of social class, she watches these unladylike—that is, animal-like—women who incongruously demand reform of the Law—Divorce Laws, taxation, Minimum wage, maternity policy, Trades Board and Education Acts, and Adult Suffrage. She appreciates their frame-breaking, she even thinks that the paternalistic frame is wrong, yet they are humorous, she must admit, because their specific frame was not hers. "Something was always creeping in from a world that was not their world and making the picture false. . . . One sat in an armchair or read a book. One saw landscapes and seascapes, perhaps Greece or Italy, where Mrs. Giles or Mrs. Edwards must have seen slag heaps and rows upon rows of slate roofed houses . . . the game [was] too much of a game (xxi)." "Therefore," Woolf concludes, "however much we had sympathised our sympathy was largely fictitious" (xxvi) and she passes on to describe the differences between ladies and working women, differences that lead to criticism of a set of cultural and intertextual frames, so that the outcome is that Woolf is empowered by watching working women break their own frames, codes, or sets of social premises.

Conversely, according to Woolf, the women of the Congress find humorous ladies' "mincing speech and little knowledge of what it pleases them to call 'reality'" (xxvi)—presumably because such speech would be inaudible and such reality absent in the lives of working women. Working women find humor in cross-class transgressions, as when their soi-disant superiors enter their world of necessity to make ludicrous trivial gestures or when they try to imagine themselves in middle-class situations. The midwife Mrs. Layton recalls an absurd image of a lady, a complete stranger, looming out of Victoria Park to assail her with bourgeois values when she was a child. The alien lady "asked my age and if I went to school and a lot of other questions. She said I was a bright, intelligent little girl, and asked if I could read a few verses out of a nice Testament she had in her hand . . . and made me promise that I would never neglect to wash myself before leaving home . . . and never miss an opportunity of improving myself if only I had more time" (*Life as We Have Known It* 5). Then, Mrs. Layton recalls, the lady vanishes. The Bohemian dancer Betty May was sold on the white slave market as a child and spent her adolescence in Apache Gangs in Paris. She wryly records the incongruity between herself and the parents of her gentle barrister fiancé in Cornwall when she attempted to assimilate herself at the rectory: "I was not regarded as the interesting person I had expected to be, as someone who had been through experiences they would never encounter, who had seen sides of life that they had only read of in novels. . . . But I tried: I even used to go to lectures on potatoes and that sort of thing" (May 86). As a child, Emma Smith had been abused regularly. Leaving the penitentiary, she is advised by a nun to marry and tries to imagine domesticity: "A wife and mother? Was it possible? Suddenly, in my mind's eyes, I saw a little home, furniture, curtins, a cradle—and I tried to imagine (only this was more difficult) a man in slippers" (Smith 151).

In none of the hundreds of working women's autobiographies I have read have I found jokes about sex or jokes at the expense of unfortunates: the sole source of humor is real or imaginary transgressions relating to social class. The form these humorous transgressions take is not disparagement or release, nor brief laughter, but rather a process of imaginative engagement. Woolf's confrontation with the Co-Operative Working Women is one of the most penetrating class confrontations in modern British discourse precisely because Woolf allows herself to imagine a full intertextuality or exchange of frames. As she muses on the working women challenging the laws of privilege, she writes, "This force of theirs . . . is about to break through and melt us together so that life will be richer and books more complex and society will pool its possessions instead of segregating them—all this is going to happen" (xxviii). Most women of her class, however, simply believed that the rules were different for working women and for ladies, that ladies could break their own rules but that extrasystemic transgression was out of the question.

To the extent to which this "separate spheres" view prevailed, there was comparatively little humor in working women's autobiographies. For the rules that concerned working women—at least the majority of working women who had not begun to undergo embourgeoisement—were the rules of survival and necessity, not polite society, and writers seldom break or see others break the rules of survival without providing pathos rather than humor. Similarly, in order to protect their own status, upper-class women seldom let social inferiors see them breaking rules, so working-class women could seldom learn from the example of rebellious upper-class women. And working women were aware of their relative lack of humor. In *Jipping Street* (1928) Kathleen Woodward confesses that in her reading for self-improvement she was acutely conscious of losing much of the sense of middle-class authors, especially, she imagined, in her inability to detect when they were being humorous (130), that is, breaking middle-class rules or codes that remained largely mysterious for her.

On the other hand, the significantly greater number of rules to be broken, relative to the few—and iron—rules of a worker's life, makes middle-class woman's writing rather more humorous than that of working women. In memoirs of educated middle-class women, humor is very often exclusively directed toward one thing: the rules of the school, or the education that would make them ladies. Again, faced with codes that were incongruous with women's perceived powers, women launched sustained and anarchic attacks upon those codes.

In her *Life* (1894) Frances Power Cobbe describes the 100+ ladies' schools in Brighton with their hundreds of rows of identical girls in full evening dress, facing the wall for breaking the rules. After a curriculum of—in descending order of importance—music, dancing, deportment, drawing, Continental languages, English, and Religion ("fasting will be good for our souls *and* our figures"), the young Cobbe left school secure in a position that the older philanthropist, suffragette, and antivivisectionist could only record with considerable humor. Upon leaving school, Cobbe recalls, she thought: "I know as much as any girl in our school, and since it is the best school in England, I *must* know all that it can ever

be necessary to know. I will not trouble my head ever again with learning anything; but read novels and amuse myself for the rest of my life" (vol. 1, 60–69).
Cobbe's humor, of course, turns to disparagement of what she calls "feminine
futility" by the second volume, as illustrated by the ludicrous description of a
lady attempting for three pages to uncork a bottle (vol. II, 229–32). Ladies and
labor—even such labor as opening champagne—were incongruous, but the humor for Cobbe consists in the disparity between this image of febrile femininity
and what she knows of women's capabilities.

In *A Little Learning: or A Victorian Childhood,* the educationist Winifred Peck
(née Winifred Knox) recalls the 250 rules that could not be broken daily at Miss
Quill's Day School for Christian Ladies in the 1870s. Peck recalls the rule to "Assume your underwear as modestly as possible under the covering of your night
gown" and grows riotous trying to envision some flagrant disregard of the rule
(66). Peck also mocks her childhood education from standard texts like *Near
Home and Far Off* for their ludicrous and incongruous formulae of national stereotypes (the mechanical encrusted upon the living) to be learned by rote by British
schoolchildren, such as "The Irish are a merry people and fond of pigs," or "The
Italians are a dark, revengeful race where [*sic*] the stiletto is in frequent use"
(22). And she grows hilarious at the specious rules of English grammar after the
Romans, as in "Castle: noun, accusative; third person, neuter gender, etc."

In Mary Vivian Hughes's *A London Family 1870–1900: A Trilogy* (1934–37), the
educator Hughes also finds humor the only way to describe her own education.
Her twenty-sixth edition of Brewer's *Guide to Science* (1869) presented itself in the
form of a catechism: "Q. What is heat? A. That which produces the sensation of
warmth. Q. What is light? A. The unknown cause of visibility. Q. What should a
fearful person do to be secure in a storm? A. Draw his bedstead into the middle
of his room, commit himself to the care of God, and go to bed" (43). Surrounded
by strictly enforced rules at North London Collegiate in the 1880s, Hughes
philosophically laughs at the impossibility of not breaking them: "We were forbidden to get wet on the way to school, . . . to drop a pencil-box, leave a book
at home, hang a boot-bag by only one loop. . . . One felt that if a girl were to
knock over the blackboard by mistake there would be a rule against it the next
day" (165).

Perhaps the most eloquent humor at the expense of school rules for ladies appears in my last example of this kind, Antonia White's *Frost in May* (1933), which
is only nominally fictive. In the Convent of the Five Wounds, Fernanda Grey
(Antonia White) rebels against the master narratives of Roman Catholicism that
frame every aspect of the girls' lives. Nothing can be seen "for its own sake"
(169), for things are freighted with a density of religious signification that organizes and interprets the child's experience:

> To Our Lady and the Holy Child and the saints [Nanda] spoke as naturally as
> to her friends. She learnt to smooth a place on her pillow for her Guardian
> Angel to sit during the night . . . to jump out of bed at the first beat of the
> bell to help the Holy Souls in purgatory. . . . The donkey in the paddock
> reminded her that all donkeys have crosses on their backs since the day Our
> Lord rode into Jerusalem; the robin's breast was red because one of his an-
> cestors had splashed his feathers with the precious Blood trying to peck away

the crown of thorns. The clover and the shamrock were a symbol of the Blessed Trinity, the sunflower was a saint turning always towards God, the speedwell had been white till Our Lady's blue mantle brushed it as she walked in the fields of Nazareth. When Nanda heard a cock crow, it cried "Christus natus est"; the cows lowed "Ubi? Ubi?" and the lambs down at the community farm bleated "Be-e-thlehem." (46–47)

I now want to turn to a final Victorian example, perhaps the most bitter, of women's humor: Florence Nightingale's "Cassandra," which Nightingale was advised not to publish and which remained suppressed until the twentieth century. It was part of a work within a genre much attended to by women, the spiritual autobiography, and entitled *Suggestions for Thought to Searchers after Religious Truth*. In "Cassandra" the rules imaginatively broken, the boundaries imaginatively crossed, are the rules and boundaries of gender itself. It has long been known that the story of Nightingale cannot be contained by her two rigidly dichotomized popular images. Between the *Times*'s war correspondent's image of The Nurse (with her sweet approving smile, the ideal representation of ideal woman, the angel of mercy, the bedside madonna, the lady of the lamp) and Lytton Strachey's portrait of the "Eagle," the demonic slave-driver of Cabinet ministers, poets, and masters of Balliol, is Nightingale's own representation of herself as Cassandra, the prophet who knew the truth about the future but was doomed by Apollo never to have her prophecies believed.

In her commentary on the MLA panel from which this essay derives, Nina Auerbach said that women turn their frustrations and hatred into humor and then turn their humor against themselves. Nightingale's text is the mad babble of Cassandra, representing "that perpetual day-dreaming [of women's emancipation], which is so dangerous" (397): Cassandra knows the possibilities for women in the future but due to the historical connotations of Victorian gender she is powerless to enact the changes that she knows will come. The text is of women babbling their transgressions by exchanging roles with *men*. On the restrictions on ladies' activities Nightingale writes, "But suppose we were to see a number of men in the morning sitting round a table in the drawing-room, looking at prints, doing worsted work, and reading little books, how we should laugh!" (400). Of the eternal waste of leisure-class women's time in morning calls, she asks, "If you offer a morning visit to a professional man, and say 'I will just stay an hour with you, if you will allow me, till so and so comes back to fetch me'; it costs him the earnings of an hour, and therefore he has a right to complain. But women have no right, because it is '*only* their time'" (402). In her most daring assault on the boundaries between the male and female spheres, Nightingale, a deeply religious woman, does a parodic and woman's reading of the Gospel, claiming that if Christ had been a woman, "he might have been nothing but a great complainer" (416) negligent of his duties to home and family. "For instance," she writes:

Christ was saying something to [the multitude] one day, which interested Him very much, and interested them very much; and Mary and His brothers came in the middle of it, and wanted to interrupt Him, and take Him home to dinner, very likely . . . and He, instead of being angry with their interruption of Him in such an important work for some trifling thing, answers, "Who is my mother? and who are my brethren? Whosoever shall do the will of my Father which is in heaven, the same is my brother and sister and mother." But if *we* [women] were to say that, we should be accused of "destroying the family tie, of diminishing the obligation of the home duties." (417)

Such humor challenged the law that women like Nightingale no longer had reason to obey.

In sum we can say that in nineteenth- and early-twentieth-century self-representation, what women perceive as humorous is not Hobbes's "*sudden glory* arising from a *conception* of *eminency* in ourselves by *comparison* with the *infirmity* of *others*" but rather the very terms of their confinement.[7] Working women find humor in cross-class scenarios disrupting the social order, and upper-class women in disrupting the codes and regulations of their own class. This suggests that women's humor tends toward anarchy rather than the status quo, to prolonged disruption rather than, in Freudian theory, momentary release.

My second observation concerns status. In middle-class male public school memoirs—the social equivalents of the ladies' memoirs I've just cited, rules are figured in two ways: they are either accepted and played by, in which case the boy assumes his place in the social power structure, or they are despaired of, in which case the defeated boy retreats into isolation and obscurity.[8] Perhaps because women's status was lower, women did not perceive this tragic dichotomy. Facing the rules, they tended toward anarchy rather than insecurity. That is, women's lower status permitted them a lesser investment in the rules and more ease in undertaking their imaginative disruption through humor in the relative privacy of discourse among women. The corollary, of course, is that the greater the status, the more the rules are for one's benefit and the more one's relation to them is exposed to public view and may be defined as reverent, or potentially tragic.[9] It is within this frame that I have come to interpret some friendly advice to me from an academic administrator: that if I did not control my sense of humor I could never aspire to the administrative ranks.

Kate Clinton, the radical-lesbian-feminist-humorist, has a wonderful sketch on *Debbie Does Dallas* that, like her hyphenated epithet, throws into relief multiple frames of difference in opposition to the law and thus provides my last example of anarchic humor. Not the ideal male spectator assumed by the producers of the film, Clinton muses upon Debbie and the other heterosexually-marked cheerleaders in the shower-room, washing their breasts. And washing, and washing their breasts, big circular motions. Clinton, who confesses that for her breasts are no big deal, neither here nor there, nonetheless sympathizes with Debbie and her cohort: "Well, we *do* know how dirty breasts *do* get. I, for example, sometimes change my bra three or four times a day." I will not analyze here the number of cultural frames being broken in this example or transgressions in play, but the dynamic is not unlike that between Woolf and the working women.

This frame-breaking, democratizing, and anarchic humor should by now recall the laugh of the Medusa. In her classic essay, Hélène Cixous proposes that women write *for women*. What they should write should approach the Unconscious, that place where there are no rules and where boundaries break down, and where the oppressed have managed to survive.[10] Medusa's laughter, or "women's writing" in Cixous's sense, like Bergson's "living," opposes itself to undesirable ("mechanical") rules and laws.[11] "It will be conceived of only by subjects who are breakers of automatisms," writes Cixous reflecting Bergson's terminology, "by peripheral figures that no authority can ever subjugate. . . . What woman hasn't felt, dreamt, performed the gesture that jams sociality? Who hasn't held up to ridicule the bar of separation? . . . Who, by some act of transgression, hasn't overthrown successiveness, connection, the wall of circumfusion?" (Cixous 253–258). Here some would go on to employ an analysis after the work of Nancy Chodorow of women's fluid boundaries or after the work of Judith Kegan Gardiner of fluid characterization in women's writing, but I want only to insist upon the more limited arena of Medusa's *laughter* in stratified populations. For Medusa's anarchic laughter sheds some light on why—unlike those white men secure in their absolute signification who discern in isolation the hard core of humor—the black men in the study laughed at everything and the Victorian women never laughed alone.

NOTES

1. For contemporary humor theory referred to here see Apte, Chapman and Foot, McGhee and Goldstein, and Raskin. These sources, especially Raskin and the two collections, provide compendious histories of previous work and full bibliographies of humor research. My essay is indebted to Jim English, who alerted me to much contemporary humor research and graciously commented on an earlier version of this paper; Regina Barreca, who organized the MLA panel on Women's Humor for which it was written; and to the Institute for Research on Women and Gender, Stanford University, which gave me another opportunity to present and discuss the material in its Jing Lyman Lecture Series, Spring 1987.

2. The technical formulation includes clauses of magnitude and degree:
    1. The more intense the negative disposition toward the disparaged agent or entity, the greater the magnitude of mirth.
    2. The more intense the positive disposition toward the disparaged agent or entity, the smaller the magnitude of mirth.
    3. The more intense the negative disposition toward the disparaging agent or entity, the smaller the magnitude of mirth.
    4. The more intense the positive disposition toward the disparaging agent or entity, the greater the magnitude of mirth. (Zillmann 91–92).

3. But see the weak explanation in Fine 171–72.

4. For critiques of such biological theories without reference to humor see Fausto-Sterling, especially 30–32, 44–53.

5. My major source of working-class autobiography is *The Autobiography of the Working Class: An Annotated, Critical Bibliography Vol. I: 1790–1900*, ed. John Burnett, David Vincent, David Mayall (Sussex: Harvester, 1984). For a broader analysis of some of these autobiographies see Gagnier "Social Atoms: Working-Class Autobiography, Subjectivity, and Gender" *Victorian Studies* (Spring 1987).

6. "Introductory Letter to Margaret Llewelyn Davies" by Virginia Woolf in *Life as We have Known It by Co-Operative Working Women* xvi. Further page references will be included in the text.

7. Strictly speaking, of course, there may be a little Hobbesian disparagement in women's mockery of rules that are generally followed or beliefs that are widely held, for with such mockery women implicitly elevate themselves and demonstrate at least a latent

"conception of eminency." Yet although this may be the case theoretically, women get no purchase from the elevation: humor for women as I am describing it here is an imaginative process, whereas elevation or superiority is a fixed status. In Aristotelian terms the difference is between comedy and humor, or a laugh and reflective critical engagement.

8. Specifically, they typically retreated into aesthetics. See Gagnier, "'From Fag to Monitor; Or, Fighting to the Front': Art and Power in Public School Memoirs" *Victorian Learning*, ed. Robert Viscusi vol 16 (*Browning Institute Studies: An Annual of Victorian Literary and Cultural History*), 1988.

9. For a compatible analysis of humor and status see Williams 1987, in which an anthropologist argues that humor intervenes in disputes in a rural Guyanese community in inverse proportion to the elevated status of the participants and formal litigation.

10. Cixous's term is "repressed" rather than "oppressed," but I want to emphasize the political point: women's humor in these texts allows for a continuous assault upon the social forms constraining women. See Cixous 250.

11. Bergson's seemingly narrow focus on the mechanical/living opposition in fact has a very wide range of application, his sense of the mechanical extending to "automatic" reliance on rules. For Bergson, humor's primary social function is that of offering a corrective to rigid, "automatic" behavior—a way of freeing the agent from undesirable social restraints. Thus Victorian women's humor points up the incongruity between rules (the mechanical) and women's real capabilities (the living, the *élan vital*). The question contested among Bergsonians of course is whether Bergson envisioned the kind of sustained critical process I claim for these women or the more conventional and conservative short-term releases that in the long run only serve to reinforce the status quo. Freudians debate the same question with respect to Freudian humor theory.

WORKS CITED

Apte, Mahadev. *Humor and Laughter: An Anthropological Approach*. Ithaca: Cornell, 1985.

Aristotle. "Poetics" *Rhetoric*. New York: Random House, 1954.

Bergson, Henri 1899. "Laughter" *Comedy*. Ed. Wylie Sypher. New York: Doubleday, 1956.

Chapman, Antony J. "Humor and Laughter in Social Interaction and Some Implications for Humor Research" in McGhee and Goldstein Vol. 1.

Chapman, Antony J. and Hugh Foot, eds. *It's a Funny Thing, Humor*. New York: Pergamon, 1977.

Chodorow, Nancy. *The Reproduction of Mothering*. Berkeley: University of California Press, 1978.

Cixous, Hélène 1975. "The Laugh of the Medusa" *New French Feminisms: An Anthology* Ed. Elaine Marks and Isabelle de Courtivron. New York: Schocken, 1981.

Cobbe, Frances Power. *Life*. 2 vols. London: Richard Bentley, 1894.

Co-Operative Working Women. *Life as We Have Known It*. New York: Norton, 1975.

Eco, Umberto. "The Frames of Comic Freedom" 1–9. *Carnival!* Ed. Thomas Sebeok. New York: Mouton, 1984, 1–9.

Fausto-Sterling, Anne. *Myths of Gender: Biological Theories About Women and Men*. New York: Basic Books, 1985.

Fine, Gary Alan. "Sociological Approaches to the Study of Humor" in McGhee and Goldstein Vol. 1.

Freud, Sigmund 1905. *Jokes and Their Relation to the Unconscious*. New York: Penguin, 1976.

——— 1928. "Humour." *International Journal of Psychoanalysis* vol. 9: 1–6.

Gardiner, Judith Kegan. "On Female Identity and Writing by Women" *Writing and Sexual Difference* Ed. Elizabeth Abel. Chicago: University of Chicago Press, 1982, 177–91.

Hegel, Georg W. F. 1835. *The Philosophy of Fine Art* Vol. IV. London: G. Bell, 1920.

Hobbes, Thomas 1650. *The English Works of Thomas Hobbes* Vol. IV. London: John Bohn, 1840.

Hughes, M. Vivian. *A London Family: 1870–1900: A Trilogy*. London: Oxford University Press, 1946.

Kant, Immanuel 1790. *Critique of Judgment*. New York: Hafner, 1951.

La France, Marianne. "Felt Versus Feigned Funniness: Issues in Coding Smiling and Laughing" in McGhee and Goldstein Vol. 1.

May, Betty. *Tiger-Woman: My Story*. London: Duckworth, 1929.

McGhee, Paul E. and Jeffrey H. Goldstein, eds. *Handbook of Humor Research* 2 vols. New York: Springer-Verlag, 1983.

Nightingale, Florence 1852. "Cassandra" in Ray Strachey *The Cause: A Short History of the Women's Movement in Great Britain* 1928; rpt: New York, Kennikat Press, 1969.

Peck, Winifred. *A Little Learning: or A Victorian Childhood*. London: Faber and Faber, 1952.

Plato. *Philebus*. Oxford: Clarendon, 1975.

Raskin, Victor. *Semantic Mechanisms of Humor*. Boston: Reidel, 1985.

Schopenhauer, Arthur 1819. *The World as Will and Idea*, Vol. I. London: Routledge and Kegan Paul, 1957.

Smith, Emma (pseud.). *A Cornish Waif's Story: An Autobiography*. London: Odhams Press, 1954.

Suls, Jerry M. "Cognitive Processes in Humor Appreciation," in McGhee and Goldstein Vol. 1.

White, Antonia 1933. *Frost in May*. New York: Dial Press, 1980.

Williams, Brackette. "Humor, linguistic ambiguity, and disputing in a Guyanese community" *International Journal of the Sociology of Language* 65 (Amsterdam, 1987): 79–94.

Woodward, Kathleen. *Jipping Street: Childhood in a London Slum*. New York: Harper, 1928.

Zillmann, Dolf. "Disparagement Humor" in McGhee and Goldstein Vol. 1.

men

"**M**en" may well be the most controversial subject heading in this anthology. Some readers may feel that, after all, a book called *Feminisms* should not even concern itself with "men." What does "Men" have to do with feminism(s)? The semantic difficulties of even asking this question are illustrative. Does it mean "What place do male critics have in feminism?" or "What place do men as subjects have in feminism?" Or could it mean "What does feminism have to offer toward coming to a clearer understanding of men?" Here, we take it to mean all three.

Mary Jacobus addresses the first sense of that question. She is responding to, among other things, an influential essay by Elaine Showalter, "Critical Cross-Dressing: Male Feminist and the Woman of the Year," an essay that characterizes male feminist literary critics as in some sense "academic Tootsies." Showalter expresses an anxiety shared by many that the movement of male critics into feminist criticism is less alliance than colonization (two terms we'll see repeatedly in these essays), that, like the title character of the Dustin Hoffman film *Tootsie*, these men are "wearing women's clothes" just to advance their own personal careers, a move that will exclude women from the one refuge they have found in the academy.

Jacobus refutes this position in "Reading Woman (Reading)" (1987) by addressing directly the question of what difference the sex of the reader makes to literary criticism, in particular, and to reading at large. In this chapter from her book *Reading Woman*, she critiques three essays which focus on cross-dressing and gender: Showalter's, an essay by Sandra M. Gilbert called "Costumes of the Mind: Transvestism as Metaphor in Modern Literature," and one by Shoshana Felman, "Rereading Femininity" (none of these essays is reprinted in this volume, but other essays by all three authors do appear here). Jacobus argues that the theory of reading should be grounded in a psychoanalytic theory of subjectivity that recognizes that gender is constructed through language. Psychoanalysis, she argues, does not try to *define* gender, but rather to describe where it comes from; it is therefore necessary, she argues, to any feminist explanation of women's relation to discourse. By the same token, though, she argues that feminism, with its focus on the importance of gender in culture, is necessary to any use of psychoanalysis. Jacobus critiques Showalter and Gilbert because they do not adopt this model of gender, but she praises Felman's essay because it urges a theory of reading that recognizes fluid sexual identities.

Joseph A. Boone and Susan Jeffords address the second sense of the question this section raises: "What place do men as subjects have in feminism?" Of course, men were a chief subject of much early feminist literary criticism. Kate Millett's *Sexual Politics* (1970), one of the first openly feminist works of literary criticism, addressed the patriarchal abuses by male authors, male characters, and male readers. But after Elaine Showalter proposed the idea of gynocriticism, the study of female-authored texts and women-centered issues (detailed in the "Methodologies" and "Traditions" sections), work on male-authored texts and male-centered issues almost disappeared from feminist criticism. In the last few years, though (as Elaine Showalter explains in "A Criticism of Our Own," in "Methodologies"), we have seen the beginnings of "gender theory," an analysis that, working from feminist criticism, takes gender to be one, if not *the*, decisive factor in literary meaning. Since feminist critics have argued convincingly that gender differences are constructed differences, the reasoning goes, shouldn't that mean stereotypical masculinity is as constructed—and as deforming—as stereotypical femininity? The result is a new way of examining texts, a way of looking at "masculinity" as a product of patriarchy that is potentially as damaging to those subjected to it as is "femininity." "Gender theory" does not see men as simply perpetrators of sexual oppression, but as themselves victims of it; it takes the onus of historical abuses off of men *per se*, and assigns the blame instead to patriarchy as a system.

There is, of course, much disagreement as to whether gender theory is a good thing. Skeptical feminist critics ask whether gender studies are not just a way to re-legitimate traditionally male-dominated literary studies, a way to exploit feminist critique against its own best interests. Proponents argue that it is an expansion of the feminist criticism which genuinely recognizes the discursive, constructed nature of patriarchal gender norms, a necessary step if we are ever to realign oppressive gender politics. This is, of course, a debate that cannot be resolved here—if at all. But it is a useful dialogue to keep in mind while reading the essays that follow.

In "Male Independence and the American Quest Genre: Hidden Sexual Politics in the All-Male Worlds of Melville, Twain and London" (1986), Joseph Boone challenges the two powerful views of "classic American fiction," that of Leslie Fiedler (whose *Love and Death in the American Novel* remains a standard critical work) who sees the novels as evidence of "arrested adolescence," and of feminist critics who have argued that the genre upholds patriarchal ideology. Boone argues instead that the novels' all-male worlds are the means to a radical critique of the gender-polarization of nineteenth-century society, and that their male–male couples represent the desire for non-hierarchized pairings. Although he recognizes that twentieth-century manifestations of this genre have been openly misogynistic, Boone maintains that the nineteenth-century novels not only represent an alternative to the dominant narrative structure of the time—the courtship and marriage plot—but that they offer the potential for a genuine critique of patriarchy and an alternative world-view.

Susan Jeffords examines a different aspect of the "all-male world" in "Masculinity as Excess in Vietnam Films: The Father/Son Dynamic" (1988). Jeffords's particular focus in this essay, which became part of a longer study called *The Remasculinization of America: Gender and Representations of the Vietnam War*, is the combat scene and its relation to the stabilization of a masculine identity. Using *Platoon* and the "Rambo" film series as her examples, she argues that these films are not so much about war as about the destabilization of masculinity in American culture, and about the confusion of a young man as to which of several father-figures he should emulate; "*this* is the fear, the anxiety, the threat, the violence that underlies [the] combat sequence . . . in Vietnam film—not a battle with NVA soldiers." The real focal points of the films are not war *per se* but the linear movement of power from a (white) father to a (white) son; the narrative tension arises from the threat that someone inappropriate—a woman or a man of color—will usurp that power. The resolutions of the films, she points out, are not the resolutions of the war, but of the reconstruction and stabilization of masculine identity. Within these films, the combat scenes function as "excess" in a number of ways: as warnings about the results of such gender destabilization, as distractions from the crisis of masculine identity, and as the means to re-establish that threatened identity. Jeffords reads these films not as simple maturation stories, but as powerful narratives which attempt to reconstruct a patriarchal notion of masculinity at a particular point in social history—the 1970s and 1980s—when feminism had offered a strong challenge to it.

The final essay in this section, Paul Smith's psychoanalytic study "Vas" (1988), addresses a different relation between men and feminism(s). Noting that the feminist critique of psychoanalysis has dramatically affected the understanding of female sexuality, Smith proposes to study male sexuality following the model of that feminist work, an undertaking which he hopes can provide new possibilities for alliance and collaboration between male critics and feminists through a re-examination of psychoanalysis itself. In this tentative, exploratory essay, Smith proposes that we re-evaluate our understanding of male sexuality, and consider the "lived experience" of a male body instead. Rather than the stable, monolithic sexuality symbolized by a phallus, he proposes a model of male sexuality marked by the repressed preoedipal, a sexuality which would describe male sexuality as essentially unstable. Turning his attention to pornography, Smith discusses representation and the place of the male viewer to refute contemporary feminist theories which assert that pornography encourages male viewers to identify with the men in the films; he argues instead that these films prevent identification and, in fact, make identification itself unstable, especially when it comes to gender. Smith reintroduces the issues of male hysteria and of male sexuality to psychoanalytic parlance, questioning the reason for their initial exclusion from it, in hopes of reopening the study of male sexuality itself. Smith performs the kind of double move that Mary Jacobus urges for feminist criticism in "Reading Woman (Reading)"; he uses psychoanalysis not to define gender, but to examine where gender differences originate at the same time that he uses the gender analysis provided by feminist criticism to critique psychoanalysis. As a male speaker in/with feminism, he shows that men can borrow from feminism without necessarily exploiting it.

—DPH

READING WOMAN (READING)

"It was a change in Orlando herself that dictated her choice of a woman's dress and of a woman's sex. And perhaps in this she was only expressing rather more openly than usual . . . something that happens to most people without being thus plainly expressed. For here again, we come to a dilemma. Different though the sexes are, they intermix. In every human being a vacillation from one sex to the other takes place, and often it is only the clothes that keep the male or female likeness, while underneath the sex is the very opposite of what it is above. Of the complications and confusions which thus result every one has had experience."

VIRGINIA WOOLF, *ORLANDO*[1]

Or, "it is clothes that wear us and not we them"; Woolf's *Orlando* (1928) again. Can we say the same of language—that words speak us and not we them—and hence of reading too? What would "reading woman" mean if the object of our reading (woman as text) and the reading subject (reader as already read) were gendered only as the result of the reading process? What if, to put it another way, there were no gender identity except as constituted by clothes, or by language— just as there is no "literal" meaning to oppose to metaphor, but only metaphors of literalness. As Shoshana Felman puts it,

if it is clothes alone, i.e., a cultural sign, an institution, which determine our reading of the sexes, which determine masculine and feminine and insure sexual opposition as an orderly, hierarchical polarity; if indeed clothes make the *man*—or the woman—are not sex roles as such, inherently, but travesties?[2]

In Woolf's novel, Orlando's transvestism is not simply a travesty which mimics or exaggerates the signs by which gender identity is culturally instituted and maintained; rather, Orlando might be said to dress up at (cross-)dressing, exposing the dilemma ("here again, we come to a dilemma") or impossible choice of gender; as the *OED* has it, "A choice between two . . . alternatives, which are or appear equally unfavorable; a position of doubt or perplexity, a 'fix.'" In Felman's words, transvestite roles become "transvesties of a travesty," since there is no unequivocal gender identity to render ambiguous in the first place, but only the masquerade of masculine and feminine.

If there is no literal referent to start with, no identity or essence, the production of sexual difference can be viewed as textual, like the production of meaning. Once we cease to see the origin of gender identity as biological or anatomical—as given—but rather as instituted by and in language, "reading woman" can be posed as a process of differentiation for which psychoanalysis provides a model. In Freudian terms, the subject acquires both gender and subjectivity by its passage through the Oedipus and castration complexes; in Lacanian terms, the subject's entry into the symbolic order, and hence the subject's gender, are determined by relation to the phallus and (it amounts to the same thing) by taking up a predetermined position within language.[3] In order to read as women, we have to be positioned as already-read (and hence gendered); by the same token, what reads us is a signifying system that simultaneously produces difference (meaning) and sexual difference (gender). We might go further and say that in constituting woman as our object when we read, we not only read in gender, but constitute ourselves as readers. The stabilizing, specular image of woman in the text makes reading possible by assuring us that we have women's faces too—or men's, for that matter, since "woman" serves also as a figure for or reflection of "man."[4] Reading woman becomes a form of autobiography or self-constitution that is finally indistinguishable from writing (woman). Putting a face on the text and putting a gender in it "keeps the male or female likeness" (in Woolf's words) while concealing that "vacillation from one sex to another" which both women and men must keep, or keep at bay, in order to recognize themselves as subjects at all. The monster in the text is not woman, or the woman writer; rather, it is this repressed vacillation of gender or the instability of identity—the ambiguity of subjectivity itself which returns to wreak havoc on consciousness, on hierarchy, and on unitary schemes designed to repress the otherness of femininity.

Feminist critics have traditionally concerned themselves with the woman writer, and especially with what Woolf calls "the difference of view, the difference of standard."[5] Women's writing occupies an unchallenged place in the politics of feminist criticism and in the classroom; yet the category itself remains problematic (defined by authorship? by style or by language? by refusal of the very categories "masculine" or "feminine"?). More recently, feminist criticism has concerned itself with the woman reader—with woman as the producer of her own system of meanings; meanings that may challenge or subvert patriarchal readings and undo the traditional hierarchy of gender.[6] So much so that Jonathan Culler can make the question of "Reading as a Woman" an exemplary instance for his discussion of readers and reading in *On Deconstruction* (1982). "For a woman to read as a woman," he concludes, paraphrasing Peggy Kamuf's "Writing Like a Woman," "is not to repeat an identity or an experience that is given but to play a role she constructs with reference to her identity as a woman, which is also a construct, so that the series can continue: a woman reading as a woman reading as a woman."[7] The appeal to "experience," whether reader's or writer's, short-circuits this process and creates an illusory wholeness or identity, denying the internal division which simultaneously produces the gendered subject and the reading subject. Since "reading woman" necessarily entails both a theory of reading and a theory of woman—a theory of subjectivity and a theory of gender—I want to look at the double question of reading woman (reading) or woman reading (woman) from the perspective of three feminist essays which raise these theoretical issues by way of the metaphor of transvestism ("the clothes that wear us"). The first is Sandra Gilbert's "Costumes of the Mind: Transvestism as Metaphor in Modern Literature"; the second is a review article by Elaine Showalter, "Critical Cross-Dressing: Male Feminists and the Woman of the Year"; and the third is Shoshana Felman's "Rereading Femininity."[8] Each of these three feminist critics has been highly influential in defining what "reading woman" might mean, whether for Anglo-American readers or, in the case of Felman, in a Franco-American context; yet they reveal strikingly different assumptions about both gender and textuality—so much so that the first two essays deploy the metaphor of transvestism in the context of a theory of gender identity which the third essay, Felman's, sets out to deconstruct. Perhaps this difference can be attributed to the fact that while Gilbert and Showalter have attempted to construct a feminist literary and critical "herstory," Felman situates herself at the intersection of literature and psychoanalysis. Significantly, for my purposes at least, Felman's essay takes as its point of departure a rereading of Freud's 1932 lecture, "On Femininity." The intervention of psychoanalysis in the context of feminist criticism and theory, I shall argue, makes all the (sexual) difference. Read as a history of the way in which "the difference of view" is produced, rather than an attempt to describe what it consists of, psychoanalysis frees women's writing from the determinism of origin or essence while providing feminist criticism with a way to refuse the institutionalization of sexual and textual difference as gender identity and hence as questions that cannot be posed at all.

Sandra Gilbert's "Costumes of the Mind" is an "argumentative history" (Gilbert's own phrase) designed to rewrite literary history in feminist terms. A speculative account of twentieth-century modernism based on differing uses of the transvestism metaphor by men and women, her essay champions the (female) opponents of sexual hierarchy. Whereas Joyce in the Nighttown episode of *Ulysses*, Lawrence in "The Fox," and Eliot in *The Wasteland* all portray gender disorder or the blurring of sexual distinctions either as a means of endorsing conservative views of male dominance, or as nightmare (Gilbert argues), feminist transvestism becomes a means to subvert and repudiate the hierarchical views of the male modernists. Woolf's *Orlando*, for instance, portrays gender identity as fluid, multiple, and interchangeable; in Gilbert's phrase, "insouciant shiftings" (Woolf's "vacillation from one sex to the other") replace the fixity of gender identity. Gilbert clearly privileges this vision of the happily multiform self or genderless identity beyond sexual divisions which she sees in the "utopian" androgyny of writing by Djuna Barnes and H.D. The culminating metaphor of her essay, fittingly, is the gesture by which the heroines in writing by Atwood, Chopin, and Plath all discard their clothes in order to "shatter the established paradigms of dominance and submission associated with the hierarchy of gender and restore the primordial chaos of transvestism or genderlessness."[9] Although Gilbert does not ask whether this fantasy of utopian androgyny or primordial genderlessness could ever be realized, she does ask what might account for the differing gender ideologies of male and female modernists. In the last resort, however, her inquiry is limited by a theory of gender in which the relation between body and subject remains unmediated by either the unconscious or language. The answers she provides—psychobiography on one hand, literary history on the other—reveal the unquestioned argument that underpins her "argumentative history." For all her sympathy with Woolf's transvestite metaphor, her assumptions about both identity and history are ones that finally reproduce the very fixities which *Orlando* is supposed to unsettle.

To take identity first. In order to account for the specifically male anxieties which Gilbert sees as energizing the "nightmare fantasies" of the male modernists, she invokes Joyce's ambivalent relation to mother, church, and country; Lawrence's mother-dominated childhood; and Eliot's clouded first marriage. But if psychobiography fixes gender identity thus, what price the "insouciant shiftings" of *Orlando?* And what factors in the formative years and relationships of female modernists might account for their differing view of gender arrangements? Are men constituted by their object relations, while women remain somehow immune to such identity fixes and fixations? What the answer to these questions might be we never learn, since for Gilbert the modernist writer is already unambiguously gendered, either male (hierarchical, conservative) or female (insouciantly shifting, feminist). Significantly, Gilbert quotes extensively from Robert Stoller's *Sex and Gender* (1975) on the subject of male transvestism; in Stoller's terms, gender identity is either male or female, a "core identity" that is only rendered equivocal by unsatisfactory object relations and that may in fact uncannily correspond to biological and genetic factors even where it appears anomalous, as in the case of the boy raised as a girl who effortlessly adapts to his "new" gender ("Although he would seem to fit into the category of those rare people who have no difficulty in shifting their gender identity. . . . He never did shift his identity. He always felt . . . that he was a male").[10] Like Nancy Chodorow in *The Reproduction of Mothering* (1978), which also draws on Stoller's work, Gilbert ultimately assumes (by implication at least) the possibility of what Chodorow calls "the establishment of an unambiguous and unquestioned gender identity."[11] For Stoller, in fact, there is really no shifting at all, but only mistaken identity.

Gilbert, however, is primarily a revisionary literary herstorian and interpreter rather than a theorist (or even a psychoanalytic reader); and so it is no surprise that her account of twentieth-century modernism turns on what is often seen as its crucially determining (his)torical event—the differing implications for men and women of World War I. While the war years left men figuratively and literally shattered, Gilbert argues, they offered women the chance to redress their previously disinherited state. Every white feather given to a young man thereby dispatched to the trenches might mean another job for a woman; every angel in the house—every Red Cross nurse—became an avenging angel of death. The figure of the female angel of destruction, familiar from Gilbert and Gubar's *The Madwoman in the Attic* (1979), gives Gilbert's account of literary modernism a mythic dimension which itself derives from the myths of male modernists such as Yeats (Herodias' castrating daughters in "Nineteen Hundred and Nineteen," for instance). Why should the turn to history give birth to this vision of avenging female monstrosity? Is it possible that where the text of history is concerned, women can only be monsters or aberrations, since history itself (as Gilbert duly notes) is a conspiracy to marginalize or repress them? Hence the view of history offered in Woolf's *Between the Acts* (1941) by Miss La Trobe, who seems, in Gilbert's words, "to want to fragment history in order to ruin it" rather than "shoring up fragments of history against her ruin."[12] On the face of it, Gilbert endorses Woolf's modernist and feminist theory of history both here and in *Orlando*, where "shifts in literary style, shifts in historical styles, changing modalities of all kinds . . . remind us that . . . all is in flux." Yet in the last resort her own position turns out to be closer to that of the male modernist who, in her own words, "insists that the ultimate reality underlying history . . . is and must be the Truth of Gender"[13] than to the view that the ultimate reality underlying gender is history. Perhaps it is not so much the monster, woman, to which history gives birth, as the monster flux. Like identity, the very notion of (literary) history attempts to repress ambiguity and division; and what is repressed necessarily returns, in the language of the unconscious, as an avenging monster.

If Gilbert can be seen as falling back on the disorders of history to fix the still more threatening disorders of gender identity, what of Elaine Showalter's unsettling juxtaposition of recent forays into feminist criticism by male critics, on one hand, and Dustin Hoffman's 1982 film, *Tootsie*, on the other? "Critical Cross-Dressing" asks, shrewdly and wittily, whether the conversion to feminist criticism by male theorists such as Jonathan Culler in *On Deconstruction* and Terry Eagleton in *The Rape of Clarissa* (1982) is merely a form of transvestism akin to female impersonation—an appropriation which, like cross-dressing in *Tootsie*, can be viewed as a way of promoting masculine power while ostensibly masking it. Showalter's initial question ("Is male feminism a form of critical cross-dressing, a fashion risk of the 1980s that is both radical chic and power play?")[14] leads to others that are especially germane to feminist criticism; questions such as: is reading learned, and can men learn to read as feminists? Is "reading as a woman" fundamentally differentiated from "reading as a man," and if so, by what (political, sociological, or ideological) differences? Showalter persuasively unmasks *Tootsie* as not so much a feminist film but rather a film that reveals Hoffman's sense of the actor's career as feminine—passive, vulnerable, and physically exposed. Accordingly she diagnoses its transvestism, as Gilbert diagnoses that of the male modernists, in terms once more derived from Robert Stoller's *Sex and Gender*. For Stoller, the transvestite man sets out to prove that he is better than a biological woman because he is a woman with a penis.[15] *Tootsie*, Showalter argues, has it both ways. Michael Dorsey becomes a female star while still being able to lift heavy suitcases and grab taxis. But, while this is acute and apt, what has it to do with reading? Has Showalter allowed two different questions, that of female impersonation and that of reading as a woman, to become elided? Are they really the same (or at least analogous) questions, as she implies, or are they questions whose very conflation reveals an underlying contradiction in her theory of gender?

Contrasting Eagleton and Culler, Showalter represents the first as the Dustin Hoffman of literary theory—the Marxist critic who fears (like Lovelace himself in Richardson's novel) that he is effeminized by writing, and whose appropriation of feminist criticism attempts to recuperate its "phallic" power, just as Lovelace in Eagleton's own analysis attempts to recover Clarissa's imaginary phallic power by raping her. This "phallic criticism" is for Showalter simply "another raid on the resources of the feminine in order to modernize male dominance."[16] The effect, she observes, is to silence or marginalize feminist criticism by speaking for it, while simultaneously silencing the "something equivocal and personal in

[Eagleton's] own polemic" which she sees as motivating his criticism. What is this "something equivocal"? Showalter's phrase occurs in the context of what is arguably her central thesis about reading and writing as a woman:

> Like other kinds of criticism . . . feminist criticism is both reading and writing, both the interpretation of a text and the independent production of meaning. It is through the autonomous act of writing, and the confrontation with the anxiety that it generates, that feminist criticism is both reading and writing, both the interpretation of a text and the independent production of meaning. It is through the autonomous act of writing, and the confrontation with the anxiety that it generates, that feminist critics have developed theories of women's writing, *theories proved on our own pulses*. (p. 147; my italics)

Just as *Tootsie* reveals Hoffman's sense of the actor's career as feminine, and just as *Clarissa* reveals Richardson's anxiety about the feminizing effects of writing, so for the Marxist critic (Showalter suggests) there may be something effeminate about literary criticism as opposed to revolutionary action. But if one sees writing itself as feminine—and here Showalter's view is unclear—then there can be no specifically feminist theory of women's writing as opposed to men's, and no way in which such theories can be proved experientially on the pulses of women. Showalter comes close to glimpsing that textuality at once produces gender and simultaneously produces equivocation, only to repress that insight with the language of the body ("proved on our own pulses"). By invoking the experience of being biologically female, she closes the very question which she opens in her discussion of Eagleton.

Culler's argument, as Showalter accurately recapitulates it, is precisely to "demonstrate some difficulties in the feminist appeal to the woman reader's experience, an experience and an identity which is always constructed rather than given." For Culler, "'reading as a woman' is always a paradoxical act, in that the identity as 'Woman' must always be deferred" (pp. 139, 141). With apparent approval, Showalter summarizes Culler's analysis of feminist theories of reading, including his insistence that the appeal to female experience as a source of authority is always a double or divided request since the condition of being a woman is simultaneously seen as given and as created. She then proceeds to her own question, apropos of Culler's work: namely, "can a *man* read as a woman?" Noting that while Culler never presents himself as a feminist critic, he does offer a feminist reading of Freud's *Moses and Monotheism* (1939), she asks further "whether a male feminist is in fact a man reading as a woman reading as a woman?" Showalter is ready to concede that Culler has avoided the pitfall of female impersonation by reading "not as a *woman*, but as a man and a feminist" (p. 142). But one might well ask why it matters. If reading as a woman is a paradoxical act, reading as a man must involve a similarly double or divided demand. Showalter comes close to implying that while reading as a woman may (if she accepts Culler's view of the matter) involve constructing a gender identity, reading as a man does not. In other words, her theory of gender identity remains ultimately untouched by Culler's argument. Though ostensibly careful to distinguish between the essentialist "woman" reader and the "feminist" reader (a reader who may be male or female), Showalter chooses to emphasize what she calls feminist reading because "it has the important aspect of offering male readers a way to produce feminist criticism that avoids female impersonation" (p. 143). But again, if criticism—like reading and writing—can be viewed as all a matter of cross-dressing anyway, Culler's avoidance of female impersonation is neither here nor there. Ironically, Culler's "feminist" reading of *Moses and Monotheism* is designed to show why "the promotion of the paternal" should produce patriarchal criticism's characteristic concern with legitimacy of meaning and with the prevention of illegitimate interpretations. This very preoccupation with legitimacy and illegitimacy, this very preference for unambiguous meanings and stable origins, is precisely what underlies Showalter's unease about the shiftiness of critical cross-dressing in the academy.

Showalter's energetic polemic is fueled by understandable professional anxiety about preserving an area in criticism that is specific to women. This anxiety is played out most clearly in her final paragraph, which culminates in a comic apocalyptic fantasy. "Without closing the door on male feminists," she writes, "I think that Franco-American theory has gone much too far in discounting the importance of signature and gender in authorship."[17] Though she warns against essentialist simplicities ("Culler's deconstructive priorities lead him to overstate the essentialist dilemma of defining the *woman* reader"), it is surely essentialism—whether theoretical or professional—that we glimpse here, for without essentialism identity itself comes into question, and with it "the importance of signature and gender in authorship" (what one might call the *Moses and Monotheism* principle, or the insistence on legitimate origin). "Going much too far" for Showalter means the cover of the *Diacritics* special issue of summer 1982, enigmatically entitled "*Cherchez la Femme: feminist critique/feminine text.*" Here is her description:

> On a white background is a figure in a black tuxedo and high heels, resting one knee on a bentwood chair à la Marlene Dietrich. The figure has no hands or head. On the back cover, a dress, hat, gloves, and shoes arrange themselves in a graceful bodiless tableau in space. No "vulgar" feminist, the chic Diacritical covergirl hints at the ephemera of gender identities, of gender signatures.[18]

To invoke *Orlando* once more, the cover says: "it is clothes that wear us and not we them." For Showalter this graphic display of the metaphoricity of clothes risks dispersing gender identity altogether, leaving only the headless (i.e., silent) woman, the *corps morcelé* of nightmare.

Hence the form taken by Showalter's dream of the feminist literary conference of the future: the demonic woman rises to speak, but mutates into a column of fire; the Diacritical woman rises to speak, but she is headless; and finally the third panelist, a transvestite male, takes the podium: "He is forceful, he is articulate; he is talking about Heidegger or Derrida or Lévi-Strauss or Brecht. He is wearing a dress." The phallic critic, or rather, the deconstructive or Marxist critic, has successfully usurped the feminist. Showalter is surely right to be canny about the appropriative moves of the masculine critical establishment vis-à-vis feminist criticism. But the very uncanniness of this final vision should alert the reader to what has been elided by her argument—namely, woman and text, body and subject. Showalter comes dangerously close to endorsing a position she has earlier derided, that of Lewis Lapham opposing the admission of women to the Century Club ("The clarity of gender makes possible the human dialectic"); in her own text the reemergence of gender hierarchy necessarily brings with it the accompanying specter of gender disorder. But in the last resort, her fantasy reveals what is troubling about the fashion for female impersonation—the uneasy recognition that when the text takes off its clothes, it is indeed disembodied, uncanny, and silent. In other words, the very discontinuity of (female) body and (feminine) text is the scandal that experientially based theories of the woman reader displace onto the scandal of critical cross-dressing in the 1980s.

Showalter views critical cross-dressers with all the suspicion that Joyce, Lawrence, and Eliot bring to transvestism. What theoretical argument might provide a less residually conservative theory of gender, a more revisionary reading of woman? Shoshana Felman's "Rereading Feminity" approaches the question of the woman reader (woman as other) "otherwise"; that is, in the light of psychoanalytic theory.[19] Freud's question, "What is femininity?" asks, Felman points out, "what is femininity—*for men?*" As she elaborates it, the question is rather, "what does the question—'what is femininity—*for men?*' mean *for women?*" A short answer to this longer question might be: the silencing or elimination of woman. Felman's reading of a story by Balzac, "The Girl with the Golden Eyes," in the light of Freud's lecture "On Femininity" poses, in her own words, "the double question of the reading of sexual difference and of the intervention of sexual difference in the very act of reading." Read as the story of a triangular relationship (the interference of an affair between a man and a woman in an existing affair between two women), Balzac's text, Felman argues, "at once explores and puts in question the very structure of opposition between the sexes, as well as the respective definitions of masculinity and femininity."[20] Her analysis of the way in which class struggle and gender struggle both spring from a *division* which is institutionalized as an authoritative *order* by *hierarchy* (her terms) neatly deconstructs the conservative ideology of Gilbert's male modernists. Like Eagleton's Lovelace or Showalter's Eagleton, the rake in Balzac's story can be viewed as a man in search of his own phallus—a man for whom the girl with the golden eyes is only a narcissistic reflection of his desire. In this conventional polarity of masculine and feminine, woman serves only as a metaphor for man; he alone has a proper identity, since woman is always a figurative substitute for man. Hence her final reduction to the *corps morcelé*—in Balzac's story, literally a bloody and mutilated corpse—of Showalter's nightmare. In this scheme of things, woman's only function is to mediate desire or to serve as a medium of exchange. Deprived of her function, she is expendable.

Felman's reading of "The Girl with the Golden Eyes" is also designed as a lesson in how not to read—"how to *stop reading* through the exclusive blind reference to a masculine signified" (p. 27). But just as the rake, Henri, reads Paquita (the girl with the golden eyes) in terms of a masculine signified, so Paquita herself can only read "in the feminine." Bound erotically to a Marquise whom we later learn is Henri's half-sister, Paquita loves Henri for his ambiguous resemblance to a woman. In the famous transvestite scene from Balzac's story, she dresses Henri in the Marquise's clothes so that he may better resemble her beloved. For Felman, in fact,

> Balzac's text could be viewed . . . as a rhetorical dramatization and a philo-
> sophical reflection on the constitutive relationship between transvestism and
> sexuality, i.e., on the constitutive relationship between sex roles and clothing.
> If it is clothes, the text seems to suggest, if it is clothes alone, i.e., a cultural
> sign, an institution, which determine masculine and feminine and insure
> sexual opposition as an orderly, hierarchical polarity; if indeed clothes make
> the *man*—or the woman—are not sex roles as such, inherently, but trav-
> esties? Are not sex roles but travesties of the ambiguous complexity of real
> sexuality, of real sexual difference? (p. 28)

Henri and Paquita, Felman concludes, "are thus but transvestisms of the other
sex's deceptively unequivocal identity; that is, they are travesties of a travesty."
Like words, gender identity can be travestied or exchanged; there is no "proper"
referent, male or female, only the masquerade of masculinity and femininity.
At the climax of her ecstatic sexual intercourse with Henri, Paquita cries out:
"Oh! Mariquita"—as Felman points out, a name which links that of Henri (de
Marsay), Paquita herself, and the Marquise, thereby subverting the conventional
opposition of masculine and feminine and staging "the ambiguous complexity of
real sexuality." In addition, the name "Mariquita" means in Spanish, according
to Felman, "an effeminate man"; we are told that Paquita's ecstatic cry pierces
Henri's heart. The challenge here is not just to sexual hierarchy (Henri finds a
woman installed in his place) but, Felman argues, to the smooth functioning of
representation. Where Henri had previously found his ideal self—an imaginary,
unequivocal sexual identity—reflected in Paquita's golden eyes, he now finds
only division and the evidence of ironic misrecognition. The betrayer that must
be cast out is the principle of difference, here redefined as femininity itself. Although the jealous Marquise forestalls Henri's revenge on Paquita, brother and
sister come face to face over her dead body with the principle of ambiguity which
each embodies for the other. Henri's discovery, that his rival is not other, but the
same, installs his double as feminine. In Felman's words, "Since Henri himself
has a woman's face, the feminine, Henri discovers, is not *outside* the masculine,
its reassuring canny *opposite*, it is *inside* the masculine, its uncanny *difference from
itself*" (p. 41). Inside every transvestite man, a woman is struggling to get out (a
view of transvestism radically opposed to that of Stoller).

Femininity, in Felman's terms, "*inhabits* masculinity" as otherness or disruption; it is the uncanny of repression itself. Another name for it, though Felman
does not invoke it, might be "bisexuality"—a bisexuality that necessarily returns as monstrosity. Henri first describes the girl with the golden eyes as "the
woman of [his] dreams":

> She is the original of that ravishing picture called *La Femme Caressant sa
> Chimère*, the warmest, the most infernal inspiration of the genius of antiquity;
> a holy poem prostituted by those who have copied it for frescoes and mosaics;
> for a heap of bourgeois who see in this gem nothing more than a gewgaw and
> hang it on their watch-chains—whereas, it is the whole woman, an abyss of
> pleasure into which one plunges and finds no end. . . . And here I am today
> waiting for this girl whose chimera I am, asking nothing better than to pose
> as the monster in the fresco.[21]

What can we make of this strange allusion to "La Femme Caressant sa Chimère," seemingly an antique Pompeian fresco? Balzac apparently has in mind a passage from Henri Latouche's Neapolitan novel, *Fragoletta* (1829) where, during a visit to the Palazzo Studii, Latouche's characters discuss this and other paintings:

> "Et cette femme caressant une Chimère . . . c'est donc là une idée de tous les temps? Ce monstre aux ailes de colombe at aux nageoires de poisson est un bien bizarre objet d'affection; mais que de grâces dans l'attitude et particulièrement dans les bras de cette femme!" "Et que d'amour dans son regard. . . . On sent que rien de réel n'obtiendra jamais un tel culte de sa part."[22]

Balzac himself described the central character of Latouche's novel as "cet être inexprimable, qui n'a pas de sexe complet, et dans le coeur duquel luttent la ·timidité d'une femme et l'énergie d'un homme, qui aime la soeur, est aimé du frère, et ne peut rien rendre à l'un ni à l'autre. . . ."; "comme *l'Hermaphrodite*," he concludes, "*Fragoletta* restera monument."[23] The reference here is to Polyclitus's hermaphroditic statue, a discussion of which follows closely after that of the fresco and provides the centerpiece for Latouche's representation of the bisexual as an emblem of love. Elsewhere in Balzac's writing, "ce monstre" is, of course, the bisexual;[24] and the monster whom Henri views in his imagination as the object of Paquita's desire is himself—monstrous not by contrast with her ideality, but because, as we duly discover, his own gender identity is ambiguous. When Henri vows vengeance on Paquita for daring to love a woman in the guise of a man, he attempts to destroy the monster of bisexuality that always lurks within. Ironically, her death confronts him more surely with what she screens, the woman who is his monstrous or ambiguous double—with the femininity which he must deny if he is to maintain the illusion of unequivocal gender identity on which his masculinity depends.

Balzac's rake and his half-sister are alike in seeing Paquita as an object of exchange to be possessed or discarded at will (like her mother, "She comes from a country where women are not beings, but things—chattels, with which one does as one wills, which one buys, sells, and slays").[25] Whether viewed as an object of exchange or as the mediator of desire, Paquita transgresses the system in which she is inscribed by daring to be a desiring subject in her own right, and one whose desire disrupts the hierarchical opposition of masculine and feminine. As she intervenes in Balzac's story to reveal the scandalous interchangeability of man and woman—each standing for the other—so Felman herself, she points out, intervenes in Freud's lecture "On Femininity." Felman disrupts Freud's text as Paquita ruins representation in Balzac's story by daring to be at once a desiring and a speaking subject. Freud had posed the problem of femininity as a problem for men; the question *of* women is opened in a manner which closes it *for* them. As Felman writes,

> In assuming here my place as a speaking subject, I have then *interfered*, through female utterance and reading, in Freud's male writing. I have *enacted* sexual difference in the very act of reading Freud's interrogation of it; enacted it as precisely difference, with the purpose not of rejecting Freud's in-

terrogation, but of displacing it, of carrying it beyond its *stated* question, by disrupting the transparency and misleadingly self-evident universality of its male enunciation.[26]

But—one might ask—is Freud's text so misleadingly, so self-evidently and universalizingly "male" after all? Doesn't textuality itself (like Eagleton's writing) always contain "something equivocal"?

Freud's fictive "lecture" actually starts a paragraph earlier than Felman's opening quotation implies ("Today's lecture . . . may serve to give you an example of a detailed piece of analytic work"). It begins conventionally enough, at first sight, with the time-honored words, "Ladies and Gentlemen"—only to announce a problem: "All the while I am preparing to talk to you I am struggling with an internal difficulty" (*SE* 22 : 112). What is this "internal difficulty"? Surely nothing else but the recognition by Freud of his own ambiguous relation to discourse (Felman's "enunciation"), and hence to gender as well. He is, he confesses, "uncertain . . . of the extent of [his] license"; how far can he go? (Like Franco-American theory in Showalter's polemic, could he go "much too far"?) Should an introduction to psychoanalysis such as these *New Introductory Lectures* have been left "without alteration or supplement" (*SE* 22 : 112), he asks? One might ask, in turn, why a lecture "On Femininity" should take the appearance of "alteration or supplement." *Alteration* (an everyday euphemism for the neutering of domestic pets) and *supplement* (après Derrida, an academic euphemism for writing-as-masturbation) are terms that suggest unmanning effects, as if both theory and writing reenact the internal division by means of which sexual identity is constituted (or should I say, "fixed"?).

Freud proposes, he tells his imaginary audience, to bring forward "nothing but observed facts." But it is precisely the evidence of observation—the empiricism of scientific inquiry—that his lecture dismantles at the outset:

> When you meet a human being, the first distinction you make is "male or female?" and you are accustomed to make the distinction with unhesitating certainty. Anatomical science shares your certainty at one point and not much further. The male sexual product, the spermatozoon, and its vehicle are male; the ovum and the organism that harbours it are female. . . . [But] Science next tells you something that runs counter to your expectations and is probably calculated to confuse your feelings. It draws your attention to the fact that portions of the male sexual apparatus also appear in women's bodies, though in an atrophied state, and vice versa in the alternative case. It regards their occurrence as indications of *bisexuality*, as though an individual is not a man or a woman but always both. (*SE* 22 : 113–14)

If anatomical science can provide only an ambiguous answer to the riddle of gender, then, Freud writes "you are bound to . . . conclude that what constitutes masculinity or femininity is an unknown characteristic which anatomy cannot lay hold of" (*SE* 22 : 114). Could "psychology" provide an answer, perhaps? No, since it merely reinscribes in the realm of mental life either anatomy or conventional attributions of gender to qualities such as activity or passivity. If "psychology too is unable to solve the riddle of femininity" (*SE* 22 : 116), what of psychoanalysis? For Freud, psychoanalytic inquiry would take the form of an aporia, refusing the idea of a secret or "essence" altogether. Instead of demanding an answer to the riddle against which so many heads have knocked—"Heads in hieroglyphic bonnets, / Heads in turbans and black birettas . . ." (*SE* 22 : 113n.)[27]—psychoanalysis asks how differentiation itself comes about: "In conformity with its peculiar nature, psychoanalysis does not try to describe what a woman is—that would be a task it could scarcely perform—but sets about enquiring how she comes into being" (*SE* 22 : 116). The "peculiar nature" of psychoanalysis, Freud suggests, is not to describe what is, knocking its head against the opaque reality of observation or representation, but rather to uncover the process by which that reality or set of representations is constructed.

The outlines of what Freud calls "the prehistory of women"—a process of sexual differentiation founded on the differing operations on boy and girl of the Oedipus and castration complexes—forms (in Gilbert's phrase) an "argumentative history" with which feminists in turn have argued; arguing, that is, both with Freud and among themselves.[28] Rather than rehearsing here that (pre)history or the debate which surrounds "On Femininity," I want simply to invoke the crucial but problematic thesis of bisexuality put forward in Freud's lecture. Though he at first thought of bisexuality in terms of an undifferentiated sexual nature prior to the institution of sexual difference, Freud came to see bisexuality, in the words of Juliet Mitchell and Jacqueline Rose—whose *Feminine Sexuality* (1983) contains the most sustained account of a revised, Lacanian Freud—as standing for "the very uncertainty of sexual division itself" and as inseparable from "the division and precariousness of human subjectivity."[29] This Lacanian reading of sexual difference would emphasize in particular what Rose calls "the availability to all subjects of both positions in relation to that difference itself." Lacan and language simultaneously install the subject in sexual difference, and sexual difference in the subject: "For Lacan, men and women are only ever in language. . . . All speaking beings must line themselves up on one side or the other of this division, but anyone can cross over and inscribe themselves on the opposite side from that to which they are anatomically destined."[30] But as Stephen Heath points out in *The Sexual Fix* (1984), bisexuality works both ways in theoretical arguments, functioning "as the beginning of an alternative representation, as an insistence against the one position, the fixed sexual order, man and woman"; but also returning "as a confirmation of that fixity, a strategy in which differences . . . are neutralized into the given system of identity."[31] On one hand, bisexuality as crossing over or shifting: on the other, bisexuality as the old fix. Though he seems to start by dissolving the opposition between masculine and feminine, Freud ends by reaffirming the old order; masculinity provides the measure for the feminine. For Sarah Kofman in *The Enigma of Woman* (1985), Freud first masters sexual difference by positing an original masculinity in women, making the girl's bisexuality more pronounced than the boy's, and then establishes a norm of bisexuality which predisposes women to hysteria; the sign of feminine sexual difference becomes the sign of feminine neurosis.[32] The binary opposition returns to obliterate sexual difference while restoring sexual hierarchy.

Yet a resourceful reading of Freud's "On Femininity" (such as Kofman provides) might reveal that the very bisexuality posited for women makes them, not a derivative of man, but rather, in their complexity, a model for sexuality in general. As Culler puts it, "the moves by which psychoanalysis establishes a hierarchical opposition between man and woman rely on premises that reverse this hierarchy."[33] Reversal becomes the first and necessary step, the point of leverage for dismantling a theoretical structure in which the feminine is produced only as a negative term: as lack. If, from a Lacanian point of view, "masquerade" (crossdressing?) "is the very definition of 'femininity' precisely because it is constructed with reference to a male sign,"[34] that definition, in turn, is itself clearly a form of masquerade, an imposture. Freud's account of the "peculiar nature" of psychoanalysis ("psycho-analysis does not try to describe what a woman is . . . but sets about enquiring how she comes into being," *SE* 22:116) could well be rephrased as Rose's Lacanian account of the "peculiar nature" of femininity: "Psychoanalysis does not produce that definition. It gives an account of how that definition is produced."[35] Hence the importance of psychoanalysis for any account of women's relation to, and constitution by, discourse. But there is another side to it. Reread, not as given, but as produced, "femininity"—woman—also demands a rereading of the text of psychoanalysis. Hence the importance of feminist criticism for any account of the constitution of psychoanalytic discourse. The theoretical reversal reveals the role played by woman in sustaining Freud's theory of gender. But it also reveals how that theory can be reread to produce a theoretical formulation in which the emphasis shifts from "woman" to "reading."

Orlando too might be called an "argumentative history"—the history of a woman writer. Orlando's gender shift from masculine to feminine occurs during the reign of Charles I at approximately the moment when (according to Woolf's literary-historical scheme) it was possible for the first time to become a woman writer and not the suicidal Judith Shakespeare of *A Room of One's Own* (1929). Though at once lover and beloved, Orlando is also a poet whose writing provides history of literary possibilities from 1500 to Woolf's own age. Indeed, like *A Room of One's Own*, *Orlando* can be read as the history of its own writing. Though she lightheartedly takes issue with essentialist notions of gender—such as "(1) that Orlando had always been a woman, (2) that Orlando is at this moment a man"[36]— Woolf's underlying concern is with questions of writing. The convergence of Orlando and authorial concerns, or gender and writing, is most clearly marked when Orlando, having married and so met the requirements of the spirit of her age (at this point, the Victorian age) "could write, and write she did. She wrote. She wrote. She wrote." With this, Orlando's biographer, and text, break off for a long digression on the mind of the writer at work. The life of a writer refuses to be written. Woolf as biographer can only invoke processes that are at once Orlando's and her own: "this mere woolgathering; this thinking; this sitting in a chair day in, day out, with a cigarette and a sheet of paper and a pen and an ink pot."[37] Writing and thinking, Orlando neither thinks of a gamekeeper (like Lady Chatterley) nor pens him a note (the only forms of thinking and writing nobody objects to in a woman); she is, Woolf observes, "one of those monsters of iniquity who do not love." This monster who will neither love nor (like Henri de Marsay) kill, is "no better than a corpse," a mere body: "if . . . the subject of one's biography will neither love nor kill, but will only think and imagine, we may conclude that he or she is no better than a corpse and so leave her."[38] Looking out of the window, the only resource left, the biographer searches for other signs of life;

returning from her year's imaginative absorption, Orlando-as-writer similarly pushes aside her pen, comes to the window with her completed manuscript, and exclaims: "Done!" Life is most fully present when the life of the writer and the writing of the life merge, breaking down the distinction between subject and object; between woman as writer or woman as written, woman as reader or woman as read. Orlando and her biographer, in other words, create each other by mutual substitution; the masquerade—Orlando's transvestite progress through the literary ages—is that of writing, where fictive and multiple selves are the only self, the only truth, the writer knows.

What Gilbert calls "a revisionary biography"[39] can be seen as autobiography; specifically, as female autobiography. Woolf wrote to Vita Sackville-West apropos of *Orlando,* "it sprung upon me how I could revolutionise biography in a night."[40] In a review of Harold Nicolson's biography, *Some People* (1927), written while she was at work on *Orlando,* Woolf described "the new biography" as one in which we realize that the figure which has been most completely and most subtly displayed is that of the author"; one in which we realize that "Truth of fact and truth of fiction are incompatible" and "the life which is increasingly real to us is the fictive life."[41] *Orlando* culminates—or rather, fails to culminate—with a mock peroration in which the (auto)biographical subject meditates inconclusively on herself as woman writer; on the "true self" that is "a woman. Yes, but a million other things as well." In the face of such irrepressible diversity, such multiplicity of shifting selves, the biographer throws in her hand:

> But (here another self came skipping over the top of her mind like the beam from a lighthouse). Fame! (She laughed.) Fame! Seven editions. A prize. Photographs in the evening papers (. . . we must here snatch time to remark how discomposing it is for her biographer that this culmination and peroration should be dashed from us on a laugh casually like this; but the truth is that when we write of a woman, everything is out of place—culminations and perorations; the accent never falls where it does with a man).[42]

"When we write of a woman, everything is out of place." Or, as Barbara Johnson has written apropos of women and autobiography, "the monstrousness of self-hood is intimately embedded within the question of female autobiography. Yet how could it be otherwise, since the very notion of a self, the very shape of human life stories, has always, from St. Augustine to Freud, been modeled on the man."[43]

Orlando "discomposes" or undoes her (auto)biographer because the displaced accent also displaces the writing subject. "When we write of a woman everything is out of place"; displacement, not hierarchy, becomes the order of the day. These multiple displacements—from one self to another, from masculine to feminine, from biography to autobiography, from reader to writer—constitute the "insouciant shiftings" of writerly non-identity or otherness which simultaneously preclude both closure (culminations and perorations) and certainty (truth). "If you want to know more about femininity," Freud inconclusively concludes his lecture, "enquire from your own experience of life, or turn to the poets" (*SE* 22:135). When literature turns from experience to psychoanalysis for an answer to the riddle of femininity, psychoanalysis turns the question back to literature, since it is in language—in reading and in writing woman—that femininity at once discloses and discomposes itself, endlessly displacing the fixity of gender identity by the play of difference and division which simultaneously creates and uncreates gender, identity, and meaning. "The difference (of view)" which we look for in reading woman (reading) is surely nothing other than this disclosure, this discomposition, which puts the institution of difference in question without erasing the question of difference itself.

NOTES

1. Virginia Woolf, *Orlando, A Biogrpahy* (New York and London: Harcourt Brace Jovanovich, 1928), pp. 188–89.

2. Shoshana Felman, "Rereading Femininity," *Yale French Studies* (1981), 62:28.

3. Juliet Mitchell and Jacqueline Rose, eds., *Feminine Sexuality: Jacques Lacan and the école freudienne* (London and New York: Norton, 1989). See the introductions, pp. 1–57 *passim* for the evolution of Freudian and Lacanian theories of the gendered subject.

4. "Defined by man, the conventional polarity of masculine and feminine names woman as a *metaphor of man*. Sexuality . . . functions . . . as the sign of a rhetorical convention, of which woman is the *signifier* and man the *signified*. Man alone has thus the privilege of proper meaning"; Felman, "Rereading Femininity," p. 25.

5. Virginia Woolf, "George Eliot," *Collected Essays of Virginia Woolf*, 4 vols. Leonard Woolf, ed., (London: Hogarth Press, 1966–67), 1:204.

6. See, for instance, Annette Kolodny, "A Map for Rereading: Or, Gender and the Interpretation of Literary Texts," *New Literary History* (Spring 1980), 11(3): 451–67, and Jean E. Kennard, "Convention Coverage or How to Read Your Own Life," *New Literary History* (Autumn 1981), 13(1): 69–88, as well as Judith Fetterley, *The Resisting Reader: A Feminist Approach to American Fiction* (Bloomington: Indiana University Press, 1978).

7. Jonathan Culler, *On Deconstruction: Theory and Criticism after Structuralism* (Ithaca: Cornell University Press, 1982), p. 64, and in this volume in "Reading"; cf. Peggy Kamuf, "Writing Like a Woman," in Sally McConnell-Ginet, Ruth Borker, and Nelly Furman, eds., *Women and Language in Literature and Society*, p. 298 (New York: Praeger, 1980).

8. Sandra Gilbert's essay was first published in *Critical Inquiry* (Winter 1980), 7(2): 391–417 and republished in Abel, ed., *Writing and Sexual Difference*, pp. 193–219; Elaine Showalter's review article appeared in *Raritan* (Fall 1983), 3(2): 130–49; and Shoshana Felman's essay appeared in *Yale French Studies* (1981), 62: 19–44.

9. Gilbert, "Costumes of the Mind," p. 218.

10. Robert J. Stoller, "A Contribution to the Study of Gender Identity," *International Journal of Psycho-Analysis* (April–July 1964), 45(2–3): 223. Stoller's concept of "core gender identity" is also elaborated in "Facts and Fancies: An Examination of Freud's Concept of Bisexuality," in Jean Strouse, ed., *Woman and Analysis*, pp. 343–64 (New York: Grossman, 1974). Cf. Gilbert, "Costumes of the Mind," pp. 199–200 and *n*. for citation of Stoller's work on transvestism.

11. See Nancy Chodorow, *The Reproduction of Mothering: Psychoanalysis and the Sociology of Gender* (Berkeley: University of California Press, 1978), p.158, and cf. Mitchell and Rose, *Feminine Sexuality*, p. 37*n*. for a brief analysis of Chodorow's displacement of "the concepts of the unconscious and bisexuality in favour of a notion of gender imprinting . . . which is compatible with a sociological conception of role."

12. Gilbert, "Costumes of the Mind," p. 214.

13. *Ibid.*, pp. 207, 214.

14. Showalter, "Critical Cross-Dressing," p. 134.

15. See Robert J. Stoller, *Sex and Gender*, 2 vols. (New York: Jason Aronson, 1975), 1:177, and cf. Showalter, "Critical Cross-Dressing," p. 138, and Gilbert, "Costumes of the Mind," p. 199.

16. Showalter, "Critical Cross-Dressing," p. 146.

17. *Ibid.*, p. 149; cf. the debate between Peggy Kamuf, "Replacing Feminist Criticism" and Nancy Miller, "The Text's Heroine: A Feminist Critic and Her Fictions," in *Diacritics* (Summer 1982), 12(2): 42–47, 48–53.

18. Showalter, "Critical Cross-Dressing," p. 149.

19. Cf. the subtitle of Felman's "Literature and Psychoanalysis," special issue of *Yale French Studies* (1977), 55/56, "The Question of Reading: Otherwise."

20. Felman, "Rereading Femininity," pp. 21, 22.

21. Honoré de Balzac, "The Girl with the Golden Eyes," *The Thirteen*, Ellen Marriage and Ernest Dowson, trans. (London: Society of English Bibliophiles, 1901), pp. 308–9.

22. "And this woman caressing a Chimera . . . is this, then, an idea for all time? This monster with the wings of a dove and with the fins of a fish is a rather bizarre object of affection; but such grace in the attitude and particularly in the arms of this woman!" "And such love in her look . . . one senses that nothing of reality will ever be reached by such worship on her part." Henri Latouche, *Fragoletta: Naples et Paris en 1789* (Paris: Pour la Societé des Médecins Bibliophiles, 1929), p. 42.

23. "This inexpressible being, who does not have a complete sex, and in whose heart the timidity of a woman and the energy of a man are in conflict, who loves the sister, and is loved by the brother, and can return nothing to one or to the other. . . ."; "like *The Hermaphrodite*," "*Fragoletta* will remain a monument." Honoré de Balzac, "Du roman historique et de *Fragoletta* (1831)," *Oeuvres Complètes de Honoré de Balzac: Oeuvres Diverses*, 3 vols., Marcel Bouteron and Henri Longnon, eds. (Paris: Louis Conard, 1935–40), 1:207.

24. See, for instance, Honoré de Balzac, *Peau de chagrin* (Paris: Editions Gallimard, 1974), p. 204, and for another chimera in Balzac's *Sarrasine*, cf. Roland Barthes, *S/Z*, Richard Miller, trans. (New York: Hill and Wang, 1974), pp. 63–64.

25. Balzac, "The Girl with the Golden Eyes," p. 356.

26. Felman, "Rereading Femininity," p. 21.

27. See Jane Gallop, *The Daughter's Seduction: Feminism and Psychoanalysis* (Ithaca: Cornell University Press, 1982), pp. 59–62, for a reading of the role played by these lines in Freud's text.

28. See, for instance, Luce Irigaray, *Speculum of the Other Woman*, Gillian C. Gill, trans. (Ithaca: Cornell University Press, 1985), pp. 13–129, for an extended reading of "On Femininity"; cf. also Jane Gallop's reading of Irigaray in *The Daughter's Seduction*, pp. 56–79, and reprinted in this volume, pp. 411–29; and Part Two of Sarah Kofman's *The Enigma of Woman: Women in Freud's Writings*, Catherine Porter, trans. (Ithaca: Cornell University Press, 1985), pp. 101–225; Kofman's reading of Freud also takes issue with Irigaray's.

29. Mitchell and Rose, *Feminine Sexuality*, pp. 12, 29. Mitchell and Rose's book should be read in the context of Gallop's less sanitized, more diacritical reading of Lacan on femininity; see *The Daughter's Seduction*, pp. 1–42, where Gallop's point of departure is Mitchell's earlier reading of Freud in her *Psychoanalysis and Feminism* (Harmondsworth: Penguin, 1974).

30. Mitchell and Rose, *Feminine Sexuality*, p. 49 and note. Cf. also the discussion in Parveen Adams and Elizabeth Cowie, "Feminine Sexuality: Interview with Juliet Mitchell and Jacqueline Rose," *m/f* (1983), 8:13.

31. Stephen Heath, *The Sexual Fix* (New York: Schocken Books, 1984), p. 142.

32. See Sarah Kofman, *The Enigma of Woman: Woman in Freud's Writings*, trans. Catherine Porter (Ithaca: Cornell University Press, 1985), pp. 122–42, 202–10.

33. See Culler, *On Deconstruction*, p. 171.

34. Mitchell and Rose, *Feminine Sexuality*, p. 43.

35. *Ibid.*, p. 57.

36. Woolf, *Orlando*, p. 139.

37. *Ibid.*, pp. 226, 267.

38. *Ibid.*, p. 269.

39. Gilbert, "Costumes of the Mind," p. 208.

40. Nigel Nicholson and Joanne Trautman, eds., *The Letters of Virginia Woolf*, 4 vols. (New York and London: Harcourt Brace Jovanovich, 1975–79), 3:429.

41. Virginia Woolf, "The New Biography," *Collected Essays*, 4:233–34.

42. Woolf, *Orlando*, pp. 310, 312. Cf. the later, more explicit text, with its reference to "this culmination to which the whole book moved, this peroration with which the book was to end"; *Orlando: A Biography* (Harmondsworth: Penguin, 1963), p. 220.

43. Barbara Johnson, "My Monster/My Self," *Diacritics* (Summer 1982), 12(2): 10.

JOSEPH A. BOONE

MALE INDEPENDENCE AND THE AMERICAN QUEST GENRE

hidden sexual politics in the all-male worlds of melville, twain and london

The absence of women, courtship and marriage in classic American fiction—the absence, that is, of precisely those hallmarks of theme and form distinguishing the English tradition—has been a literary commonplace since the 1960 publication of Leslie Fiedler's *Love and Death in the American Novel*. It is, however, a commonplace in need of some rethinking. In the first place, as recent feminist critics have reminded us, those "classic" texts of men-without-women represent a minority deviating from a popular tradition in which women, courtship and marriage are very much in evidence.[1] And in the second place, as the hindsight of twenty-five years makes clear, Fiedler's argument is fueled by an unquestioning allegiance to certain Freudian assumptions about "normal" or "correct" male psychological development that predispose him, as a critic, to judge the quester's prototypical gesture of escape from society as a negative example of "arrested adolescence." I would propose a more positive interpretation of the male quester's search for freedom than that offered by Fiedler, or, conversely, by those feminist critics who have assumed that the genre—as a literature written by men and about men—must inevitably valorize ideological concerns culturally designated as "masculine" or "patriarchal." Rather, concealed beneath the quest-romance's male-defined exterior there often exists a fascinating if sometimes ambivalent exploration of sexual politics, including a *potentially* radical critique of the marital norms, sexual roles and power imbalances characterizing nineteenth-century American familial and social life. What has been even less noted in studies of quest fiction—and which I will attempt to demonstrate in the cases of Melville, Twain and London—is the degree to which the experimental form of this "aberrant" fictional mode often corresponds to the presence of such a hidden sexual politics.

The complex relation of gender to genre in the American quest is anticipated by Fiedler's study in two important ways which merit review at the onset of my own argument. First, Fiedler explains the rise of the American genre not merely as a reaction to the formal realism of everyday life espoused by the early English novel, but also as a rebellion against the ethos of sexual polarity pervading the countless tales of love and seduction that followed Richardson's achievement. The sentimental debasement of love ensuing shortly thereafter in early American fiction, Fiedler argues, sent the serious American writer scurrying in pursuit of alternate subject matters and modes—whence the accomplishments of authors ranging from Cooper and Hawthorne to Melville and Twain. Second, Fiedler forcefully argues that the bonding of males repeated throughout the American canon came into being as an explicit alternative to the antagonistic heterosexual relationships emanating from the "sentimental love religion" dominating the conventional novel. However, in tracing the paradigmatic movement of the male quester away from societal structures—including marriage—Fiedler betrays the bias to which I have already referred: for, in his eyes, the freedom sought by the male protagonist "on the run" from society *necessarily* constitutes an adolescent avoidance of mature love, as epitomized in marital responsibility, and of adult identity.[2] Despite the partial truth of this assertion when applied, for instance, to figures such as Rip Van Winkle or Natty Bumppo, it does not follow that every unattached or independent quester lacks personal fulfillment simply because he avoids the constraints of patriarchically conceived marriage or traditionally defined manhood.

Indeed, several examples of the quest genre—*Moby-Dick* (1851), *The Adventures of Huckleberry Finn* (1884), *Billy Budd* (c. 1891) and *The Sea Wolf* (1904)— point in the opposite direction: the quester's linear projection outward from the closed circle of societal circumspection into undefined geographic and textual space "liberate[s] him," to paraphrase Henry James' definition of American romance, "from the conditions that we usually know to attach to [experience],"[3] and the consequence of that liberation, for a few of these unconventional protagonists, is the discovery of an affirming, multiform self that has broken through the strictures traditionally imposed on male social identity. Thus, the outward-bound voyage to confront the unknown that by definition constitutes quest narrative simultaneously traces an inner journey toward a redefinition of self that defies social convention and sexual categorization. Lines from Melville's poem "After the Pleasure-Party" eloquently evoke the hidden or subconscious goal of many such quests:

> Could I remake me! or set free
> This sexless bound in sex, then plunge
> Deeper than Sappho, in a lunge
> Piercing Pan's paramount mystery!
> For, Nature, in no shallow surge
> Against thee either sex may urge,
> Why has thou made us but in halves—
> Co-relatives? This makes us slaves.
> If these co-relatives never meet
> Self-hood itself seems incomplete.[4]

Adopting Melville's terminology, we might say that the yearning to be "set free" from those inner and outer "bounds in sex" which threatens to stultify the self leads to a "plunge" into the "mystery" of sexual identity, the psychological terrain of Pan, that is analogous to the physical act of questing itself.

This goal, moreover, helps distinguish the American genre from archetypal patterns of quest-romance, such as those described by Northrop Frye. For in the

traditional model the mythic wanderer most often returns from his perilous journeys to the world of the known as a culture-hero, his discovery of identity serving a *social* good that heals the wasted kingdom.[5] In spirit if not always in reality,
the prototypical American quester remains a rebel-figure or social outcast whose
true self can only exist *outside* the parameters of his culture; unlike the hero of
the mythic pattern, he strives not so much for the reintegration into society as for
the reintegration of his often fragmented identity, a leveling of the reductively
constructed hierarchies of heart and mind as well as those severed "halves" of
personality associated in "After the Pleasure Party" with the two sexes. The
following pages will attempt to measure the radical implications—and psychic
dangers—of the questing figure's departure from his prescribed sexual role by
examining four fantasies of male freedom and escape in which the format's provisional, "unfixed" organization facilitates an unusually probing inquiry into the
social and psychological problematic of masculine identity. Instead of uncovering
a univocal paen to traditional norms of manhood, we will find inscribed in the
trajectories of these specific American quest narratives visions of individuality
and mutual relationship that attempt to break down conventional sexual categorization by breaking through the limiting forms of culture and the conventions
of love-literature at once. In a sense, the questing vision was ultimately limited
by its chosen field of representation; for the decision to forgo the world of male–
female relations necessarily involved an absence of female reality that, in replicating women's metaphoric invisibility in patriarchy, could be used to support a
misogynistic world-view. Nonetheless, the early *potential* of the mode was immense, for by presenting the figuratively all-male world as an *imaginative* alternative to existing social and literary constructs, the quest writer found himself
empowered to express in "a bold and nervous lofty language" (*Moby-Dick* 71),
perhaps for the first time, a questioning of the dominant sexual order within
which he too was trapped.

I

The male quest in American fiction represents only one branch, of course, of the
larger fictional category self-consciously labeled the "Romance" by early pro-
moters of the form. The quest formula shared with American romance the
latter's repudiation of the strictly realistic methods associated with conventional
English fiction;[6] but the quest variant went further in *also* repudiating the love
emphasis of traditional fiction—an inheritance from which few general American
romancers were exempt. So the frequently stereotypical images of women, high
degrees of etherealized eroticism, and reliance upon conventional love-plot mechanisms in writers as diverse as Cooper, Poe and Hawthorne indicate.[7]

The writer of quest-romance, in contrast to the general romancer, dealt by
definition with a world largely void of women or normal social regulations, a
world in which the male exploration of sea or desert provided a subject ideally
suited for the novelist interested in working outside the thematic strictures of the
literary marriage tradition. Historically, as Frye has demonstrated, the questing
hero's physical movement away from civilized realms, often alone, makes the

development of his independent, singular identity a paramount focus, and American adaptations continue this emphasis. What is different—and hence revealing—about American versions of the quest-romance formula is the extent to which the fair lady who typically figured as the medieval quester's goal or reward has been displaced by the more metaphysical objects of truth, absolute reality, the nature of authority and similar lofty issues. Implicit in this shift, whether of conscious or unconscious design, are several very significant factors: first, having less reason to promulgate the objectification and idealization of woman inherent in most other literatures of the time, the quest skirts the historical perception of woman as man's opposite, leaving the universe instead to play the antagonistic role of "Other"; second, since the quester's virility is therefore less dependent on genital than heroic contact (as Fiedler puts it), his acquisition of adult male identity is freed from usual connotations of reproductive function and social good; and third, the "forward thrust of inquiry, the dynamic assertion of self in a progressive line of exploration" that John Seelye defines as the genre's underlying structural principle dissociates it from the closural constraints that the finality of return-and-marriage, if only as symbol, would impose.[8]

The quester's journey *into* the unknown simultaneously implies an escape *from* the known—that is, the context of nineteenth-century American culture. As we have seen, Fiedler argues that the quest writer's avoidance of themes of passion and marriage was a direct result of his society's extreme degree of sentimentalization and sexual bifurcation. This assumption is corroborated by Ann Douglas in *The Feminization of American Culture*, which analyzes the sentimental myth of absolute connubial love and of the wife's domestic role that took root in early nineteenth-century America and rapidly became *the* middle-class ideal.[9] The widely preached doctrine of the wife's sacred "influence" within the home arose as a response to the period's increasingly severe dichotomization of male and female spheres and roles: the more that the growth of capitalism encouraged "masculine" aggression and drive in its fledgling male entrepreneurs, the more society venerated traditional "feminine" values, which in turn kept women in their place. Given the importance of the marriage institution in maintaining these hierarchical roles, it is small wonder that the unmarried male, having freely chosen his independence from the blandishments of marriage and the "softer sex," came under attack by the moral guardians of society. "Does not your soul become chilled," the hero of the tract *Married and Single* warns a bachelor hero, "at the soul-revolting idea, that all the noble deeds . . . of a Washington would have been lost . . . to the world, if his father had acted the strange, unnatural, criminal part you propose to yourself?"[10]

If the quester sought to flee this marital ethos, the romance-quest writer also sought escape from the seeming banalities of much popular "women's fiction"—literature generally written by and for women that served as a tool for socialization into often unwittingly proper "feminine" roles.[11] The tendency of these sentimental writers to employ pat formulas to convey their messages of domestic and social order hinged on the shared belief that the marriage vow, as the novelist Mrs. E.D.E.N. Southworth put it, was "the most sacred tie on earth"; unravel that knot and not only "the peace of families, [but] the social welfare of the whole community" might fall apart.[12] Hence, as Herbert Ross Brown explains in the standard work on the sentimental tradition, these writers coerced the structural paradigms of courtship, seduction and marital trials inherited from English love fiction into serving their aims with unabashed fervor:

> The final solution was neatly reserved for the last chapter where the punish-
> ment was made to fit the crime, and the reward to equal the virtue. To
> achieve it, authors subjected the long aim of coincidence to the rack of expe-
> diency where it was stretched and fractured to suit every need of the plot.[13]

The domination of the American fictional market by these formulaic productions—inspiring Hawthorne's unkind reference to that "damned mob of scribbling women"[14]—intensified the sense of exclusion felt by those writers in search
of unsentimental themes and uncontrived forms.

Rather than directly challenge the falsifying stereotypes of the sexes promoted
by this fictional system and its parent realist tradition, the prototypical romance
writer simply abandoned the subject of "realistic" romantic involvement altogether; some romancers like Hawthorne and Poe turned to largely allegorical
modes of narrative whose dichotomized images of light/dark heroines, in particular, were as "unreal" as those mythologized by sentimental fiction, while the
quest writer sidestepped the social and literary problematic of the sexes by imagining worlds without women, hence ostensibly free of the gendered system creating a sexually bifurcated society. As we have noted, there may be at times
a fine line separating innovative and conservative impulse in the writer's choice
of the quest as narrative subject. By examining *how* the male world is used,
however, whether it gives voice to dominant values, as in Cooper, or attempts
through indirection to give voice to a hitherto silenced reality and alternative
world, as in Melville, we can begin to filter the wishfully escapist from legitimately progressive variations within the genre. In the latter case, moreover, it is
important to realize that the socially subversive content of the fiction is, as in
much marginalized women's fiction, filtered first through the private realm of individual desire: rather than confronting the politics of sexuality head-on or in a
public context, such texts often limit their explorations of the impingements of
social and fictive structures of power to the personal level—a focus nonetheless
opening up, for the quest writer, a hitherto unexplored geography of possibility
underlying social myths of male identity and relationship.

A later and contrasting literary context that sheds light on the exploration of
masculine identity in the quest-romance is the male adventure story of the frontier or wild West, with its prototype in Cooper's wilderness tales. Only superficially resembling the romance-quests in which I am interested, this late-century
development served the same ideological function for its male readers as the sentimental treatise did for the female audience: through its romanticized fantasies
of supervirile heroism and strength, the western novel validated accepted notions
of sexual hierarchy and male authority.[15] Telling in this regard—and radically at
odds with the quest genre—is the fact that the frontier hero's rough-and-ready adventures are almost always governed by a crude manifestation of the courtship pattern. As one also finds in the Leatherstocking Tales, it is the inspiriting presence of
women—as frail vessels to rescue and protect from the menacing wilderness
environment, as signifiers of a civilization whose values can only be maintained
by male prowess—that gives the frontier novel's hyper-masculine ethos its

whole point.[16] From opposing vantage points, then, the western and sentimental genres—along with most "Romance" narrative in general—maintained an essentialist myth of sexual dichotomization from which the protagonists of Melville, Twain and London's quest novels attempt to escape.

II

While these various literary and social contexts help explain the genesis of the quest format, certain repeating thematic and formal tropes peculiar to the genre underline the uncommonness of its attempt to redefine masculine sexual identity. Paramount among three distinguishing characteristics is the ever-present male bond in the world of the quest. Fiedler first deduced that the genre's "manly friendships" represent "a kind of counter-matrimony":[17] whence the relationships of Ishmael and Queequeg, Huck and Jim, Van Weyden and Wolf Larsen. As symbolic alternative to the conventions and constrictions associated with the social ideal of wedlock, the "pure marriage of males" facilitates bonds that are deeply committed yet—unlike hierarchically-ordered marriage—not detrimental to either partner's sense of personal freedom.[18] The mutuality of gender, it would appear, permits a level of equal interchange and individualism that the dualistic assumptions underlying conventional marital union negate. Unlike the male pairs represented in the British tradition of master and servant (one thinks of Crusoe and Friday, Pickwick and Sam Weller, Holmes and Watson, whose "unions" reflect the hierarchical order of society), American comrades often present a more multifaceted model of loving relationship: their bonds simultaneously partake of brotherly, passionate, paternal, filial, even maternal qualities, without being restricted to one definition alone. Even when the paired questers comprise a racial duality—which Fiedler interprets as a symbolic union of the "primitive" or instinctual life and the questing ego[19]—the fact remains that the black–white opposition is only "skin-deep," as it were, since the true source maintaining the male bond is its mutuality—of spirit, of gender, of democratic fraternity.

The theoretical absence of women in the quest narrative provides a second indication of its untraditional status, but not in an expected fashion. For, although the male quest by definition excludes woman as major protagonist (the second half of London's *The Sea Wolf* will prove an instructive exception), her traces nonetheless resurface in the world of the quest to play a crucial role as symbol and image, as inner principle in the individual quester, and as external role imposed on weaker or androgynous men by repressive figures of authority.[20] As the lines cited from Melville's "After the Pleasure Party" indicate, the quest not only reaches "beyond" for a metaphysical explanation of existence, but may also reach "within" for a psychogenic truth that reveals the falsity of the constructs of gender used to differentiate the sexes and distribute power unequally between them.[21] *Moby-Dick, Huckleberry Finn, Billy Budd* and *The Sea Wolf* all to some extent participate in a dialectic between those obsessed questers, filled with a will to power that blinds them to this truth, and those expansive selves—like Ishmael, Huck, Billy—whose inner equanimity rests upon their unselfconscious acceptance of the love and compassion traditionally associated with the female sphere and the heart. The dangers besetting such "openness" of personality are best illustrared in *Billy Budd*, where the eponymous hero's "androgynous" attributes become a "feminine" weakness to those authorities who fear loss of their male-identified powers and thus force the "handsome sailor" to assume a role analogous to that of woman's in society. The very existence of such "female-substitute" figures in the quest genre becomes a powerful textual signifier of the oppressiveness and potential destruction associated with an ethos equating power with masculinity.

A third distinguishing trait of the American male quest—noted by Chase, Brodhead, Seelye and other—is its unique narrative structure. What has gone unmentioned, however, is the degree to which the mode's textual organization, in replicating the quester's search for unboundaried self-definition, evolved as an important correlative of the radical thematic departures outlined above. In essence, the rejection of restrictive cultural formats that triggers the protagonist's desire to escape society simultaneously operates as a rejection of the concept of stable narrative centers: that is, the forward movement of the quest into unknown *geographic* space is so orchestrated as to create a linear projection into undefined *textual* space. Instead of a symmetrically unified pattern based on conflict, separation and resolution, the narrative organization of the quest novel is characterized by an open series of often jarring or startling narrative expansions and transformations. Related to Romantic theories of the organically proliferating text, the quest narrative thus has an effect of being always already in process, of forever reaching after new and unexpected plateaus of meaning. As Richard Brodhead has demonstrated, this effect is often achieved by the linking together of disparate representational modes (or sub-genres) of fiction, so that the reader gains the sense not merely of several types of narrative strung together, but of one mode after the other being left behind, traveled beyond, as the evolving quest carries both reader and protagonist into increasingly uncharted realms of discourse and plot.[22] These transitions from one mode of narration to the next are often marked (1) by threshold moments that serve as springboard from which the narrative, like the quest itself, launches forward into the unknown, or (2) by symbolic moments of rebirth that propel the protagonist into new contexts and new identities.

Often accompanying these shifts in mode are abrupt refocusings of perspective, exemplified by the frequently discussed movement in *Moby-Dick* from Ishmael's narrating voice to omnisciently narrated scenes to which he has no access. This process of juxtaposing voices and viewpoints is not simply authorial idiosyncrasy or pyrotechnical display: more importantly, the technique reenacts a process happening on the psychological level as the hero's identity undergoes successive expansions towards an ideally inclusive openness. The representational and perspectival strategies structuring the quest thus function in concert with its thematic content; its innovative format embodies *both* the quester's escape from restrictive sexual convention and his subsequent expansion into a multiform sense of maleness. In the process, as the following examples of *Moby-Dick*, *Huckleberry Finn*, *Billy Budd* and *The Sea Wolf* will show, the movement of the quest forms an emphatic rejection of the narrative stability and fortuitously merging plot lines associated with nineteenth-century fiction in general and with the love-plot in particular.

III

A major secondary theme—and target of criticism—running throughout Melville's canon concerns the sexual polarity that can render wedlock a life-denying prison and selfhood a state of incompletion. At the same time, his novels and stories stage an unremitting attack on fictional conventions, particularly those formal constraints inherited from the literary marriage tradition.[23] Melville's evolution of the male quest narrative can be seen as a defiant response to these concerns: his strategic reformulation of the quest-romance genre, importantly, allowed his personal vision of *vital* male identity to emerge in healthy opposition to the sentimental literary ideology that countenanced an unbridgeable separation of male and female roles, powers and spheres.[24] In Melville's world of quest, in fact, individual authenticity depends on the effort to reconcile such antimonies, and this ideal of manhood is given concrete if brief representation in the avatars of the Handsome Sailor type recurring throughout the canon; these men (Marnoo of *Typee*, Jack Chase of *White-Jacket*, Billy) are most notable for their striking physical unions of masculine and feminine beauty.[25] But it is in *Moby-Dick*, the archetypal quest narrative, that Melville most allusively and deeply explores the psychological connection between self-sufficient male identity and an acknowledgement of the "feminine" within man; in the process the issue of sexual identity becomes an inseparable part of the text's subject-matter and narrative form. The result is a completely different mode of "love story," one in which unending quest (as pursued by Ishmael) rather than ultimate conquest (Ahab's goal) defines the independent self and its relationship to others.

Despite its lack of heterosexual romance, *Moby-Dick* exudes a powerful erotic energy that is manifested in a complex network of sexual innuendo, imagery and mythic allusion.[26] Ever since D. H. Lawrence's identification of the white whale as "the great American phallos," numerous psychoanalytic readings have focused on the battle of Moby Dick and Ahab as an expression of the aggressive male libido. This emphasis, however, has tended to neglect the symbolic significance with which Melville imbues the feminine as well as the phallic.[27] Not only is the whale evoked in imagery suggesting a paradoxical union of masculine and feminine principles;[28] the encompassing universe of the novel—sea and sky—is figured in the suggestively titled chapter "The Symphony" as a primordial wedding of "hardly separable" elements iconographically represented as male and female. The polymorphous life-force at work in the natural world becomes an appropriate backdrop for Melville's depiction of a similar state existing in human nature and embodied in Ishmael, who progresses toward a psychic harmony and an elasticity of identity that is always in motion, never fixed by conventional rules of social roles. Significantly, Ishmael's bond with another man forms the text's opening paradigm of the means to inner unity. Beginning his narration in a state of self-division, Ishmael soon undergoes a "melting" that heals his "splintered heart" through the restorative influence of the self-possessed and loving Queequeg, his bed-companion in New Bedford.[29] The fact that Melville repeatedly identifies their sojourn as a kind of honeymoon (pp. 53, 54) points to the symbolic "marriage" taking place within Ishmael's psyche, as well as to the viability of the male bond in affirming the individual wholeness of the independent male quester.

Exactly *what* is being unified in Ishmael is given further symbolic representation in the "Grand Armada" chapter, which as many critics have noted presents a vision of internal union already prefigured in Ishmael's bonding with Queequeg.[30] For as his whaleboat inadvertently penetrates to the "innermost heart of [a] shoal" of gallied whales (p. 324), the young man has a revelation of the maternal love and feminine life-processes abiding at the secret heart of life. Within a circle of "enchanted calm" the boat is visited by sporting "cows and calves[,] the women and children of this routed host" (p. 324); in the translucent "watery vaults" below the craft there unfolds a "still stranger world" of "nursing mothers" (p. 325) and of "young Leviathan amours in the deep" (p. 326). What makes this glimpse of the sources of life so overpowering is Ishmael's immediate recognition of an analogous state existing within himself: "But even so, amid the tornadoed Atlantic of my being, do I myself still for ever centrally disport in mute calm . . . deep down and deep inland there I still bathe me in eternal mildness of joy" (p. 326).

Although this actual moment passes as the herd of whales disperses, its interior vision of love echoes through the rest of the novel, perhaps most vividly dramatized as external possibility in the famous "A Squeeze of the Hand" chapter. In this simultaneously rhapsodic and comic scene, where the crew lovingly join hands while squeezing whale casing or sperm, the inner "mildness of joy" experienced in the Armada becomes a joyous embrace of all fellow-men. The male bond of two equivalent selves celebrated in the New Bedford chapters is thus transformed into a principle of fraternal democracy shared among several dozen men. Yet pointedly enough, as Chase and Shulman point out, this ideal of loving community exists *outside* the "settled social order" because its all-male constituency necessarily forms a "radically unorthodox alternative" to societal— and specifically marital—norms.[31]

The degree to which Ishmael's expanding identity depends upon his unquestioning acceptance of the "maternal" or "feminine" within himself is also central to the narrative's conclusion. It is the Rachel, after all, the loving mother "in her retracing search after her missing children" (p. 470), that reclaims Ishmael from the wreck of the Pequod. In a penultimate image of rebirth, Ishmael undergoes yet one more expansion of self as he survives to tell the tale. His salvation, however, is neither fixed nor permanently secured, like that of a traditional hero, at the novel's end. It will rather depend on a continuing series of "rebirths" into progressively new worlds: selfhood is realized, paradoxically, in the perpetual act of questing for it. Ishmael's expansive textual presence and narrating voice have reaffirmed this truth time and again, suggesting in the process his capacity for transcending socially-prescribed labels and for championing a revisionary definition of his independent subjectivity as a man.

The ideal wholeness toward which Ishmael moves contrasts vividly with Ahab's one-sided definition of his masculinity, as his tragically fixed purpose and fixated personality attest. Having concentrated all his energies, both emotional and libidinal, into one singularly aggressive goal, Ahab becomes the stereotype of the destructive "male" impulse, fueled by ultimately empty shows of vengeance, power and ego. In the process, the mad captain has replaced the potential for loving contact with his fellow beings with what Martin Pops has aptly terms "violent thrusts" against an imagined foe.[32] The aim of "quest," so perverted by Ahab's monomania, has become simply "conquest."

Ahab's defiant posturing specifically reveals the self-hatred that is unleashed when the softening influences of the heart, the soul (he identifies the soul's gender as female), are subordinated to the masculine. Ahab's first mate mourns that "small touch of the human mother" and that "soft feeling of the human" which he feels that Ahab, through his assumption of absolute mastery, has "overmanned" both in himself and in his crew (p. 118); a few chapters later the reader is made privy to Ahab's nightmare-ridden sleep when this very "soul" attempts to escape the "integral" of which it is part (p. 175), an action metaphorically leaving Ahab a divided, incomplete man: in a pattern that will become increasingly familiar, will has triumphed over feeling. The degree to which patriarchal values of hatred and tumult finally supplant in Ahab the maternal ones of love and inner calm embraced by Ishmael becomes obvious when Ahab declares his satanic allegiance and "right worship" to "my fiery father" (pp. 416–17) during the terrifying storm-at-sea episode near the end of the novel. It comes as no surprise that in the shortly following "The Symphony" chapter Ahab once again rejects the momentarily softening emotions coaxed into life within him by the surrounding environment. By the time the climactic three-day chase begins, Ahab's identity has become more hardened than ever, impervious to change or emotion—the man has become a nightmarish embodiment of the erotic compulsion to subjugate lying behind the traditional male ethos that maintains its supremacy in a gender-divided world through power.

The contrast between Ishmael's acquisition of an open perspective that might be called androgynous and Ahab's imprisonment within a limited role forms a powerful critique of the male ethos ruling American society. The depth of this critique is extended, to a significant degree, by Melville's unconventional manipulation of narrative form in *Moby-Dick*. In defining the quester's pursuit of "open independence" as a rejection of the finality of port or harbor, the "safety" of home or hearthstone (p. 97), Melville suggests the manner in which the very trajectory of his text, a linear projection into the unknown, not only breaks from the closed world of shore values but also from the self-contained design and narrative ends of traditionally conceived fiction. But the structure of this narrative is not linear in a simply descriptive fashion. As Brodhead has perceived, the novel's sense of irrevocable forward motion results from the strategic arrangement of a series of continually transforming narrative modes and extending perspectival structures. As a result, the reader's sensation of traveling through and beyond a succession of texts and superimposed views of reality replicates that of the quester simultaneously plunging into the unknown in search of a new identity. Thus, the predominantly comedic mode of the initial shore chapters, ending with the "marriage" of Ishmael and Queequeg, gives way to a new form and new realm, that of supernatural romance, as the Pequod launches its mysterious quest into the "lone Atlantic" (p. 97); the world of romance is in turn interrupted and extended by a variety of representational modes—stage-drama, monologues, Montaigne-like essays, interpolated tales and more—whose shifts in format are accompanied by modulations in points of view. This organicism engenders an expansive textuality appropriate to the recording of Ishmael's growth toward inclusive, unlimited identity; for his chameleon shifts of tone, style and role—matching and accommodating the various structural modulations—attest to what Brodhead calls a "mazy dance of mind" capable of activating "a whole range of

. . . [hidden] potential within."[33] Structure, in effect, becomes as instrumental as characterization in conferring on Ishmael an identity that encompasses a radically untraditional conception of male selfhood.

The open pattern that Ishmael comes to view as more true to life and to the human personality ("There is no steady unretracting progress in this life; we do not advance through fixed gradations, and at the last one pause," he states in a famous passage [p. 406]) also becomes descriptive of Melville's textual enterprise: through Ishmael's narrating voice he constantly emphasizes the openness of a narrative technique which "promise[s] nothing complete" (p. 118). In juxtaposition to Ahab's enunciation of his madly fixed purpose in chapter 44, Ishmael declares at the beginning of chapter 45 that his own direction as narrator will be determined by impression and indirection rather than straightforward movement, and he thus voices an aesthetic credo that corresponds to the inconclusive openness of his own personality: "I care not to perform my task methodically" (p. 175). Nothing could be more removed from Ahab's desire for absolute finality—an "end" ironically attained in Ahab's final "reunion" in death with his antagonist, the White Whale. Although the literal action of the hunt reaches a close, the novel's meaning remains deliberately open. The mystery of the whale, which remains as inconclusive and enigmatic as ever, is matched by the opening affixed to Ishmael's story. His symbolic rebirth and rescue from the wreckage of the Pequod ("one did survive the wreck . . . and I was he" [p. 170]), reactivating the continuing possibilities of self-discovery, moves Ishmael toward an open future and unknown point in the time from which he narrates the Epilogue. The "portrait" of Ishmael, therefore, eludes a final framing, just as his identity escapes restrictive definitions of masculine behavior. Melville's innovative break from fictional tradition in evolving the quest narrative, it becomes clear, has helped to give voice to an alternative vision of selfhood that similarly eludes social and sexual convention.

Themes of independent selfhood, nonrestrictive sexual roles, and countertraditional male bonds also figure prominently in the voyage of self-discovery charted in Twain's *The Adventures of Huckleberry Finn*. The degree to which this "innocent" novel of "boyhood" is actually a subversive document of social and political protest has often been pointed out; Huck's quest through the contrasting worlds of shore and river provides a devastating commentary on confrontation between enslavement and freedom in American life, race and culture. Huck's quest, however, is also a response to a bifurcated sexual ethos that blocks individual wholeness or self-expression. In rejecting the shore world's negative models of masculine aggression and feminine piety alike, Huck embraces an independent truth of self, rooted in an ethos of compassionate love, that runs counter to all social hierarchies. For it is his loving relationship with the slave, Jim, above all else, that becomes the measure of Huck's status as a cultural misfit and of his unretraceable deviation from a traditional standard of manhood.

In contrast to a world enslaved in custom, Huck shares with Ishmael an innate flexibility and receptivity in face of the unknown. The multiple roles, identities, and fabricated biographies he invents during the course of his quest give him the figurative space within which to develop a more complete sense of self. Whereas the disguises donned by the charlatan Duke and Dauphin simply make clear their parasitic relationship to society, Huck's facile movement among multiple identities attests to his freedom from all fixed roles: he can cross boundaries of class, race and sex with startling ease.[34]

Like a younger Ishmael, Huck also undergoes a series of symbolic deaths and rebirths that, analogous to the various identities he assumes, illustrate his continually expanding personality. These rebirths, not coincidentally, mark progressive stages in the novel's structure, for its organization is predicated upon a series of modal and tonal shifts tracing Huck's geographic, then psychological, removal from societal structures that impede personal development. The first two stages of Huck's removal from the known define the twin sources of his oppression as sentimental and patriarchal in organization. First, Huck finds himself trapped in the "feminized" world of the Widow Douglas and Miss Watson who ply the tools of conventional morality and religious piety in an attempt to sanitize Huck's rebellious strain and thereby "fix" him within a norm of childhood predictability. With Pap's kidnapping and imprisoning of the boy in the woods at one remove from the decorous social order of St. Petersburg, Huck finds himself once again psychologically circumscribed—now by stupidly "masculine" force rather than "feminine" threats of conscience. Accordingly, the novel shifts from the genre of adolescent escape fiction to that of backwoods melodrama. But in both cases the power structure sanctioning Huck's oppression remains the same. For, antisocial as Pap may seem, he shares with the Widow Douglas a belief in familial and social hierarchy that justifies his parental brutality as well as his racial bigotry.

Staging his "death" to escape Pap's tyranny, Huck begins an odyssey—first to Jackson Island, then downriver with the runaway Jim—that inaugurates a third mode of narrative, the quest proper. The diametric opposition between Huck's values and the world he is attempting to elude becomes the text's basic structural principle from this point to the river-voyage's end in chapter 31. For the linear projection of the quest is periodically interrupted by digressive shore episodes and picaresque adventures that expose, time and again, the patriarchal and sentimental norms that have cooperated in corrupting American culture.[35] Juxtaposed with the power of oppression, however, is the potential power of love residing in the river idyll itself, an oasis of freedom to which Huck repeatedly returns after his disastrous adventures on shore.[36] As the one constant element in the fluid downriver movement, the raft comes to represent a more stable concept of "home" than its sentimentalized Victorian counterpart: "We said there warn't no home like a raft, after all," Huck comments upon escaping the gruesome aftermath of the Grangerford-Shepherdson feud, happy to feel "free and safe once more."[37]

And if this momentary paradise comprises an unconventional definition of home, its two members form an equally counter-traditional example of "family"—made as it is of two races and one sex. Similar to the bond shared by Ishmael and Queequeg, Huck and Jim's loving attachment is forged in a mutuality of spirit that, over time, becomes genuine, equitable and non-possessive: as such it transcends the structures defining the relation of man and wife, parent and child, white and black, in American society. If Huck's identity refuses to be fitted to one role, neither does this bond conform to a single need but rather embodies multiple dimensions. Fiedler rightly observes of this "counter-marriage of males" that

> Jim is all things to [Huck]: father and mother and playmate and beloved, appearing naked and begowned and bewhiskered . . . and calling Huck by names appropriate to their multiform relationship: 'Huck' or 'honey' or 'chile' or 'boss,' and just once 'white genleman.'[38]

Moreover, Jim also provides the boy with a positive model of male selfhood, the ideal goal of the quest; as he pronounces early in the text, "I owns myself" (p. 246), his words calling to mind the self-possession of Queequeg, "always equal to himself" (*MD*, p. 52). For Twain and Melville the path to individual integrity lies through heartfelt compassion, and the stages by which Huck discovers the worth of his attachment to Jim simultaneously chart his progress toward a non-conforming identity that depends, ironically, on *not* being "man enough" (p. 310) in the eyes of society to turn in Jim as an escaped slave.[39]

What, then, many critics have asked, happens to Huck's gains in self-knowledge in the final escapades at Phelps Farm? In stepping off the raft in chapter 31, Huck literally walks into another novel—one authored, in a figurative sense, by Tom Sawyer—and accordingly his character seems to transform dramatically as he becomes Tom's passive accomplice. However, if we take into consideration the modal shifts typical of the quest genre in general, we can see that the episode at Phelps Farm, rather than marking a complete departure from the social criticism that has preceded it, forms the final in a series of transforming modes of fictional representation: from its opening in a juvenile fantasy fiction that is presented as a spin-off of *Tom Sawyer*'s ending to quest idyll punctuated by the violent, the gothic, and the picaresque, the text now evolves into a scathing social satire that works to expose the "fictions" of authority by which a slave-owning society operates. For Master Tom's sadistic (and utterly ridiculous) scheme to rescue Jim from his new captivity at the Farm—worked out "regular" according to "what's in the books" (pp. 202, 203)—becomes Twain's satiric parody of the conventional plot formulas that Twain himself is violating in writing a romance-quest. The inadequacy of Tom's viewpoint is exposed when his regulated plot backfires—indeed, approaches tragedy—as Tom is shot and Jim recaptured to be hanged. Conventional novelistic form, Twain implies, may be the least effective way of "freeing" a subject—be that subject Jim or be it Twain's subversive themes.

Yet Tom's fantasies seem to carry the day, given the neatly contrived, happy ending and last-page revelation that Jim is a free man after all. But we simultaneously learn that Huck has also been "freed"—released by the death of Pap into sole possession of his named identity. Tom's earlier gripe that Huck "want[s] to be starting something fresh all the time" (p. 480), rather than going along with established conventions, becomes a prophecy of the text's final structural turn. For in the last lines Huck announces his intention of escaping the boundaries of conventional life and the closure of Tom's imposed fiction by lighting out for the Territory. With this penultimate gesture, Huck reaffirms both the forward-moving dynamic of the quest and his own countertraditional opposition to growing up to fit a "sivilized" definition of manhood. One may question whether Huck will ever succeed in attaining true or total self-expression, however far West he moves, but this closing ambiguity only enhances the radical implications of Twain's social criticism and Huck's dream of unhampered freedom.[40]

As the nineteenth century drew to a close, the sentimentalism that had long dominated American society began to give way to a more overtly masculinist ethos that venerated male power at the expense of the softer emotions of the heart celebrated by Ishmael and Huck. Melville's last and unfinished *Billy Budd, Sailor* appraises the effects of this new set of values in an allegory of life and death aboard a man-of-war ship literally and figuratively adrift at sea. With damningly calm, clear simplicity, this text presents the death of Melville's personal ideal of independent manhood—the Handsome Sailor prototype embodied in the androgynous Billy—at the hands of unfeeling justice and brute violence. In so doing, this interiorized version of the quest-romance unequivocally sets itself against a power-oriented culture whose univocal reading of "masculine" authority and "masculine" identity not only further disempowered women in general but also threatened to eclipse what Melville would identify in symbolic terms as the "feminine in man." [41]

The conjunction of masculine and feminine characteristics in Billy's appearance, coupled with his personality and its effect on others, indicates the extent to which a probing of sexual identity lies at the heart of the novella. [42] With a face "all but feminine in purity," [43] Billy also boasts a "masculine beauty" (p. 53) and fine physical "mold" (p. 51) that "in the nude might have posed for a statue of young Adam before the Fall" (p. 91). For all the marks of the "heroic strong man, Hercules," in his physical bearing, Billy also calls to mind "something suggestive of a mother" favored by the goddess of Love, Venus (p. 51), and it is this latter characteristic, feminine-associated love, that Billy's personality most abundantly conveys, as his harmonizing role as "peacemaker" aboard the merchantship Rights-of-Man illustrates (p. 47).

The floating, idyllic and all-male comaraderie of the Rights-of-Man—evocative of the Edenic paradise temporarily established aboard Huck and Jim's raft— is only a memory, however, in *Billy Budd,* which opens after the foretopman's impressment into the King's service by the officers of the Bellipotent. Billy's transition from one ship to the other, as their names suggest, outlines a crucial rite of passage as he grows from a youthful state of freedom to an adult life in which martial power stands as the controlling metaphor for a state of male domination: the shipboard world of quest, hitherto an escape from social circumscription, has become a microcosm of the hierarchical world left behind.

The psychological action culminating in the eclipse of Melville's male ideal unfolds, appropriately, as a series of confrontations between the untraditional Billy and the Bellipotent's two representatives of entrenched power, the bullying "master-at-arms" Claggart and the authoritarian captain, Edward Fairfax Vere. Both men perceive Billy as a threat because his presence subconsciously reminds them of the emotive or loving faculty within themselves that has been suppressed to insure their superiority over and control of others.

Claggart's dual feelings of attraction for and subsequent hatred of Billy's physical beauty, for instance, amount to a profound "envy" (p. 78) of Billy's sensed difference. Thus, the master-at-arms' attraction becomes a smouldering "passion" of hatred (p. 77) that renders any mutual love on the order of that experienced by Huck and Jim, or Ishmael and Queequeg, impossible. As Georges Michel Sarotte and E. Grant Watson have realized, Claggart's ensuing attempt to dominate Billy through persecution—precipitating Billy's tragedy—is a defensive mechanism to protect himself against love, that very *non-aggressive* force embodied in Billy that Claggart at once desires and fears.[44] In the sadomasochistic configuration that Claggart and Billy form—a perverse parody of the romantic ideal of complementary opposition—it is inevitable that words be replaced by physical aggression as the only mode of communication possible between the two men, for these are the terms that the "master" Claggart has imposed on his victim. "I could only say it with a blow" (p. 106), Billy thus testifies of his spontaneous rebellion against this tyranny, which results in Claggart's death.

At this moment the narrative focus shifts to Vere, who embodies an intellectualized version of the impulses underlying Claggart's brutality. For Vere's is a "resolute nature" (p. 60) founded on self-control as crippling as Claggart's repressed passions; his reasoned deliberations leave him, "the most undemonstrative of men" (p. 60), an incomplete self "lack[ing] in the companionable equality" (p. 63). Only in response to Billy's crime does the extent of Vere's allegiance to authoritarian norms surface, however, and then in a very telling substitution of terms: "The father in him, manifested toward Billy thus far . . . was replaced by the military disciplinarian" (p. 100). Although Vere may be justified in fearing mutiny, given the politically unstable climate of the times, the extreme "prudence and vigor" (p. 103) that he chooses to exercise in summoning the drumhead court is extreme. For as his amazingly explicit summary speech at Billy's trial indicates, his hardness and rejection of mercy are directly linked to a fear of the "feminine in man," and all that term connotes as dangerously subversive of masculine authority:

> But let not warm hearts betray heads that should be cool. . . . Well, the heart here, sometimes *the feminine in man* is as that piteous woman, and hard though it be, *she must here be ruled out*. (p. 111; emphasis added)

Not only is the jury being told to rule out "that piteous woman" in themselves, but they are implicitly being directed to "rule out" Billy, who has come to represent the "feminine in man," the signifier of difference that must be expelled if the hierarchical supremacy of men is to be maintained in the world of which the Bellipotent is a microcosm. For Vere also stresses that Billy's crime has been to violate the whole concept of traditional hierarchy by "strik[ing] his superior in grade" (p. 111). In a man-of-war world, as well as in society, disciplinary action for this infraction of order must "[take] after the father"—that is, the destructive principle Vere identifies as "War" itself (p. 112). The purpose, then, toward which Vere drives is nothing less than the erasure of the "feminine," yet radically insubordinate, impulse embodied in Billy.

While patriarchal rule superficially triumphs in this confrontation—for Billy is hanged—the male world without his harmonizing presence is left more incomplete than ever, a fact simultaneously registered in the novella's jagged narrative structure. Throughout the text Melville has made its formal attributes suggestive of an ever-deepening inquiry into the nature of male authority and identity. Hence the "voyage into the unknown" format presented here is depicted less as an external than psychological event, as the absence of all but minimal physical action suggests. Instead, the "movement" characteristic of the genre occurs as an intellectual or textual activity: one chapter will become an opening up, rather than linear extension, of the information conveyed in its predecessor; seeming digressions turn into the true trajectory of the narrative; the shifting of focus from Billy to Vere, then to Claggart and back to Vere, abets the disorienting sensation of an evolving movement whose destination is uncertain; Melville's use of a conjecture-filled narrative voice which can only hypothesize about but never penetrate the various characters' states of consciousness heightens the reader's experience of plunging blindly into a mystery—Billy's martyrdom—for which there is no final explanation.

The purposefully "ragged edges" (p. 128) of Melville's conclusion—a series of digressive "sequel[s]" (p. 128) that follow upon Billy's execution—therefore introduce several divergent impressions of Billy and his story in order to continue the questioning raised by the prior events; issues are refused the simplification inherent in a closed plot format.[45] As a result, the open-ended quest narrative utilized in *Billy Budd* unlocks a disturbing exploration into the far reaches of patriarchal power, revealing the all-male world to be an inferno of violence, domination and repression when traditional male authority is allowed to stamp out the "feminine in man." The tragic outcome of the confrontation between self-sufficiency and limited sexual roles, played out as psychodrama in this "inside narrative" (the novella's subtitle), foreshadows the advent of the male-oriented novel of the twentieth century, in which men bond together not to escape sexual dichomotization but to perpetuate its stranglehold on norms of identity.

The status of Jack London's *The Sea Wolf* as a quest novel falls somewhere between these extremes of male fiction. On one level London is as vitally concerned with issues of sexual identity as Melville; yet his attempt to chart a more positive ideal through male bonding is fraught with ambiguities that become not only thematically but textually problematic when, at the novel's end, the format of the quest dissolves into that of sentimental romance. The conflicting allegiances of *The Sea Wolf* offer an opportunity to assess, by way of summary, the potential and the liabilities of using the quest-romance mode as an expression of rebellion against literary and sexual norms.

London's novel shares with other male quest narratives a sea-journey into the literal and metaphysical reaches of the unknown, experienced by reader and protagonist alike as a process of defamiliarization. Opening with the shipwrecked Humphrey Van Weyden stranded "in the midst of a gray primordial vastness,"[46] the action shifts to Wolf Larsen's seal-hunter whose plunging movement "into the heart of the Pacific" seems to near the "bounds" of "the universe itself" (pp. 30, 166). Simultaneously, Humphrey is gradually divorced from the realm of the psychological familiar as the nightmarish outbreaks of violence aboard the renegade ship increase in tempo. This process of removal is matched by another element common to quest narrative—Humphrey's immersion in an all-male environment that inspires a redefinition of his own manhood and realization of a supposedly more well-rounded identity. But here we can pinpoint an important difference between London's purpose and that of the preceding authors. Whereas Billy's identity has always been unselfconsciously androgynous and both Ishmael and Huck grow to accept the "feminine" as part of their integral selves, Humphrey's task is rather to incorporate the manly element lacking in his dilettantish, effeminate upbringing. "My muscles were small and soft, like a woman's" (p. 30), he confesses to the reader, explaining that "I had not been called 'Sissy' Van Weyden all my days without reason" (p. 64). Thus, while Melville and Twain reclaim the feminine from a stereotypical context in order to make it a symbol of a universal loving capacity that transcends gender, London continues to link femininity with weakness, passivity, inertia. The goal of Humphrey's quest for identity—theoretically at least—is a blending of his initial sensitivity with virile strength, but London's emphasis on the latter, as we shall see, ultimately circles back to a traditional view of the sexes.

Fished from the sea and rubbed back to life aboard Larsen's "bruteship," Humphrey is reborn into a totally alien, all-male world where "Force, nothing but force obtained" (p. 32) and where all "Weakness is wrong" (p. 55). The hierarchy of domination that arises from this ethos of brute strength—an anarchic version of the iron-clad authoritarianism represented in *Billy Budd*—is embodied in Wolf Larsen, captain of the Ghost and Humphrey's immediate model for the elemental "potency" and "virility of spirit" (p. 16) characterizing the perfect "man-type" (p. 99). Despite Wolf's unfeeling cruelty, he is also a brooding thinker haunted by "that questing, that everlasting query . . . as to what it was all about" (p. 59). Hence he becomes Humphrey's emblem of the archetypal romantic quester as well as virile superman: "I could see him only as living always, and dominating always, fighting and destroying, himself surviving" (p. 120).

Although Humphrey's prognosis of Wolf's future turns out to be wrong, his relationship with Wolf provides the necessary spur to his own growth and survival. Metaphorically, Wolf becomes the very territory through which Humphrey's quest for manhood must lead: "I felt an elation of spirit," Humphrey says of the Captain's presence, "I was groping into his soul-stuff . . . I was exploring virgin territory. A strange, a terribly strange, region was unrolling itself before my eyes" (p. 56). So intimate a drawing together may seem to recall the affirming bonds of Ishmael and Queequeg, or Huck and Jim, but in fact Humphrey and Wolf's gravitation to each other is based on an antithetical norm of polarity and hierarchy. For Wolf is not only Humphrey's teacher but his total *master* in an arrangement closer to marital conventions than London realizes: "And thus it was that I passed into a state of involuntary servitude," Humphrey reports of the role he assumes in response to Wolf's domination. "He was stronger than I, that was all" (p. 23). The sexual undercurrents always present in Humphrey's physical attraction to Wolf also italicize the conventional dynamics implicit in their master–slave relationship. When Humphrey first sees Wolf in the nude, for instance, he is instantly mesmerized by his masculine beauty; and Wolf's "command" that the awed Humphrey feel "the great muscles [that] leapt and moved under [his] satiny skin" (p. 99) is an act of deliberate provocation, establishing Wolf's power at the same time it valorizes male virility above any other sexual expression. The homoeroticism that Melville makes a positive symbol of unconventionality in *Moby-Dick* here becomes, unconsciously for London, an extension of the destructive male–female dialectic from which Melville's questers flee.

The disquieting resonances of such a relationship inevitably mark Humphrey's development, calling into question the ideal of manhood that London has set up as the proper end of his protagonist's quest. As in most quest narrative, personal growth is measured in a succession of newly acquired identities and roles, a process initiated when the nearly drowned Humphrey is renamed "Hump" by Wolf and made to assume the role of cabin-boy with the promise that "It will be the making of you" (p. 18). Having plummeted from a privileged status in the outer world to lowest position in the shipboard hierarchy, Hump undergoes his first *rite de passage* when he beats up the bully Cooky, a man even more effeminate than—and hence hierarchically inferior to—himself.[47] Progressing to the coveted rank of "mate," Hump becomes "aware of a toughening or hardening I was undergoing" (p. 108). While he maintains enough of his former values to realize that brutality alone is wrong, he welcomes the fact that he can "never again be quite the same man" because he feels that in touching upon his masculinity he is encountering "the world of the real" for the first time (p. 108).

But simultaneous with this process is Hump's awareness of the inadequacies of Wolf's world and creed: namely, its "unnatural" exclusion of women and the crew's lack of any capacity for "softness, and tenderness, and sympathy" (p. 89). However, unlike the texts of Melville and Twain, which advocate a realization *within men themselves* of emotions and values traditionally associated with women, Hump means his solution literally: it is the *actual presence* of women as spiritual exemplars that is needed, without which the inherent "brute" in man cannot be tamed nor a "balance to their lives" be added (p. 89). This essentially conservative estimate of male and female nature anticipates the next turn of the plot as the shipwrecked Maud Brewster enters the hitherto all-male world of the Ghost and irrevocably upsets its psychological dynamics. The modal shift from quest format to erotic-seduction narrative accompanying Maud's arrival serves to underscore London's vision of "correct" male development for Hump. By becoming the "willing slave" (p. 133) of Maud rather than Wolf, Hump redirects his newly acquired "masculine" energy into the chivalric service of fragile womanhood—a sacred duty successfully carried out when he strikes a blow to Wolf, his former master, to keep him from ravishing Maud.[48]

Following this positive exertion of male strength, the narrative undergoes yet another modal shift as Hump engineers his and Maud's escape from Wolf's ship; a kind of New World narrative evolves as the two set up house on a deserted island, Maud playing Friday to Hump's increasingly resourceful Crusoe in a primitive version of the domestic plot. Hump's successes in sheltering and protecting the physically less competent Maud, confirming his new masculine identity, precipitates an inner recognition of his love for Maud and of his natural ascendance in the conventional sexual order: "instantly conscious I became of my manhood," Hump lyricizes upon embracing Maud for the first time, "I felt myself masculine, the protector of the weak, the fighting male. And, best of all, I felt myself the protector of my loved one" (p. 201). Hump's last rite of passage is accomplished when he defeats the now weakened Wolf—who has coincidentally drifted to the same island—and prepares to sail back to civilization with Maud. With this imminent return to social order, the rhetoric of the last pages of the novel, in which the lovers exchange declarations, becomes that of sentimental romance:

> 'My woman, my own small woman,' I said, my free hand petting her
> shoulder in the way all lovers know though never learn in school.
> 'My man,' she said, looking at me for an instant with tremulous lids which

fluttered down and veiled her eyes as she snuggled her head against my
breast with a happy little sigh. (p. 252)

It is telling that neither Hump's sense of himself as a "man" nor Maud's as a
"woman" stands alone: the identity of each depends on a complementary other
who is to be possessed rather than be appreciated for his or her individuality—
"my" man, "my" woman. Unlike the self-possession characterizing the independent identities of Ishmael or Huck or Billy, the "new" definition of masculinity
toward which London directs his quest becomes, in Hump's case, evidence supporting an already existing ethos. The "feminine" side of the male protagonist,
represented by Hump's initial effeminacy and aesthetic capacities as a literary
critic, is deflected to the female "half" of a literal conjunction of male and
female—for Maud is no less than a female poet by profession. The union that
takes place within Ishmael has once again become the union that takes place
externally, and in being made simultaneous with the ending of the novel it
brings to a halt the fictional movement and meaning synonymous with quest.

IV

The imminent return of Hump and Maud to civilization—transforming the text's
originally infinity-bound quest into a circular voyage of return and a recuperation
of the familiar—serves to remind us of the potential of earlier quest narrative to
move in quite the *opposite* direction—into unknown spheres where a new ideal of
manhood awaits discovery. For, at its most psychologically adventurous, the
quest novel as conceived by Melville or Twain activates a vision of male autonomy and subjectivity that engages in a covertly revolutionary sexual politics of its
time by departing from traditional sexual categories. From our vantage point, the
positive attributes of the questing hero's escape into a world without women appear threefold. First, his removal from the social and sexual expectations of a
marriage-oriented culture may set free an expansive sense of identity that, like
Ishmael's or Huck's, is multiform, fluid and affirming in its integrity. Second, the
elevation of mutuality—rather than polarity—in the male bond, rendering it a
marriage of equals, presents an alternative to the inequality governing institutionalized heterosexual relationship. And, third, an understated but powerful critique of the sexual order left behind often lingers in image, symbol, and situation
in the all-male world; thus, as in *Billy Budd*, the degree to which the world of quest
replicates the negative aspects of the society from which the quester has flown can
become the vehicle for acute social criticism of America's male-dominated structures of power. As all these analyses have indicated, furthermore, the genre's
potential for exploring the various implications of male independence exists in
proportion to the radically "unfixed," provisional status of its narrative form.
Hence, *The Sea Wolf*'s lack of success in maintaining the open-ended imperatives
of the mode—signaled in its return to the happy ending of conventional romance—also becomes a sign of its abandonment of the untraditional themes we
have seen in other quest narratives.

London's rather confused alliances—holding to both a "progressive" sexual ethic and an overtly masculinist creed—help explain the failure, by and large, of modern quest fiction to explore the unorthodox potentialities unearthed by earlier Americanists. For twentieth-century versions of the male quest—and here I largely agree with Fielder's analysis of modern American fiction—have become increasingly ambiguous and self-deceiving as the possibility of escaping into a womanless world has become only a symbolic reality. In turn, literary evocations of the male bond have ceased to function as positive expressions of alternative relationships; rather, the depiction of camaraderie among men often disguises a profoundly disturbing authorial desire to avoid female reality altogether, while the fantasy of escaping society with one's comrades becomes the protagonist's ultimate excuse for misogynist exclusivity. The underlying fear of losing power that motivates such attitudes—so well dramatized in the pathological cases of Ahab, Claggart and Wolf—has led not only to a new and destructive stereotype of femininity (the "castrating bitch" syndrome) but also to a new archetype of phallic manhood, epitomized in the supervirile and silent western hero impervious to overt displays of emotion but swift to take violent action.[49]

These negative manifestations of modern-day quest, emerging from what was initially a movement away from stereotypicality, have been complicated by another factor: the distrust, in a more self-conscious age, of the homosexual implications of relationships between men who flee women. The result has often been an increased representation of machismo in male relations, as if mere strength would allay such fears, and a shying away from the nonsexist ideal embodied in Billy, as if representing the "feminine in man" would constitute an admission of sexual "deviance." Ironically, the natural and unconscious celebration of homoeroticism in traditional quest narrative becomes the ultimate taboo in contemporary renderings of the form.[50]

It is illuminating to trace these various ambivalences at work in Hemingway's *The Sun Also Rises* (1926) and Mailer's *The Naked and the Dead* (1948), two modern adaptations of the genre preoccupied with issues of sexual identity and independence from women. The fragmented postwar world of *The Sun Also Rises* provides the setting in which Jake Barnes' aimless quest for self-renewal unfolds; his sexual war-wound, leaving him literally a man without women despite the hovering presence of Brett, becomes the symbol of a personal inner void as well as the sign of the impotence of the world at large. Counterposed with this despairing vision, however, is the center of values residing in the reduced, modern-day version of male quest—Jake's spiritually purifying fishing trip to Spain with Bill Gordon—that lies at the heart of the novel. Yet the negative effect of this necessarily momentary retreat is that it reinforces the men's tendency to see *all* the world as an exclusively male domain: Brett, indeed, can only participate in this world by playing (unsuccessfully) at being "one of the boys." The result is a misogynist universe in which any independently minded woman, because of the threat she poses to male superiority, is doomed to failure.

Mailer's novel, on the other hand, exposes a hellish underside of Hemingway's nostalgic dream of an untroubled male Eden. Set in the all-male environment of a Pacific war zone, its central action a monomaniacal quest through the defamiliarizing reaches of the island Anopopei's jungles and mountains, *The Naked and the Dead* uses conventions of the quest format to show that there is *no escape*, however far one journeys, from the power-structures that rule society and dictate human behavior. All of Mailer's characters, in attempting to leave behind their disastrous personal relationships with women at home, have only found in war another battlefield, where they can continue to vent their frustrations in acts of meaningless aggression; even their own in-group relationships are simply power plays, demonstrating a "universal" compulsion to dominate and control others. Thus, Mailer makes the quest into war—and his inquiry into the psychology of power—a scorching indictment of a destructive ethos associated with masculine aggression. But at the same time he seems to view the urge to fight and conquer as an inescapable aspect of maleness, and in the process he denigrates the alternative value of what we have been calling the "feminine" as saving inner principle or outer reality.[51] The novel's strongest point is at once its true weakness: for the oppressive vision of aggressive force that Mailer discloses simultaneously eclipses his perception of other possibilities.

These modern versions of the quest would seem to confirm Eve Kosofsky Sedgwick's thesis in *Between Men: English Literature and Male Homosocial Desire* that men form socially permissible bonds in order to perpetuate patriarchy.[52] The patriarchal order, that is, carries on its functions as if it were a "world without women," whether or not women are actually present to participate in its transactive desires. In a sense, then, even the earliest imaginings of the world of male quest are not without a certain potential ambiguity. But this is where it becomes crucial for us to distinguish between, say, the pairing of Natty–Chingachgook, who recuperate the wilderness for the white man and that of Ishmael–Queequeg, who plunge into its mystery in search of their own untapped potential. For as long as the possibility of breaking completely with the world of the known could be imagined *as actuality* by the nineteenth-century quest writer, the symbolic value of venturing into the unknown with other men held the power of meaning *differently*, other than the pattern that Sedgwick sees as pervasive. Indeed, the unlikely heroes that we find in Ishmael, Billy and Huckleberry attest to the fact that outside the boundaries of social constriction exists the possibility of re-imagining male identity; outside the boundaries of social discourse, an innovative language of the self; outside the boundaries of conventional literary texts, the forward momentum of an ever-unfolding narrative form that we now call the "quest."

By way of conclusion, I would like to turn to a fictional model that we might not suspect of drawing on the American male quest: Charlotte Perkins Gilman's utopian-feminist *Herland*, written in 1915. For in the parodic narrative action framing this fantasy in an all-*female* world, three male explorers inadvertently dash headlong into the circumference of a hidden Amazonian kingdom; this act of discovery simultaneously triggers an opposing form of narration which absorbs all forward motion and reformulates it in the nonlinear patterns that comprise the Herlanders' nonpatriarchal way of life. This brilliantly arranged opening sequence, of course, deliberately appropriates the movement associated with quest in order to debunk the aggressive ethos that Gilman categorically equates with it. But the trajectory that her own opening chapters inscribe, fascinatingly enough, reproduces on a slightly larger scale that of the psychological progress that Ishmael, the archetypal American quester, undergoes in the Grand Armada chapters of *Moby-Dick*—a linear entrance into an "enchanted circle" within which the feminine secrets of life and ongoing creation unfold. It is this prospect of interior recovery, this wedding-within of those unequal "co-relatives" without which "Selfhood itself seems incomplete," then, that forms the true goal and unorthodox "love story" of Melville and Twain's versions of the male quest. Gilman's feminist message turns out to be not so far removed, indeed, from that of questromancers who made of the symbolic act of questing a *modus vivendi* and of its literary method a countertraditional genre.

NOTES

This essay is an earlier and much shorter version of chapter 5 of my *Tradition Counter Tradition: Love and the Form of Fiction* (Chicago: University of Chicago Press, 1987).

1. See, for example, Nina Baym's *Woman's Fiction: A Guide to Novels by and about Women in America, 1820–1970* (Ithaca: Cornell Univ. Press, 1978), p. 11ff.

2. For Fiedler's description of the sexual combat or polarity inherent in sentimental ideology, see *Love and Death in the American Novel* (New York: Stein and Day, 1966), pp. 62–71; for his summary of the effect of its "debasement" on the anti-bourgeois American novelist, see pp. 74–93. Fiedler's assumptions about the immaturity of the American writer/quester's attitude toward women and sex echo throughout his analysis, reflected in generalizations such as "It is maturity above all things that the American writer fears, and marriage seems to him its essential sign" (p. 388); the theme of arrested adolescence is implicit in his diagnosis as well of the "Good Bad Boy" syndrome in much American fiction (pp. 270–90). The "anti-bourgeois" genre that Fiedler sees rising in America consists not only of quest elements, but also of a heavily gothic strain (one thinks of C. B. Brown, Poe, certain Hawthorne and Faulkner works); in regard to such "fictions of terror," Fiedler's analysis of the guilt over and evasion of sexuality as a psychologically regressive tendency seems more apt.

3. Preface to *The Americans*, quoted from *The Art of the Novel* in Michael David Bell, *The Development of American Romance: The Sacrifice of Relation* (Chicago: Univ. Press, 1980), p. 8.

4. *Selected Poems of Herman Melville*, ed. Henig Cohen (Carbondale, Ill.: Southern Ill. Univ. Press, 1964), p. 134.

5. *Anatomy of Criticism: Four Essays* (Princeton: Princeton Univ. Press, 1957), see "The Mythos of Summer: Romance," pp. 186–205.

6. The antirealist aspects of American "Romance" are presented by Richard Chase in *The American Novel and its Tradition* (Garden City: Doubleday, 1957), pp. 12–13; Lionel Trilling in "Manners, Morals, and the Novel," in *The Liberal Imagination: Essays on Literature and Society* (New York: Scribners, 1976), p. 212; and Richard Brodhead in *Hawthorne, Melville, and the Novel* (Chicago: Univ. of Chicago Press, 1973), pp. 18–24. Brodhead argues that Chase's complete separation of (English) novel and (American) romance is too extreme, since one of the strategic disunities characterizing American romance is its *inclusion* of "realism," but as only one mode and angle of vision among many.

7. My reasons for excluding Cooper's works, in particular, from the following discussion of male "quest" novels deserve a word of explanation. Despite the "masculine" adventures seeming to dominate his romances of the American wilderness, Cooper's sagas of male bonding are shot through with courtship subplots in which the protection of frail maidenhood provides the underlying structure—and proves a clue to Cooper's true ideological allegiances. For, as Nina Baym has incisively demonstrated in "The Women of Cooper's *Leatherstocking Tales*," in *Images of Women in Fiction: Feminine Perspectives*, ed. Susan Koppelman Cornillon (Bowling Green, Ohio: Popular Press, 1972), pp. 135–51, marriage is central to each of the tales, its function that of validating Cooper's conservative

social message by imprinting the codes of civilization onto the "virgin" face of the wilderness. If *The Last of the Mohicans* is the most obvious example of the importance of women and marriage to Cooper's romances, *The Pathfinder* is the most telling. For even as Natty Bumppo forfeits his chance to marry Mabel Dunham in order to remain a bachelor in a world of men, he acts in the greater service of the patriarchal order; since Mabel's father has been suddenly killed, Natty as his loyal friend must step in as her paternal guardian, and it is in this fatherly role that Bumppo hands Mabel over to a younger suitor, who has been fretting impatiently in the wings since the story opened and now steps forward to frame the courtship action.

Poe's view of the sexes, akin to that of the English Romantic poets, was particularly stereotypical in its view of women as spiritual beings or destroyers of men; his stories reveal an obsession with sex as a means of possession and self-destruction. Hawthorne, as America's literary heir to the Puritan and Miltonic vision of holy marriage as a positive good, promotes in countless "Romances" marriage as the means by which "man and woman together can momentarily restore Paradise on earth" (Fiedler, p. 223). Thus, the allegorical trajectories of romantic involvement in *The Blithedale Romance, The House of the Seven Gables* and *The Marble Faun* achieve equilibrium in "mitigated happy endings" that echo the last lines of *Paradise Lost:* innocence is a sad but fortunate fall as long as it culminates in the salvation of bourgeois marriage.

8. Seelye, *Melville: The Ironic Diagram* (Evanston, Ill; Northwestern Univ. Press, 1970), p. 5.

9. *The Feminization of American Culture* (New York: Knopf, 1977), pp. 10–13, 45–46. Nancy F. Cott in *The Bonds of Womanhood: "Women's Sphere" in New England 1780–1835* (New Haven: Yale Univ. Press, 1977) documents a similar process occurring in the earliest years of the century.

10. T. S. Arthur, *Married or Single* (1813), quoted in Herbert Ross Brown, *The Sentimental Novel in America, 1789–1860* (Durham: Duke Univ. Press, 1940), p. 282.

11. Some critics of the sentimental genre include Brown; Henri Petter, *The Early American Novel* (Columbus: Ohio State Univ. Press, 1971); Henry Nash Smith, "The Scribbling Women and the Cosmic Success Story," *Critical Inquiry,* 1 (1974), 47–70; and Baym, *Woman's Fiction;* which argues for a less pernicious influence of the genre upon its readers: in Baym's view, the heroine achieves a relative degree of self-autonomy, signified by the successful accomplishment of marriage, that presented its female audience with a positive model of individual development. I would, however, counter that the admitted "formulaic constraints" (p. 12) structuring the genre similarly limited the "feminine" roles its heroines were allowed to represent or experience.

12. *The Minister's Wooing,* quoted in Brown, p. 285.

13. Brown, p. 176.

14. Letter, dated Jan. 19, 1855, Liverpool, in *Letters of Hawthorne to William D. Ticknor,* 2 vols. (Newark, N.J., 1910), 1:75.

15. For descriptions of the frontier of western genre, see Ann-Janine Morey-Gaines, "Of Menace and Men: The Sexual Tensions of the American Frontier Metaphor," *Soundings,* 4 (1981), 133–47, and Fritz H. Oehlschlaeger, "Civilization as Emasculation: The Threatening Role of Women in the Frontier Fiction of Harold Bell Wright and Zane Grey," *The Midwest Quarterly,* 20 (1981), 346–59.

16. On the proximity of the frontier ethos to Cooper, see Baym, "The Women of Cooper's *Leatherstocking Tales,*" previously cited, p. 146.

17. Fiedler, p. 211.

18. Fiedler, pp. 211, 367–68.

19. Fiedler, pp. 365–66.

20. I owe the concept of the role played by the "missing woman" in the all-male world to the suggestive study of all-male casts in drama written by Robert H. Vorlicky, "Amer-

ica's Power Plays: The Traditional Hero in Male Cast Drama," Diss. Univ. of Wisconsin, 1981; see especially chapter 2, "The Power of the Invisible Woman."

21. Martin L. Pops applies such a Jungian method to Melville's canon in *The Melville Archetype* (Kent, OH: Kent State Univ. Press, 1970), pp. 7–9, 17.

22. Brodhead, pp. 18–22.

23. Pierre the would-be writer acknowledges precisely these formal constraints when faced with the "unravelled plot" of Isabel's past: "By infalliable presentiment he saw . . . that not always doth life's beginning gloom conclude in gladness; that wedding-bells peal not ever in the last scene of life's fifth act . . . [but] have no proper endings." See *Pierre, or The Ambiguities*, ed. Harrison Hayford, et al. (Evanston: Northwestern Univ. Press and the Newberry Library, 1971), p. 141. Examples of Melville's critique of wedlock roles include the satiric portrayal of the native couple, Samoa and Anatoo, in *Mardi*, and the truly disturbing marital warfare in the story, "I and My Chimney."

24. Douglas, in comparing Melville's achievement with that of Margaret Fuller, notes that because "genuine sexual identity becomes . . . illicit" in any society prone to sexual stereotyping, "Melville conceived masculinity, as Fuller understood feminism, essentially as resistance to sentimentalism, as an effort at a genuinely political and philosophical life" (p. 284).

25. Richard Chase elaborates on this point in *Herman Melville: A Critical Study* (1949; rpt. New York: Hafner, 1971), p. 17.

26. The pioneering study of sexual reference in the novel is that of Robert Shulman, "The Serious Functions of Melville's Phallic Jokes," *American Literature*, 33 (1966), 179–94.

27. For such Freudian readings, see Lawrence, *Studies in Classic American Literature* (1923; rpt. New York: Anchor, 1951), pp. 156–74; Harry Slochower, "Freudian Motifs in *Moby Dick*," *Complex*, 3 (1950), 20; Newton Arwin, *Herman Melville* (n.p.: William Sloane, 1950), 128; and Henry A. Murray, "In Nomine Diaboli," *Moby Dick Centennial Essays*, (ed. Tyrus Hillway and Luther S. Mansfield (Dallas: Southern Methodist Univ. Press, 1953), pp. 3–21. Two critics employing a Freudian method yet focusing on the "feminine" are Fiedler and Mark Hennelly, "Ishmael's Nightmare and the American Eve," *American Imago*, 30 (1973), 274–93. Noting that although it is true that "on the surface the novel seems almost totally lacking in reference to things feminine," Hennelly correctly directs the reader to trace the "various mutations [of feminine reference] through the novel's structure, imagery and characters" (p. 278).

28. In "The Battering Ram," the whale's impervious forehead, destroying all enemies, first seems a personification of masculine aggressive force; yet this surface member actually protects an inner sanctum filled with the "effeminacy" of a "most delicate oil." If the whale's head is described in rather startling bisexual imagery, so too is its opposite anatomical member, the tail, which combines Titanic strength and delicate grace in one consistent movement.

29. *Moby-Dick*, ed. Harrison Hayford and Hershel Parker (New York: Norton, 1967), p. 53. All further references to this edition will appear in parenthesis in my text.

30. For instance, see Fiedler, p. 382, and Julian Rice, "Male Sexuality in *Moby Dick*," *Amerian Transcendental Quarterly*, 39 (1978), p. 244.

31. These quotations are from Chase, *Herman Melville*, p. 106, and Shulman, p. 184, respectively.

32. Pops, p. 73.

33. Brodhead, pp. 154, 156.

34. When Mrs. Loftis discovers he isn't "Sarah Williams," Huck becomes "George Peters" and when that fails, "Sarah Mary Williams George Alexander Peters" (p. 263): to the raftsmen in chapter 16 he proclaims himself the "Charles William Allbright" of Ed's ghost-tale, then admits he is "really" only "Alex James Hopkins" (p. 306). The Grangerfords know him as "George Jackson," he parades as the English valet "Adolphus" in the

Wilks home, and Tom's rescue-scheme calls for him again to impersonate a woman as the "yaller servant-girl" (p. 511). Kenneth Lynn equates Huck's spontaneous fictional biographies with his search for identity in "Huck and Jim," *The Yale Review*, 47 (1958), 427.

35. The feud waged by the Grangerford-Shepherdson men, for example, exposes meaningless aggression as a component of Southern-style patriarchy, while their womenfolk illustrate lives of domestic triviality; the Duke and Dauphin provide an example of absolutely corrupt power; the Pokeville revival scheme, like Peter Wilks' funeral scene, ridicules the sentimental piety of the indiscriminately sobbing crowd that can just as easily turn into a senseless mob howling blindly for blood and vengeance, as in the Colonel Sherburne incident.

36. Tom Towers in "Love and Power in *Huck Finn*," *Tulane Studies in English*, 23 (1978), 17–37, makes the dialectical alternation between these two forces the subject of his study, citing Huck's exchanges with Pap, the Grangerfords, and the Duke and Dauphin as significant markers of this rhythmical pattern.

37. *The Adventures of Huckleberry Finn*, in *The Portable Mark Twain*, ed. Bernard DeVoto (1946; rpt. New York: Viking, 1972), p. 340. All further references to this edition will appear in parentheses in my text.

38. The lines I have quoted from Fiedler's excellent analysis of the Huck–Jim bond are preceded by these equally illuminating observations:

> . . . In Jim, Huck finds the pure affection offered by Mary Jane without the threat of marriage; the escape from social obligations offered by Pap without the threat of beatings: the protection and pettings offered by his volunteer foster-mothers without the threat of pious conformity; the male companionship offered by the Grangerfords without the threat of combat of honor; the friendship offered by Tom without the everlasting rhetoric and make-believe. (pp. 352–53)

39. Here I refer to the episode in chapter 16 in which Huck has a chance to prove his loyalty to Jim's love—and thus his nonconforming individuality—when he lies to a group of slave-hunters about the race of his raft-companion. The terminology used to express this snap decision suggests the extent to which Huck's nonconformity is a disavowal of traditional norms of masculinity: "*I warn't man enough*, hadn't the spunk of a rabbit, I see *I was weakening;* so I just give up trying, and up and says 'He's white'" (p. 310; emphasis added). Likewise, Huck's famous decision in chapter 31 to "go to hell" rather than "pray a lie" comes as the result of being overwhelmed by a series of memories of his and Jim's idyllic life together that figuratively "unman" the boy: "somehow I couldn't seem to strike no places *to harden me* against [Jim]" (p. 450; emphasis added). Again, Huck's growth toward nonconforming identity expresses a rejection of traditional masculine associations (strength, hardness) and a simultaneous awareness of the depth of his love for Jim.

40. An excellent article regarding the "future" growth of Huck is Paul Delaney's "You Can't Go Back to the Raft Ag'in, Huck Honey! Mark Twain's Western Sequel to *Huckleberry Finn*," *Western American Literature*, 11 (1976), 215–29, which evaluates the failure of Twain to finish the "Huck Finn and Tom Sawyer Among the Indians" manuscript (begun 1884) because of the particularly brutal sexual realities, along with a growingly bleak existential dilemma, that must face Huck as a maturing young adult in a vicious world.

41. On this subject, see the Epilogue to Douglas' previously cited *The Feminization of American Culture*, pp. 327–29.

42. Mary E. B. Fussell's research into the novella's composition in "*Billy Budd:* Melville's Happy Ending," *Studies in Romanticism*, 15 (1976), 43–47, undercovers several reasons for assuming that Melville's earlier investigations into sexual identity were on his mind during its conception. For one, the early manuscript leaf upon which Melville plotted his essential creative "breakthrough" by inventing the mediating figure of Vere

("Look at it. Look at it," Melville exclaimed in the margin) is inscribed on its reverse with the dedication to that "great heart," Jack Chase, an avatar of the Handsome Sailor apotheosized in *White Jacket* as "the man who, in a predominantly masculine world, has successfully integrated the 'female' side of his nature with his more overtly 'male' side, losing by neither, gaining by both" (Fussell, p. 47). In addition, Melville composed three of the most provocative later leaves on the backs of the holograph copy pages of the poem, "After the Pleasure Party," which as we have seen contains a crucial articulation of Melville's belief in the need to break through restrictive sexual roles in order to achieve individual harmony (pp. 45–46). Hence, it is not unreasonable to assume, along with Fussell, that the associations roused by this poem and the memory of Chase may have helped spark Melville's creation of *Billy Budd* as an investigation into the nature of masculine identity and authority.

43. *Billy Budd, Sailor (An Inside Narrative)*, ed. Harrison Hayford and Merton M. Sealts, Jr. (Chicago: Univ. of Chicago Press, 1962), p. 50. All further references to this edition will appear in parentheses in my text.

44. Sarotte, *Like a Brother, Like A Lover: Male Homosexuality in the American Novel and Theatre from Herman Melville to James Baldwin*, trans. Richard Miller (New York: Anchor-Doubleday, 1978), and Watson, "Melville's Testament of Acceptance," *New England Quarterly*, 6 (1933), 324–25.

45. These "sequels" not only precipitate a series of modal transformations (from quasi-scientific explication to newspaper account to verse ballad) typical of quasi-structure, but also underscore the issues of sexual identity and authoritarian power raised throughout the text. This series of five "endings" has been analyzed well by Mary Foley in "The Digressions in *Billy Budd*," in *Melville's Billy Budd and the Critics*, ed. William T. Stafford (San Francisco: Wadsworth, 1961), pp. 220–22.

46. *The Sea Wolf* (New York: Bantam, 1963), p. 7. All further references to this edition will appear in parentheses in my text.

47. For this exercise of physical force, Humphrey earns Wolf's words of approbation, "You've got *spunk*" (p. 65; emphasis added)—which, ironically, is that very quality that Huck feels guilty for lacking in not betraying Jim to the slave-hunters (*HF*, p. 310).

48. Also telling is the fact that Hump's *chivalrous* love comes into being the instant he realizes Wolf's *sexual* desire for Maude; that is, Wolf's sexual desire awakens Hump's "purer" love, in a paradigmatic situation of mediated or triangular desire with the woman as mediator between men. See pp. 147–48.

49. Morey-Gaines provides a telling example of the equation of virility, violence and selfhood in the western genre by citing the moment in *Shane* when the hero, who has been in disguise, puts his "guns" back on. Simultaneously his identity as a "real" man resurfaces: "They were part of him, part of the man . . . for the first time this man was complete, was himself, in the final effect of his being" (p. 140).

50. Another product of the modern quest writer's homophobia is the tendency to make the "villain" in the all-male world a homosexual: hence General Cummings' repressed homosexual yearnings in *The Naked and the Dead*. Melville, of course, also exploited this stereotype in his depiction of Claggart in *Billy Budd*, but with a qualitative difference since the psychological motivations underlying Claggart's repressed desires are regretted rather than condemned.

The writer's fear of the homosexual implications of the male bond is tied to a larger narrative problem, namely, the limited fictional possibilities of representing men together in interpersonal situations other than those traditionally "male" ones of exploration, sports or war. As Robert Kiely insightfully notes of *Women in Love* in *Beyond Egotism: Fiction of James Joyce, Virginia Woolf, and D. H. Lawrence* (Cambridge: Harvard Univ. Press, 1980), pp. 156–68, the narrative simply stops, has no place to go, when Gerald and Rupert find themselves alone together. The generic implications of this spatial issue are fascinating when we note that the two fictional subgenres overwhelmingly concerned with relationships between men—the American quest-romance and twentieth-century gay fiction—inscribe totally opposite trajectories; for the soaring movement of quest narrative contrasts vividly to the symbolic center of much gay fiction—the room or circumscribed space where all important action takes place (see, for example, Baldwin's *Giovanni's Room*, the prison cell of Puig's *The Kiss of the Spiderwoman*, the largely interior scenes of Mary Renault's "war" novel, *The Chairioteer*, from which the battlefields are never glimpsed).

51. The women of the novel, only "present" in the "Time Machine" flashbacks, are almost always seen as antagonistic "Others" who are either stereotypically naive, frigid, lascivious or conniving and whom Mailer seems to hold equally responsible for the inherent sexual warfare that drives men to violent extremes. And the one male character explicitly linked with "feminine" feelings, General Cummings (whose father used to beat him for acting "like a goddam woman") is depicted as a homosexual fascist whose repressed desires are directly responsible for the doomed mission on which he sends the recon team. The "villain" wrecking the quest, that is, is the "feminine" in man, personified by Mailer as homosexual and antithetical to his conception of masculinity.

52. *Between Men* (New York: Columbia University Press, 1985), pp. 21–27.

SUSAN JEFFORDS

MASCULINITY AS EXCESS IN VIETNAM FILMS
the father/son dynamic of american culture

American filmic representations of the Vietnam War narrate the exchange, transference, or continuation of power between father and son, the defining parameters for the definitions and determination of the masculine subject in American
social relations. From *The Green Berets* (1966), in which a primary subplot tells the
story of a marine "adopting" a Vietnamese boy; to *Uncommon Valor* (1983), in
which an Army Colonel returns to Vietnam to rescue his son from a POW camp;
to *Rambo III*, in which Rambo is befriended by an orphaned Afghani boy—these
narratives record as their primary tension the stabilization of relations between
figures who are positioned as "father" and "son."[1] Whether those relations are
failed, as in *The Deer Hunter*, corrupted, as in *Apocalypse Now*, or fulfilling, as in
the Rambo series, the dynamic and intention of the father/son relation remains
the same: to define and determine power as existing only in and through the
exchange between father and son, and to insure that alternate sources and forms
of power—in Vietnam films, women, Vietnamese, and blacks; feminism, communism, and revolution—are denied and defeated. This is what American wars—
whether fought "at home" or "in country"—are about.

Moments of exchange and transfer of power are clouded and deferred by
scenes of violence in Vietnam narration, scenes that function to distract from recognitions that power is not absolute (i.e. is situational) or that it can be "stolen"
by someone other than a "son" (i.e. by the "enemy"). For example, in *First
Blood*, Rambo begins the film alone, drifting, and powerless; he is easily apprehended and jailed by Sheriff Teasle and his deputies. At the film's close, after
multiple scenes of violence against both men and property, Rambo has disrupted
an entire town and has demonstrated his ability to kill or maim at will. Though
handcuffed and subdued in the last scene, surrounded by police cars and expec-
tant rifles, we know that his power is only controlled, not absent. He could, and
as subsequent films will show, does, strike again at any moment.

Presentations of violence like these perform two simultaneous functions: first,
to distract from recognition that power is being exchanged—importantly, not
gained or lost—here, between Teasle and Trautman/Rambo; second, to suggest
to the viewer that a consequence of power disconnected from the apparently
stable subject positions of father/son is destruction, death, and confusion, and

that without the narrational reinstatement of the son/father's control/identity, that destruction would continue. Finally, scenes of violence serve as intimidation/entertainment for the viewer. Intimidation in suggesting that "war" is a game we as viewers are unable to play and, more importantly, win (Rambo would catch us too); entertainment in that, as we identify with the hero, we repress our own helplessness before that hero (here recall the significance of Claudia Springer's recognition [in "Anti-war Film as Spectacle: Contradictions of the Combat Sequence," *Genre* 21.4 (1988): 479–86] that in these scenes "we could die; we do not die"). I will refer to these scenes of violence as moments of excess, not of power, but of the father/son dynamic.

The specific point I want to argue in this essay is that scenes of violence—combat sequences in war films—are products of a destabilization of the father/son dynamic, moments when the masculine subject being constituted in the film is made ambiguous or contradictory *as* and *by* its movement along the father/son continuum, i.e. as power is transferred—from father to son (who becomes father) or from one father to another—it is not connected to a stable identity. It is important to recognize that these moments of destabilization are *not* moments when either the masculine subject or the father/son dynamic are being directly challenged for their sufficiency, but instead are necessary disruptions that occur in the process of exchanging power. Consequently, to interpret Vietnam films, or, as I will later suggest, any dominant cultural representations of violence, through their "political" positions—as in the numerous discussions of whether *Platoon* is "liberal" or "conservative"—is to accept as significant a specific location along that continuum—one can overturn the father/ one can imitate the father—and not examine the fact of the paradigm itself, i.e. that "liberal" and "conservative" are defined by and have meaning only within the father/son dynamic. By examining moments of excess—points of exchange—I believe we can best read the operation of that dynamic and propose possibilities for its negation.

Jeanine Basinger, in her definitive study of the World War II combat film as a genre, remarks, "The best antiwar film has always been the war film,"[2] and later, "a film which says 'war is hell,' but makes it thrilling to watch, denies its own message" (95). The contradictions embedded in such arguments underscore the necessity of Claudia Springer's astute comments on combat sequences as excess. As she concludes, "Combat sequences have to be analyzed in relation to their narrative frameworks" (12) in order to determine how their "excess" will be read by viewers, as pro- or antiwar, for example, in the case of *Platoon*, or as conservatively militaristic or subversive in the case of the Rambo films. While it can be stated that combat sequences *can* be interpreted in multiple ways due to their narrative position as excess, it is clear that they are not generally so interpreted, due to general cultural codes that influence how we view violence, as well as to the specific narrative context established by the film for understanding the significance of the combat sequence as a particular occasion. I will argue in this essay that the narrative context within which those sequences are controlled and interpreted is the father/son dynamic.

The combat film is, first and foremost, a film not simply about men but about the construction of the masculine subject, and the combat sequence—or, more generally, scenes of violence in combat films, whether as fighting in battle, torture, prison escapes, or explosions—is the point of excess, not only for the filmic narrative, but for masculine subjectivity. Because the continuous progression of (social) narrative depends upon the stable positioning of power as affiliated with the father, exchanges of power between fathers and sons or transferences of power in which the son becomes the father cannot be openly articulated. As breaks in that narrative continuity through productions of excess as spectacle, combat sequences provide deferring arenas from such exchanges and allow transferences of power to occur, at the close of which power relations, though altered, appear continuous and stable. Combat sequences are produced by and relieve moments of crisis in the construction of the masculine subject, and function narratively to enable exchanges of power within and between the father/son dynamic that stabilizes that subject.

There are two films that exhibit these points most clearly and that will be the focus for my discussions here: Oliver Stone's *Platoon* (1987) and the Rambo series, particularly *Rambo: First Blood, Part II.* I choose them not only for their combat displays, but for their openly political positions: Stone's film as a type of antiwar statement from the point of view of the man in battle, and Stallone's as a pro-vet/antigovernment bureaucracy statement that asks for social recognition of the Vietnam veteran's strength and achievements; in other words, both are films that do not take as their proposed messages the promotion of combat or warfare but have in both cases clearly foregrounded political issues. But as Basinger says of the World War II combat film: "The combat film pieces can be put together as a propaganda machine or as an anti-propaganda machine, as an 'America is beautiful' or an 'America is an imperialist dog' message. 'War is necessary' or 'war is never necessary'" (16). Such confusions of political "message" should not be attributed, as they are by Basinger, to the "flexibilities" of the genre, or, as they are by Richard Corliss, *Time*'s reviewer of *Platoon*, to the "cunning" and "complexity"[3] of the directors. Instead, they should be recognized as indications that these films are not chiefly *about* their stated political messages or historical reviews or revisions, but about something altogether different, something that discussion of combat films as political statements functions only to cloud and defer: the constructions, reproductions, and reshapings of the masculine subject within the father/son dynamic that structures patriarchy.

Because Kristin Thompson's definitive essay on cinematic excess insists so emphatically upon the *materiality* of filmic elements as excess, I want to pause briefly to discuss how I intend to use the concept of "excess" to delineate a cultural and not a filmic formation, specifically, to refer to the construction of "masculinity" as excess.

In her study of the materiality of filmic narrative, Kristen Thompson defines excess: "a film can be seen as a struggle of opposing forces. Some of these forces strive to unify a work, to hold it together sufficiently that we may perceive and follow its structures. Outside any such structures lie those aspects of the work which are not contained by its unifying forces—the 'excess.'"[4] Specifically, Thompson identifies material elements such as sound, textures of costumes, acting style, unclear items, etc., as providing "a perceptual play by inviting the spectator to linger over devices longer than their structured function would seem to warrant" (133). Functioning as they do in the narrative structure, such elements "may serve at once to contribute to the narrative and to distract our perception from it" (134). Consequently, excess "is precisely those elements which escape unifying impulses" (141).

Elsewhere,[5] I have argued that this notion of "excess" depicts the production of gender itself, as the production and enforcement of gender relations requires a constant reaffirmation and enactment of its structures in order to maintain its "existence." This argument stems from statements like those by Susan Brownmiller, who says of "femininity" that "it always demands more. It must constantly reassure its audience by a willing demonstration of difference."[6] How can these two forms of excess—one referring to the materiality of filmic narratives and the other to the ideological enactments of gender relations—be compared and combined?

In her essay, Thompson turns to the Russian Formalist concept of "motivation" to explain how excessive elements may be noticed in some narratives and not others: "Strong realistic or compositional motivation will tend to make excessive elements less noticeable. . . . But at other times, a lack of these kinds of motivations may direct our attention to excess. More precisely, excess implies a gap or lag in motivation" (134). Motivation would here apply to the "unifying structures" (134) of a filmic narrative function of the individual elements within a film in their relation to the overall "motivation" that links those elements together to create the appearance of a unified structure.

"Motivation" and "demand" are, as I am using them here, equivalent. It is, for example, the demand for the illusion that cinema depict "reality"—a demand that, to use Brownmiller's words, "must constantly reassure its audience"—that sets up the motivation for cinematic "realism,"[7] the inclusion of the very material elements that Thompson identifies as incidents of excess. The textures of costumes, the appearance of unexplained items, the pressures of sound—all participate in the overdetermination of realism that marks classic Hollywood cinema and the productions of dominant culture. Thompson's material analysis identifies the ways in which these "demands" become visually identifiable.

As I want to use these terms here, the "unifying structures" of cultural narratives are the primary arguments of a patriarchal system—the father/son dynamic; the "motivation," to make that system appear coherent, and, in Thompson's words, "reasonable"; the "demand," constantly to reaffirm the sufficiency of that system and its exhaustion of that motivation; the "excess," the multiple ways in which that demand can never be met.

It is the presence of excess that "motivates"—requires—the constant reproduction of narrative. At the same time, such excess is a necessary product of narrativization as an attempt to reconcile contradictions and oppositions within the social network, disjunctions that can never be fully reconciled or "explained" by or through representational productions. In this way, the excess of masculinity—finally of gender itself—as I am using it here is the point at which we can be "distracted," in quite the way Thompson suggested for material aspects of film, from the "unifying structure" of patriarchal narratives, a version of what Antony Easthope calls making masculinity "visible": "Social change is necessary and a precondition of such change is an attempt to *understand* masculinity, to make it visible."[8] In different terms, the excess of masculinity can lead to what Paul Smith has posed as the concept of "resistance," not simply conscious resistance to inadequate positions of identification offered by narrative, but resistance as a structural feature of representational productions, "a notion of resistance which would be able to recognize it as, in fact, a veritable *product* of ideological interpretation."[9]

In the terms I am suggesting here, the father/son dynamic that formulates and is one of the primary mechanisms for reproducing patriarchal systems simultaneously offers a "unifying narrative" to explain the processes of social relations *and* produces excess that distracts us from accepting that narrative as wholly "our" story. It is out of *both* of these processes that the tensions surrounding the exchange of power between fathers and sons arises: on the one hand, showing the linear and stable passage of power as "unifying," and, on the other, because power is being exchanged at all, revealing that exchange as possibly unstable and vulnerable to failures and mistakes. The father/son dynamic then identifies one of the principal locations for "resistance" to patriarchal systems in the very definition of its narrative process, i.e. though the son may replace the father, the son is not the father. It is in response to and as a deterrence of this contradiction that narrational violence is produced.

To say that masculinity is excess is then to argue that the gender system of American culture cannot fulfill the motivation of a patriarchal system to establish itself as exhaustive.[10] Because gender has no material existence, must enact itself through and upon bodies, it can only be *affiliated* with material elements, and because this affiliation can never be a complete identification, there is a constant slippage between gender and materiality in subject experience. Consequently, any attempt to enact gender through material formations—and gender can be *only* so enacted—must produce excess, moments during which the materiality of those formations asserts itself as separate from gender (think here of the extreme close-ups of Rambo's arm, shots that are unidentifiable until we can place them in the larger context of Rambo's body). The reproduction of gender through material formations is both a consequence and a denial of this separation.

There are several consequences of defining "excess" in gender terms, specifically in this argument, as masculinity. Let me list a few of them:

> It will be assumed that there will be no dominant narrative in a patriarchal system that does not include gender as excess, or, more typically, masculinity as excess.

> Though Thompson's definition of excess stems from her analysis of cinema, and I will be discussing filmic narratives here, these arguments apply equally to any dominant cultural production, any articulation of cultural narrative that participates in a patriarchal system.

> In order to fulfill the "constant demand" of patriarchy to insist upon its materiality, gender must constantly be reproduced and renegotiated to fit the specific terms of a particular culture and historical moments. As I will argue in this essay, those terms are now ones that depict the resurgence of power in and through the father, or in which the son willingly (if sometimes perversely) adopts the father's role and position. These are the most visible articulations of the reproduction of gender relations, suggesting in the interplay between constructions of the father and the son that such positions exhaust simultaneously the subject relations of masculinity and of gender.

> That such dominant structures are constructed to deny what Smith calls the "multiple interpolations" of subjects and, therefore, the resistance that rises from contradictions between these positions. That the goal of such analyses

is, like that of Thompson's analysis of cinematic excess, to offer "an awareness of excess [that] may help change the status of narrative in general for the
viewer."[11]

In the following pages, I will offer an analysis of the combat sequences in two
dominant narratives in which the constructions of productions of masculinity are
key aspects of the filmic "motivation"—Oliver Stone's *Platoon* and the *Rambo*
sequence—in an effort to delineate the operation of masculinity as excess. As I
hope to show, it is at the point of the narration of combat sequences that we can
best recognize the excess of masculinty, primarily because it is there that the
father/son relations that form the motivation for dominant narratives are transferred and negotiated. It is also there that the tensions aroused by the excess of
the production of the masculine subject are relieved and deferred through the
spectacle of combat (i.e. "this is not what we are fighting about").

There are three combat sequences in *Platoon:* the first, while Chris Taylor
(Charlie Sheen) is still a "cherry," a battle in which he receives his first injury, a
superficial neck wound; the second, when the platoon is ambushed by the NVA,
a battle during which Taylor exhibits bravery and competence as a soldier and
after which Sergeant Elias is killed by Sergeant Barnes; and the third, the final
and longest battle scene of the film, in which the battalion's position is overrun
by NVA and Taylor is wounded, and after which Taylor kills Barnes. Preceding
each of these scenes is dialogue that shows Taylor's uncertainty about his identity and purpose; as that uncertainty increases, and *in direct response to it,* the
combat scenes become increasingly longer and more violent. Following each
scene is a reshaping of the depiction of masculinity, specifically, of paternal
father/son relations, until at the film's conclusion, Taylor takes over the father's
position as a way of stabilizing that identity and controlling the excess of its production or the resistance to it.

Before the first battle, Taylor has his initial exposure to Vietnam and the war.
There is confusion, and the camera during the first patrol is placed in such a way
that we never see Taylor's face clearly, are unable to establish firm connections
with him as a focus for our identification; the camera positions thus exemplify
the ways in which we are positioned as viewers to experience as our own these
crises in subjectivity, and then to instill in us a desire for a return to stability, for
a stable and distant camera. He speaks of "Hell [as] the impossibility of Reason"
and admits in a letter to his grandmother that he "made a big mistake coming
here." He then claims that he "just want[s] to be anonymous. Like everybody
else," and then hopes that "maybe from down here I can start up again and be
something I can be proud of, without having to fake it, maybe . . . I can see
something I don't yet see, learn something I don't yet know." He wakes Junior
for his watch, goes to sleep himself, and is awakened by the sound of approaching NVA.

Stone wants us to see this character as someone confused, disoriented, beginning to question his reasons for being in Vietnam. These are all overt political
impressions that are translated into the visual and verbal narrative of the film.
But more than this, Taylor's monologue, coming as it does immediately before
the first combat sequence, can be read as an increasing deterioration of his sense
of himself as subject, in which he is "anonymous," has no individuality, and is

seeking for an identity that he "can be proud of," someone he can become "without having to fake it," i.e. an "authentic" subject position. In the midst of this ambiguity of identity, Taylor finds that his paternal connections—his grandfather fighting in WWI and his father in WWII—are no longer meaningful as a means of solidifying that identity. Instead, he must start all over again, "way down here in the mud," and produce a "new" personality that will not depend upon theirs. More specifically, he must discover a "new" father in relation to whom he can establish his own identity, i.e. a father who, unlike his own, has power: "[my parents] wanted me to be just like them—respectable, hardworking, making $200 a week, a little house, a family. . . . I didn't want my whole life to be predetermined by them." Though Taylor speaks here of his parents, it is clear he is speaking only of his father, who, in 1967, would most likely be the one who is "hard-working, making $200 a week." In addition, by writing to his grandmother, he severs any connections to any male line in his family. His last words before the combat scene are to his mother, not his father: "tell Mom I miss her too," an affinity that will be completely denied by the film's close.

The ensuing combat scene is a product of this disjunction between continuous father/son identities. Abandoning both his grandfather and father, Taylor maintains connections only to the women in his family, and instead chooses to immerse himself into the "anonymity" [12] of the male community that is the combat situation in American culture. [13] Because those new ties are insecure—Taylor is still a "cherry," i.e. a son [14]—and the old ones intact through women, Taylor's wound is a surface one, i.e. the damage to his subjectivity is superficial because he has not wholly severed himself from his previous masculine identity.

Before the second combat scene, Taylor's confusion increases. Following the near-massacre of the Vietnamese village, during which Taylor finds his own limits for behavior brought into question as he taunts a retarded Vietnamese boy, Taylor voices more ambiguity: "It's a struggle to maintain my sanity—it's all a blur. I don't know what's right and what's wrong anymore. There's a civil war in the platoon. . . ." Not only has he lost his previous social identity by rejecting his father's lifestyle and seeking for "anonymity," he now is forced to abandon all prior notions of moral valuation, even the very "reason" upon which he was able to judge that war is like hell, "the loss of reason." In his anonymity, "it's all a blur."

Taylor recites these lines in a voiceover as the platoon wades through a waist-high stream during monson rains. Big Harold, angry that he didn't get his assignment to a laundry detail that would take him out of combat, says, "Shit, got to paint myself white get one of dem jobs. Get ma request in for a circumcision." Taylor then pulls a leech off of his cheek.

Importantly, Stone eliminates several lines from the screenplay here. The scene begins with Big Harold pulling a leech "out of his open crotch area," saying, "Shit, lookit this little fucker trying to get up ma glory hole." After his remark about the circumcision, Francis says to Harold, "Gonna cut your pecker down to size huh Big Harold?" who answers, "Dat's okay wid me, better to have a small one den no one at all," to which King replies, "Your girlfriends gonna look for new lovers, man. Best thing a bro's got's his flap." [15]

While the film's juxtaposition of Big Harold's comments on circumcision and Taylor's leech seems merely coincidental, the screenplay shows these scenes to be intimately linked through an imagery of castration. The leech that is trying to enter Big Harold's penis prefaces circumcision as literal castration—"Gonna cut your pecker down to size"—and ties this to a fear of/for women—"Your girl-friends gonna look for new lovers." At the close of this discussion, Taylor's appar-ently blithe move to pick a leech off of his cheek takes on a greater meaning as a hint at his own pending castration, both at the hands of the war and the powerful father.

Such scenes enable us to read how the structure of the father/son dynamic and the masculine subject it stablizes are intimately linked to racial difference in Vietnam films. Stone's screenplay shows how the threat of castration that under-lies the exchange of power between father and son (i.e. that the son could not become the father) is more readily articulated in relation to black rather than white men: the leech that is in Big Harold's penis is only on Taylor's cheek. The white penis is here both mythified as unseeable and made unavailable for com-parison with the mythically larger black penis.[16] As in other Vietnam films, this threat is translated through a fear of the responses of women, not men, in an effort to suppress the tensions of racial difference between men.[17]

Big Harold's line about circumcision must, I think, also be read in relation to an earlier joke of the film. The lieutenant, whom Stone's screenplay describes as having a "false masculinity" (53), i.e. cannot be a father, declines playing poker with Barnes and his group by saying, "Nah, I wouldn't want to get raped by you guys. . . ." (53). O'Neill replies, "What are you saving up to be Lieutenant—Jewish?" (53). There are complex racisms voiced here—only white men get out of combat, white men are circumcised, Jews are circumcised, Jews are virgins/feminine, "false masculinty" belongs to Jews and those like them who can't play poker with men like Barnes, Jews hoard money, etc.—that overlap race, class, and gender issues. Without trying to unwind these knotted articulations of dif-ference, it is clear that Big Harold's brief comment refers to this complex set of prejudices that are otherwise denied by the comraderie of scenes like those in the "Underworld," where men bond together regardless of backgrounds. Big Harold's single line here hints at the explosion of that collective image as dic-tated in its most threatening terms—castration ("Get ma request in for a circum-cision"). Taylor's leech makes him vulnerable to this threat.

Racial difference as constructed in *Platoon* insures that the father/son dynamic will have meaning only for white men.[18] As these scenes show, Jews and blacks are argued as "non-men," not simply "feminized," but men who *willingly* cas-trate themselves—Big Harold requests circumcision, Lt. Wolfe chooses not to play poker for fear of being "raped," and later, at the end of the final battle scene, Francis, who has survived the battle unharmed, stabs himself in the leg rather than face more combat. Much of this argument is directed against reading, as Clyde Taylor suggests, King as "actually more of a father-figure to Charlie than Elias." Taylor explains that, "deprived of the moral authority that neither the film nor its primary audience will grant him, [King's] characterization tips toward the familiar role of black male mammy to innocent white youth. . . . Where Elias' affirmation is an activist, apocalyptic salvationism, King's is a broth-erly accommodationism."[19] King's relationship to Taylor is structured in such a way that he *cannot* be seen as a father, must be seen as at best a "brother," ra-cially neutralized through self-castration. The black soldiers in *Platoon* are negated as well as possible enemies through their companionship with Taylor and their relative separation, both physically and emotionally, from the interests and concerns of white soldiers. Denied both the possibility of being fathers or sons-who-could-become-fathers, black soldiers in *Platoon* are situated to insure their non-participation in the father/son dynamic that defines these films and therefore their non-participation in the exchange of power.

The second combat sequence of the film occurs immediately after this scene. As the platoon walks through a wooded area, they are ambushed, the enactment of castration in combat.[20] Unlike the first combat scene, where the American patrol was staging an ambush of the Vietnamese, here the Americans are vulnerable, they are being killed, and they may soon be trapped. As Elias describes it, "Flank's wide open, dinks get 3–4 snipers in these holds, when Third Platoon comes up, they'll get us in a crossfire with 'em. We'll shoot each other to shit, then they'll hit us with everything they got. It'll be a massacre!" (87). Previously being attacked by the Vietnamese, here men are in danger of killing themselves.

Such scenes fit in with popular interpretations of the film like Richard Corliss' "Americans were fighting themselves, and both sides lost"[21] and are very much part of how Stone wants to portray the Vietnam War as a battle within America, between Americans like Barnes and Elias, who fight wars differently and who both die in the film. But these scenes also exemplify a masculinity in peril, led into an ambush by a clever and unseen "feminine" enemy to "massacre" itself. Men like Big Harold are "requesting" their own circumcisions. Men like Wolfe are in charge. Men like Barnes are killing men like Elias, and men like Taylor are confused and "in a blur." *This* is the fear, the anxiety, the threat, the violence that underlies this combat sequence and others in Vietnam film—not a battle with NVA soldiers.

The last combat scene, the longest and most elaborate of the film, is the final explosion of masculinity in *Platoon*. With Elias, Taylor's positive role model—one of his "fathers"—now dead at Barnes's hands, and Taylor unable to act on his desires for revenge, the film is in its most complete state of disorder and confusion. Soldiers who had seemed hardened before are crying now; both O'Neill and Junior are frightened that they will die in a battle in which they know they are outnumbered, merely "bait" to draw out the NVA. Even Barnes says, "everybody gotta die sometime."[22] Taylor's despair is at its lowest: "People like Elias get wasted and people like Barnes just go on making up rules any way they want and what do we do, we just sit around in the middle and suck on it!" (106). And Taylor, whose only link to a secured identity before Vietnam was through his letters to his grandmother, has stopped writing.

> King: What's the matter wid you? . . . How come you ain't writing no more? You was always writing something home. Looks like youse half a bubble off, Taylor.
> What about your folks? That grandma you was telling me about? . . .
> (Chris shakes his head.)
> Girl?
> (Chris' eyes answer negatively.)
> Must be somebody?
> Chris: . . . . there's nobody. (105)

Now completely cut off from his past, Taylor's identity is entirely dependent upon his immediate surroundings, the war he is in and the men he is fighting with. It is at this point that we can see how the masculine subject as traditionally defined by American culture has been deteriorating (though never disappearing) throughout the film—moving from the initial confusion and disorientation of arriving in Vietnam to do this final silence of disconnection. Taylor has finally found that bottom, that spot "way down here in the mud," from which he "can start up again," the point from which the masculine subject can be reconstructed, no longer in relation to "the world," but now only in relation to the interconnected subjectivity of masculinity in Vietnam. Out of this confusion, the final battle scene occurs, in which their position is overrun and Taylor proves himself to be a rabid combat soldier, able to sense danger, to kill, and to survive.

At the peak of the battle, Barnes, red-eyed and in a fury of killing—what Stone calls "the essence of evil" (123)—is about to attack Taylor with a trenching tool when an American plane drops a bomb on their position and the screen blacks out. When the scene returns at dawn of the next day, Stone's camera signifies that a change has occurred. Shot in black and white, not color, the camera pans across the multiple bodies of soldiers and the decimated jungle, turning slowly to color again. While filmically this is meant to show Taylor's gradual return to consciousness, this single use of black-and-white film in an otherwise intensely colored and closely-shot cinema signifies more than Taylor's physical awakening. It also marks the "dawn" of a different masculine subject, Taylor's appearance as a father. During the battle, Taylor emerged from his confusion and loss of identity as a "warrior,"[23] a man who no longer knew fear. On his first patrol, he was paralyzed by the sight of the enemy, unable to act, unprepared to fight, sitting draped in a blanket and separated from his gun and Claymore ignitors. Here, he is not only prepared, but he abandons his protected foxhole and charges the enemy straight on, killing with fury and skill. No longer afraid to act, no longer threatened, Taylor emerges during this battle with a different identity. It is finally only Barnes that seems able to stop him.

Why? Let me digress for a moment to discuss *Platoon*'s portrayal of the enemy before returning to Taylor's final battle with Barnes. As the combat scenes become longer and more violent, as Taylor himself kills more and more people, as Taylor's distance from his previous identity increases, the enemy becomes more and more distinct. Only shadows against a misty night in the first combat scene, and then fleeting and hidden figures in the battle in the woods, the enemy in this final combat scene has become identifiable. We see NVA soldiers preparing booby traps, selecting weapons, examining maps. Taylor hears their voices beyond his foxhole. We see in slow-motion the firing of an RPG (rocket-propelled grenade) that explodes Taylor's abandoned foxhole. We see NVA soldiers killing Bunny point blank in his chest, and wounding Barnes and Taylor. And then finally, at the height of the battle, we see Barnes.

The increasing specificity of the enemy has now become fixed, not on the NVA soldiers whom Taylor is able to kill and who finally die from the bomb explosion, but upon Barnes. It is Barnes whom Taylor must fight in order to establish his own identity. The Vietnamese become merely a backdrop for the display of American masculinity struggling to stabilize itself in a revised environment.[24]

But the increasing specificity of the Vietnamese as enemy works both to focus our attention upon perceiving the enemy, an attention that culminates in seeing Barnes as enemy, and at the same time to distract us from seeing other American men—specifically, other white American men—as enemies. Stone wants us to conclude finally that *only* Barnes is the enemy, so that while battles against the NVA will go on, Barnes' death marks a significant ending to one particular struggle, that for Taylor's masculine identity. As a "two-timer" (soldiers who have been wounded twice), Taylor leaves this battlefield for good. In the simplest of terms, *his* war is over.

By focusing entirely upon Barnes as the "enemy," the film has succeeded in negating fears that power might be taken by someone outside the father/son dynamic, in this case by the Vietnamese. As Taylor's distance from his biological father grows, and his relation to his "new" fathers, Elias and Barnes, becomes more defined—in other words, as his identification of positions of power increases—the enemy becomes clearer, until we learn that the "real" enemy is the evil and powerful father, the one Taylor must defeat in order to secure his own power, to become a father himself. In telling the story in this way, *Platoon* shows why the father/son dynamic is the logic of patriarchy: by declaring that power exists only within the framework of the masculine arena—the war—and only by identifying and affiliating with a strong father, alternate forms of power are denied; according to *Platoon*, one can only gain power—what Stone chooses to call "experience"—by acknowledging and accepting this system as exhaustive and determinative. Consequently, that Barnes should finally be identified as the enemy does not challenge but instead confirms the father/son dynamic as system. All meaning stems from and acquires "truth" only as it becomes a character in this narration.

At the film's close, the confusion that has so haunted Taylor has disappeared. Because the war itself is not resolved, seems, at the close of this film, to have the possibility of going on forever, any sense of resolution the film offers must stem, not from a change in the war, but from a change in Taylor. The film's resolution rests then not upon the war but upon the stabilization of masculinity through acquisition of the power of the father. As the last words of the film declare, Taylor is now quietly confident that he has a knowledge to impart, a message to deliver: "those of us who did make it have an obligation to build again, to teach others what we know and to try with what's left of our lives to find a goodness and meaning to this life." [25] While the film would like us to see this change as a product of Taylor's experience in war and discovery of a part of himself that he could not know while still in college, I find another explanation more convincing.

The change in Taylor is a product of a reconstruction and stabilization of his masculine identity through his testing and rejection of various masculine models—his father and grandfather, Elias and Barnes—until in the end he establishes an identity that is separate from theirs but still part of them, "the child born of those two fathers" (129). This might sound at first like a simple maturation narrative, in which a young man struggles to separate himself from his father or father-figure. What distinguishes *Platoon* from such narratives and marks it as a product of contemporary gender concerns in American culture is Taylor's relationship to multiple fathers, [26] each of whom represents a different aspect of previously denied notions of manhood: Taylor's father, the middle-class breadwinner; his grandfather and father, the dutiful patriots who served their country and could fulfill their commitment to the *polis;* Elias, the peace-loving, compassionate, and sensuous man; and Barnes, the ruthless, law-breaking renegade who kills to survive. Taylor tests himself as each of these heroes—goes to college, enlists in the Army, rescues young girls from rape, and kills lustfully in battle—and accepts none of them as satisfactory. But instead of offering a "new" and alternate model, Taylor integrates these into a single character: he will return home having fulfilled his commitment as a "patriot" and having become a "warrior"; he maintains his compassion as he shows concern for Francis' wounds; and he has established his own law in killing Barnes and suffering no recrimination for it. His is not a "new" masculinity but a revised version of the old ones. What knowledge has he gained? That none of these masculine characters can continue independently in American culture, but that joined together in a revised character, they can "survive." [27] This is the coalescence of a masculinity that had become dispersed; by gathering itself under the umbrella of the "god/father," it can achieve a restabilized position of power.

With all other fathers dead or neutralized in the film, Taylor becomes the "new" father at its close, able "to teach to others what we know" and to "build again." Stone's screenplay is especially instructive here, as he describes Taylor's departing helicopter as "now rising to meet God" (128). Through his experiences in war, Taylor has gained a perspective that enables him to see what others cannot, a perspective that is "god-like," authoritative, and powerful. As the closing position of the film from which Taylor narrates his new goals of "teaching" and "building," it can be described as nothing less than paternal.

The combat scenes of *Platoon* have led emphatically to this point. The increasing violence of the combat sequences can be seen as a direct result of the increasing ambivalence of the masculine character as it is severed from previous forms of stability and identification. The combat sequences are eruptions of the anxiety about this ambivalence as well as forums within which the tension of that anxiety can be dispelled and "new" masculine roles can be tried on. That anxiety decreases and is arrested as the masculine subject becomes stabilized through the adoption of the position of father. The resolution of the father/son tension is not then coincidentally but structurally tied to combat scenes because it is through combat sequences that the son is enabled (often through the literal death of the father) to adopt an altered paternal role. The deterioration of the masculine subject is halted only by the son becoming the father; only through restabilization of the position of the father is violence arrested.

It is here that Springer's discussion of the spectatorial security in viewing death becomes again relevant. Identifying as we do with Taylor, a character who we know will not die in the film, we share that security of witnessing and causing death, being twice wounded, and yet not being vulnerable to death. It is as well the "security" of the masculine character within patriarchy, enabling experimentation with the "death" of previous masculinities along with "wounds" to present ones, and yet not being vulnerable to the "death" of masculinity itself. [28] By inviting the viewer to take Taylor's character at its point of identifiction, we are being asked to share, not simply this conclusion, but the system that enabled its production.

This is the cultural appeal of the combat film, explains its rise, as now, during

periods when cultural conceptions of masculinity are being brought under examination. In American culture, such periods have often coincided with postwar
years during which men who have been in combat must return to a society that
has altered its gender roles during their absence,[29] but it is not necessarily the
case that combat films are linked to actual wars or combat scenarios.[30] To make
this kind of gender/genre elision is to misperceive the operation of violence in
culture. Combat narratives are linked to efforts to produce restabilized images of
masculinity during historical moments when gender roles are being renegotiated,
but they are only the most apparent and not the exclusive means by which such
renegotiation occurs. In representations of the Vietnam War, those images are
most generally oriented toward producing and promoting a paternal masculinity.[31]

The Rambo films show how this promotion takes place historically, shifting its
relations and representations during the past decade. The three films, *First
Blood* (Kotcheff, 1982), *Rambo: First Blood, Part II* (Cosmatos, 1985), and *Rambo
III* (Macdonald, 1988), display different stages in the historical development of a
reconstructed American masculinity that has occurred in recent years. First,
these films sequentially display the rejection of various forms of masculine identification, progressively triumphing over traditional middle-class roles (*First
Blood*), institutionalized forms of paternity (*Rambo: First Blood, Part II*), and finally global/international political authorities (*Rambo III.*). But more importantly, in addition to distancing its own presentations of masculinity from these
positions, the Rambo films reinscribe masculine relations within a revised father/
son dynamic that confirms masculinity as the relevant framework for subjective
and social relations in American culture. The Rambo films offer this paternity
in its most compact forms, not only in Rambo's rejected relationships to the
American government and the military as paternal figures, but in relationship to
Rambo's mentor and teacher, Colonel Trautman.

First Blood shows Rambo struggling unwillingly against a town sheriff who is a
Korean War veteran. This is the fairly straightforward battle with a traditional
father figure that Chris Taylor is able, five years later, to dismiss so readily in his
epistolary rejection of his father's way of life. Sheriff Teasle is shown to have
middle-class concerns and prejudices, judging Rambo a hippie, and wanting only
to keep his town of Hope, Oregon a quiet and safe place for its citizens. The ease
with which Rambo disrupts that quiet and destroys that town are only the most
superficial evidences that Teasle's masculinity and the middle-class ethic he represents are no longer sufficient in a post-Vietnam world. But in spite of this easy
rejection of Teasle, Rambo's character at the close of the film is firmly subordinated to that of Colonel Trautman, Rambo's leader and teacher in the Army.
When Rambo walks away from a final pending gun battle (the fact that this kind
of full-scale combat scene is *avoided* in *First Blood* marks its early participation in
masculine revision; anxieties about masculinity are here repressed rather than
explored and exploded), it is under Trautman's protective arm. It is clear that
Trautman still has control over Rambo, is, in fact, the only man—the only type
of masculinity—that can stop him. Rambo does not, in this first film, gain the
kind of "god-like" independence that Chris Taylor inhabits at the end of
Platoon.

In the second film, *Rambo: First Blood, Part II*, Rambo has a distinctively different paternal figure to react against. Not the conservative middle-class figure of

Sheriff Teasle, Rambo here must work against Marshall Murdock, government representative in charge of a POW rescue mission that can gain Rambo a pardon from the jail sentence he is serving as a result of his actions in *First Blood*. Murdock's is a technologically sophisticated, bureaucratized, professional, and powerful paternal figure whose influence and abilities far surpass those of Sheriff Teasle. Also a World War II veteran, but one who has moved beyond that time into a corporate era, Murdock is politically wise and economically clever. His power as paternal authority figure is made most clear at the moment when he singly decides to abandon Rambo and a rescued POW to a pursuing Vietnamese patrol by declaring to the helicopter pilots who could rescue Rambo, "Abort the mission!"

But again, as in *First Blood*, Rambo triumphs over this adversary, returning with the POWs Murdock said did not exist, destroying Murdock's computers (the source of his virility), and threatening to return and "find" him if Murdock fails to find other POWs (this threat is visually articulated as castration, when Rambo, laying Murdock across a desktop, stabs his foot-long knife into the table by Murdock's ear). As in the first film, *Rambo* closes with his relation to Trautman, though here Rambo is moving out of the subordiante position that confined him in *First Blood*. Instead of accepting Trautman's offer to "come home," Rambo walks deliberately away from Trautman and off into the jungles of Thailand. Though it is still clear that Trautman is the only man who retains any link to Rambo, the only one to whom he will speak, there is a decided distance between them as Rambo separates himself from Trautman.

In *Rambo III*, Rambo's entire mission is defined by a now clearly altered paternal relationship with Trautman. The early advertisements for *Rambo III* make this shift clear. On subsequent pages of film sections of newspapers, Rambo's motivations are declared, in bold print, without context or ascription (as if everyone understands the context for their meaning): "The first time was for himself/ The second was for his country/ This time is for a friend." Naming Trautman as Rambo's "friend" suggests the distance traveled between this film and *First Blood*, where it is clear that Rambo and Trautman are not on a level to be "friends." Here, though Rambo refuses to accompany Trautman on a mission to help Afghan rebels, he quickly offers to rescue Trautman when he is captured by Russian soldiers. The incentive for action here is straightforwardly linked to this paternal tie, with masculine roles reversed; now Rambo must save the "father" who first saved him. The authority figure of the film is a Russian colonel renowned for his torture techniques and ruthlessness. This is the "evil" father-figure that was Barnes in *Platoon*, a man who survives by making his own rules and eliminating all who disrupt his power. But instead of the moral evil that formed the center of Stone's concerns, Colonel Zaysen's is the multinational corporate power that does not respect national boundaries, is interested not in justice or political position but careerist maneuvering (he excels at his job so that he can be promoted out of Afghanistan), and is focused upon destroying the family unit and traditional way of life that "subvert" his enforcement of power.

To mark the clear shift in paternal relations that has taken place in representations of the 1980s, Rambo not only succeeds in rescuing his "father" but then proceeds to fight beside and outdo him on the battlefield. The close of *Rambo III* shows its distance from *First Blood:* instead of walking out to a waiting police force under the protection of Trautman's raincoat and sheltering arm, Rambo and Trautman drive away from the celebrating Afghan tribes, exchanging quips about their military successes. They are no longer father and son but buddies.[32] Rambo has taken the place of the father (he is "adopted" by a small Afghan boy as evidence of his own ability to stand as father) and the father has been "wounded," infantilized, and had to depend upon the son for his own survival.

What a look at the combat sequences of the Rambo films reveals is that these multiple battles with successively more powerful and threatening father-figures are *not* the focus of the narrative force in these films; instead, these plot strains are diversions to distract us from recognizing the actual source of tension and intensity in these narratives—the restructuring of the father–son relation and the production of the masculine subject within that frame.

Rambo—a film about the rescue of American POWs, of "lost men"—records the story of the son's recognition that the father is not all-powerful, and of the son's exchange of power with and in support of the father. Trautman, who taught Rambo how to survive in war, who rescued Rambo from his first "battle" at home, and who promises Rambo a pardon for volunteering for this mission, is shown in this film not to be in charge. Instead, his power is subordinated to that of Murdock, the man who heads the rescue mission. During successive scenes of the film, Trautman's remaining power is increasingly cut away by Murdock, until he finally is unable to help Rambo at all. When Rambo and a POW are unexpectedly sighted by the rescue helicopter, Murdock aborts the mission and recalls the ship. Though Trautman orders, "We're going down," the doorgunner, one of Murdock's assistants, points a gun at Trautman and replies, "You're not going anywhere." When Trautman screams, "There's men down there! *Our* men!" the gunner answers coolly, "No. *Your* men. Don't be a hero." As the helicopter flies away, Rambo calls out, "Colonel! Don't leave!"

The violence of the film's combat scenes increases in direct proportion to the decline of Trautman's power. More specifically, the most extended and violent scenes of the film—Rambo's single-handed defeat of his numerous Russian and Vietnamese pursuers—occur *immediately* following Murdock's emasculation of Trautman, when he tells him, "I'm in charge here. You're just a tool." The film's narration is set up in such a way that we are to see the death of Co Bao, Rambo's Vietnamese female guide, at the hands of a Vietnamese officer as Rambo's motivation for this rampage (while with Co, he had earlier agreed that they were heading to Thailand, not back to get the POWs). But there is not a continuous line between Co's death and Rambo's rampage. Instead, the death and burial are interrupted by a scene of Trautman's demanding that Murdock gather a rescue team to help Rambo. It is here that Murdock declares that he, not Trautman, is in charge. The film then cuts to Rambo's hands on Co's grave and his return to exact revenge upon his pursuers.

Framing the final emasculation of the father, Co's death and burial become diversions for the film's narration of the reconstruction of masculine identity. The immediacy of the physical and emotional ties between Rambo and Co seems to outweigh the bond between Trautman and Rambo. And the brevity and inaction of the intervening scene between Trautman and Murdock would make it appear incidental in comparison to the lengthy and action-filled scenes with Co. But the placement of these scenes reveals where the weight of the film's tension lies, as it is Trautman's "death," not Co's, that precedes the celebrated combat sequence that follows. The grave at which Rambo kneels could just as well be the grave in which Trautman's father-image has been laid to rest. It is finally the tension of Trautman's emasculation, not Co's death, that must be relieved and reoriented by the elaborate violence that follows.

Co functions as well to siphon off the tension of the homoerotic overtones in the Trautman/Rambo bond. It is immediately prior to Trautman's final displacement as father-figure that Co kisses Rambo and asks him to take her to America. (Is it perhaps this kiss that marks Trautman's downfall, as he is here rejected by the son? Such questions hint at the degree to which all events in these narrations are diversions from the tensions involved in restructuring the father/son dynamic as the focus for masculine identification.) Co's impersonation of the prostitute echoes in this kiss to confirm her as heterosexual and feminine, something her role as Rambo's guide seemed to deny ("You didn't expect a woman?"). When the father is released from his elevated and thereby nonerotic position (nonerotic because fully sexed, completely in possession of the power of castration), the possibility of homoerotic links between men comes into play. As Rambo and Trautman are exchanging power in these scenes, passing through each other's identities (Trautman held at gunpoint in the helicopter is Rambo at the end of *First Blood;* Rambo, knowing that Trautman has either betrayed him or been made helpless to assist him, must "save" himself, must become his own mentor/father; etc.), they must guard this exchange and restructuring of masculine power from recognition of the homoerotic. Co's presence serves this purpose; when the exchange is released, she must be eliminated.

Co must die in this film because her death mediates between Trautman's failure as a father and Rambo's resuscitation of Trautman's power and his own elevation as masculine strength. When Trautman is prevented from rescuing Rambo by Murdock's bureaucracy, it is Co who saves him. Her entrance into the camp as a disguised prostitute underscores her position as feminine, making Trautman's helplessness all the more demeaning. It is thus not accidental that Co's death would be linked so intimately to the final negation of Trautman's power by Murdock. It is as if, abandoned by the father, she has taken his place while Rambo is in the camp, i.e. taken over the power of the father in rescuing the son. In order for Rambo to revive his own masculinity as well as that of Trautman, Co, as reminder of that substitution, must be eliminated in order for the bond between father and son to be reaffirmed and restructured, to be reintroduced into a world outside the imagery of failure and loss associated with the POW camp. This is the strongest anxiety that the ensuing combat sequence must dispel—that a woman could take the place of the father in rescuing the son from his tormentors.

After the combat scene, when Rambo has defeated the Russians and the Vietnamese, Rambo announces over a helicopter radio that he is returning with POWs. As the men in the receiving room begin to cheer, they halt and look questioningly at Murdock, waiting for his response. When Murdock leaves the room in silence (supposedly from Rambo's threat to come back and "get" him), Trautman takes over, saying "You heard him! Let's go!" Though again in charge and in a position superior to Murdock's, it is only through Rambo that Trautman has regained his power, to the point that his "orders" are only references to Rambo's own orders to prepare for their arrival. And when Rambo returns to the base, Trautman only follows him as he first destroys the computers, threatens Murdock, and then walks off toward Thailand. Though Trautman is still the significant figure in relation to whom we are to view Rambo, he is no longer the powerful mentor of *First Blood*, but is now a product of Rambo's own strength and activity.

The most spectacular combat sequence in *Rambo III* (a film that is almost entirely combat scenes of various kinds, a result of the father's kidnapping—the threat of his disappearance and death, and of the final and most complete exchange of power) is the culmination of this exchange of power between father and son, and the confirmation of Rambo's reconstruction as father-figure. As the film's most celebrated dialogue indicates, this paternal imagery, like Chris Taylor's, is god-like: When Zaysen hears that Rambo is coming to rescue Trautman, he asks, "Who do you think this man is? God?" and Trautman replies, "No, God would have mercy. He won't." After having rescued Trautman from his Soviet torturers and apparently evaded their pursuers, Rambo and Trautman find themselves surrounded by a large and technologically sophisticated Soviet force. When they are told to surrender, and Trautman asks Rambo what they should do, Rambo replies, "Fuck 'em," and they decide to fight. When it seems that they will be easily killed, Afghan rebels ride to their rescue on horseback, and they collectively defeat the Russian soldiers.

The triumph of Rambo and the Afghan rebels in the ensuing scenes validates the value of the personal versus the impersonal, the individual versus the corporate, and the paternal versus the bureaucratic[33] line. Rambo's valiant but hopeless desire to fight the Russian army is evidence of his commitment to the paternal and masculine characters that define him. Having gone to such lengths to rescue the father—to insure the father's "survival"—Rambo would rather die than relinquish that image. More to the point, without the figure that represents and insures that system, without that system itself, Rambo would himself be powerless, "defeated." What saves him is his own portrayal as father-figure to the Afghan soldiers, emblematically shown in the boy who is drawn to Rambo as his mentor and father-image. It is finally as if the Afghan rebels are fighting—not for political, national or religious independence from the Soviet occupation forces (there is no discussion in the film of reasons for rebellion other than to protect wives and children from Soviet torture and murder, again constructing the Afghan characters in a solely patriarchal vocabulary)—but for the possibility of confirming that a father-figure—a "savior"—continues to exist. As in *Rambo*, before this final threat to the father's power, the rebels were prepared to leave the area and seek safety elsewhere. But the threat of emasculation, here so much stronger because *both* white father-figures will be eliminated, brings the "rebels" back to the battlefield and to victory.

The Rambo sequence shows then the gradual progression and translation of power from father to son, as the son is reconstructed as father and the production of masculinity is, momentarily, assured. Clearly, there are displayed shifts in the purported values and "beliefs" of father and son, so that Rambo's apparent independence and rejection of the military institution that Trautman still participates in seems a radical change, along with Rambo's altered definition of patriotism and individual responsibility to national demands. Because the son does not replicate the father in any of these cases, significant change in power relations and definitions seems to have occurred. But such issues function only to distract our attention from the repetition, not of the father himself, but of the father's position and significance as stabilizer for social meaning. Such repetition serves to maintain the structural features of subject construction in patriarchy while altering its specific characteristics.

The elaborate and distracting displays of combat sequences help to suggest that actual change has occurred, as we visualize the literal destruction of the very landscape of previous meaning production and must, as we are visually instructed to do, "start over again." It is here that we recognize the spectatorial value of overhead shots like that at the end of *Platoon*, which function to convince us of the destruction of the "old order" and the apparent start of a "new." And while the spectacular display of combat scenes may yield a kind of exhilaration and euphoria of power not linked to a subject position and available for assumption by the spectator, we are clearly instructed as to the consequences of such exhilaration—death and destruction. As *Platoon* shows most emphatically, by the end of a lengthy combat scene, we are, designedly, exhausted by uncontrolled displays of power and are positioned to *desire* a return to order, a reinstallation of ourselves as stable subjects in relation to a stabilized subject order. This may then be *the* key function of the combat sequence in narrative: to encourage our desire for a return of the father and the stable order he represents.

The importance of films like *Platoon* and the Rambo narratives is then that they provide an arena within which it appears that *only* the father/son dynamic determines meaning and that masculinity is the only arena for the definition and recognition of the subject. The only relevant question of these and films like them is not *if* the father/son dynamic is significant, but of *how* it will be played out. In such terms, the masculine subject is presented as moving only between these two poles, being either father or son, but not daring to be neither (this position is relegated to the feminine in all of these films). The cultural function of these narratives is to display at large the tensions surrounding masculine subjectivity and to resolve them through the depiction of active and powerful father figures.

Combat sequences thus function in this project in two ways: First, to relieve tensions aroused by the filmic narration or brought to the film by the audience about the stability, place, and power of the masculine subject. Second, to provide a means by which the masculine subjectivities portrayed in the film can change, shift emphasis, and exchange roles without having to reveal those roles as themselves suspect or in peril. To portray a masculine subject in transition would suggest that this subject is neither stable nor sufficient; combat scenes distract us from seeing these exchanges occur. The increasingly spectacular nature of these scenes in contemporary film is evidence of how risky such sights would be as well as of how unstable that subjectivity is felt to have become.

Combat sequences reveal that the structural excess of contemporary American culture is the construction of the masculine subject within the frame of the father/son dynamic. The comments made here about combat sequences can be applied to various aspects of contemporary American culture, in fact, to the structure of that culture itself. The recent resurgence of the popularity of action films is only one indication of how this structure is being enacted. Films like *Lethal Weapon*, *The Big Easy*, *Road Warrior* and *Mad Max*, *Star Wars*, and *The Empire Strikes Back*, and many others show how scenes of violence are resolved by the stabilization of a father-figure at the end of the film. Much of the popularity of the issue of "male-bashing" (discussed in such forums as "The Oprah Winfrey Show," "Donahue," "Geraldo," and the television special "Of Macho and Men") stems, I suspect, not only from a backlash to feminism, but from an anxiety that too much criticism and alteration of masculine roles may lead, not to a replacement of the father with a "new" man, but with the disappearance of the father and the stable subject positions he designates altogether (in such ways, the father/son dynamic dovetails with terrorism). And certainly political fears about having a woman or a black man as vice-president are linked to this logic.

The question that must be asked is this: Is the apparent resurgence of cultural violence, both on film and in social relations, an indication that the father/son dynamic has suffered from challenges to its sufficiency and needs to be reaffirmed, or simply that it is, as is said of the Death Star in *The Empire Strikes Back* (the ultimate emblem of phallic destructive power), "fully operational"? Though a detailed answer to this question would require more space than I can take here, and obviously neither of these situations would be absolutely applicable at any single moment, let me suggest a general rule for reading the historical stability of the father/son dynamic and the patriarchal structure it enacts: that during periods in which the father/son dynamic and its confirmation and definition of the masculine subject are being challenged and altered, dominant representations focus on narrations of the son; during periods when those challenges have been addressed and constructions of the masculine subject have been restabilized in relation to those challenges, dominant representations offer the narration of the father. For example, during the 1970s, a period when constructions of masculinity were being challenged and reshaped, films focused on sons rather than fathers: *Easy Rider*, *Butch Cassidy and the Sundance Kid*, *Midnight Cowboy*, *The Graduate*, etc. Though shown primarily battling and being defeated by insurmountable external and indifferent social forces (the Father)—the military, corporations—these sons were shown to be rejecting positions as fathers, sharing and altering power relations rather than confirming them. Neither necessarily more "progressive" nor "subversive" than films of the 1980s, these narratives indicate how the father/son dynamic is able to respond to local historical conditions while maintaining its determination of the structure of social relations and, at the same time, reformulating those structures to adapt to different social circumstances.

Finally, it is excess that enables alterations in the construction of the masculine subject in particular historical settings. What this suggests, to return to Thompson's argument, is that excess is *both* the moment at which the narrative structure, the "unifying system," can be read *and* the point at which that structure alters itself. This is the problem presented by Thompson's insistence on reading excess within individual films; by expanding the concept to see its function *between* films, as in the Rambo series, we can recognize that the excess of one narrative provides material for a subsequent narratives's renegotiation of gender relations. What is overdetermined as "style" in one setting can be incorporated as coherent "character" in another. The "son" of one film is adopted as "father" in the next. Thus, while the concept of excess enables us to read individual narrative arrangements, it enables us to see as well how cultural narratives are negotiated, reformulated, and "adopted."

As so often, I would like to thank Robyn Wiegman for a helpful reading of an early draft of this essay.

NOTES

1. I choose to describe these relations through "positions" rather than depictions or imagery to emphasize that the same character can, and in many cases does, occupy both positions during a single narrative, moving from son to father or vice versa.

2. Jeanine Basinger, *The World War II Combat Film: Anatomy of a Genre* (New York: Columbia University Press, 1986), xi.

3. Richard Corliss, "Platoon: Viet Nam, The Way it Really Was, On Film," *Time* 129.4 (January 26, 1987):59.

4. Kristen Thompson, "The Concept of Cinematic Excess," in *Narrative, Apparatus, Ideology: A Film Theory Reader.* ed. Philip Rosen. (New York: Columbia University Press, 1986), 130.

5. *The Remasculinization of America: Gender and Representations of the Vietnam War* (Bloomington: Indiana University Press, 1989).

6. Susan Brownmiller, *Femininity* (New York: Fawcett Columbine, 1984), 15.

7. Anthony Easthope defines succinctly how realism functions in cultural representations: "Realism aims to naturalise ideology. That is, it seeks to change the effect and force of constructed meanings so that they do not appear constructed but rather as obvious, inevitable and part of how things really are" ("Realism and Its Subversion: Hollywood and Vietnam," in *Tell Me Lies About Vietnam: Cultural Battles for the Meaning of the War,* eds. Alf Louvre and Jeffrey Walsh (Milton Keynes, England: Open University Press, 1988).

8. Anthony Easthope, *What a Man's Gotta Do: The Masculine Myth in Popular Culture* (London: Paladin, 1986), 7.

9. Paul Smith, *Discerning the Subject* (Minneapolis: University of Minnesota Press, 1988), xxxi.

10. Gender and the patriarchal system are not to be seen as equivalent or interchangeable. Gender relations are one of the primary ways in which patriarchal structures are enacted, but they are not the only way. Delineations of other forms of difference—particularly race, class, age and sexuality—are historically varied and foregrounded in relation to gender as mechanisms for the specification of patriarchies.

11. Thompson, 140.

12. Where masculinity was previously assumed to be equivalent to the universal, it is now marked as equivalent to the "anonymous," a strategy that is designed to take away an aura of privilege from the masculine position by rephrasing it as non-position.

13. In spite of the increasing numbers of women in the American military, all services still adhere to the rule that women are to be excluded from combat situations (though many women medical veterans of the Vietnam War point out the hypocrisy of this position, as women were frequently exposed to shellings, mortar barrages, and direct attacks while working in field hospitals).

14. Because "cherry" is a gendered term derived from female sexuality, it might seem that I am undermining my own argument here. At this point in time, Taylor, as occupying

the position of the son, is, in relation to the father (who is fully masculine), affiliated by difference with the non-masculine, i.e., the feminine, and therefore can be likened to the female body. Significantly, such likening applies only to a part of that body that can "change" and "disappear," the hymen, suggesting that the son's potential ascendancy to the position of the father via "experience" will enable him to leave any and all affiliations with the female body and the feminine. As Jacques Derrida has shown (*Spurs: Neitzche's Styles*, trans. Barbara Harlow [Chicago: University of Chicago Press, 1979]1), this is not the case, and the hymen will leave its "trace," posing another site for resistance.

15.   Oliver Stone, *Platoon* (New York: Vintage, 1987), 82.

16.   Stanley Kubrick's *Full Metal Jacket* (1987) is even more explicit about this threat of racial comparison of the male penis. As the other squad members look on, a Vietnamese prostitute who had first said she would not have sex with Eightball because he was "too beaucoup" changes her mind when he actually shows her his penis. Through a non-white woman's eyes, the black man's penis can be seen and judged as like that of the white man. For a discussion of white male anxieties about the black penis see Trudier Harris' *Exorcising Blackness: Historical and Literary Lynching and Burning Rituals* (Bloomington: Indiana University Press, 1984).

17.   For a fuller discussion of race and gender in American culture, see Robyn Wiegman's *Negotiating the Masculine: Configurations of Race and Gender in American Culture* (doctoral dissertation, University of Washington, 1988).

18.   *Platoon* has been charged with racism by numerous critics. Acel Moore says, for example that "the black characters in the film are all peripheral. All the main characters are white" ("Vietnam Film Deserves Another 'Award': For Racism," *Seattle Times*, February 18, 1987: A8). It is what Richard Corliss calls a "passive racism. The black soldiers are occasionally patronized and sentimentalized; they stand to the side while the white soldiers grab all the big emotions" (58). Clyde Taylor identifies it most concisely when he asks, "What kind of rupture would have been made if Charlie had been cast as black. . . ?" and answers, "[I]f Charlie were black, his blowing away of Barnes would burst the repressive limits of colonialist myth-making. . . . [W]hen a black infantryman in A Soldier's Story kills a black sergeant as fascist as Barnes, the film's text condemns him" ("The Colonialist Subtext in Platoon," *Cineaste* 15.4:9).

19.   Taylor, 9.

20.   In Donald Pfarrer's *Neverlight* Katherine Vail tells her husband, Richard, whose platoon was ambushed in Vietnam, "I have never been ambushed, thank god, and you, thank god, have never had a miscarriage at five months" (New York: Laurel, 1982:74). The Sustained linkage in Vietnam representation between combat actions and reproduction makes a reading of ambush as castration all the more feasible: the loss of a foetus for the female is, in this logic, the equivalent of castration for the male. In such ways the female subject is presumed to be constructed in similar manners and terms as the male.

21.   Corliss, 55.

22.   Stone, 109.

23.   As Judith Hicks Stiehm insightfully reminds us, the "only unique role men have had in society is a social one—that of warrior—a role that is risky, unpleasant, and often short in duration. During peacetime modern men lack a specific way of proving that they are men" (*Bring Me Men and Women: Mandated Change at the U.S. Air Force Academy* [Berkeley: University of California Press, 1981], 296).

24.   Richard Corliss makes explicit the racism of this thinking in Platoon: "The nearly 1 million Vietnamese casualties are deemed trivial compared with America's loss of innocence, of allies, of geopolitical race. And the tragedy of Viet Nam is seen as this: not that they died, but that we debased ourselves by killing them" (58).

25.   Stone, 129.

26. If we think, for example, of earlier English and American novels that narrate the son's development—*Tom Jones, Humphrey Clinker, For Whom the Bell Tolls, Catcher in the Rye*—none shows this multiple depiction of fathers nor the full ascendence of the son to the father's role through an integration and adoption of the paternal position. It is at this juncture that class issues would become most relevant to arguments about the constructions of masculinity.

27. Though there is not a space to discuss this here, it is in such positionings of sons taking the positions of several fathers that we can see the link between patriarchy and capitalism, as the imagery of multiple fathers combining to form a single more unified and powerful figure ties in with contemporary corporate structures and multinational corporations.

28. James G. Frazer's *The Golden Bough* (New York: Macmillan, 1984) explains the ways in which "primitive" societies sustained the myths of an immortal masculinity through killing kings who showed any signs of weakness, wounds, or aging, so that their kings would have the illusion of perpetual youth, strength, and virility (265–274). Though space does not permit, it is easy to see how such needs are met in contemporary culture through the "immortality" of the filmic image on the one hand and the invulnerability of the characters within the film on the other. Rambo is the most obvious case in point.

29. Though many have discussed the effects of the soldier's return on women's position in American and British society, Peter G. Filene in particular discusses these effects on the construction off a masculine character in *Him/Her/Self: Sex Roles in Modern America* (Baltimore: Johns Hopkins University Press, 2nd ed., 1986).

30. Though Jeanine Basinger suggests that combat films are adapted to address different interests during non-combat periods, in particular the maintenance of military readiness (107), and the revisionary treatment of previous wars (99), her dependent definition of the combat film as generated by World War II prevents recognition of the extent to which these films are merely part of an overall argument to negotiate and reproduce masculine imagery in patriarchal interests.

31. For a fuller discussion of those presentations of fathering and fathers in Vietnam representation, see my "Reproducing Fathers: Gender and the Vietnam War in American Culture" (in *The Cultural Legacy of Vietnam: Uses of the Past in the Present*, ed. Peter Ehrenhaus and Richard Morris [1990]).

32. Robin Wood identifies what he calls the "male duo" film, such as *Butch Cassidy and the Sundance Kid, Easy Rider*, and *Thunderbolt and Lightfoot*, of the 70s, explaining their appearance as "a response to certain social developments centered on the emancipation of women and the resultant undermining of the home," in which the films' "implicit attitude is 'You see, we can get along pretty well without you'" (*Hollywood From Vietnam to Reagan* [New York: Columbia University Press, 1986], 24). Such examples show the historical shift that has taken place from the 70s to the 80s in relation to alterations in gender positions. Whereas the characters in these films are invariably "pals," with both sharing flaws and heroic qualities, the father/son films of the 80s are much more oriented toward discrepant relations between men; where "buddy" films relate exchanges of power between these men and the society they oppose, inevitably in such a way that the society, however malevolently displayed, retains power through the elimination of the duo, the father/son films show how that exchange has been internalized so that power is exactly a relation between men and not between marginalized men and society-at-large. Though power relations may be briefly destabilized in 80s films, it is always clear in what terms those relations are to be restabilizied, i.e. only within the terms of masculine relations.

33. In "The New Vietnam Films: Is the Movie Over" (*Journal of Popular Film and Television* 13.4 [1986]: 186–95), I describe how the U.S. government is depicted in recent Vietnam representation as "feminine," not only being represented by women, but being

as well weak, interested in negotiation rather than action, indecisive, and passive. In similar ways, the bureaucratic is opposed to the paternal as an almost maternal organization: Rambo must cut himself free from the technological equipment that threatens to kill him as he dangles from the plane that is to drop him in Vietnam in *Rambo*, a clear metaphor of severing an umbilical cord that attempts to kill its foetus. That Rambo cuts his own "cord" is significant of the portrayed self-sufficiency of the masculine subject in this film.

VAS

"It is not going to be easy to write about masculinity," says Anthony Easthope near the beginning of his book about what he calls the "myth" of male sexuality in popular culture.[1] It might well be difficult. On the other hand, it might prove all too easy, in approaching the topic of male sexuality, to think to have adequately located it in its manifestations in the popular culture—and then automatically condemn it. All too easy, as well, to read it almost unmediatedly through the paradigms of a psychoanalysis which has chronically revolved around and devolved onto the central metaphor of the phallus—and then predictably have to disown masculine sexuality as "phallocentric." All too easy to guiltily take to heart the often repeated femininist charge that men have yet to speak about their sexuality—and then give forth a few heartfelt mea culpas.

In fact (or as experienced, rather), male sexuality is both difficult and deadly easy. One of the assumptions underpinning this essay will be that male sexuality is overt and obvious; it is not something hidden nor anything mysteriously authentic residing beneath its cultural forms and representations—it *is* spoken in and through those forms and representations. One must assume that it exists quite fully in the everyday and needs to be dealt with as such. There seems to me, in other words, to be no particular call to think of masculinity primarily as a cultural "myth," as Easthope does, and in any case not as a myth which can be exhaustively explained by reference to the further myth of the phallus as it resides in most forms of psychoanalytical interpretation.

This essay will try, not to displace that metaphorical mechanism of the phallus, but to provisionally work alongside it in order to try to explore—heuristically at least—another idea and another emphasis: the articulation of the male body and male imaginary in the construction of a preoedipal register for masculinity. That idea will at some points take up the word "vas," which in Latin means a variety of things: "vas," vessel, container, baggage, gear. "Vas" is another metaphor, to be sure, but one which will be used to address notions which are left aside by the metaphor of the phallus. "Vas" might, then, hold on to some aspects of the male imaginary and the male body which have been underplayed because of (men's) frequent emphasis on the difficulty of talking about male sexuality.

But "vas" also tries to avoid reducing male sexuality to the body itself: it does not figure or suggest any specific organ in the way the word "phallus" ultimately does. It will be used instead to describe a nexus of imaginary effects—some of which might well be somatic in origin and in connection, but all of which I take to be imaginarily "spoken" through particular cultural representations. Another assumption here, then, will be not only that male sexuality can be understood in or as its cultural manifestations, but importantly that these representations involve and are part of personal agency too insofar as they address the experience of living a male body.

Part of the aim of this article will thus be to try to talk about some of the ways in which male sexuality can be sensibly said to exist, and to speak (of) itself. Along the way I want to look at some of the critical paradigms and mechanisms which in my view have obstructed or still obstruct to some degree the discussion of male sexuality. Psychoanalysis is my main object here, but some of those paradigms will be specifically feminist ones. I'll want to enter into some kind of dialogue with them to begin to answer the feminist complaint that men haven't yet spoken about their sexuality but rather have been content to examine femininity only.

There have, of course, been other attempts to answer such a complaint and this essay will probably appear quite faltering in comparison to most of them.[2] However, one difference here will be that I want to take a particular first step that much other work does not: that is, I want to avoid—provisionally, at any rate—speaking of male sexuality as inevitably or irredeemably condemnable across all its possible forms, modes, and representations. On one level, that will certainly entail an implicit resistance to some feminist assertions, such as the claim that all male penetration of female bodies is tantamount to rape, or that there is a direct analogue to be made between pornographic and other patriarchal representations. But more important to me, the engagement with feminist thinking in this essay searches ultimately for possibilities of collaboration and alliance. That is, it might be useful to approach masculine sexuality in terms which owe at least something to the way in which feminism has attempted to understand feminine sexuality. This is not to say that I want to render masculine sexuality as identical to feminine sexuality. Nor do I wish simply to repeat the truism that sexuality is ultimately a matter of bisexuality—although that notion will certainly be implicit. Rather, one emphasis will be on the fact that feminism has offered ways of understanding sexuality itself and that these have not yet been usefully applied to masculine sexuality.

Of course, it might also be all too easy for men to turn to feminism to find some kind of self-righteous comfort. Judith Mayne has carefully addressed this issue in her contribution to the anthology, *Men in Feminism*. Her article there ends with a particular kind of call: "the intersection between feminism and male desire needs to be thought and rethought by submitting theory to the test of narrative."[3] That is, the injunction I extrapolate from her article is that theory needs to evolve from an understanding not just of theory itself but also of the lived experience of desire and sexuality.

For men, in that experience, there is still a kind of ache that has everything to do with men's imaginary, the baggage that we carry around. But we men can perhaps now, partly as a result of what feminism has taught us and demanded of us, at least examine that baggage. This is not to construe femininity and/or feminism as a kind of gigantic phallic mother; and certainly not to expect that feminism can provide some sort of absolution; and probably not to expect that the ache will go away just yet. But rather more simply to propose a job to be done: our work on our experience of sexuality could help, cooperate with, and even form alliances with feminism as we try to find out the reality of our sexuality in the way that feminists have tried to find out the reality of theirs.

ACHE

As a sufferer myself from classic migraines that sometimes give me two or three days of quite amazing pain, preceded by many hours of hallucination and nausea, I've always admired Freud when he managed to turn his migraine symptoms to some account. One particular onset of migraine that he records is described as something akin to a mystical experience, or an almost literal flash of genius:[4]

> I was suffering from that degree of pain which brings about the optimum condition for my mental activities[.] The barriers suddenly lifted, the veils dropped, and everything became transparent—from the details of the neuroses to the determinants of consciousness. (146)

This is late in 1895 in a letter to Wilhelm Fliess, and is one of many references in that correspondence to Freud's migraines. Indeed, migraines are actually part of the network of symptoms which Freud uses, with himself as subject, to formulate what can feasibly be considered the very beginnings, the ur-insights, of psychoanalytical theory.

By 1893 Freud was for all intents and purposes certain about the sexual etiology of neuroses, and simultaneously was toying with the idea that society's conventional ways of dealing with sexual desire meant that "society [was] doomed to fall victim to incurable neuroses, which reduce the enjoyment of life to a minimum, destroy marital relations, and bring hereditary ruin on the whole coming generation" (44). Freud here seems quite anxious about the fate of his male patients—especially those for whom the familiar nineteenth-century problem with the control of sexuality caused, in his view, serious neuroses. Masturbation, coitus interruptus, problems and worries about contraception, and the ever-present danger of venereal disease all enter Freud's discourse as the factors of various debilitating neuroses in his male patients.

Much of Freud's thinking on these matters is predicated upon what might be called a "substantialist" theory of sexuality wherein understanding sexuality is a matter of recognizing the economy of substances in the body and in the brain. Symptoms and illnesses are, for him at this point, often signs of a derangement in such economies, and the migraine is a particularly important symptom of this sort. Freud's 1895 paper on migraines talks in general of the neuronic buildup and release or "discharge in tonic tension," and specifically notes both the "complicated etiology" of migraine and its "frequency in people with disturbed sexual discharge (neurasthenia, coitus interruptus)" (142–143).

The link between the body's economy and the sexual etiology of migraine as a symptom is made explicit at various points, but perhaps nowhere with such determination as in another letter to Fliess (Jan 1st, 1896) where it is given the full weight of a nineteenth-century scientific account of the phenomenology of migraine, and where the "paths" for all the "neuronal motion" which is supposedly characteristic of migraine are described as being "also, of course, the paths for sexual energy" (159). At this point then—while his investigations of hysteria are proceeding apace—one of Freud's abiding concerns is with what he had come to see as a preeminent symptom of male (and one is led to infer, his own) sexual disturbances. His preferred mode of explanation relies upon the idea of a kind of substantialist economy in the body and brain.

Freud's own migraines are marked throughout the years of the Fliess letters by very particular epiphenomena, both somatic and psychical: suppurations and secretions from the left side of his nose, "the most touching substitute relationship between my migraine and my cardiac symptoms and the like" (316), "attacks of fears of dying" (181), fears of his own homosexuality (295), and so on. These are all part and parcel of, or they all contribute to, Freud's thinking about sexuality and the origins of the neuroses.

However, the further his parallel investigations of hysteria and dreams go, the more inclined Freud becomes to allow the puzzle of the migraine headache to begin to give way to a puzzle of what is by now for us a more familiar kind: the puzzle of the feminine symptom and of the female sexuality in general—a problem which "throughout history people have knocked their heads against," of course.[5] The descriptions of Freud's own headaches begin to take on a tellingly different cast: they become "gorgeous" (382), or "splendid" (400), or might be followed by moods that are "downright merry" (386). Remarkably, a migraine which Freud suffered in June 1899 coincides with his daughter Mathilde's making "her entry into womanhood. . . . I had a migraine from which I thought I would die" (357). And by the time of Freud's last letters to Fliess, the transformation is complete: migraines have become simply synonomous with "hysterical headaches" in women patients.

One particular instance of what might well amount to a process of projection is particularly significant, when Freud proposes to Fliess that

> hysterical headaches rest upon an analogy in fantasy which equates the top with the bottom parts of the body (hair in both places—cheeks [*Backen*] and buttocks [*Hinterbacken*]—lips [*Lippen*] and labia [*Schamlippen*]—mouth = vagina), so that an attack of migraine can be used to represent a forcible defloration, and yet the entire ailment once again represents a situation of wish-fulfillment. The necessary conditions of the sexual become clearer and clearer. (340)

Apart from now no longer being Freud's own symptom, the headache here is also no longer to be explained by reference to somatic tensions, quantities, neuronal activity, and so on. Instead it has become the matter of fantasy. Not irrelevantly of course, it is now also being described through the psychoanalytical modes, procedures, and vocabulary that mark the mature Freud: word-association, considerations of representability, and wish-fulfillment.

Perhaps it would be possible to consider the shift that the above passage represents—away from Freud's general "scientific" and social worries about male symptoms, male neuroses, and male hypochondria, towards the condition of femininity and towards the fuller expression of what will become Freudian meta-psychology—as in some ways a loss. That isn't to suggest that the earlier Freud-ian method is in any sense preferable, but rather to surmise that in the shift from male to female object of investigation something apparently irredeemable oc-curs. Perhaps what psychoanalysis comes to repress is masculinity, or rather a particular experience of masculinity which is uncomfortably close to hysteria.

Freud's dropping the investigation of migraine headaches with himself as pri-mary subject can be catachretically suggestive about the beginnings of psycho-analysis. Of course, the actual reasons for this turn can be matter for speculation merely—especially if one wishes to avoid the rather academic occupation of psy-choanalyzing Freud through his texts, biographies and letters. However, two possibilities present themselves. First, for Freud the prospect of isolating the sexual origins of psychic and somatic symptoms in a male body might have been too radically upsetting, something too threatening to the patriarchal male ego which, we are told so often, Freud epitomized.

A second (neither more nor less likely) interpretation could take account of another possibly relevant phenomenon: that is, Freud's own well-documented sense of powerlessness and alienation in the scientific and academic fields. Freud's anxieties about his place and that of his work (for which the locus classi-cus might, I think, be the botanical monograph dream) are rampant across the pages of the Fliess correspondence and in Freud's own dream interpretations. In the light of that anxiety, Freud's sensation of not having full access to the power of his discipline could have enforced a decision about sexuality itself and the as-signation of gender. Perhaps Freud is not really a man (that is, not already in the preconstituted patriarchal male position). As a Jew, and a worried one at that, and so already associated by popular theories of the time with womanliness and thus with sexuality itself, Freud perhaps threw himself and his energy across the bodies and psyches of those proper bearers of sexuality—women. As male sub-ject he is not at all clear that real power does not reside in the other, or that it cannot be attained by taking advantage of the conflation woman/Jew/sexuality.

This reading would lead to a reconsideration of Michèle Montrelay's and other feminists' suggestion that psychoanalysis was invented to repress femininity. Rather, we might take seriously Freud's knocking his head against the puzzle of femininity as a displacement, or even a *hystericization*, of the problem of his own sexuality and power. Importantly, this is a gesture that pre-assumes that gender assignations are not pre-fixed. This is not to say that all critiques of Freud's later monosexual libido theory aren't correct, but to suggest that the origin—this par-ticular origin—of psychoanalysis might be less a way of repressing femininity than actually deploying it for his own benefit. Another way of saying this is that Freud *identifies* here with femininity. Identification, for all of its aggressive con-notations, bespeaks a desire for access to the power of the other. Thus it can be suggested that here Freud makes a strange (very likely colonizing) alliance with femininity. In that sense, for Freud the replacement of the migraine's ache by the headache of the puzzle of femininity constitutes a flight from a particular condition of masculinity.

Roland Barthes, another man very interested in presenting himself as mar-ginalized, interprets his migraine headaches as a "psychosomatic sign of man's

mortal malady: *the failure of symbolization.*" [6] It is perhaps in that particular identification with femininity that the ache of the migraine becomes most intolerable.
The bodily secretions and suppurations of Freud's own migraine might not so
much bespeak some kind of castration anxiety, but rather subsist as exactly real
substances that escape sexual repression and therefore speak directly of the malady of sexuality itself. Thus the turn away from masculinity and towards an identification with the marginality, the puzzle, or the ache of femininity is more than
a displacement, and more than an attempted alliance with femininity: here psychoanalysis has begun what will become its twentieth-century role of creating
the theoretical and practical conditions under which it will be not easy to talk of
male sexuality anymore. This fundamental symptom of exchanging one ache for
another has led psychoanalysis to a particular contradiction: it is, as Alice Jardine
points out, a knowledge based on women's bodies but with a male subject as its
norm; and "this gap," says Jardine, is "itself hysterical." [7]

VAS(A)

The Latin dictionary that was school issue for me as a teenager (a third edition of
Sir William Smith's 1855 work) is a precious archival artefact for me now. One of
the words that is underlined—I don't recall whether by me or someone else,
though I remember particularly seeing the word in Cicero and being fascinated
by it—is "*vas*, vasis (*vasum*, NOM sing.; Pl., and pl. regularly, *vasa*, orum)." In
the singular "vas" is a vessel, a utensil, or a container of any kind. In the plural,
"vasa" means packs, baggage, gear and equipment of various sorts (but especially military). One of the reasons it was an interesting word, no doubt, was its
connotation of the "vas deferens" of the male sexual gear, and the—I suppose—
castratory idea of "vasectomy."

But I was reminded of the word again quite recently while reading Michèle
Montrelay's article "L'Appareillage" (the only—so far as I know—published excerpt of her psychoanalytical seminars on male sexuality in the early 1980s), since
the various meanings of the word "vas" seem quite akin—in ways to which I'll
return—to some of Montrelay's ideas about the male sexual apparatus and the
male imaginary. [8]

It's signal that, just about a hundred years after Freud makes his turn away
from masculinity, it is a feminist who returns there by way of continuing her earlier important work on hysteria and female sexuality. Montrelay's *L'Ombre et le
nom*, [9] while dependent upon Lacan's return to Freud, can be read as its own kind
of return—not exactly to Lacan's Freud, but to the earlier Freud of *Studies in
Hysteria*—and thus to the point where Freud begins the psychoanalytic probing
of femininity. It is clear that Montrelay intends a kind of reworking of those areas
where Freud might have gone astray. In that book, and armed with a Lacanian
notion of the imaginary, she investigates Freud's writing on hysteria in order to
theorize a specifically feminine imaginary. This she adumbrates by reference
to perhaps her best known contribution to psychoanalytical feminism in the
1970s—her notion that femininity can be defined as "the ruin of representation."
(*L'Ombre . . . ,* 89)

That notion is discovered through a theorization of the respective positions of masculinity and femininity in relation to primary repression: femininity, she claims, is not dealt with by repression and therefore has specific access to the "abyss of non-meaning which is opened in every discourse and which is the real of every discourse." The propinquity of femininity to such "blind spots of the symbolic" (29) is the basis for her description of a feminine imaginary and is related to the concentric drives—those so-called "archaic" drives posited by Grunenberger, Jones and others as a way of trying to counter the phallocentrism of Freud's theories of the drives centered around the Oedipal moment.

Montrelay's project of trying to discover or define a specifically feminine imaginary has, of course, proven to be an extremely problematic one for feminism and this has been especially the case where she appears to found such an imaginary on the specificity of the female body. Thus it might well seem less than helpful to replicate those problems at this point in relation to masculinity. First of all, I'd want to argue that the exploration of the idea of a specific feminine imaginary has in fact been a crucial moment for feminism's work on sexuality; that it has produced a useful resistance to utter acceptance of the Oedipal schema of psychoanalysis; and also that it has provoked necessary reconsideration of the ways in which the body figures into psychical structuration. In relation to male sexuality, both those theoretical emphases still need to be made—not, to be sure, as the final word on masculinity, but rather as a provisional and heuristic gesture.

One of the problems with those sorts of emphases in Montrelay and other feminist writers is, of course, that they seem often to have led to forms of essentializing gender. But this is actually where I think Montrelay is of some help. It seems to me that Montrelay has often been misconstrued as an essentialist for whom all forms of psychic representation are predicated upon some crude biologism.[10] But it's important to distinguish her work on femininity from apparently similar feminist attempts to speak (of) "woman." In *L'Ombre et le nom*, femininity is described as a *function*, culturally controlled and constructed, and it is not equivalent to (or even necessarily attached to) the female body or psyche—indeed, many of her discussions of femininity take discourses by men as their explanatory object. Montrelay is thus in fact committed to the notion of sexuality as bisexuality, and furthermore as nonessential.

Montrelay's project of looking for and at the representations of a male imaginary begins with the simple recognition that repression is never perfect even for men, and with one particular consequence of that: that the male imaginary too must contain unrepressed material, material which would by definition be unsymbolizable. "L'appareillage" is the heuristic device by which she tries to recover and figure some of that material of masculinity. The word is used to evoke at least some subset of the multiple functionings of the representatives of the drives and their failure in the imaginary.

She unpacks the word into four significations. First, *appareillage* contains the word *appareil:* "appearance," or the external deployment of preparations so as to produce a pleasing appearance. In French the word *appareillage* has been extended from this sense to refer to various functional apparatuses or gear—"electronic equipment or gear," for instance. In a third meaning, *appareillage* designates all the operations necessary for getting a ship ready for departure. Finally, the fourth meaning refers to the actual departure of a ship from port.

"The masculine imaginary," Montrelay says, "takes account of and plays with these four meanings" in relation to the experience of sexuality: (1) the externally visible formations and deformations of the male genitalia, its appearance (and disappearance); (2) the idea and perception of the male genitalia as a set of "equipment" or "gear"—as an apparatus, in other words; (3) "appareillage" in the sense of getting ready, systematically preparing for a transportation, or a taking off of sexual pleasure; and (4) the taking off itself, the orgasmic experience of having taken off" (36–7). Montrelay concentrates mostly on the fourth meaning—the departure metaphor—and on the way in which her male analysands will speak of the "floating [*flottement*]" and the "jumping off [*saut*]" aspects of their sexual experience. While such representations might at first sight appear to be suspect biological metaphors, still part of Montrelay's point in analyzing these strands of the male imaginary is to distance psychoanalysis from a literalizing view of the body and specifically the phallus. Her unpacking of *appareillage* heuristically attempts to turn discussion of the male imaginary towards a more *dynamic* mode of operation and description. Specifically, this path leads her to take more seriously than any analyst on male sexuality—except Wilhelm Reich, of course—the importance and crucial place of ejaculation in the male imaginary. Ejaculation is thought of here as a structure of sensation, or as something more akin to an ontological than a biological event:

> Endlessly, throughout his whole life, the male subject affirms the fact that he is losing, that he is giving up his sperm, this seed that's not just any old thing. . . . (38)

The loss that Montrelay locates here, and which she assumes produces a certain kind of anxiety in the male sexual subject, relates to much of her previous work on the drives and specifically to what she has called the "projectiles of the drive." In *L'Ombre et le nom*, she had examined Lacan's theory of the *objet petit a*, the phallic fantasy that is supposed to represent the drives' relatively seamless return to the body. *L'Ombre et le nom* posits for female sexuality a kind of supplement to the *objet petit a* in the form of "projectiles of the drive" which mark the "lack of castration" and the escape from primary repression which characterize femininity. In this earlier work, these "projectiles" help explain sexual difference itself, in that for male analysands they seemed susceptible to the standard processes of repression; but for women, Montrelay claimed, the same processes of repression do not operate and those escapees of the drive remain unsymbolizable—thence the notion of femininity as the ruin of representation. In the later work on male sexuality, she examines the incidence of these "projectiles" in the discourses of her male analysands and posits the idea that there too they are not completely repressed and thus must form part of the structuring material of the psyche.

It is important to recognize that she is dealing here with an area of masculinity which, if it has escaped repression, would therefore properly be unspeakable and unfixable. Its unfixed or vascillating character might well help explain why the usual figure through which she glimpses its symptomatic matter is something detachable, movable—the male imaginary figures a departure, a leaving, a floating in the air. This "departure" Montrelay links to the experience and sensation of ejaculation ("another launch or take off" as she describes it). She thus understands the male imaginary as having in part "the function of deploying and mark-ing out a possible space to prevent ejaculation from leading to a destruction of the subject" (38) through flight or evanescence, thus preventing the subject's having to confront the abyss of the Other or of non-meaning (to adopt Lacan's vocabulary).

Whatever the virtues and powers of Montrelay's notions here as she attempts to produce a dynamic notion of male sexuality loosed from unmediated readings of the phallic, her theory nonetheless eventually defers to the metaphor of the phallus as its central and driving mechanism—returns, therefore, to insist on the repressed and defensive function of the male imaginary. The loss that she claims the *appareillage* bespeaks is, of course, a loss of subjectivity in relation to the phallus. It's almost as if, for Montrelay, the ejaculatory sensation of departure is simply a moment or a point of vulnerability in a male subjectivity which is other-wise firmly constructed in its relation to the Oedipal moment. In other words, the *appareillage* ultimately has no structuring effect in and of itself. There is something of a contradiction here since the very presence of the unsymbolizable material which she stresses—the marks of a psychic time where castration has not yet happened—would seem to suggest an area outside of that paradigm. But it's here that the notion of "vas" might be of help. While Montrelay's schema is absolutely obliged to offer the figure of the phallus as the sovereign instance in the interplay between such defense and threat, it might be just as useful at this point, not quite to do away with, but to provisionally ignore that particular psy-choanalytical ogre, and move towards a less defensive model. The evanescent effect that the *appareillage* trope points to might be considered less as an aberrant or irrational moment of male sexuality and its defence, but more as something profoundly *constructive*.

I'm not proposing here simply the kind of shift in thinking about the phallus that Moustafa Safouan suggests.[11] Safouan has recommended what he calls a "relativization of the Oedipus"—and thus of its central term, the phallus—on the grounds that that figure is only one possible variation of representations of castration anxiety: other cultures and other times might well produce other analogous representations, he says. All or any of these, however, would still serve to promote the function of castration in the psyche. The important point for Safouan is that there must always be such a finality—a ruling third term to the dialectic of self and Other. I'm not wishing to dispute that necessarily, but just want to shift attention from it and to add another term which would reside in the male imaginary not as so fundamental a figure of defense, but perhaps equally as a registration of the lived reality of male sexuality.

Vas marks the flexible and movable container where accumulations of imagi-nary "substance" are built up and from which they can be lost. But the loss here is not that of a bodily part, or of an organ: the phallus and castration are not the primary referents. Rather, vas both points to the imaginary schema of a drive (where any drive is itself always understood as a representation), and also acts as a further, specific representation in the imaginary of the experience of living in a male body.

Understood in these terms, vas might be taken to connote two particular pre-established psychoanalytical notions. First, it might respond to the somewhat underdeveloped psychoanalytical notion of the genital drive, and thus serve as an effort to grasp simultaneously an aspect of the male imaginary which has a direct linkage to the substantial experience of the body (rather than to the ambiguous phallus/penis). As Jacqueline Rose points out, in Lacan (and thus in some of his followers like Montrelay) the function of "the phallus and castration [is to] testify above all to the problematic nature of the subject's insertion into his or her sexual identity, to an impossibility writ large over that insertion at the point where it might be taken to coincide with the genital drive."[12] In other words, the genital drive cannot be taken to be in itself constitutive of sexuality or sexual identity as such—in part because the genital drive is perhaps all too readily conflated with a crude biologism—even though it is not so fully elaborated in Lacan, for instance, as the oral, anal, scopic and, to some extent, the invocatory drives are.

The drives are always a matter of representation, but for Lacan they also mark "the relation between the living subject and that which he loses by having to pass, for his reproduction, through the sexual cycle." Thus there is an "affinity of every drive with the zone of death. . . . the drive makes sexuality present to the unconscious and represents, in its essence, death."[13]

Here we can perhaps return to Montrelay's idea that the male imaginary holds out a space where the threat of the destruction of the subject can be warded off. If one understands, after Lacan, the death of the subject as a metaphorical way of talking about what it would mean to be unable to symbolize, then the loss of symbolization at the point where the drives return incompletely or unsuccessfully to the body becomes a crucial instance of male sexuality; and this is what Montrelay aims at with her notions of incomplete repression and the opening out of the subject's experience onto non-meaning or non-sense.

Secondly and relatedly, vas might point to something akin to the preoedipal organization of sexuality which feminist psychoanalysis—including Montrelay's work—has sometimes claimed for women in the hope of reaching a view of the specificity of female sexuality away from the phallus. While the search for that kind of specificity for female sexuality has, as I remarked above, turned out to be politically unsatisfying to many feminists, it has nonetheless constituted an important step in the theorization of sexuality and I think that it might not be unproductive to think through similar notions in relation to male sexuality. The aim here would be to extend the theory of male sexuality, rather than reduce it. Such a move in relation to male sexuality would involve not only—as it does for female sexuality also—positing a particular version of the genital drive (self-consciously taking the concomitant risk of biologism), but also deprivileging the phallic schema (with a concomitant recognition of the unsymbolizable in sexual organization for both men and women). I want to stress that such a preoedipal account for male sexuality cannot discard the phallic schema. It would, however, locate an area of concern or serve as a heuristic device to account for the peculiar nature of the genital drive and the residues it leaves of somatic experience.

The characteristic feature of the preoedipal in the male imaginary would then be its va(s)cillation. Vas: that which men carry around in the real and which at the same time contains the unsymbolizable; it represents that which we consist in *and* that which we don't symbolize; that which we both carry and lose; or, to use an older vocabulary, that which we both accumulate and spend.

One place where all this has already some resonance is in Klaus Theweleit's book, *Male Fantasies*.[14] There, analyzing the production of sexuality in the writings of the German Freikorps and the genesis of fascism in the 1920s, Theweleit proposes in effect an area of what he calls "fantasies" that is disjunct from the standard accounts of fantasy in object relations psychoanalysis. In my opinion, one of his main insights is to notice that male sexuality in these proto-fascistic writings cannot be wholly accounted for by object relations theories of the unconscious. That is, he wants to suggest that the "fantasies" of these males exist in a less mediated form than psychoanalysis allows: that is, they exist as the de facto reality of a particular lived sexuality.

In Theweleit's view male "fantasies" are not a question of men's being thereby "blinded to reality," but rather of their having access to a form of reality which exceeds the binds of object relations mediated through the third term. Indeed, throughout his book Theweleit insists on invalidating as far as possible any fantasy/real distinction within sexuality, and he thus has recourse—as I think is appropriate—to the notion of a somatic real which is directly tied to a preoedipal imaginary. In keeping with his general tendency to not elaborate overmuch on his theoretical and methodological procedures, Theweleit will not explore the terminology of the preoedipal, but prefers to think of his insight as contributing to an *anti*-Oedipal argument.[15] Nonetheless, it seems to me that his continual stress on the somatic and representational reality of male sexuality can be useful even if one does not wish to discredit the phallic schema altogether. The proposition of a somatic reality and the stress on the actually effective representations of lived sexuality are expressed in terms which recognize the vacillation of affect in the body and the imaginary: there is both anxiety and desire, but neither is subjected to the mediating effect of the Oedipus and so each remains properly unsymbolizable. Theweleit finds in his subjects a continual vacillation between anxiety about and desire for what he calls "fusion, explosion," and for a loss of the boundaries of the body. This vacillation signifies that defensive states are also sites for the production of pleasure and he specifically notes the lack of repression associated with such states. Here he is describing something, some area of sexuality in its relation to lived reality which is not, strictly speaking, unconscious in the object relations sense.

Theweleit's subjects are, of course, fascists. But I don't want by any means to suggest (as I think Theweleit has to) that this preoedipal scenario is necessarily constitutive of authoritarian and fascistic subjects only; nor, certainly, that all male sexuality is, contains, or entails this particular political signification. Another large effort of Theweleit's book is to mark the historical specificity of all forms and modes of sexuality, and this is an emphais that one can only endorse. The preoedipal should not be thought of as some fixed and timeless essence: it will inevitably take on different shapes and forms, different imaginary figuration, across history and culture. Indeed, the task of historicizing the preoedipal must take on the same importance as the task of historicizing the monolithic psychoanalytical metaphor of the phallus: the imaginary is only ever constructed through phenomenologically available matter which is variable across history, and the body itself is also variably constructed across history.

Theweleit's stress on the need to construct a somatics of male sexuality seems to me important for the following reasons.[16] Sexuality itself, as a signified, has chronically been feminized. It is construed as a quality, as an immanence, that femininity embodies. Samuel Delany thus talks of a veritable substantialist ideology of sexuality, where the woman's body contains substance, or "stuff."[17] Within this substantialist ideology masculine sexuality is perceived inversely: it has been taken only as an action—or more precisely a reaction—and is nonsubstantial, being merely an array of behavioral epiphenomena. Theweleit's work suggests that the body, or indeed a whole somatics, might need to be reintroduced into the theory of male sexuality. Or in other words, perhaps it would be useful to see what might happen if some more substantialist notion of male sexuality were pulled—heuristically and provisionally—away from the phallus.

PORN

Pornography is often understood, as much in recent feminist theory as in the juridical arena, to be in some sense a generalizable instance of masculine sexuality at work through cultural representations. That is, pornography often seems to act as the analogue from which the very structures and modes of masculinity can be read off; masculinity is at its most visible there. I want to look briefly both at that notion and also consider a specific kind of pornographic text. The texts that I'll refer to here constitute a large subsection of all texts that could possibly be understood as pornographic: that is, there would probably be little disagreement about their pornographic nature, even if one didn't want to limit the notion of the pornographic to such texts alone. These texts have become, since the so-called video revolution, probably the most readily available form of hardcore pornography in the USA: videotapes that can be easily purchased in stores or mail-ordered, seen in the peep shows of "adult bookstores," and which also tend to constitute the collections of those neighborhood video stores which offer "adult" products.

While I largely agree with the theoretical point made by Beverly Brown[18]— that explicitness is not the real issue with pornography and cannot per se be used to define the pornographic—it nonetheless remains the case that, where we live now, explicitness defines access to such texts and is a defining factor in both the legal codes which dictate availability and also the codes of self-censorship deployed by the Hollywood and TV industries. That is, even cable subscribers currently never see on their pay channels an erect penis, an open vagina, or any kind of penetration, heterosexual or homosexual, of any male or female body. Most importantly for my purposes here, they will not see what the industry calls "cum"—the sexual suppuration of the body.

For me as viewer (by predilection and circumstance confined to those mainly heterosexual texts which form the majority of the videos available in my local stores), one of the most unexpected features about these kinds of texts is that just about universally they can be read to defy or resist two prejudicial views of them: first, the assumption that they are more or less unmediated representations of male violence against women; and second, that they offer the male viewer ready identification with the male protagonists.

These videos feature both male and female bodies enjoying sex, hands, mouths, breasts, vaginas, penises actively operating to produce both male and female orgasm. One important aspect of these images—beyond the notion that they demean women, elide them, "misrepresent" them, or act out obvious anxieties around them—is that they usually try to posit some kind of equivalence and coincidence of both desire and power in men and women. Now, this is not to go so far as to say that these texts are socially progressive; nor indeed that they are not damaging (though I would suggest that any attempt to call them damaging would do well to be very specific in its reading of them). It could, of course, be said of them that their representation of women is nothing but a way either (a) of imaginarily allaying male fears about women's active sexual being; or (b) of repeating the masulinist fantasy that all women are whores. Now, neither of these elements is absent from these texts, but I'd suggest that they might also be "about" something else too.

I want to broach what that might be by looking for a moment at a particularly sophisticated and insistent feminist attack on pornography, Susanne Kappeler's *The Pornography of Representation*.[19] As the title suggests, Kappeler's book is not only an attack on specifically pornographic representations, but also an argument for regarding them as the extension of, or the model for all forms of patriarchal representation. The central argument for that position is Kappeler's insistence on the idea that the pleasure pornography offers is best considered as an instance of voyeurism—the spectator being positioned outside the image and controlling it. That objectifying and controlling positioning she takes to be an exemplary device in the service of the so-called transcendental male subject of patriarchy, and thus to be exhibited repetitiously everywhere in all other representational genres of patriarchal culture.

Kappeler's book in fact contains no analysis at all of any actual visual pornographic representation (indeed, the only real analysis in her book of a pornographic text is of some sections of D. M. Thomas's *White Hotel*). But she does address herself to a particular kind of viewing situation: the peep show of the sort that one might find in London's Soho, or on New York's 42nd Street. She argues a familiar point: that the male subject in our culture(s) is the only legitimated subject, alone authorized to have access to self-expression and to social action. And for her, viewing and self-expression are conflatable—for all intents and purposes they are identical kinds of action in the world. Thus she argues against men and other feminists who would claim that pornography is "only fantasy" and therefore not directly or "really" harmful to women. Kappeler's sense is more that these representations *are* reality:

> the place of the action-subject, the place of the hero, is the locus of identification for the viewer. Man the action-subject is identical with man the viewing subject. The ultimate symbol of this are the hundreds of thousands of men ejaculating into a bucket in their booths at the peep shows: subjectivity of viewing goes over seamlessly into agency in the world. The plot, the action between the imaginary male and the represented woman-object spills over into the structure of representation: the viewer has to imagine himself into the plot vacancy, play the hero and represent the action to himself. (58)

It's difficult for me to imagine that Kappeler has actually looked at any of the kinds of texts that I'm calling pornographic here. But more to the point, I think it's in any case far too simple to assume that the mode of reception of such texts is that of *identification*. This particular term of analysis is in general much abused, in my view; but in Kappeler's book, where all analysis of the rhetoric of the image is lacking, it is especially inappropriately used. The ways in which a "subject"—male or female—becomes "agency in the world" through and by means of representations will depend heavily on the actual nature of those representations. The formal structures of the Hollywood apparatus work very specifically for the possibility of a viewer identifying with the supposed protagonists of a "realist" filmic narrative. But porn video is emphatically not of the realist mode, and the positioning of the spectator in porn video is a problematic issue.

For instance, the use of reaction shots in this kind of video does not follow any easily discernible or conventionalized formal patterning. Male and female actors on the porn video screen are often shown in tight close-up reaction shots at what would seem to be the most arbitrary and disruptive moments in terms of identification. Also, reactions are very rarely shot from the point of view of the male protagonists in a heterosexual encounter. At the same time, the familiar structure of the fetishistic gaze of Hollywood movies is undercut in porn video, where both male and female bodies are fragmented and divided; while in the Hollywood mode the irruption of women's bodies into the diegesis stands in for the phallus, in porn video a literal representation of the phallus appears along with women's bodies. Equally, the spectator's point of view is normally subject to continual variation and movement: cameras and editing don't respect any kind of 180-degree rule—in fact, the space of the porn scenario is often a space in the round, broken down ageometrically by edited close-ups and so on. Furthermore, the use of a static camera for long periods at either close or medium shot range is standard. The viewer's "identification" is thus never with the subject of the diegesis, but is more likely a momentary identification with the static voyeuristic camera—and even that identification is rendered fundamentally unstable by the camera's variable positioning in 360 degrees and by the plethora of disruptive ("illogical" by Hollywood standards) close-ups, jump cuts, and so on. The narratives themselves usually operate with several male and female protagonists so that the major plot lines and the subplots offer identical kinds of sexual encounter and make identification with any major figure problematic. Such identification is made even more problematic by what I call the two-prick syndrome (the quite frequent depiction of one woman with two men) where the assumed male spectator's identificatory urge is divided. That identificatory urge also has the further and confusing option of identifying with the female protagonists who continually exceed the position of mere spectacle.

In short, these videos are rarely in that Hollywood realist vein which would foster the kind of identificatory position for the male viewing subject that Kappeler assumes. Beyond that, the psychoanalytical theory of identification has recently been given a particular twist by Parveen Adams's article, "Per Os(cillation)" (*Camera Obscura* 17 (May 1988): 7–29). There Adams argues the fundamental instability of identificatory positions, and tries—successfully, in my view—to untie identification from its role as the producer of particular object choices and particular gendered positionings. Dora, for instance, identifies with Frau K. *and/ or* her father. Adams's article might be taken as license not just to question particular uses of the process of identification, but even to question the processes and consequences of identification itself in more general productions. The instability of identification as she proposes it points to the possibility that all identification can be described as "hysterical identification," suggesting once again the incomplete repression of the oscillation and vacillation of preoedipal sexuality and thence, by Montrelay's logic, pointing to the necessary figuration of the projectiles of the drives, to the residue of reality in the imaginary and its discourses.

Using the kind of notions which Adams and Montrelay make available, perhaps a particular claim about these representations can be made. Pornographic images produce exactly an instability of identificatory positioning in the male spectator. One function of porn video is to produce and reproduce that instability, along with the fundamental hystericization of sexual identity that it entails. Furthermore, the orgasmic excitement (and sometimes, feasibly, the boredom) that these images produce for the male imaginary might be enhanced by a sensation akin to Roland Barthes's recognition that in photography the thing shown was once really there.[20] I think that pornographic images of the type I'm looking at here are, at least in part, read as real in that sense. They respond to and figure a male imaginary about the body, and its history and its present: they figure that unsymbolizable reality of the preoedipal through a hystericization of the present. Most importantly for the claims that I'm putting forth in this essay, these texts are not—as another feminist, Jacquelyn Zita unequivocally describes them, for instance—"seen as pure fantasy (it isn't really happening to those women)."[21] Nor are they unmediatedly "real" (as Kappeler would have it) and thus simply condemnable on moralistic grounds. On the other hand, they do figure some part of the reality of living a male body.

I want to claim further that one particular feature of these representations can be read as a symptomatic figuration of that reality. They continually replay and refigure the release, the *flottement*, the launching, that Montrelay claims is a fundamental figure in the male imaginary. In this kind of pornography, the rarest thing is for a man to have an orgasm inside a woman's body. The moment of ejaculation, that is to say, is always visible. One might want to suggest that this is in part the allaying of some kind of anxiety about orgasm—the imaginary solution to a contradiction around sexuality. But what would the contradiction be? Perhaps the one embedded in the most romantic (and indeed, most Freudian) notions of our culture: the dialectic of eros and thanatos, orgasm and evanescence. Thus one might claim that these representations, so often repeating the image of cum scattered across a woman's body, speak not to a masculinity which fears women's bodies, fears its own lack of control over those bodies, or even fears repetition of castration. Rather, they speak to a masculinity for which the hysterical desire for somatic loss, the death of the body in an efflux of bodily substance, is a paramount element in its constitutive reality. Perhaps porn video figures in some measure an overcoming, around and on the bodies of women, of the terrible finality of the male orgasm of which Wilhelm Reich spoke.

If this is indeed any part of the content of porn video, it is clearly something which is readily historicizable, arriving as it does in this particular representation with the advent of the video revolution, and pointing to a specifiable figuration of the reality of male sexual experience. In this regard, Kappeler's book does make an important emphasis that I think is helpful. One of her most insistent arguments is that all representations help construe an effective and affective reality. For her, a representation has real effects on real subjects in a real world and has, therefore, to be understood as component of "agency in the world." This is an emphasis that, to me, seems worth making, though in a perhaps slightly different way. To conflate "fantasy" and "reality" in the way that Kappeler does will actually leave no space for the mediation of agency. It's perhaps more helpful to suggest that the male viewer's imaginary mediates the relation of fantasy and reality but registers both.

That's to say that, at least in part, porn video points to a sliver of reality: these texts are, for me, "about" that reality rather than *solely* "about" the production of fantasies around women's sexuality or around male control and domination over women. I certainly don't discount those other elements and aspects of pornography—nor indeed the corollary and perhaps most crucial consideration of the means of production and control of the pornography industry in capitalism. But there is perhaps this other element: the container broken open, the baggage or gear put down, pornography affectively and effectively addressing the boundaries and limitations of the male body and extending and complicating the peremptory simplicity of male sexual experience.

LONDON

One of my recurrent memories of London (as an Englishman in America, I suffer from such memories frequently) is of sitting in the railway station bar at Charing Cross, talking to a lover, saying goodbye to her; and then, after our separation, being overcome by an exceptionally sudden and vicious set of migraine hallucinations. In the ensuing headache my only clear thought was the recollection that Charing Cross had been erected to commemorate the last stop of the funeral cortège of Edward I's queen, Eleanor ("Charing" supposedly being a corruption of the words *chère reine*). That information might have come (though it didn't, in fact) from Freud. At Clark University in 1909 Freud gave the talks that are now called "Five Lectures on Psycho Analysis." [22] There, as part of his explanation of hysteria, he asks his audience to take an imaginary trip to a couple of the sights of London—Charing Cross and the monument. He reminds them that Charing Cross marks the passage of Queen Eleanor's dead body in the thirteenth century; and that the Monument marks the destruction of London by fire in 1666. Freud asks his audience,

> what should we think of a Londoner who sheds tears before the Monument that commemorates the reduction of his beloved metropolis to ashes although it has long since risen again in far greater brilliance? (17)

What, it turns out, we should think of such a Londoner is that he (Freud uses the masculine pronoun) is hysterical because he clings unreasonably to traumatic moments of a past long gone. "Abnormal attachment to the past is very clear" in hysterics.

The place of cathexis to the past—to history itself, and also to one's psychic past—is a problematic one in psychoanalysis. In this first Clark University lecture Freud himself seems to condemn such an attachment: the male hysteric he describes in his parable has "abnormal" attachments and he attends to these instead of "going about his business . . . or instead of feeling joy over the youthful queen of his own heart;" he "neglect[s] what is real and immediate." Psychoanalysis here takes the hysterical man, caught up in the present reminders of his traumatic past, as a patient and as paradigmatically neurotic. The melancholy Londoner has become the epitome of what Freud's invention of psychoanalysis allows Freud himself to repress.

The hysteric in Freud's little illustrative story is overtly a male—even though the case study that goes along with the story is, predictably enough, that of a female patient. This is nicely symptomatic of the constitutive *décalage* in psychoanalysis between male subject and female body that I mentioned before. But more than that, it is also a simple reminder that, theoretically or in the abstract, psychoanalysis can quite easily assume that hysteria belongs as much with the male body as the female body. However, the assumption is scarcely ever operative since to be a male hysteric is to have reneged upon responsibilities in the world, to have abandoned to some degree the here and now—or, in short, to have failed to live up to the demands of the Oedipalized world. And this is not what "men" are assumed to do. The Oedipus divides those of us who are assumed to obey—and to be able to obey—the law from those who are assumed to be unable. In this sense the Oedipus entails the demand that men forget a past in favor of access to the law.

I've been suggesting so far in this essay that one aspect of that past of masculinity is preoedipal. That past is repressed, but never completely and so its residues—its projectiles—are structured into and help structure the male imaginary. Those projectiles might be figured as the residue of the drives as they miss their return to the body, and as they escape the castratory stand-ins, the *objets petit a*, of the phallic imaginary. I've suggested too that these projectiles are unsymbolizable by dint of being incompletely repressed; but that nonetheless and indeed inevitably, their mutism finds figuration as part of the lived experience of male sexuality. I've followed somewhat Montrelay's suggestion that in the imaginary the figure of ejaculation is tied to this experience and this past. At the same time, I've wanted to avoid mapping the imaginary production onto the actual biological event of the male orgasm. That is what the term "vas" is intended to do. Vas is itself a vascillating term, implying both container and emptying of container, both body and not the body, both movement and immobility, both past and present: it stands in some sense between body and imaginary.

Vas is, obviously, not a genuine psychoanalytical term (whatever one of those would be), and it arises only at many removes from any actual psychoanalytical practice. But it is presented here as a kind of wishful addendum to the vocabulary to which and by which discussion of male sexuality is usually confined. Indeed, it might be appropriate to call vas by the metaphor of a foreign body in the sense that it points to a hysterical body. As I suggested at the start of this article, I don't intend the introduction and discussion of male hysteria to constitute a criticism of male sexuality—not just yet, anyway. If there is a criticism here it's primarily of psychoanalysis itself which, as feminists discovered long before I did, has chronically elided some part of the lived experience of sexed bodies.

NOTES

1. Anthony Easthope, *What A Man's Gotta Do* (London: Paladin, 1987). As Easthope does de facto in his book, I assume in this article that there is little to be gained by making a rigorous distinction between "maculinity" and "masculine sexuality." At the same time it can readily be said that my work here is more about masculine sexuality (the masculinity of the sexed subject) than Easthope's, which is more about masculinity as a cultural ideology.

2. I haven't attempted a particularly extensive bibliography here. But in addition to a wide array of relevant psychoanalytical material (from Freud himself through writers as various as Reich, Stoller, or Hocquenghem), the following books of relatively recent vintage offered material that was useful or relevant or provocative: Anthony Easthope (see note 1); *Feminist Review* editors, *Sexuality: A Reader* (London: Virago Press, 1987); Stephen Heath, *The Sexual Fix* (London: Macmillan, 1982); Andy Metcalf and Martin Humphries, eds., *Male Sexuality* (London: Pluto Press, 1985); Eileen Phillips, ed., *The Left and the Erotic* (London: Lawrence & Wishart, 1983); J. H. Pleck, *The Myth of Masculinity* (Cambridge, Mass: MIT Press, 1981); Emmanuel Reynard, *Holy Virility* (London: Pluto Press, 1987); Peter Schwenger, *Phallic Critiques* (London: Routledge & Kegan Paul, 1984); Eve Kosofsky Sedgwick, *Between Men* (New York: Columbia Univ. Press, 1985); Jon Snodgrass, *For Men Against Sexism* (San Rafael: Times Change Press, 1977); Klaus Theweleit, *Male Fantasies* (Minneapolis: Univ. of Minnesota Press, 1987); Jeffrey Weeks, *Sexuality and Its Discontents* (London: Routledge & Kegan Paul, 1985).

3. Judith Mayne, "Walking the Tightrope of Feminism and Male Desire," A. Jardine and P. Smith, eds. *Men in Feminism* (New York: Methuen, 1987) 70.

4. *The Complete Letters of Sigmund Freud to Wilhelm Fliess, 1887–1904*, J. Moussaieff Masson, trans. and ed. (Cambridge, Mass.: Harvard Univ. Press, 1985).

5. Sigmund Freud, "Femininity," *Standard Edition* vol. 22.

6. *Roland Barthes par lui-même* (Paris: Seuil, 1975) 128.

7. Alice Jardine, *Gynesis* (Ithaca: Cornell Univ. Press, 1985) 160.

8. Michèle Montrelay, "L'Appareillage," *Cahiers Confrontations* 6 (printemps 1982): 33–43.

9. Michèle Montrelay, *L'Ombre et le nom* (Paris: Minuit, 1977).

10. See my "Femininity According to Montrelay," *enclitic* vol. 9, nos. 1–2 (1987), where I argue some of these points.

11. See Moustafa Safouan, "Is the Oedipus Complex Universal?", *m/f* nos. 5–6 (1981), and "Men and Women—A Psychoanalytical Point of View," *m/f* no. 9 (1984).

12. Jacqueline Rose, "Introduction II," Juliet Mitchell and Jacqueline Rose, eds. *Feminine Sexuality* (London: Macmillan, 1982) 41.

13. Jacques Lacan, *The Four Fundamental Concepts of Psycho-Analysis* (Harmondsworth: Penguin, 1977) 199.

14. Klaus Theweleit, cited in note 2, above.

15. In fact, Theweleit specifically aligns himself with the project of Gilles Deleuze and Félix Guattari to displace the phallic schema of psychoanalysis; see their *Anti-Oedipus* (Minneapolis: Univ. of Minnesota Press, 1983).

16. Some of the same reasons, along with other interesting suggestions, will be found in one of the more adventurous reviews of Theweleit's book: Chris Turner and Erica Carter, "Political Somatics," in Victor Burgin, James Donald and Cora Kaplan, eds. *Formations of Fantasy* (London: Methuen, 1986).

17. Samuel Delany, "De la sexualité masculine considerée comme bien de consommation," *Cahiers Confrontations* 6 (printemps 1982): 5–12. Delany is not, by the way, endorsing such a "substantialist" ideology.

18. Beverly Brown, "A Feminist Interest in Pornography—Some Modest Proposals," *m/f* nos. 5–6 (1981).

19. Susanne Kappeler, *The Pornography of Representation* (Minneapolis: Univ. of Minnesota Press, 1986).

20. Roland Barthes, *La Chambre claire* (Paris: Gallimard/Le Seuil, 1980) 120.

21. Jacqueline Zita, "Pornography and the Male Imaginary," *enclitic* vol. 9, nos. 1–2 (1987).

22. Sigmund Freud, *Five Lectures on Psycho-Analysis* (New York: Norton, 1977).

autobiography

Autobiography is ubiquitous in feminist literary criticism. As subject matter, autobiography seems specially suited to the study of women's literature in Western culture, since so many women have written (though not always published) letters, journals, diaries, or stories of their lives. Two women writers in particular, Virginia Woolf and Maxine Hong Kingston, have recently come into prominence as authors of texts that take the writer's "self" as subject matter. In this section of *Feminisms* we include essays focusing on Woolf's and Kingston's autobiographical works as illustrations of new theories about ways a writer's gender can affect her writing of this genre.

In addition to being a popular subject area, autobiography touches on "subject" in another sense in feminist scholarship: feminist theorists and critics—breaking with the conventions of objectivity that dominate traditional Anglo-American criticism—often evoke themselves as the "speaking subjects" of their own writing. When the writer's presence seems to tear through the fabric of the academic text—revealing glimmers of the lived experience that forms the context for scholarly writing—"confessional" moments occur in otherwise conventional prose. (See, for an example, Regenia Gagnier's anecdote in her essay in our section on "Class," where she interrupts a highly formal analysis of the ideological function of humor in British women's autobiography to mention that someone warned her she would never rise in the administrative ranks if she did not curb her irreverent sense of humor.) The confessional mode can also govern an entire essay, as it does here in the selections by bell hooks and Jane Tompkins, or in Rachel Blau DuPlessis's "Washing Blood" essay in *For the Etruscans*, an influential precedent for this kind of feminist work. In this new form of academic writing, autobiography merges with scholarship, and a personal voice begins—if only tentatively—to take shape in expository prose.

Whether their focus is autobiography-as-a-subject-matter or the essayist's own subjective experience of living and writing about life, the four essays in this section circle around themes that have become central to much feminist literary criticism: the controversial relation between authorship and authority, and the related quest for a "voice"; the bonds and divisions between the individual woman and the family, community, and culture around her; and the sense of a double or divided self, common in postmodern writing but especially problematic for women. As essays in the "Institutions" and "Discourse" sections of *Feminisms* indicate, the "self" poses a set of vexed questions for feminist theory: if a "self" is always a social or institutional construct, if it is indeed (as Gayatri Chakravorty Spivak argues in "History" and Paula Gunn Allen explains in "Ethnicity") an instrument of patriarchal and imperialist oppression, how can a feminist writer come to terms with looking for a "self" in another woman's writing, or constituting a "self" in her own? Feminist theories of autobiography resort to various strategies—from psychoanalytic models to personal anecdotes—to confront these difficulties.

bell hooks's examination of "writing autobiography" (from *Talking Back: Thinking Feminist, Thinking Black*, 1989) articulates each of these issues, without recourse to the literary-theoretical apparatus so often brought to bear upon them. In a style that demonstrates her commitment to a broadly based intelligibility, hooks writes of the drive to represent herself in prose, as well as the terrors of its attendant dangers. She begins with a confessional moment that is startling in its violence: she wanted, she says, to "kill the self that I was"—the self named Gloria Jean, whose troubled childhood is so briefly but so vividly rendered here—by writing her life. In the course of the essay, hooks imagines the form Audre Lorde called "biomythography," combining the story of a woman's life with a "recaptured" sense of a disappearing past, in this case, the mythologies and folk traditions of southern black culture. Thinking about her place in that broader context, hooks comes to see that past not as horrific, but rather in terms of "these glorious memories." In the process of writing and rereading pieces of her life, she ends up rescuing Gloria, rather than killing her off. The rhetoric of her essay mirrors that process of giving form and significance to a life, moving from the opening paragraph's violence to the conclusion's expression of faith that reconciliation with the past can bring release from its constraints upon one's present self.

Although the contrast in style and approach is striking as we turn from hooks to Shari Benstock, the issues are familiar. Benstock's essay "Authorizing the Autobiographical" (1988) elucidates Jacques Lacan's psychoanalytic model of "the mirror stage" to explain the complexities involved in writing autobiography, especially for women. Contrasting the Lacanian idea of the self with the version of selfhood that dominates androcentric theories of autobiography, Benstock shows how helpful psychoanalysis can be to the study of women's autobiography, through the example of Virginia Woolf. Instead of seeing the self as a unified entity whose depths can be plumbed and whose essence could be transmitted through carefully crafted prose, as traditional autobiographical theory sees it, Lacan views the self as fundamentally split between the "I" that one holds to be an ideal and the "I" that one sees reflected back from others. As Benstock explains, Lacan locates the individual's awareness of this split at "the mirror stage," the moment when the child first recognizes its own reflection, and realizes that "I" is—from another perspective—also an "other." Not coincidentally, this developmental moment occurs during the stage in which the child also acquires language.

Written and spoken words, then, come to represent (or to occupy) the slippage, the gap between the two selves, for—as Benstock explains—language is "both internal and external." To the autobiographer, language is "the . . . symbolic system that both constructs and is constructed by the writing subject." Benstock builds upon Lacan's abstract and universalizing theory to think in terms of individual social development and lived experience. Glancing back at bell hooks, we could say—from Benstock's point of view—that her double self represents her being a "split subject": "Gloria" is the external cosntruction she saw reflected back from the people around her; "I" (bell?) is the ideal she recognizes and wishes to embrace as her own.

Benstock uses Virginia Woolf's most informal writing, her diaries and fragments of memoir, to show how a woman autobiographer can explore the unconscious. Looking at Woolf's earliest memories of mirror reflections, sexual abuse, and family members (especially her mother), Benstock focuses on Woolf's feminine awareness of her own "otherness," even from herself. For Benstock, Woolf's earnest endeavor to avoid shaping, censoring, or editing her journal-writing leads the texts into the realm of the unconscious. Rather than choosing significant contextual details to recreate in language, Woolf tries to include "everything that forms the background of perception and action," everything traditionally left out of autobiography. In this light, Woolf becomes a model for feminist autobiographers, having reconfigured "authority" in a way that allows for a split subjectivity.

"Otherness" is an issue, too, for Maxine Hong Kingston, as Sidonie Smith explains in the selection reprinted here from *A Poetics of Women's Autobiography* (1987). Smith's book traces women's autobiographical writing back five hundred years, beginning with Margery Kempe. Identifying patterns in women's writing about their lives, Smith holds those patterns up against androcentric histories and theories of autobiography to show how that scholarly field has overlooked female-written texts. Smith's study culminates in her analysis of Kingston's *The Woman Warrior*, which—as Smith observes—complicates the already marginal position of the female autobiography by adding ethnicity (Chinese American) and social position (working class) to the mix. According to Smith, Kingston's book is "meta-autobiography," as much "about" its own process of being written as it is "about" its writer's life. Kingston intertwines stories of her own memories with legends her mother told her, so that her "self" gets represented always within the context of her familial and cultural heritages.

As Smith sees it, Kingston's book is full of doublings: the author's voice intertwines dialogically (that is, in dialogue) with her mother's; the daughter's experience is contrasted with that of the older women in her family; the daughter sees herself mirrored in a "dumb" Chinese American girl at school who will not speak. In the end, says Smith, Kingston overcomes familial and minority/majority–cultural bans on women's speaking, reaching "total identification" with her storytelling mother as "woman poet." The mother's stories served initially to induct the daughter into her filial role in an oppressive family structure, but function ultimately to empower her to find a voice.

In academic writing as in autobiography, finding a voice is a challenge for women, as Jane Tompkins demonstrates in her 1989 essay "Me and My Shadow." As conscious of doubleness as any autobiographer, Tompkins represents her writing self as split between two voices, that of an academic critic who knows how to use all the critical terminology, all the moves, and that of "a person who wants to write about her feelings." Oscillating fearlessly between the public side of her working life (as in her direct scholarly response to the Ellen Messer-Davidow essay that inspired this piece) and the private side (as in allusions to her husband, Stanley Fish, or to her stockinged feet, her childhood conflicts, her anger at men, her present need to go to the bathroom), Tompkins goes as far as any academic feminist has dared to go in pushing out the boundaries of academically appropriate writing. As she explains, the public/private split is a fiction anyway, perpetuated by a system that assigns the private realm of emotions to women in order simultaneously to devalue both females and feelings (for an explanation of the historical context in which this split occurred, see the introduction to our section on "History"). In her call for "love," not "anger," as a dominant academic mode (and her recognition that such a call is *embarrassing* because it is "mushy" and "sentimental"); in her evocation of the voices of poststructuralist theorists alongside her "own" voice's questioning, musing, even humming; Tompkins is redefining the way autobiography might inform the feminist theory and criticism of the future: the way it might have its effect—like some of its sources—in the world of experience outside texts.

—RRW

WRITING AUTOBIOGRAPHY

To me, telling the story of my growing up years was intimately connected with the longing to kill the self I was without really having to die. I wanted to kill that self in writing. Once that self was gone—out of my life forever—I could more easily become the me of me. It was clearly the Gloria Jean of my tormented and anguished childhood that I wanted to be rid of, the girl who was always wrong, always punished, always subjected to some humiliation or other, always crying, the girl who was to end up in a mental institution because she could not be anything but crazy, or so they told her. She was the girl who sat a hot iron on her arm pleading with them to leave her alone, the girl who wore her scar as a brand marking her madness. Even now I can hear the voices of my sisters saying "mama make Gloria stop crying." By writing the autobiography, it was not just this Gloria I would be rid of, but the past that had a hold on me, that kept me from the present. I wanted not to forget the past but to break its hold. This death in writing was to be liberatory.

Until I began to try and write an autobiography, I thought that it would be a simple task this telling of one's story. And yet I tried year after year, never writing more than a few pages. My inability to write out the story I interpreted as an indication that I was not ready to let go of the past, that I was not ready to be fully in the present. Psychologically, I considered the possibility that I had become attached to the wounds and sorrows of my childhood, that I held to them in a manner that blocked my efforts to be self-realized, whole, to be healed. A key message in Toni Cade Bambara's novel *The Salteaters*, which tells the story of Velma's suicide attempt, her breakdown, is expressed when the healer asks her "are you sure sweetheart, that you want to be well?"

There was very clearly something blocking my ability to tell my story. Perhaps it was remembered scoldings and punishments when mama heard me saying something to a friend or stranger that she did not think should be said. Secrecy and silence—these were central issues. Secrecy about family, about what went on in the domestic household was a bond between us—was part of what made us family. There was a dread one felt about breaking that bond. And yet I could not grow inside the atmosphere of secrecy that had pervaded our lives and the lives of other families about us. Strange that I had always challenged the secrecy, always let something slip that should not be known growing up, yet as a writer staring into the solitary space of paper, I was bound, trapped in the fear that a bond is lost or broken in the telling. I did not want to be the traitor, the teller of family secrets—and yet I wanted to be a writer. Surely, I told myself, I could write a purely imaginative work—a work that would not hint at personal private realities. And so I tried. But always there were the intruding traces, those elements of real life however disguised. Claiming the freedom to grow as an imaginative writer was connected for me with having the courage to open, to be able to tell the truth of one's life as I had experienced it in writing. To talk about one's life—that I could do. To write about it, to leave a trace—that was frightening.

The longer it took me to begin the process of writing autobiography, the further removed from those memories I was becoming. Each year, a memory seemed less and less clear. I wanted not to lose the vividness, the recall and felt an urgent need to begin the work and complete it. Yet I could not begin even though I had begun to confront some of the reasons I was blocked, as I am blocked just now in writing this piece because I am afraid to express in writing the experience that served as a catalyst for that block to move.

I had met a young black man. We were having an affair. It is important that he was black. He was in some mysterious way a link to this past that I had been struggling to grapple with, to name in writing. With him I remembered incidents, moments of the past that I had completely suppressed. It was as though there was something about the passion of contact that was hypnotic, that enabled me to drop barriers and thus enter fully, rather re-enter those past experiences. A key aspect seemed to be the way he smelled, the combined odors of cigarettes, occasionally alcohol, and his body smells. I thought often of the phrase "scent of memory," for it was those smells that carried me back. And there were specific occasions when it was very evident that the experience of being in his company was the catalyst for this remembering.

Two specific incidents come to mind. One day in the middle of the afternoon we met at his place. We were drinking cognac and dancing to music from the radio. He was smoking cigarettes (not only do I not smoke, but I usually make an effort to avoid smoke). As we held each other dancing those mingled odors of alcohol, sweat, and cigarettes led me to say, quite without thinking about it, "Uncle Pete." It was not that I had forgotten Uncle Pete. It was more that I had forgotten the childhood experience of meeting him. He drank often, smoked cigarettes, and always on the few occasions that we met him, he held us children in tight embraces. It was the memory of those embraces—of the way I hated and longed to resist them—that I recalled.

Another day we went to a favorite park to feed ducks and parked the car in front of tall bushes. As we were sitting there, we suddenly heard the sound of an oncoming train—a sound which startled me so that it evoked another long-suppressed memory: that of crossing the train tracks in my father's car. I recalled an incident where the car stopped on the tracks and my father left us sitting there while he raised the hood of the car and worked to repair it. This is an incident that I am not certain actually happened. As a child, I had been terrified of just such an incident occurring, perhaps so terrified that it played itself out in my mind as though it had happened. These are just two ways this encounter acted as a catalyst breaking down barriers enabling me to finally write this long-desired autobiography of my childhood.

Each day I sat at the typewriter and different memories were written about in

short vignettes. They came in a rush, as though they were a sudden thunder-
storm. They came in a surreal, dreamlike style which made me cease to think of
them as strictly autobiographical because it seemed that myth, dream, and reality had merged. There were many incidents that I would talk about with my
siblings to see if they recalled them. Often we remembered together a general
outline of an incident but the details were different for us. This fact was a constant reminder of the limitations of autobiography, of the extent to which autobiography is a very personal story telling—a unique recounting of events not so
much as they have happened but as we remember and invent them. One memory that I would have sworn was "the truth and nothing but the truth" concerned
a wagon that my brother and I shared as a child. I remembered that we played
with this toy only at my grandfather's house, that we shared it, that I would ride it
and my brother would push me. Yet one facet of the memory was puzzling, I
remembered always returning home with bruises or scratches from this toy.
When I called my mother, she said there had never been any wagon, that we had
shared a red wheelbarrow, that it had always been at my grandfather's house because there were sidewalks on that part of town. We lived in the hills where there
were no sidewalks. Again I was compelled to face the fiction that is a part of all
retelling, remembering. I began to think of the work I was doing as both fiction
and autobiography. It seemed to fall in the category of writing that Audre Lorde,
in her autobiographically-based work *Zami,* calls bio-mythography. As I wrote, I
felt that I was not as concerned with accuracy of detail as I was with evoking in
writing the state of mind, the spirit of a particular moment.

The longing to tell one's story and the process of telling is symbolically a gesture of longing to recover the past in such a way that one experiences both a
sense of reunion and a sense of release. It was the longing for release that compelled the writing but concurrently it was the joy of reunion that enabled me to
see that the act of writing one's autobiography is a way to find again that aspect of
self and experience that may no longer be an actual part of one's life but is a
living memory shaping and informing the present. Autobiographical writing was
a way for me to evoke the particular experience of growing up southern and black
in segregated communities. It was a way to recapture the richness of southern
black culture. The need to remember and hold to the legacy of that experience
and what it taught me has been all the more important since I have since lived in
predominately white communities and taught at predominately white colleges.
Black southern folk experience was the foundation of the life around me when I
was a child; that experience no longer exists in many places where it was once all
of life that we knew. Capitalism, upward mobility, assimilation of other values
have all led to rapid disintegration of black folk experience or in some cases the
gradual wearing away of that experience.

Within the world of my childhood, we held onto the legacy of a distinct black
culture by listening to the elders tell their stories. Autobiography was experienced most actively in the art of telling one's story. I can recall sitting at Baba's
(my grandmother on my mother's side) at 1200 Broad Street—listening to people
come and recount their life experience. In those days, whenever I brought a
playmate to my grandmother's house, Baba would want a brief outline of their
autobiography before we would begin playing. She wanted not only to know who
their people were but what their values were. It was sometimes an awesome and

terrifying experience to stand answering these questions or witness another play-mate being subjected to the process and yet this was the way we would come to know our own and one another's family history. It is the absence of such a tradition in my adult life that makes the written narrative of my girlhood all the more important. As the years pass and these glorious memories grow much more vague, there will remain the clarity contained within the written words.

Conceptually, the autobiography was framed in the manner of a hope chest. I remembered my mother's hope chest, with its wonderful odor of cedar and thought about her taking the most precious items and placing them there for safekeeping. Certain memories were for me a similar treasure. I wanted to place them somewhere for safekeeping. An autobiographical narrative seemed an appropriate place. Each particular incident, encounter, experience had its own story, sometimes told from the first person, sometimes told from the third person. Often I felt as though I was in a trance at my typewriter, that the shape of a particular memory was decided not by my conscious mind but by all that is dark and deep within me, unconscious but present. It was the act of making it present, bringing it into the open, so to speak, that was liberating.

From the perspective of trying to understand my psyche, it was also interesting to read the narrative in its entirety after I had completed the work. It had not occurred to me that bringing one's past, one's memories together in a complete narrative would allow one to view them from a different perspective, not as singular isolated events but as part of a continuum. Reading the completed manuscript, I felt as though I had an overview not so much of my childhood but of those experiences that were deeply imprinted in my consciousness. Significantly, that which was absent, left out, not included also was important. I was shocked to find at the end of my narrative that there were few incidents I recalled that involved my five sisters. Most of the incidents with siblings were with me and my brother. There was a sense of alienation from my sisters present in childhood, a sense of estrangement. This was reflected in the narrative. Another aspect of the completed manuscript that is interesting to me is the way in which the incidents describing adult men suggest that I feared them intensely, with the exception of my grandfather and a few old men. Writing the autobiographical narrative enabled me to look at my past from a different perspective and to use this knowledge as a means of self-growth and change in a practical way.

In the end I did not feel as though I had killed the Gloria of my childhood. Instead I had rescued her. She was no longer the enemy within, the little girl who had to be annihilated for the woman to come into being. In writing about her, I reclaimed that part of myself I had long ago rejected, left uncared for, just as she had often felt alone and uncared for as a child. Remembering was part of a cycle of reunion, a joining of fragments, "the bits and pieces of my heart" that the narrative made whole again.

WORKS CITED

Bambara, Toni Cade, *The Salteaters* (New York: Random House, 1980).
Lorde, Audre, *Zami: A New Spelling of My Name* (New York: Crossing Press, 1983).
Petry, Ann, *The Street* (New York: Pyramid Books, 1946).

SHARI BENSTOCK

AUTHORIZING THE AUTOBIOGRAPHICAL

> I suggest that one could understand the life around which autobiography forms itself in a number of other ways besides the perfectly legitimate one of "individual history and narrative": we can understand it as the vital impulse—the impulse of life—that is transformed by being lived through the *unique medium of the individual and the individual's special, peculiar psychic configuration;* we can understand it as *consciousness, pure and simple, consciousness referring to no objects outside itself, to no events, and to no other lives;* we can understand it as *participation in an absolute existence* far transcending the shifting, changing unrealities of mundane life; we can understand it as the *moral tenor of the individual's being.* Life in all these latter senses does not stretch back across time but extends down to the roots of individual being; *it is atemporal, committed to a vertical thrust from consciousness down into the unconscious rather than to a horizontal thrust from the present into the past.*
>
> JAMES OLNEY, "SOME VERSIONS OF MEMORY" (EMPHASIS ADDED)

In this extended definition of "the life around which autobiography forms itself," James Olney has accounted for nearly all the concerns addressed by the essays in this book. In one way or another each contributor has taken up the issues enumerated here: the assertion that autobiography is "transformed by being lived through the unique medium of the individual"; the assumption that the individual bears a "special, peculiar psychic configuration"; the belief that autobiography represents "consciousness, pure and simple . . . referring to no objects outside itself, to no events, and to no others" and that it transcends "the shifting, changing unrealities of mundane life"; the supposition that "life . . . does not stretch back across time but extends down to the roots of individual being," moving in "a vertical thrust from consciousness down into the unconscious rather than to a horizontal thrust from the present to the past." These essays take up such premises in order to revise them, to rethink the very coincidence of "ontology" and "autobiography." That each of these premises should prove an "issue" in the essays that follow derives, I think, from the primary contexts of their writing—the concerns with gender, race, class, and historical and political conditions in the theory and practice of women's autobiographical writings.

How does writing mediate the space between "self" and "life" that the autobiography would traverse and transgress? One definition of autobiography suggests that it is an effort to recapture the self—in Hegel's claim, to know the self through "consciousness" (Gusdorf 38). Such a claim presumes that there is such a thing as the "self" and that it is "knowable." This coming-to-knowledge of the self constitutes both the desire that initiates the autobiographical act and the goal toward which autobiography directs itself. By means of writing, such desire presumably can be fulfilled. Thus the place to begin our investigation of autobiography might be at the crossroads of "writing" and "selfhood."[1]

INITIATING AUTOBIOGRAPHY

> The autobiographical perspective has . . . to do with taking oneself up and bringing oneself to language.—Janet Varner Gunn, *Autobiography*

If the autobiographical moment prepares for a meeting of "writing" and "selfhood," a coming together of method and subject matter, this destiny—like the retrospective glance that presumably initiates autobiography—is always deferred. Autobiography reveals gaps, and not only gaps in time and space or between the individual and the social, but also a widening divergence between the manner and matter of its discourse. That is, autobiography reveals the impossibility of its own dream: what begins on the presumption of self-knowledge ends in the creation of a fiction that covers over the premises of its construction. Georges Gusdorf has argued that "the appearance of autobiography implies a new spiritual revolution: the artist and model coincide, the historian tackles himself as object" (31). But in point of fact, the "coincidence" of artist and model is an illusion. As Jacques Lacan has noted, the "mirror stage" of psychic development that initiates the child into the social community and brings it under the law of the Symbolic (the law of language as constituted through society) serves up a false image of the child's unified "self." This unity is imposed from the outside (in the mirror reflection) and is in Ellie Ragland-Sullivan's words, "asymmetrical, fictional, and artificial." As Ragland-Sullivan continues, the "mirror stage must, therefore, be understood as a metaphor for the vision of harmony of a subject essentially in discord" (26–27). The "discord" that gives the lie to a unified, identifiable, coterminous self has been built up out of the images, sounds, and sensory responses available to the child during the first six months or so of its life; it is called the unconscious, or that which derives from an experience of "self" as fragmented, partial, segmented, and different. The developing child drives toward fusion and homogeneity in the construction of a "self" (the *moi* of Lacan's terminology) against the effects of division and dissolution. The unconscious is thus not the lower depths of the conscious (as in Olney's description of it) but rather an inner seam, a space between "inside" and "outside"—it is the space of difference, the gap that the drive toward unity of self can never entirely close. It is also the space of writing, which bears the marks and registers the alienating effects of the false symmetry of the mirror stage.

[Here I bracket some considerations about a developing self with particular reference to divisions between the soma and psyche and to mirrors.

In Virginia Woolf's "A Sketch of the Past," her effort at writing her own memoirs, she comments at length on her relation to mirrors, remembering crucial events from her childhood in which mirrors played some part:

> There was a small looking-glass in the hall at Talland House. It had, I remember, a ledge with a brush on it. By standing on tiptoe I could see my face in the glass. When I was six or seven perhaps, I got into the habit of looking at my face in the glass. But I only did this if I was sure that I was alone. I was ashamed of it. A strong feeling of guilt seemed naturally attached to it. (*Moments of Being* 67–68)

Woolf lists various reasons for this shame—that she and Vanessa were "tomboys" and that "to have been found looking in the glass would have been against our tomboy code" (68); or that she inherited "a streak of the puritan," which made her feel shame at self-regard or narcissistic behavior. From a readerly perspective, neither of these reasons seems adequate to the kind of shame she clearly felt before the looking glass, a shame that lasted her entire life. Further on in this memoir, she continues her commentary on female beauty: "My mother's beauty, Stella's beauty, gave me as early as I can remember, pride and pleasure" (68). She declares that her "natural love for beauty was checked by some ancestral dread," then clarifies and qualifies her perceptions: "Yet this did not prevent me from feeling ecstasies and raptures spontaneously and intensely and without any shame or the least sense of guilt, so long as they *were disconnected with my own body*" (68; emphasis added).

Slowly, as though with dread, Woolf comes to "another element in the shame which I had in being caught looking at myself in the glass in the hall" (68). She declares that she was "ashamed or afraid" of her own body. The memory of the hallway with its looking glass is overlaid by another memory of that same hallway, a scene that may well have been reflected for her in the very looking glass of which she speaks. This memory is of George Duckworth raising her onto the slab outside the dining room and "there he began to explore my body":

> I can remember the feel of his hand going under my clothes; going firmly and steadily lower and lower. I remember how I hoped that he would stop; how I stiffened and wriggled as his hand approached my private parts. But it did not stop. His hand explored my private parts too. I remember resenting, disliking it—what is the word for so dumb and mixed a feeling? It must have been strong, since I still recall it. This seems to show that a feeling about certain parts of the body; how they must not be touched; how it is wrong to allow them to be touched; must be instinctive. (69)

Sexual abuse adds itself to the shame of looking at the face in the mirror. Or perhaps sexual abuse actually preceded the shame of looking in the glass. Woolf's memories, we shall see, do not announce their sequence; their timing always contradicts the logical sequence of conscious thought and action, escaping the dating of calendars and clocks. In recounting the scene with George Duckworth, Woolf does not claim to have discovered the reason for her shame at looking at her own face, she admits to having "only been able to discover some possible reasons; there may be others; I do not suppose that I have got at the truth; yet this is a simple incident; and it happened to me personally; and I have no motive for lying about it" (69). The layers of conscious recall and justification overlap each other, their movement inexorably marked by the semicolons of these clauses that march her back to the moment in the hallway, just as her circuitous "tunneling" method of finding her way back to the past had brought her to the scene with George Duckworth from another direction—from the reflection of her own face in the mirror.

Woolf has one more comment on the "mirror stage" of her own sexual and psychic development:

> Let me add a dream; for it may refer to the incident of the looking-glass. I dreamt that I was looking in a glass when a horrible face—the face of an animal—suddenly showed over my shoulder. I cannot be sure if this was a dream, or if it happened. Was I looking in the glass one day when something in the background moved, and seemed to me alive? I cannot be sure. But I have always remembered the other face in the glass, whether it was a dream or a fact, and that it frightened me. (69)

Two things presumably occur at the mirror stage: a realization (even if it cannot yet be verbalized) of wholeness, completeness, in an image that contradicts the intuited understanding that the child is still fragmented, uncoordinated, and not yet experiencing bodily reactions through a kind of psychic "wholeness"; and a shock of awareness that the image (which may be seen not in a mirror, but rather in a parent's or a sibling's face) is that of an *other*—someone or something unlike and unconnected to the infant. The mirror stage marks a differentiation that is potentially frightening, a moment that cannot be recaptured through memory as such, a moment that hangs in a space that is neither dream nor fact, but both. The mirror stage marks both the exceptional and the common; it is a stage common to us all, but within our experience—and this experience exists outside and beyond memory—this stage marks us as exceptional, differentiated. What should be communicated in this moment is a wholeness, an integration that is present in the image but not yet apparent in experience. For Woolf such an experience— really an aftershock of trauma—recorded both differentiation and a psychic/ somatic split. A mysterious, frightening, unknown shame clouds the mirror; the other face in the mirror marks dread.]

In a definition of the autobiographical act that strikingly recapitulates the effects of Lacan's mirror stage, Georges Gusdorf has written: "Autobiography . . . requires a man to take a distance with regard to himself in order to reconstitute himself in the focus of his special unity and identity across time" (35). The effect of such a distancing and reconstituting is precisely the effect of the mirror stage: a recognition of the alienating force within the specular (the "regard") that leads to the desperate shoring-up of the reflected image against disintegration and division. What is reinforced in this effort is the *moi*, the ego; what is pushed aside (or driven into the darkened realms of the repressed) is the split in the subject (who both "is" and "is not" the reflected image) that language effects and cannot deny. Man enforces a "unity and identity across time" by "reconstituting" the ego as a bulwark against disintegration; that is, man denies the very effects of having internalized the alienating world order. One such "denial" is autobiography itself, at least as it is defined by Gusdorf, who would place random reflections on self and society, such as diaries, journals, and letters, in a category separate from (and prior to—the sources for) the *self-conscious* autobiography in which the writer "calls himself as witness for himself" (29).

For Gusdorf, autobiography "is the mirror in which the individual reflects his own image" (33); in such a mirror the "self" and the "reflection" coincide. But this definition of autobiography overlooks what might be the most interesting aspect of the autobiographical; the measure to which "self" and "self-image" might not coincide, can never coincide in language—not because certain forms of self-writing are not self-conscious enough but because they have no investment in creating a cohesive self over time. Indeed, they seem to exploit difference and change over sameness and identity: their writing follows the "seam" of the conscious/unconscious where boundaries between internal and external overlap. Such writing puts into question the whole notion of "genre" as outlined by the exclusionary methods of Gusdorf's rather narrow definition of the autobiographical. And it is not surprising that the question of "genre" often rides on the question of gender.[2]

Psychic health is measured in the degree to which the "self" is constructed in separateness, the boundaries between "self" and "other" carefully circumscribed. From a Gusdorfian perspective, autobiography is a re-erecting of these psychic walls, the building of a linguistic fortress between the autobiographical subject and his interested readers: "The autobiography that is thus devoted exclusively to the defence and glorification of a man, a career, a political cause, or a skillful strategy . . . is limited almost entirely to the public sector of existence" (36). Gusdorf acknowledges that "the question changes utterly when the private face of existence assumes more importance" (37), but he suggests that "the writer who recalls his earliest years is thus exploring an enchanted realm that belongs to him alone" (37). In either kind of autobiography, the writing subject is the one presumed to *know* (himself), and this process of knowing is a process of differentiating himself from others.[3] The chain-link fence that circumscribes his unique contributions is language, representative of the very laws to which this writing subject has been subjected; that is, language is neither an external force nor a "tool" of expression, but the very symbolic system that both constructs and is constructed by the writing subject. As such, language is both internal and external, and the walls that defend the *moi* are never an entirely adequate defense network against the multiple forms of the *je*.

If the linguistic defense networks of male autobiographers more successfully keep at bay the discordant *je*, it may be because female autobiographers are more aware of their "otherness." Like men, we are subjected to the phallic law, but our experience of its social and political effects comes under the terms of another law—that of gender. Ragland-Sullivan comments that "the early mother is internalized as the source of one's own narcissism, prior to the acquisition of individual boundaries, while the father's subsequent, symbolic role is that of teaching these boundaries—he is a limit-setter. As a result, the father is later both feared and emulated, since his presence has taught the infant about laws and taboos" (42). Language itself, as Lacan has shown, is a defense against unconscious knowledge (179). But it is not an altogether successful defense network, punctuated as it is by messages from the unconscious, messages that attempt to defeat this "fencing-off" mechanism; indeed, there is no clearly defined barrier between the conscious and the unconscious. Fenced in by language, the speaking subject is primordially divided.[4]

This division is apparent as well in writing, and especially in autobiographical writing. Denial of the division on the part of some theoreticians of autobiography, however, is itself a symptom of autobiographical writing—a repeated but untranslated, unconscious message. This message is directed at the culture from the position of the Other, by those who occupy positions of internal exclusion within the culture—that is, by women, blacks, Jews, homosexuals, and others who exist on the margins of society. A frequent spokesperson for those who have been denied full rights within the society on the grounds of gender, Virginia Woolf also questioned the limits of genre, with particular regard to autobiography. In 1919, at age thirty-seven, she was particularly concerned with these issues, thinking to what use she might put her diary and at what point in her life she would begin writing her memoirs. She begins by suggesting that "this diary does not count as writing, since I have just re-read my year's diary and am much struck by the rapid haphazard gallop at which it swings along, sometimes indeed jerking almost intolerably over the cobbles" (20 January 1919). But the next sentence justifies this fast-paced method as preserving that which "if I stopped and took thought . . . would never be written at all," that which "sweeps up accidentally several stray matters which I would exclude if I hesitated, but which are the diamonds of the dustheap." Thinking of her future self at age fifty, Woolf conjures up on the diary page an image of herself, wearing reading glasses, poring over the pages of the past in preparation for the writing of her memoirs. Many years later, when Woolf was fifty-eight, she placed her memoir writing even further in the future, commenting in her diary: "I may as well make a note I say to myself: thinking sometimes who's going to read all this scribble? I think one day I may brew a tiny ingot out of it—in my memoirs" (19 February 1940). The "brewing" method would seem to be reductive—to eliminate the dross and save the gold.

Woolf did not live to write her memoirs, and the bulk of the autobiographical Virginia Woolf exists in her diary and letters, forms whose generic boundaries she extended and reconstructed. The diary, for instance, was constantly reexamined as a cultural artifact, as a living presence, as a necessary exercise for her fatigued mind, as a secret place (she found it impossible to write in it, for instance, if anyone else were in the room). She used the diary to pose theoretical and practical questions of *writing*, a place where the very definitions of writing might be reexamined:

> There looms ahead of me the shadow of some kind of form which a diary might attain to. I might in the course of time learn what it is that one can make of this *loose, drifting material of life;* finding another use for it than the use I put it to, so much more consciously and scrupulously, in fiction. What sort of diary should I like mine to be? Something loose knit and yet not slovenly, *so elastic that it will embrace anything, solemn, slight or beautiful that comes into my mind.* I should like it *to resemble some deep old desk, or capacious hold-all,* in which one flings a mass of odds and ends without looking them through. I should like to come back, after a year or two, and *find that the collection had sorted itself and refined itself and coalesced,* as such deposits so mysteriously do,

> into a mould, transparent enough to reflect the light of our life, and yet steady, tranquil compounds with the aloofness of a work of art. The main requisite, I think on re-reading my old volumes, *is not to play the part of censor*, but to write as the mood comes or of anything whatever; since I was curious to find how I went for things put in haphazard, and found the significance to lie *where I never saw it at the time*. (20 April 1919; emphasis added)

Setting aside momentarily the question of what Woolf might have done with the materials she later rediscovered in the "hold-all" of the diary, we can readily see that her efforts at defining the diary's form in the broadest terms possible ("so elastic that it will embrace anything, solemn, slight or beautiful that comes into my mind") and assigning the sorting, refining, and coalescing of such deposits into "a mould, transparent enough to reflect the light of our life," radically redefine the whole autobiographical project. Woolf does not conceive of such an undertaking in terms that Augustine, Rousseau, Montaigne, Proust, or Sir Leslie Stephen would recognize. She removes herself—that is, herself conceived as a censor—from this enterprise, discredits the notion of "self-consciousness" (indeed, she argues for the importance of the thoughtless, the loose, the unrestrained, the *un*conscious, and refrains from all efforts to shape, sort, or subordinate this material to her will. She rather systematically cuts out from under herself the props that hold up her authority as an *author*, turning authority back to the matter that constitutes her "subject"—and that subject is not necessarily the "self" of traditional autobiography. Woolf gives power to conscious artifice through fiction, a creation that also bears a relation to the "loose, drifting material of life." But for the purposes of memoir writing, she wishes to conceive of a different form and purpose—a conception that is infinitely deferred, as her own death puts an end to the project. That such a project would have followed the unconscious, would have followed the seam of writing itself, is undeniable, as the sections from *Moments of Being* discussed in the second part of this essay demonstrate.

> It took me a year's groping to discover what I call my tunnelling process, by which I tell the past by installments as I have need of it. This is my prime discovery so far; and the fact that I've been so long finding it proves, I think, how false Percy Lubbock's doctrine is—that you can do this sort of thing consciously. (*Diary*, 15 October 1923)

Later she comments, "as far as I know, as a writer I am only now writing out my mind" (20 March 1926), in a turn of phrase that suggests multiple relations between "mind" and "writing." In 1933, she notes "how tremendously important unconsciousness is when one writes" (29 October 1933). Such commentaries on the workings of the mind ally themselves with others that address questions of narrative method and artistic systems. On 25 September 1929, she writes in the diary: "Yesterday morning I made another start on *The Moths* [later retitled *The Waves*] . . . and several problems cry out at once to be solved. Who thinks it? And am I outside the thinker? One wants some device which is not a trick." And on 2 October 1932, in an entirely different context, she writes in irritation at reading D. H. Lawrence's published letters of what she calls his "preaching" and "systematizing": "His ruler coming down and measuring them. Why all this criticism of other people? Why not some system that includes the good? What a discovery that would be—a system that did not shut out." The relation of the conscious to the unconscious, of the mind to writing, of the inside to the outside of political and narrative systems, indicate not only a problematizing of social and literary conventions—a questioning of the Symbolic law—but also the need to reconceptualize form itself.

In other words, where does one place the "I" of the autobiographical account? Where does the Subject locate itself? In definitions of autobiography that stress self-disclosure and narrative account, that posit a self called to witness (as an authority) to "his" own being, that propose a double referent for the first-person narrative (the present "I" and the past "I"), or that conceive of autobiography as "recapitulation and recall" (Olney 252), the Subject is made an Object of investigation (the first-person actually masks the third person) and is further divided between the present moment of the narration and the past on which the narration is focused. These gaps in the temporal and spatial dimensions of the text itself are often successfully hidden from reader and writer, so that the fabric of the narrative appears seamless, spun of whole cloth. The effect is magical—the self appears organic, the present the sum total of the past, the past an accurate predictor of the future. This conception of the autobiographical rests on a firm belief in the *conscious* control of artist over subject matter; this view of the life history is grounded in authority. It is perhaps not surprising that those who cling to such a definition are those whose assignment under the Symbolic law is to *represent* authority, to represent the phallic power that drives inexorably toward unity, identity, sameness. And it is not surprising that those who question such authority are those who are expected to submit to it, those who line up on the other side of the sexual divide—that is, women.[5] The self that would reside at the center of the text is decentered—and often is absent altogether—in women's autobiographical texts. The very requirements of the genre are put into question by the limits of gender—which is to say, because these two terms are etymologically linked, genre itself raises questions about gender.[6]

FISSURES OF FEMALE DISCONTINUITY

> Alas, my brothers,
> Helen did not walk
> upon the ramparts,
> she whom you cursed
> was but the phantom and the shadow thrown
> of a reflection
> —H.D., *Helen in Egypt*

How do the fissures of female discontinuity display themselves, and what are their identifying features? On what authority can we ascribe certain forms of discontinuity to the female rather than to the male, assigning them as functions of gender rather than of social class, race, or sexual preference? One might remark that such issues are not raised—either directly or indirectly—by those texts that form the tradition of autobiographical writings in Western culture. The confessions of an Augustine or a Rousseau, the *Autobiography of Thomas Jefferson*, or the *Education of Henry Adams* do not admit internal cracks and disjunctures, rifts and ruptures. The whole thrust of such works is to seal up and cover over gaps in memory, dislocations in time and space, insecurities, hesitations, and blind spots. The consciousness behind the narrative "I" develops over time, encompassing more and more of the external landscape and becoming increasingly aware of the implications of action and events, but this consciousness—and the "I" it supports—remains stable. The dissection of self-analysis premises the cohesion of a restructured self. Any hint of the disparate, the dissasociated, is overlooked or enfolded into a narrative of synthesis. This "model" of autobiography, a product of the metaphysic that has structured Western thinking since Plato, repeated itself with unsurprising frequency until the early twentieth century—until the advent of what we now term Modernism put into question the organic, unifying principles of artistic creation that had reasserted themselves with such force in the nineteenth century.

The influence of Freud's discovery of the unconscious cannot be discounted in the unsettling of the "I" that had heretofore stood at the center of narrative discourse. (In accounting for this "unsettling" of self-unity, one must also consider the political and social effects of World War I, the advent of industrial mechanization, the loss of belief in God, the fall of colonial empires, and the changing status of women and minorities, all of which altered the cultural landscape against which literature was produced in the early years of the twentieth century. We live today in a world that has been constructed out of these changes; nearly all the changes that discomposed the complacent world of 1910 have been culturally assimilated, except perhaps the full force of Freud's discoveries. Predictably, its effects are most tenaciously resisted precisely where they are most evident: in language—in speech and writing.) The instability of this subject is nowhere more apparent than in women's writing of this period, in texts by Djuna Barnes, Isak Dinesen, H.D., Mina Loy, Anaïs Nin, Jean Rhys, Gertrude Stein, and Virginia Woolf, writing that puts into question the most essential component of the autobiographical—the relation between "self" and "consciousness." The simultaneous exploration of the autobiographical and probing of self-consciousness in works by each of these writers suggests not that they knew their Freud better than T. S. Eliot, James Joyce, Ezra Pound, or W. B. Yeats, but that as women they felt the effects of the psychic reality Freud described more fully than did men. Gender became a determining issue at the point at which culture (broadly defined in both its psychic and social terms) met aesthetic principles.

As I have argued elsewhere, female Modernism challenged the white, male, heterosexual ethic underlying the Modernist aesthetic of "impersonality" (e.g., the transformation of the textual "I" from the personal to the cultural).[7] It is this white, male, heterosexual ethic that poststructuralist critics have exposed behind the facade of a supposedly apolitical artistic practice.[8] Poststructuralism has taught us to read the politics of every element in narrative strategy: representation; tone; perspective; figures of speech; even the shift between first-, second-, and third-person pronouns. In identifying the "fissures of female discontinuity" in a text, for example, we also point toward a relation between the psychic and the political, the personal and the social, in the linguistic fabric.[9]

Although Virginia Woolf did not publish her memoirs, she did leave behind fragments of a memoir collected under the title *Moments of Being*. These five pieces ("Reminiscences," "A Sketch of the Past," and three readings done for the Memoir Club—"22 Hyde Park Gate," "Old Bloomsbury," and "Am I a Snob?") retrace the same material: that portion of her young adulthood between the deaths of her mother in 1895 and her father in 1904. In addition, much of this material is incorporated into two of her novels, *To the Lighthouse* and *The Years*. While the "content" of the fictions and the reminiscences is strikingly similar, the variations of perspective, through a shift of prounouns both between texts and within texts, signal discontinuities. In the memoirs in particular, these discontinuities are striking. They suggest that the entire project is poised over an abyss of selflessness, or, to put it differently, that the entire project is posed on the question of self and its relation to language and storytelling strategies.

She begins with "the first memory" of "red and purple flowers on a black ground—my mother's dress." The flowers, seen close up (she is on her mother's lap), are assumed to be anemones; the conveyance is either a train or an omnibus; the light suggests that it is evening and "we were coming back to London" (*Moments of Being* 64). As soon as this scene is suggested, however, it reverses itself, giving life to a second scene:

> But it is more convenient *artistically* to suppose that we were going to St. Ives, for that will lead to my other memory, which also seems to be my first memory, and in fact it is the most important of all my memories. If life has a base it stands upon, if it is a bowl that one fills and fills and fills—then my bowl without a doubt stands upon this memory. (64; emphasis added)

This second memory diverges both in time and place from the first. Comprised of sound rather than sight, it translates the former memory into a different medium:

> It is of lying half asleep, half awake, in bed at the nursery at St. Ives. It is of hearing the waves breaking, one, two, one, two, and sending a splash of water over the beach; and then breaking, one, two, one, two, behind a yellow blind. It is of hearing the blind draw its little acorn across the floor as the wind blew the blind out. It is of lying and hearing this splash and seeing this light, and feeling, it is almost impossible that I should be here; of feeling the purest ecstasy I can conceive. (64–65)

We know that the unconscious is comprised of just such "memories"—of images and sounds—and that later identity reflects these first sensory experiences.[10] Virginia Woolf's writing is characterized by the recurrence of such experiences; indeed, *The Waves* reflects the images and repeats the rhythms of precisely these two moments: "The sun sharpened the walls of the house, made a blue fingerprint of shadow under the leaf by the bedroom window. The blind stirred slightly, but all within was dim and unsubstantial" (*The Waves* 8). As a writer, Woolf knew how to make such experiences work toward aesthetic coherence; as critics, we know how to read such textual effects, working sound against image to make the metonymic metaphoric. But what is most striking from the "Sketch" itself is not the self-reinforcing aspect of the two memories, but the disparity between them: juxtaposed to each other within the same paragraph, they mark not only different psychic moments, but difference itself. Later in the text Woolf herself comments on this discovery of difference, but not before she has discussed artistic considerations, the place of the self in memoir writing, and the peculiarities of her social education.

The "first memory"—which is not a memory at all, strictly speaking—is displaced by an "other memory, which also seems to be my first memory." This displacement is effected for "artistic convenience," a change that reverses the narrative direction—toward St. Ives rather than toward London. But this change enforces another: although the first memory is conditioned by the light (which seems to be evening), the second memory can be reached by reversing not only the direction of the train but by inverting evening and morning: if they are leaving London for St. Ives, then the scene is lit by morning rather than evening light. Although the second memory is not dependent on light—as its "focus" is sound—the "yellow blind" of the room suggests visibility. The time of day in this second memory is unclear from an initial reading (it could be either morning or evening), and the confusion is cleared up only later, when Woolf apparently realizes the "connection" between the two scenes. Both are occasioned by displacement, and they shadow forth a doubling and displacement of "self."

Having remarked on the "pure ecstasy" that the second memory conveys, Woolf stops the narrative to comment on autobiography itself:

> I could spend hours trying to write that [the scene of the second memory] as it should be written, in order to give the feeling which is even at this moment very strong in me. But I should fail (unless I had some wonderful luck); I dare say I should only succeed in having the luck if I had begun by describing Virginia herself. (65).

The writer's "luck" becomes dependent on conventional literary forms—here the requirement that the autobiographical begin with a description of the central character. Woolf sets aside the evidence that her method, adopted at random, "without stopping to choose my way, in the sure and certain knowledge that it will find itself" (64), has already provided crucial elements not of the *self* but of the elements out of which the unconscious is constructed. She has tapped the unconscious, and the effect has been to split the "subject" that her autobiography struggles to delineate. She has stumbled against "one of the memoir writer's difficulties—one of the reasons why, though I read so many, so many are failures. They leave out the person to whom things happened" (65). At this juncture, "Adeline Virginia Stephen, the second daughter of Leslie and Julia Prinsip Stephen, born on the 25th January 1882" is inserted into the text. But this historical Virginia Stephen is of little help to Virginia Woolf the memoirist, as neither knows how history and lineage "made them," or—more important—"what part of this" history "made me feel what I felt in the nursery at St. Ives." Woolf confesses to not knowing "how far I differ from other people." A crucial factor in this "not knowing" has been her social and educational conditioning: "Owing partly to the fact that I was never at school, never competed in any way with children of my own age, I have never been able to compare my gifts and defects with other people's" (65). Elsewhere—in her diaries and letters, in *A Room of One's Own*, in *Three Guineas*—Virginia Woolf wrote at length, with passion and anger, against the strictures of her Victorian upbringing, against its isolation, against the intellectual and emotional hardships of its expectations for women. Of whatever else this social setting deprived her, its cruelest denial was a community in which she could learn and against which she could measure herself.

Two sentences in this paragraph from "A Sketch of the Past" are linked, and they lead to an explanation for the second memory. The first sentence is the one on which the paragraph is premised ("They [memoirs] leave out the person to whom things happened"); the second is the realization that because of the circumstances of her upbringing Woolf does not know "how far I differ from other people." That is, she has been absent in her own memoir—thus committing the sin of so many memoirs—because she cannot measure her own *difference* from others. And it is precisely this difference, this individuality, on which the traditional memoir premises itself. This problem of difference suggests to Woolf "another memoir writer's difficulty." Unlike others, she has no standard of comparison, and it is this lack that leads to a rationale for the kinds of reminiscences she has already delineated:

> But of course there was one external reason for the intensity of this first impression: the impression of the waves and the acorn on the blind; the feeling, as I describe it sometimes to myself of lying in a grape and seeing through a film of semi-transparent yellow—it was due partly to the many months we spent in London. The *change of nursery was a great change*. And there was the long train journey; and the excitement. I remember the dark; the lights; the stir of the going up to bed. (65; emphasis added)[11]

The memory of the waves at St. Ives is specifically marked here as "this first impression," perhaps blotting out, or at least circumventing, that prior "first memory" of the flowers on the "black ground" of the mother's dress. The explanation for the feeling that results from this impression uses elements from both memories: although the impression of the waves and the acorn on the blind reside in hearing ("It is of hearing the blind draw its little acorn across the floor as the wind blew the blind out"), Woolf's description relies on sight ("the feeling . . . of lying in a grape and seeing through a film of semi-transparent yellow"). The two impressions belong to different sensory orders, and their coincidence (one explained in terms of the other) is the result of "a great change"—a registering of difference between the London and St. Ives nurseries. It is significant that this registration occurs in a section of the text in which individual difference is denied and made the excuse for the failure of memoir writing: "I do not know how far I differ from other people." The "I" in this sentence is absent precisely to the extent that it is doubled ("I . . . I"): selfhood registered in difference from others is demonstrated on *social* grounds to be nonexistent; coexistent selfhood across time and space is shown to be nonexistent even under the auspices of memory. These impressions displace hierarchies (first, second), refuse synthesis, and resist distinctions between external and internal, conscious and unconscious.

In these fragments from what would have become her memoirs, Woolf attempts to come to terms with the notion of "memoirs" itself. She examines carefully the two presumed essential ingredients ("personal history and narrative"), posing difficult theoretical questions through her own autobiographical practice.

Despite the claim that the "subject of the memoir" must be central to it—must provide not only the "I" but the "eye" of its telling—she finds it impossible to place herself in that position. Indeed, she finds it nearly impossible to name herself; "Adeline Virginia Stephen" was never a name she was known by, and in the late 1930s, when she began constructing her reminiscences, her name—the one by which she was called and by which she called herself, the name that provided the signature to her texts, including this one—was something different. The central figure of the early years of her development was her mother, the woman who—until after the writing of *To the Lighthouse*—"obsessed" Virginia Woolf.

> I could hear her voice, see her, imagine what she would do or say as I went about my day's doings. She was one of the invisible presences who after all play so important a part in every life. This influence, by which I mean the consciousness of other groups impinging upon ourselves; public opinion; what other people say and think; all those magnets which attract us this way to be like that; or repel us the other and make us different from that; has never been analyzed in any of those Lives which I so much enjoy reading, or very superficially. (80)

Such "invisible presences" keep "the subject of this memoir" in place, according to Woolf. And it is the question of place—of space—that absorbs the autobiographical writer's attention as much as the proverbial issue of time. The mother, who occupied "the very centre of that great Cathedral space which was childhood" (81), becomes an "invisible presence" in Woolf's later life. Indeed, it is her removal from temporal and spacial existence that provides the central trauma of Woolf's narrative, an absence over which scar tissue knots this narrative and refuses to let the story unwind itself over the years. Like Gertrude Stein's obsession with the year 1907 (the year Alice B. Toklas entered her life, changing its contours and directions), Virginia Woolf's continual return to the morning of her mother's death, the morning she awoke to news of this loss and was led to her mother's bedroom to kiss her goodbye, constitutes a symptom of the writing, or a scab that is picked until it bleeds and forms again. Significantly, this scene is repeated twice in the memoir fragments, is reconstructed in *The Years*, and marks the moment of temporal absence ("Time Passes") in *To the Lighthouse*. For Virginia, Julia Stephen was "the creator of that crowded merry world which spun so gaily in the centre of my childhood. . . . She was the centre; it was herself. This was proved on May 5, 1895. For after that day there was nothing left of it" (84).

The centrality of the mother to this lost world of childhood, the nearness of her presence, prevents Woolf from describing her "in the present" of the past. All that becomes available are "those descriptions and anecdotes which after she was dead imposed themselves upon my view of her" (83). That is, the action of memory has been translated through narrative (description and anecdote), leaving a hole where once there was a center: "Of course she was central. I suspect the word 'central' gets closest to the general feeling I had of living so completely in her atmosphere that one never got far enough away from her to see her as a person" (83). A first memory of this mother centers on the flowers on the black ground of her dress: "I . . . saw the flowers she was wearing very close" (64). The point is not that Woolf's mother became an "invisible presence" after her death, but that she was always an invisible presence—too central, too close, to be observed: "If we cannot analyze these invisible presences, we know very little of the subject of the memoir; and again how futile life-writing becomes. I see myself as a fish in a stream; deflected; held in place; but cannot describe the stream" (80).

Thus the workings of memory, crucial to the recollection implicit in life writing, are found to be suspect. They slip beyond the borders of the conscious world; they are traversed and transgressed by the unconscious. Every exercise in memory recall that Woolf tries in these autobiographical efforts demonstrates the futility and failure of life writing. What is directly gazed upon in the memory remains absent; what is "revealed" comes by side glances and hints, in the effects of sound, light, smell, touch. Returning to the peculiar power of the "two strong memories" that initiate "A Sketch of the Past," Woolf comments, "I am hardly aware of myself, but only of the sensation. I am only the container of the feeling of ecstasy, of the feeling of rapture" (67). She wonders whether "things we have felt with great intensity have an existence independent of our minds" and whether "some device will be invented by which we can tap them" (67). She believes that "strong emotion must leave its trace" (67). Finding a way to tap these resources, to rediscover these traces, becomes both the overriding desire in her memoir writing and the cause of its failure. She is forced to discount memories: "As an account of my life they are misleading, because the things one does not remember are as important; perhaps they are more important" (69). Woolf attempts to explain away the intellectual difficulties posed by the problem of remembering and not remembering by dividing life into "moments of being" and "moments of non-being." She constructs a tapestry in which there is "hidden a pattern" that connects both the being and nonbeing of everyday life. She tries to find a means by which to include in the "life" that which is excluded in life writing: everything that forms the background of perception and action.

Woolf's effort leads to the construction of a series of metaphors by which to image the relation of present to past, of perception to action, of writing to living. She first builds a platform, a base on which to stand in recollecting the past, and decides to "include the present—at least enough of the present to serve as a platform to stand upon. It would be interesting to make the two people, I now, I then, come out in contrast" (75). There is no intention of reconciling these two people seen from the platform of the present ("I now, I then"). Woolf's project is nothing like the one James Olney describes for Richard Wright in *Black Boy:* "This double-reference 'I' delivers up a twofold *bios*—here and now, there and then, both the perpetual present and the historic past—and it is the tenuous yet tensile thread of memory that joins the two 'I's, that holds together the two *bioi*, and that successfully redeems the time of (and for) Richard Wright" (248).

Redemption and the action of recollection (in the sense of "gathering again") by which it claims to be achieved are shown by Woolf to be the deadly temptations of the autobiographical. On 25 October 1920 she had admitted to her diary the happiness that writing gave her: "and with it all how happy I am—if it weren't for my feeling that it's a strip of pavement over an abyss." Her fictional narratives (all of which could be termed "autobiographical" to some degree) were the strip of pavement over the abyss of self. While these fictions were in some sense a pretense against the primordial split subject (and were created "out of" that split), the memoir posed the question of selfhood directly; it forced Virginia Woolf to look into the abyss—something she could not do. Using a metaphor that explores surface and depth, the "experience" of present and past, along narrative movement, Woolf writes: "The past only comes back when the present runs so smoothly that it is like the sliding surface of a deep river. Then one sees through the surface to the depth" (98). This "sliding surface" is not available to conscious thought and practice; indeed, it demands an *unconsciousness* of the present. The present cannot call attention to itself (the "pavement" or "platform" of the present must be invisible). That is, "to feel the present sliding over the depths of the past, peace is necessary. The present must be smooth, habitual." Later in the same paragraph, Woolf reverses this process in an effort to restore a "sense of the present": "I write this partly in order to recover my sense of the present by getting the past to shadow this broken surface" (98).

Woolf concludes her contemplation of the autobiographical act and its relation to writing, memory, and self-consciousness by returning to its initial impetus—what she calls "scene-making":

> But, whatever the reason may be, I find that scene-making is my natural way of marking the past. Always a sense of scene has arranged itself: representative; enduring. This confirms me in my instinctive notion: (it will not bear arguing about; it is irrational) the sensation that we are sealed vessels afloat on what is convenient to call reality; and at some moments, the sealing matter cracks; in floods reality; that is, these scenes—for why do they survive undamaged year after year unless they are made of something comparatively permanent? (122)

It is the very admission of "irrationality" that interests here. Woolf views the past not as a "subject matter"—a content as such—but rather as a method, a scene making. Such scenes arrange themselves (much as the matter in the "hold all" composed itself) in moments when the "sealing matter" of identity and selfhood cracks. Unable to argue logically the ontology of autobiography by means of self-consciousness, Woolf moves toward an "instinctive notion" that the "sealed vessel" of selfhood is an artificial construct, that it "cracks" and floods, allowing access to that which in conscious moments is considered wholly separate and different from self—"what it is convenient to call reality."

But Woolf's notion of reality would share little with T. S. Eliot's. Hers is not a shock of recognition in the mirror but rather a linguistic space (a "scene") that conceals—and tries to seal itself against—the gap (the "crack") of the unconscious. Language, which operates according to a principle of division and separation, is the medium by which and through which the "self" is constructed. "Writing the self" is therefore a process of simultaneous sealing and splitting that can only trace fissures of discontinuity. This process may take place through "the individual's special, peculiar psychic configuration," but it is never an act of "consciousness, pure and simple"; it always refers to "objects outside itself, to . . . events, and to . . . other lives"; it always participates in "the shifting, changing unrealities of mundane life"; it is never "atemporal" (Olney 239). There is no grid whose horizontal axis represents a "thrust from the present into the past" and whose vertical axis constitutes a "thrust from consciousness down into the unconscious" (Olney 239). Instead, this scene forms itself as a kind of writing:

so it seemed to me
that I had watched
as a careful craftsman,

the pattern shape,
Achilles' history,
that I had seen him like the very scenes

on his famous shield,
outlined with the graver's gold;
true, I had met him, the New Mortal,

baffled and lost,
but I was a phantom Helen
and he was Achilles' ghost.
(*Helen in Egypt*, 262–63)

NOTES

1. Olney's "Some Versions of Memory" examines the *bios* at the center of this word without attention to the terms that enclose it—auto/graphy. In particular, this essay fails to mention that without *graphé* autobiography would not exist—that is, it is known only through the writing.

2. Gusdorf's essay "Conditions and Limits of Autobiography" opens with the declaration: "Autobiography is a solidly established literary genre" (28). James Olney's later essay in the same volume suggests "the impossibility of making any prescriptive definition for autobiography or placing any generic limitations on it at all" (237). Indeed, whether autobiography can be circumscribed within generic definitions is an important issue in autobiography studies. To date, however, there has been no rigorous investigation of the question of genre in relation to autobiography.

It is important to note that for Gusdorf autobiography is a genre that belongs to men, whose public lives it traces. Women are denied entrance to this writing for reasons examined in Susan Friedman's essay in Benstock, ed., *The Private Self*.

3. The "subject presumed to know" is a Lacanian construction belonging not, as one might expect, to the conscious realm of thinking (as "the one consciously in control") but to the unconscious. This subject is "supposed" precisely because the speaking (or writing) subject senses a lack in itself, and supposes, in Ellie Ragland-Sullivan's terms, that "'something' somewhere knows more than he or she. That 'something' furnishes the speaker with the authority for a given opinion" (172). The sense of an internal division, the claim of an authority from "elsewhere" (in the Other residing in the unconscious), problematizes the assigning of authority in the speaking/writing situation. Both meanings of "suppose" are at work here: to believe, especially on uncertain or tentative grounds; to expect or require, to presume.

4. This division cannot be "healed"; identity itself rests in this division, the effects of the working of the unconscious. Ragland-Sullivan comments: "Humans have an unconscious because they speak; animals have no unconscious because they do not speak. Since Lacan views repression and verbal symbolization as concurrent processes, which both mark the end of the mirror stage and create a secondary unconscious, we can look for answers to the self/ontology riddle in the transformational processes that mark repression" (173). For a particularly cogent reading of the effects of this division in women's writing, see Buck.

5. Not only women are included in this group, but all humans who—for whatever reasons—are not seen to represent authority. Psychosexual identity often does not coincide with biological sexuality, and thus male homosexuals fall into this grouping (and female homosexuals resist its effects), as do all others considered powerless and marginal—blacks, Jews, the economically deprived, and so on.

6. For an exhaustive analysis of the relation of *genre* and gender, see Jacques Derrida, "La Loi du Genre/The Law of Genre," which traces the etymological transferences of the two terms, and my essay, "From Letters to Literature," which traces the effects of this law on one literary *genre.*

7. See Benstock, "Beyond the Reaches of Feminist Criticism" and *Women of the Left Bank;* DeKoven, *A Different Language;* DuPlessis, *Writing Beyond the Ending;* Friedman, "Modernism of the Scattered Remnant" and *Psyche Reborn;* Friedman and DuPlessis, "'I Had Two Loves Separate'"; Gubar, "Blessings in Disguise" and "Sapphistries"; Kolodny, "Some Note on Defining a 'Feminist Literary Criticism'"; Marcus, "Laughing at Leviticus" and "Liberty, Sorority, Misogyny"; and Stimpson, "Gertrice/Altrude."

8. Special reference needs to be made to the work of Roland Barthes, Hélène Cixous, Jacques Derrida, Jacques Lacan, Michel Foucault, and Julia Kristeva. Interestingly, each of these people is excluded in one way or another from the dominant national discourse (French, white, male heterosexual); each sees himself or herself as (or is seen as being) an "outsider." This outsidership—which takes various forms and exerts varying effects over the "subjects" that these writers choose to discuss and the ways in which they discuss them—has been overlooked entirely by those critics who claim that collectively these people constitute a hegemonic power.

9. Lacan's reading of Freud teaches us that the social constructs the personal: "In 'The Agency of the Letter' (1957) Lacan says that there is no original or instinctual unconscious. Everything in the unconscious gets there from the outside world via symbolization and its effects" (Ragland-Sullivan 99). This discovery by Freud and its patient explication by Lacan have been systematically disregarded by most American interpreters of this work, especially by American feminists who ground their objections to Lacan's reading on the presumption that it separates the unconscious and the social or that it gives the unconscious the power (through the phallic signifier) to construct the external environment.

10. The unconscious is composed of these initial perceptions. Because of its physical helplessness and dependency, the child spends much of its early months listening and looking, taking in the environment around itself. Although it cannot use language, it assimilates sounds and rhythms. Ellie Ragland-Sullivan writes: "earliest perception is inseparable from the effects of the outside world, both linguistic and visual. . . . Since the primordial subject of unconsciousness is formed by identification with its first images and sensory experiences, it will thereafter reflect the essence of these images and objects in identity" (18).

11. The first summer that the Stephen family spent at St. Ives was 1882, the summer following Virgina's birth on January 25. She would have been six or seven months old that summer, and it is possible that the memories she "recalls" here are not memories at all but initial impressions of her environment—impressions that preceded use of language.

WORKS CITED

Benstock, Shari. "Beyond the Reaches of Feminist Criticism: A Letter from Paris." *Tulsa Studies in Women's Literature* 3 (1984): 5–27. Rpt. in *Feminist Issues in Literary Scholarship.* Ed. Shari Benstock. Bloomington: Indiana University Press, 1987. 7–29.

———. "From Letters to Literature: *La Carte Postale* in the Epistolary *Genre.*" *Genre* 18 (Fall 1985): 257–95.

————, ed. *The Private Self: Theory and Practice of Women's Autobiographical Writings*. Chapel Hill: University of North Carolina Press, 1988.

————. *Women of the Left Bank: Paris, 1900–1940*. Austin: University of Texas Press, 1986.

Broe, Mary Lynn, ed. *Silence and Power: Djuna Barnes, A Revaluation*. Carbondale: Southern Illinois University Press.

Brown, Cheryl L. and Karen Olson, eds. *Feminist Criticism: Essays on Theory, Poetry and Prose*. Metuchen: Scarecrow, 1978.

Buck, Claire. "Freud and H.D.—Bisexuality and a Feminine Discourse." *m/f* 8 (1983): 53–66.

DeKoven, Marianne. *A Different Language: Gertrude Stein's Experimental Writing*. Madison: University of Wisconsin Press, 1983.

Derrida, Jacques. *"La Loi du Genre*/The Law of Genre." Trans. Avital Ronnell. *Glyph* 7 (1980): 202–32.

Doolittle, Hilda [H.D.] *Helen in Egypt*. New York: New Directions, 1961.

DuPlessis, Rachel Blau. *Writing beyond the Ending: Narrative Strategies of Twentieth-Century Women Writers*. Bloomington: Indiana University Press, 1984.

Friedman, Susan Stanford. "Modernism of the 'Scattered Remnant': Race and Politics in H.D.'s Development." In *Feminist Issues in Literary Scholarship*. Ed. Shari Benstock. Bloomington: Indiana University Press, 1986. 208–31.

————. *Psyche Reborn: The Emergence of H.D.* Bloomington: Indiana University Press, 1981.

Friedman, Susan Stanford, and Rachel Blau DuPlessis. "'I Had Two Loves Separate': The Sexualities of H.D.'s *Her*." *Montemora* 8 (1981): 7–30.

Gubar, Susan. "Blessings in Disguise: Cross-Dressing as Re-Dressing for Female Modernists." *Massachusetts Review* 22 (1981): 477–508.

————. "Sapphistries." *Signs* 10 (1984): 43–62.

Gunn, Janet Varner. *Autobiography: Toward a Poetics of Experience*. Philadelphia: University of Pennsylvania Press, 1982.

Gusdorf, Georges. "Conditions and Limits of Autobiography." In Olney, *Autobiography* 28–48.

Heilbrun, Carolyn G., and Margaret R. Higgonet, eds. *The Representation of Women in Fiction*. Baltimore: Johns Hopkins University Press, 1983.

Kolodny, Annette. "Some Notes on Defining a 'Feminist Literary Criticism.'" In Brown and Olson, 37–58.

Marcus, Jane. "Laughing at Leviticus: *Nightwood* as Woman's Circus Epic." In Broe.

————. "Liberty, Sorority, Misogyny." In Heilbrun and Higgonet, 60–97.

Olney, James, ed. *Autobiography: Essays Theoretical and Critical*. Princeton: Princeton University Press, 1980.

————. "Some Versions of Memory/Some Versions of *Bios:* The Ontology of Autobiography." In Olney, *Autobiography*, 236–67.

Perry, Ruth, and Martine Watson Brownley. *Mothering the Mind*. New York: Holmes and Meier, 1984.

Ragland-Sullivan, Ellie. *Jacques Lacan and the Philosophy of Psychoanalysis*. Urbana: University of Illinois Press, 1986.

Stimpson, Catharine R. "Gertrice/Altrude: Stein, Toklas, and the Paradox of the Happy Marriage." In Perry and Brownley, 123–29.

Woolf, Virginia. *The Diary of Virginia Woolf*. Ed. Anne Olivier Bell. 5 vols. New York: Harcourt Brace Jovanovich, 1977–84.

————. *Moments of Being*. Ed. Jeanne Schulkind. New York: Harcourt Brace Jovanovich, 1976.

————. *The Waves*. New York: Harcourt Brace Jovanovich, 1959.

MAXINE HONG KINGSTON'S *WOMAN WARRIOR*

filiality and woman's autobiographical storytelling

> It is hard to write about my own mother. Whatever I do write, it is my story I am telling, my version of the past. If she were to tell her own story other landscapes would be revealed. But in my landscape or hers, there would be old, smoldering patches of deep-burning anger.
> —ADRIENNE RICH, *OF WOMAN BORN*

Since Harriet Martineau wrote her autobiography in 1856, many hundreds of women have contributed the story of their lives to the cultural heritage. Writers, artists, political figures, intellectuals, businesswomen, actors, athletes—all these and more have marked history in their own way, both as they lived their lives and as they wrote about them. A tradition so rich and various presents a challenge to the critic of twentieth-century autobiography. There is much to be written about the works; indeed, studies of twentieth-century autobiography are beginning to emerge. Articles now abound. I do not want to conclude this study of women's autobiographies without attention to a contemporary work; but I also realize that there are many choices that would have served my critical purposes. Nonetheless, for me at least, no single work captures so powerfully the relationship of gender to genre in twentieth-century autobiography as Maxine Hong Kingston's *Woman Warrior*.

And so it is fitting to conclude this discussion of women's autobiography with *The Woman Warrior: Memoirs of a Girlhood among Ghosts*, which is, quite complexly, an autobiography about women's autobiographical storytelling. A postmodern work, it exemplifies the potential for works from the marginalized to challenge the ideology of individualism and with it the ideology of gender. Recognizing the inextricable relationship between an individual's sense of "self" and the community's stories of selfhood, Kingston self-consciously reads herself into existence through the stories her culture tells about women. Using autobiography to create identity, she breaks down the hegemony of formal "autobiography" and breaks out of the silence that has bound her culturally to discover a resonant voice of her own. Furthermore, as a work coming from an ethnic subculture, *The Woman Warrior* offers the occasion to consider the complex imbroglios of cultural fictions that surround the autobiographer who is engaging two sets of stories: those of the dominant culture and those of an ethnic subculture with its own traditions, its own unique stories. As a Chinese American from the working class, Kingston brings to her autobiographical project complicating perspectives on the relationship of woman to language and to narrative.

Considered by some a "novel" and by others an "autobiography," the five narratives conjoined under the title *The Woman Warrior* are decidedly five confrontations with the fictions of self-representation and with the autobiographical possibilities embedded in cultural fictions, specifically as they interpenetrate one another in the autobiography a woman would write.[1] For Kingston, then, as for the woman autobiographer generally, the hermeneutics of self-representation can never be divorced from cultural representations of woman that delimit the nature of her access to the word and the articulation of her own desire. Nor can interpretation be divorced from her orientation toward the mother, who, as her point of origin, commands the tenuous negotiation of identity and difference in a drama of filiality that reaches through the daughter's subjectivity to her textual self-authoring.

Preserving the traditions that authorize the old way of life and enable her to reconstitute the circle of the immigrant community amidst an alien environment, Kingston's mother dominates the life, the landscape, and the language of the text as she dominates the subjectivity of the daughter who writes that text. It is Brave Orchid's voice, commanding, as Kingston notes, "great power" that continually reiterates the discourses of the communty in maxims, talk-story, legends, family histories. As the instrument naming filial identities and commanding filial obligations, that voice enforces the authority and legitimacy of the old culture to name and thus control the place of woman within the patrilineage and thereby to establish the erasure of female desire and the denial of female self-representation as the basis on which the perpetuation of patrilineal descent rests. Yet that same voice gives shape to other possibilities, tales of female power and authority that seem to create a space of cultural significance for the daughter; and the very strength and authority of the maternal voice fascinates the daughter because it "speaks" of the power of woman to enunciate her own representations. Hence storytelling becomes the means through which Brave Orchid passes on to her daughter all the complexities of and the ambivalences about both mother's and daughter's identity as woman in patriarchal culture.[2]

Storytelling also becomes the means through which Kingston confronts those complexities and ambivalences. In dialogic engagement with her mother's word, she struggles to constitute the voice of her own subjectivity, to emerge from a past dominated by stories told to her, ones that inscribe the fictional possibilities of female selfhood, into a present articulated by her own storytelling. Her text reveals the intensity of that struggle throughout childhood and adolescence and the persistance of those conflicts inherent in self-authoring well into adulthood; for, not only is that effort the subject in the text; it is also dramatized by the text. In the first two narratives she re-creates the stories about women and their autobiographical possibilities passed on to her by her mother: first the biographical story of no-name aunt, an apparent victim and thus a negative model of female life scripts, and then the legendary chant of the warrior woman Fa Mu Lan, an apparent heroine and positive model. But as she explores their fates, Kingston questions the very basis on which such distinctions are predicated. Uncovering layer by layer the dynamics and the consequences of her mother's interpretations as they resonate with the memories of her past, the daughter, as she too passes them on to posterity, circles around them, critiquing them, making them her own. Next she reconstructs out of the autobiographical fragments of Brave Orchid's own Chinese experience a biography of her mother, discovering by the way the efficacies of powerful storytelling for the woman who has fallen in status with her translation to another culture. In the fourth piece, an elaborate fabrication played on actual events, she becomes even more keenly attentive to all autobiographical and biographical representations, including her own. Looking back to the beginnings of her own struggle to take a voice, she traces in the final narrative the origins of her own hermeneutics. The apparent line of progress, which as it ends returns us to the beginning, becomes effectively a circle of sorts, a textual alternative to the constricting patriarchal circle Kingston has had to transgress.

"'You must not tell anyone,' my mother said, 'what I am about to tell you. In China your father had a sister who killed herself. She jumped into the family well. We say that your father has all brothers because it is as if she had never been born.'"[3] With that interdiction of female speech, uttered in the name of the father, Kingston's mother succinctly elaborates the circumstances of the sister's suicide. The concise maternal narrative concludes with forceful injunctions and powerful maxims inscribing the filial obligations of daughters in the patriarchal order: "'Don't let your father know that I told you. He denies her. Now that you have started to menstruate, what happened to her could happen to you. Don't humiliate us. You wouldn't like to be forgotten as if you had never been born. The villagers are watchful'" (5). Kingston thus situates the origins of her autobiography in her recollection of the story her mother used to contextualize the moment of transition ineradicably marking female identity and desire. That event, as it proclaims woman's sexual potency, proclaims also woman's problematic placement within the body social, economic, politic, and symbolic.[4] While her body, the locus of patrilineal preservation, will be contracted out to male authority to serve as the carrier of legitimate sons and of the order those sons perpetuate, it will always remain a potential source of disruption and disintegration in the community: It may provide no sons for the line of descent; or it may entertain strangers and thus introduce illegitimate children and an alternative genealogy into the order.[5] Should a daughter opt for the latter (unfilial) alternative, warns the mother, the patriarchal order will work efficiently to punish her transgression of the contract, eliminating her body and name from the world of things and of discourse. Kingston's aunt has suffered this fate: Her family, like the villagers, has enacted its own cleansing ritual; and Kingston's mother has perpetuated the ritual in the very way she tells the story. The aunt's name remains unuttered; and her interpretation of events is sacrificed, within the mother's text, to concern for the villagers' actions. Only her body assumes significance as it reveals the sign of its transgression, as it plugs up the family well.

The mother's cautionary tale at once affirms and seeks to cut off the daughter's kinship with a transgressive female relative and her unrepressed sexuality.[6] Kingston acknowledges the effectiveness of that strategy by revealing later in the narrative that for a long time she accepted her mother's interpretation and kept her counsel, thereby colluding in the perpetuation of both her own silencing and the erasure of her aunt's name:

> I have believed that sex was unspeakable and words so strong and fathers so frail that "aunt" would do my father mysterious harm. I have thought that my family, having settled among immigrants who had also been their neighbors in the ancestral land, needed to clean their name, and a wrong word would incite the kinspeople even here. But there is more to this silence: they want me to participate in her punishment. And I have. (18)

Now, however, at the moment of autobiographical writing, Kingston resists identification with mother and father by breaking the silence, returning to the story that marked her entrance into sexual difference and constituting her own interpretation of events. She comes to tell another story, seeking to name the formerly unnamed—the subjectivity of her aunt. As she does so, she imagines her aunt in a series of postures toward that excess of sexuality signified by the growth of her womb. Initially dismissing the probability that "people who hatch their own chicks and eat embryos and the heads for delicacies and boil the feet in vinegar for party food, leaving only the gravel, eating even the gizzard lining— could . . . engender a prodigal aunt" (7), she imagines her aunt the victim of rape, fearful, silent, and vulnerable before her victimizer. But she suspends that narrative line, apparently dissatisfied with its unmitigated emphasis on female powerlessness and willlessness. Beginning again, Kingston enters her aunt's subjectivity from another perspective, preferring to see her as a willful woman after "subtle enjoyment." Contemplating this posture, she finds herself increasingly aware of the gaps in her mother's tale, which motivate her to ask further questions of the story and to piece together an alternative textual genealogy.[7]

Instead of imagining her aunt as one of "the heavy, deep-rooted women" who "were to maintain the past against the flood, safe for returning" (9), and thus as victim, she imagines her as a woman attuned to "a secret voice, a separate attentiveness" (13), truly transgressive and subversive. The fruit of her womb becomes the mark exposing the priority of her desire for sexuality and autobiographical inscription. Indeed, the expansion of her very body and of her sense of her own authority to define herself ultimately challenges the ontological roots of her culture—"the real"; for publicized female subjectivity points to the fundamental vulnerability of the patrilineage by exposing it as a sustained fiction.[8] The alternative genealogy thus engendered breaks the descent line, subverting the legitimacy of male succession that determines all lines in patriarchy—descent lines, property lines, and lines of texts.[9] "The frightened villagers, who depended on one another to maintain the real," writes Kingston, "went to my aunt to show her a personal, physical representation of the break she had made in the 'roundness.' Misallying couples snapped off the future, which was to be embodied in true offspring. The villagers punished her for acting as if she could have a private life, secret and apart from them" (14).

While her journey across the boundaries that circumscribe the patriarchal order takes the aunt into the unbounded spaces of self-representation, Kingston acknowledges also that this "rare urge west" (9) leads her into the vast spaces of alienation, fearfulness, and death. Expelled from the family circle, her aunt becomes "one of the stars, a bright dot in blackness, without home, without a companion, in eternal cold and silence" (16). While the endless night proposes limitless identities beyond the confining borders of repetitious patriarchal representations, it promotes the "agoraphobia" attending any move beyond the carefully prescribed boundaries of ancestral, familial, and community paradigms of female self-representation. Overwhelmed by the vast spaces of possibility, the aunt returns to the genealogical source, reestablishing her cultural "responsibility" by giving birth in the pigsty—"to fool the jealous, pain-dealing gods, who do not switch piglets" (16)—and then by killing herself and her child—"a child with no descent line would not soften her life but only trail after her, ghostlike, begging her to give it purpose" (17). From one point of view, then, the aunt enacts on her own body and her own alternative genealogical text the punishment of the tribe, fulfilling her filial responsibilities to her circle by eliminating the source of contamination from its center and thereby restoring it to its unbroken configuration. She thus returns to the silence that defines her condition and her identity. From another point of view, however, the aunt's suicide continues her rebellion in a congeries of ways.[10] First, she brings back with her to the center of her natal circle the two loci of greatest pollution in Chinese culture—the moments of birth and death.[11] Second, by jumping back into the circle—the family well—she contaminates, in a recapitulated gesture of disruption, the water that literally and symbolically promises the continuance of patrilineal descent and the symbolic order it nourishes. Third, she takes with her the secret of paternal origins, never revealing the name of the father. Saving the father's face, she paradoxically erases the paternal trace, betraying in yet another way the fundamental fragility of undisputed paternal authority. Finally, by withholding from her natal family the name of the offender whose actions have caused such disgrace, she denies them the means to recover face by enacting their own revenge on the violator.[12] Thus, while she seems to capitulate before the monolithic power of the order against which she has transgressed, Kingston envisions her as a "spite suicide," an antiheroine whose actions subvert the stability of an order that rests on the moral imperatives of filial obligations, including sexual repression. Her very silence becomes a powerful presence, a female weapon of vengeance. Toward the end of this imaginative portrait, Kingston returns once again to her mother's tale by repeating the earlier refrain: "'Don't tell anyone you had an aunt. Your father does not want to hear her name. She has never been born'" (18). Yet while Kingston repeats her mother's words, she does so with a critical difference. Unlike her mother, she engenders a story for her aunt, fleshing out the narrative and incorporating the subjectivity previously denied that woman. Individualizing her mother's cautionary and impersonal tale, she transforms in the process both her aunt's text and her aunt's body from a maxim (a mere vessel to hold patriarchal signifiers) into a "life." Moreover, she ensures that she herself becomes more than a mere vessel preserving her mother's maxims, however deeply they may be embedded in her consciousness. For the story of this "forerunner," her "urge west" and her agoraphobia, becomes a piece in the puzzle of her own erased and erasable identity: "Unless I see her life branching into mine, she gives me no ancestral help" (10). And so, the filiations of her own story stretch backward to her aunt's, and the filiations of her aunt's story stretch forward to her own, as the two lives interpenetrate, crossing narrative boundaries in the text as Kingston interweaves her childhood experiences in the immigrant community encircling her with the imaginative biography of her aunt.

Kingston retrieves her aunt from the oblivion of sexuality repressed and textuality erased by placing her in an alternative narrative: the line of matrilineal descent to which she traces her origins and through which she gives voice to her subjectivity. Like her aunt's before her, this transgression of the injunction to filial silence challenges the priority of patrilineal descent. Allowing her imagination to give voice to the body of her aunt's text, Kingston expresses in her own way the excess of narrative (textuality) that links her intimately to that earlier excess of sexuality she identifies in her aunt. Indeed, her aunt becomes her textual "child," product of the fictions through which Kingston gives "birth" to her, and, by the way, to herself. Her story thus functions as a sign, like her aunt's enlarging belly, publicizing the potentially disruptive force of female textuality and the matrilineal descent of texts.

On the level of her mother's tale, then, the originating story of Kingston's autobiography testifies to the power of the patriarchy to command through mothers the silence of daughters, to name and to unname them, and thereby to control their meaning in discourse itself. On another level the opening piece displaces the mother's myth with the daughter's, thereby subverting the interpretations on which patrilineal descent and filial responsibilities are predicated and establishing a space in which female desire and self-representation can emerge. Yet Kingston concludes with a word of caution:

> My aunt haunts me—her ghost drawn to me because now, after fifty years of neglect, I alone devote pages of paper to her, though not origamied into houses and clothes. I do not think she always means me well. I am telling on her, and she was a spite suicide, drowning herself in the drinking water. The Chinese are always very frightened of the drowned one, whose weeping ghost, wet hair hanging and skin bloated, waits silently by the water to pull down a substitute. (19)

As the final sentence suggests, the identification may not be fortuitous, for autobiographical journeys and public self-representations are problematic adventures for daughters to pursue. Kingston does not yet know her aunt's name; and the subjectivity she has created for her remains only another interpretation, a fiction. Nor, by implication, can she be sure that she will ever know the truth about her own past. Her name is never uttered in the text; and her memories and stories may only be fictions too. This maternal trace, disruptive of the patriarchal order, may be potentially as threatening to Kingston as it was to her aunt. Indeed, she may be the child—"it was probably a girl; there is some hope of forgiveness for boys" (18)—that her aunt takes with her to the grave. Ultimately, the full, the "real" story of woman may lead to madness and to self-destruction rather than to legitimate self-representation.

Kingston in the second piece engages another of her mother's representations of female autobiography, a story from which she learned that Chinese girls "failed if we grew up to be but wives and slaves." Here she does not distinguish in quotation marks the words of her mother; rather, she moves directly to her own elaboration of Fa Mu Lan's chant.[13] But she goes further, appropriating not only the chant but also the very body of that legendary woman warrior: The identities of woman warrior and of woman narrator interpenetrate until biography becomes autobiography, until Kingston and Fa Mu Lan are one.[14] Through this fantasy of mythic identification, the adult daughter inscribes an autobiography of "perfect filiality" through which she fulfills her mother's expectations and garners her mother's unqualified love. Simultaneously, this "life" enables her to escape confinement in conventional female scripts and to enter the realm of heroic masculine pursuits—of education, adventure, public accomplishment, and fame. Ironically, however, Kingston's mythical autobiography betrays the ontological bases on which that love, power, and compliance with perfect filiality rest.

The woman warrior gains her education beyond the engendered circle of community and family in a magical, otherworldly place where male and female difference remains undelineated. Her educators are a hermaphroditic couple beyond childbearing age whose relationship appears to be one of relative equality; and the education they offer encourages her to forge an identity, not through conventional formulations of woman's selfhood, but through a close identification with the creatures of nature and the secrets of natural space.[15] In such a space female sexuality, signaled by the onslaught of puberty, remains a "natural" event rather than a cultural phenomenon situating the girl in a constellation of attitudes toward female pollution and contamination. Nonetheless, that education, while it appears to be liberating, presupposes Fa Mu Lan's total identification with the desires of her family, ubiquitously present even in its absence. For instance, she passively watches in the gourd as her own wedding ceremony takes place despite her absence, the choice of husband entirely her parents' prerogative. Ultimately, woman can be trained as warrior only in a space separate from family; but she can enter that space only because her sacrifice to the circle is the basis on which her education takes place at all. Consequently, her empowerment does not threaten to disrupt the representations of the patriarchal circle; on the contrary, it serves both the family and the discourse of gender.

When she returns home, Fa Mu Lan takes her place, not as "woman," but as extraordinary woman—as, that is, man: "My parents killed a chicken and steamed it whole, as if they were welcoming home a son" (40). As surrogate son, she replaces her father in battle, eventually freeing her community from the exploitation and terrorization of the barons. Yet she must do more than enact the scenario of male selfhood. She must erase her sexual difference and publicly represent herself as male, a "female avenger" masquerading in men's clothes and hair styles. And while her sexual desire is not repressed altogether, as in the case of the virginal Joan of Arc to whom Kingston alludes, it must remain publicly unacknowledged. Hidden inside her armor and her tent, her "body" remains suppressed in the larger community.[16] It also bears the marks of her textual and sexual appropriation by man: "Now when I was naked, I was a strange human being indeed—words carved on my back and the baby large in front" (47). The lines of text on her back are not her own creation: They are the words by which the father has inscribed his law on her body, wounding her in the process. And her belly is full of a male heir whose birth will ensure the continuance of the patrilineage she serves in her heroism.[17] Finally, and most telling, the narrative's closure asserts the ultimate limitations of the warrior woman's autobiographical possibilities. Fa Mu Lan's story breaks roughly into two parts: the narratives of preparation and public action. It thus reinscribes the traditional structure of androcentric self-representation, driven by a linear-causal progression. Once the revenge carved on her back has been enacted, however, both her life as woman warrior and her autobiography end. Having returned home to unmask herself and to be recuperated as publicly silenced wife and slave, she kneels before her parents-in-law: "'Now my public duties are finished. . . . I will stay with you, doing farmwork and housework, and giving you more sons" (53–54). There is nothing more to be said by her and of her.

Fa Mu Lan's name, unlike the name of no-name aunt, is passed on from generation to generation, precisely because the lines of her story as woman warrior and the lines of her text as woman autobiographer reproduce an androcentric paradigm of identity and selfhood and thereby serve the symbolic order in "perfect filiality." Since both life and text mask her sexual difference and thereby secure her recuperation in the phallic order by inscribing her subjectivity and her selfhood in the law of the same representation, they legitimate the very structures man creates to define himself, including those structures that silence women.[18]

The heroic figure of Fa Mu Lan thus represents a certain kind of woman warrior, a culturally privileged "female avenger." Embedded in Kingston's fantasy autobiography, however, lies a truly subversive "story" of female empowerment. Imaged as tiny, foot-bound, squeaky-voiced women dependent on male authority for their continued existence, the wives of warriors, barons, and emperors who haunt the interstices of the textual landscape are, in one sense, conventional ghosts. Yet those apparently erased ciphers become, in another sense, the real female avengers:

> Later, it would be said, they turned into the band of swordswomen who were a mercenary army. They did not wear men's clothes like me, but rode as women in black and red dresses. They bought up girl babies so that many poor families welcomed their visitations. When slave girls and daughters-in-law ran away, people would say they joined these witch amazons. They killed men and boys. I myself never encountered such women and could not vouch for their reality. (53)

Such "witch amazons" are figures of all that is unrepressed and violent in ways both sexual and textual, in the narrator herself as well as in the social order. Wielding unauthorized power, they do not avenge the wrongs of fathers and brothers; they lead daughters against fathers and sons, slaying the source of the phallic order itself.[19] Moreover, they do so, not by masking, but by aggressively revealing their sexual difference. Paradoxically, Fa Mu Lan has liberated the women who subvert the order she serves, just as Kingston the narrator has released the rumor that subverts the story she tells.

Kingston's memories of the real, rather than mythical, childhood also subvert the fiction she has created out of her mother's expectations. Juxtaposing to this autobiography of androcentric selfhood another self-representation that undermines the priority of the fantasy of "perfect filiality," Kingston betrays Fa Mu Lan's story as a fragile fiction only coterminous with the words that inscribe it as myth. And the jarring texture of her recollected experience—its nervous, disjointed, unpoetic, frustrated prose—calls into question the basis for the seamless elegance and almost mystical lyricism of Fa Mu Lan's poetic autobiography.

Kingston recalls the repetition of commonplace maxims that deny female significance ("Feeding girls is feeding cowbirds"; "When you raise girls, you're raising children for strangers"; "Girls are maggots in the rice"); the pressures of a language that conflates the ideographs representing the female "I" and "slave"; the images "of poor people snagging their neighbors' flotage with long flood hooks and pushing the girl babies on down the river" (62). All these signs and stories of her culture equate her identity as "girl" with failed filiality and engender in her a profound sense of vulnerability and lack. Thus she remembers how she tried to fulfill her filial obligations in the only way imaginable to her: She works at being a "bad" girl—for, as she asks, "Isn't a bad girl almost a boy?" (56). She rejects the traditional occupations of femininity: refusing to cook, breaking dishes, screaming impolitely as maxims are mouthed, defiantly telling her parents' friends that she wants to become a lumberjack, bringing home straight As, those signs from another culture of her extraordinary public achievements. She adopts, that is, the cultural postures of a "son" by generating signs imitative of male selfhood. But her efforts to be the phallic woman do not earn the love and acceptance of her mother and community, as they do Fa Mu Lan. And so her experience gives the lie to that other autobiography: Everywhere the legend is betrayed as a misleading fiction.[20]

In the end, there remains only one residual locus of identity between Kingston and Fa Mu Lan: "What we have in common are the words at our backs. The ideographs for revenge are 'report a crime' and 'report to five families.' The reporting is the vengeance—not the beheading, not the gutting, but the words. And I have so many words—'chink' words and 'gook' words too—that they do not fit on my skin" (63). Her appropriation of the pen, that surrogate sword, and her public inscription of the story of her own childhood among ghosts become the reporting of a crime—the crime of a culture that would make nothing of her by colonizing her and, in so doing, steal her authority and her autobiography from her as her mother's legend would do. In the tale the forces of exploitation remain external to her family; but in her own experience they remain internal, endemic to the patriarchal family whose existence is founded on the colonization and erasure of women in service to the selfhood of men and boys and whose perpetuation is secured through the mother's word. By simultaneously enacting and critiquing that legendary story of female power, Kingston manages to shatter the complacencies of cultural myths, problematic heroines, and the illusory autobiographical possibilities they sanction. By "slaying" the stories of men and boys and phallic women warriors, she allies herself with the true female avengers of her tale. Fa Mu Lan may have denied her identity with such women; Kingston does not.

Whereas the first two narratives explore the consequences of Kingston's appropriation of her mother's stories, the third goes through the stories to the storyteller herself. Three scrolls from China serve as the originating locus of this biography of her mother pieced together with "autobiographical" fragments. Texts that legitimate her mother's professional identity as doctor, the scrolls stimulate biography because they announce public achievements, a life text readable by culture. They also announce to the daughter another mother, a mythic figure resident in China who resisted the erasure of her own desire and who pursued her own signifying selfhood. In her daughter's text, Brave Orchid becomes a kind of "woman warrior," whose story resonates with the Fa Mu Lan legend: both women leave the circle of the family to be educated for their mission and both return to serve their community, freeing it through many adventures from those forces that would destroy it. Both are fearless, successful, admired.

Kingston's biography accretes all varieties of evidence testifying to her mother's bravery and extraordinariness. Portrayed as one of the "new women, scientists who changed the rituals" (88), Brave Orchid bears the "horizontal name of one generation" that truly names her rather than the patronym signifying woman's identity as cipher silently bonding the patrilineage. Thus Kingston's awe-filled narration of her mother's confrontation with the Sitting Ghost takes on such synecdochic proportions in the text: "My mother may have been afraid, but she would be a dragoness ('my totem, your totem'). She could make herself not weak. During danger she fanned out her dragon claws and riffled her red sequin scales and unfolded her coiling green stripes. Danger was a good time for showing off. Like the dragons living in temple eaves, my mother looked down on plain people who were lonely and afraid" (79). The ensuing battle between woman and ghost unfolds as a primal struggle with the dynamics and the rhythms of an attempted rape. A physically powerless victim of the palpably masculine presence who "rolled over her and landed bodily on her chest" (81), Brave Orchid is initially unable to challenge his strength. But she ultimately prevails against the Boulder, defeating him with the boldness of her word and the power of the images she voices to taunt him into submission and cowardice. Such fearlessness and verbal cunning characterize subsequent adventures the daughter invokes: the coexistence with ghosts and strange monsters populating the countryside through which she travels on her way to administer to the sick; the bargain she drives with the slave dealer; her response to the birth of monster babies; and her bold orientation toward food.[21]

Embedded in the daughter's representation of her mother's extraordinariness, however, lies another, a palimpsest that tells of her mother's preoccupation with autobiographical interpretation. Even more important than the story of Brave Orchid's confrontation with the Sitting Ghost is the re-creation of her narrative of the encounter. Skillful in creating compelling stories of her experience, Brave Orchid makes of the ghost a vividly ominous antagonist, thereby authoring herself as powerful protagonist. Such imaging ensures the emboldening of her presence in the eyes and imaginations of the other women (and of her daughter): "'I am brave and good. Also I have bodily strength and control. Good people do not lose to ghosts" (86). Kingston also suggests that her mother secured the same admiration in other ways. By studying in secret, "she quickly built a reputation for being brilliant, a natural scholar who could glance at a book and know it" (75). Returning to her village, she "wore a silk robe and western shoes with big heels"; thereafter she maintained that posture by never dressing "less elegantly than when she stepped out of the sedan chair" (90). By avoiding treatment of the terminally ill, she ensured that her powers as doctor were magnified. In linguistic and behavioral postures, Brave Orchid orchestrates her public image, inscribes, that is, her own autobiography as extraordinary woman.

The mother's mode of self-authoring complicates the daughter's effort to reconstruct her mother's biography. Brave Orchid's stories about China become the only archival material out of which Kingston can create that "life"; and yet the stories are already "representations" or "fictions" of her experiences before she reaches an America where she is no doctor, where she works daily washing other people's laundry or picking fruit and vegetables in the fields, where she is no longer woman alone but a wife and mother, where she is no woman warrior dressed elegantly in silk. "You have no idea how much I have fallen" (90), she confesses and therein suggests the efficacy of stories and storytelling as means to preserve her extraordinariness. Significantly, the dynamics of the mother's fate recall those of Fa Mu Lan's: Adventures concluded, both return to the home of the husband as wife and slave, there to become the subject of wonderful tales of an earlier glory in a faraway place.

Kingston's narrative, as it interpenetrates her autobiography with her mother's biography, reveals how problematic such stories can become for the next generation. From one point of view, they can be exhilarating, creating in children the admiration that is so apparent in Kingston's text. But from another, they generate confusions and ambiguities, since as a child Kingston inflected the narratives with her own subjectivity, attending to another story within the text of female heroism. For Brave Orchid's tales of bravery and exoticism are underwritten by an alternative text of female vulnerability and victimization. The story elaborating the purchase of the slave girl reaffirms the servile status of women and actually gives legitimacy to Kingston's fears her parents will sell her when they return to China. The stories of babies identify femaleness with deformity and suggest to the daughter the haunting possibility that her mother might actually have practiced female infanticide. The story of the crazy lady, scurrying directionless on bound feet, encased in the mirror-studded headdress, caught in her own self-destructive capitulations, dramatizes communal fear of the anomalous woman who embodies the threat of uncontrolled female sexuality and subversive alliances between women—always strangers within the community—and the enemy outside.

All these tales from her mother's past, by reinforcing the representation of women as expendable, resonate with Kingston's sense of displacement in her family and in the immigrant community in America, her confusion about her sexuality, and her fears of her own "deformities" and "madnesses." They leave her with food that suffocates her, a voice that squeaks on her, and nightmares that haunt the long nights of childhood. They also complicate Kingston's sense of identification with her mother by betraying the basis on which her tales of extraordinariness are founded, that is, the powerlessness of ordinary women and children and their cruel and insensitive victimization, even at the hands of Brave Orchid herself. In fact, in her self-representation Kingston identifies herself with the "lonely and afraid," a victim of her mother's stories, and thus no true heroine after her mother's model. Paradoxically, her mother, the shaman with the power of word and food, has, instead of inspiring her daughter to health and heroism, made the daughter, sick, hungry, vulnerable, fearful.

In the closing passage of this third narrative, Kingston re-creates her most recent encounter with her mother and, through it, her continuing resistance to her mother's victimizing presence. Ironically, the scene recapitulates the earlier scene of her mother's biography. The dark bedroom, the late hour recall the haunted room at the medical school. Here Brave Orchid is herself the ghost who would continue to haunt her daughter: "My mother would sometimes be a large animal, barely real in the dark; then she would become a mother again" (118).

Like Brave Orchid before her, Kingston grasps the only weapon effective in over-coming that ghost—the words with which she resists her. In the syncopated rhythm of statement and rebuttal, she answers her mother's vision of things with her own, challenging unremittingly the power of her mother to control inter-pretations. She also offers an alternative representation of her mother in this clos-ing scene, portraying her as an old woman, tired, prosaic, lonely, a woman whose illusions of returning to China have vanished, whose stories have become pee-vish, repetitious. In creating a portrait of her mother as neither fearless nor ex-otic, the daughter demystifies Brave Orchid's presence and diffuses the power of her word.

For all the apparent rejection of her mother as ghost, the final passage points to a locus of identification between mother and daughter and a momentary rap-prochement between the two. In saying goodnight, Kingston's mother calls her Little Dog, a name of endearment unuttered for many years, and, in that gesture of affection, releases her daughter to be who she will. As a result, Kingston expe-riences the freedom to identify with her; for, as the daughter makes evident in her biography, her mother before her had strayed from filial obligations, leaving her parents behind in pursuit of her own desire: "I am really a Dragon, as she is a Dragon, both of us born in dragon years. I am practically a first daughter of a first daughter" (127). At this moment of closure, Kingston affectionately traces her genealogy as woman and writer to and through her mother in a sincere gesture of filiality, acknowledging as she does so that her autobiography cannot be inscribed outside the biography of her mother, just as the biography of her mother cannot be inscribed outside her own interpretations. Mother and daughter are allied in the interpenetration of stories and storytelling, an alliance captured in the ambig-uous reference of the final sentence: "She sends me on my way, working always and now old, dreaming the dreams about shrinking babies and the sky covered with airplanes and a Chinatown bigger than the ones here" (127). As the motifs of the final pages suggest, both mother and daughter are working always and now old.

In the fourth narrative Kingston does not take the word of her mother as her point of narrative origin. She will reveal at the inception of the next piece that the only information she received about the events narrated in the fourth piece came from her brother through her sister in the form of an abrupt, spare bone of a story: "What my brother actually said was, 'I drove Mom and Second Aunt to Los Angeles to see Aunt's husband who's got the other wife'" (189). Out of a single factual sentence, Kingston creates a complex story of the two sisters, Brave Orchid and Moon Orchid. She admits that "his version of the story may be better than mine because of its bareness, not twisted into designs" (189); but the "designs" to which she alludes have become integral to her autobiographical interpretations.

In Kingston's designs Moon Orchid, like Brave Orchid in "Shaman," embod-ies her name: She is a flower of the moon, a decorative satellite that revolves around and takes its definition from another body, the absent husband. Mute to her own desire, attendant always on the word of her husband, she represents the traditional Chinese wife, a woman without autobiographical possibilities. "For thirty years," comments her niece, "she had been receiving money from him from America. But she had never told him that she wanted to come to the United States. She waited for him to suggest it, but he never did" (144). Unlike Brave Orchid, she is neither clever nor shrewd, skilled nor quick, sturdy nor lasting. Demure, self-effacing, decorative, tidy, refined—she is as gracefully useless and as elegantly civilized as bound feet, as decoratively insubstantial as the paper cutouts she brings her nieces and nephews from the old country. Having little subjectivity of her own, she can only appropriate as her own the subjectivity of others, spending her days following nieces and nephews through the house, describing what they do, repeating what they say, asking what their words mean. While there is something delightfully childlike, curious, and naive about that narration of other people's lives, there is a more profound sadness that a woman in her sixties, unformed and infantile, has no autobiography of her own.

When her husband rejects her, giving his allegiance to his Chinese-American wife, who can speak English and aid him in his work, he denies the very ontological basis on which Moon Orchid's selfhood is predicated and effectually erases her from the lines of descent. He also undermines with his negation of her role what autobiographical representations she has managed to create for herself. "'You became people in a book I read a long time ago'" (179), he tells the two sisters, dramatically betraying the elusiveness of the "fictions" on which Moon Orchid has sustained her identity as first wife. Once having been turned into a fairy-tale figure from a long time past, this woman loses the core of her subjectivity and literally begins to vanish: She appears "small in the corner of the seat" (174); she stops speaking because the grounds for her authority to speak have been undermined—"All she did was open and shut her mouth without any words coming out" (176); later she stops eating, returning to Brave Orchid's home "shrunken to the bone." Ultimately, she vanishes into a world of madness where she creates repetitious fictions, variations on a story about vanishing without a trace. Thus she fantasizes that Mexican "ghosts" are plotting to snatch her life from her, that "'they' would take us in airplanes and fly us to Washington, D.C., where they'd turn us into ashes . . . drop the ashes in the wind, leaving no evidence" (184). The tenuousness, evanescence, and elusiveness of identity press on her so that everywhere she sees signs (sees, that is, evidence of the legitimacy of her own interpretations) that alien males threaten to erase her from the world, leaving no trace of her body as her husband has left no trace of her patrilineal existence. To protect herself she withdraws into the "house" of her sister, that edifice that has supported her construction of an identity as first wife. There she literally makes of the house what it has always been metaphorically— a living coffin—windows shut and darkened, "no air, no light," and she makes of storytelling itself a living coffin. As Brave Orchid tells her children, "'The difference between mad people and sane people . . . is that sane people have variety when they talk-story. Mad people have only one story that they talk over and over'" (184). Only after Brave Orchid commits her to a mental institution does she find a new fiction to replace the old one, a renewed identity as "mother" to the other women ("daughters") who can never vanish. In the end the story of vanishing without leaving a trace becomes the only trace that is left of her, an impoverished autobiographical absence.

Her mother Kingston now represents, not as the "new woman" of "Shaman," but as a traditional woman intent on preserving her family from harm by maintaining the old traditions against the erosions of American culture. Through the conventions of speaking (Chinese), eating, greeting, chanting, storytelling, she keeps China drawn around her family in a linguistic and gustatory circle. More particularly, she seeks to preserve the old family constellation and, with it, the identity of woman. Thus, from Brave Orchid's "Chinese" perspective, her sister is a first wife, entitled to certain privileges and rights, even in America. Yet, in her allegiance to the old traditions of filial and affinal obligations, Brave Orchid becomes shortsighted, insensitive, and destructive. She succeeds only in making other women (her niece, who remains trapped in a loveless marriage; her sister, who dies in a mental institution) unhappy, sick, even mad; and she does so because, failing to anticipate just how misplaced the traditions and myths have become in the new world, she trusts her word too well. The stories she tells create illusions that fail of reference to any reality.

The story of the Empress of the Western Palace is a case in point. "'A long time ago,'" Brave Orchid tells her sister on the drive to Los Angeles,

> "the emperors had four wives, one at each point of the compass, and they lived in four palaces. The Empress of the West would connive for power, but the Empress of the East was good and kind and full of light. You are the Empress of the East, and the Empress of the West has imprisoned the Earth's Emperor in the Western Palace. And you, the good Empress of the East, come out of the dawn to invade her land and free the Emperor. You must break the strong spell she has cast on him that has lost him the East." (166)

The myth, however, is an inappropriate text through which to interpret Moon Orchid's experience. The Empress of the West is not conniving; the Emperor does not want freeing; and the Empress of the East cannot break the spell. Moreover, for all Brave Orchid's forceful narratives of the projected meeting among Moon Orchid, the husband, and the second wife, the actual scene is pitifully humorous, squeezed as it is in the backseat of the car. "'What scenes I could make'" (146), she tells her sister; but the only scenes she makes are in her fantasies of them (and her daughter the storyteller is the one who actually makes the scene). Though she is not entirely speechless when they confront Moon Orchid's husband, she is obviously awed by the wealthy, successful, and much younger man, and by the pressure of his young, efficient wife. Kingston creates a Brave Orchid bested in the game of fictionalizations. The husband has turned the two sisters into characters from a book read long ago, a devastating recapitulation of their efforts to turn him into the fictional Emperor. While the power of her myths to help define and situate identities has been eroded by another cultural tradition, Brave Orchid herself has not been destroyed because, unlike Moon Orchid, she is willful, hardworking, clever, intelligent, shrewd, stubborn, "brave"—all those qualities that have enabled her to cope with and to survive in her translation to another cultural landscape. Moreover, she can always fabricate another story, as she does when she urges her children to sabotage any plans her husband, now in his seventies, might have to marry a second wife. Nonetheless, other women are victimized by her words, their autobiographical possibilities cut off.

Through the "designs" in "At the Western Palace," Kingston confronts explicitly the problematics of autobiographical "fictions." Both Moon Orchid and Brave Orchid serve as powerful negative models for the perils of autobiography. Moon Orchid, bereft of the husband who defines her place and who sets the limits of her subjectivity within the structures of the patrilineage, succumbs to an imagination anchored in no-place, an imaginative rootlessness threatening Kingston herself. Overwhelmed by repetitive fantasies, her aunt vanishes into a world where alien males continually plot to erase her from existence, a preoccupation that resonates with Kingston's childhood fears of leaving no culturally significant autobiographical trace. A woman of no autobiography, Moon Orchid cannot find a voice of her own, or, rather, the only subjectivity that she finally voices is the subjectivity of madness. Brave Orchid, too, serves as a powerful negative model. She would write a certain biography of her sister, patterned after traditional interpretations of the identity of a first wife. In preserving her interpretations, however, she victimizes other women by failing to make a space in her story for female subjectivity in unfamiliar landscapes, by remaining insensitive to her sister's fears and desires, as she remains insensitive to her daughter's desires. Giving her unquestioning allegiance to language, she fails to recognize the danger in words, the perils inherent in the fictions that bind.

In the end Kingston, too, has created only a fiction, an elaborate story out of the one sentence passed by her brother through her sister; and she, too, must beware the danger in words as she constructs her stories of those other women, more particularly her mother. To a certain extent she seems to do so in this fourth narrative. For all the negative, even horrifying, aspects of Brave Orchid's fierce preservation and Moon Orchid's repetitive fantasies, both women come across in this section as fully human. Her mother, especially, does so; and that is because, releasing her mother to be her own character, under her own name "Brave Orchid," rather than as "my mother," the daughter penetrates her mother's subjectivity with tender ironies and gentle mercies. In doing so, she effaces her own presence in the text as character, her presence implied only in the reference to Brave Orchid's "children." Unlike her mother, then, who does not imagine the contours of her sister's subjectivity, Kingston here tries to think like her mother and her aunt. Yet even as she creates the fullness of her mother out of her word, she recognizes the very fictionality of her tale—its "designs" that serve her own hermeneutical purposes. She, too, like her mother within her story, negotiates the world by means of the fictions that sustain interpretations and preserve identities. In the persistent reciprocities that characterize Kingston's storytelling, her mother becomes the product of her fictions, as she has been the product of her mother's.

Kingston represents in the final piece, "A Song for a Barbarian Reed Pipe," her adolescent struggle to discover her own speaking voice and autobiographical authority. This drama originates in the memory of her mother's literally cutting the voice out of her: "She pushed my tongue up and sliced the frenum. Or maybe she snipped it with a pair of nail scissors. I don't remember her doing it, only her telling me about it, but all during childhood I felt sorry for the baby whose mother waited with scissors or knife in hand for it to cry—and then, when its mouth was wide open like a baby bird's, cut" (190). Notably, Kingston remembers, not the actual event, but the reconstruction of the event in language, a phenomenon testifying to the power of the mother's word to constitute the daughter's history, in this case her continuing sense of confusion, horror, deprivation, and violation. Her mother passes on a tale of female castration, a rite of passage analogous to a clitoridectomy, that wounding of the female body in service to the community, performed and thereby perpetuated by the mother.[22] It is a ritual that results in the denial to woman of the pleasure of giving voice to her body and body to her voice, the pleasure of autobiographical legitimacy and authority.

In her re-creation of the confrontation with the Chinese American girl in the bathroom of the Chinese school, Kingston evokes her childhood confusion about speechlessness: "Most of us," she comments, "eventually found some voice, however faltering. We invented an American-feminine speaking personality, except for that one girl who could not speak up even in Chinese school" (200). A kind of surrogate home, the Chinese school functions as the repository of old traditions and conventional identities within the immigrant community; and the bathroom is that most private of female spaces—only for girls, only for certain activities, which, as it locates the elimination of matter from the body, ultimately becomes associated with female pollution and shame. In that space, Kingston responds cruelly, even violently, to the female image before her, abhorring the girl's useless fragility: her neat, pastel clothes; her China-doll haircut; her tiny, white teeth; her baby-soft, fleshy skin—"like squid out of which the glassy blades of bones had been pulled," "like tracing paper, onion paper" (206). Most of all, she abhors her "dumbness," for this girl, who cannot even speak her name aloud, is ultimately without body or text. "'You're such a nothing,'" Kingston remembers yelling at her. "'You are a plant. Do you know that? That's all you are if you don't talk. If you don't talk, you can't have a personality. You'll have no personality and no hair. You've got to let people know you have a personality and a brain. You think somebody is going to take care of you all your stupid life?'" (210).

Yet, while the girl stands mute before the screaming Kingston, they both weep profusely, wiping their snot on their sleeves as the seemingly frozen scene wraps them both in its embrace. Kingston remembers feeling some comfort in establishing her difference from the girl, taking pride in her dirty fingernails, calloused hands, yellow teeth, her desire to wear black. But the fierceness with which she articulates her desire for difference only accentuates her actual identity with the nameless girl: Both are the last ones chosen by teams; both are silent and "dumb" in the American school. An exaggerated representation of the perfect Chinese girl, this girl becomes a mirror image of Kingston herself, reflecting her own fears of insubstantiality and dumbness (symbolized for her in the zero intelligence quotient that marks her first-grade record). In the pulling of the hair, the poking of the flesh, Kingston captures the violence of her childhood insecurity and self-hatred. Striking the Chinese American girl, she strikes violently at her own failure to take a voice and at all her mother's prior narratives of female voicelessness. Tellingly, her aggressive attack on that mirror image eventuates, not in the girl's utterance of her name, but in Kingston's eighteen-month illness, which ensures that she indeed does become like the other girl. Confined to bed, isolated inside the house, she is literally silenced in the public space, a fragile and useless girl. Attended always by her family, she too becomes a plant, a nothing. Ironically, she says of that time: "It was the best year and a half of my life. Nothing happened" (212). The admission betrays the tremendous relief of not having to prove to people she has "a personality and a brain," the powerful enticement of succumbing to the implications of her mother's narratives and her culture's maxims, the confusing attractiveness of not having to find a public voice, of not struggling with shame.

For, as her narrative recollection reveals, taking a voice becomes complicated by her sense of guilt. She is ashamed to speak in public with a voice like those of the immigrant women—loud, inelegant, unsubtle. She is ashamed to speak the words her mother demands she say to the druggist ghost because she considers her mother's words, as they exact compliance with traditional beliefs, to be outdated. She is ashamed to keep the same kind of silences and secrets her mother would keep because such secrets command her duplicity before the teachers she respects. For all these reasons she would not speak like her mother (and Chinese women) in her American environment; but her own efforts to take the appropriate American-feminine voice fail, and that failure too gives her cause for shame. In public her voice becomes "a crippled animal running on broken legs" (196), a duck voice; her throat "cut[s]" off the word; her mouth appears "permanently crooked with effort, turned down on the left side and straight on the right" (199). Her face and vocal chords continue to show the signs of her prior castration, the physical mutilation and discomfort that mark her relationship to language and to any public enunciation of subjectivity.

The landscape of her childhood, as she reconstructs it, reveals the underlying logic in Kingston's failure to overcome her symbolic disability. Seeing around her the humiliating representations of woman, hearing words such as "maggots" become synonyms for "girls," suspecting that her mother seeks to contract her out as the wife and slave of some young man, perhaps even the retarded boy who follows her around with his box full of pornographic pictures, she negotiates a nightmare of female victimization by adopting the postures of an unattractive girl, the better to foil her mother's efforts and to forestall her weary capitulation. Cultivating that autobiographical signature, she represents herself publicly as the obverse of her mother's image of the charming, attractive, practical young girl by becoming clumsy, vulgar, bad-tempered, lazy, impractical, irreverent, and stupid "from reading too much" (226). She becomes, that is, a kind of fiction; and the psychic price she pays for orchestrating such a public posture is high. Publicly appearing as the "dumb" and awkward girl, she does not earn the affection and respect of her family and community. Moreover, she must convince herself of the reality of her mind by constantly attending to the grades she earns in the American school, those signs, unrecognized in her Chinese culture, that signal her access to other discourses. She remains "dumb" in another sense, for she recognizes even in childhood that "talking and not talking made the difference between sanity and insanity," in that "insane people were the ones who couldn't explain themselves" (216). Since she cannot give voice to her subjectivity except by indirection and dissimulation, externalizing in an awkward masquerade the text of publicly unexpressed desires, she finds commonality with the anomalous women such as Pee-A-Nah and Crazy Mary, who retreat into imaginary worlds, there to haunt the outskirts of the immigrant community and the imaginations of its children.

The culmination of this struggle with voice comes when Kingston finally attempts to "explain" her silenced guilts, the text of which lengthens daily, and to represent her repressed desires to her mother, believing that by doing so she will establish some grounds for identification and overcome her profound isolation and dumbness: "If only I could let my mother know the list, she—and the world—would become more like me, and I would never be alone again" (230). Recapitulating the earlier castration, her mother cuts her tongue by refusing to acknowledge the daughter's stories as legitimate: "'I can't stand this whispering,' she said looking right at me, stopping her squeezing. 'Senseless grabbings every night. I wish you would stop. Go away and work. Whispering, whispering, making no sense. Madness. I don't feel like hearing your craziness'" (233). In response, Kingston swallows her words, but only temporarily. The tautness of her vocal cords increasing to a breaking point, she later bursts the silence, uttering in a cathartic moment the text of her inner life before her mother. Finally, this girl takes on a voice, albeit in great confusion, and thereby authors a vision, textualizes her subjectivity, and legitimizes her own desires. She embarks, that is, on the autobiographical enterprise, articulating her interpretations against her mother's.

In this battle of words, mother and daughter, products of different cultural experiences, systems of signs, and modes of interpretation, speak two different "languages" and inscribe two different stories—graphically imaged in the sets of quotation marks that delimit their separate visions and betray the gap in the matrilineage as the circle of identity, of place and desire, is disrupted. Unable to understand the mother, unwilling to identify with her, the daughter would, in ironic reciprocity, cut off her mother's word: "'I don't want to listen to any more of your stories; they have no logic. They scramble me up. You lie with stories. You won't tell me a story and then say, 'This is a true story,' or 'This is just a story'" (235). But her mother's reluctant admission—"'We like to say the opposite'" (237)—forces Kingston to question, at the moment of their origin, her own interpretations and thus the "truth" or "fictiveness" of the autobiography she would inscribe through her memories of the past. As a result, the young Kingston comes to recognize the relativity of truth, the very elusiveness of self-representation that drives the autobiographical enterprise. "Ho Chi Kuai" her mother calls her; and, even to the moment in her adult life when she writes her autobiography, she cannot specify, can only guess, the meaning of the name her mother gave her from that culture she would leave behind. In the end she can only try to decipher the meaning of her past, her subjectivity, her desire, her own name: "I continue to sort out what's just my childhood, just my imagination, just my family, just the village, just movies, just living" (239).

Kingston closes *The Woman Warrior* with a coda, returning it to silence after telling two brief stories, one her mother's, one hers. She starts with the former: "Here is a story my mother told me, not when I was young, but recently, when I told her I also talk-story. The beginning is hers, the ending, mine" (240). Notably, her mother's story is now a gift. Passed from one storyteller to another, it signals the mother's genuine identification with the daughter. Yet the two-part story also functions as a testament to difference, the simple juxtaposition of two words rather than the privileging of one before the other. Here, at last, Kingston lets her mother's word stand without resisting it.

Her mother's story, set in the China of the previous generation, presents Kingston's grandmother as a willful and powerful woman who, convinced "that our family was immune to harm as long as they went to plays" (241), loves to attend theater performances. Unfolding in the ironies of the unexpected, the contingencies of opposites, the absence of linear logic, the story is emblematic of Brave Orchid's individual narrative style and vision, of the kinds of stories she tells. It speaks both of the horrifying vulnerability of women and of their fierce and commanding power; and it tells of the power of art to sustain the continuity of life and the power of interpretations to turn adversity and victimization to triumph. Through her "gift," mother places daughter in the line of powerful "Chinese" women whose source of inspiration and whose very survival in the midst of vulnerability lie in the word of the creative imagination.

Kingston follows her mother's words with what she imagines might be the story on the stage at one of those performances. Turning toward rather than resisting her Chinese roots, she takes as her protagonist a Chinese poet who lived in the second century.[23] Forced to live among barbarians for twelve years, during which time she bears two children who cannot speak Chinese, Ts'ai Yen remains isolated beyond the boundaries that sustain her sense of place and identity. Nonetheless, she eventually discovers that even barbarians make music of life and longing, reflecting civilized, rather than merely primitive, sensibilities. In the midst of cultural difference, the poet finds a commonality of experience and subjectivity through the language of art, which enables her to give voice to her own desire for self-representation and, in doing so, to join the circle of humanity. Eventually, Ts'ai Yen is ransomed, returning to her home "so that her father would have Han descendants" (243); but the more momentous "birth" she contributes to posterity is the song of sadness, anger, and wandering created out of her experience in the alien land. Speaking of human yearning, it "translates well" through the generations and across communal boundaries. Ultimately, the story of Ts'ai Yen, the woman of words, is the tale of Brave Orchid, who finds herself hostage in the barbarian land of America where even her children, born like Ts'ai Yen's among the aliens, cannot "speak" her native language, cannot understand her. Yet the tale is simultaneously that of Kingston herself, whose sense of alienation is doubly complicated, since, as a product of two cultures, she remains outside the circle of both. Mother and daughter sing the songs of sadness, loneliness, and displacement, finding their common sustenance in the word. Thus through her storytelling Kingston can create the total identification of mother and daughter as they both become Ts'ai Yen, woman poet.

In that final juxtaposition of two stories, Kingston asserts the grounds of identification with her mother, affirming continuities rather than disjunctions in the line.[24] She is her mother's daughter, however much she may distance herself geographically and psychologically, learning from her the power and authority that enable her to originate her own storytelling. Carrying on the matrilineal trace, she becomes like her mother a mistress of the word in a culture that would privilege only the lines, textual and genealogical, of patrilineal descent.[25] With her text she gives historical "birth" to Brave Orchid, creating for her a textual space in the genealogical record, and she gives "birth" to herself as the daughter who has passed through the body and the word of the mother.

NOTES

1. Albert E. Stone comments that Kingston's autobiography joins others in "this terrain of contemporary autobiography which abuts the continent of fiction" (Albert E. Stone, *Autobiographical Occasions and Original Acts.* [Philadelphia: Univ. of Pennsylvania Press, 1982], p. 25).

2. For a review article on recent literature on mothers and daughters, see Marianne Hirsch, "Mothers and Daughters," *Signs: Journal of Women in Culture and Society* 7 (Summer 1981): 200–222. See also Adrienne Rich, *Of Woman Born* (New York: Norton, 1976), esp. ch. 9.

3. Maxine Hong Kingston, *The Woman Warrior: Memoirs of a Girlhood among Ghosts* (New York: Random House, 1977), p. 3. Subsequent citations appear in the text.

4. At this moment the female body, emitting the menstrual flow and promising the subsequent discharge of childbirth portended in the blood, becomes one powerful and primary source of pollution in the community: The blood emitted reaffirms the association of woman with the dangerous powers of life and death, those two events that bring into play the processes of disintegration and integration within the patrilineal group and the forces of disorder and order in the community. See Emily M. Ahern, "The Power and Pollution of Chinese Women," in *Women in Chinese Society,* ed. Margery Wolf and Roxane Witke (Stanford: Stanford University Press, 1975), pp. 193–214. See also Mary Douglas, *Purity and Danger: An Analysis of Concepts of Pollution and Taboo* (New York: Praeger, 1966), esp. pp. 114–28.

5. For a discussion of the subversive power of woman's womb, see Susan Hardy Aiken, "Dinesen's 'Sorrow-acre': Tracing the Woman's Line," *Contemporary Literature* 25 (Summer 1984): 165–71.

6. For a discussion of *The Woman Warrior* with an attention to certain dynamics in the work that is similar to my own, see Paul John Eakin, *Fictions in Autobiography: Studies in the Art of Self-Invention* (Princeton: Princeton Univ. Press, 1985), pp. 255–75. As Eakin comments on this first "cautionary" tale, he focuses on the relation of woman to her community. I find Eakin's analysis throughout stimulating. Although we read the work in similar ways, we often give different emphases to the details.

7. Margery Wolf, "Women and Suicide in China," in *Women in Chinese Society,* ed. Wolf and Witke, p. 112. Why, for instance, was this married aunt living with her own parents rather than with her in-laws? And who had been the stranger, or was he a stranger, who had entered her house/womb? Kingston notes that a woman pregnant by someone near to, perhaps even in, her natal family would lay bare the vulnerability of the patrilineage to violations by incest.

8. Aiken, p. 167. See also Gayle Rubin, "The Traffic in Women: Notes on the 'Political Economy' of Sex," in *Toward an Anthropology of Women,* ed. Rayna R. Reiter (New York: Monthly Review Press, 1975), pp. 157–210; and Tony Tanner, *Adultery in the Novel: Contract and Transgression* (Baltimore: Johns Hopkins Univ. Press, 1979), pp. 58–66.

9. See Ahern, pp. 199–202.

10. See Wolf, pp. 113–14.

11. See Ahern, p. 198.

12. See ibid., p. 113.

13. Florence Ayscough, *Chinese Women: Yesterday and Today* (Boston: Houghton Mifflin, 1937), pp. 214–22.

14. Suzanne Juhasz makes this point also in her essay, "Towards a Theory of Form in Feminist Autobiography: Kate Millet's *Flying* and *Sita;* Maxine Hong Kingston's *The Woman Warrior*," in *Women's Autobiography: Essays in Criticism*, ed. Estelle C. Jelinek (Bloomington: Indiana Univ. Press, 1980), p. 234.

15. She does not succumb to the agoraphobia that presses so heavily upon her no-name aunt. Indeed, despite cold and hunger, she prospers in the midst of illimitable space and possibilities.

16. Kingston/Fa Mu Lan recognizes that her very life depends on this successful era-sure of her true identity: "Chinese executed women who disguised themselves as soldiers or students, no matter how bravely they fought or how high they scored on the examina-tion" (46). In that way traditional Chinese culture effecitvely denied women access to the power signified by the sword and the power signified by the surrogate sword, the pen and the knowledge it inscribed.

17. In the original legend Mu Lan remains chaste during her years as the woman war-rior. Kingston does make a space in her interpretation and her text for female sexuality, but, as I note above, it remains suppressed in the larger community.

18. Josette Féral, "Antigone or the Irony of the Tribe," *Diacritics* 8 (Fall 1978): 4.

19. The baron whom Kingston/Fa Mu Lan finally slays mistakes her for this kind of warrior. In response to his query about her identity, she tells him she is "a female avenger." His response—"'Oh, come now. Everyone takes the girls when he can. The families are glad to be rid of them'" (51)—suggests that he understands her to be an avenger of the wrongs of woman. Kingston/Fa Mu Lan specifies that the crime she seeks to avenge is, however, his impressment of her brother.

20. Her heroic space is far larger than that which provided the canvas for Fa Mu Lan's adventures: "Nobody in history has conquered and united both North America and Asia" (58). The public gestures of heroism she attempts are not uttered in a dazzling display of swordsmanship but in a self-effacing, tentative, "squeaky" voice that identifies her, not with the woman warrior, but with the "wives and slaves" tucked into the interstices of the mythical narrative. In her modern American space, the martial arts are not the grandiose gestures of heroic action; they are merely exercises "for unsure little boys kicking away under flourescent lights" (62). Moreover, in Communist China her relatives, instead of being identified with the exploited peasants, are identified as exploiting landowners and punished as the barons in the myth.

21. As the daughter knows, "all heroes are bold toward food" (104). They demonstrate by their gustatory feats their power over the natural world, their high degree of aristocratic cultivation, and their association with the sacred. See Claude Lévi-Strauss, *The Raw and the Cooked*, trans. John and Doreen Weightman (New York: Harper & Row, 1969).

22. See Mary Daly, *Gyn/Ecology: The Metaethics of Radical Feminism* (Boston: Beacon Press, 1978), pp. 153–77.

23. For a brief biography of Ts'ai Yen, see Wu-chi Liu and Irving Yucheng Lo, eds., *Sunflower Splendor: Three Thousand Years of Chinese Poetry* (Garden City: Anchor, 1975), pp. 537–58.

24. For a discussion of the narrative rhythms of identification and differentiation in *The Woman Warrior* and *China Men*, see Suzanne Juhasz, "Maxine Hong Kingston: Narrative Technique and Female Identity," in *Contemporary American Women Writers*, ed. Catherine Rainwater and William J. Scheik (Lexington: Univ. Press of Kentucky, 1985), pp. 173–89.

25. See Aiken, pp. 175–84.

ME AND MY SHADOW

I wrote this essay in answer to Ellen Messer-Davidow's 'The philosophical bases of feminist literary criticisms,' which appeared in the Fall 1987 issue of *New Literary History* along with several replies, including a shorter version of this one. As if it weren't distraction enough that my essay depends on someone else's, I want, before you've even read it, to defend it from an accusation. Believing that my reply, which turns its back on theory, constituted a return to the 'rhetoric of presence,' to an 'earlier, naive, untheoretical feminism,' someone, whom I'll call the unfriendly reader, complained that I was making the 'old patriarchal gesture of representation' whose effect had been to marginalize women, thus 'reinforcing the very stereotypes women and minorities have fought so hard to overcome.' I want to reply to this objection because I think it is mistaken and because it reproduces exactly the way I used to feel about feminist criticism when it first appeared in the late 1960s.

I wanted nothing to do with it. It was embarrassing to see women, with whom one was necessarily identified, insisting in print on the differences between men's and women's experience, focusing obsessively on women authors, women characters, women's issues. How pathetic, I thought, to have to call attention to yourself in that way. And in such bad taste. It was the worst kind of special pleading, an admission of weakness so blatant it made me ashamed. What I felt then, and what I think my unfriendly reader feels now, is a version of what women who are new to feminism often feel: that if we don't call attention to ourselves *as* women, but just shut up about it and do our work, no one will notice the difference and everything will be OK.

Women who adopt this line are, understandably, afraid. Afraid of being confused with the weaker sex, the sex that goes around whining and talking about itself in an unseemly way, that can't or won't do what the big boys do ('tough it out') and so won't ever be allowed to play in the big boys' games. I am sympathetic with this position. Not long ago, as organizer of an MLA session entitled 'Professional politics: women and the institution,' I urged a large roomful of women to 'get theory' because I thought that doing theory would admit us to the big leagues and enable us at the same time to argue a feminist case in the most unimpeachable terms—those that men had supplied. I busily took my own advice, which was good as far as it went. But I now see that there has been a price for this, at least there has been for me; it is the subject of my reply to Ellen. I now tend to think that theory itself, at least as it is usually practiced, may be one of the patriarchal gestures women *and* men ought to avoid.

There are two voices inside me answering, answering to, Ellen's essay. One is the voice of a critic who wants to correct a mistake in the essay's view of epistemology. The other is the voice of a person who wants to write about her feelings (I have wanted to do this for a long time but have felt too embarrassed). This person feels it is wrong to criticize the essay philosophically, and even beside the point: because a critique of the kind the critic has in mind only insulates academic discourse further from the issues that make feminism matter. That make *her* matter. The critic, meanwhile, believes such feelings, and the attitudes that inform them, are soft-minded, self-indulgent, and unprofessional.

These beings exist separately but not apart. One writes for professional journals, the other in diaries, late at night. One uses words like 'context' and 'intelligibility,' likes to win arguments, see her name in print, and give graduate students hardheaded advice. The other has hardly ever been heard from. She had a short story published once in a university literary magazine, but her works exist chiefly in notebooks and manila folders labelled 'Journal' and 'Private.' This person talks on the telephone a lot to her friends, has seen psychiatrists, likes cappuccino, worries about the state of her soul. Her father is ill right now, and one of her friends recently committed suicide.

The dichotomy drawn here is false—and not false. I mean in reality there's no split. It's the same person who feels and who discourses about epistemology. The problem is that you can't talk about your private life in the course of doing your professional work. You have to pretend that epistemology, or whatever you're writing about, has nothing to do with your life, that it's more exalted, more important, because it (supposedly) *transcends* the merely personal. Well, I'm tired of the conventions that keep discussions of epistemology, or James Joyce, segregated from meditations on what is happening outside my window or inside my heart. The public–private dichotomy, which is to say, the public–private *hierarchy*, is a founding condition of female oppression. I say to hell with it. The reason I feel embarrassed at my own attempts to speak personally in a professional context is that I have been conditioned to feel that way. That's all there is to it.

I think people are scared to talk about themselves, that they haven't got the guts to do it. I think readers want to know about each other. Sometimes, when a writer introduces some personal bit of story into an essay, I can hardly contain my pleasure. I love writers who write about their own experience. I feel I'm being nourished by them, that I'm being allowed to enter into a personal relationship with them. That I can match my own experience up with theirs, feel cousin to them, and say, yes, that's how it is.

> When he casts his leaves forth upon the wind [said Hawthorne], the author addresses, not the many who will fling aside his volume, or never take it up,

but the few who will understand him. . . . As if the printed book, thrown at
large on the wide world, were certain to find out the divided segment of the
writer's own nature, and complete his circle of existence by bringing him into
communion with it. . . . And so as thoughts are frozen and utterance, be-
numbed unless the speaker stand in some true relation with this audience—
it may be pardonable to imagine that a friend, a kind and apprehensive,
though not the closest friend, is listening to our talk. (Nathaniel Hawthorne,
'The Custom-House,' *The Scarlet Letter*, pp. 5–6)

Hawthorne's sensitivity to the relationship that writing implies is rare in academic prose, even when the subject would seem to make awareness of the reader
inevitable. Alison Jaggar gave a lecture recently that crystallized the problem.
Western epistemology, she argued, is shaped by the belief that emotion should
be excluded from the process of attaining knowledge. Because women in our
culture are not simply encouraged but *required* to be the bearers of emotion,
which men are culturally conditioned to repress, an epistemology which excludes emotions from the process of attaining knowledge radically undercuts
women's epistemic authority. The idea that the conventions defining legitimate
sources of knowledge overlapped with the conventions defining appropriate gender behavior (male) came to me as a blinding insight. I saw that I had been socialized from birth to feel and act in ways that automatically excluded me from
participating in the culture's most valued activities. No wonder I felt so uncomfortable in the postures academic prose forced me to assume; it was like wearing
men's jeans.

Ellen Messer-Davidow's essay participates—as Jaggar's lecture and my précis
of it did—in the conventions of Western rationalism. It adopts the impersonal,
technical vocabulary of the epistemic ideology it seeks to dislocate. The political
problem posed by my need to reply to the essay is this: to adhere to the conventions is to uphold a male standard of rationality that militates against women's
being recognized as culturally legitimate sources of knowledge. To break with
the convention is to risk not being heard at all.

This is how I would reply to Ellen's essay if I were to do it in the professionally
sanctioned way.

The essay provides feminist critics with an overarching framework for thinking
about what they do, both in relation to mainstream criticism and in relation to
feminist work in other fields. It allows the reader to see women's studies as a
whole, furnishing useful categories for organizing a confusing and miscellaneous
array of materials. It also provides excellent summaries of a wide variety of books
and essays that readers might not otherwise encounter. The enterprise is carried
out without pointed attacks on other theorists, without creating a cumbersome
new vocabulary, without exhibitionistic displays of intellect or esoteric learning.
Its practical aim—to define a field within which debate can take place—is fulfilled by *New Literary History*'s decision to publish it, and to do so in a format
which includes replies.

(Very nice, Jane. You sound so reasonable and generous. But, as anybody can
tell, this is just the obligatory pat on the back before the stab in the entrails.)

The difficulty with the essay from a philosophical, as opposed to a practical, point of view is that the theory it offers as a basis for future work stems from a confused notion of what an epistemology is. The author says: 'An epistemology . . . consists of assumptions that knowers make about the entities and processes in a domain of study, the relations that obtain among them, and the proper methods for investigating them' (p. 87). I want to quarrel with this definition. Epistemology, strictly speaking, is a *theory* about the origins and nature of knowledge. As such, it is a set of ideas explicitly held and consciously elaborated, and thus belongs to the practice of a sub-category of philosophy called epistemology. The fact that there is a branch of philosophy given over to the study of what knowledge is and how it is acquired is important, because it means that such theories are generated not in relation to this or that 'domain of study' but in relation to one another: that is, within the context of already existing epistemological theories. They are rarely based upon a study of the practices of investigators within a particular field.

An epistemology does not consist of 'assumptions that knowers make' in a particular field; it is a theory about how knowledge is acquired which makes sense, chiefly, in relation to other such theories. What Messer-Davidow offers as the 'epistemology' of traditional literary critics is not *their* epistemology, if in fact they have one, but her description of what she assumes their assumptions are, a description which may or may not be correct. Moreover, if literary critics should indeed elaborate a theory of how they got their beliefs, that theory would have no privileged position in relation to their actual assumptions. It would simply be another theory. This distinction—between actual assumptions and an observer's description of them (even when one is observing one's own practice)—is crucial because it points to an all-important fact about the relation of epistemology to what really gets done in a given domain of study, namely this: that epistemology, a theory about how one gets one's knowledge, in no way determines the particular knowledge that one has.

This fact is important because Messer-Davidow assumes that if we change our epistemology, our practice as critics will change, too. Specifically, she wants us to give up the subject–object theory, in which 'knowledge is an abstract representation of objective existence,' for a theory which says that what counts as knowledge is a function of situation and perspective. She believes that it follows from this latter theory that knowledge will become more equitable, more self-aware, and more humane.

I disagree. Knowing that my knowledge is perspectival, language-based, culturally constructed, or what have you, does not change in the slightest the things I believe to be true. All that it changes is what I think about how we get knowledge. The insight that my ideas are all products of the situation I occupy in the world applies to all of my ideas equally (including the idea that knowledge is culturally based); and to all of everybody else's ideas as well. So where does this get us? Right back to where we were before, mainly. I still believe what I believe and, if you differ with me, think that you are wrong. If I want to change your mind I still have to persuade you that I am right by using evidence, reasons, chains of inference, citations of authority, analogies, illustrations, and so on. Believing that what I believe comes from my being in a particular cultural framework does not change my relation to my beliefs. I still believe them just as much as if I thought they came from God, or the laws of nature, or my autonomous self.

Here endeth the epistle.

But while I think Ellen is wrong in thinking that a change of epistemology can mean a change in the kinds of things we think, I am in sympathy with the ends she has in view. This sympathy prompts me to say that my professionally correct reply is not on target. Because the target, the goal, rather, is not to be fighting over these questions, trying to beat the other person down. (What the goal is, it is harder to say.) Intellectual debate, if it were in the right spirit, would be wonderful. But I don't know how to be in the right spirit, exactly, can't make points without sounding rather superior and smug. Most of all, I don't know how to enter the debate without leaving everything else behind—the birds outside my window, my grief over Janice, just myself as a person sitting here in stockinged feet, a little bit chilly because the windows are open, and thinking about going to the bathroom. But not going yet.

I find that when I try to write in my 'other' voice, I am immediately critical of it. It wobbles, vacillates back and forth, is neither this nor that. The voice in which I write about epistemology is familiar, I know how it ought to sound. This voice, though, I hardly know. I don't even know if it has anything to say. But if I never write in it, it never will. So I have to try. (That is why, you see, this doesn't sound too good. It isn't a practiced performance, it hasn't got a surface. I'm asking you to bear with me while I try, hoping that this, what I write, will express something you yourself have felt or will help you find a part of yourself that you would like to express.)

The thing I want to say is that I've been hiding a part of myself for a long time. I've known it was there but I couldn't listen because there was no place for this person in literary criticism. The criticism I would like to write would always take off from personal experience. Would always be in some way a chronicle of my hours and days. Would speak in a voice which can talk about everything, would reach out to a reader like me and touch me where I want to be touched. Susan Griffin's voice in 'The way of all ideology.' I want to speak in what Ursula LeGuin, at the Bryn Mawr College commencement in 1986, called the 'mother tongue.' This is LeGuin speaking:

> The dialect of the father tongue that you and I learned best in college . . . only lectures. . . . Many believe this dialect—the expository and particularly scientific discourse—is the *highest* form of language, the true language, of which all other uses of words are primitive vestiges. . . . And it is indeed a High Language . . . Newton's *Principia* was written in it in Latin . . . and Kant wrote German in it, and Marx, Darwin, Freud, Boas, Foucault, all the great scientists and social thinkers wrote it. It is the language of thought that seeks objectivity.
>
> . . . The essential gesture of the father tongue is not reasoning, but distancing—making a gap, a space, between the subject or self and the object or other. . . . Everywhere now everybody speaks [this] language in laboratories and government buildings and headquarters and offices of business. . . .

> The father tongue is spoken from above. It goes one way. No answer is expected, or heard.
>
> . . . The mother tongue, spoken or written, expects an answer. It is conversation, a word the root of which means 'turning together.' The mother tongue is language not as mere communication, but as relation, relationship. It connects. . . . Its power is not in dividing but in binding. . . . We all know it by heart. John have you got your umbrella I think it's going to rain. Can you come play with me? If I told you once I told you a hundred times. . . . O what am I going to do? . . . Pass the soy sauce please. Oh, shit . . . You look like what the cat dragged in. (pp. 3–4)

Much of what I'm saying elaborates or circles around these quotes from LeGuin. I find that having released myself from the duty to say things I'm not interested in, in a language I resist, I feel free to entertain other people's voices. Quoting them becomes a pleasure of appreciation rather than the obligatory giving of credit, because when I write in a voice that is not struggling to be heard through the screen of a forced language, I no longer feel that it is not I who am speaking, and so, there is more room for what others have said.

One sentence in Ellen's essay stuck out for me the first time I read it and the second and the third: 'In time we can build a synchronous account of our subject matters as we glissade among them and turn upon ourselves.' (p. 79)

What attracted me to the sentence was the 'glissade.' Fluidity, flexibility, versatility, mobility. Moving from one thing to another without embarrassment. It is a tenet of feminist rhetoric that the personal is political, but who in the academy acts on this where language is concerned? We all speak the father tongue, which is impersonal, while decrying the fathers' ideas. All of what I have written so far is in a kind of watered-down expository prose. Not much imagery. No description of concrete things. Only that one word, 'glissade.'

> Like black swallows swooping and gliding
> in a flurry of entangled loops and curves . . .

Two lines of a poem I memorized in high school are what the word 'glissade' called to mind. Turning upon ourselves. Turning, weaving, bending, unbending, moving in loops and curves.

I don't believe we can ever turn upon ourselves in the sense Ellen intends. You can't get behind the thing that casts the shadow. *You* cast the shadow. As soon as you turn, the shadow falls in another place. Is still your shadow. You have not got 'behind' yourself. That is why self-consciousness is not the way to make ourselves better than we are.

Just me and my shadow, walkin' down the avenue.

It is a beautiful day here in North Carolina. The first day that is both cool and sunny all summer. After a terrible summer, first drought, then heat-wave, then torrential rain, trees down, flooding. Now, finally, beautiful weather. A tree outside my window just brushed by red, with one fully red leaf. (This is what I want you to see. A person sitting in stockinged feet looking out of her window—a floor to ceiling rectangle filled with green, with one red leaf. The season poised, sunny and chill, ready to rush down the incline into autumn. But perfect, and still. Not going yet.)

My response to this essay is not a response to something Ellen Messer-Davidow has written; it is a response to something within myself. As I reread the opening pages I feel myself being squeezed into a straitjacket; I wriggle, I will not go in. As I read the list 'subject matters, methods of reasoning, and epistemology,' the words will not go down. They belong to a debate whose susurrus hardly reaches my ears.

The liberation Ellen promises from the straitjacket of a subject–object epistemology is one I experienced some time ago. Mine didn't take the form she outlines, but it was close enough. I discovered, or thought I discovered, that the post-structuralist way of understanding language and knowledge enabled me to say what I wanted about the world. It enabled me to do this because it pointed out that the world I knew was a construct of ways of thinking about it, and as such, had no privileged claim on the truth. Truth in fact would always be just such a construction, and so, one could offer another, competing, description and so help to change the world that was.

The catch was that anything I might say or imagine was itself the product of an already existing discourse. Not something 'I' had made up but a way of constructing things I had absorbed from the intellectual surround. Post-structuralism's proposition about the constructed nature of things held good, but that did not mean that the world could be changed by an act of will. For, as we are looking at this or that phenomenon and re-seeing it, re-thinking it, the rest of the world, that part from which we do the seeing, is still there, in place, real, irrefragable as a whole, and making visible what we see, though changed by it, too.

This little lecture pretends to something I no longer want to claim. The pretense is in the tone and level of the language, not in what it says about post-structuralism. The claim being made by the language is analogous to what Barthes calls the 'reality effect' of historical writing, whose real message is not that this or that happened but that reality exists. So the claim of this language I've been using (and am using right now) lies in its implicit deification of the speaker. Let's call it the 'authority effect.' I cannot describe the pretense except to talk about what it ignores: the human frailty of the speaker, his body, his emotions, his history; the moment of intercourse with the reader—acknowledgment of the other person's presence, feelings, needs. This 'authoritative' language speaks as though the other person weren't there. Or perhaps more accurately, it doesn't bother to imagine who, as Hawthorne said, is listening to our talk.

How can we speak personally to one another and yet not be self-centered? How can we be part of the great world and yet remain loyal to ourselves?

It seems to me that I am trying to write out of my experience without acknowledging any discontinuity between this and the subject matter of the profession I work in. And at the same time find that I no longer want to write about that subject matter, as it appears in Ellen's essay. I am, on the one hand, demanding a connection between literary theory and my own life, and asserting, on the other, that there is no connection.

But here is a connection. I learned what epistemology I know from my husband. I think of it as more his game than mine. It's a game I enjoy playing but which I no longer need or want to play. I want to declare my independence of it, of him. (Part of what is going on here has to do with a need I have to make sure I'm not being absorbed in someone else's personality.) What I am breaking away from is both my conformity to the conventions of a male professional practice and my intellectual dependence on my husband. How can I talk about such things in public? How can I *not*.

Looking for something to read this morning, I took three books down from my literary theory shelf, in order to prove a point. The first book was Félix Guattari's *Molecular Revolution*. I find it difficult to read, and therefore have read very little of it, but according to a student who is a disciple of of Deleuze and Guattari, 'molecular revolution' has to do with getting away from ideology and enacting revolution within daily life. It is specific, not programmed—that is, it does not have a 'method,' nor 'steps,' and is neither psychoanalytic nor marxist, although its discourse seems shaped by those discourses, antithetically. From this kind of revolution, said I to myself, disingenuously, one would expect some recognition of the personal. A revolution that started with daily life would have to begin, or at least would have sometimes to reside, at home. So I open at a section entitled 'Towards a new vocabulary,' looking for something in the mother tongue, and this is what I find:

> The distinction I am proposing between machine and structure is based solely on the way we use the words; we may consider that we are merely dealing with a 'written device' of the kind one has to invent for dealing with a mathematical problem, or with an axiom that may have to be reconsidered at a particular stage of development, or again with the kind of machine we shall be talking about here.

> I want therefore to make it clear that I am putting into parentheses the fact that, in reality, a machine is inseparable from its structural articulations and conversely, that each contingent structure is dominated (and this is what I want to demonstrate) by a system of machines, or at the very least by one logic machine. (p. 111)

At this point, I start to skip, reading only the first sentence of each paragraph.

> 'We may say of structure that it positions its elements. . . .'
> 'The agent of action, whose definition here does not extend beyond this principle of reciprocal determination. . . .'
> 'The machine, on the other hand remains essentially remote. . . .'
> 'The history of technology is dated. . . .'
> 'Yesterday's machine, today's and tomorrow's, are not related in their structural determinations. . . .'

I find this langugae incredibly alienating. In fact, the paragraph after the one I stopped at begins: 'The individual's relation to the machine has been described by sociologists following Friedmann as one of fundamental alienation.' I will return to this essay some day and read it. I sense that it will have something interesting to say. But the effort is too great now. What strikes me now is the incredibly distancing effect of this language. It is totally abstract and impersonal.

Though the author uses the first person ('The distinction I am proposing,' 'I want therefore to make it clear'), it quickly became clear to me that he had no interest whatsoever in the personal, or in concrete situations as I understand them—a specific person, at a specific machine, somewhere in time and space, with something on his/her mind, real noises, smells, aches and pains. He has no interest in his own experience of machines, or in explaining why he is writing about them, what they mean to him personally. I take down the next book: *Poetry and Repression* by Harold Bloom.

This book should contain some reference to the self, to the author's self, to ourselves, to how people feel, to how the author feels, since its subject is psychological: repression. I open the book at page 1 and read:

> Jacques Derrida asks a central question in his essay on 'Freud and the Scene of Writing': 'What is a text, and what must the psyche be if it can be represented by a text?' My narrow concern with poetry prompts the contrary question: 'What is a psyche, and what must a text be if it can be represented by a psyche?' Both Derrida's question and my own require exploration of three terms: 'psyche,' 'text,' 'represented.'
> 'Psyche is ultimately from the Indo-European root. (p. 1)

—and I stop reading.

The subject of poetry and repression will involve the asking and answering of questions about 'a text'—a generalized, non-particular object that has been the subject of endless discussion for the past twenty years,—and about an equally disembodied 'psyche' in relation to the thing called 'a text'—not, to my mind, or rather in view of my desires, a very promising relation in which to consider it. Answering these questions, moreover, will 'require' (on whose part, I wonder?) the 'exploration' of 'three terms.' Before we get to the things themselves—psyches, texts—we shall have to spend a lot of time looking at them *as words*. With the beginning of the next paragraph, we get down to the etymology of 'psyche.' With my agenda, I get off the bus here.

But first I look through the book. Bloom is arguing against canonical readings (of some very canonical poems) and for readings that are not exactly personal, but in which the drama of a self is constantly being played out on a cosmic stage—lots of references to God, kingdom, Paradise, the fall, the eternal—a biblical stage on which, apparently, only men are players (God, Freud, Christ, Nietzsche, and the poets). It is a drama that, although I can see how gripping Bloom can make it, will pall for me because it isn't *my* drama.

Book number three, Michel Foucault's *History of Sexuality*, is more promising. Section One is entitled 'We "other Victorians."' So Foucault is acknowledging his and our implication in the object of the study. This book will in some way be about 'ourselves,' which is what I want. It begins:

> For a long time, the story goes, we supported a Victorian regime, and we continue to be dominated by it even today. Thus the image of the imperial prude is emblazoned on our restrained, mute, and hypocritical sexuality. (p. 3)

Who, exactly, are 'we'? Foucault is using the convention in which the author establishes common ground with his reader by using the first person plural—a presumptuous, though usually successful, move. Presumptuous because it presumes that we are really like him, and successful because, especially when an author is famous, and even when he isn't, 'our' instinct (I criticize the practice and engage in it too) is to want to cooperate, to be included in the circle and the author is drawing so cosily around 'us.' It is chummy, this 'we.' It feels good, for a little while, until it starts to feel coercive, until 'we' are subscribing to things that 'I' don't believe.

There is no specific reference to the author's self, no attempt to specify himself. It continues:

> At the beginning of the seventeenth century . . .

I know now where we are going. We are going to history. 'At the beginning of the seventeenth century a certain frankness was still common, it would seem.' Generalizations about the past, though pleasantly qualified ('a certain frankness,' 'it would seem'), are nevertheless disappointingly magisterial. Things continue in a generalizing vein—'It was a time of direct gestures, shameless discourse, and open transgressions.' It's not so much that I don't believe him as that I am uncomfortable with the level or the mode of discourse. It is everything that, I thought, Foucault was trying to get away from, in *The Archaeology of Knowledge*. The primacy of the subject as the point of view from which history could be written, the bland assumption of authority, the taking over of time, of substance, of event, the imperialism of description from a unified perspective. Even though the subject matter interests me—sex, hypocrisy, whether or not our view of Victorianism and of ourselves in relation to it is correct—I am not eager to read on. The point of view is discouraging. It will march along giving orders, barking out commands. I'm not willing to go along for the march, not even on Foucault's say-so (I am, or have been, an extravagant admirer of his).

So I turn to 'my' books. To the women's section of my shelves. I take down, unerringly, an anthology called *The Powers of Desire* edited by Christine Stansell, Ann Snitow, and Sharon Thompson. I turn, almost as unerringly, to an essay by Jessica Benjamin entitled 'Master and slave: the fantasy of erotic domination,' and begin to read:

> This essay is concerned with the violence of erotic domination. It is about the strange union of rationality and violence that is made in the secret heart of our culture and sometimes enacted in the body. This union has inspired some of the holiest imagery of religious transcendence and now comes to light at the porno newsstands, where women are regularly depicted in the bonds of love. But the slave of love is not always a woman, not always a heterosexual; the fantasy of erotic domination permeates all sexual imagery in our culture. (p. 281)

I am completely hooked, I am going to read this essay from beginning to end and proceed to do so. It gets better, much better, as it goes along. In fact, it gets so good, I find myself putting it down and straying from it because the subject is *so* close to home, and therefore so threatening, that I need relief from it, little breathers, before I can go on. I underline vigorously and often. Think of people I should give it to to read (my husband, this colleague, that colleague).

But wait a minute. There is no personal reference here. The author deals, like Foucault, in generalities. In even bigger ones than his: hers aren't limited to the seventeenth century or the Victorian era. She generalizes about religion, rationality, violence. Why am I not turned off by this as I was in Foucault's case? Why don't I reject this as a grand drama in the style of Bloom? Why don't I bridle at the abstractions as I did when reading Guattari? Well?

The answer is, I see the abstractions as concrete and the issues as personal. They are already personal for me without being personal*ized* because they concern things I've been thinking about for some time, struggling with, trying to figure out for myself. I don't need the author to identify her own involvement, I don't need her to concretize, because these things are already personal and concrete for me. The erotic is already eroticized.

Probably, when Guattari picks up an article whose first sentence has the words 'machine,' 'structure,' and 'determination,' he cathects it immediately. Great stuff. Juicy, terrific. The same would go for Bloom on encountering multiple references to Nietzsche, representation, God the father, and the Sublime. But isn't erotic domination, as a subject, surer to arouse strong feeling than systems of machines or the psyche that can be represented as a text? Clearly, the answer depends on the readership. The people at the convenience store where I stop to get gas and buy milk would find all these passages equally baffling. Though they *might* have uneasy stirrings when they read Jessica Benjamin. 'Erotic domination,' especially when coupled with 'porno newsstands,' does call some feelings into play almost no matter who you are in this culture.

But I will concede the point. What is personal is completely a function of what is perceived as personal. And what is perceived as personal by men, or rather, what is gripping, significant, 'juicy,' is different from what is felt to be that way by women. For what we are really talking about is not the personal as such, what we are talking about is what is important, answers one's needs, strikes one as immediately *interesting*. For women, the personal is such a category.

In literary criticism, we have moved from the New Criticism, which was anti-personal and declared the personal off-limits at every turn—the intentional fallacy, the affective fallacy—to structuralism, which does away with the self altogether—at least as something unique and important to consider—to deconstruction, which subsumes everything in language and makes the self non–self-consistent, ungraspable, a floating signifier, and finally to new historicism which re-institutes the discourse of the object—'In the seventeenth century'—with occasional side glances at how the author's 'situatedness' affects his writing.

The female subject *par excellence*, which is her self and her experiences, has once more been elided by literary criticism.

The question is, why did this happen? One might have imagined a different outcome. The 1960s paved the way for a new personalism in literary discourse by opening literary discussion up to politics, to psychology, to the 'reader,' to the effects of style. What happened to deflect criticism into the impersonal labyrinths of 'language,' 'discourse,' 'system,' 'network,' and now, with Guattari, 'machine'?

I met Ellen Messer-Davidow last summer at the School of Criticism and Theory where she was the undoubted leader of the women who were there. She organized them, led them (I might as well say us, since, although I was on the faculty as a visiting lecturer, she led me, too). At the end of the summer we put on a symposium, a kind of teach-in on feminist criticism and theory, of which none was being offered that summer. I thought it really worked. Some people, eager to advertise their intellectual superiority, murmured disappointment at the 'level' of discussion (code for, 'my mind is finer and more rigorous than yours'). One person who spoke out at the closing session said he felt bulldozed: a more honest and useful response. The point is that Ellen's leadership affected the experience of everyone at the School that summer. What she offered was not an intellectual performance calculated to draw attention to the quality of her mind, but a sustained effort of practical courage that changed the situation we were in. I think that the kind of thing Ellen did should be included in our concept of criticism: analysis that is not an end in itself but pressure brought to bear on a situation.

Now it's time to talk about something that's central to everything I've been saying so far, although it doesn't *show*, as we used to say about the slips we used to wear. If I had to bet on it I would say that Ellen Messer-Davidow was motivated last summer, and probably in her essay, by anger (forgive me, Ellen, if I am wrong) anger at her, our, exclusion from what was being studied at the School, our exclusion from the discourse of 'Western man.' I interpret her behavior this way because anger is what fuels my engagement with feminist issues; an absolute fury that has never even been tapped, relatively speaking. It's time to talk about this now, because it's so central, at least for me. I hate men for the way they treat women, and pretending that women aren't there is one of the ways I hate most.

Last night I saw a movie called *Gunfight at the OK Corral*, starring Burt Lancaster and Kirk Douglas. The movie is patently about the love-relationship between the characters these men play—Wyatt Earp and Doc Holliday. The women in the movie are merely pawns that serve in various ways to reflect the characters of the men, and to advance the story of their relationship to one another. There is a particularly humiliating part, played by Jo Van Fleet, the part of Doc Holliday's mistress—Kate Fisher—whom he treats abominably (everybody in the movie acknowledges this, it's not just me saying so). This woman is degraded over and over again. She is a whore, she is a drunkard, she is a clinging woman, she betrays the life of Wyatt Earp in order to get Doc Holliday back, she is *no longer young* (perhaps this is her chief sin). And her words are always in vain, they are chaff, less than nothing, another sign of her degradation.

Now Doc Holliday is a similarly degraded character. He used to be a dentist and is now a gambler, who lives to get other people's money away from them; he is a drunk, and he abuses the woman who loves him. But his weaknesses, in the perspective of the movie, are glamorous. He is irresistible, charming, seductive, handsome, witty, commanding; it's no wonder Wyatt Earp falls for him, who wouldn't? The degradation doesn't stick to Kirk Douglas; it is all absorbed by his female counterpart, the 'slut,' Jo Van Fleet. We are embarrassed every time she appears on the screen, because every time, she is humiliated further.

What enrages me is the way women are used as extensions of men, mirrors of men, devices for showing men off, devices for helping men get what they want. They are never there in their own right, or rarely. The world of the Western contains no women.

Sometimes I think *the world* contains no women.

Why am I so angry?

My anger is partly the result of having been an only child who caved in to authority very early on. As a result I've built up a huge storehouse of hatred and resentment against people in authority over me (mostly male). Hatred and resentment and attraction.

Why should poor men be made the object of this old pent-up anger? (Old anger is the best anger, the meanest, the truest, the most intense. Old anger is pure because it's been dislocated from its source for so long, has had the chance to ferment, to feed on itself for so many years, so that it is nothing but anger. All cause, all relation to the outside world, long since sloughed off, withered away. The rage I feel inside me now is the distillation of forty-six years. It has had a long time to simmer, to harden, to become adamantine, a black slab that glows in the dark.)

Are all feminists fueled by such rage? Is the molten lava of millenia of hatred boiling below the surface of every essay, every book, every syllabus, every newsletter, every little magazine? I imagine that I can open the front of my stomach like a door, reach in, and pluck from memory the rooted sorrow, pull it out, root and branch. But where, or rather, who, would I be then? I am attached to this rage. It is a source of identity for me. It is a motivator, an explainer, a justifier, a no-need-to-say-more greeter at the door. If I were to eradicate this anger somehow, what would I do? Volunteer work all day long?

A therapist once suggested to me that I blamed on sexism a lot of stuff that really had to do with my own childhood. Her view was basically the one articulated in Alice Miller's *The Drama of the Gifted Child*, in which the good child has been made to develop a false self by parents who cathect the child narcissistically. My therapist meant that if I worked out some of my problems—as she understood them, on a psychological level—my feminist rage would subside.

Maybe it would, but that wouldn't touch the issue of female oppression. Here is what Miller says about this:

> Political action can be fed by the unconscious anger of children who have been . . . misused, imprisoned, exploited, cramped, and drilled. . . . If, however, disillusionment and the resultant mourning can be lived through . . . , then social and political disengagement do not usually follow, but the patient's actions are freed from the compulsion to repeat. (p. 101)

According to Miller's theory, the critical voice inside me, the voice I noticed butting in, belittling, doubting, being wise, is 'the contemptuous introject.' The introjection of authorities who manipulated me, without necessarily meaning to. I think that if you can come to terms with your 'contemptuous introjects,' learn to forgive and understand them, your anger will go away. But if you're not angry, can you still act? Will you still care enough to write the letters, make the phone calls, attend the meetings? You need to find another center within yourself from which to act. A center of outgoing, outflowing, giving feelings. Love instead of anger. I'm embarrassed to say words like this because I've been taught they are mushy and sentimental and smack of cheap popular psychology. I've been taught to look down on people who read M. Scott Peck and Leo Buscaglia and Harold Kushner, because they're people who haven't very much education, and because they're mostly women. Or if not women, then people who take responsibility for learning how to deal with their feelings, who take responsibility for marriages that are going bad, for children who are in trouble, for friends who need help, for themselves. The disdain for popular psychology and for words like 'love' and 'giving' is part of the police action that academic intellectuals wage ceaselessly against feeling, against women, against what is personal. The ridiculing of the 'touchy-feely,' of the 'Mickey Mouse,' of the sentimental (often associated with teaching that takes students' concerns into account), belongs to the tradition Alison Jaggar rightly characterized as founding knowledge in the denial of emotion. It is looking down on women, with whom feelings are associated, and on the activities with which women are identified: mother, nurse, teacher, social worker, volunteer.

So for a while I can't talk about epistemology. I can't deal with the philosophical bases of feminist literary criticisms. I can't strap myself psychically into an apparatus that will produce the right gestures when I begin to move. I have to deal with the trashing of emotion, and with my anger against it.

This one time I've taken off the straitjacket, and it feels so good.

NOTES

Parts of this essay are reprinted from *New Literary History* 19 (Autumn 1987), by kind permission.

WORKS CITED

Benjamin, Jessica 1983. 'Master and slave: the fantasy of erotic domination,' in *The Powers of Desire: The Politics of Sexuality*, ed. Ann Snitow, Christine Stansell, and Sharon Thompson. New York: Monthly Review Press: 280–9.

Bloom, Harold 1976. *Poetry and Repression: Revision from Blake to Stevens*. New Haven, Conn.: Yale University Press.

Foucault, Michel 1980. *The History of Sexuality, Volume I: An Introduction*. Trans. Robert Hurley. New York: Vintage Books. Copyright 1978 by Random House, Inc. [Originally published in French as *La Volonté de Savoir*. Paris: Editions Gaillimard, 1976.]

Griffin, Susan 1982. 'The way of all ideology,' in *Made from the Earth: an Anthology of Writings*. New York: Harper and Row: 161–82.

Guattari, Félix 1984. *Molecular Revolution: Psychiatry and Politics*. Trans. Rosemary Sheed, intro. David Cooper. New York: Penguin Books. [First published as *Psychanalyse et transversalité* (1972), and *La Révolution moléculaire* (1977).]

Hawthorne, Nathaniel 1960–1. *The Scarlet Letter and Other Tales of the Puritans*. Ed. with an intro. and notes by Harry Levin. Boston, Mass.: Houghton Mifflin Co.

LeGuin, Ursula 1986. 'The mother tongue,' *Bryn Mawr Alumnae Bulletin* (Summer): 3–4.

Miller, Alice 1983. *The Drama of the Gifted Child*. New York: Basic Books.

ABOUT THE AUTHORS

Paula Gunn Allen is a leading scholar in the field of Native American Studies. She is the author of *The Sacred Hoop: Recovering the Feminine in American Indian Traditions* (1986) and editor of *Spider Woman's Granddaughters: Traditional Tales and Contemporary Writing by Native American Women* (1989). Recipient of the 1990 Santa Cruz Native American Literature Prize, she is author of the 1983 novel *The Woman Who Owned the Shadows*, as well as several collections of poetry, including *Skins and Bones* (1988) and *Shadow Country* (1982). Allen is currently Professor of English at UCLA.

Nancy Armstrong, Professor of Comparative Literature at the University of Minnesota, is the author of *Desire and Domestic Fiction: A Political History of the Novel* (1987) and co-author, with Leonard Tennenhouse, of *The Imaginary Puritan: Literature, Intellectual Labor, and the Origins of Personal Life* (forthcoming, 1992). In addition, Armstrong has co-edited two recent anthologies with Leonard Tennenhouse, *The Violence of Representation: Literature and the History of Violence* (1989) and *The Ideology of Conduct: Essays on Literature and the History of Sexuality* (1987). She is co-editor of the journal *Genders*.

Dale Bauer, Associate Professor of English and Women's Studies at the University of Wisconsin, Madison, is the author of *Feminist Dialogics: A Theory of Failed Community* (1988), one of the first major attempts to adapt Bakhtinian theory to feminist criticism. Her articles include work on Edith Wharton and reproductive technology, which is part of a book in progress on Wharton's late fictions, and essays on feminist pedagogy and American culture.

Nina Baym, Professor of English and Jubilee Professor of Liberal Arts and Sciences at the University of Illinois at Urbana-Champaign, has written extensively about nineteenth-century American women's literature. She has edited a recent edition of Maria S. Cummins's novel *The Lamplighter*, and has also written *Novels, Readers, and Reviewers: Responses to Fiction in Antebellum America* (1984) and *Woman's Fiction: A Guide to Novels By and About Women in America, 1820–1870* (1978). Baym is also an editor of the *Norton Anthology of American Literature*.

Catherine Belsey is Professor of English at the University of Wales College of Cardiff, where she chairs the Centre for Critical and Cultural Theory. Her publications include "Towards Cultural History—In Theory and Practice" (1989), "Disrupting Sexual Difference: Meaning and Gender in the Comedies" (1985), and "Re-Reading the Great Tradition" (1982). Her book-length works include *John Milton: Language, Gender, Power* (1988), *The Subject of Tragedy: Identity and Difference in Renaissance Drama* (1985), and *Critical Practice* (1980), a study of poststructuralist theory.

Shari Benstock, Professor of English at the University of Miami, has written on such diverse topics as feminist scholarship, James Joyce, and autobiography. She has edited *The Private Self: Theory and Practice of Women's Autobiographical Writings* (1988) and *Feminist Issues in Literary Scholarship* (1987). She is also the author of *Women of the Left Bank: Paris, 1900–1940* (1986), a study of American and English expatriate women in literary Paris.

Joseph A. Boone is Associate Professor of English at the University of Southern California. His 1987 study *Tradition Counter Tradition: Love and the Form of Fiction* explores the relationship between sexual ideology and narrative structure in the novel. Boone has recently co-edited *Engendering Men: The Question of Male Feminist Criticism* (1990), and he is now working on two book-length projects, "Authority's Anxieties: Sexuality and Modern Narrative" and "The Homoerotics of Orientalism: Male Writers and the Near East."

Hazel Carby, Professor of English, African American Studies, and American Studies at Yale University, is the author of *Reconstructing Womanhood: The Emergence of the Afro-American Woman Novelist* (1987). Her recent publications include "The Politics of Fictive Anthropology and the Folk: Zora Neale Hurston" (1991), "The Politics of Difference" (1990), and the introductions to reprints of *Seraph on the Sewanee* (1990), *The Magazine Fiction of Pauline Hopkins* (1988), and *Iola Leroy* (1987).

Barbara Christian is a Professor of Afro-American Studies at the University of California, Berkeley, where she is the first black woman to have received tenure. She is the author of *Black Feminist Criticism: Perspectives on Black Women Writers* (1985), *Black Women Novelists: The Development of a Tradition, 1892–1976* (1980), and such recent articles as "The Race for Theory" (1988) and "But Who Do You Really Belong To—Black Studies or Women's Studies?" (1989). Professor Christian is also currently an editor of the journal *Feminist Studies.*

Hélène Cixous is the Head of the Centre d'Etudes Féminines and Professor of English Literature at the Université de Paris VIII—Vincennes. Cixous is the author of numerous books, essays, novels, and plays. Her novels include *Dedans* (1969, awarded the Prix Médicis), *Manne aux Mandelstams aux Mandelas* (1988), *Jours de l'an* (1990), and *L'Ange au secret* (1991). Her critical works include *L'Exil de Joyce ou l'art du remplacement* (1968), *Entre l'Écriture* (1986), and *L'Heure de Clarice Lispector* (1989).

Jonathan Culler, Professor of English and Comparative Literature at Cornell University, is the author of numerous critical works, including *Structuralist Poetics: Structuralism, Linguistics, and the Study of Literature* (1975), *The Pursuit of Signs: Semiotics, Literature, Deconstruction* (1981), and *On Deconstruction: Theory and Criticism After Structuralism* (1982). He has also written studies of Flaubert, Roland Barthes, and Ferdinand de Saussure. Among his recent works are *On Puns: The Foundation of Letters* (1988) and *Framing the Sign: Criticism and Its Institutions* (1988).

Shoshana Felman is the Thomas E. Donnelley Professor of French and Comparative Literature at Yale University. She is the author of *Jacques Lacan and the Adventure of Insight: Psychoanalysis in Contemporary Culture* (1987), *Writing and Madness* (1985), and *The Literary Speech Act: Don Juan with J. L. Austin, or Seduction in Two Languages* (1983, English translation), and the editor of *Literature and Psychoanalysis: The Question of Reading: Otherwise* (1982). Her most recent work is a book co-authored with Dori Laub, M.D., entitled *Testimony: Crises of Witnessing in Literature, Psychoanalysis, and History* (1991). "Women and Madness" is part of a forthcoming book, *What Does the Woman Want?: Reading and Sexual Difference.*

Judith Fetterley is Professor of English at the State University of New York at Albany and author of *The Resisting Reader: A Feminist Approach to American Fiction* (1978) and *Provisions: A Reader from 19th Century American Women* (1985), as well as numerous articles examining questions of gender and sexual politics in the works of such writers as Elizabeth Stuart Phelps, Charlotte Perkins Gilman, F. Scott Fitzgerald, Louisa May Alcott, and Willa Cather.

Susan Stanford Friedman is Professor of English and Women's Studies at the University of Wisconsin, Madison. Friedman has written extensively about Hilda Doolittle in such works as *Psyche Reborn: The Emergence of H.D.* (1981) and *Penelope's Web: Gender, Modernity, H.D.'s Fiction* (1990). She is co-author of *A Woman's Guide to Therapy* (1979) and co-editor of *Signets: Reading H.D.* (1990). She has published articles on gender and genre, pedagogy and women's studies as well as on such writers as Virginia Woolf, Adrienne Rich, Elizabeth Barrett Browning, Sigmund Freud, James Joyce, and Julia Kristeva. She is at work on a book entitled *Return of the Repressed in Modernist Narratives.*

Regenia Gagnier is Associate Professor of English at Stanford University. Her recent works include *Subjectivities: A History of Self-Representation in Britain, 1832–1920* (1991) and *Idylls of the Marketplace: Oscar Wilde and the Victorian Public* (1986). She teaches feminist and social theory and nineteenth-century literature and politics. For 1991–92 she has a Guggenheim Fellowship for her work on private property.

Jane Gallop is Professor of English and Comparative Literature at the University of Wisconsin, Milwaukee. She is the author of *Thinking Through the Body* (1988), *Reading Lacan* (1985), *The Daughter's Seduction* (1982), and *Intersections: A*

Reading of Sade with Bataille, Blanchot, and Klossowski (1981). Her most recent work is *Around 1981: Academic Feminist Literary Theory* (1991).

Sandra M. Gilbert, Professor of English at the University of California, Davis, has published numerous collaborative works with Susan Gubar, including a recent multivolume work entitled *No Man's Land: The Place of the Woman Writer in the Twentieth Century,* as well as *The Madwoman in the Attic: The Woman Writer and the Nineteenth-Century Literary Imagination* (1979), runner-up for the 1980 Pulitzer Prize in General Nonfiction. Gilbert is also the author of numerous volumes of poetry, including *Emily's Bread* and *Blood Pressure* (1988), as well as a book-length study of the poetry of D. H. Lawrence.

Susan Gubar is Professor of English and Women's Studies at Indiana University. She is co-editor, with Sandra M. Gilbert, of *The Norton Anthology of Literature by Women: The Tradition in English* (1985) and *Shakespeare's Sisters: Feminist Essays on Women Poets* (1979). She has written numerous critical works, including "Feminism and Utopia" (1986) and "Representing Pornography: Feminism, Criticism, and Depictions of Female Violation" (1987). Gubar is also the editor of *For Adult Users Only: The Dilemma of Violent Pornography* (1989).

bell hooks (Gloria Watkins) is Associate Professor of English at Oberlin College. She has lectured extensively on the issues of race, class, and gender, and is the author of such works as *Yearning: Race and Gender in the Cultural Marketplace* (1990), *Talking Back: Thinking Feminist, Thinking Black* (1988), *Feminist Theory from Margin to Center* (1984), and *Ain't I a Woman: Black Women and Feminism* (1981). Among her recent articles are "Writing from the Darkness" (1989) and "Zora Neale Hurston: A Subversive Reading" (1989). hooks is the author of "Sisters of the Yam," a column that appears monthly in *Zeta.*

Luce Irigaray has two doctorates, one in linguistics and one in philosophy. Since leaving the Université de Paris VIII—Vincennes, Irigaray has been writing and practicing psychoanalysis. Her publications, from *Speculum of the Other Woman* (English translation, 1985) to *This Sex Which is Not One* (English translation, 1985), have explored the relationship between language, psychology, and gender. Among her other works are *Parler n'est jamais neutre* (1985), *Ethique de la différence sexuelle* (1984), and the recent article "L'Ordre sexuel du discours" (1987).

Mary Jacobus is the Anderson Professor of English at Cornell University. Her recent publications include *Reading Woman: Essays in Feminist Criticism* (1986), *Romanticism, Writing, and Sexual Difference: Essays on "The Prelude"* (1989), and *Women Writing and Writing About Women* (1979). In addition, she is the author of numerous critical articles examining such topics as Sigmund Freud's essays on screen memory, Melanie Klein, and breast-feeding during the French Revolution. Jacobus is co-editor of *Body Politics: Women and the Discourses of Science* (1990).

Susan Jeffords, Associate Professor of English at the University of Washington, is the author of numerous works examining gender and militarism, including *The*

Remasculinization of America: Gender and the Vietnam War (1989). She is currently completing a study of the Persian Gulf war, *Rape and the New World Order*, portions of which have been published in *Discourse, Cultural Critique*, and *The Women's Review of Books*. Professor Jeffords is also founding member and co-editor of the journal *Genders*.

Myra Jehlen is Professor of English at the University of Pennsylvania. She is the author of *American Incarnation: The Individual, the Nation, and the Continent* (1986) and *Class and Character in Faulkner's South* (1976). Co-editor of *Ideology and American Literature* (1986), Jehlen is also the author of such recent articles as "The Family Militant: Domesticity versus Slavery in *Uncle Tom's Cabin*" (1989) and "The Ties That Bind: Race and Gender in Mark Twain's *Pudd'nhead Wilson*" (1990).

Barbara Johnson is Professor of English and Comparative Literature, and the Mellon Professor of Humanities, at Harvard University. She is the author of numerous books including *A World of Difference* (1987), a study of difference "in the real world," *The Critical Difference: Essays in the Contemporary Rhetoric of Reading* (1980), and *Défigurations: du langages poétiques* (1979). Recent shorter works have dealt with such diverse topics as the Yale School of Criticism, Charlotte Perkins Gilman, Stéphane Mallarmé, translation theory, and Zora Neale Hurston. Professor Johnson is also the translator of *La Dissemination* by Jacques Derrida.

Ann Rosalind Jones, Professor of Comparative Literature at Smith College, has written extensively about both sixteenth-century literature and French feminism. Her recent articles include "Nets and Bridles: Early Modern Conduct Books and Sixteenth-Century Women's Lyrics" (1988), "Surprising Fame: Renaissance Gender Ideologies and Women's Lyric" (1986), "Inscribing Femininity: French Theories of the Feminine" (1985), and "Inside the Outsider: Nashe's Unfortunate Traveller and Bakhtin's Polyphonic Novel" (1983). Her most recent book-length study is entitled *The Currency of Eros: Women's Love Lyric in Europe, 1540–1620* (1990).

Cora Kaplan, Professor of English at Rutgers University, is the author of *Sea Changes: Culture and Feminism* (1986), and editor of a critical anthology of women poets, *Salt and Bitter and Good: Three Centuries of English and American Women Poets,* as well as an edition of Elizabeth Barrett Browning's *Aurora Leigh* (1988). Her recent articles include " 'Like a Housemaid's Fancies': The Representation of Working Class Women in Nineteenth-Century Writing" (1988) and "New Colours and Shadows: Feminist Literary Criticism."

Linda Kauffman, Professor of English at the University of Maryland, is the author of *Discourses of Desire: Gender, Genre, and Epistolary Fictions* (1986) and *Special Delivery: Epistolary Modes in Modern Fiction* (1991). She is the editor of *Feminism and Institutions: Dialogues on Feminist Theory* (1989) and *Gender and Theory: Dialogues on Feminist Criticism* (1989). Professor Kauffman is also the author of numerous articles, including "Special Delivery: Twenty-first-Century Epistolarity in

The Handmaid's Tale" (1989), which won the Florence Howe prize as the best feminist essay of the year in 1988. Her work-in-progress is *Masked Passions: Pornography, Politics, and Feminism 1976–1990*.

Annette Kolodny is Dean of the Faculty of Humanities at the University of Arizona. She is the author of *The Land Before Her: Fantasy and Experience of the American Frontiers, 1630–1860* (1984), "The Integrity of Memory: Creating a New Literary History of the United States" (1985), and *The Lay of the Land: Metaphor as Experience and History in American Life and Letters* (1975). Kolodny has also written a follow-up piece to her important essay "Dancing Through the Minefield" (1980), entitled "Dancing between Left and Right: Feminism and the Academic Minefield in the 1980's" (1988).

Julia Kristeva is a psychoanalyst, writer, and Professor at the Université de Paris VII. Her works have covered a wide breadth of topics, from clinical depression to semiotics to Bakhtin to the situation of women in China. Among her publications which are translated into English are *Language: The Unknown; Desire in Language: A Semiotic Approach to Literature and Art; Tales of Love, Powers of Horror: An Essay on Abjection;* and *Revolution in Poetic Language*.

Susan S. Lanser, Associate Professor of English and Director of Comparative Literature at the University of Maryland, has written on feminism and narratology in *The Narrative Act* (1981) and *Fictions of Authority: Women Writers and Narrative Voice* (forthcoming, 1992). Her most recent essays include "Feminist Criticism, 'The Yellow Wallpaper,' and the Politics of Color in America" (1989), and "Feminist Literary Criticism: How Feminist? How Literary? How Critical?" (1991). For a response to "Toward a Feminist Narratology," see Nilli Diengott, "Narratology and Feminism" and Lanser's reply, "Shifting the Paradigm: Feminism and Narratology" in *Style* 22 (1988).

Paul Lauter is the A. K. and G. M. Smith Professor of English at Trinity College in Connecticut and author of numerous works examining canon formation and politics in the United States. His most recent book is *Canons and Contexts* (1991). Among his other publications are "Race and Gender in the Shaping of the American Literary Canon: A Case Study from the Twenties" (1983) and (with Louis Kampf) *The Politics of Literature* (1972). Professor Lauter is also the coordinating editor of the *Heath Anthology of American Literature* (1990) and director of the MELUS project to create a new multicultural and gender-fair series of secondary school readers.

Amy Ling is Associate Professor of English and Director of Asian American Studies at the University of Wisconsin, Madison. She is the author of numerous critical articles including "Asian-American Literature: A Brief Introduction and Selected Bibliography" (1985), "Winnifred Eaton: Ethnic Chameleon and Popular Success" (1984), "Thematic Trends in Maxine Hong Kingston's *The Woman Warrior*" (1984), and "Edith Eaton: Pioneer Chinamerican Writer and Feminist" (1983). *Chinamerican Reflections*, a chapbook of her poems and paintings, appeared in 1984. Ling's most recent work is *Between Worlds: Women Writers of Chinese Ancestry* (1990).

Jane Marcus is Iris Howard Regents Professor of English and Comparative Literature at the University of Texas, Austin. Author of numerous studies of Virginia Woolf, including *Art & Anger: Reading Like a Woman* (1988), *Virginia Woolf and the Languages of Patriarchy* (1987), and *Virginia Woolf and Bloomsbury: A Centenary Celebration* (1987), Professor Marcus has also written extensively about such topics as feminist criticism, autobiography, and war. Her other publications include "The Asylums of Antaeus: Women, War, and Madness—Is There a Feminist Fetishism?" (1989), "Daughters of Anger/Material Girls: Con/Textualizing Feminist Criticism" (1988), and "Invisible Mediocrity: The Private Selves of Public Women" (1988).

Nellie McKay, Professor of Afro-American and American Literature at the University of Wisconsin, Madison, is editor of *Critical Essays on Toni Morrison* (1988) and co-editor, with William L. Andrews, of a special issue on "20th-Century Afro-American Autobiography" for *Black American Literature Forum* (Summer 1990). Among her most recent works are "Crayon Enlargements of Life: Zora Neale Hurston's *Their Eyes Were Watching God*" (1990) and "Alice Walker's 'Advancing Luna—and Ida B. Wells': A Struggle Toward Sisterhood" (1990). She is the Associate General Editor of the *Norton Anthology of Afro-American Literature* (forthcoming) and is at work on book-length studies of Afro-American women's autobiographies and the novels of Toni Morrison.

Helena Michie is Associate Professor of English at Rice University. Her works include *The Flesh Made Word: Female Figures and Women's Bodies* (1987), "'There is No Friend Like a Sister': Sisterhood as Sexual Difference" (1989), "Mother, Sister, Other: The 'Other Woman' in Feminist Theory" (1986), and "The Battle for Sisterhood: Christina Rossetti's Strategies for Control in Her Sister Poems" (1983). Professor Michie is currently at work on a book exploring the figure of "the other woman" and the anxieties of sisterhood.

Laura Mulvey is the Senior Lecturer in Film Practice at the London College of Printing. A filmmaker and a media and cultural theorist, Mulvey has co-directed a number of films with Peter Woollen, including "Riddles of the Sphinx" and "Crystal Gazing." Mulvey is also the author of such works as *Visual and Other Pleasures* (1989) and essays on film and narrative theory, Italian cinema, and the films of Jean-Luc Godard.

Judith Lowder Newton, Associate Professor and Director of Women's Studies at the University of California, Davis, is the author of *Women, Power, and Subversion: Social Strategies in British Fiction 1778–1850* (1981). She is co-editor of *Sex and Class in Women's History* (1983) and, with Deborah Rosenfelt, of *Feminist Criticism and Social Change: Sex, Class and Race in Literature and Culture* (1985). Among her more recent works is the essay "History as Usual? Feminism and the 'New Historicism'" (1988), a feminist examination of new historicist criticism.

Diane Price Herndl is Assistant Professor of English at New Mexico State University, Las Cruces, and the author of "The Writing Cure: Charlotte Perkins Gilman, Anna O., and 'Hysterical' Writing" (1988) and "The Dilemmas of a Feminine (Dia)Logic" (1991). Her most recent work is *Invalid Women: Figuring Feminine Illness in American Fiction and Culture, 1840–1940* (forthcoming).

Leslie W. Rabine is Professor of French at the University of California, Irvine. She is the author of *Reading the Romantic Heroine: Text, History and Ideology* (1985), "Ecriture féminine as Metaphor" (1988), "No Lost Paradise: Social Gender and Symbolic Gender in the Writings of Maxine Hong Kingston" (1987), "Searching for the Connections: Marxist-Feminists and Women's Studies" (1983), and "History, Ideology, and Femininity in *Manon Lescaut*" (1981).

Janice Radway is the author of *Reading the Romance: Women, Patriarchy, and Popular Literature* (1984). Among her shorter works are "The Book-of-the-Month Club and the General Reader: On Uses of 'Serious' Fiction" (1988), "Reading is Not Eating: Mass-Produced Literature and the Theoretical, Methodological, and Political Consequences of a Metaphor" (1986), "Interpretive Communities and Variable Literacies: The Functions of Romance Reading" (1984), and "The Aesthetic in Mass Culture: Reading the 'Popular' Literary Text" (1982). Radway is Professor of Literature at Duke University.

Lillian S. Robinson is Affiliated Scholar at the Institute for Research on Women and Gender, Stanford University, and Visiting Professor of English and American Studies at the University of Texas at Austin. She is the author of *Monstrous Regiment: The Lady Knight in Sixteenth-Century Epic* (1985) and *Sex, Class, and Culture* (1978), and co-author of *Feminist Scholarship: Kindling in the Groves of Academe* (1985). Many of Professor Robinson's latest publications, which include "Canon Father and Myth Universe" (1987), "Feminist Criticism: How Do We Know When We've Won?" (1988), and "What Culture Should Mean" (1989), deal with issues of canon formation and the politics of feminist criticism.

Joanna Russ, Professor of English at the University of Washington, is also a noted author of feminist science fiction. Her fictional works include *The Zanzibar Cat* (1984), *The Adventures of Alyx* (1983), and *The Female Man* (1975). Among her critical publications are *Magic Mommas, Trembling Sisters, Puritans & Perverts: Feminist Essays* (1985), *How to Suppress Women's Writing* (1983), "Amor Vincit Foeminam: The Battle of the Sexes in Science Fiction" (1986), and "Recent Feminist Utopias" (1981).

Patrocinio P. Schweickart is Associate Professor of English at the University of New Hampshire. She is the author of *A Theory for Feminist Criticism* (1980), "Add Gender and Stir" (1985), "Reading a Wordless Statement: The Structure of Doris Lessing's *The Golden Notebook*" (1985), and co-editor of *Gender and Reading: Essays on Readers, Texts, and Contexts* (1986). Her essay "Reading Ourselves: Toward a Feminist Theory of Reading" won the Florence Howe Award for Outstanding Feminist Scholarship in 1984.

Eve Kosofsky Sedgwick is Professor of English at Duke University. She is the author of *Between Men: English Literature and Male Homosocial Desire* (1985) and *The Coherence of Gothic Conventions* (1980). She has also written numerous articles exploring gender relations in such diverse writers as Willa Cather, Denis Diderot, William Wycherley, Laurence Sterne, and Walt Whitman. Her essay "The Beast in the Closet: James and the Writing of Homosexual Panic" (1986) was awarded the Crompton-Noll Prize in Gay Studies by the Modern Language Association.

Elaine Showalter is Chair of the English Department at Princeton University. She is the author of *A Literature of Their Own: British Women Novelists from Brontë to Lessing* (1977) and *The Female Malady: Women, Madness, and Culture in England, 1830–1980* (1985), and editor of several anthologies of feminist criticism, including *The New Feminist Criticism: Essays on Women, Literature, and Theory* (1985) and *Speaking of Gender* (1989). Her most recent books are *Sexual Anarchy: Gender and Culture at the Fin de Siècle* (1990) and *Sister's Choice: Tradition and Change in American Women's Writing* (1991).

Barbara Smith is a Black feminist writer, activist, and co-founder of Kitchen Table Press. She is editor and co-editor of three major collections of writing by Black women: *Conditions: Five, The Black Women's Issue* (1979); *All the Women Are White, All the Blacks Are Men, But Some of Us Are Brave: Black Women's Studies* (1982); and *Home Girls: A Black Feminist Anthology* (1983). She is also co-author, with Elly Bulkin and Minnie Bruce Pratt, of *Yours in Struggle: Three Feminist Perspectives on Anti-Semitism and Racism* (1984) and is currently completing a collection of her own short stories.

Paul Smith is Associate Professor of Literary and Cultural Studies at Carnegie Mellon University. Professor Smith is the author of *Pound Revised* (1983), *Discerning the Subject* (1987), "Julia Kristeva Et Al.: Or, Take Three or More" (1989), "Visiting the Banana Republic" (1988), and "Action Movie Hysteria, or Eastwood Bound" (1989). He is also co-editor, with Alice Jardine, of *Men in Feminism* (1987).

Sidonie Smith is Professor of English and Comparative Literature at the State University of New York at Binghamton. She is the author of *A Poetics of Women's Autobiography: Marginality and the Fictions of Self-Representation* (1987) and *Where I'm Bound: Patterns of Slavery and Freedom in Black American Autobiography* (1974) and co-editor, with Julia Watson, of *De/Colonizing the Subject: The Politics of Gender in Women's Autobiography* (forthcoming, 1992). Her recent essays include "The Autobiographical Manifesto: Identities, Temporalities, Politics" (1991) and "The Other Woman and the Racial Politics of Gender: Isak Dinesen and Beryl Markham in Kenya" (1992).

James J. Sosnoski, Professor of English at Miami University, in Oxford, Ohio, has published various articles on literary theory and ciritism. He is a co-founder of the Society for Critical Exchange and was its Executive Director from 1982 to

1988. Having recently completed a book-length manuscript entitled "The Magister Implicatus: The Call to Orthodoxy in Literary Studies," he is now at work on another entitled "Coming to Terms with Terms"—a study of the uses of literary terminology.

Gayatri Chakravorty Spivak is Professor of English at Columbia University. She is the author of *The Post-Colonial Critic: Interviews, Strategies, Dialogues* (1990), *Selected Subaltern Studies* (1988), and *In Other Worlds: Essays in Cultural Politics* (1987). Spivak is the author of several studies of Yeats, as well as translator of Jacques Derrida's *Of Grammatology*. Among her more recent publications are "Theory in the Margin: Coetzee's *Foe* Reading Defoe's *Crusoe/Roxana*" (1991), "The New Historicism: Political Commitment and the Postmodern Critic" (1989), "Imperialism and Sexual Difference" (1986), "Feminism and Critical Theory" (1985), and "Speculation on Reading Marx: After Reading Derrida" (1984).

Catharine R. Stimpson is presently the Dean of the Graduate School at Rutgers University, New Brunswick. She was the founding editor of the journal *Signs: Journal of Women in Culture and Society*. Dean Stimpson is also the co-editor of *Women—Sex and Sexuality* (1980) and the author of the novel *Class Notes* (1979), as well as editor of *Women and the American City* (1981). She is the editor of several anthologies of feminist criticism and author of numerous short stories and reviews. Her most recent work is *Where the Meanings Are: Feminism and Cultural Spaces* (1988).

Jane Tompkins, Professor of English at Duke University, is the author of *Sensational Designs: The Cultural Work of American Fiction, 1790–1860* (1985) and editor of *Reader-Response Criticism: From Formalism to Post-Structuralism* (1981) and *Twentieth-Century Interpretations of The Turn of the Screw* (1970). Among her other publications are "'Indians': Textualism, Morality and the Problem of History" (1986), and "Susan Warner (1819–1885)" (1985). She has just completed *West of Everything*, a study of Westerns in American life with an emphasis on gender (forthcoming, 1991), and is at work on a book about teaching in higher education.

Robyn R. Warhol is Associate Professor and Director of Graduate Studies in English at the University of Vermont. The author of *Gendered Interventions: Narrative Discourse in the Victorian Novel* (1989), she has published essays on such topics as feminist narratology, the body in/and the text, and nineteenth-century women novelists. Currently she is co-editing *Women's Work*, an anthology of American women writers from the seventeenth century to the present.

Susan Willis is Associate Professor of English at Duke University. She is the author of *Specifying: Black Women Writing the American Experience* (1987) and *A Primer for Daily Life* (1991). Professor Willis is the author of numerous essays exploring Afro-American identity, French Caribbean, Guatemalan, and Cuban literature, and cinematic adaptations of Shakespearean drama. Her recent publications include "I Shop Therefore I Am: Is There a Place for Afro-American Culture in Commodity Culture?" (1989), "Alice Walker's Women" (1985), and "Eruptions of Funk: Historicizing Toni Morrison" (1982).

Yvonne Yarbro-Bejarano is Associate Professor of Romance Languages and Comparative Literature at the University of Washington. Her editorial work includes co-editing the recent exhibition catalogue *Chicano Art: Resistance and Affirmation* (UCLA). Professor Yarbro-Bejarano has written extensively about sixteenth- and seventeenth-century Spanish literature, contemporary Chicana writers, and feminist criticism. Among her recent publications are "The Female Subject in Chicano Theatre: Sexuality, 'Race,' and Class" (1986), "De-constructing the Lesbian Body: Cherrie Moraga's *Loving in the War Years*" (1991), and "Masquerade, Male Masochism, and the Female Outlaw: A Feminist Analysis of Lope's *Embustes de Fabia*" (1991).

Bonnie Zimmerman, Professor and Chair of Women's Studies at San Diego State University, is the author of " 'The Dark Eye Beaming': Female Friendship in George Eliot's Fictions," "The Politics of Transliteration: Lesbian Personal Narratives" (1984), and "Exiting from Patriarchy: The Lesbian Novel of Development" (1983). Professor Zimmerman's most recent publication is *The Safe Sea of Women: Lesbian Fiction, 1969–1989* (1990).

ALTERNATIVE ARRANGEMENTS FOR *FEMINISMS*

As our introduction explains, the arrangement of
Feminisms is meant to be neither prescriptive nor
definitive. We offer this index as a set of suggestions
toward other ways of organizing the material. We
include references to a few literary authors and works
that appear repeatedly in these essays, to help in-
structors select primary texts they might teach with
this book.

AUTHOR/TITLE INDEX

TEXT PERMISSIONS